A HISTORY OF
TECHNOLOGY

A HISTORY OF
TECHNOLOGY

EDITED BY

CHARLES SINGER · E. J. HOLMYARD

A. R. HALL and TREVOR I. WILLIAMS

ASSISTED BY

Y. PEEL · J. R. PETTY · M. REEVE

VOLUME V

THE LATE NINETEENTH CENTURY
c 1850 TO *c* 1900

OXFORD
AT THE CLARENDON PRESS

Oxford University Press, Walton Street, Oxford OX2 6DP

OXFORD LONDON GLASGOW
NEW YORK TORONTO MELBOURNE WELLINGTON
KUALA LUMPUR SINGAPORE JAKARTA HONG KONG TOKYO
DELHI BOMBAY CALCUTTA MADRAS KARACHI
NAIROBI DAR ES SALAAM CAPE TOWN

First published 1958
Reprinted 1965, 1967, 1970, 1979

Printed in Great Britain
at the University Press, Oxford
by Eric Buckley
Printer to the University

PREFACE

WITH this fifth volume *A History of Technology* ends, at the opening of the modern age of scientific industry. It was clear to the Editors from the inception of the work that for a number of reasons it would be impracticable to extend its range to include the twentieth century. The amount of additional space that would be required would be excessive, and it would moreover be impossible to present the recent development of technology in the relatively non-technical manner adopted in these present volumes. A further difficulty lies in the nature of technological history—and perhaps of all history—for this must be based on the selection from an immense number of events of those that have proved most significant for future ages. The choice of such events from the distant past is a very different operation from the semi-prophetic selection of the significant happenings of a recent generation.

For such reasons it was decided to terminate this *History* at approximately the turn of the century, a date conveniently coinciding with the beginnings of modern transport on the road and in the air, and of the great growth of the heavy electrical industry; with the origins of commercial radio-telegraphy; and with the inauguration of a new age of mechanical power in which the century-old supremacy of the reciprocating steam-engine was rapidly terminated. Although all these developments had yet to make their great social impact, their technological basis had been firmly established and they are discussed at some length.

The new century also opens a new era with the development of manufacture and the progress of invention in Germany, America, and later Russia. The emergence of the United States and Russia in the forefront of technology during the twentieth century indeed signalizes a leap from one order of magnitude in production to another. Again, modern physics began about 1900, with all its immense implications for technology and for the relation of science to industry. Now for the first time abstract scientific thought, carried on without concern for its practical consequences in the life of man, was to offer as an incidental reward a mastery of natural resources totally different in kind and scale from anything contemplated in the older technology grown from remote empirical roots.

Even in the present volume, terminating before the beginning of these tremendous changes, it is in most cases possible to offer only the barest outline of the processes and methods used in the various industries. This is partly because their complexity makes heavy demands on the available space; more important, however, is the growth in depth of their scientific and economic background. To describe adequately the way in which chemists used their theoretical insight to enable them to perform a new synthesis and to turn it to practical account in industry; to discuss the reasons for the use of one machine for a given purpose in one region, and of another in a second; to study the causes of a higher rate of invention and technological progress appearing now here, now there, would be to suppose both in our readers and in ourselves a combination of specialized departments of knowledge which no one can possibly possess. The need for broad scientific and technological synthesis, as well as interpretation, is not least among the requirements of our age, and for its satisfaction it is hoped this *History* will provide some foundation.

The importance of applied science is the outstanding theme of this volume, for few branches of manufacture or production were left unchanged by the fruits of scientific discovery. These are most evident in the newer industries, as in chemical manufacture (chs 11 and 14) or electrical engineering (chs 9 and 10), and in the new manifestations of old industries, as in the novel processes evolved for the extraction of metals, whose applications were becoming increasingly important. Nevertheless, the dependence of industry on science was still somewhat fortuitous. In some fundamental manufactures, such as the steel-industry (ch 3) and shipbuilding (ch 16), vast improvements, economy in labour, increase of scale, and so on took place, and the product was rendered far more suitable for its purpose than formerly. Yet the empirical element remained large, and progress was achieved rather through the accumulated experience of craftsmen, the enterprise of management, and the skill of individual designers, than through scientific insight. Few scientists were employed in connexion with such manufactures, and in investigating the design of product and plant they were rarely consulted. Factors other than scientific bearing upon the growth of industry are discussed in chapter 33. Even where a scientific discovery was consciously exploited for industrial purposes, as with synthetic dye manufacture, accident could still play a very large part. In the history of telegraphy scientific analysis of problems and methods of solving them were from the first essential, but other new developments like those of the internal combustion engine (ch 8) and of the aeroplane (ch 17) owed more to creative empiricism and to persistent trial-and-error than to the availability of scientific theory. Theory might still follow, rather than precede, a major technological accomplishment.

In the second half of the nineteenth century the technical proficiency of any nation—and hence its capacity to compete industrially—was becoming ever more directly related to the numbers of its scientists and technicians, and to the general educational level of its population. A large share in the responsibility for the relative decline of Britain at this time must certainly be ascribed to those who failed to see the basic importance of education, and above all of technical education, because intellectually they were still living in the first stage of the Industrial Revolution. Here there is surely a lesson for our own times. The greater the extent to which scientists and technicians assumed control of an industry, the more rapidly the need for them expanded. Hence the development of technical education, and its relevance for the progress of industry, have been specially studied in chapter 32.

Educational changes are one instance of the way in which the infiltration of industry by science affected society in general, and perhaps unexpected, ways; there were many others. Thus, the application of science created many new industrial nuisances, as in the chemical industry. A symptom of the end of the *laissez-faire* attitude was the introduction of legal control in such cases—though often the manufacturer's own reluctance to waste potentially valuable materials exerted a no less beneficent influence. The dangers and inconveniences of life in the greatly enlarged towns were mitigated by the application of science to problems of water-supply and sanitation (ch 23), of furnishing adequate stocks of food (chs 1 and 2), and of transport. Science both revealed perils and abuses in manufacturing processes and designed ways of avoiding their occurrence. Had space permitted, we would have devoted more attention to the interrelationship between medicine and scientific technology in an industrialized society, but it has been possible to refer only briefly to some outstanding examples of this, and to offer some early instances of the debt of medicine to the new chemical industry.

The second phase of the industrial revolution impinged far more directly and beneficially on the lives of the majority of the inhabitants of western Europe and the United States than did the first. The first social effect of the Industrial Revolution was to make life in the factory and mine almost unbearably harsh; life in the home was impoverished. Scientific industry, even during the second half of the nineteenth century, did much to diminish danger, hardship, and squalor. Cheap transport made it possible for millions to leave the depressed areas of Europe, Russia, and even Asia for new lands of promise. Labour was eased by the greatly extended use of power and machinery—though much old craft skill was sacrificed. The régime of sunlight was ended by the development of cheap and powerful artificial illuminants. Printed matter was made accessible to all (ch 29), and may be said to have laid the foundations of popular democracy.

Even the poorest benefited from new materials, more and better food, and improved housing. For the wealthy, new developments like photography (ch 30), ballooning (ch 17), and mechanical road transport (ch 18) offered diversion as well as being useful.

Though few yet recognized the fact, daily life was assuming a technical colour. For this reason, it has seemed appropriate to the Editors to step a little beyond the limits of the former volumes of this *History* to discuss the human aspects of the new technology, and this has been done in ch 34.

Another important theme in world-wide technological history is the establishment of western technology and methods of production in non-European countries; this again took place in the later nineteenth century, most strikingly in Japan after 1868. Adhering to their former policy, however, the Editors have decided to omit deliberate discussion of this historically significant process, which during the period with which we are concerned was very largely one of direct imitation. It is, however, important to note the evidence of the increasing importance of invention and development in technology outside western Europe, above all in the United States but not inconspicuously in Russia, that will be found in every chapter of this volume.

The selection of suitable illustrations for the relatively more technical processes described in this volume has been greatly facilitated by the ready co-operation of the various authors concerned, and the Editors again express their thanks to the officials of the British Museum Library, the Cambridge University Library, the London Library, the Patent Office Library, and the Science Library, from whose rich stores so many illustrations have been copied, and who have otherwise assisted the detailed editorial work. The librarian of Imperial Chemical Industries Limited has also supplied much material otherwise difficult to obtain. For the execution of most of the art-work, which adds so much to the informative value of the text, we are again indebted to the skill and technical accomplishment of Mr D. E. Woodall. As with volumes III and IV, the indexes have been compiled by Miss M. A. Hennings, whose unfailing attention to detail revealed several minor discrepancies in time for them to be rectified.

The Editors have again to record the essential part played in the completion of this volume by the other members of their team—Mrs D. A. Peel, Miss M. Reeve, Miss J. R. Petty, and Miss J. V. Woodward.

To mark the conclusion of the entire work rather than of this particular volume, it is the pleasure as well as the duty of the Editors to express their warmest thanks to all who have made it possible. First and foremost these thanks must be expressed to Imperial Chemical Industries Limited, without whose generous financial support the project could never have been undertaken. In this considerable publishing venture the Editors have inevitably had a heavy responsibility, which could never have been discharged without much assistance from many sources. We remember with appreciation of our contributors and their readiness to consider editorial suggestions, former as well as present members of our staff, the Secretary and members of the staff of the Clarendon Press, our illustrators, and the many who have given freely of their time when we have consulted them on points of difficulty. Finally, our thanks are due to Sir Walter Worboys, who, as a director of Imperial Chemical Industries Limited, has given this project his most active support and encouragement throughout the eight years taken for its completion.

CHARLES SINGER
E. J. HOLMYARD
A. R. HALL
TREVOR I. WILLIAMS

CONTENTS

PART VIII. THE THRESHOLD OF THE TWENTIETH
CENTURY

ILLUSTRATIONS

Scene in the electricians' room of the Great Eastern, *1 September 1866. The broken transatlantic cable of 1865 has been recovered and the ends have been reunited. After a quarter of an hour's anxious delay, the needle of the galvanometer moves, showing that telegraphic communication between the Old World and the New has been restored. Among those portrayed are Cyrus W. Field, J. Temple, D. Good, J. Griffith, S. Anderson, S. Camerling, Augustus Hamilton, W. Thompson, H. Moriety, Willoughby Smith, R. Dudley, H. Clifford, C. Deane, Oliver Smith, and H. Sawyer.* Painting by Robert Dudley, reproduced by courtesy of the Metropolitan Museum of Art, New York, and the Smithsonian Institution, Washington   FRONTISPIECE

TEXT-FIGURES*

* The names at the end of entries are those of the artists who drew the illustrations.

9. THE GENERATION OF ELECTRICITY *by* C. MACKECHNIE JARVIS

10. THE DISTRIBUTION AND UTILIZATION OF ELECTRICITY by C. MACKECHNIE JARVIS

16. SHIP-BUILDING *by* A. M. ROBB

17. AERONAUTICS *by* PETER W. BROOKS

18. MECHANICAL ROAD-VEHICLES *by* D. C. FIELD

19. CARTOGRAPHY AND AIDS TO NAVIGATION *by* D. H. FRYER

20. BUILDING MATERIALS AND TECHNIQUES *by* S. B. HAMILTON

21. BRIDGES AND TUNNELS *by* H. SHIRLEY SMITH

22. HYDRAULIC ENGINEERING *by* J. ALLEN

29. PRINTING AND RELATED TRADES *by* W. TURNER BERRY

30. PART I. THE PHOTOGRAPHIC ARTS: PHOTOGRAPHY *by* HELMUT and ALISON GERNSHEIM

30. PART II. THE PHOTOGRAPHIC ARTS: CINEMATOGRAPHY *by* ANTHONY R. MICHAELIS

31. PRODUCTION AND UTILIZATION OF RUBBER *by* S. S. PICKLES

PLATES

ABBREVIATIONS OF PERIODICAL TITLES

(AS SUGGESTED BY THE WORLD LIST OF SCIENTIFIC PERIODICALS)

Agric. Hist.	Agricultural History. Agricultural History Society. Washington
Amer. Mach., Lond.	American Machinist; Magazine of Metal-working Production (European Edition). London
Amer. Mach., N.Y.	American Machinist; Magazine of Metal-working Production. New York
Ann. Chim. (Phys.)	Annales de Chimie (et de Physique). Paris
Arch. Sci. phys. nat.	Archives des Sciences physiques et naturelles. Geneva, Lausanne, Paris
Archit. Rev., Lond.	Architectural Review. London
Atlant. Mon.	Atlantic Monthly. Boston
Ber. dtsch. chem. Ges.	Bericht der Deutschen Chemischen Gesellschaft. Berlin
Bitumen, Berl.	Bitumen. Arbeitsgemeinschaft der Bitumenindustrie. Berlin
Bull. Ill. Engng Exp. Sta.	Bulletin. Illinois University Engineering Experimental Station. Urbana
Bull. Instn Metall.	Bulletin of the Institution of Metallurgists. London
Bull. Soc. Enc. Industr. nat.	Bulletin de la Société d'Encouragement pour l'Industrie Nationale. Paris
Bull. Soc. industr. Mulhouse	Bulletin de la Société Industrielle de Mulhouse. Mulhouse
Bull. U.S. geol. Surv.	Bulletin of the United States Geological Survey. Washington
Business Hist. Rev.	Business History Review. Boston
C. R. Acad. Sci., Paris	Compte Rendu hebdomadaire des Séances de l'Académie des Sciences. Paris
Chem. & Ind.	Chemistry and Industry. Society of Chemical Industry. London
Civ. Engng, N.Y.	Civil Engineering; Magazine of engineered Construction. American Society of Civil Engineers. New York
Concr. constr. Engng	Concrete and Constructional Engineering, including prestressed Concrete. London
Dinglers J.	Dinglers polytechnisches Journal. Berlin
Dyer, Lond.	Dyer, Textile Printer, Bleacher, and Finisher. London
Econ. Geogr.	Economic Geography. Worcester, Mass.
Econ. Geol.	Economic Geology and the Bulletin of the Society of Economic Geologists. Urbana
Econ. J.	Economic Journal. Royal Economic Society. London
Edison Mon.	Edison Monthly. New York
Electrician	Electrician. London

Emp. Surv. Rev.	Empire Survey Review. London
Engineer, Lond.	Engineer. London
Engineering, Lond.	Engineering. London
Engng Insp.	Engineering Inspection. London
Fm & Home, Lond.	Farm and Home. London
Glass Ind.	Glass Industry; devoted to Glass Technology, Engineering, Materials and Glass Factory Equipment and Operation. New York
Ill. Lond. News	Illustrated London News. London
Impl. Mach. Rev.	Implement and Machinery Review. London
India Rubb. J.	India Rubber Journal. London
Ingenieur, 's Grav.	De Ingenieur. The Hague
Inst. Petrol. Rev.	Institute of Petroleum Review. London
Iron Age	Iron Age. Philadelphia
J. Buchdruck.	Journal für Buchdruckerkunst, Schriftgießerei und die verwandte Fächer. Berlin
J. chem. Soc.	Journal of The Chemical Society. London
J. dom. Appl.	Journal of Domestic Appliances, Sewing and Washing Machines and Pram Gazette. London
J. Inst. Met.	Journal of the Institute of Metals. London
J. Inst. Navig.	Journal of the Institute of Navigation. London
J. Instn elect. Engrs	Journal of the Institution of Electrical Engineers. London
J. Instn Loco. Engrs	Journal of the Institution of Locomotive Engineers. London
J. Iron St. Inst.	Journal of the Iron and Steel Institute. London
J. phys. Chem.	Journal of Physical Chemistry. American Chemical Society. Washington
J. R. agric. Soc.	Journal of the Royal Agricultural Society (of England). London
J. R. Instn	Journal of the Royal Institution of Great Britain. London
J. R. sanit. Inst.	Journal of the Royal Sanitary Institute. London
J. R. Soc. Arts	Journal of the Royal Society of Arts. London
J. Soc. Arts	Journal of the Society [afterwards Royal Society] of Arts. London
J. Soc. chem. Ind., Lond.	Journal of the Society of Chemical Industry. London
J. Soc. Dy. Col.	Journal of the Society of Dyers and Colourists. Bradford
J. Soc. telegr. Engrs	Journal of the Society of Telegraph Engineers and Electricians. London
J. Text. Inst. (Proc.)	Journal of the Textile Institute [containing Abstracts, Proceedings and Transactions]. Manchester
Liebigs Ann.	Liebigs Annalen der Chemie. Leipzig
Matières grasses	Les Matières grasses. Le Pétrole et ses Dérivés. Paris

Mber. preuß. Akad. Wiss.	Monatsberichte der Königlich-Preußischen Akademie der Wissenschaft zu Berlin. Berlin
Mém. Acad. R. Sci. Sav. étrang.	Mémoires présentés par divers Savants [étrangers] à l'Académie Royale des Sciences de l'Institut de France. Paris
Mem. Manchr lit. phil. Soc.	Memoirs and Proceedings of the Manchester Literary and Philosophical Society. Manchester
Mem. R. Accad. Torino	Memorie della Reale Accademia delle Scienze di Torino. Turin
Metal Ind., Lond.	Metal Industry; Journal of non-ferrous Metals. London
Metals & Alloys	Metals and Alloys. Easton, Pa.
Min. Proc. Instn civ. Engrs	Minutes of Proceedings of the Institution of Civil Engineers. London
Murex Rev.	Murex Review. Murex Limited. Rainham
Nuovo Cim.	Nuovo Cimento. Società Italiana di Fisica. Bologna
Pharm. J.	Pharmaceutical Journal and Pharmacist. London
Phil. Mag.	Philosophical Magazine; a Journal of theoretical, experimental and applied Physics. London
Phil. Trans.	Philosophical Transactions of the Royal Society. London
Print. Reg.	Printers' Register. London
Proc. Instn civ. Engrs	Proceedings of the Institution of Civil Engineers. London
Proc. Instn mech. Engrs, Lond.	Proceedings of the Institution of Mechanical Engineers. London
Proc. Instn Rly Sig. Engrs, Lond.	Proceedings of the Institution of Railway Signal Engineers. London
Proc. phil. Soc. Glasg.	Proceedings of the Philosophical Society of Glasgow. Glasgow
Proc. roy. Soc.	Proceedings of the Royal Society. London
Proc. Scottish Shipb. Ass.	Proceedings of the Scottish Shipbuilders' Association. Glasgow
Proc. Staffs. Iron St. Inst.	Proceedings of the Staffordshire Iron and Steel Institute. Dudley
Prof. Pap. Ordn. Surv., Lond.	Professional Papers. Ordnance Survey. London
Rep. Brit. Ass.	Report of the British Association for the Advancement of Science. London
Rep. Smithson. Instn	Report of the Board of Regents of the Smithsonian Institution. Washington
Research, Lond.	Research: a Journal of Science and its Applications in Industry. London
Rly Gaz., Lond.	Railway Gazette; a Journal of Management, Engineering and Operation. London
S. Afr. Surv. J.	South African Survey Journal. Cape Town
Schweiz. polyt. Z.	Schweizerische polytechnische Zeitschrift. Winterthur
Sci. Amer. Suppl.	Scientific American Supplement. New York

Science	Science. American Association for the Advancement of Science. Washington
Sheet Metal Ind.	Sheet Metal Industries. London
Struct. Engr	Structural Engineer. Institution of Structural Engineers. London
Tech. et Civil.	Techniques et Civilisations. Saint-Germain-en-Laye
Text. Color.	Textile Colorist and Converter. Philadelphia
Text. Mfr, Manchr	Textile Manufacturer. Manchester
Text. Rec.	Textile Recorder. Manchester
Trans. Amer. Inst. min. (metall.) Engrs	Transactions of the American Institute of Mining (and Metallurgical) Engineers. New York
Trans. Camb. bibliogr. Soc.	Transactions of the Cambridge Bibliographical Society. Cambridge
Trans. Instn Engrs Shipb. Scot.	Transactions of the Institution of Engineers and Shipbuilders in Scotland. Glasgow
Trans. Instn Min. Metall.	Transactions of the Institution of Mining and Metallurgy. London
Trans. Instn nav. Archit., Lond.	Transactions of the Institution of Naval Architects. London
Trans. Newcomen Soc.	Transactions. Newcomen Society for the Study of the History of Engineering and Technology. London
Wire & Wire Prod.	Wire and Wire Products; devoted to the production of Wire, Rod and Strip, Wire and Rod Products and insulated Wire and Cable. Wire Association. Stamford, Conn.
Wire Ind.	Wire Industry; the British Wire Journal. London

I

GROWTH OF FOOD PRODUCTION

G. E. FUSSELL

I. GENERAL CHANGES IN FOOD SUPPLIES

BETWEEN 1800 and 1900 the population of Europe approximately doubled. The inhabitants of England and Wales numbered 10 m in 1811 and 37 m in 1911; those of the German Empire 40 m in 1871 and 70 m in 1914; everywhere (save in France, where the population remained almost stationary after 1870) there were comparable increases. Thus, despite much migration to North America and elsewhere, 200 m more people had to be fed in Europe at the end of the nineteenth century than at its opening.

In other parts of the world, such as India, the effect of a growing population in depressing the standard of living has been notorious. No such effect was felt in Europe in the nineteenth century; on the contrary, the standard of living generally rose, and the diet became more varied and more healthful than in the past.[1] Life at the barest level of subsistence became steadily less common. It is natural to ask how this was possible, for the agricultural land of Europe was certainly not greatly augmented. Moreover, there was in many countries a pronounced drift to the towns, so that the ratio of producers of food in the country to consumers of food in the town was continually diminishing. And towns can live only on the countryman's labour.

There are four answers to this question, two of which will be discussed in more detail later. The first was the growth of industrial production, which was even more rapid than that of population and which enabled the inhabitants of Europe to exchange their manufactures for foodstuffs and the raw materials of industry. Secondly, the development of methods of transportation enabled surplus food from remote parts of the world to be brought to Europe cheaply and plentifully; in this connexion, progress in methods of preservation (ch 2) is of the first importance, since the kind of meat, for example, that could have been brought from as far as Australia before 1850 would have been a very poor addition to the diet of Europe. In the third place, there was an enormous increase in the area of land

---

[1] Ireland provides an exception to this statement; there the precarious balance of people and potatoes was destroyed by the blight from 1845 onwards. The result was starvation and mass emigration.

farmed by Europeans overseas, not only in the newly opened territories of North America, Argentina, Australia, New Zealand, and South Africa, but in Egypt, India, Ceylon, West Africa, Malaya, and other tropical regions where native inhabitants had long been tilling the soil. In the new countries virgin soil was tilled or grazed, and, in the main, yielded textile fibres, meat, and cereals which found an expanding market in Europe; in them labour was scarce, and machinery took its place. In tropical plantations native labour worked under European management, with relatively little elaborate mechanical equipment, raising larger and better crops of rice, sugar, tea, coffee, and so on, as well as industrial crops such as rubber and vegetable oils. Wherever the European influence dominated overseas, there was not only an insatiable demand for consumer goods, but for capital equipment—for the railways, bridges, ships, machines, and plant that European industry alone could supply. Hence the economies of the colonized countries and of the mother-continent were complementary, each supplying the wants of the other.

Finally, the productivity of European agriculture was itself brought to a higher level. Generally, this may be attributed partly to better systems of land-tenure and land-use, partly to the introduction of new aids such as machines and fertilizers, partly to improvements in the quality of plants and animals brought about by selective breeding. The major fraction of Europe's increased food requirements between 1800 and 1850 was in fact supplied by more intensive exploitation of Europe's own resources: after 1850, however, these increased requirements were largely met by supplies from overseas, particularly with respect to the basic foods—cereals and meat. As will be shown in greater detail below, this changing structure of European agriculture imposed great hardship, whose results are felt even to this day. In some countries, such as Denmark and Holland, where overseas competition in the food-market was most rapidly countered by an effective and rational reorganization of agricultural practice, the catastrophe of falling food-prices produced less calamity than, for example, in Britain, where not only had industrialism advanced farthest (so that the demand for cheap, shop-bought food was most pressing) but where also agriculture did not occupy a foremost place in social and political policy

In 1850, when the population of western Europe was still largely fed on the produce of its own farm-lands, there was a fairly extensive trade in grain, cattle, and dairy products between the different countries, but little or no overseas competition in these commodities. Some grain was imported from North America, and wool from the Antipodes had already had some effect on sheep-rearing in Europe. As yet, however, most imported foodstuffs were tropical or sub-tropical products, such as coffee, tea, cocoa, sugar, and rice. The first two it was not possible to grow in Europe, but beet-sugar was already competing with cane-sugar, and rice was cultivated to some extent in Italy and Spain. Tobacco also was grown in most European countries, though the bulk of that consumed came from America and Asia.

Fifty years later these conditions had changed completely. Whereas European farmers had formerly sold their produce in a local market for the supply of their own and neighbouring countries, by 1900 the local or national market had been absorbed into a world market. The European farmer, whose crops were procured by intensive methods involving the use of high-quality seeds, expensive fertilizers, careful cultivation, and a mixture of arable and pasture farming, found himself confronted by imported supplies of cheap meat and cereals produced at a minimum cost and on the most extensive scale in newly occupied lands, whose fertility had not previously been exploited.

These new countries were the middle west of the United States and Canada, the great spaces of Australia, the uplands of New Zealand, and the pampas of the Argentine. All but the last of these regions had previously been non-productive, except in their indigenous flora and fauna used by scattered populations of aborigines. They had known little systematic tillage or grazing, but by the end of the century they were producing largely for export. Moreover, during the same half-century the renowned black soils of the Ukraine were brought under the plough for the cultivation of wheat.

II. THE UNITED STATES AND CANADA

In the United States the settled area had reached the eastern fringe of the Great Plains by 1850, when they had already been crossed by the pioneers who had established settlements in California, in Oregon, and in Utah. During the following four decades almost the whole of this region was occupied and cultivated. The Union Pacific Railway was completed in 1869, the working crews living on the buffalo (bison), which they almost wiped out. Other transcontinental lines were built in the twenty years after the Civil War (1861–5), and the vast ranges, no longer populated by herds of bison, could be used for grazing cattle. Between 1860 and 1900 it is estimated that over 400 m acres were added to the farm-lands of the United States: more than ten times the total area of England and Wales.

The earliest settlers on the eastern seaboard of North America brought with them the farming ideas of their homeland, although they were forced to adapt themselves to the cultivation of new crops—maize, tobacco, cotton, and sugar—

especially in the hot climate of the southern states. Later, in Revolutionary days, and about the beginning of the nineteenth century, the new rotations practised in England were investigated by such progressive farmers as George Washington (1732–99) and Thomas Jefferson (1743–1826). For even by this time yields were falling in the older settled regions, particularly where, as in Virginia, the soil had been partially exhausted by the continued cultivation of tobacco without the use of fertilizers. The rotations practised in Europe were tried, clover, beans and peas, and occasionally turnips being grown; but these crops did not meet with the same success in America. Clover-grazing and hay were less important in a country where maize was generally grown and formed the staple fodder-crop. Turnips were not successful in the field. Gypsum, marl, lime, and Peruvian guano were all used in the nineteenth century to enhance soil fertility.

By 1850 large numbers of factory-made machines were being used on the farms. McCormick's reaper, designed in 1834, was selling at the rate of 1000 a year in 1850 (vol IV, figure 5); Wood's iron ploughs and Deere's steel ones sold at 10 000 a year by 1857. The wheat-drill was in general use before the outbreak of the Civil War. Then the demands of the armies for men reduced the supply of labour, and forced the increased use of machines.

The most striking development of the years after the war was that of the open range, which had its golden age in the period 1866–86. Here the cattle, descendants of stock imported by the Spaniards, roaming freely and controlled only by cowboys, multiplied rapidly in the room of the almost exterminated bison. Great herds were driven northwards from Texas to the railways and as far as Montana. On them was founded the meat-packing industry, centred on Chicago, which by the seventies was already supplying the European market. The quality of this beef was at first low—the animals were hardy, but lean and heavy-horned, yielding little meat or milk—and remained so until European strains were used to improve it. The Jersey, Hereford, Ayrshire, Galloway, and Devon breeds had been imported before 1861, and others followed. The cattle-population of the range was doubled in two decades, to reach 45 m about 1886.

There was also a large extension of grazing in other parts of the United States. In the later days of the range, as stocks improved, cattle were fattened in Iowa, Illinois, Indiana, Arkansas, and other states instead of being taken direct to the slaughter-house. In the first two of these states—each as large as England and Wales—they fed on the famed 'blue grass' (*Poa pratensis* and *P. compressa*), popularly associated with horse-breeding Kentucky. Maize, however, was widely used to fatten beef for the market, 75 bushels of corn and five months being required for the purpose. In Iowa, timothy-grass[1] was sown to give a hay crop after the corn had been harvested. Horses, sheep, and pigs also became more numerous in this age of fantastically rapid growth in the area of farmed land and in the human population it supported. Some herds flourished on the edges of the range, but the greater expansion was in livestock kept domestically. Maize and other feeds were used, and in this area wheat, oats, rye, barley, buckwheat, and potatoes were grown as well. In the farms, as on the range, attention was given to the

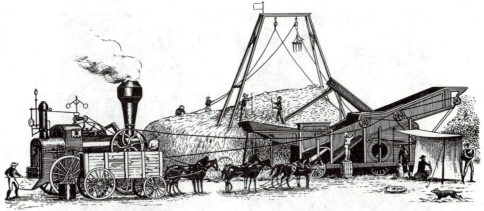

FIGURE 1—*Threshing in California, 1883. The work was done on a large scale, requiring many men. In the figure, two 'tablers' are continuously employed in feeding material into the 'self-feeder'. At the right of the machine another team is continuously employed hauling away the straw, part of which is used in the furnace of the steam-engine.*

improvement, of stock by breeding. Cotswold, Southdown, and Leicester rams were used, for example, as well as the famous merinos. Herd-books began in the seventies, a sign of a new attitude.

Elsewhere, in the new states formed after 1850—mainly west of the Mississippi —climate and soil for a time favoured intense concentration on wheat as a cash-crop. Such states were Kansas, Nebraska, and, later, North and South Dakota. Railways carried the grain to the huge elevators in the east; by way of the Great Lakes and other routes (vol IV, figure 304) it crossed the Atlantic and steadily depressed the relative cost of bread. These 'bonanza' farms suffered many vicissitudes—a dry season when the soil, deprived of binding grass-roots, blew away; hail-storms; plagues of grasshoppers that could wipe out a crop— but when conditions were propitious large quantities could be exported. The cultivation of these vast areas was rapidly becoming mechanically elaborate (figure 1), though it remained agriculturally primitive. No manure was used: none was available for use. The seed was drilled into a shallow furrow and left to grow.

---

[1] *Phleum pratense*, the cultivation of which was fostered by Timothy Hanson (fl 1720).

After one or two crops, a bare fallow was allowed to restore to the soil such fertility as it might.

The impact of this flood of grain and meat was felt not only in the long-settled eastern states—where much poor land passed out of cultivation, and a tendency towards dairy-farming and market-gardening was further stimulated by rapid urbanization and ceaseless immigration from Europe—but even more in Europe itself. In turn, in the last two decades of the century, American wheat-farmers

FIGURE 2—*Large-scale ploughing in Dakota, c 1880.*

suffered from the competition of other newly opened areas in Australia, the Ukraine, and Canada.

The wide prairies stretch far north of the 49th parallel. These western provinces of Canada were settled somewhat later than the corresponding regions of the United States, but the farming practice was similar, being a restless exploitation of inherent fertility. Wheat was the almost universal crop, especially in Manitoba, as it has largely remained since; two crops were taken, then a crop of oats, followed by a fallow. Ploughing was light (figure 2). The prairie grass was broken in June and 'back-set' a month later. This land was sown first (figure 3); next came that which had been summer-fallowed, and finally that which had been ploughed in the preceding winter. As a result the harvest did not all fall at the same time. In western Canada the same problems of soil-erosion and declining fertility were encountered as in the western United States, but less quickly and less severely. Meanwhile, large quantities of wheat were produced for export at comparatively low cost.

Some cattle, too, were kept everywhere in this region of Canada, especially in the area just east of the Rocky Mountains, where they ranged freely on wild grass as in the United States. The export of meat, however, was never on a comparable scale. Here, too, there was a useful improvement in stock, by Shorthorn, Angus, and Dutch cattle. Some stock was exported live to Europe, but this trade was replaced by that in refrigerated meat well before the end of the century. As dairy-farming became more important, particularly in the easterly provinces, its products also reached the European market to the embarrassment of the native farmer.

FIGURE 3—*Mass sowing of wheat on the Canadian prairie, c 1880.*

III. AUSTRALIA, NEW ZEALAND, AND ARGENTINA

The rapidity of the growth of food-exports from the antipodes was even more striking. At the close of the eighteenth century the Europeans in Australia were confined to a few penal settlements; by the beginning of the twentieth there was a European population of several millions producing large quantities of meat and wheat for export. New Zealand, colonized even more recently, had become a great sheep-grazing and dairy-farming country.

Merino sheep, grazing on natural herbage, had proved exceptionally successful in the early days of Australia, and their wool provided the settlers with their first export. Wheat also was exported from South Australia in 1843, when the European population of the continent was about 200 000. The discovery of gold brought about a six-fold increase in numbers during the next two decades, while the repeal of the Corn Laws and other tariff reforms in Britain favoured the importation of food there. Cultivation developed more tardily in Australia than on the flat, open prairies of America. The soil was often difficult to work, lying in pits and troughs that had to be made level before crops could be grown successfully. Years of tillage were necessary before it became adequately fertile. Besides suffering from low rainfall, in many parts of Australia the land lacked phosphates; but superphosphate was not imported until 1882. Yields were as low as in medieval Europe, being no more than 10–15 bushels to the acre. New implements, however, such as the stripper (a type of combine-harvester) and the stump-jump plough for use in burned-over or partly cleared forest lands, assisted in the hard work of raising crops. The incentive to use machines was all the greater because land was far more freely available than labour. The development of a railway system also promoted the exportation of bulky primary products, so that already in the 1880s Australian wheat was a significant factor in the world's markets. Its full impact came at the turn of the century.

Large numbers of cattle were kept on open ranges, but the meat was mainly eaten at home. Since all the cattle were of much more recent stock than the Spanish Longhorn cattle that formed the foundation of the American prairie herds, they were probably of improved breeds. However, the methods of keeping were little different; the animals grazed on what they could find, and bred quite indiscriminately. Before refrigeration was practised some salt beef, hides, and tallow were exported. Refrigeration (p 45) permitted a large expansion of this trade; frozen or chilled beef, mutton, and lamb were sent to Europe from the eighties. Successful as this trade was, Australian beef could not compete with Argentine chilled beef, which began to capture the market in the years towards 1914.

The development of dairying followed a characteristic course, spreading from South Victoria to New South Wales, New Zealand, and Tasmania. The forest was cleared by felling, burning, and ring-barking. Rye-grass, cocksfoot, and clovers were sown on the partly cleared land, and these roughly-made pastures proved excellent for fattening stock or for dairying, in spite of the sporadic invasion of grasshopper plagues and the results of the introduction of the starling. There were indigenous snakes and other pests such as the dingo, which destroyed sheep and would on occasion attack cattle.

The introduction of the refrigerator, of the separator, and of the Babcock testing-machine simplified and encouraged the production of dairy products (p 33). The first butter-factory was established in 1892. Refrigerated holds made it possible to export an improved and uniform butter after 1890. The season, too, was an advantage. The peak period of production with the spring growth of pastures came from September to November, when in Europe the milk-yield was declining. Thus a surplus could be sent to Britain at the right time of the year for a good market. Australian dairy cattle are of well known breeds—Shorthorn, Ayrshire, Red Poll, Friesians, and Guernsey—and each breed has its Australian herd-book.

Two methods were used to make up for a summer shortage of pasture. Some paddocks were grazed lightly during the heavy spring growth. Their grasses ran to seed and this remained as roughage during the next few months. It was considered that there was enough scattered green material to enable the cows to digest it. This practice was not sound, for it was very likely to cause deterioration of the pasture. Elsewhere, the lack of grass was remedied by growing other fodder crops as the dairy industry developed. Maize, millet, sudan grass, sorghums, and roots were all cultivated, and either grazed or cut green for silage. More recent improvement in the pastures has tended to increase the amount of hay or grass silage while reducing that available for cropping. That much more butter than cheese was made from the milk was an effect of local taste.

Sugar-cane was first grown in Australia during the 1860s in the north coast area of New South Wales and southern Queensland. By about 1875 some 11 000 acres had been planted, and this area was increased northwards during the next twenty years. Viticulture, begun by the early settlers, occupied 60 000 acres in 1900, when it was estimated that some $3\frac{1}{2}$ m gallons of wine were made. Fruit-growing for export came only at the turn of the century.

In the agricultural expansion of New Zealand, too, pastoral farming dominated the first phase. Sheep were kept on a rapidly multiplying scale on the large Crown leases. In North Island tracts of bracken and forest were cleared by fire, and English grasses were sown. South Island developed as a mixed farming area with large-scale wheat-growing for export, and with artificial grasses grown as fodder-crops. Here the double-furrow plough, the binder, and the grain-drill were used, but little artificial fertilizer was applied until after 1880. At a slightly later date, and especially after 1890 when dairy-production for export began, some farmers began to top-dress the pastures with fertilizers and lime, a practice that slowly became more general as agricultural education progressed after the founding of Canterbury Agricultural College in 1880, and of the Department of Agriculture in 1892.

The agricultural wealth of New Zealand increased as rapidly in proportion to its area as did that of other newly exploited virgin lands. The number of sheep rose from 762 000 in 1855 to nearly 13 m in 1881, wheat yields from 325 000 bushels in 1870 to $16\frac{3}{4}$ m in 1891 and $19\frac{1}{4}$ m in 1899. The making and export of butter and cheese became more and more important after 1890.

The Argentinian pampas were more densely settled after immigration was allowed in 1850, and were utilized for the production of range sheep and cattle. From the 1870s some frozen mutton was exported, but Argentine beef, which is today so important, was not sent out in any quantity until after 1900, when the country became one of the leading exporters of agricultural produce.

IV. FARMING IN BRITAIN, c 1840–90

The effect upon European farming of this growing flood of food from land that before 1850 had never been farmed, or indeed fully explored, was profound. Yet without such food European industrial development could not have taken place and the needs of a population rapidly outgrowing its own food-producing resources could not have been met. Britain, because she was foremost in industrialization, and because her population increased most swiftly, was most in need of these supplies. Her farmers were perhaps the most sorely tried as overseas competition became keener, but the competition was felt by farmers all over western Europe.

Besides the relatively slow development of the intercontinental trade in foodstuffs before about 1880, several circumstances combined to delay its full impact on British farming until about that time. The effect of the repeal of the Corn Laws in 1846, so dreaded by farmers, had been mitigated not only by the growth of the population but by its enhanced prosperity. People demanded more food for more mouths, as well as a more varied diet, more meat and milk, more fruit and vegetables. Again, the Crimean War of 1854–6, the American Civil War of 1861–5, and the Franco-Prussian War of 1870–1 tended to maintain the prosperity of the British farmer, so it was not until the physical catastrophes of 1879 had occurred that the economic disasters, vividly foreseen and described in 1846, were realized—in a time of peace. These were in fact the results of a combination of inimical circumstances added to foreign competition.

The farmers' own efforts had contributed much to the maintenance of their position between 1840 and 1880, the period of so-called 'high farming'. In effect these involved the use of very intensive methods and a general raising of the standard of farming practice.

Many developments combined to make such a result possible. First, new fertilizers (ch 11) improved crop-yields. Bone-dust, or dissolved bones, had been obtainable since the beginning of the century. Peruvian guano and Chilean nitrate were imported from the 1840s, at which time also Lawes and Gilbert began the manufacture of superphosphate at Barking. Mineral phosphates were dug in Cambridgeshire, in continental Europe, and in north Africa; potash was mined in Germany and Alsace from the 1860s. Secondly, ingenious plant-breeding placed more productive varieties of cereals at the farmers' disposal. Among these were Squarehead Master wheat and Chevalier barley. Thus corn-growing was ameliorated in two ways; the plant could be fed more effectively and the seeds were in themselves better suited to reproduction.

A problem tackled by a variety of methods, yet incompletely solved, was that of relieving land of superfluous water. The mole-plough had been known in Essex for half a century and variously shaped tiles had been used for at least that time, but not until a machine to make tubular drain-pipes had been designed was any very great progress possible, particularly on the heavy lands. Government loans assisted this work in accordance with the Act of 1846 and its successors, and large areas of land were drained by private and unsubsidized effort. In agreements prevailing between many landlords and their tenants the former

FIGURE 4—*One type of steam-driven reaping machine,* c *1876.*

supplied the tiles or pipes, while the latter provided the labour for laying them. Unfortunately the mechanics of soil-drainage were not then well understood, and many pipes were laid at depths of four feet and more, much too deep to be really effective for their purpose.

New agricultural machines were designed, and introduced even into the small British fields. The Americans McCormick and Hussey showed their reapers at the Great Exhibition of 1851, and Bell tried to revive the interest in his machine that had lapsed a decade or more before. Many new types of cultivating machines —horse-hoes, seed- and manure-drills, rollers, harrows, and reapers (figure 4)— were offered to the farmer. The portable steam-engine had already been applied to driving barn-machinery, in which there was equally rapid development, and in 1858 John Fowler was awarded a prize of £500 for his method of steam-ploughing (figure 5). This and similar systems were widely employed during the half-century, both by ploughing- and threshing-contractors and by individual owners.

Though overseas trade naturally lowered the prices of native grain and meat, its disadvantageous aspects were offset a little (it would be difficult to say how much) by the importation of more liberal supplies of feeding-stuffs. Maize, beans, and barley were brought in to help to feed the animals, and thus increased the supply and quality of organic manure. Moreover, industrial wastes such as rape-cake and linseed-cake, long used in the Low Countries, came into increasing use in Britain. After about 1850 their value to the farmer was enhanced by the

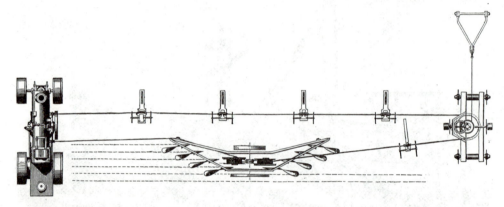

FIGURE 5—*Steam-ploughing apparatus, with two sets of ploughs used alternately across the field, made by John Fowler & Company, Leeds. Extensive development of steam-ploughing depended upon the availability of steel rope, as chains were too heavy and hemp was too easily frayed. In the 1860s it was usual to use a rope of 24 steel wires of No 14 gauge.*

addition of imported products such as palm nuts and sesame seeds to form a compound cake. As the prices of grain fell, and the advantages of grazing and dairying increased, grain also was fed to livestock. A variety of dried products came on to the market, such as brewers' grains, blood, and fish, and all were used for the same purpose. These feeding-stuffs were used to supplement the roots and clover that still formed the basis of the Norfolk four-course system, devised in the eighteenth century to improve mixed husbandry. This system and its modifications, with some attempts to improve the ley, whether short or long, lasted throughout the period. It had, however, to be greatly modified, or even abandoned, after the physical disasters of the 1870s.

Animal diseases had caused serious losses throughout the early years of Queen Victoria's reign, and in 1865 an epidemic of rinderpest compelled the government to take stringent action. The decision to slaughter affected herds was taken; by this means rinderpest was overcome and foot-and-mouth disease and pleuro-pneumonia were much reduced. Despite outbreaks of disease, breeders made great progress during the twenty-five years between 1850 and 1875. Many cattle herd-books were begun at this time. New breeds of sheep were developed, such as the Oxford and Hampshire Down, and the old were maintained. Farmers both increased the numbers of their herds and flocks and improved the quality of the animals composing them. An important trade in the exportation of fine breeding-stock to the new countries flourished.

Then came the succession of bad seasons culminating in the disastrous year 1879. The hay rotted in the fields in continuous rain, the grain sprouted in the stook, sheep died from liver-rot, cattle were afflicted by foot-and-mouth disease and pleuro-pneumonia. As if this were not enough, calamity-stricken farmers were called upon in the next few years to face an increasingly intense competition from cheaply produced cereals and meat coming from the new lands overseas. In spite of animal disease those farmers who were predominantly graziers suffered less than those whose main cash-crop was grain; yet during the last years of the nineteenth century British farmers generally encountered low prices, fixed by the new world market in agricultural produce, which impelled them to modify both their methods and their products. It was a fortunate circumstance that the industrial towns provided a rising demand for milk and dairy produce. Overseas producers could not compete in the market for fresh liquid milk, though they could, and did, send in condensed milk (p 35), margarine,[1] butter, and cheese. Consequently farmers began to expand their yield of liquid milk, especially after the 1865 outbreak of rinderpest had devastated the urban cow-keepers' stocks. The railways played an important part in this development, making the rapid transport of milk possible. The trend towards dairy-farming continued until the end of the century. As a result some types of land, such as the heavier clays of Essex and the lighter soils of Norfolk, were hardly cultivated at all.

Though the climate was a little more favourable in the 1890s the state of British agriculture aroused political concern because of the increasing volume of imported produce and the continued fall in prices and rise in costs. Some ameliorative legislation had been passed after 1879, and other measures became law after a further inquiry in 1893. A Board of Agriculture was established in 1889 in place of the committee of the Privy Council that had earlier dealt with agricultural questions.

By 1900 the system of farming had been greatly modified. There were still large farms where a correspondingly large capital was successfully devoted to the

[1] Margarine was invented in the 1860s by the French chemist Mège-Mouriès. Its manufacture and improvement, particularly at first in Holland, proceeded rapidly in the last decades of the century.

production of grain, meat, and milk at a profit, but cereal-growing had been much reduced throughout the country. Now farmers had also begun to concentrate upon market-garden crops, such as potatoes and green vegetables, which they grew in the field for the townsman. They continued to breed good animals, for there was always a home market for fine home-grown beef and mutton. The dairy industry was more fully organized, sometimes co-operatively, and fruit was more extensively grown. Once again British farmers had demonstrated their ability to adapt their methods to meet new and changing circumstances, and in the decades before the first world war they were beginning to recover.

V. CONTINENTAL FARMING, 1850–1900

Germany. In Germany development proceeded steadily along lines familiar since the beginning of the century. Justus von Liebig (1803–73) and his pupils had great influence, and farm schools and institutes were founded to teach the best practice. Some measure of the progress in arable farming is provided by the diminishing proportion of bare fallow; forming about 15 per cent of the cultivated area in 1850, it had fallen to about 7 per cent in 1883, and to 2 per cent in 1913. The superficial area under crop was therefore steadily increasing, and because of its better condition, improved manuring, and the use of selected seeds, this larger area also gave a higher average yield per acre than was obtained in earlier days.

Ancient methods of draining land by bush- or stone-filled drains had been practised for centuries. The new English method of using tubular clay pipes was being discussed and tried in Belgium, France, Germany, and Austria by 1852. This was an important element in the improvement of the moorland in north-east Germany, a process greatly encouraged by the Bremen research station, founded in 1877. The so-called 'high moor' was improved by draining, irrigation, and chalking, and by adding artificial nitrogen, potash, and phosphorus to the soil before cultivating legumes. The 'low moor' was drained, sand dug from the subsoil or neighbouring deposits was spread on the surface, and artificial fertilizers were used.

The amount of artificial fertilizers used in 1850 was small, but more was used as such substances became easier to obtain. Peruvian guano was first imported in 1842. Bone-meal was already used and became more important. It was the first phosphatic fertilizer before superphosphate, and was used as raw crushed bones, steamed bones, and limed bones. Other new fertilizers were Chilean nitrate of soda, poudrette prepared from town sewage, ammonium sulphate obtained as a waste-product from gas-works, the Stassfurt potash (1868), and basic slag. Sherrif's new wheat, Squarehead Master, reached Denmark by 1874 and Germany by 1879. In 1890 von Petkus produced Petkus rye, and Rabbethge and Geisecke their higher-yielding varieties of sugar-beet. As in Britain, however, the breeding of grass and fodder-crops was not studied to any appreciable extent during this half-century.

The making of the seed-bed was facilitated by new machines. The first steam-ploughing set was used in 1868, and English ring-rollers and clod-crushers were imported. More farmers used seed- and manure-drills, while reaping- and mowing-machines proved as useful in Germany as elsewhere. Barn-machinery became a feature of the larger estates and farms. On many peasant holdings, however, the older methods—broadcast hand-sowing on a seed-bed prepared by ox- or cow-draught, manual mowing, and reaping with scythe and sickle—persisted, as they do in some places today.

Animal breeding was intensified after 1850. Deeper ploughing in the new way required more powerful horses, and it has been said that there was an 'invasion' of Belgian horses. They were crossed with German horses, to the great benefit of the latter breed. There were many changes in the feeding and breeding of cattle, as well as experiments in crossing, and attempts were made to fix the characters of breeds suited to the local soil and climate. Some increase in bovine tuberculosis and other diseases was thought to be associated with the confinement and lack of exercise incidental to stall-feeding. Open-air grazing was accordingly resumed, animals spending the months from May to September in the pastures, which were fenced with plain or barbed wire. A consequence of this revival of an older custom was the need for more grass-land, which was met by making longer leys, or by putting land down to permanent pasture, a process generally most successful on heavy land. Grass was supplemented by imported feeding-stuffs. Much maize was grown; it was both imported and exported, but imports were larger than exports by 1900. Potato-waste and that from sugar-beet factories were used. Rich feeding deserves good cattle, and selected breeds were imported to improve the local stocks. Since 1850 the Low Countries cow has spread over the whole of north Germany, but the Simmentaler is now the most widespread, representing 44 per cent of the total.

Though there was still a large sale of merino sheep abroad, the total flock declined between 1860 and 1900, because of the competition from overseas wool. As the demand for mutton grew, Rambouillet and English sheep were used to add weight to German breeds. Pigs, fed on dairy wastes, increased in number even more rapidly than cattle.

The thirty years between 1850 and 1880 were the happiest in the history of

German agriculture. After 1880 German farmers faced much the same critical situation as the British. Russia joined with the new overseas countries in sending her agricultural produce to Germany in increasing quantities. The price of cereals fell, while the cost of production, chiefly in wages, rose. The German farmers tried to counter foreign competition by growing more fodder-crops, by using purchased feeding-stuffs, and by developing more productive livestock. The yield of animal products was materially raised, as were the numbers and weight of cattle and pigs. The German farmer also tried to increase crop-yields by more efficient cultivation and harvesting, richer manuring, and careful seed-selection —in a word, both their crop and their animal husbandry became more intensive.

France. French farmers were equally affected by the new developments. Pipe-drainage, introduced by Count Dumanoir, proved too expensive for the peasant proprietors and was therefore confined to large estates and farms until 1897, when associations were formed in the Seine-et-Marne department to enable the peasants to effect it. Large-scale drainage was carried out in Brie, Sologne, and Champagne.

Artificial manures were manufactured in France, and importation of guano began about 1855. Animal charcoal from sugar-factories all over the world was shipped to Nantes from about the same date. Chilean nitrate was not imported till 1870. Mining for phosphates near the Somme and in the Ardennes had been carried out for several years before the north African phosphates were discovered during the conquest of Tunisia in 1881. Basic slag began to be generally used after the Lorraine peasants farming near the ironworks had discovered its beneficial effect. As in England, the sale of impure and ineffective fertilizers had to be controlled by legislation.

Towards 1860 France took the lead in the production of vegetable and fodder crops, and French plant-breeders became active. Le Couteur had produced his wheat in 1823; Bon Fermier and others were developed later. Chevalier barley was another French product. Vilmorin greatly improved some strains of sugar-beet.

Between 1862 and 1892 the number of seed-drills in use rose from 9400 to 38 000, mowers from 18 800 to 52 000, and reaping-machines from 8900 to 51 000. Oil-engines were coupled to barn-machinery and steam-ploughing sets were to be seen. The reaper-binder was first used in 1885.

More attention was paid to animal breeding. Miscellaneous crossing was less favoured, and after 1860 breeders took to studying native breeds instead of seeking fine animals in England. Careful selection and better feeding developed Norman, Limousin, Flemish, and Dutch cattle, and Berrichon sheep. The

Boulonnais, Ardennes, Percheron, and Breton horses were treated in the same way. Herd-books for the principal breeds were instituted after 1880, in addition to the Durham book started in 1855. The results were increased weight and productivity of cattle, earlier maturity, more manure, and better traction.

Animal nutrition was steadily becoming more scientific. Liebig had divided aliments into three groups: nitrogenous (protein) for blood and muscle, non-nitrogenous (carbohydrates and fats) for heat, and minerals. Claude Bernard (1813–78) discussed digestion in 1847, and in 1852 Wolff, a German investigator, published nutritional tables in terms of content of protein, carbon, fat, and cellulose. By 1895 Lawes and Gilbert had calculated rations based on digestible nitrogen, fat, and carbohydrates. For ordinary purposes the starch-equivalent was regarded as a measure of the value of a feeding-stuff.

Nor should it be forgotten that Louis Pasteur (1822–95), by his work on bacteria between 1857 and 1881, set on foot a revolution in agricultural methods comparable with that which occurred in veterinary and human medicine. His investigation of anthrax, for example, pointed the way to a relief from one of the greatest scourges afflicting sheep and pigs.

The economic crisis caused by oversea competition between 1878 and 1898 stimulated an increase in the production of meat and dairy products and an expansion of the area devoted to market gardens, fruit, and flowers. In addition, more land was devoted to potatoes, roots, and fodder crops (of which the yield per acre steadily increased), while the area devoted to industrial crops such as the fibre- and oil-plants was reduced.

Belgium, divided between the heavier land in the Walloon country of the south and the lighter soils of the Flemish north, did not greatly modify its farming methods in this period. The famous Flemish husbandry (vol IV, pp 14 ff) was still practised, with the dairy cattle stall-fed and the arable under complex intensive rotations with many catch-crops.

The farmers were just as careful as their fathers in preserving their supplies of organic manure, and some used a sprinkling of artificial fertilizers as well. Beet for the sugar-factories, potatoes for starch as well as food, and barley for the distilleries were cash-crops. Towards France, in the south-east, large quantities of hops were grown. In the Ardennes a form of *Koppelwirtschaft*[1] still prevailed in the 1880s. The larger farms of the Walloon area were farmed on a mixed system, including longish rotations and larger herds of cattle, numerous horses, and comparatively few sheep. Some blood manure, superphosphate, and nitrate of soda or sulphate of ammonia were used to supplement manure.

[1] A system of rotation of crops; see p 19.

A proportion of the cattle-feed was waste from breweries, distilleries, and sugar factories, but there were everywhere fields of clover for cutting green and for hay; some beans were grown, and buckwheat was still a normal crop. Cake and meal were fed. A kind of soup of turnips, weeds, and grass, with bits of oil-cake, boiled overnight, was a popular morning feed at milking-time. As in other countries, the urban demand for liquid milk was growing, but a sufficiency of cheese and butter was still made. The dairy-work is reputed to have been somewhat slipshod, though the better farmers had adopted up-to-date systems of cooling the milk and used new designs of churns and so forth. Fine heavy horses were bred, the Flemish mare having been famous for centuries. Belgium did not, however, produce enough grain to meet her requirements.

Holland was in the same position. In spite of some arable farming, the country had not been self-sufficient in cereals for centuries, and in 1880 an Englishman thought that it might be described as wholly a dairy country. Liquid milk was sold to the towns, and cheese and butter were produced for export as well as for home consumption. Pigs were fed on the dairy waste-products. Where available, distillers' waste and brewers' grains were used as supplements to the grazing, with summer stall-feeding on green fodder of various kinds, and hay and roots in winter. The horses of Walcheren and the Dutch cows, especially those of Friesland, are world-famous, and have been exported to many countries, including Britain and the United States. Until about 1870 live cattle for slaughter were exported to England and to France, but this industry declined in face of the competition of chilled and frozen beef (ch 2). Market-gardening and flower-culture became more important. The dairy farmers were wise enough to form co-operative factories at a fairly early date, and by 1882 there were at least three in operation, at Leiden, at Winkel in north Holland, and near Hoorn. Besides seeking uniform quality in the products of such co-operative factories, some dairy farmers—for example, those of Friesland—were trying to improve their methods by adopting equipment of Danish pattern and the Swartz method of cooling milk.

The reclamation of the peat lands by well established methods continued, mainly in north and south Holland. The surface-soil and a little peat were pared off, the peat was excavated and used for fuel, and the spoil was added to a little peat at the bottom of the cut, mixed with the clay subsoil. The large-scale reclamation carried out in the east Netherlands made land available for forestry, farming, or market gardening. On the higher peat lands, a canal was usually cut as a preliminary step, and after the peat was extracted the land was brought under cultivation. Sand and large quantities of farmyard manure were mixed with the residual peaty earth. A rotation of (i) oats and clover, (ii) clover, (iii) rye, and (iv) swedes, mangolds, and potatoes was then followed. Each crop was manured. Cattle were kept for the dairy. Some farmers acquired flocks of German sheep and fattened them under cover during winter on beet-pulp, oats, linseed-meal, and so on.

Agricultural education was not as well developed in Holland and Belgium as in some other European countries, but was being expanded at the end of the century.

Denmark. Danish farmers had made steady progress from the beginning of the century, developing a system of mixed farming based on corn-growing much like that of Britain; but they proceeded along different lines. In Britain, the live-stock essential to the success of this system had largely been bred for meat. In Denmark the farmers bred for the dairy, and as a result their farming bore some resemblance to that of the Low Countries—especially after about 1860, when the Danes realized that all the world could compete with them in cereal production, but that they had a foremost place amongst the producers of milk and meat. By choosing to strengthen this tendency the Danish farmers were well equipped to meet the difficulties aroused by the sea of grain from the new countries, and they made much of agricultural co-operation in butter, cheese, and bacon factories. The first co-operative dairy factory was founded in 1875, but that at Hjedding, established in 1882, is usually regarded as the starting-point of the movement. Co-operation was probably encouraged by the fact that the farmers had the benefit of a carefully designed system of agricultural education.

The farming was of two main types, dairy husbandry and meat husbandry. On both types of farm some corn was grown. The arable was farmed on a *Koppelwirtschaft* system: bare fallow, followed by three years of corn and then three years of grass. Some farmers used very complex seed-mixtures for the ley. Other rotations comprised up to ten changes of crop. Tares and oats were sometimes grown together, and sometimes peas and oats, both mixtures being used for fodder. Most farmers used only farmyard manure in 1876, but the large farmers had already begun to use calcium superphosphate and improved seeds, such as Squarehead Master wheat (p 15).

In another respect the two types of farm resembled one another. The dairy farmers slaughtered all bull calves that they could not sell, and all heifer calves that they did not need for replacements. The meat farmers killed all heifers, and the bull calves that they did not intend to fatten. Dairy cows were fed on bran or coarse meal besides hay, straw, carrots, rape-cake, and palm-cake. Permanent pasture was not essential to the system because the dairy stock was largely wintered on spring corn. The cows were tethered on the leys in May and during the summer. Dairy work was facilitated by carefully designed utensils. Pigs were fed on the waste dairy-produce; some large White Yorkshires were used for crossing.

The meat-producing farms were in north and north-west Jutland. Many Danish cattle were sent to Schleswig and Holstein to reach maturity. These two provinces were said to be the home of *Koppelwirtschaft*, but the larger farmers had already adopted a more enlightened system in 1876, without bare fallow. Winter feed of cattle here was hay and corn with some linseed-cake. The marshes carried cattle and sheep, the latter generally crossed with Cotswolds, Leicesters, or Lincolns, and the former having a good deal of Shorthorn blood. The milk-yield was about 700 gallons a lactation.

Sweden. After the intermixed-strip system had been changed by legislation in Sweden about 1800 (as it had been a few years earlier in Denmark), the cultivation of new land was actively carried on until about 1870, and the acreage trebled. As elsewhere in Europe, cereal-growing decreased in face of world competition after that date, and dairy and animal husbandry increased. The prevailing method, as in Norway, was that of arable dairying, broadly similar to that practised in Denmark. In detail, agricultural progress in Sweden and Norway was on the same lines as elsewhere in western Europe, save that somewhat modified breeds of cattle and horses were found better suited to the climate and terrain.

Italy. The landowners and peasants of Italy were little affected by the stirring events of the *Risorgimento*, culminating in the unification of the country (1861–70). Political changes did not alter the social structure, and life remained hard for the land-worker. The agricultural output was composed of cereals, fodder crops, wine, and oil, in that order. The most important crop was wheat, though imports were required to make up the balance of consumption. Rice was important in Piedmont and was also grown in Lombardy. Maize was widely grown everywhere, while beans played a large part in the extensive agriculture of central and southern Italy. Potato-growing spread during the period, as did that of sugar-beet, but the greater expansion of the area under the last crop took place after 1900.

From about 1850 the area under hemp and flax declined, though a little flax was exported in the 1880s. Cotton was grown in Sicily, Calabria, and Apulia in 1850, but diminished in face of oversea competition as the century advanced. Oil-plants were very important in this area.

The cattle of the north had long been famous, and animal husbandry continued on the more extensive farms, above all in the Po valley. Here the dairy products were excellent. The famous Italian cheeses, such as Parmesan, had been well known for centuries. Near the large towns fresh milk and butter were sold to meet the local demand. There were some 9 m sheep in the country in 1850, Apulia being a centre of sheep-husbandry. Some merinos had been imported earlier by the king of Naples. In spite of overseas competition, shepherding did not decline in Italy as it had done in other countries, and there was a larger sheep-population in 1900 than in 1850. Goats were kept everywhere, but particularly in the south. The silk industry was ancient, but declined in the nineteenth century through disease.

At first the government of united Italy took little interest in farming, but here, as elsewhere, experimental and research stations were expanded and some attempts were made to provide agricultural education. The coming of the world market for grain caused a fall in prices from about 1870 onwards, and the difficulties which thenceforward faced the peasants caused large-scale emigration, mainly from the north in the 1880s, and from the south in the 1890s. It can hardly be said that Italian farming made sufficient progress in this critical half-century to enable the country to meet the new conditions.

VI. TROPICAL AGRICULTURE

We have seen that the development of transport enabled the farmers of the new countries of the temperate zone to send the products of their extensive farming to Europe; similarly, the products of tropical countries, most of which had long been densely populated, could be imported in far greater volume. Tea, coffee, and cocoa, drinks that were first introduced in the seventeenth century (vol III, ch 1), were regarded as necessities in the nineteenth. Sugar from the East and West Indies also was consumed in larger and larger quantities, requiring the development of substantial machinery for processing it (figure 6). The tropical sugar-cane faced the competition of the temperate sugar-beet from the beginning of the nineteenth century, but beet-sugar did not begin to oust cane-sugar until after its end. Rice, long grown in parts of Italy and Spain, was imported from the Far East. Spices were another ancient import from that area, and oil was extracted from several tropical plants. Bananas from the West Indies and elsewhere were a novel fruit, soon to be followed by others. Most tropical farming remained quite primitive in character, however, except perhaps where reformed by Chinese and white planters. The export of tea was as notable as the clippers that carried it. But the Far East was soon to be challenged by India, Ceylon, and Java. Assam began to export tea in 1869, Ceylon soon after 1875. Java had 50 000 acres under the crop in 1909. When the white planters were first able to settle the empty highland areas of Ceylon, after the highways were built, they embarked upon coffee-growing. West Indian methods were adopted by a planter arriving thence in 1837; it was anticipated that a good market would be found for all that could be grown, because the West Indian production fell owing to shortage of labour after the slaves were emancipated in 1843. Consequently there were large plantings in Ceylon, but unfortunately the coffee-plant was attacked by diseases and pests. Exports reached one million cwt in 1870, but had

FIGURE 6—*Robinson and Russell's steam sugar-cane crushing-mill, c 1850. The engine, gearing, and mill were all combined upon the same base to render the equipment movable.*

fallen to negligible quantities by 1905. It is possible that the trees were planted in unsuitable soil and unskilfully cultivated. Cinchona was an alternative crop but had been abandoned by 1900. Tea had become the new staple.

Cocoa, indigenous to tropical America, was grown there and in the West Indies during the second half of the nineteenth century. The plant was intro-duced to the Gold Coast in 1879, and a further supply was imported by the government in 1887. In 1893 about 3500 lb of cocoa was exported, and by 1900 the annual production had risen to $1\frac{1}{4}$ m lb. A native chief introduced the plant from Fernando Po into Nigeria in 1874, where a similar development took place just before the outbreak of war in 1914.

Sugar-cane cultivation produced about the same quantity of sugar as the sugar-beet. The sugar-cane was grown in widely separated parts of the tropics. It was very general throughout the West Indies and the Guiana coast of South America, and was a staple in Louisiana, Java, Queensland, and Hawaii. In 1852 there were large estates and sugar-factories in Cuba, Java, and Hawaii; but in the British West Indies small estates were the rule, each with its own factory. By the end of the century India no longer exported sugar.

Improvements in sugar-cane technique taking place during these fifty years were mainly in the manufacture, not in the growing, though some progress was made in that. Captain Bligh of the *Bounty* brought the 'Otaheite' or Bourbon sugar-cane to the West Indies in 1791, but the Demerara was the standard cane in 1892. The Otaheite failed, or suffered from what was called 'running out', from 1840 onwards in the West Indies, and a little later in Brazil and Puerto Rico. Other varieties remained healthy. New varieties of cane were bred at the government institution in Barbados in 1866, and others in Java, but, as previously mentioned, the emancipation of the slaves had rendered planters in the West Indies short of labour. The negroes had long lost any idea of peasant farming, and the landlords wanted free labourers. The planters had not modified their original ideas and made poor examples. Some of the sugar-plantations were turned into cattle-ranches, but others continued to grow sugar, encouraged for a time by a practical monopoly of the home market owing to high duties on foreign sugar. The labour shortage was also troublesome in Guiana and elsewhere. In East Africa it was supplied by labour from India, and in Queensland by 'blackbird' kanakas and some Chinese.

Bananas were first exported from Jamaica in 1870. It is thought that this fruit may have originated in India. The inhabitants of the Canary Islands were using it in 1516 as a staple in place of the barley their forefathers had cultivated, and it was well distributed in the West Indies before 1550. By 1900 it was grown in several so-called 'banana republics' in tropical Central America.

Regular imports of palm-oil were brought into Britain from West Africa through Liverpool in 1772. The oil was obtained from the wild palms that flourished in the forests. These imports had reached 30 000 tons in 1851, but from about 1860 the trade was confronted with the competition of American paraffin. The collection of the palm-oil was entirely in the hands of the natives, who were said to waste much of it in the process. A botanical garden was established in Lagos in 1887 and others followed. Experimental stations were founded in 1889–90.

Gambia dispatched its first consignment of ground-nuts in 1830. These nuts were grown partly outside Gambia, or by farmers who came into the area to grow a couple of crops and then went away again. For many years the bulk of the output went to France. The total exports reached 15 000 tons in 1859. Other oil-plants, such as the citronella of Ceylon, and many plants yielding perfumes and spices, were produced in the tropics and sub-tropics.

VII. SUMMARY

There were many technical advances in the period 1850–1900. New and more effective methods of land-drainage were developed, new and better strains of seed were bred and multiplied, animal breeding progressed, new means of providing for plant and animal nutrition and control of disease were discovered, new sources of fertilizer in the islands of Peru, in Chile, in Europe, and in Africa were exploited, and new and more effective farm implements and machinery were designed. Steam was used for traction and for driving the numerous barn-machines. Stronger animals provided better traction on some of the farms where steam-engines were not used, but in spite of these advances there were many peasant holdings all over western Europe, and small farms in Britain and parts of the United States, where simple, traditional, laborious methods involved arduous work for small returns.

The occupation of the vast, but formerly empty, spaces of North and South America and the antipodes resulted in the production of immense supplies of grain, meat, and, later, dairy produce that could readily be shipped to Europe in the steamships that gradually superseded sail. Tropical resources were developed and former luxuries from those lands became necessities for the growing industrial populations. The farmers of the Old World found themselves faced with searching competition that had previously been non-existent. Many of them, with the help of science and engineering, were able to meet the challenge successfully.

BIBLIOGRAPHY

BARRETT, O. W. 'The Tropical Crops.' Macmillan, New York. 1928.
CARRIER, ELSÉ H. 'The Pastoral Heritage of Britain, a Geographical Study.' Christophers, London. 1936.
FABER, H. 'Co-operation in Danish Agriculture' (Eng. adaptation of 'Andelsbevægelsen i Danmark' by H. HERTEL). Longmans Green, London. 1918.
'Farmers in a Changing World.' U.S. Department of Agriculture Year Book. United States Government Printing Office. 1940.
'Farming in New Zealand.' Department of Agriculture, New Zealand. 1951.
FRAUENDORFER, S. VON. 'Agrarwirtschaftliche Forschung und Agrarpolitik in Italien. Entwicklung vom 18. Jahrhundert bis zur Gegenwart.' Parey, Berlin. 1942.

FUSSELL, G. E. "The Dawn of High Farming in England." *Agric. Hist.*, **22**, 83–95, 1948.

Idem. "Home Counties Farming, 1840–1880." *Econ. J.*, **57**, 321–45, 1947.

Idem. " 'High Farming' in Southwestern England, 1840–1880." *Econ. Geogr.*, **24**, 53–73, 1948.

Idem. " 'High Farming' in the North of England, 1840–1880." *Ibid.*, **24**, 296–310, 1948.

Idem. " 'High Farming' in the West Midland Counties, 1840–1880." *Ibid.*, **25**, 159–79, 1949.

Idem. " 'High Farming' in the East Midlands and East Anglia, 1840–1880." *Ibid.*, **27**, 72–89, 1951.

GOLTZ, T. A. L. G. VON DER. 'Geschichte der deutschen Landwirtschaft', Vol. 2. Cotta, Stuttgart. 1903.

GRAS, N. S. B. 'A History of Agriculture in Europe and America' (2nd ed.). Crofts, New York. 1940.

GROMAS, R. 'Histoire agricole de la France dès origines à 1939.' Prolibro, Paris. 1948.

GULLANDER, A. 'Farmers' Co-operation in Sweden.' Crosby Lockwood, London. 1948.

JENKINS, H. M. Reports on farming in Belgium and Holland to Royal Commission on Agriculture, 1880, and various essays on Scandinavia and the Netherlands in *J. R. agric. Soc.*, 1875–87.

KRZYMOWSKI, R. 'Geschichte der deutschen Landwirtschaft.' Ulmer, Stuttgart. 1939.

LONG, J. 'Canadian Agriculture. A Report of a Visit to the Dominion in 1893.' London. 1894.

MACDONALD, J. 'Food from the Far West, or American Agriculture.' London. 1878.

MASEFIELD, G. B. 'A Short History of Agriculture in the British Colonies.' Oxford University Press, London. 1950.

MOORE, O. K. 'Argentine Farming and the Farm Trade.' U.S. Department of Agriculture, Foreign Agricultural Reports, No. 25. United States Government Printing Office. 1948.

PROTHERO, R. E. (LORD ERNLE). 'English Farming Past and Present.' Longmans, London. 1932.

SEEBOHM, M. E. 'The Evolution of the English Farm.' Allen & Unwin, London. 1952.

SNELLER, Z. W. 'Geschiedenis van de Nederlandse landbouw, 1795–1940.' Wolters, Groningen. 1951.

TROW-SMITH, R. 'English Husbandry.' Faber, London. 1951.

WADHAM, S. M. and WOOD, G. L. 'Land Utilization in Australia.' Melbourne University Press, Melbourne. 1939.

WALLACE, R. 'Special Report on the Agricultural Resources of Canada.' Ottawa. 1894.

WATSON, J. A. S. and HOBBS, MAY E. 'Great Farmers.' Faber, London. 1937.

WILLIS, J. C. 'Agriculture in the Tropics.' University Press, Cambridge. 1909.

Idem. 'Recent Progress in Tropical Agriculture. . . . A Course of Lectures given at Harvard University in 1909.' 'Ceylon Observer' Press, Colombo. 1910.

2

MANAGEMENT AND PRESERVATION OF FOOD

T. N. MORRIS

1. FOOD MANAGEMENT

MOST raw foods soon deteriorate under ordinary conditions unless they have a low moisture-content, like grains and pulses; or firm flesh and skins, like apples; or hard, dry shells, like nuts. The chief causes of this deterioration are moulds, yeasts, bacteria, and spontaneous or oxidative chemical changes in the foods themselves, usually accompanied by physical changes. Other causes—which will not be discussed here, although they are often important—are infestation by insects and destruction by rats, mice, and other animals. For this reason mankind has always been faced with the task of preparing and preserving foods and, without fully understanding the problems, has evolved various empirical methods for meeting them. The scope of this task has, however, been increased since the industrial revolution, with its urbanization, generally accompanied by a rapid increase in population, especially in western Europe,[1] the United States, and in those countries of the British Commonwealth whose people are mainly of European stock.

This development has meant that while the proportion of people with direct access to the land and to the means of providing themselves with the bulk of their individual and family food-requirements has progressively diminished, the total number of mouths to be fed has increased. Thus, to take an extreme example, the total population of England in 1801 was just under 9 m but had doubled by 1851. At this stage, the beginning of our period, rural and urban populations were about equal, and only about a quarter of the grain required for our bread was imported. By 1901 the population was $32\frac{1}{2}$ m, the increase being almost entirely urban: in fact, some rural areas showed a decrease.

The grading, processing, preserving, packaging, and storage of foods for distribution in convenient forms, and with their wholesomeness and nutritive values unimpaired, have recently been described collectively as food management, and, whereas such management was formerly done in households and small establishments, it has now been more and more transferred to large factories. This applies to the handling of raw foods, including milk, and to traditional

---

[1] France is an exception.

processes like bacon- and ham-curing and the manufacture of milk-products (chiefly cheese and butter), as well as to the more modern processes like canning, refrigeration, and dehydration which, from the first, have required special plant and equipment.

In modern food-factories scientific research and mechanization are as fully employed as in any other industrial activity, and so varied is the nature of foods that their study has now assumed the stature of a special science, food science— a composite of chemistry, physics, biology, physiology, and nutrition. Food technology is, therefore, essentially the application of food science to food management, especially, although not necessarily, on a large scale. It involves not only the discovery of new techniques and processes but the operation of traditional methods with more complete understanding and control.

In 1850 food technology in this sense was embryonic; the Great Exhibition of 1851 probably marks the beginning of an era. Apart from the facts that foreign trade had to some extent increased the variety of foods available, while improved agricultural methods at home had made it possible to produce fresh meat all the year round instead of slaughtering most of the cattle in the autumn and preserving the meat in salt, food management was more or less the same as it had been for a long time. Meat would be brought into the towns on the hoof and slaughtered; milling was still largely carried out in small or moderately sized country mills for which the motive power was provided by wind or water; much bread was baked at home or in small bake-houses; cows for milking were kept in and around large towns; and many hostelries as well as private householders and farmers brewed their own beer. The canning of food, although invented during the Napoleonic wars, had not yet made any impact on the ordinary civilian population, being used only for the armed forces and by explorers. Mechanical refrigeration, although its principles were known, had not been applied to foods.

On the other hand, considerable progress had been made in inorganic and organic chemistry and in physics, especially during the 1830s and 40s. There were also intense activity and widespread interest in biological studies. Steam-engines had given great impetus to the construction of other machines; railways were being laid down; steam-navigation had begun; and many factories were being built. The United States of America and the British colonies had reached a point where they could export food in return for manufactures (ch 1), and the corn laws which regulated the importation of wheat into this country in relation to home supplies and in favour of home producers had been repealed (p 10).

In food technology, however, empiricism still ruled. Food management, in many of its branches, is a very ancient art. The properties of our foods are fixed by Nature, and practical experience through the centuries had taught men how to deal with them in ways which have to a great degree satisfied their tastes as well as their bodily needs. Fortunately, as practical experience and researches on vitamins have shown, these two are linked together. What looks good, smells good, and tastes good is usually good nutritionally. This being so, it is only natural that the chief emphasis, particularly at first, was on applying mechanical aids and on devising equipment suitable for adapting well tried methods and recipes to large-scale production, all of which is hardly food technology in the true sense. This was true even with the newer processes like canning and refrigeration when once the conditions for reasonable success had been ascertained empirically: in short, it was the engineer and the practical man who at first held chief sway. Indeed, science was hardly in a position to take the lead, for the foremost scientists of the time were mainly preoccupied with building up a body of scientific information for its own sake rather than for the sake of its immediate practical value.

During the last quarter of the nineteenth century the City and Guilds of London Institute for the Advancement of Technical Education conducted examinations in scientific subjects, and technical schools and colleges began to function after the Technical Instruction Acts of 1889. Before this, however, the [Royal] Society of Arts had done much to encourage the application of scientific knowledge through lectures and discussions. There were also bodies like the Institute of Brewing, founded in 1886 largely for scientific research into the brewing-processes, and the National Association of Master Bakers and Confectioners of Great Britain and Ireland, who employed chemists and consultants. Before 1900, however, few, if any, food firms had their own laboratories or employed chemists on their permanent staffs, and it was not until after the first world war that research into food problems was undertaken on a systematic scale, either by government departments or by associations of food manufacturers.

Since then, food technologists with a training in the natural sciences, and particularly in chemistry, have more and more assumed managerial status, and every food firm of repute has its laboratory. But in 1900 empiricism and rule of thumb were by no means dethroned, and even in 1911, in their monumental work 'The Technology of Bread-making', W. and W. C. Jago, after quoting a personal communication from a leading flour-miller to the effect that he found laboratory work 'one of the absolute essentials for successful and economic operation and for the maintenance of a uniform product of high quality', wrote of chemists as constituting a 'new wheel in the machinery which is not keenly welcomed by those responsible for its general running', that is, by mill foremen and others. They urged patience and sympathetic support on the part of employers and tact on the part of the chemists.

After this general survey we turn to the various processes for dealing with foods. These processes may be classed roughly as 'traditional' and 'modern'. The former comprise drying in sun and wind; salt-curing and smoking, sometimes combined with drying; pickling in vinegar or in salt and vinegar, sometimes with added sugar; preservation in sugar; and preservation by acidic or alcoholic fermentation as in cheese, sauerkraut, wines, and beers. In all these processes the finished products are usually very different from the raw materials in appearance and flavour, but the treatment they have received not only preserves them but renders them more attractive to the palate.

The 'modern' processes are canning, refrigeration, dehydration (that is, drying under scientifically controlled conditions in specially constructed plant by heat derived from fuel), and preservation by means of toxic chemicals. In these processes, success is usually measured by the degree of resemblance of the finished article to the fresh, raw material or to some form in which the raw material is normally eaten after being cooked or otherwise prepared.

The foregoing, it should be noted, are all, essentially, methods for preserving the more perishable foods; that is to say, they aim either at suppressing or destroying or excluding the various spoilage-agents. In addition, we have ancient processes like the milling of cereals, the brewing of beer, bread-making, and the making of cakes, biscuits, and confectionery. The raw materials in these cases are already well preserved: the processes are designed to bring them into a suitable condition for eating or drinking.

II. FLOUR-MILLING

It will be most convenient to start our more detailed survey with the older processes and to close with those whose development falls entirely, or almost entirely, within our period.

In 1850 stone-milling was the only method used in England, and, at about this time, many improvements in driving, balancing, and cooling the mill-stones were introduced. Bolting-cloths of silk gauze were also substituted for those of linen and wool for separating the finest flour. In the English style of milling, known as 'low milling', the mill-stones were in close contact from the first, and grinding was one continuous process. This yielded a fine, reasonably white flour with good English wheats, which have a soft endosperm (85 per cent of the grain) and tough bran-coats ($13\frac{1}{2}$ per cent). Over-grinding, or the use of inferior wheats, could lead to inclusion of bran and breaking up of the starch grains, and such flour made a dark loaf which was also heavy and sticky owing to the action on the starch of diastatic enzymes released from the embryo. With the hard, flinty wheats of Hungary and North America, in which both bran-coats and endosperm are brittle, low milling also gave a dark flour full of bran particles. In all stone-milling, the embryo and scutellum, which constitute $1\frac{1}{2}$ per cent of the grain and contain the wheat-oil and most of the vitamin B_1, find their way into the flour and so into the bread. If kept too long, however, stone-milled flour tends to go rancid owing to oxidation of the oil.

On the continent of Europe, and particularly in Hungary, the problem of brittleness was overcome by 'high milling', in which the stones are at first set far enough apart merely to break or 'end' the wheat and are brought closer together in stages, the products of grinding being sifted away at each stage. This process yielded fine white flours which were much in demand.

About 1840, roller-milling was introduced into Hungary and began to supersede 'high milling'. Roller-milling is carried out by passing the grain between pairs of special spirally fluted rollers arranged in a series and followed by pairs of plain rollers. As in high milling, the grinding is in stages ('breaks') and it is possible to produce five or six different qualities of flour from the same wheat. The net result is that the bran-coats are obtained practically free from flour. The embryo and scutellum, being of a different texture from the endosperm, also appear as a separate fraction and are thus lost to the bread. Roller-milling was rapidly adopted in the United States and the flour thus manufactured, being whiter than that produced from stone-milled English wheat, became popular and was soon imported into England in large quantities. It is generally 'stronger' than flour made from English wheat, that is, it forms a stiffer dough, absorbs more water (thus yielding more loaves per sack), and, being free from oil and from the diastatic enzymes of the embryo, it does not become rancid and malted; usually, also, it makes taller and better 'piled' loaves.

Popular demand, and the fact that England was becoming less and less self-supporting in wheat, forced English millers who could afford to make the change to adopt roller-milling: those who could not went bankrupt or were absorbed by larger concerns. This process began in the late 1870s, and by 1891 J. Harrison Carter, in a lecture to the [Royal] Society of Arts, could show that roller-milling, cleaning, and purifying were very far advanced in this country, and claimed that British mills were the best in the world. Apart from continual improvements in cleaning and dressing (sifting) and in blending wheats in accordance with bakers' requirements, there were no major changes in milling operations between 1890 and 1900, and it was only after the turn of the century that patents began to be taken out for bleaching flour and adding 'improvers' to increase its strength. It had, however, long been known that alum had this effect and it had been claimed that some flours could not be made into bread without it; but the quantities required are such that its use was forbidden in Britain (1875 Food Act).

III. BREAD-MAKING

Changes in milling and the importation of foreign wheats have naturally affected the quality of bread and, from about 1880 onwards, bakers were preoccupied with obtaining flours suitable for their various products. For bread, they wanted flour of a strength that would enable them to produce high, well-piled loaves with a fine white crumb. So far as actual baking operations were concerned, even up to 1900 mechanization was unknown in the smaller bakehouses but, in large town bake-houses, sponge-setting and kneading machines appeared about 1850 and were adopted in other countries. Automatic machines for dividing, weighing, and moulding the loaves before baking presented greater difficulties and came much later. About 1850, also in large bakeries, the Perkins oven, heated by steam-pipes, began to supersede the older types of coal- or coke-heated ovens. These steam-heated ovens, which are cleaner and afford better control of temperature, still persist with minor modifications. One improvement has been the introduction of a draw-plate to form the bottom of the oven; this plate can be drawn in and out for charging and emptying, and is most useful when the oven is to be charged with a homogeneous batch of material. Formerly, charging and emptying had always been carried out by means of a long-handled flat shovel or peel. This took longer, and, to avoid uneven baking, the front of the oven was usually heated to a higher temperature than the back.

In addition to research on the strength of flours and the devising of strength-tests which could be carried out by bakers, much was done to improve the purity and the activity of the yeast employed and to make it available in convenient forms. This yeast, which was originally imported mainly as distillers' yeast from Holland and France, at first contained starch, added as a drying-agent and as an aid in consolidating it. With improved methods of manufacture and purification the difficulty of compressing yeast into blocks was overcome, and most of the yeast on the market at the end of our period consisted of yeast cells only.

IV. SALT-CURING AND SMOKING

The methods for preserving meat and fish by curing with salt and smoking are very ancient and widespread (vol I, ch 11); in fact, directions for curing bacon dating from Roman times read very much like some of the older recipes for dry-salting in this country. In these there is no mention of saltpetre, which was, however, included in the salting-mixture before 1850. Its use in the west probably dates from the early days of the British connexion with India, where it occurs as an efflorescence on the surface of the soil. The pink colour of bacon is due to the use of saltpetre, which no doubt gained esteem for that reason.

Before the great expansion of the bacon-curing industry that occurred in the late 1920s most of the bacon produced in Great Britain was dry-salted, except for the Ayrshire cure, which was effected by soaking the pork in a tank of brine. Tank-curing has always been favoured in Denmark as being the quickest process and the one most suitable for large-scale work; it has now become almost universal.

Before 1850, bacon- and ham-curing had been restricted to the cold time of the year and all bacon was hard-cured, that is, it contained about 9 per cent of salt, more being in the lean than in the fat. This was necessary for its preservation, but about 1850 bacon began to be cured all the year round in cellars cooled by ice, and later (about 1880) by mechanical refrigeration. This made possible the production of mild-cured and leaner bacon, containing only about 5 per cent of salt, all the year round, thus suiting the general taste and also the nutritional requirements of townspeople leading sedentary lives, for whom much fat is unnecessary.

Up to about 1925 there had been no systematic investigation of bacon-curing in this country and little elsewhere; in 1900 everything was traditional, although to a great extent organized on a factory scale.

V. DAIRY PRODUCTS

Before dealing with dairy products individually, mention should be made of events affecting all of them. In the 1870s, when the great depression struck British agriculture—especially corn-growing, which had hitherto been its mainstay (p 10)—many farmers turned their attention to such activities as dairying and fruit-growing for jam-making, which seemed to offer better prospects. In 1876, therefore, the first annual Dairy Show was held in London and, at the same time, the British Dairy Farmers' Association was founded. These two institutions have done much to stimulate the dairy industry by demonstrating new methods and appliances and spreading the latest information on all aspects of the subject.

Liquid milk. The main problem presented by milk is to distribute it before it goes sour. Before 1860 the transport of milk from country to town was just beginning, following the growth of the railways; also, so far as England was concerned, the result of the cattle plague of 1865 (p 12) was to stimulate the milk-traffic, for the plague compelled the dairymen of London and other large towns to seek milk all over the country. The invention at about this time of the refrigerator, a form of water-cooler by means of which the milk was cooled at or near the place of origin, greatly helped to ensure its arrival in good condition. For a long time, milk was delivered to dairymen in large cans of tinned steel plate; these were satisfactory until the tin coating was worn off, but about 1900 there began to be a demand for pasteurized milk in bottles.

Pasteurizing was designed primarily to prevent the spread of tuberculosis, of which milk can be a carrier. Research in America showed that heating milk for 20 minutes at 140° F in a closed pasteurizer gave a good margin of safety without ruining the flavour and the creaming-properties. Cream after pasteurization can still be made into butter.

Butter. Probably the greatest advance in the mechanical part of butter-making during our period was the invention by the Swedish engineer and scientist Gustav de Laval, in 1877, of the centrifugal cream-separator. These machines came into use about 1880 and were quickly adopted in the larger dairies, where they effected enormous savings in labour and space. They were further improved by von Bechtolsheim in 1890 by the addition of the so-called Alfa disks arranged one above another within the bowl. These had the effect of dividing the contents of the bowl into a number of shallow layers, thus giving more rapid and complete separation of the cream. Another mechanical advance was the use of a centrifuge instead of the 'butter-worker' for removing whey from butter. This was considered to improve the grain, besides being quicker in action.

Before the arrival of the centrifugal cream-separator, the milk was allowed to stand in large shallow pans of porcelain, tinned iron, or enamelled iron until all the cream had risen. The cream was transferred to a cream-crock by means of a perforated dish or skimmer and allowed to stand for one to three days to ripen before being churned. Butter made from unripened cream is insipid, and by the end of our period culture-starters were being used for butter as well as for cheese (p 34).

On the strictly technological side, perhaps the most important advance was the introduction about 1890 of a quick and easy test whereby the content of butter-fat in milk can be determined in a few minutes. This was first proposed by S. M. Babcock of the Wisconsin Agricultural Experiment Station and was improved later by N. Gerber of Zürich. These tests have been extremely useful both for evaluating milk and as a safeguard against adulteration with water.

Cheese. Most of the local cheeses existed long before 1850, and the methods for making them were entirely traditional. Even in the same locality quality could vary greatly, depending on the skill and judgement of the makers and on their adherence to well tried formulae.

One of the most famous makers of 'cheddar' cheese[1] in the 1850s was Joseph Harding of Marksbury, Somerset, who was induced to teach his methods to producers in Ayrshire. Harding's most important rule was to use day-old whey as a starter for the next batch before adding the rennet to produce curd, and he succeeded in making Scottish cheddar famous.

It is remarkable that the factory system made no headway in the west of England, the home of true Cheddar cheese; yet the factory-made cheese of Canada, the United States, and Australia was all of the cheddar type. In 1889 R. J. Drummond was engaged by the Ayrshire Dairy Association to teach them the Canadian methods. By this time there was some knowledge of bacteriology, and Drummond was critical of Harding's method of always adding the sour-whey starter. He considered that not only was this often done when the milk was already sour enough, but that it was a method by which faulty batches could reproduce themselves. He also criticized the methods of temperature control and of measuring the quantity of rennet added. Drummond used a standard rennet, and did not at first use a starter but depended entirely on securing the correct acidity for ripening by controlling the temperature of the milk while maturing. To determine ripeness he relied on the hot-iron test, which was carried out by applying a hot iron to a piece of curd from which the whey had been squeezed. If conditions were right the curd would stick to the iron and, when pulled apart, would draw out into long silky threads. It was not until 1899 that the acidity was determined by titration.

Careful studies of the ripening of cheese began in Ayrshire in 1895. These arose through an investigation of cases of discoloration of Scottish cheddar by Drummond and J. R. Campbell, of the Glasgow Technical College, who discovered that discoloration was caused by invasion of the curd by foreign bacteria during ripening. They prevented the trouble by using pure cultures of lactic acid organisms as starters before adding the rennet.

While this discovery of how to suppress undesirable by desirable bacteria was valuable because it showed how to secure correct conditions for ripening, it did not prove that the lactic acid bacteria were responsible for ripening. Later studies by Babcock and Russell in America indicated that enzymes rather than bacteria

---

[1] So called because it is made by the same method as that used to make cheese in the Cheddar district of Somerset. Genuine farmhouse Cheddar is now difficult to procure, but is different from, and superior to, the factory or creamery cheddars.

are the main ripening-agents. In 1897 they found in milk an enzyme that could act upon casein to give decomposition products similar to those occurring in ripened cheese. They also found that the pepsin in rennet hastens ripening through its proteolytic action. These enzymes, unlike the bacteria, could work at temperatures ranging from 25° to 45° F, although at these low temperatures the resulting flavour was milder than usual. It became more pronounced, however, when the cheeses were transferred to ordinary temperatures. This is in line with the old practice of ripening 'cheddar' cheeses in caves where possible. It is said that genuine Cheddar cheese used to be ripened in the caves for which the village is famous and from which its name is derived.

Other milk-products. In addition to butter and cheese there are evaporated milk, dried whole milk, dried skim-milk, milk-sugar from the whey, and the industrially useful casein. All these products were being manufactured during this period.

The condensed-milk industry was established at about the same time as the factory system of butter- and cheese-making, although a British patent had been taken out as early as 1835 by Newton, and in 1849 E. N. Horsford had prepared condensed milk with the addition of lactose. In 1853, after ten years of experimentation, Gail Borden of Litchfield County, Connecticut, applied for a patent for evaporating milk in a vacuum, the air being excluded from the beginning to the end of the process. This was granted in 1856 and, after two failures, a factory was started by Borden in New York State in 1860. Borden advertised his product as 'fresh country milk from which the water is nearly all evaporated and nothing added. The Committee of the Academy of Medicine recommend it as an article that for purity, durability and economy is unequalled in the annals of the milk trade.'

The process was rather crude and the product imperfect, but it was found extremely valuable during the American Civil War and from that time its manufacture expanded rapidly. Borden also packed a sweetened condensed milk as early as 1856, and before the 1880s this was the only form of condensed milk packed in hermetically sealed cans. It is not sterile microbiologically, but contains sufficient sugar to preserve it. The unsweetened condensed milk, which was sold open, like ordinary milk, was first sterilized in cans by J. B. Meyenberg, a native of Switzerland, where a factory had been built in 1866 by the Anglo-Swiss Condensed Milk Company. Working for this firm, Meyenberg experimented from 1880 to 1883 and finally succeeded in producing a satisfactory product by sterilizing condensed milk in a revolving pressure-cooker, for which he took out a patent in 1884. In 1885 he emigrated to America where, after a short time at the Helvetia Milk Condensing Company in Illinois, he promoted numerous factories in the Middle West and on the Pacific Coast. By 1900, evaporated milk was becoming an important product. It still had a 'cooked' flavour, however, and up to 1900 the vacuum pan (figure 7) was the only type of evaporator used.

Dried milk. The first patent for dried milk powder was granted in England in 1855. In this process sodium carbonate was added to fresh milk, which

was evaporated in an open steam-jacketed pan to a dough-like consistency. After adding cane-sugar, the dough was pressed to a ribbon between rollers, dried further, and ground into powder. The alkali was added to make the casein more soluble, the sugar to cause granulation in the final stages. A later improvement was the use of vacuum pans instead of open pans for evaporating the milk. Dried skim-milk, made in this way, keeps better than dried whole milk.

Malted milk is a popular form of dried milk invented in 1883 and first marketed in 1887. It consists of milk with a proportion of malt-extract and wheat-flour.

Dried milk without any additions appeared on the American market in 1898 and patents were taken out for various types of film (roller) driers at about this time. Spray driers soon followed, and with these, and improved methods of packaging, the quality of milk powders has continually improved.

FIGURE 7—*Vacuum pan for condensing milk,* c *1890.*

VI. BISCUITS

The manufacture of biscuits is much more of an exercise in the handling of materials on a large scale than anything we have considered so far. There is little or no question here of deviating from a recipe that has been decided upon by small scale trials, or of the control of a biological process as in bread-making, or of exploring unfamiliar fields as in canning and refrigeration: what has become familiar and acceptable to the public taste must be reproduced accurately year in year out, no matter what the scale of production.

Advances in the industry have consisted in increasing the efficiency and scale of manufacture while maintaining standards, and in devising novel and attractive recipes, this last being more the province of the skilled chef than that of the food technologist—although it is not always easy to say where the one begins and the other ends.

During the fifty years of this period there were introduced machines for mixing the ingredients and preparing the dough, which then passes to rolling-out machines bringing it to the correct thickness, and after that to machines which cut it to the required sizes and shapes and impress patterns, lettering, and so forth. The shaped and cut pieces, generally loaded on trays, then pass at a controlled rate in a continuous stream through ovens heated to the appropriate temperature, and thence to packing-rooms.

In such a process the uniformity of the product depends entirely on maintaining uniform conditions and using uniform materials. The flour for biscuits is best derived from soft English wheats and is of low extraction; much skill is required in choosing and blending it. The other materials—butter, sugar, milk, and so on—must also be up to specification and, as we have seen already, it was only towards the end of our period that human judgement in these matters and human controls of mechanism began to be assisted by tests in the laboratory and by means of instruments and automatic appliances.

VII. PICKLES, RELISHES, SAUCES, AND SUGAR PRESERVES

In 1850 such preserves as these were generally made in the home, except for those prepared on a comparatively small scale by a few high-class firms. The products of the latter included certain pickles and sauces which were often based on famous old recipes or on the masterpieces of distinguished chefs, and were packed in elaborate and ornamental containers. Later, as world conditions changed and suitable raw materials became more readily available, preserves were gradually produced on a larger scale and at more popular prices.

As already mentioned (p 10), the factory production of sugar preserves received a great impetus in the 1870s, when corn-growing and general farming declined and hard-pressed farmers were forced to look for other sources of income, such as fruit-growing and dairying. They were indeed advised to do so by political leaders like Gladstone, and it is no accident that some of the first jam-factories were started by ardent Liberal nonconformists. They found their customers largely in the industrial areas, particularly in the north of England, and, as these grew, so their business expanded.

At first, their manufacturing activities were largely confined to the season of fruit-harvest: they sold in the winter what they produced in the summer and autumn. But in order to maintain permanent staffs, they soon turned to additional lines such as orange marmalade (first manufactured by a Scottish firm in 1797), mincemeat, Christmas puddings, table jellies, lemon curd, and salad creams, and finally, near the end of our period, to canned fruits. They also preserved quantities of fruit-pulp, by heat-treatment in large stone jars and barrels which could be sealed, for jam-making out of season, although jam made from such pulps is seldom as palatable as that made from fresh fruit.

As with biscuits, these products were either based on well tried recipes similar to those used in the kitchen, or on demonstrations and information provided by consultants and by persons who were anxious to sell their ideas and experience or to secure permanent employment. Although by 1900 most of the firms making these products had their own staffs of trained engineers and were well advanced in mechanization, very few, if any, employed trained chemists or possessed laboratories where they could test their raw materials or finished products and carry out investigations and experiments. Makers of excellent jams had probably never heard of pectin, the substance in fruits that causes jams and jellies to set, but they knew by experience the kinds and conditions of fruits which would make the best jam; and that strawberries and raspberries, however good, usually needed to be fortified with juice obtained by boiling gooseberries or apples. In making their jams, the jam-boilers had nothing to guide them in choosing the right moment to stop boiling, except their observation of the changes in the appearance of the jam as it boiled, and the manner in which it dripped from their long-handled metal spoon or skimmer. Nevertheless, so proficient did they become that, when jam-boiling thermometers were introduced, about 1900, to indicate when the correct concentration of sugar for maximum jelly-formation had been reached, they often preferred to trust their customary methods and were seldom wrong. In fact, the thermometer could lead them astray through sudden changes in the barometric pressure, unless such changes were allowed for.

VIII. MODERN PROCESSES OF PRESERVATION: CANNING

The modern processes of food preservation have contributed far more than the older ones to the development of modern ways of life and, moreover, to the waging of war on the modern scale. With the exception of dehydration, which did not approach perfection until the second world war, these processes all became established and important entirely within the period here considered; hence we are entitled to treat them in somewhat more detail than those which were already established, although not on mass-production lines.

By 1850 two considerable advances had been made on the original technique of François Appert (1750?–1841), the Paris confectioner who first preserved many different kinds of foods by enclosing them in containers which could be sealed hermetically and heated (*appertisation*). Appert filled glass bottles and jars with the food he wished to preserve, corked them loosely, and immersed them in a bath of hot water for periods found by experience to be long enough, after which the corks were hammered in tightly and luted with suitable material.

The most important advance was the adaptation in England in 1811 of Appert's methods to tin-plate canisters (cans). The first patent for using tin-plate was taken out in 1810 by Peter Durand (B.P. no 3372), but there is no evidence that he ever took part in the business of canning. Others did, however, and by 1814 Donkin and Hall were supplying vegetable soups and preserved meats to the Royal Navy. Canned food had been taken on Parry's third Polar voyage in 1825 (figure 8 and plate 4 B). A typical canning factory of the 1850s is seen in figure 9.

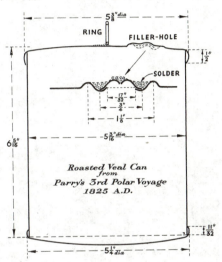

FIGURE 8—*Veal can, seen in section, taken on Parry's third Polar voyage, 1825.*

The second advance was in cooking cans containing meat at temperatures higher than that of boiling water. This was achieved in two ways: by means of autoclaves and by the use of the calcium chloride bath. Appert himself used autoclaves, but it is not known whether he was the first to do so. Judging from the reliability of their products, it is also possible that some of the early English canners may have used them, but, according to the official catalogue of the 1851 Exhibition, the firm of J. H. Gamble had adopted the method of cooking in a bath of calcium chloride at temperatures above that of boiling water, which had been patented in 1841 by S. Goldner (B.P. no 8873) and J. Wertheimer (B.P. no 8874). The early autoclaves were primitive and dangerous, being merely enlarged Papin digesters,[1] and therefore liable to blow up. The explosions of over-filled cans that occurred in the chloride bath were generally less serious (but see p 41): hence this method became established and was preferred by many canners until near the end of our period, despite the fact that, in 1854, Raymond Chevallier Appert, the successor of François, had fitted pressure-gauges on autoclaves. These were

[1] Papin in 1681 first cooked food in an iron pot, called a *marmite* (saucepan), the cover of which could be clamped on to withstand moderate pressure. It was fitted with a safety-valve.

soon followed by safety-valves and thermometers, and in 1874 autoclaves were attached to independent boilers.

Gamble's process is thus described in the Exhibition catalogue:

The process consists in placing the partially cooked provisions into tin canisters, with a little bouillon or juice of the meat, then soldering on the covers, which have a small hole perforated therein. The tins after this are immersed to a great portion of their depth in a

FIGURE 9—*Interior of a Houndsditch cannery, 1852.*

saline bath heated above the boiling point of water, and left therein until the air has been expelled as completely as possible by the air generated within them; the hole in the cover is now hermetically closed with a little solder, the tin being momentarily touched with a damp sponge to stop the egress of steam. The minute portion of oxygen still remaining in the tins enters into combination with the animal or vegetable matter at the induced temperature and thus further change is prevented. After sealing of the tins, they are submitted to the ordeal of the testing room, heated to a temperature above 100° F; if putrefaction takes place, the generated gases burst the tins, but those which pass uninjured remain perfectly good.

There is no indication here that heating in the bath was continued after closure with solder, but this is no doubt an omission on the part of the reporter (Sir Warren de la Rue), as Wertheimer, in his patent of 1841, had described a method of closing the hole while heating was in progress, and Goldner states that he continued heating for some time after soldering. This is also confirmed in a description following an illustration of a London cannery in the 'Illustrated London News' of 31 January 1852, where it is stated that 'after soldering the steamhole, the canister is not immediately removed from the source of heat, but its contents are raised under pressure to a degree of temperature considerably above the boiling point'. What follows has a somewhat gruesome humour:

This last operation is essential to success and by no means devoid of danger. We well remember having recited to us the relation of an operator who was killed most ridiculously and ignobly by a boiled turkey. The canister in which the bird had been soldered was exposed to this process of heating under pressure and steam was generated beyond the power of the canister to endure. As a natural consequence, the canister burst, the dead turkey sprang from his coffin of tinplate and killing the cook forthwith, made him a candidate for a leaden one. . . . Now on account of the air soldered into lead coffins, their contents decompose, gas is generated and the coffin sides bulge out. Well, the sides of a canister of preserved meat will bulge out too if any decomposition is going on within and by this infallible sign may a good canister be known from a bad one. . . . This takes time, hence it is far from a safe plan to purchase these preserved provisions immediately after they have been prepared.

There was at this time scarcely an inkling of the part played by micro-organisms in putrefaction, and of the ability of some of them to survive the conditions necessary for what would normally be considered adequate cooking; thus, notwithstanding the improvements in canning mentioned above, the period around 1850 was notable for some disasters. In 1845, Goldner, who canned foods in Moldavia as well as in England, had been accepted as a contractor to the Board of Admiralty; he obtained an order for 22 000 pints of soup, 5500 lb of vegetables, and 31 000 lb of meat for Franklin's expedition with H.M. ships *Erebus* and *Terror*. Being in danger of failing to fulfil this contract within the agreed time, Goldner sought and obtained permission to supply the soups in larger canisters than those specified. Much of this consignment went bad, and later inquiry by a royal commission showed that the change of can had been ill advised. Possibly the failure was partly attributable to hasty preparation, but it is significant that it was at this time that containers capable of holding more than 6 lb first began to be used. In 1849 there were further adverse reports, and in the following year 111 108 lb of Goldner's tinned meat was condemned. A correlation was traced between the introduction of large tins (9–32 lb) and the sudden increase in condemnation, and although the trouble was then ascribed to the difficulty of eliminating air from such large containers and to inadequate cooking, there is now no doubt that Goldner's process did not sterilize the innermost layers of the meat.[1]

It was, in fact, not until the work of Pasteur (1822–95) in 1861 and later that it became possible to establish the canning process on a truly scientific basis; but progress in assimilating this new knowledge was slow. Judging from a report on preserved meat made to the [Royal] Society of Arts in 1884 by J. J. Manley, interested parties were still arguing as to whether the presence of oxygen was the 'sole cause of putrefaction', or whether it is caused by 'microscopic germs'. The author gave it as his opinion that, whichever view was correct, 'it may be taken for granted that, without a perfect expulsion of air and the creation of a perfect vacuum, preservation is not effected'. As A. J. Howard has remarked: 'The early canners [meaning those operating up to 1890 or even later] had little knowledge of bacteriology and probably even less regard for it. Their sterilization methods were arrived at entirely by trial and error and losses due to spoilage [by micro-organisms] were often heavy.'

In 1895 there were important developments in the United States of America. There, Appert's methods of packing food in glass had been introduced in 1819, and tinned cans came into use only in 1840. Thus in the early days America lagged behind Europe; in fact, she even lagged behind Australia, where meat was being canned and exported to England in 1847. From the time of the Civil War, however, canning in America made rapid strides, and the great meat-packing factories in Chicago and elsewhere began to function in 1868 (p 4). Considerable advances had been made in bacteriology, and when H. L. Russell of the University of Wisconsin investigated the cause of the 'blowing' of cans of peas, he showed that the 'blown' cans contained gas-producing bacteria which had not been destroyed by the cooking process. He further demonstrated that they could be killed by longer times of processing and higher temperatures.

Two years later (1897) S. C. Prescott and W. L. Underwood of the Massachusetts Institute of Technology made systematic studies of the bacterial flora of blown cans and identified many of the organisms concerned. They also compared the merits of autoclaves with those of baths for the process of cooking, much to the advantage of the former. By placing maximum-registering thermometers in the centres of cans of various sizes filled with different products, they were able to ascertain the rate of heat-penetration into solid packs and so to identify the types of foods for which cooking at high temperatures in autoclaves was essential.

[1] The article from the 'Illustrated London News' quoted above may well have been inspired by Goldner, as it ends by asking whether Goldner's cans may not have gone bad because they were badly stowed and became perforated from the outside.

They were also able to specify times and temperatures for cooking which, while not excessive, would allow a sufficient margin of safety from the risk of bacterial spoilage. In general, they found that for products of high acidity, like fruits, the boiling-water bath is sufficient; products of low acidity, like meats, vegetables, and fish, were found to require autoclave cooking at 240–250° F for times depending on the size of the cans and the nature of the pack.

Similar work, concentrated on the canning of lobsters, was carried out at about the same time by Macphail in Canada, and the first private laboratory specializing in canners' problems was opened in the United States by E. Duckwall in 1905. Thus the end of our period can be said to mark the beginning of that scientific control of the canning process which has since rendered negligible the risks of waste and loss and, more serious, of food-poisoning. After many years, canned foods have been freed from the suspicion with which they were once regarded, often justifiably.

FIGURE 10—*Interior of tinsmith's workshop, mid nineteenth century.*

The history of canning is, to a great extent, bound up with the history of the evolution of the tinned can, without which the usefulness of the process would have been enormously restricted. There is no material other than tin-plate that is at once so readily available and so amenable to rapid fabrication into containers which are light, very strong, easy to seal hermetically, resistant to external corrosion and, with suitable precautions in the case of certain products (p 44), to internal corrosion, and non-poisonous. Its only rivals are glass, which is brittle and has to be rather thick and heavy to withstand handling and processing, and aluminium, which is less robust than tin-plate and not suitable for acid foods.

The early cans were all hand-made; a tinsmith's shop of the 1860s is seen in figure 10. Sheets of tinned iron were cut to the required size and bent into shape on a roller, the edges being overlapped and soldered together to form a cylinder or 'body'. Disks for the ends had the edges turned over to fit the bodies closely and were attached by solder. The top disk had a circular aperture for filling which was closed by soldering a smaller disk on after cooking. The next step was to make cans with only one end attached. These were filled and the top end, which had only a small vent hole, was soldered on before cooking, the hole being closed by solder afterwards. The progress of the mechanization of can-making was probably rather sporadic and seems to follow two lines: the line of the can with lapped seams and that of the can with locked side seams and double seams at the ends. In the former, the first step seems to have been the American invention (1847) of the drop-press forming the flanges on the disks. Later, a combination press cut out the disks, flanged them, and cut out the filler-holes in the same operation. By 1866 machines were being devised to solder the side-seams and, by the end of the century, the manufacture of cans with lapped seams had become entirely automatic (plate 4 c).

The evolution of the can with locked seams, which is now almost universally used, is peculiar. As far back as 1824, the firm of Joseph Rhodes, of Wakefield, England, was making machines that formed locked seams, and in a catalogue published about 1870 they stated that 'these machines . . . are suitable for double seaming on the bottoms or tops of round . . . canisters, one end at a time, without solder. If the bodies are well made, notched [that is, lapped at the tops and bottoms only] and uniformly flanged the seams are quite airtight. But, for liquids and other substances, we recommend a composition of caoutchouc being placed in the recesses of the tops and bottoms.' From this point it would seem to be no more than a step to the modern 'sanitary' open-topped type of can, but this step does not seem to have been taken at all generally until the Ams's patents for preparing and applying to can-ends a rubber composition suitable for making a perfect joint appeared in America in 1896 and 1897.

The next improvement was the coating with appropriate enamels of the inner surfaces of cans intended for fruits, especially those containing soluble red and purple pigments, and for various meats, fish, and vegetables which contain unstable sulphur compounds. This is necessary because, although tin is not attacked by the acids of fruits in the absence of air or oxidizing agents, it is not practicable to eliminate air from cans completely; and many fruits themselves contain oxidizing agents. Traces of tin will thus always be dissolved, in sufficient quantity to turn fruit-syrups cloudy, and to change bright red and purple colours into an objectionable, muddy blue. Traces of iron taken up at defects in the tinning cause darkening of tannins in fruits and vegetables; they also form, with the unstable sulphur compounds mentioned above as present in some meats, fish, and vegetables, a black sulphide of iron which not only stains the insides of the cans but may even penetrate into the contents. Also, certain fruits can react with the iron to form sufficient hydrogen to make the ends of the cans bulge outwards ('hydrogen-swells'), or even to become perforated. A perfect coating of lacquer or enamel would prevent all these troubles, and experiments with internal lacquering began in France in 1868. Unfortunately, perfection proved hard to achieve, and an imperfect coating of lacquer can make matters worse rather than better, especially as regards hydrogen-swells and perforations. It was, in fact, a

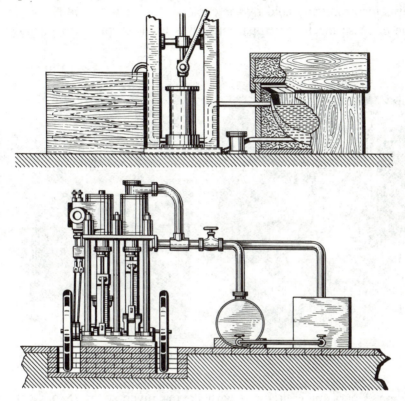

problem that remained unsolved until some considerable time after the close of this period.

IX. REFRIGERATION

It has always been known that foods keep longer in cold than in warm weather. This is because all chemical changes, including life-processes, become slower as the temperature falls. From the earliest times, advantage has been taken of natural cold, and of natural ice, for cooling food-stores, but low temperatures were available only on a very limited scale before the invention of refrigerating machines. Such machines were beginning to appear at the outset of our period.

In 1834, a patent for the manufacture of ice by an air-compression process was taken out by L. W. Wright (no 6665), and another for the production of cold by the expansion of volatile fluids (figure 11) by Jacob Perkins (1766–1849) (no 6662). In 1839 the astronomer Piazzi Smyth (1819–1900) also constructed an apparatus for producing cold by the expansion of compressed air.

None of these machines, apparently, was used for practical purposes. John

FIGURE 12—*The Atlas compression ice-making machine, c 1875.*

Gorrie, an American, is credited with having invented in 1849 a cold-air refrigerating machine such as was used there in the early stages of the frozen-meat trade. Patents for producing cold and making ice, either by expansion of compressed air or by the evaporation of volatile liquids, began to follow one another at fairly frequent intervals in the 1850s, and probably the first refrigerating plant to be applied to a manufacturing process (in a paraffin factory) was due to James Harrison (B.P. no 749 of 1856—see figure 11—and no 2362 of 1857) who improved upon the Perkins machine. Harrison was a native of Glasgow but emigrated to Australia in 1837. He became editor of the 'Melbourne Age' and is reported to have been the first to see the 'enormous source of wealth that lies still undeveloped in the export of meat from the Australian pastures'. It will be remembered that Australia was the first country to export canned meat. Harrison interested himself in refrigeration and erected an ice-factory at Rodey Point in Victoria at a cost of £1000. In 1851 he installed a refrigerating machine for a brewing firm at Bendigo, which was the world's prototype of such machines. Later, Harrison devoted himself to meat-freezing and, at Melbourne in 1873, several carcasses of sheep, sides of beef, poultry, and fish, which he had kept frozen for six months, were consumed at a public banquet. An ice-making machine of the 1870s is shown in figure 12.

The first works in the world for freezing meat, however, had been set up at Darling Harbour, Sydney, in 1861 by Thomas Sutcliffe Mort who, with E. D.

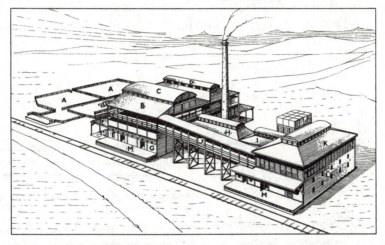

FIGURE 13—*View of the Riverina freezing-works, Deniliquin, New South Wales, c 1895.* (A) *Receiving and drafting yards;* (B) *slaughter-house;* (C) *digester-house;* (D) *preserving-rooms;* (E) *and* (G) *stores for by-products;* (F) *cooperage;* (H) *boiler-house;* (I) *engine-room;* (J) *inclined passage;* (K) *cooling-rooms;* (L) *chilling-rooms;* (M) *loading-platforms.*

Nicolle, a French engineer, had been working on the subject for several years. In 1874, Mort founded the New South Wales Fresh Food and Ice Company, using ammonia-compression machinery, and set up a slaughter-house alongside his cold store in 1875. A New South Wales freezing-works of the period is seen in figure 13. These ventures, which operated successfully, were designed for local trade, but the idea of sending meat to England was not forgotten. In his address at the inauguration of his enterprises Mort told his guests: 'There is no work on the world's carpet greater than this in which I have been engaged. . . . Before long France and England will look to us almost entirely for their supplies of food. . . . God provides enough and to spare for every creature . . . He sends into the world: but the conditions are not often in accord. Where the food is the people are not, and where the people are the food is not. It is however . . . within the power of man to adjust these things. . . .'

In the light of later events, it might have been better to have concentrated more on letting the people find their way to the food, but the other idea prevailed, and both Harrison (1873) and Mort (1876) attempted to ship frozen meat to England: both failed, however, owing to the breakdown of plant under the strain of maritime conditions.

A distinction must here be drawn between storage in the frozen state at 14° F or below, and storage unfrozen, or only very slightly frozen, at 29–30° F (chilling or cool storage). About 1870, chilled beef was being carried successfully from the United States to England in ships' holds cooled by ice-salt mixtures. In 1877, at about the same time as Mort's attempt at frozen shipment from

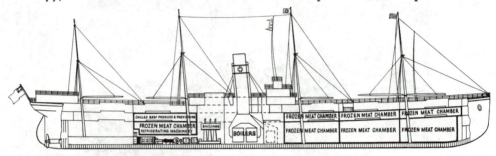

FIGURE 14—*Section of frozen-meat carrier, s.s.* Oswestry Grange. *This ship was registered in 1902.*

Australia, a partially successful experimental shipment of chilled meat under mechanical refrigeration was made from Rouen to Buenos Aires in the *Frigorifique*, a slow vessel fitted out by the French engineer Charles Tellier. The return voyage with a cargo of meat took 104 days and, when landed, the meat was in poor condition; it was, however, considered that sufficient information had been gained to solve the problem. Early in 1879 the first really successful shipment of mechanically chilled beef was brought to England from the United States in the *Circassia*, a vessel fitted with a Bell–Coleman compressed-air machine. Owing to the relatively short voyage, cargoes from the United States generally arrived in good condition, and a very large trade developed—more than that with all other countries put together. It did not begin to decline until after 1907 when, as the population of the United States increased, more was consumed there and trade between Argentina and Europe took its place.

Turning again to frozen meat, we find that in 1877 there was for the first time a very successful shipment of frozen mutton from Buenos Aires to Le Havre in the s.s. *Paraguay*, fitted with a Carré ammonia-compression machine. The voyage took six months, owing to a collision, but the meat, which was frozen hard at −17° F, is said to have arrived in excellent condition. This showed what could be done, and stimulated the Australians to further efforts. A vessel, the *Strathleven*, was fitted with a Bell–Coleman refrigerating plant in Great Britain and sailed from Plymouth to Australia in 1879. She arrived back in London on 2 February 1880, with 40 tons of beef and mutton in such good condition that 'neither by its appearance in butchers' shops nor by any peculiarity of flavour could it be distinguished from freshly killed English meat'.[1] After this, frozen beef and mutton continued to be exported from Australia, although the companies concerned experienced vicissitudes due either to drought or to the poor quality of the meat, which was not always taken from high-grade animals slaughtered alongside the refrigerators, as it was in New Zealand and Argentina. A typical frozen-meat carrier of the turn of the century is shown in figure 14.

In 1880, pioneers in New Zealand, where flocks had grown from 233 000 in 1851 to over 11000 000, fitted out the sailing-ship *Dunedin* with the Bell–Coleman plant and successfully delivered a cargo of frozen mutton and lamb in London after a voyage of 98 days. By 1892, the trade amounted to 2 000 000 carcasses, and 10 years later to 4 000 000. At first the meat was frozen on board ship, but later it was placed in cold storage on land ready for immediate loading.

The figures for Argentina, too, are impressive. In 1880 only 3571 carcasses of mutton and lamb, and no beef, were sent, but in 1900 there were 2 332 837 carcasses of mutton and lamb, 412 262 cwt of frozen beef, and 2114 cwt of chilled beef. The last was soon to increase rapidly and take the place of the chilled beef from North America already mentioned.

While the history of refrigeration during our period is largely that of the frozen- and chilled-meat trades, it was continually being brought into use for other purposes. Fish was one of the earliest commodities to be frozen, but unless it is frozen very rapidly it becomes soggy and quickly deteriorates when thawed. This effect of the rate of freezing was not understood until 1933; hence, for a long time, the chief use of refrigeration in the fish industry was to provide ice and cool conditions for short-term storage, that is, until the fish could be brought to shore and transported inland to consumers. In the dairying industry refrigeration was used to cool milk and for shipment of butter from Australia and New Zealand. Eggs in shell do not lend themselves to frozen storage, although they were early subjects for cool storage, and as soon as the building of mechanically cooled stores began in the United States (about 1890) the freezing of liquid egg seems to have started. No doubt freezing and chilling were applied to poultry also.

Special techniques are required for freezing fruits and vegetables and these

[1] Contemporary 'Daily Telegraph' report.

have been developed since 1900, but cool storage was used long before this date. The first long shipment of apples in cool storage was from Tasmania to London in 1884, but failures with both Tasmanian and Australian apples were numerous throughout our period. Apples are living things and some varieties can suffer damage if stored little above freezing-point; some can also be suffocated or otherwise damaged in ill-ventilated stores, although others benefit from closed conditions. Behaviour of this kind is not confined to apples, and much research has been required since 1900 to discover the storage conditions necessary to give the best results in each case.

It is not within the scope of this chapter to discuss the theory of refrigeration or the various systems and machines by which it is achieved. The installations here mentioned have since been superseded for reasons of space, weight, and economical working rather than because they were incapable of producing the conditions required in cold stores. These conditions are:

For chilling or cool storage at 29·5–30° F or higher: a steady and even temperature throughout the store, with, where possible, some control of humidity to minimize the drying-out and withering of the material stored. As we have already seen, chilling temperatures slow down, but do not prevent, the growth of moulds, yeasts, and bacteria. With meat, spoilage of this kind shows itself before other forms.

For frozen storage: a temperature low enough to freeze the food solid, stop the growth of micro-organisms entirely, and render other forms of deterioration so slow as to be negligible over the period of storage. For prolonged frozen storage, the lower the temperature the better the final result, but 14° F was found by experience to be satisfactory for ordinary purposes and served as the recognized commercial storage-temperature for many years. Initial temperatures were often lower, however, to induce rapid freezing. Good insulation and extensive cooling-surfaces make it possible to keep the temperature of the refrigerant near that required for the store, an arrangement which minimizes 'freezer-burn' (surface-drying) of stored material and formation of ice on the cooling-pipes.

These conditions were largely attained by practical experience, but it must be recognized that, by the time refrigeration began to be applied, a considerable body of scientific information had been built up. From the first, thermometers were available for registering conditions in cold stores and for regulating the working of refrigerating-machinery. By the end of our period, these had taken the form of long-distance and recording thermometers, whereby the whole story of the temperature conditions in a store during a voyage was recorded automatically on a chart. An early device was an alarm thermometer which gave warning when the temperature of a store rose or fell outside certain limits. Not so very long after the end of our period (1912) Critchell and Raymond could write: 'So exact have the regulating devices in the brine circulatory systems of ships' installations now become that the makers' claim to be able to keep the temperature of a meat hold within a degree Fahrenheit or less is justified.'

X. DEHYDRATION

Although sun-drying is probably the most ancient method of food-preservation, dehydration as defined on p 29 is modern. Dried milk has already been dealt with. Patents for drying eggs were sought in the United States by C. A. La Mont as early as 1865, but, so far as is known, he did not operate a plant until about 1878, by which time another inventor, W. O. Stoddard, was also drying eggs commercially. From 1895 onwards, egg-drying expanded rapidly in the United States, but it declined later under competition from China, where it was started just before 1900 with plant installed by German engineers.

Sun- or wind-dried meat, called charqui in South America, biltong in South Africa, and pemmican in North America, is a typical food of hunting and migratory peoples. The sun-drying of fish is also very ancient. But the nearest approach to dehydrated meat during our period was the meat-powder produced about 1870 by Hassall and others, who dried lean meat on steam-heated plates and ground it to be made into soups, or to be mixed with flour and made into biscuits.

Apart from dehydrated potato, which has been used as an ingredient in bread, and, possibly, dried onions, dehydrated vegetables have never been commercially successful except for special purposes and in special circumstances. Unsuccessful attempts were made over a long period in Europe to use them for troops and on board ship to combat scurvy. Desiccated vegetables, and dried apples and peaches, were also used for this purpose in the American Civil War and, many years later, in the Boer War, as a basis for soups, stews, and other dishes. Success was always very mixed and problematical, however, until the second world war, in spite of the fact that the key had existed, forgotten and neglected, since 1780, when a British patent was granted for scalding vegetables before drying them. Scalding has the effect of destroying enzymes and therefore preventing their action during and after drying; but, even when scalded, most dried vegetables require rather elaborate precautions and expensive packaging-materials to prevent them from deteriorating in storage, especially in the tropics. Dehydrated foods have, however, obvious advantages in wars and for expeditions; and in nutritive value, flavour, and appearance when prepared for the table they can now take their place beside canned and frozen foods.

XI. CHEMICAL PRESERVATIVES

Substances like borax or boric acid, formalin, and salicylic and benzoic acids were used much too freely in Britain as preservatives in such foods as potted meats, fish, and various beverages until the passing of the Food Act of 1875. The same remark applies to 'improvers', such as alum, in bread, and to artificial colouring matters, sometimes of a poisonous nature. A previous Act of 1860 had proved unworkable and was a dead letter. That of 1875 was more carefully framed and, consequently, more effective in some respects. It contained many loop-holes, however; for instance, it banned alum in bread but permitted it in baking-powders. There were also injustices; thus a small retailer might be held responsible for offences of which he was not aware, while the wholesaler and manufacturer might escape scot-free.

The great objection to the use of this group of preservatives, and what distinguishes them from sugar, vinegar, and the salts used in curing, is that while very small proportions of them in foods inhibit the activity of micro-organisms, they are also harmful to human consumers, and some of them are cumulative. The least objectionable of them is sulphurous acid, which has long been used and is very effective with acid products like fruits and fruit-beverages. It has the advantage of being readily removed by boiling or cooking, with almost complete restoration of the original colours where these have been bleached by it. The Act of 1875 was subjected to considerable review and amendment in 1899, and the proportions of the few preservatives permitted in certain classes of foods were defined. All of them except sulphurous acid have since been disallowed, and the law has been tightened in respect to artificial colours and 'improvers', except those still regarded as harmless.

BIBLIOGRAPHY

BITTING, A. W. 'Appertizing; or, the Art of Canning; its History and Development.' Trade Pressroom, San Francisco. 1937.

CRITCHELL, J. T. and RAYMOND, J. 'A History of the Frozen Meat Trade.' Constable, London. 1912.

HUNZIKER, O. F. 'Condensed Milk and Milk Powder Prepared for Factory, School and Laboratory' (5th ed.). Published by the author, La Grange, Illinois. 1935.

JAGO, W. and JAGO, W. C. 'The Technology of Breadmaking.' Simpkin, Marshall, Hamilton, Kent, London. 1911.

KENT-JONES, D. W. and AMOS, A. J. 'Modern Cereal Chemistry' (4th ed.). Northern Publishing Company, Liverpool. 1947.

TREVELYAN, G. M. 'English Social History.' Longmans, London. 1942.

3

THE STEEL INDUSTRY

H. R. SCHUBERT

I. THE BESSEMER CONVERTER

BETWEEN 1850 and 1900 the production of iron and steel increased very considerably all over the world. The foundations of this development had been laid in the first half of the century, when a growing demand for iron evolved. It was caused by the development of machinery and engineering, the increasing use of iron for structural purposes and, above all, the railway boom of the 1830s and 1840s. The demand was met almost exclusively by the production of wrought and cast iron: in comparison with those two materials, the production of steel was very small. About 1850 Britain, at that time the biggest producer in the world, turned out approximately $2\frac{1}{2}$ m tons of iron, but not more than about 60 000 tons of steel. The reason for the difference was the high cost of steel. At that time it was mainly produced by cementation or by the crucible process, which despite improvements remained laborious and uneconomical: as a result, steel was still a comparatively rare and expensive material. Then a most remarkable change occurred, brought on by the invention of processes which made it possible to produce steel at considerably lower cost and in greater quantities, so that ultimately it could be substituted for wrought and cast iron as the principal ferrous material.

These great inventions, which after many trials and failures finally provided the world with a new material suitable for mass-production at a cheap rate, were developed almost simultaneously in the United States of America and in England, about the middle of the century. William Kelly (1811–88), a native of Pittsburgh, Pennsylvania, began the process with experiments in his iron-works at Eddyville, Kentucky, in 1847. Originally, he was concerned with the manufacture of sugar-kettles for farmers. The iron of which these kettles were made was produced by the usual finery process in which pig iron was converted into malleable (wrought) iron by burning out the excess of carbon with a current of air. The fuel employed for generating the required heat was charcoal, the rising cost of which was a matter of great concern to the ironmasters of the day. One day Kelly noticed that some molten pig iron in the finery hearth not covered with charcoal became very much hotter when air was blown on it than if it had been so covered. This experience taught him that the carbon contained in pig iron could be blown out by air-blast alone, the carbon itself acting as a fuel and producing a much higher temperature. By decarburizing the metal in the finery process to a lesser degree than is necessary for making wrought iron—a method which had been familiar to iron-makers for centuries—steel could similarly be produced.

The novel feature of Kelly's 'air-boiling' process was, then, that the temperature was raised through the rapid combustion of the carbon contained in the pig iron. When Kelly enthusiastically proclaimed his discovery of making steel 'without fuel', the ironmasters completely rejected his idea and even his wife thought him mentally unbalanced. Kelly was forced to proceed with his experiments at a secluded spot in a forest, where in 1851 he built the first of seven converters for producing steel by his newly discovered method, all secretly erected within the next five years. He did not apply for a patent until 1856, when he learned that an Englishman, Henry Bessemer (1813–98), had been granted an American patent for the same process. Able to convince the officials of his priority, Kelly obtained a patent on 23 June 1857. On this occasion he was officially declared to be the first inventor, and Bessemer's application for a renewal of his patent was rejected. Kelly's final success came too late, however, for in the same year he became bankrupt.

In England, Bessemer, who independently worked on the same lines, was more successful, and the process ultimately became everywhere associated with his name. There was, however, a difference in the methods adopted. Kelly's aim in the early years was to obtain a better product than that obtained from the finery and the puddling processes, but without liquefying the metal. Bessemer's aim, on the other hand, was to keep the metal completely liquid at a very high temperature.

On 11 August 1856 Bessemer presented a paper 'On the Manufacture of Malleable Iron and Steel without Fuel' to the annual meeting at Cheltenham of the British Association for the Advancement of Science. The invention he disclosed was welcomed enthusiastically by the audience, but the results of its subsequent practical application were 'most disastrous', to use Bessemer's own words. In his very early experiments, Bessemer had been fortunate enough to employ a pig iron remarkably free from phosphorus. When phosphoric iron was used, his process failed. Phosphorus, which makes steel brittle, was very commonly present in iron, since it is contained in the majority of iron ores exploited both in Britain and on the continent. Failure to remove the detrimental element greatly limited the application of the process in the early years.

The first Bessemer steel was brittle and contained many blow-holes, but a remedy was discovered in the same year as that in which Bessemer announced his invention. It was due to Robert Forester Mushet (1811–91), son of an iron-master in the Forest of Dean. Mushet had realized the essential fact that addition of spiegel, an alloy of manganese and iron which had a de-gasifying effect, would remove the excess of oxygen introduced into the metal in Bessemer's process. Moreover, addition of spiegel, which was also a recarburizer, could be used to adjust the carbon-content of steel, which could not be satisfactorily achieved in Bessemer's process alone. After initial differences, Mushet's contribution was acknowledged by Bessemer himself as 'a most useful and valuable' invention, supplementary to his own. Mushet's discovery, however, was only partly an answer to Bessemer's difficulties, since the use of spiegel was limited to the making of products with a relatively high carbon-content.

The first real success of the process was achieved in Sweden through the efforts of Göran Fredrik Göransson. It was mainly due to the use of iron made from the pure Swedish Dannemora ores, which are almost free from phosphorus and sulphur. Göransson bought part of Bessemer's Swedish patent in 1857, and obtained from England a fixed Bessemer converter and a steam blast-engine, which were set up in Sweden by an English engineer. After many initial failures, success was achieved in July 1858. Göransson's important contribution to the development of the process appears to have consisted in controlling the blowing, that is, stopping it just at the moment when the carbon-content required for varying grades of steel was attained.

The improvements contributed by Mushet and Göransson do not in any way diminish Bessemer's merit as an inventor, or the greatness of his work. Whatever the contributions made by others, there is little doubt that Bessemer 'was the real accoucheur of the infant industry which grew to strident manhood in such a short period of time'. [1]

Bessemer's initial experiments were made in a fixed vertical converter established in his London workshop at Baxter House, St Pancras, in 1855 (figure 15). The converter was a small upright cylinder, about 4 ft high internally, with six *tuyères* through which air was blown in horizontally at the foot. A blast at 10–15 lb per sq in was applied. The molten iron was run into the converter by a movable spout direct from the cupola furnace in which the pig iron had been remelted. When conversion was completed, the metal was tapped from a hole at the bottom of the converter and conducted into a movable shallow pan or receiver.

The disadvantage of the fixed converter was the loss of heat during the running-in of the metal and again during its discharge. Bessemer found a remedy. It consisted in mounting the converter on axes, which made it possible to keep the *tuyères* above the metal until the charge of molten iron was run in. It also allowed the blowing to be stopped during the discharge of the converted

FIGURE 15—*Bessemer's fixed converter.* (Centre rear) *Cupola furnace on the usual principle;* (foreground) *the Bessemer furnace;* (extreme left) *vessel in which the crude iron is received from the smelting furnace and then passed into the refining chamber.*

metal. Bessemer's movable or tilting converter was first put into operation in his own steel-works at Sheffield. This new type, patented in 1860, has remained virtually unchanged ever since (figure 16). (A) shows the converter in the elevated position before charging begins. It is then turned horizontally (B) and retained in that position, while the charge of molten iron, brought in ladles, is poured in. (C) shows the position during the blow. The air-blast is turned on, and enters through the *tuyères* passing through the bottom: at C, G, H, the bottom of the converter and the form of the *tuyères* are shown. The converter is then turned up, and the blast is increased and forces its way through the molten metal. At the end of the process the steel is poured from the converter, which has been turned down again (D) into a ladle (E and F) and taken to the casting-bay.

The converter has the advantage of being a very fast producer of steel, but

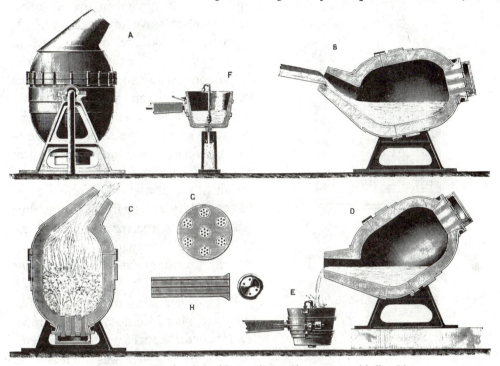

FIGURE 16—*The first form of Bessemer's movable converter and ladle, 1860.*

compared with other processes the loss of iron, some of which is carried away with the blast, is fairly high.

Outside Britain, the Bessemer converter was introduced first in France, about 1858, at Saint-Seurin in the Gironde. In Germany, Alfred Krupp erected a Bessemer plant at Essen: this was first operated in 1862. In the next year Austria followed with a Bessemer converter established at Turrach, in Styria. In the United States, Bessemer steel was first blown (under Kelly's patent) at Wyandotte, Michigan, in 1864.

II. THE SIEMENS OPEN-HEARTH PROCESS

In the same year as that in which Bessemer disclosed his process of steel-making in a converter, Frederick Siemens (1826–1904), a naturalized Englishman of German origin, obtained an English patent for his newly invented method of heat-regeneration. The regenerative principle became the essential characteristic of steel-production by the open-hearth process developed by Frederick and his brother Charles William Siemens (1823–83). In iron-making, the prin-

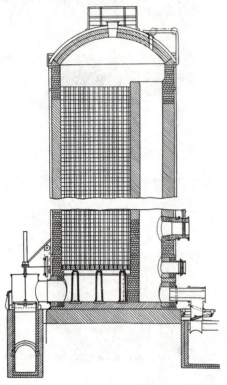

FIGURE 17—*Cowper's hot-blast stove. Sectional plan and elevation.*

ciple was first applied in the regenerative hot-blast stove invented by E. A. Cowper, an associate of Siemens, in 1857 (figure 17). In the Cowper stove, the air on its way to the blast-furnace was driven through, and heated by, a checker-work of firebricks heated by the waste gases of the same blast-furnace; the furnace was thus made to heat its own blast. During the generation of hot air in the first stove, a second stove was heated by waste gases, and was thus made ready to receive the flow of air and heat it. Alternation of the flow assured a constant supply of hot air for the blast.

The Cowper stove was introduced at Ormesby, near Middlesbrough, in 1860. The immediate effect was that the temperature of blast-air was increased to 620° C; this had never before been achieved. As a result, the output of pig iron rose by 20 per cent. Improved Cowper stoves are still in use for heating the blast-air of furnaces.

Siemens's furnace, which like the Cowper stove was operated on the principle of heat-regeneration, differed from Bessemer's converter in its source of heat. In the converter, the heat of the process itself provided the necessary working temperature. In the open hearth, the heat required for melting the charge came from outside the process. In the beginning, Siemens used solid fuel; the next important step, taken in 1861, was the conversion of the solid fuel into gas in a gas-producer entirely separate from the furnace. The gas-producer made it possible to use low-grade coal.

The patent granted in 1861 to C. W. Siemens for the gas-producer shows the open-hearth furnace on the bed of which steel could be melted. In the same year the complete invention was applied at a glass-works in Birmingham, and soon afterwards to various other industrial processes (figure 18).

Inside the furnace, air and gaseous fuel combine to form a flame which stretches about two-thirds of the length of the hearth and above the surface of its contents. The function of the ports (1 and 2) is to control the direction of the flame. The bath or hearth through which the flame passes is a shallow oblong box built of heat-resisting material. To prevent the waste gases from depositing all their solid content in the checkers, they are first passed through slag-pockets (3 a and 3 b) in which some of the solid material is deposited. On their way from the furnace to the chimney the waste gases give part of their heat to the incoming gaseous fuel and air as they pass through the checker-chambers (4 a, gas; 4 b, air).

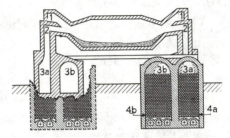

FIGURE 18—*Diagrammatic cross-section of the open-hearth furnace.*

As a result, the temperature of the flame in the hearth is increased considerably, to about 1650° C. The flow of air and gas is reversed in direction at intervals.

For decarburizing pig iron melted in the open-hearth furnace, Siemens added iron ore, the oxide of which reacted with the carbon of the pig iron and reduced it to the desired degree. The possibility of dilution by adding scrap metal to the bath of molten iron first occurred to Pierre Martin, who with his father owned a small steel-works at Sireuil, near Angoulême. In 1864 the Martins succeeded in producing steel by the addition of scrap. The pig iron they employed was particularly suitable, because it was obtained from high-grade haematite ores mined on Elba. The Martins used a regenerative furnace built by Siemens's engineers. Two years later they made a contract with Siemens that laid the foundations for the subsequent expansion of the so-called Siemens–Martin process, which was conducted in open-hearth furnaces.

The possibility of treating large quantities of metal at a very high temperature and of keeping it molten throughout the process, combined with the economic advantage of using scrap-iron and cheap low-grade coal, ensured the success of the open-hearth process. This success is indicated by the fact that shortly after 1900 it had become more widely practised than Bessemer's.

Towards the close of the century, open-hearth furnaces of considerably increased dimensions began to be built, as well as movable furnaces that could be tilted. The American steel industry led in this respect. In 1895 Benjamin Talbot of Leeds invented the process of continuous blowing, in which only a part of the metal contained in the open hearth was tapped at a time; in this way the temperature was kept constantly at a very high level. Four years later, the process was put into practice at Pencoyd, near Philadelphia. In Europe it was not introduced until 1902, at Frodingham, Lincolnshire.

III. THE BASIC PROCESS

The problem of eliminating phosphorus was finally solved by a Londoner, Sidney Gilchrist Thomas (1850–85), who was assisted by his cousin Percy Gilchrist. Bessemer's converter was lined with 'acid' materials, rich in silicic acid. The silica bricks of the lining made it possible to remove carbon, silicon, and manganese, but not phosphorus. Thomas succeeded in dephosphorizing the metal by using a basic lining in the converter, with the addition of limestone. The lining was made of calcined dolomite, one function of which was to combine with phosphorus and to remove it from the metal. The limestone, which was principally concerned with this effect, was pulverized and converted into a valuable agricultural fertilizer. Thomas offered a paper describing the successful application of his invention to the British Iron and Steel Institute in 1875, but it was rejected: several years elapsed before the process became a commercial success. Either a basic or an acid lining could be applied to both the Bessemer converter and the open-hearth furnace; which was used depended upon the nature of the pig iron employed and on the grade of steel desired.

The practical advantage of Thomas's invention was that it made possible the use of phosphoric ores. Britain was less affected by it than some other countries, since she had a fair supply of non-phosphoric ores; after his first failures, Bessemer concentrated on pig iron made from haematite ores mined in Cumberland and in the peninsula of Furness in the north of Lancashire. Cumberland ore became known as 'Bessemer ore': it was practically free from phosphorus and sulphur. In addition, high-grade ores were imported from Sweden and the north of Spain. In consequence, Thomas's basic process did not become popular in Britain until towards the end of the century. The countries which derived the greatest benefit from it were those on the continent which had large quantities of phosphoric ores: Belgium, France, and, above all, Germany. In the province of Lorraine, annexed from France in 1871, Germany had a valuable phosphoric ore known as *minette*. As a consequence of Thomas's invention a great increase in German steel-production took place.

IV. THE USES OF STEEL

The 1870s, which saw all the major advances in steel-making accomplished, were a period of industrial change which affected the iron and steel industries of the whole world. The most remarkable feature was the tremendous increase in the production of steel that took place in the last three decades of the century. The world's annual output of steel increased from a little more than half a million tons in 1870 to almost 28 m tons in 1900. Nowhere was this growth more significant than in the United States. There the annual output grew from approximately 22 000 tons in 1867, when steel-making was well established, to 11·4 m tons in 1900. From 1889 onwards the United States led the world in steel-production, and has done so ever since, greatly surpassing Britain. In 1873 British steel-production was 653 500 tons, more than three times as much as that of the United States, which at that time produced rather less than 200 000 tons a year. By 1900, Britain's annual output had risen to about 4·9 m tons, which was less than half the production in the United States. Second to the United States was Germany, which also had surpassed Britain by then. At that time Germany produced more than 8 m tons of steel a year; a remarkable increase, since in 1850 the total output had been less than 12 000 tons.

The increase in steel-production was accompanied by a proportionate reduction in the output of puddled iron. In 1883, for example, 70 per cent of all the pig iron made in England was converted into puddled bar iron, but in 1897 not more than 5 per cent was so treated. Wrought iron, from the puddling-furnaces, was reverting to its original uses—by the blacksmith, the anchor-smith, the chain-maker, and others. The change, however, proceeded very gradually, and took longer in Britain than in America. A significant factor was the substitution of steel for iron in the construction of railways.

At the time of Bessemer's invention railway construction was expanding rapidly. Railways began to be built in India and other British dependencies. In Russia, railway construction was begun on a large scale in 1857, in which year considerable contracts were for the first time placed in Britain. About 1869 the building of railways on the continent increased considerably, but it was interrupted by the Franco-German war of 1870–1. After the conclusion of peace both France and Germany desired to proceed with their railways and placed very large contracts in Britain. From 1862 to 1872 Britain was the world's principal supplier of rails, but only a part of the demand was met by rails rolled from Bessemer acid steel; the rest were made from puddled iron.

Real appreciation of the importance of steel for railway construction did not begin until after 1870. At that time the puddling-furnaces in south Wales, the midlands, and the northern counties of England, still supplied iron for rails. In the 1880s a steady decline took place in the production of puddled iron, the fall marking the victory of the steel rail. Steel was not only the less expensive material: it had the additional advantage of reducing the costs of replacement, since steel rails lasted fifteen to twenty times as long as those made from puddled iron.

In the United States the first rail made of Bessemer steel was rolled in 1865. Production increased tremendously in the great railroad boom of the 1870s and 1880s. For rails Bessemer steel was used almost exclusively until 1902, when steel made by the open-hearth process was found to be a superior material. For the axles of rolling-stock, however, puddled iron remained the preferred material until 1900.

For the manufacture of boilers steel proved particularly suitable, since steel plates could be thinner than iron ones. Boiler-makers in Lancashire began to use steel plates in 1859. A few years later, plates made from Bessemer steel were used for the first time in ship-building. The pioneer work was undertaken by a Liverpool firm which in 1862 built a small paddle-steamer named the *Banshee*. This ship, which sailed from Liverpool to America in March 1863, was the first steel vessel ever to cross the north Atlantic. In 1864 the *Clytemnestra*, a clipper ship of 1250 tons built of steel plates three-eighths of an inch thick, was launched by the same firm. In the same year she successfully withstood a cyclone off Calcutta [2]. More than any other country, Great Britain was particularly affected by the growing demand for iron and steel in ship-building, since up to the first world war more than half of the world's tonnage was British-owned. Although steel ships were built in steadily increasing numbers in the second half of the nineteenth century, the major change from wrought or puddled iron to steel in ship-building did not take place until about 1890.

The use of structural steel developed in the last quarter of the century. Eads Bridge, across the Mississippi River at St Louis, constructed in 1874 by the Carnegie Steel Company, was the first bridge ever built in which steel replaced iron in part of the structure. The first bridge made completely of steel was built in 1883–90 across the Firth of Forth (pp 476, 505–7).

From 1888 steel gradually became the structural material for tall buildings (p 477). In that year the first sky-scraper was built at Chicago. In the framework of the upper floors Bessemer steel was substituted for the wrought iron used lower down. As the principal attraction for the great exhibition of 1889 the French engineer Gustave Eiffel (1832–1923) built the Eiffel Tower in Paris (p 476). It is 984 ft high, almost double the height of any building previously erected. The constructional material was wrought iron produced in France by the Siemens–Martin process.

V. METHODS OF WORKING

Increasing demand for iron and steel led to improvements in the finishing process, in particular in the technique of rolling. Reversing-mills, in which the hot metal was passed backwards and forwards, are supposed to have been used first at Crewe in 1866. In the following year they were certainly in use at Sheffield. The so-called three-high mills, in which a third roller was placed above the top roller of the first pair, made it possible to pass the iron back again without reversing the engines. The first mill of this kind was erected by O. E. Carlsund at Motala in Sweden, in 1856. The idea, however, had already been conceived by the great Swedish civil engineer Christopher Polhem (1661–1751) (vol III, pp 342–3). In England it was introduced in 1862 by Bernhard Lauth in his works at Birmingham (figure 19).

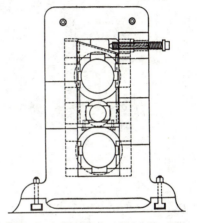

FIGURE 19—*Lauth's three-high mill, 1862.*

The continuous mill, consisting of a number of roller-stands placed one behind the other and decreasing in size and power, came into use about the same time. This idea, too, had been conceived as early as the eighteenth century. In 1798, William Hazeldine (1763–1840) had obtained a British patent for it, but no practical use was made of his invention. It was not until 1862 that another Englishman, George Bedson of Manchester, took up the idea and constructed a continuous-rolling mill; this was patented in the same year. Seven years later a continuous mill of this type was built in England and sent to the United States, where it was erected at Worcester, Massachusetts. Both the continuous and the three-high mill were developed to a very high level by American engineers.

A sensation was caused amongst the ironmasters when the Mannesmann process of tube-making, patented in 1885, was published (p 629). The process, widely used today, made it possible to make seamless tubes, which are more accurate than welded tubes. The idea had been conceived about 1860 by Reinhard Mannesmann, a steel-manufacturer at Remscheid in Germany (figure 20). A hot metal rod is inserted between two rollers which are mutually inclined and rotate in the same direction. By the action of the rollers the rod is drawn forward, away from its centre, so that a cavity is formed. This hole is made circular by a nose-piece placed on a mandrel just beyond the rollers. When T. A. Edison, the American inventor, was asked what impressed him most at the World Exhibition at Chicago in 1893, he replied immediately that it was the seamless steel tube made by Mannesmann.

The last quarter of the nineteenth century was characterized by a change in the economic relationship between Britain and the industrial countries of Europe.

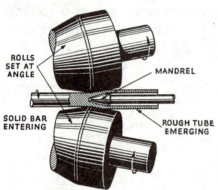

FIGURE 20—*Mannesmann process of making seamless tubes.*

For more than a century up to 1870, British technical knowledge had helped to promote the expansion of engineering and transport on modern lines in the main manufacturing regions of the continent. By 1875, however, the annual rate of increase in Britain's output of iron, steel, and engineering products began to show signs of slowing down. Until then Belgium, the first nation on the continent to be industrialized, had been Britain's only serious rival, but now new competitors were arising and industrial output outside Britain was increasing rapidly. Home industries able to replace imports from Britain had been developed on the continent, principally in Germany.

Britain's role of schoolmaster to industrial Europe came to an end. Men educated in such excellent technical colleges as those of Charlottenburg in Germany, Zürich in Switzerland, and the *Montanistische Hochschule* at Leoben in Austria, could replace British engineers and skilled operatives. In the steel industry of the 1870s England in all likelihood 'learned more than she taught' [3].

VI. SPECIAL ALLOY STEELS

The difficulty of imparting uniform hardness to carbon steels, in particular to massive blocks, was overcome by the use of alloy steels containing specially added amounts of other elements, such as chromium, tungsten, manganese, and nickel. Alloy steels were, and still are, employed for many purposes; for example, for cutting-tools, heavy guns, and the steel parts of motor-car engines.

Alloy steels had been produced accidentally in the smelting of mixed ores. The first prepared deliberately was the chromium steel made by Michael Faraday. Stimulated by reports on the famous Indian wootz steel, he began experiments in 1819 at the Royal Institution and at a steel-works. There experiments were made jointly with J. Stodard, a cutler. The quantities of chromium steel they produced were, however, too small for mechanical tests. Production on a large scale and for commercial use began very much later. Not before Julius Baur, in New York, had obtained a patent in 1865 was the attention of the steel-manufacturers drawn to chromium steel. It was first produced on a commercial scale in 1877 at Unieux, in France, by Jacob Holtzer, who recommended it for the manufacture of armour-plate and shells.

The invention of alloy steels for tools is frequently associated with the name of Mushet in England, but he had a forerunner in the Austrian chemist Franz Köller. In 1855 Köller invented tungsten steel, which was produced in subsequent years at special works at Reichraming on the river Enns, in Austria [4]. As the invention was made widely known by the Austrian metallurgist Peter Tunner, who was an authority of international reputation, it is not impossible that Mushet obtained some knowledge of it. At Coleford, in the Forest of Dean, he began in 1868 to manufacture his alloy steels (high-carbon tungsten-manganese steels). The alloy attained hardness merely by being left to cool in air, thus dispensing with the hardening by quenching formerly required. Tools made from the alloy outlasted by at least five or six times those previously made. This was of particular importance for manufacturing processes which required continuous machining (p 640). In 1871 Mushet assigned the manufacture and marketing of his steel to the firm of Samuel Osborn at Sheffield, who within a few years introduced 'R. Mushet's special steel' into almost all engineering workshops in the world. Mushet's belief that tungsten was of special importance in tool-steels was confirmed by further experiments at Sheffield and elsewhere. In the 1890s his improved special steels were able to cut mild steel at 150 ft per minute without any lubricant and without breaking down.

The year 1882, in which Sir Robert Hadfield (1859–1940) of Sheffield announced his discovery of manganese steel, may be regarded as a landmark in the history of alloy steel. Manganese had been used long before as an adjunct to the making of steel (p 55), but not in quantities sufficient to constitute an alloy steel. When the proportion of manganese was increased the steel became extremely brittle. Hadfield discovered that the embrittling effect disappeared when the proportion of manganese was further increased to 12 or 13 per cent. Such a steel can be brought to an unusual degree of hardness by heating it to 1000° C and quenching it in water. Steel of such toughness is used for purposes requiring a very hard metal, such as rock-breaking machinery and railway points and crossings.

Besides discovering chromium steel, Faraday is also credited with having prepared nickel steels, but his invention had no practical consequences. Nickel steel
was re-invented by Johann Conrad Fischer, who in the winter of 1824-5 produced nickel steels in his steel-works at Schaffhausen, in Switzerland, and subsequently obtained an Austrian patent [5]. Nickel steel began to be produced
for industrial use and was introduced into the market by the French firm of
Schneider, of Le Creusot, in 1888. It was followed immediately by the nickel-
chromium group of alloy steels. American firms were quick to see the advantages
of high-speed steels, but even in the United
States they were employed to only a very
moderate extent before 1906.

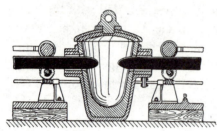

FIGURE 21—*Siemens's indirect arc furnace.*

VII. LATER TYPES OF FURNACE

Although most alloy steel is produced
in open-hearth furnaces, high-grade alloys
are manufactured in electric furnaces.
Steels used for many cutting-tools and
dies, and stainless steel, are made in furnaces in which the heat is generated
by an electric arc instead of by fuel. In this way impurities, inevitably introduced when coke is used as a fuel, are reduced to a minimum. Working with
electricity, however, was expensive, so that about 1900 the number of electric
furnaces in operation was still very small, apart from those used for experimental purposes.

The first electric furnace applied to the smelting of iron-ores or metallic iron
was constructed by the French chemist Pichou, demonstrator at the École de
Chimie Pratique in Paris. In 1853 a patent for the application of electricity for
metallurgical purposes, and especially for the metallurgy of iron, was granted to
him in France, and simultaneously in England (in the name of Johnson, who was
probably a patent agent). Pichou intended to construct such furnaces on a large
scale, but he was not able to realize his ambitious plans, for he was very much in
advance of his time.

In 1878 and 1879 new furnaces were patented and constructed by Charles
Siemens. They were small indirect arc furnaces consisting of a melting-crucible
of non-conducting material with laterally adjustable electrodes, one of which was
hollow so that by introducing a suitable gas a reducing or inert atmosphere could
be obtained (figure 21).

In contrast to the output of wrought or puddled iron, which was adversely
affected by the growing demand for steel, production of pig iron, large quantities

of which were converted into steel, rose considerably. In 1850 world output of pig iron was approximately 4·75 m long tons; in 1900 it was little less than 39 m. In the production of pig iron, also, Britain was outstripped by the United States during the period with which we are now concerned; a few years after 1900 she was outstripped by Germany, too. From about 1840 to 1865 Britai 1 had produced more than half the world's pig iron. After 1865 growth continued, but a very moderate one in no way comparable with the swift upward rush in America and Germany. Britain lost her leading position in the iron trade. Her share in world production decreased, and sank to less than one-quarter of the total in 1900. In the same period production showed a rapid increase in the United States, rising to more than one-third of the world's production in the last decade of the century. German production of pig iron increased slowly but constantly from 1850 onwards. Her share in world production was one-fifth in the middle of the century, but exceeded one-quarter in 1900. Of the other iron-producing countries, Russia showed the greatest increase. By the end of the century production of Russian pig iron was more than fourteen times as great as it had been in 1850, and amounted to approximately 7 per cent of the world's production.

Britain's reduced share in total production was mainly due to economic factors, such as the raising of tariffs in America and the growth of competitive industries on the continent: it was in no way a result of technical inferiority. Britain contributed as much as any country to improvements in furnace-practice and to the development of the blast-furnace towards its modern form, as with Cowper's regenerative hot-blast stoves (p 58). But the principal characteristic of the blast-furnace, which from its inception in the late Middle Ages distinguished it from all other types of furnace, was retained even after 1850. This characteristic was the fore-hearth. The ironmasters tenaciously retained it, since it facilitated the ladling of liquid iron from the hearth for casting. The principal argument for the retention of the fore-hearth was that it was considered indispensable to have unimpeded access to the interior of the hearth in order to keep it clear from slag, which tended to attach itself to the walls and around the *tuyère*. The danger of slag becoming attached in this way was, however, practically eliminated by the hot blast introduced after Nielson's invention of it in 1828 (vol IV, p 109): the higher temperature generated by hot blast promoted liquefaction of slag.

Tunner (p 65), who had much experience in the working of Austrian furnaces in which the proportion of slag was very low on account of the use of high-grade and fusible ores, was the first to advocate abandoning the fore-hearth and closing the hearth completely. It was, however, not until 1867 that a German engineer, F. W. Lürmann, broke with tradition by constructing a closed hearth at the blast-furnace of Georgsmarienhütte, near Osnabrück. The furnace was equipped with four *tuyères*. The extraction of slag, which formerly had been effected by letting it run out periodically through a notch in the dam of the fore-hearth, was effected by a water-cooled pipe invented by Lürmann, which was placed a short distance below the *tuyères* (figure 22). By closing the hearth a better retention of heat was achieved. Previously, a good deal of heat had been lost each time the fore-hearth was opened for the tapping of metal and slag. Lürmann's innovation made it possible to generate a higher temperature, and, as a result, to obtain a greater production of pig iron in furnaces of increased height. Before 1860, the average height of blast-furnaces had been not more than 50–60 ft. Higher furnaces, with an average height of 75 ft, began to be built in the 1860s and 1870s in the Cleveland district of England. Despite the increase in the height of the furnace, the hearth was kept small.

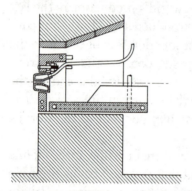

FIGURE 22—*Lürmann's water-cooled slag-pipe, 1867.*

American ironmasters were the first to ignore the old prejudice against a wider hearth. By introducing this type of hearth, and by further improvements, they created the modern type of blast-furnace. Their object was to increase production as much as possible: this was the general aim in the period of 'rapid driving' which began in the American iron industry in 1880.

The first blast-furnace in which the hearth was made larger was Furnace B, built in 1880 at the Edgar Thomson Works, near Pittsburgh, owned by Andrew Carnegie. The height of the furnace was 80 ft, and the diameter of the hearth 11 ft and that of the boshes[1] 20 ft. The walls of the hearth were surrounded by cast iron plates, but originally no cooling-plates were used. The brickwork of stack and boshes was held together by a crinoline of six iron bands supported by staves. In the following year the crinoline was replaced by an iron jacket. The larger dimensions of the hearth made it possible to increase the number of *tuyères* to eight. They protruded slightly into the hearth and were placed in a much more elevated position than in former furnaces. Owing to these alterations, the output of the furnace rose to 1200 tons a week against a former maximum of 800–900 tons.

[1] The tapering portion of the furnace between the bottom of the stack and the top of the hearth.

At the same works a mixer was introduced in 1889. The idea of using a mixer for stirring liquid iron before it was poured into the steel-converter had been conceived by William Deighton in England and patented in 1873. The first two mixers at the Edgar Thomson Works had a capacity of not more than 80 tons each, which, however, was soon increased. A mixer not only ensured a uniform supply of molten iron ready for the steel-converter; it provided an opportunity of removing impurities and making the metal more homogeneous by blending the

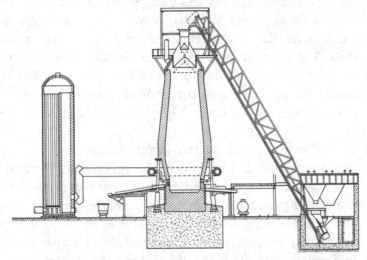

FIGURE 23—*Blast furnace* (centre), *stove for production of hot blast* (left), *and ramp for raising the charge of coke and ore* (right). *The slag was discharged to the left and the iron to the right.*

flow from several furnaces. By the early years of the present century the use of mixers had become almost universal.

Other improvements made before 1900 increased the efficiency of the blast-furnace still more, with the result that production-figures became higher than ever before. The principal improvements consisted in lowering the boshes, further increasing the dimensions of the hearth and the number of *tuyères*, and introducing water-cooled plates, with an internal coil, for cooling the walls of the hearth and boshes. The height of furnaces ultimately increased to 100 ft and even more (figure 23).

By the close of the century the modern iron and steel industry, based on pig iron production in blast-furnaces operated with coke, had been introduced into the major iron-producing countries of the world. Britain had taken the lead long before 1800, followed by European countries and, around 1850 by the United

States. In Russia, where lack of wood became a difficulty comparatively late because of the vast forests, the first coke-operated blast-furnaces were erected in 1869–70. They were situated in the Donetz coal basin. In India attempts to create an iron industry on the European pattern were greatly impeded by the difficulty of obtaining suitable labour, since the climate was so trying to Europeans. The first Indian coke-furnace, erected by the Bengal Ironworks Company in 1875, was in operation for not more than four years. The plant was taken over by the British Government in 1881 and enlarged by the addition of two more furnaces. Effective development in India, however, did not begin until 1903, when J. N. Tata, a Bombay manufacturer, started to erect an extensive ironworks, in which Indians only were employed. It was situated at Chanda in central India. The first modern iron-works in China was erected at Han-Yang, opposite Hankow, in 1893. In Japan the iron- and steel-works at Yawata was started as a government enterprise in 1897; the first blast-furnace was completed in 1901.

By 1900 all the major inventions and improvements had been made that determined the general line of development and progress for the iron and steel industries. The most remarkable period, however, was that in the middle of the century from about 1850 to 1865. In these few years the great pioneers of steelmaking—Kelly in the United States; Bessemer and Mushet in England; the brothers Siemens, natives of Germany; Émile and Pierre Martin in France; and Göransson in Sweden—laid the foundations of the age of steel.

REFERENCES

[1] MITCHELL, J. *J. Iron St. Inst.*, **183**, 179–89, 1956.
[2] LORD, W. M. *Trans. Newcomen Soc.*, **25**, 171, 1945–7.
[3] BURN, D. L. 'The Economic History of Steelmaking, 1867–1939', pp. 43–44. University Press, Cambridge. 1940.
[4] WALZEL, R. *J. Iron St. Inst.*, **168**, 369, 1951.
[5] SCHIB, K. and GNADE, R. 'Johann Conrad Fischer, 1773–1854', pp. 50–51. Fischer, Schaffhausen. 1954.

BIBLIOGRAPHY

BESSEMER, SIR HENRY. 'An Autobiography.' Offices of *Engineering*, London. 1905.
BORCHERS, W. 'Electric Furnaces' (trans. from the German by H. G. SOLOMON). Longmans, London. 1908.
BOUCHER, J. N. 'William Kelly: a True History of the So-called Bessemer Process.' Published by the author, Greensburg, Pa. 1924.

CLAPHAM, SIR JOHN H. 'An Economic History of Modern Britain', Vols 2 and 3. University Press, Cambridge. 1932, 1938.

DAVIES, M. E. 'The Story of Steel.' Burke Publishing Company, London. 1950.

DESCH, C. H. "Metals as Engineering Materials." *J. R. Soc. Arts*, **88,** 599–606, 1940.

JEANS, J. S. 'The Iron Trade of Great Britain.' Methuen, London. 1906.

JOHANNSEN, O. 'Geschichte des Eisens' (3rd ed.). Verlag Stahleisen, Düsseldorf. 1953.

The Clydach Iron Works, 1813.

4

NEW EXTRACTION PROCESSES FOR METALS

R. CHADWICK

I. GENERAL CONSIDERATIONS

IN the early part of the nineteenth century the range of metals extracted from the earth was in the main confined to those which had been known from antiquity. Iron, copper, lead, zinc, tin, and mercury were made by smelting the ores with charcoal or coal, as they had been from early times, while silver was parted from copper and lead after smelting. Gold was found in elementary form and separated by simple hand-washing operations. Antoine Laurent Lavoisier (1743–94) had postulated the existence of many other metals, but no process by which these could be extracted from the so-called 'earths' had been suggested until Sir Humphry Davy (1778–1829), using the newly discovered galvanic cell, succeeded in preparing sodium and potassium as well as magnesium and some of the alkaline earth metals. In 1825 H. C. Oersted (1777–1851) isolated aluminium. Throughout the nineteenth century the diligence of the chemist added more and more new metals to the list, and it became apparent that the industrially available metals represented but a small fraction of those provided by nature. Even so, the laborious means by which very small quantities of these new metals had been prepared gave no indication of the prospects so soon to be realized.

The second half of the nineteenth century was characterized by tremendous advances both in the method and scale of operation of metallurgical processes for the established metals, and in the invention and development of methods of extracting metals hitherto regarded as chemical curiosities. The scale of this advance is shown by some figures of world production for 1850, 1875, and 1900 (p 73). All the common metals showed a faster rate of increase in the fourth quarter-century than in the third, the major increase in nickel and aluminium being in the last decade.

Chemistry and engineering each had a share in transforming the old and in developing the new methods. Chemistry provided basic understanding of the ancient metallurgical processes involving reduction by charcoal or coal. Because of this better understanding, it became possible to change methods of operation logically and to find new and more powerful agents of reduction. Chemistry also made possible accurate analytical methods for determining and controlling the metal content of intermediate products as well as of discarded gangue and slag. It also provided knowledge of refractories, so that operations could be carried to higher temperatures, while the resistance of furnace-linings to slagging was improved. Not least, chemical science made possible methods of separating pure metallic oxides from their ores, without which the manufacture of such metals as aluminium and tungsten could not have succeeded.

World Production of Metals (metric tons)

	1850	1875	1900
Copper . . .	55 000	130 000	525 000
Lead	130 000	320 000	850 000
Zinc	65 000	165 000	480 000
Tin	18 000	36 000	85 000
Nickel . . .	20	500	8000
Aluminium . . .	negligible	2½	7300

Engineering played its part in providing the means for handling ores in vast quantities. Apart from mining operations (vol IV, ch 3), plant was constructed for grinding and comminuting, and for pumping ore concentrates in the form of slurries. Metallurgical operations themselves were accelerated by the availability of powerful mechanical blowers. Finally, the period 1850–1900 saw the introduction of electrical power generation for industry (ch 9), and by the turn of the century it became possible to translate the electrolytic preparations of Davy and Oersted from a laboratory scale to a manufacturing one. This, within a short period of time, was to add completely new metals to mankind's many raw materials for manufacturing, as well as to provide new processes for the extraction and purification of the older metals.

II. ORE CONCENTRATION

The existence of secondary ore deposits in rich veins near the earth's surface was a fortunate circumstance for early metallurgical technology, and indeed it was only because of the opportunity thus afforded of achieving an adequate concentration by hand-picking that primitive smelting operations were possible. As the world's requirements of metals increased, the scale of operation reached a level at which hand-picking became impracticable. Before this stage was reached, the rich secondary veins began to be worked out, and it became imperative to find means of utilizing primary ore deposits of lower metal content.

The oldest ore concentration process is washing with water, but in its simplest form this method is applicable only to precious metals and to certain heavy metallic oxides and sulphides, such as the tin ore cassiterite. In primitive methods, as in early tin-mining, washing was carried out in a series of wooden enclosures usually constructed in the bed of a stream, or by hand 'panning'; the latter was used especially for gold. With the advent of steam-power, mechanical jigging was adopted to keep the lighter constituent in suspension. The Rittinger shaking-table was perhaps the first scientifically designed jigging machine. It employed a shallow layer of finely ground ore to increase the efficiency of separation.

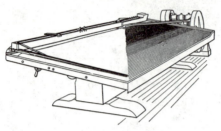

FIGURE 24—*Wilfley table for ore concentration.*

A major advance in ore beneficiation was made in 1895 by Arthur R. Wilfley, who introduced a table with parallel grooves. These grooves or riffles were deep at the feed end, becoming progressively shallower towards the exit end, the level of which was very slightly raised (figure 24). Water passed transversely over the riffles and washed away the lighter particles of gangue from the tops of the grooves. As the ore passed towards the shallower parts of the grooves, so heavier particles tended to be removed; by careful adjustment it was possible to separate a number of constituents along different sections of the table.

Magnetic separation was the second ore concentration method to be developed in the late nineteenth century. In this the finely crushed ore is carried on a belt between the poles of a powerful electromagnet. This method was first used to separate ferrous from non-ferrous constituents, but by the end of the century it was being used to separate minerals differing only slightly in magnetic susceptibility.

Flotation eventually became the dominating process for ore enrichment, and by the early twentieth century was in use for the separation from gangue of most low-grade sulphide ores such as copper pyrites (copper iron sulphide), blende (zinc sulphide), and galena (lead sulphide), and for removing unwanted and harmful components of gold ores. The forerunner of ore flotation was a process suggested by William Haynes in 1860, in which finely ground ore is mixed with water and a viscous oil. Mineral sulphide particles treated in this way are not wetted by water and become concentrated in the oil, so that the gangue can be washed clear by water. This, and various modifications, proved to be of limited value because of the large amount of oil used and the inefficient separation. In

1901 C. V. Potter and G. O. Delprat carried out the first modern flotation operation, in which a small amount of oil was employed and the mixture was agitated by air. The sulphide particles adsorb the oil, and as a result resist wetting by water; in other words, they acquire a high surface tension so that they are readily carried up by bubbles of air. Flotation by this method was first used in 1901 at Broken Hill, New South Wales, for the production of zinc concentrates. From there its use spread rapidly, and the technique was elaborated and developed so that, by the use of special surface-active additives, and by careful control of pH

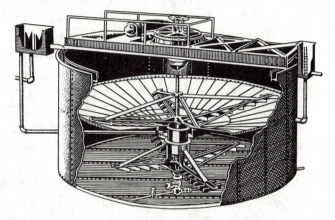

FIGURE 25—*Dorr thickener for increasing the solids content of a water suspension.*

in the aqueous component,[1] it became possible to separate most of the heavy metal sulphide from lean ores, and also to separate selectively constituents such as galena and blende.

In the practical application of flotation, the ore is finely ground in a ball-mill with water. It is then passed through a classifier, in which coarse particles are separated by centrifugal force and returned for regrinding. The pulp is next diluted, treated with the appropriate oils, and run into the uppermost of a series of wooden tanks. Air is blown in through perforated pipes in the base of the tank and forms a froth which overflows at the side; the aqueous residue is run into the next lower tank, where treatment is repeated to separate further amounts of the same or a different constituent. The ore is thus stripped of its valuable mineral content before reaching the bottom tank, from which the residue is pumped to waste. The final step is to remove as much water as possible from

[1] pH is a symbol used to define the degree of acidity or alkalinity of an aqueous liquid. It denotes the logarithm of the reciprocal of the hydrogen ion concentration.

the concentrate. This is carried out in an ingenious machine known as a Dorr thickener (figure 25). Here the suspension of solids is gently agitated by rakes which cause the solid particles to settle in the centre of the conical base, from which they are drawn off as a slurry containing up to 70 per cent solids.

III. NEW OR IMPROVED PROCESSES

To describe all the major changes and advances in the technology of extraction, even for the common metals, would require a much larger treatise than the present. The following sections relate, therefore, only to those metals for which the methods developed involved completely new principles, or for which industrial extraction was undertaken for the first time. Copper is given special prominence because, after iron, it was by far the most important metal of the late nineteenth century, and was the first metal to be refined electrolytically. Within the period nickel became of industrial importance from very small beginnings, while aluminium and tungsten were made for the first time and achieved commercial significance by about the end of the century. Gold and silver are included because of their derivation as by-products of copper and nickel refining. The completely novel process of alumino-thermic reduction was important to the production of many of the less common metals, and is briefly mentioned. The extraction metallurgy of zinc, lead, and tin has not been treated, for, although new processes were introduced, they did not involve major changes of principle. Furthermore, the main developments in technology occurred early in the period and are dealt with elsewhere (vol IV, ch 6).

IV. COPPER—THE CHANGING INDUSTRIAL SCENE

At the beginning of the nineteenth century, world production of copper was about 9000 tons,[1] and three-quarters of this total was smelted in south Wales, where the industry was located mainly in the Swansea valley along the banks of the river Tawe, into which ships brought ores from the mines of Cornwall and Anglesey. By mid-century, when world output had reached 55 000 tons, Swansea was still the centre of the world's copper industry, with an annual production of some 15 000 tons, and metallurgical industry reached its zenith in this area about 1860. At that time, on the banks of the Tawe there were as many as 600 furnaces engaged mainly in copper-smelting. From then on copper smelting in south Wales declined, but although after about 1870 its copper production in relation to the world total was insignificant, Swansea had important contribu-

[1] Nicol Brown and Charles C. Turnbull (1900) quote a world production of 16 000 tons. The additional amounts are ascribed to Russia, Japan, and South America, but the amounts are estimated and unsupported by evidence.

tions still to make to technology. Leadership in copper production was held successively by Spain, Chile, and North America, with the United States producing more than half the world total by the end of the century.

The main feature of these new enterprises in copper smelting was the complete integration of mining, smelting, and refining on one site, thus saving the cost of transporting ores over long distances. Additional economies were secured from the increased scale of working based on the vast ore bodies of Chile and of Michigan, Arizona, and Montana. So many and diverse were the methods adopted that any summary is bound to be incomplete, but methods were mainly

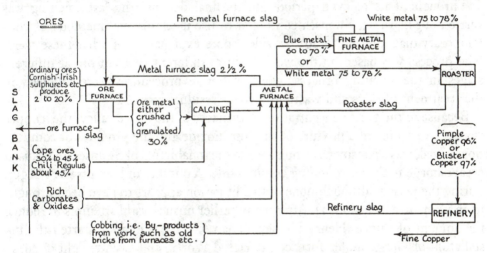

FIGURE 26—*Flow-sheet of Welsh copper-smelting process.*

based on and developed from the Welsh process. The principal change was that some of the separate stages were eliminated and operations were simplified, with very considerable shortening of the time necessary to complete smelting and consequent reduction in fuel consumption. Perhaps the greatest advantage derived from smelting at the mine was that only one type of ore was treated, and so the process could be 'tailored' to suit the ore and the method of working standardized and controlled. The Swansea smelters, on the other hand, found themselves treating ores in ever-increasing variety, with metal contents ranging from 5 per cent in the leaner pyritic ores to more than 70 per cent in precipitates from the Rio Tinto mines of Spain. As copper production became less profitable, the Swansea industry concerned itself to an increasing extent with the development of by-products and with fringe activities, and its output included silver, gold, nickel, and cobalt. The sulphur extracted from the flue gases was used to build up an extensive industry in heavy chemicals. Zinc smelting also became of some importance. However, none of these new enterprises could save the smelting industry from ultimate extinction.

Ores and concentrates arriving at Swansea were taken over by the smelters after public auctions or 'ticketings'. Each parcel or shipment of ore was dumped in a yard, where it was sampled and analysed by the various firms of smelters, who submitted sealed tenders; the ore went to the highest bidder. Later, this system came into disrepute because of collaboration in tendering by some of the larger firms, and much ore was imported privately.

Throughout its halcyon period and its final decline (the last smelting was carried out in 1921), Swansea continued to use its traditional methods. A contemporary diagram (figure 26) provides some explanation of what these were. The process was based on the working-in of different types of ore at different stages in the smelting process, while elaborate procedures were followed in the treatment of slags and waste to recover residual copper.

Because of the great concentration of furnaces in the Tawe valley, the 'copper smoke', consisting of a mixture of sulphur dioxide and the products of combustion of coal, was a considerable nuisance to the inhabitants of Swansea and caused great damage to the surrounding country-side. A number of lawsuits were begun during the period, although none of this litigation appears to have been brought to an ultimate conclusion [1]. After many earlier unsuccessful attempts to reduce the amount of smoke, Henry Hussey Vivian (1821–94) in 1865 started the installation of Gerstenhöfer furnaces at Hafod Works, and twenty-eight of these were eventually installed [1, 2]. The reverberatory furnaces previously used for calcining were replaced by these vertical furnaces (figure 27). Here the finely ground product of roasting was fed into hoppers at the top of the furnace, whence it fell down over horizontal bars triangular in section. Once the furnace had been started, the heat of combustion of the sulphur maintained the temperature, the red-hot ore being divided at each layer of bars. These furnaces were erected at the foot of old slag-heaps, the gases being led up ducts to chambers for sulphuric acid manufacture built on the flattened-out summits of the heaps [1]. The acid thus produced was utilized in other new manufactures: for example, copper sulphate was made on a considerable scale and exported to the continent for the treatment of vines against phylloxera. Then phosphatic rock was imported and converted to superphosphate fertilizer (p 254) [1]. The manufacture of hydrochloric acid, bleaching-powder, and soda crystals was also undertaken, while by-product salt-cake was utilized in metallurgical operations.

The smelting of nickel and cobalt ores was undertaken in Swansea from about 1870, although the amounts produced were small. At that time there was little demand for nickel, but cobalt was of considerable importance, the oxide being used extensively for colouring glass and china. Swansea was probably the first place in which the copper and nickel constituents were successfully separated from *Kupfernickel* (p 87). Silver and gold were extracted by chemical methods from argentiferous ores, silver concentrates were purchased for treatment, and

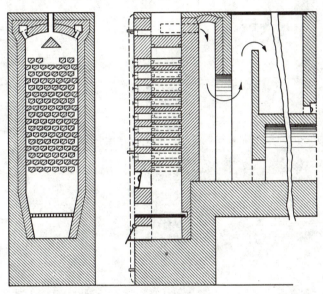

FIGURE 27—*Section of Gerstenhöfer kiln for calcining copper ore, with sulphur dioxide recovery.*

later the precious metals were extracted in the electrolytic refining of copper. These matters are more fully considered under the appropriate metals.

Although the large-scale smelting of ores at the mine was first undertaken in South America, and then in the Michigan or Lake Superior region of North America, the main advances in technology came about in Montana and Arizona. In the first development of this rich mineral area individual prospectors dug out ore and smelted it in small reverberatory or blast furnaces, roughly constructed from stone or brick, using charcoal as fuel. The industry may be regarded as originating in 1879 with the construction of a 14-ft reverberatory furnace at Butte by the Colorado Smelting and Mining Company. This furnace produced a matte, assaying 60 per cent copper and from 700 to 800 oz silver to the ton, which was shipped abroad, presumably to Swansea, for further treatment [3]. By the end of the century, Arizona and Montana between them were producing at a rate of some 200 000 tons a year, little short of half the world's copper output.

According to W. Gowland [4], Japan used its old traditional processes until at least 1884. In these the ore was mixed with charcoal and smelted to matte; an

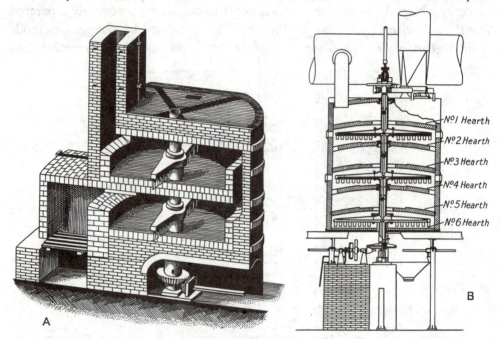

FIGURE 28—*Sections of roasting furnaces for sulphide ores.* (A) *Parkes's roaster with rotating rakes, 1850.* (B) *MacDougall's roaster, 1873 (reduced scale).*

air blast was then played on the metal surface, and the reduction to copper effected in the same furnace. Finally, the molten bath was sprinkled with water and the metal removed in the form of rosettes.

V. COPPER—NEW TECHNIQUES

A classic paper presented to the Society of Arts by J. Hollway [5] in 1879 made an important contribution to the chemistry of copper smelting. His main purpose was to point out the possibilities of using the heat of combustion of the sulphide by burning pyritic ore in a confined space rather than roasting it in an open reverberatory furnace, although it should be noted that this was ten years after the installation of Gerstenhöfer furnaces in Swansea. Pyritic smelting, which developed directly out of Hollway's proposals, adopted the blast-furnace in place of the reverberatory furnace for ores containing a high proportion of pyrites (iron sulphide) as well as copper sulphide. Successful operation depended on careful grading of the burden and became impracticable with the increasing use of lean ores derived from primary deposits, since ore concentration processes invariably necessitated grinding the ore to a fine powder.

The early stages of treatment of these finely powdered ores depended on a totally different development. In 1850 A. Parkes (1813–90) introduced the first multi-hearth roasting furnace (figure 28 A). In this furnace the ore is loaded on to the top hearth and is raked by rotating arms towards the centre, whence it drops through slots to the second hearth where it is worked to the outside. This was followed by the greatly advanced furnace of J. S. MacDougall. In the original installation of 1873 (figure 28 B) this had six hearths with a height of 18 ft and diameter of 16 ft [2], later increased to twelve hearths, the whole construction being of steel with the walls, arches, and hearths lined with brick. The rotating arms on this furnace were of steel, with internal water-cooling. Temperature in a rotary furnace of this type could be very effectively controlled, and in one short operation it was possible to produce a reduction of sulphur content which required several days of slow roasting in the old Welsh calcining furnaces.

In all these smelting processes, roasting to burn off sulphur is followed by the production of matte. This is the first liquid metallic product. The composition of matte has varied little over the years or from one smelter to another. For example, eight separate published examples are in the range copper 32–46 per cent, iron 25–36 per cent, sulphur 22–27 per cent. Matte furnaces throughout all changes and developments continued to be of the reverberatory type, although they increased in size and in efficiency of operation. As an example of this development, figure 29 shows furnaces at Anaconda, Montana, of 1880 and 1902. The earlier type had a length of 16 ft, a maximum width of 10 ft, and using wood as fuel smelted 12 tons of ore in 24 hours. The later type had a length of 50 ft and a daily burden of some 100 tons of ore; fuel consumption, in terms of calorific value, was less than half that of the earlier furnace [3].

It was in the conversion of matte into blister, involving the elimination of most of the sulphur and iron to produce a metal of some 98·5 per cent copper content, that the biggest revolution occurred. Henry Bessemer (1813–98) had pointed out in 1856 how malleable iron and steel could be manufactured from pig iron by burning out the carbon in an air blast without the use of fuel (p 52), and by 1860, after certain metallurgical difficulties had been overcome, a practical converter was successfully installed. The analogy with copper matte oxidation was obvious, and the saving to be achieved by eliminating the prolonged treatment in the 'metal furnaces' of the Welsh process equally attractive. First attempts to use the Bessemer converter were unsuccessful, because, as a result of the high thermal conductivity of copper, solidification of the bottom layers invariably put an end to the reaction. In 1880 Pierre Manhès of France invented the side-blown converter which bore his name; four years later this was adopted in the Anaconda smelter, with immediate success.

The converter was charged directly with liquid matte, with a small amount of

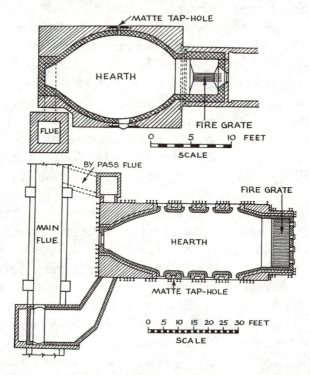

FIGURE 29—*Sections of Anaconda reverberatory furnaces producing copper matte.* (Above) *Wood-burning furnace,* c *1880;* (below) *coal-fired furnace,* c *1902.*

added coke in inverse proportion to the sulphur content. As the reaction proceeded, the sulphur was oxidized away and formed a fluid slag with silica from the lining of sand and fire-clay. Fresh matte was sometimes added, and the reaction usually took some two hours to complete, when the blister copper, averaging 98·5 per cent copper content, was poured off by tilting the converter. In the typical early converter (figure 30), the initial capacity had to be small, but the lining slagged away so rapidly that after two to three days' operation the capacity increased from 2 tons to some 4–5 tons. Relining then became necessary. The need for a basic lining was recognized from an early date, but no suitable material was available. It was not until 1909 that W. H. Peirce and E. A. C. Smith developed durable refractory bricks of magnesia. These were soon adopted for converter linings, silica sand then being added to the charge in the correct amount to slag away the iron content.

The refining of blister copper (or the slightly less pure metal known at Swansea as pimple copper), to produce 'tough pitch' metal of a quality suitable for manufacture into wrought forms, is a process that has remained unchanged in principle and in its major technological practice over many centuries (vol II, ch 2; vol III, ch 2). The impure copper is melted in a reverberatory furnace, and blown with air to oxidize it up to about 1 per cent oxygen content and burn out the last traces of sulphur. The iron and other impurities are also oxidized, forming a slag with sand thrown on to the charge. The copper is then reduced by thrusting under the surface a stout pole of green wood, a procedure for which no effective substitute has been found (cf vol I, p 587). The tough pitch is reached when a sample of copper solidifies with a level surface. Molten copper contains both oxygen and hydrogen in solution, as shown in figure 31. When the copper solidifies, these two gases

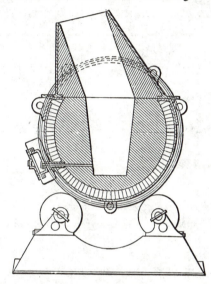

FIGURE 30—*Section of copper converter, c 1885.*

combine to form steam; this is evolved inside the casting and forms microscopic pores which counteract the shrinkage of the metal on solidification. The amount of steam evolved depends on the hydrogen content, because excess oxygen is always present as oxide in the metal. If oxygen is reduced too far the hydrogen content increases (figure 31), large amounts of steam are formed, and the metal is porous. However, the more complete the elimination of sulphur and other impurities, the lower the oxygen content associated with the tough pitch condition. Early samples of copper contained at least 0·1 per cent of oxygen and often much more, lead being frequently added to combine with traces of sulphur which might otherwise have caused brittleness. The purest copper manufactured at the end of the century contained as little as 0·015 per cent oxygen.

Perhaps the most significant advance in copper technology was the introduction of electrolytic refining as an industrial operation. With the invention of the dynamo the end-uses of copper were completely changed. No longer did the prime requirement arise from such miscellaneous applications as the sheathing of ships' bottoms, the manufacture of domestic cooking-pots and other utensils, or fire-box construction for steam locomotives, which had become important from 1840 onwards. Copper, because of its high electrical conductivity and the ease with which it could be drawn into wire, was in great demand as an electrical conductor, and very soon this became its principal use. Only the best qualities of copper had the necessary electrical conducting properties. Commercial fire-refined copper, although perfectly satisfactory for all other purposes, displayed only 50–70 per cent of the maximum possible conductivity, because of impurities such as arsenic, nickel, iron, and other elements, even though these might amount in total to less than 0·1 per cent (excluding oxygen, which has a slightly beneficial effect on electrical conductivity). Although Lake Superior ores were capable of producing high-grade copper by normal fire-refining methods, in general high-conductivity copper could be produced solely by electrolytic refining, and this became commercially feasible only with the advent of cheap electric power, while, conversely, efficient power generation called for electrolytically refined metal for dynamo windings and bus-bars.

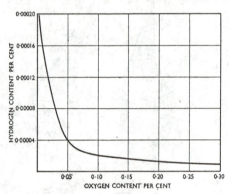

FIGURE 31—*Hydrogen–oxygen equilibrium in molten copper.*

James Balleny Elkington, in a patent [6] of 1865 remarkable for its perspicuity, described a process of electrolytic refining of copper which was to remain basically unaltered in subsequent years. Elkington proposed to start from a series of cast plates of either blister or pimple copper 18 in square and $\frac{3}{4}$-in thick, with cast-on lugs by means of which they were to be suspended vertically from conductor bars resting on wooden supports. These plates, constituting the anodes of an electrolytic cell, were suspended in a trough in pairs in three parallel rows, 6 in apart. Between, and also outside, these were sixteen smaller negative, or cathode, plates of rolled copper arranged in four rows of four each. These were to be $\frac{1}{32}$-inch in thickness and fitted with lugs for mounting on copper conductor bars. It was proposed to have about twenty-five troughs in the installation, the negative plates of one trough being connected to the positive plates of the next, and so on, so that there would be in all twenty-five separate cells in series in an electrical circuit. Electricity was supplied by a magneto-electric machine de-

scribed as having '50 permanent magnets weighing 28 lb each and fully mag-
netised, the other parts of the machine being in proportion'. A saturated aqueous
solution of copper sulphate was to be used as electrolyte and current was to be
passed until the cathodes reached $\frac{3}{4}$–1 inch in thickness; the electrolyte was retained until the content of ferrous sulphate became excessive, when it was
discarded and the copper contained in it recovered. The importance of recovering silver, gold, tin, and antimony from the anode sludge was referred
to in Elkington's patent. A subsequent patent [7] of 1869 proposed that the
copper should be deposited on gutta-percha sheets made electrically conducting
by a coating of bronze powder. As soon as a coating was formed, the gutta-percha
was stripped off, leaving the copper to receive further deposits. Starter sheets
prepared by stripping in this or some similar way formed the basis of all subsequent installations, thus avoiding the use of expensive rolled sheets.

The first electrolytic refinery was constructed in 1869 at Pembrey, near
Swansea, in the copper-smelting plant of Mason & Elkington. This plant was
subsequently taken over by the Elliotts Metal Company. Vivian and other industrialists erected electrolytic plants, small by present standards, in the Swansea
area. The economic operation of these plants was based on the high value of the
silver and gold recovered from the anode slimes when using blister coppers
derived from ores rich in precious metals, mined chiefly in Spain and South
America. Electrolytic refining was continued in Wales until about 1912.

The first electrolytic refinery on the American continent was at Laurel Hill,
New York, in 1892 [8]. This refinery also was designed to operate with blister
copper, which was purchased from various sources, a high precious-metal content
being the basis of choice. Later, with the increasing demand for copper of high
conductivity, electrolytic refining plant was installed by most major copper producers, and the refinery tank-house was eventually to become a principal world
source of precious metals, as well as of some of the other less common metals,
including bismuth and cobalt.

The practice of refining blister copper ceased by the end of the century, because the iron and other impurities contained in it produced a rapid deterioration
of the electrolyte, while the uneven solution of the anode resulted in a low yield.
Instead, the metal was first subjected to fire-refining and the tough pitch copper
was cast into anodes. After electrolytic refining, the cathodes were for the most
part remelted and subjected once more to the refining cycle of oxidation and
poling with green wood to tough pitch. Other modifications in electrolytic refining have been of a minor character, designed in the main to secure closer spacing
of the electrodes and so to increase current efficiency, upon which the economic

success of the operation so largely depends, but the broad principles laid down by Elkington are still employed. The deleterious effect of impurities on the electrical conductivity of copper was first realized about 1850, but the copper used in the transatlantic cable of 1856 had only half the conductivity of the purest available copper. A. Matthiesen carried out extensive experiments to establish the effect on the conductivity of copper of different metallic impurities and proposed a system of rating in which the purest copper was regarded as having 100 per cent conductivity [9]. This basis of assessment was adopted generally from about 1890, but it was not until 1913 that agreement was reached on an international standard of conductivity. This called for a minimum resistance of 1·7241 microhms/cm cube at 20° C. Material of this minimum resistance is described as 100 per cent I.A.C.S. (International Annealed Copper Standard).

VI. NICKEL

Nickel was being extracted in small quantities quite early in the century, and was used from about 1824 in the so-called German silvers, that is, brasses to which up to 20 per cent of nickel was added to give a white silvery colour. Much earlier examples of these alloys are, however, found in ornamental work imported from China. The metal itself was originally regarded as useless because of its brittleness. The cause of this defect was not then understood, but it is now known to be due to an impurity, sulphur, which forms nickel sulphide films over the boundaries of the minute crystalline grains of which the metal is composed.

Rudolf Böttger in 1843 showed that coatings of nickel could be produced on other metals by electrodeposition [10], but the time was too early for practical exploitation of the process. Theodore Fleitmann in 1879 showed that nickel itself was rendered tough and ductile by the addition of magnesium [11], so that it could be wrought. Later, manganese was used in preference to magnesium, both metals having the property of combining preferentially with sulphur and preventing its deleterious effect. Nickel sheet was being rolled in 1881, its first use being in twenty-centime pieces for Switzerland [12].

From about 1820 nickel was worked in small quantities in various countries, using both wet methods of separation and conventional smelting based on the Welsh process. For example, in 1874, the Morfa Works at Swansea was producing about 5 tons of nickel and 1 ton of cobalt per month, using the Welsh process of smelting [13]. In 1865 Jules Garnier discovered large deposits of silicate ores in New Caledonia, a French possession in the Pacific. Mining was started in 1875 and this soon became the main source of nickel, the price falling within three years to about one-third.

In 1883, during the construction of the Canadian Pacific railway, the vast Sudbury ore deposits were discovered. Many prospectors were attracted to the district, and large-scale mining operations commenced in 1886. At first these ores were worked for their copper, but it was soon realized that they resembled the German *Kupfernickel* (p 79) and presented the same difficulties in smelting.

FIGURE 32—*Orford 'tops and bottoms' process for separating copper and nickel.*

Because of this, most of the original mining schemes were abandoned, but a limited amount of nickel-bearing matte was produced and shipped abroad for treatment. Hussey Vivian operated the Murray Mines at Sudbury between 1889 and 1894, the ores being smelted at Swansea for nickel and copper.

Nickel extraction lagged because world demand for the metal was small, and its price soon dropped to an unprofitable level, but this situation changed with the publication in 1889 of a classic paper by James Riley [14] describing the improvements in the properties of steel conferred by the addition of nickel (p 66). The study of the extraction of nickel was taken up by R. M. Thompson of the Orford Copper Company, and the Orford 'tops and bottoms' process was announced in 1893. This was based on the use of salt-cake (sodium bisulphate), a substance which had been in use in copper smelting at Swansea since 1844 (vol IV, p 128). The salt-cake, together with some coke, was added to the molten matte containing some 48 per cent nickel and 17 per cent copper, giving a mixture of sulphides of sodium, copper, and nickel. The mass was then poured into large pots, copper sulphide (which is soluble in sodium sulphide) floating, while nickel sulphide collected at the bottom; after solidification the two parts could be separated with a sledge-hammer (figure 32). The treatment was repeated so that the 'second bottom' contained 72 per cent nickel, 1·5 per cent copper, and 25 per cent sulphur. The process is shown schematically in figure 33. After leaching with water to remove soluble sodium salts, the mass was subjected to a roasting or sintering operation which burned off the bulk of the sulphur, giving an oxide containing about 0·5 per cent sulphur. This was crushed, mixed with coke, and charged into reverberatory furnaces, where it was reduced to nickel, melted, and cast into anodes containing approximately 95 per cent nickel. This crude metal was refined in electrolytic tanks similar to those used for copper. As in electrolytic copper-refining, precious metals were recovered from the anode slimes, which were particularly rich in platinum.

The outstanding discovery in the technology of nickel extraction was announced in a paper to The Chemical Society in 1890. Ludwig Mond (1839–1909), then working at Winnington Hall on the ammonia-soda process (p 243), found that nickel valves were being attacked by traces of carbon monoxide present in the carbon dioxide used to purge certain vessels. The attack was shown to be due to the formation of a new compound, nickel carbonyl, a gas which was formed at one temperature range and decomposed at a higher one, nickel being deposited [15]. Mond appreciated how valuable this reaction would be in carrying out the very difficult separation of nickel. Patents were filed, and Mond and his assistant, Carl Langer, together undertook research which led to the erection of a complete experimental plant in 1892 at the works of Henry Wiggin and Company, who at that time were smelters of nickel ores at Smethwick, near Birmingham. Most of the technical difficulties of the carbonyl process appear to have been solved by 1895 [16], but several years elapsed in negotiations over mining rights, and it was not until 1900 that it was possible to begin mining and smelting operations in Canada. A refining plant based on the carbonyl process was built at Clydach in the Tawe valley, where a high-grade anthracite coal was available for making producer-gas, and operations started in 1902.

In the original process, matte from the Canadian smelters was calcined to

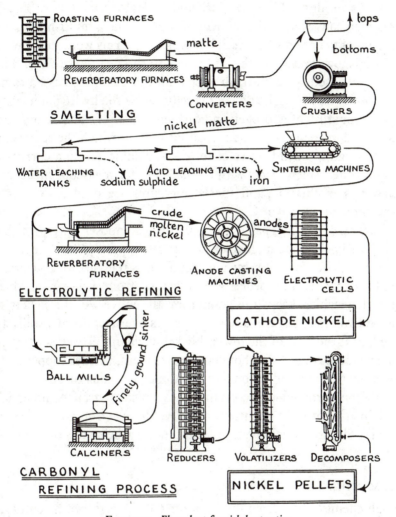

FIGURE 33—*Flow-chart for nickel extraction.*

remove the remaining sulphur, and then leached with sulphuric acid to dissolve out the copper, while the insoluble nickel-bearing residue passed to the Mond carbonyl plant proper (figure 33). Later, the Orford 'tops and bottoms' process was adopted as an intermediate stage to separate the bulk of the copper. In the Mond plant the sinter is very finely ground in a ball-mill, the powder from which is sized in a classifier and discharged into a cyclone separator, the coarser material falling back into the mill. This fine powder is again calcined, to remove the last traces of sulphur, in a double-deck furnace fitted with ploughs which work the powder outwards along the upper deck and back along the lower. The calcined powder is then conveyed to the reducer towers, having a multi-hearth construction made up of twenty double-deck boxes. Rabble arms work the powder down the 40-ft high towers from each upper deck to the one next below. The lower deck has an enclosed space through which hot flue gases are passed to maintain a temperature of 400° C. The powder is reduced by the hydrogen in a stream of water-gas—a mixture of hydrogen and carbon monoxide. The carbon monoxide released is used in the next process, volatilization, in which the reduced powder is passed through a second series of towers and subjected to a current of pure carbon monoxide, which reacts with the nickel to form gaseous nickel carbonyl. The reaction is exothermic, and special measures are needed to maintain the optimum temperature of 50° C.

The nickel carbonyl then passes through the decomposer tower, which is filled with nickel seed pellets maintained at a temperature of 180° C. Pure nickel is deposited on the pellets and the carbon monoxide is released for re-circulation in the volatilizer towers. The pellets are prevented from welding together by an elevator system which keeps the column on the move. As the pellets grow in size, the total volume increases and some pellets overflow down a spillway into a collecting box at the base of the tower. Nickel made in this way is 99·95 per cent pure. The residues from the carbonyl process contain, besides copper and nickel, some 4 per cent cobalt and 30 ounces per ton of precious metals.

Although the carbonyl process rapidly established itself commercially and continued in use into the twentieth century, the electrolytic process was not superseded and substantial tonnages continued to be made by both of these methods.

VII. ALUMINIUM

Although chemists had, from the beginning of the eighteenth century, recognized the probable existence of a new metal, aluminium, attempts to prepare it by chemical reduction failed because of its high energy of oxidation. Oersted was the first to prepare an impure metallic powder by heating anhydrous aluminium chloride with potassium amalgam. It was not, however, until 1845 that Friedrich Wöhler (1800–82), by allowing aluminium chloride to react with potassium vapour, produced pin-head globules of the metal, with which he demonstrated its light weight and malleability. Another chemist, Henri Étienne

Sainte-Claire Deville (1818–81), under the patronage of the Emperor Napoleon III of France, undertook a study of possible methods of making the metal commercially. In 1854, he first developed a method of manufacturing his two raw materials, aluminium chloride and sodium. By heating sodium carbonate with charcoal, sodium was made at the then low cost of about 5s per oz. Pure alumina was made from the mineral bauxite, a widely distributed ore originally found at Les Baux, Provence. The bauxite, containing between 50 and 65 per cent alumina, was crushed and digested with caustic soda, the sodium aluminate leached out with water and the solution filtered, and pure alumina precipitated by blowing in carbon dioxide. The calcined alumina was then heated with charcoal in a stream of chlorine to produce aluminium chloride, a volatile solid.

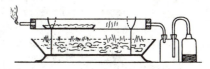

FIGURE 34—*Deville's apparatus for the reduction of aluminium chloride to aluminium.*

At the Salindres foundry near Paris, Sainte-Claire Deville produced aluminium by virtually laboratory methods. The reaction was carried out in a series of Bohemian glass tubes heated over burning charcoal (figure 34). Pure dry hydrogen was passed through the tubes and over the aluminium chloride, the vapour of which was led over boats containing liquid sodium. Some 50 tons of aluminium were made by this process [17] in Sainte-Claire Deville's factories at Salindres, and later at Nanterre, between 1855 and 1888, during which period the price of the metal fell from £12 to 50s per lb, the average purity being about 97 per cent. Its use was confined to ornamental and luxury articles, among those commissioned by Napoleon III being a breast-plate, spoons for use at state banquets, and a rattle for his infant son.

Several other manufacturers undertook the production of aluminium by Sainte-Claire Deville's process, the most notable being James Fernley Webster, who founded the Aluminium Crown Metal Company in 1877; this produced up to 500 lb per week of metal at plant installed close to the sodium works at Oldbury, near Birmingham. The process received a great fillip in 1886 with the introduction of the Castner process for the manufacture of sodium (p 248–9). All processes based on reduction with sodium soon became obsolete, however, because studies by electrochemists, which were being actively undertaken in consequence of the availability of electric power from the dynamo, soon led to a successful and much more economic process for the direct production of aluminium by electrolysis.

In 1886 Charles Martin Hall in America and Paul Louis Toussaint Héroult in France, who were both born in the year 1863 and who both died in 1914, independently and simultaneously discovered the process of direct electrolysis which has been used ever since for the production of metallic aluminium (p 249). The importance of the Hall–Héroult process depends upon two important and essential factors. The first is the use of an electrolyte consisting of alumina dissolved in molten cryolite, a double fluoride of sodium and aluminium originally mined in Greenland, but later made synthetically. On electrolysis the alumina only is decomposed, the relatively expensive cryolite remaining available for

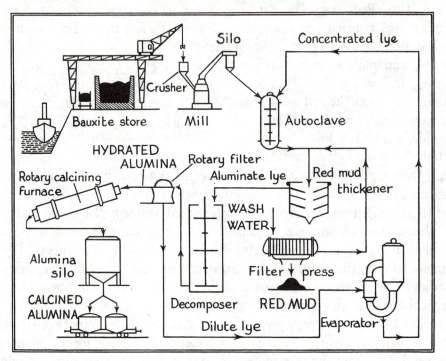

FIGURE 35—*Flow-sheet for Bayer process of alumina purification.*

further use. The second factor is that the molten electrolyte is of such a density that aluminium generated at the cathode sinks to the bottom of the bath and is thus protected from atmospheric oxidation.

Although Sainte-Claire Deville had recognized the need for chemically purified ore in aluminium manufacture, his process was expensive because the soda had to be heavily diluted and reconverted from carbonate to caustic by the use of lime. Fortunately, within a short time of the discovery of the electrolytic process, Karl Josef Bayer put forward a new method of purification remarkable for its elegance; this has since continued unchanged, none of the many suggested alternatives offering serious rivalry.

Important deposits of high-grade bauxite ore are found in France, Italy, Yugo-slavia, and Greece; in British Guiana and Jamaica; and in the Gold Coast. Workable ores contain 50 per cent or more of aluminium, and must have a low silica content for economical extraction. The crushed and washed ore is usually shipped to the site of the reduction plant where the Bayer purification is carried out. After grinding, it is digested in large vessels with strong caustic soda solution. The process thereafter depends upon the ore composition; if it is monohydrate a single extraction at a temperature of 165° C is sufficient, but

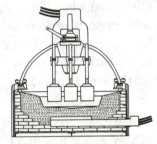

when both mono- and tri-hydrates are present a first extraction in cold caustic soda is followed by a second at 168° C under a pressure of 180 lb to the sq in. After reaction, the charge is blown into a second vessel and brought down to atmospheric pressure, whereupon impurities, which include silicates and iron oxides, settle and the fine suspended matter is removed by filtration. The critical step is the one that follows. The liquid is pumped into decomposers, diluted slightly with water, and seeded with alumina crystals from previous production. Crystalline alumina hy-

FIGURE 36—*16 000-amp Héroult cell for the production of aluminium by electrolysis.*

drate slowly separates, but several days are required for completion of the process. When precipitation is complete the liquid is run off into multiple-stage evaporators, where it is concentrated for re-use, and the alumina crystals are washed, dried, and calcined at a temperature of 1300° C to drive off combined water. A flow-sheet of the Bayer process is illustrated in figure 35. Alumina pre-pared in this way is a coarse, white free-flowing powder, very easy to handle and free from impurities deleterious to the reduction process.

Héroult cells were first operated commercially in 1887 at Neuhausen, Switzer-land, by the Swiss Metallurgical Company, using electric power generated at the famous falls of the Rhine [18]. Shortly afterwards, plant was installed by Péchiney at Froges in France. Production was first undertaken in America in 1888 by the Pittsburgh Reduction Company and by the British Aluminium Company in 1896, but for many years the Swiss aluminium industry was the main producer. The form of cell construction, which has remained fundamentally unchanged since those early days, is shown in figure 36. The base consists of a steel or cast iron casing within which the cathode is built up from carbon blocks, with some back-ing of fire-bricks for economy of construction. This carbon-lined cell contains the molten electrolyte, consisting of alumina dissolved in cryolite and main-tained at about 950° C. The anode in the first furnaces was a single carbon block;

it was rotated continuously, but this was found to be unnecessary. Subsequently the furnaces were made larger, with several carbon blocks forming the anode, attached by steel bars to the overhead conductor. Aluminium is formed at the cathode as a liquid pool protected from oxidation by the electrolyte, while oxygen evolved at the anode results in the burning away of the carbon. A cover of bauxite is maintained and provides very effective heat insulation over the molten electrolyte. When the bauxite in solution is exhausted there occurs a sudden increase in resistance, producing a sharp rise in cell voltage. This is known as the anode effect, and when it occurs the bauxite cover, which has consolidated into a semi-solid mass, is broken down with crowbars and sinks into the electrolyte. A fresh layer of bauxite is then shovelled on to the surface of the electrolyte and the cell is put back into circuit. Aluminium is removed periodically, being either tapped off through a siphon or withdrawn into a mobile vacuum vessel from which it is discharged to moulds.

Theoretically, to decompose alumina requires 2·1 volts, but Héroult cells operate at 5 volts; the overall efficiency is about 36 per cent, the remaining energy being used to maintain the cell temperature, in which the combustion of the anode block also plays a part. A 'pot-line', as it is called, may consist of up to 100 cells in series connected by heavy aluminium bus-bars (plate 6 A). The first cells to be installed at Neuhausen were of 4000 amps, but an amperage of 8000 was usual by the end of the century. Some 18 000–20 000 kilowatt-hours are required for each ton of aluminium, together with about half a ton of carbon. For this reason most plants have been installed near sources of water-power.

Carbon for the electrodes was originally produced from finely ground coke mixed with pitch and fired at a high temperature, but special cokes made from oil-refinery residues were employed later because of their greater freedom from ash. The purity of the metal depends upon the efficiency of purification of aluminium in the Bayer process and upon the use of pure carbon anodes. Residues from either source may contain iron and silicon which enter the aluminium, but the usual commercial metal produced by electrolysis contains only 0·25 per cent or less of each of these elements.

VIII. GOLD, SILVER, AND PLATINUM

With the expansion of industry and commerce in the late nineteenth century, gold and silver came into great demand. Both were in universal use as currency, while gold had become established as an essential basis for credit and banking systems, which were concerned in financing the great new projects overseas for which European civilization was mainly responsible. Furthermore, new demands for silver and gold arose during this period from the invention of plating and its application to cheap silver ware and jewelry, for which very large markets quickly developed.

In the middle of the nineteenth century alluvial concentrations of gold were being panned in the newly discovered Californian gold-fields, while the Patio process of amalgamation was still in use in Mexico and South America. Amalgamation was the only process then available for dealing in bulk with the low concentrations of dispersed gold in quartzite rocks or silica gravels. From lean ores amalgamation extracted not more than about 75 per cent of the gold, while much of the expensive mercury was lost because of the high vapour pressure of this metal, and the operation was barely profitable.

Although it had long been known that metallic gold was dissolved by an aqueous solution of sodium or potassium cyanide in the presence of oxygen, cyanide was not applied to gold extraction until 1887, when J. S. MacArthur and R. W. and W. Forrest pointed out in a patent that extraction could be effected by a very dilute solution of cyanide [19]. At first, potassium cyanide, but within a few years sodium cyanide, became the standard chemical for gold and silver extraction (p 249). Whereas amalgamation was barely profitable on ores averaging 4 oz per ton, cyanide could be effectively used with as little as 5 dwt of gold per ton. After this discovery, West Africa and the Rand became the main sources of the world's gold, although Russia continued to be a significant producer.

For extraction with cyanide, the ores are crushed and coarsely ground, then mixed with an aqueous solution containing 0·05 per cent sodium cyanide and sufficient lime to neutralize natural acid in the rock, which would otherwise decompose the cyanide and evolve a dangerous gas, hydrogen cyanide. Grinding of the wet mixture is carried out in ball-mills and then in rod-mills; the slurry thus produced is treated in classifiers, the coarse particles being returned for regrinding. The fine suspension or slime, containing 25 per cent of solids, is then thoroughly aerated by blowing in air until all the gold is dissolved. The liquid is separated in Dorr thickeners (p 75) or by filtration, and after removal of dissolved oxygen the gold is liberated from the cyanide by reaction with zinc shavings, the cyanide being regenerated. Subsequent melting oxidizes the zinc, leaving gold of 850–900 (85–90 per cent) fineness.

In early times silver was obtained mainly from the refining of lead, although the lead and copper-bearing ores of Spain had been worked from Roman times purely for their silver content: extraction methods have been described already, in vol IV. Many copper ores contain both silver and gold. In smelting and refining, these metals concentrate in the copper, and in the early nineteenth century they were sometimes recovered by melting the copper with lead and allowing the two liquids to separate, the silver being thereby transferred into the lead fraction. About 1840 the Augustin process was developed in Germany, and in 1845 it was introduced into Wales [1]. In this, the sulphide ore is roasted with salt and the silver chloride so produced is extracted with saturated sodium chloride solution. Shortly afterwards this process was supplanted by the Ziervogel process, in which the sulphide ore, after roasting, is extracted with water. The silver sulphate is dissolved, along with some copper sulphate, and the silver is re-precipitated by scrap copper. Gold appears to have been extracted by the Plattner method, in which the roasted ore is treated with chlorine water. In 1880 Vivian's works at Swansea produced an average of 30 000 oz of silver and 300 oz of gold a month from copper ores, as well as about 50 000 oz of silver from silver-bearing lead or lead ores [20]. Chemical methods of separating silver and gold were superseded shortly afterwards by electrolytic refining, which had been introduced in Wales in 1869. In those early days of the Welsh refineries it seems probable that copper with 100 oz or more per ton of silver, and as much as 2 oz per ton of gold, was available for treatment. Laurel Hill, New York, later in the century was handling copper with up to 60 oz per ton of silver and 3 oz per ton of gold.

However, these larger amounts were exceptional, and, when in the twentieth century electrolytic refining became more general, it was more usual to find a silver content of 2–3 oz per ton and no more than a fraction of an ounce of gold. The electrolytic refining of nickel (p 88) was also an important source of precious metals, but here, in addition to silver and gold, platinum metals were commonly present in recoverable amounts. Precious-metal residues were also derived from the carbonyl process of nickel extraction. With the rapid increase in copper production, and the general adoption of electrolytic refining in the early twentieth century, anode slimes became a major source of precious metals.

In the separation of precious metals from such slimes, wet chemical methods have been generally adopted. Briefly, the slimes are treated with *aqua regia* to dissolve platinum and gold, leaving silver in the residue, and the platinum is precipitated from solution as ammonium chloroplatinate by the addition of ammonium chloride.

For the refining of silver and gold, electrolytic methods displaced the old chemical methods at about the turn of the century. The possibility of the electrolysis of gold in chloride solution was first discovered by Charles Watt in 1863, and the process was first used to refine bullion by Emil Wohlwill in 1874. The main difficulty experienced was that silver chloride became deposited on the anodes, so preventing solution; this was overcome by superimposing an alternating component in the direct current electrolysis. Silver is electrolytically refined in nitrate solutions in which copper and gold, the principal impurities, are retained in solution. Very complex sequences are involved in the electrolytic refining of these metals in order to recover all the various components, including nickel and cobalt, as well as selenium, tellurium, and metals of the platinum group.

IX. ALUMINOTHERMIC PRODUCTION OF MANGANESE AND CHROMIUM

Towards the end of the nineteenth century, the value as additions to iron of several metals, such as manganese and chromium, was beginning to be realized. Salts or oxides of these metals were already in use for a variety of purposes, and in the first instance metals were prepared by established metallurgical processes, principally reduction with coke in a blast furnace to give ferro-alloys.

Production in this way had many disadvantages. High temperatures were generally required, so that the fuel consumption was high; moreover, since metals such as manganese, chromium, and titanium are themselves readily oxidized, it proved difficult to obtain a correct balance of fuel and air, with the result that carbon was often present in large excess. Chromium and titanium both form stable carbides which are objectionable in steel-making.

Sodium and potassium were employed by early chemists for reducing various metals from their oxides and Sainte-Claire Deville had shown that finely divided aluminium could be similarly used. In the 1890s, C. Vautin carried out some work on the use of aluminium powder for the production of ferro-alloys and in 1898 ferro-vanadium was being produced by this means. An exhaustive study of the so-called thermo-reduction of metal oxides by aluminium powder was carried out by Hans Goldschmidt (1861–1923) [21], and the aluminothermic process of metal reduction became established industrially in the early years of the twentieth century.

In this process the purified metal oxide is intimately mixed with finely powdered aluminium and the mixture is ignited, whereupon a vigorous reaction takes place with the formation of alumina and liberation of the metal. In spite of the relatively high cost of aluminium powder as the fuel in such a reaction, the process was technically and economically attractive because (i) it is capable of producing a metal free from major impurities, especially carbon; and (ii) it depends on an exothermic reaction, so that the necessary high temperatures are reached quickly, with the expenditure of a relatively small amount of aluminium fuel, whereas very large amounts of coke or coal would be needed to obtain the requisite thermal conditions were the heat applied externally.

Successful operation of the process depends upon a number of factors, such as particle-size, ratio of free oxygen to aluminium, and the free energy of dissociation of the various oxides comprised in the charge. For example, in the reduction of manganese by aluminium the reaction is almost explosive in violence if the dioxide is used. On the other hand, reduction of manganous oxide provides insufficient thermal energy to complete the reaction. It is therefore necessary to carry out a preliminary roasting of the dioxide in a reducing atmosphere to obtain a mixture of oxides. In the case of chromium, where again the chromic oxide has too great an energy of reaction and the chromous oxide too little, the most satisfactory solution is to use the chromous oxide and provide additional energy by pre-heating the charge. With other metals, it may be necessary to slow down the reaction by the introduction of an inert powder, or to provide additional thermal energy by the addition of potassium nitrate or some other oxidizing agent.

Successful working demands that the temperature attained shall exceed 2200° C so that the alumina slag is sufficiently fluid to separate completely from the metal. The reaction is started by a piece of magnesium ribbon immersed in a mixture of aluminium powder and a metallic peroxide. Once started, it quickly spreads to the main charge and thence throughout the mass, which soon becomes molten. Before combustion of the first charge is complete, further quantities of mixture are added. Finally, when the reaction ceases, the liquid products fill the pot. After a short interval to permit the separation of metal and slag, the upper layer of liquid alumina is poured off, and the underlying metal may then be cast into pigs.

X. TUNGSTEN

Tungsten is important historically as the first metal to be made industrially by methods of powder-metallurgy. Tungsten trioxide was isolated in the eighteenth century, and the crude metal was prepared in powder form by reducing it with charcoal. The industrial importance of the metal dates from 1857, when Oxland took out a patent for the manufacture of iron-tungsten alloys. From these developed the high-speed steels in which tungsten, in amounts up to 20 per cent, is used to confer strength at high temperatures (p 65).

Following the introduction of the carbon-filament lamp in 1878 (p 214), attempts were made to find a metallic element of sufficiently high melting-point from which more durable wires might be prepared. Carl von Welsbach (1858–

1929) made filaments from osmium, but this metal was too scarce to be seriously considered, and at the beginning of the twentieth century tantalum, melting at 2996° C, was used to some extent. The development of tungsten, melting at 3410° C, as a lamp filament began about 1904, and this metal has been used almost exclusively since 1911.

Chemical methods are used to separate tungsten from its ores and to purify it. In simplified form, the treatment of the principal ore, wolframite (ferrous tungstate) is as follows. The ore is finely ground and digested with hot caustic soda solution. A soluble sodium tungstate is formed, and after dilution to precipitate iron and manganese salts and addition of sodium peroxide to oxidize sulphides, the liquid is filtered and the oxide reprecipitated by acidification. Further purification follows by the formation of ammonium paratungstate. To obtain this compound, the precipitate is digested with aqueous ammonia, and on standing crystals of the paratungstate separate out.

After redissolving and reprecipitation, a high degree of purity is obtained, the paratungstate being converted to oxide once more by reaction with hydrochloric acid under carefully controlled conditions, the size and shape of the oxide particles being most important for the subsequent metallurgical process. Heating in air to drive off ammonia is sometimes preferred to treatment with acid. The compressed oxide is reduced to tungsten by carefully heating it in hydrogen. For this reaction, the powder is placed in refractory boats in a metal tube-furnace, the rate of heating being important in its effect on grain size and on the consolidation of the metal powder. After cooling and removing from the furnace, the tungsten powder is crushed, and placed in shallow steel dies some $\frac{1}{2}$-in square and 6 in long, in which it is compressed at some 20–30 tons per sq inch in a powerful hydraulic press. The next stage is to sinter the bar; this is effected by placing it in a vertical position between clamps constituting the terminals of a source of powerful low-tension current, the bar being heated as a result of its own electrical resistance. The heating is carried out in an enclosed furnace in an atmosphere of hydrogen, the clamps being free to move so as to accommodate the considerable shrinkage which occurs in sintering. Subsequently, the bar is hot-worked by rolling and swaging, pre-heating being carried out in an atmosphere of hydrogen, but after reducing to rod about an eighth of an inch in diameter it may be cold-drawn to wire of the finest sizes.

REFERENCES

[1] GRANT-FRANCIS, G. 'The Smelting of Copper in the Swansea District of South Wales from the Time of Elizabeth to the Present Day.' London. 1881.

[2] GOWLAND, W. Presidential Address. *Trans. Instn Min. Metall.*, **16**, 265, 1906–7.

[3] LAIST, F. *Trans. Amer. Inst. min. (metall.) Engrs*, **106**, 23, 1933.

[4] GOWLAND, W. "Metals and Metal Working in Old Japan" in Report of the 147th Annual Meeting of the Society of Antiquaries, London. 1915.

[5] HOLLWAY, J. *J. R. Soc. Arts*, **27**, 248–63, 1879.

[6] British Patent No. 2838. 1865.

[7] British Patent No. 3120. 1869.

[8] HARLOFF, C. S. and JOHNSON, H. F. *Trans. Amer. Inst. min. (metall.) Engrs*, **106**, 398, 1933.

[9] FITZPATRICK, T. C. *Rep. Brit. Ass.*, 60th meeting, 120–30, 1890.

[10] BÖTTGER, R. *Pharm. J.*, **3**, 358–9, 1843.

[11] FLEITMANN, T. *Ber. dtsch. chem. Ges.*, **12**, 454–5, 1879.

[12] STURNEY, A. C. 'The Story of Mond Nickel.' The Mond Nickel Company, London. 1951.

[13] WILLIAMS FOSTER AND COMPANY, SWANSEA. Private records.

[14] RILEY, J. *J. Iron St. Inst.*, no. 1, 45–55, 1889.

[15] MOND, L., LANGER, C. and QUINCKE, F. *J. chem. Soc.*, **57**, 749–53, 1890.

[16] MOND, L. *J. Soc. chem. Ind., Lond.*, **14**, 945–50, 1895.

[17] SAINTE-CLAIRE DEVILLE, H. E. 'De l'aluminium, ses propriétées, sa fabrication et ses applications.' Paris 1859. (Eng. trans. by R. T. ANDERSON. Sherwood Press, Cleveland, Ohio. 1933.)

[18] 'Geschichte der Aluminium-Industrie-Aktien-Gesellschaft, Neuhausen, 1888–1938' (2 vols). Aluminium-Industrie-Aktien-Gesellschaft, Chippis. 1942, 1943.

[19] MACARTHUR, J. S. *J. Soc. chem. Ind., Lond.*, **24**, 311–15, 1905.

[20] VIVIAN AND SONS, SWANSEA. Private records.

[21] GOLDSCHMIDT, H. and VAUTIN, C. *J. Soc. chem. Ind., Lond.*, **17**, 543–5, 1898.

BIBLIOGRAPHY

AITCHISON, L. "A Hundred Years of Metallurgy, 1851–1951." *Sheet Metal Ind.*, **28**, 405–24, 519–26, 530, 1951.

BROWN, N. and TURNBULL, C. 'A Century of Copper' (2 vols). Wilson, London. 1899, 1900.

CLENNELL, J. E. 'The Cyanide Handbook.' McGraw Hill, New York. 1910.

'Copper Metallurgy' (Rocky Mountain Fund Volume). *Trans. Amer. Inst. min. (metall.) Engrs*, **106**, 1933.

LEVY, D. M. 'Modern Copper Smelting.' Griffin, London. 1912.

LOUIS, H. 'The Dressing of Minerals.' Arnold, London. 1909.

MORRISON, W. M. "Aluminium and Highland Water Power." *J. Inst. Met.*, **65**, 17–36, 1939.

PERCY, J. 'Metallurgy: Fuel; Fire-Clays; Copper; Zinc; Brass, etc.' London. 1861.

Idem. 'Metallurgy: Refractory Materials and Fuel.' London. 1875.

Idem. 'Metallurgy: Silver and Gold.' London. 1880.

PETERS, E. D. 'Practice of Copper Smelting.' McGraw Hill, New York. 1911.

ROBERTS-AUSTEN, SIR WILLIAM CHANDLER. 'An Introduction to the Study of Metallurgy' (6th ed.). Griffin, London. 1910.

ROSE, SIR THOMAS KIRKE and NEWMAN, W. A. C. 'The Metallurgy of Gold' (7th ed.). Griffin, London. 1937.

SMITHELLS, C. J. "Three Cantor Lectures on Aluminium." *J. R. Soc. Arts*, **98,** 822–63, 1950.

Idem. 'Tungsten: a Treatise on its Metallurgy, Properties and Applications' (3rd ed.). Chapman & Hall, London. 1952.

STURNEY, A. C. 'The Story of Mond Nickel.' The Mond Nickel Company, London. 1951.

'The Refining of Non-Ferrous Metals: a Symposium.' The Institution of Mining and Metallurgy, London. 1950.

WADHAMS, A. J. "The Story of the Nickel Industry." *Metals & Alloys*, **2,** 166–75, 1931.

WARK, I. W. 'Principles of Flotation.' Australasian Institute of Mining and Metallurgy, Melbourne. 1938.

WEST, E. G. "The First Century of Aluminium." *Bull. Instn Metall.*, **5,** 5–14, March, 1955.

ZEERLEDER, A. VON. 'Aluminium.' Akademische Verlag Gesellschaft, Leipzig. 1955.

Idem. "Attempts to Improve Aluminium Reduction Since Héroult and Hall." *J. Inst. Met.*, **83,** 321–8, 1955.

The Old Forest works at Swansea, c. 1800.

5

PETROLEUM

R. J. FORBES

I. EARLY KNOWLEDGE OF MINERAL OILS

THE bitumen industry of ancient Mesopotamia (vol I, p 250) lay beyond the pale of the Roman Empire. In Roman times there was little interest in petroleum products, and demand for them was small. The bituminous products required for medicaments, caulking ships, or coating the trunks of fruit-trees were found in wood-tar or wood-tar pitch, obtained in large quantities as by-products of charcoal burning. This does not mean that the various seepages in western Europe were unknown, or even that they were not exploited on a minor scale. The printed technical works of the sixteenth century show that some of them were renowned and that their modest production was marketed for all manner of purposes [1]. From various broadsheets which specify in detail the excellent medicinal properties of petroleum, we learn [2] that since as long ago as 1400 *oglio de sasso* or 'St Catharine oil' was being extracted from seepages near Modena, in competition with the 'St Quirinus oil' of Tegernsee, Bavaria, where a few years later about 42 litres a day were being skimmed from the water that welled up there. The oil from Lampertsloch, Alsace (1498), and from Wietze, Hanover, was already known. In an illustration depicting the extraction of oil near Modena about 1540 we can see that the oil was transported in standard bottles like large hip-flasks (figure 37). In 1576 Abraham Schnitzer obtained a licence from the authorities to exploit the ichthyol shales of Seefeld in the Tyrol.

Explorers began to bring back reports of seepages outside Europe. In 1526 Oviedo described the seepages of Puerto Príncipe, Havana, which provided the so-called 'carine' often used to caulk careened ships. According to Sahagun, seepages near Tampico, Mexico, produced bitumen which provided the Aztecs with a kind of chewing-gum known as *tzictli*. Zarate reported seepages on the coast of Peru, close to the present Lobitos oil-fields (1555), and Sir Walter Ralegh visited the asphalt lake of Tierra de Brea, Trinidad, for the first time in March 1595. Barbados tar was first described by Hughes in 1753. In Asia, Marco Polo had visited Baku in 1272 and had described the burning natural gas (figure 38) and the neighbouring seepages; but the best description of Baku was provided by Kämpfer [3]. Other seepages known in antiquity from Mesopotamia, Persia, and Afghanistan are re-encountered in the travel literature of the sixteenth and seventeenth centuries.

In the twelfth book of his *De re metallica*, Agricola describes how the crude oil was carefully skimmed from the seepages and inspissated by heating in large pots, and how bitumen was separated by melting (*destillatio per descensum*) out of rock asphalt. A more detailed description of the processing of the oil from Pechelbronn is found in a small pamphlet written in 1625 by Johann Volck [4], an apprentice of the alchemist Thurneisser zum Thurn. Volck carefully distilled this crude oil and investigated the properties, especially the medicinal properties, of the fractions. He found the oil suitable as a basic material for axle-grease, paints and varnishes for wood and ships' hulls, products for dressing leather, ointments and plasters, and lamp-oil. From other writers we learn that the oil from the new seepages near Monte Chiaro and Piacenza

FIGURE 37—*Oil was extracted at Modena about 1540, and transported in large flasks.*

(1640), and from the hand-dug shafts in Galicia (1649), was used in the same way, although they do not give details about the processing, as Volck does. In England, Eele, Portlock, and Hancock took out a patent in 1694 for 'A way to Extract and Make great Quantities of Pitch, Tarr and Oil out of a sort of stone' (vol III, pp 687–8) [5]. They built a factory at Pitchford[1]-on-Severn, Shropshire, and there extracted bitumen from bituminous sandstone by boiling, afterwards distilling the bitumen. The residue was sold as a substitute for tar for caulking ships, and the light fractions came on the market as 'Betton's British oil' for medicinal purposes.

Apart from some local exploitation of seepages and processing of the oil to make grease or medicinal products, the position remained unchanged for some time. The production of rock asphalt and natural asphalt alone showed a sharp rise early in the nineteenth century, when asphalts began to be used in roadbuilding (vol IV, p 539). An urgent demand for petroleum or petroleum products was needed to bring life to the industry: this stimulus, too, came in the nineteenth century, and brought about the birth of the modern petroleum industry. It resulted from the demand at the end of the eighteenth century for better and cheaper sources of light, to which the development of the gas-industry also owed its origin (vol IV, ch 9). In 1783 the first step was taken with the invention of the

---

[1] First element from OE *pic*, pitch, indicating that the presence of bitumen there was known in early times.

flat woven wick [6]; then Argand introduced the circular oil-burner with a round wick and a cylindrical lamp chimney; and in 1836 Franchot introduced the principle of the 'moderator lamp', in which a spring exerted pressure on a float on the oil and thus forced the latter up to the burner. Other inventors used the principles of Argand and Franchot in their own constructions, of which numerous examples were on the market by 1850. The quality of house- and street-lighting improved considerably in consequence, but the use of the new lamps was limited by the supply of suitable fuels. In general, rapeseed, colza, whale, lard, sperm, and rosin oils were considered suitable, but all were having a hard struggle in competition with the new gas-lighting. There was, therefore, an urgent need for better and cheaper fuels for oil lamps.

FIGURE 38—*Burning gases at Baku, eighteenth century.*

'Coal oil' and later kerosene (paraffin oil) provided the answer to this challenge. The pioneer of 'coal oil' was James Young (1811–83), a brilliant scientist who assisted Faraday in his experiments at the Royal Institution and later became manager of a chemical works at Manchester [7]. In 1847 his attention was drawn to a petroleum 'spring' producing about 300 gallons a day of crude oil in a coal-mine at Riddings in Derbyshire. With the owners, he started to manufacture lubricants, industrial naphthas for use as solvents, and paraffin wax, but the source of supply was soon exhausted. Young erroneously believed that this oil was formed from neighbouring coal-deposits by the effect of subterranean heat, and he filed a patent (B.P., 17 October 1850; U.S. patent, 23 March 1852) for the production of 'paraffin oil' from coal by dry distillation and refining. In 1850 he moved to Bathgate, West Lothian, to produce this oil from the torbanite deposits found near by. The paraffin oil and the solid paraffin wax thus produced were not sold until 1856, but by 1859 they had found a considerable market. These deposits, too, soon gave out, and Young immediately started work on the oil-shales which occurred in large quantities in the same region, thus becoming the founder of the Scottish shale-oil industry.

In the meantime Abraham Gesner (1797–1864) had prepared the first kerosene from petroleum [8]. Gesner qualified as a physician in London in 1827, and afterwards became interested in geology. What led him to his lamp-oil enterprise is a matter for speculation. Its origin may possibly lie in his friendship, formed during a stay in Halifax, with Thomas Cochrane, tenth Earl of Dundonald, who carried out numerous experiments with natural asphalt from Trinidad, and on the basis of his results filed several patents for applications of bituminous products. In 1853 the Asphalt Mining and Kerosene Gas Company was founded in order to work patents granted to Gesner [9]. In these he describes how the liquid obtained by dry distillation of asphalt rock was to be treated to remove undesirable impurities. This was done by mixing it thoroughly with 5–10 per cent by volume of sulphuric acid, to remove any tars present. The purified oil was then treated with freshly calcined lime, about 2 per cent by volume, to absorb any water present and to neutralize the effect of the acid. Following this treatment, the oil was redistilled. Gesner called the oil kerosene, from the Greek *keros*, wax.[1]

Works for the manufacture of kerosene were established on Newton Creek by the North American Kerosene Gas Light Company (later called the New York Kerosene Oil Company) in 1854. Its sale was placed in the hands of John H. & George W. Austen of New York, who also supplied a cheap, flat-wick kerosene lamp with a glass chimney (the so-called Vienna burner). By 1856 this oil was so well known that Gesner's expectation that 'kerosene would make possible a long and lasting holiday . . . for . . . the finny monsters [whales] of the sea' seemed likely to come true.

At about this time (1856–7) Gesner's chief competitors were James Young at Bathgate and Samuel Downer Jr at South Boston. Both had first turned their attention to the manufacture of lubricants from bituminous substances such as shale or coal-tar. Luther Atwood, one of Downer's experts, had demonstrated that refined naphtha from Young's works was an excellent illuminating oil. Young acted on this hint and started to sell a 'paraffin illuminating oil' both in England and in the States; and as early as 1856 he shipped part of his first batch to Vienna. In 1857 Downer and his United States Chemical Manufacturing Company started to sell for lamps 'coal oil' made from albertite (a bituminous mineral), and by 1859 large profits were being made on it. However, the battle between these competing lamp-oils was soon decided when an oil-well developed by E. L. Drake (1819–80) started to produce on 27 August 1859 (figure 39).

While these developments took place in North America the situation in Europe had by no means remained static. The rise of organic chemistry since the beginning of the century (vol IV, ch 8) had thrown much light on the composition and

---

[1] This kind of light hydrocarbon mixture is generally known in the United Kingdom as paraffin (oil), but the name kerosene is still used in the United States.

properties of crude oil from the numerous known seepages. Many constituents of tar, which is related to petroleum, had gradually yielded up their secrets, and new methods of research dating from the first decades of the century now enabled scientists to determine the chemical nature of petroleum. It was found to be a mixture of various hydrocarbons belonging to the paraffin series, together with naphthenes, aromatics, and sometimes also some olefines: de Saussure, Dumas, Boussingault, and von Liebig were among those who took part in these investigations [10].

FIGURE 39—*The Drake well in 1866.*

In the 1860s, this research was carried further by scientists such as Schorlemmer, Pelouze, Cahours, and Sainte-Claire Deville [11], who also began to pay attention to the economics of processing oil, and sought for and suggested profitable uses for the various oil fractions. At the time, American research workers contributed little to this increase of scientific knowledge: they applied themselves wholly to the practical processing of oil. Yet the American oil industry was based on an excellent scientific report on the Pennsylvanian oil, which provided the incentive for drilling down to oil-bearing strata far below the surface.

The methods of drilling applied by the pioneers of the petroleum industry were not original. As early as the eighteenth century they were being used in mining and quarrying, and in soil-testing for civil engineering works. Rotary drilling, in which a bit is forced into the soil as if it were a screw, additional drilling-rods being screwed in as the depth increased, was a very old system used for drilling artesian wells in the Middle Ages; in quarrying and mining, however, percussion-drilling was preferred for making holes to contain explosives (vol IV, pp 67–72). By these means it was possible to drill holes to a depth of some 300 ft. Drilling was, however, costly: the main source of power was animal or human (figure 40), and, as steel was still expensive, wrought iron drilling-rods were used, but they proved to be too easily broken. In these circumstances the reports brought back by French missionaries from China concerning the centuries-old drilling-methods of the Chinese created a sensation [12].

II. DRILLING FOR OIL

Cable-drilling with hempen cables, a system soon known as the Pennsylvanian system, was tried out as early as 1830, but here, too, the lack of appropriate materials retarded its general introduction. The innovation which Fauvelle made at Perpignan in July 1846, when he drilled a well 550 ft deep with hollow drill-pipes, was of far greater importance, for it enabled him to pump water through the drill-pipes down to the bit; when the water rose along the pipes it entrained the drilled cuttings and flushed them from the hole. This flush-drilling, which later came into general use in the petroleum industry, enabled Fauvelle to attain an average drilling-speed of 3 ft an hour.

FIGURE 40—'*Kicking down*' *a well by the spring-pole drilling method.*

von Oehnhausen's invention of the drilling-jar (1834) and Kind's free-fall jar (1843) prevented the rebound of the bit on to the drilling-rods and thus initiated a temporary revival of percussion-drilling, which, as the ' German' drilling-system or *système prussien*, made rapid progress, but notably in drilling for brine.

The derrick, as an assembly centre for all machinery and power-engines at the mouth of the drill-hole, dates back to 1830. In the derrick the pulley could be placed high up, and the drill-pipes could be raised well out of the boring. Drilling apparatus and drill-pipes could be stored vertically in the derrick. At first the necessary power was provided by man-power or horses: not until about 1850 was steam-power introduced, at first as a locomotive, later as a stationary, steam-engine (figure 41).

Reliable materials for making deep wells and for breaking up hard formations were not on the market until long after the sixties. In 1859 Drake still had to depend on wrought iron bits with steel cutting-edges. Only after Bessemer and

Siemens had made mass-production of cast steel possible did efficient materials gradually become available (ch 3). Fortunately, up to the end of the nineteenth century, the demand for petroleum products was not such as to make deep drillings imperative.

It was not until the days of Drake that a new method for piercing hard formations, namely diamond-drilling, was developed and found its place in the petroleum industry. It was invented by Rudolf Leschot in 1864. When it was demonstrated at the Great Exhibition in Paris in 1867, a visitor from the United States was very much impressed and drew the attention of American experts to it. In 1870 the sale of such gear was started by the firm of Severance & Holt in New York, and it was from America that the invention reached England and Sweden. One of the English examples was sold to Germany in 1872; there the state mining-engineer Köbrich greatly improved it and used it in exploratory drill-holes for salt, coal, and other materials. In 1886 the Schladebach boring reached a depth of 5735 ft, and later records of 6570 ft (1893) and 7230 ft (1909) were not broken by the petroleum industry until about 1924.

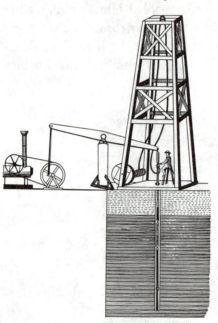

FIGURE 41—*Early well being drilled by a mechanical successor to the spring-pole method.*

The development of drilling-methods not specific to quarrying and mining was due to the increasing demand for water and brine early in the nineteenth century. In France artesian wells were required for agriculture, but in central Europe, especially in Germany, circumstances were very different. There attention was focused on the production of rock-salt and the exploitation of strata bearing other salts, to supply the demands both for common salt and for raw materials for the expanding chemical industry. There was, however, also a search for water, and many German spas owe their rise to springs discovered by drilling.

The beginnings of the American oil industry. In America, as in Europe, there was a constant search for salt and for water. As early as 1841 petroleum was struck at a depth of 475 ft near Duck Creek, Ohio, when drilling for salt was in progress; Goodrich mentions no fewer than fifteen borings for salt, made between 1840 and 1860, which struck petroleum [13]. This frequent occurrence of salt and petroleum together finally led to deliberate drilling for oil.

Samuel M. Kier of Pittsburgh had a 400-ft salt-well at Tarentum, on the Allegheny, but he 'was ruined as a salt producer because of infiltration of oil into the brine'. Necessity became the mother of invention, and Kier began to skim the oil from the brine and to sell it in small bottles as 'Kier's Petroleum or Rock Oil, celebrated for its wonderful curative powers as a natural remedy'.

The picture of the derrick over Kier's brine-well on the label of the bottles of petroleum made a deep impression on George H. Bissell (1821–84), an industrialist, who perceived from it a new possibility of producing oil. In 1854 Bissell and Jonathan G. Elvereth, promoters and founders of the Pennsylvania Rock Oil Company, the oldest petroleum firm in the world (founded 30 December 1854), sent a sample of crude oil from a seepage on Hibbard Farm near Titusville, Pennsylvania, to Benjamin Silliman Jr, then professor of general and applied chemistry at Yale. On 16 April 1855 Silliman finished his report [14], which is now one of the historic documents of petroleum.

In this report, Silliman first described the general properties of the crude oil and those of the fractions he had prepared by distillation. He determined the boiling-point range and specific gravity of each fraction. Even at this early date he pointed out the possibilities of new products being formed while the crude oil was being heated—products not originally present in it. He investigated the 'stiffening or liquidity' at low temperatures before and after treatment with various acids and decolorizing earth; prepared illuminating-gas by heating the fractions strongly; and obtained lighter, quickly darkening, fractions by superheating heavier fractions—by 'cracking' them, as we should now say. He also separated paraffin wax, which was found very suitable for candles. The lighter fractions, or naphtha, furnished an excellent lamp-oil which Silliman burnt in various lamps, carefully measuring the candle-power produced. He noted the high price of the sperm and rapeseed oil then used as illuminants. He also pointed out that certain fractions of petroleum might be useful lubricants because 'they form no resins, nor become rancid, nor form acids'. Silliman evidently knew little of the contemporary European manufacture of lubricants from crude oil.

This first survey of the technical and economic possibilities of the constituents of crude petroleum closes with the words:

In conclusion, gentlemen, it appears to me that there is much encouragement in the belief that your Company have in their possession a raw material from which, by a simple and not expensive process, they may manufacture very valuable products. It is worthy of note that my experiments prove that nearly the whole of the raw product may be manufactured without waste, and this solely by a well-directed process which is in practice one of the most simple of all chemical processes.

Bissell acted on this report and started drilling for petroleum. The contractor was Drake, who struck oil at a depth of 69½ ft near Oil Creek, Pennsylvania, on 27 August 1859. This date is usually mentioned as marking the modern phase of the petroleum industry—though in point of fact G. C. Hunäus had struck both gas and oil at Wietze, Hanover, two years earlier (April 1857–May 1859) in a series of five wells drilled for the specific purpose of producing crude oil. This development dealt a death-blow to the manufacture of coal-oil and kerosene from bituminous coals, natural asphalts, albertite, and shales. Crude oil offered a much more economical source for the production of lamp-oil. From then on the oil industry, founded on apparently inexhaustible underground deposits, developed in America and soon afterwards in other parts of the world. Plate 6B shows a characteristic American oilfield of about 1870. We shall not trace the economic and political fortunes of the industry here [15].

Drake's success stimulated the development of drilling methods. The older methods evolved into the Pennsylvanian drilling system, which was later to be improved upon as the Californian system. A Canadian system, which from the outset was designed to drill for oil, was developed at Petrolia, Ontario. The effects of American progressiveness were soon felt in Europe; in Galicia, European and American drilling methods met, and the contact and exchange of ideas were profitable to both.

The oil industry in Galicia. In Galicia, after many decades of production from hand-dug shafts, percussion-drilling was first introduced about 1862. In 1867 experiments were made with the Pennsylvanian system; these, however, were not successful because of the peculiar local structure of the oil-strata, with their steep dip and greatly varying hardness. In 1882 the Canadian system was introduced by the Canadian firm of Bergheim & MacGarvey: it was an unqualified success and ousted the older systems for a long period. It was also adopted in Germany.

From Galicia the newer drilling techniques spread to Rumania, where the Canadian system was introduced about 1882 and the Pennsylvanian system a year later. In Baku and Grozny, where the first derricks were built in 1869, these systems were not entirely successful: in 1878 American drillers tried in vain to introduce the Pennsylvanian system in Baku. The Romanians clung to the system of free-fall drilling with very heavy tools, and only in the 1890s was there competition from rapid percussion-drilling, and percussion-drilling with rotation. After the turn of the century these methods were finally superseded by rotary drilling.

The last had not yet been heard of the hand-dug shaft, however. In 1897 de Chambrier experimented at Pechelbronn with a system consisting of a deep shaft into which a system of galleries debouched, so that all the oil was led from the strata to the bottom of the shaft. This system was successful and was adopted at Wietze (1919) and at Sarata-Monteoru, Rumania (1923), but in the end it was forced to give way to drilling.

Galicia was for long the country whence drillers were engaged for other fields, as European production then depended mostly on the oil-fields of Galicia, Rumania, and Russia. One of the Galician drillers was A. Fauck, who invented several important drilling machines and other tools; another, Anton Raky (1868–1943), worked in Germany as manager of the *Internationale Bohrgesellschaft* and in 1895 invented the *Schnellbohrkran*, a rapid-drilling machine, which was very successful.

Applications of geology. The early drillers were practical men who drilled for oil where surface seepages indicated its presence in the subsoil. But these sources of supply soon proved inadequate to meet the enormous demand, and it was realized that the services of the scientist, especially the geologist, would have to be enlisted to provide a sounder basis for prospecting and deep drilling.

The controversial question of the origin of oil was closely related to the search for new sources of it. Towards the end of the eighteenth century rational theories began to be propounded, the theory that attributed a vegetable origin to oil being the one most generally accepted. In the nineteenth century the evolution of organic chemistry led to new theories, which temporarily eclipsed the older ones. Impressed by Berthelot's work on the formation of various hydrocarbons from acetylene at high temperatures, both D. I. Mendeleev and J. A. Le Bel held that crude oil had originated from the reaction of water with metallic carbides in the depths of the earth. This theory was not acceptable to the geologists studying the structure of oil-fields; they preferred the theory of animal origin advanced by Quenstedt and Sterry Hunt. This theory seemed to be supported by the experiments of C. Engler, who converted fish-oil into a product very similar to Pennsylvanian crude oil [16]. The problem appeared to be solved: crude oil had been formed from animal remains under the influence of pressure and temperature over a period of thousands of centuries, during which reaction occurred with salts dissolved in the water present. Observations in the Caspian Sea and the Gulf of Suez seemed to corroborate this hypothesis, but it was of little importance for the discovery of new oil-fields before the drilling-bit revealed the structure of the underground formations. Seepages and shallow hand-dug shafts failed to provide sufficient information.

Both the European and the North American geological reports supported the view that crude oil was usually to be found in the pores of folded strata enclosed by non-porous strata which prevented the escape of the gases and oil formed. The foundations of this 'anticlinal theory' were laid by observations made by Thomas Young, father of the Geological Survey of India, who observed the joint occurrence of oil-accumulations and anticlinal structures in the strata of Burma in 1855. E. B. Andrews and Sterry Hunt independently worked out a similar theory for the American oil-fields in 1861 and later. The first theoretical discussion devoted to this subject was contained in an essay by J. C. White, published in 1885 [17]. It proved helpful in choosing the right places for profitable drilling.

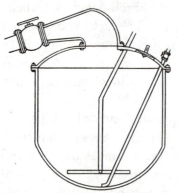

FIGURE 42—*Section of early steam-heated still for crude oil, 1861. The largest stills of this kind were about 8 ft in diameter.*

III. OIL REFINING

Oil was now being discovered and produced in ever-growing quantities all over the world; in consequence, refining-methods had to be evolved, for it was soon realized that the composition of the crude oils varied greatly from one oil-field to another and even according to the depth of the stratum from which the oil was obtained. The market for lamp, fuel, and lubricating oils, however, demanded a much smaller variation in composition and quality.

The refining of crude oil was based on two related techniques, which were applied in various combinations according to the type and composition of the crude material. These two techniques were distillation and chemical refining; cracking was not added until after 1890.

Distillation is essentially a thermal fractionation according to boiling-point. The evolution of the theory of heat in the latter half of the eighteenth century and the early part of the nineteenth was of vital importance to distillers. During this period the development of better distillation-apparatus was still closely associated with the production of alcohol [18]. Cellier Blumenthal devised the first good rectifying column in 1813. The invention of the steam-regulator by Savalle (1857) made possible the use of superheated steam as a source of heat (figure 42). The old idea of vacuum distillation was revived and effectively achieved. The columns, condensers, and other apparatus used in producing large quantities of alcohol from wine or potato-mash (p 304) were adopted and improved by the tar industry, and were taken over unmodified by the petroleum industry until experience taught the refiners how to design columns more specifically suitable for the refining of petroleum products. The early stills (figure 43) were not based on exact scientific data: the first attempts at chemical engineering in this field were made by Hausbrand and Sorel [19].

Samuel Kier built his first still, of 800 litres, in 1855. American distilling-apparatus had then hardly outgrown the pharmaceutical stage. Refiners were usually content to use horizontal cylindrical stills (or even box-shaped 'cheese-box' stills), in which the contents were distilled off as with alcohol; at regular intervals the hot residue had to be drained off and the still cooled, before refilling for the next distillation became possible (figure 44). This batch-process took no heed of heat-economy; it did not use fractionating columns, because its sole aim was to obtain the middle fraction, kerosene. The first runnings, which we now call petrol or gasoline, were useless and even dangerous; the high-boiling residue was usually sold as fuel, and was

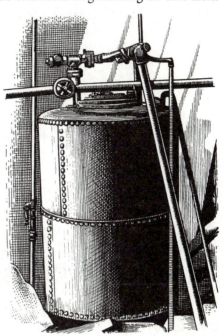

FIGURE 43—*Five-barrel still, used in the 1850s.*

seldom fractionated to yield lubricants. The American refiners for some time continued to distil petroleum wastefully: efforts made by Samuel Van Sickle to introduce a battery of continuous stills at Titusville in 1877 had no success.

In Europe, where distillation on a large scale had a much longer history, fuel was costly and economy in its use was of prime importance. Le Bel, Wurtz's assistant and later manager of the Pechelbronn refinery for twenty-two years, had studied this problem. As knowledge of distillation techniques spread to Galicia, Romania, and Russia from France and central Europe, it was found that batch-distillation was too expensive, and means of economizing were sought.

As early as 1871 Galician refiners used a system of two stills, one on top of the other; the upper had the form of a horizontal boiler and was used for distilling off the light fractions. The residue then flowed down to the lower still, where the

heavier fractions were removed. Perutz succeeded in rendering this flow continuous, which enabled him to make runs of three or four days; at the end of this
time the operation had to be stopped to drain the residue from the lower vessel.

In 1875 Fuhst built a series of stills in which an ingenious set of floats and
overflow-pipes caused the residue in each still to flow into the next. The condensers also were built in series, in order to use the cooling-water as economically
as possible. Fuhst's intention was to eliminate rectification of the distillates; up
to that date the primary distillates were so crude that they had to be redistilled in
Coffey (p 306) or Lugo (1867) columns in order to produce fractions with a fairly
narrow boiling-range. In Russia, columns derived from the Glinsky laboratory
column and the Heckmann column were used. Tube-condensers built on the
Grimble principle were commonly used by the petroleum industry after the publication of their description by Pelouze and Auduin (1873).

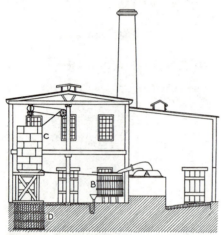

FIGURE 44—*Refinery for crude petroleum or coal-tar,*
c 1860. (A) *Stills;* (B) *worm tanks;* (C) *washers or*
agitators; (D) *receivers.*

Though continuous or bench distillation had great advantages, there were
many obstacles to its introduction. When
Tawrisow wished to introduce it at
Baku in 1873 he had to rearrange his stills as batch-stills, because the customs
officers believed that bench distillation would facilitate evasion of taxes. Progress
could not be checked, however, and in 1880–81 Nobel had a bench of seventeen
stills built and patented. Bench distillation had proved its merits and Russian
and Rumanian scientists improved it. From eastern Europe this system found
its way to the Far East, though for many years it was not favoured by the
American experts who worked there.

Minor inventions also contributed their share to more efficient refining. Pre-
heating the intake of crude oil by utilizing the heat of the residue drawn from the
last still was patented for petroleum distillation in 1880 (French Patent no
395,108), though the principle had long been applied in the alcohol industry.
The use of superheated steam for the distillation of high-boiling constituents
came from Gustave-Adolphe Hirn (1815–90), who used it in his small refinery
at Logenbach, near Colmar. In 1855 he improved the steam-superheater which
had been invented in 1827 by Becker, of Strasbourg, and applied Savalle's steam-

regulator. This method of blowing hot, dry steam into the still, avoiding over-heating of the contents, was introduced by Perutz into Germany and Galicia, whence it travelled to Russia.

The idea of vacuum distillation was derived from sugar-refining. P. Wage-mann introduced this system in his Augustenhütte refinery near Bonn about 1855 [20]; the distilling of valuable high-boiling lubricants in this way slowly gained ground. Independently, the earliest American experiments with a high-vacuum distillation were made about 1879, which shows how closely trade secrets continued to be guarded in those days.

Close co-operation between the universities and the refineries existed only in Europe, and there mainly in Russia, where Count Witte (1849–1915) had ordered the universities to direct their research in organic chemistry to the pro-motion of the Caucasian oil industry. This collaboration resulted in con-siderable progress in distillation and refining technique and apparatus. At the turn of the century the handbooks of Ragosin [21], Ipatieff, Gurevitch, Stepanoff [22], and Chercheffsky were of even greater importance to the European refiner than the works of Engler and Höfer and their schools. Admittedly, American refiners had published practical manuals on refining much before this, the earliest being a little booklet by Thomas Gale [23], which was soon followed by the treatises of Gesner and Antisell [24]. However, it took them a long time to realize that progress was intimately related to scientific research, which in the United States did not start in earnest until the period of the first world war.

Chemical refining-methods for petroleum were also adopted from older indus-tries. Sulphuric acid was commercially available in large quantities early in the nineteenth century and was used in the manufacture of soap and fats. It was from this source that Hirn got his information when, about 1850, he refined petroleum products at Logenbach with sulphuric acid, using water and caustic soda to wash the remains of the acid out of the oil [25]. In 1864, lubricating oil was refined by treatment with hot concentrated sulphuric acid. Moldenhauer, formerly an assistant to von Liebig, brought sulphuric acid refining to Baku from central Europe. There it was found that the addition of about 0·25 per cent of alcohol promoted the coagulation of the acid tar derived from hot oil. In America, hydrochloric acid had at first been used in refining petroleum, but Gesner (1854) and Joshua Merrill (1857) suggested the use of sulphuric acid, which was much cheaper. This acid treatment was effected in vessels with mechanical stirrers, but about 1870 Gmelin in Budapest had introduced air-stirring; in this much more economical method a stream of air-bubbles ensured better mixing.

Acid treatment was often followed, or even replaced, by treatment with caustic

soda or with a decolorizing earth. Theodor Lowitz had discovered the decolorizing properties of charcoal in 1785, and this form of carbon was extensively used
for the refining of glycerine, and even of paraffin wax, about 1868. In 1870
Floridin was first used; this is a natural clay which has been treated with the
waste water from the manufacture of certain cyanides, a treatment which increases its decolorizing effects. Certain other clays, when chemically treated,
show a similar enhancement in decolorizing power; the original observation, on
Floridin, was made in 1867. Such clays were to prove of great value to the
petroleum industry. Experiments were started soon afterwards in France and
England, but it was not until the end of the century that other serviceable processes were found.

Up to 1900, the petroleum industry made paraffin oil mainly, by these simple
methods. In Europe, various refiners had already preceded Gesner. In 1816
Joseph Hecker had distilled lamp-oil from crude oil from Truskawiec, Poland;
this was used to light a few streets in Prague in 1817, but the arrangement did
not last. Lukasiewicz was more successful, with lamp-oil prepared from Galician
crude oil in 1853; in that year this oil was used to light the hospital at Lwow. In
Rumania in 1856–7 production from hand-dug shafts amounted to some 275 tons
a year; from 1 April 1857, the city of Bucharest was lit by oil lamps. Other
examples could be mentioned, but the production of this lamp-oil was limited
because it was not based on the regular supply of crude oil from drilled wells.
The American production of lamp-oil had a good lead in this respect, and it
expanded enormously after Drake's success. The oil was shipped to California,
and even to Australia by way of Cape Horn, in tins packed in wooden cases.
About 1860 imports of American kerosene began to have a distinct effect on the
European market. This was due in part to the demonstration, on the initiative
of Joseph de Keyzer, of paraffin lamps at the Ghent Flower Exhibition of 1859.

IV. THE USES OF MINERAL OIL

Heating. In addition to its use for illumination, the importance of paraffin for
the kitchen was now becoming clear. It was not until the great Paris Exhibition
of 1878, however, that the prototype of the modern paraffin oil-stove could be
shown to the public by Besnard and Maris, the latter being already famous for
an excellent and popular paraffin lamp. The result was spectacular. Within ten
years over 500 000 of these stoves were sold, despite discouraging measures
taken by the authorities in a number of countries—who soon learned, however,
to regard paraffin as an excellent object for taxation.

The marketing of kerosene did not proceed without serious competition. The use of gas for lighting and cooking increased by leaps and bounds (vol IV, ch 9). Bunte, the father of modern gas manufacture and analysis, applied his talents to the creation of new household uses for gas and did much to promote its use in the kitchen. Then in the 1880s a second competitor, electricity, entered the lists, especially in those countries which were so fortunate as to have an ample supply of water-power and could thus produce electricity cheaply in large quantities. It was no longer economic merely to market the middle fraction of crude oil as kerosene; many of those engaged in the industry soon became convinced of the possibilities of using the heavy fractions, often distillation residues, as fuel, in competition with coal.

The earliest applications of such material as a fuel were very simple: the oil was run into a pan, or over a metal sheet, and fired. Many variations of this basic conception appeared on the market. Thus Edward John Biddle took out an American patent (1862) for a burner consisting of a sheet with long parallel channels sunk into it. These primitive burners were unsatisfactory, and in 1865 a Russian, Schpakofsky [26], proposed spraying the hot oil with compressed air and igniting the mist of oil thus formed; this would make it possible to adjust and regulate the flame much better. In the same year an Englishman, Aydon (with Wise and Field), had a similar idea, but preferred to atomize (a term adopted in 1860 by Benjamin F. Isherwood, head of the bureau of steam engineering of the U.S. Navy) the fuel with superheated steam.

The importance of this atomizing process was that it enabled the boiler of a locomotive or ship, as well as the stills of a refinery, to be heated with the residues of crude oil. The idea took root and, at Baku, Otto Lenz heated stills and locomotive boilers with such material, using a boiler of his own design. The residue hitherto called *astatki* (dregs) was renamed *mazout* (fuel-oil). The next step in the evolution of the oil-burner was the mechanical atomization of the fuel. Frederick Cook's American patent (January 1868) seems to contain the first suggestion along these lines [27], but we owe the earliest practical burner of this type to Koerting and Schutte (1902) [28].

In the meantime a promising market for fuel-oil had been found. *The Times* of 6 April 1865 contained an article enumerating the advantages of fuel-oil over coal and stressing its suitability for burning under ships' boilers. Stover, enlarging on this article in the technical journals, agreed that the author was right in principle, but stated that his own experiments had shown that fuel-oil was still much too expensive in Europe to be used as a marine fuel, although in America economic conditions were very different. Trial runs with French, British, and American vessels followed. American submarines were generally using fuel-oil by about 1903; the Royal Navy was somewhat later in recognizing the superiority of the new fuel. Changes in the economic situation, affecting the relative costs of oil and coal, encouraged the change to oil: at the present time 90 per cent of ships are oil-fired.

Lubrication. For centuries crude oil had been used as a lubricant, together with fats, tallow, and vegetable oils, but only on a small scale. The systematic use of lubricants dates from the end of the eighteenth century, when the industrial revolution created a demand for faster traffic and better vehicles. Thenceforward, greater attention was paid to the rational construction of vehicles, which meant that a closer study had to be made of friction. The first systematic experiments go back to Charles Augustin de Coulomb (1736–1806) [29]. His laws of friction were almost unquestioned for over a century, though his coefficients of friction turned out to be from six to sixty times too high. Morin raised a critical voice in the thirties, but Coulomb's figures, and some of his theories, were not disbelieved until the experimental work of Beauchamp Tower, who was commissioned by the Institution of Mechanical Engineers in 1879 'to study friction at high velocities, especially with references to bearings and pivots, friction of brakes, etc.'. His four reports (1883, 1885, 1888, 1891) were backed by Osborne Reynolds (p 547), who provided the theoretical background and the mathematical formulae for Tower's work, and by Rüllmann's book. These publications can be said to constitute the foundation of modern lubricant-testing [30].

On 29 June 1831 Charles Dolfuss addressed the Société Industrielle de Mulhouse, and demonstrated an instrument for testing lubricants; this was a vessel with a small hole in the bottom from which the lubricant could escape. By measuring the number of seconds necessary for a measured volume of lubricant to leave the vessel, he obtained an index for its 'liquidity'. This instrument Dolfuss dubbed a *viscosimètre*. It was very useful, for everywhere means were being sought of replacing the then costly and unstable lubricants by better ones.

Several decades before James Young's time, mineral lubricants were being prepared by dry distillation of shales and asphaltic rocks in small plants in France and central Europe. In 1835 Selligue and de la Haye had begun to distil oil from the Autun shales, to make lubricants. In 1839 establishments were set up at Igornay, Surmoulin, and Cordesse. In 1843 there were similar plants at Vagnas, Fréjus, and other places, including Lobsann and Travers.

In 1845 Le Bel had isolated oil from oil-sands by boiling them in water, and had found it to be an excellent lubricant. His successor as manager of the Pechelbronn refinery was Gustave-Adolphe Hirn (p 114), who continued Le Bel's research work. Hirn aimed at substituting distilled mineral oils for the vegetable or fatty oils then commonly used. He thus began making lubricants, which in turn compelled him to investigate the principles of friction. An account of this work, which according to his notes must have been begun in 1847, was sent to the Académie des Sciences for publication. It was refused, the secretary, Fourneyron, writing that the results 'were contrary to the well known principles of mechanics', meaning the laws of Coulomb. Hirn stopped neither his experiments nor his attempts to publish them, and finally had his work printed [31]. We have proof that Hirn produced lubricants by distillation of mineral oils in his refinery at Logenbach at least as early as 1853. From then onwards lubricating oils were always among the products of every oil-refinery in America and Europe. Besides the heavier machine-oils, spindle-oil was used fairly early in Europe as a lubricant. It was a very thin lubricant used in spinning to make the fibres supple before they entered the spinning-machines. For this purpose, mineral oils replaced products derived from bog-head coal or shale. They were manufactured especially in France, from crude oil imported from the United States.

Petrol and gas-oil. A scientific background to the application of petrol or gasoline scarcely existed in 1880 or 1890. The motor-car (ch 18) and the aeroplane (ch 17) were in the experimental stage and held out only the vaguest promise of a worth-while market for petrol in the distant future. There were soldering-lamps and pressure-stoves which used petrol, and some naphtha was used for dry-cleaning and the extraction of oil from seeds. For some time it was thought that petrol might be used to enrich or carburize coal-gas. For this purpose the petrol was evaporated, according to a patent of Bolley, of Zürich [32], by spraying it into heated brick-lined retorts, in which it vaporized and mixed with town gas. A much handier, portable apparatus was designed by Richardson and Morse and introduced into France about 1864.

Water-gas had been made in England since 1828 by blowing steam through red-hot coke; this water-gas also was carburized with petrol according to a process invented by Thompson and Hind. It was felt, however, that cheaper and less dangerous petroleum products could be found for this purpose. Gas-oil, isolated from the fraction intermediate between kerosene and the lubricants, appeared to offer the solution. It was cracked, like petrol, in red-hot retorts, forming gases which were mixed with town gas or industrial gases to enrich them [33]. This, however, did not greatly increase the market for petrol, and in the United States natural gases were often used for carburizing.

In 1794 Robert Street of London, following up Huygens's work of 1680 on the gunpowder engine (vol IV, p 171), took out a patent (B.P. no 1981) for 'an engine operating by the explosion of spirit of tar or turpentine'. For many generations afterwards work continued on the perfecting of the internal combustion engine, and Otto's 'silent gas-engine' of 1877 and Diesel's experimental engine of 1893 at length arrived (ch 8). By the end of the nineteenth century there were several promising engines [34] burning petrol, kerosene, or Diesel oil, but the cost of the fuel and the price of the engines themselves limited development. Only in the first decade of the twentieth century did circumstances become such as to

FIGURE 45—*Transporting oil at Oil Creek, 1875.*

make these engines economic propositions; this enabled the petroleum industry to turn a worthless and highly inflammable by-product into its most valuable asset.

As long as there was still no large market for petrol, cracking was not an integral process of the petroleum industry. Admittedly, this process was used in the dry distillation of shales and bituminous rocks, and even on a modest scale in the older primitive stills, in which the oil was sometimes superheated for the purpose of distilling off more paraffin, but this was scarcely regarded as a separate process. Yet the first patent for cracking, filed by Benton of Titusville, dates from as far back as 1886 [35]. He proposed to subject residual or heavy oil to superheating in pipes placed in a furnace, and then to vaporize the resulting light constituents in a chamber installed behind the furnace. The oil was heated in the furnace at 370–540° C, at a pressure of 20–35 atm. This proposal was followed shortly afterwards by the ingenious patents of Carl M. Pielsticker [36], creator of the pipe-still. He drove the oil at high speed and under pressure through a spiral 60 m long built into a furnace; the light fractions were afterwards separated under pressure in a vaporizing chamber from the heavy uncracked fractions, which could then be led back. During these years (1890–2) there was, however, no market for cracked petrol; the natural product from crude oil already caused the refiner enough trouble; thus Pielsticker's patents were neglected, and were later declared 'paper patents'.

V. TRANSPORT OF OIL

No serious attempt was made to organize the transport of oil before 1890. In the pioneering days wooden barrels (figures 45 and 46) were used; these were followed, for overland transport, by tin cans or sheet iron drums. For ocean transport similar receptacles were used, but the tins were usually packed two by two in wooden cases. Shipment was made as general cargo, usually on deck.

FIGURE 46—*Early rail tank-cars with two round wooden vats mounted on each. Total capacity about 1700 gallons.*

The first cargo of petroleum to cross the Atlantic was carried in wooden barrels stowed in the hold of the brig *Elizabeth Watts* in 1861. It was soon felt, however, that shipment in bulk offered the only solution to the transport problem. Large iron tanks were placed in the holds of the vessels; later the wooden hulls were lined with cement.

This led to the design of special ships. The first tanker, the *Zoroaster*, was built in 1877 and was employed in the Caspian Sea trade. The *Glückauf*, built by Armstrong Whitworth & Company on the Tyne in 1885, was the first European tanker. It was followed by a large number of smaller vessels of the same type; they were divided by bulkheads into a number of compartments so as to be able to carry several kinds of oil at the same time. For river transport, too, special types of tankers were designed. By 1890 some fifty or sixty tankers were in service, sailing under the British, American, or Russian flags.

Special tank-cars for rail transport were first introduced in Russia about 1881, but the future of bulk transport on land lay with the pipe-line. The first pipe-lines were built, after several failures with wooden lines, when steel piping became available in the 1870s: the old cast iron pipes used for water-mains in the early nineteenth century were not strong enough to stand the high pumping-pressures necessary. In America, Van Sickle was the pioneer in this field (1874); in Russia, Nobel (1876). In the United States the pipe-line soon became a most important factor in Rockefeller's oil policy.

The storage of oil products presented no difficulties, for other industries had developed the equipment. Sheet iron (later steel) tanks had long been used in the tar, gas, alcohol, and chemical industries. New forms specially designed for the petroleum industry emerged only when the light, low-boiling hydrocarbons of natural petroleum were recovered and stored under pressure.

REFERENCES

[1] FORBES, R. J. "Bitumen and Petroleum in Antiquity" in 'Studies in Ancient Technology', Vol. 1. Brill, Leiden. 1955.
     Idem. 'Studies in Early Petroleum History.' Brill, Leiden. 1957.
[2] *Idem. Ingenieur, 's Grav.*, Special Number: III World Petroleum Congress, pp. 1–3. June, 1951.
[3] KÄMPFER, E. *Amoenitates exoticae politico-physico medicarum.* Lemgo. 1712.
     MEIER-LEMGÖ, K. and SCHMITZ, P. M. E. *Bitumen, Berl.*, **9,** 76–79, 1939.
     SCHMITZ, P. M. E. *Matières grasses*, **30,** 252–3, 1938.
[4] VOLCK, J. 'Hanawischen Erdbalsams, Petrolei oder weichen Agsteins Beschreibung.' Jozua Rihel, Strasbourg. 1625.
[5] British Patent No. 330. 1694.
     EELE, M. *Phil. Trans.*, **19,** 544, 1697.
[6] BLOCH, W. 'Vom Kienspan bis zum künstlichen Tageslicht.' Dieck, Stuttgart. 1925.
     ROBINS, F. W. 'The Story of the Lamp and the Candle.' Oxford University Press, London. 1939.
[7] BAILEY, E. M. *Inst. Petrol. Rev.*, **2,** 180–3, 216–21, 249–52, 1948.
     Idem. Ibid., **2,** 357–60, 1948.
     Idem. 'The Oil-Shales of the Lothians' (3rd ed.), pp. 240–65. Memoirs of the Geological Survey, London. 1927.
[8] BEATON, K. *Business Hist. Rev.*, **29,** 28–53, 1955.
[9] U.S. Patents Nos 11,203, 11,204, and 11,205. 1854.
[10] SAUSSURE, N. T. DE. *Ann. Chim. (Phys.)*, **4,** 314, 1817.
     DUMAS, J. B. A. *Liebigs Ann.*, **6,** 257, 1833.
     BOUSSINGAULT, J. B. J. D. *Ann. Chim. (Phys.)*, **64,** 141–51, 1837.
[11] SCHORLEMMER, C. *Liebigs Ann.*, **127,** 311, 1863.
     PELOUZE, J. and CAHOURS, A. *Ann. Chim. (Phys.)*, fourth series, **1,** 5, 1864.
     SAINTE-CLAIRE DEVILLE, H. E. *C.R. Acad. Sci.*, Paris, **66,** 442, 1868.
     Idem. Ibid., **68,** 349, 485, 686, 1869.
     Idem. Ibid., **69,** 933, 1869.
[12] IMBERT, P. *Dinglers J.*, **34,** 72, 1828.
     LOTZKY, J. *Ibid.*, **38,** 109, 1830.
[13] GOODRICH, H. B. *Econ. Geol.*, **27,** 160–8, 1932.
[14] SILLIMAN, B. (Jr). 'Report on the Rock Oil or Petroleum from Venango County, Pennsylvania, with Special Reference to its Use for Illumination and Other Purposes.' New Haven. 1855.

[15] GIDDENS, P. H. 'The Birth of the Oil Industry.' Macmillan, New York. 1938.
    Idem. 'The Beginnings of the Petroleum Industry.' Pennsylvania Historical and Museum Commission, Harrisburg. 1941.
    Idem. 'Pennsylvania Petroleum, 1750–1872.' Pennsylvania Historical and Museum Commission, Harrisburg. 1947.
    Idem. 'Early Days of Oil, a Pictorial History of the Beginnings of the Industry in Pennsylvania.' Princeton University Press, Princeton, N.J. 1948.
    TARBELL, I. M. 'The History of the Standard Oil Company' (2 vols). McClure Phillips, New York. 1904.
    GERRETSON, F. C. 'History of the Royal Dutch' (4 vols). Brill, Leiden. 1957.
[16] ENGLER, C. and HÖFER, H. 'Erdöl und seine Verwandten.' Brunswick. 1888.
[17] SWEMMLE, J. 'World Geography of Petroleum', p. 300. Princeton University Press, Princeton, N.J. 1950.
    WHITE, J. C. *Science*, **5**, 521–2, 1885.
[18] FORBES, R. J. 'Short History of the Art of Distillation.' Brill, Leiden. 1948.
    Idem. *Trans. Newcomen Soc.*, **24**, 105–12, 1947–8.
[19] HAUSBRAND, E. 'Die Wirkungsweise der Rectificier- und Destillierapparate.' Berlin. 1893.
    SOREL, E. 'La rectification de l'alcool.' Paris. 1894.
    Idem. 'La distillation.' Paris. 1895.
    Idem. 'Distillation et rectification industrielle.' Paris. 1899.
[20] WAGEMANN, P. *Dinglers J.*, **139**, 42, 1855.
[21] RAGOSIN, J. V. 'Le naphte et l'industrie du naphte.' Paris. 1884.
    Idem. 'Traité sur la distillation rationnelle des pétroles bruts.' Paris. 1889.
[22] STEPANOFF. 'Les principes fondamentaux de la théorie de la lampe.' St Petersburg. 1905.
[23] GALE, T. 'Rock Oil in Pennsylvania and Elsewhere.' Erie. 1860.
[24] GESNER, A. 'A Practical Treatise on Coal, Petroleum and other Distilled Oils.' New York. 1861.
    ANTISELL, T. 'The Manufacture of Photogenic or Hydro-Carbon Oils.' New York. 1860.
[25] SCHMITZ, P. M. E. 'L'Épopée du pétrole.' Pichon & Durand-Auzias, Paris. 1947.
[26] British Patents of 27 June, 1865, and 16 October, 1865.
[27] ROMP, H. A. 'Oil Burning.' Nijhoff, The Hague. 1937.
[28] PEABODY, E. H. 'Oil Fuel.' Newcomen Society of North America, New York. 1942.
[29] COULOMB, C. A. 'Théorie des machines simples.' Paris. 1779.
[30] REYNOLDS, O. "On the Theory of Lubrication and its Application to Mr Beauchamp Tower's Experiments, including an Experimental Determination of the Viscosity of Olive Oil." *Phil. Trans.*, **177**, Pt I, 159, 1886.
    RÜLLMANN, O. 'Über die Wichtigkeit der Reibung.' Berlin. 1885.
[31] HIRN, G. A. *C.R. Acad. Sci., Paris*, **99**, 127, 1884.
    Idem. *Bull. Soc. industr. Mulhouse*, **26**, 128, 1854.
[32] *Schweiz. polyt. Z.*, **8**, 1863.
[33] ARMSTRONG, H. E. *J. Soc. chem. Ind., Lond.*, **3**, 462, 1884.
[34] YOUNG, J. W. *Trans. Newcomen Soc.*, **18**, 109–29, 1936–7.
    LE GALLEC, Y. *Tech. et Civil.*, **2**, 28–33, 1951.
    SCHULZ-WITTHUHN, G. 'Von Archimedes bis Mercedes. Eine Geschichte der Kraftfahrzeuge bis 1900.' Int. Motor Edition, Frankfort. 1952.
[35] U.S. Patents Nos 342,564 and 342,565. 1886.
[36] British Patents No. 6,466 of 1890; and No. 1,308 of 1891.
    U.S. Patent No. 477,153. 1890.
    French Patent No. 209,809. 1890.

6

THE STATIONARY STEAM-ENGINE, 1830–1900

A. STOWERS

I. INTRODUCTION

SOME of the early experiments on atmospheric pressure made in the middle of the seventeenth century, and the first attempt to move a piston with steam by Denis Papin (1647–1714) in 1690, from which the earliest idea of a steam-engine may be said to have emanated, have been described earlier in this work (vol IV, ch 6). To pick up the thread of the story, however, we must briefly recapitulate this earlier work.

Savery was the first to construct a practical steam-pump, and in 1698 he obtained his master patent for 'The Raiseing of Water ... by the Impellent Force of Fire'. This steam-pump had no piston but depended on a pressure of steam for which the existing materials and methods of manufacture were not then suitable; hence, progress along this path was severely checked.

Newcomen's stroke of genius was to combine the cylinder, with its piston attached to one end of an overhead wooden beam, and the familiar reciprocating pump, connected to the other end, and to work the combination by condensing steam, at no more than atmospheric pressure, under the piston. Newcomen, about 1712, was thus the first to establish the steam-engine as a practical machine, sufficiently powerful and reliable to save tin- and coal-mines in Britain from flooding and consequent bankruptcy. Smeaton made several improvements in the design and manufacture of the Newcomen engine, which had no rival for sixty years.

A great step forward in the development of the steam-engine was made by Watt in 1765 when he invented the separate condenser, patented in 1769. This could be kept at a constant low temperature, while the cylinder remained at approximately the same temperature as the incoming steam. In 1782 Watt patented two further outstanding improvements. The first was to double the power obtained from the cylinder by making the piston double-acting, that is, with the steam pressing on either side alternately. The second was to use the steam expansively by cutting off the supply to the cylinder before the end of the stroke; this led to an economy of consumption that became more marked when steam-pressures were raised later.

The partnership of Boulton and Watt, which lasted from 1775 to 1800, may have stifled the efforts of other inventors, but it undoubtedly placed the steam-engine industry on a sure foundation. It led to the establishment of the double-acting rotative beam engine, with its condenser and centrifugal governor, which had become more or less standardized by 1787, as the most important, reliable, and efficient source of power for industry. It remained so up to the expiry of the patent for the separate condenser and the end of the partnership, and indeed for many years afterwards.

From 1800 onwards new types of steam-engine began to be made by inventors who were now unfettered by the patent. Many variations were born, only to die immediately, but during the nineteenth century designs began to be guided into distinct categories. These came to be known as Cornish engines; compound beam engines; horizontal engines, simple and compound; vertical non-condensing engines working with higher steam-pressures; and condensing engines, simple, compound, or triple expansion, running at much higher speeds than the others. The development of these types will be described later. As demands were made for larger powers, engines needed more steam, and consequently there were concurrent developments in the design of land boilers. But in the last sixteen years of the period now under review, that is from 1884 to 1900, a rival form of prime mover, the steam-turbine, appeared and developed with such amazing rapidity that the stationary steam-engine was obsolescent for many purposes at the beginning of the twentieth century.

The position regarding the steam-engine in 1830 can be stated briefly as follows. The Watt jet-condensing beam engine, supplied with steam at not more than 2 or 3 lb per sq in pressure above atmospheric, was the standard source of power for large factories and mills; water-wheels were, of course, still used in many places, but were becoming inadequate, and were liable to reduction of power in times of drought, flood, or frost. In small works, the more convenient table-engine of Maudslay, and the grasshopper engine invented by Freemantle, were often used. For pumping water out of mines and for public water-supply, Trevithick's high-pressure Cornish beam engine, working with steam supplied by Cornish boilers at 50–70 lb per sq in, was unrivalled. The Woolf compound steam-engine (vol IV, p 191) had not developed in England to the extent that might have been expected, owing to the favouring of low steam-pressures, the abundance of coal, and the greater complication and cost of the Woolf as compared with the simple engine. It was, however, made in France, and became a success on the continent because the cost of coal there was much higher. In fact, for many decades, the compound engine was generally known abroad as a Woolf engine. However, the true course of development, with higher steam-pressures and speeds, greater ranges of expansion, and lighter parts, had been rightly indicated by Richard Trevithick in England and Oliver Evans in America (vol IV, ch 6).

II. THE CORNISH BEAM ENGINE

After Boulton and Watt severed their connexion with Cornwall, because they had such trouble in getting the Cornish Adventurers to pay the agreed royalties on the fuel savings effected by their engines, the Cornishmen had to rely on their own efforts and set up some large foundries. The efficiency of the existing Watt engines deteriorated, owing to neglect and bad management, until the system of monthly reports was inaugurated by the mine-captains Davey and Lean: this introduced a spirit of competition. As a result of higher steam-pressures in Trevithick's Cornish cylindrical single-flue boiler, working up to 50 lb per sq in or more, and the persistent efforts of Cornish engineers led by Woolf, the duty[1] of the single-acting Cornish pumping engine had by 1840 been increased approximately two and a half times as compared with the Watt engine.

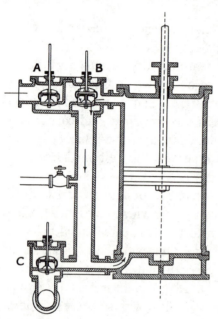

FIGURE 47—*Section through cylinder and valves of single-acting Cornish engine.*

The Cornish cycle was such an outstanding success that it is worth considering in more detail. Figure 47 shows a section through the cylinder and valves of a single-acting Cornish pumping engine. Starting with the piston at the top, steam at 40–50 lb per sq in passes from the boiler through the inlet valve A, valve B remaining closed, and drives the piston down. The cylinder space below the piston is at the same time in communication with the condenser through the exhaust valve C. Steam is cut off by closing valve A at from one-tenth to one-fifth of the stroke, the rest of the stroke being effected by its expansion. After a pause, regulated by the cataract governor, to allow the pump barrel to become

[1] The duty was a convenient measure of the performance of pumping engines, being the quantity of water in pounds raised 1 ft high by 1 bushel (84 lb) of coal.

filled with water, the equilibrium valve B opens at the end of the stroke, and valves A and C are closed. Steam now flows from above the piston to the space below it through B, and not directly to the condenser. The piston, being in equilibrium, is raised again by the weight of the pump-rod and ram. When it nearly reaches the top, B is closed and the remaining steam is compressed to give a cushioning effect, while the exhaust steam is discharged through C into the condenser. Double-beat valves, invented by Harvey and West in 1839, were used to eliminate the shock due to the sudden closing of the earlier type of clack valves. The main reasons for the increased economy of the Cornish engine were as follows: (a) the early cut-off; (b) the expansive working; (c) the fact that the fall of temperature from admission to exhaust was made in two stages, namely, above the piston from admission to release, and below the piston from release to exhaust, so that the clearance space above the piston was never in direct communication with the condenser; (d) the lagging of the cylinder, steam-pipes, and boiler to prevent loss of heat to the surrounding air.

Figure 48 gives a good idea of Taylor's Cornish pumping engine, built in 1840 at Perran Foundry for the United Mines. Its size will be realized from the height of the engine-man in charge. The cylinder was 85 inches in diameter by 11 ft stroke, and the greatest power it developed was 220 hp at $7\frac{1}{2}$ double strokes a minute; this was obtained in 1851 when pumping 500 gallons of water a minute. The iron beam was made of two parallel castings, each 34 ft long, fixed together. The skill involved in making and erecting such large engines with the limited facilities available in 1840 cannot fail to arouse our admiration and respect for the outstanding achievements of Cornish engineers of those times.

At first, the economical results claimed were regarded with suspicion in other parts of the country by engineers in charge of large waterworks. Such engineers had to meet the demand of an expanding industry and a rising population for a greatly increased water-supply (ch 23), and were at the same time handicapped by the high cost of coal, which often had to be transported over long distances. However, Thomas Wicksteed, engineer to the East London Waterworks Company, was sent to Cornwall by his directors to investigate the claims made for the Cornish engine. As the result of his favourable report, the company in 1837 bought a second-hand engine similar to that then working at Fowey Consols; this had achieved a duty of no less than 95 millions, the highest recorded up to that time. The engine was re-erected at Old Ford Pumping Station and tested in 1838, attaining a duty of 90 m, compared with 40 m of the Watt engine. The engine worked there until it was dismantled in 1892. Use of the Cornish engine became standard practice for half a century, and when old boilers had to be renewed, existing Watt engines were frequently altered to work on the Cornish cycle. The Cornish engine was not introduced into the Northumberland collieries until about 1860, because plenty of cheap, though poor quality, coal was available and there was consequently not the same incentive to economize.

The size of engines increased as more experience was gained in their manu-

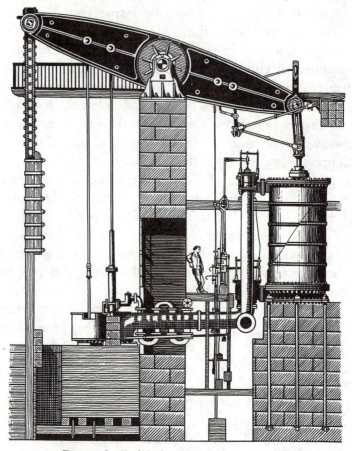

FIGURE 48—*Taylor's Cornish pumping engine, 1840.*

facture and as the mines, which required so many of them, became deeper. Harvey & Company of Hayle built an engine with a cylinder 112 inches in diameter by 10 ft stroke for the Battersea pumping station of the Southwark and Vauxhall Water Company in 1856.

A few fine examples have been saved from destruction, thanks to the successful efforts of the Cornish Engines Preservation Society. An example is the engine designed by Captain Samuel Grose and built in 1854 by Sandys, Carne, & Vivian at Copperhouse Foundry, Hayle. The cylinder was 80 inches in diameter by 10 ft 4 in stroke. It is one of the oldest Cornish engines in existence, and was moved twice before it was finally re-erected at Robinson's Shaft, South Crofty, in 1903; there it worked continuously for fifty years, and it is now honourably retired. An even larger engine, and one of the last of its type to be made in Cornwall, was built by Harvey & Company, Hayle Foundry, to the designs of Nicholas Trestrail for Carn Brea Mine. With a 90 in cylinder and 10 ft stroke, the engine weighed 125 tons and was re-erected in 1924 at East Pool and Agar Mine.

As London had the largest urban population in Britain, its demands for water were a constant anxiety to the various water undertakings, which developed in the nineteenth century before the Metropolitan Water Board was established in 1902. One of the most powerful Cornish engines manufactured for London, named Victoria, was built by Harvey & Company for the East London Water-works Company and erected in 1854 at Lee Bridge pumping station. The cylinder, 100 inches in diameter by 11 ft stroke, was supplied with steam at 40 lb per sq in pressure from eight Cornish boilers.

It is interesting to note that Cornish beam engines were made in Cornwall even in the twentieth century. Holman Brothers Limited of Camborne, for example, built an engine with a 68 in diameter cylinder for the Dorothea Slate Quarry Company Limited, Caernarvon, as recently as 1904.

Another engine that worked on the Cornish cycle, though it looked very different, was named the Bull engine after Edward Bull, who introduced it in 1792, though he infringed Watt's patent for the separate condenser. The steam cylinder was supported over the pump-shaft by beams extending across the engine-house, and the piston rod, which passed through the bottom cylinder cover, was directly connected to the pump spears. Bull thus dispensed with the heavy beam and utilized a smaller engine-house. In the nineteenth century manufacturers were free to make this type of engine. Harvey & Company built several, including two with a 66 inch diameter cylinder in 1855, one 70 inch in 1857, and one 90 inch in 1871, all for the Southwark & Vauxhall Water Company.

The Metropolitan Water Board preserves at its Kew Bridge pumping station, near London, a 70 inch Bull engine made by Harvey & Company in 1859, and four other large historic engines. These comprise a 64 in Watt and a 64 in Maudslay beam pumping engine of 1820 and 1838 respectively, both converted later to the Cornish cycle, and two Cornish pumping engines, a 90 in by Sandys, Carne

& Vivian of 1846, and a 100 in by Harvey of 1871. The latter worked for the last time in May 1946.

Although the Cornish engine was so strongly built that it would practically never wear out, its fate was sealed by the constant rise in boiler pressures. When the economic limit of expansion of steam in one cylinder was reached, the compound engine with two or three cylinders was adopted in its place.

III. THE HORIZONTAL STEAM-ENGINE

For nearly one hundred years engineers had built and worked with engines having vertical cylinders; consequently the introduction of the horizontal engine

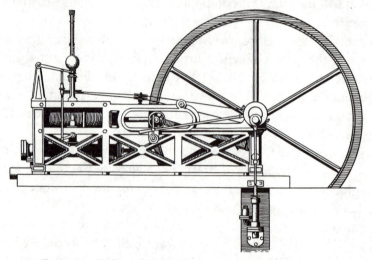

FIGURE 49—*Taylor and Martineau's horizontal steam-engine, 1826.*

was not easy. One reason for this was the fear that the lower half of the cylinder would wear more quickly than the upper owing to the weight of the piston, and another the impracticability of constructing without the appropriate machine tools a flat surface for a crosshead to slide on. The stationary horizontal engine began to be manufactured about 1826 for driving machinery in factories and mills. It is known that a London firm, Taylor & Martineau of City Road, had by then built one of the earliest types, for it is shown in an engraving published in 1826 (figure 49). The cylinder was held horizontally between two cast iron side frames, which also supported the crankshaft bearings and the guides for the rollers attached to the crosshead; the horizontal piston-valve and condenser were underneath the cylinder.

Many thousands of horizontal engines, supplied with steam from Cornish and

Lancashire boilers, were built during the nineteenth century by well known companies such as Hornsby, Robey, Tangye, Marshall, Galloway, Musgrave, and Hick, Hargreaves. A typical horizontal engine for small powers made by the Hornsby company is shown in plate 7 A. The steam-jacketed cylinder was supported on a cast iron bed, the guides being cast with the bed and bored out. The crankpin was attached to an overhanging crankplate, the outer end of the crankshaft being carried by an independent bearing. The governor automatically regulated the degree of expansion in accordance with the load on the engine. Two eccentrics on the crankshaft drove the main slide-valve and the back cut-off or expansion valve. When running at 95 rpm with steam at 60 lb per sq in, the engine developed 50 indicated hp with a cylinder 12·25 inches in diameter by 22 in stroke. The same design was used for a range of engines up to 185 hp, the largest by this maker being 22 inches in diameter by 40 in stroke.

In America the trend was towards much higher speeds. In 1863 the Porter-Allen engine was made by the Southwark Foundry & Machine Company, Philadelphia, to the designs of C. T. Porter. It had an overhung cylinder and ran at the comparatively high speed of 350 rpm, developing about 168 hp. About 1881 another engine of American origin, the Armington Sims, which was also manufactured in England by Greenwood & Batley of Leeds, was specifically designed for driving dynamos direct, without using intermediate ropes or belts (p 134). A speed of 350 rpm was in this case obtained by using a short stroke and connecting-rod, and strengthening the bed. An engine with a cylinder 6·5 inches in diameter by 8 in stroke developed 18 indicated hp.

The numerous horizontal engines with one double-acting cylinder were fundamentally the same, but there were many variations in valve-gears and governors, all designed to produce more power with higher speeds and steam-pressures, and at the same time to be more economical in steam-consumption. As the variety and quality of machine tools (vol IV, ch 14) developed, so the component parts of engines could be manufactured more accurately and at less cost. In America slide-valves began to be superseded by drop-valves for steam and exhaust. Frederick E. Sickels patented his drop-valve cut-off gear in 1841. George H. Corliss patented his gear with cylindrical rocking valves in 1849, and this was much used later. It became known to a wider public after large vertical engines fitted with it were displayed at the Paris Exposition of 1867 and at the Centennial Exhibition at Philadelphia in 1876.

In Great Britain, however, the simpler and cheaper horizontal slide-valve engine was by 1855 competing with the beam engine and was widely used until 1864, when the firm of Hick, Hargreaves at Bolton, founded in 1833 by Benjamin

Hick, made the Corliss valve-gear there. A Corliss engine had been imported into Scotland in 1859. The success of this type was due to its economical steam consumption, and to steady governing, an essential desideratum in the textile industry, where constant breakage of thread would seriously hamper production. Simple engines, in which expansion of steam was carried out in one stage only, made to standardized designs, were adequate for most requirements up to about 1880. For example, a horizontal single-cylinder condensing Corliss engine of 1500 hp was built in that year with a cylinder 52 inches in diameter by 6 ft stroke. It worked at a steam-pressure of 80 lb per sq in. The fly-wheel alone weighed 90 tons.

The demand for still more power led to the development of the compound engine with higher steam-pressures. Plate 7 B shows a typical compound condensing mill-engine, with the two cylinders arranged in tandem and the piston-rods driving a single overhung crank. The cylinders were mounted on one bedplate and the crankshaft carried a crank-disk and grooved fly-wheel. The high-pressure cylinder was fitted with double-beat inlet valves actuated by the variable expansion trip-gear patented by W. R. Proell in 1881. The valves, under the control of the Porter governor, were closed sharply by the action of springs. The exhaust valves of the high-pressure cylinder, and the inlet and exhaust valves of the low-pressure cylinder, were of the Corliss type. A wrist-plate, loose on each valve spindle, carried a spring catch engaging with an arm on the spindle. The wrist-plate was oscillated by an eccentric; when the spring catch was disengaged from the valve arm by an adjustable roller the valve was released, and closed under the action of a spring and dash-pot. One eccentric worked the inlet valves and another all the exhaust valves. With steam at 100 lb per sq in pressure, and cylinders 12 and 21 inches in diameter by 30 in stroke, the engine developed 185 hp at 110 rpm. The jet condenser was below floor level; the air-extraction and feed pumps beside it were driven by the L-shaped lever from the tail-rod of the low-pressure cylinder. In 1881 a 4000 hp cross-compound Corliss engine was manufactured with a high-pressure cylinder 50 inches in diameter, a low-pressure cylinder 84 inches in diameter, and a common stroke of 8 ft, the boiler pressure being 100 lb per sq in.

To cope with such increased powers the old-fashioned system of transmission, using cast iron spur and bevel wheels transmitting power from engines at ground level to the upper floors of factories, was too cumbersome and noisy. Moreover, heavy foundations and bearings were essential to secure correct alignment of the numerous vertical and horizontal shafts. Belts were substituted for bevel gears about 1877; soon afterwards ropes were used, leading later to the rope-race system.

An interesting horizontal engine, conceived by Jacob Perkins in 1827 and patented by Todd in 1885, was later known as the uniflow engine. In this, the steam was introduced through slide valves to each end of the cylinder and flowed out through a belt of exhaust ports in the middle. The piston acted as exhaust valve and was equal in length to the stroke minus the clearance space. The advantage was realized of keeping the ends hot and the common outlet cool at exhaust temperature, but construction was difficult. It became a successful and economical engine in 1908 when J. Stumpf patented a more suitable valve gear.

IV. THE VERTICAL HIGH-PRESSURE STEAM-ENGINE

Although the Cornish cycle was so important, as already explained, it must be remembered that many beam engines did not work on it. When the original boilers were condemned, they were replaced by new boilers working at higher pressures. The life of many Watt engines was prolonged and their power increased by compounding, that is, by the addition of a small high-pressure cylinder, usually at the other side of the beam, the original cylinder becoming the low-pressure one. This system was patented by William MacNaught in 1845 and such engines were said to be 'MacNaughted'. New compound engines, however, were normally manufactured with the two cylinders adjacent. Jonathan Hornblower had patented a double-cylinder engine in 1781, and Woolf repatented the compound engine in 1804 and built many of that type.

By the middle of the nineteenth century the compound engine was becoming established. Plate 10 A shows a small and elegantly designed double-acting compound condensing beam engine built by Thomas Horn of Westminster about 1860. This engine drove a flour-mill at Ifield, Sussex, until 1914, and developed 16 hp at 50 rpm with steam at 45 lb per sq in.

Engines without beams had been made by Trevithick at the beginning of the nineteenth century, and by the middle of it numerous types were being manufactured. Examples are the columnar and vertical winding-engines by William Fairbairn & Company of Manchester, and the table engines of Maudslay, Sons & Field previously mentioned. About 1850 James Nasmyth invented a vertical engine (figure 50), similar in design to his famous steam-hammer; it had the cylinder at the top and the crankshaft below in place of the anvil. For many years engines having this new arrangement were called 'inverted' engines, but later it was regarded as standard practice; it was very widely adopted during the latter half of the nineteenth century in stationary engines for driving pumps and for blowing blast-furnaces.

When T. A. Edison built the first central electric power station in 1881 at

Pearl Street, New York, one of his most important innovations was to drive the Edison dynamos by high-speed engines direct-coupled to them. These were Armington Sims horizontal engines, each producing 175 hp at 350 rpm. With the development of electric lighting, many attempts were made to drive dynamos at increased speeds by using belts from the existing slow-running engines or from shafting, but they were unsuccessful because long belt-drives occupied much floor space and were dangerous, and because the governing was not precise enough to eliminate flickering of the arc lamps (p 208).

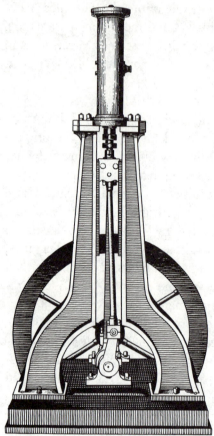

FIGURE 50—*Nasmyth's 'inverted' or steam-hammer type of engine, c 1850.*

The problem was, however, solved more satisfactorily by the introduction of high-speed vertical engines coupled directly to dynamos specially designed to work at the same speed; both were mounted on a single baseplate, forming a much more compact and safe arrangement. One of the first successful engines was that invented by George Westinghouse and made by the Westinghouse Company in America and by Alley & MacLellan Limited of Glasgow. This was a vertical single-acting engine, always made with two cylinders and a two-throw crankshaft. The connecting rods were directly attached to trunk pistons as in an internal combustion engine, the weight of the reciprocating parts being reduced by eliminating the piston rods and cross-heads. The moving parts were enclosed in the crank-case and lubricated by the splash system. Steam was distributed by a piston valve either above or between the cylinders and driven by an eccentric on the crankshaft.

In the year 1871 Peter Brotherhood in England patented a new type of steam-engine for directly driving machinery at much higher speeds than had been used previously. It had three cylinders in the vertical plane, fixed radially at angles of 120° to one another. It was manufactured in a range of sizes from 1·25 hp, at 1000 rpm, to 55 hp, at 500 rpm.

An important advance in the development of high-speed steam-engines was made by P. W. Willans, who designed and manufactured several types before he was killed in an accident at the early age of 42. His best-known stationary engine was the single-acting central valve engine, the main patents for which are dated

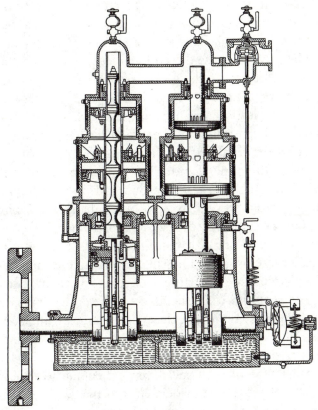

FIGURE 51—*Two-crank compound Willans engine, c 1888. As usual in this type of engine, the high-pressure cylinders are at the top.*

1884 and 1885. The idea had been in his mind since 1880, for his sketches exist showing valves inside piston rods. The first engine was made in 1885 at the Ferry Works of Willans & Robinson at Thames Ditton, and within two years Willans had designed a range of nine engines with low-pressure cylinders increasing from 5 inches in diameter at 750 rpm to 20 inches at 350 rpm. The four smaller sizes were abandoned, but the five larger ones were redesigned to develop from 25 to 100 indicated hp. These engines could be erected as simple, compound, or triple-expansion engines, with single, double, or triple cranks.

Figure 51 shows a typical two-crank compound engine of this type. The high-pressure cylinders were always at the top, and the guide pistons at the bottom worked in trunks to give an air-cushioning effect. The engine was single-acting, and as there were no reversals of stress in the reciprocating parts, which were in constant thrust, it ran smoothly and free from knocking. A novel feature was the distribution of steam by a series of interconnected vertical piston valves, shown on the left of the figure, working up and down inside the hollow piston rod with ports cut in its wall. This system reduced port clearances and consequent losses. The valve line was driven by an eccentric on the crankshaft. The pistons were attached direct to the hollow piston rod, which rotated the crankshaft by means of two connecting rods with big-end bearings surrounding the crankpin. Splash lubrication was used in the enclosed crank-chamber, and the engine-speed was controlled by the spring-loaded centrifugal governor on the opposite end of the crankshaft to the fly-wheel.

Many engines of this type, for driving generators, were made at Thames Ditton and later at Rugby. Between 1890 and 1900 the power of engines manufactured rose from 300 hp to 2400 hp. Willans was a pioneer in works organization, and he introduced a system of standardization whereby the high-pressure cylinder of one size was the same as the low-pressure cylinder of the next smaller size but one. Thus interchangeable cylinders, pistons, rings, valves, and so on were made in quantity for stock; when an order for an engine was received, the requisite components could be drawn immediately from the stores. Willans also insisted on very close manufacturing limits, and many parts had to be machined to within 0·001 in. The central-valve engine on which his classic economy trials were made is still preserved.

The more usual type of high-speed vertical engine was, however, double-acting; for small powers it was made well into the twentieth century. One of the most successful manufacturers was G. E. Belliss of Birmingham, especially when he applied the new system of forced lubrication, patented in 1890 by A. C. Pain, a designer on his staff, to the main moving parts. Previously, if the speed of double-acting engines was raised, very close adjustment of bearings was essential for quiet running. Owing to the expansion when hot exceeding the clearance when cold, crank pins and bearings were liable to seize as the temperature rose, resulting in serious damage. Forced lubrication made possible the successful running of double-acting engines at high speed without the risk of excessive wear and knocking. The system was, in fact, subsequently applied to practically all engines, turbines, and other high-speed machinery. Plate 8 B shows the first steam-engine with forced lubrication; it was made in 1890 by Belliss & Morcom Limited, and is still preserved. It developed 20 hp at 625 rpm, and the lubricating oil was circulated at a pressure of about 15 lb per sq in by a small oscillating pump, without packing or valves, situated in an oil-sump in the base and driven by an eccentric.

Many compound engines of this type, with the high-pressure and low-pressure cylinders side-by-side and with cranks at 180° apart, were built by this firm and by others, such as Allen, Brotherhood, Browett Lindley, and Sisson. Powers up to 1000 hp at 250 rpm were popular and, eventually, large triple-expansion condensing engines, supplied with superheated steam, developed up to about 2900 indicated hp. By 1900, however, the steam-turbine was established on land for driving the alternators of the then newly created electrical industry (ch 9), and the decline of the large steam-engine had begun. Several manufacturers of engines therefore started producing steam-turbines, but before these are considered the development of the boiler must be discussed.

V. STEAM-BOILERS FOR USE ON LAND

The steam-engine could not have progressed without a corresponding development of boilers. The wagon-type boiler with stays, used for Watt engines, survived until the middle of the nineteenth century, but after about 1812 the Cornish cylindrical shell boiler with one flue, invented independently by Trevithick in England and by Evans in America, came into general use. For greater capacities, the Lancashire shell-type boiler with two flues, patented in 1844 by W. Fairbairn and J. Hetherington of Manchester, was widely adopted. Both boilers were at first constructed of rolled wrought iron plates riveted together; but after 1865 mild steel plates began to be utilized. The two types were widely used until the end of the nineteenth century for steady steaming, as there was no sudden demand for higher pressures. With improved fittings and strengthened flues, the Lancashire boiler has survived well into the twentieth century.

Apart from the locomotive multiple fire-tube boilers, invented by Seguin in France and by the Stephensons in 1829 in England, and small vertical boilers, the important class of water-tube boilers, designed to meet the demand for higher pressures, was developed more quickly in America than in Europe. In 1859 J. Harrison of Philadelphia introduced his sectional boiler with inclined rows of hollow cast iron spheroids held together by wrought iron tie rods; differential expansion, however, gave trouble. In 1865 J. Twibill patented in England a boiler having straight wrought iron tubes, slightly inclined to the horizontal, but they could not be cleaned. The first sectional water-tube boiler made commercially in England was that of J. and F. Howard of Bedford in 1868; this had inclined wrought iron tubes for pressures up to 140 lb per sq. in.

The superiority of the water-tube type with natural circulation was established by the boiler patented in 1867 by G. H. Babcock and S. Wilcox of America. It had straight tubes to facilitate cleaning, a great improvement on an earlier design of 1856 by Wilcox and Stillman which had curved tubes. The straight tubes had cast iron headers at each end, connected to a steam-and-water drum above (plate 8 A), and this successful design was standard for many years. In 1889 A. Stirling in America introduced his improved boiler, which had steeply inclined tubes expanded into three cylindrical steam-and-water drums above and two cylindrical mud drums below; any sediment in the water was deposited in the latter. A typical boiler at the end of the nineteenth century generated 12 000 lb of steam an hour at 160 lb per sq in pressure. By that time water-tube boilers were successfully meeting demands for higher pressures and rapid steaming in power stations; much progress was also being made with mechanical stokers, feed-water heaters, and superheaters.

VI. STEAM-TURBINES

The steam-turbine had long engaged the attention of inventors, and up to 1880 some hundred patents had been lodged, though none had led to the making of a satisfactory machine. As early as 1784, for example, Wolfgang von Kempelen proposed a turbine which was sufficiently promising to give Watt some anxiety as a possible rival to his own engine. Trevithick, too, experimented in this field and built a 15-ft 'whirling engine' in 1815.

In 1884 the Hon. Charles A. Parsons, appreciating that one of the most urgent engineering needs of the day was for an engine that would drive dynamos directly and that a limit to the speed of the traditional steam-engine was set by its reciprocating action, invented a successful steam-turbine. He used the water-turbine as a basis for his design. He was the first to realize that if the total drop of steam-pressure was divided into many small stages, and an elemental turbine was placed at each stage, each individual turbine of the series should have an efficiency between 70 and 80 per cent, as in a water-turbine. A high efficiency should therefore result for the whole series. Furthermore, in order to reach maximum efficiency the speed of rotation necessary would be moderate, as compared with the extreme speed obtained by allowing the whole drop of pressure to take place in one stage.

Parsons, at that time with Clarke, Chapman & Company of Gateshead, therefore constructed a series of small elemental turbines, each consisting of a ring of blades mounted on one long shaft inside a fixed circular casing which carried rows of similar blades projecting inwards between the rows of blades on the shaft. The shaft with its blades is called the rotor, and the stationary casing with its blades the stator. When steam at boiler pressure was admitted to one end of the stator, it flowed parallel to the horizontal axis of the turbine between the blades of the stator and rotor alternately, until it escaped to atmospheric pressure. Thus the rotor was driven.

Parsons planned from the start that his turbine should drive a direct-coupled electrical generator, but as the maximum speed of dynamos at that time was only about 1200 rpm he had to design a new high-speed direct current generator and this was as revolutionary as the turbine. His two patents granted in 1884—no 6735 for 'improvements in rotary motors actuated by fluid pressure and applicable also as pumps' and no 6734 for high-speed generators—were of supreme importance. In the same year he built his first direct-current turbo-generator, shown in plate 9 A. It was non-condensing, generated 7·5 kw at 100 volts, and ran at the astonishing speed of 18 000 rpm. Steam was admitted at the centre and flowed axially in equal proportions to eliminate unbalanced axial thrust on the rotor.

As soon as Parsons had proved that his design was correct in practice rapid development followed, although many difficult problems had to be solved in the manufacture of large turbo-alternators. In 1887 he made a compound reaction turbine with high- and low-pressure stages, and in 1888 the first turbine-driven generating set was installed in a public power station; this was the first of four 75 kw turbo-alternators running at 4800 rpm for the Forth Banks Power Station of the Newcastle and District Electric Lighting Company.

On leaving Clarke, Chapman & Company in 1889 to found his own firm of C. A. Parsons & Company, at Heaton Works, Newcastle upon Tyne, Parsons lost the right to use the earlier patents for axial flow, and was therefore obliged to adopt radial flow. In 1891 he built a radial flow 100 kw turbo-alternator running at 4800 rpm for the Cambridge Electric Lighting Company. This was the first condensing turbine (plate 9 B)[1] and was tested by A. Ewing, who demonstrated that its steam consumption was less than that of a steam-engine of equal capacity. The steam-turbine was thus established as the best prime mover for electrical power stations on account of its economy in fuel and space, its reliability, and its freedom from vibration.

In 1893 Parsons regained by agreement his patents for axial flow, and from then onwards concentrated on the manufacture of turbines of this type. Much progress was made, leading to the important and successful installation in 1900

---

[1] Both this machine and the original steam-turbine of 1884 are preserved in the Science Museum, South Kensington.

of two 1000 kw turbo-alternators for the city of Elberfeld, Germany. They were the first tandem-cylinder turbines made, and their size was outstanding.

In the last decade of the nineteenth century other inventors were also busy on the design of different types of steam-turbine, the most noteworthy being C. G. P. de Laval in Sweden, C. G. Curtis in America, and C. E. A. Rateau in France, all of whom achieved success.

BIBLIOGRAPHY

CLARK, D. K. 'The Steam Engine' (2 vols). London. 1891.

DICKINSON, H. W. 'Short History of the Steam Engine.' University Press, Cambridge. 1939.

Idem. 'Water Supply of Greater London.' Newcomen Society, London. 1954.

DICKINSON, H. W. and TITLEY, A. 'Richard Trevithick, the Engineer and the Man.' University Press, Cambridge. 1934.

HUTTON, F. R. 'The Mechanical Engineering of Power Plants.' New York. 1897.

LEAN, T. (and brother). 'Historical Statement of the . . . duty performed by the Steam Engines in Cornwall.' London. 1839.

MATSCHOSS, C. 'Die Entwicklung der Dampfmaschine' (2 vols). Springer, Berlin. 1908.

PARSONS, R. H. 'The Development of the Parsons Steam Turbine.' Constable, London. 1936.

POLE, W. 'Treatise on the Cornish Pumping Engine.' London. 1844.

RIGG, A. 'A Practical Treatise on the Steam Engine.' London. 1878.

WESTCOTT, G. F. 'Pumping Machinery' (2 vols). H.M. Stationery Office, London. 1932–3.

Idem. 'Mechanical and Electrical Engineering; Classified List of Historical Events.' H.M. Stationery Office, London. 1955.

WICKSTEED, T. 'An Experimental Enquiry concerning . . . Cornish and Boulton & Watt Pumping Engines.' London. 1841.

Many papers and articles dealing with steam-engines, boilers, and turbines have been published in the *Proceedings of the Institution of Civil Engineers* (1818–) and the *Proceedings of the Institution of Mechanical Engineers* (1847–); also in *The Engineer* (1856–) and *Engineering* (1866–).

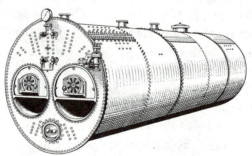

A typical Lancashire boiler, 1900.

7

THE MARINE STEAM-ENGINE

H. PHILIP SPRATT

ONE of the earliest proposals for the steam-propulsion of a vessel with paddle-wheels was that made in 1690 by Denis Papin (1647–1714), in which the pistons were to be fitted with toothed racks to obtain rotary motion. Later, in 1702, Thomas Savery (1650–1715) wrote with reference to his direct steam-pressure water-pump, that 'it may be made very useful to ships, but I dare not meddle with that matter'. He meant, however, that it might be useful in pumping ships dry.

The first mechanical use of steam-power on land, by Thomas Newcomen (1663–1729) about 1712, depended for its action on the pressure of the atmosphere, and was confined to an up-and-down movement of the piston. In 1736, Jonathan Hulls (1699–1758), of Gloucestershire, patented a steam-propelled tug-boat, in which a paddle-wheel at the stern was to have been driven by a Newcomen atmospheric engine, with a ratchet mechanism to obtain rotary motion. This scheme, however, never had a practical trial. So heavy were the engines of that time in relation to their power that successful results could not be expected.

I. THE PADDLE-WHEEL

Papin and Hulls both contemplated the use of paddle-wheels, and most of the later steam-boat experimenters tried this mode of propulsion, the invention of which has been ascribed to the Romans (vol II, p 607). The earliest reference to paddle-wheels occurs in a manuscript probably written about A.D. 370, which is illustrated by a picture of a war-vessel with three pairs of paddle-wheels, each driven by two oxen (vol II, figure 549).[1] Man-operated warships with paddle-wheels are also reputed to have been used in China about the seventh century.

Paddle-wheels reappear towards the close of the Middle Ages: for example, in a manuscript of 1335 (vol II, figure 594), and again in the *De re militari* of Roberto Valturio, of Rimini, printed in 1472. The latter contains pictures of two boats, one with five pairs of paddle-wheels on coupled crank-shafts. Leonardo da Vinci (1452–1519), about 1500, produced various mechanical schemes for

[1] The oldest surviving example of this illustration is a much later copy.

paddle-wheel propulsion. In one of them, two pedals were used to drive a pair of paddle-wheels, each with two blades. A Chinese woodcut dating from about 1522 shows a warship with two pairs of paddle-wheels and armoured with cowhide. William Bourne (fl 1565–83), an English writer on naval affairs (vol III, ch 20), proposed in 1578 the use of side paddle-wheels.

Another scheme, put forward in 1588 by Ramelli (vol III, p 330), proposed a flat-bottomed boat with a paddle-wheel on each side and a winch-handle turned by man-power. Windmills on board ship to drive paddle-wheels were suggested in 1664 and later, and in 1682 a tug-boat with paddle-wheels, driven by a horse-whim, is said to have been used at Chatham. Another horse-operated paddle-boat was made by Prince Rupert (1619–82), and tried on the Thames at London; later, in 1732, such a vessel was constructed by the Maréchal de Saxe, who hoped to travel up the Seine from Rouen to Paris in 12 hours.

II. EXPERIMENTAL STEAM-PROPULSION

The first boat to be moved by the force of steam was that used in 1775 by J. C. Périer (1742–1818) for an experiment on the Seine near Paris. The steam-cylinder was only 8 inches in diameter, and insufficiently powerful. Three years later, the Marquis Claude de Jouffroy d'Abbans (1751–1832) made some abortive experiments with 'palmipede' paddles on the river Doubs; but real success came in 1783, when his paddle-wheel steamboat, the *Pyroscaphe* of 182 tons displacement, ascended the river Saône near Lyons.

Pioneer work on marine steam-propulsion was, however, by no means confined to Europe. In 1785 the American inventor John Fitch (1743–98) proposed the use of a steam-powered endless chain of paddle-floats, and later fitted a boat with twelve vertical oars or paddles, in the manner of a canoe. About 1796 he turned his attention to screw-propulsion, and experimented with a small boat on Collect Pond, New York, without achieving practical success. Another pioneer in America was James Rumsey (1743–92), who in 1787 tried a steamboat on the river Potomac, fitted with a pump to draw in water at the bow and force it out at the stern.[1] Later he came to London; and in 1793 a steamboat of 101 tons, built on his principle, was successfully tested on the Thames.

Meanwhile important developments had taken place in Britain, as the result of some experiments in mechanical propulsion made by Patrick Miller (1731–1815) with double- and triple-hulled vessels. These were manually powered paddle-ships, and with 30 men at the capstans a speed of 4·3 knots could be maintained. The rapid exhaustion of the crew in these tests caused Miller to

---

[1] An early example of jet-propulsion!

consider the use of steam-power. His first atmospheric steam-engine was constructed by William Symington (1763–1831) in 1788, and was successfully tried
in a boat on Dalswinton Lake, Scotland, with the poet Burns on board.

Later, in 1801, Symington was commissioned by Henry Dundas (1742–1811),
then Secretary of State for War, to engine a steam tug-boat, the *Charlotte Dundas*,
for experiments on the Forth and Clyde canal. Her performance was satisfactory,

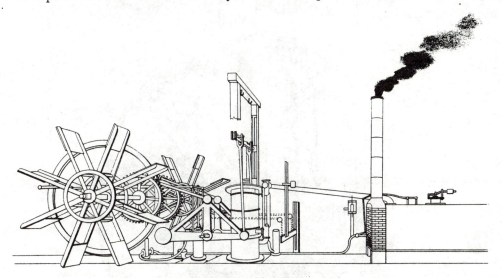

FIGURE 52—*Machinery of p.s.* Clermont, *1807.*

but the canal-owners decided that the wash from the paddles would be detrimental to the banks. The trials of the *Charlotte Dundas* in 1802 were attended
by the American pioneer Robert Fulton (1765–1815), who in the course of the
next year built his first experimental steamboat in Paris, where he tested it on
the Seine.

III. PADDLE-STEAMERS

Fulton achieved commercial success in 1807 with the paddle-steamer *Clermont*, on the river Hudson between New York and Albany. The machinery
(figure 52) for this vessel was constructed by Boulton & Watt of Birmingham.
In Europe the first paddle-steamer to run commercially was the *Comet*, built in
1812 to the order of Henry Bell for service on the Clyde. Her low-pressure engine
(figure 53), constructed by John Robertson of Glasgow, is still preserved at the
Science Museum in London. Some of the earliest steamers in Russia and Germany were also fitted out by British engineers.

One notable vessel on the Thames in 1818 was the *London Engineer*, driven by internal paddle-wheels. The first British-built steam-driven privateer, the *Rising Star* (1821), was of similar construction, the internal disposition of her

FIGURE 53—*Engine of p.s.* Comet, *1812.*

paddle-wheels being intended to protect them from enemy shot. This vessel was also the first to use steam-power on the Atlantic in the westerly direction.

The first steam-propelled vessel to cross the Atlantic (from west to east) was, however, the famous American auxiliary *Savannah* in 1819. Her low-pressure steam-engine was used merely to assist her considerable spread of sail when there was so little wind that her speed was reduced to 4 knots. At other times her collapsible paddle-wheels were folded up, detached from the shaft, and stowed on deck.

The circular paddle-wheel continued to provide the only successful means of propulsion for steamships until about 1837. Some of the earliest paddle-steamers were fitted with adaptations of the overhead beam-engine, which had already been developed by Boulton and Watt for use on land. This proved eminently suitable in America for the shallow-draught river-steamers plying on the Hudson and the Mississippi, but was never much favoured for ocean service.

In Britain, a modification known as the side-lever engine became the most popular in marine use. The overhead beam was replaced by two beams, one on either side of the engine, placed low down near the foundation-plates. This improved the stability of the vessel, and saved a considerable amount of head-room (plate 12 A). Most of the paddle-steamers on the Atlantic and other ocean routes were fitted with side-lever engines, which reached their final development in the *Scotia* (1861), the last paddle-driven vessel of the Cunard Line.

Various attempts were made to design a less cumbersome arrangement, and in 1837 the first direct-acting vertical marine engine was fitted by Seaward & Capel, of Limehouse, in H.M.S. *Gorgon*. In view of the limited vertical distance between the bottom of the hold and the paddle-wheel shaft, however, this arrangement enforced an undesirable shortening of the connecting-rods. To avoid this drawback, a modification of the direct-acting engine was introduced by Seaward & Capel in 1839. In this modified engine the cylinders were open at the top, and the connecting-rods were attached close to the upper face of the trunk piston; the necessary length of connecting-rod was thus obtained by elimination of the piston-rod.

The marine 'steeple' engine, introduced about 1831, overcame in a different manner the difficulties that arose from the limited vertical distance between the bottom of the vessel and the paddle-shaft. In this arrangement, the crankshaft was driven by a connecting-rod which returned downward from a cross-head above. The guides for the cross-head protruded above the decks, and it was their appearance which led to the term 'steeple' engine (plate 12 B).

In one form, patented by Joseph Maudslay (1801–61) and Joshua Field (1787–1863) in 1839, there were two piston-rods, both on the same side of the crank-shaft. This lack of symmetry caused a considerable difference in the timing of the two strokes. Another form, which was extensively used, was that patented by David Napier (1790–1869) in 1842. This had four piston-rods, symmetrical with respect to the axes of the cylinder and crankshaft, and became popular for river-steamers.

The twin-cylinder or 'Siamese' engine, patented in 1839 by Maudslay and Field, also enabled a long connecting-rod to be used in a limited height. The piston-rods of the twin cylinders were both connected to a double cross-head, the vertical tail of which descended between the cylinders; to this was attached the lower end of the connecting-rod. The two cylinders were placed fore-and-aft of the crankshaft. This arrangement involved a loss of hold-space, and the increased cost of two cylinders, instead of one, to each crank. Another modification, in which each unit consisted of only one cylinder, was the annular engine, patented by Maudslay in 1841. The piston was annular, and had two rods secured to a double cross-head. The tail of this cross-head descended into the central aperture of the cylinder and carried the connecting-rod at its lower end.

The form of paddle-engine which later became most popular was the oscillating engine, in which the piston-rod was directly connected to the crank, and the connecting-rod was eliminated. This had been proposed by William Murdock (1754–1839) as early as 1785, and was used in 1822 on the first iron-built paddle-steamer, the *Aaron Manby*. In 1827 the arrangement was adopted by Maudslay, who patented the construction and provided an efficient form of valve-gear for use with oscillating cylinders. The first vessel so fitted by Maudslay, Sons & Field was the Thames steamer *Endeavour* (1828); but it was only when reintroduced with improvements by John Penn (1805–78), of Greenwich, that this form became a favourite one for paddle-vessels.

The largest oscillating engines ever constructed for a ship were those made in 1858 for the famous paddle-and-screw steamer *Great Eastern* (plate 13 A, and pp 361–5). The cylinders, four in number, were 74 inches in diameter by 14-ft stroke, and developed a total of 3410 indicated hp at 10·75 rpm. The paddle-wheels were 56 ft in diameter. The calculated speed of the vessel with both screw and paddle-wheels in action was 15 knots; a special trial under paddle-propulsion alone produced a speed of 7·25 knots.

With the introduction of higher steam-pressures the oscillating engine, which could not be conveniently adapted to compound expansion, was superseded by the inclined direct-acting engine first patented in 1822 by Marc Isambard Brunel (1769–1849). This construction was fitted in 1888 to the cross-Channel paddle-steamer *Princesse Henriette* (plate 13 B), and in 1892 to the famous pleasure-steamer *Isle of Arran*.

IV. SCREW-PROPULSION

The Archimedean screw is more than two thousand years old, but its application to marine propulsion is of much more recent date. Screw-propellers had been proposed by the mathematician Daniel Bernoulli (1700–82) in 1753, and by James Watt (1736–1819) in 1770. The first British patent for screw-propulsion was that of Samuel Miller in 1775. Some of the earliest trials were made in New York, by John Fitch in 1796, and by John Stevens (1749–1838) in 1802, but without much success.

In 1837 Francis Pettit Smith (1808–74) of Hendon, Middlesex, experimented with his first screw-propelled steam-launch. The screw was of wood, and on one of the trials about half of it was broken off. It was noticed with much surprise that this accident materially increased the speed of the boat. The success of these experiments led in 1838 to the construction of the screw-steamer *Archimedes*, of 237 tons, which in turn inspired the British Admiralty to commission the *Rattler* (1843), the first naval vessel to be equipped with the screw.

After the practicability of screw-propulsion had thus been demonstrated, it was the convenience and efficiency of the screw in comparison with the paddle-wheel that led to its subsequent extensive application. But the screw required a higher speed of rotation than the slow-running paddle-engines which were then available; hence the earliest screw-steamers were fitted with geared engines, in which ropes, pitch-chains, or toothed wheels were used to obtain the necessary multiplication of speed. The machinery (plate 14 A) fitted in 1843 on the *Great Britain*, the first screw-steamer to cross the Atlantic, furnishes a notable example of the use of pitch-chains. Geared engines, of various forms, continued to be used for more than a decade in the merchant service.

In warships the need to place the machinery below the water-line, for protection, soon promoted the introduction of special screw-engines. The first instance was in the United States warship *Princeton* (1842). She was fitted with the vibrating or pendulum engine patented by John Ericsson (1803–89). The steam-chambers were segmental, while the pistons were rectangular and swung on bearings like doors on their hinges. The bearings were continued outside the chambers, and carried vibrating cranks connected by rods to the crankshaft. It appears that Ericsson adopted this construction by reason of an unfounded fear, prevalent at the time, that the ordinary form of piston was unsuitable for the increased speeds required.

About 1845 a modification of the twin-cylinder Siamese engine (p 145) was proposed by Maudslay, Sons & Field, to suit the requirements of screw-propulsion; but it never won much favour. The Bishopp disk-engine was also used in some early screw warships. It was first patented in 1836, and applied later to marine propulsion by J. and G. Rennie, with successful results in H.M.S. *Minx* (1849).

With the ordinary form of piston, however, the restricted transverse space available in vessels rendered it very difficult to accommodate the horizontal piston-rod and connecting-rod, and occasioned the introduction of the 'return connecting-rod' engine. In 1844 such engines were fitted on H.M.S. *Amphion*, and the type continued to be much used in the Royal Navy up to about 1876. The engines fitted by J. and G. Rennie in that year to the unarmoured corvettes *Boadicea* and *Bacchante* were compound expansion, with three cylinders, and worked at a steam-pressure of 70 lb per sq in.

Another method extensively used to save transverse space was the complete elimination of the piston-rod in the 'trunk-engine'. The connecting-rod was here attached direct to the piston, which was made annular and fitted with a trunk. Such engines, as patented in 1784 by James Watt, were used much later on the S.S. *Candia* in 1854. The form of double-trunk engine patented in 1845 by John Penn was fitted in 1861 on H.M.S. *Warrior*, notable as the first iron-built armoured warship, and in 1868 on H.M. Ships *Minotaur* and *Northumberland* (plate 14 B). The defects of the trunk-engine included loss of heat from the trunks, increased friction, heavier pistons, difficulty of access, and the larger size of cylinder required.

The ordinary form of horizontal direct-acting screw-engine, with a simple connecting-rod between the cross-head and crank, was first used in the Royal Navy on H.M.S. *Ajax* in 1848. It was a simple construction, often adopted for horizontal screw-engines in spite of its drawbacks, which mainly arose from the lack of adequate space athwartship, and consequent shortness of the connecting-rods. In the case of the *Great Eastern*, however, her exceptional breadth enabled horizontal direct-acting screw-engines (plate 15 A) to be conveniently installed. These were constructed by James Watt & Company and developed 4890 indicated hp.

There were four steam-cylinders, each 84 inches in diameter by 48-in stroke, driving two cranks at right-angles on the shaft, the mean speed of which was 38·8 rpm. Each cylinder had two piston-rods, and a cross-head that moved in guides; from the cross-head of each of the starboard engines proceeded one connecting-rod to a crank-pin, while from the cross-head of each of the port engines two connecting-rods proceeded, so that there were three connecting-rods to each of the cranks.

Steam to these screw-engines was supplied at a pressure of 25 lb to the sq in by six double-ended tubular boilers of the rectangular or box pattern, each 18·5 ft long, 17·5 ft wide, and 14 ft high, having altogether 72 furnaces and a heating surface of 5000 sq ft. The propeller was a four-bladed cast iron screw, 24 ft in diameter, of 44-ft pitch, and weighing 36 tons.

The final form of reciprocating screw-engine was the inverted vertical, which from about 1860 became the common type in the mercantile service. Its economy in athwartship-space enabled two sets of engines to be used, side by side, in twin-screw vessels. After the introduction of side armour, it was also used in battle-ships. The earliest types employed simple expansion; but later, with increased steam-pressures, it was found desirable for thermodynamic reasons to expand the steam successively in two or more cylinders. In 1854 the S.S. *Brandon* was the first sea-going vessel to be fitted with compound expansion engines, by John Elder on the Clyde. The first Atlantic steamship to be so fitted was the *Holland* of the National Line in 1869.

Triple-expansion was patented in France in 1871, by Benjamin Normand, and installed two years later. The first British triple-expansion engines were fitted in 1874 by A. C. Kirk, of John Elder & Company, in the S.S. *Propontis* of 2083 tons. The boilers of this vessel developed a steam-pressure of 150 lb per sq in, as did those of the S.S. *Flamboro*, fitted in 1885 with triple-expansion engines (plate 15 B). To obtain the most economical use of fuel with steam-pressures greater than c 180 lb per sq in, quadruple expansion became necessary about the end of the nineteenth century.

V. THE MARINE STEAM-TURBINE

The ideal of rotary motion obtained directly from steam-pressure was realized by Hero of Alexandria in his aeolipile, about A.D. 50. More mature plans for a steam-turbine came from Giovanni Branca (1571–1640), an architect of Loretto, who in 1629 published the description of such a machine (vol IV, p 168). The water was heated in a closed vessel, and the steam was directed from a tube with impulsive effect on to radial vanes formed on the rim of the wheel. This was mounted on a vertical shaft, with a toothed pinion at its lower end. There is no record, however, that Branca ever considered the problems of ship-propulsion.

John Stevens, of Hoboken, New York, a famous American steamboat pioneer, had in 1802 fitted a 25-ft flat-bottomed boat with a screw-propeller at the stern. To avoid the 'mischievous' inertial effects of a reciprocating piston, the screw-propeller was direct-coupled to a small rotary steam-machine. This consisted of a cylindrical chamber of brass, about 8 inches in diameter and 4 inches long, in which (mounted on the screw-shaft) ran a simple form of two-bladed rotor. With this small craft Stevens obtained a speed of 4 mph.

About this time the millwright Oliver Evans (1755–1819), of Philadelphia, another steamboat pioneer, experimented with an aeolipile on the same prin-ciple as Hero's. Supplied with steam at a pressure of 56 lb to the sq in, the machine made between 700 and 1000 rpm, and, in the inventor's own words, it

exerted 'more than the power of two men'. In 1815 the Cornish inventor Richard
Trevithick (1771–1833) patented an aeolipile or 'recoil' steam-turbine, on the
same principle as Hero's, to be used for marine propulsion.

The achievement of a practical steam-turbine on the impulse principle of
Giovanni Branca was due to the partners James Jamieson Cordes and Edward
Locke, both of Newport, Monmouthshire, who in 1846 constructed their small
rotary machine at the Surrey Docks, Rotherhithe, for experimental purposes.
It developed 32 brake-hp on trial. Their marine turbine proposal, also of 1846,

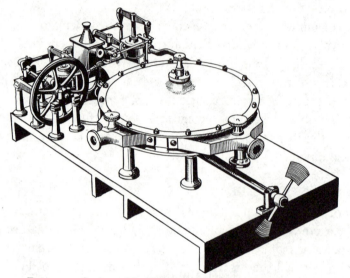

FIGURE 54—*Cordes and Locke's proposed marine steam-turbine, 1846.*

is represented in detail by the authentic model (figure 54). This shows a rotor
19 ft in diameter, intended to develop 150 brake-hp at 300 rpm.

The practical success of Cordes and Locke's experimental turbine must have
raised their hopes of its application to marine propulsion. No record has been
found, however, that it was ever fitted into a vessel. At a much later date, in
1892, Carl Gustav de Laval (1845–1913), of Stockholm, proposed to fit a small
steam-turbine of 15 hp into an experimental launch. It has been stated that the
turbine was in fact constructed, but there is no evidence that it was ever installed
in a vessel and tried on water.

The successful development of the steam-turbine and its application to marine
propulsion are due to Sir Charles Parsons (1854–1931), who in 1894 made and
tested a 6-ft experimental model hull to determine what power would be needed
to drive his *Turbinia* of 44·5 tons displacement. The first machinery tried in this

vessel consisted of a turbine with outward radial flow (figure 55), to drive one propeller-shaft. The trials with this turbine in November 1894 proved unsatisfactory; the maximum speed attained after several modifications of the propeller was 19·75 knots. As a result of the phenomenon known as 'cavitation', the propeller hollowed out cavities in the water, which was unable to sustain the thrust necessary to drive the vessel at the speed desired. The remedy was to increase the surface of the propeller.

The radial-flow turbine was replaced in 1896 by a three-shaft installation, in which a separate Parsons turbine with parallel flow was directly coupled to each

FIGURE 55—*Radial-flow turbine from the* Turbinia, *1894.*

shaft, and each shaft carried three screw-propellers. The three turbines were connected in series, steam from the boiler being first led into the high-pressure turbine on the starboard side, then passed to the intermediate-pressure turbine on the port side, and next to the centrally disposed low-pressure turbine, from which it was exhausted to the condensers. On the central shaft there was also a separate turbine to drive the vessel astern.

Steam was supplied by a double-ended Yarrow water-tube boiler at a pressure of 210 lb to the sq in, reduced to about 155 lb to the sq in at the turbine-inlet. The three turbines developed a total of about 2000 shaft-hp. As thus modified, the *Turbinia*, the first vessel ever to be propelled by turbine-machinery, made its dramatic appearance at the naval review held at Spithead in 1897 (tailpiece). Spectators were thrilled to see this tiny vessel race down the lines at 34·5 knots, a speed never before attained on water.

In these experimental marine applications, the turbines were at first direct-coupled to the propeller-shafts. To attain their maximum efficiency, however, it later became necessary to run the turbines at much higher speeds than would be suitable for the screws. Toothed reduction-gearing was therefore introduced between the turbines and the propellers. The first geared-turbine vessel was a small twin-screw launch, fitted out in 1897 by the Parsons Marine Steam Turbine Company at Wallsend. The turbine, of 10 hp, ran at about 20 000 rpm and was geared at a 14 : 1 ratio by single-helical spur-wheels to the two propeller-shafts, which ran at 1400 rpm.

In naval vessels, where speed is of paramount importance, and for merchant steamers on fast services, screw-propellers of comparatively small diameter and rapid rotation may be used with single-reduction gearing; such transmission has a mechanical efficiency of about 98·5 per cent. For slow-speed merchant vessels, whose propellers turn at fewer than 100 rpm, double-reduction geared turbines have been used. In this form, the double-helical pinions on the turbine-shaft gear with a double-helical wheel mounted on an idle shaft, which also carries another pair of pinions. These in turn gear with a second wheel on the propeller-shaft.

VI. MARINE BOILERS

In the experimental period of marine steam-propulsion almost the only form of boiler available was that introduced by James Watt about 1780 for use on land. It consisted of a water-tank with semi-cylindrical top and concave bottom, and was externally fired. The American pioneers appear to have found it unsuitable for marine purposes; both John Fitch and James Rumsey invented 'pipe' boilers, of the type used by the latter in 1787 on the river Potomac. Another early form of water-tube boiler was used by Robert Fulton in 1803 in his first steamboat experiment on the river Seine.

The simple form of boiler used on land was, however, adopted in the paddle-steamer *Comet* (p 143) in 1812; it was set in brickwork, and was fired externally. Such boilers were later improved by the addition of an internal fire-box, and developed about 1820 into the marine 'box' boiler with flat-sided flues and furnaces. This permitted an increased evaporative surface within the limited space available on a ship, and was suitable for the low steam-pressures of about 5 lb per sq in then in use.

Sea-water feed was used, and the boilers had to be emptied at frequent intervals to avoid concentration of the salt. In some cases the boilers were made of copper, which was found to resist corrosion better than iron. The invention by Samuel

Hall (1781–1863) of the surface-condenser in 1834, however, enabled boilers to be fed with pure distilled water and thus maintained in continuous operation. The earliest Atlantic steamer to be so fitted was the *Sirius*, which in 1838 crossed the ocean under sustained steam-power, and was the first ship to do so.

The next important development, which occurred from about 1835 onwards, was the replacement of the flat-sided flues in 'box' boilers by fire-tubes, which had already been introduced into locomotive practice on land (ch 15). One of the

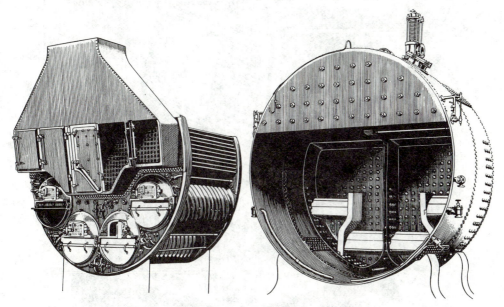

FIGURE 56—'*Scotch*' *marine boiler, 1890.*

most prominent advocates of the fire-tube marine boiler was Admiral Thomas Cochrane, tenth Earl of Dundonald (1775–1860), who in 1844 fitted such boilers in H.M.S. *Janus*. The multi-tubular box boiler was, however, never suitable for pressures above about 35 lb per sq in, and its construction was discontinued soon after a disastrous explosion on board H.M.S. *Thunderer* in 1876.

Meanwhile the use of compound expansion, with boiler-pressures of 60 lb per sq in and more, had called for cylindrical shells and flues. This led to the ultimate disappearance of the old box-shaped boiler, and to the introduction in 1862 of the 'Scotch' marine boiler (figure 56), with its cylindrical shell and furnaces and internal fire-tubes, which from about 1870 was generally adopted in naval and mercantile vessels.

Marine water-tube boilers were introduced on the Thames about 1842 by

John Penn, who used them on some small paddle-steamers. Another pioneer of this development was J. M. Rowan, who fitted water-tube boilers to the S.S. *Thetis* in 1857, with the then exceptional steam-pressure of 115 lb per sq in. These boilers suffered from rapid corrosion of the iron tubes, and further development had to await the use of mild steel. In 1878 a form of pipe boiler

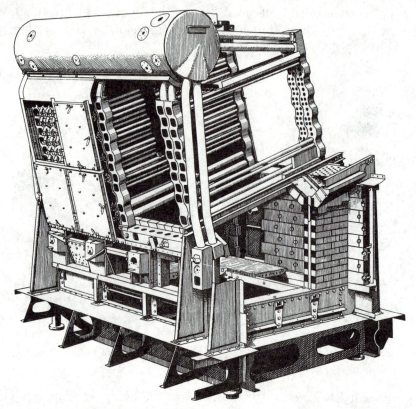

FIGURE 57—*Babcock & Wilcox marine water-tube boiler*, c 1900.

with horizontal water-tubes for a pressure of 500 lb per sq in was fitted by Loftus Perkins on the S.Y. *Anthracite*.

In the form of water-tube boiler developed in France by Julien Belleville vertical iron coils were at first used; but trials in 1856 proved unsuccessful. Inclined tubes were adopted in 1872, and as thus improved the Belleville boiler was introduced into the Royal Navy on H.M.S. *Sharpshooter* in 1893. Later it was used on H.M. cruisers *Powerful* and *Terrible* for a pressure of 250 lb per sq in; but difficulties were encountered in service, and after 1901 its use was not extended.

The first water-tube boiler to be used in the Royal Navy, however, was the Thornycroft, with small-diameter tubes, fitted in 1886 on a second-class torpedo-boat. In 1892 this form of boiler, with two lower water-barrels, was tried on H.M.S. *Speedy* at a pressure of 200 lb to the sq in. It had curved water-tubes of 1·25 in external diameter, secured at their ends to the water-barrels and the steam-drum above by means of roller tube-expanders. Another form of small-tube boiler was patented by Alfred Yarrow in 1889, and was used at first in small naval vessels and later in the mercantile marine. The Reed boiler was also used for a time in the Royal Navy, on torpedo-boats. It had an upper steam-drum and two lower water-barrels of flattened section.

The Niclausse boiler, used in the French Navy, had a form of double water-tube similar in principle to the Field tube patented in 1862. The adaptation for water-tube boilers was patented in 1878 by A. Collet, but its practical success was due to J. and A. Niclausse, of Paris. This boiler was later tried on H.M.S. *New Zealand*. The Babcock & Wilcox boiler (figure 57) was introduced into the U.S. Navy in 1889, and extensive trials were later made with it in H.M.S. *Sheldrake*. In this boiler the inclined water-tubes were expanded at their ends into vertical headers of sinuous or wavy form, so that the water-tubes were displaced sideways relatively to one another for the better absorption of heat. The Babcock & Wilcox boiler, for steam-pressures of some 250 lb to the sq in, became one of the few standard forms used in the Royal Navy about the end of the nineteenth century.

BIBLIOGRAPHY

APPLEYARD, R. 'Charles Parsons: His Life and Work.' Constable, London. 1933.
BERTIN, L. E. and ROBERTSON, L. S. 'Marine Boilers.' Murray, London. 1906.
BILES, J. H. 'The Steam Turbine as applied to Marine Purposes.' Griffin, London. 1906.
BOURNE, J. 'Practical Treatise on Steam Navigation and the Screw Propeller.' London. 1856.
DROVER, F. J. 'Coal and Oil Fired Boilers.' Chapman & Hall, London. 1924.
FERRIS, C. R. 'Steam Propulsion Developments.' Birchall, Liverpool. 1933.
FINCHAM, J. 'History of Naval Architecture.' London. 1851.
GALLOWAY, E. 'History and Progress of the Steam Engine.' London. 1833.
MAIN, T. J. and BROWN, T. 'The Marine Steam-Engine.' London. 1865.
MURRAY, R. 'Treatise on Marine Engines and Steam Vessels' (4th ed., rev. by E. NUGENT). London. 1868.
NYSTROM, J. W. 'Treatise on Screw Propellers and their Steam-Engines.' London. 1861.
OTWAY, R. 'Elementary Treatise on Steam Navigation.' Plymouth. 1837.
POWLES, H. H. P. 'Steam Boilers, their History and Development.' Constable, London. 1905.
PULL, E. 'Modern Steam Boilers.' Benn, London. 1928.
REED, S. J. 'Turbines Applied to Marine Propulsion.' Constable, London. 1913.

RICHARDSON, A. 'The Evolution of the Parsons Steam Turbine.' Offices of *Engineering*, London. 1911.

RUSSELL, J. S. 'Treatise on the Steam Engine.' Edinburgh. 1846.

SCIENCE MUSEUM LIBRARY, London, MS 'The Field Papers' (1811–72), Vol. 1: 'Ships, Marine Engines, etc.' by J. FIELD.

SEATON, A. E. 'Manual of Marine Engineering' (20th ed.). Griffin, London. 1928.

SENNETT, R. and ORAM, H. J. 'The Marine Steam Engine.' Longmans, Green, London. 1917.

SMITH, E. C. 'Short History of Naval and Marine Engineering.' University Press, Cambridge. 1938.

SOTHERN, J. W. M. 'The Marine Steam Turbine' (7th ed.). Crosby Lockwood, London. 1932.

SPRATT, H. P. 'Transatlantic Paddle Steamers.' Brown, Son & Ferguson, Glasgow. 1951.

TAYLOR, D. W. 'Resistance of Ships and Screw Propulsion.' Macmillan, New York. 1907.

THAMES IRONWORKS AND SHIPBUILDING COMPANY. 'Historical Catalogue.' London. 1911.

THURSTON, R. H. 'History of the Growth of the Steam-Engine.' London. 1878.

TOMPKINS, A. E. 'Marine Engineering.' Macmillan, London. 1921.

TREDGOLD, T. 'Steam Navigation.' London. 1851.

WHEELER, S. G. 'Marine Engineering in Theory and Practice' (2 vols). Crosby Lockwood, London. 1928.

WOODCROFT, B. 'Sketch of the Origin and Progress of Steam Navigation.' London. 1848.

YEO, J. 'Steam and the Marine Steam-Engine.' London. 1894.

The Turbinia *at speed, in 1897.*

8

INTERNAL COMBUSTION ENGINES

D. C. FIELD

I. GAS-ENGINES

THE conception of the internal combustion engine is even older than that of the piston steam-engine. In the latter part of the seventeenth century the Dutch scientist Christiaan Huygens (1629–95) was interested in the application of atmospheric pressure to yield useful power. He devised a machine in which a small quantity of gunpowder burning in a cylinder raised a balanced piston; when the gases cooled again atmospheric pressure forced the piston down, and it was proposed to obtain work from the down stroke. Huygens's experiments were continued by Denis Papin (1647–1714), but it was not until the expansive force of steam was substituted for that of burning gunpowder that a practicable engine resulted.

Despite these and other endeavours, until 1859 there was no engine of any kind, other than the steam-engine, that was capable of working continuously under industrial conditions. In that year the Frenchman Étienne Lenoir (1822–1900) designed an engine that ran on an explosive mixture of gas and air (figure 58). This closely resembled a horizontal double-acting steam-engine, with a cylinder, piston, connecting-rod, and fly-wheel, in which the gas merely took the place of steam, the mixture being fired by means of an electric spark passed between two points inside the cylinder at the appropriate moment. Ignition took place when the piston reached the mid-stroke position, the necessary high tension spark being obtained from a battery and induction coil. On the return stroke of the piston the exhaust gases were expelled, while a further charge of gas and air was fired on the opposite side of the piston, the engine being double-acting. Slide-valves like those of a steam-engine were employed and the engine was water-cooled. The running costs were found to be excessive when compared with those of a steam-engine of equal power, 100 cu ft of gas being consumed per hp-hour.

However, the partial success of the new engine augured well, and as a result many other investigators were encouraged to develop their ideas on the subject. One of these was M. Hugon, who in 1862 made an engine in which a fine spray of water was injected into the cylinder after the explosion to assist cooling. This was found to reduce the gas-consumption and lower the temperature of the exhaust gases, in comparison with the Lenoir engine, but the true weakness of engines of this type lay in the fact that there was no initial compression of the mixture.

An important stage was reached early in the same year, 1862, when another Frenchman, Alphonse Beau de Rochas (1815–91), obtained a patent in which are described the essential conditions that must be fulfilled in every practical gas-engine if efficient results are to be obtained. This patent protected the invention of the four-stroke cycle, which afterwards became almost universal and

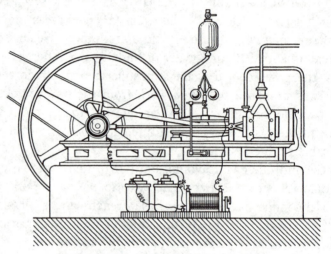

FIGURE 58—*The first Lenoir gas-engine of 1860.*

virtually superseded all other methods of operation. In the Beau de Rochas cycle, during the first stroke of the piston towards the crankshaft the explosive mixture is drawn into the cylinder; it is compressed on the return stroke. Ignition is then effected at or about the dead centre position and the burning mixture drives the piston during the third stroke of the cycle. Finally, on the fourth stroke, the burnt gases are driven out of the cylinder; the cycle is then repeated. Having demonstrated the principles of his invention, Beau de Rochas left it to others to devise the mechanical means whereby his theory might be translated into practice, and before long the patent was allowed to lapse.

Several years later the idea of the four-stroke cycle was revived by the German engineer N. A. Otto (1832–91), who had already designed a successful vertical atmospheric gas-engine in 1867. In 1878 he introduced a horizontal gas-engine (figure 59), the operation of which was based upon the cycle of Beau de Rochas.

It is, however, arguable that Otto had never heard of the earlier patent, and the system has ever since been referred to as the 'Otto cycle'.

The superiority of the new engine above other types was soon apparent; more than 35 000 of them, manufactured by the German firm of Otto & Langen, were installed all over the world in a very few years. Other types of engine were still made, such as the Bisschop engine, in which expansion of the exploded gases raised the piston, which was then driven downwards by atmospheric pressure during its working stroke, in accord with Huygens's conception. It was a low-power vertical engine and is said to have given very satisfactory results.

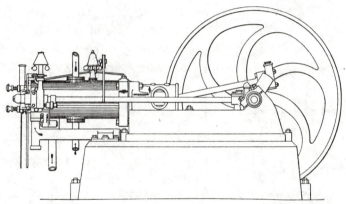

FIGURE 59—*Otto horizontal gas-engine, c 1878.*

Following steam-engine practice to a large extent, the early gas-engine designers naturally adopted the idea of the slow-speed horizontal engine, but this was a serious mistake, as will be seen subsequently. While some engines used electric ignition, a great many relied upon ignition by means of a flame drawn into the cylinder at the correct moment. An internal flame was kept burning inside the body of a cock-key, in front of a slot in the cylinder wall. When the firing-point arrived the slide-valve was so arranged as to open the slot, thus enabling the flame to ignite the mixture, the slot then being closed again. As the internal flame was at once extinguished by the explosion it was necessary to have a second, external flame outside the body of the cock in order to re-ignite the internal flame. At the moment of ignition the external flame was shut off from the internal one (figure 60).

A later idea was the hot-tube method, in which a small tube of platinum or other non-combustible material was inserted in the cylinder, its outer end being closed. The tube was kept at a bright red heat by an external Bunsen flame, and upon compression a portion of the charge was forced into the tube and promptly ignited.

By 1878 the gas-consumption of these engines had been reduced to about 28 cu ft per hp-hour. Other systems extant in the period which followed were the two-stroke engine of Dugald Clerk (1879), the single-acting Lenoir engine (1883), and the six-stroke engine of Griffin. From about 1885 onwards the Otto four-stroke cycle was generally adopted, and so superior was its performance that four years later, in 1889, all but four engines out of a total of fifty-three shown at an international exhibition used this cycle.

Thereafter, with many detailed improvements and with steadily increasing horse-power, the gas-engine was able to compete successfully with the steam-engine. Crossley Brothers of Manchester built large numbers of gas-engines of many types and sizes under the Otto patents (figure 61). The development of gas-producing plant to generate special gases for such engines at an economic rate played a great part in their subsequent success.

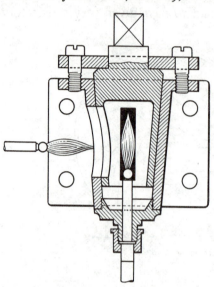

FIGURE 60—*Diagram of early flame-ignition, showing internal and external flames.*

II. OIL-ENGINES

Although the gas-engine proved to be a valuable substitute for the steam-engine in many circumstances, it was not suitable where a supply of gas was not readily available or was too costly. Other notions were now being developed, however, among them that of operating an engine upon what was then known as ordinary illuminating oil, that is paraffin (kerosene) (p 104). This mixture of hydrocarbons does not give off an inflammable vapour until a temperature of between 30° and 50° C is reached, and it has therefore to be vaporized or finely divided before an explosive mixture of it with air can be formed.

In 1873 J. Hock of Vienna patented such an engine, in which air under pressure broke up a jet of oil into a fine spray. Incomplete combustion rendered this device unsatisfactory. In the same year Brayton of Philadelphia invented an engine having two cylinders, one for compression of the mixture and the other for the actual working. Air was compressed and forced through absorbent materials soaked with the oil, so that it became charged with vapour suitable for combustion. This mixture was then admitted to the working cylinder and fired; expansion occurred and drove the piston to the end of the cylinder, the exhaust gases being expelled on the return stroke. The engine was double-acting and worked on the two-stroke cycle. To facilitate starting, a reservoir of compressed air, kept charged by the engine itself, was provided. In 1890 a much-improved type of Brayton engine, single-acting and working on the Otto cycle, was introduced and gave more economical results.

In 1886 Dent and Priestman patented an engine using the vapour of heavy oil

FIGURE 61—*An early Crossley gas-engine.*

(figure 62). Air compressed by a pump driven from a shaft running at half the speed of the crankshaft was stored in a reservoir. The jet of compressed air sprayed the oil in another reservoir and carried it in a state of fine division into a vaporizer heated by the exhaust gases. More atmospheric air was then added, to form an explosive mixture which was admitted to the combustion chamber. The engine operated on the Otto cycle, and both horizontal and vertical types, the latter of up to 100 hp, were built. A portable model mounted on wheels and entirely self-contained was made in 1889; it was intended for service on farms and gained the silver medal of the Royal Agricultural Society.

The Campbell oil-engine, made by the Campbell Gas Engine Company of Halifax, was a well built horizontal type of good design, having very few working parts. A centrifugal governor controlled the admission of the mixture and consequently the power developed. An oil-lamp was used to heat the vaporizer, and a special starting-reservoir was provided. Another engine designed to run on paraffin was the Grob, this being a vertical type working on the Otto cycle. An engine-driven pump injected the oil into the atomizer, which broke it up into fine globules. The mixture of air and oil then passed into a tube exposed externally to the action of a flame which gasified it before it entered the cylinder. The oil was thus vaporized without the use of any complex method, and was ignited by contact with an incandescent tube. A 'hit-and-miss' system of governing prevented ignition of the charge whenever the speed rose above a certain maximum. Water-cooling was used, a special form of cooler incorporating a fan being provided.

A similar type of engine was the Capitaine, developed by Émile Capitaine between 1879 and 1893. In his final design, by carefully controlling the tempera-

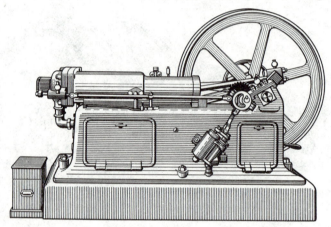

FIGURE 62—*The Dent and Priestman oil-engine, 1886.*

ture of the vaporizer the use of a heating-lamp was avoided and excellent results were obtained. The vaporizer was actually incorporated within the combustion chamber, but required heating by external means for a few moments when starting the engine from cold.

The Hornsby horizontal oil-engine employed a vaporizer situated at the end of the combustion-chamber and a special portable oil-lamp was provided for heating the former when starting; in this case a period of about 10 minutes was needed to raise the temperature sufficiently to ensure ignition of the explosive mixture (figure 63). A small pipe connected the cylinder with the vaporizer-chamber, and during the return stroke of the piston air was driven into the latter, thus filling it with compressed air. Near the end of the same stroke the precise quantity of oil required to produce an explosive mixture was injected into the chamber by means of a pump driven from the half-speed shaft of the engine. A means of adjusting the quantity of oil injected was provided, and a governor on the engine controlled the delivery valve of the pump. The oil was instantly vaporized upon being injected into the compressed air, and the mixture then at once exploded from contact with the heated walls of the vaporizer. After the initial heating it was necessary to turn the fly-wheel by hand until the first combustion occurred, when the lamp could be extinguished, the succeeding firings being sufficient to maintain the temperature of the vaporizer. Water-cooling of the cylinder was provided.

In the Crossley oil-engines a special type of vaporizer was used, incorporating a spiral passage encircling the lamp-chimney. Air was forced through this spiral

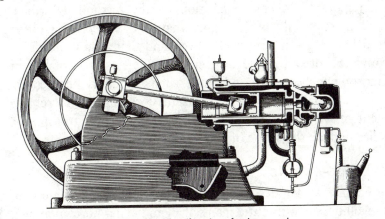

FIGURE 63—*Hornsby oil-engine, showing vaporizer.*

by means of a pump before coming into contact with the oil, and, as in other designs, the lamp was not required once the engine was properly started.

III. THE DIESEL ENGINE

In 1892 Rudolf Diesel (1858–1913), a German engineer born in Paris, took out his first English patent, his object being to produce 'motive work by means of heated air . . . compressed to so high a degree, that by the expansion subsequent to the combustion the air is cooled to about atmospheric temperature, and that into this quantity of air, after its compression, fuel is gradually introduced . . . at this compression the temperature becomes so high that the fuel employed is spontaneously ignited when it comes into contact with the compressed air'.

His principal aims were to circumvent the two main sources of heat-loss in an internal combustion engine: by controlling the maximum temperature, through the gradual introduction of the fuel, and by lowering the temperature of the exhaust gases. To these ends he designed an engine working on the Otto cycle in which pure air only was compressed by the rising piston to a very much higher degree than the mixture in any former type of oil-engine. An injector-pump then forced a minute but accurately determined quantity of oil into the combustion chamber, where it ignited spontaneously on contact with the compressed air. It was found that the engine would work well with almost all forms of petroleum oils, and that its maximum thermal efficiency was about 11 per cent greater than that of any other form of prime mover.

Its principal disadvantages were that, owing to the much higher degree of compression required to ensure ignition by the method described, a much heavier and more solidly built engine than a corresponding oil-engine was needed to deliver a given output of power, and that at low speeds there was a certain roughness of running. However, these defects were of less importance at the time of which we are speaking, when stationary engines of relatively large size were visualized as the most useful form of the Diesel engine. The development of the modern high-speed Diesel for road transport and other purposes lies outside the scope of this chapter.

IV. THE PETROL-ENGINE

All the engines so far described ran at slow speeds, not more than a few hundred revolutions per minute, many of them having horizontal cylinders like the early steam-engine.

It was left to Gottlieb Daimler (1834–1900), of Württemberg, to realize that what was needed was a small and light, high-speed motor, capable of developing power by reason of its high speed of rotation. For some years he had been engaged in gas-engine construction, and in 1884 he patented a small high-speed gas-engine, using hot-tube ignition. Early in 1885 he patented a vertical single-cylinder engine with enclosed crank-case and fly-wheels; this was the prototype of all subsequent Daimler engines made under various names. A suction-operated inlet valve and a mechanically worked exhaust valve were used, a governor being arranged to prevent the latter from opening when the speed exceeded a predetermined rate. The engine was cooled by air circulated round the cylinder by means of an enclosed fan.

To enable the engine to run on light petroleum spirit, which vaporizes readily in the presence of air, Daimler devised his surface-carburettor of 1885. It consisted of a vessel about two-thirds full of petrol, containing an annular float attached to which was a tall vertical tube having perforations near its base. Above the main vessel was a smaller chamber, which formed a reservoir for carburetted air. From this, the cylinder of the engine could draw its supply of explosive mixture by means of a pipe, but as soon as it did so more air was sucked in through the vertical tube and bubbled through the petrol above the float, thus becoming heavily charged with vapour before entering the reservoir at the top.

In 1889 Daimler patented a V-type twin-cylinder engine having two cylinders inclined to one another at about 15° with both connecting-rods working on a

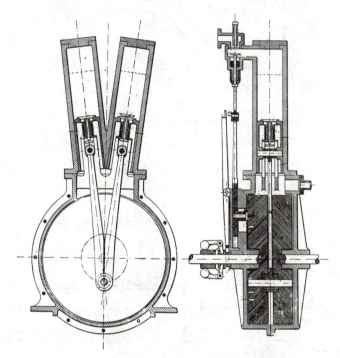

FIGURE 64—*Daimler V-type twin-cylinder petrol-engine as patented in 1889. The valves in the pistons were never fitted in practice.*

common crank (figure 64). This engine was subsequently built and sold in considerable numbers, being applied to motor-cars by several continental manufacturers; it was also used as a stationary engine, as well as for motor-launches.

The precise method of operation of the Daimler engine is of such fundamental importance that, at the risk of repeating much which has already been said in connexion with gas-engines, it is now necessary to describe its action in detail. The engine operates on the Otto or four-stroke cycle. Upon the first down stroke of the piston carburetted air is forced into the cylinder by atmospheric pressure, through the mushroom inlet valve which is opened automatically by the suction. This valve is closed by the action of a light spring at or shortly before the end of the stroke. On the return stroke the mixture is compressed into the small space above the piston, the final pressure being about 45 lb to the sq in (compression-ratio about 3 : 1). At about the top dead centre position the charge is fired by hot-tube ignition. Expansion of the charge follows, since the rise in

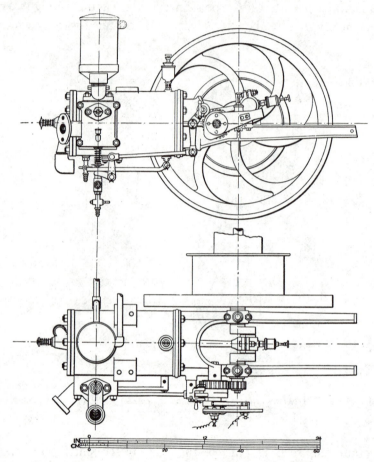

FIGURE 65—*Elevation and plan of Benz 3½ hp single-cylinder horizontal petrol-engine as used 1893–1901.*

temperature causes the gases to increase in pressure by approximately twenty times, and the piston is therefore driven downwards. Near the end of the power stroke the exhaust valve is opened by mechanical means and the products of combustion escape into the exhaust pipe and thence to the silencer. Since the valve remains open during the following up stroke, they are driven out by the piston almost completely. The valve is then closed by its spring and the whole cycle is repeated. It will thus be seen that there is one power stroke for every two revolutions of the crankshaft. In order to cause the exhaust valve to open only once every two revolutions, two-to-one reduction gearing is employed, the momentum of the fly-wheel being relied upon to keep the engine going during the non-power strokes.

The speed of the engine is controlled by a governor which causes the exhaust valve to remain closed should the speed exceed the desired maximum. This results in slowing it down, and prevents a further charge from being admitted until the speed has been sufficiently reduced for the governor to permit the resumption of normal working. In order to reduce the very high temperature of

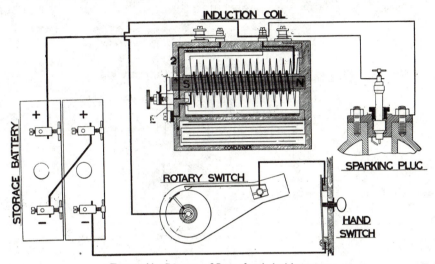

FIGURE 66—*Diagram of Benz electric-ignition system.*

the engine, caused by the combustion of the charge, the cylinder- and valve-casting is water-jacketed; cold water is constantly circulated through the jacket, being itself cooled by passing through a radiator, water-tank, or other cooling apparatus.

In 1885, at the time when Daimler was designing his high-speed vertical engine, Karl Benz of Mannheim was building his first motor-vehicle (p 427). This incorporated a horizontal engine running on petroleum spirit and using the Otto cycle (figure 65); its speed, however, was very low, as in gas-engine practice. A primitive form of surface-carburettor was used, consisting of a vessel containing the fuel, through which the exhaust pipe passed in order to heat it slightly and assist evaporation. Air was admitted to an annular chamber surrounding that containing the petrol, and was drawn through the latter in its passage to the engine. Between the carburettor and the engine a device called a mixer was arranged; this consisted of a finely perforated pipe, through which the mixture from the carburettor passed, surrounded by a larger tube with perforations to admit air from the atmosphere. A sliding shutter over the latter enabled the strength of the resulting combustible mixture to be regulated.

In the Benz car, the electric ignition involved a high-tension system consisting of an induction coil and accumulator (figure 66). It was one of the first cars so equipped, and as the arrangement was afterwards used by many makers, a full description of it will now be given.

A four-volt accumulator was connected in series with the primary winding of

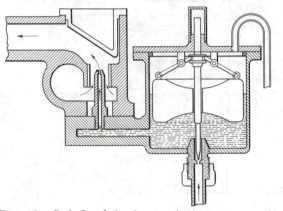

FIGURE 67—*Early float-feed carburettor, showing arrangement of jet.*

an induction coil, having incorporated in it a device known as a trembler. This was simply a laminated metal spring which became attracted to the core of the coil as soon as the latter was energized, and in moving towards it automatically interrupted the circuit. This resulted in the blade springing back to its former position and making contact again. The whole cycle was thus repeated rapidly, making a loud buzz and causing the secondary or high tension winding of the coil to deliver a series of sparks at the sparking-plug in the cylinder. The plug was similar in construction to a modern one, but considerably larger, and was attached to the cylinder-head by a flanged joint instead of being screwed in. A rotating contact-breaker driven at half the speed of the engine was connected in series with the battery and primary coil winding, thus ensuring that ignition took place only when required. By controlling the position of the finger of the contact-breaker the time of ignition could be varied over wide limits. The contact-breaker itself consisted of a disk of insulating material having let into it a metal segment occupying about one-eighth of its circumference. Each time this passed beneath the tip of the contact-finger the circuit was completed, the coil was energized, and a spark was made at the plug. Also in series was an interrupter or hand-switch to enable the circuit to be broken when required, as when stopping the engine. A condenser was connected across the contacts of the trembler to reduce sparking at this point.

A highly important invention was the float-feed carburettor patented by Wilhelm Maybach in 1893 and used on the Daimler engines. In this device petrol was fed either by pressure or by gravity to a chamber containing a float, from which chamber a pipe, terminating in a very small hole or jet, led it to a suitable point in the inlet-pipe of the engine, where the suction caused the incoming air to mix with a fine spray of petrol from the jet (figure 67). The float controlled a needle-valve governing the admission of petrol from the tank to the float-chamber, the level of petrol in which was thus maintained at the correct height. This principle was ultimately adopted by almost all manufacturers of carburettors, but Maybach protected it by patents which were not revoked for several years.

In 1895 the Comte de Dion and G. B. Bouton, at their Puteaux works near St-Denis, France, turned their attention to the production of a light high-speed petrol-engine, after having constructed steam-

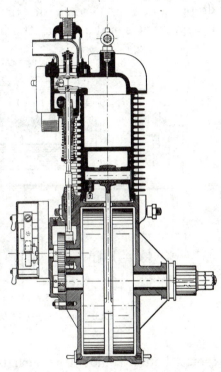

FIGURE 68—*Section of 1¾ hp air-cooled De Dion Bouton engine of 1899, showing valve mechanism and ignition device.*

driven vehicles for some years. So satisfactory were the results obtained that the engine was fitted in a motor-tricycle and great developments followed (ch 18). This little single-cylinder air-cooled engine was the precursor of many thousands built on similar principles, and merits a description (figure 68).

It worked on the Otto cycle and was fundamentally similar to Daimler's first vertical engine of ten years before. It had a vertical cylinder and twin internal fly-wheels, and an automatic or suction inlet valve, the exhaust valve being mechanically operated. Its maximum speed was about 1500 rpm. A surface-carburettor was employed, together with the special electric ignition that was afterwards used on De Dion engines for many years (figure 69). A primary battery was adopted with a plain induction coil, that is to say one not incorporating a trembler as used by Benz. In place of the simple wipe contact-breaker of the latter, a special form of cam was mounted on the half-speed shaft of the engine, having a V-shaped notch cut in its periphery at one point. The end of the contact-finger carried no current but rested upon the circumference of the cam, a small head dropping into the V-notch each time this came round, being caused to do so by the springiness of the finger. At a point about half-way along the finger a small

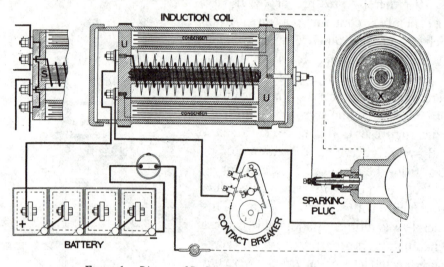

FIGURE 69—*Diagram of De Dion Bouton electric-ignition system.*

contact-button could then touch the end of an adjustable contact-screw, to which one of the wires of the primary circuit was attached; contact could take place only when the V-notch was in the right position. In theory the finger was intended to vibrate and make contact several times during each passage of the notch, thus ensuring a stream of sparks from the high-tension winding of the coil, but whether in fact there was time for this vibration to occur when the engine was running fast is a matter of considerable doubt. However, the system worked—and worked well, giving very satisfactory results. In all other respects the method was identical with the Benz system already described.

When the English Daimler company of Coventry began the manufacture of cars in 1897 an engine known as the Phoenix-Daimler was used (figure 70). It was a later development of the V-twin type already described, and consisted of two vertical single-cylinder engines mounted on a common crank-case with a common crankshaft, the cranks being set at 180° to one another. Hot-tube ignition and the Daimler float-feed carburettor (figure 71), based on the May-bach patent of 1893, were used, with 'hit-and-miss' governing on the exhaust

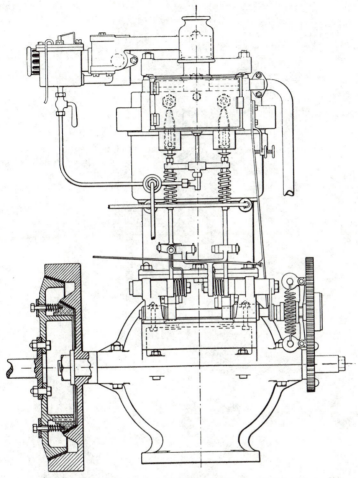

FIGURE 70—*The 6 hp Phoenix-Daimler twin-cylinder petrol-engine of 1899, showing 'hit-and-miss' governing on exhaust valves.*

valves, one of these being arranged to cut out before the other. Engines of this design were used on Daimler vehicles until 1901, a four-cylinder version—in effect two twin-cylinder engines placed end to end—being introduced in 1899.

In 1896 Peugeot Frères ceased to use the Daimler V-twin engine, which had been mounted at the rear of their vehicles, and adopted instead a new horizontal motor of their own design. This was of the parallel twin-cylinder type in which both pistons moved in and out together, the exhaust valves being worked by means of an ingenious grooved cam mounted on the crankshaft. The inlet valves of this engine were suction-operated, with, in addition, adjustment of the

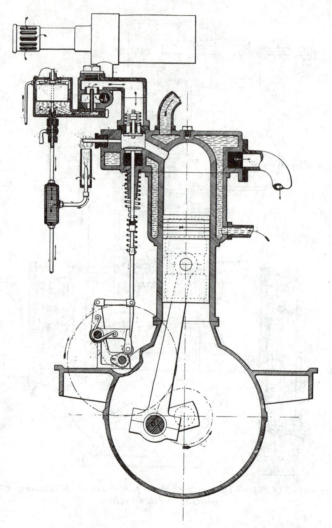

FIGURE 71—*Section of Daimler petrol-engine of 1899, showing float-feed carburettor and hot-tube ignition.*

tension of the valve-springs at the appropriate moments by a cam-and-roller mechanism. The advantage of this complication appears open to question. Hot-tube ignition and water-cooling were used. The engine was used on all Peugeot cars until 1902, when a more normal, vertical engine was adopted.

Many problems arose when multi-cylinder engines using the four-stroke cycle were introduced. At first glance the mechanical balance appears to be good. if, in a twin-cylinder engine, the cranks are arranged so that when one piston is at the top of its stroke the other is at the bottom, but unfortunately the firing-order also must be considered. Owing to the fact that each cylinder has only one power stroke for every two revolutions of the crankshaft, it follows that with

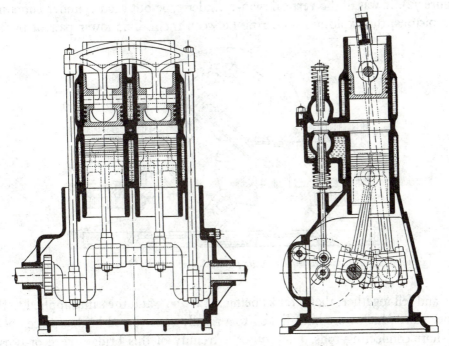

FIGURE 72—*Gobron-Brillié opposed-piston engine of 1899*

cranks as described it is impossible to avoid having the two firing strokes immediately succeeding one another during two successive half-revolutions of the crankshaft, while the next two half-revolutions will produce no power strokes.

If, on the other hand, the two pistons are made to rise and fall together, the firing periods will be perfectly symmetrical, but it is by no means easy to balance such an engine mechanically. A very good solution to this problem is that of arranging the two cylinders on opposite sides of the crankshaft, in the design known as horizontally opposed. In this case there are combined the good balance of the 180° engine and the even firing of the 360° type, and the solution appears perfect. However, the necessity of using horizontal cylinders brings certain disadvantages in its train, and the design has not been used to the extent that its merits would seem to justify. Four- and even six-cylinder engines on the same system have, however, been used quite successfully, but not until after the period with which we are now concerned.

Designed with the idea of securing improved balance of the moving parts, the engine of the Gobron-Brillié car of 1899 possessed many points of interest (figure 72). It was of the vertical twin-cylinder type but each cylinder contained two pistons, the explosion occurring between them. The lower pair of pistons

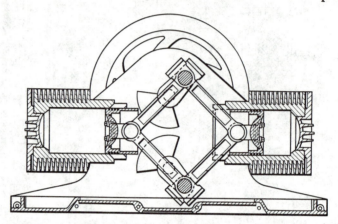

FIGURE 73—*The twin-cylinder Lanchester engine, showing method of balancing. 1897–1904.*

rose and fell together, their cranks being set at 360°, and the same applied to the upper pair, which were both linked to a rigidly constructed bridge-piece above by short connecting-rods. Each outer extremity of this bridge-piece or cross-head had attached to it a very long connecting-rod, the lower end of which had its big-end bearing on a further crank. These two outer cranks were at 180° to the inner pair for the lower pistons, a single four-throw crankshaft being used. The normal speed of the engine was 800 rpm, a somewhat complicated system of governing being employed by which the petrol supply was interrupted at the carburettor. Automatic inlet valves were used. This basic design was still employed for Gobron-Brillié cars even ten years later, in four- and six-cylinder versions.

Another engine that aimed at perfect balance was that of the early Arrol-Johnston car. Here two parallel horizontal cylinders were placed transversely across the car, one immediately behind the other. The crankshaft lay beneath them, at right-angles to the axes of the cylinders. Each cylinder had two pistons, as in the Gobron-Brillié engine, the connecting-rods from which drove the

180° cranks through a system of rocking levers mounted at the ends of the cylinders. Low-tension magneto[1] ignition and automatic inlet valves were used, the normal speed being 800 rpm. The design was employed from about 1900 to 1906, with considerable success.

Before closing this review of the development of the internal combustion engine up to the end of the nineteenth century, there is one engine that deserves to be described in some detail, since it did to a very great extent overcome the problem of balance, although at the expense of considerable complication. This was the engine designed by F. W. Lanchester in 1897. In it, two horizontally opposed cylinders were employed, but instead of the usual single crankshaft two were used, placed one above the other and geared together so that they revolved in opposite directions. The piston in each of the two cylinders had a connecting-rod to both crankshafts, the result being a degree of mechanical balance not obtained by any other means (figure 73). This engine had many other ingenious features, including mechanically operated inlet valves, low-tension magneto ignition with the magneto built into one of the fly-wheels, and instantly removable 'igniters' incorporating mechanical interruption of

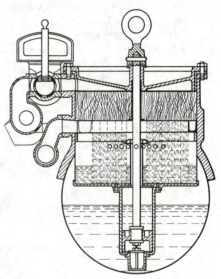

FIGURE 74—*The Lanchester wick-carburettor.*

the circuit actually within the cylinders, the inductive spark so caused igniting the charge. The Lanchester patent wick-carburettor (figure 74) was employed, in which petrol was pumped into a chamber containing a series of wicks which absorbed it, the air supply being taken through the top of this chamber; a combustible mixture was thus formed very readily, with none of the disadvantages of the usual jet- or surface-carburettors. 'Hit-and-miss' governing was used and the engine was mechanically lubricated. It says a good deal for this system of carburation that it was used successfully on all Lanchester cars before the first world war. The twin-cylinder engine described was initially air-cooled, a fan being driven by each of the two fly-wheels, but later forms were water-cooled. The design was not superseded by that of a more conventional engine

[1] With the low-tension type of magneto a spark is caused by mechanical interruption of the primary circuit within the cylinder.

until 1905, and then more because of popular, and largely unfounded, prejudice against horizontal engines than for any other reason.

BIBLIOGRAPHY

BEAUMONT, W. W. 'Motor Vehicles and Motors' (2 vols). Constable, London. 1900, 1906.

DUNCAN, H. O. 'The World on Wheels.' Published by the author, Paris. 1926.

FRENCH, J. W. 'Modern Power Generators.' Gresham Publishing Company, London. 1908.

HASLUCK, P. N. 'The Automobile' (trans. from 'Manuel théorétique et pratique de l'automobile sur route' by G. LAVERGNE). Cassell, London. 1902.

JENKINS, R. 'Motor Cars and the Application of Mechanical Power to Road Vehicles.' Fisher Unwin, London. 1902.

KENNEDY, R. 'The Book of the Motor Car.' Caxton Publishing Company, London. 1913.

ROBINSON, W. 'Gas and Petroleum Engines.' London. 1890.

SMITH, G. G. 'The Modern Diesel.' Iliffe, London. 1944.

YOUNG, A. B. F. 'The Complete Motorist.' Methuen, London. 1904.

The petrol horse: a novel form of tractor patented in France in 1897.

9

THE GENERATION OF ELECTRICITY

C. MACKECHNIE JARVIS

I. EARLY SOURCES OF ELECTRICAL ENERGY

THE sources of electricity before 1800 were frictional machines using glass cylinders or plates (vol III, figure 374); much work had been done with the aid of such apparatus, notably in electrochemistry and in creating an elementary theory of electrostatics. Joseph Priestley (1733–1804) was one of the first to make a systematic investigation of the chemical effects of an electric current, and about 1784 Henry Cavendish (1731–1810) synthesized water by means of a spark discharge through a mixture of hydrogen and air. Similar work was carried out by the Dutch chemists Van Troostwijk and Deiman.

In his experimental investigations Stephen Gray (d 1736) explored the electrical properties of many materials. In collaboration with others he demonstrated the transmission of an electric discharge over considerable distances through a metallic wire suspended on silken threads.

With the aid of large frictional machines and Leyden jars metal wires had been fused and the thermal effect of the electric current thus discovered. The discharge from such machines was difficult to control, and although they remained until the end of the eighteenth century the only source of electrical energy available to man and were extensively used in laboratories, no commercial application could be found for them.

The momentous discovery of Alessandro Volta (1745–1827), that electricity could be generated in a battery of plates of dissimilar metals in the presence of an alkaline, saline, or acid electrolyte, was described by him in a letter to Sir Joseph Banks, president of the Royal Society, in March 1800, and was published shortly afterwards. The advent of Volta's battery or 'voltaic pile' (figure 75), as it was called, could not have been more opportune. The 'electricians' working in the laboratories of the major European scientific institutions had long exhausted the possibilities of the frictional machine, and the invention of Volta was developed with alacrity. Within a matter of months William Cruikshank (1745–1800) had converted the pile into an efficient battery, employing the trough principle. He is usually credited with having planned the first of the large primary batteries built for the laboratory of the Royal Institution in London.

In the early years of the nineteenth century Sir Humphry Davy (1778–1829) several times referred in correspondence to the nature of 'the spark produced between the extremities of Signor Volta's Pile' and in 1802 commented that 'when instead of metals, pieces of well-calcined carbon are employed, the spark is still larger and of a clear white'. From the year 1809 onwards the display of the electric arc was a regular feature at public lectures and, as will be seen later, as early as 1845 determined efforts were being made to establish electric lighting on a commercial scale. All such attempts failed because the only known source of electricity suitable for the purpose was the primary battery, whose maintenance was found to be prohibitively expensive.

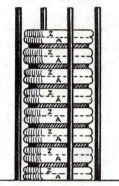

FIGURE 75—*Volta's pile. Pairs of zinc* (z) *and silver* (A) *or copper disks were separated by disks of flannel or paper soaked in brine. On connecting the top disk of zinc with the lowest disk of silver by means of a wire, an electric current flowed through the wire.*

The discovery of the magnetic field surrounding a conductor carrying electricity was announced in the year 1820 by the Danish scientist H. C. Oersted (1777–1851), in a small Latin pamphlet describing his observations on the movement of a magnetic needle in the vicinity of a conductor through which a current was passing.

The work of Oersted at once suggested to the minds of many other scientists the possibility of further discoveries. For A. M. Ampère (1775–1836) it was the revelation that inspired his original theory of the electrodynamic interaction of electric currents and magnets. To Arago, Seebeck, and others it pointed the way to the construction of primitive electromagnets. With Faraday it prompted the entry in his notebook: 'convert magnetism into electricity'. D. F. J. Arago (1786–1853) knowingly produced the first electromagnet in his laboratory in September 1820, and similar results were almost simultaneously announced in other quarters. Credit for producing the first practical electromagnet has been claimed for W. Sturgeon (1783–1850), who exhibited his invention in London in the year 1825, and for it received a prize of the [Royal] Society of Arts. Michael Faraday (1791–1867), working in the laboratory of the Royal Institution, not only confirmed Oersted's experiments but reasoned that if a pivoted magnetic needle tended to move in the presence of a 'live' conductor, it ought to be possible to observe similar motion in such a conductor, freely mounted, when brought into the field of a fixed magnet. To this end, towards the close of 1821, he devised apparatus with which he was able to demonstrate both forms of movement.

Faraday was familiar with the experiments conducted in 1825 by Arago, who, among other things, rotated a flat disk of copper beneath a magnetic needle suitably screened to eliminate the possibility of movement due to air disturbance, and noticed that the needle followed the rotating disk. Between 1825 and 1831 Faraday had made several unsuccessful attempts to achieve conversion of magnetism into electricity, but in the latter year, bringing a fresh mind to bear upon the subject, he achieved success within a relatively short time.

The discovery of electromagnetic induction was announced by Faraday in a paper read before the Royal Society on 24 November 1831. Thereafter he turned his attention to research in other directions, being characteristically uninterested in anything suggestive of commercialism, and left it to his contemporaries to apply the promising new principle. Inventors were not lacking, and from the year 1832 there was a steady stream of suggestions for magneto-electric machines of varied designs.

II. THE FIRST MECHANICAL GENERATORS OF ELECTRICITY

The position in 1832 may be simply summarized as follows. It was known that the passage of an electric current through a conductor set up a magnetic field surrounding it and that, if the conductor were coiled around a piece of soft iron, the iron would be temporarily magnetized during the flow of the current; similarly, if the iron were hardened by hammering it would become more or less permanently magnetized. The concept of lines of force had been established, and it was known that the rotation of a coil of wire within the field of a permanent magnet would cause a voltage to be generated in it. In addition, Faraday had demonstrated 'transformer' action (p 198), but this was probably less well understood.

It is familiar knowledge that electric generators of the type under review are composed of two parts, namely a field system, which in the early machines consisted of simple or compound permanent magnets, and a system of coils in which the generation takes place. Relative movement of the two systems is essential, but whether it is the magnets or the coils that revolve is immaterial, and in fact both types of construction have been used.

Magneto-electric machines. After Faraday's laboratory demonstrations, the first magneto-electric machine exhibited to the public was that shown in Paris in 1832 by Hippolyte Pixii. In this machine (figure 76) the field magnet revolves with respect to the coils. It was hand-driven and little more than a working model, yet it was the first practical generator constructed on Faraday's principle.

Many other inventors followed in quick succession; they cannot all be mentioned here, but the sketch that follows serves to illustrate the development of the magneto-electric generator.

After Pixii, Saxton in 1833 exhibited at the Cambridge meeting of the British Association a similar hand-driven generator in which the arrangement of the components was reversed, the coils rotating in the field of a fixed magnet—a system which has since been largely adopted.

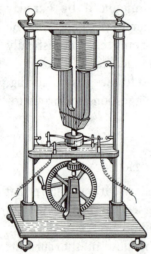

FIGURE 76—*Hand-driven magneto-electric generator of Hippolyte Pixii, c 1833. The machine illustrated is fitted with a commutator of the type proposed by Ampère.*

About this time a simple commutator was fitted by Pixii to an improved version of his machine, as suggested by Ampère. Its object was to convert the oscillating or alternating output from the coils into a unidirectional or direct current. The current obtained from such machines was necessarily pulsating, and in the larger types this caused trouble through heating.

The first manufacturer of these early generators on a commercial scale was probably E. M. Clarke, who in the 1830s was in business in London as a maker of scientific instruments. Clarke's design (figure 77) differed from its predecessors in that the coils were caused to rotate in a plane parallel with the side of the magnet. Clarke's first machine was made about 1834. It was probably intended to serve as a convenient source of electricity for laboratory experiments, at voltages higher than those readily obtainable from chemical batteries. Clarke seems to have been the first to experiment with different types of windings, and soon found that he could vary the output to suit the requirements of the user.

From the earliest days of electrical science the 'electric fluid', as it was known in the eighteenth century, was, in common with other more material substances, credited with possessing properties beneficial to health. Renewed therapeutic claims on behalf of magneto-electric machines became current in early Victorian times, and it is therefore not surprising that these hand-driven generators were manufactured in large numbers by Clarke and his contemporaries.

The quantity of electricity passed through the patient, who held a pair of metal handles, could be controlled by varying the rate at which the handle was turned, and also, on some machines, by a strip of ferrous metal forming a magnetic shunt which, when moved across the poles of the magnet, varied the strength of the external field and thus the output from the generator. Many older readers will recall childhood encounters with these 'electric batteries', as they were termed.

Improvements embodied in a series of machines made by Stoehrer of Leipzig from 1843 onwards involved the use of three horseshoe-type compound magnets instead of one, so placed as to act in multiple in conjunction with a six-polar armature, the coils on which swept the magnetic field at the extremities of the poles. A generator of this type, made in or about 1846, is now in the Science Museum in London (figure 78).

The foundation having been truly laid, it was clearly only a matter of time before mechanical construction and electrical efficiency improved sufficiently to justify the coupling of such generators directly or indirectly to one of the several forms of motive power available at this period.

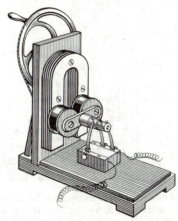

FIGURE 77—*Hand-driven magneto-electric generator with commutator. E. M. Clarke, c 1834.*

Lighthouse illumination. F. Nollet (1794–1853) was probably the first to contemplate making a power-driven magneto-electric machine to supply a relatively large output. About the middle of the nineteenth century determined efforts were being made in both England and France to improve the lighting-power of lighthouses. The lime-light, later known as the Drummond light, had already been invented, and by 1850 was established as an illuminating agent for optical ('magic') lanterns. It is a whitish light of great intensity, produced by rendering a block of lime incandescent in an oxy-hydrogen flame. Nollet thought of applying the lime-light to lighthouses, and required for the purpose oxygen and hydrogen in considerable quantities. These gases he planned to generate by means of the electrolysis of water, employing a heavy-current generator. From 1850 onwards several patents were taken out in this country on Nollet's behalf for a magneto-electric generator in which a rotating member carrying coils would rotate between or adjacent to the poles of horseshoe-magnets spaced radially with respect to the rotating member.

After the death of Nollet in 1853 those supporting him financially formed the *Compagnie de l'Alliance* with the object of developing Nollet's patents. Difficulty was experienced with the generators, and an Englishman, Frederick Hale Holmes, was invited to assist. Experiments were continued for several years, but eventually the enterprise proved a failure, in spite of the fact that the performance of the generators was regarded as satisfactory. Although the Company was liquidated, it was later revived for the manufacture of the generators and continued in this business for many years (figure 79). During his work with the company Holmes gained valuable experience with these early generators. Returning to England he took out a number of patents in 1856 and subsequent years for magneto-electric generators and associated equipment. Holmes felt

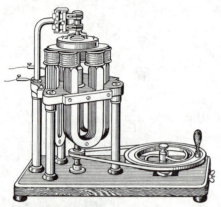

FIGURE 78—*Hand-driven magneto-electric machine, constructed by Stoehrer of Leipzig. The model illustrated probably dates from 1846, although it is known that similar machines were made for demonstration purposes from 1843 onwards.*

certain that, by substituting generators for chemical batteries, satisfactory use could be made of the illuminating properties of the electric arc, and to this end he placed definite proposals before the Corporation of Trinity House (1857). Faraday, as scientific adviser to the Corporation, was consulted, and as a result Holmes's proposals were tested on a small scale between Trinity House Wharf, near Blackwall, and Woolwich on the opposite bank of the Thames.

A description of the generator used for this test has survived; it was of the rotating-magnet pattern and employed thirty-six U-shaped magnets. These were regularly spaced, in sets of six, around the periphery of separate disks with their poles outwards. These disks were mounted on a steel shaft, and in the intervals between them were fixed the stationary coils, the spacing between them corresponding to that of the magnets. Current was induced in the coils as the field of the rotating magnets swept across their faces, and a commutator was fitted to give direct current. The machine was bulky—some 5 ft square and weighing 2 tons—and very inefficient. When driven by a steam-engine at a speed of 600 rpm the power output was rather less than $1\frac{1}{2}$ kw. This generator enabled Holmes to prove his claims, and upon receipt of Faraday's enthusiastic report the Brethren of Trinity House ordered that full-scale trials should take place at the South Foreland lighthouse. Faraday reported that the light produced from the Duboscq arc-lamp used by Holmes at Blackwall was 'so intense, so abundant, so concentrated and focal, so free from under-shadows and from flickering that one cannot but desire that it should succeed'.

The illumination of lighthouses is further discussed in chapter 10; here it is sufficient to note that the magneto-electric generator was enormously developed by Holmes. In the machines he designed for the famous trial at South Foreland, which was started in December 1858, Holmes reverted to the more satisfactory arrangement of rotating coils and fixed magnets used by Nollet. The large D.C. magneto-electric generators manufactured under his direction for further trials which began in June 1862 at Dungeness lighthouse were 8 ft in diameter.

Other machines, for the lighthouse at Souter Point, near Sunderland, were rather smaller: they stood 5 ft 6 in high, measured 6 ft by 4 ft 4 inches in plan, and weighed 3 tons. In spite of their considerable size, the output was less than 2 kw from each. These generators consisted of seven groups of eight fixed compound magnets, between the poles of which rotated six disks, each carrying sixteen bobbins equally spaced around the periphery of the disk. Commutators were not fitted and the alternators thus delivered their output in a series of pulses. They were in operation in the lighthouse from 1870 to 1900, and still survive.

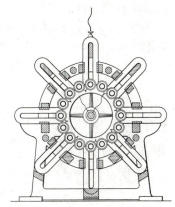

FIGURE 79—*Diagrammatic arrangements of the* Alliance *multi-polar magneto-electric generator, dating from 1855.*

Meanwhile, on the continent, the *Compagnie de l'Alliance* was supplying the French *Administration des Phares*, as it did until about 1870. By then Gramme machines (p 188) were winning favour on account of their relatively small dimensions and lower first cost.

III. DYNAMO-ELECTRIC GENERATORS

To continue logically with the history of the electric generator it is necessary to return to the year 1855 in order to consider the implication of a British patent (No 806 of 11 April 1855) granted to Sóren Hjorth of Denmark for 'An improved Magneto-Electric Battery'. The machine described is an electric generator whose main excitation derives from electromagnets. The specification is, however, of special importance because from its phrasing it is clear that Hjorth was nearer to the principle of self-excitation than any of his predecessors. The relevant passage reads:

By the mutual action between the electro-magnets and the armatures an accelerating force is obtained, which in the result produces electricity greater in quantity and intensity than has heretofore been obtained by any similar means.

There is no evidence that this machine was ever made and its specification does not appear to have aroused comment, possibly because the design prescribed was complex by contemporary standards and doubtless imperfectly understood.

Hjorth had recognized the advantages obtainable from an electromagnetic field-system. The drawings accompanying his patent indicate a machine in which a rotating disk carrying a series of coils is made to revolve between two banks of electromagnets, to which are added permanent magnets supplying the initial excitation.

Siemens's armature. E. W. von Siemens (1816–92) appears to have first appreciated the advantages of keeping the armature-coils within a field of high intensity; this he achieved with the H or 2-polar shuttle armature. In Britain the shuttle armature was patented provisionally in September 1856, as a feature of a hand-driven magneto–electric machine included in an omnibus electric-telegraph specification. The patent application was not taken further, but, as was the practice at that time, the specification was later published. The shuttle armature (figure 80) was used in many small contemporary generators; it permitted higher working speeds and hence smaller relative dimensions than those of machines of the Holmes and *Alliance* type. In later years von Siemens must have regretted the lapse of his first application—which, however, did not debar him from threatening with legal proceedings for infringement at least one of those who had adopted the shuttle armature.

FIGURE 80—*Section through the H or shuttle armature introduced by E. W. von Siemens, c 1856.*

The self-excited field. Henry Wilde (1833–1919) became famous as a patentee and manufacturer of electrical machines, of which his best known and most important is that described in a British specification (No 3006 of December 1863) describing a combination of an electromagnetic generator with a magneto-electric exciter. Generators of this pattern (figure 81) were made in some numbers by Wilde & Company of Manchester and were found particularly useful in the electroplating industry.

By 1865 events were moving towards a realization of the principle of self-excitation. Early in 1866, Wilde presented a paper to the Royal Society in which he referred to 'A new and powerful generator of Dynamic Electricity'. He wrote:

The Author directs attention to some new and paradoxical phenomena arising out of Faraday's important discovery of magneto-electric induction, the close consideration of which has resulted in the discovery of a means of producing dynamic electricity in quantities unobtainable by any apparatus hitherto constructed. He has found that an indefinitely small amount of dynamic electricity or of magnetism is capable of evolving an indefinitely large amount of dynamic electricity.

Today it seems difficult to believe that Wilde was unaware of the magnetism residual in the poles of his electromagnets, and that he should have failed to perceive that his machine possessed inherently the 'indefinitely small amount of magnetism' requisite for his purpose.

Other men also were closely studying developments in electrical science, and by December of the same year S. A. Varley had discovered the secret of self-excitation (figure 82) and had filed an application for a patent for 'Improvements in the Means and Apparatus for Generating Electricity', in which he described a self-excited electromagnetic generator the action of which was shown to depend upon the residual magnetism of the field system. The patent explains that before using the apparatus 'an electric current, passed through the coils of the electro-magnets, secures a small amount of permanent magnetism to their cores'.

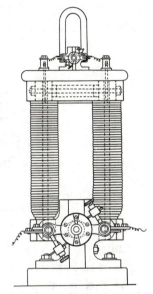

FIGURE 81—*Wilde electromagnetic generator with magneto-electric exciter, dating from 1863.*

Unfortunately the patent specification was not published until July of the following year. Meanwhile E. W. von Siemens submitted (December 1866) a paper to the Berlin Academy of Sciences describing the conversion of mechanical into electrical energy without the use of permanent magnets, citing in it the same principle as that invoked by Varley. Siemens's paper was not printed for several months, but on 14 February 1867 his brother William Siemens communicated its contents to the Royal Society and exhibited a hand-driven model generator demonstrating the self-excitation principle.

On the same evening Charles Wheatstone (1802–75) also contributed a paper on this subject and similarly produced a working model (figure 83). Wilde was present at this meeting, and it is on record that he later commented 'that having himself sometime ago made similar experiments to Siemens and Wheatstone, he came to the conclusion that in the present state of our electrical knowledge the difficulty of utilizing current after it had passed through the coils of the electromagnet when excited by intermittent currents was insuperable'. The reference to intermittent currents arose from the fact that the generators of this period were made with Siemens armatures and two-segment commutators, which produced a pulsating unidirectional current. This pulsation increased the impedance of the field windings, especially at the higher speeds which were found to be possible with the H armature. Wilde's attitude to the problem was justified by his experience as a manufacturer of electric generators, and in fact it became the practice to use separate exciters for the field of the main generator on most machines built for commercial purposes until those of the Gramme type became general.

There can be no doubt that Wilde's paper to the Royal Society in April 1866 gave a stimulus to his contemporaries which led, as we have seen, to the almost

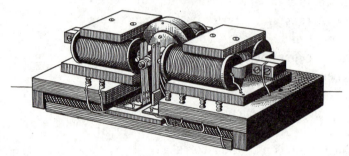

FIGURE 82—*The self-excited electromagnetic generator of S. A. Varley, 1866.*

simultaneous discovery by several independent inventors of the important principle of self-excitation.

At this point there occurred an interesting development in terminology. Several writers of the period, including Wilde, had referred to the concept of 'dynamic electricity', meaning electricity generated by rotary motion. In 1867 Charles Brooke (1804–79), in a paper read before the Royal Society, first used the compound term dynamo–electric. He used it in a generic sense to embrace machines capable of converting mechanical into electrical energy and, in connexion with the converse action, applied the term electro-dynamic to define the action of an electric motor. Brooke's paper gave examples of what he regarded as dynamo-electric machines, and instanced the glass-plate machines of Holtz 'and the cognate machines of Wilde, Wheatstone, Siemens, and Ladd'.

In the succeeding years self-excited generators were used to a greater extent and by general consent became known as dynamo-electrics, or, more briefly, dynamos. The majority of the earlier machines were of the direct-current type and so the term dynamo became exclusively associated with this type of generator in contrast with the later term alternate-current generator—or, still later, alternator—used for another type. Gradually it became the practice of technical writers to use the expression dynamo-electric to distinguish electrical generators with electromagnetic or wound field systems from those of the permanent-magnet pattern, which continued to be known as magneto-electric.

Some forty years later considerable controversy arose over the question of priority in the invention of the self-excited generator and the first use of the term dynamo-electric, which had been claimed by both E. W. von Siemens and Henry Wilde. It must not be supposed, however, that progress in electrical techniques at this period was wholly due to the pioneers named above. There is abundant evidence that the classical experiments of Faraday and his contemporaries were regularly repeated in laboratories on the European continent and in America, and it is to be expected that discoveries were made anticipating those more celebrated ones discussed already.

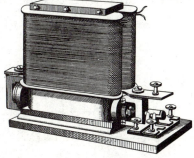

FIGURE 83—*The self-excited electromagnetic generator made by A. Stroh for Wheatstone, 1867.*

Other early designers. The history of science abounds with instances of men who failed to recognize the importance of their work, or whose reluctance to publish its fruits cost them their fame. Within recent years the work of Anyos Jedlik (1800–95) has become known through the efforts of his compatriot Verebely and the Hungarian Electro-Technical Society. Jedlik was a member of the Benedictine Order who later became professor of physics in the university of Budapest. It is asserted that he discovered the dynamo-electric principle about 1861 and employed it in a self-excited unipolar generator constructed for him in the same year. Although Jedlik published a number of scientific papers, some dealing with electrical topics, his work on electric generators appears to have been unknown to his contemporaries.

Another early pioneer was Moses G. Farmer of Massachusetts, who later became one of the early electrical manufacturers in the United States. Farmer was a correspondent of Wilde, to whom he disclosed (9 November 1866) that he also had discovered the principle of self-excitation:

I have built a small machine in which a current from the thermo battery excites the electro-magnet of your machine to start it, and after the machine is in action, a branch from the current of the magneto [that is, the armature] passes through its own electro-magnet, and this supplies the magnetism required.

The first use of the shunt connexion in a dynamo is usually attributed to Wheatstone, but this letter indicates that Farmer was at least some months ahead.

It was pointed out above (p 186) that the Siemens two-polar or H armature with a two-segment commutator, exclusively used in the dynamos of this period, yielded a unidirectional current consisting of a series of pulses, such as is today obtained from half-wave rectification. This rapidly fluctuating current gave rise to eddy or circulating currents in the solid metal cores of both field and armature, and the eddy currents in turn caused deleterious heating. It was thus not unusual for these early machines to be water-cooled.

As early as 1860 an alternative form of armature had been invented by Antonio Pacinotti (1841–1912), who became professor of physics in the university of

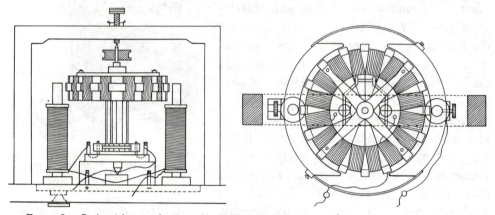

FIGURE 84—*Pacinotti dynamo-electric machine* (left) *with ring armature and multi-segment commutator, 1860;* (right) *plan view showing toothed wheel armature construction.*

Pisa. Pacinotti's machine (figure 84) was intended to demonstrate to students the reversible action of a device working on the dynamo-electric principle. The model exhibited novel features, including an armature of toothed wheel or ring construction, multiple armature coils, and a multi-segment commutator. The field system was designed for separate excitation from an electric battery and the machine could thus be run either as an electric motor or as a dynamo. The apparatus was described in an Italian journal in 1864, but at the time does not appear to have aroused more than casual interest.

IV. THE GRAMME ARMATURE AND ITS SUCCESSORS

Today it is generally conceded that Zénobe Théophile Gramme (1826–1901) deserves the credit for constructing the first dynamo of practical dimensions capable of producing a truly continuous current (figure 85). A native of Belgium, Gramme lived and worked in Paris for many years. His first generator, described in 1870, employed a ring armature like Pacinotti's. The core consisted of a coil of soft-iron wire, insulated with bitumen during winding in order to reduce eddy currents. Around the annulus so formed was wound a series of coils of insulated copper wire, the adjacent ends of which were connected together to form a continuous winding, the junctions of the coils being brought out to the segments of a commutator. The armature rotated in a two-polar magnet system and in this respect did not differ appreciably in principle from its predecessors.

Early in his career as a manufacturer, Gramme became associated with capable business interests. His success was undoubtedly due to the sound mechanical construction he employed, together with the indispensable factor that the market had long awaited the advent of a satisfactory continuous-current machine which could be run for indefinite periods without overheating. The success of the Gramme machine was immediate, and his dynamos were produced in a variety of forms for such diverse applications as lighthouse illumination, electroplating, and factory lighting. It may be fairly said that in electrical illumination considerably more progress was made in France at this time than in any other country. The

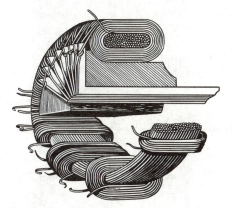

FIGURE 85—*Gramme ring armature, 1870, cut away to show method of winding coils over a soft-iron core.*

majority of Gramme machines were intended to be driven by steam-engines, but hand-driven models, using both permanent-magnet and electromagnetic field systems, were made for laboratory purposes.

By 1873 such progress had been made as to permit the Gramme Company to supply a machine for public trial in the clock-tower at Westminster (figure 86). The trials extended over several months, during which the electric arc was in competition with Wigham's improved gas-light. In 1874 Gramme dynamos (figure 87) were in use in at least two capital ships of the French navy and in some vessels of the Russian navy.

The drum armature. The success of the Gramme dynamo caused concern to the Siemens interests in Germany, which at this period were still using the shuttle armature. In 1872 the drum armature was invented by F. von Hefner Alteneck (figures 88 and 89), then chief designer to the firm of Siemens & Halske. As originally constructed the armature consisted of drums of wood carrying a surface-winding held in position by pegs. In a later type the wooden drums were over-wound with iron wire before the windings were attached. The drum armature possesses technical advantages over Gramme's ring in that the greater part of the winding is usefully employed, whereas in the ring armature the inner portion of every turn is ineffective. It must not be imagined that the early drum armatures were free from troubles, for at this stage in dynamo-design practice was in advance of theory and trial-and-error methods were commonly used. The principal troubles encountered were excessive sparking at the brushes

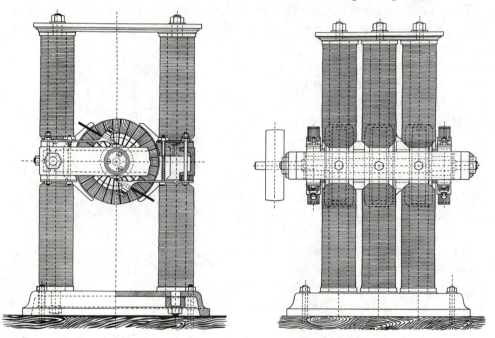

FIGURE 86—*Gramme dynamo-electric machine with triple ring armature, used in 1873 for the signal light in Westminster clock-tower.* (Left) *Side view;* (right) *end view.*

on the commutators and heating of the armature windings. Gradually the drum armature superseded the ring armature because it was more simple to manu-facture, but many years elapsed before the best combinations of windings and other details were worked out.

Another of the early dynamos deserving special notice is that designed by Emil Bürgin of Basel (figure 90). Its armature was in effect a multiple version of the ring armature, in which a series of four or more rectangular cores formed of iron wire carrying on each side a separate coil were assembled on a common spindle. This machine enabled dynamos of the Gramme type to be constructed much more efficiently, since, as the armature coils were smaller in diameter and the winding was broken into a series of sections, the heating of the windings in service was reduced. The Bürgin dynamo was developed in Britain in the early 1880s by R. E. B. Crompton (1845–1940), in whose designs the armature core became hexagonal in shape and the number of 'rings' was increased up to ten (figure 91).

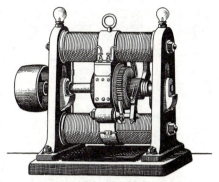

Dynamos were by now being manufactured in considerable numbers in Europe and America: all these machines were either variants of the Gramme design, if not direct copies, or designs which, owing to their inherent complexity of construction or troublesome performance, could not survive. Among the first to perceive the importance of an effective magnetic circuit in the armature was Jonas Wenström, a Swedish inventor and chief designer of the Electrical Company of Sweden. Wenström was the first to embed the armature conductors in slots or channels in the armature core (figure 92), a practice which is almost universal today. This invention, of July 1880, was patented in England in 1882.

Although the first of the magneto-electric machines made by H. Pixii of Paris in 1832 was of the alternating-current type it was afterwards fitted with a commutator (p 180), the function of which was to rectify (render unidirectional) the pulses of electricity generated when the machine was operated. Later machines, such as the early generators employed for lighthouse illumination, were largely of the direct-current or commutator type. The commutator and its brush-gear were often unreliable, and following experiments by F. H. Holmes and others, c 1862, demonstrating that an arc-lamp fed with alternating current could be as effective an illuminator as one fed with direct current, the generators for Souter Point lighthouse were constructed for A.C. working (plate 10 B).

The considerable dimensions and weight of large magneto-electric generators of the

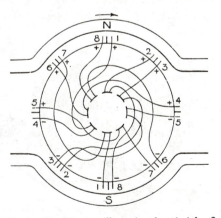

FIGURE 88—*Diagram illustrating the principle of the drum armature introduced by von Hefner Alteneck, 1872.*

Holmes type, mentioned on p 182, are further emphasized in the following table:

	Type	Speed	Approx. output	Weight	Cost
		rpm	kw	cwt	£
Magneto-electric:					
Holmes	A.C.	400	2	51	550
Alliance	A.C.	400	2·3	36	494
Dynamo-electric:					
Gramme 1873 model . .	D.C.	420	3·2	25	320
Siemens 1873 model . .	D.C.	480	5·5	11	265

V. THE ALTERNATOR

Naturally enough, dynamos of the Gramme and Siemens type were adopted for lighthouse illumination in various parts of Europe; yet within ten years the position was again reversed, for the following reasons. The early dynamos needed constant attention to their commutators and brush-gear and, unlike the later Holmes and *Alliance* machines, could not at this period be designed for alternating-current working. Another French pioneer, the Baron A. de Meritens, entered the field with an alternating-current machine of the magneto-electric type employing a distributed winding and giving an output of vastly improved wave-form (figure 93).

These generators, first manufactured about 1880, were prominently displayed at the Paris Exhibition of 1881. They soon became standard throughout France and were installed by Trinity House in the South Foreland and Lizard light-

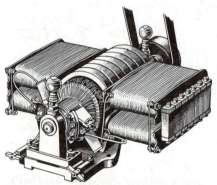

FIGURE 89—*Siemens & Halske dynamo with von Hefner Alteneck drum armature, 1876.*

FIGURE 90—*Bürgin dynamo as made by Crompton & Company, 1881-2.*

houses; they were reported to be still in use in 1947. de Meritens's generators were rather smaller than those made by Holmes for Souter Point and delivered an output of 4·5 kw at 830 rpm. Generators of this type remained at least twice as expensive as Gramme dynamos and for this reason ultimately went out of use.

FIGURE 91—*Armature for the dynamo illustrated in figure 90, showing the arrangement of the multiple hexagonal 'ring' windings. There were sometimes as many as ten rings.*

The first alternators independent of excitation from permanent magnets were those of Wilde (*c* 1867), in which a shuttle armature carried a double winding. The main winding fed the external circuit through slip-rings, and the subsidiary winding excited the field-windings through a two-part commutator. The development of these machines was limited by the heating created in their solid cores by eddy currents accentuated by the pulsating nature of the excitation current.

Both Gramme and Wilde made alternators of the ring-winding type about 1878, and others followed. The Gramme construction employed a rotating field: the exciter, a 2-polar dynamo with a ring armature, was built into the alternator carcass (figures 94 and 95). Wilde, on the other hand, retained an arrangement of armature-coils carried on bobbins mounted between two disks in the tradition of Holmes.

The disk-armature, or rotor as it is termed today, remained in favour for a number of years. Siemens, for example, followed the lead of Wilde (figure 96), though omitting from the centres of the rotating bobbins the iron cores that Wilde used.

About 1881 William Thomson (later Lord Kelvin) (1824–1907) proposed modifications to the rotor-winding which, in the hands of Sebastian Ziani de Ferranti (1864–1930), became a continuous winding of insulated copper ribbon. In other respects the Ferranti–Thomson alter-

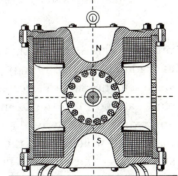

FIGURE 92—*A section through the dynamo of Jonas Wenström, showing slotted armature, c 1881.*

nator superficially resembled that of Wilde (1878); being of a sound electrical design it attained considerable success. In the Ferranti alternator the zigzag rotor-windings were free to expand outwards, thereby avoiding a source of difficulty encountered in similar machines by other makers (figures 97 and 98).

About 1882 J. E. H. Gordon (1852–93) designed and constructed some of the largest alternators then known; they were far from typical of contemporary

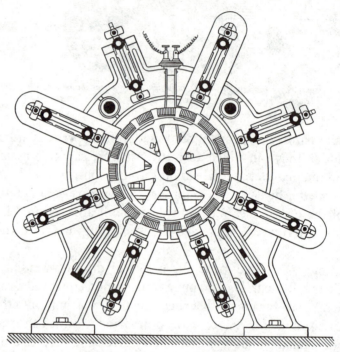

FIGURE 93—*Magneto-electric generator by de Meritens, 1881. Machines of this type were extensively used in French lighthouses.*

practice. Three such machines were built for the Great Western railway terminus at Paddington (figure 99). As operated about 1885 they were driven by steam-engines said to be capable of developing 600 indicated hp at 146 rpm from steam at 160 lb to the sq in. The alternators, of the rotating-field type, were approximately 10 ft in diameter and weighed 22 tons. The heating of these machines—which, when they were first installed, was sufficient to burn out the stator coils—caused much trouble. An improvement was effected by employing laminated cores.

A unique design by W. M. Mordey (1856–1938) was manufactured about 1886 by the Anglo-American Brush Corporation (figure 100). In this machine a

field-coil supplied from a separate exciter was
located between two steel pole-pieces. The pole-
pieces, which rotated with the field-coil, were
spaced apart, and in the air-gap thus created was
positioned the non-rotating member or stator,
carrying the main windings of the machine. This
generator produced unidirectional pulsations of
good wave-form and was for some years extremely
popular. As with the Ferranti generator, it could
conveniently be manufactured for high-voltage
working, so that 2000-volt machines for multiple
arc-lamp circuits were not unusual. Mordey 'alternators' gave considerable trouble on account of the

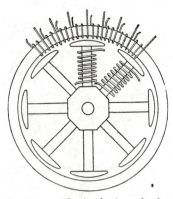

FIGURE 94—*Sectional view, showing
the arrangement of the Gramme single-
phase alternator, c 1878.*

heat developed in the stator-coils when working under conditions near full load.
These coils could not expand outwards and so tended to distort sideways, foul-
ing the rotor.

VI. ELECTRIC LIGHTING

As we have seen, the construction of a generator of adequate capacity rendered practicable the illumination of lighthouses by electric arc-lamps, in
England from 1857 onwards. Public demonstrations of arc-lighting became increasingly common, but commercial development was still limited by the high

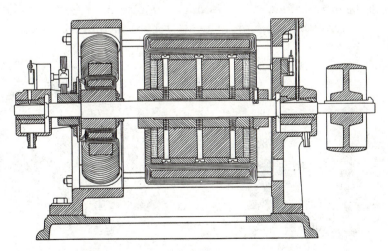

FIGURE 95—*Section through Gramme single-phase alternator, showing the exciter with ring armature on
the left and rotating field, c 1878.*

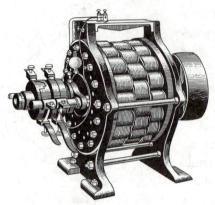

FIGURE 96—*H. Wilde's rotating field alternator,
1867.*

cost and restricted output of magneto-electric generators, and later by the imperfections of the early Siemens and Wilde machines.

The Gramme ring dynamo, which became generally available in the early 1870s, was a relatively cheap source of electricity, and for the first time rendered general-purpose arc-lighting practicable. The first installations of this type were on the continent, among the earliest being the lighting of a mill at Mülhausen and of the Gare du Nord in Paris (1875). In Britain one of the first arc-lighting installations was that of the Gaiety Theatre (1878). These developments will be reviewed more fully in chapter 10; here it is convenient to add that arc-lamps known as 'Jablochkoff candles', introduced into Britain from Paris in 1878, greatly accelerated the development of electric lighting and hence the demand for generating-equipment.

Towards the end of 1878, several municipal authorities in London indicated their willingness to install arc-lamps on an experimental scale. This situation created a demand for high-voltage machines capable of supplying numerous lamps connected in series. Even the smallest arc-lamp was too powerful for domestic purposes, however, and electric illumination of low intensity originated with the introduction of the Swan filament lamp (1881). Then the demand for electrical illumination became general, and was met initially by the establish-

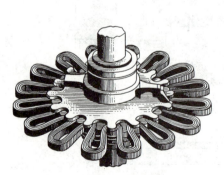

FIGURE 97—*Rotor of Ferranti high-voltage single-phase alternator.*

FIGURE 98—*Ferranti single-phase alternator,
1884.*

ment of private plants designed to meet the requirements of individual factories and buildings.

VII. ELECTRIC POWER-STATIONS

By this time the potentialities of electricity, both as a source of power for

FIGURE 99—*Interior of the power-house at Paddington Great Western railway station* c *1885, showing large Gordon alternators.*

industrial purposes and as a medium for illumination generally, had been recognized, but opinions were sharply divided on whether it should be generated in units of small or large capacity. The first electric power-station erected for the supply of private consumers was set to work in January 1882. This was the

Holborn Viaduct station of the Edison Company, originally constructed for supplying street lighting, and later extended to serve private consumers in the vicinity. Other small stations were established at Godalming and Brighton (figure 101) about the same time. One of the most famous power-stations of this epoch was that established by Sir Coutts Lindsay in 1883 for the lighting of the Grosvenor Gallery and for supplying private consumers. The network was fed with alternating current at high voltage, and each consumer was provided with a series transformer,[1] operating on the Gaulard and Gibbs system in which the

FIGURE 100—*Mordey alternator, manufactured by the Anglo-American Brush Corporation, 1886.* (Left) *Rotating field magnet;* (right) *stator.*

primary windings of all transformers were connected in series on each circuit of a ring main. This station, however, gave so much trouble in 1885 that Ferranti was consulted and, in 1886, became chief engineer of the undertaking. At this period Ferranti, in his early twenties, was manufacturing the alternators already described (p 193), and his first action was to replace the two existing Siemens alternators by 2400-volt machines of his own manufacture. He also replaced the series transformers by others of his own design arranged for parallel connexion across the single-phase distributing mains, thus initiating a practice that has since become universal.

Transformers. Faraday had, as usual, left others to develop his discovery of the principle of the A.C. transformer, and within some ten years many were familiar with the properties of induction coils. In these devices a make-and-break or interrupter mechanism produced the necessary pulsation of current in the

---

[1] The principle of the alternating-current transformer—mutual induction between distinct windings or portions of windings—was first demonstrated by Faraday in 1831.

primary winding, which in turn induced a high voltage in the secondary winding. Several suggestions for the employment of induction coils in electrical distribution were put forward, but Gaulard and Gibbs probably made the earliest practical use of transformers in a power system, in a series circuit (figure 102). Although Ferranti was not original in proposing the constant-potential or parallel connexion of transformers, his system was the first to demonstrate its possibilities on a practical scale. Westinghouse, the pioneer of alternating-current practice

FIGURE 101—*Brighton power-station, 1887.*

in the United States, was keenly interested in the Gaulard and Gibbs system. At about this time he imported from Europe, for his own experiments, a Siemens alternator and several Gaulard and Gibbs transformers. His engineers judged that the parallel connexion should be adopted, in confirmation of Ferranti's opinion.

Deptford power-station. In 1887 the London Electricity Supply Corporation was founded, with a capital of a million pounds, to take over the Grosvenor Gallery station and to put into effect Ferranti's scheme for a huge generating-plant at Deptford, which was intended to supply a large area of London. Ferranti shared with certain courageous financiers the belief that the satisfactory development of electric power must be linked with generation in quantity. Almost alone among engineers he advocated transmission at high voltages. His figure for the Deptford station was 10 000 volts, when neither generating-plant, nor transformers, nor cables for more than 2500 volts had yet been constructed. Ferranti designed his power-station himself, and had the electrical machinery built there under his supervision (figure 103). The plant included two Ferranti alternators, designed for 5000-volt working and driven by 1250-hp engines, supplying the day-time load; and four Ferranti alternators with 10 000-volt windings each directly coupled to a 10 000-hp steam-engine.

The first of the main cables for the transmission of power at 10 000 volts having failed, Ferranti designed a system of concentric conductors separated by spirally-wound waxed paper. The use of this material, admittedly an improvisation in the first place, originated a practice that has since become standard in the cable industry. For various reasons the large generators were never completed, but the smaller sets were interconnected with the Grosvenor Gallery station, and to the surprise of his many opponents Ferranti successfully demonstrated the practicability of 10 000-volt transmission. Sections of the original Ferranti main comprising 20-ft lengths of copper tubing—an inner and an outer tube separated by paper insulation and jointed under hydraulic pressure—continued in use in London for over forty years. The first current was transmitted from Deptford in 1889; success was not immediate and the station was not regularly operated until 1891. Although this station can be considered as the forerunner of all large modern central power-stations, its design was by no means accepted as rational by many contemporary electrical engineers. It is therefore not surprising that the construction of power-stations of relatively small capacity, designed to serve consumers in their immediate vicinity, continued until well into the present century, and, of these, Maiden Lane, 1889, is typical (figure 104).

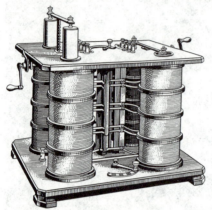

FIGURE 102—*Gaulard and Gibbs's adjustable core transformer*, c 1883.

D.C. or A.C.? Opinion was sharply divided, moreover, on the relative merits of direct current and alternating current. In this 'battle of the systems' in Britain, Ferranti, Gordon, Mordey, and S. P. Thompson, and in America Westinghouse, Tesla, Sprague, and C. P. Steinmetz were advocates of A.C. generation. They were opposed by Lord Kelvin, Crompton, A. B. W. Kennedy, and John Hopkinson in England, and by Edison in the United States, who championed the cause of D.C.

In England, the weapons were scientific argument and economic facts; in the

United States the battle was fought with allegations of positive danger from the use of A.C. First, H. P. Brown, a consulting engineer associated with Edison, strongly sponsored the legal adoption of A.C. for state electrocution and in 1889 recommended successfully the purchase of Westinghouse alternators for the purpose. Secondly, Edison and Brown attacked the use of A.C. by intensive propaganda on a national scale, alleging grave danger, claiming a relatively high

FIGURE 103—*Interior of Deptford power-station when under construction, 1889.*

rate of fatal accidents, and using as an argument in their favour its official use as a lethal agent. Westinghouse replied in articles and pamphlets and was so angered by what he took to be gross misrepresentation that he seriously contemplated instituting proceedings for conspiracy.

A victory for Westinghouse was assured when, in 1893, his company was awarded the contract for the first of the alternators and auxiliaries for the Niagara Falls power scheme. It was conceded that high-voltage transmission had much to commend it, on account of reduced mains losses, and at this time D.C. machines could not be built for high-voltage working. Nevertheless, the advocates of D.C. could rightly claim that a large storage-battery, peculiar to D.C. working, markedly increased the operating efficiency of their stations under light load conditions—during which periods the steam-engines could be shut down—and formed a valuable adjunct at times of peak load. The maintenance of storage-batteries was, however, a serious item of expenditure, and the losses in them could be considerable.

It was years before opinion became unanimous in favour of A.C., by which

FIGURE 104—*A. & S. Gatti's generating station in Bull Lane Court, Strand, known as the Maiden Lane power-station, 1889.*

time there were in existence at least as many D.C. stations as A.C. The result was a legacy to succeeding generations of a task of change-over and co-ordination which, some half century later, has not yet (1958) been completed. In England parts of London, and of some provincial towns, are still supplied with direct current.

Parallel operation of alternators. As early as 1868 Wilde had discussed the parallel operation of two alternators and had described in general terms the synchronizing of their phases. The problem seems to have been next revived in a paper of 1884 by John Hopkinson (1849–98), in which for the first time it was given adequate mathematical treatment. Difficulty in the synchronization of alternators appears to have been a major obstacle in the early days of A.C. working. According to J. E. H. Gordon:

they did not work together until they had jumped for three or four minutes . . . which might take a month's life out of 20 000 lamps, and that loss was rather a serious difficulty. Therefore . . . they could not couple alternating current machines. . . .

Ultimately the obstacle, which related to the prime-movers rather than to the alternators, was overcome, but for some years it was deemed preferable to run separate alternators, each to supply a separate section of the load, than to attempt a parallel connexion.

It has been remarked that the design of electrical machinery was for a long time mainly empirical, and it is proper to give due honour to the pioneers in this branch of technology. S. P. Thompson, J. Hopkinson, Gisbert Kapp, and Sir James Swinburne were among those who dealt more particularly with the theoretical design and testing of electrical generators, as distinct from general theory. Hopkinson, as consulting engineer to the English Edison Company, was responsible for the redesigning of the inefficient dynamos manufactured by the Edison parent company. The Hopkinson dynamos were manufactured in this country by the firm of Mather & Platt. Hopkinson's name is also associated with two other matters of great importance in this field. These are the method of determining generator-efficiency known as the Hopkinson test, and the system of electrical distribution known as the three-wire system. By means of the latter enormous savings of copper in street mains were effected.

FIGURE 105—*The Grenet potassium dichromate flask-battery.*

Kapp and Swinburne were prominently associated with Crompton & Company, of Chelmsford, and thus with the development of dynamos and instruments. Kapp designed some of the early slow-speed dynamos for direct connexion to steam-engines, and his name is associated with a system of dynamo construction embodying ventilation ducts in the armature which immediately secured a considerable saving in size and weight for a given electrical output. To Kapp also is due the term 'shell', as descriptive of a certain class of transformer. S. P. Thompson was an authority on the design of electric generators, and his textbooks, among the first to deal adequately with problems of design, ran to many editions.

VIII. BATTERIES

In the early days of the voltaic cell (p 177), many attempts were made to remedy its principal troubles, which were wasting of the metal plates when the batteries were not working and polarization during use. Sturgeon (p 178) introduced in 1830 the practice of surface amalgamation of the zinc. The treated metal, like chemically pure zinc, resists corrosion by an acid electrolyte.

Primary batteries—those generating electricity from a non-reversible chemical reaction—belong either to the single-fluid or to the two-fluid class. The simplest of the single-fluid cells is the original voltaic, in which alternate plates of dissimilar metals are used with an alkaline, saline, or acid electrolyte. A simple battery of this description is very subject to polarization, that is, retardation of the chemical action as a result of the evolution of hydrogen at the positive pole. Many attempts were made to defeat polarization, which causes a marked fall of voltage after the battery has been in operation for a short time, and some remarkably successful results were achieved.

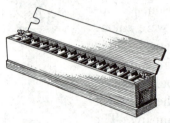

FIGURE 106—*Fuller trough battery for telegraph service.*

The replacement of costly copper plates in the early batteries was obviated by Helm, who about 1850 used carbon cylinders for the positive electrode; this also considerably reduced polarization. Warren de la Rue (1815–89) achieved similar results with lead dioxide, and subsequently in 1868 perfected the silver-chloride cell which provides an extremely constant potential. The most notable contribution towards a commercial cell at this period was, however, that of G. Leclanché (1839–82), a French railway engineer, who introduced in 1866 the form of cell still widely used.

Another family of single-fluid batteries is that in which chromic acid or chromium salts are used. Among the better-known cells of this pattern are those of R. W. Bunsen (1811–99) in which carbon and zinc plates are used with chromic acid (1844), and the potassium dichromate flask-battery, also with carbon and zinc plates, introduced by Grenet in 1859 (figure 105). All these batteries possess to a greater or lesser degree the defect of variable voltage; the voltage is affected by the varying concentration of the electrolyte, which controls the internal resistance of the cell.

The earliest of the practical two-fluid cells was that devised by J. F. Daniell (1790–1845). The object of the Daniell cell was to produce a constant electromotive force, and it undoubtedly proved to be the most popular of its class, especially for telegraphic purposes. In its original form, described in 1836, it consisted of a copper cylinder, forming the positive plate, and an inner porous cell within which was fixed a zinc rod, acting as the negative. The liquid in the inner cylinder was dilute sulphuric acid, and in the outer cylinder was a saturated solution of copper sulphate. Apart from the merit of its constant electromotive

force, it was claimed for the Daniell cell that
the plates did not waste, that the battery did
not produce unpleasant fumes, and that it would
remain active for long periods without attention.
The first notable modification to the Daniell
cell was made by J. C. Fuller (1853), who substituted a solution of zinc sulphate for the
sulphuric acid used by Daniell in the inner
cell. By this modification, it was claimed, the
life of the zinc element was considerably ex-

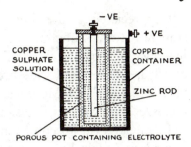

FIGURE 107—*Vertical section through a
typical Daniell cell.*

tended. Fuller constructed a 12-cell battery on the trough principle (figure 106)
which was extensively employed in the telegraphic service until 1875, when it was
superseded by the mercury-dichromate battery patented by the brothers J. C.
and G. Fuller. This new cell yielded a constant electromotive force of two volts;
three cells in series were reputed to be equal in service to a 10-cell Daniell
battery on account of lower internal resistance, and were said to operate at one-
third of the cost.

Another important modification of the Daniell cell was due to Jean Minotto
(1862). The essence of his patent was the replacement of the porous pot of the
Daniell cell by a layer of sand (figures 107 and 108). The container of the cell
consisted of a jar of glass or other suitable insulating material, on the bottom of
which was placed a thin disk of copper with an insulated connector attached to it.
Alternate layers of copper sulphate powder or crystals and sand were added
successively, concluding with a disk of zinc serving as the second plate. To bring
the battery into service it was necessary only to add water above the zinc plate
and within an hour or so the battery would be in working order, continuing in
operation until the copper sulphate had been exhausted. The Minotto cell, sometimes known as a 'gravity cell', was used extensively for the telegraph in India
and other tropical countries. Many other primary
cells have been proposed, but proved to be too
complicated in maintenance or too expensive in first
cost to be of lasting value.

The first apparatus to demonstrate the effect of
a secondary battery, otherwise known as a storage-
battery or accumulator because it can be charged
from another source, was constructed by J. W. Ritter
(1776–1810), a native of Leignitz, Bavaria, about
the year 1803, but the significance of his work was

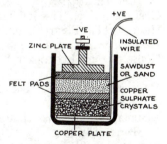

FIGURE 108—*Vertical section of the
Minotto cell, based on the principle
of Daniell.*

not appreciated at the time and it was forgotten. The father of the modern storage-battery is undoubtedly R. L. G. Planté (1834–89), of Paris, who began his work well before 1870. His batteries were first exhibited towards the end of 1878, and aroused widespread interest. Other inventors in France, notably C. Faure and A. de Meritens, took up the subject, and the names of all three are associated with particular forms of lead-plate construction.

In England Sir Joseph Swan (1828–1914) fully appreciated the value of the secondary battery, but considered the examples of Planté and Faure cells (p 418) he had seen in Paris to be much too large and clumsy to be of commercial interest. Swan carried out considerable research and by 1881 had invented the cellular lead plate, designed to receive a filling of spongy lead. This modification enabled the storage-capacity for a given size of cell to be greatly increased. Batteries embodying this improvement were widely adopted in the early direct-current generating-stations.

Acknowledgment.

The Table on p 192 is reproduced by courtesy of the Institution of Electrical Engineers.

BIBLIOGRAPHY

'Allmänna Svenska Elektriska Aktiebolaget, 1883–1908.' Privately printed, Gothenburg. [1909.]
APPLEYARD, R. 'The History of the Electrical Engineers.' Institution of Electrical Engineers, London. 1939.
BOWEN, J. P. 'British Lighthouses.' Longmans, London, for the British Council. 1947.
'Correspondence in the Matter of the Society of Arts and Henry Wilde, D.Sc., F.R.S.' Published privately, Manchester. 1900.
CROMPTON, R. E. B. 'Reminiscences.' Constable, London. 1928.
DAVY, H. "An Account of some Experiments on Galvanic Electricity." *J. R. Instn*, **1**, 166, 1802.
DOUGLAS, J. N. "The Electric Light applied to Lighthouse Illumination." *Min. Proc. Instn civ. Engrs*, **57**, Pt III, 77, 1878–9.
DREDGE, J. (Ed.). 'Electric Illumination', Vol. 1. London. [1882.]
FERRANTI, G. Z. DE. 'Life and Letters of Sebastian Ziani de Ferranti.' Williams & Norgate London. 1934.
GORDON, J. E. H. 'Practical Treatise on Electric Lighting.' London. 1884.
HIGGS, P. 'The Electric Light.' London. 1879.
Idem. Electrician, **10**, 179, 1883.
HUDSON, D. and LUCKHURST, K. W. 'The Royal Society of Arts, 1754–1954.' Murray, London. 1954.
MACKECHNIE JARVIS, C. "The History of Electrical Engineering", Pts 2, 3. *J. Instn elect. Engrs*, **1**, 145, 280, 1955.
NIAUDET, A. 'Machines électriques à courants continus, systèmes Gramme et congénères.' Paris. 1881.
PACINOTTI, A. "Descrizione di una macchinetta elettro-magnetica." *Nuovo Cim.*, **19**, 378, 1864.
PARSONS, R. H. 'The Early Days of the Power-Station Industry.' University Press, Cambridge. 1940.

PASSER, H. C. 'The Electrical Manufacturers, 1875–1900.' Harvard University Press, Cambridge, Mass. 1953.

"Report of Ordinary Meeting." *Mem. Manchr lit. phil. Soc.*, **6**, 103, 1866–7.

SIEMENS, C. W. "On the Conversion of Dynamical into Electric Force without the aid of Permanent Magnetism." *Proc. roy. Soc.*, **15**, 367, 1867.

SIEMENS, W. "Über die Umwandlung von Arbeitskraft im elektrischen Strom ohne permanente Magnete." *Mber. preuss. Akad. Wiss.*, 56, 1867.

THOMPSON, JANE S. and THOMPSON, HELEN G. 'Silvanus Phillips Thompson, His Life and Letters', p. 99. Fisher Unwin, London. 1920.

THOMPSON, S. P. 'Dynamo-Electric Machinery' (3rd ed.). London. 1888.

Idem. Electrician, **52**, 60, 1903.

WILDE, H. "Experimental Researches in Magnetism and Electricity." *Proc. roy. Soc.*, **15**, 107 1866.

See also:

Journal of the Institution of Electrical Engineers, London, Vols. 11–, 1882–.

Journal of the Society of Telegraph Engineers and of Electricians, London, Vols 1–10, 1872–82.

Telegraphic Journal and Electrical Review, London, 1872–.

Transactions of the Newcomen Society, London, 1920–.

*The electric fluid displayed. In Abbé Nollet's experiment,
c 1750, the lady lies on an insulated plate which is charged
by a cylinder machine. The bystander is amusing herself by
drawing a spark from the lady's nose.*

THE DISTRIBUTION AND UTILIZATION
OF ELECTRICITY

C. MACKECHNIE JARVIS

I. THE ARC-LIGHT

AFTER much experiment with frictional electricity, involving spark discharges and the fusion of wires, the first useful potentialities of the electric current were disclosed by the invention of the voltaic cell (p 177). As soon as large batteries were assembled it was likely that arc-ing would be noticed, and as early as 1802 carbon electrodes were deliberately substituted for metal ones in order to improve the arc; from this the science of electrical illumination arose. The brilliant light from the arc was immediately impressive, but early experiments towards its practical use for illumination failed because it was impossible to obtain a steady light (p 134). It proved difficult to procure carbon for the electrodes in a satisfactory state of purity and hardness, and to regulate the arc automatically. After twelve years of experiment W. E. Staite (1809–54) was able, from 1846 onwards, to give reasonably satisfactory public demonstrations of electric arc-lighting. Patents for carbon-purification processes were granted to Jabez Church in 1845, and to W. Greener and Staite in 1846.

Many experiments with incandescent metallic filaments showed that their life in air must be brief, as a result of oxidation. Such men as Warren de la Rue (1815–89) and Sir William Grove (1811–96) realized that the success of the filament lamp was intimately linked with the problem of operating the filament in an oxygen-free atmosphere. In the experiments of de la Rue and of Grove (c 1840), directed towards the use of filaments of platinum wire enclosed in glass bulbs as highly evacuated as possible (figure 109), the lamps were found to possess only a short life, mainly owing to the imperfection of the vacuum but partly to the narrow margin between the temperature at which a platinum wire begins to glow and its melting-point.

Staite in the mid-1840s made similar experiments with a platino-iridium alloy, but was unable to prevent the filament from disintegrating. He exhibited a lamp of this type (figure 110) at a lecture on electrical illumination which he gave at Sunderland, Durham, in October 1847. Among the audience was a young chemist, Joseph (later Sir Joseph) Swan (1828–1914), whose work is described below (p 213). Swan has left us an account of the state of artificial lighting in the early nineteenth century, which today is somewhat difficult to appreciate:

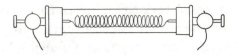

FIGURE 109—*de la Rue platinum filament incandescent lamp, 1820.*

The days of my youth extend backwards to the dark ages, for I was born when the rushlight, the tallow dip or solitary blaze of the hearth were the common means of indoor lighting. . . . In the chambers of the great, the wax candle, or exceptionally a multiplicity of them, relieved the gloom on state occasions; but as a rule, the common people, wanting the inducement of indoor brightness such as we enjoy, went to bed soon after sunset.

This was untrue of large cities, where lighting by coal-gas was introduced from about 1812 (vol IV, p 269), but it must be borne in mind that before the invention of the Welsbach incandescent mantle (1886) gas-lighting depended upon the fish-tail and similar burners.

To Staite belongs the credit for the first practical automatic-feed mechanism for the carbon arc. His lamp of 1846 embodied a clockwork mechanism whereby the carbons were advanced at a fixed rate. This had obvious disadvantages, and in 1847 Staite introduced his 'pyrometric principle', employing the fact that the heat radiated by the arc increases with its length as the carbons are consumed. In Staite's device, the heat thus generated caused a copper wire to expand and raise a detent, thus allowing a weight-loaded gear train engaging with rack-work to raise the lower carbon. Arc-lamps operating on this principle were made again by both Siemens and Edison some thirty years later. W. Petrie (1821–1904), an engineer, considerably improved the mechanism of the lamp, and participated with Staite in many public demonstrations and lectures on electric lighting in different parts of the country. The improved lamp was exhibited in London for the first time in October 1848, arousing much interest—though not invariably enthusiasm—among 'artists, scientists, engineers, gas directors, proprietors of patent lights of every kind, and a multitude of intelligent and respectable persons'. Figure 111 shows an 1853 example of the lamp.

Great as the popular interest in their invention was, however, Staite and Petrie failed to gain

FIGURE 110—*Staite's metal filament lamp, 1847.*

financial backing and to convince industrialists and others of its merits. The inventors were forced to realize that, although they had solved the problem of the lamp, they were defeated by the limitations of the Daniell cells which

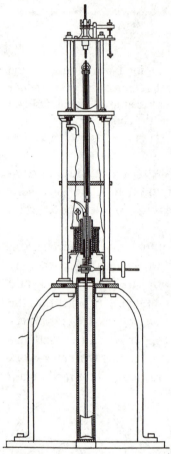

were their only source of current. Public exhibitions of the new wonder continued nevertheless. Among those associated with arc-lighting experiments at this period, Foucault, Serrin, and Duboscq should be mentioned. J. B. L. Foucault (1819–68) was approximately contemporary with Staite and his activities in Paris followed a similar course, though his apparatus (figure 112) was markedly inferior to Staite's. Serrin persevered in perfecting arc-lamps (figure 113) after most of his contemporaries had lost interest; although his first patent was taken out in 1857, his lamps did not come into general use until some fifteen years later, by which time Gramme dynamos (p 188) were freely available. Duboscq's lamp (figure 114) was of approximately the same period as that of Serrin, and is of interest in that it was used by F. H. Holmes for the Blackwall and South Foreland experiments in lighthouse illumination which started in 1858 (p 182). Later (1862) Holmes designed his own lamps to replace those of Duboscq.

FIGURE 111—*Staite's early carbon arc-lamp, 1853.*

Holmes's improved arc-lamps were used in a number of English lighthouses, notably in the South Foreland High and Low lighthouses, and in those at Dungeness and Souter Point, near Sunderland. In France, Serrin lamps were used extensively, first with *Alliance* and later with de Meritens generators, for a similar purpose (p 192).

The advent of the Gramme ring dynamo in 1871, and the successful operation of the arc-lamps installed in Gramme's Paris factory in 1873, reawakened public interest in arc-lighting, and from 1875 onwards many municipal and private installations were completed.

Among the first was that in the mill of Heilmann, Ducommun, & Steinlein at Mülhausen, where four Gramme dynamos and four Serrin arc-lamps were working in August 1875. It was not found possible to operate more than one arc-lamp from one dynamo, which rendered the installations expensive. The lighting of the Menier chocolate factory at Noisiel-sur-Marne, and of the Menier rubber factory at Grenelle, followed in 1875, and that of Ricard's cotton-mills soon after.

In 1876 it was announced that in France the Nord railway company had adopted arc-lighting for platforms at its La Chapelle station, the lamps being supplied by Gramme dynamos driven by compressed-air engines. Simultaneously it was announced that the Paris–Lyon–Marseille company was adopting it also, and a further advance was made in 1877 when in September of that year the completion of a 12-lamp installation at Lyons railway-station, supplied from one generator, was reported.

In Britain the adoption of arc-lighting lagged behind, for two reasons. The most likely explanation for the delay was the necessity to import both machines and arc-lamps from the continent, but there must also have been many who could recall the unsuccessful experiments of an earlier generation and the financial losses sustained by several companies formed to sponsor arc-lighting from electric batteries.

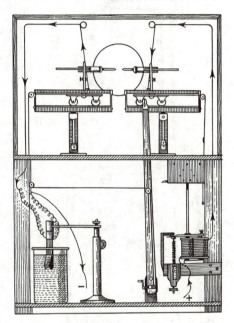

FIGURE 112—*Regulator for Foucault's early arc-lamp, c 1850.*

This lack of progress was publicly deplored on more than one occasion, until in the autumn of 1878 public and private schemes were announced in rapid succession. The first English installation was that at the Gaiety Theatre, London (p 196), where in August 1878 an installation consisting of six Lontin lamps to illuminate the façade of the building was completed. This work was carried out by French contractors, but about the same time R. E. B. Crompton (1845–1940) (p 191) installed two Gramme alternators and imported arc-lamps at the Stanton Ironworks near Derby.

Crompton, like other British engineers, had studied arc-lighting in Paris, and was aware that in factories which had changed from lighting by oil-lamps and gas-flares to arc-lighting complaints of eye-strain from the glare were numerous.

He carried out many experiments about this time on indirect lighting by means of arc-lamps (1881) and a little later with Swan incandescent lamps. An illustration of an early Crompton lamp is shown in figure 115.

Arc-lamps in which the gap between the pair of vertical carbons in the same line was automatically regulated were expensive. The problem was, however, rendered much easier by the invention in 1876 of the 'electric candle' by Paul

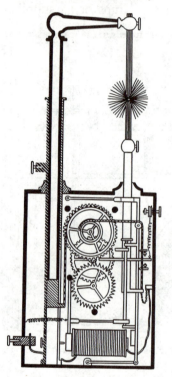

FIGURE 113—*Serrin arc-lamp, c 1857.*

Jablochkoff (1847–94), a telegraph engineer in the Russian army, who later lived in Paris. Jablochkoff candles consisted of two parallel rods of carbon, usually 4 mm in diameter, mounted vertically with a kaolin separator between them and bridged at the apex by a strip of graphite (figure 116). When the current was first switched on the graphite strip was consumed and an arc formed between the two pencils of carbon which gradually burned down. With this device it was necessary to use alternating current, in order to prevent unequal consumption of the electrodes such as occurs in a D.C. arc. The success of the electric candle was immediate; thus the various departments of the Grands Magasins du Louvre, in Paris, were equipped with eighty of them in the spring of 1877.

The Jablochkoff method was tested in England at the West India Docks in the same year, but the first small permanent installation, consisting of six electric candles fed from a single Gramme machine, was completed at the Shoreditch iron-works of Wells & Company in 1878. A little later this illumination was to be seen at Billingsgate fish-market, and as experimental street-lighting along the Thames Embankment and Holborn Viaduct. Jablochkoff was fortunate in that he had secured immediate and substantial financial support in Paris. His designs were developed and the lamps marketed by the *Société Générale d'Électricité* (later the *Compagnie Générale d'Électricité*), an organization responsible for carrying out many of the early English installations.

The use of copper-plated carbons, originally patented in France in 1859 by de Fontaine-Moreau and reintroduced by E. Carré, a Paris manufacturer, was found to reduce the rate of their consumption and enhanced the value of this type of lamp, which required only 8–9 amp against 17–20 for arc-lamps of conventional design. By 1881 the number of Jablochkoff candles in service is said to have exceeded 4000, but they fell into disuse as the inherent defects of a non-regulating lamp became more apparent. Yet Jablochkoff had successfully taken the first step towards the wide diffusion of electric lighting; his work inspired numerous competitors in attempts to invent the perfect low-current arc-lamp.

In the United States, one of the earliest names associated with electrical illumination was that of C. F. Brush (1849–1929), who by 1878 was ready to supply dynamos and arc-lamps (figure 117). In this year he completed at Wanamaker's Store in Philadelphia an arc-lighting installation which consisted of five independent dynamo sets, each supplying four arc-lamps connected in parallel, and not in series as was the practice in Europe at this time. Brush's achievement in operating arc-lamps in parallel was a prime reason for the success he enjoyed, a success enhanced by his introduction in 1879 of an automatic voltage-regulator, which worked on the carbon pile principle (figure 118).

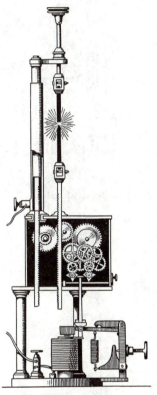

FIGURE 114—*Duboscq arc-lamp,*
c 1858.

II. THE INCANDESCENT FILAMENT LAMP

Although Joseph Swan had been familiar since 1847 with both the primitive filament lamp and the then more promising arc-lamp, he was convinced that the future of electrical illumination depended upon the perfection of the former. Pursuing his own investigations, he came across a patent of 1845, taken out on behalf of J. W. Starr (1822?–47) of Cincinnati, who claimed 'the application of continuous metallic and carbon conductors, intensely heated by the passage of a current of electricity, to the purposes of illumination'. Starr used a thin sheet of platinum foil or carbon, and remarked that when carbon was used, 'it should be enclosed in a Torricellian vacuum'. Swan was probably aware of the brevity of the life of lamps made with platinum filaments, and the idea of using an incandescent carbon filament in a vacuum appealed to him. Soon after 1848 he succeeded in making strong and flexible strips of carbonized paper, and in ensuing years was able to render incandescent a strip of carbon about $\frac{1}{4}$ in wide and $1\frac{1}{2}$ in

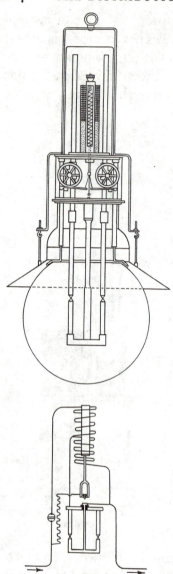

FIGURE 115—*Crompton's arc-lamp,*
c 1880. The regulator is seen above and
the feed mechanism below.

long. This lamp, made in 1860, still had only a short life, but Swan had learnt that success was unattainable so long as high exhaustion of the bulb was hindered by the imperfections of the vacuum-pump and while the current had to be derived from chemical batteries. He took up other work and did not return to the problem of the incandescent lamp until 1877, by which time the mercury vacuum-pump invented by Hermann Sprengel in 1865 had been used by Sir William Crookes and others in experiments on the phenomena of high vacua. Swan acknowledged that it was the publication of Crooke's researches that caused him to resume work on the incandescent lamp. His successful carbon-filament lamp (figure 119) was first exhibited at a meeting of the Newcastle upon Tyne Chemical Society on 18 December 1878, though not in operation.

Swan was reluctant to patent his methods, on the ground that the basic features of an incandescent lamp—a carbon filament working in an evacuated glass bulb—had been anticipated and were not patentable. Instead he directed himself wholly towards getting his lamp into production, and this for all practical purposes began early in 1881. Meanwhile, in America, Thomas Alva Edison (1847–1931) was attacking the same problem. Initially Edison held that the construction of lamp filaments from carbon in any form was impossible, and at one point he thought he had attained his goal with platinum. However, by the end of 1879 Edison was experimenting with carbon, and later, in 1880, adopted strips of bamboo suitably carbonized. Experimental lamps of this type reached London from America in February 1880. Edison's policy, unlike that of Swan, was to patent everything, and as a result the English inventor soon found himself restricted by five patents granted in Britain to his rival; the earliest of them (December 1878) covered an incandescent lamp with a metallic platinum or platinum-alloy filament.

Swan's associate Stearn repeatedly urged him to protect his ideas. During his initial experiments with Stearn in 1877 Swan had discovered that his carbon filaments retained air, which was released by their first incandescence. This caused early deterioration of the filament and blackened the interior of the bulb. To overcome the defect Swan

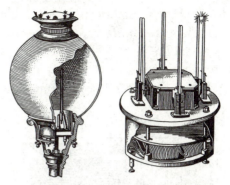

FIGURE 116—(Left) *Jablochkoff's candle arc-lamp using two parallel carbon rods, 1876.* (Right) *Jablochkoff's four-candle lamp, with the globe removed.*

initiated and patented (1880) the practice of rendering the filament incandescent during exhaustion before sealing the bulb (figure 120).

Swan was not entirely satisfied with his filaments, which in 1881–2 were made from mercerized cotton thread. He felt that it should be possible to evolve a more uniform filament from a non-fibrous material. His further research led him to adopt a plastic substance, such as nitrocellulose dissolved in acetic acid, and to extrude it as fine threads through metal dies under pressure. This process,

patented in 1883, not only revolutionized the manufacture of carbon-filament lamps, but was an early link in the chain of discoveries that led to the manufacture of artificial silk some twenty years later.

Even in England, Swan was not without rivals. St George Lane-Fox took out a series of patents for filament lamps (figure 121) from 1878, using for the filaments first a platino-iridium alloy and later a plumbago refractory composition as a carrier for a carbonaceous coating. Lane-Fox was a prolific inventor; he devised a simple and effective mercury vacuum-pump, an automatic voltage-regulator, and several integrating energy-meters (figure 122), all before 1882. By this time he had disposed of his patents

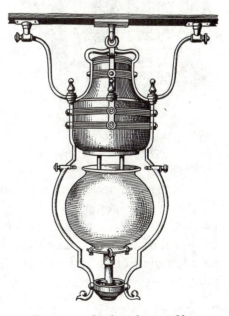

FIGURE 117—*Brush arc-lamp,* c *1880.*

to the Anglo-American Brush Electric Light Corporation, by whom his apparatus was manufactured in Britain, and to the Brush parent organization for exploitation in the United States, where events were moving forward with great rapidity.

When the incandescent lamp first attracted attention it provoked considerable adverse comment Some Americans thought little of the Edison lamp, while in 1878 the English physicist Silvanus P. Thompson (1851–1916) expressed the view 'that any system depending on incandescence will fail'. By the end of 1880 Edison lamps, known as 'burners', were being manufactured in quantity (figure 123 A), and in the first fifteen months some 80 000 were sold; yet even in 1881 Werner Siemens shared the uncertainty in the future of the incandescent lamp, and declined to take up a European licence for the development of Edison patents.

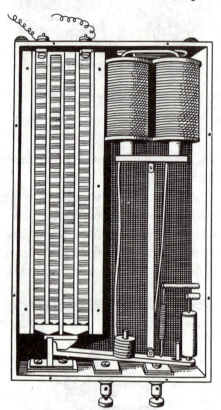

FIGURE 118—*Automatic regulator for Brush arc-lighting dynamos,* c 1880.

Swan's factory near Newcastle rivalled Edison's in prosperity, and in its early days received an American order requiring 25 000 lamps to be supplied within a fortnight! Swan lamps were graded after manufacture according to the characteristics of their filaments, since wide deviation occurred. They were sold according to their working voltage and approximate candle-power, and Swan records that the performance of each was noted at the factory before dispatch. In 1882 Swan's company was sued by Edison for infringement of his English patents. After Edison failed to obtain an injunction to restrain Swan from his lamp-manufacture, the action was settled amicably by an amalgamation which founded the Edison and Swan United Electric Light Company Limited. This joint company was registered in October 1883 with an authorized capital of £1 m.

The first incandescent-lamp installation, after that at Swan's own house at Gateshead-on-Tyne, was in Sir William Armstrong's house near Rothbury, where current was obtained from a generator driven by a water-turbine; this was said to be the first hydro-electric plant in England (December 1880). Lord Kelvin was also quick to employ the new method of lighting in his private residence, and had it installed in his old Cambridge college, Peterhouse, in 1884. The House of Commons, however, had enjoyed the amenity of incandescent electric lighting since June 1881.

In June 1881 also the first British ocean-going ship to be provided with the new lamp was so equipped. This was the Inman Line's *City of Richmond*. Nor was the Royal Navy far behind, with H.M.S. *Inflexible* selected

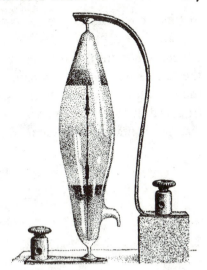

FIGURE 119—*Swan's experimental carbon-filament glow-lamp publicly exhibited in December 1878.*

for the initial trials. Swan lamps were used experimentally on a special train running from London to Brighton in 1881; the power was obtained from Faure secondary cells. One of the most remarkable installations completed at the end of 1881 was that of the Savoy Theatre, London (figure 124), where according to

Swan's account the stage was lit by 824 lamps; a further 370 were used in other parts of the building. Figure 125 shows a stage-light regulator used in Germany about the same time. Among the public buildings to adopt Swan lamps in 1882 were the Mansion House, the British Museum, and the Royal Academy.

At this period the lamps were manufactured to give approximately 16 candle-power at 36 volts, 18 cp at 41 volts, and 20 cp at 46–54 volts. A lamp rated for 20 cp took about 1·34 amps. The bayonet cap, which became characteristic of British practice, was introduced by the Anglo-American Brush Corporation about 1884, but the screw-cap (still the normal fitting

FIGURE 120—*Mercury air-pump in use in a lamp factory, c 1883.*

in the United States) was a feature of Edison's lamps from the outset (figures 121 and 123 B, C). C. H. Gimingham's fitting is shown in figure 126.

From 1885 until the close of the century there was steady improvement in the technique of manufacturing incandescent lamps and a gradual lowering of the initially high production costs. Successful osmium-filament lamps were introduced in 1898 by Auer von Welsbach, the inventor of the incandescent gas-mantle. Tantalum filaments followed in 1905 and tungsten a few years later.

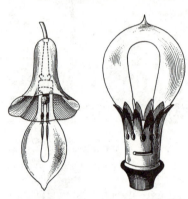

Technical improvement is reflected by the figures for lamp-efficiency, expressed in lumens per watt, which rose from about 1·4 in 1881 to 4·0 in 1900.

III. TELEGRAPHS

The origin of the electric telegraph and its development in Britain by Sir William Cooke (1806–79) and Sir Charles Wheatstone (1802–75) are described in volume IV, chapter 22. By 1850 the first of many telegraph companies had been registered under the title of the Electric Telegraph Company Limited, and to it Cooke had transferred his patents on becoming a

FIGURE 121—(Left) *Lane-Fox glow-lamp, c 1881.* (Right) *Lane-Fox Brush lamp with bayonet cap, 1884.*

director. By 1855 this company owned and operated some 4500 miles of telegraph line in Great Britain, as compared with 2200 miles belonging to the largest of their competitors, the English and Irish Magnetic Telegraph Company, founded in 1850.

When the first telegraph line was opened in the year 1839, between Paddington and West Drayton, the instruments used were of the five-needle type, in which the character transmitted was indicated at the receiving end on a dial at the point of intersection of the axes of any two of the needles. Such a system possessed the merit of direct reading, but the cost of laying five insulated wires, some £165 per mile, inhibited further development. Cooke and Wheatstone thereupon introduced their twin-needle instrument, and at a somewhat later date single-needle instruments were employed. With the abandonment of the original intention to use direct-reading instruments a signalling code became necessary. It was decided that needle-movements to the right and left of the vertical axis should represent the dot and dash equivalents of the letters of the alphabet, according to the code of Samuel Morse (1791–1872). The Morse code, though not the first of its kind, became the best known.

Both Cooke and Wheatstone had separately devised A B C or direct-reading dial telegraphs. Others associated with this type of apparatus were Siemens, whose instruments were adopted in England, and Breguet, whose apparatus found favour in continental countries. In 1850 the telegraph was still in its infancy, and both apparatus and methods were changing rapidly. It is remarkable,

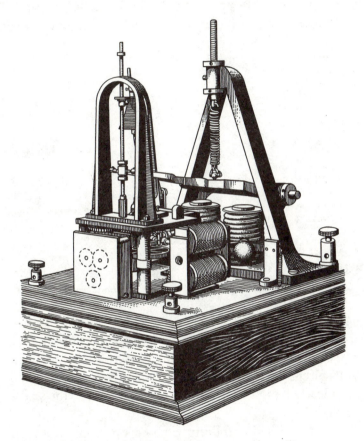

FIGURE 122—*Lane-Fox integrating energy-meter, c 1880.*

however, how closely the practices evolved within the first twenty years or so of practical telegraphy are followed even today.

The first telegraph line consisted of five hemp-covered copper wires, assembled in the form of a multi-core cable; it was made by Enderby Brothers of Greenwich in 1838 and was termed a telegraphic rope. The maintenance of underground cables proving too expensive, Cooke patented in 1842 a method of aerial suspension, in which wires of iron or copper, or a stranded conductor comprising a number of iron wires twisted round a central core of copper, were stretched between wooden posts. This method of erection had been proposed by Morse in the United States, and it is possible that Cooke was inspired by him. Cooke found paint or tar 'an expensive and ineffectual mode of protecting the iron wire from rust' and resolved to try the then new process of galvanizing. In 1845 Cooke and Wheatstone proposed 'the application of leaden tubes formed over covered wires', and in the same year another patent was granted to Young and McNair

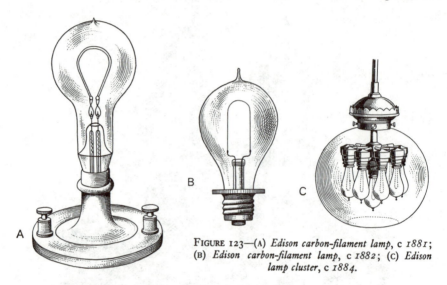

FIGURE 123—(A) *Edison carbon-filament lamp*, c *1881*; (B) *Edison carbon-filament lamp*, c *1882*; (C) *Edison lamp cluster*, c *1884*.

for an improved method of manufacturing electric conductors by covering metallic wires with plaited cotton threads and introducing them into a leaden pipe filled with pitch. The patent specification is fully detailed and includes a description of a lead press. The inventors proposed to use the lead sheath as an earth return.

Towards the end of 1845 Jacob Brett patented a printing telegraph, which at a later date became known in America as 'House's Telegraph'. In the same patent, he included an 'oceanic line', in which the wires were first varnished, 'bound with waxed or sere cloth, platted with waxed or greased twine and around the whole a platted cable saturated with tar is formed'. A further patent of his (1848) includes, among specifications for many other devices and telegraphic accessories, the first clear reference to rubber (caoutchouc) as a medium for the insulation of wires for telegraphic purposes; the rubber was to be applied in the form of a solution in benzene, toluene, or some similar solvent.

Cooke, in a patent of 1842, had referred to the use of india-rubber in con-

nexion with the protection of copper wires laid along
the tops of railway-carriages, but it is not clear
whether he intended to use this material as an insulating medium or merely as a protection from the
weather. In 1848 a machine was patented by Barlow
and Foster for covering telegraph wire with a compound of gutta-percha, cowrie gum, and sulphur by
a process of vulcanizing, and in the same year the
chairman of the Electric Telegraph Company, J. L.
Ricardo, secured a patent for combining two or more

FIGURE 124—*Swan lamp bracket,
as used at the Savoy Theatre,
London, 1881.*

wires for telegraphic purposes 'by enclosing them between two fillets of gutta-
percha in such a manner as to insulate one wire from the others and from external matters'.

The introduction of rubber into European industry is described elsewhere
(ch 31). Although an insulator, it could not at first be rendered fit for electrical
use. Meanwhile, in 1843 William Montgomerie, then resident at Singapore, sent
a detailed account to the Royal Society of Arts of the properties of a material
known in Malaya as gutta-percha,[1] which he considered was superior in many
ways to South American rubber and which possessed the great advantage of
emanating from a source within the Empire.

Faraday, after examining samples of gutta-percha, expressed the opinion that
it might prove useful as an electrical insulator. Thomas Hancock, an early pioneer
in the rubber industry, quickly appreciated the importance of the newly discovered material for his own business, and in 1845 the Gutta-percha Company
of London (later the Telegraph Construction and Maintenance Company
Limited) was formed.

The Electric Telegraph Company turned
its attention to the use of this new material
for line-insulation. Owing to objections
made to the use of overhead wires in cities
it was very desirable that, where possible,
subterranean cables should be employed.
At first (1847) the attempt was made to
roll gutta-percha upon a copper wire, passing the wire and the soft insulation material
between a pair of rollers having a semi-

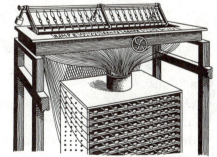

FIGURE 125—*Electric stage-lighting controller
used in Germany, c 1887.*

[1] Malay *getah percha* = 'gum of the percha [-tree]'. Several trees yield this juice, especially *Isonandra* (or
Dichopsia) *gutta*.

circular profile. It was found, however, that the insulation tended to break open at the junctions of the two rollers. At length, in July 1848, Hancock invented the machine subsequently used for the manufacture of all subterranean gutta-percha-covered wires; after this patent was taken other experiments were made in covering several wires in one gutta-percha core. A typical cable made in this way consisted of seven wires enclosed in a core of about $\frac{5}{16}$-in diameter.

The earliest cables laid under the streets of London consisted of three copper wires in one gutta-percha core. As such cables proved costly, the Electric Telegraph Company sought to cheapen them either by substituting iron wire for copper, or by increasing the number of wires to four, the weight of the cable so made being about 415 lb to the mile. In many cases, the expense of repairing multiple cables, involving the disturbance of several circuits to repair a single wire, prompted a return to single wires insulated with two or more coatings of gutta-percha (1861). On the European continent cables were insulated with gutta-percha to which sulphur had been added. This may have improved its

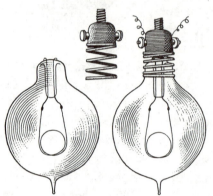

FIGURE 126—*Swan carbon-filament lamp, showing contact hooks and spring-loaded holder. This type of lamp holder, devised by C. H. Gimingham, was employed until the introduction of the bayonet cap, c 1884.*

dielectric properties, but in a short time the sulphur made the gutta-percha very brittle, and in contact with the copper it caused formation of copper sulphide with consequent corrosion of the wire. Some underground wires laid before 1853 failed because they were laid in leaden troughs. This was especially so with the London and Brighton and the South-Eastern railway telegraphs, where it was found that the lead in time dissolved the gutta-percha, so that the wires short-circuited. Another unexpected source of trouble was the decay of the gutta-percha covering of wires laid in the ground when attacked by fungi under certain conditions.

One of Siemens's patents describes this treatment of gutta-percha with sulphur. 'Gutta percha, entirely freed from water, is mixed (by means of rollers) with pulverized sulphur, and their chemical combination is effected by heating the mixture in a steam chamber.' In the same patent (1850), the use of an implement similar to a 'mole plough' for laying underground wires is described. It consisted of a frame carrying a coulter in front of a hollow cutter or 'mole', through which the insulated wires (from reels on the frame) were threaded by means of guides on the mole. 'The device could be hauled along by a fixed engine, or propelled by steam or animal power.' Modifications of this instrument, to be employed with a locomotive, and for various soils, are described and shown. 'In stony or sandy soils, the wires are enveloped in sheet lead, wound in helical form from bobbins on the wire as it is deposited in the ground. . . . A similar instrument may be used to deposit the wires under water; it is drawn through by means of a cable, wound on a crab engine on shore, a diver being in attendance; or the cable may be attached to the stern of a steam-boat carrying coils of wire.'

The use of 'bitumen, petroleum or natural pitch of Trinidad' for insulating and covering telegraph cables was patented in 1851 by Thomas, Earl of Dundonald, who held an interest in the pitch lakes of Trinidad. This material was tested but found liable to crack after short exposure to air, and was therefore regarded as less satisfactory than gutta-percha. At a later date bitumen was successfully employed in insulating electric power cables.

A further improvement in the method of insulating telegraph wires was effected by H. V. Physick in 1852; in this a fibrous material, such as calico, was used as a medium to carry the gutta-percha, tar, pitch, or other insulating material. Physick also introduced (1854) the use of differently coloured strands to identify the wires in a multi-core cable. The first mention of an external armouring of iron wires is that occurring in the January 1853 patent of W. T. Henley for the protection of both 'subterranean and submarine' cables.

The invention of the telegraph relay was due to Edward Davy (1806–85), in whose patent of July 1838 it is described. Apparently, however, Faraday had hit upon the concept of relay action, for Cooke records a conversation (1836)—which obviously he did not understand—in which Faraday 'would not give me an opinion as to the distance the fluid [voltaic electricity] might be passed in sufficient quantity, but observed that if it were only for twelve or twenty miles, *it can be passed on again*'. Another notable development (1854) was Robert Walker's system whereby messages could be sent in both directions simultaneously over a single telegraph line. The object of this 'duplex telegraphy' was to increase the speed of transmission, but the invention was born before its time. In 1854 there was no problem arising from the density of traffic, and thus, although experiments were carried out by the Electric Telegraph Company, duplex telegraphy was not adopted. It was forgotten until revived or reinvented some twenty years later, when it became a development of major importance.

The first intimation of a telegraphic exchange appears in the patent granted early in 1851 to F. M. A. Dumont, who claimed 'a particular combination of electric wires for the conveyance of intelligence in the interior of large towns whereby a central station has connected with it a certain number of houses in order that each house or subscriber may communicate privately with the central station. Any subscriber wishing to communicate with any other would be connected directly via the central station.' This patent envisaged the possibility of giving notice of an outbreak of fire, or a burglary, and contains a number of ideas that seem more appropriate to a telephone system. Dumont seemed well aware of the social potentialities of electrical communication.

IV. AUTOMATIC TELEGRAPHY

The first step in the direction of automatic telegraphy was the invention of the first practical chemical telegraph by E. Davy in 1838. This instrument, in which electrified needles were brought into contact with rolls of chemically treated paper turned by clock-work, was publicly demonstrated in London for some months before the inventor was forced by financial difficulties to abandon his work and emigrate to Australia. Alexander Bain took up the idea, and in 1864 was granted a patent for an automatic transmitting apparatus, in which perforated paper was fed into a transmitting mechanism and the messages were recorded at the distant end of the line by means of a chemical recorder. At the time, experimental transmissions of up to 400 messages an hour were demonstrated, but for reasons now difficult to establish the trials and the invention were abandoned. Other pioneers secured patents for improved devices of this description, but none won real success.

The use of perforated paper for operating automatic machines was taken up, however, as in the Wheatstone automatic system (1866), adopted in the same year by the Electric Telegraph Company. It was found capable of handling from 55 to 80 words per minute over a circuit about 280 miles long, according to the cross-section of the conductor employed. By 1879 improvements in the mechanism resulted in speeds of at least 200 words a minute under optimum conditions over similar distances, and by this time there were about 170 such instruments in use. The principles of Wheatstone's inventions are still employed.

In submarine telegraphy automatic operation was secured with the aid of the ingenious siphon-recorder invented by Lord Kelvin in 1867. This came into general use around 1870 and at a later date was greatly simplified by Muirhead.

V. SUBMARINE TELEGRAPHY

The history of submarine telegraphy began in 1845, when the brothers Jacob and John Watkins (1805–63) Brett founded the General Oceanic Telegraph

Company, to establish telegraphic communication between England and France. A concession was obtained from the French Government and in 1850 the first submarine cable was laid. This failed almost immediately, and was replaced in the following year by one of a different type, which lasted nearly twenty years. Thereafter other submarine telegraph projects followed in rapid succession. The Oceanic Company early conceived the ambition 'to form a connecting mode of communication by telegraphic means from the British Islands and across the Atlantic Ocean to Nova Scotia and the Canadas, the Colonies, and Continental Kingdoms'.

The next submarine cable was that from Port Patrick, Wigtownshire, to Dublin, which was laid in 1853 under the direction of Sir Charles Bright (1832–88), at that time engineer to the English and Irish Magnetic Telegraph Company. The success of this project encouraged Bright to contemplate an Atlantic cable. Between 1853 and 1855 he organized an extensive series of experiments, whereby existing telegraph lines up and down the country were connected in series to provide a total length exceeding 2000 miles, and from the results obtained he was able to anticipate some of the transmission difficulties that subsequently arose.

The Atlantic Cable Company, with Bright as engineer, was registered in 1856, and preparations went ahead rapidly with the promise of support in the event of success from the British and United States governments. The manufacture of the 2500 miles of cable required for the line between Ireland and Newfoundland, completed within six months, was itself a great achievement for the period, involving as it did the drawing and stranding of over 17 000 miles of copper. Laying was begun in August 1857 from the west coast of Ireland, but before 300 miles of the cable had been laid the line parted and the end was lost in 2000 fathoms. With great disappointment it was realized that the project must be postponed until the following year, while sufficient cable to make good the loss was manufactured. On the second attempt the *Agamemnon*, carrying half of the cable, was all but lost in a severe storm. Laying on this occasion began with a splice between two ships in mid-Atlantic, the vessels proceeding in opposite directions. The cable parted on no fewer than five occasions, each necessitating a return by both cable-ships and their escorts to the starting-point. After six weeks at sea the vessels again returned to port without having been successful; there seemed every likelihood that the project would be abandoned. A third attempt, however, ended triumphantly on 5 August 1858.

The working of the cable was soon found to be attended by unexpected difficulties, the most important of which was the retardation of signals caused by the high capacitance between the conductor and the surrounding sea. Moreover, after the cable had been in service for a few weeks its insulation deteriorated so greatly that it became unserviceable. It was subsequently discovered that the electrician, in a misguided attempt to apply land-signalling methods, had enlarged the battery to 500 cells, which, being used with induction coils, caused the insulation of the cable to be subjected to a potential of about 2000 volts! Several years elapsed—those of the American Civil War—before sufficient capital was raised to repeat the attempt to establish telegraphic communication with America. After further failures in 1865, success was realized in the following year (vol IV, p 661). Lord Kelvin's ingenuity did much to make it possible.

VI. THE TELEPHONE

The noun 'telephone'[1] was originally applied to any device for transmitting sound over a distance, and it was well known that sound could be conveyed through solid bodies and water, or along taut wires and speaking-tubes. Robert Hooke (1635–1703) remarked after experiments on the transmission of sound over a taut wire, ''Tis not impossible to hear a whisper a furlong's distance, it having been already done; and perhaps the nature of the thing would not make it more impossible though that furlong should be ten times multiplied.'

The first practical electrical telephone was that made and demonstrated by J. Philipp Reis (1834–74) of Frankfurt-am-Main in the year 1861, but this does not appear to have been more than a scientific toy. The work of Alexander Graham Bell (1847–1922) is generally considered to have been based upon the researches of the German physicist and physiologist, Hermann Helmholtz (1821–94), who for many years studied the reproduction of sound and invented an apparatus for producing artificially the vowel sounds of the human larynx. Bell repeated these experiments and those of other contemporary scientists, and eventually devised the instrument with which his name is associated, first patented in England and the United States in 1876. The earliest examples of the Bell telephone to reach England were exhibited at the Plymouth meeting of the British Association in 1877.

Following wide demonstrations in London and elsewhere, in 1878 the first commercial telephone undertaking in Britain was launched; it began operations, with imported instruments, at Chislehurst in Kent. At first the telephone was employed purely as a means of private conversation between two points, but, after developments in the United States, the first telephone exchange was established in London in 1879.

Bell's instrument incorporated an electromagnetic microphone virtually iden-

---

[1] Attributed to 1835 in the 'Oxford English Dictionary'.

tical with the ear-phone, which was of the pattern still used, but in 1878 Edison's carbon microphone reached London. Operation of telephone systems remained in private hands until 1912, when the assets of the National Telephone Company were acquired by the Post Office, after which all private ownership ceased.[1] In Britain, long-distance telephony began with an experiment made in 1878 over a private line between Norwich and London. This demonstrated that long-distance speech was practicable, and from then on inter-urban lines were established, at first in the provinces and later linking provincial towns with London. Such distant communication has been greatly transformed by the introduction of electronic equipment in the twentieth century.

VII. WIRELESS TELEGRAPHY

While the great development of radio-communication and of electronic equipment of all kinds is a feature of the twentieth century, it is worth recording that much of the basic theory of electromagnetic radiation was worked out before 1900, and that experiments had already demonstrated the utility of the theory.

It was a corollary of Clerk Maxwell's theoretical electromagnetic system that 'waves' should be generated by an electrical disturbance, comparable to and travelling with the same velocity as light waves—which, indeed, he took to be electromagnetic themselves. Heinrich Hertz (1857–94) turned to the experimental verification of this prediction, demonstrated the existence of the radiation (1887), and determined many of its characteristics. His transmitter was a spark oscillator with two metal plates acting as resonator and aerial, and his receiver was similarly constructed. Sparks across a small gap in the receiving circuit indicated reception of the waves radiated by the transmitter. Hertz's system had a wave-length of about 24 cm, and he was therefore able to demonstrate the 'optical' properties (such as reflection and polarization) of electromagnetic radiation.

Although there was no tremendous immediate development of Hertz's discoveries and apparatus, his results were not wholly neglected. Ernest (later Lord) Rutherford, for example, succeeding in 1895 in transmitting signals at Cambridge over a distance of three-quarters of a mile, with the aid of a new detector he had invented in New Zealand. Another pioneer was Sir Oliver Lodge (1851–1940), who recognized the usefulness of an induction coil as a means of tuning an electrical resonator (1897), and developed the coherer detector of wireless waves. By far the most successful of all these early workers was Guglielmo Marconi (1874–1919), who came to England after initial experiments in Italy and took out

[1] There is, however, a municipal telephone undertaking in operation at Kingston upon Hull.

his first patent in 1896. Marconi founded commercial radio-communication, by painstaking attention to the perfection of workable apparatus and by demonstrating its useful potentialities. In particular, he exploited radiations of a far longer wave-length than those discovered by Hertz, and at first wave-lengths of the order of 300–3000 metres proved far more serviceable in communication than the short waves. With relatively sensitive electronic detectors long-distance signalling at wave-lengths of 10–100 metres became possible in the 1920s; wave-lengths of Hertz's magnitude were not usefully employed until more recent years.

In 1895 Marconi sent signals over a mile; in England the range was extended to 2, 4, and 9 miles. Marconi's Wireless Telegraph Company was founded in 1897; an installation for communication between the East Goodwin lightship and the South Foreland lighthouse was erected in the following year, and soon wireless telegraphy had for the first time intervened in (the Boer) war. Marconi's spectacular success just falls in the new century: on 12 December 1901, at his first attempt, Marconi succeeded in sending and receiving transatlantic signals between Poldhu, Cornwall, and St John's, Newfoundland.

VIII. TRANSMISSION AND DISTRIBUTION OF ELECTRIC POWER

Much experience gained in the development of the electric telegraph during the period 1840–80 was turned to good account when electrical power became generally available. The manufacturing processes associated with rubber insulated, lead-covered, and wire-armoured cables were established and the factors responsible for the deterioration in underground cables were understood. Admittedly, there is a vast difference between the insulation required for telegraph cables and that needed for power cables for 110- and 220-volt systems, but the difference in insulation is one of degree; in any event, for telegraphic purposes the thickness of rubber employed was dictated by mechanical rather than electrical considerations.

Reference has already been made (ch 9) to the manner in which the early central generating stations were established. Distribution at first was by D.C. two-wire mains at voltages up to a maximum of 110. A notable contribution to the theory of distribution by cable networks was made by Lord Kelvin in a paper entitled 'The Economy of Metal Conductors of Electricity', read before the British Association in 1881. In this paper the author examined the criteria affecting the cost of transmission systems and enunciated a relationship since known as Kelvin's Law.[1]

---

[1] Namely, that the most economical cross-section area for a conductor is that for which the cost of energy-losses in a given time is equal to the interest on, and depreciation of, the capital involved in that time.

One of the greatest advocates of direct current systems was John Hopkinson, professor of electrical engineering at King's College, London. Hopkinson was retained as a consulting engineer by the English branch of the Edison organization of America, but his contributions to the success of the Edison system of machines and apparatus are little appreciated in this country or in America. An example is the three-wire system of D.C. distribution which Hopkinson invented and patented in July 1882, but which was proclaimed as the invention of Edison, who merely publicized it widely in America from 1883 onwards.

The three-wire system provides a means of supplying two two-wire main circuits from a single generator of double the voltage of either circuit. Originally, the voltages were 220 between outers or 110 volts between each outer wire and the middle wire. As systems expanded, it was soon found desirable to raise the voltages to 440/220 respectively, and it became the custom to connect electric motors between the 440-volt wires. A great advantage of the three-wire system is the saving in copper, varying from about 25 per cent to 50 per cent according to the rating chosen for the middle wire. Since it was impossible to ensure equal loading of the two two-wire circuits in such a system, hand or automatic balancing equipment became necessary. This consisted of two D.C. machines of the reversible type, each connected between one outer wire and the middle wire. The machines were coupled mechanically, and when the voltages between each outer wire and the middle wire were equal they would be idle. A condition of unbalanced voltage would cause the machine connected to the outer wire of higher voltage to run as a motor, driving its fellow as a dynamo, so that its output would tend to restore the balance. An extension of the three-wire system is the five-wire, which was operated in Paris about 1889 and at Manchester in 1893, but it is generally agreed that any financial advantage from the saving of copper is at least offset by the difficulty of maintaining a reasonably balanced voltage across each of the component two-wire circuits.

Upon examining the details of the early supply undertakings, one is struck by their great variety of voltages. The explanation is at least partially as follows. Swan lamps were first manufactured to operate at about 50 volts, to adapt them to existing arc-lamp circuits, but it soon became apparent that distribution from a central station at this voltage would be uneconomical. In the United States, Edison lamps were made for 100-volt working, and Swan was soon able to produce a similar filament, although neither of the pioneers was yet prepared to consider a higher voltage. In designing the systems, opinion was divided upon whether the generator voltage should be 100, or whether an allowance for voltage-drop should be made, making the generator voltage 105 or 110 to maintain the consumer's voltage at or near 100. With increasing loads on all circuits the problem of voltage-drop became more acute, and the practice of adding 10 per cent to cover distribution losses was adopted as standard. Within a few years, the majority of high-voltage systems and a great many operating at low voltages were selected as multiples of 110.

As the numbers of consumers of electric power increased, the current flowing in the mains became heavier, the mains themselves became longer, and the loss of power through voltage-drop became more serious. For the engineers in charge of the central generating systems there were four possible remedial measures. (i) By changing from D.C. to A.C. and distributing at a high voltage the losses would be reduced: the high voltage would be reduced by local transformers for the individual consumer's use. This was the solution pioneered by Ferranti and ultimately adopted (p 200). Otherwise, (ii) the number of D.C. generating-stations in a system could be increased—a very uneconomical procedure; or (iii) the principal mains could be fed with high-voltage A.C., which would be converted at local sub-stations, by rotary machines, into low-voltage D.C. for use. Such rotary converters, however, are much less than 100 per cent efficient. Finally, (iv) D.C. generated at a high voltage could be broken down to a low-voltage D.C. in sub-stations with the aid of a rotary transformer. This machine, invented by Gramme (1874), has two sets of armature-windings and two commutators on a single rotor, which spins in a single field-system. One set of armature-windings drives the machine as a motor, while the other generates electricity at a different voltage.

Large rotary converters were used in the United States for operating electrolytic processes, and were adopted for some British supply networks in the late 1890s. They have also been much used to provide D.C. for railway and tramway circuits; thus the Central London railway used 900 kw converters as early as 1897. In the twentieth century the rotary converter has been to some extent replaced by mercury-vapour and other rectifiers for industrial purposes where D.C. is required but only A.C. is available.

Rotary transformers were employed in England by the Chelsea electricity undertaking. They were 40-kw Elwell Parker machines designed to run at 500 volts and delivering 100 volts to the consumer's mains. Other rotary transformers operated by the Oxford Electrical Company ran at 1000 volts and delivered 40 kw at 100 volts, while at Wolverhampton 2000-volt sets were installed.

IX. THE ELECTRIC MOTOR

The conspicuous attribute of electrical energy is its mobility. It can be taken to any point along a pair of wires. Other methods of conveying energy from a central plant to smaller consumers were tried, but none was as convenient or efficient as the electrical method, by which the heat-energy of a boiler-furnace, or the kinetic energy of falling water, is converted into electrical energy and then again transformed into mechanical energy by the consumer's electric motors. Technologically this is by far the most important role of electricity. Electrical energy as a source of light and more recently of heat, as a means of communicating information, and as an agent in chemical processes, has clearly transformed industrial practice; but its chief significance has been to place power, great or small, in the workman's hands or at his elbow.

This was realized but slowly, and the development of the electric motor was therefore tardy. It was perceived almost at once that, however efficient the motor might be, mechanical energy could never be economically derived from chemical batteries, save in special circumstances. Even when efficient dynamos and alternators were available, it seemed that the mechanical energy obtainable from an electrical system might be much less than that put into it, because of the losses involved at each stage. When, therefore, distribution systems with central generating stations grew up in the wake of the incandescent lamp, it was the convenience rather than the efficiency of the electric motor that first commended it. Since then, however, it has been appreciated that more of the energy latent in the fuel can be obtained from large, highly efficient generating plants than if the same fuel were burnt in a multitude of little stationary heat-engines or railway locomotives. Water-power, moreover, could never be turned to full advantage except by using it to generate electricity.

The principle of the electric motor was demonstrated by Faraday in 1821 and exemplified very simply in 'Barlow's wheel' (1823). Early devices for converting electromagnetic forces into rotary motion were clumsy in construction and inefficient in practice, so that no motor of commercial significance was available before 1873, when Gramme and his associate Fontaine exhibited in Vienna a reversible combination of two Gramme machines acting as generator and motor respectively. Thus the D.C. electric motor could be seriously considered for industrial use as soon as practicable dynamos were available (p 188). Gramme motors could be used on D.C. only, and after the establishment of A.C. distribution networks from about 1882 the lack of a suitable A.C. motor became acutely felt. The first A.C. motor, employing the induction principle, was invented in America in 1888 by Nikola Tesla (1856–1943). To Tesla is due the discovery of the rotating A.C. field and of polyphase systems of A.C. working. Tesla's first motors were manufactured by Westinghouse, but it is probable that the first consistently successful induction motors were those made by C. E. L. Brown at the Oerlikon Works at Zürich, and those designed by M. von Dolivo-Dobrowolsky, chief engineer of the *Allgemeine Elektrizitäts Gesellschaft* of Berlin. Examples of both machines were shown at the Frankfurt Exhibition of 1891.

These early induction motors, though constructed without commutators, were of the wound-rotor pattern. In its most robust and popular form the induction motor employs a special form of rotor, the 'squirrel cage', so called from the arrangement of rigid conductors spanning two end-rings, regularly spaced to form a cylindrical 'cage'. This rotor was the invention of Dolivo-Dobrowolsky.

The induction motor possessed certain limitations in the then prevailing state of design, rendering it unsuitable for some applications, notably electric traction.[1] A great deal of theoretical research on electric motors was done between 1880 and 1900, and subsequently, in England, France, Germany, and America. From this there ultimately emerged the A.C. commutator motor. Those first in the field were probably E. Wilson in Britain (1891), to whom the series-wound motor is due, and H. Georges, who patented a motor with shunt characteristics in Germany in the same year.

Another machine, the synchronous motor, patented in Germany and the United States in 1887, first appeared in commercial form at the Frankfurt Exhibition of 1891. Examples shown were made by the German firms of Lahmeyer and Schuckert. About this period also Dolivo-Dobrowolsky, after investigating the starting characteristics of the squirrel-cage induction motor, proposed the ingenious adaptation known today as the double squirrel-cage, which finds special application where high starting torque is required, as in crane- or traction-motors. Motors of this type were little used before the close of the century, and as a result they are today principally associated with the name of Boucherot, who exploited them at a later date.

The development of D.C. motors also was by no means neglected during this period, for until 1900 and for some years afterward D.C. systems predominated. The efforts of designers were directed to the improvement of mechanical construction and commutation, and to reduction in size and weight in relation to horse-power. Many early D.C. motors were 'open', that is, the windings and commutator were unprotected. They were in effect dynamos fed with current from other dynamos or from the mains. It was soon found that such machines were unsuitable for general industrial applications, and thus a demand for en-

---

[1] Electrically powered transport developed slowly from 1881. A few electric tramways were working in the United States and Europe by 1887, but the great extension of this form of urban transport came later. Electric traction on normal railways developed rapidly from 1890 onwards.

closed motors arose. The first completely shielded heavy-duty electric motors were developed for tramway and railway use; they were available from several manufacturers by the year 1900. The first public electric railway, apart from small-scale experimental lines, such as those laid down at exhibitions, was probably that constructed by Siemens & Halske at Lichterfelde in Germany in 1881. The rolling-stock was drawn by a locomotive, and the line operated on the three-rail system. In the United Kingdom the electric railway at Portrush in Northern Ireland, operating in 1883 with Siemens's machinery and equipment, is of great interest in that the power was obtained from water-turbines.

The greatest single improvement in the performance of D.C. machines was effected by the introduction of the supplementary magnetic pole known as the interpole, but this innovation was not made until about 1906. The replacement of copper-gauze commutator brushes by carbon ones had been proposed in 1889, but the latter, which greatly reduced commutator wear, did not come into general use until about 1893.

BIBLIOGRAPHY

BRIGHT, A. A. 'The Electric-Lamp Industry.' Macmillan, New York. 1949.

BRIGHT, E. B. and BRIGHT, C. B. 'The Life Story of Sir Charles Tilston Bright' (2 vols). London. 1899.

'Correspondence and Reports on the Subject of Comparative Trials of Electric Lighting at South Foreland—August, 1876 to July, 1877.' Trinity House, London. 1877.

CROMPTON, R. E. "Cost of Electrical Energy." *J. Instn elect. Engrs*, **23**, 396, 1894.

CUTHBERTSON, J. 'Practical Electricity and Galvanism.' London. 1807.

DREDGE, J. (Ed.). 'Electric Illumination', Vols 1, 2. Offices of *Engineering*, London. 1882, 1885.

"Electric Light at the British Museum." *J. R. Soc. Arts*, **27**, 990, 1879.

FAHIE, J. J. 'A History of Electric Telegraphy.' London. 1884.

HOPKINSON, B. (Ed.). 'Original Papers by the late John Hopkinson' (2 vols). University Press, Cambridge. 1901.

MACKECHNIE JARVIS, C. "The History of Electrical Engineering", Pts 2, 5. *J. Instn elect. Engrs*, **1**, 145, 1955; **2**, 130, 584, 1956.

PREECE, G. E. "On Underground Telegraphs." *J. Soc. telegr. Engrs*, **2**, 369, 1873.

PREECE, W. H. "Telegraphy: its Rise and Progress in England." *Ibid.*, **1**, 228, 1872.

Report to the Trinity House on Lighthouse Illuminants. Ref. C. 4551. Pts I, II. Board of Trade, London. 1885.

SABINE, R. 'The Electric Telegraph' (2nd ed.), p. 9. London. 1869.

SWAN, M. E. and SWAN, K. R. 'Sir Joseph Wilson Swan, F.R.S.' Benn, London. 1929.

'The Telcon Story.' Telegraph Construction and Maintenance Company, London. 1950.

THOMPSON, S. P. 'Life of Lord Kelvin' (2 vols). Macmillan, London. 1910.

WATSON, J. J. W. 'A few Remarks on the Present State of Electrical Illuminators.' London. 1853.

WEBB, F. H. (Ed.). 'Extracts from the Private Letters of the late Sir William Fothergill Cooke (1836–9), relating to "The Invention and Development of the Electric Telegraph".' London. 1895.

WEBBER, C. E. "Electric Lighting from Central Stations." *J. Instn elect. Engrs*, **20**, 54, 1891.

WOLF, A. 'A History of Science, Technology, and Philosophy in the Eighteenth Century.' Allen & Unwin, London. 1938.

See also:

Lumière électrique, Paris. 1879–.

Telegraphic Journal and Electrical Review, London. 1872–.

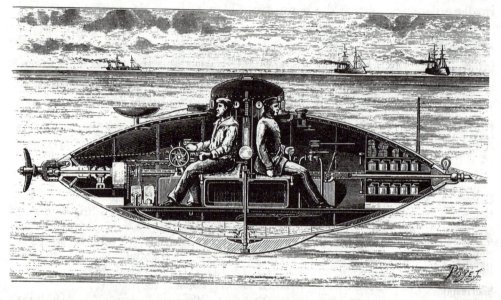

The electric motor quickly found many applications. This first electrically-propelled submarine of Goubet underwent trials at Cherbourg in May 1889. In telegraphic communication with the surface, it remained submerged in 33 ft of water for 8 hours.

HEAVY CHEMICALS

TREVOR I. WILLIAMS

ALTHOUGH the latter half of the nineteenth century saw a tremendous expansion of the chemical industry in both the variety and the total quantity of its products, two developments overshadow all others and claim our special attention. One was the birth and growth of the synthetic organic chemical industry as a result of W. H. Perkin's discovery of the first synthetic dyestuff, mauveine, in 1856: some aspects of this development are discussed at length in following chapters (12, 14). The other was the obsolescence of the Leblanc process for soda manufacture, which at the beginning of this period must have seemed a permanent feature of the industrial chemical scene, and its replacement by the Solvay or ammonia-soda process.

The immense industrial importance of soda (sodium carbonate), especially in relation to the textile industry, needs no emphasis here, for it has already been discussed in connexion with an earlier account of the development of the Leblanc process (vol IV, ch 8). In view of this importance, it is not surprising that a long struggle for supremacy between two alternative methods of soda manufacture had very far-reaching consequences both within and without the chemical industry. It is thus appropriate to begin this chapter with an account of the main features of this struggle, for they will of necessity have to be referred to in discussing other industrial chemical developments of the period.

To provide a general background to what follows, it may be remarked that in principle the Leblanc process was from the outset at a great disadvantage compared with the ammonia-soda process. In its original form it was dirty, productive of much offensive waste whose disposal was difficult, and heavy in its requirement of fuel. By comparison, the ammonia-soda process is clean, leaves no insoluble residue, and requires less than half as much fuel as the Leblanc process does. It may therefore seem surprising that for over thirty years the two processes were competitively operated side by side. The reason for this co-existence lies partly in the fact that the ammonia-soda process presented many technical difficulties, which took a long time to overcome, and more particularly in the fact that the Leblanc operators learned to work more efficiently—both technically and managerially—and to utilize profitably the waste products which in the early days were so great a nuisance and embarrassment to them. Rather paradoxically, it originally required an Act of Parliament—the Alkali Act of 1863—to compel the Leblanc operators in Britain to prevent the escape of noxious waste, whereas before many more years had passed it would certainly have required a further Act to have stopped them doing so.

I. LATER DEVELOPMENTS OF THE LEBLANC SODA INDUSTRY

For present purposes no more than the main stages of the original Leblanc process need be recalled. It consisted in treating salt with sulphuric acid, thus forming sodium sulphate and, as a then very unwelcome concomitant, clouds of hydrochloric acid gas. Roasting the sodium sulphate with a mixture of coal and limestone yielded what was known as 'black ash', consisting mainly of soda and calcium sulphide. From this the soda was extracted by lixiviation with water, leaving behind a residue of alkali waste, or 'galligu'. The latter—produced at the rate of 2 tons for every ton of soda—presented from the outset a serious problem. Not only was it a most noxious product, constantly involving the manufacturers in litigation with offended neighbours, but it was a serious source of loss, for irrecoverably locked up in it was most of the expensive sulphur originally contained in the sulphuric acid used in the first stage of the process.

The problem of the disposal of hydrochloric acid was relatively simply, though not quickly, solved. Attempts by James Muspratt (1793–1886) to disperse it by means of tall chimneys—one almost 300 ft high—were only partially successful, but in 1836 William Gossage (1799–1877) invented towers in which the gas was absorbed in a stream of water. He specified the 'application of a deep bed of materials furnishing extensive surfaces, over which water is caused to pass in the same direction as the smoke and gas'. The towers themselves were built of 'stone or brickwork made tight by a casing of clay' [1]. This invention proved of far-reaching importance, for it established a general principle for the absorption of gases, an operation frequently necessary in industrial chemical operations. Gossage showed that it was essential to present a large surface of water to the gas for the absorption to take place. This was an important step forward, for only a few months previously Thomas Lutwyche had lodged a patent for the absorption of hydrochloric acid which shows that he considered the volume, and not the surface area, of the water to be the important factor.

Gossage's towers were so effective that they made feasible the first Alkali Act (1863), which required manufacturers to absorb at least 95 per cent of the hydrochloric acid in their waste gases. But they did more than remove a very serious nuisance: they provided a useful by-product, for the acid so recovered was potentially valuable. Apart from having chemical uses of its own, it contains chlorine, which is extensively required for the textile, paper, and other industries as bleaching powder; the latter is made by the combination of lime and chlorine.

Two major processes were devised for the liberation of this chemically bound chlorine from hydrochloric acid. In a process invented by Henry Deacon (1822–76) the hydrochloric acid gas was mixed with air and passed over a catalyst—a substance which facilitates a chemical reaction without being consumed in it—commonly consisting of earthenware balls that had been soaked in a solution of cupric chloride and then dried at about 225° C [2]. Under these conditions the acid is oxidized with liberation of chlorine, but it is not practicable to make the reaction go to completion, and so the product is diluted with air, unchanged acid, and water vapour. Another patent by Deacon [3], filed in 1870, described a chamber in which strong bleaching powder could be made from such dilute chlorine gas.

In the process perfected in 1869–70 by Walter Weldon (1832–85) the oxidation of the hydrochloric acid to chlorine was effected by manganese dioxide. This process had already been used for some years, but suffered from the disadvantage that at the end of it the expensive manganese was left as the chloride, from which the dioxide could not easily be regenerated. Weldon's manganese-recovery process consisted in treating the chloride with a mixture of limestone and lime and then blowing air through it. In this way a mud was formed in which almost all the manganese was once again present as the dioxide, ready for a further cycle of operations.

Weldon's process had far-reaching effects. The output of bleaching powder was quadrupled, and its price in Britain was reduced by £6 per ton. Within five years there were reported to be only two chlorine works in the world in which it was not in use. Presenting to him the gold medal of the *Société d'Encouragement*, J. B. A. Dumas (1800–84), the great French chemist, remarked: 'By Mr Weldon's invention, every sheet of paper and every yard of calico has been cheapened throughout the world.' The handling of the bleaching powder was hazardous work and demanded the use of protective clothing and a thick oakum 'muzzle' to safeguard the nose and throat.

Although great quantities of chlorine were made into bleaching powder, it found other important uses. It was, for example, made into sodium and potassium chlorates, principally the latter, which is required for the match industry (p 252). A common method was to pass chlorine into a suspension of lime or magnesia: the resulting calcium or magnesium chlorate was decomposed with potassium chloride, giving potassium chlorate and calcium or magnesium chloride.

The problem of utilizing the vast quantities of alkali waste was a much more difficult matter, the main problem being to recover from it the valuable sulphur. In 1861 Ludwig Mond (1839–1909), later one of the pioneers of the ammonia-soda process in Britain, devised a process, patented in France in 1861 and in England [4] in 1862, by which, in a complicated series of operations, about one-third of the sulphur could be recovered. This process, not entirely novel, consisted essentially in oxidizing the waste with air, lixiviating the product, and separating the sulphur by treating the resulting liquor with hydrochloric acid. Coming to England, Mond entered into partnership with John Hutchinson (1825–65), one of the founders of the chemical industry, who in 1847 had established a Leblanc soda factory on the east bank of the Sankey Navigation at Widnes. The collaboration between Mond and Hutchinson was not a happy one, and difficulties arose about the drawing up of a contract specifying how the rights in Mond's process—which Hutchinson maintained had been virtually invented in his factory—should be allocated. Hutchinson died before agreement was reached, and not until 1866 was the plant for working the final form of Mond's process completed at Widnes. It was adopted also by Muspratt at Wood End, by Tennant at St Rollox, and at a number of other works in Britain and abroad, some sixty licences in all being issued. Despite various modifications, however, it was never a great success and was later eclipsed by the process devised by Alexander Chance (1844–1917).

Before discussing this latter process, however, mention must be made of another one devised by Gossage [5] in 1857, after some thirty years of struggling to solve the problem of alkali waste disposal. In this respect he was in a numerous company, for many industrial chemists—M. Schaffner in Germany and J. Mac-Tear in Scotland, to mention but two—had investigated it closely. In 1882 the process was aptly described as 'a sort of will-o'-the-wisp in the Alkali Trade, and [one that] had lured many a good man to serious discomfiture, if not to ruin'. Gossage showed that carbonic acid gas (carbon dioxide), obtainable from flue gases, would convert some of the sulphur in the waste into hydrogen sulphide (sulphuretted hydrogen), the combined sulphur in which could be used, but his high hopes were disappointed. Nevertheless he deserves honourable mention, which indeed he received in the following terms from Chance, after the latter's process had been perfected. 'I feel pretty confident that if Mr Gossage, during the course of his prolonged investigations, had had at his disposal the modern machinery and appliances and the powerful carbonic acid gas pumps which the progress of science placed within our reach in 1887, he, and not we, would have hit upon the process which I am about to describe' [6].

Like Gossage's, Chance's process was based upon the fact that if carbon dioxide is blown through the alkali waste, hydrogen sulphide is liberated. His success depended upon the fact that he devised what amounted to a double enrichment process, which yielded a gas sufficiently rich in hydrogen sulphide to be satisfactorily treated further for the extraction of the sulphur. This second stage was made possible by the timely patenting, in 1882, of the Claus kiln, devised primarily for a different purpose, namely the removal of sulphur from coal gas.

The kiln devised by C. F. Claus [7] was a stumpy tower, about 25 ft wide by 10 ft high, packed with bog iron ore. The gas from Chance's carbonators, rich in hydrogen sulphide, was passed through the kiln, in which it was partially oxidized to water and to elementary sulphur, which collected in a well at the bottom. Although the Chance–Claus process kept the Leblanc process going for a number of years, it could do no more than stave off the end. By 1893, however, the process was being worked on a scale large enough to produce 35 000 tons of sulphur annually in Britain.

As has been noted, the success of Chance and the failure of Gossage hinged in the main upon the improvements which, in the interval between their attacks on the problem, had been made in the pumping of carbon dioxide. It is an interesting point, indicative of the spirit of the day in the chemical industry, that much of Chance's information on this point was derived from Ludwig Mond, who had encountered the same problem in developing the competitive ammonia-soda process. Chance said of Mond: 'I desire to acknowledge our indebtedness for his courtesy in placing at my disposal the results of his vast experience in the production and in the pumping of carbonic acid. Let no one say that the days of chivalry are passed and gone, in the face of so distinguished a manufacturing chemist thus assisting a competitor, by freely giving him valuable personal technical experience, in such a struggle for survival as that which is now so keenly contested between ammonia soda makers on the one hand and Leblanc soda makers on the other' [6].

A variety of other technical improvements assisted in prolonging the life of the Leblanc process. Thus the lixiviation of the black ash, seemingly a simple process, proved capable of much improvement. Originally a crude counter-current extraction process, involving tiers of tanks, was used. In this method the water was moved from tank to tank as the black ash was laboriously shovelled from one to the other in the opposite direction. In France, Nicolas Clément-Désormes (1770–1842) and his stepfather C. B. Désormes devised a method in which the black ash was placed for extraction in perforated containers which could be suspended in tanks of water; in Britain, however, only Muspratt used this method, which also was laborious and expensive. Shanks's vats, named after

James Shanks (1800–67), to whom they are probably rightly attributed [8], were introduced in 1861 and were a great improvement; their action is based on the principle that the hydrostatic pressure of a column of weak lye is less than that of a column of strong lye of the same height, and if two such columns are balanced against each other a flow of liquid will occur (figure 127).

In the early Leblanc factories the mixture of saltcake, limestone, and coke was 'balled' in a furnace by stirring it with long iron rods, but later this process was mechanized. In 1853 George Elliot and William Russell patented a black ash

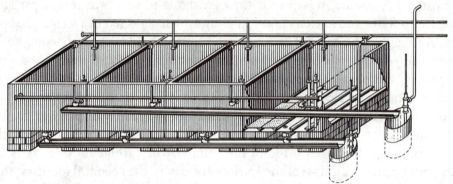

FIGURE 127—*Shanks-type lixiviating-vats for extracting soda from black ash.*

'revolver' [9], although this type of equipment did not come into general use until some twenty years later. The revolver consisted of an iron drum, generally about 10 ft in diameter and 20 ft long, lined with fire-brick, which could be rotated mechanically. The incandescent gas from the furnace was drawn away through a chimney and the molten ash was discharged when the reaction was complete (figures 128 and 129).

The first revolvers used in Britain were cast by Thomas Robinson (1814–1901) of St Helens, one of the first specialists in heavy castings for the chemical industry. Like most iron-founders of the day he had little scientific training, though he was apprenticed to an apothecary, but he was nevertheless a shrewd judge of the particular kinds of pig iron which would yield vessels sufficiently resistant to corrosion to meet the exacting needs of the alkali and other chemical industries. Two of his revolvers are still functioning at Widnes, where they are used for the manufacture of sodium sulphide by what amounts to the second stage of the old Leblanc process, the limestone being omitted.

II. THE AMMONIA-SODA PROCESS

Having thus traced the main technical developments in the Leblanc process during our present period, it is time to turn to the story of its successful rival, but to do this one must go back many years before 1872, the year in which the ammonia-soda process was first successfully worked by Ernest and Alfred Solvay in Belgium. As long ago as 1811 the French engineer and physicist A. J. Fresnel (1788–1827) seems to have known that if a concentrated solution of salt is saturated with ammonia, and carbon dioxide is passed into it, sodium bicarbonate is precipitated: the latter is easily converted into soda by heating. In essence, the reaction takes place in two stages. First, the ammonia combines with water and carbon dioxide to form ammonium bicarbonate, which then reacts

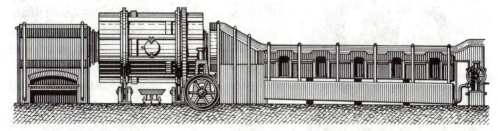

FIGURE 128—*Black-ash 'revolver' of a type built for a number of alkali works about 1870–80.*

with salt (sodium chloride) to form ammonium chloride and sodium bicarbonate; the latter, being relatively insoluble, is thrown out of solution as a precipitate. Ammonia can be regenerated from the ammonium chloride, and carbon dioxide is regenerated if the sodium bicarbonate is heated. As has already been indicated, the simplicity of this reaction conceals many practical difficulties; among them is the fact that regeneration of the ammonia results in the formation of calcium chloride, a product that was for long unmarketable.

Georg Lunge (1839–1923), a nineteenth-century authority on the chemical industry, questioned claims made on Fresnel's behalf—saying that they are 'based on some entirely indistinct allusions in a private letter'—but it is certain that not long afterwards many chemists were giving serious attention to ammonia-soda processes of this kind. In 1836 John Thom, in the works of Turnbull & Ramsay at Camlachie, made soda at the rate of 2 cwt daily by treating salt with ammonium bicarbonate, but after a year operations ceased. A little later, in 1838, two London chemists, H. G. Dyar and J. Hemming—evidently unaware of Thom's work—patented a process for making soda by interaction between salt and ammonium bicarbonate [10]. They attempted, with indifferent success, to operate it commercially at their Whitechapel works; the main difficulty, as with later attempts, seems to have been loss of ammonia, a very light and volatile gas. There they were visited by James Sheridan Muspratt (1821–71), who eventually persuaded his father, James Muspratt, that the process offered the possibility of relief from the harassing litigation then inseparable from operation of the noxious Leblanc process. A considerable works was built at Merton, and Muspratt lost more than £8000 over it. Plants to operate the Dyar and Hemming patent were built also in Berlin and Leeds; soda from the last was marketed for several years.

By this time it was clear that success was entirely a matter of efficient plant design, particularly in avoiding loss of ammonia, but nevertheless success was long in coming, and there were many further disappointing and expensive failures. Gossage took out a patent in 1854. Henry Deacon, in partnership with William Pilkington, seriously tackled the Dyar–Hemming process, but Pilkington lost heart and withdrew. Deacon then went into partnership with Holbrook Gaskell (1813–1909), who financed more trials of the ammonia-soda process at Widnes. Gaskell in turn became disillusioned as thousands of pounds were spent to no practical advantage, and eventually the Gaskell–Deacon works went over to the orthodox Leblanc process.

FIGURE 129—*Drawing a charge from a revolving black-ash furnace.*

A number of patents appeared in 1852–5. Grinus, of Marseilles, proposed to increase the yield by refrigeration, so lowering the volatility of the ammonia. Also in France, Turck patented a modification which he attempted to work at Sommervillers, near Nancy, but without success. About 1854 Rolland and Schlösing set up a works at Puteaux, near Paris, to work what they claimed to be a continuous process, in which the ammonia was regenerated by treating the ammonium chloride with lime. Again, however, it seems to have been impossible to keep the loss of ammonia within economic limits, despite attempts to reduce it by working at low pressures, and the factory was closed in 1857, after having made only some 300 tons of soda. Despite its failure, this was the most notable venture since that of Dyar and Hemming. In 1858 F. Heeren made an important theoretical study of the ammonia-soda process [11], but unfortunately his practical proposals were not of equal merit.

Further discussion of these early attempts could be almost indefinitely prolonged, but technologically they were of no great significance. Historically the next great, and indeed decisive, technical step forward was made by Ernest

Solvay (1838–1922) in Belgium; the development of his discoveries as a practical business proposition owed much to his brother Alfred.

It is a very remarkable circumstance, but undoubtedly true, that Solvay for some considerable time believed himself to be the original inventor of the basic chemical reaction of the ammonia-soda process. In 1903 he recounted: 'Convinced of the importance of my discovery, I hastened to patent it in Belgium on April 15th, 1861. Having worked alone and having obtained a patent, I believed that I alone knew of the reaction, and that I had the power to claim all rights in connection with it. Today, such ignorance would be inexcusable, but forty years ago there were neither so many technical publications nor such efficient patent offices.'

Solvay's principal contribution was that of a carbonating tower (figure 130) by means of which the process was made continuous. Other important contemporary developments were in the kilns for making carbon dioxide (figure 131) and for calcining the sodium bicarbonate (figure 132). The *Société Solvay et Cie* was formed in 1863 and works were built at Couillet, but despite the improvements some four years elapsed before it was working satisfactorily. From then on, however, progress was very rapid, and the Dombasle works was built in France in 1873. In 1872 Ludwig Mond—with characteristically far-sighted perception of the future course of events in the chemical industry—acquired the British rights in a further patent [12], embodying many improvements, which Solvay had filed in Britain that year. Mond and his partner John Brunner (1842–1919) experienced great difficulties in getting their plant at Winnington to work satisfactorily—and indeed came near financial failure before they did so—but success was ultimately achieved. At about the same time licences were issued in many other countries: the United States, Russia, Germany, Austria, Hungary, Spain, Italy, and Canada. From then onwards the success of the ammonia-soda process was never in question.

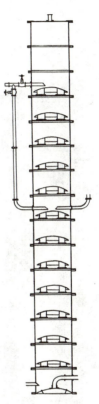

FIGURE 130 — *Solvay carbonating tower. This tall tower, patented in 1872, was a characteristic feature of ammonia-soda factories throughout the world at the end of the nineteenth century. Ammoniacal brine enters the tower at a point about two-thirds of the way up.*

The fortunes of the struggle between the Leblanc and the Solvay process, as well as the growth of the soda industry as a whole, are strikingly illustrated by some world production figures given on the next page.

Year	Total world soda production	Leblanc	Solvay
	(tons)		
1863	300 000	300 000	—
1874	525 000	495 000	30 000
1885	800 000	435 000	365 000
1902	1 800 000	150 000	1 650 000

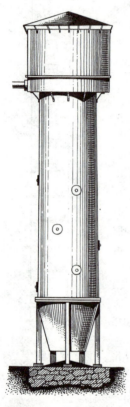

FIGURE 131—*Schreib kiln for making carbon dioxide for the ammonia-soda process. This kiln was 43 ft high and of 7 ft internal diameter. It required about one cwt of coke for every ten cwt of limestone.*

Our final words on the ammonia-soda process may appropriately be those of Solvay himself: 'Never before was the industrial realization of any process attempted so frequently and for such a long period of time as that for making ammonia-soda.'

III. CAUSTIC SODA

For many purposes—such as soap-making—a more powerful alkali than ordinary washing soda is required. In time, the production of caustic soda (sodium hydroxide) became an important adjunct of the Leblanc process. Causticization was effected by treating with lime the liquor with which the black ash had been extracted. The liquor was run into deep cast iron vessels, which could be heated by means of steam, and in it the lime was suspended in a cage. When causticization was complete the liquor was concentrated in large iron vessels and finally evaporated to dryness in smaller finishing pots. Towards the end of this period, however, an electrochemical process was introduced for making caustic alkali (p 250).

IV. SULPHURIC ACID

The first step in the Leblanc process was, it will be recalled, the treatment of salt with an equivalent quantity of sulphuric acid. Consequently the great expansion of the Leblanc industry called for a proportionate increase in sulphuric acid production: the latter was also required in very large quantities for many other purposes, particularly the manufacture of superphosphate as a fertilizer (p 254). During most of the period now under consideration much the greater part of the sulphuric acid required was made by the lead-chamber process (vol IV, ch 8). In the main this changed very little during the second half of the nineteenth century, but some important improvements were introduced.

In the lead-chamber process, sulphur dioxide, usually produced by burning either sulphur or pyrites, is oxidized by air to form sulphur trioxide, which in combination with water forms sulphuric acid. The conversion of the dioxide to the trioxide takes place in the presence of oxides of nitrogen, then derived from sodium nitrate imported from the vast natural deposits in Chile. Originally the spent oxides of nitrogen were allowed to escape into the air, but in 1827 J. L. Gay-Lussac (1778–1850) invented absorption-towers in which they were dissolved in concentrated sulphuric acid. It was more than thirty years, however, before this invention became generally

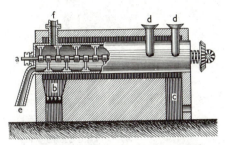

FIGURE 132—*Solvay's apparatus (1879) for calcining sodium bicarbonate to form sodium carbonate. Steam, ammonia, and carbon dioxide were drawn off through f. The first two were condensed and the carbon dioxide was returned to the carbonating tower. Calcined material was discharged through e.*

used, its introduction following the invention, by John Glover, of a denitrating tower which enabled the absorbed oxides of nitrogen to be returned to the lead chambers for further use. The Glover tower was first used in 1859 at the Washington chemical works near Durham. Thence, in conjunction with the Gay-Lussac tower, its use spread to Lancashire (1864), and soon became common practice. This important innovation much improved the economy of what was afterwards called the English process of sulphuric acid manufacture.

Pyrites came largely to replace sulphur as a source of sulphur dioxide. In 1838 Ferdinand II, King of the Two Sicilies, gave a monopoly for the export of sulphur to a French firm in Marseilles: the result was an increase in price from £5 to £14 per ton. It was soon found that iron pyrites—which for British manufacture was available in abundance in Cornwall and Wicklow—was an excellent and cheaper substitute as a source of sulphur dioxide.

Other developments, too, favoured more efficient working. The size of the lead chambers was increased—in 1864 Muspratt built one 140 × 24 × 20 ft, and by the end of the century one of twice this capacity was in use—and continuous instead of intermittent working was introduced. Acid emerging from the chambers is too dilute for many purposes and must be concentrated by removing water by evaporation: the highly corrosive nature of the acid makes this process one of some difficulty. Early in the century the work of William Hyde Wollaston (1766–1828) made it possible to employ platinum vessels for this purpose, and in the latter half of the century extensive use was made of them. Originally the platinum concentrators were constructed by a process of gold-soldering the joints, and about 160 vessels were made in Britain by this process. About 1860, however, platinum concentrators for sulphuric acid began to be made by welding the joints with the oxy-hydrogen blow-lamp.

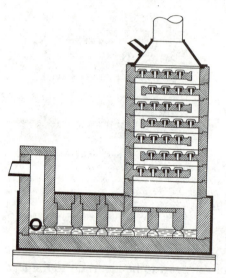

Other kinds of concentrator, utilizing waste furnace gases, were also used. For example, in the Kessler concentrator (figure 133), patented in 1891, descending streams of acid meet an uprising current of hot gas. The upper part of this concentrator, the recuperator, consists essentially of seven perforated trays, ranged one above the other and made from lava blocks. The lower part, or saturex, is constructed from lava blocks encased in lead; in it can be collected acid of 98 per cent purity if the relative rates of flow of gas and dilute acid are properly controlled.

FIGURE 133—*Kessler sulphuric acid concentrator.*

However, just as the old-established Leblanc soda process found a serious rival, so also did the lead-chamber process for sulphuric acid, although in this instance the rivalry was not so bitter—for it was originally proposed to make a form of sulphuric acid different from that obtained from lead chambers—nor did it result in the total eclipse of the older process. Again, too, it is possible to trace the origins of the new process back for many years before it became of practical significance in industry.

The basis of the new process was very simple, namely that in the presence of a catalyst (p 237) sulphur dioxide can be almost instantaneously oxidized by air to form sulphur trioxide, instead of relatively slowly, through the intermediary of oxides of nitrogen, as in the lead chamber. The first to draw attention to this was Peregrine Phillips, a Bristol vinegar manufacturer, who in 1831 patented a process in which finely divided platinum was to be used as a catalyst [13]: the combination of the sulphur trioxide with water to form sulphuric acid was to be effected in towers, packed with pebbles, down which water trickled. A number

of similar observations followed, but from these it was evident that some difficulty would arise from the fact that the catalyst gradually became 'poisoned' and
ineffective. H. G. Magnus and J. W. Döbereiner confirmed Phillips's experiments, and in 1852 Wöhler and Mahla showed that materials less expensive than
platinum, notably iron oxide, could also serve as catalysts.

However, the contact process found no application, partly because of the
various improvements made in the lead-chamber process and partly because of
the difficulties arising from the poisoning of the catalyst. It was the development
of the organic chemical industry that was mainly responsible for changing this
situation. The rapidly growing synthetic dyestuffs industry (ch 12) required large
quantities not only of pure sulphuric acid but of the form known as oleum, or
fuming sulphuric acid, which contains a considerable excess of sulphur trioxide.
The making of oleum was at that time virtually a monopoly of works in Bohemia,
where it was made by the dry distillation of iron sulphate derived from a particular form of local slate: as it required from 12 to 40 tons of slate to make 1 ton of
oleum, the price of the product was high. The contact process was potentially
well suited to supply large quantities of oleum, hence the great interest it excited.

About 1870 a German chemist, Rudolf Messel (1847–1920), found that
poisoning of the catalyst could be avoided—and the reaction in consequence
made to run for a considerable time—if the reacting gases were first carefully
purified. After the Franco-Prussian war Messel joined the firm of Squire, Chapman & Company in England, and with W. S. Squire developed a satisfactory
form of contact process which was worked at Silvertown, output eventually
rising to 1000 tons weekly. Almost on the day on which Squire filed his first
patent [14] for the contact process, Clemens Winkler published a paper [15] on
the process which excited much interest. Winkler believed that the successful
operation of the process depended upon having the sulphur dioxide and the
oxygen present in the stoichiometric ratio of 2 : 1 by volume. This belief was
erroneous, but, according to Lunge, Winkler's paper 'acted upon the industrial
chemical world like a sorcerer's wand upon pent-up spirits', for it seemed to
point the way to the manufacture of urgently needed oleum without recourse to
Bohemia.

Although Squire's patent closed development in England, Winkler's ideas
were not patented in the individual German states. In Germany, therefore,
which was rapidly becoming the world's centre for the dyestuff industry, the
making of oleum by the contact process flourished, and important works were
established, among others, by Meister Lucius and Brüning; their factory at

Hoechst-am-Rhein worked a form of the process devised by Emil Jacob. At Ludwigshafen, a careful study of the basic principles of the contact process was carried out by the *Badische Anilin-und-Soda Fabrik* as part of their extensive programme of research on the synthesis of indigo. This study led to several improvements, notably in the control of temperature, but it appears that not until after the turn of the century was it generally recognized that the composition of the gas ought not to be exactly two volumes of sulphur dioxide to one of oxygen, as Winkler had postulated.

Interest in the contact process was originally fostered by the desire to break the Bohemian monopoly in oleum, and it was not at first imagined that the process could be economically used for manufacturing ordinary sulphuric acid. Indeed, in many works the mixture of sulphur dioxide and oxygen used in the contact process was obtained by the pyrolysis of ordinary lead-chamber sulphuric acid.

V. SOME ELECTROCHEMICAL PROCESSES

Other important industrial chemical developments of the latter half of the nineteenth century stemmed from a process for the manufacture of sodium devised by an American chemist, Hamilton Young Castner (1858–99). In 1824 the Danish chemist H. C. Oersted (1777–1851) discovered that sodium, which Humphry Davy had first isolated in 1807, would reduce aluminium chloride to metallic aluminium. Three years later the German chemist, F. Wöhler (1800–82), discovered that metallic potassium would effect the same reduction, and an industrial process of aluminium manufacture was developed on this basis: the cost of the potassium was so high, however, as to make the cost of aluminium prohibitive—about £55 a pound.

In 1854 R. W. von Bunsen (1811–99) and H. E. Sainte-Claire Deville (1818–81) developed a similar process using sodium, which, although expensive, could be made more cheaply than potassium. Despite the financial support of Louis Napoleon this venture, too, failed owing to the high cost of the aluminium produced. Nevertheless, the remarkable properties of aluminium and the abundance of its principal ore, bauxite, stimulated the search for a cheap method of producing sodium. Deville's method was to reduce caustic soda with charcoal at a high temperature, but it proved difficult to mix these two substances uniformly owing to the relative lightness of the charcoal, and the reduction was slow and inefficient.

Castner overcame this difficulty by literally weighing down the charcoal with iron. He melted together pitch and fine iron filings and converted the product to coke by pyrolysis in a crucible. This coke mixed readily with molten caustic soda. The reduction was effected in a furnace (plate 11 A) at a little below 1000° C, and the sodium was distilled off and collected. Castner's process produced sodium at about 9*d* a pound, compared with 14*s* by Deville's method.

The way seemed clear for the cheap production of aluminium, but Castner failed to secure the interest of American industrialists. Coming to England, he obtained the support of the Webster Crown Metal Company at Solihull, then manufacturing small quantities of aluminium at about £3 a pound. This led to the formation of a new company—The Aluminium Company Limited—to work Castner's process, and in 1888 a factory was built at Oldbury designed to produce 100 000 lb of aluminium yearly. After some early difficulties, due to iron being carried over into the aluminium, success seemed assured, but in 1886 C. M. Hall (1863–1914) in America and P. L. T. Héroult (1863–1914) in France independently patented a process for the manufacture of aluminium by electrolysis of aluminium oxide in molten cryolite (p 91). Castner could not compete with this at all, nor could he work the new process under licence as it demanded cheap electricity, which was not available to him at Oldbury.

Castner was thus in an unenviable position, for his only remaining asset was a cheap process for manufacturing metallic sodium, for which there was now little demand. From this situation, however, a variety of important developments arose as Castner turned his attention to the conversion of sodium into useful compounds.

First he began to manufacture sodium peroxide, in considerable demand as a bleaching agent for woollens and the then very fashionable straw hats, by burning sodium in a current of air in aluminium trays. At first disastrous explosions occurred, but the process was eventually brought under control by carefully regulating the temperature. He then began to manufacture sodium cyanide by a process involving the passing of ammonia over molten sodium. This resulted in the formation of sodamide, which in the molten state was poured over red-hot charcoal. Sodium cyanamide was formed and then sodium cyanide. Later, in 1894, Castner patented a better process in which sodium cyanide was made in one stage by reaction between ammonia, charcoal, and sodium. A very large market for sodium cyanide was established as a result of gold-mining developments in Australia, America, South Africa, and elsewhere, where the Forrest–MacArthur process (patented in 1887) was, after initial scepticism, being widely used for the extraction of gold and silver from ores (p 95). For this purpose potassium cyanide was originally used, but weight for weight sodium cyanide

is more effective. Nevertheless, it took the gold-mining industry some time
to appreciate this point, and at first Castner was driven to the subterfuge of
marketing his sodium cyanide as '130 per cent potassium cyanide'.

However, Castner already had an interest in the manufacture of potassium
cyanide, which was then made by fusing potassium ferrocyanide with sodium.
This process was worked by the *Deutsche Gold- und Silber-Scheide Anstalt*,
to whom the Aluminium Company, by an agreement reached in 1891, supplied
all the necessary sodium. In 1893, however, the Cassel Gold Extraction Company of Glasgow, which had acquired the
rights in the Forrest–MacArthur process,
began to manufacture potassium cyanide
by a process invented by George Beilby
(1850–1924): in this, ammonia was passed
over a molten mixture of potassium carbonate and charcoal. This process proved
not so satisfactory as Castner's, however,
and in 1900 the Cassel Gold Extraction
Company began to work the latter, using
sodium manufactured by the Aluminium Company.

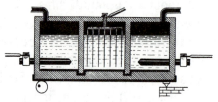

FIGURE 134—*Castner–Kellner cell for manufacture
of caustic soda by electrolysis of brine. The three
compartments are mechanically separated, but kept
in electrical contact, by a layer of mercury at the
bottom. The cell is rocked by the cam on the left.*

All these developments had an unforeseen consequence: far from having an
embarrassing quantity of sodium available, the Aluminium Company now found
it difficult to keep up with the demand. Accordingly, Castner investigated the
possibility of making the metal by the electrolysis of caustic soda. He achieved a
measure of success, but found that impurities, particularly silica, in even the
best caustic soda then available imposed severe limitations upon him. With
characteristic determination, he decided to seek a new industrial method for
making very pure caustic soda.

Again he turned to the possibility of an electrochemical process, made feasible
by the rapidly growing electrical industry (ch 10). It was at that time well known
that electrolysis of a solution of common salt yielded chlorine at the anode and
sodium hydroxide (caustic soda) and hydrogen at the cathode, but there was no
satisfactory method of separating the caustic soda from residual salt. Castner
overcame this difficulty by using a cell containing mercury (figure 134). The cell,
made originally of slate, was divided into three compartments by two partitions
reaching almost to the bottom. In the bottom was placed mercury, which formed
the cathode, sufficient to reach a point just above the bottoms of these partitions,
thus forming three separate compartments. The two end compartments were
filled with brine, into which passed carbon anodes: the middle compartment

contained water. As electrolysis proceeded, sodium ions were discharged at the mercury cathode, and dissolved in it as an amalgam. This amalgam was made to circulate by rocking the whole cell by means of a rotating cam at one end: early attempts to circulate it by pumps proved unsuccessful. When the sodium amalgam came into contact with the water in the centre compartment the sodium reacted to form caustic soda. By adding more brine to the end compartments, and periodically removing the caustic soda solution from the middle compartment and replacing it by fresh water, the process could be made continuous. A battery of cells of this kind was first successfully worked at Oldbury in 1894 (plate 11 B). The product was almost 100 per cent pure caustic soda, a product then unknown in the alkali trade. It was valuable to Castner for the manufacture of sodium, but also had great possibilities for the manufacture of paper, textiles, oils, and soaps. A profitable by-product was chlorine, which could be converted into bleaching powder, for which there was a very large market.

The idea of the mercury cell was not, however, entirely novel. It had been investigated in 1883 by the Belgian chemist A. L. Nolf, and by E. A. Le Sueur in 1889. The latter's cells, which contained a porous diaphragm, met with a good deal of success, especially at Berlin, New Hampshire. At about the same time as that during which Castner was carrying out his investigations, an Austrian chemist, Carl Kellner (1850–1905), became interested in electrochemical processes. When, in the summer of 1894, Castner began to take out international patents for his mercury rocking-cell he found that in Germany he had been anticipated by Kellner, who had patented an apparently similar process and had formed the *Konsortium für electrochemische Industrie* to work it at Golling, near Salzburg. The other European rights he sold to Solvay & Company in Brussels. Rather than face long and expensive litigation, Castner reached an agreement with Kellner to exchange their patents and processes. However, the process has in fact always been worked according to Castner's patents, and never according to Kellner's. The latter's process is at first sight very similar to Castner's, but in fact the halves of the cell are not electrically balanced and if an attempt were made to work it cumulative difficulties would arise through oxidation of the mercury. Nevertheless, the process is generally known as the Castner–Kellner process.

It was impossible to work the process on a large scale at Oldbury, owing to the difficulty of obtaining brine and the high local cost of electricity. Eventually a suitable site was found at Runcorn, in the Cheshire salt area. A new company, the Castner–Kellner Alkali Company, was formed, and a works was built which began operation in 1897. Its capacity was nearly 20 tons of pure caustic soda per day, and 40 tons of bleach. Power was supplied by three 200 hp steam engines. In the United States the Mathieson Alkali Company built a pilot plant at Saltville, Virginia, and its success in 1896 led to the immediate building of a bigger plant at Niagara Falls, where cheap electricity was available.

VI. PHOSPHORUS

The element phosphorus was discovered in 1669 by Brand, who made it by pyrolysis of a mixture of sand and concentrated urine. Exactly a century later

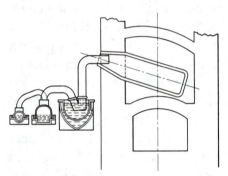

J. G. Gahn showed that the element was an essential constituent of bones, and this paved the way for C. W. Scheele (1742–86) to prepare it from bone ash.

Until about 1890 the general method of preparation was to treat bones, or mineral phosphates such as apatite, with hot sulphuric acid in large wooden vats lined with lead. This yielded a syrupy solution of phosphoric acid, which was mixed with some form of carbon (ground coal or charcoal) and dried in iron pots.

FIGURE 135—*Coal-fired phosphorus retort, and condensers.*

The resulting black mass was powdered and loaded into fireclay retorts, each about 4 ft long and 8 in wide, into which short cast iron stems were luted. The charged retorts were loaded into a furnace fired by coal, in such a way that the ends of the iron stems dipped beneath the surface of water in a long trough (figure 135). During the course of some sixteen hours the phosphorus distilled over and condensed at the bottom of the troughs. From this stage onward the phosphorus had to be kept under water, since it is spontaneously combustible on exposure to air. The crude phosphorus was refined by treatment with sodium dichromate and sulphuric acid, and was then soldered into tins for dispatch.

A considerable demand for phosphorus arose in the first half of the nineteenth century for the making of matches. Phosphorus-containing matches are said to have been invented by Charles Sauria, a French chemistry student, who tipped his matches with a mixture of phosphorus, potassium chlorate, antimony sulphide, sulphur, and gum. He did not patent his invention, however, or seek to manufacture matches: the first to do so was a German, J. F. Kammerer, in 1833.

The manufacture of phosphorus for making matches was primarily established in France and Germany. Until 1844 production in England did not exceed three-quarters of a ton annually, but in that year manufacture was begun by Arthur

Albright and Edmund Sturge at Selly Oak, Birmingham. In 1849 a bigger works was built at Oldbury, to meet the immense popular demand for matches.

The highly poisonous nature of phosphorus gravely affected the health of those who worked in the match factories, and Albright, a staunch Quaker, had serious misgivings about the propriety of continuing to supply them. It was, therefore, with great interest that he learned that in 1845 Anton Schroetter, in Vienna, had discovered that if ordinary (white) phosphorus is heated in a closed iron pot it is converted into an 'amorphous' (actually microcrystalline) form which is neither poisonous nor spontaneously combustible. It demands great care in its manufacture, however, as the process is liable to be violently explosive.

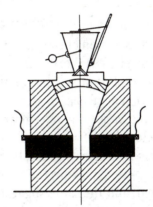

Albright acquired Schroetter's patent and began to manufacture amorphous phosphorus, but he found great difficulty in using it for the manufacture of 'strike anywhere' matches. However, some of the amorphous form, which had been displayed at the Great Exhibition of 1851, was taken back to Sweden by the Lundström brothers, who solved the problem of making 'safety' matches with it and purchased large quantities of Albright's product. The principle of the safety match was

FIGURE 136—*Original electric phosphorus furnace, worked at Wednesfield.*

that amorphous phosphorus was incorporated in the striker on the box but there was no phosphorus in the head of the match.

In 1855 Albright's partnership with Sturge ended, probably because the latter was not optimistic about the future of amorphous phosphorus, and he entered into partnership with John Wilson, thus founding the firm of Albright & Wilson, which subsequently became so well known as phosphorus manufacturers.

In the latter part of the century various improvements in phosphorus manufacture were effected. Gas-fired furnaces were introduced by Coignet et Cie in France, but a much more revolutionary development was the introduction of the electrothermal process in 1888, patented by J. B. Readman and T. Parker. This process signified more than a change in the method of heating; it converted a basically uneconomic batch process into a continuous one, an innovation allowing much more efficient working. The electric furnace (figure 136) is charged with a mixture of lumps of mineral phosphate, coal, and sand. Slag is removed periodically and there is continuous evolution of vaporized phosphorus, which is condensed.

The electrothermal process satisfactorily made the manufacture a continuous one, but it was not the first such attempt to be made. In 1887 J. B. Readman attempted manufacture in a blast-furnace near Edinburgh, but this was un-successful as it proved impossible to keep the furnace hot enough for the slag to be removed. Successful operation of the blast-furnace process depends on working on a really large scale—of the order of 15 000 tons per year—but this was not achieved until very much later.

VII. CALCIUM SUPERPHOSPHATE AND OTHER FERTILIZERS

Discussion of the manufacture of calcium superphosphate appropriately follows that of phosphorus, for the first stages of the two processes are very similar. Superphosphate, one of the most valuable of all agricultural fertilizers, came into general use in the latter half of the nineteenth century, although its pos-sibilities seem to have been appreciated a great deal earlier. As early as 1808 some field trials of vitriolized bones were made near Belfast, and it is recorded that this treatment yielded luxuriant crops. In 1835 Escher, a Brünn schoolmaster, suggested making the phosphate of bones soluble by treatment with sulphuric acid, and the same suggestion was made by Liebig in 1840. Neither Escher nor Liebig, however, sought to put this idea to practical use, although it became fairly widely known. The first to make superphosphate commercially was James Murray (1788–1871), a Dublin physician [16], who carried out his earliest experi-ments about 1817. In 1835 he pointed out that superphosphate could be made by treating with sulphuric acid not only bones but mineral phosphate rock. Six years later he was actively engaged in the production of mixed fertilizers containing superphosphate, guano, and Chilean nitrate. Murray's method of manufacturing superphosphate, patented in 1842, consisted in mixing mineral phosphate with an equal weight of sulphuric acid in an earthenware vessel, and well agitating the mixture for two or three days. At the end of this time, it was mixed with some absorbent material, such as bran or sawdust. This yielded a dry, powdery fertilizer, easy to handle, which was sold in 280-lb casks.

Although the first in the field, Murray did not make a success of his venture, and the first to manufacture superphosphate successfully on a large scale was John Bennet Lawes (1814–1900), who from 1834 onwards carried out extensive agricultural experiments on his estate at Rothamsted. In 1843 Lawes established a large superphosphate factory near London, which by the 1870s was manufactur-ing some 40 000 tons annually.

Phosphorus, very conveniently applied to the land as superphosphate, is only one of several essential plant nutrients. No less important are compounds of nitrogen, which today are made synthetically in enormous quantities by the fixation of atmospheric nitrogen. Up to the end of the nineteenth century, however, the principal accessory source of nitrogen as plant food was *caliche* (p 320), natural sodium nitrate. Small beds of this occur in many places, but the only industrially important ones are those in the province of Tarapacá on the west coast of Chile. There it occurs in beds some 1–5 ft in depth, overlaid by a few feet of rock. After mining, the *caliche* is crushed and then extracted with hot water, in open tanks, until a saturated solution is obtained. This is allowed to cool, when sodium nitrate of about 95 per cent purity crystallizes out. World consumption of sodium nitrate in 1900 was 1 350 000 tons, of which European countries, mainly Germany, consumed 1 152 000 tons and the United States 170 000 tons. A great deal of this went as fertilizer, and much of the remainder as a source of nitrous fumes for making sulphuric acid. Potassium nitrate, an essential ingredient of gunpowder (p 285), was made by double decomposition of sodium nitrate and potassium chloride. If a hot saturated solution of these two salts is allowed to cool, sodium chloride separates out, leaving the much more freely soluble potassium nitrate in solution. Before the development of methods of fixing atmospheric nitrogen, nitric acid was made by distilling a mixture of sodium or potassium nitrate and sulphuric acid in cast iron retorts. The condensers and receivers were made of glass or of some acid-resistant alloy.

The latter half of the nineteenth century also saw an important change in the source of the third principal element, potassium, necessary for the growth of plants. Up to about 1870 the traditional source of potassium salts, both as fertilizers and for manufacturing purposes, was the ash of plants. A century ago the world's principal source of plant ash was Canada, where in 1871 there were 519 asheries, consuming well over 4 m tons of wood a year. The process of potash production was simple: the ashes were extracted with water and the solution was evaporated, after filtration through straw, in iron pots. If pearl ash, the best grade, was required, the crude potash was calcined in a reverberatory furnace at the ashery. Similar processes were worked wherever there was an abundance of wood, pulp, or other easily combustible plant material.

About 1870, however, the vast deposits of potassium salts at Stassfurt, near Magdeburg, began to be worked. The effect on the wood-ash industry was immediate. By 1891, for example, the number of Canadian asheries had fallen to 128. At the turn of the century the industry was almost extinct, although it enjoyed a temporary revival during the first world war.

REFERENCES

[1] British Patent No. 7267. 1836.
[2] British Patent No. 1403. 1868.
[3] British Patent No. 2476. 1870.
[4] British Patent No. 2277. 1862.
[5] British Patent No. 518. 1857.
[6] CHANCE, K. M. *Chem. & Ind.*, **22**, 298, 1944.
[7] British Patent No. 3608. 1882.
[8] ALLEN, J. F. 'Some Founders of the Chemical Industry', pp. 213–20. Sherratt & Hughes, London. 1906.
[9] British Patent No. 887. 1853.
[10] British Patent No. 7713. 1838.
[11] HEEREN, F. *Dinglers J.*, **149**, 47, 1858.
[12] British Patent No. 1525. 1872.
[13] British Patent No. 6096. 1831.
[14] British Patent No. 3278. 1875.
[15] WINKLER, C. *Dinglers J.*, **218**, 128, 1875.
[16] ALFORD, W. A. L. *Chem. & Ind.*, **31**, 852, 1953.

BIBLIOGRAPHY

ALLEN, J. F. 'Some Founders of the Chemical Industry.' Sherratt & Hughes, London. 1906.
BARKER, T. C. and HARRIS, J. R. 'A Merseyside Town in the Industrial Revolution: St Helens 1750–1900.' University Press, Liverpool. 1954.
'Fifty Years of Progress; the Story of the Castner–Kellner Alkali Company.' Imperial Chemical Industries Limited, London. 1947.
HABER, L. F. 'The Chemical Industry during the Nineteenth Century.' Oxford University Press, London. 1958.
HARDIE, D. W. F. 'A History of the Chemical Industry in Widnes.' Imperial Chemical Industries Limited, London. 1950.
HAYNES, W. 'American Chemical Industry', Vol. 1 (1609–1911). Van Nostrand, New York. 1954.
KINGZETT, C. T. 'The History, Products, and Processes of the Alkali Trade.' London. 1877.
LUNGE, G. 'A Theoretical and Practical Treatise on the Manufacture of Sulphuric Acid and Alkali' (3rd ed.). Gurney & Jackson, London. 1903.
MIALL, S. 'History of the British Chemical Industry.' Benn, London. 1931.
MORGAN, SIR GILBERT T. and PRATT, D. D. 'British Chemical Industry; its Rise and Development.' Arnold, London. 1938.
'The Struggle for Supremacy; being a Series of Chapters in the History of the Leblanc Alkali Industry in Great Britain.' Walmsley, Liverpool. 1907.
THRELFALL, R. E. 'The Story of 100 Years of Phosphorus Making, 1851–1951.' Albright & Wilson, Oldbury. 1951.
WARRINGTON, C. J. S. and NICHOLLS, R. V. V. (Eds) 'A History of Chemistry in Canada.' Pitman, Toronto. 1949.
WILLIAMS, T. I. 'The Chemical Industry Past and Present.' Penguin Books, Harmondsworth. 1953.

12

DYESTUFFS IN THE NINETEENTH CENTURY

E. J. HOLMYARD

I. INTRODUCTORY

IN spite of the rapid development of both pure and applied chemistry in the first half of the nineteenth century, there was during that time no significant addition to the palette of dyes available. With the exception of picric acid, which was discovered in 1771 by Woulfe and independently in 1788 by Hausmann and Klaproth, and which was later used as a yellow dye for silk and wool, dyestuffs were all of vegetable or insect origin and their number had not increased since the Middle Ages. That fact does not imply stagnation in the art of dyeing: on the contrary, the vast extension of textile manufacture during the industrial revolution had led to intense efforts at the improvement of methods of dyeing. These efforts were not confined to professional dyers, or to such exceptional figures as C. L. Berthollet (1748–1822), an accomplished French chemist who was also director of the Gobelins tapestry establishment, but were shared by many scientists interested in the fascinating problems presented by the subject. The discovery of chlorine and other bleaching agents (vol IV, p 247), and Nicolas Leblanc's invention of a method of manufacturing soda (sodium carbonate) from salt and limestone (vol IV, p 239), greatly assisted the work of the dyer. The standardization of auxiliary chemicals and a more scrupulous attention to the details of procedure, following upon the growing realization that dyeing rested very largely on a chemical basis, resulted in much greater reliability. At the same time versatile—though empirical—ingenuity widened the range of effects that could be obtained.

When so much has been said, however, the fact remains that the contemporary repertoire of useful dyes still comprised scarcely more than a dozen. The most important of them were cochineal and kermes, madder, indigo, logwood and brasil-wood, old and young fustic, weld, cutch or catechu, and the yellow dyes saffron, safflower, and annatto. These had already been in use for centuries, and have been mentioned earlier in this work (vol III, pp 692–5), but in view of their enormously increased application in the nineteenth century some further reference to them is necessary in the present volume. It is too often assumed that the nineteenth century was wholly the century of man-made dyes, when in point of fact the 'natural' dyes were pre-eminent for about three-quarters of the period.

II. COCHINEAL AND KERMES

Cochineal and kermes (vol II, p 366) were very widely used as bright red dyes, especially when mordanted (p 280) with a tin salt to give scarlet. They are both obtained from the dried bodies of female scale-insects parasitic on certain plants, kermes being native to the Old World and cochineal to the New. The cochineal insect (*Dactylopius coccus*) hails from Mexico, where it lives on the cactus known as prickly pear or Indian fig (*Opuntia fico-indica*) and other species. Plantations of such cacti were established in Mexico for the purpose of breeding the insects, of which two or three generations were obtained annually. The females, which are wingless, were collected, killed by heat, and then dried; about 200 000 of them are required to give a kilogram of the dye.

Towards the end of the eighteenth century, when the demand for cochineal was rising rapidly, attempts were made to breed the insects in India. These attempts failed, but a somewhat similar insect, *Tachardia lacca*, had long been used in that country as a source of the red pigment known as lac (vol II, p 362). Greater success attended the introduction of the cochineal insect into Spain (1820) and particularly the Canary Islands (1826); in the latter the plantations organized by Santiago de la Cruz brought in a considerable revenue. In 1828 an agent of the Dutch government covertly studied the methods of cochineal-growing practised at Cadiz, secured about a thousand of the insect-bearing cacti, bribed one of the experts to accompany him, and was conveyed to Java with his spoils by a Dutch gunboat. However, this piratical venture was not strikingly successful; neither were subsequent French attempts to grow cochineal in Algeria. On the other hand, good results were obtained in Guatemala, Nicaragua, and other Central American countries, the production in Guatemala finally out-stripping that of Mexico itself. Later on in the century the Canary Islands became the chief producer of cochineal, exporting in 1869 no less than 2 717 000 kg.

The price of cochineal varied considerably, but the average was about 9s or 10s a pound: high enough to occasion a good deal of adulteration with vegetable refuse, inferior kermes, sand, white lead, and other materials. It is said that sophistication went so far as to produce 'cochineal grains' consisting of nothing more than powdered glass, resin, and clay.

Upon the discovery of synthetic red dyes soon after the middle of the nineteenth century the price of cochineal fell considerably, though for a time the production was maintained or even increased; but by 1880 the competition of the artificial dyes had made the cultivation of cochineal uneconomic. Only small quantities are now produced, mainly for colouring foodstuffs.

Kermes (vol II, p 366), like cochineal, consists of the dried bodies of female scale-insects (*Coccus ilicis*). These insects infest the kermes oak (*Quercus coccifera*) which grows abundantly in Mediterranean countries, particularly Syria, Lebanon, and Palestine; they are about the size of a small pea. When dried and pounded they yield a red dye, soluble in water and in alcohol. Kermes is one of the most ancient of all dyes, and is mentioned in the Old Testament; the Hebrew name for it was *tola'at shani*, or worm-scarlet.

The kermes 'berries' are gathered annually by hand-picking at the season when the insects themselves are dead but contain viable eggs. They are treated with a weak acid, such as vinegar, to kill the eggs, and are then packed in kegs.

The bright red colour imparted to fabrics by kermes was popular over a very long period, the centre of the trade in the Middle Ages being Venice. Cloth dyed with *écarlate de Venise*, made from kermes and cream of tartar with alum as mordant, was highly prized throughout Europe, and in 1498 Vasco da Gama presented a quantity of it to the king of Calicut. In

FIGURE 137—*The madder plant*, Rubia tinctorum *L.*

later centuries kermes was used to dye the fez, at one time *de rigueur* in much of the world of Islam; this use was in itself the basis of a large industry, reaching its peak about 1850. In that year, for example, Austria derived an income of over 12 m florins from the manufacture and export of fezes. Yet the days of kermes were nearly over; competition from cochineal at first, and from synthetic dyes subsequently, soon resulted in the virtual extinction of the age-old trade in this venerable scarlet colouring-matter.

The red substances in both cochineal (carminic acid) and kermes (kermic acid) are derivatives of anthraquinone (p 276).

III. MADDER

Madder is another dyestuff with a history stretching back beyond the written word. It is obtained from the madder plant, *Rubia tinctorum* L (figure 137), which was cultivated for at least two thousand years and which, though not native to Britain, may still be met with here as a casual. Madder is mentioned in the 'Saxon Leechdom' of *c* 1000, and in one of his minor poems, written about 1374, Chaucer says of bygone times:

> *A blisful lyf, a paisible and a swete*
> *Ledden the peples in the former age. . . .*

when there were, among other things lacking,

> *No mader, welde, or woad . . .*

and where

> *. . . the flese was of his former hewe.*

In the Middle Ages madder was used on a large scale for the dyeing of wool, the centre of the English madder trade being at Norwich, as the Maddermarket Theatre of that city may serve to remind us. Some English place-names, such as Matterdale ('madder valley') in Cumberland and Mayfield ('madder field') in Staffordshire, indicate that the plant was cultivated in many different parts of the country. Madder was also widely grown on the continent, and Charlemagne gave orders that the women's workshops on his rural estates should be well furnished with wool, linen, woad, madder, wool-combs, teasels, soap, and other necessaries for the weaving and dyeing of textiles.

The importance of madder continued to increase with the passage of time, the bulk of the crop being produced in Holland until the Revolution in France; then the French government sponsored its cultivation in Alsace and Provence and the Dutch quasi-monopoly was broken. Patronage was continued by later governments, Louis Philippe (1830–48) providing a colourful stimulus by dressing his infantry in the famous *pantalon garance* or madder-red trousers. He may have recollected that an English sovereign, Henry II (1154–89), applied a similar stimulus, for the same purpose, by ordering red coats to be worn in the hunting-field.

The madder plant is a perennial evergreen shrub with lanceolate leaves, yellow flowers, and reddish-brown berry-like fruits. The dye is obtained chiefly from the cortex of the long, slender roots, which contain the glucoside ruberythric acid. On hydrolysis, this yields the dye proper, alizarin, together with the two sugars glucose and xylose. It was customary to take the roots of one- or two-year-old plants, wash and dry them, and then powder them; the powder was put on the market in tubs or linen sacks.

When the chemical constitution of alizarin was discovered by Graebe and Liebermann in 1868–9 (p 276), the madder industry was doomed. Synthetic alizarin came into industrial use two years later, and the trade in the natural product expired after a very short interval. Dyeing with alizarin is considered on p 278.

IV. INDIGO

Many plants, but particularly the indigo plant (*Indigofera tinctoria* L) (figure 138) and woad (*Isatis tinctoria* L), contain a glucoside known as indican. When indican is hydrolysed with acids or by fermentation it yields glucose and indoxyl, the latter being readily oxidized by atmospheric oxygen to the blue dye indigotin or 'indigo' (vol II, pp 364–5). Prepared from the indigo plant or from woad in this way, the indigo is always mixed with a certain amount of impurities, such as indigo red, indigo brown, and a glutinous substance. Synthetic indigotin (p 278) is free from these contaminants.

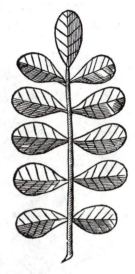

FIGURE 138—*The indigo plant*, Indigofera tinctoria *L.*

Woad gives a much smaller yield of indigo than that obtained from the indigo plant, but was extensively cultivated in England and other European countries before import of indigo from India reached a level that made woad-growing unprofitable. The growers did not succumb without a struggle, and in 1577 imported indigo was denounced in England as a 'newly invented, harmful, balefully devouring, pernicious, deceitful, eating and corrosive dye'. Similar condemnation was made of it by Henri IV of France, who commanded that those who used indigo should suffer the penalty of death, while at Nuremberg the dyers were required to take an oath that they would eschew it. It is strange that the identity of Indian indigo with the blue substance obtained from woad, and even its vegetable origin, were not realized: in 1705 English letters-patent were granted for mining it.

In spite of opposition, however, Indian indigo continued to win popularity, and by the middle of the seventeenth century its success was assured. About a hundred years later an enterprising American woman, Eliza Pinckney, started growing the indigo plant in Carolina and met with such success that the British government granted a bounty of 6*d* a pound on the American indigo; but the industry did not last long, since crops of cotton and rice gave bigger profits.

In the extraction of indigo from the indigo plant, the freshly cut plants were fermented under slightly warm water, when a yellowish solution was obtained. This was rendered alkaline and aerated by vigorous stirring, the indigo then settling out as a blue precipitate which was allowed to collect as a sludge at the bottom of the vat. The sludge was afterwards boiled with water, to prevent further fermentation, and filtered and dried, the dried product being made up

into cakes for marketing (vol III, figure 422). As with cochineal, there was often much adulteration and the dyer had to rely on his experience and acuteness of observation in judging the quality of the indigo offered for sale.

Indigotin is insoluble in water and has to be converted into a soluble derivative before it can dye. This derivative is known as the 'leuco' form of indigotin, because it is colourless (Greek *leukos*, white). In chemical terms it is a reduction product of indigotin, and the reduction was formerly effected by adding the indigo to a vat of fermenting woad containing also lime, bran, and a little madder. The cloth to be dyed was dipped in the vat and then exposed to the air, when the leuco-indigotin (indigo white) absorbed in the fibres was oxidized back to indigotin; this was precipitated in the fibres which were thus coloured blue. With synthetic indigotin (p 278) the reduction to the leuco form is now carried

FIGURE 139—*Woad*, Isatis tinctoria *L.*

out much more simply and satisfactorily by the use of alkaline sodium dithionite or proprietary substances such as Rongalite C (sodium formaldehyde-sulphoxylate). Leuco-indigo is an article of the export trade on account of the ease with which dyeing may be effected with it.

Indigofera tinctoria is a leguminous plant, but woad (*Isatis tinctoria* L) (figure 139) belongs to the Cruciferae. It is herbaceous in habit, with sessile stem-leaves and an inflorescence in the form of a corymbose panicle of yellow flowers. Though no longer cultivated it still occurs sporadically, as, for example, near Tewkesbury

in the Severn valley and in Somerset, where woad-growing was once an important industry—Glastonbury, indeed, derives its name from the Old Celtic *glasto-*,
woad.

The woad leaves were picked by hand, and while still fresh were crushed by
wooden rollers in a woad-mill (figure 140). The pulp was shaped into balls (vol II,
figures 325, 332), which were allowed to dry and then powdered. The powder
was mixed with water and left to ferment for some weeks, a process accompanied
by the emission of such a revolting stench that Elizabeth I banned woad-mills

FIGURE 140—*Woad-mill at Wisbech.*

within a radius of five miles of any of her country residences. The liquid expressed
from the leaves was similarly objectionable, and there are numerous records of
complaints that it fouled the streams into which it was allowed to run.

In spite of the competition from Indian, and later synthetic, indigo, especially
after the introduction of dithionite reduction, woad continued in use until well
into the twentieth century, the last two woad-mills in England not being closed
down until the 1930s.

V. LOGWOOD AND BRASIL-WOOD

In 1517 Hernández de Córdoba landed in Mexico at the site of the pre-
Columbian town of Kimpech. Not many years afterwards (1540) the Spaniards
founded a new town there, the modern Campeche. In the neighbouring forests
they discovered certain gnarled and ribbed trees the wood of which when steeped
in water gave a solution that would dye fabrics dark blue, purple, or black. This

wood was known as Campeche wood or campeachy wood, acquiring later the more generally used name of logwood. Logwood trees belong to the Leguminaceae, the botanical name being *Haematoxylon campeachianum*; they occur native in much of Central America and have long been cultivated in Cuba, Jamaica, and other parts of the Caribbean region. The use of the wood as a dye-source was introduced into Spain about the middle of the sixteenth century.

The colouring-matter of logwood, haematein, is obtained from the heart-wood. When freshly cut, this wood is colourless, but on exposure to the air it turns dark in colour, a colourless substance in it, haematoxylin, being quickly oxidized to the dark purple haematein. Haematoxylin is in fact the leuco form of haematein.

To extract the dye, the wood is converted into small chips which are heated in steam under pressure and then left in heaps for a varying time. The mass is subsequently treated with hot water and the haematein obtained by evaporation of the solution.

In dyeing with logwood, various shades can be produced by the use of different mordants, but the most valuable is black, which is obtained with a mordant of iron and tannin. Though largely superseded by synthetic black dyes, logwood is still unequalled for producing beautiful black shades on silk and is commonly used for that purpose. On a minor scale it finds application as a stain for biological work (p 281), particularly in histology, and as an indicator (p 282).

Brasil-wood comes from another leguminous tree, *Caesalpinia braziliensis*. It contains a leuco compound, brazilin, very similar to haematoxylin in constitution, and on exposure to air the brazilin is oxidized to the corresponding colouring-matter, brazilein. Brasil-wood trees grow in both the Old World and the New and were therefore well known to Europeans. When a Portuguese expedition reached the eastern coasts of South America in 1500, under Pedro Alvarez Cabral, its members were so much impressed by the number of brasil-wood trees growing there that they nicknamed the district *tierra de brasil*. Cabral would have preferred 'Tierra de Vera Cruz', but the nickname won. Brazil is thus the land of brasil-wood (vol II, p 367); but the origin of the word brasil is unknown.

Brazilein is still used to some extent, but mainly in admixture with other dyes to produce variations of shade.

VI. FUSTIC

Two kinds of wood used for dyeing yellow are known as fustic, from the Arabic *fustuq* and ultimately from the Greek *pistake*, pistachio. The one that has been employed by far the longer of the two is paradoxically called 'young' fustic;

it is botanically quite unrelated to the other variety, 'old' fustic. Young fustic, otherwise Zante fustic, is the wood of the Venetian sumach, *Rhus cotinus*, belonging to the Anacardiaceae (which natural order also includes the cashew). Chips of the wood are steeped in water, and the solution, which contains the colouring matter fisetin, is used with various mordants to produce on cotton and wool shades ranging from yellow through orange to a dark green; in conjunction with logwood it gives black.

Old fustic is more important than young fustic and has continued in use to the present day. It is the wood of *Chlorophora tinctoria*, a tree belonging to the mulberry order, Moraceae, and native to Central America and the West Indies. Its colouring-matter, morin, is extracted as for fisetin, and the solution is used for dyeing cotton and wool, principally mixed with logwood. Chemically, both fisetin and morin are derivatives of flavone, an interesting compound that occurs naturally as a white coating on the leaves and flower-stalks of certain species of *Primula*.

VII. WELD AND CUTCH

Weld, or dyer's rocket (figure 141), has the botanical name *Reseda luteola* L, and

FIGURE 141—*Weld*, Reseda luteola L.

is a member of the mignonette family, Resedaceae. As a source of yellow dye it has been used since prehistoric times and according to J. G. D. Clark was gathered by the Neolithic lake-dwellers of Switzerland, presumably for that purpose. It is indigenous in much of Europe, west Asia, north Africa, and the Canary Islands, and was introduced into America. Weld was early cultivated, the plants growing wild not being nearly sufficient to meet the demand in such countries as ancient Rome, where the yellow colour it imparts to fabrics was much prized. In later times it was used in England, in conjunction with woad, to give the celebrated Lincoln green.

Weld is a biennial herbaceous plant, some 3 or 4 ft high. The stems and leaves were cut, dried in the air, and made up into bundles for sale. The yellow colouring-matter was extracted by infusion in water; like fisetin and morin it is a flavone derivative and is known as luteolin.

Cutch or *catechu* is a brown dye obtained from various trees in India, Malaya, and Burma; they include species of mimosa and acacia. The colouring-matter is obtained by extracting the leaves with water, followed by evaporation. It is yet another flavone derivative, namely catechin. Though not of wide application, cutch is used in conjunction with certain metallic salts to dye fishing-nets, sails, canvas tents, and the like, as it not only gives an attractive shade of brown but adds to the life of the fabric.

VIII. SAFFRON, SAFFLOWER, AND ANNATTO

Until the advent of synthetic dyes in the second half of the nineteenth century yellow colouring-matters were very limited in number and not of the same tinctorial value as madder and indigo. The principal varieties were saffron, safflower, and annatto. All three remained in use throughout the period and still find limited employment.

Saffron is obtained from the stigmas of the saffron crocus, *Crocus sativa*, a member of the Iridaceae native to Greece, Persia, and Asia Minor. It was formerly cultivated in England near Saffron Walden, Essex, and in Spain, where it was probably introduced by the Moors; the word saffron is derived from the Arabic name of the plant, *za'farān*. According to Hakluyt (1552?–1616) it was brought to England in the fourteenth century by a pilgrim who, returning from Tripoli and thinking to do his country a good turn, 'hid two saffron corms in his staff, made hollow for that purpose, all this at some danger to his safety, for had he been apprehended he had died of the fact'. However this may be, saffron was a regular crop in England until towards the end of the eighteenth century, the growers being known as crokers: still a common patronymic in some parts of the country.

The stigmas are dried in sieves over charcoal stoves, about 4000 of them being required to yield an ounce of the dyestuff; this contains the colouring-matter in the form of a glucoside. At the present time saffron is used chiefly in cookery, medicine, and perfumery, but it is even yet not quite extinct as a dye.

Safflower is a plant belonging to the Cynareae tribe of the very large natural order Compositae; botanically it is known as *Carthamus tinctorius* L. A native of the Middle and Far East, it was cultivated in the Mediterranean region long before Roman times; and later in western Europe. In England it may still be encountered as a casual. The Spaniards introduced it into America not long after the discovery of the New World. In habit it is an annual or biennial herb

18 inches or 2 ft in height, with bright reddish-orange florets. The inflorescences are picked when fully mature and dried in the sun. They contain both a saffron-yellow and a red colouring-matter, the former being easily removed, to the extent of about two-thirds, by soaking in water. The insoluble reddish residue is used in acid or alkaline media to give a variety of shades varying from yellow through orange and pink to red, but the colours are not very fast. In spite of this disadvantage, safflower is still cultivated in India for purposes of dyeing.

Annatto is obtained from shrubs or small trees known as *Bixa orellana,* believed to be native to India or Brazil but now commonly found throughout the tropics. The colouring-matter, known as orleans or bixin, is obtained from the fleshy pulp of the fruit. This is macerated in water, and the solution is filtered and evaporated to the consistency of a paste. In this form annatto is used as a colouring-agent for such foodstuffs as butter and cheese, but before the discovery of suitable synthetic dyes it was also employed as a direct or substantive dye (p 280) for cotton. It is an interesting fact that bixin, the chemical constitution of which has been elucidated, is closely related in structure to the yellow colouring-matter, crocetin, of saffron.

IX. THE FIRST ANILINE DYES

Most generalizations contain a modicum of truth. Many are easily remembered. One that possesses both attributes may quickly assume the status of a truism, whether that status is deserved or not. An example is provided by the statement, repeatedly made by economic and social historians, that nineteenth-century chemical science was a child of the textile industry. The facts of history do not support this contention. Earlier in this work (vol IV, ch 8, I) it was pointed out that the modern science of chemistry had its principal origin in the work of Joseph Black, a professional chemist, Joseph Priestley, a Unitarian minister, Antoine Laurent Lavoisier, a Parisian man of affairs, and John Dalton, a mathematical tutor and meteorologist: none of them connected with the textile industry except Priestley, and even he only very remotely.[1] It is true that that industry greatly stimulated manufacturing chemistry, but its influence on the development of the pure science was small. Unless this fact is realized, it is difficult to understand why the art of dyeing was forced to rely on 'natural' dyes for the greater part of the nineteenth century. Chemistry had not sufficiently advanced, before about 1850, to unravel the usually complicated structures of colouring-matters, and there was therefore no obvious road along which chemists might

---

[1] Priestley's father was a cloth-dresser who went bankrupt; his grandfather, who died when Priestley was a boy of twelve, was a woollen manufacturer.

advance towards the production of new ones. When for the first time a useful synthetic dyestuff was discovered it was as the accidental result of an unsuccessful attempt to synthesize a natural febrifuge.

Before describing this momentous but fortuitous event, we may take a glance at what had been happening in chemistry since the discovery of oxygen, the determination of the composition of the atmosphere, and the establishment of the atomic theory. From the present point of view, the significant advances were in the investigation of those substances derived either directly or indirectly from plant and animal organisms and therefore known as organic compounds. A pioneer in this field was the Swedish chemist Carl Wilhelm Scheele (1742–86), who prepared tartaric acid, isolated glycerine, showed that uric acid was present in urinary calculi, discovered hydrocyanic (prussic) acid, and in the last two years of his life conducted researches upon oxalic, citric, malic, and gallic acids.

Scheele's work, though brilliant, was mainly preparative; the first to analyse organic compounds was Lavoisier, who proved that their essential constituent was carbon, while hydrogen and oxygen were usually present as well, and occasionally nitrogen, sulphur, and phosphorus. Quantitative analysis of some organic substances was carried out by J. J. Berzelius (1779–1848), and a general method of analysis was invented by Justus von Liebig (1803–73) in 1830. This consisted in taking a known weight of the substance and finding the weights of carbon dioxide and water produced on burning or 'combusting' it. The results of such combustions, taken in conjunction with the atomic weights of carbon and hydrogen, enabled the atomic population of molecules of compounds consisting of those two elements only to be ascertained; if the compound contained oxygen as well its proportion could be obtained by difference. Later, methods of estimating nitrogen and other elements in organic compounds were elaborated, and by the middle of the nineteenth century the constitutions of very numerous organic compounds had been established, as far as the numbers and kinds of atoms in their molecules were concerned.

A curious, but fundamental, phenomenon of organic chemistry was discovered in 1828 by F. Wöhler (1800–82), who observed that urea and ammonium cyanate, though quite distinct compounds, had molecules consisting of the same numbers of the same atoms. This phenomenon has innumerable parallels and is explained by the fact that given numbers of atoms of carbon, hydrogen, oxygen, and so on may arrange themselves to yield more than one molecular species and therefore more than one kind of compound. Basically, it depends upon the power of carbon atoms to join with one another to give an immense variety of skeletal structures upon which the atoms of other elements may, so to speak, be

draped. Compounds consisting of the same numbers of the same atoms are said
to be isomers of one another—a name due to Berzelius—and though at first such
isomerism proved a very puzzling matter, its study gradually led to a remarkable
insight into the molecular architecture of organic compounds (figure 142). Specifically, it rendered necessary the use of 'structural' formulae, which represented
not merely how many atoms of each element were present in the molecule of a
compound but the actual pattern in which they were believed to be arranged.

Two other important features of organic compounds gradually came to light.
The first was that whole families of
closely related substances exist, forming
series in which each member of the
family differs from those immediately

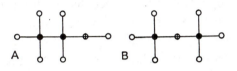

next to it on either side by possessing one

FIGURE 142—*An example of isomerism. Both ethyl*
(ordinary) alcohol (A) *and dimethyl ether* (B) *have*
molecules consisting of two atoms of carbon, six atoms
of hydrogen, and one atom of oxygen. They are quite
different substances, however, because the atoms of
the two substances are differently arranged. ○, *hydro-*
gen atoms; ●, *carbon atoms;* ⊕, *oxygen atom.*

carbon atom and two hydrogen atoms
more, or one carbon atom and two
hydrogen atoms less, respectively. All
the members of such a series have many
properties in common. The second
feature was that the presence in a compound of a particular group of atoms
manifests itself in particular kinds of chemical activity; hence the way was open
to build up or synthesize compounds which should behave in predetermined
ways.

Concurrent with these advances in theoretical knowledge was a rapid extension of the range of organic compounds isolated from natural sources or prepared in the laboratory. For the development of the synthetic dyestuff industry
later in the century, one of the most important of these compounds was benzene,
a colourless inflammable liquid discovered by Faraday (1791–1867) in 1825 in a
cylinder of compressed illuminating oil-gas. A few years afterwards the same
liquid was obtained by a chemical process from benzoic acid (from the aromatic
resin gum-benzoin), and in 1842 it was found by Leigh to be present in coal-tar.
Its effective presence on the scene, however, did not occur until 1845, when it
became the fruitful subject of research by A. W. von Hofmann.

August Wilhelm von Hofmann (1818–92) was born at Giessen, where, after
studying philosophy and law at Göttingen, he became assistant to Liebig. When
the Royal College of Chemistry, London, was established in 1845 Hofmann was
appointed superintendent there, and such were his chemical genius, enthusiasm,
and teaching ability that he very soon attracted a notable group of young research chemists. He became chemist to the Royal Mint from 1856 to 1865, and

was president of The Chemical Society in 1861–3. In 1865 he was called to the chair of chemistry in Berlin, and was instrumental in founding the German Chemical Society in the following year.

Hofmann was the first to realize that in coal-tar was a rich treasure for the organic chemist. He and his assistants set to work to investigate and separate its various ingredients by making use of the fact that these ingredients possess varying boiling-points and may therefore be at least partially separated by fractional distillation. One of the assistants, Charles Mansfield (1819–55), was so keen on the project that he fitted up a private laboratory at his lodgings in order to carry on with the work in his spare time; but by misfortune one day the tar he was distilling caught fire and he was fatally burned while carrying the retort out to the street. Such was the spirit of Hofmann's disciples.

Among the substances that Hofmann isolated from tar was benzene, the starting-point of many of his subsequent researches. It had been known for some years that when benzene is treated with nitric acid a yellow oil called nitrobenzene is formed, and that this substance in turn when reduced yields another oil, aniline, so named because it was first prepared from indigo, the Portuguese word for which is *anil*. Hofmann, however, found a much better way of reducing nitrobenzene than had previously been available and was able to make aniline in quantity. It soon appeared that aniline was only one member of a group of somewhat similar compounds, and Hofmann and his collaborators found plenty of exciting material to engage their attention.

One of the aniline-like substances was that known as allyl-toluidine, which on analysis appeared to have a chemical constitution recalling that of quinine. The possible connexion between the two substances led another of Hofmann's research students, William Henry (later Sir William) Perkin (1838–1907), to try to prepare quinine from allyl-toluidine. At that time Perkin was a youth of 18, but, like Charles Mansfield, he was not content with the hours of work at the college and set up a private laboratory at home. Of it he says:

My own first private laboratory was half of a small but long-shaped room with a few shelves for bottles and a table. In the fireplace a furnace was also built. No water laid on or gas. I used to work with old Berzelius spirit lamps and in a shed I did combustions with charcoal. It was in this laboratory I worked in the evening and vacation times. . . .

The idea at the back of the attempt to prepare quinine was quite simple and is worth examining here. In the molecule of allyl-toluidine there are 10 carbon atoms, 13 hydrogen atoms, and 1 nitrogen atom; a fact more concisely expressed in the chemical formula $C_{10}H_{13}N$. Similarly, in the molecule of quinine there are

20 carbon atoms, 24 hydrogen atoms, 2 nitrogen atoms, and 2 oxygen atoms, and the formula is thus $C_{20}H_{24}N_2O_2$. Perkin thought that by acting on the allyl-toluidine with a substance that readily yielded oxygen he might cause two molecules of it to lose a hydrogen atom each and make the residues join together with the addition of two atoms of oxygen, the hydrogen atoms being removed in the form of water. Expressed as a chemical equation, this would be:

$$2C_{10}H_{13}N + 3O \rightarrow C_{20}H_{24}N_2O_2 + H_2O.$$

Even for those days the expectation of success was rather naïve, but at least the plan had a reasonable basis.

Having prepared his allyl-toluidine, Perkin treated it with sulphuric acid and potassium dichromate, the latter to provide the necessary oxygen. No quinine was formed, however, but merely a dirty reddish-brown precipitate. Disappointment at the failure did not quench Perkin's interest in the result actually obtained, and he resolved to carry out a similar experiment upon aniline. Here again the product was not promising; it consisted of a black sludge. But on boiling this sludge with water he found that part of it dissolved, giving a purplish-coloured solution from which purple crystals could be obtained. This was a much more attractive substance, and Perkin wondered whether it would dye silk. Experiment showed that it did so, giving the silk a brilliant mauve shade that was not removed on washing and did not readily fade. It was, in fact, the first 'aniline dye'.

Perkin, with some encouragement from friends, sent a specimen of his dyed silk to Pullars of Perth, a leading firm of dyers, and in June 1856 received the following reply:

If your discovery does not make the goods too expensive, it is decidedly one of the most valuable that has come out for a very long time. This colour is one which has been very much wanted in all classes of goods, and could not be obtained fast on silks, and only at great expense on cotton yarns. I enclose you a pattern of the *best* lilac we have on cotton—it is dyed only by one house in the United Kingdom, but even this is not quite fast, and does not stand the tests that yours does, and fades by exposure to air. On silk the colour has always been fugitive. . . .

This very satisfactory report decided Perkin to take out a patent for his new dye and to start manufacturing it. At first the back garden served, but the success of the product soon seemed sufficiently assured to warrant the erection of a factory. Perkin's father advanced the necessary capital and his elder brother, Thomas Dix Perkin (1831–91), a builder, agreed to join forces, with the result that a works was erected at Greenford Green, near Harrow, in 1857.

While dyeing silk with Perkin's 'aniline purple' was a simple matter, especially —as Perkin discovered—from a dye-bath containing soap, satisfactory results could not at first be obtained on the much more important cotton fabrics. After many experiments, however, he found that this defect could be overcome by mordanting the cotton with tannic acid, and from that time production could scarcely meet the demand. One of the Pullars wrote to Perkin, 'I am glad to hear that a rage for your colour has set in among that *all-powerful* class of the Community—*the ladies*. If they once take a mania for it and you can supply the demand, your fame and fortune are secure.'

Perkin's violet soon became equally popular in France, where it was known as mauve. His French patent for its manufacture proved to be *entaché* or void, and the French producers naturally took advantage of this fact; however, the vogue that the colour attained in Paris reacted favourably upon the sales in Britain. Queen Victoria wore a mauve dress at the Great Exhibition of 1862, penny postage stamps were dyed with mauve, and according to 'Punch' the London policemen directed loiterers to 'get a mauve on'. Seldom can a single observation, even though followed up with great diligence and perspicuity, have had such widespread consequences.

By the time he was 35, Perkin had amassed a sufficient fortune to retire from business and resume chemical research; but dyes still continued to interest him and we shall have occasion to mention some further work of his (p 277).

The theoretical problems presented by mauve, no less than its commercial success, quickly attracted other workers to the investigation of aniline and its congeners, and several more dyestuffs were soon forthcoming. In 1859 Verguin discovered magenta, which has had a useful life ever since, and Hofmann himself—though he had been vexed at Perkin's temporary defection from pure chemistry—showed that magenta (otherwise known as fuchsine) could easily be converted into violet dyes, the rosanilines or Hofmann's violets. About the same time a compound of the same class, rosaniline blue, was prepared by Girard and de Laire in France, and independently by Nicholson in England; this was a useful dye but not very soluble in water, which limited its application. Nicholson therefore tried to modify it in such a way as to increase its solubility, and at length hit upon the device of treating it with concentrated sulphuric acid. In the resulting reaction, part of the sulphuric acid molecule entered into the molecule of the dye, or, as we should now say, the dye was sulphonated. Nicholson had achieved his aim, for the sulphonated dye was readily soluble. He had, however, done more than this, for the method of sulphonation was afterwards found to produce similar results on many other dyes; moreover, the sulphonated dyes were strongly acid, which from the technical point of view had considerable advantages.

In 1863 an important black dye, first observed in 1834, was rediscovered by Lightfoot. It is known as aniline black, and is of historical interest in that it was produced directly on cotton fabrics by oxidizing aniline salts with which the fabrics had been impregnated. Various substances were used to effect the oxidation, among them potassium dichromate and chlorate and ferric chloride; addition of small quantities of certain other metallic salts was found to increase the rate of formation of the dye. The first aniline black was inclined to turn dark green after a time in the presence of air and light, and cassocks, academic gowns, and other garments dyed with it gradually assumed this unattractive and shabby hue. Other types of aniline black were discovered later which did not share this defect.

Meanwhile a new type of reaction that was to prove very fruitful in dyestuffs chemistry had been observed by a young German named Peter Griess (1829–88). It was called the diazo reaction because the characteristic group of atoms concerned in it consisted of two atoms of nitrogen or *azote*. Griess had made this discovery before, attracted by Hofmann's fame, he came to England in 1858 to work at the Royal College of Chemistry. On the morning of his arrival at the college, the porter refused admission to the 'queer figure' wearing 'a reddish-brown overcoat surmounting a pair of sea-green unmentionables, a bright red knitted muffler, and a massive top-hat of a size and shape rarely seen in Oxford Street before or since'. Not until Hofmann himself came to the door to see what the resulting commotion[1] was about was Griess allowed to enter; then within an hour he was hard at work. Four years later he moved to Burton-on-Trent as research chemist to Allsopp & Sons, the well known brewers.

Aniline and its fellows proved very amenable to the diazo reaction, yielding products that when treated with phenol (carbolic acid), and other substances of a similar character, produced highly coloured bodies. Some of these coloured compounds proved very satisfactory as dyes. Several were prepared by Griess himself, but the first fully successful azo dye (to use the name given to this class) was Bismarck brown, first prepared by Martius in 1863 and already in manufacture at Manchester in the following year. In the same year another valuable azo dye, induline, was discovered; this gives shades varying from violet-blue to greenish-blue. At first it was obtained in a form that would dissolve in alcohol but not in water, and though the alcoholic solution was suitable for dyeing cotton mordanted with tannin it did not serve for silk. A water-soluble induline deriva-

---

[1] Griess shouted at the porter, *'Ich heiße Griess und bleibe hier!'* ('My name is Griess, and here I stop!').

tive was therefore made by sulphonation, and in this form it gave very good results on silk. Another contemporary dyestuff was chrysoidine (Witt, 1876), which, with a tannin mordant, dyes cotton brownish-red.

Perkin was not the only young man to perceive the commercial possibility of synthetic dyes, and in 1864 Ivan Levinstein (1845–1916) started the manufacture of magenta, violets, Bismarck brown, and other dyestuffs at Blackley,

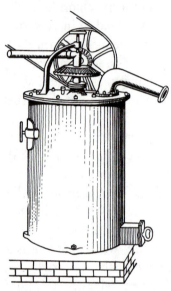

Manchester, where another firm of dyestuffs manufacturers, Roberts, Dale, & Company, was already well established. The latter company was fortunate in having on its research staff a German calico-printer named Heinrich Caro (1834–1910), who, though not trained in chemistry, proved to have a very marked flair for the subject and to whom we shall have occasion to refer again (p 277). Both these and other firms flourished, and the increasing demand for dyes rendered it necessary to improve the manufacture of intermediates, that is, substances prepared from the raw materials not for direct use but for subsequent conversion into finished products. In the dyestuffs industry one of the principal raw materials was benzene from coal-tar. By treatment with nitric acid and sulphuric acid benzene was converted into nitrobenzene, and this in turn was reduced to give aniline (p 270), the chief of the dye intermediates. Perkin

FIGURE 143—*Perkin's apparatus for preparing aniline. The reactants were heated with high-pressure or superheated steam and stirred by means of a steam-engine.*

manufactured his own nitrobenzene and aniline, effecting the reduction of the nitrobenzene by means of iron and acetic acid; the reaction was carried out in steam-heated vessels provided with mechanical stirrers (figure 143).

X. KEKULÉ'S BENZENE FORMULA

During these early years of the dyestuffs industry considerable progress was being made in the theory of organic chemistry. It would not be germane to the purpose of this narrative to attempt to describe the new conceptions, but a brief reference must be made to one of them in view of the great influence it exerted upon subsequent work upon dyes. Though benzene was the parent substance of the earliest artificial dyes, the structure of its molecule was still uncertain at the time of their discovery. It was known that the molecule consisted of six carbon atoms and six hydrogen atoms, but the way in which these atoms were arranged remained a mystery. This lack of information was not at first a serious hindrance, but as the investigation not only of dyes but of other benzene derivatives became increasingly important and systematic the need for an elucidation of the structure became correspondingly urgent. Without it, chemists could certainly advance, but the advance was largely *à tâtons*.

It was very fortunate, then, that in 1865 Friedrich August Kekulé von Stradonitz (1829–96) arrived at a conception of the benzene molecule that has stood the test of time and experiment and, with some elaboration, is still accepted.

Earlier work on the carbon 'skeletons' of organic molecules had always assumed that the carbon atoms were arranged in simple or branched chains with free ends. Benzene, however, had quite different properties from those it would be expected to have if its carbon atoms were arranged in such a way. Like other chemists, Kekulé was much puzzled by the problem, but at length an idea came to him when, tired after working at his textbook, he turned his chair to the fire and dozed. In his half-waking dreams he saw the benzene carbon atoms gambolling, twisting, and twining in snake-like motion, when suddenly one of the snakes seized hold of its own tail, 'and the form whirled mockingly before my eyes'. That was the solution of the puzzle. Instead of forming a chain with free ends, the six benzene carbon atoms had arranged themselves into a closed ring, and Kekulé was able to formulate the benzene molecule as shown in figure 144. A frivolous contemporary German cartoon suggested an alternative (tailpiece, p 283), though, as James Kendall has pointed out, if the monkeys represent the carbon atoms, each should hold a banana in its free 'hand' to represent a hydrogen atom.

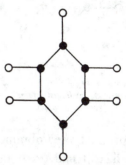

FIGURE 144—*Kekulé's conception of the benzene molecule.* O, *hydrogen atoms;* ●, *carbon atoms.*

Kekulé's formula is often simplified, for the sake of convenience, into a plain hexagon, each corner being understood to represent a carbon atom with an attached hydrogen atom. Its usefulness was immediately apparent, and the closed chain or cyclic structure of the benzene molecule explained much that had previously been enigmatic. On this foundation much more systematic research could be planned, and at the same time the molecular structure of other coal-tar products, important in the dyestuffs industry, became apparent. Such were the white crystalline solids naphthalene and anthracene. Naphthalene was shown to have a molecule consisting, as it were, of twin benzene rings but with two carbon atoms in common (figure 145), while anthracene consists of three such rings, the middle one having two carbon atoms in common with each of the outer ones (figure 146).

These fundamental facts paved the way to the successful accomplishment of two feats that only a few years earlier would have seemed impossible, namely the synthesis of alizarin and, more difficult still, that of indigotin.

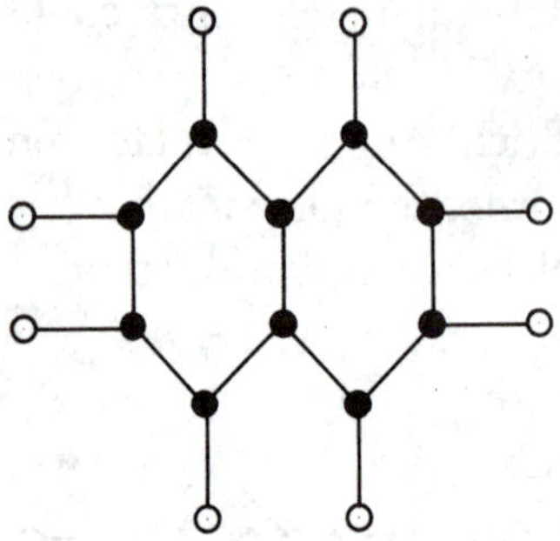

XI. ALIZARIN

FIGURE 145—*The molecule of naphthalene.* ○, *hydrogen atoms;* ●, *carbon atoms.*

European cultivation of madder in 1868 yielded a crop of some 70 000 tons; the artificial production of the red colouring-matter of madder, namely alizarin (p 260), thus held out the prospect of a rich prize. Chemists had already set out on the quest, and in this same year, 1868, the German chemists Graebe and Liebermann tried the effect of heating alizarin with zinc dust. The product they obtained proved to be anthracene, a surprising fact inasmuch as alizarin had previously been assumed to be a derivative of naphthalene. From further investigations they drew the conclusion that the immediate parent of alizarin was anthraquinone, an oxidation product of anthracene; and from still further work they made the calculated guess that alizarin itself was anthraquinone in which two hydrogen atoms had been replaced by two hydroxyl groups, —OH. It was a simple matter to put this guess to the test of experiment. By acting upon anthraquinone with bromine they were able to replace two hydrogen atoms by bromine atoms, and by fusing the product with alkali the two bromine atoms were replaced by hydroxyl groups. One can imagine the tension with which the last operation was watched, but the outcome was a happy one: their guess had been right, and the last operation yielded alizarin. This was in 1869.

A method of synthesizing alizarin had thus been worked out, but it was impracticable as a manufacturing process owing to the high cost of bromine. Graebe and Liebermann therefore tried to sulphonate (p 272) the anthraquinone instead of brominating it, since they knew that a sulphonate group can be replaced by a hydroxyl group on fusion with alkali, just as a bromine atom can. The anthraquinone, however, proved very recalcitrant to sulphonation, and the solution to the difficulty came from Caro (p 274)—again, as with Perkin's mauve, as the result of a fortuitous circumstance. The German dyestuffs firm for which Caro now worked, the *Badische Anilin-und-Soda Fabrik*, had accumulated a quantity of anthraquinone for which no use could be found, and Caro speculated as to whether he could make a dye from it by heating it with oxalic acid and sulphuric acid. Mixing the three substances in a porcelain basin, he set a flame underneath, but the only apparent result was that the oxalic acid decomposed and vanished. At that moment Caro was sent for, and went away without turning out the flame. When he returned, he found that the residue had partly charred, but that there was a pink crust which he recognized to be alizarin. The secret of the sulphonation of alizarin obviously lay in using very concentrated sulphuric acid at a high temperature, and this deduction was confirmed by subsequent experiments. Meanwhile, Perkin also had solved the problem, quite independently. Both he and Caro (with Graebe and Liebermann) hastened to take out patents for what was clearly a very valuable process, but Caro won by a day, getting his patent on 25 June 1869

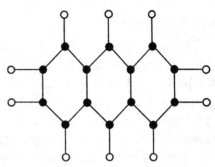

FIGURE 146—*The molecule of anthracene.* O, *hydrogen atoms;* ●, *carbon atoms.*

while Perkin's was granted on 26 June. However, matters were amicably arranged, for Caro made over his patent to the *Badische Fabrik* and they in turn gave Perkin licence to manufacture alizarin in England.

Perkin next set to work to ensure a regular supply of anthracene from the gasworks. Up to that time it had been a more or less useless substance, and Perkin had to overcome considerable difficulties in arranging a steady collection. In the meantime he devised and patented another method of synthesizing alizarin, easier to carry out on a manufacturing scale. In this new process the starting-point was anthracene itself. By the action of chlorine the anthracene was converted into dichloro-anthracene, two atoms of hydrogen in the anthracene being replaced by chlorine atoms. The dichloro compound was then sulphonated and the product was oxidized to the sulphonated anthraquinone. The sulphonate groups were finally replaced by hydroxyl groups, thus forming alizarin, by treatment with alkali.

The successful manufacture of alizarin spelt ruin to the madder industry, for the price of the synthetic dye was very much lower than that of the natural one. In consequence, large areas of madder-growing land had to be used for other crops.

Alizarin will dye fabrics different shades according to the mordant used (p 280). The brilliant red for which madder first became celebrated is obtained with alum as mordant, the fabric being first treated with special oils. The 'Turkey red' (vol IV, p 249) of pre-scientific times was obtained in this way, the oil being rancid olive or castor oil mixed with a lye of potash; but, as noted earlier in this work, the precise details of the dyeing operation still remain somewhat obscure. With an iron salt as mordant, alizarin gives violet shades, and with a chromium salt brownish-red tones.

XII. INDIGOTIN

The success achieved by attempts to synthesize alizarin stimulated research directed towards the artificial production of indigotin. Many workers attacked the problem of the constitution of its molecule, for before synthesis could become feasible chemists required to know exactly what they were required to synthesize. The task proved a formidable one, but after many years of patient investigation, in which the principal figure was that of Adolf von Baeyer (1835–1917), it was satisfactorily completed. A little later (1880) von Baeyer published a method of synthesizing the dye, but the procedure was too complicated and costly to form the basis of commercial preparation.

However, the fact that synthesis of indigotin had been effected encouraged the *Badische Anilin-und-Soda Fabrik* to spend money lavishly on further research, even though progress turned out to be extremely tardy. It took seventeen years and the expenditure of, it is said, about a million pounds, before a commercially successful synthetic process was worked out by K. Heumann (1850–93). Even then there was a grave difficulty: the starting-point in the synthesis was a substance known as phthalic anhydride, which is not an available raw material but has itself to be prepared from naphthalene (p 275) by the action of hot concentrated sulphuric acid. The rate at which this action takes place under normal conditions is tediously slow, which made the cost of the product correspondingly high. Once again chance took matters in hand, and during the heating of one batch of material the mercury thermometer placed in it broke. To the amazement of the chemist in charge, Herr Sapper, the rate of the reaction was enormously increased, the mercury sulphate formed from the mercury and sulphuric acid having acted as a catalyst.

This lucky observation enabled large quantities of phthalic anhydride to be made very cheaply and did much to render the commercial synthesis of indigotin economically successful; the synthetic product was first put on the market in 1897 and within ten years had almost entirely superseded natural indigo. At first, dyers were rather suspicious of the factory-made indigo and a vigorous publicity campaign was necessary to overcome their reluctance to use it. Their attitude was not altogether unreasonable, for, as was mentioned on p 261, natural indigo contains small quantities of substances other than indigotin and thus gives somewhat different results from the synthetic dye, which is not so contaminated. The advantages of using a pure dye, however, which could always be depended upon to behave consistently, quickly became apparent, and once the initial aloofness had been broken the use of synthetic indigotin made rapid strides. The export of Indian indigo fell from about 19 000 tons in 1895–6 to about 1100 tons in 1913–14. Over 200 000 acres of land devoted to the cultivation of the indigo plant lay idle for a time; and many of the Indian indigo-growers went bankrupt. There was a temporary revival of the industry during the first world war, when synthetic material was unavailable, but nowadays its extent is negligible.

XIII. SOME OTHER DYES

An important class of dyes is that of the 'sulphur dyes', made by heating various organic substances with an alkaline sulphide. Certain other dyes containing sulphur but prepared in other ways are not included in the class. The first sulphur dye was discovered in 1873, by Croissant and Bretonnière, who fused bran with sodium sulphide and obtained a product that would dye cotton green. In 1893 Vidal obtained a very useful black dye by heating a nitrogen derivative of phenol (p 273) with sodium sulphide, and a little earlier Green had prepared primuline yellow by heating *para*-toluidine, an aniline-like compound, with sulphur. Though the sulphur dyes could not, in the nineteenth century, compete with their rivals they deserve mention as the forerunners of other dyes of the same class which have since proved extremely valuable; the world production of one modern variety, 'sulphur black', is some 6000 tons a year.

Of dyes containing sulphur but not classed as sulphur dyes, methylene blue provides a good example. This was discovered by Caro in 1876, and is still used for dyeing cotton mordanted with tannin. Its derivative, methylene green, is widely employed for the same purpose, giving a colour with a good fastness to washing and light. Malachite green, discovered by O. Fischer in 1878, gives a deep green shade to tannin-mordanted cotton; sulphonation products of it are marketed as 'patent blues'. It is not a sulphur dye.

Congo red, discovered in 1884 by Böttiger, is of interest as the first synthetic dye that would dye cotton directly. Many of its derivatives possess the same valuable property. Indanthrene, first prepared by R. Bohn at the turn of the century, is a very fast blue dye and has several congeners of comparable worth, but they did not come into general use until after the end of the period now under consideration.

XIV. CLASSIFICATION OF DYES

While the chemist classes dyes according to their constitutions, the dyer classes them according to the methods that have to be employed in using them. On this basis he distinguishes between (among others) vat dyes, substantive dyes, mordant dyes, sulphur dyes, and ingrain dyes.

Vat dyes are exemplified by indigo. They are insoluble in water and have to be converted into a soluble derivative, such as leuco-indigotin or indigo white (p 262), before they can be absorbed by the fibres of the fabric. After the fibres have been so impregnated the leuco form of the dye is reconverted to the original form, which is thus deposited within the fabric. The formation of the leuco modification—which in spite of its designation is not always white—is usually effected by reduction (p 262), and the reconversion by oxidation with atmospheric oxygen. The principal vat dyes other than indigo are those of the indanthrene class.

Substantive dyes are those which dye a fabric directly, an example being Congo red. They are consequently easy to use and are popular for domestic dyeing, but they are apt to wash out and are generally rather lacking in brightness.

Mordant dyes or *adjective dyes* have to be 'fixed' in the fibres by previous application of substances known as mordants, which 'bite' (Latin *mordere*) or hold them. The action is a chemical one, and mordants are either acidic or basic. The commonest acidic mordant is tannic acid or tannin, while the basic mordants are provided by various metallic salts such as alum. In using a basic mordant it is customary to soak the fabric in a solution of the metallic salt and then expose it to steam; this hydrolyses the salt to the metallic hydroxide, which is the effective mordant. When the mordanted fabric is treated with the dye solution a solid complex of the dye and mordant, known as a 'lake', is formed within the fibres, and as the lake is insoluble the dye is fixed. By the use of different metallic salts, different lakes can be formed from the same dye and their shades may, and generally do, vary. Tannic acid, used in mordanting cotton, forms an insoluble complex with a basic dye.

Sulphur dyes are direct dyes for cotton and are usually applied from a solution containing soda and sodium sulphide. In some cases the sodium sulphide reduces the dye to the leuco form which is subsequently reoxidized in the air; such sulphur dyes thus resemble vat dyes.

Ingrain dyes are insoluble azo dyes produced on the fabric itself. The fabric is soaked in a solution of some compound capable of reacting with a diazo salt to form an insoluble dye, and a solution of the diazo salt is prepared ice-cold. On dipping the fabric into this second bath the dye is precipitated on the fibres. Most diazo salts readily decompose on even gentle heating, hence the necessity for keeping the temperature low.

XV. BRITISH AND GERMAN DYESTUFFS INDUSTRIES

Though Britain got off to a flying start in the manufacture of synthetic dye-stuffs, the foregoing account will have revealed that much of the work carried out in this country was due to German chemists, including Griess, Caro, Witt, and Hofmann. Most of these temporary residents (though not Griess) returned to Germany between about 1865 and 1880 and there helped to found the German dyestuffs industry. For a variety of reasons, one being the greater availability of essential raw materials, the German industry soon overtook the British, and by the time war broke out in 1914 only 20 per cent of the dyes used in Britain were made at home, the remainder being imported mainly from Germany. This was due not to any inferiority of British chemists to German, but to economic factors. When hostilities cut off the German supplies of dyestuffs British chemical skill, both academic and industrial, quickly rose to the occasion, and Britain is now among the foremost dye-manufacturing countries as she was in the days of Sir William Perkin.

XVI. SUBSIDIARY USES OF DYESTUFFS

Although the principal use of dyestuffs is for the colouring of textiles they have found numerous minor applications, some of which are of much importance both technically and scientifically. One such application lies in the field of bio-logical research, where the staining of organisms and tissues has been productive of great advances in knowledge. A pioneer in this technique was H. C. Sorby, who about the middle of the nineteenth century prepared stained specimens of jellyfish and other small animals, using carmine (cochineal), damson juice, bilberry juice, and even port wine as stains. Many of these preparations were mounted as lantern slides and are still preserved in the Art Gallery and Museum at Sheffield. The value of staining in the study of the fine structure of organisms can scarcely be over-estimated. Many structural details of the highest significance are invisible in the material in its natural state but can be revealed by the use of appropriate dyes, which may also throw light on physiological changes.

When synthetic dyestuffs became available it was not long before they were pressed into service. Weigert employed them in histological investigations, and in 1877 Robert Koch (1843–1910) published an account of his methods of fixing and staining film-preparations of bacteria—a landmark in the history of bacteriology. Seven years later the Danish physician Hans Christian Joachim Gram (1853–1938) described a staining-method of very great importance in differentiating between various groups of bacteria. This method depends upon the fact that when certain bacteria are dyed and then treated with a solution of iodine in potassium iodide they cannot be decolorized by subsequent treatment with alcohol; such bacteria are known as Gram-positive. Other groups of bacteria when subjected to the same series of operations lose their colour on the addition of alcohol; these are Gram-negative. The distinction between Gram-positive and Gram-negative groups is accompanied by a distinction in other characters, so that this very special use of dyestuffs has an importance out of all proportion to the actual quantity of dye used. A somewhat similar observation was made in 1882 by Paul Ehrlich (1854–1915), who found that while most bacteria stained with fuchsin were decolorized by the addition of a mineral acid, tubercle bacilli so treated retained their colour. This fact proved extremely useful in the early bacterial study of tuberculosis, and Ehrlich's technique, as modified later by Ziehl and Neelsen, is still widely employed in bacteriology.

Extensive use is made of dyes in photography, where as early as 1875 Waterhouse discovered that the sensitivity of the photographic emulsion to green light could be increased by the addition of eosin. Later, a mixture of dyes was used in order to widen the range of sensitivity sufficiently to include the whole visible spectrum, as in panchromatic plates and films. In the colour-photography process invented by the brothers L. J. and A. M. L. N. Lumière the essential feature was a system of dyed starch grains.

An early chemical use of dyestuffs was based on the fact that many of them change colour when treated with acids or alkalis. Thus methyl orange is pink in acid solutions, but changes to yellow or orange in alkaline solutions. Substances of this kind are known as indicators, since they indicate whether a liquid is acidic or alkaline. Degrees of acidity or alkalinity may be measured in this way by the use of suitable colour-changing dyes.

Further applications of dyes are in the colouring of paper, soap, wood, fur, hair, foodstuffs, perfumes, cosmetics, leather, candles, plastics, linoleum, and a thousand and one other commodities. Even the speleologist turns them to account: it is related that some fluorescein dropped into a swallet on Mendip after a time tinged the water of the moat of the bishop's palace at Wells, several miles away, thus settling the disputed question of a subterranean connexion.

BIBLIOGRAPHY

GARDNER, W. M. (Ed.). 'The British Coal-Tar Industry.' Williams & Norgate, London. 1915.

HURRY, J. B. 'The Woad Plant and its Dye.' Oxford University Press, London. 1930.

JOHNSON, A. and TURNER, H. A. "Synthetic Dyes from the Time of Perkin." *Dyer, Lond.*, **115,** 765–9, 1956.

KARRER, P. 'Organic Chemistry' (trans. by A. J. MEE, 3rd ed.). Elsevier Publishing Company, London. 1947.

LIPPMANN, E. O. VON. 'Zeittafeln zur Geschichte der organischen Chemie.' Springer, Berlin. 1921.

MIALL, S. 'A History of the British Chemical Industry.' Benn, London. 1931.

MORGAN, SIR GILBERT T. and PRATT, D. D. 'British Chemical Industry: its Rise and Development.' Arnold, London. 1938.

PARTINGTON, J. R. 'A Short History of Chemistry.' Macmillan, London. 1937.

ROUSSEAU, P. 'Histoire des techniques.' Fayard, Paris. 1956.

ROWE, F. M. "The Life and Work of Sir W. H. Perkin." *J. Soc. Dy. Col.*, **54,** 551–62, 1938.

SACHS, A. P. "A History of Dyestuffs." *Text. Color.*, **65,** 487–9, 517–18, 1943.

SCHORLEMMER, C. 'The Rise and Development of Organic Chemistry.' Manchester. 1879.

SPRINGER, J. F. "Pre-modern Dyeing." *Text. Color.*, **50,** 87–89, 1928.

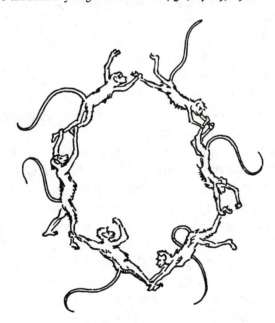

Contemporary cartoon of Kekulé's benzene formula.

13

EXPLOSIVES

J. McGRATH

I. EXPLOSIVES IN 1850

THE modern explosives industry was nascent at the beginning of the second half of the nineteenth century. The basic explosives of the industry, nitroglycerine (glyceryl trinitrate) and nitro-cotton or gun-cotton, had been discovered, but their development had scarcely started; the only explosive available for all ordinary civil and military purposes was gunpowder, otherwise known as black powder, of various compositions. In the military field it was used as a propellant, as a bursting-charge in shells, and for blowing up enemy walls and fortifications. The first recorded blasts with gunpowder were made in Hungary and Germany in the early part of the seventeenth century. The practice of blasting is said to have been introduced into England in 1629, but 1670 is a more probable date. The use of gunpowder for blasting was started in the Cornish mines in 1689. Many fatalities occurred owing to the crude nature of the methods available for igniting the charge, but the invention of the miner's safety fuse by William Bickford in 1831, and subsequent improvements, considerably reduced the number of accidents.

Gun-cotton is a highly explosive substance, formed by the action of nitric acid on cotton and other forms of cellulose. It was discovered by C. F. Schönbein (1799–1868) [1] in 1845–6 and independently by Böttger in 1846, although T. J. Pelouze [2], following the work of H. Braconnot (1780–1855) [3], had shown in 1838 that nitric acid reacted with paper and other cellulosic materials to give a highly inflammable product. Schönbein came to Britain in 1846 and took out a patent for his invention in the name of John Taylor [4]. He entered into an agreement with John Hall & Sons that they should have the sole right to manufacture gun-cotton at their powder works at Faversham, but on 14 July 1847 there was an explosion of gun-cotton which destroyed the factory and killed twenty-one men. The manufacture in Britain was then stopped. There were also gun-cotton explosions at Vincennes and Bouchet in France, and in other countries. These produced such an effect that the manufacture was discontinued in western Europe for some sixteen years, but it was still carried on in Austria, where some improvements in the process were developed by von Lenk.

Nitroglycerine, which is formed by the action of nitric acid on glycerine, is a highly explosive oily liquid. It was discovered by A. Sobrero (1812–88) in 1846 [5], but little practical application had been made of it by 1850, probably because of its dangerous nature and the inconvenience of working with a liquid explosive. There was also great difficulty in obtaining controlled explosions with nitroglycerine, owing to the lack of a safe and reliable means of firing it. This difficulty was not overcome until Alfred Nobel (1833–96), between 1859 and 1866, showed that nitroglycerine, alone or absorbed in kieselguhr, could safely be made to explode with great violence if a small quantity of mercury fulminate, contained in a suitable tube, was exploded in contact with it.

Fulminates of gold and silver had been known for many years before 1850, but they were too sensitive and dangerous for any practical use to be made of them. The less sensitive mercury fulminate, which was first prepared pure by E. C. Howard [6] in 1800, was also well known, but the commercial detonator did not come into use until after Nobel's discovery.

II. GUNPOWDER

At the middle of the nineteenth century the methods of manufacturing gunpowder had long been well established. It was also fully realized that slight variations in its composition, according to the particular uses envisaged for it, could be of distinct advantage. Progress in the next fifty years was confined mainly to improvements in the plant and machinery: examples are the abolition of stamp-mills for grinding the ingredients and their replacement by crushers, ball-mills, and similar apparatus, and the introduction of edge-runner mills for mixing, first of stone, then of iron. Hydraulic pressure was applied instead of screw-pressure in the presses; steam-power was used instead of water-power for driving machinery, and steam for heating stoves and buildings. Safety measures were studied and improved.

In 1788 Claude L. Berthollet had found that the substitution of potassium chlorate for potassium nitrate (saltpetre) in gunpowder gave a more powerful explosive, but his first attempt to manufacture the new powder ended in disaster. Repeated attempts to manufacture satisfactory explosives containing potassium chlorate were unsuccessful because of the extreme sensitiveness of the mixtures to shock and friction. Chlorate explosives may therefore be regarded as not in commercial use at the beginning of the second half of the nineteenth century.

III. NITROGLYCERINE

The method used by Sobrero for the preparation of nitroglycerine consisted in adding a half-part of glycerine drop by drop to a cooled mixture of 2 parts concentrated sulphuric acid and 1 part concentrated nitric acid, the whole being stirred by hand. This method was adopted in manufacture, using various proportions of nitric and sulphuric acids to glycerine. One of the first processes was that developed by H. F. M. Kopp (1817–92); this was designed with a view to simplicity, so that nitroglycerine could be prepared in quarries and used immediately or soon afterwards. The apparatus used (figure 147) consisted of a large earthenware vessel for cooling and washing the nitroglycerine; a cast iron vessel

FIGURE 147—*Apparatus for the manufacture of nitroglycerine by Kopp's method.*

for nitrating, with an index-mark on the outside and inside; a measuring vessel of sheet iron or china for the glycerine; a glass funnel with india-rubber tube, pinch-cock, and outlet-pipe for separation; and an iron rod for stirring. Five to six litres of ice-cold water were put in the earthenware vessel, in which stood the nitrating vessel containing 2·8 kg of mixed acid, and 350 g of glycerine were run into the acid from the measuring vessel, the mixture being constantly stirred with the iron rod. Stirring was continued for five minutes after all the glycerine had been run in, and the mixture was then drowned in the water in the earthenware vessel. The crude nitroglycerine was washed with water in the same vessel, and the water was finally separated from it with the aid of the funnel. Three to four operations an hour were said to have been possible by this process, and the yield varied between about 140 and 200 per cent by weight, calculated on the glycerine. The nitroglycerine was not pure and was suitable only for immediate use.

Nitroglycerine was manufactured by a similar method in some continental factories until as late as 1880, a number of pots standing in a trough filled with water being used for the nitration. As the demand increased, larger nitrators were introduced in which the stirring was done by paddles or agitators driven mechanically. One of these, erected by Engels at various factories, is illustrated in figure 148. In this plant the charge of mixed acids consisted of 28 kg of nitric acid and 56 kg of sulphuric acid; 10 kg of glycerine were nitrated. The stirrer was given 25 double strokes by hand every minute. When the nitration was finished, the plug in the discharge-pipe was withdrawn and the mixture was run into an oval oaken tank containing a large volume of water. The water was discharged and changed by means of decanting-tubes, and the nitroglycerine was drawn off by a rubber tube fitted to a pipe in the bottom of the tank. The nitration took about an hour, and the average yield was 195 per cent, that is, 10 kg of glycerine gave 19·5 kg of nitro-glycerine.

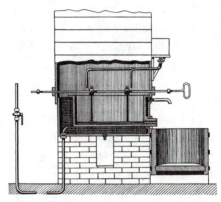

FIGURE 148—*Glycerine nitrator, and nitroglycerine drowning and washing tank, after the design of Engels.*

Further developments in the design of nitrators included mechanical stirring combined with stirring by compressed air. The nitrators generally consisted of large lead vessels closed with a conical cover and standing in a wooden vat. They were provided with an agitating helix turned by a shaft driven by a water-wheel. A horizontal disk was fitted on the shaft of the agitator; on this the glycerine ran and, as a result of centrifugal force, was thrown from it in fine drops on to the surface of the acid. An air-pipe leading to the bottom of the nitrator, and internal cooling-coils of lead, were also provided. The temperature during the nitration was shown by a thermometer passing through the cover, which also carried a fume-pipe for removal of gases and vapours formed during the reaction. The plant was generally arranged on the side of a hill, so that the materials flowed under gravity from one stage of the process to the next.

Mechanical stirring was gradually abolished altogether in Britain, air stirring alone then being used. The water for cooling was generally drawn, through storage-tanks, from the nearest natural sources; in the summer it became rather warm, thereby reducing the rate at which the nitration could be safely carried out. In nearly all factories the maximum temperature permitted during the nitration was 25° C; this was obtained by altering the rate of flow of glycerine or cooling-water as required. If the reaction could not be thus controlled, the entire charge was allowed to run out through a cock in the bottom of the nitrator into a drowning tank containing a large volume of water.

In the early processes, separation of the nitroglycerine was effected by drowning the entire charge at the end of the nitration, allowing it to settle, and drawing off the nitroglycerine from the bottom of the drowning-vessel. The waste acids were thereby greatly diluted with water and so were entirely lost. Much poisonous fume was also formed in the drowning, rendering the process inconvenient and dangerous to the workmen. Direct separation was therefore adopted. This process consisted in running the charge, on completion of the nitration, into a separator where it was allowed to stand till the bulk of the nitroglycerine had separated on top of the residual acid. The time required for the separation varied considerably. When the best-quality glycerine and acids free from suspended matter were used, the separation took place rapidly, but with low-quality glycerine or dirty acids, scums and emulsions were formed which seriously interfered with the separation. Even at best, separation was never complete, and the acid still retained some nitroglycerine in suspension and solution. The acid was therefore transferred by gravity to another separator, known as an after-separator, in another building; there it was kept until a further quantity of nitroglycerine had separated, the quantity thus obtained being added to the main yield.

At first, the separated nitroglycerine was washed by simply churning it with water in a wooden barrel, using a wooden plate fixed to a rod, but later it was washed successively in two wooden vats provided at first with hand-driven, but later with mechanically-driven, stirrers similar to those used in churns. Mechanical stirring was in time replaced by air stirring, and lead-lined vats were introduced similar in design to the preliminary washing-vessel described above. An apparatus used at Ardeer (on the Firth of Clyde) consisted of a lead-lined vessel from which the wash-water was withdrawn by means of a skimmer; this consisted of a funnel to the lower end of which was attached a rubber tube connected to a pipe passing through the side of the vessel near the bottom. A similar apparatus is illustrated in figure 149. For the final wash a solution of sodium carbonate, in slight excess, was employed, and the washing was performed at temperatures up to 50° C. The wash-waters were passed through various settling-tanks and labyrinths to remove all traces of suspended nitroglycerine before being finally passed to the drains.

As a rule, the nitroglycerine was then filtered to remove scum, a bed of salt usually being placed on the filter to remove water. In some factories, however, it was merely allowed to stand in a suitable vessel, when most of the water rose to the surface and the nitroglycerine could be drawn off fairly free from it. In an apparatus suggested by Hagron, in use at Vonges, a sponge-filter was employed, but this apparatus was useful only for small-scale work.

The residual acid from the after-separators still contained nitroglycerine in solution and suspension, together with lower nitrated products, which had to be removed before the acid was sent for recovery for further use. This was originally effected by allowing the acid to settle for long periods in open vats or glass carboys and skimming off the nitroglycerine at intervals, but several accidents occurred with this process. Vessels similar to the nitrators were then adopted; these were stood in a trough of cold water or were provided with internal cooling-coils, and the nitroglycerine that separated out was removed as required by upward displacement through a glass tube at the apex of the conical lid of the separator.

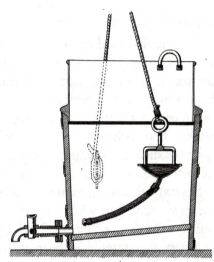

FIGURE 149—*Nitroglycerine washing-vessel.*

In the early stages of the manufacture of nitroglycerine the operations of nitration, separation, and washing were all executed in one room, transfer of the explosive from one vessel to the next being effected by comparatively short lengths of piping. As the scale of manufacture increased it became necessary first to carry out the washing in a separate building and later to separate all three stages. The nitroglycerine was transferred by pipes and gutters, but these, particularly the pipes, were liable to freeze in winter and to allow nitroglycerine to lodge in bends, cracks, and joints. The use of pipes in consequence largely ceased, and the gutters were enclosed in covered galleries and conduits. It was also found to be quite safe to transfer the nitroglycerine by gravity. This was most conveniently effected by arranging the buildings on the side of a hill, the nitrating-house being at the top and the separator- and washing-houses at successively lower levels.

The floors of the first nitroglycerine buildings were covered with sand or an absorbent earth such as kieselguhr to absorb any spilled nitroglycerine or acids. At Ardeer, where the factory was built on ground naturally covered with fine beach sand, no floor was provided, the upper layer of sand being renewed from time to time. Gradually wooden floors were installed, but it was not until the passing of the Explosives Act of 1875 in Britain, and of similar acts in other countries, that flooring became universal, and cleanliness and freedom from grit of the benches and fittings of buildings where danger existed were made compulsory.

IV. GUN-COTTON AND NITRO-COTTON

The method used by Schönbein (p 284) for the preparation of gun-cotton consisted of dipping one part of cotton in 20–30 parts of a mixture containing 3 parts by weight of concentrated sulphuric acid and 1 part of concentrated nitric acid, maintaining the temperature between 10° and 15° C. The reaction was allowed to proceed for one hour. The liquid was poured off, and the gun-cotton was washed first with water and then with dilute potash to remove the acid. It was again washed with water, squeezed out, soaked in a 0·6 per cent solution of saltpetre, squeezed out again, and finally dried at 65° C.

Several modifications were made in this process, including purification of the raw cotton, introduced by W. Crum [7], and more intensive nitration and washing, introduced by von Lenk of the Austrian army. Many difficulties were, however, encountered in the manufacture and several serious accidents occurred. The manufacture was therefore abandoned throughout Europe until Frederick Abel [8] showed that stability of the gun-cotton could be ensured only by complete removal of all traces of free acid, and that this could be effected only by a thorough disintegration of the gun-cotton to enable the wash-liquids to penetrate the fibres. On this principle he developed the process of stabilization that was generally used throughout the latter part of the century and is still employed.

In the method of manufacture of gun-cotton practised at Waltham Abbey, which incorporated Abel's method, the cotton was hand-picked to remove nails and other foreign bodies, then teased and treated with caustic soda solution to remove oil and grease, washed with water to remove the caustic soda, and finally dried at 90–95° C. After drying, the charges of cotton were weighed into suitable containers which were tightly closed and allowed to stand until the cotton had completely cooled.

The nitration was carried out in dipping-pots of cast iron or reinforced lead. These stood in a larger tank or trough through which cold water was passed to control the temperature of nitration. The mixed acid had approximately the same composition as von Lenk's, and was previously mixed in large quantities and drawn off as required. Owing to the bulk of the cotton a high ratio of mixed acid to cotton had to be employed, generally about 30 to 1; but even higher ratios were used in some factories. The dipping-pots were charged with the required weight of acid, and the cotton was rapidly introduced and submerged in the acid by means of a 3-pronged wrought iron fork. The pots were then closed with lids, in which were outlets through which the fumes were withdrawn. When cast iron pots were used, the cotton, after nitrating for 5–6 minutes, was transferred to an earthenware pot where it was allowed to stand, with its adhering acid, for about 24 hours to complete the nitration. When lead pots were used the cotton was left in the acid for 2–3 hours, after which the nitration was considered to be complete. Various other types of nitrating vessel were tried from time to time—including more elaborate dipping-pots, nitrating centrifuges, and vacuum nitrators—but none of these was extensively used, mainly because of high initial and maintenance costs.

On completion of the nitration the gun-cotton was separated from the residual acid by centrifuging the whole charge, and the acid-wet material was quickly drowned in a large volume of water. It was then washed with water in machines, similar to the beating-machines used in paper manufacture, until the wash-water was no longer acid. The wet gun-cotton was then transferred to large wooden vats fitted with perforated false bottoms and steam-coils. In these it was boiled with water, or sodium carbonate solution of about 2 per cent concentration, to remove the greater part of the acid. The boiling was continued for periods ranging from 8 hours to 4 days according to the quantity treated. After this treatment the gun-cotton still retained traces of acid, the complete removal of which was ensured by treating it in a pulping-machine. This consisted essentially of a large iron roller, on which steel knives were fitted parallel to the axis, and a bed-plate provided with similar knives. As the roller revolved, the gun-cotton, suspended in the water, passed between the two sets of knives and was reduced to pulp. The fineness of the pulp was controlled by altering the distance between the roller and the bed. Some machines were fitted with cylindrical filters, so that a continuous stream of water could be passed through the machine during the pulping, the gun-cotton thereby being pulped and washed simultaneously. The pulped gun-cotton was transferred to large vessels, known as 'poachers', which held about 10 cwt of gun-cotton and 1000 gallons of water and were fitted with power-driven paddles for stirring. The material was there washed at least three times with water, with settling between the washes. It was then transferred first to blenders, similar to the poachers, then to 'stuff chests', where calcium carbonate was added if the explosive was required for certain purposes, and finally centrifuged. The wet material thus obtained, containing about 40 per cent of water, was then pressed into blocks for demolition work or blasting, or dried for incorporation into other explosives.

In the above process cotton-waste or linters were used and 'insoluble' gun-cotton was produced. For production of the so-called 'soluble' gun-cotton or 'collodion cotton'—the form of nitro-cotton used in the manufacture of collodion and some types of propellant explosives—mixed acids containing more nitric acid and water were used and the nitration was carried out at temperatures up to 40° C. At Ardeer, when the 'blasting soluble nitro-cotton'—the form of collodion cotton used in the manufacture of blasting gelatine—was required, cotton-cop bottoms were nitrated with a mixed acid containing relatively less sulphuric acid and more water, and the nitration was effected at the ordinary temperature. Otherwise the preparation of the cotton and the treatment of the nitro-cotton were the same as in the manufacture of gun-cotton.

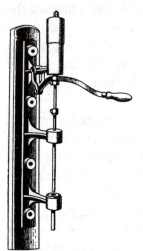

FIGURE 150—*Dynamite cartridging machine.*

V. BLASTING EXPLOSIVES

The earliest demonstration of the use of modern high explosives for blasting was made with gun-cotton in 1846 by Schönbein, who estimated that 1 lb was equivalent to about 4 lb of gunpowder. In the same year John Hall & Sons, licensees of Schönbein's patents, published short descriptions of gun-cotton cartridges manufactured by them and issued instructions for their use in blasting; the cartridges were to be fired with a fuse only. They stated that 4 oz of gun-cotton were equal in power to 24 oz of blasting powder.

For the reasons already mentioned (p 285), the use of nitroglycerine for blasting made little progress until Nobel's discovery that it could be absorbed by an inert material, such as kieselguhr, to give a mixture which was much less sensitive to shock than nitroglycerine itself, but which could be exploded when fired with a detonator containing mercury fulminate [9]. The mixture containing 3 parts of nitroglycerine and 1 part of kieselguhr was called dynamite. F. A. Abel and E. C. Brown later showed that dry compressed gun-cotton also could be exploded with a fulminate cap or detonator. These discoveries made the use of high explosives for blasting much safer, and the industry began to expand rapidly throughout Europe and America.

In the manufacture of dynamite the kieselguhr was first roughly mixed with the appropriate quantity of nitroglycerine, drawn direct from the filter in the nitro-glycerine washing-house. The mixture was then transferred to the mixing-houses proper, where it was thoroughly mixed by hand and sieved several times to ensure that it was quite homogeneous. It was then made up into cartridges in appropriate machines (figure 150). The latter consisted essentially of a plunger working through guides in a circular tube, in which was inserted a wrapping paper rolled into a cylinder and closed at the lower end. The requisite weight of explosive was added to the tube in small quantities which were pressed down by means of the plunger. When all the explosive had been added and compressed the cartridge was pushed out of the tube, and the open end was closed by folding the wrapper over the explosive charge. Other powder ex-plosives were similarly made and cartridged, and mechanical mixing processes were gradually introduced.

FIGURE 151—*McRoberts's incorporator for blasting gelatine.*

In 1875 Nobel invented blasting gelatine, which consisted of about 92 per cent of nitroglycerine gelatinized with 8 per cent of collodion cotton [10]. The initial difficulties of manufacture were rather great, however, and it was not until 1884, when blasting soluble nitro-cotton (p 292) was used, that production on a large scale began. In manu-facture, the nitro-cotton was dried until it contained less than 1 per cent of water, and was then sieved. A weighed quantity was placed in a brass-lined box, and the requisite quantity of nitroglycerine was added. The materials were given a preliminary mixing by hand, and were allowed to stand for several hours, or overnight, after which the mixture was transported to the mixing-house, where the mixing was completed at about 50° C. A little methylated spirit was added if necessary to accelerate the gelatinization. At first the final mixing also was done by hand, with wooden stirrers, but mechanical mixers were soon introduced; the McRoberts incorporator, used at Ardeer, is an example (figure 151). The time of mixing was usually about one hour, after which the explosive was allowed to cool and to become somewhat stiffer.

Blasting gelatine was usually cartridged by first passing it through a machine consisting essentially of an Archimedean screw working in a conical chamber. The explosive was fed into the hopper as the handle was turned, and the screw forced it forward and out through the nozzle, the diameter of which corresponded with the size of the cartridge to be filled. The issuing material was cut to the required length and weight before wrapping by hand in a cartridge-paper. A machine of this type is illustrated in figure 152.

In 1871 H. Sprengel (1834–1906) took out patents for a new type of explosive.

In this, an oxidizing agent, such as concentrated nitric acid or potassium chlorate, and a fuel, such as nitrobenzene, carbon disulphide, or petrol, were to be mixed on the site immediately before use, and the mixture exploded with a detonator [11]. These explosives, especially those in which potassium chlorate was the oxidizing agent, were used to a considerable extent, but both types had many disadvantages which rendered them unsafe and unreliable.[1]

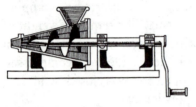

FIGURE 152—*Cartridging machine for gelatinous explosives.*

VI. PROPELLANTS

In 1846 Schönbein showed that his gun-cotton could be used as a propellant for artillery and that practically no smoke was formed when the gun was fired: von Lenk later tried to adapt it for use in small-arms, but the experiments were unsuccessful. The first successful nitrocellulose explosive for use in shot-guns was that of Schultze, who made it from nitrated wood [13]; this also was practically smoke-less. Other powders for use in small-arms were invented by Reid and Johnson (1882) and by Judson and Borland, but it was not until the invention of *Poudre B* by P. M. E. Vieille (1854–1934) in 1886, and of ballistite by Nobel in 1887, that the modern propellant explosives industry was really established.

Vieille's *Poudre B* originally consisted of about 68 per cent 'insoluble' gun-cotton containing about 13 per cent nitrogen, 30 per cent 'soluble' nitro-cotton containing about 12 per cent nitrogen, and 2 per cent paraffin wax; it was gelatinized by means of ethyl acetate. The composition was modified several times, but a mixture of the two nitrocelluloses only, gelatinized with ether, was finally adopted. Addition of about 2 per cent amyl alcohol to improve the stability was subsequently introduced; this was later increased to 8 per cent but was finally abandoned, 1 per cent of diphenylamine being added instead. Originally the mixture of nitrocelluloses was dried before adding the solvent, and the incorporation was carried out in flat ebonite vessels; when ether was adopted as the solvent, however, the mixture of wet nitrocelluloses was dehydrated by treating it with alcohol and pressing out the excess. The pressed cake was then broken up and incorporated with ether in kneading-machines, the stabilizer being added

---

[1] Another form of Sprengel explosive was invented by Linde in which at first liquid air, and later liquid oxygen, were used as the oxidizing agent; and various forms of carbonaceous matter, such as carbonized cork and wheat flour, paraffin wax, petroleum, and various kinds of oil, were used as the fuel. The carbonaceous matter was soaked in the liquefied gas immediately before use. Where oils were used they were first absorbed in kieselguhr before addition of the liquefied gas, and when paraffin wax was used it was mixed with kieselguhr at such a temperature that the wax remained liquid during the mixing. Explosives of this kind, which were known as Oxyliquit, were used in the boring of the Simplon tunnel in 1899 [12].

at this stage. On completion of the incorporation, the dough was passed through rollers to form thin sheets; these were partly dried by exposure to warm air in a drying-stove and then rolled again on steam-heated rollers to reduce the thickness still further and to remove blisters. The final sheets were cut with a guillotine to flakes of the desired size, and glazed with graphite in a drum.

Ballistite, invented by Nobel [14], consisted originally of a mixture of nitroglycerine, collodion cotton, and camphor, in which the nitrocellulose and nitroglycerine together formed a hard gel. In the original process of manufacture 150 parts of collodion cotton were mixed with 100 parts of nitroglycerine, 10–12 parts of camphor, and about 150 parts of benzol; the resulting mixture was spread out in thin layers in a suitable apparatus until the bulk of the benzol had evaporated. The mass was then rolled into thin sheets at about 50° C and cut into flakes of the desired size. Later, the camphor was omitted because of its volatility, which caused the properties of the explosive to change during storage. The process was improved by suspending the nitro-cotton in hot water, adding the appropriate amount of nitroglycerine, and stirring, usually with compressed air. The powder thus obtained was freed from water by pressing, and then passed between steam-heated rollers at 50–60° C. The nitro-cotton completely dissolved and the water was eliminated either mechanically or by evaporation; the sheet thus obtained was cut into flakes as above [15].

Cordite was invented by F. A. Abel and J. Dewar as a result of investigations carried out to overcome the disadvantages of ballistite. It consisted of a mixture of 37 per cent 'insoluble' gun-cotton of high nitrogen-content and 58 per cent nitroglycerine gelatinized with acetone; 5 per cent of petroleum jelly was added as a stabilizer [16]. In the manufacture, the dry gun-cotton was weighed into brass-lined wooden boxes and sent to the nitroglycerine weighing-house; there the appropriate quantity of nitroglycerine was added and the contents of each box were thoroughly mixed. The mixture, at this stage called cordite paste, was transferred to a kneading machine in an incorporating-house, the appropriate quantity of acetone was added, and the mixture was kneaded for $3\frac{1}{2}$ hours. The petroleum jelly was then introduced and the kneading continued for a further $3\frac{1}{2}$ hours. During the kneading the acetone gradually dissolved all the ingredients, yielding a uniform dough; this was formed into cords of various diameters by forcing it through dies in presses (figure 153). The thinner cords were usually wound on drums, but the thicker ones were cut into convenient lengths by machinery. They were then removed to the drying-stoves, where they were dried at about 38° C for times varying according to their size.

Sporting powders, which burn faster than those used in rifles and artillery, were generally made by mixing wet nitro-cotton with barium and potassium nitrates and other materials, drying, and granulating. The grains were then hardened by treatment in a rotating drum with a solvent, usually ether, and finally dried. Some powders were made by first forming fully gelatinized grains containing a fairly high proportion of barium or potassium nitrate; the salt was then partly dissolved out by steeping the powder in water, thereby forming porous grains.

VII. PICRIC ACID

Picric acid, first observed by P. Woulfe in 1771, was rediscovered in 1788 by J.-M. Hausmann, who obtained it by treating indigo with nitric acid. Its original application was as a dye, but when Turpin, in 1886, showed that it could be detonated it was used, first as a powder and then in the cast form, for filling shells. It was known in France as *mélinite*[1] and in Britain as lyddite.[2] The method of manufacture consisted of treating 1 part of crystallized carbolic acid (phenol) with 1 part of concentrated sulphuric acid at 100–120° C, then cooling the mixture and diluting it with about twice its volume of water. To the resulting solution were added 3 parts of nitric acid (sp gr 1·4). On completion of the reaction the mixture was allowed to cool and the crystals of picric acid were separated by centrifuging and washing with water. The product was purified by recrystallization from hot water.

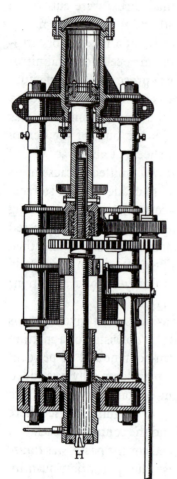

FIGURE 153—*Cordite press (front elevation). The cordite was extruded through the die (H) at the bottom of the press.*

VIII. MERCURY FULMINATE AND DETONATORS

Mercury fulminate, as previously mentioned (p 285), was prepared in a state of purity[3] by Howard in 1800, but it was used in only comparatively small quantities in percussion caps, until it was found that nitroglycerine and gun-cotton could be made to explode with great violence

---

[1] From its colour, quince-yellow (Greek *mēlinos*).   [2] Because first tested at Lydd, Kent.
[3] Impure specimens had been obtained by Kunckel as early as 1700.

when the process was initiated by a detonator containing fulminate. The method of preparing mercury fulminate consisted in dissolving mercury in nitric acid (sp gr 1·4) and then adding the solution to 90 per cent alcohol contained in a suitable vessel. The reaction was vigorous and the vapours evolved were trapped in a series of absorption vessels filled with water. When the mercury fulminate had crystallized out, the mixture was filtered and the crystals were washed with water until the washings were no longer acid. Owing to the sensitivity of the dry material to shock, only small batches were made at a time, and the product was kept wet until it was required.

Cap and detonator compositions consisted essentially of mercury fulminate to which potassium chlorate, antimony sulphide, and other materials, including ground glass, were added to increase the sensitivity to shock or flame. In the earliest stages of manufacture the caps and detonators were loaded and pressed singly, but later, with increasing demand, machines capable of loading and pressing up to 100 detonators at a time were developed. These were operated in closed compartments by remote control.

REFERENCES

[1] SCHÖNBEIN, C. F. *Arch. Sci. phys. nat.*, **7**, 26, 1846.
[2] PELOUZE, T. J. *C.R. Acad. Sci.*, *Paris*, **7**, 713, 1838.
[3] BRACONNOT, H. *Ann. Chim.* (*Phys.*), **52**, 290, 1833.
[4] British Patent No. 11407. 1846.
[5] SOBRERO, A. *Mem. R. Accad. Torino*, **10**, 195–202, 1844.
[6] HOWARD, E. *Phil. Trans.*, **90**, 204–38, 1800.
[7] CRUM, W. *Proc. phil. Soc. Glasg.*, **2**, 163, 1847.
[8] ABEL, F. A. *Phil. Trans.*, **156**, 269, 1866; **157**, 181, 1867.
[9] British Patent No. 1234. 1867.
[10] British Patent No. 4179. 1875.
[11] British Patents Nos 921 and 2642. 1871.
     SPRENGEL, H. *J. chem. Soc.*, **26**, 796, 1873.
[12] German Patent No. 100 146. 1887.
[13] British Patent No. 900. 1864.
[14] French Patents No. 185179, 1887; and No. 199091, 1889.
     British Patent No. 1471. 1889.
[15] British Patent No. 10376. 1889.
[16] British Patents Nos 5614 and 11664. 1889.

BIBLIOGRAPHY

BÖCKMANN, F. 'Die explosiven Stoffe.' Vienna. 1880.
BRUNSWIG, H. 'Die Explosivstoffe.' Göschen, Leipzig. 1907.
CHALON, P. F. 'Traité théorique et pratique des explosifs modernes et dictionnaire des poudres et explosifs.' Paris. 1889.

'Coton-poudre, nitroglycérine et dynamites.' Conférence de M. Pellet, École Centrale des Arts et Manufactures. Paris. 1881.

DUMAS-GUILIN, M. 'La dynamite de guerre et le coton-poudre.' Paris, Limoges. 1887.

EISSLER, M. 'A Handbook of Modern Explosives.' London. 1890.

ESCALES, R. 'Die Explosivstoffe', Pts 1–8. Fock, Leipzig. 1904–17.

GODY, L. 'Traité théorique et pratique des matières explosives.' Namur. 1896.

GUTTMANN, O. 'The Manufacture of Explosives.' London. 1895.

Idem. 'The Manufacture of Explosives. Twenty Years Progress.' Whittaker, London. 1909.

'Imperial Chemical Industries and its Founding Companies', Vol. 1: 'The History of Nobel's Explosives Co. Ltd. and Nobel Industries Ltd., 1871–1926.' Imperial Chemical Industries, London. 1938.

KNOLL, R. 'Das Knallquecksilber und ähnliche Sprengstoffe.' Hartleben, Vienna. 1908.

MACDONALD, G. W. 'Historical Papers on Modern Explosives.' Whittaker, London. 1912.

MARDEL, L. 'Pólvoras, Explosivos Modernos e suas Applicações.' Lisbon. 1893.

MARSHALL, A. 'Explosives.' Churchill, London. 1917.

MEYER, E. VON. 'Die Explosivkörper und die Feuerwerkerei.' Brunswick. 1874.

MILES, F. D. 'Cellulose Nitrate.' Oliver & Boyd, London. 1955.

MOLINARI, E. and QUARTIERI, F. 'Notices sur les explosifs en Italie.' Società Italiana Prodotti Esplodenti, Milan. 1913.

NOBEL, A. "On Modern Blasting Agents." *J. Soc. Arts*, **23**, 611, 1875.

'Report from the Select Committee on Explosive Substances, 26th June, 1904.' H.M. Stationery Office, London. 1904.

'Report on the Thirty-third Meeting of the British Association for the Advancement of Science, 1863.' London. 1863.

ROMOCKI, S. J. VON. 'Geschichte der Explosivstoffe', Vols 1, 2. Berlin. 1895.

'The Rise and Progress of the British Explosives Industry.' Published under the auspices of the VIIth International Congress of Applied Chemistry, Explosives Section. Whittaker, London, New York. 1909.

'Treatise on Service Explosives.' London. 1895.

UPMANN, J. 'Schießpulver, dessen Geschichte, Fabrikation, Eigenschaften und Proben.' Brunswick. 1874.

WORDEN, E. C. 'Nitrocellulose Industry.' Constable, London. 1911.

A stage in the manufacture of mercury fulminate at Westquarter, Scotland, c 1890.

14

FINE CHEMICALS

ARTHUR W. SLATER

I. GENERAL CONSIDERATIONS

THE distinction between fine and heavy chemicals is easy to recognize but difficult to define. In general, fine chemicals are those which have a high unit value, are produced in relatively small quantities, and are of high purity, or fulfil one or more of these conditions [1]. Fine chemicals tend to have more complex molecular structures than heavy chemicals, but this is by no means an infallible diagnostic. Some are highly purified forms of substances met with in a cruder state as heavy chemicals.

Although numerous fine chemicals have been made since very early times, as has been shown in earlier volumes, their manufacture on any considerable scale dates from the last decades of the eighteenth century. Most of the output then, and in the early half of the following century, went to satisfy the demand for mordants and other auxiliaries used by the rapidly expanding textile industry, and for medicinal substances, such as quinine, borax, camphor, and ether, employed in pharmacy. In the second half of the nineteenth century great progress was made in the technology of fine chemicals, owing to the following circumstances.

The enormous industrial expansion in Britain, and the rapid developments in western Europe and the United States, created extensive new demands for industrial chemicals. Inevitably the increased output was most obvious in the heavy chemical industry, but there was also a significant increase in the output of fine chemicals. New methods had to be devised for producing on the manufacturing scale chemicals that had hitherto been encountered only in laboratories.

At the same time there was an astonishing increase in the number of synthetic compounds evolved by chemists. Some of these were synthetic forms of natural substances; others were entirely new compounds that did not exist in nature at all. Many of these new synthetic compounds were derivatives of coal-tar, a by-product of coal-gas manufacture previously regarded as a nuisance and embarrassment, but now to become the source of an apparently endless series of chemical compounds. From the distillation of coal-tar were derived benzene, toluene, naphthalene, anthracene, and phenol ('carbolic acid'). From these derivatives were obtained, as a sequel to Perkin's discovery of mauve in 1856, a whole range of entirely new and fascinating dyestuffs (ch 12); synthetic perfumes, of which coumarin was an early example; antiseptics derived from phenol or cresol; saccharin and other substitutes for natural products; and drugs such as salicylic acid.

These developments in organic chemistry reflected to some extent the current developments in theoretical chemistry, as well as a great deal of empirical laboratory research into chemical reactions. Contemporary research itself gave a great stimulus to the manufacture of inorganic and organic compounds of the high degree of purity essential for most laboratory work and for use as analytical reagents. A further demand for very pure chemicals came from the photographic industry, especially after the introduction of the dry-plate process (ch 30). The introduction of anaesthetics at the beginning of this period called for increasing supplies of chloroform and ether, both of which were made from ethyl alcohol, a product of the fermentation industry. The discovery of the antiseptic properties of phenol by Lister in 1865 led to increased production of pure phenol from crude carbolic acid, procured from coal-tar.

The expansion of the fine chemical industry was assisted by improvements in chemical engineering. The basic processes of all chemical manufacture—solution, filtration, evaporation, distillation, crystallization—are essentially simple and many of them were, and continued to be, carried out with very simple apparatus. Often such apparatus was adequate when output was small, but as the scale of operations increased it became necessary to install more complicated forms and to adopt mechanical aids.

When setting up plant for the manufacture of fine chemicals on any considerable scale two major considerations have to be borne in mind. First, a process that is perfectly suitable in the laboratory may, because of technical difficulties, prove to be quite impracticable on the manufacturing scale. Thus, in the laboratory, distillation is usually carried out in glass apparatus; on the large scale, metal stills and condensers may have to be employed, and this introduces the risk of corrosion of the plant by the chemicals used and consequent contamination of the final product.

Secondly, economic factors must be taken into account. This was particularly important in the latter half of the nineteenth century, when the fine chemical trade was in the hands of a number of comparatively small firms competing intensively with each other.

The chemical industry generally made increasing use of such aids to production as filter-presses (figure 154), centrifugal machines (hydro-extractors) (figure 155), dialysers, and vacuum pans. In making fine chemicals, many of which are liquid, improvements in distillation apparatus were of particular importance.

Power, when required, was supplied from a variety of sources. In Lancashire almost every bleach-works had a water-wheel or water-turbine, even in the 1880s, and water-power was commonly used in the chemical works in the United States. In London one eminent firm of fine chemical manufacturers was using a water-wheel for grinding chemicals as late as 1901, but this was a special case: the

FIGURE 154—*Dehne's filter-press, late nineteenth century.*

original wheel had been installed in the thirteenth century and the partners had a proper regard for tradition.[1] Steam was required for many purposes, such as heating stills, and the reciprocating steam-engine was the most important source of power. Towards the end of the century other prime movers—the steam-turbine, the gas-engine, the diesel-engine, and the electric motor—were introduced into the industry (chs 6, 7, 8).

The range of fine chemicals is technologically far too complex to be easily classified, but they can conveniently be treated by considering them according to the methods by which they were produced or the purposes for which they were required. Thus we can distinguish chemicals produced by the fermentation industries, notably ethyl alcohol; those produced from wood by destructive distillation or other means; anaesthetics, antiseptics, and other substances required for medicinal purposes; essential oils; and a whole series of fine chemicals for special and general purposes, such as photographic chemicals, solvents, and analytical reagents. These categories are not, however, by any means exclusive of one another: many important chemicals fall into more than one group. Ethyl

[1] This mill was situated at Stratford; at the end of the eighteenth century it was leased to a firm of maltsters, who in 1806 sold it to the chemical manufacturing firm.

alcohol, for example, is a valuable industrial solvent, forms the basis of the manufacture of many hundreds of organic chemicals, and has numerous applications in pharmacy. In this chapter, chemicals are included as far as possible under the category in which they have a particular significance; the remainder are dealt with individually.

FIGURE 155—*Centrifugal machine for separation of solids from liquids. In this type, the solid material was discharged into bags at the bottom.*

II. THE FERMENTATION INDUSTRIES

Although fermentation processes have been used since the earliest times, the foundation of the modern fermentation industries can be said to have been laid by the French chemist Louis Pasteur (1822–95) in the middle of the last century. He clearly showed that, as the German botanist F. T. Kützing (1807–93) had supposed, fermentation was due to the action of microscopic living organisms, such as yeast, which are present in the atmosphere at all times and which multiply extremely rapidly when conditions are favourable to them. Such organisms contain a variety of enzymes or 'ferments', each acting in a specific way and giving rise to different products, such as lactic and acetic acids and alcohol. Later researches, such as those of E. Buchner (1860–1917) in 1897, showed that the living yeast cell is not necessary for fermentation but that an appropriately prepared extract will serve equally well: this is due to the fact that the actual agent of fermentation is not the yeast cell as a whole but an enzyme, zymase, contained in it.

Alcoholic fermentation depends on the fact that zymase is capable of converting sugars into ethyl alcohol (C_2H_5OH). Starchy raw materials must first be converted into sugar. The first stage in this process is the production of malt, which is obtained by steeping barley in water and keeping it in a moist atmosphere until it begins to germinate. When the barley is malted it develops an active enzyme, diastase, which has the power of converting starch into sugar. The material to be fermented is then mashed with the requisite quantity of water, usually about 5 per cent, at about 140–150° F. During the process of mashing, the starch is converted by the diastase into a mixture known as wort, which is fermentable by yeast. The wort is cooled, yeast is added, and fermentation begins; the sugars in the wort are converted into alcohol and carbon dioxide. The fermentation is carried as far as possible in order to produce the maximum amount of alcohol. The fermented wort, known as wash, is then distilled in order to separate the alcohol from the water. The resultant spirit may be further purified by redistillation.

The precise nature of the spirit obtained in this way varies with the raw material used as the original source of starch or sugar. The materials fermented are many, since man has in all ages and all countries displayed the utmost ingenuity in converting the fruits of the earth into potable drinks. Thus, brandy is obtained from grapes by distilling wine, and whisky is distilled from malted barley. Gin, however, is a semi-synthetic product made by redistilling alcohol with suitable flavouring essences.

During the period under review the industrial production of ethyl alcohol, both for consumption and for manufacturing purposes, was much increased by two important innovations. First, Pasteur's investigation of the general nature of fermentation, and E. C. Hansen's researches into the properties of various yeast strains in Copenhagen between 1870 and 1880, enabled manufacturers to obtain a greatly improved yield of alcohol from a given quantity of raw material. Secondly, the introduction of the Coffey still (p 306) provided a method of making a highly concentrated spirit by a process of continuous distillation.

The raw material used in alcoholic fermentation was different in different countries. English distillers preferred to make grain spirit from a mixture of raw and malted grain (usually barley or maize); later, molasses was extensively used. Sugar-beet and sugar-beet molasses were used in France; in Germany potatoes were the chief raw material, but sugar-beet also was utilized.

When grain was the raw material employed, the first process was to saccharify the starch moiety of the grain, which was at first crushed, but not ground into flour unless maize was used. The whole grain might be malted, by causing it to germinate, but most distillers used a mixture of crushed raw grain and malted grain, in a proportion of between 6 and 10 to 1. This mixture was placed in the mash-tub, mixed with a little warm water by mechanical stirrers, and kept warm for from 1 to 4 hours by the admission of hot water or steam. The object of this operation was to convert the whole of the starch into maltose or malt-sugar, which is directly fermentable by yeast; the temperature was kept just below 146° F, at which point maltose production begins to fall. The wort was then drawn off and fresh water was run into the mash-tub at about 190° F. The residue was allowed to infuse for an hour or two, and the second wort was then added to the first. A third wort was often similarly obtained.

When potatoes were used less malt was required, since the starch content of potatoes is lower than that of grain. In order to expose the starch to the action of the diastase in the malt, the cells must be ruptured by subjecting the potatoes to heat. This was formerly done by boiling them to swell the cell membranes. The boiling took place in tall, narrow cylinders hermetically closed (with the exception of a valve for the escape of steam and condensed water) and the softened potatoes were then crushed between rollers before being passed to the mash-tub, where they were stirred up with malt. This method had the disadvantage that some of the cell membranes escaped rupture, so that a quantity of starch was not acted upon by the diastase and the yield was correspondingly reduced.

A great improvement in the yield of alcohol was effected by Hollefreund's method of steaming the potatoes under very high pressure in a strong iron cylinder connected to a boiler by one pipe and to an air-pump by another. Steam was turned on and the potatoes were mechanically stirred for about 20 minutes; then the steam was turned off and the air-pump connected. The low external pressure thus produced caused the cell membranes to burst, and the simultaneous cooling of the mass brought it to the correct mashing-temperature. The maximum quantity of starch was thus exposed to the action of the diastase when the malt was admitted into the cylinder, after which the stirrer was again set in motion. Steaming, disintegrating, and mashing took place in the same vessel.

When the mashing of grain or potatoes was completed, the wort was cooled, yeast was added, and the fermentation started. The details of procedure varied according to the type of mash, and the time of fermentation from 3 to 9 days.

When sugar-beet was used, as in France, the juice was extracted either by rasping and pressure or by slicing and maceration: the former yielded the better spirit. The juice was then slightly acidified with sulphuric acid and a small quantity of brewer's yeast was added. In Leplay Dubrunfaut's method, introduced just after the middle of the nineteenth century, the sugar was fermented in the beet-slices themselves by immersing them in bags in the fermenting-vats; the slices, charged with alcohol, were then distilled.

Molasses obtained from sugar-beet was available in large quantities in France, Germany, the Ukraine, and other continental countries; the crop was not established in Britain until the 1920s. The concentrated molasses was mixed with water, and sulphuric acid was added to neutralize any lime or alkali present and to convert the sugar into a fermentable form. Yeast was then introduced, and fermentation proceeded rapidly.

The design of stills varied greatly, from extremely simple apparatus to complicated stills and rectifiers designed to obtain the most concentrated alcohol from the crude fermentation products by a continuous operation. The number of different designs in use was far too large to be dealt with individually here, but three main types can be distinguished. There were, first, simple pot-stills heated by direct firing; secondly, stills of the closed or rectifying type fitted with a wash-warmer; thirdly, stills with wash-warmer, rectifying, and dephlegmation apparatus for either intermittent or continuous working.

Simple stills of the first type were in use everywhere throughout the century; they were no different in principle from the crude earthenware stills used by the natives of Ceylon to make arrack (figure 156). In Ireland, where illicit whiskey distilling reached the proportions of an industry, an acceptable poteen whiskey was produced with the crudest apparatus. The distillery was often a thatched cottage. There was a hearth at one end; a

FIGURE 156—*Primitive Sinhalese still for making arrack. Similar stills on this principle were widely used in the nineteenth century for distilling alcoholic liquors.*

hole in the roof served as a chimney. On the fire stood a 40-gallon tinned vessel supported on a semicircle of large stones. This was the combined wash-heater and still. The still-head, a large tinned pot with a tube in its side, was inverted on the rim of the still and luted to it with a paste made of oatmeal and water. The spirit passed through a condenser in the form of a copper coil into the receiver.

The legitimate Scotch whisky distiller used simple flat-bottomed pot-stills of 6–12 thousand gallons capacity. They were fitted with agitators to prevent the solid matter in the wash from settling on the bottom of the still and charring. These stills produced an excellent spirit but they were extremely wasteful of fuel; and although distillation was very rapid a strong spirit could be obtained only by repeated distillation.

In stills of the second type a wash-warmer, that is, a vessel filled with the liquid awaiting distillation, was interposed between the still and the condenser. The pipe conveying the hot vapour from the still to the condenser passed through it and heated up the wash, which in consequence was already hot when it entered the still. A further improvement was made in Dorn's still—used mainly in small distilleries in Germany—in which a vessel divided horizontally into two compartments by a copper diaphragm was interposed between the still and the condenser. The upper compartment served as a wash-warmer, and the tube conveying the vapours from the still passed through it into the lower compartment, where the distillate at first condensed. As the wash warmed up this distillate gave off alcoholic vapours which passed on and condensed in a worm; the watery fraction was allowed to flow back into the still by a side tube. This rectifying action could be increased by the interposition of two or more such

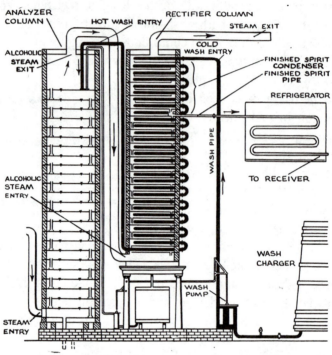

FIGURE 157—*The Coffey still, invented about 1830, was used throughout the remainder of the nineteenth century for the preparation of concentrated spirit.*

vessels between still and condenser, enabling a distillate much richer in alcohol to be obtained.

In the third type of still, fractional distillation was effected by a long established process of dephlegmation, which consisted in chilling the vapour by contact with metal diaphragms. The portion containing the most water was condensed and separated, while vapour rich in alcohol passed on to the rectifier or condenser.

The Coffey still (figure 157), invented by Aeneas Coffey about 1830, was recognized as the best and most economical apparatus for preparing a very concentrated spirit from grain-mashes in one operation. It was not, however, so well adapted for the preparation of malt whiskey, which depends for its flavour on the retention in the distillate of some volatile constituents of the wash. The

Coffey still produced a spirit containing between 86 and 95 per cent of alcohol; about 0·4 per cent of higher alcohols and related impurities, collectively termed fusel oil;[1] and a small amount of aldehydes. In this apparatus, the steam and the wash flow in opposite directions. The wash is pumped through the zigzag pipe (shown sectionally) in the rectifier, being heated in the process by rising steam. Discharging into the analyser, it falls from diaphragm to diaphragm through the dropping pipes. During the descent, the alcohol in the wash is carried off by the steam which is ascending the analyser through perforations in the diaphragms. The alcoholic steam then passes into the rectifier, where most of the alcohol is condensed by contact with the pipes carrying the cold wash, in the upper part of the column. It then passes into the receiver.

Alcohol for pharmaceutical and many industrial purposes was prepared from this spirit by further purification. It was mixed with an equal quantity of water and filtered through wood charcoal, to oxidize the fusel oil present. It was then rectified in a columnar still of the Savalle type (figure 158). The first run-

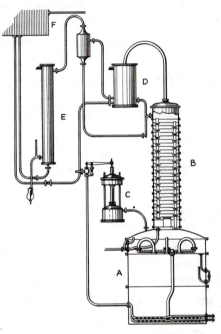

FIGURE 158—*Savalle's still with rectifying column for concentration of alcohol.* (A) *Still heated by steam coils;* (B) *rectifying column;* (C) *steam regulator;* (D, E) *condensers;* (F) *cold water reservoir.*

nings from the rectifier were impure but could be used for burning or for manufacturing processes in which the presence of impurities was unimportant. The second runnings were free from fusel oil and were largely used for pharmaceutical purposes, for the extraction of essential oils, and the manufacture of other organic chemicals. 'Absolute', or 100 per cent pure, alcohol was made by dehydrating the second runnings by means of quicklime and redistilling.

In many countries alcoholic liquors were subject to high duty and this seriously restricted their use in industry. In Britain the Board of Inland Revenue in 1855 sanctioned the sale of duty-free alcohol for manufacturing purposes, provided that it was denatured with methyl alcohol to render it unpotable. The product was known as methylated spirit. Similar concessions were made in other countries.

---

[1] Fusel comes from the German *fuseln*, to bungle; cf foozle, from the same source.

Among the by-products of the fermentation industry is tartaric acid. This was produced from argol, a crude material containing potassium hydrogen tartrate, which is deposited on the sides of the vessels during vinous fermentation. The argol was boiled with chalk, forming insoluble calcium tartrate. The calcium tartrate was filtered off, washed, and then heated with diluted sulphuric acid, thus forming insoluble calcium sulphate and a solution of tartaric acid. The solution was evaporated to dryness in vacuum pans to obtain the pure acid, which was used as a mordant in dyeing, for the making of effervescent salts and baking powder, and in pharmacy.

III. CHEMICALS FROM WOOD

Vinegar was manufactured by further fermentation of wine, cider, malt, and other similar raw materials, but acetic acid, its active constituent, was obtained by the destructive distillation of wood out of contact with air. This yields pyroligneous acid, which consists largely of acetic acid and methyl alcohol (wood-naphtha), together with allyl alcohol, acetone, a number of other chemicals, and a good deal of tarry material. Charcoal is left in the still.

The distillation was carried out in retorts of various kinds. It was found convenient in large works, where distillation was continuous, to have a number of separate retorts connected with one condensation apparatus and heated by the same flues; this allowed individual retorts to be removed and recharged without interrupting the process.

The retorts were heated slowly at first, to obtain the maximum yield of the low-temperature products, acetic acid and methyl alcohol. The temperature was then increased until gas came off freely; at the end of this stage the heat was further intensified to drive over high-temperature products. Superheated steam was often used for heating, as it furnished means of accurately controlling the application of the heat. This method was largely employed in works manufacturing charcoal for gunpowder. The distillate was allowed to stand, and soon separated in two layers—the lower one a thick dark tar, and the upper, much the larger, the crude pyroligneous acid. The yield of liquid products was affected not only by the temperature of distillation but by the variety of wood used. Deciduous trees in general gave more acid than coniferous trees, but the latter yielded more tar. The yield of methyl alcohol varied from 0·5 to 1 per cent of the weight of the dry wood.

Pyroligneous acid was also manufactured from such materials as sawdust and spent bark from tanneries, with Halliday's apparatus (figure 159). This consisted of a horizontal cylindrical retort within which revolved an endless screw.

The material to be pyrolysed was fed through a vertical pipe and was kept moving at a uniform speed along the entire length of the retort by the screw. At the farther end of the retort the products of distillation passed through an ascending pipe into the condenser, and the powdered charcoal dropped into water, where it was quenched. If sawdust is distilled in ordinary retorts they become coated with a hard crust of carbon that inhibits conduction of the heat.

Fry's process (1869) consisted of steam-distillation of wood in order to extract

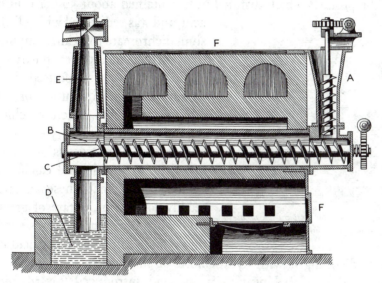

FIGURE 159—*Halliday's apparatus for preparing pyroligneous acid by the pyrolysis of sawdust, spent bark, or other vegetable waste material.* (A) *Hopper;* (B) *cylindrical retort;* (C) *revolving screw;* (D) *cistern;* (E) *outlet to condenser;* (F) *furnace.*

the desired products without carbonizing the wood, which could then be used for paper-making. The wood was cut into small chips and placed in zinc or copper cages inside a boiler, which was then filled with water and heated, by means of a steam-jacket at a pressure of 70–100 lb per sq in, for from 3 to 5 hours. The liquid in which the wood had been boiled was distilled.

The first step towards purification of the distillate in both these operations was to separate the wood-naphtha (the fraction containing the methyl alcohol) from the wood-vinegar (the fraction containing the acetic acid) by distillation. There were two methods. The crude pyroligneous acid could be neutralized with milk of lime and the wood-naphtha distilled off, when the tarry impurities would remain with the calcium salt of acetic acid in the still; on evaporation a dark mass known as brown acetate of lime was obtained. Alternatively, the pyroligneous acid was distilled without first neutralizing it with lime. The wood-naphtha distillate was collected first; the receiver was then changed and the crude acetic acid, now free largely from tar, was collected. It was neutralized with milk of lime and on evaporation yielded a salt known as grey acetate of lime. This evaporation was carried out in iron pans; impurities rose as a scum and were skimmed off. The acetate was then distilled with hydrochloric acid in copper retorts. If brown acetate was used it had first to be roasted to drive off the tar. The product which distilled over contained about 50 per cent of acetic acid, and was redistilled with a little potassium dichromate to oxidize impurities.

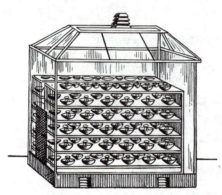

FIGURE 160—*Apparatus for preparation of acetic acid by catalytic oxidation of alcohol.*

A further method of purifying crude acetic acid was introduced by H. B. Condy in 1868. A solution of brown or grey acetate and calcium chloride in equivalent proportions yielded on slow evaporation large crystals of a double salt of calcium chloride and calcium acetate. Condy found that these crystals were readily formed in a state of great purity even when brown acetate was used. From this double salt pure acetic acid could be obtained by distilling it with hydrochloric or sulphuric acid.

A better method of making pure acetic acid, introduced towards the end of the century, was to neutralize the pyroligneous acid with soda instead of lime. Sodium acetate, unlike calcium acetate, can be purified by recrystallization and fused without decomposition. Glacial (100 per cent) acetic acid was always made by distilling fused anhydrous sodium acetate with concentrated sulphuric acid.

In Germany and other continental countries, where the duty on alcohol was not so high as in England, acetic acid was obtained during this period by an entirely different process—the oxidation of ethyl alcohol vapour by air in the presence of a platinum catalyst (figure 160). This was done in a closed box, in which were a large number of shallow porcelain dishes, each containing a porcelain tripod carrying a watch-glass holding spongy platinum. Alcohol was poured into the dishes and the temperature of the box was raised to 32° C while air was drawn through. Pure acetic acid was condensed from the current of air.

Acetic acid found many uses; the commercial product could, for example, be substituted in various processes for the more expensive vinegar. Many of its metallic salts were used in considerable quantities. Calcium acetate was used as an intermediate for making aluminium acetate, important as a mordant in dyeing and calico-printing. Basic copper acetate or verdigris was a valuable pigment. Among the uses of sodium acetate was that of filling foot-warmers in railway carriages, for which a saturated solution was used. Ammonium acetate was a traditional diaphoretic, known in medicine as Mindererus's spirit.

With alcohols, acetic acid reacts to form compounds known as esters. Amyl acetate was made by distilling a mixture of potassium acetate, sulphuric acid, and amyl alcohol, the latter derived from fusel oil. Under the name of 'essence of Jargonelle pears' it was widely used for flavouring confectionery; it was also commonly employed as a solvent in making lacquers.

Crude wood-naphtha always contains some acetone, which is also formed on the pyrolysis of many metallic acetates. Acetone was made on a large scale by distilling grey acetate of lime at about 290° C in iron stills provided with mechanical agitators. When pure it is a colourless liquid with a pleasant odour. It is an excellent solvent and was used in the manufacture of chloroform and of the antiseptic iodoform.

Methyl alcohol, as already noted, is present in crude wood-naphtha, of which it forms 75–90 per cent. To obtain it, the wood-naphtha was treated with milk of lime and then distilled in a columnar still. The distillate contained methyl alcohol, acetone, and small quantities of other impurities. It was diluted with water and redistilled over lime. It still contained acetone, from which it could be freed by several methods; this was not necessary, however, if it was to be used in the manufacture of aniline dyes or for denaturing ethyl alcohol. Pure methyl alcohol was obtained by passing chlorine through boiling wood-naphtha; any acetone present was converted into chlorine compounds of high boiling-point, from which the methyl alcohol could be separated by fractional distillation.

Oxalic acid also was made from wood, by mixing sawdust with caustic potash and spreading the mixture on heated iron plates. The resulting mass was lixiviated with water and the solution evaporated until sodium oxalate crystallized out; the crystals were separated centrifugally. The crude sodium oxalate was boiled with milk of lime for some time and the resulting calcium oxalate was decomposed with an excess of sulphuric acid; the insoluble calcium sulphate was then filtered off and the oxalic acid purified by crystallization.

Oxalic acid was largely used in calico-printing, as a bleach, for cleaning articles made of copper or brass, in the manufacture of leather, and for making formic acid.

IV. ANAESTHETICS

Scarcely a century has passed since the nightmare of surgical operations performed on fully conscious patients was ended by the introduction of anaesthetics. As early as 1799 Sir Humphry Davy wrote: 'As nitrous oxide in its extensive operation appears capable of destroying physical pain, it may possibly be used during surgical operations.'

The intoxicating effects of nitrous oxide were well known: 'laughing-gas parties' were fashionable in the early nineteenth century. The medical profession ignored Davy's discovery for nearly half a century, although Henry Hill Hickman, a surgeon at Ludlow, who in 1824 had successfully anaesthetized animals with carbon dioxide, spent years in an unsuccessful campaign to persuade surgeons in England and France to experiment with nitrous oxide as an anaesthetic. In December 1844, Horace Wells (1815–48), a dentist at Hartford, Connecticut, had a tooth extracted under nitrous oxide—having previously taken the precaution to make his will—and subsequently conducted a number of dental operations with this gas.

A little earlier, in March 1842, an American surgeon, Crawford W. Long (1815–78), had used ether to anaesthetize a patient while conducting a minor operation; the operation was successful, but that ether had been employed was not generally known.

On 30 September 1846, W. T. G. Morton (1819–68), a former pupil of Wells, extracted a tooth with the use of ether, and in October, at the Massachusetts General Hospital, administered ether to a patient upon whom J. C. Warren (1778–1856) operated for the removal of a tumour. The success of this operation while the patient was under an anaesthetic was rightly hailed as the great discovery of the age. Later that year Liston used ether as an anaesthetic at University College Hospital, London.

The use of ether as an anaesthetic in childbirth was initiated by the celebrated gynæcologist James Young Simpson (1811–70) in 1847. It was not altogether satisfactory, and, as the result of a deliberate search for a substance that would act more rapidly, he discovered the anaesthetic properties of chloroform in the same year. His use of chloroform in obstetrics involved him in acute controversy,[1] which, however, died away with remarkable suddenness when John Snow (1815–58) administered it to Queen Victoria at the birth of Prince Leopold in 1853.

Once the anaesthetic properties of nitrous oxide, ether, and chloroform were

[1] To an opponent who quoted, from Genesis, 'In sorrow thou shalt bring forth children', Simpson retorted that, before the creation of Eve, 'The Lord God caused a deep sleep to fall upon Adam'.

established the fine chemical industry was called upon to supply both these and, subsequently, other substances to meet a new and urgent demand. Nitrous oxide was prepared by cautiously heating pure ammonium nitrate and compressing the gas into cylinders. Ether had been manufactured since the eighteenth century for pharmaceutical purposes and for use as a solvent, and therefore ample supplies were available when it was introduced as an anaesthetic.

Ether was usually manufactured on a large scale by Soubeiran's process, which

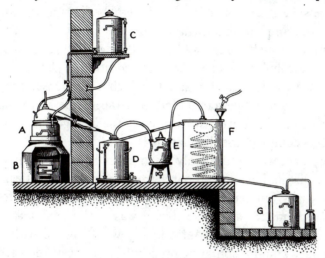

FIGURE 161—*Soubeiran's ether rectifier. Because of the very high inflammability of ether, the furnace and retort are separated from the rest of the apparatus by a brick wall.* (A) *Retort;* (B) *furnace;* (C) *alcohol reservoir,* (D) *first condenser;* (E) *purifier;* (F) *worm-condenser;* (G) *receiver.*

had the great advantage that it could produce reasonably pure ether in a single operation, thus economizing in labour and fuel and minimizing handling—the latter an important point in the preparation of a dangerously inflammable substance like ether. A diagram of the apparatus is shown in figure 161. A mixture of about 30 lb of sulphuric acid and 20 lb of 85 per cent alcohol is heated rapidly in a copper still, to the bottom of which two tubes carry alcohol from a tinned copper reservoir. The neck of the still, which is of lead, is connected with a first condenser, a copper vessel kept warm by allowing the waste water from the worm tub (where the ether is finally condensed) to flow over it. Here the steam and alcohol vapour are condensed, and the liquid formed can be drawn off by means of a stop-cock. The vapour of the much more volatile ether then passes on to the purifier. This consists of a vessel filled with wood-charcoal saturated with caustic soda; its purpose is to remove sulphur dioxide. The pure ether vapour is condensed in the well cooled worm-condenser.

The danger in handling ether arises from its volatility and its inflammability; the vapour forms a highly explosive mixture with air. For these reasons great care has to be taken in its manufacture and handling. Ether vapour is liable to creep along the ground or floor of a workshop to a surprising distance, and if it should come into contact with a naked flame an explosion is almost inevitable. The furnaces or fire-places in ether works were therefore isolated from the main apparatus by a brick wall (figure 161). Alternatively, and preferably, coils filled with high-pressure steam or a liquid of high boiling-point, such as coal-tar phenol, were used in place of a furnace.

Chloroform was usually prepared by distilling a mixture of bleaching-powder with water and alcohol, with or without the addition of slaked lime. The dilute alcohol solution was warmed in a still to which a condenser was attached, the bleaching powder and lime were added, and the temperature was raised until chloroform began to distil over; subsequently the heat generated in the reaction itself sufficed to complete the distillation.

Since chloroform was used mainly as an anaesthetic it was essential that the product of the distillation should be free from harmful impurities. This requirement was not easily fulfilled in an age when the adulteration of food and drugs was accepted as a matter of course: bread was adulterated with alum, vinegar with sulphuric acid, and sugar confectionery was coloured with red lead. The analytical sanitary commission appointed by the 'Lancet' reported that 'nearly all the most useful and important articles of the *materia medica* were grossly and systematically adulterated, often to an enormous extent'. For this reason, contemporary works on applied chemistry dealt at some length with the tests to be applied to chloroform to ascertain its standard of purity, since much of the chloroform supplied for medical use was contaminated with unchanged alcohol, acetaldehyde, methyl alcohol, and hydrochloric acid.

A good deal of chloroform was made from methylated spirit instead of pure ethyl alcohol, and this caused serious doubts to be expressed about its suitability for anaesthetic purposes unless it had been subsequently purified. However, the difficulty was overcome by a new process, introduced in the 1870s, by which a dilute solution of chloral was decomposed by caustic potash or soda and distilled. Chloroform obtained by this method is normally quite safe for use as an anaesthetic.[1]

Nitrous oxide, ether, and chloroform are all inhalation anaesthetics. The first local anaesthetic, producing anaesthesia at the site of the operation only, was

---

[1] Even so, however, it should be kept in the dark in tightly stoppered bottles, as it slowly oxidizes on exposure to air and light with formation of the very poisonous substance phosgene.

introduced in 1884 by Carl Koller (1857–1944), who first used cocaine, an alkaloid extracted from the leaves of the coca plant (*Erythroxylon coca*), in ophthalmic surgery. Cocaine, however, has toxic properties and it was not long before a search for substitutes for it began. In 1897 Einhorn and Heintz discovered that the esters of aminobenzoic and some related acids possessed marked local anaesthetic properties. This led to the discovery of a whole series of synthetic local anaesthetics, such as novocaine.

V. ANTISEPTICS AND DISINFECTANTS

The introduction of anaesthetics opened up a new era in surgery, and made it possible for surgeons to attempt operations that they could not previously have undertaken. Among the immediate results, unhappily, was an increase in post-operational mortality owing to sepsis, the cause of which was not then understood.

The problem of the nature of sepsis was eventually solved by Joseph Lister (1827–1912), who grasped the significance of Pasteur's discoveries in relation to fermentation and deduced that suppuration was due to the presence of living organisms in the tissues. He believed that they were introduced from the air, and experimented with carbolic acid (phenol) as an antiseptic in surgery, with pronounced success. Lister realized that it was better to employ antiseptics before an operation than afterwards. In 1867 he published a paper which was to establish his method of antiseptic surgery and to effect a further revolution in medical practice.

Although Lister was the first to realize clearly the role of microbes in causing infections, the value of certain substances as disinfectants was empirically known long before the nineteenth century. Thus the ancient Egyptians were aware of the preservative effects of natron (sodium sesquicarbonate), which they used in embalming. In the nineteenth century many substances were tried as disinfectants and antiseptics with varying success. In the early decades of the century the use of bleaching-powder (chloride of lime) was strongly advocated, especially in France, where it is still popular. Experiments were carried out on the disinfection of ships by gaseous chlorine, and a similar experiment was made during the cholera epidemic at Paisley in 1832, when a procession of six large tubs filled with a mixture of chloride of lime and dilute acid—yielding gaseous chlorine—was escorted through the streets of the stricken town, the inhabitants opening all windows to admit the cleansing fumes [2].

Iodoform, discovered in 1822 by Serullas, was not used as an antiseptic until 1878. Boric acid (p 320), zinc chloride, cresols, mercuric chloride, thymol, and various permanganates (Condy's fluid), were among the many antiseptics advocated in the second half of the nineteenth century. Carbolic acid, however, retained much of its popularity, and was particularly important during this time as a basis of a whole range of compounds.

Carbolic acid or phenol, one of the first compounds extracted from coal-tar, was prepared by distilling the tar and collecting the fraction that came over between 170° and 230° C. The distillate was allowed to cool, when naphthalene crystallized out, and the residual liquid was treated with caustic soda or potash in a tank in which it could be stirred. The solution of 'carbolate of soda' was acidified with sulphuric acid, and was at once decanted from the crystals of sodium sulphate which began to form in the tank. The crude carbolic acid was then allowed to stand for a few days to allow any remaining sodium sulphate to separate out. It was washed with water and distilled from small retorts. Three fractions were obtained—first, water and oil; secondly, an oil from which carbolic acid crystals could be obtained; thirdly, non-crystallizable phenols, or 'liquid carbolic acid'.

Many processes were devised further to purify the crude carbolic acid, but the most usual was to distil it in wrought iron stills, the acid which came over being then redistilled from a columnar still after treatment with potassium dichromate and sulphuric acid. Phenol, when pure, crystallizes in long colourless needles, but the commercial product was liable to have a pink or red colour. Apart from its application as a disinfectant, it was used extensively as a raw material in the manufacture of many dyestuffs (p 273), and in the manufacture of picric acid (p 296), itself a yellow dye and the basis of many high explosives.

Another substance found to possess useful antiseptic properties was salicylic acid; a method for preparing it from phenol on the commercial scale was devised by Kolbe. Crystalline phenol was dissolved in caustic soda and the solution evaporated to dryness in shallow iron vessels, stirring thoroughly. The resulting sodium phenolate was then heated in a retort in a current of carbon dioxide and the temperature gradually raised. A greyish-white mass of sodium salicylate was left in the retort. This was dissolved in water, freed from colouring matter by fractional precipitation with sulphuric or hydrochloric acid, and the salicylic acid itself then precipitated by further addition of acid. It was purified by repeated recrystallization from water. Salicylic acid was used also as a febrifuge and antirheumatic; in food-preserving; and for the manufacture of a number of dyes.

VI. ESSENTIAL OILS

Essential oils for cosmetic purposes have been prepared since the most remote times, and the three principal methods—*enfleurage*, maceration, and expression—

were practised in the nineteenth century in much the same way as in ancient Egypt (vol I, p 289) and so need no further description here. The method of steam-distillation, which depends on the fact that the essential oils are both volatile and immiscible with water, also has been known for centuries, but it received some notable improvements in the nineteenth century as a result of the general improvement in the design of stills. In its simplest form the method consists in boiling the crushed plant-material with water in a still heated by a direct fire. The distillate consists of a mixture of oil and water, from which the oil is easily separated since it floats on the surface. By the end of the century elaborate stills with a capacity of 16 000 gallons, treating a ton or more of plant-material in each operation, were in use. Another new development was the extraction of the oils with volatile solvents such as ether, alcohol, or carbon disulphide, which could subsequently be removed from the oils, and recovered for further use, by distillation.

Developments in theoretical chemistry made it possible both to establish the chemical identity of many of the constituents of essential oils and, in many cases, to synthesize them from simpler and cheaper substances. A notable example was Perkin's synthesis of coumarin from salicylaldehyde in 1868. This substance gives tonka beans their characteristic odour. Vanillin, one of the most widely used flavouring essences, is the active principle of vanilla pods; it was synthesized first from eugenol, itself obtained from cloves, and later from guaiacol.

The essential oils found many uses, most of them traditional. They were used for perfumes, toilet preparations, and soaps, and as flavourings in the culinary arts. Some, such as oils of eucalyptus, camphor, and wintergreen, found medicinal applications. Oil of turpentine was made on a very large scale for the paint industry.

VII. DRUGS AND PHARMACEUTICALS

In 1851 drugs were still largely of vegetable origin, but the tenth edition of the 'London Pharmacopoeia', published in that year, reflected the growing tendency towards using specific chemical substances in medicine. Among the new remedies introduced into this edition were morphine salts, tannic acid, sulphur iodide, zinc chloride, ferrous ammonium citrate, and chloroform.

Researches begun in the early years of the century had indicated that the action of vegetable drugs was due to the presence of definite chemical individuals, many of which had since been isolated. Among them were certain alkaloids, notably morphine and quinine.

Morphine, the active principle of opium, and the first known vegetable alkaloid, was isolated by Sertürner in 1806 and its manufacture had been developed on an appreciable scale. Quinine, the active principle of cinchona bark introduced into Europe from the New World about 1630, was isolated by P. J. Pelletier (1788–1842) and J. B. Caventou (1795–1877) in 1820; three years later its manufacture was begun at Stratford, London.

The isolation of these active compounds in a pure state had far-reaching consequences in medicine and in the fine chemical industry. First, it enabled accurate dosages of the drug to be established: this had been impossible in the past when patients had to be treated with crude drugs of unknown and variable composition.[1] Secondly, harmful effects due to the presence of impurities in the crude drugs could be avoided. Thirdly, investigation of the chemical composition of the active principles led to attempts to synthesize them and related substances.

The output of synthetic drugs increased greatly after 1860, and especially between 1885 and 1890. In 1875 it was found that salts of salicylic acid (p 316) were effective febrifuges. Aspirin (acetylsalicylic acid) was first prepared in 1899. Phenacetin, often compounded with it, was introduced in 1887. Saccharin, a valuable synthetic sweetening agent, was produced from toluene by Ira Remsen (1846–1927) in 1879. Liebreich, in 1868, discovered the soporific properties of chloral hydrate, the first synthetic hypnotic to be introduced into medicine. Paraldehyde was introduced as a hypnotic in 1882, and sulphonal in 1889. Barbitone (veronal[2]) was discovered by Nebelthau in 1898, and a wide range of similar drugs, the barbiturates, has since been prepared.

The advent of these synthetic products did not diminish the large-scale extraction of drugs from plant material by means of solvents, usually water or alcohol; this was still a function of the pharmaceutical manufacturer at the end of the century. In the preparation of such drugs as senna, liquorice, and cascara, which were extracted with water, the crude raw material was disintegrated before being fed into the digesters. These were usually long rectangular vessels, either copper tanks or wooden vats lined with sheet copper, furnished with a cold-water supply for cold extraction or with steam-coils for hot extraction. The liquid extract was usually concentrated in vacuum pans.

Alcoholic extraction was often necessary: for example, with alkaloids, resins, or essential oils. In the manufacture of alcoholic extracts the design of the plant was mainly governed by the necessity of conserving the expensive spirit used. Thus filters and filter-presses were sealed to prevent evaporation.

[1] The importance of using drugs free from contaminants was realized by Paracelsus (1493–1541) and his followers, but contemporary methods of purification were inadequate.

[2] The name is due to von Mering, who considered Verona to be the most restful city in the world.

VIII. BROMINE AND IODINE

Bromine is a red, fuming liquid with a pungent smell: it is one of the only two elements which are liquid at normal temperature, the other being mercury. Discovered by A. J. Balard (1802–76) in 1826, it remained a scientific curiosity until 1860. Then developments in photography and medicine created a demand for bromides, and bromine itself was required for the manufacture of coal-tar dyes.

Bromine was obtained from the mother-liquor remaining after the crystallization of salt from sea-water (which contains about 2 oz of bromine, as bromide, per ton) or from the Stassfurt carnallite deposits (which contain about $5\frac{1}{2}$ lb per ton). The concentrated mother-liquor, rich in magnesium bromide, was trickled down a tower packed with earthenware balls. Chlorine entered the tower from below, and reacted with the solution, liberating the bromine and forming magnesium chloride. Bromine vapour left the top of the tower at the upper end and was condensed. Any bromine left in the liquor was expelled by steam. The gas leaving the condenser was led into a small tower packed with moist iron filings, in which any further bromine was absorbed.

Bromine was chiefly used for the production of eosin dyes; for the production of potassium bromide, used in medicine as a sedative; and in the manufacture of silver bromide for the rapidly growing photographic industry. Potassium bromide was made by dissolving bromine in caustic potash, evaporating to dryness, and heating strongly with charcoal. Silver bromide, which is insoluble in water, was obtained as a precipitate by adding silver nitrate to a solution of potassium bromide. Liquid bromine was sometimes used as a disinfectant, for which purpose it was absorbed in kieselguhr to make it easier to handle.

Iodine occurs in small quantities in certain seaweeds and was formerly obtained from kelp, the ash obtained from burning them. Kelp was at one time an important source of soda (vol IV, p 236). To obtain iodine, the kelp was lixiviated with water, and the solution was run off and concentrated by evaporation in cast iron pans, when many of the dissolved salts crystallized out. By repetition of the process a mother-liquor rich in potassium iodide was obtained. This liquor was mixed with sulphuric acid and allowed to settle, filtered to remove any deposit, and run into an iodine still (figure 162). A set of stills consisted of a series of hemispherical iron pots, heated by open fires, each retort being connected by lead pipes to two sets of flat earthenware condensers known as udells or aludels, about ten in each set. Manganese dioxide was then added to the contents of the still and the liberated iodine distilled over with the steam. Distillations went on continuously until the udells were full of iodine, which was obtained in a dry crystalline form ready for the market. Iodine required in a pure state, especially for medicinal purposes, was resublimed in small earthenware pots.

This process had the merit of yielding directly a product pure enough to be sold, but towards the end of the century iodine was largely obtained as a by-product in the purification of Chilean saltpetre or *caliche* (sodium nitrate) (p 255). The mother-liquor remaining after the recrystallization of *caliche* contained about 0·5 per cent of iodine. It was run into wooden vats coated with pitch, and the iodine was precipitated with the calculated amount of sodium bisulphite.

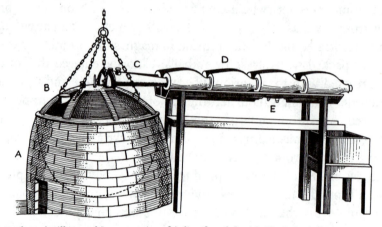

FIGURE 162—*A still as used in preparation of iodine from kelp.* (A) *Hemispherical iron pot set in brickwork fireplace;* (B) *lid with hoisting chains;* (C) *lead pipes;* (D) *udells;* (E) *drainage stoppers for removing water from udell.*

The iodine was washed with water, pressed into cakes, and purified by sublimation from an iron retort.

The main use of iodine was as an antiseptic, but some was used in making coal-tar dyes, such as erythrosin, and silver iodide for photographic purposes.

IX. BORIC (BORACIC) ACID AND BORAX

Boric acid occurs naturally in many parts of the world, but for many years Tuscany was the chief source. There, in the province of Pisa, jets of volcanic steam (*soffioni*) issuing from the ground are charged with this acid to the extent of about 0·06 per cent by weight, and the acid remains dissolved in the small lagoons formed when the vapour condenses. The boric acid was obtained by building walls round the crevices or fumaroles from which the jets of steam issued (figure 163), and the water so condensed and collected was acidified and run into a common reservoir, where it was allowed to settle. Thence it passed to iron or lead pans heated by the *soffioni* themselves, no additional heat being necessary. On concentration by evaporation, calcium sulphate and other in-soluble impurities were deposited in the pans; the boric acid crystallized when the hot concentrated solution was allowed to cool. It was further purified by treatment with charcoal, followed by recrystallization.

Borax (sodium pyroborate) occurs in solution in salt lakes in Transylvania, Peru, India, and Tibet. In the earlier part of the century it was imported in large

FIGURE 163—*Method of preparing boric acid in Tuscany.*

quantities from India as tincal, a crude salt obtained by the evaporation of the water of borax lakes. The crude tincal, which was very impure, was treated with lime, filtered, and purified by crystallization.

Later, borax was largely obtained from Searles Lake in California. The bed of this lake, which is in a volcanic region, was covered with borax crystals: these were recovered by sinking caissons, pumping out the water, and digging out the borax. The crude salt was purified by dissolving in water, decanting from insoluble matter, and crystallizing. It was purified by recrystallization. A very pure borax was also obtained by treating boric acid with sodium carbonate.

REFERENCES

[1] WILLIAMS, T. I. "Chemicals" in 'A Century of Technology' ed. by P. DUNSHEATH. Hutchinson, London. 1951.
[2] CLOW, A. and CLOW, NAN L. 'The Chemical Revolution.' Batchworth Press, London. 1952.

BIBLIOGRAPHY

BLOUNT, B. and BLOXAM, A. G. 'Chemistry for Engineers and Manufacturers' (2 vols). London. 1896.
'Chemistry, Theoretical, Practical, and Analytical as Applied to the Arts and Manufactures', by writers of eminence (2 vols, 8 pts). London. 1882.
DAVIS, G. E. 'A Handbook of Chemical Engineering' (2nd ed., 2 vols). Davis, Manchester. 1904.
GILDEMEISTER, E. and HOFFMANN, F. 'The Volatile Oils' (trans. from the German by E. KREMERS). Pharmaceutical Review Publishing Company, Milwaukee. 1900.
PAUL, B. H. (Ed.). 'Payen's Industrial Chemistry.' London. 1878.
SADTLER, S. P. 'A Handbook of Industrial Organic Chemistry' (2nd ed.). Philadelphia. 1895.
THORPE, T. E. 'A Dictionary of Applied Chemistry', (3 vols). London. 1890, 1891, 1893.

15

THE DEVELOPMENT OF RAILWAY ENGINEERING

C. HAMILTON ELLIS

I. GENERAL

THE use of railway transport is at least medieval, if not earlier. Vehicles running on flanged wheels, with a track made of poles, are described in Agricola's *De re metallica* (1556) and were used then in the mountains of Transylvania (vol II, tailpiece, p 562). Guidance of vehicles by ruts was much older (vol I, p 499); this arrangement may be said to have invented itself originally. Early railways were therefore of two kinds with, respectively, the plain wheel bearing on rut-bottom—or, later, on a flanged plate—and the Danubian flanged wheel on a plain rail.

It was not until the early nineteenth century that the flanged wheel running on what was contemporaneously called the edge-rail came into general use for railway track. Variations still persist to meet special conditions. In some funicular mountain railways, one set of wheels is flangeless and the other double-flanged; aerial cable-ways and suspended mono-rails, such as the Langen type, necessarily involve double-flanged wheels on the single rail; the street tramway employs narrow flanged wheels running on a grooved rail-head. The former Kingston upon Hull tramways used a medial flange.

Until reliable motive power was available, railways remained of only local importance. Richard Trevithick's application of his high-pressure engine in the first decade of the nineteenth century (tailpiece, and plate 20 A) made possible the commercial steam railway, and much valuable work was done by Matthew Murray, Timothy Hackworth, and George and Robert Stephenson, and by Marc Seguin in France. The latter's multi-tubular boiler, Hackworth's refined use of exhaust steam to create a strong, even draught, and the mechanical flair and business acumen of the Stephensons, combined to produce the archetype of the steam locomotive as it was to be known for more than a century.

Early locomotives caused continual trouble by breaking the brittle cast iron rails, and it was not until malleable iron rails were produced, and then improved, that main-line steam railways became a commercial possibility. The tractive

weakness of the locomotives necessitated very gentle gradients on the new railways, which had to be as nearly level as possible. This was the reason for the
magnificently easy grading of such early main lines as the London and Birmingham and the Great Western between London and Swindon. By 1866, however,
Joseph Mitchell could confidently build the Inverness and Perth Junction Railway with very long stretches as steep as 1 in 70, and even as far back as 1840 the
Birmingham and Gloucester Railway had built, and worked, two miles over the
Lickey Hills at more than 1 in 38.

The now vanished race of navvies (the 'navigators' who built the canals)

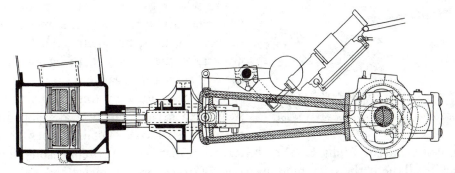

FIGURE 164—*Stephenson link motion and slide-valve, with steam reversing gear, London and South Western
Railway. It is shown in neutral or mid-gear with the engine on dead-centre. The marine-type big-end, visible
beyond the excentrics, was characteristic of Dugald Drummond's work both in Scotland and on the South Western
Railway.*

furnished the heavy labour needed for early railway construction. There were no
means of mechanical excavation; railways were built by pick and spade, shovel
and barrow. There was arduous work indeed in all railway building, whether the
technique were that of Joseph Locke, which was to go up and round, or that of
Robert Stephenson, which was to go as nearly as possible straight through.

The world's first public railway to handle both goods and passenger traffic on
the main line by steam locomotives was the Liverpool and Manchester Railway,
opened in 1830; it was followed at the end of the decade by the first of the great
trunk lines. By 1850, following the boom and slump called the 'railway mania',
railway transport was firmly established. The ensuing half-century saw it progress towards methods still familiar. In 1850 British and many foreign railways
were laid with double-headed iron rails keyed into chairs on transverse wooden
sleepers. Some lines, such as the Great Western, used flat-footed or inverted-
U-section rails on longitudinal baulks kept in place by cross-ties. This form had
an American poor relation, the strap rail, which showed a disastrous tendency to

curl up and pierce the floors of the cars. Much better, and extensively used abroad, was the inverted-T rail, with its flat foot resting directly on the sleepers. Today it is the world-wide form, though now of much heavier section and used in conjunction with spring clips or bolts, and with sole-plates between sleeper and rail.

The world's commonest rail-gauge, 4 ft 8½ in, derived from that of the Tyneside colliery tram-roads. The broadest, used on parts of the Great Western down to 1892, was 7 ft 0¼ in. This gauge has been exceeded only by travelling crane tracks. Other gauges still in considerable use today are 3 ft 6 in (sometimes called the Cape gauge), one metre, the Russian 5 ft gauge, the Irish 5 ft 3 in gauge, and the Indian 5 ft 6 in gauge.

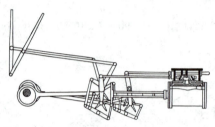

FIGURE 165—*Gab valve-gear and slide-valve, forms of which were widely used before the adoption of expansive link motions in the 1840s.*

Valve-gears for admitting and using the steam expansively had been developed in the eighteen-forties, notable types being those of Daniel and John Gooch, of Alexander Allan, and the Stephenson–Howe gear. In all these, the valve motions were controlled by excentrics and a sliding reversing-link, hence the generic term 'link motion' (figure 164). Earlier valvegears had been used solely for the admission and exhaust of steam to and from the cylinders, with no means of varying the cut-off through a reversing link. Very early gears were usually indirect, the excentric rods engaging by means of gabs[1] with rockers which conveyed their motion to the valve rods (figure 165).

There were at this time two classic types of locomotive, both British in origin. That of Edward Bury (1794–1858), with bar frames, was exported to the United States where it was enthusiastically accepted; much modified, elaborated, and enormously enlarged, it remained the orthodox steam railway-engine there for well over a century. The plate-framed or slab-framed engine, in various forms, became the characteristic British type, and even the most recent steam locomotives of British Railways are all plate-framed. Two typical British and American locomotives of about 1880 are compared in figures 166 and 167. Engineers throughout the world copied either the bar-framed or the plate-framed type. There were numerous variations, some important, some freakish. Akin to the plate-framed engine, but now long obsolete, was the sandwich-framed engine. In this the main frames, outside the wheels but supplemented by inside plate

---

[1] Hooks or forks designed to drop over a rod or lever to make a temporary connexion.

frames, were of hardwood planking enclosed between iron plates. Thomas Russell Crampton (1816–88), an English engineer more honoured abroad than in his own country, originated the now general practice of placing not only the cylinders but the valve-gear outside, with raised platforms to improve access. Though design was generally simple, drawing-office standards were very high; many surviving drawings are unsurpassed in their meticulous beauty.

Locomotive speeds in the mid-nineteenth century were very variable. On the

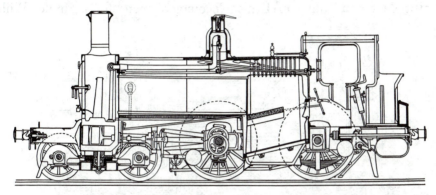

FIGURE 166—*Fast passenger tank engine by Dugald Drummond for the North British Railway, 1879. It has Stephenson link motion, Adams bogie, and Ramsbottom safety-valves. The drawing shows the brick arch in the fire-box, but all save two of the flue tubes, of which there were 220, are omitted. (Cf figure 167.)*

Great Western, which then used broad gauge and engines that were relatively large even by much later standards, 60 miles an hour was commonplace. Elsewhere, however, especially in other countries, speeds were generally much lower. Locomotive performance was already being scientifically studied, Daniel Gooch (1816–89) of the Great Western having built the first dynamometer cars for running tests. A later example of a locomotive following Gooch's basic design is the 'Swallow' (plate 21 A).

The passage of feed-water into the boiler under pressure was at first accomplished entirely by force-pumps, which might be worked by a crank or by an extension-rod off the cross-head. In either case, the engine could replenish loss by evaporation only while in motion, or at any rate with the wheels revolving. During idle periods, unless these were spent on a special roller-bed, it was necessary to steam a locomotive backwards and forwards on a siding for this purpose alone. To the French engineer Henri Giffard (1825–82) goes the credit for production of the first practical injectors, in which the energy of live steam issuing from a jet draws feed-water from the tank. The steam condenses with the fresh feed-water, and the mixture of the two passes through a second jet and thence through a widening passage, the pressure of the water then being sufficient to pass through a clack-valve against the boiler pressure; in this way the necessary water-level is maintained in the boiler. Giffard's original injectors were installed experimentally during the middle years of the century, and were thereafter improved, but many British engineers were at first shy of them. To a certain conservative type of mind the injector, compared with the simple though inconvenient force-pump, seemed to entail a sort of mechanical cheating. All too often this attitude was a failing of British locomotive men; for example, William

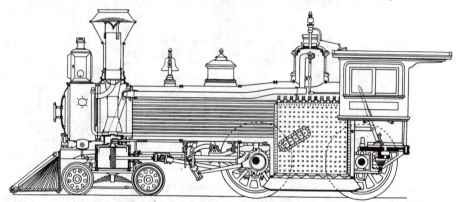

FIGURE 167—*American engine built for the Old Colony Railroad in 1883. The slide-valves are on top of the cylinders, worked through rockers; there is a complex spark arrester, an extended smoke-box, and a water-bridge in the fire-box, which has a large grate for burning low-grade fuel.* (*Cf figure 166.*)

Stroudley of Brighton, often held up as a pattern of the Victorian locomotive engineer, and certainly an apostle of careful design and superb workmanship, clung to his old force-pumps (plate 21 C).

Other appliances connected with boiler feed, which saw application as far back as the 1860s, were apparatus for its pre-heating and purification. Schau in Austria, and Wagner (Bergisch–Märkische Railway), removed scale-producing impurities by passing the injected feed-water down through a series of trays placed in an extra dome on the barrel of the boiler, the clack-valves being mounted on this dome and the water introduced at the top. This arrangement was the earliest practical form of what we know today as top-feed, and in Germany it is still called the Wagner purifier. Joseph Beattie, of the London and South Western Railway, patented and used various forms of feed-water heater. The oldest was a jet-condenser using exhaust steam, which resulted in oil and other impurities getting into the boiler. Beattie superseded this with an arrangement of concentric tubes, in which exhaust steam warmed the feed-water without direct contact. As Giffard injectors could not deal with hot feed-water, both the old force-pumps and steam-driven donkey-pumps were used, the latter in conjunction with the heater.

One of the most important developments of the late 1850s and 1860s was the substitution of coal for coke as fuel. Coke was smokeless, but expensive; on the other hand early legislation required that locomotives 'must effectively consume their own smoke' and coke provided the only sure preventive of smoke-emission and consequent prosecution of the railway companies. Complex boilers were devised by Joseph Beattie, J. I. Cudworth (South Eastern), and J. E. McConnell

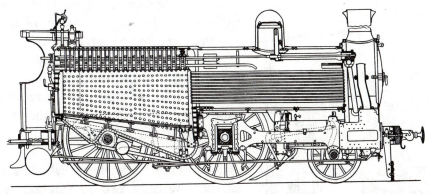

FIGURE 168—*Section of a Belgian express locomotive by M. L. Bika, 1885. Note the large sloping grate for burning poor-quality small coal and slack. The main frames are outside and steam distribution is by Walschaerts's valve-gear (partly visible). The chimney has been broken in the drawing; it was considerably higher than the dome. (See also figure 169.)*

(London and North Western) to achieve complete, and therefore smokeless, combustion of coal. Beattie used combustion chambers, water-filled firebox partitions, and even a form of thermic syphon, and his fuel economies have never been surpassed by orthodox locomotives. His 'St George' averaged 23 lb of coal to the mile with express trains over a heavy road. These complicated boilers were vulnerable, hence the need for hot feed-water mentioned above.

Experiments carried out on the Midland Railway under the direction of Matthew Kirtley produced a much simpler coal-burning firebox by the simple means of a brick arch and a deflector plate. Though less economical in fuel, it was far more durable and cheaper to maintain than the other, very complex, designs. In the United States James Millholland, of the Philadelphia and Reading Railroad, carried out various interesting experiments on the burning of anthracite. His work culminated in the design of a very wide grate, copied in many countries; this is often, though erroneously, called the Wootten firebox. Quite properly, firebox design varied according to the nature of the fuel burnt.

Belpaire's long-grate, flat-topped firebox (figures 168 and 169) served equally well in its native Belgium and on the Great Western Railway, which burned Welsh coal, at the very end of the nineteenth century and later. It is indeed still in general use.

Throughout mid-Victorian years, express passenger engines usually had a single driving-axle, but four-coupled and six-coupled wheels were used for ordinary passenger and heavy goods engines respectively. The first in Britain to abandon single-drive for coupled express engines was Joseph Beattie in 1859. He also produced the prototype British tender of later years, with slotted plate frames, the springs over the axle-boxes and below platform level, and the tank of maximum width: it was perpetuated as the British Railways standard tender about ninety years later.

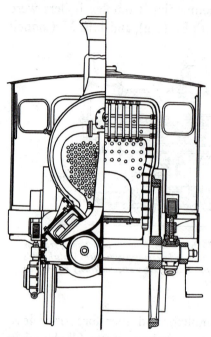

FIGURE 169—*Cross-section of a Belgian locomotive by M. L. Bika, 1885. It has a Belpaire firebox with characteristic flat crown and flat-topped casing. (See also figure 168.)*

On ordinary locomotives, cylinders were almost invariably two in number, either inside or outside the frames, the latter position being most favoured in America and in central Europe. John Haswell, an English engineer in Vienna, built a four-cylinder simple-expansion locomotive in 1861, with all cylinders outside, arranged diagonally and driving a single axle through double Hall cranks. Joseph Hall, another Englishman, went to the firm of J. A. Maffei in Munich. His cranks were outside the main frames, which were themselves outside the wheels; the excentrics and link-motion were likewise outside, between crank and axle-box (figure 170). This form was very rare on British railways; an exception was an experimental locomotive designed by J. E. McConnell for the London and North Western Railway. It made a locomotive unduly wide, and some trouble with platform copings earned for McConnell's engine the nickname of 'Mac's Mangle'. With the low platforms of Austria and South Germany, as of many other continental countries, however, this feature caused no trouble.

The influence of British engineers such as Crampton, Hall, Haswell, and others in western and central Europe had a parallel farther east, for the American engineers Winans, Eastwick, and Harrison founded the Russian locomotive and rolling-stock industry. Both British and American engineering contractors were responsible for a very large proportion of the earlier mileage of Russian railway construction.

FIGURE 170—*Crampton patent locomotive 'Komet', built by the Karlsruhe Engine Works for the Baden State Railway in 1854. It had Hall cranks with outside Gooch link motion and the valves on top of the cylinders. The bogie was equalized. Boiler feed was by force-pumps worked by the piston tail-rods.*

II. SIGNALLING

Early signalling on British railways depended on a combination of simple fixed signals and the observance of time intervals. The normal position of the former, except at junctions, was at 'clear'; each was placed at 'danger' for a variable interval after the passage of a train. The perils of such a system in heavy traffic are obvious, though provided that speeds were not too high and that rules were observed it was not so potentially dangerous as it sounds. The fixed signals themselves were of various types according to the several companies, which followed their own preferences. The earliest consisted of movable banners and flags, with coloured lights at night. Rotating disks were much employed, especially by the Great Western and its allies in Britain, and abroad. The quarter-rotating chequer-board is still widely used in France. But the semaphore, invented in France by Chappe in the late eighteenth century as a form of visual telegraph (vol iv, p 645), was peculiarly suited to railway signalling, and was introduced at the beginning of the 1840s by Hutton Gregory.

Use and improvement of electric telegraphs made possible what was called the block system; the up and down roads were divided into block sections, none of which might be entered until the previous train had been cleared by telegraph from the succeeding block post. At first, it was employed only on exceptional sections, such as very long tunnels, and a misunderstanding with the old single-needle telegraph led to a very bad collision in Clayton Tunnel, Brighton, in 1861. This was due to a combination of circumstances. First, the dangerously short time-intervals on the preceding section; secondly, the failure of a very early form of automatic signal, which was supposed to return to danger when a train depressed a treadle, and in fact did not. A signalman became flustered and sent ambiguous messages on the telegraph with the result that two trains got into one block section, which was the tunnel.

Following this accident came an interesting divergence of opinion. The government inspector advised a complete block system: the railway company countered with the theory that too many mechanical safeguards led to more human lapses, giving this particular signalman's failure as an instance. Advances in electric telegraphy made for better and less cumbersome working of the block system, which later in the century was enforced on all British and most other European main-line railways.

Interlocked points and interlocked signals, with the levers in a single long locking-frame, were installed by Saxby at the Bricklayers Arms junction, London, in 1856. Four years later, at Kentish Town, Chambers installed the first complete interlocking of points and signals, ensuring that the latter could not give indications at variance with the position of the former. In America, a form of interlocking was first installed at Spuyten Duyvil, New York, in 1874; a year later a complete Saxby and Farmer installation was made at East Newark Junction, New Jersey.

Though coloured lights were used to give night indications from very early days, and special colour-light signals were used on the underground Metropolitan railway in the 1860s, the day of electric automatic colour-light signalling was still far away. Even mechanical automatic signalling by semaphores did not come until the turn of the century: the Pennsylvania Railroad used it, and the first British installation was made on the South Western main line at Grateley, Salisbury Plain, in 1903. In many countries abroad, railway signalling was for long years far behind British practice.

America depended chiefly on a telegraph train-order system, far from proof against human mistakes, and for decades Russian practice was backward. Germany and France led continental Europe, but even in France attempts by the government to enforce uniformity on the different railway companies were largely frustrated by a mechanical isolationism on their part.

In North America traffic in both directions over a vast network of single track was governed purely by train-order, but as early as 1860 the London and North Western Railway began to safeguard such movements from head-on collision by a train-staff system, in which an inscribed staff or baton permitted movement over each single-track section. A ticket would be issued to a train preceding that on which the staff was carried, or several tickets to successive trains, but no train might proceed in a contrary direction until the staff had come in. In theory it was faultless, but it was not proof against blunders or criminal negligence. From this simple token system evolved the more advanced tablet and electric train-staff systems, worked in conjunction with the block apparatus. Tyer's electric tablet system was patented in 1878, and is supposed to have been inspired by the scandalous circumstances of a single-line collision at Radstock, on the Somerset and Dorset Joint Railway, two years before.

III. PERMANENT WAY

During the second half of the century, permanent way improved in quality and solidity. Originally, rail-joints had been formed simply by the rail-ends being keyed into a common chair. A heavy or rough-riding locomotive could work havoc with such a road. Fish-joints formed of narrow plates on each side of, and bolted through the web of, each pair of rail-ends were patented by Bridges Adams in 1847. Peter Bruff, of the Eastern Counties railway, obtained the patent, and fish-plates were generally used from the 1850s onwards. It was a simple arrangement, and made the permanent way very much safer.

Successful use of steel instead of iron for rails was an important British contribution, and was possible only after the introduction of Bessemer's process in 1856 (p 54). First use of Bessemer steel for rail-manufacture was claimed by the London and North Western Railway, which made its own steel and rolled its own rails at Crewe, where it had the largest railway-owned engineering works in the world. Iron rails continued to be made for many years; the first American steel rails were made in Pennsylvania in 1867, but two years later the Baltimore and Ohio Railroad was placing its first steel-rail contracts with a Sheffield firm. Rails gradually increased in weight, for a given length, proportionately to the weight and speed of trains, but even at the turn of the century, when American locomotives had become very heavy indeed, flat-bottom rails weighing 100 lb to the yard were regarded as heavy; in Great Britain, with much lighter rolling-stock, bull-head rail at 90 lb to the yard was massive by contemporary standards.

IV. STATION DESIGN

The barn-like stations of very early days were intended to act as carriage sheds as well as passenger shelters, but the huge arched roofs of iron and glass, characteristic of later Victorian times, were among the railway's unique contributions to architectural development. Classic examples in London were Barlow's St Pancras, Brunel's Paddington, and Hawkshaw's Cannon Street stations. There were many splendid foreign stations, such as Broad Street, Philadelphia, and the Central Station, Frankfurt-am-Main. The vast glazed roofs served a double purpose; they kept most of the place dry and reasonably draught-proof in all weathers, and they prevented the stations from becoming too dark. Being very large, they allowed the dispersal of the heavy exhaust vapours emitted by the locomotives.

Station lay-out was at first extremely simple, at the expense of rapid movement. Points were kept to a minimum, and in large stations ranges of turn-plates, or very short turn-tables, allowed the movement of vehicles from one road to another. The turn-table is of considerable antiquity; as early as 1719 Louis XV of France appears to have had one on his pleasure line at Marly-le-Roi, near Versailles. Movement by turn-plate was cumbersome, crude, and not regulated by proper signals. Further, it could be used only while coaches remained small, with very short wheel-base; even a Pullman car of the early seventies would have needed something like a locomotive turn-table for shunting in such a fashion. By the end of the century, turn-plates were used only in certain large goods depots, where movement of wagons was by capstan or horse-traction.

At the end of the century the simplest country station, on double track, usually comprised up and down passenger platforms, with trailing points from one or other of the roads to give access to the goods yard; the latter would contain several tracks, a covered goods shed with crane and loading-dock, and a separate coal depot. Between the up and down through roads would be a trailing cross-over—or two, one at each end—to provide running-round facilities for any train that had to terminate there. Many much larger through-stations were still basically on this plan, but at major centres goods and passenger stations would be quite separate and often in different parts of the town. Island platform stations were already quite common—indeed, certain very large stations were laid out on the island principle. The largest example is Edinburgh Waverley, rebuilt between 1892 and the end of the century. Here the island comprises two terminal portions, end-on to one another and with the offices between; the through lines by-pass the island to north and south, and there is a separate island suburban station on the south side. When this station was laid out, suburban traffic was of great importance, but in the early part of the twentieth century much of it was lost to cable tramways and never recovered. Another Scottish station on the same plan is Perth General. Comparable English stations are Carlisle, Preston, and Darlington, and this form of giant island lay-out is characteristically British. Foreign instances are usually at international frontiers. There is a fine example at Salzburg.

City terminal stations, whether by design or prevailing circumstances, may be of fan-shaped design, like the South Western part of Waterloo in London (built in the present century), or parallel, with generous approach roads, as in the case of Paddington. An interesting continental example is Munich Central, the lay-out of which somewhat resembles that of Paddington, but to which have been added two 'wing' stations for the exclusive handling of local traffic. Medium-sized semi-terminal stations, with through tracks on one side, are typified by Blackfriars, London, and Westland Row, Dublin, both built during the Victorian era and with many features in common. Amiens Street, Dublin, and London Road, Manchester, are technically the same sort of station.

Large terminal stations placed end to end, with through roads and a long through platform in common, are rare. Manchester Victoria and Exchange stations provide the best example; they owe their separation to the former independence of the Lancashire and Yorkshire and the London and North Western companies. Inter-company differences were, indeed, responsible for most of the apparently illogical divisions of large British stations. Noteworthy is London Bridge, which has a through high-level section; a terminal low-level section; and another terminal section, much larger but still on the low level, which was originally the City terminus of the London, Brighton and South Coast Railway. Divisions of this sort were uncommon in foreign cities, owing to the prevalence of state ownership from an early date, but in such different cities as Buenos Aires and Gothenburg there were termini more or less in line but without connexion.

V. LOCOMOTIVE DESIGN

London, like most big cities, acquired a perimeter of railway-stations, and during the fifties the internal road-traffic became unbearably congested. It was this circumstance that led to the building and expansion of the world's first underground railway system, opened early in 1863 (p 346 and plate 22). Unlike later, deep-level, underground lines, it involved no revolutionary technique; construction was by cut-and-cover. Mechanical innovations were necessary, however, for the locomotives had to be provided with surface condensers to prevent the tunnels from becoming completely fogged. By means of two-way valves in the exhaust-passages, the exhaust steam was turned into the tanks, which were supposed to be emptied and replenished with fresh, cold water at the end of each trip, a process easier in conception than in practice. In fact, under heavy traffic conditions, the water was brought nearly to boiling-point and was practically useless for condensing purposes.

Various improvements were made in the general design of British and foreign locomotives from the sixties onwards. Hitherto, a low centre of gravity had been striven for; some of Crampton's patents went to extremes of freakishness to gain this end. But on the London and North Western, McConnell raised the centre

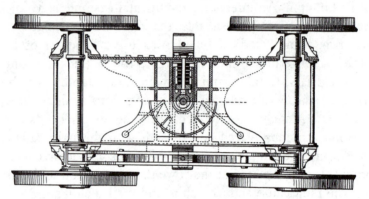

FIGURE 171—*Plan of Great Eastern Railway bogie by William Adams, late 1870s, with side control of the laterally sliding pivot by india-rubber springs.*

of gravity considerably, anticipating by a long time the practice of later years. His engines were not at all top-heavy, as critics had foretold; moreover they were altogether steadier and easier on the road. With a low-pitched boiler, lateral motion was sometimes excessively rough.

Excessive lateral movement occurred, too, with engines having archaic short-wheel-base bogies,[1] with a central pivot but no side-play to the pin; but the old pivoted bogie, it should be noted, was intended to allow for inequalities in the surface of the track rather than for facility in rounding curves. William Adams (1823–1904) patented the familiar four-wheeled engine bogie (figure 171), and first applied it on locomotives which he designed for the North London Railway in the sixties. The wheel-base was made fairly long, to give steady running, and the pivot moved in a transverse slot; lateral movement was controlled by inclined planes or, later, by springs. This design made a superb bogie, still in use all over the world. Radial trucks and axle-boxes provided an alternative to the

---

[1] Bogie: a pivoted truck under the frame of a locomotive or vehicle; an old Northumbrian word for a trolley.

Adams bogie, but have rarely given such satisfactory results, least of all in high-speed running. The Bissell truck, swinging radially from a pin at the rear, was nevertheless liked by many designers.

Four-wheeled Bissell trucks, outwardly resembling true bogies, were much used on the Metropolitan railway in the days of steam, and a form with longer wheel-base was employed by Francis Webb on the London and North Western at the end of the century. Webb, an original but obstinate man, intensely disliked bogies and never would put one under a locomotive. The radial axle-

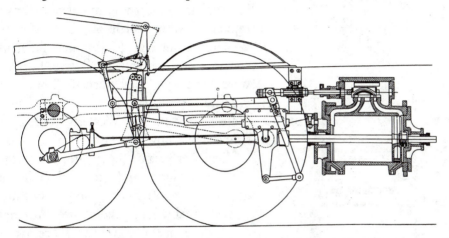

FIGURE 172—*Égide Walschaerts's valve-gear. It had its origins in Belgium in the mid-nineteenth century. A most satisfactory gear, it is the standard form on British Railways today, and is used on railways all over the world. Excentric motion is derived from a return crank outside the driving-wheel crank and big-end.*

box was shorter-lived; Bridges Adams made a form which was satisfactory at moderate speeds, and a North London engine so fitted was in service for about ninety years.

In general, a true locomotive bogie could be described as a pivoted frame containing two carrying-axles, with wheels of equal diameter. At the end of the century von Helmholtz, manager and chief designer of the Krauss works at Munich, produced a bogie which contained both the single leading carrying-axle and the leading coupled axle, suitable play being allowed in the side-rods. The Krauss–Helmholtz bogie was thereafter widely employed in various countries of continental Europe, and in several countries it is compulsory on all locomotives that are used on passenger or other fast services but are not equipped with the four-wheeled Adams bogie. The Krauss–Helmholtz bogie has never been used in Great Britain.

John Ramsbottom, in command of Crewe on the London and North Western, produced two notable accessories: a safety-valve proof against reckless attempts to obtain a high but dangerous pressure by screwing down the lever, and water-troughs from which locomotives could replenish their tanks at speed. Rams-bottom's safety-valve was widely used until well into the present century; it was a very simple appliance, with the valves on top of two columns, loaded through a lever by a common spring between them. Water-troughs and pick-up apparatus

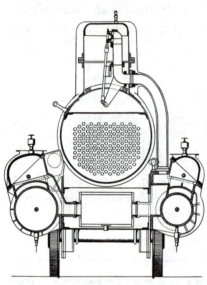

on tenders were first introduced by Rams-bottom on the Chester and Holyhead line in 1860; the object was to cut out stops to replenish water north of Crewe for the very important Irish Mail trains. Their use spread to many British railways, but they were little employed abroad. They were used on certain lines in the eastern United States, and on the Western Railway of France, but nowhere else.

FIGURE 173—*Cross-section of von Borries loco-motive, taken from the rear, showing the regulator, high-pressure steam-pipe, high-pressure cylinder, receiver, and low-pressure cylinder. The valve-gear was of Heusinger von Waldegg's type, a close relation of the Walschaerts gear. (See also figure 177.)*

The latter part of the nineteenth century saw experiment and innovation in the design of valves and valve-gears. Slide-valves remained in general use. Attempts to produce piston-valves were premature, but various radial valve-gears were de-signed, one of the most successful being that invented and developed by Égide Walschaerts in Belgium (figure 172); this was adopted in various foreign countries. It was many years before British railways took up Walschaerts's gear, save in isolated instances, though it was much used on locomotives built for export. It is, however, the standard gear on British Railways steam locomotives today.

Walschaerts's gear differed considerably in arrangement from established link-motions, and this was enough to make Victorian locomotive engineers cautious of it. Excentric motion is derived from a single return crank each side. The accompanying figure shows its design; the connecting-link and combination lever from the cross-head give constant lead at all positions of the link, whereas in the older link-motions this lead gradually increased from full-gear to mid-position. Valve-gears of the Walschaerts family include the German Heusinger von Waldegg gear (figure 173) and certain American types.

David Joy's valve-gear (figures 174, 175) was another radial valve-gear of the later nineteenth century, and one which, unlike Walschaerts's, was considerably employed on certain British railways in those years, notably on the London and North Western and the North Eastern Railways. Its weak point, which became uncomfortably apparent when it was applied to larger engines, was that its arrangement involved a piercing of the connecting-rod; there were some bad break-downs through the fracture of the latter while running.

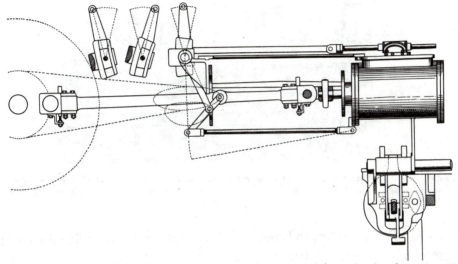

FIGURE 174—*David Joy's radial valve-gear without excentrics, arranged for an American locomotive with the valves on top of the cylinders. The drawing shows how the excentric motion was derived from a pin passing through the connecting-rod near the small-end, an arrangement that became vulnerable on large engines.*

The use of compound expansion in steam locomotives was for long a goal of engineers both at home and abroad, though the principle was only slowly adopted on railway engines, as compared with marine and stationary engines. As early as 1850, John Nicholson, of the Eastern Counties Railway, devised a 'continuous expansion' locomotive with two cylinders, high- and low-pressure respectively, but it differed from the true compound engine of later days in that the steam, first admitted to the high-pressure cylinder only, then worked expansively in both cylinders.

The object of compounding was to economize on fuel by making fuller use of a given supply of steam, and its most extensive application in nineteenth-century England was by Francis Webb on the London and North Western Railway. The most familiar Webb compound type had two high-pressure cylinders outside, driving the trailing-axle, and a single large low-pressure cylinder inside, driving the middle axle, the two pairs of driving-wheels being uncoupled (figures 175 and 176). Joy's gear was employed to work the high-pressure valves with link motion for the low pressure, but later examples had an inside slip-excentric gear, which was supposed to make a sympathetic reversal of its own accord when the high-pressure portion of the engine was put into, and moved, in reverse. Sometimes it did not act. The engines were erratic, but the later ones were capable of good work and hundreds were built. Later Webb com-

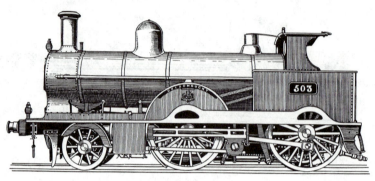

FIGURE 175—*Elevation of three-cylinder compound express engine by Francis Webb, London and North Western Railway, 1884. It has outside Joy radial valve-gear serving the high-pressure cylinders. (See also figure 176.)*

pounds had four cylinders and coupled wheels; they were generally reliable, but sluggish and expensive to maintain.

Thomas Worsdell's two-cylinder compound engines on the North Eastern Railway (plate 21 B) in the eighties followed the German von Borries system, with one high- and one low-pressure cylinder, both inside (figures 173 and 177). They were more reliable than Webb's engines, but less so than various existing simple expansion locomotives on the same and other railways. von Borries compounds worked satisfactorily for years in central and northern Europe. Two relevant circumstances should be noted. First, the standard lateral dimensions of British engines were very severely restricted by the high platforms, while the German and other continental designers had, relatively, plenty of room. Secondly, while the English engines earned a reputation for sluggishness, scheduled train-speeds in Germany at that time were without exception moderate: the same was true of Sweden and Ireland, where von Borries compound locomotives ran for many years.

One other British compound locomotive of the nineteenth century is important historically. It was a North Eastern engine, rebuilt in 1898 from a Worsdell two-cylinder compound, according to W. M. Smith's system. It had one high-pressure cylinder inside and two of low-pressure outside—a complete reversal of Webb's arrangement. Furthermore, the wheels were four-coupled and all three cylinders drove the leading coupled axle. In the Smith engine, a reducing-valve admitted boiler steam to both the high- and low-pressure steam-chests, so that on starting it worked as a three-cylinder simple locomotive of considerable tractive power. The reducing-valve was controlled by a spring-loaded regulating-valve, and the locomotive went over to compound expansion when it was under way. It could be worked 'simple' all the time, in an emergency, by altering the regulating valve-spring; or 'semi-compound' under severe conditions of load or gradient.

Smith's three-cylinder compound locomotive was taken up by Samuel Johnson on the Midland Railway, and modified by Richard Deeley on the same system, where it became the most successful of all British compound locomotives. Examples were built in large numbers as late as the 1920s and worked, with apparent ease, far heavier trains than their prototypes had been called upon to draw on the old Midland services.

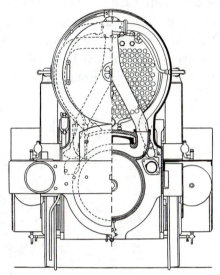

FIGURE 176—*Cross-section of Francis Webb's three-cylinder engine, 1884, showing the arrangement of the high-pressure cylinders, with the steam-chests and valves underneath, and the single very large low-pressure cylinder between the frames. The low-pressure receiver, serving the large cylinder, is formed of large pipes in the smoke-box, intended to dry the steam on its way to the low-pressure steam-chest. (See also figure 175.)*

Many arrangements of compounding were successfully carried out abroad. Noteworthy were Gölsdorf's engines on the several railways of the Austro-Hungarian empire, which worked very satisfactorily under such varying conditions as those of the Bohemian plains and the mountains of Tyrol and Carinthia. The Vauclain system in the United States deserves mention; it comprised four cylinders, all outside, with high- and low-pressure superimposed in pairs, driving a single connecting-rod each side through a common cross-head. Its mechanical weakness arose from the size and weight of these doubled reciprocating masses; this applied especially in a big ten-wheeled American locomotive of the 1890s, such as the Atlantic type used in the eastern states. In a slow-moving heavy freight locomotive, this weakness was less serious. The same disability applied to tandem compound engines, in which each pair of high- and low-pressure cylinders had a common piston-rod. Examples were built in America and in continental Europe; three British experimental engines of this type were unsuccessful.

There was no more fortunate system of locomotive compounding than that of de Glehn, used at one time in many parts of the world but achieving its outstanding success in France. There the four-cylinder de Glehn engines of the Northern Railway, stemming from an experimental machine of the eighties, achieved in the earlier years of the present century some of the finest express work in the world. France was, indeed, for many years the main home of the

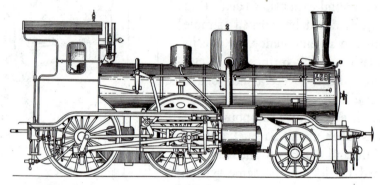

FIGURE 177—*Elevation of a von Borries two-cylinder compound locomotive for the Hanover lines of the Prussian State Railways, c 1885. (See also figure 173.)*

compound locomotive, just as Prussia was the birthplace of the fire-tube superheater, which next deserves our attention.

The idea of 'dried' steam had long appealed to locomotive men, and early modifications of the steam-pipe had usually been made in the smoke-box. A live-steam chamber in the smoke-box, with smoke-tubes passing through it, was fitted on an engine designed by R. and W. Hawthorn for the Newcastle and North Shields Railway as early as 1840, but efforts to 'burn' the steam had been made earlier than this. It was, however, not until the very end of the century that Wilhelm Schmidt of Kassel conducted experiments in true superheating which were to influence boiler-design during the ensuing half-century. It is true that, in England, John Aspinall produced a highly efficient smoke-box steam-drier, but the superheater of Schmidt's inspiration was quite different. Very briefly described, the principle was that the steam-pipe from the dome, or from a perforated steam-collecting pipe in domeless boilers, passed to a header whence the live-steam passages were split up into a large number of small-diameter hairpin tubes. Each of these passed into, and out again from, a series of enlarged flues to a second header, whence the steam flowed on to the steam-chests. The design was conceived in the nineteenth century; its advantage was proved in the twentieth, but in Britain its application was tardy. Noteworthy British modifications of the Schmidt system were Churchward's 'Swindon' superheater, Robinson's superheater, and Urie's 'Eastleigh' superheater.

The characteristic locomotive of 1900, however, ran on saturated steam. It was, in all countries, many times larger than its forerunners of the mid-nineteenth century. The first six-coupled bogie express engines in Europe appeared on the Upper Italian Railway in 1884; this 4-6-0 type made its British début under David Jones on the Highland Railway ten years later. But little mechanical advance had been made, apart from a new conception of the proper ratio of boiler-power to cylinder-capacity, together with much higher working-pressures and various admirable accessories. Bridging the gap of some forty years between a McConnell 'Bloomer' on the London and North Western and a McIntosh 'Dunalastair' on the Caledonian Railway, it is not entirely unreasonable to describe the 'Dunalastair' as a giant 'Bloomer' with coupled wheels and an Adams bogie. William Buchanan's magnificent locomotives on the New York Central Lines in the nineties were, basically, of the same type as those which had helped to win Sherman's Georgia campaign in the mid-sixties. There was much of Crampton's hand in French locomotives of 1900, and Haswell and Hall had lasting influence in Austria-Hungary.

VI. ROLLING-STOCK

In all countries, increased size of locomotives had been dictated by the greater quantity of freight handled, by the greater number of passengers carried, and by the improved standards of comfort with a consequent increased weight of passenger coaches *per capita*.

In 1850 the first-class coach in Great Britain and other western European countries was still of the sort that Hilaire Belloc described as resembling three stage-coach 'insides' stuck together on one frame. Figure 178 shows a larger, four-compartment, variety on the Great Western. Carriages of inferior class were lighter and carried more passengers. They were four-wheeled, or, exceptionally, six-wheeled. The extra axle usually went with one more compartment to a first-class body. Travelling Post Office carriages, with apparatus for the exchange of mail pouches, had been introduced as far back as 1838 on the Grand Junction Railway. America adopted them much later, in the sixties.

Apart from freaks and a few special vehicles, the first eight-wheeled carriages for British main-line service were some broad-gauge composites, called 'Long

Charleys', built by the Great Western in 1852; twenty years later, however, eight-wheelers were still rare. America had built long coaches, eight-wheeled and mounted on bogies, with central passage-ways, since the forties. The American coach body derived to some extent from the cabin of a canal boat, whereas the European type derived from the stage-coach or diligence. The use of

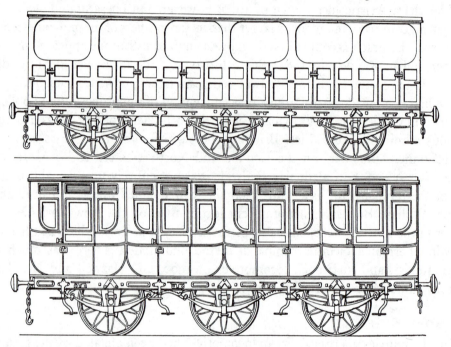

FIGURE 178—*Second- and first-class carriages, 7 ft 0¼ in gauge, Great Western Railway, 1839. The second-class, roofed but open above the waist, had a seat for the guard, with a hand-brake working through toggles. The first-class carriage exemplifies the derivation of railway coaching design from Georgian carriage building. Compartments were just over 6 ft high inside.*

bogies for American coaches was necessitated by the very rough-and-ready methods of track-construction, which would have entailed frequent derailment of short, rigid vehicles. Through American influence, the long bogie coach soon came into general use on Russian railways.

Because of the great distances involved, both Russia and America were necessarily much earlier users of sleeping-cars than other nations. Russia put the berths transversely, with a side gangway; America, in George M. Pullman's classic type, made them longitudinal (plate 20 B and C). Both countries saw the earliest general installation of water-closets, or at least of their equivalent, on ordinary long-distance trains. Structurally these resembled the 'heads' of an eighteenth-century ship. The first British sleeper was built by the North British Railway in 1873; it contained two sleeping-compartments with three longitudinal sleeping-berths in each.

Dining-cars appeared in Canada in 1867, and had spread to Great Britain by 1879, where imported American Pullman cars, both 'parlour' and sleeping, had been in service since 1874. By the end of the century, British sleeping-cars were of extraordinary variety—adapted family saloons, reduced American Pullman cars, and carriages that offered a modification of ships' state-rooms. The proto-

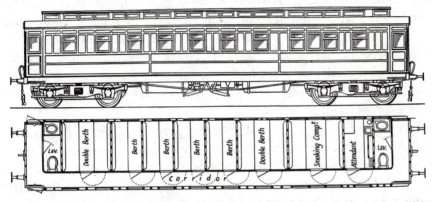

FIGURE 179—*Elevation and plan of a sleeping car built by the North Eastern Railway, 1894. With five single-berth, two double-berth, and one smoking compartment, reached by end vestibules and side corridor, it was the forerunner of the standard British sleeper of today. The body was entirely of wood, with gas-lighting and a clerestory roof.*

type for the next half-century and more, however, had appeared in 1894 on the North Eastern Railway; this was a side-corridor carriage with single-berth compartments, still the standard British and continental first-class sleeping-car (figure 179).

In 1882 the Great Northern Railway produced what was to be the standard British coach of later years. It was a small version of a type already running in Austria, having compartments connected by a side corridor with lavatories at each end. The first completely gangwayed side-corridor trains in Great Britain appeared practically simultaneously on the Great Eastern and Great Western Railways in 1891. Of the two, that of the Great Western was the more imposing and more nearly 'modern', but the Great Eastern train was better in that it provided dining arrangements for all classes.

All carriages at this time were wooden, often with clerestories to the roofs. Lighting was generally by vegetable oil or by compressed oil-gas. The world's first electrically-lit carriage was an imported American Pullman car on the

Brighton line in 1881; it was equipped with Swan incandescent lamps supplied by a large battery of Faure cells. Pullman cars were generally lit by Argand lamps burning paraffin; these gave a good light, but could be, like gas, highly dangerous in the event of an accident. In 1896 J. Stone patented his electric lighting system for trains, with a belt-driven dynamo beneath the coach. The arrangement was quickly adopted by the Great Northern Railway of Ireland.

General standards of comfort had for long remained static, but in 1875 Thomas Clayton on the Midland Railway provided soft seats for all classes of passenger, and other British railways were obliged to follow suit. The wooden third-class was perpetuated in continental Europe; the highest foreign concessions to comfort were the stiff leather seats of certain French third-class carriages, and the reversible 'day-coach' seats of North America, rather deceptively trimmed in plush. All countries had their superior classes of carriage, but in 1900 no land conveyance offered better comfort to all classes of passenger than a British express train.

The progress of goods vehicles during this period was slight. North America adopted enormous freight-cars, double-bogied; Europe carried its goods in small four-wheeled wagons, the descendants of which are still with us. America had introduced the automatic central coupler, whereas main-line railways throughout Europe relied, as most of them do today, on screw-couplings and side buffers, themselves dating back to the 1830s.

The braking systems of trains were for long a disgrace. Various forms of continuous brake were devised, both manual and power-driven, but the essence of good train-brakes is that they should be not only continuous but automatic. Both the Westinghouse automatic air-brake (figure 180), an American design, and the automatic vacuum, were tried and proved by the late eighties. In the Newark brake-trials of June 1875 the former had stopped a Midland Railway train weighing 203·2 tons, travelling at 52 mph, in a distance of 913 ft and in a time of 19 seconds. Nevertheless, it was not until a major disaster near Armagh in 1889 agitated public opinion that automatic continuous power-brakes, proof against both runaway and breakaway, were made compulsory on all British railways. Such brakes not only facilitated rapid stopping in an emergency, but made possible great improvements in the timing of express trains.

Faster timing was stimulated by exhibitions of competitive running between London and Scotland in 1888 and again in 1895. A curious feature of the first outburst of 'racing' was the considerable age of some of the locomotives employed. E. L. Ahrons ascribed the improved performance of these old engines to the use of steel tyres, and there is certainly some corroboration of this. At this time, the Midland Railway in particular achieved wonderful performances with old Kirtley locomotives dating back to the sixties. However, less reliance was placed on steel in Britain than in America. Dugald Drummond tried steel fire-boxes on the Caledonian Railway in the 1880s, but copper is still preferred by British locomotive engineers.

In concluding our survey of locomotive design, attention should be paid to several types of articulated steam locomotive. In the 1860s Robert Fairlie patented a double engine with twin boilers, each end being supported by a motor bogie. It was powerful and flexible, but slow, and its most successful

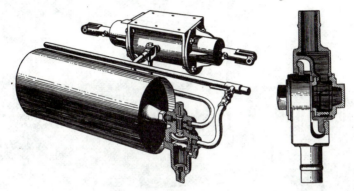

FIGURE 180—*Westinghouse automatic air-brake; an early application for railway coaches. On the left are the reservoir, valve, and train-pipe connexion, with the brake cylinder above and behind. On the right, on a larger scale, is one of the flexible couplings in the train-pipe.*

application was on the mountain division of the Mexican Railway. Anatole Mallet of France designed a compound type in which also there were two sets of coupled wheels, of identical dimensions, but with the forward set forming a long bogie; one set used high-pressure and the other low-pressure steam. This type was employed to some extent in France and Germany, most successfully on narrow-gauge lines such as those of Corsica and the Harz. It found its principal use in the United States, however, where giant articulated Mallet compounds, and simple expansion engines also, have been at work to the present time on lines serving the eastern coalfields, as well as in the sierras of the far west.

During construction of the Mont Cenis tunnel, railway traffic was handled on Napoleon's military road over the pass by a form of railway patented by J. B. Fell, in which horizontal driving-wheels on the locomotive gripped a central double-headed rail laid on its side. The system was used until quite recently on the Rimutaka incline in New Zealand, and is still used for braking on the Snaefell line in the Isle of Man. Most steep mountain railways adopted a rack-and-pinion system, one of which, Riggenbach's, with the engine's spur-wheel engaging a ladder-like steel rack between the rails, originated in the sixties and had its first important application on the Vitznau–Rigi Railway in Switzerland in 1871. It is still employed on the mountain, though with electric traction in recent years. The Abt rack, equally efficacious, consists of parallel toothed

FIGURE 181—*Electric line between Frankfurt-am-Main and Offenbach, 1884, by Siemens & Halske. The leading car had a single driving axle to which the motor was geared down. The overhead conductor- and return-lines consisted of slotted gas-piping in which ran shuttle-shaped runners with lugs projecting downwards through the continuous slot and attached by light frames and cables to the car.*

rails, close together, with the teeth staggered, and double spur-wheels for traction and braking.

VII. UNDERGROUND AND ELECTRIC RAILWAYS

In the London clay, tunnelling was relatively easy, and during the nineties new, deep-level underground railways were built to relieve the congestion of surface and sub-surface transport. These were made possible by the evolution of satisfactory electric traction. The first practical electric railway in the world was a miniature line demonstrated at a Berlin exhibition in 1879; on this a small Siemens & Halske locomotive hauled cars with back-to-back seats round the grounds. German experimental electric tramways followed (figure 181), and in 1883 the first British electric railway was opened; it was built and operated by

Magnus Volk on the beach at Brighton, where it is still in use. It was closely followed by the partially electric Giant's Causeway, Portrush, and Bush Valley Tramway in Ireland, the first electric railway in the world to derive its current from water-turbines.

More important was the construction of the City and South London Railway,

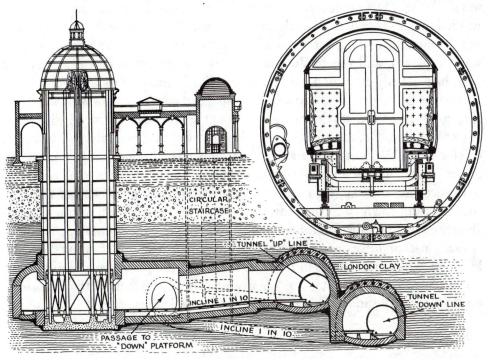

FIGURE 182—*Section of Oval Station, City and South London Railway, 1890. This was the first deep-level electric city railway in the world, and was on a smaller scale than later lines, with 10 ft 6 in tubes. Haulage was by small electric locomotives and access by hydraulic lifts. (Inset) Section through tunnel and passenger car.*

the first of the London 'tubes', between 1887 and 1890 (figure 182). J. H. Greathead, a South African engineer who had gained experience under P. W. Barlow in the construction of the little Tower Subway, London, in 1870, undertook the building of this line. It was excavated with the Greathead shield, the tunnel being built up, ring by ring, from iron segments as the shield advanced. Electric traction was decided upon, with direct current at 500 volts, and the three-car trains were hauled by small four-wheeled locomotives having a pair of series-wound motors, each developing 25 hp at 310 rpm with a 50 hp aggregate at 25 mph. The motors were mounted directly on the axles, though an alternative design, not proceeded with, had rod-drive through cranks. In spite of the lack of precedent and experience, the line was an outstanding success, and before the end of the century three more 'tubes' had been built: the Waterloo and City Railway, the Central London Railway, and the Glasgow District Subway. The last had cable traction until the middle 1930s.

Electric traction was clearly in the ascendant for city and underground railways. The first electrification of a section of main-line steam railway took place in 1895, in the Camden–Waverly tunnel of the Baltimore and Ohio Railroad, nearly four miles of track lying beneath Baltimore. Heavy twin electric locomotives were employed, and the conductors were overhead. The overhead trolley and wire had already appeared on tramways, but a more substantial form was adopted at Baltimore. This had a light, suspended conductor rail with which the locomotive made contact through a single pantograph collector mounted diagonally at one side. Each locomotive consisted of two units mounted on two rigid driving-axles, the units being articulated or pivoted to one another under the driver's cab, forming an 0–4–0+0–4–0 engine. It was not, outwardly, an ambitious conversion; the reason for it was the elimination of smoke and fumes in the long tunnel, which for its time carried very heavy traffic. Nevertheless, this Baltimore line was the forerunner of the great electric main lines of the world.

Electric locomotive design did not quickly assume a definite form as the steam locomotive had done in the forties, but in view of the present popularity of the double-bogie locomotive it is worth remarking that this was used, though briefly, on the Central London Railway at the very end of the century.

BIBLIOGRAPHY

Ahrons, E. L. 'The British Steam Railway Locomotive 1825-1925.' Locomotive Publishing Company, London. 1927.
Idem. 'Development of British Locomotive Design.' Locomotive Publishing Company, London. 1914.
'Catalogue of the Centenary Exhibition of the Baltimore and Ohio Railroad.' Baltimore and Ohio Railroad, Baltimore. 1927.
Cooke, C. J. Bowen. 'British Locomotives.' London. 1893.
Deakin, W. H. "Early History of Railway Signalling." Proc. Instn Rly Sig. Engrs, Derby, Session 1928-9, 22–43, 1930.
Ellis, C. Hamilton. 'Nineteenth Century Railway Carriages in the British Isles from the 1830s to the 1900s.' Modern Transport Publishing Company, London. 1949.
Forward, E. A. 'Railway Locomotives and Rolling Stock Exhibits at the Science Museum.' H.M. Stationery Office, London. 1931.
Helmholtz, R. von and Staby, W. 'Die Entwicklung der Dampflokomotive.' Oldenbourg, Munich. 1930.
Lascelles, T. S. 'The City and South London Railway.' Oakwood Press, Godstone. 1956.

LEE, C. E. 'The Evolution of Railways.' *Railway Gazette*, London. 1943.

MARSHALL, C. F. DENDY. 'Centenary History of the Liverpool and Manchester Railway.' Locomotive Publishing Company, London. 1930.

Idem. 'Early British Locomotives.' Locomotive Publishing Company, London. 1939.

Idem. 'Two Essays in Early Locomotive History.' Locomotive Publishing Company, London. 1928.

MOREAU, A. 'Traité des chemins de fer.' Paris. 1899.

NOCK, O. S. 'The Railway Engineers.' Batsford, London. 1955.

SHIELDS, T. H. "Evolution of Locomotive Valve Gears." *J. Instn Loco. Engrs*, **33**, 368–460, 1943.

SPOONER, C. E. 'Narrow Gauge Railways' (2nd ed.). Spon, London. 1879.

WARREN, J. G. H. 'A Century of Locomotive Building by Robert Stephenson and Co.' Reid, Newcastle upon Tyne. 1923.

WESTINGHOUSE BRAKE AND SIGNAL COMPANY. 'A Century of Signalling. John Saxby, 1821–1913, and his Part in the Development of Interlocking.' Westinghouse, London. 1956.

WILLIAMS, A. 'Life in a Railway Factory.' Duckworth, London. 1915.

YOUNG, R. 'Timothy Hackworth and the Locomotive.' Locomotive Publishing Company, London. 1923.

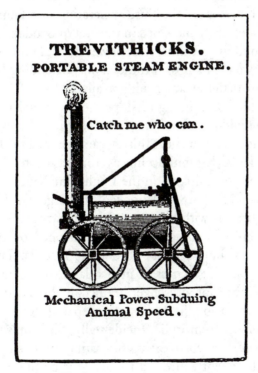

The first passenger locomotive, 1808.

16

SHIP-BUILDING

A. M. ROBB

I. THE FIRST IRON VESSELS

'SETTLED to commence iron shipbuilding': with this sentence Alexander Stephen on Clydeside closed his diary for 1851. It indicates the trend of the industry about the middle of the nineteenth century, when this ship-builder was a new-comer to the Clyde, although not to the business of ship-building. Stephen represented the third generation of a family concerned with the building of wooden craft and ships in the east of Scotland for a century. The use of iron for the building of ships was, however, beginning to develop rapidly, and the builder of wooden ships in the east was extending his activities to the west, where the new material was readily available.[1]

The use of iron for the building of ships, however, did not begin on Clyde-side or so late as the middle of the nineteenth century. But intense development started about that time, and the next thirty years spanned the hey-day of the iron ship; there followed a fairly rapid decline as iron was ousted by steel. The use of iron in place of wood was initiated in the English midlands as far back as 1787, when John Wilkinson (1728–1808) launched the barge *Trial*, 70 ft long, having a shell of $\frac{5}{16}$-in plates but with some wood in the structure. It is believed that similar craft were built in succeeding years and plied on the Severn and on canals in the midlands, but there are no definite records. There is, however, a good record of the pioneer iron craft in Scotland, the barge *Vulcan*, built at Airdrie, in Lanarkshire, for passenger traffic on the Forth and Clyde canal (figure 183). The design for the barge was prepared during 1816 by Sir John Robison, a retired officer from India. Incidentally, Sir John's father, as a student at Glasgow University, formed an early, and lasting, friendship with James Watt, whose genius he subsequently directed towards the steam-engine. Construction of the barge began in 1818 and was completed in the next year. It was carried out by Thomas Wilson, a carpenter in the employment of the canal company, with the assistance of two blacksmiths for the shaping and connecting of the iron

[1] Descendants of his family still control the firm, which has now been associated with ship-building for more than two centuries.

plates. There is no record of the service of the *Vulcan* as a carrier of passengers, but she was sailing as a coal-barge on the Firth of Clyde during 1864, and it is believed she had been in service for more than fifty years by the time she reached the breaker's yard.

Although Clydeside has been called 'the home of iron ship-building' it was not the cradle of the industry; more pioneering work was done in England. Thus the first iron steam-ship was built in England. She was a precursor of the modern process of pre-fabrication, for the material was prepared at Horsley Iron Works,

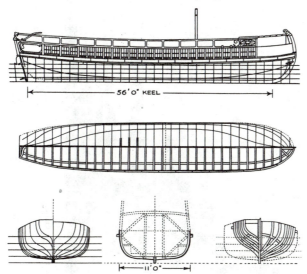

FIGURE 183—*Constructional diagrams of the barge* Vulcan, *built to the design of Sir John Robison in 1819.*

in Staffordshire, and sent to the Thames for erection. This ship, the *Aaron Manby*, completed in 1821, crossed the Channel to Le Havre, *en route* for Paris, in 1822. Further construction of iron ships was not put in hand for some years. William Laird, and his son John (1805–74), of Clydeside origin, started a succession of them at Birkenhead in 1829; their family connexion with ship-building at Birkenhead ceased not very long ago. It was a ship built by the Lairds that first indicated the reliability of iron as a material of construction. On her first voyage the *Garry Owen*, built in 1834, was driven ashore in company with several wooden ships; the destruction of several of the latter, the severe damage to others, and the slight injury to the iron vessel, justified the advocates of iron. The most ardent and probably the most effective of those who supported the use of iron, William Fairbairn (1789–1874), had started to build iron ships on the Thames in 1836. A millwright at Manchester in his younger days, his interest in naval architecture and his belief in the suitability of iron for the construction of ships were stimulated by problems on which he was asked to advise the Forth and Clyde canal company. There followed, in 1831, the building of a small steam-ship in Manchester, launched into a canal after carriage through the streets on a wagon; thereafter, for wider scope, ensued the establishment of the Millwall Iron Works on the Thames.

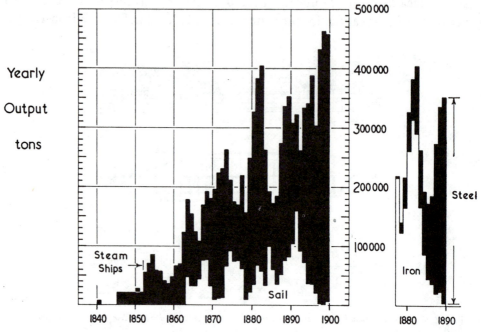

FIGURE 184—*Production of ships on the Clyde during the nineteenth century. The diagram to the right shows the tonnages of iron and steel ships.*

Uninterrupted production of iron ships did not begin on Clydeside until 1839, a year after the steam-engine had proved itself on transatlantic service, but it was some years before the use of iron was fully established there. The four pioneer ships of the fleet now known as the Cunard Line, initiating the company's transatlantic service in 1840, had wooden hulls; indeed, so late as 1852 a ship for the fleet was built of wood. It does, however, appear that the active development of the iron ship began about the middle of the century. This is indicated in figure 184, charting the production of ships on Clydeside during the nineteenth century; statistics for the whole country are not readily available. There is some doubt as to the basis of the earlier records; the figures do not show clearly how far they are confined to steam-ships, and more particularly to iron steam-ships. From 1864 onwards, however, the figures include steam- and sailing-ships, and the small number of craft with wooden hulls; the era of the iron ship had been established. A point of interest emerging from the diagram is that the large production of sailing-ships in the early nineties shows that even then the steam-engine had not become supreme on the 'long hauls'.

II. THE STRENGTH OF SHIPS

The period of rapid growth in production was also a period of intense development in the technical aspects. The foundations of technical knowledge had been laid a century before—not in Britain, nor even in Europe—but high up in the equatorial Andes. They were laid by Pierre Bouguer (1698–1758), geographer and mathematician, joint leader of an expedition to measure a degree of latitude in Peru. His *Traité du Navire*, published in Paris in 1746, was the fruit of leisure activity during the expedition. It embodies nearly all the roots of the naval architect's knowledge. Bouguer devised the trapezoidal rule for the mensuration of areas, and checked the results against those obtained by the use of the rules devised by Isaac Newton and Roger Cotes; Simpson's simplification of Newton's rules was unknown to Bouguer, for it was published while he was in the Andes. On the basis of the simple trapezoidal rule he outlined most of the hydrostatic calculations that now enter the daily business of the naval architect.

More important in the present context, Bouguer outlined the principle that underlies the analysis of the strength of ships. Wooden ships suffered from 'arching' or 'hogging'—a tendency for the ends to droop in relation to the midship portion—and Bouguer showed that the tendency arose from differences in distributions of weight and buoyancy over the portions before and abaft the middle. The circumstances are illustrated in diagram (a) of figure 185; the equal and opposite forces of weight and buoyancy constitute a couple acting on the structure which must be resisted by a couple created by forces acting in the structure. To strengthen the vessel internally Bouguer proposed the fitting of a trussed girder along the centre-line plane of the ship, with tension-members of wrought iron and compression-members of wood.

Bouguer offered only a crude approximation to the distribution of weight, but in 1811 a closer approximation, akin to approximations in current use, was offered by Thomas Young (1773–1829), physician, physiologist, physicist, linguist, Egyptologist, and ornament of London society. Neither Bouguer nor Young took into account the variation in the distribution of buoyancy accompanying the passage of a ship through waves, but in 1860 Fairbairn presented a statement of the circumstances to be taken into consideration:

If we take a vessel . . . we shall approximate nearly to the facts by treating it as a simple beam; actually a vessel is placed in this position, either when supported at each end by two waves or when rising on the crest of another wave, supported at the centre, with the stem and stern partially suspended. Now in these positions the ship undergoes alternately a strain of compression and a strain of tension along the whole section of the deck, corresponding with equal strains of tension and compression along the whole section of the keel, the strains being reversed according as the vessel is supported at the ends or the

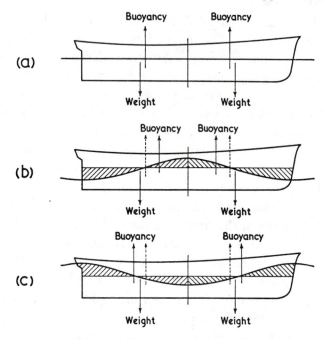

FIGURE 185—*Diagram of forces acting on the hull of a ship.*

centre. These are, in fact, the alternate strains to which every long vessel is exposed, particularly in seas where the distances between the crests of the waves does not exceed the length of the ship.

Soon afterwards W. J. M. Rankine (1820–72) published a diagrammatic treatment of the same analysis, and offered an extension of it. Diagram (b) of figure 185 shows a ship poised on the crest of a wave of her own length. As compared with the still-water condition shown in diagram (a), some buoyancy, indicated by hatching, has been transferred from the ends toward amidships. Accordingly the separation of the lines of action of weight and buoyancy has been widened, and the bending-moment causing hogging has been increased. In diagram (c) the ship is shown poised across the trough of the wave. In this case sufficient buoyancy has been transferred from amidships toward the ends to bring the line of action of the buoyancy to the other side of the line of action of the weight. Accordingly the direction of the external couple has been reversed, and the tendency is now for the middle portion of the ship to droop relatively to the ends —the circumstance termed 'sagging'. Rankine separated the total external couple, or bending-moment, into two elements: a still-water moment, almost invariably a hogging-moment, and a wave-moment, due to the transference of buoyancy. For the ship on the wave crest the transference is such as to increase the initial, still-water, moment whereas for the ship across the wave trough the transference is such as to reduce, and sometimes to reverse, the initial moment.

III. THE STRUCTURE OF IRON SHIPS

In broad outline there was no difference in disposition of structure between the early iron ship and the wooden ship. In both there were transverse members —the ribs or frames—branching from a backbone, or keel, along the centre-line. In both there was a skin, or shell, clothing the transverse members and making the hull watertight. There was, however, a fundamental defect in the structure of the wooden ship; it was impossible to provide end-to-end connexions. The narrow planks, or strakes, of the skin were fitted in relatively short lengths, and the only approach to continuity lay in the fact that ends of planks in neighbouring strakes were kept as far apart as possible. Accordingly the structure was not suited to withstand the 'strains of tension' to which Fairbairn referred in the above quotation.[1] It was this consideration that imposed an upper limit, in the region of 300 ft, on the length of the wooden ship; beyond such a length the deformation due to the differing distributions of weight and buoyancy became excessive, with consequent difficulty in maintaining the hull watertight. The adoption of iron, and the ability to connect the ends of plates by rivets, offered the possibility of overcoming the defect of the wooden hull; but this possibility was not at once fully exploited, as may be seen by examining the plans of the barge *Vulcan* (figure 183).

In the *Vulcan* the backbone, or keel, was formed by two plates, 12 in deep by ¾-in thick, running fore-and-aft. From it branched the ribs, or frames, spaced 24 in apart, extending round to the gunwale. They were formed from strips of plate, hammered on a special anvil into an L-shape. The flanges of the angle were about 3 in wide over most of the length, but across the bottom of the barge the vertical flange was gradually increased in depth to about 5 in where the frame

---

[1] The wooden keel also, though massive, was built in relatively short sections scarfed together, and therefore lacked stiffness.

was riveted to the keel; the horizontal leg was turned round vertically to provide the attachment, and the frames on the two sides of the keel were riveted together through the two thicknesses of the keel (figure 186 a). The skin or shell was generally $\frac{1}{4}$-in thick, but at the bow the thickness was increased to $\frac{3}{8}$-in. It was

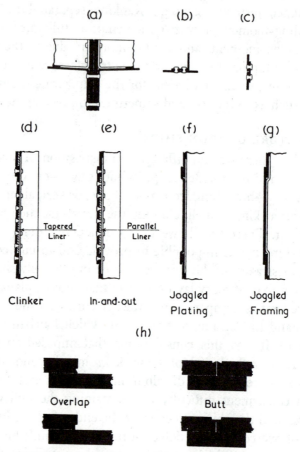

(a)   (b)   (c)

(d)   (e)   (f)   (g)

Tapered Liner   Parallel Liner

Clinker   In-and-out   Joggled Plating   Joggled Framing

(h)

Overlap   Butt

FIGURE 186—*Arrangements of shell plating.*

arranged in a series of panels, each extending from the keel to the gunwale, and over the distance between neighbouring frames. The edges of adjacent plates ran down the middle of a frame, two rows of rivets through the frame providing the end-to-end connexion of the plates (figure 186 b). It was, however, not possible to fit each panel in one piece, and therefore a joint had to be made at about half-width. The adjacent edges, running fore-and-aft, were covered by a strip of plate about 3–4 in wide, extending between consecutive frames (figure 186 c).

It was a defect in the structural design of the *Vulcan* that at each frame there was a joint right round the ship from gunwale to gunwale; the riveted attachment provided by the flange of a frame was not nearly so strong as the unpierced iron plating. The defect was not significant in a canal barge, but the arrangement of the plating in panels would not serve in a sea-going vessel. Accordingly it became common to arrange the plating of iron ships like the planking in wooden ships, namely, in strakes running fore-and-aft. There was, however, the major difference that the end-to-end fastening absent in the wooden ship was provided in the iron ship; the ends of adjacent plates in a strake were tied together by rivets. Following a practice very commonly adopted in small wooden craft, and occasionally in large wooden ships, the strakes of plating were arranged with overlapping edges (figure 186 d). In small wooden craft the planks were 'clenched' together at the edges; hence the application of the terms clencher or clinker to this form of the plating. There is no record of the origin of clinker-plating, but it seems to have persisted for about twenty years, that is, until about the middle of the century.

There was, however, a serious objection to clinker-plating. Between each plate and the frame running across it there was a triangular gap which had to be filled before the rivets joining the outer plate and the frame could be hammered up; a rivet can be made good only if there is no 'spring' between the parts to be connected. On occasion, ill-fitting washers were fitted in the gap around the rivets, but more usually a tapered 'liner'[1] was used. Such liners were difficult to make, and commonly not very well made. A simple improvement seems to have been suggested by John Scott Russell (1808–82), who will be mentioned again (p 361). In this the strakes were arranged alternately 'in' and 'out', (figure 186 e). The space between frame and outer plate was filled by a simple parallel liner of the same thickness as the inside strakes. This procedure had the further advantage that the inside strakes could be fitted first, and then templates, or patterns, of the various outside plates could be obtained from the ship, with increased accuracy in the matching of the rivet-holes.

Towards the end of the century, even the parallel liners were eliminated. There were two ways of doing so. One is illustrated in figure 186 f: the edges of the outside strake were 'joggled' to allow the plating to bed on the frame. The other, and more widely adopted, method is illustrated in figure 186 g. Here the frame is 'joggled' outward to bed against the outside plate. The arrangement of plating as 'in' and 'out' strakes persisted almost universally throughout the days of the riveted ship; an occasional reversion to clinker-plating is considered later (p 369).

[1] A narrow strip of plate to fill in between a frame and an outer strake.

The mere connexion of plate to plate by rivets did not by itself make the shell watertight, and it was necessary to caulk the seams and butts.[1] Close to the edge of the plate a V-groove was cut parallel to the adjacent plate (figure 186 h). Then with the same tool held in a different manner the ridge so formed was hammered down. In the case of a butt joint the metal of the adjacent plates was thus hammered together in the bottom of a shallow rectangular trough. In the case of an overlapped joint there was also a shallow trough, with the metal of one plate hammered hard against the surface of the other. It is not known whether this process was adopted on the *Vulcan*. It was, however, probably introduced to ship-building by the boiler-makers who were employed to shape and prepare the material for erection by the ship-wrights—craftsmen in wood—and the process has persisted, without significant change. This demarcation of the crafts concerned has persisted, and until fairly recent years it was common to class all the iron-workers in a ship-yard as boiler-makers.

The rolling of iron was introduced in 1784, but rolled iron plates did not become available until a later date. It is therefore probable that the plates of the *Vulcan* had been manufactured under a tilt-hammer. But the building of iron ships required more than the provision of flat plates, whether hammered or, as later, rolled; frames or ribs of iron, corresponding in function to the frames of a wooden ship, were still necessary. Strength equivalent to that of a wooden frame rectangular in section could be obtained from a thin iron rib lying transversely; but such a rib could not be attached to the iron shell. Hence the need for a member lying fore-and-aft, and thus for angle-iron such as was hammered out of plate for the *Vulcan*. It is not known when the first angle-irons were produced by rolling, but by the middle of the nineteenth century the iron-works were able to supply a variety of them in different sizes and proportions, as well as some other sections.

Figure 187 shows stages in the development of framing for ships. The simple angle-iron adequate for the smaller ships is illustrated at (a). To provide the greater strength required for large ships a reverse-bar was fitted to the frame bar, as shown at (b); this arrangement had the merit that the reverse-bar could be attached for that distance only where the reinforcement was considered to be necessary. A Z-bar (c) was virtually a frame and reverse-bar rolled in one piece; this section was much used by the Admiralty but, for a reason to be given later (p 368), was not much favoured by builders of merchant-ships. A channel-bar (d) is a Z-bar with the inner flange turned round, while a bulb-angle (e) may be described as a channel-bar with the inner flange compressed and rounded.

---

[1] A seam is a joint running fore and aft, whereas a butt is a joint running athwartships.

For years the bulb-angle has been the most widely used section in ship-building, though weight for weight it is not quite so resistant to bending-moments as a channel-bar. The reason commonly given for the choice of the bulb-angle is that it is more likely to receive the proper painting necessary for protection against corrosion; there is the fear that the painter's brush will never properly reach the inside flange of the channel. The adoption of a single rolled section such as the channel or bulb-angle in preference to the built-up frame and reverse-bar entailed the carrying of some excess weight, insofar as the section that was strong enough in the region of heaviest loading was stronger than neces-

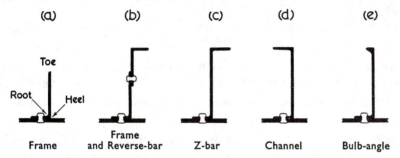

FIGURE 187—*Types of frame.*

sary in the regions of lighter loading; the strength of the member could not be varied in the manner possible with the frame and reverse-bar. It had, however, been appreciated that economy in cost of construction could best be achieved by reduction in the number of parts to be handled and fitted, and this consideration was dominant.

In the wooden ship it was not possible to fit a frame in one piece from keel to gunwale, for timber of approximately the desired shape and sufficiently great length was not obtainable. Accordingly a frame was composed of several timbers arranged end to end, with other similar pieces alongside, so disposed that the common ends of one succession of pieces lay between the common ends in the other succession. That manner of construction was carried over to the early iron ships. It was described, and criticized, by Scott Russell in a book published in 1865:

. . . it was truly curious to notice the early ship-builder . . . most assiduously putting together short pieces of angle iron, and regularly scarfing their ends together, to form from their assemblage a single iron frame, all formed out of little pieces. Happily there came an end of this, for he found it easier, cheaper, and stronger, to have his frame rolled in one piece, or at most in two; and in a short time he found out how, out of an angle iron of moderate dimensions, to bend or weld a complete frame, all in one length.

But it was a long time before he could reconcile his mind to this fine simplicity; and even to this day there are rude ways of patching one angle iron on to the back of another, to give something like a rough imitation of the graduation in strength, which used to run from keel to gunwale, in a timber ship.

The fitting of angle-bar frames in relatively short pieces, either welded together or scarfed by riveting another bar at the back to bridge—and make good—the break, was initially forced on the builder of iron ships by the inability of the rolling-mills to provide angle-bars of adequate length. That inability was, however, fairly soon overcome and bars became available in lengths adequate for frames in one piece from keel to gunwale.

Scott Russell's criticism was but a prelude to his advocacy of a radical departure from accepted practice. A passage in which Fairbairn describes the creation of alternating 'strains of tension and compression' within the structure of a ship has already been quoted (p 354). The following quotation, from Fairbairn's book of 1865, indicates the distribution of material best suited to withstand the strains:

The material . . . should be, as far as practicable, accumulated at the top and bottom of the sections at midships, that at the sides being merely sufficient to form a rigid connection between these two parts.

Scott Russell carried the argument a stage farther. He questioned the desirability of fitting frames:

One good alone can the frames of an iron ship be said to do to the structure when complete, and one while it is building. In the process of building the frames are a convenient support on which to hang the plates of iron which form the skin, before they have been fastened to one another. After that they cease to be of any such value, and have served only as a temporary scaffolding. The benefit they confer upon the structure, when completed, is, that they give it some stiffness against an external force, tending to change its form; but for this purpose they are feeble in force, and wasteful in materials. We shall see how stiffness, and power to maintain the shape of the ship against local forces, are much more effectually given in other ways.

The method of construction proposed by Scott Russell and sometimes, but not invariably, adopted by him is illustrated in figure 188. On every strake of plating there was a stiffener running fore-and-aft, in the shape of a Z formed by a plate and two angle-bars. Under the deck were two similar stiffeners, as well as others formed merely of angle-bars. The shape of the ship was maintained by a series of transverse partitions or bulkheads, one of which is shown in the figure. In addition, a series of webs, or partial bulkheads, was spaced between the complete bulkheads; one of these is also shown in the figure. This system of construction was not, however, widely adopted. The explanation is found in Scott Russell's words given above. Transverse frames afforded a means of suspending the shell plating in preparation for the riveting; convenience of construction required their adoption.

IV. 'THE GREAT IRON SHIP'

The early days of the iron ship also witnessed a most spectacular conception

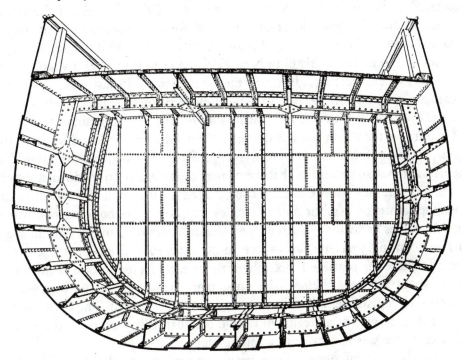

FIGURE 188—*Scott Russell's longitudinal framing, as used in the* Annette.

and an unsatisfactory achievement: they were the days of the *Great Eastern*—'the great iron ship'. The two men most prominently associated with the conception and its execution were Isambard Kingdom Brunel (1806–59), son of an *émigré* of the French Revolution,[1] and John Scott Russell, son of the minister of a parish on the outskirts of Glasgow. Both were versatile. Brunel had been trained as a civil engineer during association with his father's work, and when he was 27 years old he was appointed engineer for a proposed railway from Bristol to London, soon to be known as the Great Western Railway. Scott Russell had

[1] The father, Sir Marc Isambard Brunel (1769–1849), was also a notable engineer, who drove the first Thames tunnel.

initially been destined for the ministry, but an aptitude for affairs mechanical rather than clerical led him into engineering workshops during his vacations from university studies. Instead of becoming a professor at Edinburgh he became manager of a ship-building yard at Greenock. While manager of the yard he built a steam-carriage that ran successfully on the road between Greenock and Paisley. In 1844 he moved to London, and in 1850 took over the establishment at Millwall which had been founded by Fairbairn. Brunel's association with ship-building is said to have begun at a meeting of the directors of the Great Western Railway in 1835, when one of them spoke of the enormous length of the proposed railway. To which Brunel retorted: 'Why not make it longer, and have a steam-boat to go from Bristol to New York, and call it the *Great Western*.' In those days of engineering adventure the remark made in jest was considered in earnest; and the 'steam-boat' was built under Brunel's superintendence.

The *Great Western* was the first steam-ship to cross the Atlantic in fulfilment of the purpose for which she was designed. She did so in 1838, and initiated the regular crossing of the Atlantic by steam-ships. She had a wooden hull and paddle-engines, and was so successful that the owners soon decided to lay down a second vessel. For the new ship Brunel recommended an iron hull. At a later stage, when the construction of the hull was under way, he took the bold step of discarding the paddles in favour of a screw. The *Great Britain* went into service in 1843. In the following year she ran ashore in an exposed position on the coast of Ireland, where she remained throughout the winter. As in the case of the *Garry Owen*, about ten years before, the satisfactory behaviour of the iron hull in abnormal circumstances engendered faith in the new material. The *Great Britain* remained in service as a steam-ship for more than thirty years; and for some years more she was in service as a sailing-ship.

It may be that his service for a period as engineer to the Australian Mail Company, in connexion with the building of two ships by Scott Russell, directed Brunel's thoughts towards the problems of constructing a ship large enough to carry sufficient fuel for a very long voyage. It is, however, certain that in 1851 and 1852 Brunel was turning over such problems in his mind. In 1852 he had decided that the ship should have a 'cellular bottom', and that the main frames should be longitudinal instead of transverse. In that year he discussed the project with Scott Russell and with the directors of the Eastern Steam Navigation Company. The initial proposal was for a ship to sail to Calcutta, but subsequently the project was extended to the provision of a ship large enough to carry fuel for a round voyage to Australia, outward by way of the Cape of Good Hope and homeward by way of Cape Horn. Early in 1853 Brunel had made the note: 'The ship, all iron, double bottom, and sides up to waterline, with ribs longitudinal like the Britannia Tube' [the bridge over the Menai Straits built by Robert Stephenson, pp 503-7, plate 28].

After consideration of a variety of designs, including one for a ship 730 ft long, the contract for the new vessel was signed in December 1853. It called for a ship 680 ft long by 83 ft broad by 58 ft deep, with an engine of 4000 hp driving a screw, and another of 2600 hp driving paddles; Brunel was satisfied that the necessary power could not be obtained from screw-propulsion alone. In addi-

tion there were to be six masts carrying an ample spread of sail, to take advantage of the prevailing winds on the long passages between the Capes. The building of the hull and of the paddle-engine was entrusted to Scott Russell, and the building of the engine to drive the screw to James Watt & Company, of Birmingham.

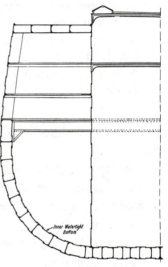

Brunel's first ship was 212 ft long between perpendiculars, and 35 ft 4 in broad; she displaced 2300 tons at a draught of 16 ft 8 in. His first iron ship was 322 ft long overall and 51 ft broad, and displaced nearly 3000 tons at a draught of 16 ft. His great ship displaced about 11 800 tons when floating light at 15 ft 6 in draught, and about 27 400 tons when loaded to 30 ft draught.

An elevation and a plan of the fifth deck of the *Great Eastern* are reproduced in plate 24, and

FIGURE 189—*The* Great Eastern (*constructional section*).

a cross-section indicating the character of the structure is shown in figure 189. There were five boiler-rooms, each containing two boilers, the design assuming the use of four boilers for the paddle-engine and six for the engine driving the screw; but a common steam-line, running fore-and-aft along a gallery, permitted the steam to be distributed to the engines to suit requirements. The bunkers, arranged across the ship, and abreast of and above the boilers, were intended for the stowage of 12 000 tons of coal, the amount reckoned to be necessary for the round voyage. It is apparent that the greater portion of the lower regions of the ship was occupied by the engines, boilers, and fuel. In the upper regions there was accommodation for 4000 passengers.

Brunel's decision and his note on the general character of the structure have been given above. These guiding principles were developed in detail by Scott Russell. The section reproduced in figure 189 shows the double bottom and part-double side, as well as the double skin along the upper deck. By virtue of the two bulkheads running fore-and-aft over the length of the machinery and bunker spaces the structure was akin to two 'Britannia Tubes', connected together by the double bottom under the engines and boilers. Between the double skins there were the longitudinal frames, fitted generally on alternate strakes of plating and formed of plates connected to the skins by angle-bars.

A general principle followed by Scott Russell in the detail design was indicated by him in his book:

> I recommend for general use that you should have the least possible variety and shapes of iron in your ships. . . . The work made uniform will thus be cheapest and best, if the design be consistently carried out in this way. In the *Great Eastern* there is one thickness of plates ($\frac{3}{4}$ in.), for skin, outer and inner, one thickness of internal work ($\frac{1}{2}$ in.), one size of rivet ($\frac{7}{8}$ in.), one pitch (3 in.), and one size of angle-iron (4 in. $\times$ 4 in. $\times \frac{5}{8}$). The exceptions that happen to have got in . . . were accidental, and formed no part of the design. . . .

It is not known how far Scott Russell was guided by Fairbairn's experience and inquiries.

In a paper of 1850,[1] Fairbairn had provided information vitally necessary for the successful construction of iron ships. Along with a wealth of general information he had shown that for end-to-end connexion of iron plates a single row of rivets was inadequate, and that at least two rows were necessary. In the *Great Eastern* the butt joints were made with double rows of rivets, whereas all the edge-connexions were made with single rows. Incidentally, the degree of standardization sought by Scott Russell is no longer necessary, although the present-day ship-builder is fully alive to the disadvantages of using too great a variety of rolled sectional material.

The construction of the *Great Eastern* was put in hand early in 1854 and the ship was ready for launching late in 1857. To this stage the work had been a marvellous achievement. An iron hull weighing about 6250 tons had been constructed from about 30 000 small plates connected by about 3 m rivets; apart from a few specially large plates associated with the stern-frame, no plate exceeded 10 ft in length and 33 inches in width. It has been recorded that when the ship was broken up in 1889 the hull was found to be in excellent condition.

The launching disclosed the first major defect in the ambitious conception. On the advice of Scott Russell the ship had been built broadside-on to the Thames because of the restricted width of water. After the failure of the first attempt

---

[1] 'An Experimental Inquiry into the Strength of Wrought-Iron Plates and their Riveted Joints as applied to Ship building and Vessels exposed to severe strains'. *Phil. Trans.*, 140, xxxv, 677–725, 1850.

to launch, Brunel devised the arrangements for transferring the ship down to the water; the operation took months, and involved an expenditure of about £120 000. The ship was afloat early in 1858, and was completed late in 1859, without all the elaboration initially intended, for the cost of the launching had led to severe financial stringency.

Late in 1859 the *Great Eastern* made a coastal trip to Holyhead, and some misgivings were expressed about her performance. After a winter in port while various repairs and alterations were effected, the ship sailed for New York in mid-1860, and the doubts were soon confirmed. In his book Scott Russell wrote:

When the ship shall pass into the hands of skilful owners and managers, there will be no difficulty, with a much less expenditure of fuel, in maintaining the 14 knots an hour for which the ship was designed, and which, with a much larger expenditure of fuel, she has already performed; but it would be unsafe to entrust such skilful working to any but owners and managers who have shown by a long term of capacity and ability their trustworthiness for such work.

The management does seem to have been inefficient, but no change at that level could have eradicated the fatal defect. The consumption of coal had been gravely underestimated. At the speed of 14 knots mentioned by Scott Russell the ship would have required a steaming-time of almost 75 days for the round-the-world voyage. Without any margin for contingencies, and with no allowance for use of coal in port, the burning of the whole 12 000 tons of coal in 75 days would have permitted a daily consumption of only 160 tons. On the basis of the 6600 hp noted above the daily consumption could not have been less than about 280 tons; some published figures suggest that the rate was indeed in the region of 250–300 tons. An abounding faith in an inadequately developed technology was betrayed by lack of guidance from matured experience.

On the north Atlantic run, for which she had not been designed, the *Great Eastern* was a failure. From 1865 she was frequently used for cable-laying (p 226), and in 1889 she was broken up for scrap.

V. METAL-WORKING IN THE IRON SHIP

In building a wooden ship some shaping and trimming of material could be done after erection, and the relatively flexible strakes of planking could be bent round into position against the robust framing. On the iron ship no such shaping after erection was possible, and there could be no bending of plating against the relatively slender framing. Scott Russell—who had been a lecturer in geometry at Edinburgh University—saw that the change in the nature of the material of construction demanded a fuller consideration of the geometry of the hull in order that the shapes of plates could be more accurately determined. Others saw in the change the invasion of the ship-yard by the machines of the engineer. It is probable that the boiler-makers called in to shape and fit the new material brought with them their early machines for shearing the edges of plates and for punching holes. In a book on iron ship-building published in 1858 there are illustrations of such machines, as well as of machines for shearing angle-bars and for drilling and countersinking holes; and there is an illustration of a portable fire for heating rivets. The same book has an illustration of a machine for rolling flat plates into cylindrical form. Fairbairn is credited with the manufacture of such a machine, but it is not known whether he was the first to do so; early boilers for marine use did not require plate rolls, since they were commonly rectangular. In this book there is, too, an illustration of a steam-riveter, with a plunger squeezing down the point of a rivet held in place against a 'bolster'. It is believed that Fairbairn introduced riveting by steam-pressure for the construction of the tubular bridges over the river Conway and the Menai Straits carrying the railway from London to Holyhead. A machine for planing the edges of plates was introduced in 1874.

The early machines were driven by belts from overhead shafting, with steam-engines providing the power, although individual steam-engine drive was adopted in some instances. Operation of the machines by hydraulic power was introduced in 1879. This development was accompanied by the production of more powerful machines, and the provision of additional machines for flanging, joggling, and the punching of large man-holes; before the provision of the man-hole punch it was necessary to pierce out the outline with a rivet-hole punch, and then chisel away the remaining rough projections.

There is one major process which has been little affected by the development of machines—the bending of the frames. There is no record of the manner in which the frames of the *Vulcan* were bent to the shape required. Nor is it known when the process in common use today was originated, though it is described in early books on the building of iron ships. The first stage in the process is the delineation of the whole shape of the hull in chalk on the floor of the 'mould-loft' (vol III, p 490)—a vast shed in which one branch of the craft of the ship-wright is exercised in the highest degree. The delineation is based on information furnished by the design office. It is carried out at full size as regards breadth and depth, but for a large ship may be made on reduced length. From this delineation the outline of every frame is determined and shown on the 'scrieve-board'—an assembly of flat planks clamped together. The outlines are 'scrieved-in' with a grooving-tool to prevent erasure; the men using the scrieve-board walk over it, and mere chalked or painted lines would soon be obliterated. Much information besides the outlines of the frame is given on the scrieve-board, presented in the symbolism of the ship-wright. The frame-outlines marked on the scrieve-board are those of the 'heels' (figure 187 a).

The frames are bent on a flat floor formed of large cast iron slabs, in front of the furnace in which the bars are heated, and with the scrieve-board alongside. The slabs are pierced with holes of $1-1\frac{1}{2}$ in diameter, spaced 5–6 in apart in lines at right-angles. In the earlier days a pattern was made from the scrieve-board to the 'toe' of the frame (figure 187 a), and from this pattern the outline was chalked on the slabs. Pegs were then inserted in the holes in the slabs near to the chalked outline, and washers of such a size as to touch the outline were fitted over the pegs; a refinement was to use washers with excentric holes as an alternative to using a wide range of sizes. In more modern practice a light 'set-iron' is bent to the desired outline, laid on the slabs, and secured by 'dogs' hammered into the holes and holding down the set-iron. Whatever be the method of marking the outline, the red-hot frame is squeezed and levered round to its shape. The only machine used in the process is a hydraulic ram on a wheeled carriage, which can be locked in position by the use of the holes in the slabs and also readily shifted to the positions where pressure is required. This is a relatively modern application of hydraulic power, developed as frames increased to dimensions so large that they could not be shaped by hand-leverage alone. The frames are not actually bent to the exact shape required, since they tend to straighten during cooling; the allowance for this change of shape reflects the experience and skill of the 'frame-turner'.

In figure 187 the various types of frame have their legs or flanges at a right-angle. Convenience in construction demands that the flange projecting inboard toward the centre-line of the ship—the standing-flange—shall lie, from top to bottom, in a plane making a right-angle with the axis of the vessel. The other flange—the faying-flange—must lie along the shell plating. On the flat side amidships the two flanges are at a right-angle, but elsewhere they must be at an angle which varies all the way from top to bottom; in other words, the frame must be bevelled. In order that the riveters may have access to the rivets connecting the frame to the shell, the angle between the flanges may be obtuse, but it must never be acute; in other words, the frame may have 'open' bevel, but must never have 'closed' bevel. This is achieved by arranging the frames so that in the forward part of the ship the standing-flange is at the fore end of the faying-flange, whereas in the after part the standing-flange is at the aft end of the faying-flange. This disposition of the frames is illustrated in a book on iron ship-building published in 1858, but the desirability of adopting it was not appreciated by the designer of the barge *Vulcan*.

The determination of the angle between the flanges at any position—the determination of the amount of bevel—is a simple matter of geometry on either the scrieve-board or the floor of the mould-loft. In the early days the frame was always bevelled during the process of bending, by fitting a 'fork' over the faying-flange standing vertically up from the slabs, and levering the flange over to the desired angle. For many years a bevelling-machine has been available. It consists essentially of two bevelled rollers making contact at such an angle that the bevels on the rollers are initially at a right-angle; the rollers meet in the 'root' of the frame (figure 187 a). The angle of the lower roller can, however, be continuously reduced so that the bevelled portion squeezes down the flange of a frame passing under the twin rollers; the upper roller keeps the other flange vertical. The machine is mounted at the mouth of the furnace, and the straight frame is bevelled as it is pulled out on the way to the bending slabs.

The objection to the Z frame (figure 187 c) is that it does not lie flat on the bending-slabs, and must be raised on special blocks during the processes of bending and bevelling.

Another process little affected by the introduction of machines was the joining of parts by rivets. Early books on the building of iron ships describe methods that have persisted with only relatively minor changes. The rivet is heated in a portable fire-hearth blown by a bellows, and passed—sometimes thrown—by the rivet-heating boy to the holder-on. There is skill in the accurate throwing of a red-hot rivet from a pair of tongs. The holder-on knocks the rivet through the hole, and holds it in place with a heavy hammer; the head of the rivet is commonly of 'pan' shape, as indicated on the insides of the frames in figure 187. The point of the rivet—the end of the parallel shank projecting from the head—is hammered up by two riveters striking alternately, if the rivet is to fill a counter-sunk hole as shown in the shell plating in figure 187. If the point of the rivet is too large for the countersinking the surplus material is removed by a cutting-tool held by one riveter and struck by the other. If the point is not to fill a counter-sunk hole it is partially hammered up by the two riveters, and then shaped with a die held by one of the riveters and struck by the other; a rivet of this type is shown connecting the frame and reverse frame in figure 187 b. A riveting-hammer operating by compressed air was available by 1865; the head of the hammer was actuated by a piston within a cylinder. This machine does not seem to have been a success, since about half a century elapsed before compressed-air drive was widely adopted in tools for riveting, caulking, chipping, drilling, and trepanning. When a 'wind-hammer' is used the rivet-point can be formed by one riveter, since the blows from the tool are in as rapid succession as the blows from two riveters with hand-hammers.

The steam-riveter also, to which reference has been made, does not seem to have been widely adopted. Since it was fixed in position it could be used only to connect parts that could be taken to it, and the amount of riveting which could be done with advantage before the erection of the parts was but a small fraction of the whole. A hydraulic riveter became available in 1871, some years before the general adoption of hydraulic power for the driving of ship-yard machines. Like the steam-riveter, the hydraulic riveter formed the point of the rivet by pressure, not by hammering. In the ultimate development of the hydraulic riveter the dies to take the head and form the point are at the ends of pivoted arms, with an interval of 6 to 8 ft between the dies and the pivot, and with the operating cylinder on the side of the pivot remote from the dies; the outward movement of the hydraulic ram causes the dies to squeeze the red-hot rivet.

The first hydraulic riveter was described as portable, but the term was only relative. By virtue of flexible connexions from the main pipe the riveter could be moved about, provided it were slung from an adequate support. Even in its ultimate development it is considered, in general, to be too heavy and too awkward for use on the topsides of ships, although on large ships it is necessary to use it to ensure satisfactory closing of the heaviest rivets. When, on occasion, it has been used for the closing of rivets in shell plating on the bottom it has necessitated a reversion to the earlier clinker arrangement of the strakes. With in-and-out strakes only the inside strakes could be riveted hydraulically, but with clinker strakes, put on in succession from the centre, the riveter could deal with each in turn; the width of the strakes was determined by the length of the jaws of the riveter. The most common use of the hydraulic riveter (figure 265) was for the riveting of minor parts to a major part, on 'skids'—a series of angle-bars forming a platform—at the head of the building-berth; this was found to be economical, although it does not seem to have been adopted with the steam-riveter.

VI. THE LAST IRON SHIPS

Figure 190 shows constructional cross-sections of the *City of Rome*, built in 1881, 546 ft long, and almost the last of the large iron ships. Apart from the number of decks appropriate to a large ship, the general features of construction are fairly well representative of all iron ships. In the *Vulcan* the keel was formed by two plates 12 in deep and $\frac{3}{4}$-in thick (figure 186 a). In the *City of Rome* the keel was formed of one slab 12 in deep and $3\frac{3}{4}$ in thick. In both cases the shell plating was flanged to bed on the keel, and was riveted through the keel. In the *Vulcan* the frame, hammered from a flat plate, was increased in depth across the bottom of the barge to become 5 in deep where it was attached to the keel. Such a depth was not nearly adequate for a large ship, and a varying depth could not be obtained with a rolled angle-bar. The necessary depth at the centre-line was attained by interposing a vertical plate—the floor-plate—between a frame and a reverse frame, so forming a deep Z. In the *City of Rome* the floor-plates were

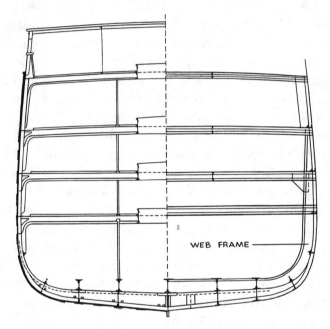

FIGURE 190—City of Rome (*constructional midship sections*).

34 in deep at the centre-line, whence they were tapered toward the sides and round the bilge to the 7-in depth of the frames; there was no direct connexion between the floor-plates and the keel as there was between the frames and the keel of the *Vulcan*. The floor and frames were spaced 28 in apart, and additional stiffness was conferred by arranging, at intervals, a deep 'web' floor and frame across the bottom and up the sides. A web floor and frame is shown on the right-hand side of figure 190; the webs were probably spaced about eight to twelve frame-spaces apart, and were associated with deep cross-beams under the deck.

The bottom was further stiffened by fitting above the floors, and running continuously fore-and-aft, a centre keelson and four side keelsons, formed by plates and angle-bars riveted together in the form of an ⊥. Below each keelson, and connected to it, a piece of plate was fitted between the floors, connected to them by angle-bars in the case of the centre keelson, and to the shell plating in the case of the side keelsons. There were also two 'stringers' fitted on each side, the lower one consisting of a plate and two angle-bars running continuously fore-and-aft near the ends of the floors, and the upper one of two angle-bars running fore-and-aft on the insides of the reverse frames. Support was given to the decks by two rows of round iron pillars, arranged from top to bottom fore-and-aft along the lines of the inner side keelsons; the pillars were probably fitted at alternate beams (figure 190).

An unusual feature of the *City of Rome* was the flush fitting of the shell

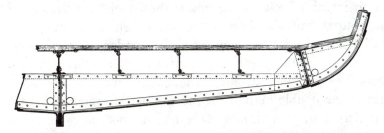

FIGURE 191—*Cross-section through a McIntyre tank for water ballast.*

plating, neither in-and-out nor clinker, the seams being covered generally by strips fitted on the outside, not on the inside as on the *Vulcan*. Around the bilge and between the two top decks the strips were replaced by wide plates, so that in these regions there were two complete thicknesses of plating. The majority of the shell plates were $\frac{3}{4}$-in thick.

The only major development in the structure of the iron merchant-ship was introduced in the colliers running between the Tyne and the Thames. For the northward run in ballast it had been the custom to carry gravel, entailing considerable expense in the purchase, loading, discharging, and disposal; the ballast was necessary to ensure adequate immersion of the ships. Weight could be cheaply obtained by using water as ballast, and it was at first carried in canvas sacks; at the end of the northward trip the sacks were emptied into the hold and the water pumped out. Wastage of the sacks, and on occasion their rupture during a trip, led to a ship being built in 1854 with iron tanks fitted on top of the floors across the bottoms of the holds. Soon afterwards the separate tanks were replaced by a large tank arranged as an integral part of the structure. A cross-section of such a tank is illustrated in figure 191; the particular arrangement is known as a McIntyre tank, from the name of the inventor. The figure shows the almost universal bar-keel, with the two strakes of shell plating at the centre-line riveted to it. It shows the usual floor-plate, but in this case the plate is stopped at, and connected by a bracket to, the fore-and-aft boundary of the tank, set normal to the shell plating. Outside the boundary the frame and reverse frame extending up the side are connected to the boundary by a large bracket. The centre keelson is of the same type as that in the *City of Rome* (figure 190). There are also three side keelsons on each side, somewhat similar to those on the *City of Rome*, but lacking the connexion to the shell plating. The keelsons form a foundation for the top plating of the tank.

A double bottom had been a feature in the construction of warships, sometimes associated with a double skin on the sides; the inner skin limited the danger of an inrush of water occurring if the vessel were damaged in action. A double bottom had also been fitted years before in the *Great Western*. Brunel had arranged deep fore-and-aft girders under the machinery, and had completed the structure by fitting plating over them; this was probably the prototype of the double-skin arrangement adopted in the *Great Eastern*. But the advantages of the double bottom for the carriage of water as ballast, and the security conferred by an additional skin over the bottom, were not commonly appreciated in the building of large ships until about 1880; as shown in figure 190, a double bottom was not fitted in the *City of Rome* (1881).

VII. STEEL SHIPS

In 1860 there was founded the Institution of Naval Architects, an enterprise in which a large part was played by John Scott Russell. The 'Transactions' of the Institution, published annually since 1860, embody practically the whole record of progress in ship-building and marine engineering since then. Moreover, the Institution has had an indirect effect on progress by virtue of its concern with technical education. At the meetings of the Institution in 1863, Scott Russell called attention to the lack in Britain of facilities for the technical education of naval architects and engineers such as were available in France. As a result, the Royal School of Naval Architecture and Marine Engineering was established at South Kensington in 1864; it was transferred to Greenwich in 1874, to form part of the Royal Naval College.

The story of the great change in the construction of ships during the latter part of the nineteenth century—the change from iron to steel—is well recorded in the Institution's 'Transactions'. Ships had been built of steel before 1860; in 1859 a paddle-steamer for service on the Black Sea had been built on the Thames, and a paddle-steamer for the Pacific Steam Navigation Company had been built on the Clyde. Moreover, during the American Civil War some steel steamers were built to run the Northern blockade. In these cases the use of steel was probably imposed by the need to save weight in order to gain speed; in one case the thickness of steel components was about half that of equivalent iron ones. Steel had been tested in Chatham dockyard in 1864; yet for years it was viewed with suspicion. If early steel was over-heated and too slowly cooled, it became soft and weak, and if too quickly cooled became hard and brittle. The annealing proposed for the correction of some of the undesirable characteristics was not practicable. In 1875 the position was summed up by Nathaniel Barnaby, Chief Naval Architect to the Admiralty, in a paper to the Institution of Naval Architects:

No doubt excellent steel is produced in small quantities by the converter and the bath at a much cheaper rate than it could be produced ten years ago; and where the management is strict and careful considerable quantities may be delivered of trustworthy material. Nevertheless our distrust of it is so great that the material may be said to be altogether unused by private shipbuilders, except for boats and very small vessels, and masts and yards; . . .

Toward the end of the paper he wrote:

The question we have to put to the steel makers is, What are our prospects of obtaining a material which we can use without such delicate manipulation and so much fear and trembling?

The question was soon answered by the Landore Siemens Steel Company, under the management of James Riley. This company's steel, made by the Siemens-Martin process, which afforded a more sure control than the older Bessemer converter, satisfied the Admiralty and a contract was placed for the supply of steel for the construction of the fast dispatch-vessels *Iris* and *Mercury*.

The launching of H.M.S. *Iris* at Pembroke dockyard in 1877 is commonly taken to mark the beginning of the era of steel in the building of ships. The rapidity of the subsequent progress may be assessed from the graph in figure 184. This shows the tonnages of iron and steel ships built in the Clydeside ship-yards during the period from 1878 to 1900. At the end of this period the production of iron ships was as insignificant as that of steel vessels had been at the beginning.

The change in the material raised the question of the allowance to be made for the increased strength. It has been noted that in a ship built for blockade-running the thicknesses of steel were made half the thicknesses of equivalent iron. By 1868 the committee of Lloyd's Register had permitted a ship to be built of steel with thicknesses reduced by one-fourth as compared with those of an iron ship. Finally, practice became stabilized with thicknesses of steel reduced to four-fifths of the corresponding thicknesses of iron. This change was readily effected, for it had been customary to measure thicknesses of iron in sixteenths of an inch, and when steel was adopted the same figures were applied to twentieths of an inch. This habit of measuring by twentieths of an inch lasted many years, but now the ship-builder expresses thicknesses in hundredths of an inch.

The adoption of steel instead of iron did not entail any radical change in the arrangement of the structure. Figure 192 indicates the structural arrangements in the *Campania* (plate 25) and *Lucania*, the express Cunard Line steamers built in 1893. These ships may be taken to represent the highest level of British ship-building during the nineteenth century. With the exception of the *Great Eastern* they were the largest ships that had then been built. Their dimensions were, indeed, much less than those of 'the great iron ship', by about 80 ft in length, 17 ft in breadth, and 16 ft in depth. There were, however, two tiers of superstructure arranged above the upper deck in the *Campania* and *Lucania*, but none on the *Great Eastern*. The Cunard ships were designed to carry 1700 passengers each, as compared with 4000 in the *Great Eastern*. The horse-power of the engines driving the two screws, about 30 000, was nearly $4\frac{1}{2}$ times as great as the power developed by the paddle- and screw-engines of the *Great Eastern* (p 363). In fact, the engines of the *Campania* and *Lucania* were the most powerful reciprocating steam-engines ever built in Britain for merchant-ships.

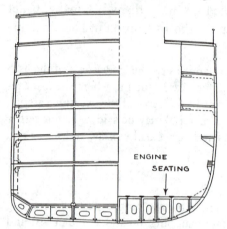

ENGINE
SEATING

FIGURE 192—*Constructional midship sections of express Cunard Line steamers* Campania *and* Lucania.

The major difference between the structural arrangements shown in figures 190 and 192 is in the provision of a double bottom in the later ships; incidentally the fitting of a complete double bottom is now compulsory in passenger ships more than 300 ft long. Moreover, the construction of the double bottom has changed from that shown on figure 191, and has taken almost its final form. The floor-plates are fitted over the whole depth between inner and outer bottoms, and are pierced by large man-holes for access during construction and for maintenance during service; they are pierced also by small holes for drainage and ventilation. The centre keelson shown running along the top of the floors in figures 190 and 191 has been replaced by a centre girder, running fore-and-aft along the centre-line between the inner and outer bottoms; the centre girder consists of a vertical plate connected to the horizontal plating at top and bottom by angle-bars. The provision of a centre girder is a convenience, but not a necessity, in the process of erection; it is essential for a ship which must be dry-docked on a line of blocks arranged along the centre-line of a graving-dock. Associated with the arrangement of the centre girder of the form indicated in figure 192 is the disappearance of the bar keel shown in figures 190 and 191. The centre girder in association with flat bottom-plating had been adopted by Brunel in the *Great Britain* and again in the *Great Eastern*; such an arrangement is also indicated in figure 188. Nevertheless the much less satisfactory arrangement of a bar keel—a relic from the days of the wooden ship—persisted for many years, and survived into the days of common adoption of the double bottom. It may have been thought that the vertical projection below the nearly flat bottom of a ship was of some benefit to the steering. In the *Campania* and *Lucania* the flat keel was formed of two thicknesses of plate.

The side keelsons shown in figures 190 and 191 have been replaced in figure 192 by side girders fitted between the floor-plates; in this figure the middle side girder on the left-hand side is actually continuous fore-and-aft, but that was not the most common arrangement. The side keelsons are connected to the floor-plates, and to the inner and outer plating, by angle-bars. The floor-plates are connected to the shell plating by a frame-bar, and to the inner bottom plating by a reverse bar. In the early days of the double bottom, following the use of the McIntyre tank (figure 191), the transverse structure within the double bottom sometimes took the form of a number of separate bracket-pieces tied together by angle-bars. It has, however, already been noted that economy in construction could best be attained by reduction in the number of parts to be handled, and this accounts for the adoption of large plate floors extending from the top to the bottom, and from the centre-line to the side, of the space. An inevitable development was hydraulic riveting of the frame-bar, reverse-bar, and minor connecting angle-bars to the floor-plate, and the erection of the whole as a unit.

In the *Campania* and *Lucania* the floors were spaced 30 in apart, and the double bottom was 56 in deep over most of the length. Under the engines the depth of the double bottom was increased to about 90 inches in order to provide a sufficiently rigid foundation. Moreover, two of the side girders were made continuous, and the floor was therefore in three pieces from centre-line to side. A cross-section in the region of the engine-room is shown on the right-hand side of figure 192.

A convenient backbone for the erection of the structural elements of a ship was provided by the combination of a flat keel-plate with a centre girder, laid on a line of closely spaced blocks running along the centre-line of the building-berth. Most commonly the floors were connected to the centre girder, with shores to support the outer ends, and then the boundary-plates of the double bottom—the margin plates—were fitted to tie together the outer ends of the floors. After that, the plates of the outer and inner bottoms were fitted. On occasion the plating on the 'flat' of the outer bottom was laid first, and then the floors were fitted on top. Commonly the erection of the whole, or nearly the whole, of the double bottom preceded the erection of the side frames.

On the *Campania* and *Lucania* the side frames were of channel-section, as

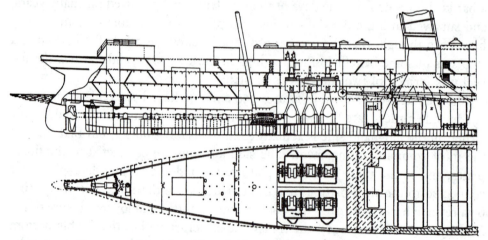

FIGURE 193—Campania *and* Lucania (*elevation and plan*). (Continued opposite.)

indicated in figure 187 d, extending from the boundary of the double bottom to the upper deck and connected to the margin plates by large brackets. Like the floors, the frames were spaced 30 in apart. Web frames, extending to the deck below the upper deck (figure 192), were fitted at intervals throughout the length. The deck-beams were bulb-angles (figure 187 e) supported by three rows of pillars extending upward from the inner bottom.

The methods of working the material were no different from those familiar in earlier days. Frames were heated, bent, and bevelled, and shell plates mainly rolled cold into their combinations of cylindrical and conical forms; in these, and in all other cases, some shell plates more severely curved than usual had to be heated and hammered to shape on moulds and cradles, but economy dictated the arranging of the plating in such a way as to reduce to a minimum the number of 'furnaced' plates. Progress was marked by the ability to deal with larger and heavier materials. It has been noted that on the *Great Eastern* the majority of the shell plates were 10 ft long and 33 in broad; with a thickness of $\frac{3}{4}$-in the weight of each plate was about 825 lb. On the *Campania* and *Lucania* the shell plates, commonly 25 ft long by 72 in broad, weighed about 2 tons, and some of the plates were nearly 96 in broad. Moreover, at the top of the shell plating, and over a considerable portion of the double bottom, hydraulic riveting was employed.

Outline arrangements of the *Campania* and *Lucania* are shown in figure 193, for comparison with the outline arrangements of the *Great Eastern* (plate 24). In the later ships as in the earlier one the engines, boilers, and coal occupy a very considerable portion of the ship along the bottom. There is, however, the

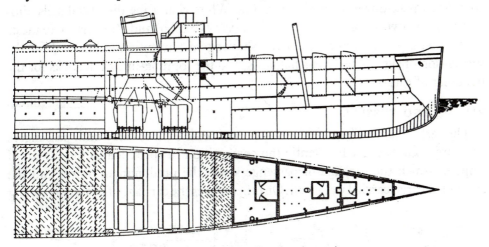

FIGURE 193 (contd). (See also plate 25.)

difference that the later ships carried sufficient coal only for the comparatively short passage across the north Atlantic, whereas the *Great Eastern* was intended to carry coal for a voyage extending around the world (p 362). The volume of the coal bunkers required for the relatively short voyages of the *Campania* and *Lucania* is a rough indication of the cost of speed. These ships crossed the Atlantic at a speed about one-and-a-half times as great as that of the *Great Eastern*, and to do so they required more than four times the power; but, thanks to improved efficiency in engines and boilers, they burned less than double the amount of coal. In his book Scott Russell stated the daily consumption of the *Great Eastern* at 13 knots to be 383 tons; the figure differs from those given on p 365 and is open to suspicion. On the *Campania* and *Lucania* the coal consumption was about 485 tons per day to yield about 30 000 hp; comparison of these figures reveals the progress of marine engineering.

A development not clearly indicated in figure 193 was the disappearance of all provision for the setting of sails. As long as ships were fitted with single screws only, the provision of sails was deemed to be a necessary precaution against a break-down of the machinery. The express Cunard liners immediately preceding the ships illustrated in figure 193, the *Umbria* and *Etruria*, built about 1884, and fitted with single screws, were fully rigged as barques, with top- and top-gallant masts on fore and main, and a top-mast on the mizzen. Even when twin screws were first adopted for north Atlantic service, in the *City of New York* and the *City of Paris*, built about 1888, yards were initially carried on the foremasts, although the fitting of twin engines and screws had minimized the risk of a complete break-down of machinery. The White Star Line discarded sails altogether in the twin-screw *Teutonic* and *Majestic* (*c* 1889) and after that date masts became bare poles, used only for the showing of navigation-lights, and for the suspension of signal-stays, flag-halliards, and the topping-lifts of derricks for the handling of cargo.

VIII. CARGO VESSELS

The early steamers for overseas voyages were all built to carry both passengers and cargo. On the north Atlantic the competition in speed led to the design of ships in which the carriage of passengers was the predominant object and the amount of cargo carried was small. On other routes the carriage of passengers along

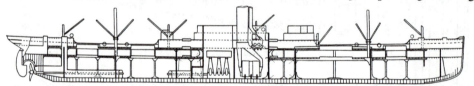

FIGURE 194—*Blue Funnel cargo liner (elevation). This represents the highest standard of British general-cargo ship in the nineteenth century.*

with considerable quantities of cargo persisted for many years. In time, however, there emerged a type of ship built for the carriage of cargo alone. The history of the development of the cargo ship has not been written. It may, however, be permissible to associate the development of the general-cargo carrier in Britain with the passage of the Merchant Shipping Act of 1894; by that Act the ship built to carry passengers was made subject to more stringent regulations than the ship intended solely for the carriage of cargo. The absence of passenger accommodation left space available on the decks for the provision of large hatches for access to the cargo-spaces, and for the installation of efficient cargo-handling gear to ensure rapid loading and discharge.

The highest standard of British general-cargo carrier during the nineteenth century is represented in the outline plan of figure 194, associated with the constructional cross-sections represented in figure 195. The ships portrayed were designed by Henry B. Wortley for the Blue Funnel Line service to the Far East. They embodied the major development in the structural arrangements of ships since the general adoption of the double bottom. In earlier ships the rows of closely spaced pillars in the holds (figures 190 and 192) imposed severe limitations on the stowage of large pieces of cargo. Pillars were occasionally removed for convenience in stowage, and commonly could not be replaced; they were frequently bent by stevedores and their usefulness was impaired. Instead of sup-

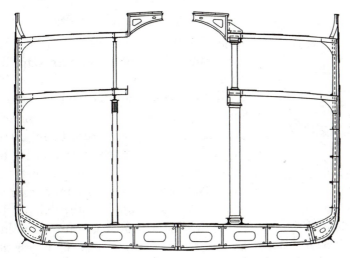

FIGURE 195—*Blue Funnel cargo liner (constructional sections).*

porting the decks by closely spaced pillars Wortley used large girders running fore-and-aft, each girder being supported by one or two substantial columns in the length of each hold. In the ship illustrated in figure 194 there was only one support to the girder on each side in the largest hold; but instead of being merely a round bar a few inches in diameter it was a steel tube with a diameter of 21 in (figure 195). In the other large holds there were two columns, either formed of steel tubes or built up from channel-bars, supporting each girder. Throughout the fore end of the ship it was possible to obtain a very satisfactory structural arrangement by incorporating the girders in the sides of the cargo hatches. The provision of girders and widely spaced columns for the support of decks soon became invariable practice.

A minor development indicated in figure 194 was the arranging of two relatively small cargo compartments immediately before and abaft the machinery space; these compartments were so fitted that water-ballast could be carried in them when necessary, to supplement the water-ballast carried in the double bottom. Another feature of the ships was the provision of derricks and winches at both ends of the four larger hatches in order to ensure the rapid handling of cargo. A characteristic feature of the cargo carrier was the elimination of all wooden covering for the steel decks, except in and over accommodation for officers and crew, a feature which was not viewed with favour by the old-time seaman with a passion for wooden decks bright after treatment by the holystone and scrubber.

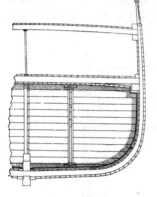

FIGURE 196—*An early oil-tanker (constructional section).*

IX. SPECIALIZED CARGO SHIPS

Long before the development of the ship to carry general cargo alone there had been ships built for the purpose of carrying only special cargoes. The earliest specialist carriers were the colliers, and they were followed by carriers of oil—the alternative fuel of a later day. Persian craft were actually carrying crude oil in bulk across the Caspian Sea so far back as the middle of the eighteenth century, but the carriage of oil in bulk across the north Atlantic from the sources of supply in the United States did not begin until after the middle of the nineteenth. At first, the oil was transported in casks and in cases, and even toward the end of the century most of it was still carried in this way. A serious objection to carriage in casks was that the stowage of a ton of oil required a space of about 80 cu ft, whereas the oil itself occupied only about 45 cu ft. A lesser objection was that the net value of the casks—the initial cost less the scrap price obtained at the port of discharge—was an appreciable fraction of the value of the oil carried in them. Carriage in cases was not so wasteful of space, but the cases—tin-plate boxes protected by wood—were as valuable as the oil they contained, and yet had to be scrapped at the port of discharge. A disadvantage common to both casks and cases was that the time spent in loading and discharging was considerable.

The first carriage of oil in bulk across the north Atlantic seems to have been in a wooden sailing-ship which was in service from 1869 until 1872. In that ship there were fitted 59 iron tanks, shaped to suit the ship. A cross-section of the first oil-tanker of which there are clear records is represented in figure 196. The ship—the *Lindesnaes*, of Norwegian registry—was adapted for the carriage of oil in 1878. Within the frames, up to the lower deck, was a double thickness of planking, with felt between, and below the beams of the lower deck there was planking to form the tops of the tanks. In addition to partitions arranged athwartships to subdivide the space into separate tanks, a division was fitted fore-and-aft

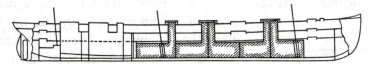

FIGURE 197—*Elevation of the* Vaderland, *the first steamship built to carry oil.*

on the centre-line of the ship; the purpose of the division was to restrict the freedom of the oil to move across the ship as she rolled, and so increase her inclination. Moreover, at about half-breadth of each of the two tanks formed by the fore-and-aft division there were 'wash-boards' to break the force of the oil travelling across the tank owing to the motion of the ship; a fluid cargo in violent motion can cause severe damage. The figure incidentally illustrates features of wooden-ship construction carried forward into the iron ship. It shows the rectangular block keel which was transformed into the bar keel. It shows also a centre keelson; in this case it was formed of rectangular logs and provided a convenient foundation for the division along the centre-line.

The first steamship specially intended for the carriage of oil in bulk was built on the Tyne in 1872. An outline elevation of the ship—the *Vaderland*—and a constructional cross-section are represented in figures 197 and 198. As in the *Lindesnaes*, and for the same purpose, the tanks were divided by a bulkhead running fore-and-aft on the centre-line. The oil was confined mainly to the space below the third deck, but at the end of each compartment there was an expansion-trunk running to the top deck, and surmounted by a hatch for access. The function of the trunks was to hold sufficient oil to ensure that in the event of minor leakage the level of the oil would not fall below the top of the main tank and so permit the oil to surge across a wide space when the ship was tossed about by waves. With the same end in view, the trunks allowed for the contraction of the oil, pumped or run on board fairly warm and then allowed to cool.

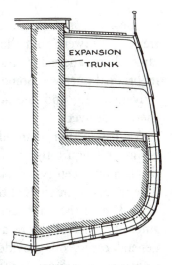

FIGURE 198—*Section of the* Vaderland.

As in all modern tankers, the machinery was arranged at the aft end of the ship.

In the *Vaderland* the boundaries of the main oil-tanks formed a complete inner skin, and for this reason an unusual arrangement of the framing was adopted. The frames were disposed transversely and ran from the usual bar keel to the upper deck around the inside of the shell plating. The reverse frames were fitted on the outsides of the tanks from the centre-line to the third deck. The floor-plates did not extend far outboard from the centre-line, but beyond them the frames and reverse frames were connected at intervals by plates spanning the gap between the shell and the tanks. With this arrangement there was adequate accessibility for construction and maintenance. On the other hand, there was the serious danger of an accumulation of gas from the oil in the space around the tanks. About fifteen years were to elapse before the shell plating was made to serve also as a boundary of the oil tanks.

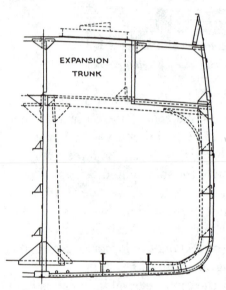

FIGURE 199—*Constructional section of late nineteenth-century oil-tanker.*

The *Vaderland* was never tested in service as a carrier of oil. She was built to trade to Antwerp, but the authorities refused to allow the erection of storage-tanks there, and a favourable contract for other service diverted the ship from its original purpose. Some succeeding ships built to carry oil in bulk were similarly diverted, and the accumulation of experience in a specialist trade was thereby delayed.

A cross-section of an oil-tanker as built at the end of the nineteenth century is shown in figure 199. Here the expansion-trunk extends vertically only over the distance between two decks, but horizontally over the whole length of the tank. The spaces at the sides of the expansion-trunks were used as bunkers for reserves of coal, then the only fuel used on steam-ships. There was no double bottom, since the oil-tanks were available also for the carriage of water-ballast; unlike general cargo, oil provides only one-way traffic. The framing was arranged transversely, subject to the consideration that no part of it should pass through an oil-tight boundary. Accordingly the main bulb-angle frames extended upward only to the lower deck, where they were connected by brackets to the beams. Above the lower deck the frames were angle-bars, connected by brackets to the lower deck and to the beams of the upper deck. The upper deck beams did not pass through either the centre-line bulkhead or the sides of the expansion-trunk; they were fitted in short lengths bridging the distances between the fore-and-aft vertical plating, and connected to it by brackets.

Experience had soon proved that in order to withstand the forces set up by even the restrained surging of a fluid cargo it was necessary to provide a very robust structure. Accordingly, in addition to the support provided by the relatively closely spaced bulkheads forming the tank-divisions, there were in each tank three or four transverse webs (p 360) on the sides and across at the level of the lower deck, associated with webs on the centre-line bulkhead. Substantial fore-and-aft keelsons and stringers were also fitted. There was no difference in the working of the material from that adopted in a dry-cargo ship, but greater care in riveting was demanded. Minor leakage of water will commonly soon come to an end, if only because a small amount of corrosion fills up the gap. An oil-leak will not corrode the metal, and efficient riveting is thus required.

The very great benefit conferred by the carriage of oil in bulk is the rapidity with which it can be run or pumped on board, and then at the port of discharge pumped ashore. Time spent in loading and discharging is unprofitable to the ship-owner.

X. STEERING-GEAR

Steam-engines had been used for the propulsion of ships for about half a century before they were used for operating their rudders. Even in the mammoth *Great Eastern* the rudder was at first operated manually. At that time the hand-steering gear commonly consisted of a fore-and-aft drum carrying several turns of wire rope or chain, with one end of the wire or chain led over to a lead-block on the port side of the ship and back to the tiller, while the other end was led over to the starboard side and back to the tiller. Rotation of the drum by means of the steering-wheels heaved in the wire or chain on one side while paying it out on the other, so swinging over the tiller and the rudder. A steam-engine was first used to rotate the drum about 1860, on an American ship. The engine was mounted with its shaft parallel to the axis of the drum, the axle of the drum and the engine-shaft being linked by gears. Slide-valves admitted steam to the cylinders in the usual way, so that the drum could be rotated in either direction, but the excentrics controlling them were mounted on a separate shaft, driven from the steering-wheel through a wheel and pinion corresponding to the pinion and wheel between the engine-shaft and the axle of the drum. This steering-gear seems to have been based on the presumption that the operation of the engine would conform exactly to the movement of the steering-wheel; there seems to have been no recognition of the intense variation of force on the rudder of a ship in a seaway. It was soon removed from the ship on which it had been fitted, presumably because of unsatisfactory operation.

The first satisfactory steam steering-gear was fitted on the *Great Eastern* in 1867. It was designed by J. Macfarlane Gray, subsequently chief engineer to the Board of Trade. As in the earlier steam-gear, the engine was used to drive a drum through a toothed pinion and wheel. The vital innovation was the method of controlling the engine, which since then has persisted almost without change.

The essential features of the Macfarlane Gray control-gear—the hunting gear as it is commonly called—are illustrated in figure 200. The bell-crank lever controls the movement of a valve arranged between the slide-valves controlling the admission of steam to the cylinders. When the valve is in the central position there is no flow of steam toward the slide-valves, but when it is displaced it admits steam to one side or the other of the slide-valve chests according to the direction of displacement, so acting both as a reversing valve and as a stop-valve. The operation of the bell-crank lever is governed by the collar on the vertical screwed shaft working in a nut combined with a bevel wheel. The screwed shaft is turned by a toothed wheel engaging with a similar wheel on the control-shaft turned by the steering-wheel. If the control-shaft is turned while the nut and bevel wheel are fixed the screwed shaft must rise or fall, according to the direction of rotation, thus raising or lowering the collar, operating the bell-crank lever, and displacing the central valve; the toothed wheel on the control-shaft is made sufficiently deep to allow vertical movement of the screwed shaft without the teeth becoming disengaged. If, on the other hand, the bevel wheel and nut rotate at the same speed and in the same direction as the screwed shaft, the collar will neither rise nor fall and the bell-crank lever will not be affected.

The bevel wheel is actually driven from the drum-shaft (as in the *Great Eastern*) or from the engine-shaft, and the operating conditions are a combination of those which have been outlined. Rotation of the control-shaft by means of the steering-wheel tends to raise or lower the collar, thus opening the central stop-valve and also determining the direction of rotation of the engine. As the engine begins to turn—slowly at first—when the stop-valve has been sufficiently opened, it causes the bevel wheel and nut to rotate in the same direction as the screwed shaft. Consequently the vertical movement of the screwed shaft, and so of the collar, is first slowed down, and then stopped when the engine has gained sufficient speed. Since, however, the engine continues to turn after the rotation of the control-shaft has been stopped, the screwed shaft and collar are set into vertical motion again but in the reverse direction, and the motion continues until the central control-valve is closed and the engine stopped. Direction

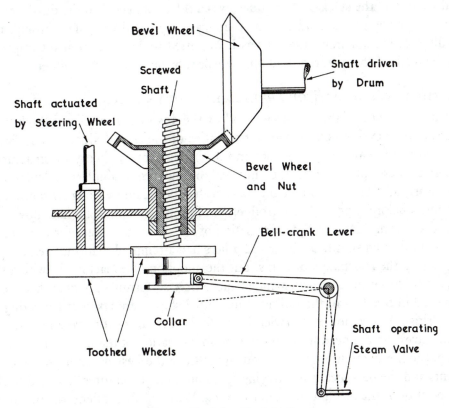

FIGURE 200—*Macfarlane Gray's hunting gear.*

and duration of the motion of the steering-engine are thus made to conform completely to the direction and duration of the motion of the steering-wheel.

The type of steering-gear fitted on the *Great Eastern* persisted for many years; the only material difference was that instead of the steering-engine being near the rudder, as in the first installation, it was moved to the engine-room, in order to permit more effective supervision by the engineers. Control of the rudder was effected by rods and chains working over rollers: rods for the straight leads and chains where there were changes of direction. At the stern the chains were connected to a quadrant on the stock of the rudder, with heavy helical springs fitted in the chains to cushion the shocks from heavy seas. Such gear was inefficient and expensive to maintain. It was not until the end of the century that an alternative arrangement of the gear, in a form commonly used later, became available. In that form a worm on the shaft of the engine engaged a toothed quadrant fitted on, but not secured to, the stock of the rudder. Immediately above the quadrant, and secured to the stock of the rudder, was a tiller connected to the quadrant by a helical spring on each side. Thus the engine operated the tiller through the medium of the quadrant, the springs being fitted to cushion the loads imposed on the teeth of the quadrant and on the worm by shocks on the rudder.

XI. THE DEVELOPMENT OF APPLIED HYDRODYNAMICS

Early volumes of the 'Transactions' of the Institution of Naval Architects indicate the development of the technicalities of the ship-designer, in so far as these are problems in hydrostatics and in the elementary theory of structures. There are descriptions of the then unusual, but now commonplace, calculations. For nearly all these matters the foundations had been laid by Bouguer more than a century before (p 353). The introduction of propulsion by steam had, however, raised a new problem—the determination of the power necessary for the attainment of a desired speed. Bouguer and others had attempted to formulate the laws expressing the resistances of ships, but the adoption of a machine in which the power could be measured demanded more precise formulation than had been achieved in the days of the sailing-ship. Initial steps were taken at a meeting of the British Association at Norwich in 1868. As a result of the presentation of a paper stressing the need for experimental investigation of the problems of ship-propulsion, a committee was formed to consider the best direction for experiments and the best means of carrying them out. The committee reported to the Association at the meeting at Exeter in 1869. With one dissentient, the members agreed that an approach should be made to the Admiralty to allow one or more of Her Majesty's ships to be towed in sheltered waters in such conditions that the associated resistances and speeds could be accurately measured. The dissentient was William Froude (1810–79), a civil engineer by profession and a friend of Brunel, who had acquired a reputation amongst naval architects by the presentation of a paper on the rolling of ships at the second of the annual meetings of the Institution of Naval Architects.

The ground for Froude's dissent lay in his belief that experiments with models, offering opportunity for economical investigation of a wide range of shapes and proportions, were much more likely to lead to assured knowledge than a limited range of experiments on ships. Experiments with models had been carried out in past years. There is a reference to some crude experiments of this kind in a book on ship-building published in England in 1765, and there may have been experiments in France at about the same time. Towards the close of the eighteenth century more precise experiments were carried out by Chapman—a Swede whose parents were English by birth. In these early experiments with models there was, however, a serious error in principle: there was no recognition of the need to relate the speeds of model and ship in a scale associated with their dimensions. It was not until about the middle of the nineteenth century that the eminent French mathematician, Joseph Bertrand (1822–1900), developed a proposition that had long before been enunciated by Sir Isaac Newton, and so laid down, once and for all, the general principles relating to the speeds and dimensions of models used for experimental purposes. In 1852 a French naval architect—Frédéric Reech (1805–74)—applied the general principle of Bertrand to the particular case of a ship-model, but he did not make any experiments because

FIGURE 201—*Froude's sketch of wave-pattern at fore end of a model.*

he appreciated the existence of frictional force that did not follow the principle developed by Bertrand.

Froude also appreciated the existence of a frictional force, but he contended that it was completely separable from the other forces, and also amenable to simple calculation. On that basis he proposed to measure the total force, deduct the calculated frictional force, and then apply the principle of Bertrand to the remainder—the 'residuary' resistance. The Admiralty refused to assist the committee of the British Association in their desire for experiments with ships. Instead, they provided Froude with funds for experiments with models. The first of the modern experimental tanks took the form of a long trench excavated in a field alongside Froude's house near Torquay. The trench was spanned by a truck running on rails and towed by a wire from steam-driven winding-gear. The model was attached to the truck through the medium of a calibrated helical spring, so permitting the towing force to be measured. Provision was made for determining the speed of the truck.

Figure 201 is a reproduction of a sketch made by Froude during one of his experiments. It illustrates the wave-pattern generated at the fore end of a model; the creation of waves had suggested to Froude that the resistance other than that due to friction might be termed the 'wave-making' resistance. At a later date Sir William Thomson, later Lord Kelvin (1824–1907), plotted the equations expressing the disturbance on the surface of water caused by a travelling 'point of pressure'; the plotting is illustrated in figure 202, with the lines representing crests of waves. The point of pressure generates an ever extending train of waves confined within two straight lines radiating from the point. There is an obvious resemblance between figures 201 and 202; indeed, careful observation from the fore end of a ship in favourable conditions permits the salient features of figure 202 to be traced. Accordingly it seemed reasonable to treat the presence of waves as the visible manifestation of the variations of pressure which are

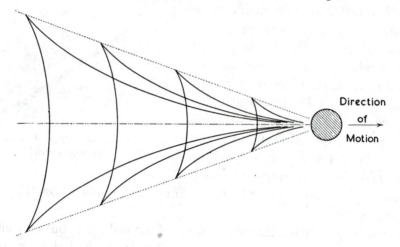

Direction
of
Motion

FIGURE 202 —*Kelvin's pattern of wave-train generated by a travelling 'pressure point'.*

associated with the passage of a ship through water; hydrodynamical considerations indicate the existence of a peak of pressure at the fore end, and the existence also in most, but not all, cases of a lesser peak at the aft end.

Froude was satisfied that the determination of the frictional force or resistance, whether for a model or a ship, involved no more than the determination of the frictional resistance of a long, thin plank in end-wise motion. Accordingly, the first use of his experimental tank was for the measurement of the resistances of a series of thin planks towed at various speeds. Thence followed the formulation of a law of frictional resistance. On the basis of that law the frictional resistance of a model could be evaluated for a series of speeds, and from this, by deduction from the measured total resistances at these speeds, followed the evaluation of the 'residuary', or wave-making, resistances. It was to these residuary resistances that the principle developed by Bertrand and extended by Reech was applied: provided that the speeds of ship and model are in the same ratio as the square roots of the linear dimensions the forces on ship and model are in the ratio of the cubes of the dimensions. In other words, if the length of the ship is 16 times the length of the model, and the speed of the ship is $4(= \sqrt{16})$ times the speed of the model, the residuary resistance of the ship is 16^3 times the residuary resistance of the model.

In spite of the refusal by the Admiralty to provide a ship, or ships, to meet the desire of the committee of the British Association, they had to provide

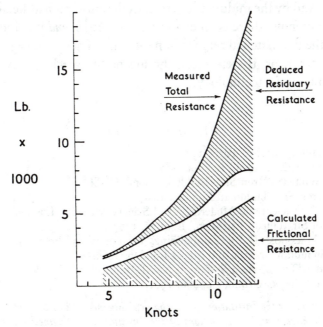

FIGURE 203—*Experimental check of Froude's method made by towing H.M.S.* Greyhound.

two ships for an experimental purpose, one as a tug and the other as the tow; but the purpose was the investigation of the reliability of the Froude method. The tow was H.M.S. *Greyhound*, and the total resistances at a series of speeds were measured by a recording dynamometer on the tow-rope. The results from one set of experiments are shown in figure 203. The top curve expresses the measured relation between resistance and speed. The upper hatched region shows the variation of the residuary resistance as derived from the evaluation of the residuary resistance of the model. The lower hatched region shows the variation of the frictional resistance as determined from the experiments on thin planks.

Froude did not present the results of the *Greyhound* experiments in the form here adopted, and the experiments were taken to afford justification of the method of determining the resistance of a ship from experiments with a model. His original experimental tank has been followed by many others, in countries over the whole globe, and the amount of money furnished to Froude for the solution of a problem has been spent many times over without sight of the exact solution. A tank under construction in 1957 was estimated to cost 1000 times the total amount allowed to Froude to cover the provision of his tank and the expense of the work in it. And by the middle of the twentieth century it had been realized that somewhere, somehow, there is an error; for the *Greyhound* it is indicated by the gap between the two hatched regions in figure 203. There is no agreement on the source of the error, or, therefore, on the means by which it may be corrected. There is no finality in technology.

BIBLIOGRAPHY

BOUGUER, P. 'Traité du navire.' Paris. 1746.
BRUNEL, I. 'Life of I. K. Brunel.' London. 1870.
FAIRBAIRN, SIR WILLIAM. 'Iron Ship Building.' London. 1865.
GRANTHAM, J. 'Iron Ship-building.' London. 1858.
HOLMES, G. C. V. 'Ancient and Modern Ships.' Science Museum, London. 1906.
POLE, W. 'Life of Sir William Fairbairn.' London. 1877.
RANKINE, W. J. MACQUORN (Ed.). 'Shipbuilding, Theoretical and Practical.' London. 1866.
REED, E. J. 'Shipbuilding in Iron and Steel.' London. 1869.
RUSSELL, J. SCOTT. 'The Modern System of Naval Architecture.' London. 1865.
WALTON, T. 'Steel Ships.' Griffin, London. 1901.

See also *Transactions of the Institution of Mechanical Engineers, Transactions of the Institution of Naval Architects,* and *Transactions of the Institution of Engineers and Shipbuilders in Scotland.*

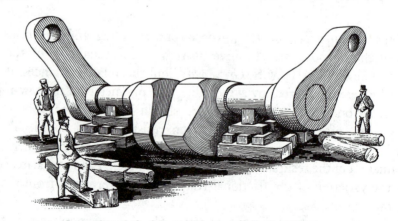

Intermediate shaft of the paddle-engines of the Great Eastern.

17

AERONAUTICS

PETER W. BROOKS

I. THE WRIGHT BROTHERS

MAN'S conquest of the air was finally confirmed on 17 December 1903 at Kitty Hawk, North Carolina, on the east coast of the United States, when a young bicycle-manufacturer, Orville Wright (1871–1948), made the first powered, sustained, and controlled flight in history (plate 23 B). Orville and his brother Wilbur (1867–1912) had built their 'Flyer'—a simple tailless pusher biplane powered by a 12 hp petrol-engine of their own design and manufacture—at their home at Dayton, Ohio, during the preceding summer (cf figure 204). The first flight was made over level sand and lasted only 12 seconds, covering a distance of 40 yds at a height of a few feet and an air speed of about 30 mph, but the aeroplane flew straight and level under the complete control of its pilot and landed undamaged at a point as high as that from which it took off. All the conditions of a successful flight were thus fulfilled. This event is now accepted by responsible opinion throughout the world as the significant landmark identifying the beginning of the era of powered heavier-than-air flight, which has become one of the most important technological developments of the twentieth century.

Orville Wright's 12-second flight in 1903 was followed on the same day by three longer flights also more or less straight and close to the ground, two by his brother and another by himself. These confirmed the initial success. The longest flight lasted 59 seconds and covered a distance of about 280 yds. Shortly afterwards, the 'Flyer' was blown over and damaged by the wind, and the Wrights were obliged to put an end to their flying for that year. In 1904 they resumed their experiments at Simms Station, near Dayton, with an improved but similar aeroplane. This flying took place over a level field and the aeroplane took off, as at Kitty Hawk, from a length of level mono-rail laid on the ground. At Simms Station, however, unlike the experiments at Kitty Hawk, where the take-offs were unassisted, the aeroplane was launched by a catapult device which consisted of a rope-and-pulley system to apply the energy provided by a falling weight. The importance of the flights in 1904, which amounted to a total flying time of about 45 minutes, lies not only in their greater duration—two lasted for about five minutes—but also in the fact that the brothers thereby showed that they had solved the problems of control in other than straight and level flight, and that they could manœuvre their aircraft at will. This had not been established in the previous year.

A third 'Flyer', similar to the first two, was built in 1905 and provided final proof of success. With it many circular flights were made, one covering a distance of $24\frac{1}{5}$ miles in 38 min 3 sec. The practical aeroplane had arrived. The Wrights then stopped flying and concentrated their energies on designing and building a number of improved aircraft and engines. At the same time they negotiated

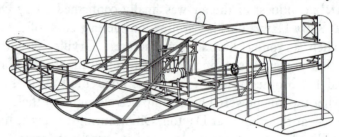

FIGURE 204—*The 1908 Wright biplane. The original 'Flyer' of 1903 was closely similar (plate 23 B). Control was by the double front elevators (on the left), wing-warping, and the double rudder at the rear.*

with various governments for financial support with which to continue their work. Incredibly, the American press entirely ignored their success, apparently because of the general scepticism at that time about the practicability of human flight. For this reason, few people knew or believed that human flight had been achieved, and the Wrights had the greatest difficulty in exploiting their invention. Two and a half years passed before the American government, early in 1908, at last signed a contract for one of their aeroplanes. At the same time a company to build from the Wrights' designs was formed in France. They then resumed their flying, first in America in May 1908 and then in Europe—at the Hunaudières race-course near Le Mans—on 8 August of the same year.

Meanwhile, successful powered, sustained, and controlled flight had been achieved independently in Europe. At Bagatelle, near Paris, a Brazilian, Alberto Santos-Dumont (1873–1932), made his first heavier-than-air flight on 23 October 1906. He achieved a straight flight of 65 yds close to the ground in the Santos-Dumont 14 *bis*, a tail-first pusher biplane with a 50 hp Antoinette petrol-engine (figure 205). Three further flights were made on 12 November, the longest of 240 yds. The Brazilian's aeroplane was, however, not nearly such a practical flying-machine as that of the Wrights, and it was left to other European designers —the Voisin brothers, Louis Blériot, Robert Esnault-Pelterie, and Alfred de Pischof—to follow up this initial achievement with fresh lines of development, including that of the monoplane, which led to successful first flights in 1907 by several designs of great promise. By 1908, when the Wrights first demonstrated in Europe the then unchallenged—but, as events were to show, short-lived—superiority of their biplane, a number of European pioneers were flying successfully, and the vital first phase of rapid development of the aeroplane, which was to be centred in Europe, and particularly in France, was under way. It continued at a high tempo until the outbreak of war in 1914 brought a new objective and emphasis to further progress.

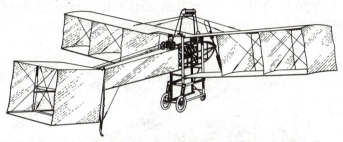

FIGURE 205—*The Santos-Dumont 14 bis, which achieved the first powered flight in Europe in 1906.*

II. THE ORIGINS OF PRACTICAL AERONAUTICS: THE FIRST BALLOON ASCENTS

During the years between 1850 and 1900 the final steps were taken that led to the emergence early in the present century of the practical heavier-than-air flying-machine as the solution to man's age-long aspiration to fly. Although the most important progress in the evolution of this branch of technology occurred during the nineteenth century, endeavours to fly can be traced back some hundreds of years. Most of the records of early thought and experiment are, however, either legendary or historically poorly documented and need not be considered in detail.

The best-known legend of flight is that which concerns the myth of Daedalus and his son, Icarus, who attempted to escape from imprisonment on the island of Crete by flying with artificial wings made from feathers secured to their arms with wax. Against his father's advice, Icarus flew too close to the Sun, which melted the wax and caused him to fall to his death in the sea. Another story concerns the legendary King Bladud of Britain, who is said to have lost his life in 852 B.C. while trying to fly. A third tells of Archytas of Tarentum (fourth century B.C.), who was reputed to have made a wooden pigeon which flew.

These stories may have had some basis in fact, but their significance lies rather in the indication they afford of man's early interest in the problem of flying. Other names which the history of flight has recorded include the 'Saracen of Constantinople' and Oliver of Malmesbury (both in the eleventh century A.D.), G. B. Danti (1503), J. Damian (1507), Besnier (1678), the Marquis de Bacqueville (1742), and A. L. Berblinger (1811). All these pioneers are remembered because, no doubt like many others who have been forgotten, they leapt from high places after providing themselves with artificial wings in the hope of achieving flapping or, possibly, gliding flight. Some survived their experiments; others did not. Significantly, however, not one of them appears to have achieved sufficient success to have inspired immediate emulation.

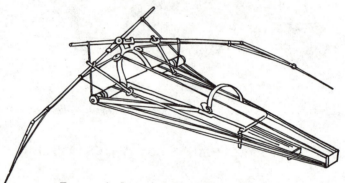

FIGURE 206—*Leonardo da Vinci's ornithopter project.*

Early thinkers, as distinct from experimenters, in the field of human flight included Roger Bacon and Albert the Great in the thirteenth century, Albert of Saxony in the next, Caspar Schott, and—by far the most important—Leonardo da Vinci, that unique fifteenth-century genius who had such a widespread impact on both art and science. Leonardo made proposals for parachutes, helicopters, and ornithopters (figure 206), and devoted much time to a study of the flight of birds. His ideas would undoubtedly have had a greater influence on subsequent events if publication of his work had not been delayed for nearly 300 years.

The next name in the prehistory of aeronautics is that of Robert Hooke (1635–1703), who apparently made several experiments with flying-machines in the second half of the seventeenth century. Details have unfortunately been lost. The Jesuit Francesco de Lana-Terzi's design for a flying ship (1670) was the first proposal to use the lighter-than-air principle based on the law of Archimedes (250 B.C.). de Lana's idea was that his ship should derive its lift from four evacuated spheres. The scheme was quite unpractical, but is important because it prepared the way for the invention of the balloon, which appears to have been the work of another Jesuit, Bartholomeu Lourenço de Gusmão, in Lisbon early in the eighteenth century. de Gusmão also built a full-sized, but unsuccessful, flapping-wing flying-machine and a model glider.

de Gusmão's balloon is believed to have been a small hot-air model which he successfully demonstrated before the king of Portugal on 8 August 1709. This important event does not appear, however, to have inspired in any way the invention by the French brothers Joseph and Étienne Montgolfier of Annonay, near Lyons, of the man-carrying hot-air balloon seventy-three years later. The Montgolfiers made their first experiment with a model balloon on 15 November 1782.

An important landmark in the emergence of practical aeronautics occurred in the following year. The first free flight by man was achieved by two Frenchmen, J. F. Pilâtre de Rozier and the Marquis d'Arlandes on 21 November 1783. They ascended from the garden of the Château de la Muette in the Bois de Boulogne, Paris, in a 'Montgolfière' hot-air balloon of 78 000 cu ft capacity and landed near

FIGURE 207—'*Montgolfière*' *hot-air balloon of the type used for the first ascents in 1783.*

the Gobelins at Le Petit-Gentilly 26 minutes later, after covering a distance of $7\frac{1}{2}$ miles and reaching a height of about 3000 ft (figure 207). The first man to fly, de Rozier, was also the first to be killed in an air accident—on 15 June 1785.

The invention of the hot-air 'Montgolfière' was closely followed by that of the much more practical hydrogen balloon, which has remained unchanged in its essentials until the present day. The famous physicist J. A. C. Charles (1746–1823), shortly after the invention of the hot-air balloon, suggested—following an earlier proposal by Joseph Black (1728–99)—that hydrogen (which had been first isolated and described by Henry Cavendish in 1766) would be a more efficient lifting-agent than hot air. The hydrogen balloon (figure 208)—or 'Charlière' as it was originally called—made its first free man-carrying flight ten days after the historic ascent of de Rozier and d'Arlandes. Charles, with the elder of the Robert brothers who constructed the balloon, made an ascent from the Tuileries Gardens in Paris on 1 December 1783 (vol IV, p 255). After a flight lasting two hours, during which 27 miles were covered, the balloon landed at Nesle. Robert then alighted from the basket and Charles ascended again alone for a further flight of half an hour, during which he reached a height of 9000 ft. The great ballooning era had begun. It was to last for 120 years,

FIGURE 208—'*Charlière*' *hydrogen balloon, 1783.*

during which many attempts were made—with little success—to improve the free balloon as a practical means of transport.

The first balloon ascents marked the beginning of practical human flight. They were, however, separated from the twentieth century, when man's discovery of means of navigating the air in heavier-than-air craft at last made possible large-scale use of the new medium for practical purposes, by a period during which experiment and progress were spasmodic and at times seemed almost completely arrested. The very method by which the much-sought objective of true aerial navigation was to be achieved remained for a long time in doubt. There was no direct line of development possible from the first balloon ascents of 1783 to the Wright brothers' final success with a heavier-than-air machine in 1903. The affinity was only in men's minds in the single objective before them and in the growing interest in, and knowledge of, the new element. The techniques and problems of ballooning were totally unlike those of heavier-than-air flight.

III. KITE-BALLOONS, KITES, AND PARACHUTES

In considering the development of aeronautics following the discovery of the free balloon it is convenient to consider practical flying-machines as of two basic types: lighter-than-air and heavier-than-air. These can be further subdivided as follows:

Lighter-than-air	Heavier-than-air
(1) Free balloons	(3) Ornithopters
(2) Airships.	(4) Helicopters
	(5) Gliders
	(6) Aeroplanes
	(7) Ballistic rockets.

In addition to the above categories of flying-machine, there are three aeronautical devices with limited and specialized applications. These are (a) kite-balloons, (b) kites, and (c) parachutes.

(a) *Kite-balloons* made their appearance as a direct military development of the free balloon. The ancestor of the kite-balloon was the normal spherical balloon moored to the ground by a cable. The first human flights were in fact made in tethered hot-air balloons. Pilâtre de Rozier's first ascent on 15 October 1783, when he rose to a height of 84 ft and stayed up for $4\frac{1}{2}$ minutes, was of this type.

The first military use of moored balloons was at Maubeuge (Nord) on 2 June 1794, when a specially formed company of the French army sent up a spherical hydrogen balloon to observe the enemy's positions. Balloons were also used in this way at the battle of Fleurus (1794) and at the siege of Mainz (1795). In the American Civil War they were again used, notably at the battle of Fair Oaks (1862). The British army used them in several campaigns during the last two decades of the nineteenth century, including the Boer War. Notably, balloons played a part during the defence of Ladysmith in 1899.

The kite-balloon proper is an elongated gas-filled balloon, usually fitted with tail-fins, designed to be more stable when moored in a wind than a spherical balloon. This type owes its origin to the suggestions of two Frenchmen, Abel Transon (1844) and Alphonse Pénaud (1874). The first practical kite-balloon was the German *Drachen*, which appeared in 1896 (figure 209). This was followed by the French *Saucisse Caquot* (1916), which set the fashion for all subsequent balloons of this type. Kite-balloons were extensively used for observation purposes during the first world war, and were employed in balloon-barrages as a defence against low-flying aircraft. The latter application continued during the second world war, when kite-balloons were also found useful for training parachute troops—a purpose for which they are still used on a limited scale—as well as for experimental work.

(b) *Kites* trace their origins to remote antiquity. The Chinese kite, which may date from about 1000 B.C., was apparently the first practical aircraft. Kites in their simplest form consist of single monoplane lifting-surfaces tethered to the ground. They were probably first flown for amusement, as they still are, but there is a possibility that the Chinese may have built and flown large kites for man-lifting purposes. If so, these were the first tethered human flights, anteceding by many hundreds of years de Rozier's first tethered-balloon ascents in

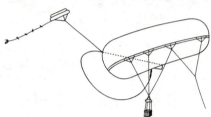

1783. The date of the first appearance of kites in Europe is obscure. The Romans may have known about them; they were certainly being flown in Europe from the fifteenth century.

The more efficient box-kite was not invented until 1893 (by L. Hargrave in

FIGURE 209—*German* Drachen *kite-balloon of 1896.*

Australia). This has tandem biplane lifting-surfaces (figure 210). Man-lifting kites were built in Europe, notably by G. Pocock (1827), E. J. Cordner (1859), J. Simmons (1876), B. F. S. Baden-Powell (1894), and S. F. Cody (1904).

(c) *Parachutes*, like kites, seem to have been known to the ancient Chinese, but they were first suggested in Europe by Leonardo da Vinci about 1500. Early illustrations of parachutes appeared in three books, *Machinae novae* by F. Veranzio (c 1595), *Ariane* by des Maretz (1639), and *La Découverte australe par un homme-volant* by Restif de la Bretonne (1781).

The first practical experiments with parachutes may have been made by the Chinese, but the earliest trials of this device in Europe appear to have taken place in the eighteenth century, shortly before the invention of the balloon. Early experimenters included François Blanchard (1777), Joseph Montgolfier (1779), and S. Lenormand (1783). The last of these three Frenchmen probably made the first human parachute descents in Europe, initially from the top of a tree and then from the tower of Montpellier observatory in December 1783.

Widespread practical demonstration of the parachute followed the appearance of the balloon. Blanchard released a small one, carrying a weight, from his balloon while ascending from Vauxhall, London, on 3 June 1785. Later he dropped animals. The first human descent from a balloon was made by A. J.

Garnerin over Paris on 22 October 1797 (plate 23 A). Garnerin later made the first human descent over England in 1802. Parachuting from balloons became a popular form of public spectacle in the nineteenth century, and many descents were made all over the world.

The first parachute-jump from an aeroplane was made by A. Berry on 2 March 1912. The first jump from an airship was by E. M. Maitland on 18 October 1913. During the first world war the parachute came to be widely used by both sides as a means of escape from observation balloons and, towards the end of the war, the Germans also used it for this purpose from aeroplanes. These parachutes, like those in the earlier experiments, were either hung unfolded from the balloon or were folded and packed in containers attached to the aircraft. In the latter case, the user pulled the parachute out of its container by his fall after jumping. In the early 1920s the first free-fall packed parachutes of the modern type, which are worn on the body and operated by the user, were introduced. Since the first world war this

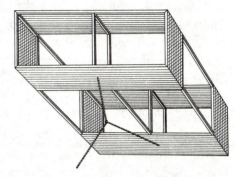

FIGURE 210—*Hargrave's box-kite of 1893. This was the ancestor of the biplanes which pioneered flight in both America and Europe.*

type of parachute has come into universal use as an escaping device for military and experimental flying. In more recent years, the packed parachute operated by a static line attached to the aircraft has been adopted for parachute troops and for the dropping of stores.

IV. FREE BALLOONING IN THE NINETEENTH CENTURY

From the time of their invention at the end of the eighteenth century until the first practical experiments with airships and gliders during the last two decades of the nineteenth, balloons were the only method by which man could explore the air. Moreover, until airships and aeroplanes began to fly in numbers in the first and second decades of the present century, the balloon remained by far the most widely used type of aircraft. For this reason, although there was almost no progress in improving the design of balloons or in making them into more serviceable vehicles, they played a vital part in man's conquest of the air by enabling him to study the many new problems associated with travel through the atmosphere.

The balloonist learnt to keep track of his path while travelling great distances across country, to fly at night and through clouds, to avoid obstructions on the earth's surface, and to choose the best types of landing-place. He made the first crossings or attempted crossings of several seas and oceans, and explored from the air various inaccessible parts of the world. Famous flights that should be mentioned include the first crossing of the Channel by F. Blanchard and J. Jeffries on 7 January 1785; the attempted crossing of the Adriatic by Count F. Zambeccari and two companions on 7 October 1804; the first crossing of the Alps by F. Arban on 2–3 September 1849; attempted crossings of the Atlantic in 1859, 1861, and 1873; and the tragic air voyage of exploration by S. A. Andrée and two companions in the Arctic on 11–14 July 1897. Balloons were also used to investigate the characteristics of the atmosphere and for other meteorological purposes, to reach the upper atmosphere (J. Glaisher and H. Coxwell's ascent to between 20 000 and 25 000 feet on 5 September 1862 was particularly notable), for aerial photography (the first air photograph was taken over Paris by F. Tournachon in 1858), and for the first air-transport service for passengers and mail (during the siege of Paris, 1870–1).

Although the balloon was used for these and other serious purposes during this period, it remained primarily a showman's device. By far its most wide-spread use was at fairs and fêtes as a popular spectacle. Balloon ascents at night with fireworks, acrobatic ascents, ascents with ballerinas, 'equestrian ascents', and parachute drops were the professional balloonist's regular stock-in-trade. The professional aeronaut became the experienced airman of the day. Men and women like Blanchard and his wife, the Godards, Charles Green (who first used coal-gas instead of hydrogen to fill a balloon), Henry Coxwell, John Wise, and the Spencers made thousands of ascents and accumulated many hundreds of hours of practical experience in the air. When, at the turn of the century, ballooning became a popular and fashionable sport for the wealthy, the new amateur enthusiasts learnt a skill handed down and extended over more than a hundred years largely by these professional practitioners. Many of these same enthusiasts later took to the aeroplane when it was sufficiently developed as a practical machine for it to become the medium of a new sport. In this way, the experience of the air accumulated with the balloon was handed on to the era of the aeroplane.

V. THE EPOCH OF THE AIRSHIP

While the balloon remained the only useful aircraft for a hundred years after its invention, its limitations as a means of transport were so obvious that the age was rich in attempts to develop from it a lighter-than-air flying-machine which would be able to navigate in any direction under the control of its pilot and independently of the wind.

The first attempts to navigate balloons were made soon after their invention. Paddles, oars, and propellers were tried by many experimenters who ascended in spherical balloons. These futile attempts were paralleled by more promising assaults on the problem by a number of pioneers who realized that an elongated

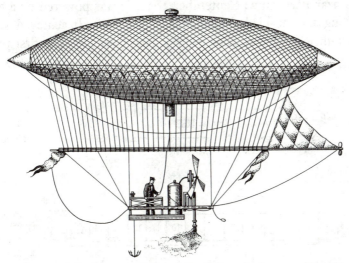

FIGURE 211—*Giffard's steam-propelled airship of 1852: the first successful airship.*

shape was essential for any workable dirigible balloon. Charles and the Roberts (p 396) made the first serious attempt on 15 July 1784, when they unsuccessfully tested an elongated hydrogen balloon provided with an air-filled ballonet contained within the main envelope—an important innovation which was later to be a feature of all pressure-airships.[1] The ballonet's function was to maintain the main envelope's shape despite variations in gas-pressure and atmospheric pressure. A second similar balloon was built by the Roberts and tested, again unsuccessfully, later in the same year.

The main problem to be solved was, however, that of providing a sufficiently light and powerful means of propulsion. Man-power was clearly inadequate, as was to be proved repeatedly during the following seventy years.[2] The first

[1] In a pressure-airship the shape is maintained by the pressure of the contained gas.
[2] Notable designs during this period were by J. B. M. Meusnier (1785), S. J. Pauly (1789), Baron Scott (1789), Lippich (1812), Sir George Cayley (1816), S. J. Pauly and D. Egg (1816), E. C. Gênet (1825), Count Lennox (1834), P. Ferrand (1835), J. S. Partridge (1843), R. Porter (1845), P. Jullien (1850, 1852), H. Bell (1850), J. Luntley (1851), P. Meller (1851), J. Nye (1852), H. Vanaisse (1863), E. Delamarne and G. Yon (1865), R. Boyman (1866), F. Marriott (1869), S. C. H. L. Dupuy de Lôme (1872), P. Haenlein (1872), Baumgarten and Wölfert (1880), and A. and G. Tissandier (1883).

successful model airship appears to have been built by T. Monck Mason and flown, at a speed of 6 mph, at the Royal Adelaide Gallery in London in 1843. Another successful model, steam-driven, was designed by Le Berrier, and was flown in Paris on 9 June 1844.

The first man-carrying airship to fly successfully—although at only about 5 mph—was that designed by H. Giffard and first flown by him for a distance of 17 miles near Paris on 24 September 1852. It was powered by a 3 hp steam-engine driving a three-bladed propeller (figure 211). It achieved steerage-way but lacked sufficient performance to be a useful vehicle. The first practical air-

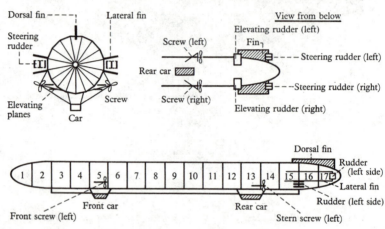

FIGURE 212—*The earliest practical form of Zeppelin rigid airship, 1900.*

ship was *La France*, designed and built by C. Renard and A. C. Krebs; it was driven by a 9 hp electric motor fed from especially light batteries. A circular flight of about 5 miles at a speed of 14 mph was achieved at Chalais-Meudon, near Paris, on 9 August 1884.

Airships appeared in numbers in various countries from about 1900. Santos-Dumont (p 392) built and flew a series of small pressure-airships in Paris between 1898 and 1906. Larger airships of the same type also appeared, notably in France where the *Lebaudy* made the first pre-planned and controlled cross-country flight in history, from Moisant to Paris (38½ miles) on 12 November 1903. Pressure-airships were greatly improved during the next fifteen years and were widely used by the Allies for coastal patrol during the first world war.

The Germans were leaders with the rigid airship, which differed from the pressure type in having a cylindrical or streamlined hull enclosing a number of separate gas-bags and supporting the engine-nacelles and passenger accommodation. The first rigid airship was built by D. Schwarz and was flown, unsuccessfully, on 3 November 1897. Rigid airships were usually much larger than those of the pressure type and were developed, in particular, by Count F. von Zeppelin (1838–1917), who launched his first airship from Lake Constance on 2 July 1900 (figure 212). Zeppelins were used with some success to run passenger services in Germany between 1910 and 1914. During the first world war they were widely employed for military purposes. A few Zeppelins and foreign airships of similar design continued to be used for military purposes and civil transport in later years, but the type had become extinct by 1940. The small pressure-airship has been used on only a limited scale since 1918, but the type does survive to this day in small numbers.

VI. ORNITHOPTERS

Flapping-wing flying-machines were the earliest type to be suggested by the pioneers of heavier-than-air flight. Imitation of birds seemed so clearly the easiest way to achieve artificial flight. Many generations of experimenters were required to establish that this is, in fact, the most difficult way to approach the problem. Successful man-carrying ornithopter flight has yet to be achieved, but a large number of model aircraft of this type have been flown.[1]

High-speed photography, modern knowledge of aerodynamics, and a clearer concept of the structure and behaviour of the atmosphere have made possible a better understanding of bird-flight in recent years (plate 44 A). It is now apparent that the wings of the majority of birds provide lift very largely, even during flapping flight, as if they were fixed surfaces; propulsion is effected by the flapping action of the outer parts of the wings. True flapping flight is, however, used by certain birds and insects while hovering, or flying at low speeds, but this type of flight is far less common. The aerodynamics are complex and are still not fully understood.

While it would appear possible that a successful man-carrying ornithopter may eventually be built, it is unlikely that this class of flying-machine will ever challenge other types as practical aircraft. Flapping wings provide the best

---

[1] The first was probably one powered by gunpowder which was made by the Frenchman, G. Trouvé, in 1870. Before and after that date, and following the original ornithopter proposals of Leonardo da Vinci (p 394), there were numerous designs for flapping-wing flying machines. These included designs by: de Gusmão (1709), E. Swedenborg (1714), Abbé Desforges (1772), C. F. Meerwein (1781), F. Blanchard (1781), A. J. Renaux (1784), L. G. Gérard (1784), R. de Goué (1788), T. Walker (1810), Count A. de Lambertyre (1818), F. D. Artingstall (1830), W. Miller (1843), Duchesnay (1845), F. von Dreiburg (1845), M. Seguin (1846 and 1864), Bréant (1854), Smythies (1860), Count F. d'Esterno (1864), Struvé and Telescheff (1864), J. M. Kaufmann (1868), W. F. Quimby (1869), A. P. Keith (1870), Prigent (1871), Jobert (1871), H. de Villeneuve (1872), F. X. Lamboley (1876), C. de Louvrié (1877), M. H. Murrell (1877), F. W. Breary (1879), I. M. Wheeler (1887), and E. P. Frost (1890 and 1902). The great majority of these projects were remarkable only for their impracticability; they merely served to distract the attention of serious thinkers from the far simpler and more promising fixed-wing approach to the problem.

solution for birds, owing to the inherent impossibility of full rotary motion in an animal organ. Fixed wings with propellers or jet or rocket thrust are more efficient mechanically, and are therefore to be preferred for machines.

The problem of man-powered flight is also, at present, unresolved. There is little doubt that none of the man-powered ornithopter or fixed-wing designs which have been put forward over the years could have solved this problem. However, modern aerodynamic knowledge suggests that it may be just possible for a man to generate sufficient power with his muscles to sustain a man-powered aircraft in level flight, although there would be little extra power available for take-off or climb.

VII. HELICOPTERS

Like the ornithopter, the helicopter[1] interested the early thinkers and experimenters more than did the much simpler fixed-wing aeroplane, but the first man-carrying helicopters to leave the ground did so as recently as 1907. Paul Cornu was responsible for one such machine, and a second was the Breguet-Richet I designed by the Breguet brothers (pioneers also of fixed-wing flight) and Charles Richet. The Cornu helicopter had two counter-rotating rotors and the Breguet-Richet four, in both cases driven by petrol-engines. Although both helicopters rose from the ground, they were not in any sense practical aircraft. The first successful helicopter was the French Breguet-Dorand 314, which had twin superimposed counter-rotating rotors and made its first flight in July 1935. It flew 540 yds in a closed circuit at a height of about 100 ft, and attained a speed of 62 mph. The Breguet-Dorand was followed by the German Focke-Achgelis Fa 61, which had twin side-by-side rotors. It first flew on 26 June 1936 and its performance soon eclipsed that of the French machine. A similar British design, the Weir W 5, flew for the first time near Glasgow on 6 June 1938. The first widely used type of helicopter, the Sikorsky V S 300, with a single main rotor and a small torque-compensating tail-rotor, was first flown by its designer at Stratford, Connecticut, on 14 September 1939.

[1] Leonardo da Vinci was the first to expound the helicopter principle in Europe. The Chinese, however, probably demonstrated it much earlier with their 'flying tops'. After Leonardo, helicopter designs were proposed by, notably, A. J. P. Paucton (1768), Launoy and Bienvenu (who flew the first successful model helicopter in Paris in 1784), Sir George Cayley (1796, 1843, and 1854), Count A. de Lambertyre (1818), V. Sarti (1828), D. Mayer (*c* 1828), W. H. Phillips (who flew a model with a tip-drive rotor in 1842 using steam as the working agent), Bourne (1843), M. Seguin (1846), Auband (1851), H. Bright (1859), Viscount G. de P. D'Amecourt (1861), L. C. Crowell (1862), G. de la Landelle (1863), J. Wootton (1866), W. Smyth (1867), A. Pénaud (1870), Pomès and de la Pauze (1871), J. B. Ward (1876), E. Dieuaide (1877), Melikoff (1877), W. Kress (1877), E. Forlanini (1878), P. Castel (1878), Dandrieux (1879), Wellner, W. R. Kimball, G. Trouvé (1887), Renard (1904), E. Berliner and J. N. Williams (1905), I. Sikorsky (1909 and 1910), Papin and Romilly (1915), T. von Karman and Petrosczy (1916), P. de Pescara (1920), E. E. Oemichen (1920), G. de Bothezat (1923), H. Berliner (1924), L. Brennan (1925), von Baumhauer (1925), V. Isaaco (1927, 1930), O. von Asboth (1928), C. D'Ascanio (1930), and N. Florine (1930).

Thirteen years before the Breguet-Dorand helicopter emerged, a Spaniard, J. de la Cierva, had flown an intermediate form of rotating-wing aircraft, the Autogiro, on 9 January 1923. The Autogiro was not a true helicopter because it employed a free-wheeling rotor, but it developed into a completely practical aircraft and was widely used in the 1930s until superseded by the true helicopter. About 500 Autogiros were built.

By the middle of the twentieth century, the helicopter had established itself as a type of aircraft second in importance only to the aeroplane. Its future development will include combination with the fixed-wing principle in the convertiplane—first suggested by Sir George Cayley in 1843. The first transition from helicopter to fixed-wing flight by an aircraft of this type, the McDonnell XV-1, took place on 29 April 1955.

VIII. THE ORIGINS OF FIXED-WING FLIGHT: THE GLIDING PIONEERS

Developments between 1850 and 1900 were to lead to the establishment of the fixed-wing aeroplane as the answer to man's long search for an effective aircraft. However, as has been shown, the early pioneers were slow to appreciate the possibilities of fixed-wing flight. They were almost invariably attracted to other more complicated solutions. A very few, such as Hooke (1655), de Gusmão (1709), and Ariès (1784) seem to have had ideas along fixed-wing lines, but it was not until the 'father of aerial navigation', Sir George Cayley (1773–1857), clarified the issues and pointed out the possibilities of the glider in 1799 (tailpiece) that experimenters were at last put on the track to ultimate success.

Cayley went much farther than merely to make proposals. In 1804 he constructed a model glider with a kite-like monoplane wing and a cruciform tail-unit. This was flown successfully from the top of a steep hill, and was the first of a succession of similar models with which Cayley experimented over a number of years. The model experiments were followed by tests which brought results towards the end of Cayley's life (in 1852/3), when at least one full-sized man-carrying glider seems to have flown for a short distance carrying on one occasion a man and on another a boy. Unfortunately, no complete record has survived of Cayley's full-scale experiments, and it was not until 1891 that his proposals at length bore fruit in the first successful glides by Otto Lilienthal (1848–96). Before that time a number of gliders had been built and flown, although in too halting a fashion for them to give any evidence of progress in obtaining stability and control with a full-sized machine—the two most important problems which remained to be solved before the glider, and hence the powered aeroplane, could emerge as a workable machine. These earlier experiments were conducted by

J. M. Le Bris (1856, 1868), L. P. Mouillard (1856, 1865, 1896), C. G. Spencer (1868), J. G. Household (1871, 1875), and Biot (1879).

The German Lilienthal and his English disciple, P. S. Pilcher, were the great exponents of actual experiments in the air. Applying the principles enunciated by Cayley at the beginning of the century, Lilienthal built a series of full-sized 'hanging gliders' (figure 213) with which he taught himself to fly, and on which he was to make more than a thousand glides before his death as a result of a flying accident in 1896. Pilcher followed Lilienthal and made his first successful glide on 12 September 1895 at Cardross on the Clyde. He also lost his life in a gliding accident in 1899. At the time of their deaths, both Lilienthal and Pilcher were working on power-plant installations for their gliders, and it is not unlikely that, if they had lived, they might have achieved successful powered flight before the Wrights. Pilcher in particular, who had achieved successful towed flight and who was interesting himself in Hargrave's ideas on box-kites at the time of

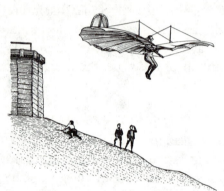

FIGURE 213—*One of Lilienthal's 'hanging gliders' with which very numerous glides were made in the 1890s.*

his death, might well have succeeded. The box-kite within a few years was to provide the basis from which the successful European biplane was to be developed, and thus set the pattern of aircraft design for thirty years.

Lilienthal and Pilcher were followed by a number of other gliding pioneers, including Octave Chanute, P. Suarez, F. Ferber, J. B. Weiss, J. J. Montgomery, and the Wright brothers themselves. For most of the nineteenth century the initiative in aeronautical development had been centred in Europe. It now switched to America. Chanute, by his gliding experiments and his active encouragement of the Wrights, played an important role in getting the brothers started on their fruitful work. He passed on to them the trussed-biplane structure, which he developed from Hargrave's box-kites. Chanute also contributed to progress by giving Europe information on the Wrights' work.

In Europe, too, after the Wrights had achieved success but before it was known on this side of the Atlantic, Hargrave's box-kite was to provide the basis for far-reaching developments which first found expression in glider designs. In 1905 the Voisin brothers—who became the world's first professional aeroplane manufacturers—designed and built two biplane gliders based on the box-kite, one for E. Archdeacon and the other for L. Blériot. These gliders were mounted on floats and in the summer of 1905 made flights from the Seine, towed by a motor-boat. Further gliding tests were made in 1906. Later, the Voisin gliders evolved into a series of powered aeroplanes which were the precursor of the successful pusher and tractor biplanes developed in later years.

The Wrights understood the importance of making gliding experiments before attempting powered flight. Indeed, five years before the developments in Europe mentioned above, they had undertaken a comprehensive programme of practical experiment. This was probably the most important reason for their ultimate success. They fully appreciated that it was essential to build, and to learn to fly, a successful glider before going forward to the more difficult undertaking of a powered aeroplane. In this vital respect they were the next to take up the torch already carried successively by Lilienthal and Pilcher. In 1900, 1901, and 1902 the Wrights built three gliders with which they progressively investigated, and solved for themselves, the problems of controlled gliding flight. By 1903 they were ready to take the final step and to install an engine. The glider had played its part in the development of the aeroplane. It has, however, survived to the present day as an aircraft in its own right, in the form of the sporting and research gliders and sailplanes of modern times, and as the military transport glider which had a brief span of utility during the second world war. The first sustained soaring flight by a glider was achieved by Orville Wright on 24 October 1911, when he made a flight of $9\frac{3}{4}$ minutes at Kitty Hawk.

IX. THE EVOLUTION OF THE POWERED AEROPLANE

Before taking up the story of the Wrights' final success, it is desirable to consider the origins of aerodynamic theory and to recount briefly the various earlier experiments with powered fixed-wing designs. The practical work followed, and was inspired by, Sir George Cayley's clear definition of the problem at the end of the eighteenth century and his forecast of the basic steps that would be needed for its solution. Aerodynamic theory after Cayley did not make any significant progress until the twentieth century. Man learnt to fly by practical methods of trial-and-error, reinforced by a minimum of recorded experimental data. Aerodynamics, when it did evolve as a science, did so on the foundations of hydrodynamical theory. The latter had been gradually built up by such men as Newton, Bernoulli, and Euler in the seventeenth and eighteenth centuries. The equivalent giant of aerodynamics was F. W. Lanchester (1868–1946), who published his work in 1907 and 1908, but only after successful powered flight had been achieved. His theories were later expanded and clarified by L. Prandtl.

Two lace-manufacturers of Chard in Somerset, W. S. Henson and J. String-fellow, were the first to act on the precepts expounded by Cayley. Henson drew up and patented a specification for a large transport aeroplane in 1842. His remarkably far-sighted design was for an 'Aerial Steam Carriage', a large 150-ft-span monoplane powered by a steam-engine driving two propellers (figure 214). It had a tail-unit to provide stability and control, and a tricycle under-carriage for take-off and landing. An 'Aerial Transit Company'—the world's first airline! —was formed to build and operate the aircraft, but the whole scheme came to nothing. Henson and Stringfellow did, however, build a steam-driven 20-ft-span model of the same basic design five years later. When tested in 1847 this proved

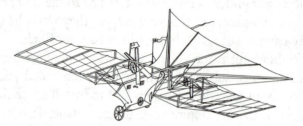

FIGURE 214—*The Henson 'Aerial Steam Carriage' of 1842.*

to be incapable of sustained flight. Henson then emigrated to the United States and Stringfellow continued the experiments alone. He built a smaller but similar model in 1848, and in June of that year, inside a disused lace-factory at Chard, it made a short flight after taking off from a wire. This has been claimed—on somewhat doubtful evidence—as the first sustained flight by a powered fixed-wing model aircraft. Stringfellow then suspended his experiments for nearly eighteen years. In 1868 he built a steam-driven model triplane which he ex-hibited at the first Aeronautical Exhibition held at the Crystal Palace in that year. This model was not flown.

The first model aeroplane to take off from the ground and make a successful flight under power was designed and built in 1857 by two Frenchmen, Félix and Louis du Temple de la Croix. It was a small tractor monoplane powered, in its initial form, by clockwork and later by a steam-engine. A third Frenchman, A. Pénaud, produced another successful model aeroplane fourteen years later. This was driven by twisted rubber and achieved flights of up to about 60 yds. It was the ancestor of every subsequent creation of the aero-modeller's art. Another successful model of this period was that built by V. Tatin in 1879. It was driven by a compressed-air engine. In the 1880s several successful models driven by rubber, clockwork, or compressed air were built by L. Hargrave in Australia.

S. P. Langley also started work at this time with rubber-driven models in America, and W. Kress did the same in Europe. Langley continued his experiments during the following decade and built a series of models, now powered by steam, until in 1896 he achieved a flight of three-quarters of a mile with his 'Aerodrome 5', a large model tandem monoplane with wings of 16-ft span. In 1901 an even larger model, driven by a small petrol engine, was flown most successfully. Langley then undertook the construction of a full-sized machine of similar configuration driven by a 53 hp petrol engine. This was tested twice during the latter part of 1903 but failed to take off.

A model project of 1867 was of particular prophetic significance. This was a

FIGURE 215—*The 1908 Voisin: prototype of thirty years of successful biplane designs.*

dart-shaped design by Butler and Edwards; it was to be propelled by a jet of steam. A rather similar proposal had been made four years earlier by a Frenchman, C. de Louvrié.

During the second half of the nineteenth century, full-scale aeroplane designs were proposed and in some cases built by, notably, M. Loup (1853), Viscount Carlingford (1856), F. du Temple de la Croix (1857), C. de Louvrié (1863), A. Pénaud (1873), T. Moy (1875), A. Mozhaisky (1882), V. Tatin and C. Richet (1890), C. Ader (1889, 1890, and 1897), H. F. Phillips (1893), and Sir Hiram Maxim (1894).

Important experimenters with power-driven aeroplanes after the turn of the century included W. Kress (1901), F. Ferber (1903, 1905, and 1906), L. Levavasseur (1903), J. C. H. Ellehammer (1904), L. Blériot (1906), T. Vuia (1906), G. and C. Voisin (1907), R. Esnault-Pelterie (1907), A. de Pischof (1907), S. F. Cody (1907), J. W. Dunne (1907), and the 'Aerial Experiment Association' formed in Canada in 1907 by Alexander Graham Bell, G. H. Curtiss, T. E. Selfridge, F. W. Baldwin, and J. A. D. MacCurdy. H. Fabre made the first successful flight of a seaplane from water on 28 March 1910.

Outstanding amongst these pioneers were the Voisin brothers and Louis Blériot. The Voisins pioneered the box-kite biplane (figure 215), which had separate mainplane and tailplane cells and was derived directly from Hargrave's box-kite, while Blériot was responsible for the tractor monoplane (figure 216). The box-kite biplane proved in time to be a more satisfactory configuration than the tailless Wright biplane. It later evolved into the tractor biplane which was to be the paramount type of aeroplane for nearly thirty years. Blériot's monoplane configuration was the more far-sighted: the monoplane became supreme as soon as there had been sufficient progress in structural design and manufacture and in aerodynamics.

FIGURE 216—*The Blériot XI in which the Channel was crossed in 1909: the prototype of the modern monoplane.*

Although these two outstanding European designs proved to be the most significant in the long run, this fact does not detract in any way from the triumph of the Wrights. The Wright biplane was the first aeroplane to fly successfully and, for nearly three years, it held the proud title of being the only design which had flown. Thereafter, it remained the most efficient type in use for two more years. To emphasize this achievement of the Wrights, it may be helpful, in conclusion, to consider the problems that they solved in producing the first practical aeroplane.

The fundamental ingredients of a successful aeroplane, and the names and dates of those who originally provided them, can be set out as follows:

(1) *The fixed-wing concept*: Cayley (1799).
(2) *Cambered wing sections for the main lifting surface(s)*: Cayley (1799), F. H. Wenham (1851), and Phillips (1884).
(3) *High aspect ratio wings*: Wenham (1866).
(4) (*a*) *The trussed-biplane structure*: Hargrave (1893), Chanute (1896), and the Wrights (1903).
    (*b*) *The wire-braced monoplane structure*: Henson (1841), Lilienthal (1891), Blériot (1907), and Esnault-Pelterie (1907).
(5) *Tandem horizontal surfaces with longitudinal dihedral* (for longitudinal stability): Cayley (1799), Pénaud (1871), and Lilienthal (1891).
(6) *Fixed vertical tail surface(s)* (for directional stability): Cayley (1799), Pénaud (1871), and Lilienthal (1891).
(7) *Setting the mainplanes at a dihedral angle* (for lateral stability): Cayley (1809), Pénaud (1871), and Lilienthal (1891).
(8) (*a*) *Rear elevator surface(s)* (for longitudinal control): Cayley (1799), Henson (1841), and Lilienthal (1895).
    (*b*) *Front elevator surface(s)* (for longitudinal control): Maxim (1894) and the Wrights (1901).

(9) *Rudder surface(s)* (for directional control): Cayley (1799) and Henson (1841).

(10) (*a*) *Wing-warping* (for lateral control): the Wrights (1901).

　　　(*b*) *Ailerons* (for lateral control): M. P. W. Boulton (1868), Esnault-Pelterie (1904), and Santos-Dumont (1906).

(11) *Streamlining to reduce drag*: Cayley (1804).

(12) *Practical piloting experience in gliding flight*: Lilienthal (1891) and the Wrights (1901).

(13) *A sufficiently light and powerful engine*: Langley (1903) and the Wrights (1903).

(14) *Airscrew(s) for propulsion*: Blanchard (1784) and Cayley (1809).

(15) *An undercarriage (or other means) for take-off and landing*: Henson (1841), Pilcher (1896), the Wrights (1903), and Santos-Dumont (1906).

(16) *Practical piloting experience in powered flight*: the Wrights (1903).

All these steps were concerned solely with the attainment of human flight, with the exception of (13). The petrol engine had been developed for other purposes (ch 18), and its application to flying-machines was of great importance in making powered flight possible. Human flight would have been possible with a light, oil-fired steam-engine; in practice, however, various forms of internal combustion engine have proved indispensable. Thus the invention of a motor with a sufficiently high power-to-weight ratio, and modest requirements in the weight of fuel to be carried, came opportunely at the end of the nineteenth century at a time when aerodynamic knowledge was able to put it to good use. The prime requirement, however, was the design of a machine that would support itself in the air, and be subject to the control of its pilot.

The above list makes it clear that the 'invention' of the aeroplane was primarily a matter of selecting the correct ingredients from among the great superfluity of information, often redundant and misleading, which had been accumulated by experimenters and thinkers during the previous hundred years. These ingredients had then to be combined successfully into a sufficiently light but strong structure. This was the great achievement of the Wrights. Many of the solutions which they adopted for the 'Flyer'—its over-all configuration, wing-warping, the starting-rail, the method of power-transmission, the interconnected warp and rudder control-system and, perhaps most serious of all, the deliberately designed instability—were actually of limited practicability and were soon to lead to the eclipse of their design. Several of the first successful aeroplanes produced independently in Europe were, in fact, superior to the Wright biplane in most of these fundamentals, but—and these are the significant issues—the European designs first flew successfully more than three years after the Wrights', and even then proved for some time to be notably less efficient flying-machines. The flight of Orville Wright on 17 December 1903 was therefore unquestionably one of the great turning-points in history, initiating a new era in transport and in war.

X. THE DEVELOPMENT OF THE ROCKET

Rockets originated in China (vol II, p 378). Their earliest recorded use as weapons was in 1232, when the Monguls employed them during the siege of Pien-king. They first appeared in Europe in 1379, being used during the battle for the island of Chiozza. Rockets have continued ever since to be used at intervals for military purposes. Important steps in development were Sir William Congreve's artillery rocket of 1805, and the fin-stabilized Hale rocket which appeared in the middle of the nineteenth century. The latter was the ancestor of all unguided rocket projectiles used since that time, including the Le Prieur rockets of the first world war and the many developments which came into widespread use in the second world war. A vital step in rocket progress was the first flight of a liquid fuel rocket on 16 March 1926. This rocket was designed by an American, R. H. Goddard.

The first proposal to use rocket propulsion for an aircraft seems to have been that of a Chinese, Wan-Hoo, who is reported to have designed a kite propelled by rockets in about 1500. This anticipated the first authenticated rocket-propelled flight by more than 400 years.

F. von Opel made a flight of some two miles in a rocket-propelled glider on 30 September 1929. The next steps in the development of this form of propulsion were the first flight of the Heinkel He 176 rocket aircraft on 30 June 1939 and the limited operational use by the Germans towards the end of the second world war of the Messerschmitt Me 163 rocket fighter. Further developments along the same lines after the war led to the rocket-propelled Bell X-1 becoming the first manned aircraft to exceed the speed of sound, on 14 October 1947.

These applications of rockets have been to the propulsion of fixed-wing aeroplanes. The rocket started to emerge, however, as an aircraft in its own right with the appearance of guided ballistic missiles, pioneered by the Germans with the V-2 rocket during the second world war. In time, such missiles may develop into manned vehicles following ballistic trajectories for the first phase of their flight paths, but converting into fixed-wing aircraft for the latter part of their journeys and for landing. Alternatively, lift for low-speed flight may be obtained from jet or rocket thrust. The future beyond this stage will be outside the realm of aeronautics—and in that of astronautics. The rocket has played a key role in the launching of Earth satellites and will ultimately—with molecular or nuclear fuels—provide the means of propulsion for interplanetary travel.

BIBLIOGRAPHY

CHAMBE, R. 'Histoire de l'aviation.' Flammarion, Paris. 1948.

DAVY, M. J. B. 'Aeronautics: Heavier-than-air Aircraft.' H.M. Stationery Office, London. 1929.

Idem. 'Aeronautics: Lighter-than-air Aircraft.' Ibid. 1934.

Idem. 'Aeronautics: Propulsion of Aircraft.' Ibid. 1930.

Idem. 'Interpretative History of Flight.' Ibid. 1937.

DOLLFUS, C. and BOUCHÉ, H. 'Histoire de l'aéronautique.' L'Illustration, Paris. 1932.

GIBBS-SMITH, C. H. 'A History of Flying.' Batsford, London. 1953.

HODGSON, J. E. 'The History of Aeronautics in Great Britain.' Oxford University Press, London. 1924.

KELLEY, F. C. 'The Wright Brothers.' Harrap, London. 1944.

NESSLER, E. 'Histoire du vol à voile de 1506 à nos jours.' Œuvres Françaises, Paris. 1948.

TAYLOR, J. W. R. 'A Picture History of Flight.' Hulton Press, London. 1955.

TURNER, C. C. 'The Old Flying Days.' Samson, Low, Marston, London. 1927.

VIVIAN, E. C. and MARSH, W. L. 'A History of Aeronautics.' Collins, London. 1921.

WARD, B. H. (Ed.). 'Flight—a Pictorial History of Aviation.' Published by Year—the Annual Picture History, Los Angeles. 1953.

Sir George Cayley's sketch of his man-carrying glider, proposed in 1799.

18

MECHANICAL ROAD-VEHICLES

D. C. FIELD

I. THE BICYCLE

THE basic idea of a two-wheeled machine astride which a man might sit and propel himself along is undoubtedly of considerable antiquity, but it did not assume a practical form until 1818. Then a German, Freiherr Karl Drais von Sauerbronn (1785–1851), constructed an improved type of hobby-horse, or dandy-horse, as such machines were called in England. It consisted of a wooden frame or backbone, to which two wheels of equal size were attached by iron brackets, the front one being capable of turning relatively to the frame by means of a handle-bar fixed to the top of the front fork (figure 217). The rider sat on a saddle mounted in the centre of the backbone and leaned forward against a padded support between the saddle and the handle-bar, propelling himself by taking long strides with each foot in turn against the ground. The wheels were wooden and no brake was fitted. To ride the hobby-horse downhill must have been an alarming experience.

About 1839 Kirkpatrick Macmillan, a Scot, built a machine incorporating a system of treadles, linked by connecting-rods and cranks to the rear wheel, which was the first bicycle to be propelled by the rider without touching the ground with his feet. A brake on the rear wheel could be applied by twisting the handle-bar. It was not until 1861 that cranks and pedals were directly applied to the wheels of a hobby-horse, and credit for the first use of these on the front wheel must go to Ernest Michaux, a Frenchman, who by 1867 had formed a company for the manufacture of velocipedes of his own design. Late in the previous year the first American bicycle patent had been taken out jointly by Pierre Lallement and J. Carrol.

During the next few years the bicycle industry in France grew rapidly. On 17 November 1869 a great international race from Paris to Rouen, a distance of 83 miles, was won by an Englishman, James Moore, riding a machine fitted with ball-bearings. He subsequently designed more efficient ball-bearings, which were soon adopted by manufacturers generally. By this time England was waking up to the fact that there was a growing demand for bicycles, and in 1869 the first machines to be made in this country were built at Coventry. James

Starley (1831–81), of that city, took out a patent for the first ladies' bicycle in 1874, and also invented the tangentially spoked wheel—a great improvement on the earlier radial-spoke design. He patented the 'Coventry' tricycle in 1876 and a year later took out another patent for the use of the differential gear in combination with chain-drive, which features he embodied in the 'Coventry' tricycle. This machine paved the way for the introduction by other manufacturers of many different designs with two, three, and four wheels. More than 200 varieties were on the market in 1884.

A typical example is the Otto bicycle, or dicycle, which consisted of a pair of

FIGURE 217—*The 'Draisine' or hobby-horse, c 1818.*

very large driving-wheels several feet apart, between which the rider sat perched on a saddle above the axle (figure 218). Treadles were connected by a belt-drive to each wheel, steering being effected by means of small spade handles on each side of the rider. When one of these was turned the drive on that side was made to slip, and possibly some braking action occurred as well, with the result that the opposite wheel caused the machine to swing in the desired direction. A good deal of confidence must have been necessary before attaining a reasonable speed on the road, and to balance correctly on the machine was an art in itself. All such designs as this suffered from the disadvantages of excessive width and general clumsiness; their popularity was short lived.

The high or 'ordinary' bicycle (figure 219) was now rapidly becoming the standard type, for a reason which is comprehensible if not immediately obvious.

In order that each revolution of the pedals attached directly to the hub of the front or 'high' wheel should cause the machine to travel a reasonable distance, it was necessary that the wheel should be from 4 to 5 ft in diameter, and in fact they were so made, with variations in steps of 2 in to suit the length of the legs of different riders. Attempts to make the front-driving machine safer were numerous, one such being the 'Kangaroo' bicycle in which the front or driving wheel was considerably smaller than in the case of the 'ordinary', the pedals being

FIGURE 218—*The Otto bicycle, 1880.*

mounted at a point about half-way between the hub and the ground and driving the former by geared-up chains. Another design was the 'Geared Facile' (plate 16 A) which incorporated a lever action and sun-and-planet gearing. A slightly inclined front fork also helped by placing the weight of the rider farther behind the centre of the wheel.

The advent of the contemporary safety bicycle was foreshadowed as early as 1876, when H. J. Lawson patented a rear-driving machine known as the 'Crocodile'. In this machine the rear wheel, rotated by a system of levers and treadles, was considerably larger than the front. It was not a commercial success. In 1879 Lawson designed the first rear-driven safety bicycle using ordinary cranks and pedals, a geared-up chain-drive to the small rear wheel being employed (cf figure 220). A large front wheel gave the machine a rather ungainly appearance.

It was left to J. K. Starley of Coventry, nephew of James Starley, to design and

FIGURE 219—*Rudge 'ordinary' bicycle, 1884.*

FIGURE 220—*A development of the first chain-driven safety bicycle, made by H. J. Lawson, 1879.*

FIGURE 221—*The Rover safety bicycle, 1885.*

FIGURE 222—*The Singer safety bicycle, 1890. Note that the steering axis passes through the point of contact of the tyre and the ground, thus improving the steering.*

manufacture the first commercially successful safety bicycle, the Rover, in 1885 (figure 221). It employed all the elements of the modern machine, having wheels of almost equal size, direct steering with inclined forks, and geared-up chain-drive to the rear wheel. It soon attained great popularity. The introduction of this machine and others constructed on similar principles (figure 222) doomed the 'ordinary' to extinction. The invention of the pneumatic tyre (p 771) very soon afterwards was the final blow, and by the turn of the century the safety bicycle, now fitted with a free-wheel, a device that had been anticipated at least thirty years earlier, reigned supreme.

II. ELECTRIC ROAD-CARRIAGES

The successful use of electricity for the propulsion of road-vehicles may be said to have originated with the improvement of the secondary battery or Planté accumulator by Camille Faure, about 1880 (p 206). Previous attempts, of which there had been a number, had all relied upon primary batteries, which were quite incapable of providing the necessary heavy current for more than a very brief time.

In 1882 Ayrton and Perry built an electric tricycle. This was fitted with an electric motor geared to one of the road-wheels, and a platform carrying the battery of cells. The weight of equipment was so great that results were not at all satisfactory. Four years later, in 1886, Radcliffe Ward constructed an electric cab capable of a maximum speed of 8 mph. It had a battery of 28 cells and an electric motor which drove the road-wheels by means of a belt and a two-speed friction-gear. The following year Magnus Volk, widely known from his construction of the electric railway along the sea-front at Brighton (p 347), built an electric dog-cart which achieved a certain degree of success. With a 16-cell battery to work the motor, which drove one rear wheel by means of a chain, it was able to travel at 9 mph under favourable conditions.

The earliest electric carriage to achieve some commercial success was that made by Pouchain in 1893. This vehicle had seats for six persons; its 3·5-kw motor supplied from a 54-cell battery drove the rear axle through a gear-and-chain transmission system. The speed of the machine was regulated by varying the grouping of the cells, with the aid of a drum-type controller rotating over a number of electrical contacts. This appears to be the earliest recorded example of such a device.

In 1894 Garrard and Blumfield constructed a vehicle having four wheels fitted with large-section pneumatic tyres. A constant-speed type of motor was employed with a variable ratio friction-drive. The machine had a 24-cell battery, and its total weight was about half a ton. A speed of 10 mph was attained.

In one type of Jeantaud electric carriage of 1898 the fore-carriage system was employed, the electric motor being mounted just behind the front axle, which it drove through reduction gearing. An ingenious arrangement of bevel-wheels at each end of the axle ensured that the action of the Ackermann steering mechanism in no way interfered with the transmission of power to the road-wheels. In 1897, when electrically propelled vehicles were successful enough to warrant

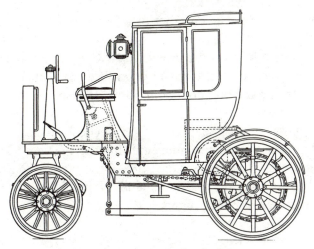

FIGURE 223—*Bersey electric cab of 1897.*

serious attempts towards commercial application, the London Electric Cab Company began a regular service of electric cabs in the streets of the capital (figure 223). The design of these cabs was ingenious, incorporating a readily removable tray containing 40 accumulator cells. The battery was said to be capable of driving the cab some 50 miles on a single charge, after which the cells had to be removed and replaced by a freshly charged set at the company's charging-station, where a system of hydraulic lifts ensured that this operation was performed very quickly.

A rear-mounted electric motor developing 3 hp drove, by means of spur-gearing, a countershaft that carried the differential gear and had chain-sprockets at each end, the latter carrying chains to larger sprockets attached to each rear wheel. A drum-type controller was provided, and, in addition to band-brakes on drums fitted to the rear wheels, electric 'regenerative' braking was effected by reversing the connexions to the motor. Steering was controlled by a vertically mounted hand-wheel, which caused the entire fore-carriage to swivel about a central pivot, the latter being fitted with a ball-race between its locking-plates.

For various reasons the enterprise did not succeed and its service ceased about two years after it had begun. One reason for its lack of commercial success was undoubtedly the excessive weight of the cabs and their very heavy and cumbersome construction, resulting in slow speed and somewhat jerky motion when starting and stopping. When business ceased in 1899 some 36 complete cabs and 41 incomplete ones were offered for sale, figures that give some idea of the magnitude of the undertaking.

The same problems face the designer of any battery-driven electric vehicle. Until an entirely new and light form of storage-battery is invented the weight of the batteries must always limit in every way the performance of an otherwise ideal type of vehicle: silent, easily controlled, and, unlike the petrol- or diesel-engined car, producing no odours and undesirable exhaust gases to pollute the atmosphere.

Probably the most remarkable electrically propelled vehicle of the nineteenth century was the cigar-shaped machine built for the Belgian, Camille Jenatzy, in 1899 and known as 'La Jamais Contente'. On 2 April 1899 he established with it a world's record for speed on land of nearly 66 mph at Achères, France, over a distance of one kilometre.

III. STEAM ROAD-CARRIAGES

The early period of the steam road-coach had ended by 1840, its development having been effectively stultified by the excessive tolls imposed by the local road authorities upon an otherwise flourishing and technically successful new industry. Interest in mechanical road-transport then lapsed, and it was many years before any serious attempt was made to develop further the use of steam power on ordinary roads. However, here and there a few far-sighted individuals, having recognized the fact that one day the obvious superiority of the mechanically propelled road-carriage over more primitive forms of transport must eventually prevail, continued their experiments. No doubt the great progress being made in the development of the railway locomotive at this period influenced them to a considerable extent, and did much to convince them that steam-driven private carriages were feasible.

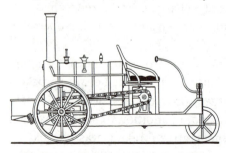

FIGURE 224—*Rickett's road-steamer of 1858.*

Thus in 1858 Thomas Rickett of Buckingham built the first of several steam-carriages (figure 224). It resembled a small railway locomotive rather than a carriage and consisted of a steam-engine mounted on three wheels, two large driving wheels at the rear and a smaller wheel in front by which the vehicle was steered. A seat for three persons including the driver was placed in front of the boiler, and the stoker was accommodated on a platform at the back. The offside rear wheel was driven by a chain from the engine, the other wheel running free on the main axle. On steep hills or under other difficult road conditions both wheels could be driven, a clutch being provided for this purpose which had to be disengaged when rounding curves. A maximum speed of 12 mph was reached, the weight of the machine being 1·5 tons. Two years later, in 1860, Rickett built a similar though rather heavier vehicle, of the same general design but incorporating spur-gear drive instead of chain (figure 225). In his final design the

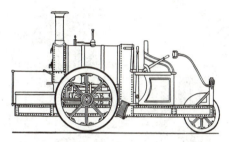

FIGURE 225—*Rickett's improved road-steamer of 1860.*

cylinders were directly coupled outside to cranks on the driving-axle, in the manner of a railway locomotive.

An engine weighing 5 tons and seating nine persons was made in 1861 by Carrett, Marshall & Company of Leeds. This was in many respects similar to Rickett's road-steamers in general design, and incorporated a twin-cylinder engine and spur-gear drive. In 1862 Yarrow and Hilditch built a steam-carriage conveying eleven people and having a vertical multi-tubular boiler. The rear driving-wheels were placed within the main frame and were both secured to the axle, the slipping of one or other wheel when turning corners being considerably less than with other designs, owing to the comparatively narrow track. In 1862 also a steam-carriage of a quite different type was built by A. Patterson. This was of the fore-carriage design, having the steam-engine and two-speed gear mounted above the front wheels on a turn-table, which was made to swivel so that the machine could be steered. The front wheels were the drivers, and a vertical boiler was placed over them with a cylinder on either side of it. The carriage portion at the rear seated six or eight persons and the weight was about 1 ton.

H. P. Holt constructed a small road-steamer in 1866. Capable of a maximum speed of 20 mph on level roads, it was equipped with a vertical boiler at the rear and two separate twin-cylinder engines, each of which drove one of the rear wheels by means of a chain and sprocket-wheels. A differential gear was thus eliminated. An ingenious method of suspending the single front wheel was devised, whereby all road shocks were transferred to the frame rather than to the front wheel steering-pivot. Eight persons could be carried and the weight was 1·5 tons. In 1869 Catley & Ayres of York built a small three-wheeled vehicle propelled by a horizontal twin-cylinder engine which drove the rear axle by means of spur-gearing; only one rear wheel was driven, the other turning freely upon the axle. A vertical fire-tube boiler was mounted at the rear, with

a polished copper casing over the fire-box and chimney; the boiler itself was lagged and enclosed in a mahogany casing. The single front wheel was used for steering and the weight was only 19 cwt.

In 1868–70 J. H. Knight of Farnham built a four-wheeled steam-carriage which originally had a single-cylinder engine, but was subsequently fitted with two cylinders. It was a heavy machine, weighing some 33 cwt in working order, and had a vertical boiler at the rear. A

FIGURE 226—*Randolph's steam-carriage of 1872.*

seat at the front accommodated three persons and there was room for two on the firing-platform at the back. Only one rear wheel was driven. A speed of 8 mph was attained on level roads. In 1871 the road-steamers of R. W. Thomson of Aberdeen won considerable repute, largely because their wheels were shod with heavy solid rubber tyres, which provided a great improvement on the traction of the usual iron tyres. These machines were in reality tractors; some were used in India to draw two-wheeled omnibuses carrying passengers and mail.

A steam-coach built by Charles Randolph of Glasgow in 1872 shows many features of interest (figure 226). Fifteen feet in length, it weighed 4½ tons when ready for the road, but its maximum speed was only 6 mph, as it was somewhat underpowered. The central carriage portion could accommodate six passengers and the box in front two more beside the driver. The rear compartment contained the vertical boiler, on each side of which was placed a vertical twin-cylinder engine; the two engines were independent of one another, and each drove one of the rear wheels by spur-gearing. The entire vehicle was enclosed and fitted with windows all round. This carriage seems to have been very fully equipped—even to a driving-mirror for observing traffic approaching from behind, the earliest recorded instance of such a device. It must have been far too heavy and cumbersome to be of practical utility, and it was not used for more than a few years.

In 1875 R. Neville Grenville of Glastonbury designed a three-wheeled steam vehicle which is of particular interest because it is still in existence and has been run quite successfully on the road in recent years. It is fitted with a horizontal twin-cylinder engine, although when first constructed a vertical single-cylinder was employed. A vertical boiler of the type used in steam fire-engines is mounted at the rear, with a platform for the stoker behind it. The two forward seats carry six persons, the driver occupying the centre of the front one with the brakesman on his right. Solid disk wheels made of teak with iron rims and tyres are fitted; the single front wheel controls the direction, and the weight is 45 cwt. Mahogany body-work is fitted, and the maximum speed is reputed to be about 15 mph. This vehicle is now preserved in the Bristol city museum.

In 1880 Amedée Bollée of Le Mans designed and built a steam-coach that ran with considerable success. It displays a number of points of interest, not the least being the general lay-out of the mechanism, which closely resembles that of much later motor cars. A vertical twin-cylinder steam-engine was mounted ahead of the front axle and drove direct to a countershaft situated a little forward of the rear axle, by means of a clutch, propeller-shaft, and bevel gearing. The countershaft embodied a differential gear, and small sprocket wheels were mounted at its two extremities. Chains then transmitted the power to further sprockets on each rear wheel, the latter revolving freely upon the ends of a fixed axle-beam which was secured to the frame by elliptic road-springs. A vertical water-tube boiler at the rear carried a chimney which just projected above the roof of the stoker's compartment. A wheel vertically mounted immediately behind the engine controlled the steering by means of a toothed sector and pinion, the front wheels being mounted on short pivoted axles from which arms projecting rearward were linked to the sector by means of rods. Screw-operated brake-blocks on the rear wheels were applied by means of a handle surmounting a shaft which passed through the hollow steering-column. There was a single front seat for the driver, protected by a hood, and between this and the boiler-compartment was a comfortable enclosed coachwork body. A speed of 18 mph is said to have been attained on the level.

At the other end of the scale, numerous attempts to design steam-driven vehicles of a much lighter type were made during this period, and a small steam-tricycle was built by the Comte de Dion in 1887. This had two wheels in front, between which was the steam-generator, and a single rear wheel driven by the engine. Pneumatic tyres were fitted to this machine, which is almost certainly the earliest example of a power-driven vehicle so equipped. In the same year Léon Serpollet constructed a coal-fired steam-tricycle which had two rear driving-wheels and the power-plant mounted between them (figure 227). Two years later, in 1889, he invented the instantaneous steam-generator which subsequently became widely known. In it a stack of flat coils of nickel-steel tubes was arranged in

FIGURE 227—*Léon Serpollet's coal-fired steam-tricycle of 1887.*

the casing, the coils being connected together in series. When a small quantity of water was pumped in at the lower end of the coils the heat of the burner and of the red-hot coils converted it instantly into steam; and by the time that the steam had passed through all the coils and thence to the engine it was not only super-heated to a considerable degree, with increased expansive force, but was also much drier than steam obtained from a fire- or water-tube boiler. Serpollet successfully applied this generator to a steam-carriage in 1894; his later models were fitted with either petroleum or paraffin burners and a four-cylinder hori-zontally opposed engine employing poppet-valve gear. In 1899 an American named Gardner supported Serpollet's venture financially, and the Gardner–

Serpollet steam-car became exceedingly well known both in England and in France, remaining so until the death of Serpollet in 1907.

A steam-van built by the old-established firm of Thornycroft in 1896 is of particular interest, for it is still extant and in working order. A double compound condensing engine drives the front wheels through chains and a differential gear. The rear wheels, of smaller diameter than the front, are the steering wheels and are controlled by a horizontal wheel with a worm and chain connexion to the turn-table at the rear. A water-tube boiler fired by coke is used, and a condenser is accommodated in the roof of the van. The van can attain a speed of 9 mph.

Another interesting steam-vehicle, built by G. S. Soame of Marsham, Norfolk, about 1897, is also in existence. This is constructed somewhat on the lines of certain of the earlier machines already described, having a horizontal twin-cylinder engine at the rear which drives the rear wheels through a two-speed sliding gear-box and two side-belts. There are a vertical boiler at the rear and a canopy over the cart-type body, which seats five persons. The machine is coke-fired and has tiller steering.

Towards the end of the year 1897 the Stanley brothers of Newton, Massachusetts, began the testing of their first steam-vehicle. This was a novel venture in steam-car design, of strong but light construction and weighing in all about 7 cwt. The tubular frame carried a wooden two-seater body, a vertical twin-cylinder engine being fitted amidships and driving the rear live axle by means of a chain, through a differential gear. A small vertical fire-tube boiler, heated by a petroleum burner, was fitted beneath the seat, and the feed-water tank occupied the boot. The car was mounted on full elliptic springs and ran on wire wheels fitted with single-tube pneumatic tyres (plate 18 B). Although the Stanley brothers sold their design to the Locomobile Company of America in 1899, they resumed the manufacture of an improved steam car in 1901, and it is from their experiments that the once flourishing steam-car manufacture of the United States may be said to have originated.

The traction engine. About the year 1850 a method of steam-ploughing was introduced, in which 'portable' steam-engines were employed to draw a plough across a field by means of wire ropes winding over drums placed on opposite sides of the field (vol IV, figure 11). These engines consisted of a horizontal boiler mounted on a pair of large rear wheels, and a small fore-carriage which could be steered. A single-cylinder engine was mounted above the fire-box. By 1856 the idea of connecting the crankshaft to the rear axle had been developed, in order to produce an engine capable of moving under its own power.

Once shown the way, many firms took up the manufacture of such traction-engines, three of the best known being Aveling, Burrell, and Fowler. At first the design closely followed that of the portable type, but by the 1860s the engine-cylinder was being placed at the front of the boiler, where it has remained ever since, and steering was often accomplished by means of an extra or fifth wheel attached to the front of the fore-carriage. By 1870 gear-transmission instead of chain, and wheel steering from the driving position, resulted in a finality of design which remained unchanged over a period of many years.

The only subsequent major developments of note were the dynamo driven by a belt from the fly-wheel and mounted on a bracket over the front of the boiler, for supplying electric power for many purposes, and the use of solid rubber tyres on the hitherto iron-tyred wheels, when used for road-haulage work. The development of the steam traction-engine may be said to have reached absolute finality in the magnificent showman's engines of the twentieth century, now unfortunately entirely displaced by less spectacular but more efficient transport with internal combustion engines.

IV. PETROLEUM MOTOR-CARRIAGES

Despite the limited success of certain of the early steam-driven road-vehicles, a number of inventors rejected the idea that the private carriage of the future would be propelled by steam. Steam-vehicles were heavy and cumbersome, and, while it was possible to design a light steam-engine, its auxiliary equipment —its boiler or steam-generator and burner—could not be made either light or compact enough to accommodate them satisfactorily in a relatively small and light road-vehicle. Furthermore, there was always the disadvantage that frequent stops to take on water must be made.

The earliest claim to have constructed a vehicle driven by an internal combustion engine burning petroleum spirit is that of the Austrian, Siegfried Marcus. He is reported to have made such an engine and to have mounted it upon a small hand-cart about the year 1864. Apart from the fact that it was a vertical engine and that its two fly-wheels replaced the rear wheels of the hand-cart, little is known of the details of its construction. It is said to have made only one short experimental journey before the inventor, being dissatisfied with the result, broke it up. Marcus is also credited with having built three other vehicles, the earliest of which is preserved today in the Technical Museum in Vienna (plate 18 A). Said to have been built in 1874, the machine incorporates a number of ingenious features but is exceedingly heavy and clumsy. The engine is a horizontal single-cylinder four-stroke, the piston rotating the crankshaft through an oscillating-beam system. There is a cone clutch with an arrangement of four belts to drive the rear axle and wheels. Steering is effected by swivelling the entire fore-carriage by means of a hand-wheel and worm and worm-wheel. A unique form of carburettor is used, in which a revolving brush sprays the atomized fuel into the induction pipe. A low-tension magneto system is fitted, which is certainly the earliest known example of such a device on a road-vehicle. The maximum speed of the car is 5 mph. Siegfried Marcus appears to have lost interest in perfecting his designs once he had satisfied himself that they were practical, even in such a crude form, and to have then devoted himself to other activities. It is not known what became of his two later vehicles.

Of a vastly different character was Karl Benz (p 167) of Mannheim, Germany, who in 1885 constructed a light three-wheeled vehicle driven by a horizontal single-cylinder petrol-engine (figure 228). The crankshaft was vertical and at the rear of the car, a large horizontal fly-wheel being fitted at its lower end. This unusual arrangement was said to be intended to overcome possible gyro-scopic effects affecting the steering of the vehicle. The power was transmitted through a pair of bevel-gears from the top of the crankshaft to a short horizontal shaft from which a belt drove a countershaft placed low down in the centre of the car and incorporating a differential gear. The belt could be moved from a fast to a loose pulley, so enabling the engine to run without driving the car; a pair of chains drove the rear wheels from the countershaft. A rack-and-pinion steering system controlled the movement of the single front wheel from a small tiller. A surface-type carburettor and coil-and-battery ignition were used. The speed of the machine was about 8 mph.

Benz made two further three-wheeled vehicles before developing a design for a four-wheeled car. This was first constructed in 1893 and, apart from the fact that the crankshaft was now placed horizontally and a two-speed belt-drive employed, the design was basically the same as that of the three-wheeler of 1885. So successful was this model that many hundreds of cars were built of almost identical 3½-hp type (plates 16B and 17A) until 1901, when the design was superseded by others. Karl Benz may be properly considered to be the father of the automobile, in so far as any one person may be so described.

In this period when Benz was testing his first vehicle, Gottlieb Daimler (p 164) of Württemberg, Germany, was inventing the first high-speed internal com-bustion engine. It was a simple, light, and compact vertical single-cylinder engine and, unlike the horizontal engines of Benz, which ran at a very low speed, it effected a large number of revolutions per minute. It was applied to a motor bicycle, the first trial of which took place in 1886 (p 434). In the same year a similar engine was placed in the rear of a four-wheeled carriage of a horse-drawn type, in which the shafts had been replaced by a steering mechanism. This was satisfactorily driven on the roads in the following year. In 1889 a motor quadricycle was designed, and built successfully. Thereafter a number of different designs for four-wheeled motor-carriages were executed. Characteristic

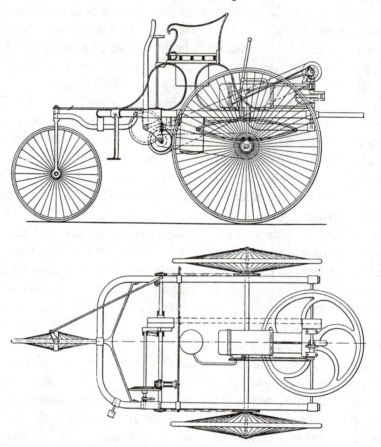

FIGURE 228—*First Benz three-wheeled vehicle of 1885: elevation and plan.*

of all of them was the use of hot-tube ignition and belt-transmission (plate 17 B). These products of the Cannstatt works from about 1894 are referred to as Cannstatt-Daimlers to distinguish them from the cars built by the English Daimler Company of Coventry (plate 19 B), which was formed in 1896 as an entirely separate concern. The Cannstatt-Daimler vehicles ultimately became known as Mercédès.

Development was also proceeding apace in other European countries. One of the earliest surviving petrol-driven vehicles is the car built in 1886 by Albert Hammel and Hans Johansen of Denmark, now owned by the Danish Technical Museum. The horizontal engine has twin cylinders placed side by side, with a surface carburettor and hot-tube ignition. Power is transmitted by gears and friction-clutches to a single chain driving the live rear axle. A differential gear is not fitted; instead, each rear wheel is driven through a leather-lined cone clutch, permitting a certain amount of slip when traversing curves. A highly ingenious feature is the provision of a reverse motion by taking the drive from the cam-shaft when it is desired to travel backwards. This automatically reduces the speed by half, as well as reversing the drive. There is only one forward speed. The steering mechanism is remarkable for two reasons: first, a wheel is fitted, not a tiller; secondly, the connexions are such that in order to turn to the left it is necessary to move the wheel to the right and vice versa!

In 1954 this car completed the London to Brighton commemoration run of 53 miles in $12\frac{1}{2}$ hours, the last four after dark, the only illumination being by candle-lamps. The average speed was $4\frac{1}{2}$ mph, and there was no major break-down, which renders this a remarkable performance for a vehicle then 68 years old.

The earliest English pioneer of a vehicle with an internal combustion engine was Edward Butler who, after preparing a design in 1884, applied in 1887 for a patent for a motor tricycle which was tested in the following year. He called it the 'Petrol cycle'—the first recorded use of the term petrol.[1] Butler used a hori-zontal twin-cylinder engine, which in the original design drove the single rear wheel directly, the axle forming the crankshaft. This arrangement was sub-sequently abandoned, the engine-speed being found to be too low, and an epicyclic gear-train was added. Two side-levers controlled the front steering wheels, and a unique feature was a pedal or foot-lever which was used to raise the rear wheel clear of the ground in order to start the machine. Electric ignition was used. Unfortunately Butler discontinued his experiments on account of the restrictive legislation against road-vehicles in force at that time in Britain.

In France, Armand Peugeot was experimenting with a light vehicle built like a cycle and driven by a V-twin Daimler engine built under licence by Panhard and Levassor of Paris. This, constructed in 1889–90, was the first petrol-driven car to be made in France. Peugeot placed the engine at the rear of the carriage, which was of light construction with large wire wheels and a form of handlebar steering. Developments of this design followed, and in 1896 a horizontal twin-cylinder engine of Peugeot's own manufacture was used instead of the Daimler

---

[1] In the modern sense (French *pétrole*, refined petroleum).

type. Not until 1902 did the firm build a car employing a vertical forward-mounted engine. The premier position among builders of cars in France must, however, be assigned to the firm of Panhard and Levassor already mentioned. In 1889 they secured the French manufacturing rights for the Daimler motor, and an experimental car was made and tested exhaustively. In 1891 a car of completely different design was put in hand and was successful enough to merit a rather detailed description.

The twin-cylinder Daimler engine was mounted vertically at the front of the vehicle and connected to a three-speed sliding gear-box by a friction-clutch. To the rear of the gear-box was a countershaft driven through bevel-gears whence a chain in the centre of the vehicle carried the power to a live rear axle incorporating a differential gear. This general lay-out subsequently became the standard one for the great majority of motor cars of nearly all other makers, except for variations of detail and the substitution of side-chains or shaft drive at a later date. Ackermann steering, controlled by a tiller, and wooden wheels shod with either iron or solid rubber tyres, were adopted. The firm was one of the first to substitute wheel for tiller steering a few years later.

An important English pioneer was John Henry Knight of Farnham, Surrey. As early as 1868 he had built a steam road-vehicle and in July 1895 he constructed a three-wheeled petrol-driven car. This had a horizontal single-cylinder engine running on benzoline, and subsequently on paraffin with the aid of a vaporizer. Originally it had hot-tube ignition, but this was later changed for the electrical type. A two-speed belt-transmission was employed, jockey pulleys being used to cause the required belt to take up the drive, the other belt then running idle. At first a single front wheel was used, but early in 1896 the machine was converted to a four-wheeler for greater stability, and at the same time the original rear wheels of wire were replaced by wooden ones fitted with solid rubber tyres. In this form the car exists today and is now owned by Farnham Urban District Council. That the inventor regarded the vehicle as an experimental one accounts for the many alterations made to it at different times. Later in 1896, for instance, a larger cylinder was fitted, and in its final form the car ran well, with a speed of 10 mph easily achieved. This car must share with the three-wheeled Wolseley car of 1895 (p 432) the honour of being the earliest extant British-built petrol-driven motor-vehicle.

One of the most important of the early English designers, F. W. Lanchester, was unlike most of the contemporary motor enthusiasts in that he was already a distinguished engineer. He perceived that a new approach to the design of self-propelled vehicles was essential, an approach based upon truly scientific principles. Hitherto inventors had all been working in terms of the adaptation of existing horse-drawn carriages to mechanical propulsion, merely substituting an engine and transmission mechanism for the horse and adding suitable steering apparatus, the result being literally a 'horseless carriage'.

Lanchester determined to begin from first principles and to design a vehicle which owed little or nothing to others, particularly to the continental pioneers, but which was to be original in almost every respect and functional to a degree. How well he succeeded may be judged from the fact that every modern car still (1958) incorporates several features displayed in Lanchester's vehicle of 1895–6 (plate 19 A). This historic machine had a frame of brazed steel tubes to which was fitted, in the centre, an inclined single-cylinder air-cooled engine of 5 hp. In order to balance the irregular impulse inherent in all single-cylinder engines, two contra-rotating crankshafts were used, geared together and each carrying its own fly-wheel. Chain-transmission connected one of the crankshafts to the live rear axle, on which was mounted an epicyclic gear-box and the differential gear. The former gave a low and reverse speed as well as a direct drive on the high gear. Specially made Dunlop pneumatic tyres were fitted to tangent-spoked wire wheels, and central tiller steering was used. A wick-type carburettor was incorporated in the fuel tank. The car made its first trial run early in 1896 and performed satisfactorily, except that it proved to be somewhat under-powered.

Soon afterwards, Lanchester designed a horizontally opposed twin-cylinder air-cooled engine of 8 hp, incorporating the same basic principles of balance as the original engine, which it replaced. The inlet valves were mechanically operated. Low-tension magneto ignition components were carried within one of the fly-wheels. The roller-bearings used in the epicyclic gear-box had to be specially made, for such bearings were not commercially obtainable at that time. This improved type of epicyclic gear and worm-drive to the rear axle replaced the chain-transmission system originally employed, the new engine being carried at the rear of the chassis. The car in its modified form was on the road again in 1897 and proved capable of a speed of 20 mph.

In the meantime a second experimental car had been designed, and was completed early in 1898. Also of tubular-frame construction, a similar twin-cylinder balanced power-unit was placed in the centre of the chassis, which was carried on cantilever springs at the forward end only, the rear end being un-sprung. This car achieved a speed of 28 mph on the level and performed many long journeys without manifesting any mechanical defect. In 1899 it was awarded a gold medal for its performance at the Automobile Club of Great

Britain and Ireland's Richmond trials, and later in the same year the Lanchester Engine Company was formed. A 10-hp model similar in basic design was subsequently placed upon the market and won considerable reputation in commerce. Not until 1905 was a more conventional engine-design adopted. Unfortunately the 1895-6 car was totally destroyed by enemy action during the second world war, but the other is preserved in the Science Museum at South Kensington. Some five examples of the twin-cylinder production model survive today in this country, and most of them are regularly run on the road.

At the time when the late Lord Austin designed his first motor vehicle, in 1895, he was employed by the Wolseley Sheep Shearing Machine Company; he had become interested in the problems of mechanical road-transport and began by constructing a three-wheeled machine. This exhibited a number of ingenious features well in advance of their time. A steel tubular frame was used, and a balanced horizontally opposed twin-cylinder engine, in which the inlet valves were operated mechanically, was mounted on the near side of the frame, the crankshaft being extended to pass freely through the hub of the single rear wheel. A fly-wheel was carried on the opposite side of the road-wheel and also a belt-pulley from which a flat belt conveyed the drive forward to a three-speed sliding gear-box beneath the driver's seat. A roller chain connected the gear-box to the rear wheel. Ackermann steering controlled by a tiller was used, the driver's seat being arranged well forward and almost over the front axle. The air-cooled engine was said to develop 2 hp.

In 1896 Austin designed a second three-wheeler which differed in almost every way from the earlier model. It had the single wheel in front steered by a long tiller, and a small dog-cart body in which the driver and passenger sat back to back. In the original design a twin-cylinder water-cooled engine and epicyclic transmission were used, but this arrangement was found unsatisfactory. It was soon replaced by another, utilizing a single-cylinder horizontal engine, water-cooled with an air-cooled cylinder-head, and belt-transmission. The latter provided two forward speeds, obtained by means of two belts and fast and loose pulleys, a roller chain conveying the drive to an axle-casing which contained both a differential and a reduction gear. A spur-gear at the extremity of each half shaft drove a gear-wheel attached to the related road wheel. Not the least interesting feature of the design was the employment of independent rear suspension of the swing-axle type, each wheel being free to move in an arc, nearly vertically, against the compression of a coiled spring, without affecting the other wheel.

It is satisfactory to record that both the first and second Wolseley vehicles are still in existence in the Company's private museum, as is also the first four-wheeled Wolseley car. Built late in 1899, this car included features found in both the earlier vehicles, and in addition incorporated others which were to become customary in all Wolseley production models of the next six years or so. The engine was a horizontal single-cylinder unit of $3\frac{1}{2}$ hp, fitted with a detachable cylinder-head and an ingeniously designed water-jacket. A system of finned tubes in the forepart of the car formed an effective radiator. Trembler-coil ignition and a single-jet carburettor were used. Transmission between engine and gear-box was by means of a flat belt, and the three-speed sliding gear-box, having its shafts mounted on roller bearings, drove the countershaft which carried the differential. At the ends of the countershaft sprocket-wheels carried chains which drove the rear wheels. A form of 'gate' change was employed, sideways movement of the gear-lever selecting the required gear, and forward movement swinging the entire gear-box and tightening the belt, thus taking up the drive. Tiller-steering operated the front wheels on the usual Ackermann system, and a comfortable two-seater body was fitted. Pneumatic tyres were used on this car, as well as on the two earlier ones. The 1899 car performed extremely well in the historic Thousand Miles trial of the Automobile Club of Great Britain and Ireland in 1900, winning a number of awards; it undoubtedly formed the basis of the many subsequent successful Wolseley production models.

In America, Henry Ford (1863–1947), who had been developing his ideas on horseless carriages for at least six years, built his first car and had it running in 1896. This fact is mentioned on account of its importance for the great developments associated with the name of Henry Ford in the early years of the twentieth century. Sometimes referred to as a quadricycle, Ford's original car was fitted with a twin-cylinder four-stroke water-cooled engine. Belt transmission was employed, as was tiller steering, and the car ran on wire wheels shod with solid rubber tyres. A speed of 25–30 mph is said to have been reached. Ford's second car was built a few years later and ran successfully; it proved to be a considerable advance upon his first attempt. The Ford Motor Company was founded in 1903, from which time it has never looked back. Subsequent developments cannot be described here, but it is worthy of mention that between 1908 and 1927 more than 15 million Ford Model 'T' cars were made and sold; so satisfactory was this design that no major change was necessary during that long period. It was an all-time world's record for the production of a single model.

This account would not be complete without some mention of the work of the Renault brothers of Billancourt, France, and more particularly that of Louis Renault. Towards the end of 1898, being dissatisfied with the performance of his $1\frac{3}{4}$-hp De Dion-Bouton tricycle, Louis removed the air-cooled engine and fitted it in a four-wheeled car of his own design. This was a very lightly built vehicle incorporating an unusual type of three-speed gear-box, and transmission by means of a universally jointed shaft to the differential gear in the live axle. On the highest speed the drive was direct between the engine and the rear axle. This system he patented on 9 February 1899, and subsequently an attempt was made to impose a one per cent royalty on the retail catalogue price of every car sold by other makers who used this system. Since the use of chain-transmission was rapidly on the decline this would have resulted in a considerable fortune for the Renault firm, had not the patent been quashed eventually in the law-courts of both France and England.

From this original car, with its small air-cooled engine, the whole of the vast Renault business was developed in the early years of the twentieth century. A standard design was soon evolved and remained basically unaltered for many years, although a great variety of different models and sizes of cars were produced, all having a strong family resemblance, and all of them incorporating the basic features embodied in the first experimental car of Louis Renault.

V. THE MOTOR CYCLE

In 1885 Gottlieb Daimler patented the application of his high-speed petrol-engine to a bicycle, thus paving the way for the world's first motor cycle. Such a machine was designed and constructed, and its first trial took place, in 1886. Controversy exists as to whether it in fact ever ran with any degree of success, but its design contained a number of interesting features. The air-cooled single-cylinder engine was mounted vertically between the two wooden wheels of almost equal size, and drove the rear wheel by means of a round leather band which could be tightened by means of a jockey-pulley worked by a cord. This was in-geniously arranged so that when the brake on the rear wheel was applied the driving-band was slackened. Hot-tube ignition was used, with a specially de-signed surface carburettor. To assist in supporting the machine, which was very heavily and solidly constructed, two small rollers were provided near the driving-wheel. These could be lowered by the feet when required, but were normally clear of the ground. A form of friction-drive was incorporated in the engine-pulley so that slip would occur under any excessive load likely to cause the engine to stop.

In 1893 Hilderbrand and Wolfmüller of Germany built a motor bicycle which was fitted with a horizontal four-stroke twin-cylinder petrol engine, the rear wheel being driven directly by means of cranks and long connecting-rods from the engine. Pneumatic tyres were used. Series production of an improved model began in France in 1895, where the patent rights had been purchased. Several novel features were introduced, including a rear wheel of solid metal to act as a fly-wheel. Heavy rubber bands, stretched at each stroke of the pistons, were intended to assist on the return stroke and in overcoming the dead centre, as both pistons moved simultaneously in the same direction. As may be imagined, the result was an extremely jerky and unpleasant ride.

Meanwhile at the Puteaux works of De Dion-Bouton the Comte de Dion was experimenting with high-speed petrol engines, and in 1895 he fitted one of $\frac{1}{2}$-hp rating to an ordinary pedal tricycle and arranged a gear-drive to the rear axle. With the engine running at a speed of about 1500 rpm the results were extremely satisfactory, and it was not long before the motor tricycle became their principal product. Improved models followed, fitted with larger engines, until by 1900 a $2\frac{3}{4}$-hp size had become standard. However, the day of the motor tricycle was nearly over, for the two-wheeled machine possessed all the advantages save only that of stability, and no De Dion tricycles were made after 1901. Nor did they attempt to manufacture motor cycles instead, except in very small numbers, preferring to concentrate on the motor car, with which they soon achieved great success. Electric ignition was a feature of all De Dion petrol engines, from the very first of 1895.

Another machine that comes more nearly in the motor cycle class than the car class was the three-wheeled vehicle invented by the Frenchman Léon Bollée, and patented late in 1895. Early in 1896 he brought his first experimental model to England, where it aroused great interest. The tubular frame carried two seats arranged in tandem, the driver occupying the rear one. A small hand-wheel and a rack-and-pinion mechanism controlled the two front wheels for steering purposes, and a spade-handled lever at the driver's left hand performed several functions, as will appear. A large horizontal single-cylinder air-cooled engine, fired by hot-tube ignition, was mounted on the near side of the frame, the crank-shaft running across the centre of the machine and an extension of it forming the primary shaft of the three-speed sliding gear-box. On the opposite end of this shaft the fly-wheel was fixed. A single flat belt drove from the gear-box to a rim on the rear wheel, which was so mounted in the frame that it could be moved forwards to a limited extent. Fore-and-aft movement of the spade-handled control lever effected a corresponding movement of the rear wheel, this movement resulting in a slackening of the driving-belt and in bringing the belt-rim in contact with a large brake-block attached rigidly to the frame in front of the wheel. An ingenious feature of this arrangement was that the weight of the machine assisted the operation, as the pivoted wheel-mounting beneath the frame was over centre when the wheel was in the forward position. A locking device secured the lever in any desired position, and a twisting motion of the spade-handle selected any of the three gear-ratios. No reverse mechanism was fitted. These vehicles were very fast, won numerous awards in continental races, and remained popular for several years.

In 1896 Major Holden invented a novel form of four-cylinder engine which he applied to a motor cycle, and two years later the machine was placed on the market. A 24-in front wheel and a 20-in rear wheel, both with pneumatic tyres, were used, and between them the engine formed part of the frame. It consisted of two parallel steel tubes each containing two pistons connected together by a piston rod. A steel cross-bar was attached to the piston rods, the former passing through slots in the sides of the two cylinders and having pivoted to its extremities two long connecting-rods which were coupled to cranks on the axle of the rear wheel. Electric ignition was used. These machines gave very smooth running at a speed of about 20 mph. They were manufactured for several years and sold reasonably well; the later models were water-cooled.

Two Russians by birth, the brothers Werner, next claim our attention. Having settled in France, they conceived the idea of producing an ordinary type of safety bicycle fitted with a small high-speed petrol motor. They patented the idea of mounting the engine above the front wheel with a belt drive to the latter, and in 1897 manufacture of the Werner Motocyclette began. Shortly afterwards they sold the patents to an English firm, which began to manufacture the machine. In 1900 an improved design was patented in which the engine was placed in what has since come to be regarded as the most suitable position, that is, low down in the frame midway between the wheels. This resulted in lowering the centre of gravity, thus greatly reducing the tendency for side-slip to occur. The machine was now a practical proposition and sold in large numbers. Although the design was anticipated by Daimler some fifteen years earlier, he did nothing to develop it, and it is the brothers Werner whom we should regard as chiefly responsible for the motor cycle as we know it today.

BIBLIOGRAPHY

Autocar, Vols 1, 2, and 3. 1895–8.
Automot. J., Vols 1, 2, and 3. 1896–9.
BEAUMONT, W. W. 'Motor Vehicles and Motors' (2 vols). Constable, London. 1900, 1906.
BERSEY, W. C. 'Electrically Propelled Carriages.' London. 1898.

Bury, Viscount and Hillier, G. L. (Eds). 'Cycling.' London. 1891.

Duncan, H. O. 'The World on Wheels.' Published by the author, Paris. 1926.

Harmsworth, A. C. (Ed.). 'Motors and Motor Driving.' Longmans, Green, London. 1902.

Hasluck, P. N. 'The Automobile.' Cassell, London. 1902.

Jenkins, R. 'Motor Cars.' Fisher Unwin, London. 1902.

Karslake, K. 'Racing Voiturettes.' Motor Racing Publications, Abingdon-on-Thames. 1950.

Knight, J. H. 'Notes on Motor Carriages.' London. 1896.

Idem. 'Light Motor Cars and Voiturettes.' Iliffe, London. 1902.

Veteran Car Club Gazette, Vols 1, 2, 3, and 4. 1938–57.

Wallis-Tayler, A. J. 'Motor Cars.' London. 1897.

'A Bicycle made for Two.' (*1869 version.*)

19

CARTOGRAPHY AND AIDS TO NAVIGATION

D. H. FRYER

THE latter part of the nineteenth century was a period of intense activity in cartography; the output of new maps and charts was prodigious. In the field the days of the private practitioner were virtually ended and all activity was directed by the national survey departments. The great firms printing and publishing maps continued to flourish, however, and new ones came into being.

By 1850 the technique of surveying both on land and at sea was well established on firm principles and but little advance was made in work ashore, though the gradual replacement of sail by steam had a marked effect on work afloat. The difference in technique and outlook of the land and the sea surveyor makes it convenient to consider them separately.

I. CARTOGRAPHY

In Great Britain the progress of triangulation and detailed mapping by the Ordnance Survey was interrupted by the transfer of the whole survey organization to Ireland in 1824. The 6 inches to the mile map of Ireland was completed in 1846, the year that saw the publication of the first sheet of the 6-in map of Great Britain, which was not completed until 1891. Similarly the principal triangulation, resumed in 1838, was not completed until 1852. When the field work of the Irish Survey was completed (1840) there followed a long period of indecision ('The Battle of the Scales') lasting until 1863, concerning the most useful publication scales for our national maps. Ireland had been mapped on a scale of 6 in to the mile, but the southern part of England—all that had been mapped in Great Britain—was on a scale of 1 inch to the mile. Finally it was decided that, except for uncultivated areas which were to be surveyed on the 6-in scale, the standard scale was to be 1/2500, approximately 25 in to the mile, and that the smaller scales, 6 in and 1 in to the mile, should be reduced from the 25-in survey. The choice of scales for the large towns was also very controversial: at the end of the century larger towns had been surveyed on four different scales, 1/500, 1/528 (exactly 10 ft to the mile), 1/1056 (5 ft to the mile), and many on 1/2500 only.[1]

The method of surveying the third dimension and its representation on maps

---

[1] The scale now (1958) adopted for large towns is 1/1250 (approx. 50½ in to the mile).

was almost equally in dispute. Until 1837 heights were determined by observing vertical angles with the theodolite (trigonometrical levelling). However, a ray of light passing from one point to another on the Earth's surface is bent by refraction in the atmosphere and follows a curved path concave to the centre of the Earth. This fact was well known, and experiments had been made even before 1800 to determine the amount of the bending. It was also realized that if reciprocal vertical angles were observed simultaneously at each end of a line the mean value would be free from error caused by terrestrial refraction and data would be provided for calculating the coefficient of refraction under the meteorological conditions then prevailing. In 1833 the Ordnance Survey carried a line of reciprocal vertical angles from coast to coast in Ireland, for the dual purpose of comparing the tidal heights on the two coasts and of determining more accurately the coefficient of terrestrial refraction. Two years earlier a long line of spirit-levelling had been run between Sheerness and London Bridge, and in 1837–8 experiments in both Ireland and England fully demonstrated the superiority of spirit-levelling over trigonometrical levelling. The desirability of using mean sea-level as a datum instead of low spring-tide (used, for reasons of safety, on nautical charts), as previously adopted by the Irish survey, was also proved. Consequently, in 1839 spirit-levelling was adopted as the official method of fixing altitudes, and in the following year the primary levelling of England was begun with mean sea-level at Liverpool as the datum.[1]

Contours were drawn on a map in Britain in 1777. By this time they were well established in France[2] as the best means of depicting heights on maps, but the Ordnance Survey debated afresh the merits of the different methods from about 1841 onwards. The original 1-in maps of England and 6-in maps of Ireland showed spot-heights obtained trigonometrically during the primary triangulation, and also those observed during the chaining of the sides of the tertiary triangles to enable the chained lengths to be reduced to their true horizontal lengths. By applying the sine instead of the cosine to the vertical angle, vertical as well as horizontal distances between theodolite stations were obtained. In 1844 contouring was sanctioned for Ireland and in 1846 it was introduced into the English survey. There was much change of policy, but, generally speaking, in addition to the 50-ft contour, contours at 100-ft vertical intervals up to 1000 ft were surveyed instrumentally (that is, marked on the ground and then inserted on the map) and thence at 250-ft vertical intervals up to 2000 ft.

[1] In 1921 mean sea-level at Newlyn, Cornwall, was adopted.
[2] Earliest known contours were drawn on a chart of the English Channel by Philippe Buache in 1737.

All European national surveys had histories somewhat similar to that of the Ordnance Survey. France was the pioneer, her survey having been well established before 1800 by Cassini de Thury, but by 1850 most European countries had national surveys employing much the same surveying techniques and producing topographical maps of approximately 1 in to the mile. No other country, however, had a basic scale as large as the 6 in to a mile of the Ordnance Survey.

The development of cartography in India was very similar in date and method to that in Britain. James Rennell (1742–1830) made so good a survey of the Ganges in 1764 that in 1767 Clive appointed him the first Surveyor General of Bengal with instructions to produce a map of the province as soon as practicable. Rennell was so skilful as a practical surveyor and in putting together existing maps that ten years later he was able to retire to England, his task almost complete. The preparation of an atlas embracing all India was proposed by the new Surveyor General and many detached surveys were put in hand with this object. Though much was done, the isolated surveys lacked cohesion until William Lambton (1756–1823) set on foot, c 1800, the triangulation of the whole subcontinent, with the dual purpose of measuring an arc of meridian for geodetic purposes and of providing the framework on which all the topographical maps would depend. Thus was begun the Great Trigonometrical Survey, carried on assiduously side by side with the topographical survey, so that by 1900 the maps of India could compare very favourably with those of Europe.

Organized cartography in the United States proceeded on rather similar lines from 1807, when President Jefferson obtained authority for a trigonometrical survey of the coasts and harbours of the United States. A plan for the work submitted by Ferdinand Hassler, a Swiss engineer who had emigrated in 1805, was accepted. Hassler's absence in England and France obtaining instruments, and the outbreak of war with Britain (1812–14), delayed the start of the field work until 1816. Two years later it ceased from lack of funds and it was not until 1832 that the work of the United States Coast and Geodetic Survey[1] fell into its stride. In 1835 this body carried out its first hydrographic survey, and since then has surveyed the coasts of the United States both at sea and on land. From the first it has been based on triangulation, of which Hassler had had considerable experience in the Canton of Berne. Since the topographic work of the Survey is confined to coastal regions, most of the States prepared their own maps in the early part of the century, though, until 1830, none of them was based on triangulation. In addition there was much military surveying. Between 1867 and 1872 four different geological and geographical surveys were organized for exploring

---

[1] Originally known as the Coast Survey; it assumed its present title in 1878.

and mapping the continent, but all were amalgamated in the United States Geological Survey in 1879, which since then has been responsible for the topographical and geological mapping of the United States.

Mapping in Africa, Asia, and Australia followed the pattern that might be expected: a coast-line remarkably well delineated by early navigator-explorers, and an interior becoming gradually filled in from travellers' tales of lesser or greater accuracy, followed later by more detailed sketch-surveys and eventually, in the second half of the nineteenth century, by triangulated survey. Sir David Gill, within a year of being appointed to the observatory in the Cape of Good Hope in 1879, prepared a detailed and comprehensive scheme for the proper survey and mapping of South Africa. With the exception of the coastal regions which had been accurately charted, following the wreck of the *Birkenhead* in 1852, the only maps were compilations from farm surveys and a military sketch-map made between 1818 and 1825. Gill pointed out the scientific advantages of having an accurate triangulation of South Africa as the beginning of a chain of triangles along the 30th meridian, which would ultimately connect the Cape with the Mediterranean (p 442). This geodetic triangulation of South Africa was finished in 1905, but owing to wars and other difficulties the topographical survey was not even put in hand until this century.

By 1850 the general technique of land-surveying, both for geodetic and for topographical purposes, was well established: into an accurate framework of triangulation the topographical detail was inserted by plane-table, detail traverse, or chain-survey methods, the last being very suitable for countries such as the British Isles using a large scale as the basic scale of the survey. The method of surveying the topographical detail varies very much from country to country, and has been modified as new instruments have been invented and developed.

II. GEODESY AND THE WORLD MAP

Modern geodesy may be said to have begun in 1615 with Willebrord Snell's triangulated measurement of (roughly) a degree of latitude between Alkmaar and Bergen op Zoom, followed half a century later by Jean Picard's measurement in France (vol III, p 544). Eighteenth-century geodesy confirmed Newton's theory that the Earth was shaped like an oblate spheroid. Long arcs of the meridian and arcs roughly along parallels of latitude were measured in many countries before 1850, and were used progressively to compute 'figures of the Earth', usually stated in terms of the equatorial radius (the semi-axis major), a, and the compression, $c = (a-b)/a$, where b is the semi-axis minor. Of these figures the best known, perhaps, are those of Delambre ($c = 1/334$) in 1806, from which the length of the metre (one-millionth of the quadrant) was derived; of Airy (Astronomer Royal) ($c = 1/299 \cdot 3$) in 1830, which has been used when computing the triangulation of this country; of Everest (who completed Lamb-ton's arc through India) ($c = 1/300 \cdot 8$), also in 1830, which has been used in Indian surveys; and of Bessel ($c = 1/299 \cdot 2$) in 1841, whose figure is the basis of much continental mapping.

When degree measurements made in different countries are to be combined it is of the utmost importance that the relationship between the various national standards of length should be known. Comparisons of the English measures with the standards of Russia, Prussia, Belgium, Spain, Austria, and (later) the United States were made over a period of four years by A. R. Clarke (1828–1914), who in 1866 published the result of his investigations and the figure of the Earth he derived from them ($c = 1/295$), which has been used for maps of the United States and Canada.

The European standards had been based on the old 'toise of Peru', the standard used in the classical degree measurements in Finland and Peru (vol III, p 553), and it was most unfortunate that the French were unable to send a metre standard to Clarke to be included in his comparisons. Unknown to him, there were two metre standards in existence, the legal metre, defined by law as a fraction ($443 \cdot 296/864$) of the toise, and the metre of the Archives, a rather poor standard made of impure platinum. Endless trouble has been caused to geodesists by these two metres, and the situation was not improved when the *Bureau International des Poids et Mesures*, established in 1875 (after an international con-ference), made a copy of the imperfect metre of the Archives for the 'International Metre' which was intended for use in all future geodetic work.

One of the most important geodetic measurements undertaken in the later nineteenth century was that of the arc of the 30th meridian. The objective was a continuous measured arc from the Cape to Cairo. By 1905 the southern end of the arc through South Africa was completed (p 441), but its northern end, in Egypt, was not started until 1907. The field work of this ambitious project was finally completed in 1954 and, by connexion across the Mediterranean, there is now a complete arc measured from the Cape in 34° South latitude to the North Cape in 71° North latitude.

The significance of timing the swing of a pendulum as an indication of the shape of the Earth dates back to Richer, who in 1672 observed that near the equator it was necessary to shorten the pendulum of his clock to make it keep correct time. Although his reasoning was faulty, Huygens deduced from Richer's observations that the Earth was probably flattened at the poles. A Russian scientist, Sawitch, timed pendulum swings in the nineteenth century and from observations made at twelve stations computed the compression of the Earth to be 1 : 309. (Hayford's determination, 1910, adopted internationally in 1924, made it 1 : 297.)

It was early realized that in the vicinity of large mountain masses the plumb bob was deflected from its normal position. The deflexion at any point can be estimated by comparing the latitude and longitude observed astronomically (that is, referred to the local direction of gravity) with the geodetic latitude and longitude as computed through the triangulation (on the selected spheroid of reference) from the origin, where astronomic and geodetic latitude and longitude are assumed to be the same. Since the level surface is perpendicular to the direction of gravity, if sufficient of these comparisons are made it is possible to deduce the shape of the equipotential surface of the Earth (that is, the surface of an imaginary ocean, inserted under the land, covering the whole world at present sea level); this irregular surface, the geoid, being defined by the height of points on it above the particular spheroid of reference used in the computation. Measuring the relative

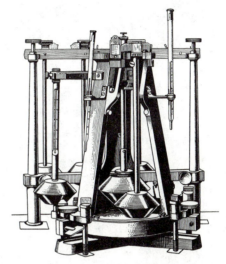

FIGURE 229—*von Sterneck's pendulum apparatus, c 1900. In use, the apparatus was enclosed to avoid draughts. The swing was recorded by light reflected from a mirror at the top of the pendulum.*

intensity of gravity by timing the swing of a standard pendulum can, if observations are made at a sufficient number of connected points, also provide data for determining the shape of the geoid.

By 1850 India had a reliable triangulation and, with the highest land mass in the world as its northern boundary, it is, perhaps, natural that the deflexion of the vertical was made the subject of early investigation. In 1854 J. H. Pratt [1], archdeacon of Calcutta, calculated that the deflexion due to the Himalayas was not so great as their visible mass would suggest, and it appeared to him as if the expected effect was compensated by some underlying deficiency of density. Sir George Airy postulated a different, flotation, theory that the Earth's crust, about 40 miles thick, floated on a liquid and that visible mountain masses were balanced by corresponding protuberances into the liquid. Of the many theories that have been advanced since then to explain the balance or compensation, probably the best known is that of 'isostasy' developed, from Pratt's, by the American geodesist J. F. Hayford in the early part of this century. From 1865 to 1872 a very thorough series of pendulum observations was made in India by Basevi and Heaviside. The apparatus illustrated (figure 229) is of a later type than that used by them. Similar work in many countries has continued and has been greatly augmented since 1920 by observations made afloat, chiefly from submarines.

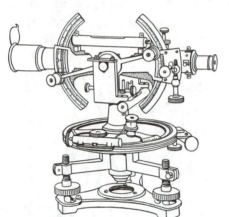

FIGURE 230—'Everest' theodolite, as used in the survey of India, introduced by Sir George Everest (c 1840).

III. LAND-SURVEYING INSTRUMENTS

Considering the intense surveying activity throughout the nineteenth century it is rather surprising that there was so little improvement in the two basic surveying instruments, the theodolite and the level.

Much good work was done from 1787 to 1853 with the 3-ft theodolite of the Ordnance Survey built by Jesse Ramsden (vol IV, p 604), but very few of these mammoth instruments were made. All the instruments used for precise work were large and cumbersome by modern standards, 10- or 12-in horizontal circles being quite common. Telescopes were invariably focused externally, and in many theodolites they could not be rotated completely about the horizontal axis; instruments permitting this rotation were designated transit theodolites. Telescope diaphragms were usually fitted with spider webs to define the line of collimation until, towards the end of the century, glass reticules with engraved cross-'hairs' were introduced. Four foot-screws were most commonly used for levelling the instruments, but the 'Everest' theodolite (largely used in the survey of India) had three foot-screws only (figure 230). Precise reading of the circles was usually by vernier, though micrometers reading to one second were frequently used for the larger instruments.

Until W. Gravatt introduced the 'Dumpy' level (c 1848), the levels in common use were Y-levels, cumbersome instruments with telescopes 20 in or more long. The innovations introduced by Gravatt were: (a) the telescope, about 12 in long, with an object glass of large aperture and short focal length and a high-power eye-piece; (b) provision of a small cross-level, at right-angles to the main level, which greatly facilitated the setting up of the instrument; and (c) fitting of a small mirror at the end of the bubble so that the observer could check its setting without moving from the observing position. It is curious that this last very desirable innovation appeared only in the original, and was discarded in the 'improved' models that followed it. In the Y-level the telescope could be rotated through 180° about its axis in the Ys, thus enabling a ready adjustment, or allowance, to be made for any error in the line of collimation. This feature, considered essential for precise work, was included later in W. F. Stanley's 'Improved Dumpy Level'.

Gradiometers—virtually levels fitted with a graduated micrometer tilting-screw under the eye-piece—were on the market before the turn of the century. Strangely, this device (though with smaller scope) was never embodied in instruments until the twentieth century, to produce the modern 'tilting level'.

IV. OPTICAL: SUBTENSE, MEASUREMENT OF DISTANCE

The subtense principle, that $S = \dfrac{D}{2} \cot \dfrac{\alpha}{2}$ (figure 231), can be utilized in instruments in several ways. In some the angle α is fixed and a variable distance D is read on a graduated staff; others employ a fixed distance D and a varying angle α, or its tangent, is measured at the instrument.

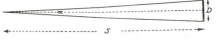

Although W. Gascoigne fitted a diaphragm with movable hairs in a telescope in 1639, the first surveying instrument for

FIGURE 231—*Subtense measurement.*

subtense measurement appears to have been that used by Brander at Augsburg in 1764. James Watt is said to have constructed such an instrument, and to have used it in Scotland in 1771. Another pioneer was W. Green, an optician, who in 1778 placed a micrometer in the focus of the eye-piece of a theodolite telescope. He devised two types of micrometer: one had lines ruled at fixed distances apart and the other had one fixed line and one adjustable one whereby the 'fixed' angle α (figure 231) could be set as desired. His book described the instrument and the method of its use, which is now known as tachymetric survey. This method of surveying never became as popular in this country as it did overseas. In 1866 D. R. Edgeworth patented his 'stadiometer' in which two hairs were placed in the diaphragm of the telescope of an instrument somewhat akin to a theodolite, 'distant from one another a hundredth part of the focal length of the object glass. . . . The hairs can be adjusted by means of screws from observation on a staff at a known distance.' Neither Green nor Edgeworth was aware of the optical problems involved, though these were known on the continent. As early as 1823 J. Porro of Milan had introduced the anallatic telescope into an instrument called a tachymeter. Briefly, an extra or 'anallatic' lens is inserted in the theodolite, whereby the subtense distance obtained is from the staff to the vertical axis of the instrument instead of to a point at a variable distance, $f+c$ (about 18 in), in front of the axis (figure 232).

Edgeworth also cautioned that when surveying over precipitous ground, that is, when the staff is at an elevation or depression exceeding 15°(!) from the

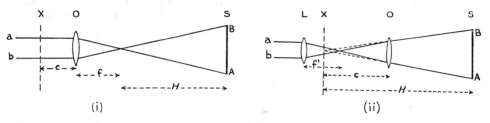

FIGURE 232—*Stadia subtense measurement.* (i) *With ordinary external-focus telescope;* (ii) *with anallatic lens.* X = *vertical axis of theodolite;* O = *object-glass with focal length* f; a, b = *stadia hairs;* S = *staff on distant object;* L = *anallatic lens with focal length* f'; c = *distance* X *to* O; H = *horizontal distance measured;*

$$LO = f' + \frac{fc}{f+c}.$$

instrument, normal procedure must be abandoned and the staff held perpendicular to the line of sight, after which the normal slope correction must be applied.

The tangent method of tachymetry can be used to obtain the horizontal distance OV by the formula $OV = \dfrac{AB}{(\tan\theta - \tan\phi)}$ (figure 233). This relation was used by the German engineer C. Eckhold in his 'omnimeter' (British patent 1859). In figure 233 AV and ZH are both perpendicular to the horizontal line OV, and it can be seen that $\dfrac{OV}{OH} = \dfrac{AB}{XY}$, or $OV = \dfrac{OH \times AB}{XY}$. The omnimeter was somewhat similar to a theodolite, with a horizontal arc and foot-screws for levelling, but instead of a vertical arc it carried a bar, OH, perpendicular to the vertical axis of the instrument and parallel to the plane of rotation of the telescope. A sensitive level attached to the bar allowed it to be set accurately in the horizontal plane. ZH was a finely graduated scale, perpendicular to OH, which was read by a microscope attached rigidly to the main telescope, their lines of collimation being parallel. AB was a rod carrying two sighting marks A and B, which was held vertically on the object being observed. In use the instrument was directed on B, and after the bar was levelled the telescope was sighted in turn on A and B and readings were taken to X and Y on the scale. A micrometer attachment enabled these readings to be made to 0·002 mm. In the original model AB was 3 metres and OH was 20 cm, so that the horizontal distance OV was given in metres by the formula $\dfrac{600}{(XH-YH)\text{ mm}}$. This instrument gave good results and survived in an improved form until the end of the century. But, as can be seen, the readings XH and YH are merely the tangents of θ and ϕ, which can be found just as readily from a table of tangents after vertical angles have been observed with an ordinary theodolite.

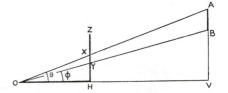

FIGURE 233—*Diagram to illustrate the 'omnimeter' tangent method of tachymetry.*

V. BASE-MEASURING EQUIPMENT

General Roy's base-line on Hounslow Heath was re-measured in 1791 by Colonel Williams using a special chain made by Jesse Ramsden; the same chain was used to measure five bases of verification before 1806. Generally, however, geodesists in the nineteenth century preferred to use rigid bars for measuring base-lines. Wooden rods and glass rods were replaced by metal bars, and all the ingenuity of invention was centred on the accurate determination of the temperature of the apparatus and hence its exact length while the measurement was being made.

Jäderin of Stockholm in 1880 revolutionized former practice by suspending steel tapes between tripods, making use of the fact that a wire extended between supports at a constant tension will always take up the same catenary curve. Consequently, other conditions being the same, the distance between the supports will be a constant.[1] By this method uneven sites, with a bare minimum of clearing, can be used without loss of precision. Tripods at set intervals are aligned along the base, and the chord-distances between fiducial marks, scribed on the measuring head of each tripod, are measured by the tape or wire kept at a constant tension either by weights or by spring balances. To overcome uncertainty about the exact temperature and length of the wire, two were used, one of brass and the other of steel, the double measurement being used as a bimetallic thermometer for the correction of the whole length.

Revolutionary as this invention has been, its value was doubled by the re-

[1] $D = L\left(1 - \dfrac{W^2}{24F^2}\cos^2\theta\right)$, where L is the length, W the weight of the unsupported tape, F the tension (in the same units as the weight) applied at the ends of the wire, and θ the angle of slope between the supports.

searches of Benoît, Guillaume, and Hopkins of the *Bureau International des Poids et Mesures*, who found (1896) that an alloy (which they named invar) of steel and nickel (36%) had an infinitesimal coefficient of expansion (less than 0·000 000 5 per °F). All modern geodetic base lines since then have been measured by invar tapes or wires supported in catenary.

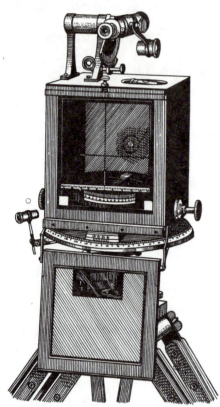

FIGURE 234—*Bridges Lee photo-theodolite* (back view).

VI. ELECTRIC TELEGRAPH. PHOTOGRAPHY

Two other nineteenth-century inventions, though primarily important for other reasons, have had a tremendous influence on surveying techniques. The *electric telegraph* (1837) covered the world with a network of cables crossing oceans as well as land. Although now rendered obsolete by radio, wire telegraphy greatly improved the reliability of all geodetic determinations of longitude. By means of the telegraph the time at the place of reference (preferably Greenwich Observatory) could be conveyed almost instantaneously to the place of observation, whereas formerly it had to be carried, literally, by means of a chronometer, whose accuracy might well be impaired by its long journey from the place of origin.

Photography was not long invented before it was used for surveying. Laussedat, of the French army, experimenting from 1851, completed a photographic survey of a small village near Versailles in 1861. This method of surveying resembles plane-table survey and field-sketching. The normal plane-table methods of intersection and resection which would have been employed in the field are applied in the drawing-office to photographs taken at various stations, and are supplemented by a few angles observed with the theodolite at each camera site. Alternatively a combined photo-theodolite may be used. Figure 234 shows a pioneer type introduced by J. Bridges Lee in 1895. In this model the appropriate part of the compass-card and an angular scale, left and right of the optical axis of the camera, appeared on each photograph. Large areas were surveyed by these methods in the Rocky Mountains after 1888, and shortly afterwards Swiss, German, and Russian surveyors made considerable photographic surveys. The chief contemporary interest of this method is that it paved the way for the modern technique of survey from the air; in fact, surveys by photography from captive balloons were made in the latter half of the century, the earliest being by Laussedat himself (1858).

VII. CHARTS AND HYDROGRAPHIC SURVEYING

The expansion of oversea trade during the nineteenth century, and, in the latter half of the century, the increase in size of ships, created a demand for more and better charts. The improvement in the technique of geodetic surveying provided, in many cases, a reliable means of relating map to chart, though in most regions, right up to the end of the century, the hydrographic surveyor was on the scene long before the land surveyor.

The Hydrographic Department of the British Admiralty. Although organized hydrography had been established in France in the middle of the eighteenth century it was not until 1795 that the Board of Admiralty decided that to require commanding officers to supply their own charts was not the most satisfactory way of safeguarding naval vessels. Alexander Dalrymple was appointed Hydrographer to the Board 'with the duty of collecting and compiling all information requisite for improving navigation, for the guidance of Commanders of H.M. Ships'. At first this was all the newly established office did; not until 1801 did it issue orders (to Matthew Flinders in the *Reliance*) for hydrographic surveys to be made. Since 1808, when Dalrymple was succeeded by Thomas Hurd, the post of Hydrographer of the Navy has always been held by a naval officer who has specialized in surveying. During Hurd's term of office the surveying service may be said to have been born; in 1814 two surveying ships appear in the Navy List for the first time; by 1823, when Hurd died, twelve ships were employed in surveying. One of the last administrative acts of Hurd was to make the Admiralty charts available to the merchant navy and the public, instead of reserving them exclusively for H.M. ships.

By 1850 the Hydrographic Department, well organized by Beaufort,[1] was able to cope with the tremendous amount of new information coming in from the surveying ships, and also to co-ordinate and publish the vast amount of data that had accumulated at the Admiralty through the years, including the valuable surveys made by the Honourable East India Company. This accumulation of

---

[1] Rear-Admiral Sir Francis Beaufort, F.R.S., Hydrographer of the Navy, 1829-55.

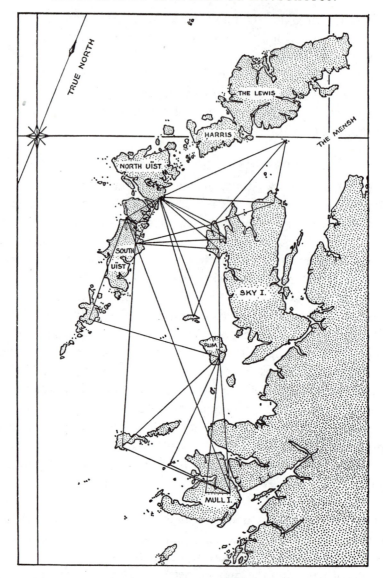

FIGURE 235—*Part of chart of the west coast and Western Islands by Murdoch Mackenzie (senior), published 1775, showing his triangulation for connecting the Inner and Outer Hebrides.*

data, and the growth of the work of the hydrographic department through the last half of the century, are indicated by the annual catalogue of Admiralty charts, which listed 1748 navigation charts in 1849 and 3413 in 1900.

Hydrographic surveying. The control of a hydrographic survey of a harbour or coastal region is very similar to that of a land survey, and is usually fixed by triangulation built up from a measured base. Where an enclosed bay enables the area under survey to be surrounded by triangulation stations the similarity is complete, but more often the hydrographic survey will extend along a fairly straight stretch of coast. In this case the control will be from a chain of coastal triangulation, necessarily confined to one side of the survey, though the triangula-

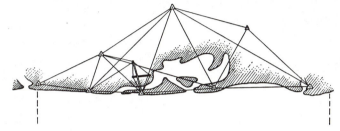

FIGURE 236—*Triangulation for a hydrographic survey off a straight stretch of coast.*

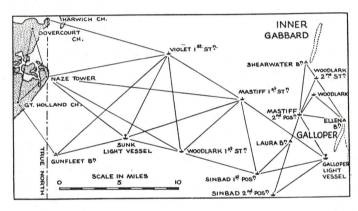

FIGURE 237—*Floating triangulation for fixing position of Galloper Shoal, 1840, by George Thomas, R.N.*

tion may be extended seaward by means of anchored ships or floating beacons (figures 235, 236, and 237). Angular measurement ashore is by theodolite, but, since this instrument cannot be used afloat, angles are observed on board the ships or boats with the sextant.

In cases where it was inconvenient or impossible to penetrate into the hinterland, the coastal chain of triangulation could be extended along the coast by using the ship as an unvisited triangulation station. Since such a station was not steady the observations ashore had to be instantaneous and were usually coordinated by a signal made from the ship. For the main triangulation no angles would be observed on board, but secondary stations might be intersected by sextant angles from the ship while anchored in the positions required by the triangulation (figure 238).

The linear measurement to determine the scale of these triangulations would be, whenever possible, either a base-line measured ashore by orthodox means, or one adopted from the local land survey, should that prove practicable; but frequently the measurements were made afloat by different methods [2]: (i) by subtense, measuring the angle subtended by the mast of the ship, anchored at one end of the base, from a boat at the other end; (ii) by sound, timing at one

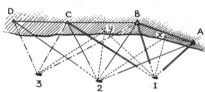

FIGURE 238—*Use of ship in triangulation when hinterland is inaccessible.* (A, B) *Known stations;* (C, D) *new stations;* (1, 2, 3) *successive positions of ship;* (x, y) *secondary stations intersected from ship.*

end of the base the interval between the flash and the report of a gun fired at the other; (iii) by log, measuring the distance between two positions afloat; and (iv) by computing the distance between two astronomically observed positions. Methods (i) and (ii) measured, of necessity, short bases that could be extended when necessary by base-extension triangulation; with (iii) and (iv), however, long bases were desirable, if possible between the extremes of the survey. Methods (iii) and (iv) were frequently combined to provide the scale for the 'running' surveys by which the coast-line was delineated by the early navigators and explorers.

The control systems outlined above were standardized during Beaufort's time as Hydrographer of the Navy and were generally followed by 1850, but in the early part of the century there was much diversity of practice. Figure 235 is from a survey of 1753, when most charts were being constructed from 'running' surveys.

Before leaving the subject of control it should again be stated that right up to the end of the century hydrographic surveying frequently preceded land survey; even when this was not so, the land-survey control points were often too distant to be of much use to the hydrographic surveyor. However, there were cases of very close co-operation between land and sea surveyors: for instance, in Shetland in 1817, between George Thomas in the *Investigator* and Colby of the Ordnance Survey.

Soundings were obtained by lead and line, in which a lead weight of 10–14 lb was attached to a hemp line marked in fathoms (and, towards the end of the century, in feet). Each cast of the lead gave a direct measurement from water-level to sea-bottom, but supplied precise information only of the area—about 4 sq in—covered by the lead. The chance of missing a pinnacle of rock was always great, and this mischance could be avoided only by close sounding and vigilance in examining any surface indication that might be caused by rocks or shoals close to the surface. The fact that so few dangers to navigation did escape the notice of the early surveyors is truly remarkable, especially since, with so much of the world uncharted, in coastal surveys quantity tended to become more important than quality. As late as 1877 the Hydrographer, Sir Frederick Evans, remarked that 'the importance of sounding is not sufficiently considered by young surveyors. They should recognise that this is the real test of a chart' [3]. As a depth of 10 fathoms is about the greatest obtainable by a good leadsman from a moving vessel, for greater depths the vessel had to be stopped for each cast of the lead. Later, in steamships, a heavy lead could be 'hove' by a winch and depths up to about 40 fathoms obtained without stopping the ship.

The leads always had a hollow in the bottom in which could be inserted an arming of tallow, which would bring to the surface a specimen of the sea bed. The nature of the bottom is always shown on the chart, since it can help the mariner to determine his position in fog, or to select a place for anchoring where holding properties are good.

From early in the century the datum used for the soundings was the depth at low-water spring tides, a safety precaution to ensure that the mariner would never (or seldom), under any conditions of the tide, encounter in any position less water than that charted.

In the second half of the century there was much interest in the depths of the oceans, both for laying transoceanic telegraph cables and for scientific purposes. Many difficulties are encountered in deep sounding, one of the greatest being that of recovering the heavy lead that has to be used. Lieutenant Brooke, U.S.N., invented a device in 1854 in which the 'lead' was a light tube with weights attached which were released automatically when the bottom was struck [4]. Other similar devices were evolved, the Baillie rod and sinker being the type eventually adopted by the Royal Navy (figure 243) [5]. Another difficulty arose from the sudden strains put on the line by the surging of the ship in the sea; these were minimized by leading the sounding line through a block secured to the yard-arm or derrick by an elastic strop [6].

These deep soundings were made with hemp lines, but in 1872 William Thomson (later Lord Kelvin) tested a sounding-machine using piano wire (p 461). He was enthusiastic about it, but the Admiralty was not at first convinced and the *Challenger*, which sailed on her celebrated oceanographic voyage at the end of 1872, carried out all her deep-sea sounding with hemp lines [4]. However, by the end of the century all deep-sea sounding was carried out by wire sounding-machines (p 461).

Until about 1860 practically all hydrographic surveying was carried out from sailing-ships, and it might be said that almost the only innovation in the art during the latter half of the century was the adaptation of steam to the service of the surveyors. While greatly expediting the work, steam-propulsion made practically no difference to the technique. Even at the end of the century most British surveying ships still carried sails as an auxiliary.

Although a sea-map is the most important product of the hydrographic surveyor's work it is not the only one. Observation of water-movements, both vertical and horizontal, provides data for the Admiralty tide tables (published regularly since 1830), and for the charts of tidal streams and currents. Sailing directions are a necessary accompaniment to a chart, giving the mariner useful information that cannot readily be gleaned from it.

The Hydrographic Department supplies details of all lighthouses in the world in the Admiralty List of Lights, published annually since 1895. In addition, new hydrographic information—the discovery of an uncharted rock or an alteration of the light characteristic of a lighthouse—is promulgated immediately in 'Notices to Mariners', the regular issue of which began in 1857.

This brief account of hydrographic surveying may appear rather insular, but in writing of the nineteenth century such an emphasis is justifiable. Apart from the seaboards of the United States, and of France and the French empire, there were few parts of the seven seas that were not charted by British seamen (including those of the Honourable East India Company, later the Royal Indian Navy), and from its foundation the Hydrographic Department set out to supply charts of the whole world.

VIII. OTHER AIDS TO NAVIGATION

Essential as the chart and other hydrographic publications are, certain other aids to navigation are equally vital. They may be divided into two groups: (i) those carried in ships, such as compass, sextant, chronometer, log, and lead line; and (ii) those set up on or from the shore for the mariner's benefit, such as lighthouses, buoys, leading-marks, and time-signals.

Compasses. Comparatively little thought seems to have been devoted to the improvement of this fundamental aid until the eighteenth century was well advanced, when Gowin Knight (1713–72) discovered how the magnetic flux of compass-needles and other magnets could be increased (vol III, pp 523–4, 555). Yet since he failed to understand the importance of equalizing the moments of inertia of the compass-card and needles about all diameters, his improved compasses, like others at that time, were very unsteady in bad weather.

It was long before it was realized how seriously the iron in a ship affected its compasses; even Captain Cook is reported to have kept iron keys in the binnacle. It was not until the early nineteenth century that Flinders (p 449) made the first scientific investigation of this 'deviation' of the compass. He discovered the effect of the soft iron of the ship, and the means of correcting it; the corrector for this component of the ship's magnetism is still called the 'Flinders bar'. Investigations continued, and in 1837 the Admiralty appointed a committee to inquire into the whole question of compasses for the Royal Navy. This committee emphasized the importance of placing the compass in such a position that errors caused by the ship's magnetic properties would be minimal; with the relatively small amount of iron used in ship-building at the time suitable positions were easy to find. The committee further recommended that compasses should not be corrected (by correcting magnets), but that the compass error should be determined at very frequent intervals during a voyage and allowed for in the normal way when laying off bearings and courses. This committee also designed a compass which was adopted by the Royal Navy and by several foreign ones, and used as the azimuth compass, that is, as the compass from which bearings of objects, terrestrial or celestial, could be observed and which was used for navigating (as opposed to steering) the ship; from this time such a compass was known as the *standard compass*. The first standard compass had a paper card, of $7\frac{1}{2}$-in diameter, stiffened with mica, set upon four parallel needles made of rectangular steel laminations, and so disposed that the moment of inertia in the east–west plane equalled that in the north–south. This card was set in a thick copper bowl.

Until about 1820 the azimuth compass was mounted on a tripod and moved about the ship as necessary; later it was mounted on a permanent pillar of wood or brass, which retained the name binnacle (from the Portuguese *bitacola*, small shelter) originally given to the cupboard in which the compasses were set.

The Admiralty standard compass, although successful for a time in the Royal Navy, was not altogether satisfactory in merchant ships which, possibly carrying a highly magnetic cargo on one voyage and a non-magnetic one on the next, needed a compass that could be adjusted. Accordingly in 1855 the Liverpool compass committee of shipowners and scientists was formed to investigate the magnetic conditions and compass errors of merchant ships. By 1862 this committee had presented three reports to the Board of Trade, one of the most important recommendations being that a thorough working knowledge of magnetism and compass-correction should be obligatory for all commanders and navigators of British merchant ships.

The modern compass dates from 1876, when Sir William Thomson patented his dry-card compass, embodying in a practical way his own findings with those of previous investigators (plate 31 C). It was chiefly remarkable for employing much lighter needles and cards than had previously been thought necessary. Thomson used eight light needles secured rather like the rungs of a rope ladder to silk threads radiating from a pivot—a small inverted aluminium cup with a sapphire crown—to a light aluminium ring 10 inches in diameter. Similar threads also supported the compass-card composed of paper sectors. The whole card, weighing only 180 grains (compared with 1525 grains of the Admiralty standard compass), revolved upon a fine iridium point soldered to the top of a thin brass wire attached to the bottom of the compass-bowl. Excellent though this new compass was, it was the binnacle in which it was supported that was most revolutionary and advantageous; it contained provision for correcting magnets, soft iron spheres, and the Flinders bar, which are necessary for compensating the effect of the ship's magnetism. The Thomson compass was speedily introduced into the Royal Navy and larger merchant ships, and gave great satisfaction. When the increased speed of ships caused sufficient vibration to disturb the compass seriously, springs were incorporated in the gimbal suspension (which had been in use since the sixteenth century).

Liquid compasses. Filling the compass-bowl with liquid steadies the card when the ship is in violent motion and, if the card be made buoyant, greatly diminishes friction on the pivot. First suggested by Ingenhousz (1730–99) in 1779, liquid compasses were in use by the Danes in 1830. In 1845 they were supplied to the Royal Navy for use in bad weather. Towards the end of the century excessive vibration in small, fast ships, and the shock of gunfire, necessitated a liquid compass, though it was not until 1906 that it superseded the Thomson compass for all ships in the Navy. In merchant ships the Thomson compass remains in use as a standard compass to this day, though many ships have adopted the steadier liquid compass as a steering compass (if they have not fitted the modern gyro-compass, which first appeared in practical form in Germany in 1906).

Throughout the nineteenth century compass-cards were graduated in points (eight points to each quadrant of the circle) and in degrees, though many compasses used by smaller ships were graduated in points only. A pointer, called the 'lubber's point', attached rigidly to the compass-bowl, indicates the position of the ship's head.

The Sextant. In general design the octant, also known as the quadrant, and navigator's sextant have remained unaltered since Hadley introduced his quadrant in 1731. Octants (vol III, p 555) made of wood, with an ivory graduated arc and a vernier reading to 30 seconds, remained in use until well into the second half of the nineteenth century, though brass ones were made before 1800. In 1757 Campbell had a metal sextant constructed, with an arc graduated to 120°, and with Ramsden's improvements the sextant gradually superseded the octant. Sextants were preferred because the 90° arc of the octant was frequently insufficient in extent for lunar observations and usually did not have sufficiently precise graduations. Sextants were invariably made of metal; throughout the century they were graduated to 10 seconds of arc and were supplied with telescopes.

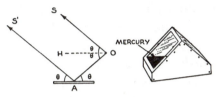

FIGURE 239—*Artificial horizon.* (Left) *Theory; observed angle* SOA = 2 SOH (*the apparent altitude*); (*right*) *mercury type with glass roof in place.*

Artificial horizons. In the latter half of the eighteenth century, particularly before the advent of reliable time-signals in all important ports, navigators would ascertain the errors of their chronometers by astronomical observations for time, made at certain observation-points whose geographical co-ordinates were accurately known and listed in books of nautical tables and other publications. Usually the Sun was observed before noon and the chronometer-time noted; after noon the chronometer-time was again taken when the Sun was at the same altitude; the mean of these times (subject to an allowance for the change in the Sun's declination) gave the chronometer-time of the Sun's meridian passage. Since the longitude of the place of observation was known, the error of the chronometer could be calculated. Such an observation when made, as was usual, with a sextant required an artificial horizon, because the sea horizon would almost certainly be obscured. Although proposed by George Adams in 1748 (vol III, p 556) the instrument was not made in practical form until the end of the eighteenth century, when it appeared as a small tray of mercury covered with a glass roof to prevent disturbances from the wind. It was used in this form throughout the nineteenth century, though simpler ones of black glass, about 4 by 3 in, levelled by spirit-levels and levelling screws, were also devised. The sextant altitude observed in the artificial horizon is, after the index error has been applied, double the true altitude, uncorrected for refraction (figure 239).

A different type of artificial horizon is desirable on board ship when the sea horizon is obscured by mist or fog. Only a year after Hadley's quadrant appeared, John Elton proposed fitting two spirit-levels to the sextant to enable the observer to hold his instrument truly horizontal; twenty years later John Robertson mentions an invention of a spinning-top with a glass upper surface (a gyroscopic artificial horizon); and, in the middle of the nineteenth century, two different pendulum devices were tried. None of these devices proved successful at sea.

Chronometers and time-signals. From the beginning of scientific navigation accurate determination of longitude was its most difficult problem (vol III, pp 551–2, 557, 672). The most profitable lines of research followed were: (i) the design and manufacture of a really reliable timepiece, and (ii) the compilation of accurate lunar tables whereby the distance of the Moon from the Sun, planets, or bright stars could be found for any time at Greenwich. By observing the 'lunar distance' with a sextant the local time of the observation as shown on the ship's timepiece (checked by solar observations) could be compared with the Greenwich time as shown in or computed from the tables, the difference between the two times giving the longitude. This solution of the problem appears to have been first suggested by Johann Werner (1468–1528) of Nuremberg in 1514, and the Royal Observatory at Greenwich was established in 1675 very largely to further it.

Harrison (vol III, p 672) produced his first timepiece, which underwent successful trials, in 1735 and his fourth chronometer, a very handy instrument rather like a large watch, in 1761. This was still more successful, and convinced thoughtful mariners that the problem was solved.[1] Yet the Board of Longitude continued to develop the lunar method. In 1755 they accepted, as accurate to one minute of arc, lunar tables prepared by J. T. Mayer (1723–62) of Göttingen, and in 1767 the first British 'Nautical Almanac', containing such information, was published. In 1800 few ships carried chronometers, but by 1850 nearly every properly equipped vessel carried and used them. However, lunar distances were still observed until the end of the century, though latterly only as a check on a possibly faulty chronometer. Tables of lunar distances were printed in the 'Nautical Almanac' until 1908.

The invention of the electric telegraph greatly increased the accuracy of longitude determinations ashore, and also facilitated the transmission of correct time from the nearest observatory to the ports; hence time-signals, from which the navigator could check and rate his chronometers, became both more precise and more numerous. Such time-signals were usually of the type erected over Greenwich Observatory: a large ball dropped down a mast, frequently in conjunction with the firing of a gun.

Logs. In the second half of the century the navigator was well equipped for

---

[1] Contemporary with Harrison's fourth chronometer were successful experiments carried out by the French with chronometers constructed by P. Leroy and F. Berthoud (vol IV, pp 409–15).

determining his position at sea, but this did not lessen the importance of keeping 'dead reckoning' of courses steered and distances run, because days—sometimes weeks—might pass with no opportunity for astronomical observation.

In 1800 two methods of estimating the distance run were in use; that favoured by the English and most others was the log (log chip or logship), a triangular piece of wood, weighted and secured to the log-line so as to float upright in the water, the log-line being a light line marked at regular intervals by knots (vol III, p 549). In well ordered ships the log was hove at the end of every hour; when thrown overboard it remained stationary in the water while the ship sailed on for the period indicated by a sand-glass. The distance travelled in this time was reckoned by the number of knots of the line that had passed over the stern of the ship, and from this the speed could be calculated. Knowing the speed at hourly intervals and also the weather conditions, a very close estimate of the distance the ship had travelled through the water during each watch could be made. Originally the knots were spaced 42 ft apart and the sand-glass ran for 30 seconds; in 1860 in ships of the Royal Navy and in most others a 28-seconds glass was used and the knots on the line were 47·3 ft apart.

In the other method, favoured by the Dutch, the time to sail past a floating object was noted. Towards the end of the eighteenth century marks 40 ft apart were placed on the ship's side and the time, in half-seconds, between the forward and the after marks passing some spume was noted, either by a watch or by reciting some doggerel verse; 48 divided by this number gave the speed of the ship in sea-miles per hour (knots).

The crude but effective logship-and-line was in use until the end of the nineteenth century, but even before 1800 search was being made for an instrument that would record the distance, rather than the speed, of travel through the water. There is record of two 'perpetual' logs being tried by Captain Phipps in 1773; both consisted of helices of copper or wood towed through the water, their revolutions being transmitted inboard by means of their towing-lines and recorded on dials. No such instruments proved popular before the 'Massey Patent Log' [7] appeared and was adopted by the Royal Navy and larger merchant ships. In this log, both rotator—a cylinder with vanes—and recorder were towed by a line sufficiently long to keep them clear of the eddies in the wake of the ship. The recorder was prevented from rotating by fish-tail vanes, and recorded the revolutions of the rotator on dials in terms of distance run (figure 240). In 1861 Walker produced another log, which had a rotator similar to that of the Massey but with a longer rotating line, so that the recording apparatus could be secured to the ship's rail. Thus the distance run could be read off the dials without having to haul the log inboard. Walker's log became the more popular, though both remained in use until about the end of the century, when they proved rather unreliable in the new high-speed ships. Soon after 1900, however, Walker invented a log of similar pattern capable of accuracy at high speeds. All self-recording logs were operated by a propeller of some kind, and it was early recognized that the revolutions of the ship's paddle-wheels or propeller, particularly in those ships which maintained a fairly constant draught, as, for example, warships and cross-channel packets, could give an equally good indication of the distances travelled through the water.

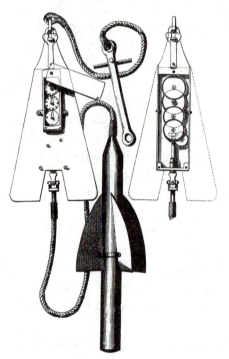

FIGURE 240—*Massey's patent log, c 1840. The log was towed by a long line attached to it.*

Lead lines and sounding machines. The lead line (p 452) is perhaps the oldest of all aids to navigation. Knowledge of the depth serves the mariner in two ways, first as a warning that he may be standing into danger, and, second, provided sufficient offshore soundings are shown on the chart, as a reliable indication of the ship's position. In bad visibility a line of soundings obtained at regular intervals can be plotted on tracing-paper and moved about until they fit those shown on the chart, giving a position which may be partially confirmed by the specimen of the bottom brought up by the arming of the lead (p 453).

The hand lead could not give reliable soundings from a moving ship in depths greater than 10 fathoms, and a device for deep-sounding from a moving ship was thus obviously desirable, since much time and labour were involved in stopping the ship for a cast of the deep-sea lead. Massey seems to have been the first with a practical solution, his 'sounding fly' [7] preceding his patent log. The 'fly', which replaced the lead, was a tubular weight to which were attached a propeller and a recorder which registered, in terms of depth, its revolutions while the fly descended from the surface to the bottom. An ingenious device released the propeller when the fly hit the water and locked it again when it hit the bottom (figure 241). A contemporary invention which was more acceptable to the

Admiralty at the time was Burt's 'buoy and nipper' [8]. The lead line was rove through a buoy; if the line was paid out quickly the buoy remained stationary in the water as the ship sailed away and the lead dropped vertically from the buoy to the bottom. A spring catch jammed the line when the lead hit the bottom, and when the apparatus was hauled on board the depth could be read off. Both devices remained in use and others were invented. In the ingenious self-registering lead of Erichsen or Ericsson (1836) [9] a glass tube, closed at one end and with a non-return valve at the other, was attached to the lead; as it descended to the bottom the hydrostatic pressure forced into the tube water whose escape was prevented by the valve. Graduations, in terms of depth (subject to a correction for any deviations from a mean atmospheric pressure), could be read off against the entrapped water. This idea was incorporated in Sir William Thomson's sounding-machine (p 453), which by the last decade of the century had superseded all other types. The slow rate of sinking of the lead with its hemp line rendered all such devices useless if the ship was travelling fast, for all the line was exhausted before the lead could reach the bottom. In 1870 Thomson suggested the use of a thin wire instead, and in 1872 he obtained successful deep

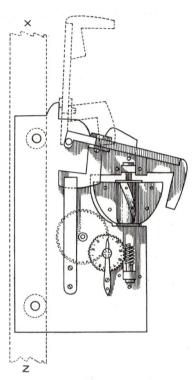

FIGURE 241—*Massey's sounding fly, c 1820.*
The line was attached at x and the lead at z.

soundings with a device rather similar to the Lucas machine (p 462). He then made a machine which consisted of a drum of wire on a galvanized frame, fitted with brake and handles. The wire, which was attached to a heavy lead, was led through a block over the taffrail; when the brake was released the lead fell quickly to the bottom, the drum having very little friction and the wire offering very little resistance to the water. By a 'feeler' on the wire it was easy to detect when the lead had hit the bottom; the brake was then applied and the amount of wire run out was recorded on a dial at the top of the machine. The lead was then hove in again. The depth could be found from tables relating the length of the wire to the speed of the ship. In depths up to 20 fathoms soundings could be obtained very quickly by this method. For greater depths, a glass tube of very narrow gauge was inserted into a brass cylinder close to the lead, and this registered the depth on Erichsen's principle. The tube, open at one end and sealed at the other, was coated internally with silver chromate; the sea-water forced into the tube discoloured the chromate to a sharp line, and this could be read off on a boxwood scale graduated in terms of depth (figure 242). Within a very few years of the introduction of this machine in 1878 it had been adopted by the Royal Navy and by all well found ships. In a similar device of a few years later the hydrostatic pressure forced a piston against a spring with a non-return

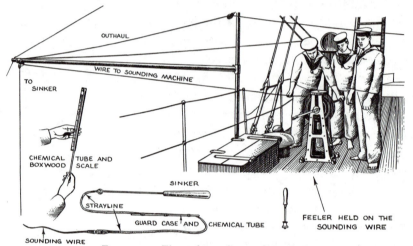

FIGURE 242—*Thomson's sounding machine, 1878.*

arrangement to ensure that it remained in position until the lead was recovered and the depth read off [8].

For great oceanic depths a different type of machine, designed by Lucas of the Telegraph Construction and Maintenance Company, came into use about 1880. Figure 243 shows a late model, but in essence this is similar to the original. The large drum A carries about 5000 fathoms of piano wire which is led by way of a hinged frame C over a pulley E to the heavy lead. The hinged frame is attached to the band-brake B so that when the weight of the lead acts on it the brake is released, but when the lead hits the bottom the tension on the wire is reduced, thus allowing the springs D to apply the brake to the drum. The amount of wire run out is read on a recorder.

The station-pointer. This useful instrument for the mechanical solution of the three-point resection problem, sometimes attributed to Joseph Huddart (1753–1816), appears to have been in use by hydrographic surveyors before the nineteenth century. By the end of the century it was also considered one of the essential tools of the navigator for plotting the position of the ship from horizontal angles observed with the sextant when sailing along the coast.

Lighthouses and buoyage. Buildings in the form of towers and beacons have been erected on the land as an aid and guide to mariners from time immemorial, as a means of identification on an otherwise featureless coast, as warnings of hidden dangers, or as leading-marks to assist in navigating a tortuous channel. From very early times some of them, such as the Pharos of Alexandria, have displayed a light. In the nineteenth century numerous lighthouses were built, many of them on outlying rocks. Winstanley had erected his wooden lighthouse on

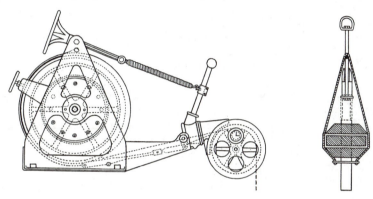

FIGURE 243—(Left) *Lucas sounding machine;* (right) *Baillie rod and sinker, improved type,* c 1920. *Weights* (shaded) *supported by slings are released by the shoulder when lead hits the bottom.*

the Eddystone Rock in 1698, but for many years this was the only offshore light round the coasts of the British Isles. In 1850 the number of lighthouses and lightships listed in the Admiralty List of Lights for the whole world was 1570, but by 1900 there were 9424. In 1956 there were over 30 000.

Wood and coal were the first illuminants, but in 1756 candles were tried in Smeaton's stone-built tower on the Eddystone, and shortly afterwards oil-lamps were used which, until 1846, burned sperm-oil. Soon after the turn of the nineteenth century many types of illuminant were in use, with incandescent lighting predominant, burning either mineral oil or acetylene gas; coal-gas had been tried in 1837 and electricity in 1855.

The first British lightship to be put on station was at the Nore (in the Thames estuary) in 1732, but by the end of the century there were at least 36 others. Buoys, both lit and unlit, are much used to mark the approach channels to large ports, and to give notice of hidden dangers. The problem of illuminating light-buoys was not solved satisfactorily until the twentieth century.

Most coastal lightships and lighthouses also carry fog-signals, but up to the present (1958) no perfect form of signal has been devised; curious areas of silence may occur quite close to the most powerful fog-signal. Before 1900 guns, horns, and bells were used, the operation of which imposed a great physical strain on the lightkeepers.

REFERENCES

[1] LENOX-CONYNGHAM, SIR GERALD (PONSONBY). *Emp. Surv. Rev.*, **7**, 146–55, 1943.

[2] MAYNE, R. C. 'Practical Notes on Marine Surveying.' London. 1874.

[3] 'General Instructions for the Hydrographic Surveyors of the Admiralty.' Hydrographic Office of the Admiralty, London. 1877.

[4] 'The "Challenger" Reports', Vol. I, by T. H. TIZARD *et al.* Hydrographic Department of the Admiralty, London. 1873–6.

[5] SHORTLAND, P. F. 'Sounding Voyage of H.M.S. Hydra.' London. 1868.

[6] WHARTON, W. J. L. 'Hydrographic Surveying.' London. 1882. (See also edition of 1898.)

[7] MASSEY, E. Massey's Sounding Machine and Patent Log. Pamphlets in the Admiralty Library, London. 1820, 1837.

[8] LAMBERT, M. A. 'Sounding Machines for the Prevention of Strandings with Special Reference to James' "Submarine Sentry". ' Pamphlet in the Admiralty Library, London. 1891.

[9] THOMSON, SIR WILLIAM. 'Popular Lectures and Addresses: Navigation.' Paper read before the United Service Institution, London, 4 February, 1878.

BIBLIOGRAPHY

ARDEN-CLOSE, SIR CHARLES F. 'The Early Years of the Ordnance Survey.' Institution of Royal Engineers, Chatham. 1926.

BRIDGES LEE, J. 'Description of the Bridges-Lee New Patent Photo-Theodolite' (2nd ed.). London. 1899.

CURTEIS, G. "The Work of Trinity House." *J. Inst. Navig.*, **4**, 1, 1951.

DEVILLE, E. 'Photographic Surveying.' Ottowa. 1895.

EDGELL, SIR JOHN A. 'Sea Surveys, Britain's Contribution to Hydrography.' Longmans, Green, London, for the British Council. 1948.

GORE, J. H. 'Geodesy.' Boston and New York. 1891.

HEWSON, J. B. 'A History of the Practice of Navigation.' Brown, Son & Ferguson, Glasgow. 1951.

HITCHENS, H. L. and MAY, W. E. 'From Lodestone to Gyro Compass' (2nd ed.). Hutchinson, London. 1955.

McCAW, G. T. "Standards of Length in Question." *Emp. Surv. Rev.*, **1**, 277–84, 1931–2.

Idem. "The Two Metres: the Story of an African Foot." *Ibid.*, **5**, 96–105, 1939–40.

PHILLIMORE, R. H. 'Historical Records of the Survey of India' (3 vols). Published by order of the Surveyor General of India. Dehra Dun. 1945–54.

RABBITT, J. C. and RABBITT, M. C. "The United States Geological Survey, 75 Years of Service to the Nation, 1879–1954." *Science*, **119**, no. 3099, 1954.

ROBINSON, A. H. W. "The Early Hydrographic Surveys of the British Isles." *Emp. Surv. Rev.*, **11**, 60–65, 1951–2.

Idem. "Captain William Bligh, R.N., Hydrographic Surveyor." *Ibid.*, **11**, 301–6, 1951–2.

Idem. "Some Hydrographic Surveyors of the early Nineteenth Century." *Ibid.*, **12**, 146–52, 1953–4.

STANLEY, W. F. 'Surveying and Levelling Instruments' (3rd ed.). Spon, London. 1901.

STIGANT, G. B. "The Hydrographic Department of the Admiralty." *Emp. Surv. Rev.*, **12**, 2–12, 1953–4.

STUDDS, R. F. A. "The United States Coast and Geodetic Survey; its Work and Products." *Ibid.*, **11**, 98–111, 146–58, 1951–2.

'The United States Geological Survey, its Origin, Development, Organization and Operations.' *Bull. U.S. geol. Surv.*, **227**, 1904.

WHITTINGDALE, W. "Maps and Survey in South Africa." *S. Afr. Surv. J.*, **3**, 276–85, 1930.

WINTERBOTHAM, H. ST J. L. "An Old File and a New Arc." *Emp. Surv. Rev.*, **2**, 7–12, 1933–4.

Idem. 'The National Plans.' *Prof. Pap. Ordn. Surv., Lond.*, **16**, 1934.

H.M.S. Challenger (*built 1858*), *whose world cruise, 1872–6, supplied so much of the data on which modern oceanography depends.*

20

BUILDING MATERIALS AND TECHNIQUES

S. B. HAMILTON

BUILDINGS of this period for which their designers or owners would have claimed architectural merit were solid and dignified but unoriginal: they were scholarly imitations of an historic style, Palladian, Grecian, or Gothic. Such buildings posed few technical problems. Constructional interest in the design of buildings was aroused by adaptation to use rather than by beauty; by the long-span roofs, for instance, of the larger railway stations and exhibition halls, the designers of which were usually engineers. The framed building that came in towards the end of the period was primarily a utility building. It might as a matter of prestige be embellished with ornament borrowed from older buildings of a quite different character, but there was a tendency for its walls to be constructed of sheets of glass and light panels; it had many allegedly 'fireproof' floors; it was divided internally by thin partitions. Such a building was developed to meet the needs of business men who wanted their offices to be as near as possible to the centre of a crowded commercial city.

Style and ornament are of little interest from the technical point of view. The subject-matter of this chapter is the techniques by which well known materials were used in a novel way, or which were developed to utilize some new material, or to apply in practice some theoretical principle suggested by scientific study rather than by the evolutionary process of trial and error. It was only in this period, and somewhat haltingly, that such application came to be made. We cannot do better than start with the use of wood, the oldest of all building materials except, perhaps, mud.

I. CARPENTRY

Wood could now be used more efficiently in large structures, through the ability of designers to resolve forces and the availability of iron fastenings (vol IV, ch 15). In the domestic building of well wooded regions, however, it was still customary to form a framework of posts mortised into plates, with much notching and halving of braces and other members at junctions. This tradition was carried to America by the early colonists. In Europe, the spaces between frame-members were usually filled with wattle-and-daub, or later with brick-nogging

(vol III, figure 171); but in the colonies, as also in Kent and Essex, these spaces were commonly fitted with light vertical studs (upright posts or timbers) and the whole façade was covered with horizontal weatherboarding, known in America as clapboarding (vol III, p 265). As the population of the United States, continually augmented by immigrants from Europe, spread westward from the At-lantic seaboard, an urgent demand arose for houses in all the new settlements. There was plenty of timber but a scarcity of carpenters. The demand was met by the invention of the 'balloon frame', derisively so called by the traditional builder on account of its light weight and apparently flimsy construction.

There is some doubt as to who really invented the balloon frame. S, Giedion stated (1943) that it was George Washing-ton Snow (1797–1870), a New England Quaker who in 1832 joined a small settle-ment at the mouth of the Chicago river. C. W. Cordit contended (1957) that it was not Snow, but a carpenter from Hart-ford, Connecticut, named Augustine Deo-dat Taylor. Both agree, however, that its development began in the little township that was destined to become Chicago[1].

It was realized that the vertical studs, serving hitherto only to hold the clap-

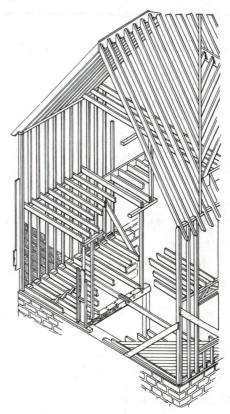

FIGURE 244—*A 'balloon frame' for a house.*

board, could also carry the roof, if plates of wood were nailed to them at the top and the bottom, since there were so many studs placed about 18 in apart. Thus the heavy frame timbers could be omitted. All mortising, halving, and other cutting and fitting could be saved as well, since all the remaining timbers were joined by nailing. This method of construction was tried in 1833 on a small church. So satisfactory was the result that the system was adapted to the construction of houses. Using long, light studs extending from top to bottom of the building, with a plate nailed on half-way up, the studs would carry not only the roof but the upper floor as well (figure 244). The timbers for the studs could be cut to length, marked, and numbered at the saw-mill, and delivered to the site together with a bag of nails and ready-made doors and windows, so that a handy man, with little more equipment than a hammer and a ladder, could assemble and erect the house for himself. The old-fashioned carpenter, having only expensive hand-made nails, had used them sparingly, mainly to fix boards to framing in floors, doors, and shutters; but by the 1830s machine-made nails were available at a fraction of the former price, and even the many long, strong nails needed to fasten together studs and floor-plates were no longer prohibitively dear. In this way was invented the type of building in which most citizens in the new townships and farms all over the west came to be housed.

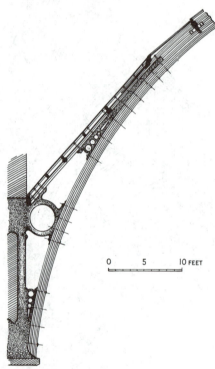

FIGURE 245—*The original interior of King's Cross station, London, with wooden arches springing from cast iron shoes.*

The opening of passenger railways in Britain, where such transport originated, created a demand for buildings of a novel character. Those which inevitably attracted most public attention were the stations in the larger cities. At first these were modest enough. The Liverpool terminus of the Liverpool and Manchester Railway, built in 1830 at Crown Hill while the deep cutting between Edge Hill and Lime Street was still unfinished, had a roof carried by queen-post trusses of 35-ft span. The trusses of the first Lime Street station, built in 1836, were of 55-ft span. On the Great Western Railway, the trusses of the first Paddington station (1837) were of only 30-ft span. At Bristol, however, Brunel erected in 1840 a much bolder and more magnificent type of roof of 72-ft span. Ostensibly a hammer-beam roof, it was structurally a tied, pointed arch. For comparison it may be recalled that Westminster Hall, built in 1388, had a hammer-beam roof of 68-ft span arranged about an arch as its principal member. Between 1842 and 1844 British engineers constructed at Rouen a station roof with a single 82-ft span. But the greatest of all the wooden roofs was at King's Cross, London, where in 1852 the station was built with two great barrel-vaults carried by semi-circular arches of 105-ft span, springing from cast iron shoes on piers that projected from the main brick walls (figure 245). In the 1850s the railway terminal station catered not only for passengers but for goods traffic, and was equipped with turn-tables and cross-tracks so that shunting could be carried out. The building was indeed a train shed as well as a passenger station.

There were two ways of building up arches in wood from small scantlings. One, introduced by Philibert de l'Orme in the sixteenth century [2], was to lay short planks side by side with the flat faces vertical and ends cut to butt along radial planes (vol III, figure 164). Joints between planks in adjacent layers were staggered and the planks were held together by trenails. This method, except that iron nails have replaced trenails, is still used in the temporary centring of arches. The alternative method is usually credited to Colonel Emy, who, about 1825, utilized long, thin planks bent to the radius of the arch to carry a roof of 60-ft span. This method was used later for bridges as well as roof-work.

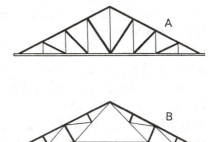

FIGURE 246—*Forms of roof truss: compression members in thick lines, tension members in thin lines.* (A) *Suitable for ceiled roof;* (B) *suitable for open roof.*

An alternative to the arch as a means of carrying a roof is the truss, a form that came into occasional use long before its mechanics were fully understood (vol II, figure 402 B). A common type of medieval roof depended for its strength on a solid tie-beam, from which ridge and purlins were supported either by vertical posts or by inclined struts (vol IV, figure 265). The rafters thus became merely carriers of the roof-covering. In the king-post roof or queen-post roof of the eighteenth century, some of the rafters again resume their original function as virtually members of an arch (vol IV, figure 265). The tie-beam is relieved of part of its beam-load and assumes the duty of tying in the feet of the principal rafters and resisting their outward thrust. This form required some iron fastenings. The next step was to insert iron ties in order to triangulate the framework in one or other of the two forms shown in figure 246. With proper tightening of the tension members, the main tie could be relieved of the whole of its beam-load. In these forms the truss came to be fabricated wholly in wrought iron, and later in steel, but in the mid-nineteenth century it was common to find only tension members of wrought iron; rafters and struts could be of cast iron or of wood, perhaps some of each.

For railway work the use of wood in roof-trusses was short-lived. Though wood is resistant to the sulphureous gases of locomotive-smoke, iron in contact with wood that tends to hold moisture is not, and the fastenings rapidly corroded, particularly where iron rods entered holes in the wood. The wooden arches at King's Cross were in 1869 and 1887 replaced by wrought iron ones, using the original sockets.[1] The Bristol hammer-beam roof, though doubtless repaired from time to time, still remains. The London and Birmingham Railway used iron throughout the roof-work of its stations from the beginning.

II. CAST IRON

In England the structural use of cast iron in buildings began with attempts to increase the fire-resistance of mill buildings (vol IV, ch 15). The use of cast iron for columns, beams, and window-frames, with external walls of brickwork or stone masonry, and stone-flagged floors carried on brick arches spanning between the iron beams, became standard practice for such buildings. In the 1850s, many shop and office buildings were constructed with interiors similar to those of mill buildings, but having façades entirely of iron and glass [3]. James Bogardus of New York, who built many (figure 247), wrote a book about them. In the United States and in Britain a number of examples still stand; for instance, Gardiner's Building in Glasgow, erected in 1855 to the design of an unknown architect, is still unaltered.

Cast iron also lent itself to the reproduction of ornament in any style. John Cragg (1767–1854) of the Mersey foundry, aided and abetted by Thomas Rickman (1776–1841), the architect whose period classification of Gothic buildings is still accepted, made the experiment between 1813 and 1818 of building three churches in Liverpool in which columns, arcades, roof-work, and window-mullions and tracery, all of Gothic outline, were of cast iron [4].

Cragg patented this system of building, the roof and walls being of slate slabs held between internal and external mouldings, much as glass is still fixed in metal glazing bars. The wall slabs were finished with sand or stone dust to look like ashlar masonry. The columns were too slender, the arches too narrow, and the walls too thin to look like true 'gothic' masonry. The castings, moreover, were too regular and too exactly alike to convey an interest comparable with that of the play of light and shade on the slightly irregular texture of hand-wrought masonry. Rickman, on aesthetic grounds, repented of the experiment, but Cragg, having obtained his patents and made his patterns, was still prepared to supply castings to any who desired them. The ecclesiastical demand was never great and soon died away, but the practice of casting columns, the frames of steam-engines,

---

[1] Several modern works refer to the 1869 arches as of steel; that is erroneous. It is clear from contemporary reports, such as R. M. Bancroft's in *The Building News* of 17 December 1869 (**xvii**, 465), that they are of wrought iron.

and parts of bridges with 'gothic', classical, or merely unclassified ornamental details persisted. The catalogues of a famous Scottish foundry continued to advertise cast iron columns in the classical orders until the first world war. The Coal Exchange, in Lower Thames Street, built between 1847 and 1849 by James Bunsten Bunning (1802–63), architect to the City of London, though conventional in its masonry exterior, possesses an inner court surmounted by a dome

FIGURE 247—*Cast iron façade, New York, 1851.*

60 ft in diameter. This dome has cast iron ribs, filled in with glass, supported by cast iron columns with brackets that carry cast iron galleries at three levels. The height to the top of the dome is 74 ft (plate 26 A) [5]. The roof of the present Houses of Parliament (1840–57) is a remarkable structure; it is mainly of cast iron, including the covering plates. The framework enclosing and covering the great clock that strikes Big Ben is also of cast iron.

A notable example of cast iron columns, arcades, and tracery in a large church is to be found in Saint-Eugène, Paris, at the corner of the rue Sainte-Cécile and the rue du Conservatoire. It was built by L. A. Boileau between 1854 and 1855, iron being chosen for economy[1] [6]. An even more striking example of ecclesiastical cast iron work is the great open-work spire, begun in 1823 but not finished until

[1] In 1868 Boileau built a French church (now demolished) in Leicester Place, London, with exposed cast iron vault-ribs.

1876, on the central tower of Rouen Cathedral. This spire, which rises 485 ft from the ground, was at the time of its completion the highest erection then

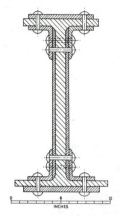

standing in the world (plate 27 B).[1]

III. WROUGHT IRON

In the 1850s and 1860s, while the fashion for cast iron construction was still at its height, there occurred a considerable extension of the use of wrought iron. By the puddling process introduced in the eighteenth century (vol IV, ch 4) wrought or malleable iron was produced from crude cast or pig iron by burning out the excess carbon in a reverberatory furnace. The process was improved in 1839 by Joseph Hall of Tipton, who 'lined his puddling furnace with a partially fusible oxide of iron and boiled instead of baked his pig' [7]. This removed

FIGURE 248 — *Fielder's patent for strengthening wrought iron beams*

phosphorus and some sulphur and so produced a better quality of iron for the smith without restricting the smelter to the use of expensive imported ores of high purity.

Wrought iron was at first used in building mainly as a supplement to wooden or cast iron members. In the 'flitch beam', for instance, a long plate of iron was sandwiched between two wooden balks, or a timber beam was sandwiched between two iron plates. In each case the combination was firmly bolted together. To strengthen or repair iron beams, Henry Fielder took out a British patent (1847) for riveting to them suitably formed plates or angles of wrought iron (figure 248). In the same year Ferdinand Zorés, a well known Parisian engineer, persuaded the rolling-mills to produce a small I-beam of wrought iron for use in floors. In 1855 two of the beams (figure 249) were exhibited in Paris at the Exposition Universelle. Their flanges were narrow and not flat. The production of both flange and web with wide flat surfaces became possible only with the invention of the 'universal mill' in which the horizontal and vertical rollers were geared to run at the same peripheral speed. Such a mill was made about 1853, but the manufacture of heavy rolled beams of wrought iron was still limited because only a small bloom, which a man could stir in the furnace and eventually remove on an iron bar, could be produced at one time. Before a long beam of heavy section could be rolled a number of blooms had to be made and hammered together into one large billet, a process expensive in labour. The economical pro-

[1] Great pyramid, *c* 2500 B.C., orig. 479 ft, now 449 ft; Old St. Paul's, London, A.D. 1315, burnt 1561, 489 ft; Beauvais Cathedral spire, A.D. 1500, fell 1573, 486 ft.

duction in quantity of rolled joists in any but small sections had to await the invention of structural mild steel, a cast product poured in large ingots. Although the universal mill was available as early as the 1850s, and has in the twentieth century become increasingly important for the rolling of heavy sections with wide flanges, it was found practicable and economical to roll common beam sections in mills fitted only with rollers with horizontal axes. Between these rollers, a white-hot billet, originally of rectangular section, was passed to and fro. The rolls were cut with a series of diminishing grooves so that after, say, eight passes the steel finally emerged as a beam with its web horizontal, the outside faces of the flanges vertical, and the inner faces of the flanges inclined at 8° to the vertical. Until these sections were commercially available, beams of large size for use in bridges or buildings were made by riveting together plates, angles, tees, and other sections. Figure 250 shows examples illustrated by Sir William Fairbairn in the second edition of his classic work on 'The Application of Cast and Wrought Iron to Building Purposes' (1857). Fairbairn's advocacy of wrought iron as a useful and economical material for construction roughly coincided with the period in which the railway companies were seized with the idea of constructing great open train-sheds with the fewest possible obstructions, such as columns, that would make it difficult

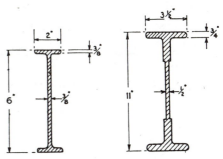

FIGURE 249—*Two wrought iron beams exhibited in Paris in 1855.*

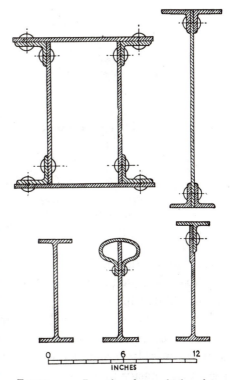

FIGURE 250—*Examples of wrought iron beams (Sir William Fairbairn).*

to rearrange tracks and platforms to meet changing needs [8]. The roof-trusses of the original (1839) Euston station (still covering platforms 4 to 7 used by local trains) were only of 40-ft span. They were of wrought iron, carried

by cast iron beams and columns. When, however, Lime Street station, Liverpool, was rebuilt between 1846 and 1849—the third terminus on its line in 15
years—the roof-trusses took the form of sickle-shaped girders of 152-ft span,
the largest at that time in the world. At New Street, Birmingham, in 1854, the
station roof was carried by sickle girders of 212-ft span. St. Pancras station,
London, was covered in 1865 by a single vault with pointed lattice-work arches
designed by W. H. Barlow (figure 251). They are of 240-ft span and 100 ft

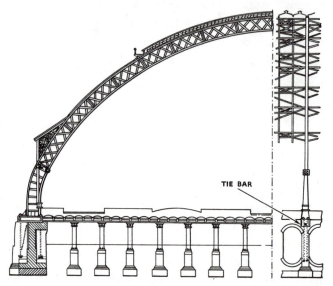

FIGURE 251—*St Pancras station, London, 1865. The area covered by this
roof, which is of 240 ft span, is 690 ft by 240 ft. The main ribs are at 29 ft 4 in
centres.*

high, and are tied under the track by wrought iron tie-beams. This span was
in 1891–3 exceeded by the 300-ft span of the pointed tied arches of Broad Street
station, Philadelphia.

Wrought iron was not used for complete load-bearing building-frames in any
but a few exceptional examples. A mixed construction of wrought iron and cast
iron that was also a remarkable example of prefabricated structural units, namely
the Crystal Palace built for the Great Exhibition of 1851 in Hyde Park, London,
was described in vol IV, ch 15. The building erected for the Menier Chocolate
Works in 1871–2 at Noisiel, by Jules Saulnier, had a complete iron frame carried
by masonry piers built in the bed of the river Marne [9]. Power was supplied by
water-wheels between the piers. Since the structure was virtually a bridge, with
one storey between the piers and four more above, the walls had to be light in

weight. They were built of hollow brickwork in panels between the members of a braced iron frame, and were covered with variegated tiles (figure 252). The load from the frame was transmitted through continuous box-girders to the masonry piers. Even earlier buildings with complete iron framework and curtain walls

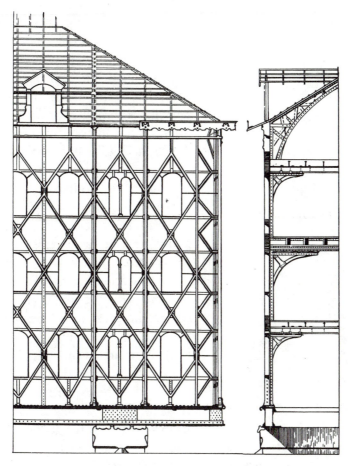

FIGURE 252—*Jules Saulnier's chocolate factory at Noisiel-sur-Marne, the earliest example of a skeleton frame, 1871-2.*

were erected in Sheerness dockyard in the 1850s.[1]

The floors of the galleries of the British Museum were carried by open-webbed cast iron girders of clear spans up to 41 ft 6 in; these girders represented a considerable feat of casting at the time (1824). Between 1854 and 1857, within the large inner courtyard of the Museum, the Reading Room was erected with a

[1] Skempton, A. W., *Trans. Newcomen Soc.*, **32**, 57-78, 1960.

dome of 100-ft internal diameter, and a height to the base of the lantern of 105 ft. The ribs of the dome were of wrought iron plates and angles, with cast iron purlins and a double cast iron ring-beam at the foot. The columns were of cruciform section each made up from three I-shaped sections, a deep one set radially directly under the rib, and others less deep, one on each side, bolted together through the web of the deep section (plate 26 B). These great castings were not machined, and would not present true meeting planes. They were erected with gaps of about an inch between the castings, the gaps being filled with rust cement, a mixture of iron borings, sal ammoniac, and water which set hard between, and adhered strongly to, the iron surfaces. The invention of this cement was attributed to William Murdock (1754–1839), the pioneer of gas-lighting (vol IV, p 261) and a close associate of Boulton and Watt, who presumably used it first in the erection of steam-engine frames.

FIGURE 253—*The Eiffel Tower, Paris, 1889.*

As a feature of the Paris Exhibition of 1889, Gustave Eiffel (1832–1923) designed the great tower bearing his name which rises to a height of 984 ft (figure 253). It is carried by beds of concrete 7 ft thick; those near the river Seine were set at 50 ft below ground, those inland at 23 ft. On these beds are masonry piers deep into which the feet of the ironwork are tied by wrought-iron rods 4 inches in diameter. 7300 tons of wrought iron were used in the superstructure. A necessary feature of this remarkable structure was the provision of mechanically operated passenger lifts.

IV. STRUCTURAL STEEL

It is somewhat surprising to find that wrought iron, not steel, was used so late as 1889 for such a structure as the Eiffel Tower, when simultaneously the Forth bridge was being built in the newer material. Before the 1850s no such choice would have been possible, for at that time steel was usually made by heating wrought iron bars with powdered charcoal in crucibles. The process was expensive and the output small. The use of steel was therefore confined to tools, springs, and objects of moderate size for which the hardness of steel was essential; it was too expensive for use in the elements of structures. The first process by which steel could be manufactured in bulk was patented by Henry Bessemer (1813–98) in 1855 (p 54).

With steel ingots replacing blooms of puddled iron, large billets of steel were available and machinery sufficiently powerful to deal with them was installed in the rolling-mills. Thus the long-desired **I**-beam of substantial section became commercially practicable. The Butterley Company of Derby had been rolling wrought beams for some years before they began in the 1880s to produce beams of mild steel. Dorman Long began rolling steel beams in 1885. In 1886 both Dorman Long and Redpath Brown opened constructional departments, and in 1887 Dorman Long published their first section book.

Other manufacturers entered this promising field, but each mill had its own range of shapes and sizes. It was not till 1904 that the British Engineering Standards Association (now the British Standards Institution) issued specifications standardizing both the range of sections to which the trade undertook to restrict their main future rollings, and the quality of the steel to be used. Structural steel-work was in 1877 admitted by the Board of Trade in Britain as a suitable material for bridges, and indeed in the superstructure of the Forth bridge (1883–90) just over 50 000 tons of steel were so used.

The development in steel of the complete skeleton framework of a building took place in the United States about 1890, in the course of solving the problem of building to unprecedented heights. Very high buildings have not found the same favour in Europe as in America, but the steel frame was widely adopted somewhat later.

In Britain, Basil Scott of the Redpath Brown firm designed in 1895 a large warehouse with steel beams and columns, but with external load-bearing walls of brickwork. In 1896 he designed a completely steel-framed furniture warehouse erected in West Hartlepool; this, he thought, was probably the first building so constructed in Britain [10]. The steel frame for other than industrial buildings was introduced to London in 1904, when the Ritz Hotel was built with steel-work designed by S. Bylander, who had studied this form in the United States. It was not, however, till 1909 that the London Building Act allowed any reduction to be made in the statutory minimum thickness of the external wall of a building, even though it was reduced functionally to a series of weather-resisting panels supported at every floor-level by steel beams.

V. HIGH BUILDINGS

Buildings more than four or five storeys high were in no great demand until reliable passenger lifts were available. Elevators for goods were installed in Boston and New York before 1850, but they were slow-moving devices. The cage, partly balanced by a counterweight attached by a rope passing over a pulley at the head of the shaft, was mounted directly on a long plunger working in and out of a cylinder that descended into a pit in the ground as deep as the rise of the cage. The power was hydraulic. Such a device was safe and silent in operation but slow. Faster motion was obtained by using a hydraulic motor of moderate length, and increasing the movement by a system of pulleys. This meant, however, that the cage must hang at the end of a rope. Ropes wear and lose their strength; should the rope break, the cage would fall to the bottom of the shaft. Before lifts could be used continuously for passenger traffic, some safety device had to be introduced. Elisha Graves Otis (1811–61) met this requirement by erecting a ratchet up each side of the shaft, with pawls on the cage held clear of the ratchets so long as the rope was in tension, but forced out by springs so that they would engage the ratchets at once if the tension failed. He exhibited this device at the Crystal Palace Exposition at New York in 1854 (tailpiece) and in 1857 installed an elevator embodying it in a five-storey store in New York. The first successful electric elevators date from about 1889.

Meanwhile from 1882 at Chicago, and shortly afterwards in New York, buildings were being constructed with many more than five storeys. Probably the last of its height to depend on load-carrying walls was the Pulitzer Building in New York, completed in 1890, with fourteen storeys and external walls 9 ft thick at the base. Queen Anne's Mansions at Queen Anne's Gate, London (plate 27 A), were begun in 1873 and built to about the same height, with external walls, cross-walls, and internal walls of brickwork. The stoutest walls, however, are only 2 ft 7½ in thick at ground-floor level. This English experiment was not repeated.

To support the weight of a lofty building on walls of brickwork they would have to be immensely thick in the lower storeys and thus occupy a large amount of space. Even with the weight of the interior carried by cast iron columns, a thick, very lofty, external wall capable of carrying its own weight could spare only a limited area for window-openings. When, therefore, William Le Baron Jenney (1832–1907) was commissioned in 1883 by the Home Insurance Company to build for them at Chicago a 10-storey block of offices that would be fireproof and let as much natural light as possible into every room, he used in the external walls cast iron columns encased in brickwork (figure 254). The six lower floors were carried by wrought iron beams, but for work above that level he used beams of Bessemer steel. This was possibly the first use of that material in quantity in an important building [11].

Other lofty buildings followed in which cast iron, wrought iron, and steel were all used in the construction, often in the same building. The first wholly steel-framed building was probably the second Rand–McNally Building at

FIGURE 254—*The Home Insurance Building, Chicago, an early example of the use of Bessemer steel in building.*

Chicago, completed in 1890. With the complete steel skeleton it was possible to build the walls at several levels independently and simultaneously. The tallest building of the period was the 21-storey Masonic Building, finished in 1892. Other American cities soon followed Chicago's lead in erecting high buildings. As external walls became virtually weather-screens in the panels between columns and beams, it was possible to make them of light construction, or, indeed, mainly of glass.

VI. THE FIRE-PROTECTION OF BUILDINGS

The risk of destruction or damage to buildings by fire has existed since man began to cook his meals and warm his body by lighting fires inside his dwelling. In due course he added further hazards by the use of artificial light, and by the practices of smoking and carrying matches. Some industrial processes involving the use of highly combustible materials led to serious fires, particularly when they were carried out on a large scale within buildings with combustible floors, stairs, and partitions.[1] About 1800 measures were taken to reduce the fire-risk in factories by making columns and beams of cast iron, and by carrying floors on brick arches in place of wooden beams and planks (vol IV, ch 15). The iron was, however, usually left exposed, and in a severe fire it lost its strength and collapsed. This risk of collapse was greatly increased when lighter and thinner sections of wrought iron and, later, steel were used instead of the more massive castings. It was soon clear that such structural members needed a cover of material that could withstand high temperatures and was also a poor conductor of heat. Without such protection for the steel framework of high buildings the risk of damage by fire, and still more the risk of loss of life, would have been excessive.

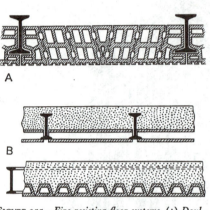

FIGURE 255—*Fire-resisting floor systems.* (A) *Doulton, 1873;* (B) *Homan, 1889.*

Concrete cast around steelwork, with a mesh of steel wire embedded in it to prevent it from cracking and parting from the steelwork at the corners of columns or the under-side of beams, is a highly efficient protective covering, provided it gives a cover of about $1\frac{1}{2}$ in at the thinnest place. Concrete also came to be used for the floor-slab spanning between main beams, with steel joists of shallow section (known as filler joists) completely embedded within the thickness of the slab. Falsework (temporary support) was required for the concrete around main beams and columns, and to support the slab until it set around the filler joists. There were, however, numerous alternatives to the solid concrete slab. Two typical fire-resistant floors are shown in figure 255, in both of which the lower part of the floor-thickness consists of hollow terracotta blocks. In

---

[1] Some materials not usually considered to be highly inflammable are actually explosive when diffused in the air as fine dust. Thus many serious explosions have occurred in old-fashioned flour-mills.

(A) they form a flat arch, in (B) a series of parallel lintels. In neither of these was continuous shuttering needed for the slab, though in (A) some light falsework was needed for the arch [12].

The manufacture in the United States of hollow-block floor-units of burnt clay is believed to date from about 1875, first in New Jersey, but shortly afterwards in many other places. From the beginning they were a machine-made product. Many were very similar to those shown in figure 255 A, but for heavily loaded floors a stronger arrangement was to run the upstanding solid divisions between the voids of the blocks at right angles to the beams instead of in the same direction as the beams as shown in the figure. To lighten the weight of hollow-floor blocks, A. D. Gilman, of Eldora, Iowa, mixed sawdust with the clay before burning. The sawdust was consumed in the kiln leaving a porous block that could be cut with a saw and, it was alleged, worked with a plane. It was described as terracotta lumber, and from 1884 onwards was produced on a large scale at New York. The proportion of sawdust to clay may be almost as high as one to one. Both dense and light-weight blocks are known as structural clay tile, and as such came to be widely used in the multi-storey buildings of framed construction that were built in Chicago, New York, and other cities in the last decade of the century.

The very high building raised several new fire-protection problems. The use of a fire-resisting structure was an obvious precaution, and the availability of light-weight structural clay tile was timely. It was particularly important to confine and isolate any outbreak of fire, for otherwise a fire in a lower storey could make it impossible for persons on higher floors to reach the ground by an interior route, and some would be trapped too high for escape by ladders erected outside. Above 80 or 100 ft it would be impossible for firemen to fight the fire from outside. For greater heights water has to be taken from hydrants fed by tanks in the building filled by private pumping machinery. In a very high building such tanks are needed at several levels, or the pressure at some of the lower levels would be too high for the hose-pipes.

It was not long before a few high buildings advertised as 'fireproof' were tested by fire; some of them were found wanting. Terracotta blocks gave protection to the steel-work so long as they stayed in place, but details of their fixing needed careful attention, or when most needed the tiles would fall off. Service-pipes were often run in chases within the casing intended to give fire-protection to a column. These might leave insufficient cover, or they might result in the remainder of the casing being insecurely fixed. Holes left or made to carry pipes through otherwise fire-resisting floors could allow smoke or

5363.5

flame to pass unless they were carefully stopped. Staircases and lift-shafts could act as flues and carry fire from floor to floor unless at each floor they were divided from rooms and corridors by fire-resisting walls and by fire-resisting doors kept closed. Bad details and careless workmanship could undo the effectiveness of an otherwise adequate design. Building legislation then in force did not provide safe requirements for the new forms of construction, but insurance companies and one or two public authorities soon realized the need for its revision. In 1890 a group of insurance companies at Boston started to test

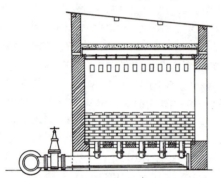

FIGURE 256—*British Fire Prevention Committee's testing furnace (roughly 10 ft square) for floors, 1897.*

safety-devices. In 1896 the Building Department of New York City started to carry out tests on the fire-endurance of allegedly 'fireproof' floors. In Germany, also, tests were carried out in 1893 in Berlin and in 1895 at Hamburg.

In London between 1889 and 1899 there were ten conflagrations each of which destroyed many buildings. Most of them started in old property that did not comply with the current building-laws, but the fire spread across narrow

lanes to newer property. London did not possess, and was not prepared to sanction, very high buildings; but the tendency in new buildings to increase window-space made them more vulnerable than many older buildings to ignition by radiant heat from fire in neighbouring buildings. One of the worst of these conflagrations broke out in the Cripplegate area north of the City on 19 November 1897, soon after midday, and though fought by 300 firemen and 50 steam fire-engines it did not die down until the evening. It served to increase considerably the membership of the British Fire Prevention Committee, a voluntary body started some months earlier by a small group of architects and others under the leadership of Edwin O. Sachs (1870–1919). This body set up a testing-station in the grounds of a house near Regent's Park and began the issue of a series of publications, some informative or advisory, others consisting of reports on tests made on various forms of floor-construction, doors, partitions, and the like. The tests were made in brick-walled furnaces (figure 256) of which, for instance, a floor under test formed the top. Firing by gas was regulated to give the required temperature for a stipulated time or till failure. The committee drew up standard test requirements for fire-resisting floors and ceilings, partitions, and doors which in 1903 were duly adopted by an International Fire Prevention

Congress held in London under the auspices of the committee. Many years were to elapse before a proper grading of buildings according to their fire-resistance, and regulations to enforce an appropriate degree of protection according to the use and size of a building, were generally adopted anywhere, but by the beginning of the twentieth century important steps in that direction had been taken.

VII. CEMENT

In the middle decades of the nineteenth century there were three types of calcareous material commercially available for use in mortar or concrete that

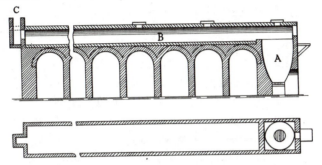

FIGURE 257—*Section of Johnson's tunnel cement kiln, 1872.*

possessed what L. J. Vicat (1786–1861) had called the 'hydraulic' property of setting in a wet situation or actually under water. The first type included various hydraulic limes and natural cements, such as Parker's 'Roman' cement, made by calcining stone that naturally contained a suitable mixture of lime, alumina, and silica. The second type included artificial cements, sold under various proprietary names, all made by mixing limestone or chalk with clay or shale in appropriate proportions (found empirically) before burning them at a temperature of about 1100–1300° C. Portland cement as described in Joseph Aspdin's original patent appears to have belonged to this second class, but by the 1850s the name Portland cement had come to be applied to a third type: artificial cements in which the mixed materials were sintered at a temperature of 1400–1500° C, and the resulting clinker ground to a fine powder. By 1850, this hard-burnt cement was being made in four manufactories in England and in one at Boulogne-sur-Mer, and the publicity given at the 1851 Exhibition to its strength, demonstrably greater than that of other cement, led to the establishment of many more.

The type of kiln used for the burning of cement was still of the form illustrated in vol IV, figure 246. The materials were mixed dry and dealt with as a batch. In 1870 W. Goreham took out an English patent for grinding the materials wet, as the French makers of hydraulic lime at Meudon, near Paris, had been doing for a century. The resulting slurry had to be dried before roasting. In 1872 I. C. Johnson patented the 'tunnel kiln' in which the slurry was dried in a

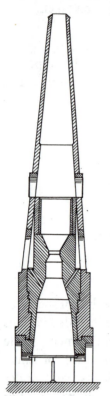

horizontal chamber 70–80 ft long through which the hot gases, hitherto liberated at the top of the kiln into the atmosphere, were made to pass on their way to a chimney. The charge pumped up from the grinder into this chamber was thus dried by the waste heat from the roasting of the previous batch (figure 257).

Attempts were made to introduce continuous working instead of batch-working. Various forms of shaft-kiln, for instance, were developed on the European continent. One form consisted of a vertical cylinder about 40 ft high and 8 or 9 ft in diameter, with a funnel-shaped top into which the mixture of limestone, clay, and coke was fed (figure 258). The shaft-kiln was introduced into Britain from Germany in the 1880s. In 1877, T. R. Crampton patented a rotary kiln; the charge was fed into the higher end of a rotating, inclined, hollow cylinder while a flame from the burning of a jet of powdered coal and air, or from producer-gas or other source, burned at the lower end. The air for combustion was drawn through a second rotating cylinder in which the clinker was cooling (Brit. Pat. No 2438 of 1877) (figure 259). Mixing, drying, roasting, and cooling were all to be carried out continuously in the way that has since become standard practice, but the proportions of the parts were not satisfactory, and Crampton's invention does not appear to

FIGURE 258—*A Danish shaft-kiln, c 1900.*

have reached the stage of commercial development. Frederick Ransome thought that by introducing the materials in the form of a powder, and keeping it agitated, no fine grinding would be necessary. He hopefully patented the idea in 1885, but the fine materials always formed a clinker. Ransome built a rotary kiln at Arlesey, near Hitchin, in 1887, but it did not work satisfactorily. He then went to the United States, where he obtained an American patent in 1886 [13].

The American Portland cement industry began later than the British, and for some years British cement was exported to the United States. The cost of transport made its use expensive, and many brands of natural cement that had been developed during the American canal boom (*c* 1820–40) continued in favour until the 1890s. A Portland cement factory was established in 1876 at Coplay, Pennsylvania, by D. O. Saylor, but he found it difficult to compete in price with the imported article until the rotary kiln was available. It was he who took up Ransome's scheme, and with others brought it to successful development. There were many practical difficulties to overcome. For one thing, the lime and cement clinker acted as a flux that melted the firebrick lining of the roasting-cylinder. Later, a lining made of cement and cement-clinker was found to serve

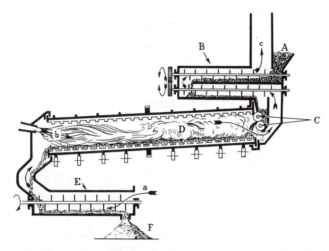

FIGURE 259—*Crampton's patent rotary kiln for cement burning. (a) Entry for cold air; (b) flame; (c) chimney; (A) hopper for mixed chalk and clay; (B) drying-chamber with rotating paddles; (C) crushing-rollers; (D) rotating tubular kiln, on rollers; (E) cooling-chamber with rotating paddles; (F) cement clinker.*

better. The early cylinders were too short for the burning-process to be completed before the contents were discharged. Their length was progressively increased to about 150 ft with beneficial results.[1] The cooling-cylinder for clinker, shown in Crampton's patent specification drawing (figure 259), had not been generally used, and cooling in a thin layer on a floor occupied considerable space and time. E. H. Hurry and H. J. Seaman reintroduced revolving cooling-cylinders, with improvements, and by the early 1890s the rotary kiln was fully successful; the American cement industry quickly became independent of foreign competition and almost drove natural cements off the market [14].

By the 1890s European manufacturers also became independent of British exported cement, and even threatened the British home market. Many of the English manufacturers were working with out-of-date plant; the output of some factories was unreliable in quality; and complaints were made that some

[1] Many modern (1958) kilns are over 300 ft long.

were adulterating their cement with inert stone-dust. Fortunately for the future of the British industry others were aware of the importance of high quality and had the enterprise to take concerted action to modernize their plant, and to reorganize their manufacturing and marketing methods.

As stated earlier in this work (vol IV, p 449), an important start had been made in the control of the quality of cement by the Metropolitan Board of Works, in the terms under which from 1859 to 1867 they purchased 70 000 tons of cement to be used in the mortar of the brickwork sewers of the London main drainage system. They made 15 000 tests [15]. To ensure that their material would meet the Board's standard of acceptance, some cement-makers carried out tests in their own works, but the practice did not, at that time, become general. In 1878, however, a few works introduced the regular use of sieves to keep a check on the fineness of their grinding, which greatly affected the strength of the cement. In 1889 G. & T. Earle of Hull began to test the physical and chemical properties of their Portland cement as a matter of routine, and from 1897 to provide their customers with certificates bearing the results of the tests.

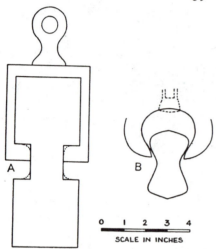

FIGURE 260—*Briquettes for testing cement in tension.* (A) *Grant (c 1860): note the sharp interior corners that encourage premature fracture, later modified as shown by dotted line;* (B) *modern (1904), shaped to ensure even distribution of stress.*

As already stated, by the 1890s Britain had lost the advantage of being first in the field with cement, and if that position were to be regained, or, indeed, if British manufacturers were not to fall still farther behind their overseas competitors, decisive action had to be taken. Consultations took place between the leading firms, and in 1900 many of them joined together to form the Associated Portland Cement Manufacturers. This organization purchased from the Americans E. H. Hurry and H. J. Seaman the rights to their improvements to the rotary kiln, and proceeded to erect such kilns in its Thames-side works. The first British Standard Specification for Portland cement was issued in 1904. The American Society for Testing Materials issued its standard in the same year, but tests had been standardized since 1884 by the American Society of Civil Engineers [14].

John Grant made his tests for the Metropolitan Board of Works on tensile

specimens of neat cement of a cross-sectional area of $1\frac{1}{2}$ in by $1\frac{1}{2}$ in. His preliminary tests on specimens 7 days old showed variations in strength from 75 to
719 lb, that is, from 33 to 320 lb/sq in. The sharp edges at the neck of the specimen no doubt exaggerated this variability (figure 260). He specified a minimum
for acceptance of 400 lb, equivalent to 178 lb/sq in. The British Standard requirement in 1904 was a minimum of 400 lb/sq in at 7 days, and 500 at 28 days,
for specimens of neat cement. An alternative was to test briquettes of cement
mixed with a standard sand, obtainable (screened as specified) from a pit at Leighton Buzzard, Bedfordshire, in the proportions of 1 part to 3 by weight. These
should not fail at less than 120 lb/sq in at 7 days and 225 lb/sq in at 28 days.
In subsequent revisions of the British Standard Specification (B.S. 12) the
minimum-strength criterion has gradually been raised, partly because the
methods of making and testing specimens have been more strictly specified,
but even more because the closer control of the manufacturing process has led
to a more reliable product. By 1940 the standard mortar briquette was expected
to stand a 300 lb/sq inch test load at 3 days and 375 lb/sq in at 7 days.

VIII. CONCRETE: PLAIN AND REINFORCED

Lime concrete was used by the Romans, sometimes in the form of a grout or
wet mortar poured into and over a layer of broken stone or brick, sometimes as a
mixture of lime, sand, and broken stone or brick and water. Its use in both
these ways continued intermittently throughout the Middle Ages. As noted in
volumes III and IV, it gained some importance as a material for the foundations
of bridges, and in the early nineteenth century for those of public buildings,
though in Britain this use was thought to be novel. French engineers widely
used concrete made with hydraulic lime or natural cement to provide mass in
sea-walls and breakwaters.

In 1835 mass concrete was used in the foundations of bridges on the Greenwich railway and in sea-walls and dry-docks at Woolwich and Chatham. About
this time a few complete buildings, mostly houses of no great size, were made
of concrete, but this did not become a common practice. The amount of wood
needed for falsework, the heavy labour of mixing and placing concrete, and the
aesthetically unsatisfactory colour and texture of concrete walls cast *in situ* between boards made it unattractive. Somewhat better results were attainable
with building-blocks made in a factory. In 1832 William Ranger took out a
patent for blocks of artificial stone made of sand, lime, and boiling water cast in
wooden moulds. He used them at Brighton and in an extension to the College of
Surgeons in Lincoln's Inn Fields, London.

From about 1850 onwards, for nearly all purposes, Portland cement came to be preferred to other artificial cements, natural cements, and hydraulic limes. Concrete was mixed by men turning the materials over on boards; in good work the whole batch was turned over three times dry and three times more while water was added through a rose. Only on very large works was mixing effected by machines driven by steam-engines. Cement concrete could not be left lying unused for long periods, as lime concrete can be, as it set hard and became unusable within an hour or so of mixing.

Concrete could be used as a substitute for, or indeed as a form of, masonry and shared with other forms a high resistance to compressive forces but a low resistance to tensile forces. Soufflot's attempt to overcome this weakness in masonry by burying iron rods in the joint-planes of masonry was cumbersome and expensive. Moreover, joints in masonry exposed to weather are difficult to keep free from moisture, with the consequent risk of corrosion and expansion of the iron leading to disruption of the masonry. The use of hoop-iron in brick-work by Brunel and others entailed a similar risk. To embed iron rods in poured concrete, however, was not difficult, and a well made Portland-cement concrete was virtually waterproof. It was to be expected that, with the growing reliance on Portland cement, its use in conjunction with iron would be tried, and so indeed it happened. In 1848 J. L. Lambot, a French engineer, built a rowing-boat of concrete reinforced with a mesh of iron bars. Its appearance in 1855 at the Exposition Universelle in Paris aroused considerable interest. Lambot patented this combined use of iron and cement as an alternative to wood in building, both in France and provisionally in England (1855), but does not seem to have developed it.

Joseph Monier (1823–1906), another Frenchman, was more persistent. He began in 1849 with tubs for orange trees, made of concrete with an embedded mesh of iron rods. He extended his interest to portable containers and other articles, and took out several patents (p 502), of which the most important (1877) covered reinforced concrete beams.

Meanwhile W. B. Wilkinson, a builder of Newcastle upon Tyne, made floors with pre-cast gypsum-plaster coffers to serve as ceilings and as permanent form-work for a concrete deck (figure 261). Between two adjacent coffers he left a gap, the bottom of which he filled with a coarse plaster; in this he embedded an iron rod. Over the whole he laid Portland-cement concrete. Main beams were of concrete with second-hand mining rope as reinforcement. He patented this system in 1854, but its application seems to have been local and temporary.

Another important pioneer was François Coignet. He was primarily interested in a concrete mixture embodying pozzolanic materials with lime and an acid phosphate of lime, the latter both to increase the hardness of the surface and, by reducing the alkalinity of the mix, to leave the surface suitable for painting. Incidentally his patent included 'burying beams, iron planks, or a square mesh of rods in concrete on falsework' to form the floors. In 1861 he wrote a memoir in which it appears that he visualized the possibility of most of the modern uses of reinforced concrete, but he had no theoretical basis to work on and could therefore only suggest, without attempting to design, the structures of which he foresaw the possibility. His son, Edmond Coignet (1850–1915), from 1890 onwards took out patents to cover the use of reinforced concrete in pipes,

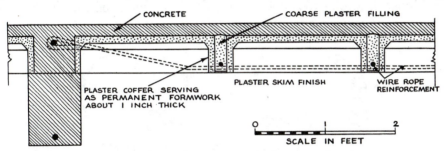

CONCRETE — COARSE PLASTER FILLING

PLASTER COFFER SERVING
AS PERMANENT FORMWORK
ABOUT 1 INCH THICK

PLASTER SKIM FINISH

WIRE ROPE
REINFORCEMENT

0   1   2
SCALE IN FEET

FIGURE 261—*W. B. Wilkinson's floor and ceiling construction, 1854.*

aqueducts, tunnels, pre-cast beams, piles, and sheet-piles. In 1892 he succeeded in persuading the authority concerned to build main sewers in Paris consisting of a shell of thin reinforced concrete, instead of the massive masonry intended. The comparison is shown in figure 262. Coignet's walls were only $3\frac{1}{8}$ in thick. They subsequently carried about 15 ft of earth [16].

Whether Monier in France would have fared better than Wilkinson is perhaps doubtful, had not G. A. Wayss (b 1851), of the firm of Wayss & Freitag of Frankfurt-am-Main, been interested in developing reinforced-concrete work. In 1885 he acquired the right to use Monier's inventions in Germany, and this no doubt encouraged Monier to go ahead. Wayss's firm developed a whole system of construction in reinforced concrete which they applied to many structures, including arched bridges of spans up to some 120 ft. Moreover, they commissioned Mathias Koenen (1849–1924) to work out the theory of such construction on sound mechanical principles. In 1887 Koenen's work was published in a book entitled *Das System Monier*. This aroused the interest of professors in several German polytechnic institutes and thus led to considerable experiment and ultimately to a workable theory. Edmond Coignet also interested himself in theory, and in 1894, jointly with N. de Tedesco, he submitted to the Société des Ingénieurs

Civils de France an essay on the design by calculation of structural members in reinforced concrete. Of those who heard the paper few were able to discuss it, and it received scant attention, though an official commission sat from 1892 until 1900 to study the methods of calculation in use.

Coignet's principal competitor was François Hennebique, who in 1892 patented a reinforced concrete beam in which the main bars were fish-tailed at the ends and shearing-force was resisted by vertical stirrups of hoop-iron, details to which he adhered for several decades. By about 1898 he had developed a complete system of construction with columns, beams, floors, and walls all of reinforced concrete. The Hennebique system was introduced to Britain by L. G. Mouchel, who in 1897 opened an office in London and had no rival until Coignet did the same in 1904. With the exception of Wilkinson, no one before

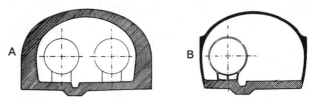

FIGURE 262—*Comparative sections of a Paris sewer.* (A) *As originally proposed in masonry;* (B) *as constructed by E. Coignet in reinforced concrete, 1892.*

Mouchel had made any serious attempt to introduce reinforced-concrete construction into Britain. Thaddeus Hyatt had had some tests made for him at Kirkaldy's laboratory in London, but then went to New York where, in 1877, he published privately a book in which he outlined a theory of reinforced concrete more advanced than any yet produced. In 1878 he took out an American patent for his system of construction, but little seems to have come of it. E. L. Ransome (1844–1917), another Englishman, was more successful. In 1870 his father, the superintendent of the Ransomes & Sims ironworks at Ipswich, sent him to San Francisco to sell reconstructed burr stones. There he found factories being built with cast iron or wrought iron beams and brick or concrete arches, as in the allegedly fireproof mills of this country. He replaced the iron beams by iron tie-bars from wall to wall embedded in concrete, to act with the concrete in the spandrels of the arches as a composite beam, and thereby saved considerably on the weight of iron in the beam. In 1888 he erected his first important building with the reinforced concrete beams, arched floors, and cast iron columns. He next developed a pre-cast beam unit of reinforced concrete with main bars in the bottom, and a helix of wire half-buried in it to bond with the slab of reinforced concrete which, when cast on the site, made with the beams a complete floor.

This was the main item in the Ransome system of unit-construction for which in 1902 he took out an American patent (No 694 577). In 1903 he erected his first fully concrete-framed building at Greenburg, Pennsylvania, and thus established his position as an American pioneer of such construction [17].

By 1900 reinforced concrete construction was well established in western Europe, and had made a promising start in the United States and Britain. Design was largely empirical, and each formulator of a system of construction had his own ideas. The civil engineering profession was only mildly interested, and indeed somewhat sceptical. Statutory authorities were everywhere taking notice, but were not yet ready to issue appropriate regulations. Reinforced concrete buildings with appropriate cover to the reinforcement were satisfactorily fire-resisting. For work exposed to the weather, it was important that the mixture should be properly made and firmly rodded into place, and that the bars should be well covered with dense concrete. In the early work, carried out by specialists on their mettle, these conditions were generally fulfilled, and much of their work is still sound after half a century and more. Some later work, done when familiarity had dulled the edge of vigilance, has proved less satisfactory.

IX. STRUCTURAL THEORY

C. L. M. H. Navier (1785–1836) embodied in a standard textbook (1826) the theory of how beams resisted loads and deflected under them, as developed by Jakob Bernoulli, Leonhard Euler, and C. A. Coulomb (vol IV, p 479). That theory of the beam is still taught. The true position in the cross-section of a beam of the neutral axis (the line that divides the part subject to tension from that subject to compression) became important only when beams were made of cast iron, a material offering great resistance to compressive forces but much less resistant to tension. In the absence of endwise forces the neutral axis passed, as Eaton Hodgkinson (1789–1861) showed in 1831, through the centroid of the section. By studying available experimental results and by carrying out many tests himself Hodgkinson also produced a workable theory of the column that, modified by Lewis Gordon and by W. J. McQuorn Rankine (1820–72), remained standard for the rest of our period. Rankine's 'Applied Mechanics' (1858) and other works provided for British engineers the first comprehensive textbooks comparable with the work of Navier in France. Their authority was not seriously challenged for the remainder of the nineteenth century.

Coulomb (1773) had shown how to test the stability of an arch, but it was necessary to assume the section and the several possible positions of virtual hinges. The best depth and profile for the arch-ring had to be found by trial.

Engineers would have preferred a method of deriving them directly, but this they could not discover. Some tables based on Coulomb's method were produced in France by Garidel, and were reproduced in an English work by Henry Moseley (1801–72) [18].

Probably, however, all the bridges built in the canal era, and nearly all the masonry and brickwork viaducts of the railway era, were designed with the aid of empirical rules having no basis in mathematical theory. Some revealing comments were made by leading civil engineers in 1846, in discussing a paper read before the Institution of Civil Engineers by W. H. Barlow (1812–1902) [19]. Barlow, realizing that Moseley's mathematical methods were too forbidding for engineers, attempted a graphical method. Robert Stephenson (1803–59) thought that 'the paper would remove many difficulties hitherto felt in examining the subject by the process laid down by Professor Moseley, whose formulae, though highly scientific, and no doubt very beautiful, were much too abstruse for the use of the practical man'. I. K. Brunel (1806–59) thought 'an arch might be considered not as composed of separate voussoirs bound together by cement, but as a homogeneous elastic mass'. In this view Brunel was prophetic, but at the time no workable method of so treating the arch was available. It is interesting to note that Barlow and others of that period, who propounded theories or advocated methods of checking the stability of an arch of known or assumed proportions, felt obliged to try out their theories and methods on the Pont-y-ty-Pridd, a remarkably slender masonry arch of 140-ft single span that was still in use after a century, though its stability defied all the empirical rules for the proportions of arches (vol III, p 435) [20].

It was mentioned in vol IV (ch 15) that several works on the design of trussed bridges appeared around 1850, explaining how the forces in the members of the trusses could be computed by resolving and combining the forces acting at each panel-point. de Belidor (1729) and others had advocated a similar treatment but in less general terms. The process was admittedly somewhat laborious. It was not long, however, before it came to be realized that, since the force in every member acts at two joints, the polygons of forces of the various points could be juxtaposed and in effect run into one diagram for the whole truss. This treatment was adopted in Rankine's 'Applied Mechanics' (p 491). Reciprocal diagrams, of which La Hire's treatment of the loaded chain and arch had been the first example (1695; vol III, p 433) were generalized by James Clerk Maxwell (1831–79) in 1864 [21]. Maxwell's treatment was difficult, and probably few engineers read the 'Philosophical Magazine' in which it was printed. It was not till R. H. Bow introduced a systematic notation for marking the corresponding points in the diagrams, and showed by examples how easy his method was to apply to familiar types of truss, that engineers began to pay attention to it. Bow's notation has remained the standard one ever since [22].

The comprehensive development of graphic statics, however, took place in Switzerland and Germany. Carl Culmann (1821–81) had mastered projective geometry, a study originated by Gaspard Monge (1746–1818) of the École Poly-technique, Paris, as early as the 1780s. Projective geometry was further developed and applied to mechanical problems by J. V. Poncelet (1788–1867), and Culmann applied it in the practical design of railway bridges. When the Federal Poly-technic was established at Zürich (1859) Culmann was appointed its first professor of engineering. In his teaching he generalized the use of force- and link-polygons and applied them to the determination of bending-moments, moments of inertia, and other properties of sections, and to the general solution of forces in a jointed triangulated framework. In this work he was greatly assisted by Wilhelm Ritter (1847–1906), who in 1882 succeeded to his chair, collected Culmann's unpublished papers, added material of his own, and so completed a comprehensive treatise in four volumes [23]. The work of Culmann and Ritter was extended by others, notably Otto Mohr and H. Müller-Breslau in Germany, Maurice Levy in France, and Luigi Cremona in Italy. Cremona's book on 'Graphic Statics', published in 1872, was translated into English by Hudson Beare (1890).

In the graphical methods of treating the forces in framed structures, no account was taken of the rigidity of the joints. In American practice, for a long time, actual pins or hinges were provided to ensure some freedom of movement. In Europe and Britain the members were fastened together by riveting or bolt-ing them to gusset plates; but it was found that with careful design there was no serious discrepancy between the actual state of stress in the members of such trusses and the stresses computed from theory ignoring the stiffness of joints. Two types of structure, however, could not be dealt with by simple graphical methods: those in which stability depended not at all on triangulation but on stiffness at joints and the associated resistance of members to bending-moments; and frameworks in which there were more members than were required for simple triangulation and where therefore, from statical considerations alone, the designer could not determine how the loads would be shared between members one or more of which was statically, though not structurally, redundant. To deal with redundant frames the actual lengthening, shortening, or bending of members under load had to be considered.

It would be impossible in this chapter even to summarize intelligibly the principal steps in the progress of various techniques for computing the internal forces in structures by considering the strains in their component members. The author has attempted this survey elsewhere [24] and S. Timoshenko has undertaken it in much greater detail in a standard work [25]. It will be obvious that the skeleton framework of a building with columns and beams but without diagonal bracing must depend for stability either upon solid walls filling some of the panels, or upon the resistance of members and their junctions to bending. The importance that such structures assumed in the closing decade of the nineteenth century compelled engineers to pay attention to mathematical theory that had previously been regarded as merely academic. Broadly speaking, most of the methods of designing partially rigid, statically redundant, or otherwise indeterminate structures were analytical; that is to say, the designer had first to determine approximate sizes and sections for the various members and then find how these would share their loads, the virtual work done by the external forces in distorting the framework being balanced by the strain-energy stored in the members.

The terms 'stress' and 'strain' had been very loosely used by English writers on structural design until Rankine clearly defined them. Stress is the load per unit area of the section over which it acts. Strain is the change in length of a unit length of the material; and in structural materials under normal working loads strain is proportional to stress, according to Hooke's law. The stress divided by the strain is therefore a constant for any given material, and is known as the 'Young's modulus' of that material.

The principle of virtual work was first applied to structures by G. Lamé, an engineer in the service of the Ponts et Chaussées, in a paper presented by him in 1833 to the Académie des Sciences in Paris [26]. Lamé was also the first to advance the theory that a material under load failed when the direct stress reaches a certain value, which we now call the ultimate stress. In this he was followed by Rankine. Other theories have, however, been advanced: that failure occurs when a maximum strain or a maximum shear-stress is reached, or when the strain-energy stored reaches a certain value. In straightforward conditions of tension or compression there is nothing to choose between these theories, but for more complicated stress-conditions, such as occur in a crankshaft subject both to twisting and bending, the choice is not simple, for the ductility or brittleness of the material has to be taken into account. The relationship of strains to stresses in cross directions is complicated by the circumstance that materials squeezed in one direction, say lengthwise, bulge sideways by an amount which varies with different materials. The sideways strain is for the most part between one-third and one-quarter of the lengthwise strain. This relationship was noticed by S. D. Poisson in 1829; hence the term 'Poisson's ratio' for it when expressed as a fraction.

The mathematical theory of elasticity was extended to a wide range of problems between 1830 and 1860, and thenceforward has influenced structural theory increasingly, though its application to practice was slight even at the end of the nineteenth century. The application of such ideas as the principle of virtual work, and the use of methods of calculation based on strain-energy, were, however, brought to the notice of engineers by A. Castigliano's treatise in 1879 [27], and by the writings of Otto Mohr and H. Müller-Breslau in the later decades of the century. Some of these continental developments were introduced to British engineers by T. Claxton Fidler's book entitled 'Bridges' (1887). It was ultimately the problems raised by the design of skeleton-framed buildings that compelled engineers, in the twentieth century, to pay serious attention to methods of computation based on the study of elastic distortions.

In describing the development of reinforced concrete, it was noted that the pioneers in the design of early structures in that material relied on intuitive structural sense and empirical application of simple tests. As the structures became larger, bolder, and more complex, such reliance had obvious limitations. If failure was to be avoided, either the material must be used in a conservative and probably uneconomical manner, or designers must know more certainly how the steel and the concrete actually behaved in combination. In Koenen's book *Das System Monier* (p 489) it was recognized that the volume-changes of steel and concrete with fluctuations of temperature are so nearly equal that for all practical purposes stress-changes from differential movement could be ignored; that the adhesion between the two materials was adequate to transfer the internal forces; and that the steel alone should be relied on to resist tensile forces, since the surrounding concrete must inevitably crack under its share of the strain. Koenen placed the neutral axis at the mid-depth of rectangular beams; but Paul Neumann pointed out (1890) that when the moduli of elasticity of steel and concrete were taken into account this central position was inconsistent with the equilibrium of tensile and compressive internal forces. More experiments on the elastic deformation of reinforced concrete members under load were made by Fritz von Emperger (1862–1942), J. Bauschinger (1834–93), and others. In 1902 E. Mörsch, on behalf of Wayss & Freitag (p 489), wrote *Der Eisenbeton*, a book which made public the whole of the firm's experimental data and put the theory of the subject on a rational basis. On this theory the Prussian official regulations covering the design of reinforced-concrete structures were based (1903). Mörsch was by this time designing bridge-arches in re-inforced concrete with spans up to 200 ft. Though Mörsch's book revealed to competitors the hitherto secret methods of design, they also enhanced public confidence in his firm's work. No other had nearly so much experience or organization.

Edmond Coignet and de Tedesco (p 489) assumed that the Coulomb–Navier theory of bending applied approximately to reinforced concrete if all tensile resistance in the concrete was ignored. That is, they supposed that plane sections before bending remained plane after bending, and that the material distorted in accordance with Hooke's law. They also assumed that the moduli of elasticity of steel and concrete were constant, and gave to the ratio between them the title 'modular ratio' which has been used ever since.

A. G. Considère (1841–1914) showed by experiment that the strength of simply reinforced columns could be markedly increased if closely spaced hoops, or a spiral of stout wire, surrounded the main longitudinal bars and so retained a core of concrete which was prevented from bursting outwards and pushing the main bars aside as it would otherwise do under a much smaller load. He worked out the relationship between the hooping provided and the increased strength. Considère collaborated with A. Mesnager, engineer to the City of Paris, in drawing up regulations for design which in 1906 were adopted officially in France.

The further development of reinforced concrete lies outside our period, but by the turn of the century a workable theory, largely based empirically upon test results, was being followed with confidence by the most experienced designers. The assumptions on which it was based were not strictly true, and did not pass without challenge; but greater refinement of theory, until very recent days, has been held to add complications which in practice were not justified, their greater accuracy in some directions being more than outweighed by the variability of the physical properties of concrete. This was undoubtedly true until much closer control came to be exercised over both the manufacture of cement and the mixing and placing of concrete.

REFERENCES

[1] GIEDION, S. 'Space, Time and Architecture', pp. 269 ff. Harvard University Press, Cambridge, Mass. 1943.
CONDIT, CARL W. "Engineering in History", *Isis*, **48**, no. 154, p. 485. History of Science Society, Cambridge, Mass. 1957.
[2] DE L'ORME, P. 'Nouvelles inventions pour bien bâtir à petit frais.' Paris. 1561.

[3] HITCHCOCK, H. R. *Archit. Rev., Lond.*, **109**, 113–16, 1951.
BOGARDUS, J. 'Cast Iron Buildings.' New York. 1856.
[4] BANNISTER, T. *Archit. Rev., Lond.*, **108**, 232, 245, 1950.
[5] HITCHCOCK, H. R. 'Early Victorian Architecture in Britain', Vol. 1, ch. 10; Vol. 2, Pl. x, 14. Architectural Press, London. 1954.
[6] LAVEDAN, P. 'French Architecture', p. 149, Pl. XXVIII. Penguin Books, Harmondsworth. 1956.
[7] HALL, J. W. *Trans. Newcomen Soc.*, **8**, 43, 1927–8.
[8] MEEKS, C. L. V. *Archit. Rev., Lond.*, **110**, 163–73, 1951.
[9] GIEDION, S. See ref. [1], p. 138.
KIRBY, R. S. *et al.* 'Engineering in History', p. 322. McGraw Hill, New York. 1956.
[10] SCOTT, B. *Struct. Engr*, new series, **7**, 102, 1929.
[11] GIEDION, S. See ref. [1], pp. 292 ff.
KIRBY, R. S. See ref. [9], pp. 464 ff.
BOSSOM, A. C. *Struct. Engr*, new series, **7**, 75, 1929.
[12] HAMILTON, S. B. 'A Short History of the Structural Fire Protection of Buildings.' National Building Studies, Special Report No. 27. H.M. Stationery Office, London. 1958.
WEBSTER, J. J. *Min. Proc. Instn civ. Engrs*, **105**, Pt III, 249–88, 1890–1.
[13] REDGRAVE, G. R. and SPACKMAN, C. 'Calcareous Cements' (3rd ed.) Griffin, London. 1924.
[14] DRAFFIN, J. O. *Bull. Ill. Engng Exp. Sta.*, **40**, no. 45, 14, 1943. (Reprint no. 27.)
[15] GRANT, J. *Min. Proc. Instn civ. Engrs*, **25**, 66–79, 1865–6.
[16] TEDESCO, N. DE. *Concr. constr. Engng*, **1**, 162, 1906.
[17] RANSOME, E. L. and SAUBREY, A. 'Reinforced Concrete Buildings.' McGraw Hill, New York. 1912.
[18] MOSELEY, H. 'Mechanical Principles of Engineering and Architecture.' London. 1843.
[19] BARLOW, W. H. *Min. Proc. Instn civ. Engrs*, **5**, 162, 1846.
[20] HAMILTON, S. B. *Trans. Newcomen Soc.*, **24**, 131, 1943–5.
[21] MAXWELL, J. C. *Phil. Mag.*, fourth series, **27**, 250, 294, 1864.
[22] BOW, R. H. 'Economics of Construction in Relation to Framed Structures.' London. 1873.
[23] CULMANN, C. 'Die graphische Statik.' Zürich. 1864.
RITTER, W. 'Anwendungen der graphischen Statik' (4 vols). Meyer & Zeller, Zürich. 1888–1906.
[24] HAMILTON, S. B. *Proc. Instn civ. Engrs*, **1**, Pt III, 374–419, 1952.
[25] TIMOSHENKO, S. P. 'History of Strength of Materials.' McGraw Hill, New York. 1953.
[26] LAMÉ, G. "Mémoire sur l'équilibre intérieur des corps solides homogènes." *Mém. Acad. R. Sci. Sav. étrang.*, **4**, 465, 1833.
[27] CASTIGLIANO, A. 'Théorem de l'équilibre des systèmes élastiques.' Turin. 1879. (See also Eng. trans. by E. S. ANDREWS. 'Elastic Stresses in Structures.' Scott Greenwood, London. 1919.

BIBLIOGRAPHY

DRAFFIN, J. O. "A Brief History of Lime, Cement, Concrete and Reinforced Concrete." *Bull. Ill. Engng Exp. Sta.*, **40**, no. 45, 14, 1943. (Reprint no. 27.)
GOODING, P. and HALSTEAD, P. E. "The Early History of Cement in England" in 'Proceedings of the Third International Symposium on the Chemistry of Cement, London, 1952', pp. 1–29. Cement and Concrete Association, London. 1955.

FAIRBAIRN, SIR WILLIAM. 'Researches on the Application of Iron to Buildings' (2nd ed.). London. 1857.

HAMILTON, S. B. "The Historical Development of Structural Theory." *Proc. Instn civ. Engrs*, **1**, Part III, 374–419, 1952.

Idem. 'A Note on the History of Reinforced Concrete in Buildings.' National Building Studies, Special Report No. 25. H.M. Stationery Office, London. 1956.

HITCHCOCK, H. R. 'Early Victorian Architecture in Britain', Vols 1, 2. Architectural Press, London. 1954.

KIRBY, R. S. *et al.* 'Engineering in History', chs 10, 14. McGraw Hill, New York. 1956.

SACHS, E. O. (Ed.). *Concr. constr. Engng*, **1**, 1906.

STRAUB, H. 'Die Geschichte der Bauingenieurkunst.' Birkhäuser, Basel. 1949. (See also Eng. trans. by E. ROCKWELL. 'A History of Civil Engineering.' Hill, London. 1952.)

TIMOSHENKO, S. P. 'History of Strength of Materials.' McGraw Hill, New York. 1953.

Elisha Otis demonstrating his original safety elevator, 1854.

21

BRIDGES AND TUNNELS

H. SHIRLEY SMITH

THE main factors that determine advances in the technology of bridging and tunnelling are the materials of construction available, the type of power and variety of machines at the engineer's command, and the extent of his knowledge both of design and of the strength of materials. When we examine the influence of these factors in the years 1850–1900 we see that marked progress was made in every field.

I. MATERIALS OF CONSTRUCTION

In the mid-nineteenth century the only materials in use were timber, stone, brick, concrete, and iron. The use of cast iron persisted for tunnel-rings, but for bridge-work it had been superseded by wrought iron, which was produced from pig iron in a vibrating puddling-furnace. Although weight for weight wrought iron was more expensive than cast iron, it had less carbon in it and was therefore tougher, much stronger in tension, and capable of being riveted instead of bolted. Wrought iron plates were rolled from 'faggots', which consisted of bundles of flat bar-iron assembled into rectangles of the same size, laid one upon the other, and bound together with iron wire to hold them during heating. The alternate layers of iron were of different quality—hard, soft, refined, and unrefined. The faggot was rolled hot to make an approximately rectangular plate which was then sheared to the size required. As more works became equipped with shearing- and punching-machines, in the first place to build ships and boilers, so wrought iron gained in favour. Then in 1856 Bessemer converted pig iron into steel by blowing jets of hot air through the molten metal to remove some of the carbon and other impurities. Nine years later the open-hearth process for producing mild steel commercially was invented by Martin and Siemens. Engineers were deeply impressed by the uniform strength, workability, and cheapness of the new material. In 1877 the Board of Trade permitted its use in bridge-work in Great Britain, and eight years later, when Dorman Long & Company rolled the first steel joists, the days of the iron bridge were numbered.

Before 1880 galvanized cast steel wire had been manufactured, and was used in the cables of the Brooklyn suspension-bridge. Although there was little if any advance in masonry work, the first reinforced concrete bridge of 52-ft span was built in 1875, thus introducing the so-called reinforced concrete age of the next century. Somewhat surprisingly, the use of timber as a permanent structural material persisted even in important bridges well after 1900.

FIGURE 263—*Pneumatic rock-drill used for excavation in the caissons of the Forth bridge.*

II. POWER AND MACHINES

The railway era was now in its prime, and steam was of course the principal motive- and driving-power. In addition to railway engines there were steam-driven locomotives and Goliath cranes, Scotch derricks, excavators, hoists, and winches. Towards the end of the period, steam was also employed to drive a variety of smaller tools used in steel fabrication, such as drilling- and planing-machines. Steam-driven air-compressors were used for pneumatic work in under-water tunnelling and in the sinking of caissons for bridge foundations. Rock-drills driven by compressed air at a pressure of 70 lb to the sq in were used for excavating inside the caissons of the Forth bridge (figure 263), and multiple drills were evolved for tunnel-boring. A wide variety of hydraulic machines such as pumps, accumulators, rams, and presses came into use, as well as clay spades (figure 264) and hydraulic riveting machines (figure 265). For lighting, gas- and oil-lamps were widely used, and in the erection of the Forth bridge 'Lucigen' lamps were employed. In these, creosote oil was forced in the form of a spray through a small nozzle by means of air-pressure, and produced a naked flame more than 3 ft long emitting a light of brilliant intensity. Before the end of the century electric arc and incandescent lamps had appeared, and the first electric motors were being developed; but in constructional work the internal combustion engine remained a prime mover of the future.

III. THEORY OF DESIGN

Considerable progress was made in this period in the theory of the design of structures. In 1845 Robert Stephenson (1803–59) had to design the Britannia bridge (p 503), connecting the Isle of Anglesey with the Welsh mainland, by following the empirical method of trial and error. Models were made and tested, strengthened where they failed, and re-tested until a reasonably economic and satisfactory result was obtained. At that date little if any theory was available, although mathematicians were at work on it. Thirty years later, however, a great deal of theory had been established, much of it on the European continent, and was set out in scientific papers and textbooks. Benjamin Baker (1840–1907) was thus able to design a mighty structure like the Forth bridge with full confidence in his knowledge of the stresses created in every part by dead loads, moving loads, wind loads, and changes of temperature.

FIGURE 264 — *Hydraulic spade for clay used in the Forth bridge caissons.*

Much credit for the application of scientific study to practical engineering to bring about this notable advance belongs to W. J. M. Rankine (1820–72), who occupied the chair of civil engineering and mechanics at Glasgow University from 1855. His works embodied a comprehensive survey of most European and American mathematical or technical monographs of importance to engineering, and embraced subjects as diverse as thermodynamics, strut-formulae, earth-pressures, and the conception of shear in beams. It was Rankine who gave currency to the words stress and strain in their precise technical senses (p 494). His theories of earth-pressure and angle of repose of materials have long been used in the design of tunnels and retaining walls.

Foremost among continental scientists was Karl Culmann (1821–81) of Zürich, who was responsible for the development of the graphic methods of structural analysis, first described in his 'Graphic Statics' (1864) and subsequently elaborated by Cremona at Milan and Mohr at Dresden. In 1863 Ritter produced his method of sections, which enabled the stresses in a truss to be calculated. The investigations of Clerk Maxwell (1831–79) and the notation devised by Bow (1873) enabled engineers to draw stress diagrams. Influence-lines for the determination of the effect of moving loads were described by E. Winkler in 1868. The elaboration of the 'Theorem of Three Moments' of Clapeyron (1799–1864) for the solution of continuous beams, and Williot's method for the graphical determination of deflexions in a frame, also belong to this period.

A considerable variety of trusses had been evolved with Warren, Pratt, 'N'-type, and other kinds of bracing. The early practice in the United States, where the first major iron-truss bridge was built in 1851, was to use pins for making the connexions at the node-points or joints; in Europe rigid connexions were made by means of bolts or rivets, but the stresses were calculated on the assumption that the joints were pinned. The effect of making them rigid was to set up secondary bending-stresses in the members, which were investigated in the 1880s by H. Manderla and C. von Abo, using strain-energy methods. In 1867 the first iron cantilever girder, consisting of a series of alternate continuous and cantilever spans, was built by H. Gerber over the Main at Hassfurt (Bavaria).

In masonry work, graphical methods were evolved by Winkler and Fuller for plotting the line of thrust in an arch, and the principle of the 'middle third'[1] was given publicity by Rankine. In 1867 Joseph Monier of France took out the first patent for reinforced concrete; but it was left to the German engineer M. Koenen, followed by P. Neumann and E. Coignet, to investigate the theory of composite structures and to devise a method of mathematical analysis and design (p 489).

In tunnel construction, the Austrian engineer Franz von Rziha (1831–97) was the first to enunciate the scientific principles underlying the work, which had formerly been largely left to the practical engineer on the site.

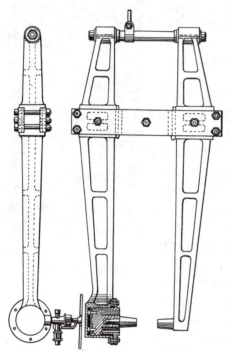

FIGURE 265—*Portable hydraulic riveting machine used on the Forth bridge steelwork.*

Experiments on wind pressure. In 1850 little if anything was known of the effect on bridges of moving loads, impact, and wind forces, and many failures resulted. The effect of wind was gravely underestimated. Engineers were still thinking in terms of wind pressures taken from a table presented by Smeaton to the Royal Society in 1759—a hundred years before:

6 lb per sq ft for 'high winds';

8 or 9 lb per sq ft for 'very high winds';

12 lb per sq ft for a 'storm or tempest'.

[1] This is the well known rule for masonry work, in which no tension is allowable, that across a rectangular joint the resultant thrust must fall within ⅙th of the thickness from the centre line of the joint, i.e. within the 'middle third'. The rule was deduced by Navier in 1826, and was introduced independently by Méry in 1840.

The failure of the first Tay bridge in 1879 revealed the deficiency of design in allowing for wind forces, and in 1883 Benjamin Baker undertook a comprehensive series of experiments in order to determine the wind pressures to be taken into account in the design of the Forth bridge. Three wind gauges or pressure boards were installed upon the old castle at Inchgarvie at the central pier of the bridge. The large board, having an area of 300 sq ft, was fixed in a north–south line, facing east and west winds; of the two smaller boards, $1\frac{1}{2}$ sq ft in area, one was fixed and one free to swivel. Records were taken for two years on these wind gauges. In addition, further experiments were carried out on models with the object of determining the degree of shelter afforded by one truss to another, and also the effect of the wind on lattice box girders and on tubular members respectively. Baker states that he 'designed a very simple pendulum arrangement, consisting in effect of a cross-bar, with a model at one end and an adjustable flat surface at the other of exactly equal weight, which bar was suspended at the centre so that the only resistance to turning was the torsion of the suspending string. On oscillating this pendulum, if the flat surface were not the exact equivalent in resistance of the model, one or the other would advance.' As a result of a careful analysis of all these tests, Fowler and Baker agreed to allow for a wind pressure of 56 lb per sq ft acting on an area equal to twice the front surface of the structure, with a deduction of 50 per cent in the case of tubes. This was in conformity with the advice of the committee set up by the Board of Trade after the Tay bridge disaster, but Fowler and Baker were of the opinion that 'the assumed pressure of 56 lb per sq ft over the whole bridge is considerably in excess of anything likely to be realized'. This opinion is supported by the results of modern investigations, which indicate that a reasonable wind pressure to adopt would have been about 34 lb per sq ft.

IV. THE DESIGNING AND BUILDING OF SOME SPECIFIC BRIDGES

(i) *The Britannia bridge*. It is instructive to examine the methods used in the design and erection of the Britannia bridge, which was completed in 1850, comparing them with those used in the building of the Forth bridge some 35 years later. In order to overcome objections by the Admiralty and shipping interests to a bridge composed of a series of arches, Stephenson came to the conclusion that a suspension-bridge, with its deck stiffened to enable it to carry fast railway traffic, offered the most promising design. From this sprang the idea of pairs of huge wrought-iron tubes through which the trains would pass, supported by suspension-chains on either side. No doubt the availability of the good-quality wrought-iron plates and sections recently produced for ship-building contributed to this idea. William Fairbairn, who collaborated with Stephenson, undertook the fabrication and testing of model tubes at his shipyard at Millwall, and Eaton Hodgkinson, a mathematician, assisted in interpreting and applying the results of the tests. Twelve experiments were made on tubes of cylindrical section, seven on tubes of elliptical section, and fourteen on tubes of rectangular section. The tubes were of various sizes and spans and were constructed of plates of different thicknesses; they were all tested to destruction by a concentrated load applied at mid-span. The experiments disclosed that the tube of rectangular section was the strongest, and a final series of tests was conducted on a model of a large rectangular tube one-sixth of full size. Six tests were made on this model, and as a result of them its carrying-capacity was increased nearly $2\frac{1}{2}$ times by an addition of material amounting to only 20 per cent in weight. The resident engineer, Clark, recorded that 'the model failed at length from the crushing of the top, after a greater weight than even a double line of locomotives throughout the whole length'.

There were to be four spans in all, consisting of pairs of tubes side by side; the two spans over the water were each 459 ft long, and the two over the land at each end 230 ft long. Each tube was 30 ft deep at the centre and had a width of 14 ft 9 in. In order to stiffen the tube against buckling, the top and bottom were built in cellular construction. Fixed bearings were provided in the Britannia tower, but in order to allow for their expansion and contraction with changes in temperature the tubes were carried on expansion bearings at the other two towers and at the abutments.

When the quotation for the cost of the suspending-chains was received it proved unexpectedly high. Stephenson had from the start been sceptical about the necessity for such chains, except to assist in the erection of the tubes, and he therefore sought another method of erection so that the chains could be dispensed with altogether. Clark then suggested that the tubes should be floated out on pontoons and raised to their final level by means of hydraulic rams, and this scheme was adopted. Workshops were built on the site. The tubes for the land spans were assembled *in situ* at their final height on temporary timber stagings; those spanning the water were constructed on a staging by the water's edge. An overhead gantry was used to lift the wrought iron plates and sections, and most of the rivets were driven by means of hydraulic riveting-machines designed by Fairbairn. After assembly each tube, weighing 1285 tons, was floated out on pontoons at high water (plate 29) and landed, as the tide fell, in recesses in the masonry towers. The tube was then slowly raised to its correct level by means of vertical hydraulic rams fixed near the top of the towers (figure 266).

The stroke of the rams was 6 ft and the tubes were lifted at the rate of 2 in per minute. On each tube this operation occupied several weeks, and the work was not without incident. While the first tube was being raised the bottom of the cylinder of one of the rams burst and broke away, and the end of the tube fell heavily through a distance of 10 inches upon the timber packings that were used to follow up the lifting. The bottom plates of the tube were buckled inwards for some 40 ft from the end, but the damage was soon repaired and after two more weeks of careful lifting the tube reached its final elevation in the bridge.

Although the theory of beams was not properly understood at this time, Stephenson knew enough to realize that the tubes would develop their full capacity as continuous beams only if a negative moment was set up initially over the supports. He therefore had the far end of the tube raised slightly, before riveting the near end to the junction-piece at the tower. When this riveting was completed the far end of the tube was lowered on to its permanent bearings, thus setting up a negative moment at the tower. Owing, however, to his inability to make accurate calculations of the moments and corresponding deflexions, Stephenson did not

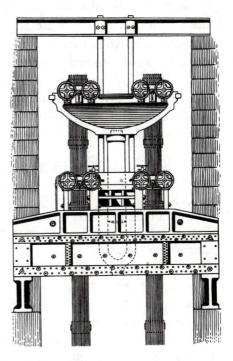

FIGURE 266—*Hydraulic ram employed in hoisting the tubes of the Britannia bridge.*

fully attain his object, and the moments at mid-span remain greater than those over the supports.

The Britannia bridge represents an amazing advance in bridge-building, the previous longest wrought-iron span having been only 31 ft 6 in. Moreover, the Britannia bridge is the forerunner of the tens of thousands of plate-girder bridges—the most useful kind of railway bridge devised—that can be seen all over the world today. Without any alteration and with only negligible repairs, the bridge is still in service and is carrying much heavier traffic than that for which it was designed more than a hundred years ago.

(ii) *The Forth bridge.* In the Forth bridge (1882–90), about 54 000 tons of Siemens–Martin open-hearth steel was used. This was the first railway bridge having a long span to be built of steel. The Board of Trade specified that the working stresses should not be more than a quarter of the ultimate strength of the material, but made no further stipulations. The designers decided that the steel for compression-members should have an ultimate tensile strength of 34–37 tons per sq in and for tension-members 30–33 tons per sq in. The steel used was thus substantially stronger than commercial mild steel as manufactured today, which has an ultimate strength of 28–32 tons per sq in. Two further advances since Robert Stephenson's day were that all rivet-holes were drilled, not punched, and the edges of every plate were planed, in order to remove the metal affected by shearing. The fabrication of the steel-work was carried out in extensive engineering shops and yards, covering an area of 50 acres, built for the purpose at South Queensferry.

In 1884 Benjamin Baker stated:

The plant includes 14 steam barges, launches and other vessels; 22 steam, 12 hydraulic and 38 hand-power cranes; 28 single and double engines for shop machines, hydraulic work, air-compressing, electric lighting, pumping and other purposes; also gas furnaces for heating the steel plates, a 2000-ton hydraulic press for bending them, and planing machines, multiple drills, hydraulic riveters and other specially-designed tools too numerous to mention.

The heaviest compression-members were designed as tubular struts 12 ft in diameter, built from plates up to $1\frac{1}{4}$ in thick, about 4 ft 6 in wide, and 16 ft long. For these members some 42 miles of plates had to be bent. The best method proved to be to bend the plates hot in the 2000-ton press and to give them a straightening squeeze afterwards when cold. The plates were planed on the sides in the usual manner, and at the curved ends by a radial machine. They were then, with the internal stiffeners, temporarily built into a tube round a mandrel, and the rivet-holes were drilled through plates, covers, and bars at one operation. Four annular drill-frames, surrounding the tubes and furnished each with ten traversing-drills, capable of attacking every hole, travelled along railway lines in the drilling-yards so laid out that four sections of tube, each having a total length of 400 ft, could be dealt with at once.

After drilling, these members were dismantled and subsequently re-erected plate by plate in the bridge. There they were assembled by a 2-ton hydraulic crane, which was supported on top of the finished part of the member, and moved along erecting the steel-work in front of it. Riveting was carried out by a hydraulic machine beneath the crane. For erection of the upper girders, which consisted of lattice box members, and the struts and ties, light steam-cranes were used. They were mounted on carriages spanning the width of the bridge, and were followed by hydraulic cranes which handled the riveting-machines.

The erection of the steel-work proceeded outwards from both sides of each main pier so that the weights on either side were kept approximately in balance (plate 28). The steel members last erected were supported by those behind them, hence no staging was required. Each main span of 1710 ft was made up of two 680-ft cantilever arms, with a 350-ft suspended span between them. It was decided to build out the halves of the suspended span as continuations of the cantilever arms until they met and could be joined in the middle. With considerable courage the engineers had relied on the heat of the sun to effect the closure, and it was calculated that at a temperature of 60° F the bolt-holes in the overlapping plates at the centre connexions would come fair, so that the bolts could be inserted and the connexions made. Owing to delays, however, the first span was not ready until October and on a sunny day when closure was attempted the temperature did not rise above 55° F. With the help of hydraulic rams the holes in the west lower chord joint were brought fair and the bolts inserted, but a chilly north-east wind was blowing and the holes in the east boom remained stubbornly blind. The engineers then showed their resource by lighting fires of wood shavings and oily waste laid for 60 ft either way along the lower chords. The steel-work, heated by the flames, quickly expanded the last quarter of an inch, the holes came fair, and the bolts were inserted. Next day the wedges to close the compression-joints in the upper chords were driven, the temporary ties at the ends of the suspended span were removed so that it hung free, and the closure was thus successfully completed.

(iii) *The Clifton suspension-bridge*. Turning now from girder and cantilever bridges to another type, the most interesting suspension-bridge built in Britain in the period under review was the Clifton bridge of 702-ft span (plate 30), designed by I. K. Brunel (1806–59) to cross the gorge of the Avon.[1] The chains, made of Low Moor wrought iron, were taken from the first Hungerford bridge over the Thames and re-erected at Clifton in 1862. Each link was tested to a stress of 10 tons per sq in. Whereas Telford's procedure in building the Menai suspension-bridge, forty years before, had been to lay out the chains full length, tow them across the waterway, and then hoist them up into position, at Clifton a temporary suspended staging was slung across the gorge, on which the chains were assembled link by link. Temporary stagings of this kind, known as 'cat-

---

[1] The bridge was designed by Brunel in 1831, but was not completed till after his death. The old Hungerford suspension-bridge was built by him in 1841–5, and was taken down in 1862 to make way for Charing Cross railway-station.

walks', are invariably used in the erection of suspension-bridges today. This staging was made of eight iron-wire ropes with cross-planking and was hung just below the position the chains would finally occupy. The links of the chains, which consisted of flat plates upwards of 24 ft in length, connected by bolts (figure 267), were assembled by beginning at the anchorages and working out to the middle of the span. They were conveyed by light travellers running on an overhead cable, and the assembled chains were supported on timber packings on the staging. After the last link in each chain had been assembled the packings were knocked out and the chain hung free. The vertical suspension rods were

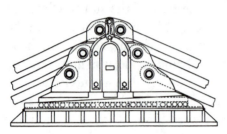

FIGURE 267—*Connexion of cable links to tower saddle on Clifton bridge.*

hung in position and the cross-girders erected by a light travelling-crane, which moved out at roadway-level erecting the deck in front of it. To support the roadway against the action of the wind, four longitudinal stiffening girders of wrought iron were provided. These were very effective, and an observer stated that even the most violent storms set up no more than 'a slow and stately movement of the structure', which manifested itself by an undulation of the roadway not exceeding 6 inches above and below the mean position.

(iv) *The Grand Trunk bridge, Niagara.* The greatest advance in the technique of suspension-bridge construction, however, was made by John A. Roebling (1806-69) in America. Before his time wire cables for suspension-bridges had always been made, following European practice, from numbers of twisted or stranded wire ropes, which were hauled across the span and erected each in one piece. Roebling, however, conceived the idea of a cable made up of a great number of parallel wires not twisted at all, but 'spun' or erected *in situ* wire by wire and subsequently formed into a compact, uniformly tensioned bunch held together with binding wire. In March 1841 he applied for a patent, and the method was successfully used on aqueducts and on short spans; but it was not until 1855, when his Grand Trunk bridge at Niagara was completed, that he was able to demonstrate the success of his invention on a major bridge.

The Grand Trunk bridge, which had a span of 820 ft between the centres of its masonry towers, was a double-decked structure, carrying a single-track railway on the upper deck and a roadway below. It was the first suspension-bridge that proved sufficiently rigid to carry the concentrated loads and impact of railway traffic with any success. The four main cables, built up from parallel wrought iron wires, were each ten inches in diameter. Stiffening girders 18 ft deep were assembled between the upper and lower decks, and inclined stays of wire rope were provided both above and below the deck to prevent it from being heaved up and down by the action of the wind.

Twelve years later, when Roebling was appointed chief engineer for the design and construction of the famous Brooklyn bridge in New York, he used the same method of forming the cables; but at the last moment he decided to make them of galvanized cast steel wire which had an ultimate strength of 71·5 tons per sq

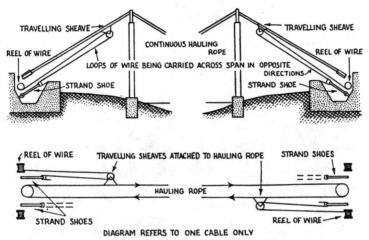

FIGURE 268—*Diagram illustrating the method of cable-spinning devised by John A. Roebling.*

in. The method of cable-spinning devised by Roebling (figure 268) has been adopted in its essentials, although with many embellishments and mechanized aids, in all the huge suspension-bridges since built in the United States. The wire, which is usually about 0·19 in thick, is delivered to the site in hundreds of large reels which are mounted in succession at the anchorages at each end of the bridge. Loops of wire are then pulled from these reels across the span, over special saddles on the tops of the towers, and down to the anchorages on the far side. This is effected by means of grooved spinning-wheels fixed to an endless hauling-rope. When each loop of wire reaches the far end of the bridge it is removed from the spinning-wheel by hand and placed round a 'strand shoe' which connects it to the anchorage. Another loop is then carried across on the return journey of the wheel and so the spinning proceeds. Men on the cat-walks adjust the wires to the correct level, at the centre of the span and in the side spans, against a fixed guide-wire, and thus ensure that they all have exactly the same sag. After all the wires have been assembled, they are squeezed together to make a solid compact bunch and bound round with binding wire. Figure 269 shows the squeezing and initial seizing being carried out on one of the cables of the Brooklyn bridge.

(v) *The St Louis bridge*. We have now seen how the spans of girder bridges such as the Britannia bridge were lifted bodily into position, how the members

FIGURE 269—*Compacting and initial seizing of cables on Brooklyn bridge.*

of a great cantilever bridge like the Forth were built out and were self-supporting from the piers, and how the cables of suspension-bridges, whether made from links or wires, were assembled. Other problems were involved in the erection of the early iron-arched bridges, such as the St Louis bridge (1867–74), designed and built by James B. Eads, over the Mississippi river. The bridge consisted of three arches, the central one having a span of 520 ft and the two at the sides of 502 ft; it was double-decked and carried a roadway on the upper deck and two railway tracks below. The St Louis bridge is noteworthy because it was the first major arch-bridge to be erected by the cantilever method (figure 270), the halves

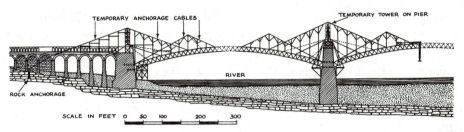

FIGURE 270—*Cantilever method of erection adopted on the St Louis bridge.*

of each arch being temporarily tied back, by means of cables passing over the tops of towers built on the piers, until they met and were joined in the middle. It is usually uneconomic, if not impracticable, to construct staging to support an iron arch of wide span, and, with the exception of the Bayonne bridge where the circumstances were most unusual, the cantilever method has been adopted for all the big steel arch-bridges subsequently built. During erection the upper chords of the cantilevers are in tension, and this method could not therefore be used for the construction of brick or masonry arches, which can resist only compressive force, and must be supported by centring.

V. BRIDGES OF MASONRY AND CONCRETE

From time immemorial it has been necessary to build masonry bridges on temporary staging or centring, which obviously cannot be removed until the arch is complete and self-supporting (vol III, ch 16). Figures 271 and 272 show an elevation of the magnificent Pont Adolphe at Luxembourg (1899–1903), and the arrangement of the temporary centring on which the masonry voussoirs of the arch-ring were placed. The main arch has a span of 84·65 m and the centring consisted of a braced timber arch, tied across by cables at each panel point (figure 272). The ends of the lower ribs of the staging were supported on temporary piers between which the centring extended as a self-supporting structure.

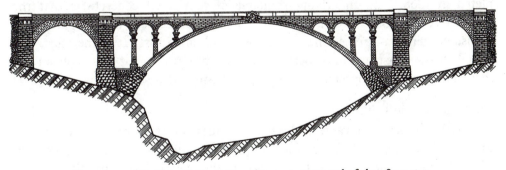

FIGURE 271—*The Pont Adolphe at Luxembourg, a masonry arch of about 85 m span.*

Centring of this kind is said to be 'suspended', and is adopted if the bridge spans a deep gorge or river that would make the provision of temporary piles or trestles too costly. Devices such as screw-jacks, sand-jacks, or folding wedges are used to enable the centring of masonry arches to be struck without difficulty. To save masonry, the Pont Adolphe was built in the form of twin arches, each 6 m wide, side by side, and joined together by a reinforced concrete deck 16 m wide above them.

Reinforced concrete bridges. Although Portland cement was in use, and the first patent for reinforced concrete was taken out in England by Ralph Dodds, long

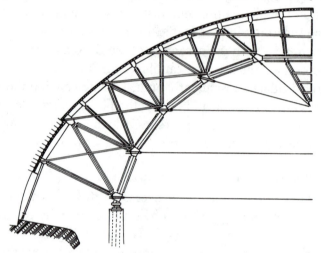

FIGURE 272—*Suspended centring used for the erection of the Pont Adolphe.*

before 1850, it was not until nearly the end of the nineteenth century that the new material was used in bridge-construction. Perhaps the first notable reinforced concrete bridge was the Pont de Châtellerault, an arch of 172-ft span, designed by the famous French engineer François Hennebique (1842–1921) and completed in 1898. The underlying principle of reinforced concrete is that the concrete resists compression, while the steel reinforcement is incorporated to withstand tension-stresses that concrete could not resist. It is therefore well suited to the construction of beam- and arch-bridges, but it was only on the threshold of its development at the end of the period under review.

VI. MOVABLE BRIDGES

The chief types of movable bridges are bascules, swing spans, and the vertical-lift type. Transporter-bridges, such as those at Middlesbrough and Newport, Monmouthshire, were not built until early in the twentieth century. Some of the first swing bridges of cast iron were erected in the London docks early in the nineteenth century, but the evolution of modern bascule and swing spans did not take place until towards the end of it. Perhaps the most famous of them is Tower Bridge in London (1886–94), which is a double-leaf, simple trunnion bascule-bridge, providing a waterway of 200 ft for shipping. A sectional elevation of one of the leaves is shown in figure 273. Each rack quadrant is engaged by two pinions rotated by hydraulic power deriving from one of two double-

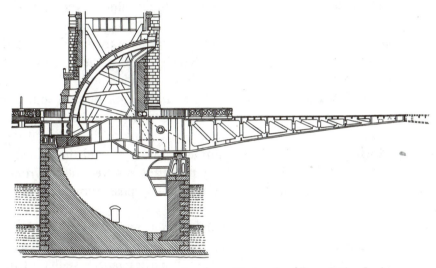

FIGURE 273—*Sectional elevation of one of the bascules of Tower Bridge, London.*

tandem, compound, surface-condensing steam-engines installed in the south abutment. The other engine is held in reserve. The pumps driven by these engines discharge into an accumulator on each pier. The plunger has a diameter of 22 in, a stroke of 18 ft, and works at a pressure of 700 lb to the sq in.

The biggest swing span built in the nineteenth century was the Harlem river bridge in New York City. This bridge carried four railway-tracks and had an overall length of 389 ft; the turning-weight was 2500 tons. The bridge was replaced by a twin-lift bridge in 1956. One of the first modern vertical lift bridges was the Halstead Street bridge, over the Chicago river, built in 1893–4. The lifting span, which is 130 ft long and 48 ft wide, is raised to give a headway of 155 ft beneath it for vessels. The counterweighted bridge is operated by two reversing steam-engines of 70 hp.

VII. FOUNDATION-WORK FOR BRIDGES

Before 1851 the usual method of building piers in mid-stream employed a coffer-dam (vol III, pp 421–7). This consisted of a box, open at the top and bottom, made by driving a double wall of sheet piling so as to surround and enclose the site in the river where the pier was to be built. To make the coffer-dam watertight, the space between the walls was filled with clay. The water inside the dam was then pumped out and the soft ground inside excavated in the dry until a firm foundation was reached. But coffer-dams have their shortcomings: the length of the sheet piling is limited; it cannot be driven into very hard ground or past obstacles; and if the ground is very soft it will squeeze up into the dam as fast as it is excavated.

To overcome these difficulties, cylinders or wells were used and sunk either by open dredging or under compressed air. Nearly all the great bridges built in India by British engineers from 1850 onwards are founded on brick wells sunk by open dredging in the sand. As the sand was grabbed or pumped out of the well, the latter sank under its own weight and the walls were built up to keep them above ground level. When the well had been sunk to the required depth it was plugged with concrete deposited through the water, and the bridge pier was erected on top of it. By this means many fine bridges were built far from the resources of civilization, and with the aid of only the most primitive plant and of unskilled labour.

Compressed-air caissons. For sinking cylinders in ground that was too hard to be grabbed, or where obstructions were likely to be encountered, compressed-air caissons were devised and first used in England in 1851 by Sir William Cubitt (1785–1861) and John Wright for the 61-ft-deep piers of the bridge at Rochester over the Medway. I. K. Brunel (1806–59) subsequently used pneumatic caissons for his bridge at Chepstow and, on a much greater scale, for the Royal Albert bridge at Saltash. Considerable improvements were introduced by Fleur Saint-Denis (who may be regarded as the pioneer of the modern system) in the foundations of the Rhine bridge at Kehl (1859), and thereafter the method came into general use in Europe and America.

The essentials of the procedure are as follows. At the bottom of the caisson there is a working chamber into which compressed air is pumped. This working chamber is enclosed above but open at the bottom, round which runs a cutting-edge, usually of iron or steel. The pressure of the air pumped in is so controlled as to be equal to or slightly greater than the hydraulic pressure at the foot of the caisson. As the caisson sinks, the hydraulic head increases and the air-pressure inside the caisson has to be raised to balance it and thus keep the water out of the working chamber. An access-shaft for men and materials leads up to the surface from the roof of the working chamber. In this shaft is an air-lock which enables men and materials to enter and leave the caisson without releasing the air-pressure inside it. In order to sink the caisson, men enter the working chamber and dig out the subsoil, which is loaded into buckets and removed through the air-shaft. Alternatively it may be pumped or dredged. As the caisson sinks, the side walls are built up in order to keep them above water-level.

Figure 274 shows a cross-section of one of the caissons used in 1870 on the St Louis bridge in America (p 510). In this caisson, sand-pumps were used to remove the subsoil, and the air-locks were located at the bottom of the shaft, whereas in modern practice they are always put at the top, above water-level, so as to be safe in the event of flooding. The greatest depth at which men can work efficiently and without considerable discomfort even in very short shifts is 120 ft, at which depth the air-pressure is 52 lb per sq in. Unless men are decompressed very slowly as they come out of the lock after working at such a pressure they are liable, like deep-sea divers, to be attacked by caisson-disease or 'bends'. This is caused by bubbles of nitrogen becoming liberated in the tissues during decompression. According to where the bubbles are liberated, a man may be attacked by symptoms varying in severity from ear-

FIGURE 274—*A sectional elevation of the east caisson for the St Louis bridge, 1870.*

ache and nose-bleeding to cramp and perhaps fatal paralysis. When compressed air was first used its physiological effects and the precautions to be observed for safety were not known, and many fatalities resulted.

On the St Louis bridge the sinkers had to work more than 100 ft down, at a pressure of 45 lb to the sq in, and although the shifts were reduced to half an hour each, the men were taking only two or three minutes to decompress, instead of an hour or more as would be needed for safety. Consequently there were fourteen deaths and many serious cases of bends. So little was the nature of caisson-disease understood that the sinkers were issued with bands of armour, made of alternate scales of zinc and silver, to be worn around the waist, ankles, arms, and wrist, and also under the soles of the feet. These were intended to give protection against the disease by means of galvanic action. Meanwhile the French physiologist, Paul Bert (1833–66), had discovered the cause of caisson-sickness and the method of avoiding it; but it was not until early in the twentieth century, after the researches of Sir Leonard Hill (1866–1952) and others, that the full nature of its dangers was understood and compressed-air work was safely controlled by regulations.

VIII. TUNNELS

The main advances in the technique of tunnelling in the dry in the period 1850–1900 were the use of mechanical drills and blasting, and the substitution of permanent cast iron rings for linings of brickwork. In 1818 Marc Isambard Brunel took out a patent covering the use of a tunnel-shield and cast iron lining. The first shield was used on the famous Thames tunnel (1825–41), but cast iron rings were not employed until the Tower subway was built under the Thames in 1869. Shields are used mainly for tunnelling under water or through relatively soft strata; they are unneces-sary for tunnelling in the dry through rock. The most important advance in under-water tunnelling, apart from the shield, was the use of compressed air to prevent the inflow of water. Although this method had been proposed and patented by Lord Cochrane in 1830, it was not employed until nearly fifty years later. Before this time prodigious feats of sealing and pumping were under-taken, as, for instance, in the construction of the Severn tunnel (p 518).

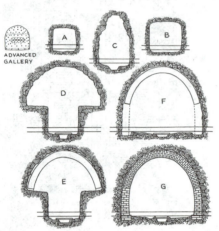

FIGURE 275—*Diagrams showing the stages of ex-cavation in the Mont Cenis tunnel.*

(i) *Tunnels built in the dry.* The first of the great tunnels under the Alps was the Mont Cenis tunnel (1857–71), nearly 8 miles long, which linked the railways of France and Italy. It was driven through hard rock consisting principally of calcareous schist, with some carbonaceous schist and a little quartz and lime-stone. The tunnel rises towards the centre, where it is a mile deep below the summit of the mountain; its section is approximately 26 ft wide and 25 ft high. The excavation was carried out in stages as shown in figure 275. A heading, or advanced gallery, about 10 ft square was driven from each end and subsequently widened out to receive the brick walls and arches of the roof. Excavation was carried out by boring the rock and blasting with gunpowder. Hand-boring was used at first, but was later superseded by rock-drills, which were driven by compressed air obtained from water-power (p 527).

The tunnels were originally lit by gas and subsequently by oil. Experience showed that the compressed air which escaped from the Sommeiller drills used for boring provided adequate ventilation in the advanced galleries; moreover, in expanding from a greatly reduced volume to its normal volume it materially reduced the temperature. In the large gallery, however, 80 ft or more behind the face, special measures had to be taken to improve the ventilation. These

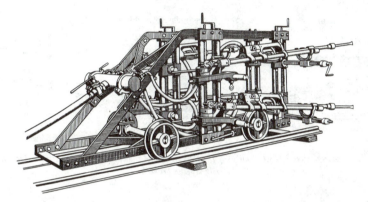

FIGURE 276—*McKean rock-drilling machine used in the St Gothard tunnel.*

took the form of a horizontal brattice, constructed inwards from each entrance, which divided the tunnel and enabled fresh air to be passed in through the lower half while the exhaust air returned overhead.

In the construction of the St Gothard tunnel (1872–81), which is 9⅓ miles long and of the same cross-section as the Mont Cenis, mechanical drills were used from the start (figure 276). Improvements in the efficiency of the drills and the substitution of dynamite for black powder enabled much quicker progress to be made. The approaches to the tunnel include seven spirals which form almost complete loops in the mountain. Nevertheless, when the two advanced galleries driven from either side met in the middle, the error was found to be only 4 in vertically and between 6 and 8 in horizontally.

Tunnels used by steam-locomotives require mechanical ventilation by fans, as otherwise the smoke tends to travel up the grade with the locomotive, and the conditions, particularly for the driver and fireman, become intolerable. In 1899 a system invented by Saccardo, an Italian engineer, was installed with marked success in the St Gothard tunnel. It is based on the principle of the ejector and is applicable only to long tunnels having no intermediate stations or shafts. At the entrance to the tunnel a brick structure 25 ft long was built, the inside line of which represented the minimum cross-section of the tunnel and extended 3 ft into its mouth. By blowing air down the sides of the tunnel, through the space between the walls of this structure and the walls of the tunnel, a current of air was induced down the axis of the tunnel, throughout its length. When an approaching train meets this draught, the volume of clean air encountered affords immediate relief to the driver and fireman.

(ii) *Under-water tunnels.* The first major under-water tunnel in Great Britain

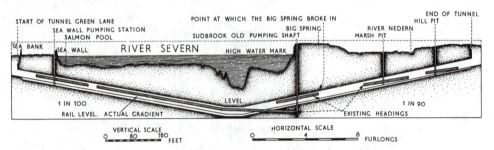

FIGURE 277—*Longitudinal section (east to west) of the Severn tunnel showing headings existing in October 1879, when the Big Spring broke in.*

was the Severn tunnel (1873–86), which is 4·3 miles long and was built for a double track of the Great Western Railway (figure 277). The strata traversed consist of conglomerate, limestone, carboniferous beds, sandstone, marl, gravel, and sand, and have a considerable dip; the least thickness of cover at the deepest part of the river is 30 ft of marl. Shafts were sunk on both sides of the crossing, from which headings 7 ft square were driven in both directions, under the river and inland. In these headings pumps were installed. Not very much water was encountered before 1879, when the headings extended under nearly the whole width of the estuary; then the engineers had the misfortune to tap the Big Spring near Sudbrook.

As water rushed in, the men fled in panic; within 24 hours all the works were flooded and it was not until fourteen months later, after extraordinary labours and innumerable disappointments, that the tunnels were at last pumped dry so that construction could recommence. To achieve this object further shafts were sunk on the landward side of the Big Spring and additional pumping-plant was installed; the flow from the spring into the old shaft was checked by means of a shield of oak fixed across the heading; and a diver named Lambert, supplied with a knapsack of compressed oxygen, at last succeeded in making his way for a distance of 1000 ft in total darkness through the flooded tunnels, to operate valves and shut an iron door which had been left open when the men scrambled for safety.

In September 1881 the headings from either side met and, in spite of water breaking into the workings on two more occasions, the last length of the tunnel across the Big Spring was completed in April 1885. Ventilation during construction was provided by a fan, 18 ft in diameter and 7 ft wide, erected above one of the deep shafts. The rock was bored by compressed-air drills, and blasting was eventually carried out exclusively by tonite,[1] which proved to be freer from noxious fumes than any other explosive. Swan and Brush electric lamps were used throughout the workings. The tunnel is lined with vitrified brickwork $2\frac{1}{2}$–3 ft thick, set in cement. Although the maximum volume of water pumped has never been greater than 30 m gallons a day, the total pumping-power provided is capable of raising more than twice this quantity. The traffic in the tunnel is heavy and permanent ventilation is effected by fans in the main shafts at each end, that in the Monmouthshire shaft being 40 ft in diameter and 12 ft wide.

IX. METHODS OF TUNNELLING

(i) *Use of compressed air*. The earliest use of compressed air on a considerable scale was in the first Hudson River tunnel between New York and Jersey City (1874–1908). From the start the work was dogged by misfortune. The tunnel consisted of two tubes, 16 ft wide and 18 ft high, which had to be driven mostly through silt beneath the mile-wide, 60-ft-deep river. A shaft 30 ft in diameter was sunk to a depth of 60 ft below high water on the New Jersey side, and from a chamber at the bottom of this shaft work on the first of the two tunnels was started under compressed air. The method adopted was to take out the excavation in terraces, relying on the compressed air to keep out the silt and water until the next section of $\frac{1}{4}$-in-thick, 30-in-wide iron lining-plates could be put in and bolted to those behind. When every fourth ring of plates had been assembled, the chamber was cleaned out and the brick lining built, thus completing a length of 10 ft.

Subsequently this method was improved by driving out a 6-ft-diameter iron pilot-tube on the axis of the tunnel, from which the lining-plates were initially strutted. Unfortunately in November 1882, when 2000 ft of the tunnel had been completed, work stopped through lack of money and six years passed before it was revived with British capital. When Sir John Fowler (1817–98), Benjamin

---

[1] An explosive consisting of gun-cotton and barium nitrate.

Baker (1840–1907), and J. H. Greathead (1844–96) were appointed as consulting engineers it was decided to build a steel shield to facilitate construction (plate 31 A), and to use a cast iron lining sufficiently strong to resist the whole of the earth-pressure.

(ii) *Tunnel-shields and cast iron rings*. The purpose of a tunnelling shield is to take the place of supporting timber-work and to hold up the surrounding subsoil during excavation. The tail of the shield affords space for building the permanent cast iron lining, which it overlaps, and from which it is jacked forward. The main advantages of a cast iron lining are its compactness, strength, speed of erection, and negligible maintenance, and the fact that it can readily be caulked watertight.

In the Hudson River tunnel the shield was 10 ft 6 in long with an outside diameter of 19 ft 11 in. The working face was divided into nine compartments, and the whole shield was jacked forward by means of sixteen hydraulic rams which butted against the last ring of cast iron erected. The segments of the cast iron rings were lifted into place by means of a hydraulic erector mounted on a travelling carriage (plate 31 B). As the shield was thrust forward, the silt in front of it was squeezed through the doors, so that there was no need to excavate by hand. The best progress made in any one week was 72 ft. However, in July 1891 the work again ceased for lack of money; the tunnels then remained flooded and were not finally completed until 1908.

Working at a pressure of 35 lb to the sq in caused considerable caisson-sickness amongst the tunnellers, and to cope with it the contractors built what may well have been the first medical lock, 'a small airtight iron hospital at ground level in which any desired pressure of air could be obtained'. By recompressing men in this lock until the cramp and pain had subsided and then decompressing them very gradually, they were in many cases cured.

Subsequently Greathead made use of cast iron rings and an improved shield in the construction of the $3\frac{1}{2}$-mile City and South London Railway (1886–90), the first underground railway in London, and these methods became standard practice. There are now more than 90 miles of tube railway below London; for the greater part of their length they are in clay, and compressed air was required only in the construction of short lengths through water-bearing gravel.

(iii) *Other methods of tunnelling*. An unusual method of tunnelling, by freezing the water in the subsoil and then excavating through the frozen material, was first used in the construction of a tunnel for pedestrians in Stockholm (1884–6). Another method, seldom adopted until recent years, is that of lowering large tubes into a previously prepared trench in the bed of the river and joining them together. A sewer-outlet tunnel, 1500 ft long, made of tubes of brick and concrete each 9 ft in diameter and 52 ft long, was constructed in Boston harbour by this means in 1893–4.

BIBLIOGRAPHY

GAY, C. 'Ponts en maçonnerie.' Baillière, Paris. 1924.

HOVEY, O. E. 'Movable Bridges' (2 vols). Wiley, New York. 1927.

SHIRLEY SMITH, H. 'The World's Great Bridges.' Phoenix House, London. 1953.

SIMMS, F. W. 'Practical Tunnelling' (4th ed., rev. and enl. by D. K. CLARK). London. 1896.

STRAUB, H. 'A History of Civil Engineering' (trans. from the German by E. ROCKWELL). Leonard Hill, London. 1952.

TYRRELL, H. G. 'History of Bridge Engineering.' Published by the author, Chicago. 1911.

Transporter bridge at Runcorn, Cheshire.

22

HYDRAULIC ENGINEERING

J. ALLEN

HYDRAULIC engineering is concerned with many aspects of design, manufacture, and construction, including water-supply and sewerage (ch 23); irrigation; machinery such as pumps and turbines; industrial processes of a wide variety; and canals, rivers, and harbours. In all of these, significant—even spectacular—advances were made during the second half of the nineteenth century. Moreover, the theoretical and experimental branches of the subject received remarkable contributions.

I. DAMS

Early nineteenth-century water reservoirs usually had earthen embankments with central puddle-clay walls, though there are notable examples of early masonry dams, such as the 135-ft-high Alicante dam (1579–94) (p 556), and the Lampy dam built in France (1780) to feed the Languedoc canal; this dam was made of quarried stone with a facing of cut stone and was strengthened by buttresses at its back.

The term 'masonry dam' has been loosely applied to (*a*) dams made entirely of natural stone or of stone and mortar; (*b*) those mainly of uncut stone but faced with dressed stone; (*c*) an artificial stone (concrete) mass with a facing of stone; and (*d*) a structure made wholly of concrete. The first high masonry dam in Britain, at Vyrnwy, is of the first type, the interior and the facing being of stone bedded in mortar (p 557, figure 295, and plate 33B). It is about 144 ft high from the lowest part of the foundation to the crest of the spill-way, and the maximum thickness at the base is nearly 130 ft. Its length is 1170 ft. A very important feature of this dam was the drainage of the foundations to prevent uplift by water-pressure which might tend to overturn it.

The French engineer Delocre (p 556) first proposed the arch form for dams blocking narrow valleys, thus enabling the thrust to be communicated to the rock at each side. The Zola dam (1843), 120 ft high, and the Furens dam (1861–6) (p 556 and figure 295) are early examples of such construction. Attempts to exploit the full arching effect in designing dams have been rare; the design presents great theoretical difficulty and important advances are of very recent date. The weight of many stone and concrete arch dams has been reduced by making a partial allowance for the arching effect.

The buttress dam of the modern type belongs to the era of dams built wholly of concrete, which gradually evolved from the original masonry designs. It consists essentially of a water-retaining membrane supported by a number of buttresses. It has been stated, however, that a dam on this principle and of considerable size was built in India as early as 1800.

The injection of cement grout to render faulty strata impervious, to avoid uneconomic depths of cut-off walls, and to seal strata at the ends of a dam has become common practice. Pressure cementation is believed to have been used by Thomas Hawksley (p 557); the first record of its use for overcoming leakage from an existing reservoir is at the Cown reservoir for Rochdale, Lancashire, in 1878.

In engineering enterprise much may be learnt from the examination of failures. The earth embankment of the Holmfirth dam, near Huddersfield, Yorkshire, failed in 1852 owing to leakage, which undermined the structure and caused settlement of the puddle core-wall and adjoining earthwork. The Dale Dyke catastrophe of 1864, involving the loss of 244 lives, appears still to be something of a mystery. The view was held at one time, however, that the 18-in cast iron outlet pipes had been disturbed and fractured by the weight of the embankment above them. When a new reservoir was constructed near the same site a few years later, the outlet was made through a tunnel in solid rock round one end of the embankment. In 1895 there was the failure of the masonry dam at Bouzey (near Épinal); it is alleged that at the time and in the region of the fracture 'the line of resultant pressure was a long way outside the middle third and the water side of the dam must have been subjected to considerable tension'.

The collapse of the Dolgarrog dam, although it occurred after 1900, deserves special mention. This was a concrete dam and its failure was attributed to its foundations not being carried deep enough to form an effective cut-off; its cross-section is believed to have been sufficient for stability. Naturally, the Dolgarrog disaster caused considerable apprehension and appears to have been partly responsible for the British Reservoirs (Safety Provisions) Act of 1930 which requires all reservoirs having a capacity of 5 m gallons or more above ground level to be inspected by a qualified engineer at intervals not exceeding 10 years. The Act also provides that only a qualified engineer may be responsible for the design and construction of such works.

In Britain, afforestation of catchment areas is said to have started at Oldham in 1885. Apart from aesthetic considerations it is a practice much favoured as a means of equalizing the discharge of water from the catchment, of holding up silt, and of reducing pollution; it also serves as a barrier against cattle. Conifers are commonly planted.

One of the most important features of reservoir design is provision for the release of flood-water. In the case of earth dams this often consists of a weir at one end of the embankment (not on the earthwork of the dam itself), the weir having a length and crest-level so arranged as to keep the water below the top of the dam at all times. With masonry and concrete dams the flood-water may be allowed to discharge over a portion of the dam itself. Among other possible devices is the bell-mouth overflow spill-way, consisting of a vertical shaft with a bell-mouth entrance at its top, the shaft joining a tunnel at its lower end and the tunnel leading the water away to the bed of a water-course below the dam. Here again the size of the shaft and of its rounded entrance are designed so that the impounded water will not rise above a safe level. In certain site conditions this form of spill-way has advantages; one was adopted in 1896 for the Blackton reservoir of the Tees Valley water board.

II. HYDRAULIC MACHINERY

The nineteenth century saw many improvements in pumps and in water-engines that had repercussions on numerous other aspects of technology: dredging, water-supply, the generation of power, and a host of industrial processes, such as the manufacture of paper, in which large volumes of water are used.

Pumps. At the beginning of the century, steam-driven reciprocating pumps were in common use, many of them designed by James Watt. In 1855 a high-pressure condensing pumping-engine (a Cornish engine) built for the East London water company had a 100-inch diameter cylinder, an 11-ft stroke, and a horse-power of the order of 380; shortly afterwards the Southwark and Vauxhall water company installed one of approximately 880 hp, raising 12 m gallons of water a day against a head of 170 ft.

Entirely different is the centrifugal pump, in which a rotating impeller generates a forced vortex. Water entering the eye or centre of this impeller has its pressure increased by the vortex and is driven through the casing of the pump and along the delivery-pipe. In many ways, this arrangement is preferable to that of the reciprocating pump: it obviates the use of working valves and gives a steady delivery. There are no reversals of motion, but a high speed of rotation is necessary. The invention of the centrifugal pump is attributed to Johann Jordan late in the seventeenth century, but it was premature. Centrifugal pumps began to appear in the mid-nineteenth century, and were shown at the Great

Exhibition of 1851 by James Stuart Gwynne (1831–1915) and John George Appold (1800–65). John Gwynne (1800–55) also patented a multi-stage pump about the middle of the century.

The arrangement of a simple, single-stage pump is shown in figure 278. Water leaves the outer rim of the impeller with a high velocity. It is possible to increase efficiency by converting part of the corresponding energy of motion into pressure-energy before the water enters the delivery-pipe. But in many pumps even today the water is simply discharged into a small chamber surrounding the impeller (as in figure 278), the delivery-pipe being coupled to this chamber. The

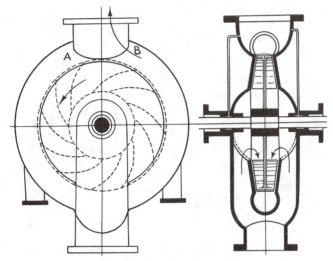

FIGURE 278—*Simple single-stage centrifugal pump.*

quantity of water passing a section of the chamber increases continuously from A (just past the delivery-pipe) to B. In consequence, much energy is wasted as heat arising from shock and the formation of eddies, since the velocity of whirl in the collecting-chamber varies from A to B and corresponds with that at discharge at only one particular section. One way of avoiding this waste is to increase the sectional area progressively from A to B. James Thomson (1822–92), a brother of Lord Kelvin, suggested the use of a much larger chamber, known as the whirlpool chamber (figure 279). In the part of this casing concentric with the impeller, the water after leaving the wheel assumes approximately the form of a free vortex, with pressure increasing radially outwards. Uniform discharge then takes place in the gradually increasing area of the outer casing. Unfortunately, in order to derive appreciably enhanced efficiency from the whirlpool chamber, it has to be of large size. It is seldom used, therefore, except in a modified form, though a pump made under Thomson's direction for drainage-works in Barbados had an impeller and a whirlpool chamber with diameters of 16 and 32 ft respectively.

As an alternative, some late nineteenth-century pumps were provided with a ring of fixed guide-vanes surrounding the rotating impeller. These were designed to receive the water from the impeller without shock and direct it through diverging passages into the surrounding chamber, whence it passed into the delivery-pipe. The contributions of Osborne Reynolds to this development and to that of the multi-stage high-lift pump are mentioned later (p 548).

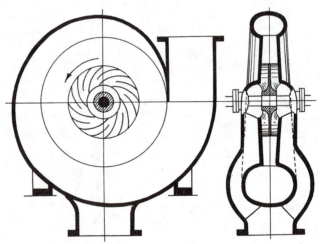

FIGURE 279—*Whirlpool or vortex chamber, seen in section.*

Although not so important as the centrifugal pump, the introduction to practical engineering of the jet-pump and of the hydraulic ram also deserves attention. The principle of the jet-pump, long known, is illustrated diagrammatically in figure 280. The jet drags the surrounding liquid along with it, causing a reduction of pressure behind the nozzle and in the suction-pipe sufficient to induce the water to rise from a sump. In its practical form this pump may be ascribed to James Thomson, who reported on his experiments with it to the British Association in 1853.

The hydraulic ram was invented by Joseph Michel Montgolfier (1740–1810) (vol IV, p 499) before the end of the eighteenth century, and was effectively introduced by Easton in 1824. In 1865 John Blake & Company began manufacturing such pumps, which rapidly gained popularity for delivering small supplies of water to a height above the source, as, for example, from a stream. The merits of the device are that it is simple and does not require an engine or drive (figure 281). Water from the source of supply can pass down the supply-pipe s into a valve-box B, which is fitted with a waste-valve V_1 opening inwards and a delivery-valve V_2 opening outwards. The waste-valve V_1 having been depressed by hand, water can escape from the valve-box and begins to flow along the supply-pipe. The velocity of flow increases under the supply-head until the dynamic pressure under the valve V_1 becomes sufficient to close it against its own weight. At this point the motion of the supply column is retarded and the pressure in the box opens the delivery-valve V_2. Water then escapes through it

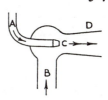

FIGURE 280—*Jet-pump. The jet reduces the pressure behind the nozzle and causes water to rise in the suction-pipe. A, jet-pipe; B, suction-pipe; C, nozzle; D, delivery-pipe.*

into the air-vessel A, compresses the air, and rises up the delivery main P. When the momentum of the supply column is exhausted, the delivery-valve closes, the water below the valve suffering a backward motion. The reflux action of the water on its rebound is followed by a reduction of pressure in the box, which causes the waste-valve to reopen, and the cycle of operations is repeated.

H. D. Pearsall subsequently effected an ingenious improvement of the hydraulic ram, enabling it to deal with large volumes of water. His invention, now obsolete, consisted essentially of opening and closing the waste-valve by mechanical means, so that a cylindrical balanced valve could be used and the periods of the various parts of the cycle of operations be regulated to suit various working-conditions. A modification of this form of hydraulic ram was made to compress air. One such (figure 282), with mechanically operated valves, was designed by the Italian engineer Germain Sommeiller to compress air for pneumatic drills in the construction of the Mont Cenis tunnel (1857–71) (p 517). The inlet-valve V_1 on the supply pipe and the waste-valve V_2 are coupled together and mechanically operated. When the valve V_2 is opened, air at atmospheric pressure is drawn in through the air-valve V_4. V_2 is then closed and V_1 opened, admitting water under pressure to the pipe A. This compresses air in the chamber B, from which it passes through the delivery-valve V_3 into the air reservoir. The valve V_1 being then closed and V_2 opened, the cycle is repeated.

Water-power engines. Prime movers driven by water may be classified under three headings: (1) water-pressure motors having a piston and cylinder with inlet- and outlet-valves: their action is analogous to that of a steam- or gas-engine with

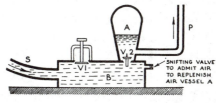

FIGURE 281—*Hydraulic ram, a non-mechanical device for raising small quantities of water to a height above the source.*

water as the working fluid; (2) water-wheels, discussed in volume II, ch 17, and volume IV, ch 7; (3) turbines deriving their energy from a high-velocity jet or jets (the impulse machine), or from water supplied under pressure and passing through the vanes of a runner which is thereby caused to rotate (the reaction type). In the piston-engine the liquid does work by virtue of its pressure; in the water-wheel chiefly by its weight; and in the impulse turbine by virtue of the kinetic energy of the jet. In the reaction turbine[1] the pressure-energy of the water is partly changed into kinetic energy within the runner.

During the nineteenth century the piston-engine was extensively adopted and gave much satisfaction when a high head was available and a slow rotation was

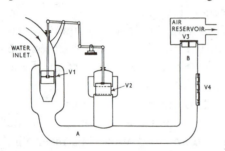

FIGURE 282—*Hydraulic air compressor, a modification of the hydraulic ram.*

required. It was adapted to the driving of hoists, capstans, winches, and small machinery requiring comparatively low power. It was sometimes made double-acting, and a three-cylinder radial engine was also developed from the design of the Brotherhood steam-engine (p 137).

Originally the name turbine[2] was applied in France to any water-motor that revolved in a horizontal plane, the axis being vertical. This definition would be satisfied by de Borda's wheel, and by Barker's mill, or Segner's turbine, or the old Scotch turbine, but Fourneyron's machine is generally recognized as opening the modern era of practical water-turbines. It was awarded a prize, which the *Société d'Encouragement* had offered for a motor of this kind, in 1827. It is essentially an outward-flow turbine (figure 283). Water passes through the fixed guide-passages P and thence into the surrounding wheel, where it impinges on the wheel-vanes B, has its direction of motion changed, and escapes around the periphery of the wheel. When completely full of water, this machine is an example of the reaction turbine, but apparently some of the early machines discharged above water and were in reality impulse wheels. One of the first turbines made by Fourneyron worked at a speed of 2300 rpm under a fall of some 350 ft. Its efficiency was improved by the addition of a diffuser, probably invented by Boyden (1844). This gradually reduced the speed of the water leaving the outside of the wheel (or runner) before discharge into the tail-race (figure 284). A portion of the energy due to velocity was thereby converted into pressure, and since

[1] The term 'reaction' arises from the fact that the change of momentum accompanying the transformation of pressure to kinetic energy necessitates an equivalent reaction on the moving vanes.

[2] Coined by Claude Burdin (1790–1873), Fourneyron's teacher, from the Latin *turbo, turbinis*, a spinning-top.

the pressure at the outside of the diffuser corresponds with its depth of immersion, this resulted in a reduction of pressure at the periphery of the wheel; consequently the effective head on the turbine was increased.

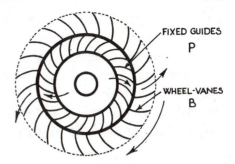

FIGURE 283—*Principle of Fourneyron's outward-flow turbine.*

Inherently, however, the Fourneyron outward-flow turbine suffered from the disadvantage that as the water flows through the fixed and the moving vanes it enters regions of successively increasing volume; that is, the flow is divergent. Such motion is essentially unstable, and is accompanied by a dissipation of energy in the creation and maintenance of turbulence. The speed-regulation, or governing, of this turbine also presented some difficulties. The Fourneyron turbine lost favour largely to the Jonval axial-flow machine (1843). By subdividing the wheel into concentric compartments and regulating the supply of water to them individually, it was possible to maintain a constant speed under varying heads, and efficiencies of 73–83 per cent are recorded. The Jonval turbine proved to be particularly well suited to many European conditions where large quantities of water were available under low or medium heads. It was introduced into the United States about 1850, but was subsequently displaced very largely both there and elsewhere by the radial inward-flow machine.

An inward-flow turbine was proposed by J. V. Poncelet in 1826 and one was built by Howd, of New York, in 1838. The latter is said to have installed several wheels 'of crude workmanship' in New England mills. In 1840 James B. Francis designed a turbine, under Howd's patent, which was of superior quality; he also carried out (1851) a fine series of experiments with two large units, one an outward-flow (Fourneyron) machine and the other a radial inward-flow wheel. Both turbines were installed in mills at Lowell, Massachusetts. Francis was largely responsible for attracting attention to the inward-flow turbine, and he formulated rules for the design of the runner. As a result his name has been attached generically to the broad class of reaction turbines having inward-flow characteristics. In such turbines (figure 285) water passes over a number of

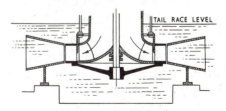

FIGURE 284—*Outward radial-flow turbine, with Boyden diffuser.*

5363.5

guide-vanes which deflect it smoothly into the passages formed between the curved vanes on the runner fixed to the shaft. After doing work on the runner, the water leaves it closer to the centre than its point of entry.

In the development of this type of turbine, great credit is also due to James Thomson (p 525). His machine (1852) is known as a vortex wheel, because in his original design the runner and guide-vanes were enclosed within a large spiral casing. Water entered the widest part of this spiral and swept around the casing with an approximately uniform velocity; it was directed into the wheel itself by guide-vanes shaped so as to follow the lines of flow in a spiral vortex. A lasting improvement introduced by Thomson was the pivoting of the guide-vanes near their inner ends so that they were approximately in balance. The pivots projected from the casing and were coupled together so that all the guide-vanes could be rotated together by hand or by an automatic governor; this arrangement of pivoted guides was later called a wicket-gate. In this way the supply to the runner could be controlled by adjusting the openings between the guide-vanes themselves, whereas regulation had previously been effected by other gates placed either between the fixed guides and the runner, or around the outer circumference of the guides. Thomson's movable guide-vanes were later modified and improved; the position of the pivots was changed and the number of guide-vanes proposed by him was greatly increased, but essentially his idea survived.

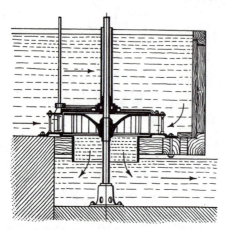

FIGURE 285—*Inward-flow turbine of the Francis type.*

A further modification of the inward-flow machine was developed in America in the form of a mixed-flow turbine, the vanes of the runner being shaped rather like spoons so that the direction of motion of the water became parallel to the shaft while the water was still inside the wheel. This design made it possible to increase both the inlet and the outlet areas within a given available space, and to deal with large volumes of water in relatively compact machines. Many of the earlier mixed-flow turbines had comparatively low efficiencies except when working under full load, but at that time American engineers were frequently dealing with rivers discharging immense volumes of water; the power available was then vastly in excess of requirements, and accordingly the economical use of the water was of less importance than the initial cost of the turbine. The object for a time, therefore, was to design a machine of given dimensions which would perform the largest amount of work, with little regard to the quantity of water consumed per horse-power. By the end of the nineteenth century, however, closer attention was being paid to the detailed design of the mixed-flow turbine in order to improve its efficiency under a wide range of loads.

The reaction turbine operates under pressure, since it is completely filled with water and is placed below the level of the water in the supply reservoir or river. It is not necessary, however, that it should be below the water in the tail-race, which receives the flow after it has done work in the machine. Frequently it is more convenient to have the machine raised above tail-water level, since this facilitates inspection and overhaul. In such cases the water is discharged from the turbine through a pipe known as the suction- or draught-tube, the design of which assumes great importance, particularly when the total head (the difference between the water-levels in the source of supply and the tail-race) is relatively small. The lower end of the suction-tube is submerged in the tail-race water and for practical reasons the turbine cannot be raised more than about 25 ft above tail-water level. The first conception of a suction-tube has been attributed to Jonval (1843), but attempts at its efficient design were influenced by that of Boyden's diffuser, as used with the outward-flow turbine (p 528). If the tube is made in the shape of a divergent cone the velocity of the water projected into the tail-race is decreased, thereby reducing the loss of energy that must occur if water flowing at a high velocity is injected into a region of lower velocity.

Important advances were also made in the design and construction of impulse turbines. Fourneyron's turbine sometimes discharged above tail-water level and so acted as an impulse machine, but it was really intended to work 'drowned'. Zuppinger's tangent wheel was one of the first turbines designed for high falls, when, for a required horse-power, the size of a reaction turbine working full of water might become impracticably small. Essentially, his idea involved directing water through a pipe and nozzle into the buckets or vanes of a wheel. The quantity of water was sufficient to act upon only a few vanes at a time; thus the turbine worked under conditions of partial admission.

About 1856 the French engineers Callon and Girard began to design impulse turbines to suit a wide range of conditions: high and low falls, large and small flows. An important innovation, by Girard, was the ventilation of the buckets to ensure that they were maintained at atmospheric pressure and thus prevented from filling and then working partly by reaction. This was effected by means of holes, in the side of the wheel, communicating with each bucket to admit the air. By the end of the century many Girard turbines were in use, with a surprising variety of axial-, inward-, or outward-flow characteristics and having vertical, horizontal, or inclined axes. They utilized flows up to about 150 cu ft/sec with falls ranging from a few feet to 1800 ft. In 1881 efficiencies varying from 59 to 79 per cent were obtained for outputs of between 82 and 400 hp, the latter being achieved by a Girard outward-flow turbine having an available head of 594 ft and running at 210 rpm.

Mechanical complication and expense prevented the general adoption of an ingenious idea of Girard's called 'hydropneumatization'. To take advantage of the full available head, an impulse turbine working at atmospheric pressure should be placed as close to the tail-race as possible, yet submergence of the machine by a rise of tail-water level in time of flood must be avoided. Raising the machine to a safe position means a sacrifice of head, which is important when the available head is already small.

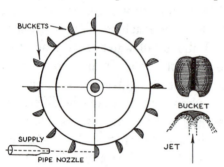

FIGURE 286—*Principle of the Pelton wheel.*

Girard's solution was to enclose the whole turbine in an air-tight casing, the lower end of which opened below the tail-water. An air-pump driven by the turbine maintained a pressure sufficient to keep the water inside the casing below the wheel whatever the tail-race level.

During the latter half of the nineteenth century the Pelton wheel came into general use for high heads. Mechanically it had many advantages over the Girard turbine, especially in its simplicity (figure 286). A jet from a nozzle at the end of a pipe strikes curved buckets mounted on a wheel. Water falls from the buckets into the tail-race. More than one nozzle may be used, acting on different parts of the wheel. The device may be controlled by means of a governor which causes a spear- or needle-valve to regulate the opening available for passage of water through the nozzle. To avoid shock in the pipe caused by a rapid restriction of the nozzle the jet may first be deflected from the wheel by a plate brought across it; thereafter the valve itself can act more slowly.

The origin of the Pelton wheel is interesting. About the middle of the century, jets of considerable power were used for hydraulic gold-mining in California. R. L. Daugherty states that:

When the gold was exhausted many of these jets were then used for power purposes. The first wheels were very crude affairs, often of wood, with flat plates upon which the water impinged. . . . The next improvement was the use of hemispherical cups with the jet striking them right in the centre [probably about 1870]. A man by the name of Pelton was running one of these wheels one day when it came loose on its shaft and slipped over so that the water struck it on one edge and was discharged from the outer edge. The wheel was observed to pick up in power and speed and this led to the development of the split bucket. [The ideal to be arrived at is a complete reversal of the direction of the jet by the bucket.]

About 1890, a 7-ft Pelton wheel, working under a head of some 400 ft at an Alaskan mine, developed 500 hp and drove 240 stamps, 96 ore-mills, and 13 ore-crushers. Another wheel was working under a head of about 2100 ft.

Briefly, the position at the beginning of the twentieth century was that either type of turbine—impulse or pressure—was considered suitable for heads up to 300 ft, though the impulse type was favoured for heads above 200 ft except for very large powers. With either type, full-load efficiencies of over 80 per cent had been attained.

The possibility of exploiting the Niagara Falls as a source of water-power appears to have been seriously considered from 1870 onwards. In 1886 a syndicate was granted authority to take sufficient water from the upper river to develop 200 000 hp. The choice of turbine to use was difficult at that time, and the help of an international commission was sought. This commission invited competitive designs; that of a famous Zürich firm which proposed twin Jonval turbines keyed to the same shaft and arranged approximately to balance the weight of the rotating parts was selected. Apparently, however, the firm declined to allow their design to be manufactured in America.

The original Niagara project envisaged a head-race starting 1½ miles above the American fall and measuring 500 ft wide by 12 ft deep. Along the edge of this supply-canal wheel-pits 160 ft deep were sunk to accommodate the turbines. From each pit a tail-race drained into a common tunnel, discharging below the Falls, which was 6700 ft long with a horse-shoe section 21 ft high by 19 ft wide. Four rings of brickwork set in cement were used to line the rock facing of the tunnel. By 1894 the Niagara Falls Paper Company had three 1100 hp inverted Jonval turbines working under a fall of 140 ft. The Niagara Falls Power Company in 1895 had two turbines each consisting of two Fourneyron wheels keyed to one shaft. They were American-manufactured from Swiss designs to yield 5500 hp each under a 132-ft head, and were said to have a full-load efficiency of 82·5 per cent. Although they earned satisfactory reports, later units of 5000 and 10 000 hp were of the inward-radial flow type. By 1903 the Canadian Niagara Power Company had a series of double Francis turbines with vertical shafts each direct-coupled to an electric generator and developing 10 250 hp at 250 rpm under a head of 133 ft (figure 287). The weight—120 tons—of rotating parts was balanced partly by the upward pressure on the bottom face of the lower run-

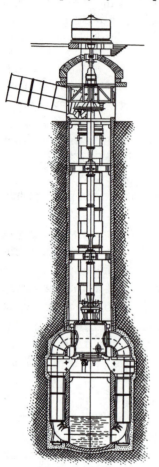

ner, beneath which water was admitted at the full pressure of the supply head, and partly by upward pressure on a rotating balance-piston. The general arrangement shown gives some idea of the strides made by the early years of the twentieth century.

Other hydraulic appliances. The nineteenth century saw many inventions and improvements in a variety of other appliances. Robert Stephenson employed hydraulic jacks to raise the girders for the Britannia bridge (p 504), as also did I. K. Brunel on his great Saltash bridge (1853–6). Sir William, later Lord, Armstrong (1810–1900), devised a hydraulic accumulator of wide application which has contributed to the use of hydraulic power for the operation of cranes, lifts, and other machines, many of which are required to do a large amount of work for a short time followed by an idle period. If such a machine is supplied by a pump, the continuous output of the pump may be considerably less than that required by the machine when working at its maximum rate (for example, during the upward motion of a hoist). During the period of peak load, the machine draws from the accumulator, which consists of a vertical cylinder fitted with a weighted ram. If the pump is delivering more water than is required, the ram rises. It may be so arranged that when the ram reaches the upper limit of its travel it actuates a linkage which shuts off the pump.

FIGURE 287—*General arrangement of double Francis turbine developing 10 250 hp at 250 rpm under 133-ft head. Canadian Niagara Power Company.*

Also important is the hydraulic intensifier, whose purpose is to provide a pressure higher than that existing in the supply mains. The simple form is illustrated in figure 288; the intensification of pressure depends on the ratio between the outer and inner diameters of the sliding ram. When the ram reaches the bottom of its stroke, the valve admitting the high-pressure water to the driven machine may be closed; the ram is then raised by opening the fixed cylinder to exhaust and admitting low-pressure water to the inside of the ram. This intensifier was often fitted to nineteenth-century machines for testing materials in tension, compression, or bending, which were supplied with water at comparatively low pressure from the town mains.

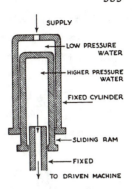

FIGURE 288—*Hydraulic intensifier, for providing pressure higher than that in the supply mains.*

The applications of hydraulic power in the nineteenth century seem to have been almost limitless. In excavating hard boulder clay for the foundations of the piers of the Forth bridge, the contractor (Sir William Arrol) devised a hydraulic spade (figure 264). The press devised by Joseph Bramah (1748–1814) utilized 'Pascal's paradox'—a hydrostatic law discovered by Simon Stevin (1548–1620). A small force acting on a small piston exerts a certain pressure on a liquid contained within a cylinder surrounding the piston; this pressure, transmitted to a larger cylinder, sustains a much larger load resting on a second piston (figure 289). Bramah's press was variously used for baling cotton, flanging boiler-plates, and forging large ingots of steel; in the last case, slow and powerful compression exerted hydraulically had advantages as compared with the steam-hammer in producing a homogeneous forging. Forces amounting to a few thousand tons could be obtained. Yet another application of hydraulic pressure on pistons, often in conjunction with the accumulator, was to riveting (pp 355, 502); both portable and fixed machines were made for this purpose.

Before the electrical transmission of energy was developed on a wide scale (ch 10), the supply of energy by water delivered under pressure from a central station had much to commend it. Sir William Armstrong played a prominent part in exploiting this system. London, Manchester, and Glasgow, among other cities, operated it, the pressure ranging from 700 to 1600 lb per sq in. In some cases the mains were used for the direct working of lifts and hoists; in others, for the operation of some form of water-motor. By the early 1900s, it was considered economic to transmit power to a distance of 15 miles from the central pumping-station.

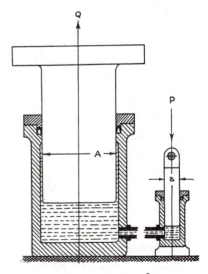

FIGURE 289—*Bramah's press.* $\frac{Q}{P}$ = *ratio of areas* $\frac{A}{a}$.

III. VALVES, METERS, AND INSTRUMENTS

To James Nasmyth (1808–90) goes the credit for one of the simplest yet most valuable examples of design in the history of hydraulic engineering. It is essential that a stop-valve on a pipe-line be easy to operate and reliable in action, producing a water-tight seal. When the crudity of the early forms was pointed out to Nasmyth, he designed (1839) a double-faced wedge-form sluice valve, which in every essential is the stop-valve commonly used today.

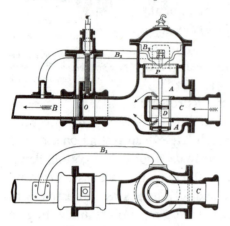

FIGURE 290—*Fleeming Jenkin's constant-flow valve.*

Another ingenious nineteenth-century invention was the constant-flow valve of H. C. Fleeming Jenkin (1833–85). Water entering from the right (figure 290) passes through the pipe C into an equilibrium valve D and then by way of the chamber A and the sluice O to the discharging-main B. The sluice O can be set for any required rate of flow in B, and the object of the arrangement is the maintenance of a constant difference of pressure between A and B so that, correspondingly, there will be a constant flow through O. This is achieved by connecting the valve D to the plunger P, free to slide inside a diaphragm which separates A from another chamber B_2: this compartment B_2 is connected to the discharging-main B by means of the pipe B_1. If the difference in pressure between A and B (which determines the discharge through O) increases, the plunger P rises and closes the equilibrium valve D; conversely, a reduction in the pressure-difference results in the valve D opening wider. In this way, the pressure-difference between A and B is continually adjusted to the value desired.

At the beginning of the nineteenth century there were no meters for measuring rates of flow along pipes conveying fluids under pressure, and it was difficult to detect waste or to measure power. Among early attempts to solve the problem were: (*a*) the piston meter, consisting of a water-pressure engine driven by the flow of water to be measured, the length and number of strokes of the piston giving the quantity; (*b*) a small reaction turbine or 'Barker's Mill' whose revolutions were recorded by a train of wheels with dial-plates; and (*c*) a small fan or propeller acting as a current-meter.

In 1873, however, G. F. Deacon (1843–1909) invented a simple rising-disk meter which showed on a drum chart the flow of water from hour to hour.

Water passes through a conical tube (figure 291) containing an axial rod carrying a circular disk D. Axial movement of this disk is resisted by a spring and is recorded on the registering apparatus by the movement of a pen over a paper fastened to a rotating drum. As the flow along the pipe varies, so does the pressure on the disk, and the device may be calibrated so that the record on the drum reads directly in, say, gallons a minute.

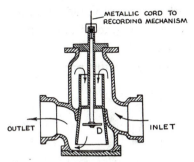

FIGURE 291—*Deacon's rising-disk meter.*

The comparatively late appearance of the Venturi meter (figure 292) is surprising, since the theorem of Daniel Bernoulli (1700–82) on which it is based had long been known. Suppose, in the figure, a liquid to be flowing from left to right. Between sections A and B the velocity increases and the pressure correspondingly decreases. A simple relationship exists between the fall of pressure (A to B) and the volume flowing per second; this arrangement may then be used as a meter, and by enlarging the section again gradually between B and C the pipe may be restored to its original size for the continuing conveyance of the liquid. If the diameter of the pipe at B were retained, the resistance to flow along the pipe as a whole would be increased. In effect, therefore, all that is necessary is to incorporate the convergent-divergent passage A B C in the pipe-line, and to provide pressure-holes in the wall at sections A and B which may be connected to a gauge registering the fall of pressure between the two points. Clemens Herschel (1842–1930) invented this meter, which he named in commemoration of the experiments of G. B. Venturi (1746–1822) on conical tubes. It was eagerly adopted by water companies and other undertakings in Britain from about 1894.

An electrical water-level recorder was installed at Rochester in 1894, and nowadays remote-reading electrical instruments are in common use for water-level meters and flow-meters. Less spectacular is the hook-gauge, used first by U. A. Boyden of Boston, Massachusetts, in 1840. It consists (figure 293) of a fixed frame with a scale and vernier; the vernier is attached to the frame and the scale slides vertically, carrying at its lower end a hook having a fine point.[1] The scale can be moved vertically by a fine-pitched screw until the point of the hook just touches the water surface; reflection from the small capillary elevation of the water surface over the hook enables this to be judged

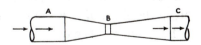

FIGURE 292—*Illustration of the principle of the Venturi meter.*

[1] It is now more usual to have the main scale fixed and the vernier movable.

with considerable accuracy ($c \pm$0·01 in). The instrument has been invaluable to many engineers and experimenters for the measurement of water-levels, as, for example, in determining the head over a weir.

For measuring pressures, nineteenth-century engineers knew various gauges depending on hydrostatic principles, such as the mercurial pressure-gauge. By the 1850s the gauge devised by the French engineer Eugène Bourdon (1808–84) was available; this can readily be attached to the pipe or vessel in which the pressure is to be measured. Inside the casing of the gauge is a flat, curved tube of metal closed at one end and communicating with the pressure at the other end. The curvature of the tube decreases or increases as the pressure exceeds or is less than the pressure surrounding the tube. The motion of the closed end is transmitted to a finger moving over a graduated scale. This convenient and compact gauge is a familiar sight on boilers, engines, pumps, and pipe-lines for indicating the pressures of steam, gases, or liquids. Yet the standard instrument for measuring boiler-pressure described in the 1838 edition of Thomas Tredgold's 'Steam Engine' consisted of a bent tube of iron, of nearly $\frac{1}{2}$-in diameter, in the shape of a letter U, with one end connected to the boiler or steam-pipe and open to it; the steam-pressure forced mercury contained in the bottom of the U up the other limb which was open to the atmosphere. A float on the mercury had a vertical stem which enabled its movement to be measured.

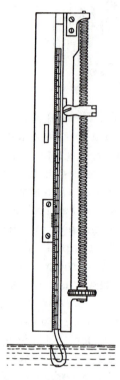

FIGURE 293—*Boyden's hook-gauge.*

The measurement of velocity and volume of flow in open channels, as distinct from closed pipes, also received much attention. One problem was the relationship between the velocity at the surface and the mean velocity through the depth; this in turn affected the interpretation of observations made by timing floats over measured distances. Many river-engineers experimented with various shapes, sizes, and materials for floats intended to indicate sub-surface velocities or, in the form of a weighted rod, mean velocities.

Frequently the most convenient method of estimating the flow in a river or canal is to measure the level of the water-surface relative to the crest of a weir. Nineteenth-century hydraulic engineers devoted much effort to the improvement of this technique by determining more accurately the relationship between the head and the discharge. At various times from 1860 onwards important determinations of the coefficient of discharge of weirs of various shapes under a wide range of flows were published. Among the points receiving special attention were: (i) the effect of the velocity of the stream approaching the weir in increasing the effective head or height over the crest, and (ii) the effect of any contractions imposed upon the overflowing sheet of water by the sides or top of the weir.

The origin of the current-meter, essentially a screw whose rate of revolution depends on the velocity of the stream, is obscure, but it was certainly improved in design and in its method of use in the field from about 1875 onwards. At various times during the century elaborations and improvements were also effected to the velocity-tube as invented or used by Henry Pitot (1695–1771); the effect of the current is to make the liquid rise in the tube above the level of the liquid in the channel. Pitot apparently expanded the submerged mouth of the tube into a funnel-shape. This, however, disturbs the normal flow of the stream. The French hydraulic expert H. P. G. Darcy (1803–58) made the mouth small, thus minimizing interference and also reducing oscillations in the column.

IV. HARBOURS

By the beginning of the nineteenth century the making of harbour works had been advanced to a remarkable degree by such men as John Smeaton (1724–92), John Rennie (1761–1821), and Thomas Telford (1757–1834). Later developments in this field were dominated by five main features: (i) the growth of sea-borne trade and of the size of ships; (ii) the creation of harbour facilities near to centres of industry and commerce, often in spite of immense natural obstacles; (iii) the application of steam-power to cranes, pile-drivers, dredgers, and other plant; (iv) improvements in materials, including concrete; (v) a growing appreciation of the importance of the study of tides, waves, and currents.

It is not possible to quote here more than a few figures and examples by way of illustration. In 1800, approximately 13 000 vessels, having a total tonnage of 1 760 000, entered the Thames in one year; by 1891 the number was approaching 52 000, with an aggregate tonnage of over 13 000 000. In the early 1800s, Telford reported that, of the vessels trading into the port of Leith, 3484 were under 200 tons and drew less than 10 ft of water; only four exceeded 400 tons, with a draught of up to $15\frac{1}{2}$ ft. By comparison, in 1891, 3749 ships entered, with an average tonnage of 333, and the available depth of $26\frac{1}{2}$ ft on the sill of the lock at spring tides was found to be inadequate for other vessels that would have used the port. A chart prepared by John Smeaton shows a depth of less than 4 ft in the Clyde at a point near the site where the *Queen Mary* was launched in 1934. The number of ships registered at Glasgow in 1810 was 24, having a total tonnage of nearly 2000; in 1891, it was 1576, aggregating over 1 300 000 tons, in addition to 309 ships (240 000 tons) at Greenock. Liverpool provides another example of re-markably rapid growth.

In many places, such as London, Liverpool, Glasgow, and Preston, great enterprise was shown during the nineteenth century (and later) in the improve-ment of approach channels. In some instances, notably in Liverpool Bay and at the estuary of the Ribble, training-walls of dumped stone have been built with the object of concentrating the currents in order to deepen the channels; but the development of steam-powered dredgers has provided the principal contribu-tion to the making and maintenance of the required depths. Late eighteenth-century attempts to deepen the Clyde—attempts that met with some success—used ordinary ploughs drawn by horses to loosen sand that dried at low water; submerged shoals were treated with special ploughs and harrows worked by hand-capstans situated on the river-bank, and the loosened material was carried away on the ebb tide (cf vol IV, p 629). The first steam dredger appeared on the Clyde in 1824 and on the Ribble in 1839. In 1890 two hopper dredgers each of 500 tons capacity were adopted for lowering the Mersey bar in Liverpool Bay. They were of the suction type, which had been made practicable by the development of the centrifugal pump (p 524); when the impeller is made large enough and has widely spaced vanes it is capable of dealing with sand, and coarser solids, mixed with water. Three years later a dredger of 3000 tons capacity was commissioned, to be followed within a short period by others, including the *Leviathan*; this had a capacity of 180 000 cu ft and was able to fill itself in 50 minutes, drawing from a maximum depth of 70 ft. Between 1890 and 1914 the depth at low spring tide over the bar was increased from 11 to 35 ft.

The application of pumps to dredgers is said to have been suggested by Henri Émile Bazin in 1867; its first American appearance (as a 'centrifugal drainage pump') was in 1871, and from 1877 onwards the suction dredger came into very wide use on the Mississippi (vol IV, p 631).

Apart from the application of steam-power (although without it most of the other developments could not have occurred) important advances were made in dredging-machinery of all kinds. The suction dredger has already been men-tioned; soft rock was removed by steel claws, and harder rock by first breaking it up with chisel-pointed rams and then removing it by grabs. About 3 m tons of hard limestone were extracted from a shoal in the Suez canal by this means: one of the dredgers had ten chisel-pointed rams or rock-cutters each 42 ft long and 4 tons in weight. Five of these were placed on each side of the well of the dredger through which the broken rock was raised by ladder and buckets. The rams were lifted by hydraulic power and allowed to fall from a height of 10–20 ft on to the rock, giving 200–300 blows an hour. The bucket-chains were driven by a four-cylinder compound steam-engine of 200 ihp. The experience gained on the Suez project had a profound influence on the development of dredging and of plant for handling materials all over the world.

Among other ingenious late nineteenth-century dredging devices was one for the pumping of water through tubes trailing in the mud deposits of a tidal basin in order to stir up the mud and keep it in suspension so that it would flow out with the ebb tide (Tilbury docks, *c* 1889). Another was W. H. Wheeler's 'eroder dredger', consisting of a cone-shaped cutter having a number of blades round its periphery; it was driven at about 100 rpm. The cutter disintegrated material on the bed of the water-way, producing a centrifugal current and encouraging the particles to be carried away by the stream.

The growth of shipping provided a demand in some harbours for pontoon- or floating-docks, in which vessels could be examined or repaired. Essentially they consist of chambers fitted with end-gates that can be closed after the ship has been towed in and securely fixed in position; the water inside the dock is then pumped away and the whole structure floats, supporting the ship. One such dock, towed across the Atlantic to Bermuda harbour in 1902, had an overall length of 545 ft and could accommodate a vessel of 32 ft draught.

V. DRAINAGE, IRRIGATION, AND RECLAMATION

In the nineteenth century European engineering skill was extensively devoted to land-reclamation in colonial territories, or in those new lands to which settlers were then migrating in large numbers. Early in the century the engineers of the East India Company made strong efforts to avert famine in India, first by reviving and improving old works, and later by the construction of 'the three classic prototype irrigation ventures of British India: the Western Jumna canal in the Punjab, the Eastern Jumna canal in the United Provinces, and the Cauvery delta system in the Madras Presidency'. The reconstruction of the Eastern Jumna system, reopened in 1830, has features of historical importance: the cross-drainage works, involving masonry weirs equipped with hinged gates that could be dropped to allow the passage of floods and raised to restore the canals, were 'possibly the first permanent canal works of any magnitude constructed during the British administration'. Silting had very often proved troublesome with these canals excavated in sandy alluvial soil, but in this case the excessive gradient of the canal resulted in heavy scour and damage to masonry works. Remedial measures thus had to be taken, including the building of locks to reduce the gradient. From this time many European engineers working in India and in Egypt investigated what is called 'the régime of canals', that is, the velocity and slope necessary to maintain a specified depth in an erosible channel of given dimensions. Similarly, the protection of weirs, sluices, bridges, and dams against scour has been the subject of special attention during the past hundred years.

The period from 1836 to 1850 has been called the golden age of irrigation works in India. The Ganges canal conceived by Colonel (later Sir) Proby Cautley (1802–71) of the Bengal Artillery was the first completely artificial canal in northern India; it was designed both for irrigation and for navigation over a 300-mile stretch between its head and Cawnpore. Survey began in 1836 and construction, interrupted by war and mutiny, lasted from 1842 to 1857. Great skill and ingenuity are evident in many crossings for torrents and drainage-channels: for example, the overbridge of masonry having a bed 200 ft wide and a flood depth of 16 ft to carry the Ranipur, and the level crossing at Dhanauri. During the monsoon, the water of the Ratman sweeps across the canal and escapes through a masonry 'weir' provided with shutters that are dropped to allow the storm-water to pass; a regulator of ten 20-ft spans keeps the excess water from flowing down the canal when the torrent is in spate. There is also the Solani aqueduct consisting of 15 arches each of 50-ft span supported on piers with foundations in the sand of the Solani river; the canal crosses the river in a channel 170 ft wide and 10 ft deep.

The Ganges canal and the Upper Bari Doab canal (opened in 1859) depended on temporary weirs annually reconstructed. Sir Arthur Cotton (1803–99) built his first permanent headworks on the Cauvery in Madras, and later, on a far greater scale, on the Godaveri delta project: these headworks consisted of $2\frac{1}{4}$ miles of weir, $1\frac{1}{4}$ miles of embankment, and three regulators each with navigation locks and under-sluices.

The experience gained in India was of benefit to Egypt. In 1826 the Pasha Muhammad Ali introduced the cultivation of cotton into Lower Egypt; this required perennial irrigation by a system of canals supplying water the whole year round. There existed some canals deep enough to take a little water from the Nile even when the river was low, about 25 ft below its flood-level. These canals were deepened and others were dug to draw off sufficient water for the crop at all times. However, at flood the canals proved to be too large for the amount required; the water in them at those times was slow-moving and the canals became heavily silted. Mechanical appliances not being then available, vast quantities of silt had to be removed by conscripted labour. In an effort to solve the problem more happily, Muhammad Ali engaged foreign engineers to build the Delta barrages, 15 miles north of Cairo, with the object of controlling the river, obstructing it, and raising its level so that the water at the head of the canals could be at a higher level in summer. Thus the canals could be reduced in depth and the annual deposit of silt decreased. Unfortunately, the problem of building such a barrage on a bed of sand was at that time even more formidable than it is today: the works were completed about 1861 but could not be used because their foundations were found to be insecure. Altogether they contained 132 sluices, to be closed during the summer months, and three regulators acting as headworks for the canals. British engineers from India later examined the bar-rage and showed that it could be brought into partial service in its existing state. In summer the level of the Nile was raised 3 or 4 ft and subsequently by as much as 10 ft, after repairs based on experience in India. By 1889 the system of forced labour for the cleaning of the canals was abolished. The Delta barrage was further strengthened by building subsidiary weirs across the river-bed below the main structures, which relieved it of some pressure.

The Aswan dam (ch 23), completed in 1902 and elevated in 1912 and 1934, is rightly regarded as one of the greatest of all civil engineering achievements. There had been many schemes for storing the excess flood-water of the Nile and using it to augment the summer flow. Sir William Willcocks's proposal for a dam at Aswan was approved by an International Commission under Sir Benjamin Baker (1894), although a member of the commission, M. Boulé, foretold that the rock downstream would not withstand the impact of falling water; protective works subsequently prevented this erosion. After due con-sideration, a straight dam was adopted in preference to Willcocks's original design for a curved one. Since the dam is $1\frac{1}{4}$ miles long and has 180 sluices, while difficulties were presented by the site and the climate, the four-year period of construction (1898–1902) is remarkably brief. The three easterly channels of the river and the central channel were dammed first; the remaining one was dammed after opening the eastern sluices in the partly completed dam. The work was facilitated by first building a bank of heavy stones, sand, cement, and sand-bags below the site and a barrier of sand-bags above it; the space between the embankments was pumped out and the foundations and lower part of the dam were constructed under the protection of the banks erected on either side. The four locks for navigation were provided with gates sliding sideways into recesses in the masonry, instead of the more common folding gates. Con-temporaneously with the Aswan works, the Asyut barrage was built with the object of raising the summer water-level of the Nile in Upper Egypt to facilitate canalization of basins and the supply of perennial water.

Knowing of the troubles experienced with the Delta barrages, the engineers took elaborate precautions over the foundations of that at Asyut. The structure was supported on a 10-ft-thick base of masonry, protected up and down stream by a continuous line of cast iron sheet-piling having cemented joints and, further, by aprons of clay and gravel faced with stone.

Both the Asyut and the Aswan dams incorporated steel gates of the Stoney type, easy to operate in spite of the pressure exerted against them. The gates open upwards, allowing the silt-laden flood waters to escape beneath them. Essentially, they consist of steel shutters; the thrust of the water against the shutter is communicated to the downstream jamb through anti-friction rollers, and a watertight joint is made on the upstream side by the pressure of the water, which forces suspended vertical staunching-rods of angle-iron between the face of the shutter and the frame. Such gates have often been used in later works of many kinds.

In Britain, the most interesting works of drainage and reclamation have been carried out in the fen country of East Anglia (vol III, ch 12). Costly schemes are still being put into effect there. During the nineteenth century many improvements were made, and many more were proposed but never carried out, either for lack of capital or on account of uncertainty as to their effectiveness, or again through the absence of an organized, overall authority with powers to attack the problem of drainage for the area as a whole. The outfalls of the rivers have long been regarded as important not only for discharging the waters brought down by them but as navigation channels, and both interests have to be safeguarded. The fact that the level of the land is always sinking adds measurably to the difficulties of drainage.

Nineteenth-century efforts in the Fens, like their predecessors, sometimes met with temporary success only to be followed by later disappointment. Among the more conspicuous events were: (i) the Eau Brink cut (1821) which removed a great bend of varying width encumbered with shifting banks of sand and silt between King's Lynn and St Germans; (ii) a new outfall for the Nene (1830); (iii) the North Level main drain (1834); and (iv) a new channel for the Welland (1838). This last required the construction of training-walls made of banks of thorn faggots about 6 ft long and 3 ft in girth laid in courses each weighted with clay or sods till the bank reached about half-tide level, the thorns interlacing and trapping silt so as to form a solid embankment. Similar fascine work was done at the Witham outfall (1841); a new channel was cut through the marshes outside the mouth of the Witham, and the Grand Sluice above Boston was enlarged (1884). In 1846 the Norfolk Estuary Company was formed, ostensibly to recover land from the Wash, but it was preoccupied for many years with attempting to induce the Great Ouse to follow a more stable and a deeper course, seawards of the Eau Brink cut.

In the Fens also a revolution resulted from the development of the steam-engine and the centrifugal pump. A 30-hp steam-driven pump was erected along the Ten Mile bank in 1819–20 and others quickly followed:

> These *Fens* have oft times been by Water drown'd.
> Science a remedy in *Water* found.
> The powers of *Steam* she said shall be employ'd
> And the *Destroyer* by *Itself* destroy'd.

The wind-driven scoop-wheel (vol III, plate 20) was doomed, though it is still a characteristic feature of the East Anglian landscape. A new marvel at the Great Exhibition of 1851 was Appold's centrifugal pump (p 525). Almost immediately it was brought into service in the Fens; by the autumn of 1853 the 1000 acres of Whittlesey Mere were fields of yellow corn.

Intensified draining was accompanied by shrinking of the peat: an iron column sunk into solid clay at one point and made level with the ground in 1851 was exposed nearly 5 ft in 1860, just over 10 ft in 1892, and 10 ft 8 in by 1932.

The foremost feat of land-reclamation of the twentieth century in Europe, following historic precedents and indeed already suggested in the seventeenth, occurred appropriately in the Netherlands (vol III, p 300). The idea of converting the Zuider Zee into an inland lake took definite shape about 1840 and was finally adopted as a result of the efforts of the engineer C. Lely (1854–1929). The main dam, 20 miles long, isolating the Ijsselmeer (as it is now called) from the North Sea, was completed in 1932; two polders having a combined area of 170 000 acres have been surrounded by secondary dikes and pumped dry; a third is well under way.

VI. THE DEVELOPMENT OF HYDRAULIC SCIENCE

In 1801 Eytelwein (1764–1848) of Berlin published his *Handbuch der Mechanik und der Hydraulik*, containing a remarkable account of studies on the flow of water in compound pipes, the motion of jets and their impact on surfaces, and the theory that a water-wheel will have its maximum effect when its peripheral velocity is half the velocity of the stream (cf vol IV, p 203).

Throughout the succeeding century the subject of water in motion excited interest in a brilliant succession of experimenters and mathematicians. In general, the earlier researchers, and some of those who followed, were content to consider the ideal frictionless, incompressible fluid, and the application of their mathematics to practical problems was necessarily limited. Characteristic of nineteenth-century progress is the development of realistic formulae based on observations, together with theories that partially explained the facts as observed and that provided some basis for extrapolation or generalization. Although great progress has been made in the present century, it remains true that the nineteenth century saw the greater and more fundamental advances.

In 1827 Poncelet (1788–1867) published his *Mémoire sur les roues hydrauliques à aubes courbes*, describing his experiments with a new type of undershot water-wheel having curved palettes (p 529). He had raised the efficiency of such wheels from the previous 25 per cent to over 60 per cent by recognizing that curved vanes would receive the water without shock and discharge it with small velocity. Poncelet is also credited with the first adequate theory of turbines (1838), and in collaboration with Lesgros he carried out extensive experiments on orifices. The quantity represented by the product of a force and the distance through which it moves was called *travail* by Poncelet and other French engineers. It was many years afterwards that the obvious translation 'work' found its way into English scientific usage. Even as late as 1841, William Whewell, afterwards Master of Trinity College, Cambridge, called it 'labouring force'.

The flow of water in pipes and channels was studied in a wonderful series of experiments by Darcy and Bazin (*Recherches hydrauliques*, 1866), and remarkable experiments on waves were described in 1837 by John Scott Russell; Russell derived empirical formulae to represent his observations, and these formulae were later justified by mathematical reasoning. Notable work was also done between 1820 and 1830 by Bidone of the hydraulic establishment in the University of Turin, and mathematical contributions to the study of waves were made by Green, Rankine, and McCowan, and by Stokes, who also considered viscous fluids and the motion of spheres through them at low velocities.

One of the most important points for the engineer concerned with the design of pipes and open channels is the fact that the friction depends not only on the material but on the shape and dimensions of the cross-section. Bazin's well known empirical formula devised to express this in quantitative terms remains as sound as any of the later formulae, although it may be less convenient than some for use in practical calculations.

About 1870 came William Froude's classic experiments at Torquay on the resistance of plane surfaces towed through water, and his introduction of the method of predicting the resistance of ships with the aid of scale models (p 387). Basically, this consists in towing a model (of scale $1:S$) through a long channel and measuring its total resistance; the velocity of towing in relation to the expected speed of the full-size ship is chosen so that what are now known as their 'Froude numbers' have equal values. This means that if v_1 represents the speed of the ship itself, its model is tested at a speed v_2 equal to $v_1/\sqrt{S}$. The skin-frictional resistance of the model, as estimated from experiments on thin boards of similar textural roughness, is then subtracted from the measured total resistance to afford an estimate of that part of its resistance due to its shape, giving rise to waves and eddies. Multiplying this by S^3, with an allowance if necessary for the different densities of water, gives the predicted drag of the ship itself due to waves and eddies, and to this is added the estimated skin-friction of its surface. In this way its total resistance can be calculated.

Fundamentally, however, the most important contribution to hydraulics—and to fluid mechanics in the widest sense—during the period under review was made by Osborne Reynolds (1842–1912), the first professor of engineering at Owens College (later the University of Manchester). In a paper of 1883 Reynolds described a series of experiments which, it is safe to predict, will always remain among the classics of science. His apparatus was simple—a tank 6 ft long by 18 in square with glass sides. Inside this tank was a horizontal glass tube having a bell-mouth; the tube projected through one end of the tank and was coupled to a vertical pipe in which was a control valve. From a flask containing dye a tube was led through the end of the tank and terminated in a fine nozzle inside the bell-mouth. A bulb floating in the water within the tank was attached by a cord to a mechanism having a pointer whose position on a circular scale measured the water-level. The method of conducting an experiment was as follows: water was admitted to the tank and allowed to settle so as to eliminate initial disturbances. The control-valve was then slightly opened and a filament of dye was caused to proceed into the bell-mouth and along the glass tube. The velocity of the flow of water along the tube could be obtained by timing the fall of the water-surface in the tank. At low velocities, the filament remained straight and steady. At higher velocities (when the control-valve was gradually opened wider) the filament was seen to break up, to become diffused through the water, and to reveal eddies.

By this simple means, Reynolds provided a visual demonstration of the two manners of motion of a fluid—laminar or truly stream-line, and sinuous or turbulent. The physical distinction may be clarified thus: suppose a fluid to be moving at a constant volume per second along a pipe, and consider a certain point P somewhere inside the pipe. If the motion is laminar, the velocity of the fluid as it passes P will be constant in magnitude and direction. On the other hand, if the flow is sinuous, the velocity at P will fluctuate in magnitude and direction even though the volume moving along the pipe per second is uniform.

Reynolds further enunciated the criteria that determine whether the motion shall be orderly or disorderly: the condition favouring turbulence in a pipe of given diameter conveying a fluid of given kinematic viscosity is that the velocity exceeds a certain critical value. Moreover, this critical velocity is reduced if either the diameter of the pipe is increased or the kinematic viscosity is decreased. The criterion that determines the manner of motion is, in fact, the dimensionless quantity vd/ν, in which v represents velocity, d diameter, and ν kinematic viscosity. This quantity has become known as the 'Reynolds number'. That is not all, for Reynolds's work served to reconcile the apparent anomaly suggested by previous investigations of pipe-resistance, namely, that sometimes the resistance appeared to increase directly with the velocity, while in others it was more nearly proportional to the square of the velocity. It was now clear that in the former case the motion was laminar, while the latter law of resistance was appropriate to turbulent motion.

These experiments have made his name immortal. . . .How fundamental [Reynolds's work is] has become increasingly evident with the development of aerodynamics, and without the Reynolds number it is doubtful if practical aerodynamics could have proceeded at all; it would have been choked by the mass of accumulated data.

The same is true of the science of hydraulics.

Nor was Reynolds's part in this golden age of hydraulics confined to the contribution already outlined. In 1875 he took out a patent for improvements in centrifugal pumps, including the idea of the multi-stage machine and that of surrounding the impeller by guide-vanes and divergent passages in order to improve the efficiency by converting a portion of the kinetic head to pressure head within the pump (p 526). The first pump exemplifying this design was built and tested in Reynolds's laboratory at Manchester.

In another connexion, Reynolds's genius had a profound, if at first sight indirect, influence upon hydraulic turbines as well as upon other machinery. His paper 'On the Theory of Lubrication' (1886) applied the equations of hydrodynamics to explain how a film of oil is maintained between two surfaces in relative motion and is able to support great pressures. His analysis aided the development of bearings, including those frequently used in large hydraulic turbines, capable of satisfying exacting conditions of load and speed.

For the testing of prime-movers, some form of brake is essential to measure the horse-power output. In many respects, a hydraulic dynamometer has immense advantages over mechanical friction-brakes; the Froude dynamometer is a well-known feature of test-beds. Reynolds himself explained on a later occasion how it would be possible to mount the casing of a centrifugal pump, or a tank in which a paddle or screw works, on the shaft of an engine in such a way as to be in balance when the shaft is at rest but so that the moment of resistance of the shaft when rotating would be equal to the moment required to turn the casing round the shaft. 'This can be readily and absolutely measured by suspending weights at a definite horizontal distance from the shaft.' He then explains that the first recorded use of such a device was by Hirn in 1865, while he himself reported in 1877 how he had used a centrifugal pump suspended on the shaft of a multiple steam-turbine for measuring powers at speeds up to 12 000 rpm. On the same occasion, William Froude (p 387) gave an account of his own hydraulic brake for determining the power of large engines; it differed essentially from previous designs, and offered a remarkable resistance in relation to its size. Accordingly, Reynolds tested a 4-inch-diameter model of Froude's brake and was led to devise an important modification. The resistance of the dynamometer was caused by the forced circulation of water in chambers formed by the vanes of the rotating wheel and the casing. The forced vortices naturally gave a lower pressure at the inside than at the outside, and under certain conditions of load and speed the pressure at the centre became sub-atmospheric; air was liberated and accumulated, displacing water and causing an irregular and disturbing reduction of resistance. This action threatened to render the device impracticable. Reynolds overcame the fault by drilling holes through the metal of the guides on the fixed casing, which communicated through a surrounding passage to the atmosphere. Thus the pressure at the centre of the vortices was atmospheric under all conditions of operation.

Reynolds utilized this modified form of Froude's brake in his redetermination of the mechanical equivalent of heat towards the close of the nineteenth century. Water at freezing-point was supplied to the brake, its volume being adjusted so that its temperature was raised to boiling-point by the internal friction of the brake. Thus measurement of temperature became independent of the accuracy of thermometer scales, since all that would be required of the thermometers was the identification of the two standard temperatures. Meticulous precautions were taken to correct for losses of heat by radiation and conduction. In a trial of an hour's duration, the quantity of water whose temperature was raised through 100 Centigrade degrees approached 1000 lb.

During the twentieth century, the study of river and harbour problems has increasingly been conducted with the aid of scale models. Laboratories have been established in many countries specifically for this purpose; one of them employs no fewer than 300 persons, and in the United Kingdom a British Hydraulics Research Station has recently been created by the Department of Scientific and Industrial Research. Osborne Reynolds was again the scientific parent of these important developments.

In 1885 he made the first model of a tidal river to be constructed on scientific principles, its time-scale being calculated on the assumption that the velocity of the tidal wave is proportional to the square-root of the depth of water in which it travels. He seems to have started only with the idea of demonstrating the circulation of the water and the accompanying eddies in the estuary of the Mersey, and discovering whether his theories concerning the circulation and its secondary effect in producing channels were correct. He observed, however, evidently with growing interest, that a flat bed of sand lying on the bottom of the model was shaped by the tides into banks and channels in such a way that the general features of the natural estuary emerged. 'And, what is as important', he wrote, 'the causes of these as well as all minor features could be distinctly seen in the model.' He reported his findings to the British Association in 1887, and pursued the matter further on its behalf with the principal objects of improving the technique and of finding how far the configuration of the bed of such models is influenced by their horizontal and vertical dimensions. In his first announcement he had stated:

In the meantime I have called attention to these results, because this method of experimenting seems to afford a ready means of investigating and determining beforehand the effects of any proposed estuary or harbour works; a means which, after what I have seen, I should feel it madness to neglect before entering upon any costly undertaking.

Sceptics have regarded the method with suspicion chiefly on the grounds that the sand used in such models is not to scale, and that the vertical scale is exaggerated in relation to the horizontal dimension, but today very few responsible hydraulic engineers would dispute Reynolds's claim. The problems of the improvement and control of rivers are often so complex, and the expenditure on remedial works so considerable, that even qualitative guidance afforded by laboratory tests is welcomed and generally acknowledged to be of real value.

BIBLIOGRAPHY

BABBITT, H. E. and DOLAND, J. J. 'Water Supply Engineering' (4th ed.). McGraw Hill, New York. 1949.

BODMER, G. R. 'Hydraulic Motors: Turbines and Pressure Engines' (2nd ed.). London. 1895.

DARBY, H. C. 'The Draining of the Fens.' University Press, Cambridge. 1940.

DAUGHERTY, R. L. 'Hydraulic Turbines, with a Chapter on Centrifugal Pumps' (3rd ed.). McGraw Hill, New York. 1920.

FLEMING, A. P. M. and BROCKLEHURST, H. J. 'A History of Engineering.' Black, London. 1925.

GIBSON, A. H. 'Hydraulics and its Applications.' Constable, London. 1908.

INSTITUTION OF WATER ENGINEERS. 'Manual of British Water Supply Practice' (ed. by A. T. HOBBS and J. E. HOBBS, 2nd ed.). Heffer, Cambridge. 1954.

KIRBY, R. S., WITHINGTON, S., DARLING, A. B. and KILGOUR, F. G. 'Engineering in History.' McGraw Hill, New York. 1956.

NEWHOUSE, F., IONIDES, M. G. and LACEY, G. 'Irrigation in Egypt and the Sudan, the Tigris and Euphrates Basin, India and Pakistan.' Longmans, Green, London, for the British Council. 1950.

NORRIE, C. M. 'Bridging the Years: a Short History of British Civil Engineering.' Arnold, London. 1956.

RANKINE, W. J. M. 'A Manual of the Steam Engine and other Prime Movers' (rev. by W. J. MILLAR). London. 1891.

ROUSE, H. and INCE, S. 'A History of Hydraulics', Iowa Institute of Hydraulic Research, State University of Iowa. 1957.

STRAUB, H. 'A History of Civil Engineering' (trans. from the German by E. ROCKWELL). Hill, London. 1952.

VAN VEEN, J. 'Dredge, Drain, Reclaim: the Art of a Nation.' Nijhoff, The Hague. 1955.

WHEELER, W. H. 'Tidal Rivers.' London. 1893.

WILLIAMS, A. 'Victories of the Engineer.' Nelson, London. 1916.

See also *The Engineer, Engineering, Proceedings of the Institution of Civil Engineers, London, Proceedings of the Institution of Mechanical Engineers, London,* and 'Encyclopaedia Britannica' (especially articles on "Hydromechanics" by W. C. UNWIN, 1876).

23

WATER-SUPPLY

F. E. BRUCE

I. INTRODUCTION

THE rapid growth of towns and industries in the second half of the nineteenth century required a corresponding increase in the supply of water, a prime necessity both of life and of many industries. The need for larger and better supplies, of which those who were concerned with public health were becoming aware in the early years of the century, was now generally recognized. Consumption increased at a remarkable rate. The water supplied by the London companies, for instance, rose from 44·4 m gallons a day in 1849 to 215 m in 1901. In Bradford, a rapidly growing industrial town, the public supply increased nearly eighteenfold between 1855 and 1873.

This increase in consumption was due not merely to the greater size of industry and of urban populations, but to changing habits. Services were extended to people who had hitherto depended on wells or other private sources, while water-closets and, to a less extent, bath-tubs, were coming into general use.

Intensive exploitation of available sources of supply near the towns proved in many instances inadequate, and the authorities had of necessity to develop distant ones. This happened, very often, both because local sources did not yield a sufficient quantity of water and because streams and rivers especially were becoming seriously polluted by the discharge of untreated sewage and industrial wastes. Some towns solved the double problem by pumping pure underground waters from deep wells. Others, unable or unwilling to find unpolluted sources, had to pay special attention to the purification of surface water, so that before the end of the century great advances had been made in filtration, the basic process of treatment. Progress in medical knowledge and the rise of the science of bacteriology produced clear evidence of the importance of clean water, and provided new standards for the assessment of its quality.

II. ORGANIZATION OF WATER-SUPPLY

The companies that had been formed in the early part of the century for the sale of water in limited localities were rarely able to raise the capital necessary for the development of major sources of new supply, especially where such sources required impounding reservoirs and long aqueducts. Many companies could serve but a fraction of the houses in their areas, and then only intermittently, the water being turned on for an hour or two each day. Even where they had the resources, as in London, they were reluctant to allow a constant supply, fearing heavy loss through leakage from faulty plumbing-systems and through the carelessness of consumers. Apart from domestic requirements, water was needed for street-cleansing, fire-fighting, and sewer-flushing, and for public baths and wash-houses (the first of which had been opened in Liverpool in 1842). For these public uses an intermittent supply was unsatisfactory, and for fire-fighting quite inadequate.

For these reasons, one after another of the larger towns took control of the water-supplies in their areas. Manchester Corporation obtained Parliamentary powers in 1847 to take over the Manchester and Salford waterworks company and set about developing supplies from the Longdendale valley in Derbyshire. Later, the corporation embarked on an ambitious scheme to raise the level of Lake Thirlmere in the Lake District and bring water to the city through an aqueduct 96 miles long. In 1848 Liverpool obtained powers to build its own waterworks, and in the 1880s constructed the Vyrnwy reservoir, 77 miles away in north Wales. Glasgow bought out two existing companies in 1855 and initiated a scheme to use the waters of Loch Katrine. Birmingham failed to gain control of its water-supply until 1875. Here, as with the other cities, local sources were becoming inadequate, and the corporation developed the catchment area of the river Elan in central Wales by means of a series of three dams built between 1893 and 1904.

These are examples from among the largest municipal undertakings in Britain, but a similar pattern was followed elsewhere. Towns often succeeded in obtaining control only after years of Parliamentary wrangling, opposition coming not merely from the existing companies but from the ratepayers, especially the smaller landlords, who foresaw heavy expenditure on new works and improvements with little direct benefit to themselves [1]. Relatively few of the water companies were strong and efficient enough to resist the prevailing tendency. Among them were those serving Bristol, the Colne Valley area in Hertfordshire, Portsmouth, south Staffordshire, and Sunderland and South Shields.

London continued to be supplied by eight companies until 1902. The General Board of Health advocated public ownership of London's water-supplies in 1850, but, because of the size and complexity of the problem, and because there was no single authority in a position to take over the elaborate works which were by then in existence, the matter was shelved. The creation in 1888 of the London County Council at last gave the capital a single governing body, but although the Council promoted several Parliamentary bills designed to bring water-supplies under public control, there was too much opposition and the attempts failed. Finally a Royal Commission, which sat from 1897 to 1900, recommended the formation of an *ad hoc* body to take over from the companies. This body, the Metropolitan Water Board, came into being in 1902 [2].

The possibility of abandoning the polluted Thames as the main source of London's water was investigated by a number of official bodies. The General Board of Health in a report published in 1850 recommended that water should be drawn from sand-beds on the Surrey–Hampshire border. Another Royal Commission (1869) rejected proposals for impounding-schemes in Wales and the Lake District, as well as several more local schemes. The 1897–1900 commission also rejected a proposal to bring water from Wales, considering that the Thames and the Lea, supplemented by wells in the south-eastern region, should continue to be used.

As supplies to the towns became more assured, distribution systems were extended and the wells on which many town-dwellers had previously relied were abandoned. Intermittent provision was gradually replaced by constant supply. 'The Engineer' commented in 1873, 'Constant water supply at pressure has long been prayed for, and the moral pressure seems happily to be proving effective in obtaining the physical pressure necessary. The most of the London companies are making arrangements to give constant supply, and some of them are giving it partially already' [3]. By the 1890s the constant supply system was effective over much of the country.

The trend in other countries was similar to that in Britain. Most, if not all, of the urban waterworks on the continent of Europe were taken over by the local authorities before the end of the century [4]. Many, including those of Amsterdam, Antwerp, Berlin, and St Petersburg, had been built and operated by British engineers.

The cities of the United States were faced with the same problems of rapidly increasing demand, sometimes even more acute than those of European cities. In the 1830s New York had impounded water in the Croton catchment area 35 miles to the north, but by 1883 the city found it necessary to build a much larger dam and an aqueduct of unprecedented size to keep pace with its totally unforeseen growth [5]. In America as elsewhere the municipalities generally bought out the water companies, and by 1860 all but four of the sixteen largest cities had municipally owned supplies [6].

III. DEVELOPMENT OF SOURCES

Searching for more ample and pure supplies of water, some communities were able to meet their requirements by harnessing springs or driving wells. The use of springs was usually confined to small towns, but some large cities, especially on the European continent, depended on them wholly or in part. An outstanding example was Paris, which in 1865 and 1871 completed aqueducts 81 miles and 106 miles long to bring water from springs at Dhuis and Villeneuve l'Archevêque. Other large cities that depended mainly on springs were Vienna and Munich, and, in Britain, Bristol and Portsmouth.

In the midlands and the south-east of England many towns and industries drew water from wells or bore-holes in the chalk- or sand-beds. Because only reciprocating pumps of large dimensions were available, wells were usually dug as open shafts with diameters up to 15 ft or more. Bore-holes of much smaller diameter, drilled by the percussion method, could be used where the ground-water was under sufficient pressure to bring it within reach of pumps. A deep bore-hole drilled at Grenelle, Paris, by H. M. J. Mulot demonstrated the importance of choosing the site carefully, in accordance with the sound geological information then becoming available. The drilling took over seven years to complete and suffered many long delays while broken tools were recovered. Finally, on 26 February 1841, water was struck at a depth of 1800 ft; Mulot's prediction was justified and his persistence rewarded. The bore yielded 800 000 gallons a day, under an artesian pressure sufficient to carry it 122 ft above ground-level. Another bore-hole at Passy, completed in 1861, was 1920 ft deep and at first yielded $4\frac{1}{2}$ m gallons a day [7].

For smaller water-supplies, tube-wells, patented by Norton and used by the British Army in the Abyssinian campaign of 1868 (and thus often known as 'Norton' or 'Abyssinian' tube-wells), were used not only for emergency or temporary purposes but also as permanent sources for town water-supplies. They were generally from 1 to 3 inches in diameter, were driven to depths not greatly exceeding 80 ft, and in suitable formations might yield up to 3000 gallons an hour.

Another way of obtaining ground-water was to drive infiltration galleries in the gravel or sand adjacent to a river-bed. This system ensured a regular yield, filtered naturally. At Perth, water was drawn from a gallery under a gravel island in the river Tay. Nottingham and Derby also made use of galleries, and many were built in Europe and America (figure 294) [8].

These developments followed established methods, for during the half-century under review there were no major advances in technique. In the exploitation of surface water, however, spectacular progress was made, and the face of Nature was changed by the creation of large impounding reservoirs in the upper valleys of rivers. In Britain the shallow valleys and absence of solid bed-rock, especially in the Pennine area close to the northern industrial towns, encouraged the building of earth dams having a central core of puddle-clay and flat outer slopes (p 522). The design of such dams improved as knowledge was gained of the properties of soils and the stability of embankments, but occasional failures, notably those of the Holmfirth dam in 1852 and of the Dale Dyke dam in 1864, were tragic reminders of the lack of precise information (p 523).

FIGURE 294—*Section of an infiltration gallery in the valley of the river Scrivia, supplying water to Genoa. The portion of the gallery illustrated was built across and beneath the bed of the river, forming an underground dam, and water from the gravel entered the gallery by pipes on the upstream side. The water was conveyed 16 miles to Genoa in two 18-in cast iron pipes, under gravity.*

French engineers had less faith in earth dams, holding that they could not be built more than about 60 ft high without risk of failure. The need in France for structures 150–200 ft high, for the control of floods, prompted theoretical investigation into the principles on which masonry dams should be designed. In 1853 de Sazilly produced the first satisfactory basis of design, when he showed that besides considering stability against overturning and sliding, as had been done hitherto, it was necessary to calculate the internal stresses in the dam and relate them to the strength of the material. Delocre a few years later worked on similar lines. Both men recommended a dam-profile in which the maximum permissible compressive stress would just be reached at the upstream face when the reservoir was empty, and at the downstream face when the reservoir was full [9].

The first dam designed on these principles was the Furens dam, which was built between 1861 and 1866 for the dual purpose of water-supply and flood protection for the town of St-Étienne. The designers, Delocre and de Graeff, showed boldness and confidence in applying the new theory to such a large structure. Exceptional care in construction was taken and the dam was a complete success; it was followed by several others designed on the same principles. Its elegant lines are compared in figure 295 with those of the massive Alicante dam (1579–94) which is representative of the earlier empirical style of dam-building.

The principles enunciated by de Sazilly and Delocre remained fundamental to the design of dams, but the calculation of internal stresses was elaborated by many engineers and mathematicians, notably W. J. M. Rankine (1820–72), who in 1870 showed that it was the inclined stress within the dam, and not merely its vertical component, which should be considered. He also emphasized the value of the 'middle third' rule in avoiding tensile stresses which might open up cracks in the masonry.

The first high masonry dam in Britain, designed by Thomas Hawksley (1807–93) and G. F. Deacon, was constructed on the Vyrnwy river in north Wales

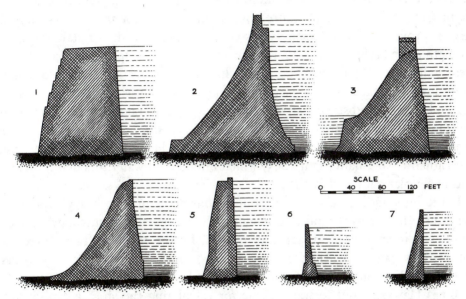

FIGURE 295—*Profiles of some notable masonry and concrete dams, with their dates of completion. (1) Alicante, Spain, 1594; (2) Furens, France, 1866; (3) Vyrnwy, Wales, 1891; (4) Caban Coch, Wales, 1904; (5) Zola, France, 1843; (6) Bear Valley, United States, 1884; (7) Lithgow No 2, Australia, 1906.*

between 1881 and 1889 for the water-supply of Liverpool (p 553). It is an over-flow dam, that is, the whole length of its crest is built as a weir to take surplus water, and a roadway is carried along its top on piers (figure 295 and plate 33 B). A very high standard of construction was imposed to ensure watertightness. The largest possible stones were used, one-third of them weighing 4–10 tons each. In describing the dam at the Institution of Civil Engineers in 1896, Deacon said: 'In 1881 there was probably no high masonry dam in Europe so far watertight that an English engineer would take credit for its construction' [10]. This cautious attitude is also reflected in the rather heavy section of the dam in comparison with the higher Furens dam, though Deacon had disagreed with Hawksley on the need for such a massive design.

Other important masonry dams in Britain were the Thirlmere dam (1894) which raised the level of an existing lake by 50 ft to provide storage for Manchester, and the three Elan valley dams built for Birmingham between 1893 and 1904 (p 553). One of these, the Caban Coch dam, is illustrated in figure 295. Like the Vyrnwy dam it is of the overflow type, but has a more economical profile [11].

In narrow steep-sided valleys where the sides are strong enough to resist an outward thrust, material can be saved by building a dam curved in plan to act as an arch. The Zola dam (figure 295), built in 1843 for the water-supply of Aix-en-Provence, was for many years the only dam relying for stability on its strength as an arch. It had a plan radius of 158 ft to the upstream face [9]. The Bear Valley dam (figure 295), built in California for irrigation in 1884, although quite low, was exceptionally slender. Its plan radius was 335 feet. It was replaced by a more substantial structure in 1911 [9]. Several other arch dams were built in California towards the end of the century. Another region in which this type of construction was adopted was Australia, where one of the highest was the Lithgow No 2 dam (figure 295) which impounded water to a depth of 78 ft and had a plan radius of 100 ft [12].

Large impounding-schemes in mountainous areas involve heavy capital expenditure and the works must be economically designed to ensure a dependable daily yield in spite of the vagaries of rainfall. By the 1860s the rainfall records collected by James Glaisher (1809–1903) and G. J. Symons (1838–1900) had given an indication of the range of variation that might be expected. In 1868 Thomas Hawksley put forward a rule for calculating the storage capacity required to ensure continuity of supply during three consecutive dry years, based on the observation that the lowest average rainfall for any three consecutive years was likely to be 'almost precisely' five-sixths of the long-term average rainfall. Further experience led Alexander Binnie (1839–1917) in 1892 to modify this rule by reducing the fraction to four-fifths, and the modified rule has since been widely used in estimation when only rainfall records are available [13]. In 1883 W. Rippl of Vienna introduced his method of calculating storage capacity when records of the flow of streams are available over a period of several years [14].

IV. AQUEDUCTS AND DISTRIBUTION

The major aqueducts carrying water from the catchment areas to the cities were as far as possible built to follow the hydraulic gradient; they then acted as 'open' channels with a free water surface. They were made either by the 'cut-

and-cover' method or by tunnelling, and were usually lined with masonry, brick, or concrete. The New Croton aqueduct, built between 1885 and 1893 to convey an additional 302 m gallons a day to New York from the Croton valley, was constructed as a tunnel for most of its 33-mile length, with a horse-shoe cross-section. Its height and width were about 13 ft 6 in and it was lined with brick up to 24 inches in thickness [5]. No European aqueducts approached this size. The Thirlmere aqueduct serving Manchester was 96 miles long and included 14 miles of tunnel and 37 miles of cut-and-cover. The section was rectangular with an arched soffit, and was approximately 7 ft high and 7 ft wide, lined with concrete [15].

Where an aqueduct had to cross a valley it was no longer necessary, as formerly, to build an elevated channel to follow the hydraulic gradient. Cast iron, wrought iron, and steel pipes were available to withstand high pressures while following the profile of the ground (cf vol II, pp 668–9). Cast iron pipes were now made by the vertical casting method, which gave greater strength, uniformity, and accuracy than the earlier 'greensand' process of inclined casting. The joints were normally of the spigot and socket type, caulked with lead, but flanged joints were used for connecting to valves and other fittings, and ball-and-socket joints had been designed to provide flexibility. Pipes were protected against corrosion by a coal-tar composition invented by Angus Smith (1818–86), which was first used in 1860 at Liverpool.

As early as 1825 wrought iron tubes had been made by drawing long strips of hot metal through a ring-die. Larger pipes were built up from wrought iron plates riveted together. A pipe of this kind, with a diameter of $11\frac{1}{2}$ in, supplying water to the gold-rush town of Virginia City, Nevada, in 1873, was under a maximum pressure of nearly 800 lb per sq in, claimed to be the highest pressure sustained by any pipeline in the world at that time [16].

With the development of the Bessemer process in 1855 and that of the open-hearth process in 1861 (pp 53–60), steel gradually took the place of wrought iron, the first steel water-mains being laid in the United States about 1860. Steel pipelines were increasingly used in America during the following years, and some of them have continued to serve for more than ninety years (plate 33 A). They were less favoured in Europe, chiefly because they were more susceptible to corrosion than cast iron. The earlier steel pipes were riveted, but welded pipes were introduced in 1887. In parts of America where timber was plentiful it was found more economical to construct timber flumes and pipes made of wooden staves than to convey iron or steel pipes hundreds of miles to the site.

For distribution within towns, cast iron pipes remained in use almost exclusively. The extension of distribution and the transition from intermittent to constant supply rendered the problem of waste more acute. Loss was caused through inferior pipes and fittings, misuse of flushing apparatus for water-closets, and, as a Parliamentary committee stated in 1867, by 'the tendency of evil-disposed persons to take away all fittings of brass and copper'. Improved fittings and a rising standard of plumbers' work did much to overcome these difficulties; and water-undertakings were authorized to inspect premises to check waste and misuse of water. Consumers gradually became accustomed to having water constantly available, and developed a sense of responsibility in its use. It was no longer necessary to leave taps permanently open for fear of missing the water when it was turned on.

To facilitate the detection and prevention of waste, G. F. Deacon invented in 1873 a recording meter (pp 536–7, figure 291) which could be placed in the mains at strategic points in the distribution system [17]. The reading of the meter during the early hours of the morning gave an indication of abnormal flow due to leakage, waste, or other causes. By closing valves to isolate in turn different sections of the town it was possible to locate faulty mains or offending houses. Another invention of economic significance was that by J. G. Appold of a pipe-scraper, which was propelled through a main by the pressure of water behind it, and removed corrosion products and incrustations that reduced the capacity of the pipe. It was first used at Torquay in 1866.

The Venturi meter (p 537, figure 292), which permitted accurate measurement of flow in a pipe with very small loss of head, was introduced in America by Clemens Herschel in 1887, and greatly simplified the task of the water-engineer in controlling treatment-works and distribution.

Few towns are so favourably placed that they can be supplied with water throughout their area without the aid of pumps, and the development of pumping machinery was an important factor contributing to the rapid expansion of distribution systems. The steam-driven reciprocating plunger- or piston-pump remained the standard equipment until the end of the century, but the power, control, and flexibility of the steam-engine were greatly improved during this period (ch 6). J. G. Appold and John Gwynne, working independently, showed in 1849 that the centrifugal pump was a practicable device for raising water (p 524), but its effective use in waterworks awaited the development of high-speed engines such as the steam-turbine and the electric motor. Consequently it was little used until the early years of the twentieth century. Gas- and oil-engines, although well established before 1900 (ch 8), were not widely adopted in waterworks practice until after that date.

V. THE QUALITY OF WATER

Before the second half of the nineteenth century the quality of the water drunk by the public was not carefully and systematically studied. It was only too evident to sight and smell that the condition of the water drawn from the Thames and other rivers was deteriorating because of the increasing volumes of sewage and other wastes discharged into them. For this reason James Simpson (1799–1869), the engineer to the Chelsea waterworks company, constructed sand filters in 1829. The filters were intended to remove visible dirt from the water, but in the following years it became apparent that they achieved more than this. During the cholera epidemics of 1849 and 1853, John Snow showed that deaths from cholera in those parts of London supplied with properly filtered water or with water drawn from the non-tidal portion of the Thames were only a fraction of those in areas using unfiltered water or water from the tidal reach. His investigation of the cholera outbreak in the Soho district in 1854, when he found that nearly every one of the hundreds of victims had drunk water from the Broad Street pump, clinched his argument that the 'poison' of cholera was conveyed from person to person by way of water polluted with human excreta. Identification of this 'poison', however, was yet to come [18].

Although Snow's theory that cholera was water-borne, and William Budd's assertion later that the same was true of typhoid, were accepted only slowly, the importance of finding pure sources of water and the value of filtration were acknowledged in the Metropolis Water Act, 1852, which required all the London water-companies drawing water from the Thames or its tributaries to remove their intakes to the cleaner non-tidal reaches and to filter all water-supplies for domestic use.

By the 1870s chemical tests for many of the impurities found in water had been standardized. The concentrations of mineral salts were readily determined, and it was recognized that the organic content was of great significance as a measure of wholesomeness. There was, however, no chemical method of distinguishing between potentially dangerous human pollution and the relatively harmless organic matter of animal or vegetable origin.

The new science of bacteriology, developed from the 1860s onwards by Louis Pasteur (1822–95), Robert Koch (1843–1910), and others, provided the key to this problem. The existence of microscopic organisms, including bacteria, had been known for two hundred years, but the role of certain bacteria as agents of disease was not understood until techniques for cultivating them on special media in the laboratory had been devised. Once these techniques were established, discoveries followed fast. In 1880 K. J. Eberth (1835–1926) isolated the typhoid bacillus, which four years later was proved by Gaffky to be the sole agent of the disease, and in 1883 the cholera vibrio was discovered by Koch. Bacteriologists were now able to trace the routes by which these and other organisms could be transmitted from person to person, and the empirical findings of Snow and Budd were confirmed beyond doubt.

In 1885 Percy Frankland (1858–1946) began routine bacteriological analysis of the water supplied by the London companies. Using gelatine plates as the culture medium he was able to show that efficient sand filtration reduced the bacterial content of water by as much as 98 per cent; he also found a correlation between his bacteriological results and the conditions under which the filters of the various companies were operated [19].

The procedures for isolating and identifying the dangerous organisms, such as the typhoid bacillus, which might be present in polluted water were too long and laborious for routine use. It was found more convenient to use simpler tests which would detect the common, harmless bacteria characteristic of the human intestine. If these bacteria were found in a supply of water, they would indicate that human contamination had occurred, with the consequent possibility that pathogenic organisms might also be present. This test, far more sensitive than contemporary chemical analysis, put into the hands of those responsible for maintaining the quality of public water-supplies an invaluable weapon in the fight against water-borne disease.

VI. THE TREATMENT OF WATER

Following Simpson's successful use of artificial sand-filters for treating Thames water at Chelsea in 1829 (p 561), numerous filters designed on the same principles were built in Britain and on the continent. They consisted essentially of a watertight basin of brick or masonry containing a bed of 2 or 3 ft of sand supported on gravel. This in turn rested on an underdrainage system constructed of open-jointed bricks, stones, or tiles to collect the filtered water (figure 296). During filtration the water stood a few feet deep over the sand and passed downwards through the bed at the rate of about 3 gallons per sq ft per hour. Solid matter from the water was held back mainly on the surface of the sand, forming a slimy growth which produced important chemical and biological changes in the water. Simpson observed 'an appearance resembling fermentation' on the surface of his filters, but the complicated processes which in fact occur there were not comprehended for many years. When the solids retained on and in the sand offered too much resistance to the passage of water, the filter was cleaned by allowing the water-level to fall below the surface of the sand, and the dirty top layer was then removed by hand (plate 32 B). To reduce the frequency of this operation it was found economical to pass the water first through settling-basins to remove the heavier solids.

Some filters included a layer of charcoal, which removed colour from the water and, it was claimed, further reduced its organic content. The filters described by Thomas Spencer in 1859 had a layer of magnetic oxide of iron; they were installed at Wakefield, Wisbech, Southport, and Calcutta [20].

Simpson's filters, known as English or 'slow sand-filters', required large areas of land (by 1903 the London water companies had nearly 150 acres of filters), and were costly to construct and to clean. Many attempts were made to devise filters

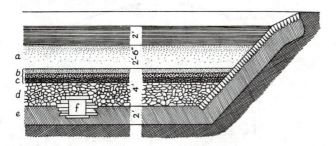

FIGURE 296—*Section of a slow sand-filter, Dublin. This shows a typical construction, but many different designs of the underdrainage system were employed, using bricks, stone, or perforated tiles. a, sand; b, fine and coarse gravel; c, broken stone, 3"; d, broken stone, 4–8"; e, puddle clay; f, dry stone collecting drain.*

which would operate more rapidly and could be cleaned mechanically. Common expedients were the enclosure of the filter in a container so that pressure could be used to force the water through the bed, and the washing of the sand by reversing the flow.

Before 1850 a number of pressure-filters designed by de Fonvielle or his rival Souchon had been installed in France, where the English filter was considered to be too expensive. Another Frenchman, H. P. G. Darcy, first studied the hydraulics of filtration, publishing his findings in his book on the public fountains of Dijon in 1856. In the same year he patented a filter that incorporated many novel features, but it does not appear to have been entirely successful—perhaps because of the extremely high rate of filtration attempted.

During the next thirty years numerous patents were granted in England and France for systems of mechanical filtration. Most of those that reached the stage of practical application were used for industrial water, where the aim was clarity rather than potability. Media other than sand were often used, including charcoal, coke, and natural sponge. The last was a convenient material because it could be alternately compressed and released by a piston while being washed by the reversed flow of water.

The modern form of rapid sand-filter emerged during the 1880s. Probably the earliest was the 'Torrent' filter introduced by the Pulsometer Engineering Company in 1880 (figure 297). In this filter the upward wash was aided by jets of compressed air admitted through the underdrains to agitate the grains of sand and loosen the dirt. The air was blown in by a steam jet, but this was later

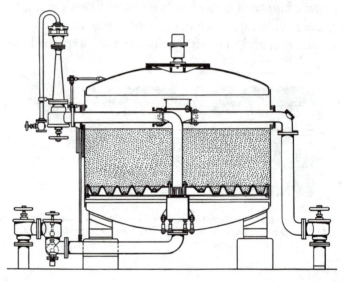

FIGURE 297—*Section of the 'Torrent' rapid sand-filter, patented in 1880. The filter was cleaned by an upward flow of water combined with air introduced by a steam injector (top left).*

replaced by a mechanical air-blower. These filters also were at first used mainly for industrial purposes, but as early as 1880 six of them were installed at the Campos waterworks in Brazil, and a further twelve were added in 1887, treating a total of 2·25 m gallons a day at a rate of over 100 gallons per sq ft per hour.

In America, filtration had a late start after a few early attempts which were only partially successful. In 1866 the city of St Louis sent its engineer, James P. Kirkwood, to Europe to study filtration practice there. His report [8], published in 1869, was a careful and valuable survey of water-treatment practice in the cities of Britain, France, Germany, and Italy. The first successful slow sand-filter in America was built at Poughkeepsie, New York, in 1872, but by 1900 no more than twenty had been constructed in the United States and five in Canada. They were less suitable for the silt-laden waters of North American rivers than for the organically polluted rivers of Europe. Attention was directed to the development of the mechanical rapid filter, which was applied to American municipal water-supplies in 1882 [20]. The general design of American rapid filters was similar to that of the British, but, instead of the air-scour which became popular in Britain, the Americans usually preferred mechanically driven agitators or high-pressure jets of water to assist the upward flow (figure 298).

Multiple filtration was employed at a number of waterworks towards the end

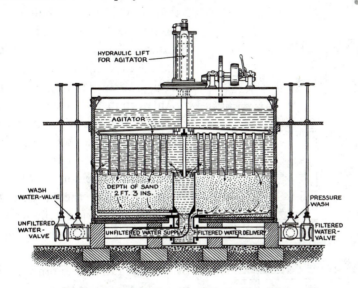

FIGURE 298—*Section of a Warren rapid sand-filter as used in the United States. The arrows indicate the direction of flow of the water during filtration. The sand was washed by an upward flow. At the same time the agitator was lowered into the sand and rotated.*

of the century. In some plants rapid filters were used as primary or 'roughing' filters to reduce the load of suspended matter coming on to the slow filters, but several systems based on the principle of filtration through successive beds of material of decreasing size were designed. Noteworthy among these was the Puech–Chabal filter (figure 299), first operated in Paris in 1899.

An important adjunct to rapid sand-filtration that quickly became firmly established in America was chemical coagulation with aluminium sulphate. This formed a flocculent precipitate which trapped suspended matter and aided its removal by settling and filtration. In this way the effectiveness of the rapid filter in purifying water was made comparable with that of the slow filter, despite a rate of filtration fifty times as great. The advantage of chemical treatment was known in Europe, and it had in fact been used experimentally by James Simpson in 1843, and on a full scale at Bolton in 1881. It was not, however, recognized as a regular form of treatment, and even after acceptance in America as an essential preliminary to rapid filtration it made only slow headway in Europe.

An alternative form of chemical treatment, using iron salts for precipitation, achieved wider use in Europe. In Medlock's patent of 1857, iron in any available form was suspended in the water for 24 to 48 hours, after which the water was

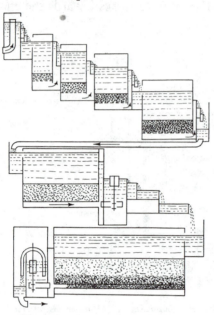

filtered. In 1870 Bischoff of Glasgow patented the use of spongy iron, made by reducing haematite ore at a low temperature. This was used as a filtering material in conjunction with sand and gravel, but the spongy-iron filters built at Antwerp in 1881 gave trouble through clogging. A more efficient way of applying iron to water was used in the 're-volving purifier' (figure 300), patented by William Anderson in 1883 [21]. After passing through the purifier, the water was aerated to oxidize the iron to the insoluble ferric form, and this was removed, along with the impurities in the water, by sedimentation and normal sand filtration. The process met with success in Europe for several years, but in the long run iron gave way to aluminium sulphate as a coagulant for water-purification.

FIGURE 299—*The Puech–Chabal system of multiple filtration, using several beds with material of decreasing size.*

The softening of water by the addition of lime to precipitate calcium carbonate was patented by T. Clark (1801–67) of Aberdeen in 1841, and the first municipal softener was built at Plumstead, London, in 1854. The filter-press, using cloth as the filtering medium, was applied to the clarification of lime-softened water by J. H. Porter in 1876, and in 1878 A. Ashby used sodium and potassium salts to remove the permanent hardness which was unaffected by the treatment with lime. More fundamental was the application, by Gans in Germany in 1906, of the principle of ion-exchange, in which ions of calcium and magnesium, the main causes of hardness, could be replaced by sodium or other 'soft' ions.

Disinfection of water as the final process for assuring its safety for the consumer was not practised until the first decade of the twentieth century. Chlorine compounds had been used for a hundred years as deodorants and to prevent or delay the putrefaction of organic matter. They were applied to sewage and raw water, but their deliberate use for the destruction of disease-producing organisms in water was not begun until 1896, when a typhoid epidemic at Pola, on the Adriatic, was stopped by the use of bleaching-powder [20]. The following year it was similarly used at Maidstone after an outbreak of typhoid. These were isolated occasions. The first permanent installation for the chlorination of water was erected at Middelkerke, Belgium, in 1902 [20]. In Britain chlorine, as a solution of sodium hypochlorite, was first applied as a regular treatment at Lincoln in 1905 (plate 32 A). This treatment was directed by Dr (later Sir) Alexander Houston (1865–1933), who subsequently became the first director of water examination to the Metropolitan Water Board, and was a pioneer of water-treatment. Both at Middelkerke and at Lincoln the chlorine was applied to the water before filtration, but the further development of the process established post-chlorination, that is, chlorination of the filtered water, as the usual practice.

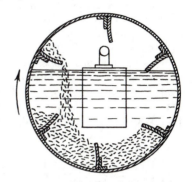

FIGURE 300—*Section of the Anderson purifier. The water passed along the revolving cylinder (seen in section), in which finely divided iron was introduced as a coagulant, and was then filtered.*

The only serious rival to chlorine as a disinfecting agent was ozone, the properties and application of which were studied by M.-P. Otto in France. The first municipal ozone plant was built at Nice in 1906, and the method has remained primarily a French interest, with relatively few installations in other countries.

VII. CONCLUSION

The developments described in this chapter brought about, in a period of fifty years, a radical change in the practice of water-supply. Technical advances had made possible the collection and distribution of the vast quantities of water which were necessary to enable men to live decently and healthily in modern cities; new fields of knowledge had been opened up, which at last showed the dangers that might lie invisible in water; and means were at hand to combat those dangers. In 1850 water-supply had been little more than a crude craft; at the beginning of the twentieth century it was a science.

REFERENCES

[1] STERN, W. M. *J.R. sanit. Inst.*, **74,** 998, 1954.

[2] CRONIN, H. F. *Proc. Instn civ. Engrs*, **2,** Pt 1, 14, 1953.

[3] Editorial. *Engineer, Lond.*, **35,** 199, 1873.

[4] HAZEN, A. 'The Filtration of Public Water Supplies' (3rd ed.). Wiley, New York. 1900.

[5] WEGMANN, E. 'The Water Supply of the City of New York, 1658–1895.' New York. 1896.

[6] BLAKE, N. M. 'Water for the Cities.' Syracuse University Press, New York. 1956.

[7] DUMBLETON, J. E. 'Wells and Boreholes for Water Supply' (2nd ed.). Technical Press, London. 1953.

[8] KIRKWOOD, J. P. 'Report on the Filtration of River Waters for the Supply of Cities, as Practised in Europe.' New York. 1869.

[9] WEGMANN, E. 'The Design and Construction of Dams' (7th ed.). Wiley, New York. 1922.

[10] DEACON, G. F. *Min. Proc. Instn civ. Engrs*, **126,** 24, 1896.

[11] MANSERGH, E. L. and MANSERGH, W. L. *Ibid.*, **190,** 3, 1912.

[12] WADE, L. A. B. *Ibid.*, **178,** 1, 1909.

[13] BINNIE, A. R. *Ibid.*, **109,** 89, 1892.

[14] RIPPL, W. *Ibid.*, **71,** 270, 1883.

[15] HILL, G. H. *Ibid.*, **126,** 2, 1896.

[16] PAINTER, C. E. *Civ. Engng, N.Y.*, **26,** 582, 1956.

[17] DEACON, G. F. *Min. Proc. Instn civ. Engrs*, **42,** 129, 1875.

[18] SNOW, J. 'Snow on Cholera.' Commonwealth Fund, New York. 1936.

[19] FRANKLAND, P. *Min. Proc. Instn civ. Engrs*, **127,** 83, 1896.

[20] BAKER, M. N. 'The Quest for Pure Water.' American Water Works Association, New York. 1949.

[21] ANDERSON, W. *Min. Proc. Instn civ. Engrs*, **81,** 279, 1885.

BIBLIOGRAPHY

BAKER, M. N. 'The Quest for Pure Water.' American Water Works Association, New York. 1949.

DICKINSON, H. W. 'Water Supply of Greater London' (Memorial volume). Newcomen Society, London. 1954.

FRAZER, W. M. 'A History of English Public Health, 1834–1939.' Bailliere, Tindall & Cox, London. 1950.

INSTITUTION OF WATER ENGINEERS. 'Manual of British Water Supply Practice' (ed. by A. T. HOBBS and J. E. HOBBS, 2nd ed.). Heffer, Cambridge. 1954.

METROPOLITAN WATER BOARD. 'London's Water Supply, 1903–1953.' Staples Press, London. 1953.

ROBINS, F. W. 'The Story of Water Supply.' Oxford University Press, London. 1946.

SNOW, J. 'Snow on Cholera: being a Reprint of two Papers by John Snow, M.D., together with a Biographical Memoir.' Commonwealth Fund, New York. 1936.

WALTERS, R. C. S. 'The Nation's Water Supply.' Nicholson & Watson, London. 1936.

24

PART I

THE TEXTILE INDUSTRY:
WOVEN FABRICS

D. A. FARNIE

I. THE DETERMINANTS OF TECHNICAL INNOVATION

TECHNICAL innovation was governed partly by such technical factors as the adaptability of the various textile fibres to spinning and weaving, the increased technical skill developed by the progressive specialization of textile engineering, and the pressure imposed by the mechanized processes on those unmechanized. It was encouraged also by economic factors, such as the increased availability of raw materials, the abundance of capital reflected in the rise of the joint-stock company, the comparative scarcity and intransigence of labour, and the varying pressures of trade. Thus the 'cotton famine' of 1861 to 1865[1] helped to oust the hand-loom weaver from the cotton industry while accelerating the mechanization of the linen, jute, woollen, worsted, and shoddy industries. The falling prices and profit-margins of the 'great depression' years, from 1873 to 1896, stimulated cost-cutting innovations in the manufacturing technique of the cotton, worsted, and carpet industries in Britain and accelerated the mechanization of the textile industries of the European continent.

II. PROCESSES PREPARATORY TO SPINNING

A vast new source of raw material was opened up by the development of techniques for the reclamation of rag-wool from used woollen material. The shoddy-industry was based on the 'devil' or rag-grinder, -tearer, or -puller invented in 1801. It was similar in principle to the 'willy' (or devil) of the woollen industry and the 'willow' of the cotton industry (relegated to the cotton waste industry in the late nineteenth century). It comprised a pair of fluted feed-rollers and a short, thick drum covered first with curry-comb blades, then, later, with thousands of curved teeth, which was revolved very rapidly. It tore rags into

---

[1] This was caused largely by the cutting-off of exports from the Southern (Confederate) States by the Federal blockade, during the American Civil War.

rag-wool (*laine de renaissance*), a fluffy fibre-mass lacking only the length, the greasiness, and some of the spinning and felting properties of new wool. The rag-wool was spun into yarn and woven into 'shoddy' at least as early as 1809 [1]; its introduction was linked with the pressure caused by the Peninsular War on the supply of raw wool, and on the demand for army uniforms. The manufacture of devils with teeth instead of blades (1834) made possible the tearing up of milled goods ('hards') and the production of 'mungo', the use of which spread more rapidly than that of shoddy. The invention of Garnett wire and the Garnett machine (1850), a woollen card with stronger and more rigid teeth, made possible the reclamation of fine hard-twisted yarns and thereby rendered thread and yarn wastes valuable, as the rag-machine had done for fabric wastes. The discovery of the carbonization process (1854–5) made it possible to re-use mixed fabric wastes: it removed the vegetable cotton fibre by acid, leaving the wool fibres untouched and producing 'extract wool'.

These innovations laid the basis of the shoddy and mungo industry, which developed rapidly from the 1850s. Its rise reflected the increasing utilization of waste material by industry, a tendency seen also in the increasing industrial use of cotton, silk, woollen, jute, and flax wastes. In turn the shoddy industry's nitrogenous waste-products (dust and refuse) were used as agricultural fertilizer, while the better sorts of shoddy cloth could be torn up and remanufactured. The heavy woollen industry of the Dewsbury–Batley–Morley district of the West Riding of Yorkshire rose on rags to riches, and clothing became cheaper, warmer, and cleaner. Rag or extract wool, mixed with carded new wool and then spun with it, entered progressively and increasingly into the composition of nearly all woollen (though not worsted) cloth: by 1880 it supplied perhaps as much as 40 per cent of the materials for the woollen industry of Britain [2]. It revived the woollen industry, by making wool more competitive in price with cotton, and cheapening the price of new wool to the benefit of the manufacturers of pure woollen goods.

The mechanical washing of wool spread, especially in the 1880s, after the improvements of J. Petrie of Rochdale (1859) and E. Melen of Verviers, Belgium (1863). The oiling of wool by a spray through fine jets, first introduced by G. Leach of Leeds in 1840, became general in the worsted industry after 1850, though some sections of the woollen industry long clung to the use of the watering can. The 'batching' of jute, whereby it was softened and lubricated with oil and water to make it spin better—a modification of the technique used in the preparation of both hemp and wool—was first successfully accomplished at Dundee in 1833, first by hand and then by machine.

The feeding of carding-machines became automatic. W. C. Bramwell's automatic feed (1876) (figure 301) eliminated the manual labour previously needed for the initial weighing and feeding of wool: it came rapidly into use, first in its place of origin, the United States, and then in Britain. In addition to the initial feed, various intermediate feeds were developed from the 1850s, to secure a

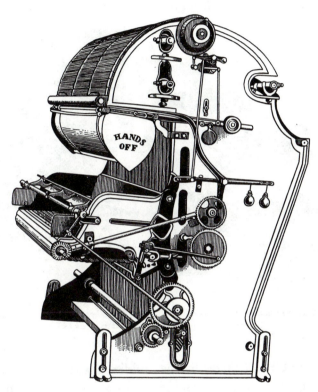

FIGURE 301—*Bramwell's automatic weighing and feeding machine, improved form, 1879. The container marked 'Hands Off' rotates periodically and automatically to deposit wool on the belt below, which feeds it to the first carding machine.*

thorough mixing of the material between the successive carding-engines. The most widely used feeds became, in Britain, the Blamire and Scotch feeds; in France and the United States, the Apperley feed invented (1849) at Stroud.

In wool-carding, the condenser, an auxiliary machine attached to the carder, was a fundamental invention. The ring doffer condenser, perfected by J. Goulding of Massachusetts in 1826, split up the web delivered by the final card into 30 to 40 narrow ribbons which were then felted and rubbed, first, from the 1830s, between rubber-covered rollers and then, from the 1870s, between two broad leather belts with a rotary and lateral motion (figure 302). The emerging condenser-rovings were stronger and more compact (condensed) than the original ribbons: wound on long bobbins they were taken to the woollen-mule and spun into yarn. Thus woollen yarn was made without the intervention of drawing-frames, and made better and more abundantly than with the slubbing-billy[1] and its attendant 'piecer' or 'tommy' (vol IV, ch 10). The condenser came into

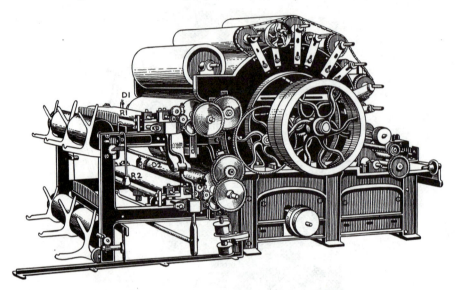

FIGURE 302—*Double ring doffer condenser card, 1888. The doffer rollers* D[1] *and* D[2] *feed the carded wool from the finisher card to the condenser rubbers* R[1] *and* R[2].

general use in the United States by the middle 1830s: in Yorkshire it was first adopted in the 1850s and spread rapidly in the 1860s with the increased use of short-stapled shoddy. It was firmly established by 1870, having largely super-seded the billy: in Lancashire it was successfully adapted (1884) to the prepara-tion of cotton-waste. On the European continent the most common type of condenser became the tape condenser, first introduced (1861) by C. Martin of Verviers. This condenser divided the web by a combined tearing- and cutting-action between leather tapes and a pair of ridged rollers: its division of the web was more minute, its suitability to fine yarns greater, and its production larger, than those of the ring doffer condenser. It was introduced rapidly in Belgium and France, but much more slowly in England and the United States.

The worsted carding-machine was used only for fine short wools, first from

---

[1] In the slubbing-billy sliver from a draw-frame was attenuated and wound on a bobbin as a coarse thread.

the 1830s as a substitute for combing, then, with the perfection of the combing-machine, in preparation for combing. Similar in principle to the woollen scribbler-card with its roller-and-clearer action, it was far gentler in its working, thus largely preventing undesirable breakage of the fibres. Flax, jute, and hemp cards were also based on the roller-and-clearer principle. The jute card was adapted

FIGURE 303—*Revolving flat card, 1887. The cotton is carded between the surfaces of the continuous chain of revolving flats and the central cylinder below.*

from the flax-tow card and benefited greatly by Worral's replacement (1853) of leather by hardwood as the material of the card-clothing: for jute-tow the teaser-card, essentially a breaker-card, was used.

For cotton the favourite machine by 1888 was the revolving flat card of J. Smith (1834) and E. Leigh (1858), which became a practical success only with the skilled engineering work of G. and E. Ashworth of Manchester (1870, 1878) (figure 303). Above the central revolving cylinder, or 'swift', and concentric with it, was a chain of wire-covered flats, travelling in the same direction but at a slower rate. Both flats and swift were clothed with flexible but durable wire teeth of hardened and tempered steel, so accurately adjusted as to present very fine points to the cotton. The revolving flat card vastly improved the quality and nearly doubled the quantity produced. It came steadily into use during the 1880s, displacing not only the roller-and-clearer card (which was relegated to the cotton-waste industry) but also the 'self top-stripping' card of G. Wellman of Lowell, Massachusetts (1853), with its stationary flats. The coiler-can and coiling-motion of D. Cheetham of Rochdale (1857) came into general use as an accessory to the carding, combing, and drawing processes in the cotton and worsted industries, but not in the linen or jute industries before 1900.

Combing was mechanized only in the 1850s. The Heilmann–Schlumberger comb (1845)[1] was suited especially to the combing of short wool and of cotton, because it broke the slivers into tufts and then pieced them together after combing. It spread rapidly in the fine-cotton spinning industry of Lancashire and Alsace from 1851: its low production and defective piecing were remedied in the Nasmith cotton comber (1901). The Heilmann comb (vol IV, p 297) was also adopted in the linen industry of Belfast and used especially for the combing of flax-tow from the 1890s. In the worsted industry it spread in the nineteenth century rather on the continent than in England, in the wool-combing establishments of Germany, Belgium, and France, especially at Rheims, where it was used for very short Botany[2] wools.

In England the machine that revolutionized wool-combing in the early 1850s was the Lister–Donisthorpe nip machine (1851), which came rapidly into use in Bradford to oust the hand-combers and acquire a dominant position in the Yorkshire worsted industry, partly because S. C. Lister, 'the great monopolist of the North' [3] acquired rival patents, thus suppressing competition with his own machine (vol IV, p 297). The Noble–Donisthorpe or circular comb (1853, 1856) (figure 304) represented the mechanical perfection of the horizontal-circle comb. It was based on the use of two revolving comb-rings, a principle first used in the Platt–Collier patent of 1827. Originally only one smaller circle worked within the larger toothed circle, but from about 1862 [4] two small inner circles were used, so producing a double machine. The inner circles touched the larger comb-ring at opposite points on its interior circumference, and rotated within it at the same speed and in the same direction. The long fibres, already straightened by their passage through the gill-combs of successive preparing-boxes, were fed from creels through special feed-boxes introduced in 1856. They fell across both circles at their points of contact and were pressed down between the pins or teeth of the circles. Then, as the circles revolved and drew apart, the fibres held in the pins of each circle were drawn 'easily and pleasantly' through the pins of the other. The long fibres left protruding from the inside of the comb-ring or from the outside of the inner circles were removed by vertical drawing-off rollers as 'tops': the 'noils' were finally retained between the pins of the inner circles and removed by inclined steel 'plough' knives and further

---

[1] It is also known as the French, the vertical circular, or the rectilinear comb.
[2] So called because they came from the merino flocks of Botany Bay, New South Wales.

drawing-off rollers. Because of its adaptability and productivity the Noble comb was adopted in the United States from the 1860s: in Yorkshire it spread after the expiry of Lister's patent monopoly in the 1860s, and by the 1880s it was supplanting the nip comb for short wools, restricting the latter to the combing of long English wools and mohairs.

The Holden–Lister or square-motion comb (figure 305), developed between

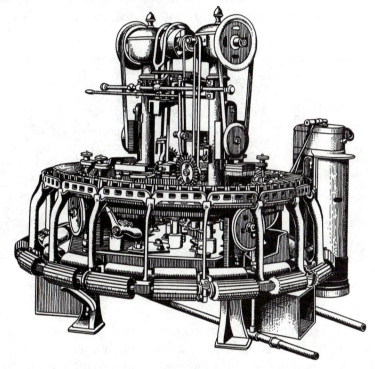

FIGURE 304—*A Noble combing machine of 1887. This type became the representative machine of the Yorkshire worsted industry in 1900, using two smaller comb-rings revolving inside the large circular comb.*

1846 and 1856, was the only combing-machine based on a close imitation of the movements of the hand-comber. It used a combination of three combs: the comb-ring itself, a gill-comb, and an intersecting comb. Pairs of feed-rollers on a movable arm fed the slivers to the comb-ring and drew the wool through its pins as they withdrew, so producing a fringe projecting outwards. The working combs were also outside the circle; they were gill-comb bars with a series of elaborately toothed fallers, tangential to the circle and therefore nearer to it at one point than at others. Using cams as pushers (1848), the fallers moved in the 'square motion' that gave its name to the comb, first upwards through the fringe of wool close to the circular comb-head and then immediately, by a quick push, backwards away from the circle to prevent the two sets of teeth from locking together. Combing the fibres progressively more thoroughly, the fallers eventually left the wool by a vertical drop and returned to their original position for further work. To complete the combing, segmental *nacteur* combs (1859), with teeth concentric to those of the comb-ring, were used, descending from above into the combed fringe, to comb the wool embedded between the pins of the carrying circle. In the worsted industry of France, located increasingly round

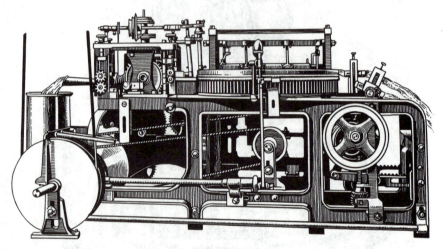

FIGURE 305—*Square-motion combing machine: a mechanical version of the movements of the hand comber in combing the wool fibres.*

Roubaix and Tourcoing, the square-motion comb became the representative machine: in England it was used only for short merino wool.

In general the combing machine cut costs substantially, and made possible the use of short fibres in the worsted, fine-cotton, and flax industries. It mechanized fine-worsted combing, replacing the hand-combers by female machine-minders. Wool-combing became a highly specialized section of the worsted industry, usually working on a commission basis. Together with the use of cheaper cotton warps and the application of the worsted card to short wools, the combing machine gave new life to the worsted industry. It also revived the fine-cotton spinning industry, distinguishing it clearly from coarse and medium spinning and thus founding Lancashire's pre-eminence therein.

In the drawing-process for cotton the electric stop-motion of J. Smalley (1875)—based on the non-conductivity of the dry cotton fibre and stopping the frame immediately on the breakage of a sliver—came into general use. In the

worsted industry, France and Belgium developed from 1856 the system of
'French drawing', which differentiated the worsted industry of the continent
more fully from that of Bradford: it used a spike-covered cylinder (or 'porcupine')
to support the sliver between the front and back drawing-rollers, and rubbing-
leathers, like those of a woollen condenser, to give firmness to the unspun
thread. It did not use fallers, like the Bradford open-drawing process. Nor did it
insert twist in the roving. It was especially adapted for the production of 'dry
spun' yarn on the worsted mule. In Yorkshire, cone-drawing, invented in 1850,
came into use from the 1890s to deal with finer yarns and to eliminate the drag
on the material evident in open drawing.

III. SPINNING

The major types of spinning-machine had been developed before 1850 (vol
IV, ch 10), both the intermittent (mule) and the continuous (flyer-throstle, cap,
and ring). The self-acting mule (1830) conquered field after field of cotton-
spinning from the 1840s as its capacity developed, and was spinning yarns
as high as 350s by the 1880s. It was introduced into Alsace from 1852, and
into Germany from 1860. The worsted mule was similar to the cotton mule,
with two pairs of fixed rollers to elongate the sliver. In Yorkshire it was
used for short wools only, long wools being spun on the throstle or cap frames.
On the continent, however, especially in France, it was used for all worsted
spinning to the virtual exclusion of other machines: its use followed on the
'French drawing' process and it spun the sliver into yarn with hardly any twist,
eliminating the drag inevitable with flyer, cap, or ring spinning. The woollen
mule employed no roller-draft but simultaneous spindle-draft and twist, as in
Hargreaves's jenny and the condenser mule for cotton-waste. The self-acting
woollen mule (1832) became common in Yorkshire between 1850 and 1870,
though hand mules survived, as in Lancashire, into the 1900s. It was generally
adopted in the large establishments of France by 1867 and began to be used
in Germany in the 1860s, though not in the United States until the 1870s.

In continuous spinning the throstle yielded place increasingly to its two offspring, the cap and ring frames. The cap spinning-frame or Danforth throstle
(1829) was introduced extensively in the Bradford district during the 1850s,
progressing with the increasing use of Australian wool in the worsted industry
and largely replacing the slower flyer-frame by 1859 for spinning Botany wools
(p 574). The invention in the United States of the ring spinning-frame (1828)
marked 'the last great step in spinning' [5], as did the combing machine in the
preparatory processes: in the twentieth century it became the dominant machine

of the world's spinning industry. It was based on a spindle revolving in the centre of a stationary ring, to which was attached a light C-shaped clip or 'traveller' in place of the heavy flyer. The yarn passed through the traveller on its way to the bobbin and so drew the traveller round the ring, the circular movement of the traveller inserting twist while the vertical movement up and down of the ring and 'ring-rail' built up the cop on the bobbin. In Britain the ring-frame spread from the 1870s, first for twisting or doubling cotton yarn and then for spinning it. It largely superseded the throstle because of its higher speed

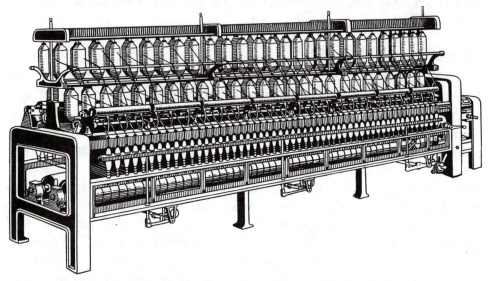

FIGURE 306—*A ring spinning-frame of 1888. The ring-frame became the representative spinning machine of the twentieth century, characterized by its high speed and continuity of production.*

and productivity, especially after the introduction of the modified Rabbeth or self-contained spindle (1878) by Howard and Bullough of Accrington. From the 1880s the ring-frame (figure 306) began to compete with the mule, because the ring-frame wound and spun continuously and required only unskilled labour. But the mule retained its dominance in Lancashire if not elsewhere, for it spun on the bare spindle with a low degree of twist, producing yarn suited for fine wefts, while ring-yarn was spun on bobbins with a high degree of twist more suitable for warps. In the worsted industry the ring-frame was used by the 1880s in England and on the continent, for both the spinning and the twisting of worsted yarn. In the woollen industry it was used extensively by 1898 in twisting, though not in spinning, woollen yarns. In the silk-throwing industry the ring-twister was based on the same principle as the ring-frame.

For the new-born viscose rayon industry C. F. Topham's 'box' (1900) pro-vided 'cakes' of continuous filament yarn spun by a centrifugal process. The automatic spooling machine of W. Weild (1860) mechanized the process of spool-winding in the sewing-thread industry, ousting the hand-spoolers and the hand-spooling machine.

IV. WEAVING

In the processes preparatory to weaving, weft-winding benefited by the doubling winding-machine of R. H. Smith (1863) and the Leeson precision pirn winder (1891) from the United States. In warping, the warper perfected by T. Singleton (1872, 1878), with its automatic stop-motion acting on the failure of an end, made the process nearly automatic and came into universal use for warping plain calicoes and linens. Sizing benefited by the invention of the Slasher sizer (1853) and the mechanical size-mixer (1856): the Slasher came into universal use for grey-warp preparation for ordinary looms, superseding the tape-sizer, and in the twentieth century proved equally suited for warp pre-paration for automatic looms. But the preparatory processes still remained slow in comparison with the weaving itself: the first machines for the 'drawing-in' of the warp threads through the eyes of the healds and through the reed of the loom were patented as late as 1882 and 1891, by Sherman and Ingersoll in the United States.

In the weaving-process proper the range of multiple-box motions, for more than one colour of weft, was progressively extended by the box-motions of Eccles (1853), Knowles (1853), Whitesmith (1857), the Wright Shaws (1868), and the circular skip-box motion (1869) of R. L. Hattersley and J. Hill. Among the looms employing shedding-motions derived from the 'dobby' (vol IV, p 303), or small jacquard, were the double or Blackburn dobby for the manufacture of bordered dhotis (loin-cloths) (1858), the Knowles positive dobby (1874), the standard type of positive dobby, the Keighley or baulk dobby for the manufacture of light fabrics (1866-7), the Lancashire and Yorkshire dobby (1885), the Burnley dobby (1888-93), and the cross-border dobby (1898). The dobby was the basis also of two important American inventions for fancy cotton and woollen weav-ing: William Crompton's 'fancy loom' (1839-40) and George Crompton's 'broad fancy loom' (1857). The greatest of all inventions for warp-shedding, the jacquard mechanism (vol IV, pp 316-19), increased its capacity with the development of the double-lift and double-cylinder jacquards and a diversity of jacquard machines for a widening range of fancy fabrics. The double-lift jacquard (1849) of A. Barlow enabled the warp-threads to be raised more than once in succession, and increased the speed of the loom while reducing the relatively excessive speeds of the jacquard operating parts. The double-cylinder jacquard (1865) with two sets of needles, each with a separate card-cylinder and set of cards, made possible still higher speeds of operation.

The power-loom had made its greatest progress by 1850 in the weaving of cotton and worsted; it was little used before 1840 in the Yorkshire woollen industry, which benefited most from the invention of the Knowles loom (1863), the first open-shed loom. This relieved the warp-threads of unnecessary strain by allowing them to remain in their highest or lowest position in the shed for as long as necessary and was thus specially suited to the weaving of woollen cloth: American in origin, the Knowles loom was adopted and modified to become the general woollen power-loom in Britain. In linen-weaving the hand-loom was still predominant in the 1840s. The linen power-loom, which first established itself in the boom of the 1850s, was heavier and stronger than the cotton power-loom; the inelasticity of the flax yarn was remedied by the application of a special dressing to the warp and of a vibrating roller to the loom, to maintain the warp under even tension. The ordinary jute power-loom, a cone overpick loom like the Lancashire cotton loom, was a lighter version of the heavy canvas loom used in the flax industry. From 1848, it wove jute yarns without sizing, and seldom used the weft-fork stop-motion because of the coarse nature of the woven fabric. The weaving of Turkish towels with a terry or looped surface was accomplished in 1851–2, first by hand and then by power. The double-pile velvet power-loom, developed in 1878, wove two fabrics face to face and cut the pile by traversing knives.

The power-loom triumphed over the hand-loom in industry after industry: in the English worsted industry by the 1850s, in the Lancashire cotton industry by the 1870s, and in the Yorkshire woollen and the Irish linen industries by the 1890s. On the continent of Europe mechanization came a generation later. By 1900 the hand-loom survived only as a curiosity in districts isolated by mountain, forest, or sea (as in the 'Celtic fringe' of the United Kingdom), as a means of weaving elaborate and expensive fabrics required only in short lengths, and as an indispensable tool of the best textile designers and pattern weavers for experimental purposes. It was, however, still employed for educational purposes in technical colleges and for giving occupation to criminals in jail.

The weaving of carpets was the most complex branch of weaving (figure 307) and the last to be mechanized. The first machine-made carpet was the ingrain or multiple-cloth carpet.[1] It comprised two or more sets of worsted warp and

[1] It was also known as the Kidderminster, Scotch, Dutch, or union carpet, and (in the seamless square form) as an 'art' carpet. Its production ceased in England during the 1930s.

two or more sets of woollen weft, drawn from different shuttles and brought to the surface according to the design, the same pattern appearing on the back but in reversed colours. The two-ply ingrain or double-cloth carpet had been manufactured at Kidderminster on the draw-loom since 1735. The three-ply Scotch or triple-cloth carpet was perfected at Kilmarnock in 1824, using to form the pattern a barrel-machine, which was being replaced by the jacquard mechanism by the 1840s. 'Tapestry ingrain', a two-ply carpet of parti-coloured threads, resembling in appearance the dearer three-ply carpet and competing success-

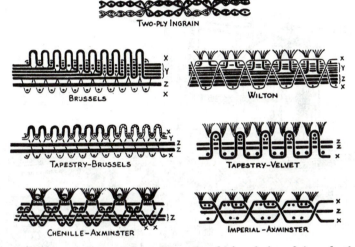

FIGURE 307—*Various carpet weaves. These sections, all made through the weft (save for the ingrain), reveal the warp and weft structures of the basic carpet weaves. X, chain- or ground-warp; Y, pile-warp; z, stuffer-warp.*

fully with it, was first patented in England in 1841 but was developed in the United States, especially by A. Smith of New York (1850).

The ingrain carpet with its flat surface was not a true carpet in the sense of the Brussels (or body-Brussels, as distinct from tapestry-Brussels) carpet, with its pile formed of uncut loops and characterized by its high resilience. The Brussels carpet contained three distinct sets of warp, the chain-warp to form with the weft a woven base, the stuffer-warp, to supply 'body', and the worsted pile-warps, up to five or six in number, which were drawn from creel-frames at the rear of the loom and ran through the whole length of the fabric. The jacquard mechanism was first applied to their manufacture at Kidderminster in 1825, to select the appropriate warp-threads for appearance on the surface and thus form the pattern, all the other pile-warp threads remaining buried in the body of the carpet. The great revolution came with the jacquard power-loom of Bigelow and

Collier for the mechanical weaving of the Brussels carpet, and of its sister-carpet the Wilton. The Brussels power-loom (figure 308) was the invention (1846–8) of Erastus B. Bigelow of Massachusetts. Introduced into England in 1851 it was perfected by G. Collier of Halifax, who had successfully applied the power-loom to linen-weaving and who patented (1852) the process whereby the set of 'wires' entered with the weft in a double shed and formed the characteristic looped pile. The terry 'wires', metal rods like ordinary meat-skewers with looped ends, were first inserted one after another and then withdrawn length-

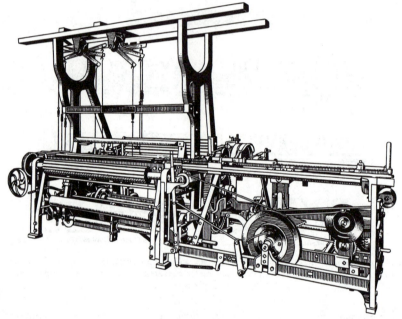

FIGURE 308—*Brussels carpet power-loom, in its perfected form, 1900. Above the loom is the framework for the pattern-controlling jacquard apparatus; to the right are the pile-forming 'wires' and their working mechanism.*

ways *seriatim* and automatically, raising and shaping the loops by their passage. For the weaving of Wilton or Tournai carpets the wires were thinner—because the fabric was woven with more rows of pile to the inch—and contained a knife-blade in their end-portion, to sever the pile-loops of worsted as each wire was withdrawn and thus form a rich, velvety surface. In England the power-loom for Brussels and Wilton carpets replaced the hand-loom in the 1850s and 1860s, well ahead of continental practice.

The Brussels carpet was limited to a maximum of six colours and was prodigal of the expensive dyed worsted pile-warp. Both these disadvantages were elimi-nated in the cheaper tinted-warp carpet, known as tapestry-Brussels or printed

Brussels, which was woven from particoloured yarn imprinted with colour on a drum (figure 309). By the process of drum-printing, invented in 1832 by R. Whytock of Edinburgh and improved in 1851 and 1855, the individual pile warp-threads were wrapped, one thread at a time, around a large printing-drum, its circumference three times the length of the design. The design was then printed in an elongated form on the threads by dye-carriages (1851), moving on rails below the drum. The process of weaving was similar to that by which the Brussels carpet was made, using wires to produce a pile but without a jacquard and without the long frames of creel-bobbins. It used only a single worsted pile-warp, wound off a single long beam and raised in loops by the wires, thus proportionately reducing the design to its desired length. The power-loom for tapestry-carpets developed (1850) by G. Collier incorporated (1851) Bigelow's improvements, and could also weave tapestry-velvets by the use of a knife-ended wire: thus tapestry-velvets bore the same relation to tapestry-Brussels as Wilton to body-Brussels. By the 1870s tapestry-Brussels were superseding five-frame body-Brussels.

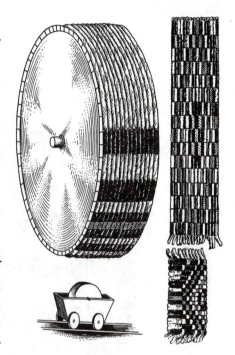

FIGURE 309—*Printing drum for tapestry carpets. The printed warp-threads before weaving have an elongated pattern (figure 307), which is reduced to the desired length in the weaving process by the use of pile-forming 'wires'.*

The tinted-warp carpet was a product of a double process: its pattern as furnished by the warp was wholly in the surface. The chenille or chenille-Axminster carpet was also a two-process fabric, with an unlimited range of colours, but its pattern was formed by the weft. The process was invented (1839) by J. Templeton and W. Quiglay of Glasgow, by an adaptation of the chenille process developed (1836) for the weaving of Paisley shawls. The chenille cloth was first woven in a weft-loom on the gauze principle, and then cut into separate strips, which were given a permanent V-shape in section by the folding upwards and steaming of the severed ends of the woollen weft: each strip resembled a furry caterpillar (French *chenille*). Then the chenille fur was woven into the carpet on a setting-loom, with catcher-, chain-, and stuffer-warps. It was woven on the hand-loom from 1839: power-weaving came by stages between 1876 and 1884. Power was first applied to the simple weft-looms and then to the more complex setting-looms, especially by the adoption of W. Adam's patent process of 1880. But the chenille fur was still combed into place by hand after each shot, making the luxurious chenille carpet 'the most hand-made of all machine-made carpets' [6].

FIGURE 310—*Northrop automatic loom (side view), 1895.*

The machine-tufted or Axminster carpet was the best machine-made carpet and the closest in character to the oriental. The Royal Axminster power-loom was developed (1876) in the United States by H. Skinner of Yonkers, New York, after twenty years of effort; it was introduced into England in 1878. The Skinner loom was a spool-loom, using a whole series of wide spools previously wound with dyed yarn according to the pattern desired and carefully arranged in rotation on carriages above the loom: each spool supplied one row of tufts for insertion in the carpet-face, around the weft, and their total number was the same as the number of rows of tufts in one complete repetition of the design. Its adaptation by Wyman in 1895 to looms containing more than one spool in width was the first of the Axminster wide-loom patents. The 'gripper' or jacquard Axminster loom was based on the English patent of Brinton and Greenwood (1890) [7], using a vertical jacquard feed to supply the necessary colours of pile-yarn drawn from creel-frames behind the loom, and a gripper insertion of the tufts between the warp-threads. This eliminated the specially prepared yarn-spools of the Skinner loom, but was restricted in its range of colours. Hand-knotted 'real Axminster' carpets were produced at Wilton from 1835. Not until 1906 was an effective loom developed by Renard of France for producing mechanically a knot-stitch carpet similar to the oriental, using special grippers and a jacquard attachment.

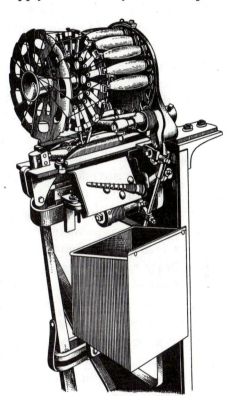

FIGURE 311—*Northrop automatic loom hopper mechanism, 1895. The insertion into the shuttle of a fresh cop of weft ejects the empty one below.*

The greatest advance in weaving was the American invention of the automatic loom: automatic in that the supply of weft was continually replenished by changing either the cop in the shuttle or the shuttle itself. The most successful was the Northrop loom, which changed the cop in the shuttle without stopping the loom. J. H. Northrop's cop-changer, more economical than a shuttle-changer, was first developed in 1890 but was not patented till 1894, because of the need to perfect an accurate warp-stop device. A cylindrical magazine or hopper was charged with cops (14 in 1895, 28 by 1911). When necessary, it pressed its lowest cop into the shuttle, ejecting the spent one into a box beneath (figures 310 and 311), and led the new weft from a stud on the hopper into the shuttle-eye. Thus the full Northrop loom comprised several basic inventions in addition to that of the cop-changer, namely, a self-threading shuttle, a weft-fork mechanism, a warp let-off motion, and a warp-stop motion. The weft-fork or weft-feeler (with a shuttle-eye weft-cutter) controlled the transfer mechanism, acting before the final exhaustion of the weft. The Roper automatic warp let-off motion maintained the warp-tension automatically. The Roper warp-stop motion, using detectors supported by the warp-threads while intact, stopped the loom when a warp-thread broke and thereby eliminated the need for constant attention on the part of the weaver.

Considered as an enterprise in mechanical engineering, the Northrop loom gave a new impetus to the development of its manufacturers, the Draper Company of Hopedale, Massachusetts, which sold its first loom in 1895 and which aimed at replacing 'the entire equipment of the most important section of one of the greatest industries in the world' [8]. As a weaving mechanism, this loom relieved the weaver of the labour of withdrawing, filling, threading, and inserting the shuttles and confined him to the repair of warp- and weft-breakages when necessary and the filling of hoppers when convenient: thus the weaver became a hopper-filler and piecer. A proportionately great increase in the number of plain looms tended by each weaver became possible—up to twenty-four in 1895, when linked with a warp-stop motion. The Northrop loom increased the weaver's production and his wages while decreasing total labour costs, since the change-over to automatic looms halved the number of weavers required in a mill. Its invention marked the highest point in the replacement of labour by capital in the weaving process.

The Northrop loom spread mainly in the new regions rather than in the old, in the United States rather than in Lancashire, where it was first introduced in 1902. In Lancashire, labour for weaving was abundant and trade unions were hostile to labour-saving devices. The capital cost of the Northrop was thrice that of the ordinary loom. It was limited at first to the weaving of plain goods and was best adapted for use in combined spinning- and weaving-mills, using weft on ring bobbins. Its speed was slower than that of the ordinary loom and the floor-space it occupied was greater. It was liable to make occasional 'double-picks' when the weft-change took place. Nevertheless such progress as it made was of the greatest significance. Like the power-loom a hundred years previously, its earliest conquests were in plain cotton weaving; by 1904 it was used in the American worsted industry, especially for the weaving of mixed fabrics with a cotton warp. The Northrop loom set in motion other innovations. Thus it aided the progress of the ring-spinning frame because of the special suitability of ring-spun wefts to automatic cop-changing looms. It led to the speeding-up of ordinary looms, to the development of shuttle-changing looms (which became the preferred type of the linen and jute industries), and to the largely increased use of self-threading shuttles and of warp-stop motions. Thus it laid down the lines of the future development of the loom: the Northrop automatic looms were truly 'the looms of the twentieth century' [9].

V. FINISHING

In the finishing processes the rotary milling machine of J. Dyer of Trowbridge (1833, 1838) came into general use from the 1840s, first in the west of England, then in Yorkshire, replacing the old fulling-stocks with their hammers in the most important finishing process for woollen cloth. The 'raising gig' of E. Moser of Bonn (1884) used fourteen high-speed small-diameter card rollers, fixed and revolving round a large drum, and permitted the raising of fabrics of light texture and thereby the production of flannelette or raised cotton cloth.

The process of mercerizing was foreshadowed though not developed by John Mercer (1791–1866), who investigated the effects of strong caustic soda on cotton cellulose in the 1840s and patented (1850) a process of 'soda-izing' or mercerizing without tension, which proved a commercial failure because caustic soda was still expensive and because the cloth shrank by 20–25 per cent in the process. P. and C. Depoully of Lyons patented (1884) a process for producing 'crimp' effects on piece-goods of worsted and cotton, or silk and cotton, based on the fact that caustic soda shrank the cotton but left the silk and wool unaffected. The shrinking-effect was used from 1890 in calico-printing for producing crimp or *crépon* effects. H. A. Lowe's patents of 1889–90 for producing a permanent lustre on cotton goods by mercerizing under tension, and thereby avoiding the shrinkage, were allowed to lapse in 1893 for lack of financial support.

The Krefeld dyers R. Thomas and E. Prévost took out (1895) German patents for a process similar to that of Lowe and made it a practical success. The process was applied first to yarn and then to piece-goods and rapidly became popular from 1898 in Britain, France, Germany, and the United States. It opened up a new era in the chemical technology of textile fibres, for mercerized cotton was a new textile material, the mechanical, optical, and dyeing properties of its fibres having been rendered by chemical means permanently different from those of untreated cotton. The application of strong caustic soda to cotton greatly reduced in size the central cavity of the fibre, and made it firmly rounded instead of band-shaped. It increased the tensile strength of the fabric and its affinity for dyestuffs. Above all—though Mercer had failed to perceive it—when cotton was mercerized under tension a permanent lustre or gloss was produced similar in appearance to, though less in degree than, that of a spun silk, a lustre unaffected by subsequent bleaching and dyeing. By the Schreiner process (1895) a satin gloss was produced on cotton cloth by the action of a very finely engraved steel roller or calender under heat and great pressure, creating a great number of small light-reflecting surfaces.

In bleaching, machine-washing was introduced from 1845 and lye-boiling under pressure from 1853. The hydro-extractor, or centrifugal dryer (invented in 1836 by Penzoldt in Paris) came steadily into use from the 1840s. In dyeing the real revolution was chemical, not mechanical (ch 12). In printing, the cylinder printing-machine (1783) generally replaced block-printing in Lancashire between 1850 and 1888, restricting block-printing to work impossible for the machine. On the continent, especially in France and Belgium, block-printing (tailpiece) was replaced by the *perrotine* process (invented in 1834 by Perrot of Rouen), a hybrid between block and cylinder printing. The ageing process whereby the colours were fixed firmly in the printed cloth by steaming was mechanized from 1856 and made continuous from 1879.

FIGURE 312—*Elias Howe's original sewing-machine, 1846. This was the first patented machine to combine the eye-pointed needle and the underthread shuttle.*

VI. SEWING

The sewing-machine did not attempt a mechanical imitation of hand-sewing, which uses only one ordinary needle and a limited length of thread. Success was achieved only by the use of a new type of needle, pointed near the eye, and a double continuous thread, and came after the mechanization of the textile industries proper. A chain-stitch was produced by the Thimonnier sewing-machine (patented in 1830 by a French tailor), which used a continuous thread and a vertically reciprocating needle. Elias Howe (1819–67), a Massachusetts mechanic, was the first American to patent, in 1846, a practical sewing-machine (figure 312). Howe's machine used a grooved and curved eye-pointed needle, and a shuttle operating on the opposite side of the cloth from the needle and carrying a second thread through the loop formed by the needle-thread to form a lock-stitch, the type of stitch peculiar to machine-sewing. However, the feed of the fabric to be stitched was imperfect and discontinuous, limiting the seam to a straight line the length of the baster-plate. The characteristic feed of the sewing-machine became the 'four-motion feed' or 'drop-feed' of Allen B. Wilson, a Michigan cabinet-maker, patented in 1854. This device used a horizontally reciprocating toothed surface, with the teeth projecting forward and moving in a rectangular motion, somewhat analogous to the basic movement of the square-motion comb and the screw-gill. It not only moved the material forward automatically and continuously after each stitch but permitted the turning of the cloth to produce a curved seam. Wilson had also patented (1851) the rotary hook-and-bobbin combination, whereby the needle-thread was seized by a revolving hook and the loop so formed was thrown over a circular spool (figure 313). It provided an alternative to the reciprocating torpedo-shaped shuttle of Howe and Singer and proved far faster because its rotary motion was continuous. It was the parent of the oscillating shuttle (1879) of Max Gritzner

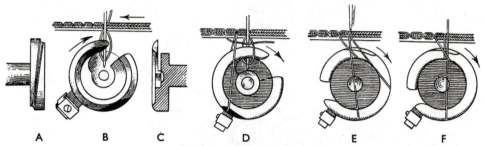

A   B   C   D   E   F

FIGURE 313—*Rotating hook. The use of continuous rotary motion to form the loops produced a great increase in speed.* A, *side view;* B, *front view;* C, *side section;* D–F, *various positions of hook and thread (back view.)*

of Germany and, with its offspring, dominated the industrial field because of its speed and durability: the simple reciprocating or vibratory shuttle was largely confined to the domestic sewing-machine.

The first practical domestic sewing-machine (figure 314) was developed and patented (1851) by Isaac M. Singer (1811–75) of Pittstown, New York. The Singer machine was characterized by a vertical standard with a horizontal arm above a horizontal work-table, a straight needle moving vertically up-and-down in place of the curved needle of Howe and Wilson, a vertical presser-foot by the needle to hold the material in place against the upward stroke of the needle, a yielding spring in the presser-foot to permit its passage over seams and its adjustment to any thickness of cloth, and a foot-treadle in place of the hand-driven crank-wheel. Such were the earliest of the minor improvements made by the firm which became the world's greatest producer of sewing-machines in the 1860s. The second main type of stitch, the chain-stitch, was also developed in America: the double chain-stitch by W. O. Grover (1851), and the single-thread chain-stitch by James E. A. Gibbs (1856) using a revolving hook, or looper, and forming a continuous series of loops, each new loop within the preceding loop.

The impact of the sewing-machine was felt throughout the world. In light engineering it created the great sewing-machine industries of the United States from the 1850s and of Germany from the 1870s, supplying machines for both industrial and domestic use. As an article of commerce 'the first consumer appliance' became the most widely advertised and distributed product of the modern world and a harbinger of mechanization in regions ignorant of any other up-to-date machinery, while the sewing-machine industry pioneered patent pooling (1856), instalment purchase (1856), and 'sale and service' [10]. The

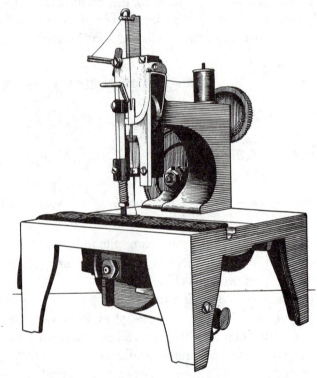

FIGURE 314—*Isaac M. Singer's sewing-machine, 1851. This was the prototype of all later domestic sewing-machines, with every main feature present.*

sewing-machine was progressively improved, and worked with regularity, precision, and 'astonishing velocity', saving time and money and enormously increasing output. The 'iron seamstress' occasioned perhaps the last machine-breaking riots: pre-eminently a labour-saving device, it effectively ended the traditional bondage of women to the needle.

Above all, it revolutionized substantial sectors of industry. In the textile sphere it became the basis of the ready-made clothing industry from the 1850s, ushering in an era of cheap clothing and setting in motion a train of further innovations, especially in the operations of cutting and marking and in certain specialized spheres of stitching. The band-knife for cutting thicknesses of cloth in bulk was adapted (1859) from the band-saw for cutting veneers in the furniture industry, the saw-edge becoming a knife-edge. The Marsden lay-marking process (1897) revolutionized stock-cutting and made possible the extraction of the maximum number of garments from a given amount of cloth. From America came the Dearborn blind-stitching machine (1899–1902), stitching half-way through the thickness of a material, and also the button-holing and buttoning machines, first produced by the Singer Company for the boot and shoe industries but perfected (1881–95) by the Reece Corporation. The sewing-machine came into use wherever fabrics were stitched or seamed, and a whole range of specialized machines was developed for use in the bleaching, carpet, lace and embroidery, hosiery, hatting, glove, umbrella, belt, corset, tent, flag, fur, and jute-bag industries. In the lace industry the sewing-machine provided the basis of the Schiffli lace-machine of 1876. In the carpet industry special machines were developed, from 1880, to move along the carpet, since the carpet was too heavy to be fed into the machine. The sewing-machine came into use also in the mattress, harness and saddlery, upholstery, and book-binding industries. Above all, the boot and shoe industries, which used the new machine first in the manufacture and then in the repair of foot-wear, were revolutionized by the McKay shoe-sewing machine (1861) and the Goodyear welt-machine (1871, 1875). Everywhere the use of the sewing-machine stimulated the growth of production and, with the application of power, the tendency towards the concentration of industry in factories.

VII. THE SIGNIFICANCE OF TECHNICAL INNOVATION

The new techniques of textile production reflected and buttressed the dominant role of Britain and America as inventive pioneers. Their contributions to progress, supplemented by lesser ones made in France and Belgium, greatly widened the field of resources effectively available for industrial use. Often in the short run the new techniques created monopolies based on patent rights, but in the long run they widened the area of competition and increased the degree of its intensity, creating a compulsion to further innovation and helping to eliminate the marginal firms incapable of maintaining the pace. With regard to the construction of machinery, technical innovation consolidated the position of the textile engineering industry as separate from the textile industries proper, reinforced the geographical concentration of the textile industries in those areas where innovation proceeded most rapidly, and led to the establishment of branch factories overseas by the textile engineering industry in quest of foreign markets.

As a factor in production, technical innovation furnished the textile industries with invaluable internal economies. It saved power and raw materials: it increased the speed and continuity of operation between processes. It hastened mechanization, more so in spinning than in weaving. Hand-work was superseded by machine-work, and domestic industry by factory industry. The new textile techniques demanded heavier fixed capital investments in plant and buildings, and by reducing wage-bills increased the ratio of capital charges to labour charges. In consequence there was temporary technological unemployment among certain unadaptable groups: thus the Chartist agitation (1837–42) in the textile districts drew its support partly from displaced block-printers, wool-combers, hand-knitters, and hand-loom weavers. Mechanization decreased the physical strain on the worker but increased his work-load and thereby the mental intensity of his work. It increased the output of manufactured textiles and the intake of raw materials, giving an impetus to the development of primary production and of world trade in general. It improved the quality and often lowered the price of manufactures, stimulating demand and creating employment. It temporarily reinforced the industrial supremacy of Europe, but paved the way for the great rise of modern manufacturing industry in America and in the rest of the world outside Europe.

REFERENCES

[1] LAW, E. *Text. Mfr, Manchr*, **7**, 248, 1881.
[2] FENTON, F. *Ibid.*, **7**, 328–9, 1881.
[3] 'Heilmann's Wool Combing Machine: Report of the Trial of an Action between J. J. Heilmann . . . and J. T. Wordsworth', pp. 8, 11. London. 1852.
[4] BRADBURY, F. 'Worsted Preparing and Spinning', Vol. 2, p. 305. Halifax, 1914.
[5] Editorial. *Text. Rec.*, **17**, 217, 1899.
[6] COLE, A. H. and WILLIAMSON, H. F. 'American Carpet Manufacture; a History and an Analysis', p. 133. Harvard University Press, Cambridge, Mass. 1941.
[7] ROTH, A. B. *J. Text. Inst. (Proc.)*, **25**, 139, 1934.
[8] DRAPER, G. O. 'Labour-Saving Looms', p. 41. Cook, Milford, Mass. 1904.
[9] UTZ, L. 'Die Praxis der mechanischen Weberei', pp. 286, 316. Uhlands technischer Verlag, Leipzig. 1906.
[10] JACK, A. B. "The Channels of Distribution for an Innovation: The Sewing Machine Industry in America, 1860–1865" in 'Explorations in Entrepreneurial History', Vol. 9, no. 3, pp. 113–41. Research Center in Entrepreneurial History, Harvard University, Cambridge, Mass. 1957.

BIBLIOGRAPHY

BARLOW, A. 'The History and Principles of Weaving by Hand and by Power' (2nd ed.). London. 1879.

BRADBURY, F. 'Carpet Manufacture.' Lord & Nagle, Boston, Mass. 1904.

Idem. 'Jacquard Mechanism and Harness Mounting.' King, Halifax. 1912.

DRAPER, G. O. 'Labor-Saving Looms. A Brief Treatise on Plain Weaving and the Recent Improvements in that Line with Special Reference to the Northrop Looms manufactured by Draper Co., Hopedale, Massachusetts, U.S.A.' Cook, Milford, Mass. 1904.

FARADAY, CORNELIA B. 'European and American Carpets and Rugs.' Dean Hicks Company, Grand Rapids, Mich. 1929.

Fox, T. W. 'The Mechanism of Weaving.' London. 1894. (See also 2nd ed., Macmillan, London. 1900.)

JUBB, S. 'The History of the Shoddy Trade: its Rise, Progress and Present Position.' London. 1860.

LEIGH, E. 'The Science of Modern Cotton Spinning' (4th ed.). Manchester. 1877.

MURPHY, W. S. (Ed.). 'The Textile Industries' (3 vols). London. 1910.

NASMITH, J. 'Modern Cotton Spinning Machinery.' London. 1890.

TAYLOR, A. 'History of the Carpet Trade.' Heckmondwike. 1874.

Sewing Machines:

BOLTON, J. "Sewing Machines" in 'Report of the Committee on Awards of the World's Columbian Commission, Chicago, 1893', Vol. 2, pp. 1405–13. Washington. 1901.

BURLINGAME, R. 'March of the Iron Men, a Social History of Union through Invention', pp. 360–77. Scribner, New York. 1938.

BYRN, E. W. 'The Progress of Invention in the Nineteenth Century', pp. 183–94. Munn, New York. 1900.

DOOLITTLE, W. H. 'Inventions in the Century', pp. 310–27. Linscott Publishing Company, London. 1902.

ERNOUF, BARON. 'Histoire de quatre inventeurs français au dix-neuvième siècle', pp. 143–80. Paris. 1884.

EULNER, K. A. 'Die deutsche Nähmaschinen-Industrie.' Schneider, Mainz. 1913.

FELDHAUS, F. M. "Nähmaschine" in 'Die Technik der Vorzeit, der geschichtlichen Zeit und der Naturvölker', pp. 739–41. Engelmann, Leipzig. 1914.

GROTHE, H. 'Bilder und Studien zur Geschichte vom Spinnen, Weben, Nähen' (2nd ed.), pp. 365–89. Berlin. 1875.

HERZBERG, R. 'The Sewing Machine: its History, Construction and Application.' London. 1864.

ILES, G. 'Leading American Inventors', pp. 338–68. Holt, New York. 1912.

"The Iron Seamstress." *Edison Mon.*, **17**, 110–13, 139–42, 1925.

KARMARSCH, K. 'Geschichte der Technologie seit der Mitte des achtzehnten Jahrhunderts', pp. 703–8. Munich. 1872.

KOHLER, W. 'Die deutsche Nähmaschinen-Industrie.' Duncker und Humblot, Munich. 1913.

LEWTON, F. L. "The Servant in the House: a Brief History of the Sewing Machine." *Rep. Smithson. Instn* for 1929, 559–83, 1930. (Reprinted New York, 1931.)

LIND, H. W. "Die Nähmaschine" in 'Das Buch der Erfindungen, Gewerbe und Industrien' (9th ed.), Vol. 8, pp. 445–70. Leipzig. 1898.

LYONS, L., ALLEN, T. W., and VINCENT, W. D. F. 'The Sewing Machine.' Williamson, London. 1924.

MATAGRAN, A. "Barthélemy Thimonnier (1793–1857), inventeur de la machine à coudre en France." *Bull. Soc. Enc. Industr. nat.*, **130**, 70–94, 1931.

MEYSSIN, J. 'Histoire de la machine à coudre: portrait et biographie de l'inventeur B. Thimonnier' (5th ed.). Lyons. 1914.

"Notice sur les machines à coudre." *Bull. Soc. Enc. Industr. nat.*, second series, **7**, 339–53, 1860.

PARTON, J. "History of the Sewing Machine." *Atlan. Mon.*, **19**, 527–44, 1867.

RICHARD, H. 'Die Nähmaschine. Ihre geschichtliche Entwicklung, Construction, und ihr jetziger Standpunkt.' Hanover. 1876.

SALAMON, N. 'The History of the Sewing Machine, from the Year 1750, with a Biography of Elias Howe, Jn.' London. 1863.

SEWELL, S. J. 'A Revolution in the Sewing Machine.' London. 1892.

URQUART, J. W. 'Sewing Machinery.' London. 1881.

WILSON, N. "The Story of the Sewing Machine" (12 articles). *J. dom. Appl.*, Vols **19, 20**; 1891, 1892.

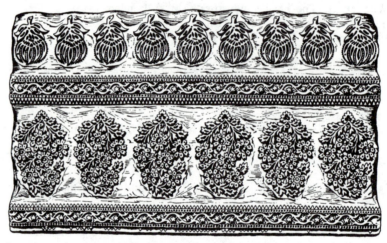

Late nineteenth-century wood block for calico printing. The very fine elements in the design are made of metal strip, and the rest is carved from wood with a felt filling.

24

PART II

THE TEXTILE INDUSTRY:

HOSIERY AND LACE

F. A. WELLS

I. THE RELATIONSHIP BETWEEN HOSIERY AND LACE MANUFACTURE

ALTHOUGH the hosiery and lace industries are now quite distinct they are closely related historically and geographically. Both owe their origin to British inventions, the former to that of the hosiery frame in the late sixteenth century and the latter to the bobbin-net machine invented in the early nineteenth; and their main centres in England are still in the east midlands, where they began.

The modern hosiery industry yields a wide range of products, including stockings, underwear, and outer wear. Its characteristic process is knitting, which in its simplest form produces fabric by way of a series of loops on a single thread, in contrast with woven material, which consists essentially of inter-crossed warp- and weft-threads. In lacemaking the characteristic operation is the twisting of threads. The simplest form of machine lace, plain net, is made from two sets of threads: the warp-threads, arranged as on a loom, and the bobbin-threads. The latter, wound on very thin bobbins, pass between the warp-threads, and after each movement the warp-threads shift sideways so that in its return passage each bobbin-thread is twisted round a warp-thread. For patterned lace more threads are introduced. The variety of production, involving the use of different types of machine, has resulted in a complicated commercial structure in which three main branches can be distinguished, that is, those concentrating on plain net, on curtain lace, and on Leavers lace respectively. The last, named after the inventor of its peculiar machine, is a patterned lace for trimmings and dresses. The same machine makes hair-nets.

In their development during the nineteenth century the two industries exhibit a marked contrast. Machine-made lace was a typical product of the industrial revolution. The manufacture was concentrated in factories almost from the start, and power was early applied. Stimulated by an ever-increasing demand for its products, the industry seemed to offer unlimited opportunities for commercial enterprise and inventive skill. Meanwhile the older hosiery industry stagnated. It was not until the middle of the century that hosiery frames began to be adapted for the application of power. Even then progress was slow, and as late as 1870 the majority of hosiery workers were framework knitters and hand seamers employed at home or in small workshops. Thus the hosiery industry, which between the 1914 and 1939 wars rose to third place among British textile trades, has passed through an industrial revolution almost within living memory.

II. HOSIERY

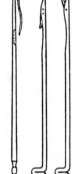

FIGURE 315—Examples of bearded (left) *and latch needles, showing open and closed position of the latter.*

The hosiery industry began with the invention of the stocking frame by William Lee of Calverton, Nottinghamshire, who completed his first model in 1589 (vol III, p 185). The inventions in textile machinery of the mid-eighteenth century that introduced the new industrial era have tended to obscure the work of the genius who, two hundred years earlier, produced this prodigy of complicated and delicate mechanism (plate 34 A). Lee seems to have realized almost at the outset that a frame-knitted fashioned[1] stocking must be made flat and afterwards seamed. This established the principle on which all hose were made for more than two hundred years. Indeed, all fashioned garments are still made in this way. The hand-frame was later adapted for making tubular or seamless work, which is cheaper but does not hold its shape when washed. The old stockingers often spoke with bitter contempt of this 'bag-work', and in the same way of 'cut-ups', that is, garments cut out of a straight piece of fabric and therefore having no selvage at the seams.

The second basic principle introduced by Lee is the manipulation of the thread by needles and sinkers. The needles are hooks with a spring barb or beard which can be pressed into a groove in order to allow the thread on the needles to be drawn through the row of loops already formed, so making a new course of fabric (figure 315). The loops are formed and moved on the needles by sinkers, operating between the needles. In the old stocking frame these movements are controlled by pedals. Two pedals move the slur-bar from side to side, this bar lifting the jacks to which the sinkers are attached. The middle pedal

[1] A fashioned garment is one shaped to fit the body. A circular machine normally knits a tube of fabric, with a constant number of loops in each row, that is, without fashioning.

operates the presser. Drawing the loops over the needle-heads to complete a course is done by hand, as is the fashioning, or narrowing and widening of the fabric.

Frames built on Lee's principles continued in general use for three centuries; there are a few still in operation. The modern power-driven machine making fully-fashioned work has the same essential features: bearded needles, sinkers,

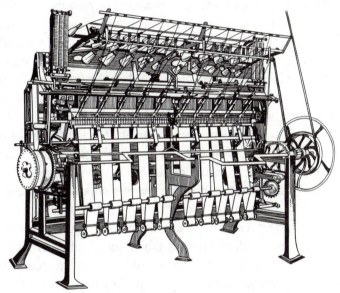

FIGURE 316—*Rotary rib-top frame. The two sets of needles, the essential feature of Strutt's machine, are shown. The knitting mechanism is similar to that of the hand frame, but it is adapted for rotary motion and lengthened to produce ten widths of fabric at once.*

and presser. The main innovations before the application of power were devices for making patterned work. In 1758 Jedediah Strutt (1726–97) patented an attachment for knitting ribbed fabric, consisting of another row of needles set vertically and operating between the original horizontal needles (figure 316). Strutt, who began as a farmer, is generally regarded as the most notable inventor in the framework knitting industry after Lee. Later he went into partnership with Richard Arkwright and helped to establish the cotton industry in Derbyshire.

From the description of its mechanism it will be evident that in the application of power the stocking frame presented much more difficulty than did spinning-machines or even looms. But mechanical difficulties were not the only obstacle, or even the main obstacle, to technical progress in this industry. In the first half of the nineteenth century framework knitting was an overcrowded occupation, employing, in addition to men, large numbers of women and children. Most of the latter were engaged in the ancillary processes of winding, seaming, and mending, but boys were often put to the frame at an early age, and sometimes girls too. Much of the trade was carried on in villages where there was little alternative employment.

The first successful experiments with power were made, not with the traditional stocking frame, but with a type of machine having its needles arranged in a circle, which obviously simplified the problem of applying rotary motion. As early as 1816 a machine of this kind, worked by turning a handle, had been patented by Marc Isambard Brunel (1769–1849). A circular frame, however, could make fabric only in the form of a straight tube, and recollecting the prejudice against bag-work and cut-ups it is perhaps not surprising that Brunel's *tricoteur* was regarded as no more than a curiosity. In any case plain fabric could be produced very cheaply on wide hand-frames. It was not until the 1840s that the possibilities of power-driven circular frames began to be realized, first at Chemnitz in Germany and later at Loughborough in England.

With the revival of interest in circular frames notable advances were made. Matthew Townsend of Leicester took out a patent for a circular rib frame in 1847, and a second in 1856 (figure 317). This gave a great impetus to the trade in seamless hose, for with an elastic ribbed fabric the absence of fashioning is less noticeable. Townsend also invented the tumbler- or latch-needle (figure 315). This was a most important innovation. In the bearded needle the spring hook must be closed by the presser, but the latch-needle has a hinged part which is opened and closed by the passage of the needle through the threads; no presser is required. All fabric of coarser gauge is now knitted with this type of needle. The latch, which pivots on a rivet through the shank of the needle, limits the fineness of the needle, so that for fine-gauge fabric the bearded needle is still essential.

The next stage in the application of power involved the adaptation to rotary motion of the flat frame producing fully-fashioned work. The pioneer in this development was Luke Barton of Nottingham, who entered into partnership with the firm of Hine & Mundella. In 1854 they brought out a machine to produce several fashioned hose at once, the narrowing apparatus being actuated by rotary motion. But the greatest advances in this type of machine must be credited to William Cotton (1786–1866), whose name has become familiar wherever hosiery is made. Cotton's early work was done while he was employed by Cartwright & Warner of Loughborough. Eventually, in 1864, he brought out the machine which became the basis of the Cotton's-patent type. The frame was remarkable for its adaptability; the later models could produce a dozen or more hose at once and could be used for all kinds of fashioned garments. Cotton is also notable as being one of the first of a new class of specialized hosiery-machine builders.

The evolution of the Cotton's-patent type has continued down to the present day. Effort has been directed, on the one hand to increasing the capacity of the machine, and on the other to producing fabric of ever finer gauge. Increased

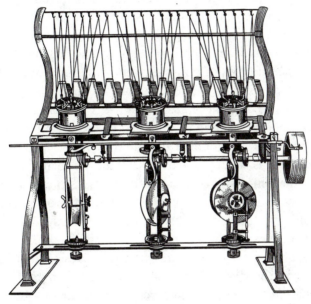

FIGURE 317—*Early example of three head circular frame, using latch needles and making tubular fabric. As the head revolves, the needles are raised and lowered by cams. As the needle rises, its latch opens. The hook then draws off thread from the feeder, and the needle is drawn downwards through the fabric. This movement closes the latch and so turns the hook into a loop. (See figure 315, latch needle.)*

capacity can be attained only by the use of larger and faster machines, and finer-gauge work requires finer needles and sinkers. A modern machine making fully-fashioned silk or nylon hose may have as many as 40 needles to the inch and may produce 32 stockings at once. The reliability of such machines obviously depends on the accuracy with which they are made, and in this respect the hosiery industry owes much to the improvement of engineering technique. Towards the end of the nineteenth century the building of hosiery machines became an important industry in Germany and the United States, and in time several of the models developed in these countries became widely used in Britain.

At first the Americans concentrated on the improvement of the circular frame for making fabric and seamless stockings. Here the best-known inventor was

R. W. Scott. In 1890 he introduced a machine capable of knitting a stocking which needed only a small seam across the toe to finish it. A woman operator could easily tend a group of such machines, so that the product was very much cheaper than the fully-fashioned article knitted by skilled men and requiring a number of sewing operations to complete it. Moreover, some semblance of fashioning was given to the seamless hose by varying the size of the loops. Although the number of stitches per course was the same down the whole length of the leg, the loops were drawn progressively tighter from the calf to the ankle.

The growth of the hosiery industry in the latter part of the nineteenth century was assisted not only by improvements in knitting-machines but by the development of special types of power-driven sewing-machines. Hand-seaming on fully-fashioned work was extremely tedious, for the selvages had to be joined together loop by loop. The mechanization of this process marks an important stage in the evolution of technique, and also in the organization of the manufacture, since it reduced the number of out-workers attached to the trade. The first linking-machine is said to have been made by Campion of Nottingham about 1858, and machines of this type are still in use. Their distinctive feature is a revolving ring set with pins corresponding to the gauge of the fabric to be sewn or linked. As the ring turns, the fabric is run on by hand, each pin through a loop, and the two edges are sewn together.

The seaming of garments cut from the piece presented further problems. Knitted fabric has the disadvantage of unroving when the loops are cut. A cut-out garment must therefore have very secure seams—but a bulky seam is unsightly and in underclothing is uncomfortable. The ordinary types of sewing-machine, making a single row of chain-stitch or lock-stitch, speeded up production but did not give a satisfactory seam. However, in 1887 the Americans introduced the 'overlock', a two-thread machine which not only made a strong seam but trimmed and covered the raw edges of the fabric. This machine, which could make 3000 stitches a minute, gave a great fillip to the cut-out trade in underwear, for which knitted fabric, with its characteristic elasticity, is especially suitable.

III. LACE

The machine-made lace manufacture is sometimes said to have grown out of the older framework knitting industry. There is some truth in this, for in the later eighteenth century many attempts were made to produce an imitation of hand-made lace on the stocking frame, but, as already explained, lace is made by twisting, not looping, threads, and it was John Heathcoat (1783–1861) who first succeeded in mechanizing this process with his bobbin-net machine, patented in 1809 (plate 34 B). Bobbin-net is also distinguished by the traversing of the threads, a process which gives the fabric firmness and durability, and this Heathcoat accomplished in the following manner. In the plain-net machine, as it is now called, the warp-threads are carried vertically. The bobbins (figure 318), made from thin brass disks between which the thread is wound, are arranged in two sets, one behind the other, and pass through the warp-threads with a pendulum-like movement on carriages working in grooves. At each passage of the bobbins the warp-threads are shogged first left then right, which twists the bobbin-threads round the warp-threads. The bobbins, however, make a further

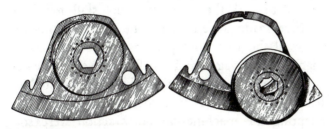

FIGURE 318—*Bobbins and carriages. The carriages move in grooves or gaits in a bar running the length of the machine. The carriages shown have notches for the catch bars which work them to and fro. But there are other methods of moving the carriages; for instance, those in the plain-net machine have teeth on the bottom which engage with the operating mechanism.*

movement. When those coming from the back have been drawn to the front by means of the catch-bar the whole set moves one space to the left; similarly, the front bobbins when transferred to the back all move one space to the right. In this way the bobbins, besides moving from back to front, gradually work their way from one end of the machine to the other. Thus the progress of the bobbin-threads is diagonally across the fabric, half to the left and half to the right.

One of Heathcoat's main problems was to get a sufficient number of bobbins into a restricted space. If they were to be placed side by side they would have to be thinner than it seemed possible to make them. He was thus led to place them in two rows. After the first set has passed through, the warp-threads are shogged one space. The second bobbins then pass through, and again the warp-threads are shogged. Thus the extra movement of the warp-threads produces the same effect as if a single row of bobbins passed through together.

It will be appreciated that the success of Heathcoat's invention depended not only on the discovery of the right mechanical principles, but on the accuracy with which the parts of the machine—especially the bobbins and carriages—were made. This same need for accurate workmanship has already been noted in describing the evolution of the stocking frame, and it is significant that Heathcoat and other pioneers of machine lacemaking were framesmiths attached to the older industry. That the lace trade originated at Nottingham is largely accounted for in this way, and although the manufacture was later established in the west of England and in southern Scotland, and in a number of foreign countries, notably France, Germany, and the United States, Nottingham has retained to the present day a virtual monopoly in lace-machine building.

The early lace machines, like the stocking frame, were operated by hand and foot, eight handles and two treadles being required to effect the complicated motions. Although the early frames made only narrow lace, considerable strength was needed to work them; so was much skill, for the order in which the movements were made depended on the operator and a mistake in the sequence would spoil the work and perhaps injure the machine. Good men therefore commanded high wages, and this fact, as well as the desire to increase productivity by using wider frames and working them faster, helps to explain the early application of power. It is surprising how quickly the mechanical problems of adapting the machine to rotary action were solved. The first attempt appears to have been made by Lindley in 1817. This was unsuccessful, but others soon followed, and Heathcoat's new factory at Tiverton (whither he removed in 1816 after his Loughborough factory had been destroyed by Luddites[1]) was early worked by power.

Few industries display a more remarkable record of invention than does the lace industry of the nineteenth century; for here we have a true handicraft, in which no machinery of any kind had been used, supplanted in a few decades by mechanical production. As might be expected, success in the manufacture of plain net was quickly followed by attempts to make patterned lace on the machine. Various devices were introduced for manipulating both bobbin- and warp-threads so as to produce simple designs such as spots on bobbin-net, but the traversing of the bobbin-threads necessarily imposed a regularity in the fabric; more ambitious designs had to be embroidered on the net by hand. What was desired was a machine capable of reproducing all the intricacies of hand-made lace, and the one that lent itself to this purpose was that brought out by John Leavers in 1813. Leavers, like Heathcoat, was a framesmith. His machine (plate 35 B), which was originally designed to make plain net, had to embody novel principles so as to avoid contravening the Heathcoat patent. Its novelty consisted in the employment of a single row of bobbins, a simplification that facilitated its adaptation for making patterned lace later on. The use of a single

---

[1] The Luddites were machine-breaking rioters, active in the midland counties in the period 1811–16.

tier of bobbins meant that, for a given gauge of net, there had to be two bobbins side by side in the space occupied by one bobbin (with another behind it) in the Heathcoat frame. The success of Leaver's method depended therefore on the ability to make bobbins and carriages twice as thin as those that Heathcoat had been able to procure. This was accomplished by Thompson and Shepperley. The latter was a watchmaker, and in time many members of this craft were drawn into Nottingham to supply the increasing demand for bobbins and carriages.

In the 1830s the Jacquard system of controlling threads according to a predetermined pattern was already widely used in weaving. After many attempts it was successfully applied to the Leavers machine by Hooton Deverill in 1841. This established the method by which Leavers lace is still made (plate 35 A). Several sets of vertical threads are used, according to the nature of the pattern, each set passing through holes in a separate guide-bar running the width of the frame. As the guide-bars, actuated by the jacquard at the side of the machine, move laterally, the threads move varying distances as required by the pattern. With every movement of the vertical threads the bobbin-threads move in between them, so tying them together at the prescribed intervals. The fact that the Leavers machine employed only a single row of bobbins greatly facilitated the application of the jacquard, for it ensured a quick passage of the bobbin-threads through the vertical threads and allowed space for the insertion of the guide-bars.

Equipped with the jacquard, the Leavers machine became an instrument of remarkable versatility (plate 36 A). It can make narrow breadths for trimmings, these being joined by threads which are drawn out after the lace is made; it can also produce wide pieces for dresses. In both these forms most of the traditional patterns of hand-made lace have been reproduced.

The third main type of lace machine, that for making curtains, is attributed to John Livesey, a Nottingham draughtsman, though several others claim a share of credit for the practical application of his ideas. The curtain machine (plate 36 B) is an adaptation of the original bobbin-net machine (plate 34 B). It uses only one tier of bobbins and, as the bobbin threads do not traverse, it produces, if not used for patterned work, a square or 'straight-down' net, distinct from the round mesh of the plain-net machine. Livesey's object, however, was to make a patterned net, though with a bolder design than could be produced on the Leavers machine. The jacquard was applied, not to the guide-bars, which had a regular lateral movement, but in such a way as to control individual threads by means of jacks. Another characteristic of the curtain machine, distinguishing it from the Leavers, is the placing of the jacquard above the frame, the jacks being linked to it by long strings.

With the use of the three types of machine now described, the lace industry expanded rapidly in the second half of the nineteenth century. Technical progress continued, but most of the innovations of this period were modifications of existing designs rather than changes of principle. Much was done to improve the action of certain parts, particularly of the carriages. The introduction of the 'go-through' method of operating the carriages in the Leavers machine is a notable example; it gave a smoother action, making for greater speed. Improvement in engineering practice and equipment made possible the production of finer-gauge machines. It will be appreciated that the progress of technique was greatly influenced by changes of fashion and by the desire for novelty in the design of lace (plate 37 B). The lace trade offered remarkable scope for mechanical ingenuity and innumerable devices were introduced, progress being accompanied by frequent litigation over patent rights. A successful innovation enabling a manufacturer to introduce a good selling line might make a fortune for the inventor or sponsoring firm, but much time and money were wasted either through technical failure or from misjudgement of the market.

In view of the versatility of what may now be called the conventional lace machine, its high initial cost and extremely long life, there was little incentive to experiment with radical changes of method. The only important exception is the Barmen machine, based on an invention of the Frenchman Malhère, which was patented in an improved form in 1894. This machine is remarkable in that it reproduces the movements of a maker of hand-made bobbin-lace. It is circular in form, the bobbins being arranged round a central crown, on which the threads are plaited by a motion like that of dancers round a maypole. The lace emerges through the crown in the form of a tube which, when opened out, is a single breadth, or perhaps two breadths, of lace. Barmen machines are relatively small and simple to work, and besides making a beautiful imitation of hand-made lace (plate 37 A) they can produce several kinds of narrow fabrics. Their rate of production is very low compared with that of a Leavers machine, while the complicated motions cause heavy wear on certain of the parts. Though extensively employed in Germany and France, the Barmen type never became very popular in Britain.

25

THE WORKING OF METALS

R. CHADWICK

I. MELTING AND CASTING METALS

IN the early nineteenth century the metals that were being produced in wrought form included iron, lead, and copper, as well as the precious metals silver and gold. Lead, readily extracted from its ores and easily worked, was in very extensive use in the form of sheet and pipe. The machines used for working lead in the eighteenth and early nineteenth centuries became the prototypes of the much more powerful machines constructed later for working copper and wrought iron. In mid-century, advances in the art of working metals were chiefly concerned with these latter metals, Britain being the largest producer of both. Wrought iron was required for all kinds of structural and engineering purposes, especially for rails for the railways which were then being rapidly developed. Copper was used mainly for the sheathing of ships' bottoms, where it had replaced lead, but it also found not inconsiderable application for domestic pots and pans, coinage, buttons, and a variety of small articles.

In the late nineteenth century the engineering arts advanced in scope and precision, and the old and primitive rolling-mills and other metal-working plants were replaced by others vastly more powerful and complex, in which metals could be worked or wrought in far greater quantities, at higher speeds, and with increased accuracy. In this period also new extraction processes were devised (ch 4), so that both ferrous and non-ferrous metals and alloys suitable for working became available in greater variety. By the end of the century, world output of mild steel, which had by then replaced cast and wrought iron as the major constructional material, had increased to 28 million tons a year. World output of copper by 1900 had increased to half a million tons, and, although not all of it was eventually converted to the wrought form, the amount is probably not very different from the total of wrought copper and copper-base alloys.

The foremost requirement for the remarkable growth in the quantity and variety of wrought metals was the ability to produce these metals and alloys as solid lumps or ingots suitable for hammering or rolling. The later increase in the size and power of mills for metal-working entailed the use of yet larger ingots or blooms.

While wrought iron remained the major material of construction, the size of the individual piece of metal was restricted to some 100–150 lb by the method of hand manipulation in the puddling furnace (vol IV, p 106). Before 1860, carbon steels were made by Huntsman's process (vol IV, p 107), in which carburized wrought iron was remelted in a crucible holding no more than about 50 lb. Limits were set by the strength of the available crucible, by the capacity of furnaces capable of achieving the requisite temperature, and by the need to lift the pot out of the coke or charcoal furnace by hand. Only iron of high carbon content could be melted on a commercial basis. In 1860 Bessemer installed the first practical furnace capable of burning out the excess carbon by a blast of air, and at the same time raising the temperature to such a level that the 'mild' steel, containing no more than about 0·1 per cent of carbon, was obtained in a molten condition (p 56). The early Bessemer furnaces had a capacity of some 2 tons of steel, and by 1865 furnaces of 4 tons capacity were in use [1].

There followed within a decade the Siemens–Martin open-hearth furnace (p 57) in which the heat is derived from outside. In this furnace the high temperature is secured by the use of regenerators, the hot waste gases preheating the incoming gas. Still larger quantities of molten steel thus became practicable, and for this reason, as well as for its technical superiority, the open-hearth furnace soon became the leading means of steel-making. Meanwhile, ingot size increased rapidly, and by the end of the century the more advanced steel mills were operating with ingots of up to 5 tons [2]. For mills laid down at the beginning of the twentieth century 4 to 5 tons was the average ingot weight in both America and Europe. The methods developed for converting steel into wrought forms were influenced to some extent by the early techniques for wrought iron, but more especially by the magnitude of the task of handling such large ingots. For mild steel, it soon became standard practice to cast large cylindrical or rectangular ingots in a vertical position, either by direct tapping from the steel-melting furnaces or by transfer with a large refractory-lined ladle. Subsequent fabrication varied according to the product required. Meanwhile, the relatively small quantities of special steels—such as carbon steel and, later, alloy steel for tool-making—continued to be melted in crucibles, large ingots being made by pouring into one mould the contents of a large number of small pots [1].

In the wrought iron period of the first half-century, copper, with its relatively low melting-point, was being produced in much larger pieces than was iron. These were cast by hand lading from the reverberatory furnace used in the final refining operation of making tough pitch copper (p 83). The various moulds already dried out and prepared for use were laid out on the refinery floor. The furnace would contain about 5 tons of molten copper, and the pouring team consisted of 6 to 8 men, each carrying a hand ladle of some 35 lb capacity, which was filled by dipping into the fore-hearth of the furnace. For making a large casting, all members of the team filled their ladles and, at a signal, simultaneously released the contents in such a way as to flood the bottom of the mould smoothly and instantaneously. Thereafter, they moved in a continuous file past the furnace hearth, each in turn filling his ladle, carrying it to the mould, and returning. Successive ladles of metal were skilfully distributed in order to maintain a constant temperature all over the solidifying ingot, the top being kept in a molten condition so that solidification took place only after filling was complete. The copper surface remained bright and metallic while molten, but the oxygen continuously dissolving from the air had to be compensated for by 'poling' (p 83) down to a lower oxygen content than would be required for tough pitch. This pouring technique was employed virtually unchanged throughout the nineteenth century. By 1850 ingots of about 2 tons in weight were being made in this way, but by the end of the century the size and form of copper ingots showed little further advance.

In the early nineteenth century metal-workers preferred the red brasses, with 10–20 per cent of zinc, to the yellow brasses, with up to 35 per cent of zinc, since additions of zinc caused the metal to become progressively harder and more difficult to work. This was an important factor, because brasses could not be worked hot, and with the relatively low power then available the size of sheets and other wrought pieces was small. As far back as 1779, James Keir had shown that by introducing a still larger percentage of zinc into copper a metal was obtained capable of being forged or wrought when either red-hot or cold, but no serious attempt was made to hot-work the brasses until 1832, when G. F. Muntz, a Birmingham brass manufacturer, took out a patent for the alloy, containing 40 per cent of zinc, that subsequently bore his name (vol IV, p 130). Muntz followed this up by manufacturing trials, and in 1837 installed works at Swansea, which in 1842 were moved to Birmingham, for the rolling of Muntz-metal sheets.

The relative ease with which Muntz-metal could be deformed, so that it could be hot-rolled into sheets almost as readily as copper, was explained only many years later, when microscopic studies of the structure of metals were undertaken, notably by H. C. Sorby, Sir W. C. Roberts-Austen, C. T. Heycock, and F. H. Neville. The first detailed study of the brasses was made by E. S. Shepherd [3]. This revealed that alloys with up to about 37 per cent zinc consist of a single phase (alpha) at room temperature. With 40 per cent zinc, a second phase (beta) is also present, and at the hot-working temperature of 800° C the structure is entirely beta. This phase is much more readily hot-worked than the alpha phase, although more difficult to deform when cold. Muntz-metal, or yellow metal as it was often termed, soon displaced copper for the sheathing of ships' bottoms (vol IV, pp 130, 581, 592). By the end of the century large quantities of yellow metal sheet were being made for the manufacture of small brass articles. This manufacture, largely carried out by hand methods, flourished particularly at Benares in India, whither sheet metal rolled in European mills was exported on a very considerable scale.

German silver or nickel silver (brass whitened by the addition of nickel), although known much earlier to the Chinese, was first made in Europe about 1824, but became of commercial importance only with the introduction of electroplating some fifteen years later. Damascus steel made from meteoric iron having been found to contain nickel, Johann Conrad Fischer in 1825 added nickel in Huntsman's process to produce carbon steel with improved strength and elasticity [4]. Nickel itself was first worked about 1880, following the discovery by Theodore Fleitmann of the toughening effect of adding a little magnesium. Shortly afterwards copper-nickel alloys (cupro-nickels) were made with a nickel content varying from 10 to 30 per cent, all having a white or whitish colour [5].

Specimens of aluminium-bronzes, as they came to be called, were first displayed by C. and A. Tissier, who described these alloys simultaneously with H. L. Debray, a collaborator of Ste-Claire Deville [6]. So great was the interest aroused by the outstanding mechanical properties, and resistance to tarnishing and chemical attack, of alloys containing about 10 per cent of aluminium that the Swiss Metallurgical Company, formed at Neuhausen in Switzerland in 1887 to exploit the Héroult cell, proposed originally to manufacture aluminium bronze. This material was thought to offer better economic prospects than aluminium itself, but commercial development of these alloys was delayed by the very considerable difficulties in their fabrication.

The tin bronzes had been used from ancient times for casting ornamental objects, and especially for statuary, because of the lower melting-point and improved castability conferred by the addition of tin to copper, but these alloys were not amenable to working. Phosphor bronze, containing about 0·1 per cent of phosphorus, together with up to 5 per cent of tin, was first mentioned in 1871 by C. Künzel, and its industrial applications were described by C. Montefiore-Levi two years later [7]. From this time, the alloy became of considerable importance in electrical applications, its high tensile strength in the cold-worked condition making it specially suitable for springs and electrical contacts.

The steel wire originally used for the electric telegraph and for electric conductors was gradually replaced by copper after the failure of the first transatlantic cable of 1858, although iron and steel continued to be used for this purpose until at least 1880. In the search for a stronger material for such applications, it is interesting to note the considerable attention given to the silicon bronzes of 2 to 4 per cent silicon content patented by L. Weiller in France in 1882. These were used for telegraph and telephone lines between Brussels and Paris, and for the first power cables for providing electric lighting in the boulevards in connexion with the Paris Exhibition of 1889.

Copper, brasses, nickel silver, and bronzes were melted in small pots in coke-fired furnaces set in the ground in the same way as for the carbon steels. The design of these furnaces changed little and their use extended well into the twentieth century. The usual type of coke pit (figure 319) accommodated clay crucibles holding from 50 to 100 lb; this was later increased to 200 lb as available

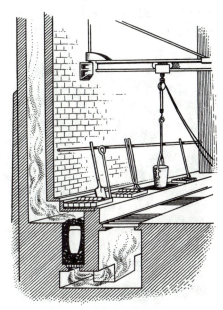

FIGURE 319—*Coke-fired crucible furnaces for melting copper and copper alloys.*

materials were improved. A simple block and tackle was then required for handling. The crucible was charged with the solid metal constituents and a handful of stick charcoal. It was then placed on the hot coke bed and, after a lid had been fitted to the crucible, coke was fed down the sides and over the top. The furnace design and proportions were such that the burning away of the coke charge, which took about one hour, brought the metal into a condition ready for pouring. Basket-tongs were then fixed to the rim of the crucible and it was pulled out with a chain and tackle ready for pouring. The mould consisted of two cast iron segments, previously dressed with oil or resin and held together by rings and wedges. It was placed in an inclined position for the pouring, although later the vertical position was preferred. The crucible of metal, manipulated with the basket-tongs, was placed in a stand and tilted so as to pour directly into each of the several moulds in turn (figure 320). During pouring the metal stream was enveloped by a shroud of burning gas due to the volatilization of mould dressing.

II. FORGING

Forging, or battering as it was originally termed, was employed before the advent of the rolling-mill, and as long as wrought iron remained in general use the hammer was essential for shaping the metal. The ball, as it was brought from the puddling furnace in a white-hot lump, was first hammered to weld it into a solid mass and to expel entrained pockets of liquid slag, and then fashioned

FIGURE 320—*Casting brass ingots in iron strip moulds.*

into shape for the subsequent rolling process. In the early days of steam, forge hammers were mounted on a fixed bearing at one end, the head being lifted by a cam or by a steam piston and allowed to fall by gravity, sometimes assisted by a spring [8]. The cast iron heads were generally quite small, about 1 to 5 cwt, and might be driven at considerable speed, but much larger hammers were made for special purposes. The introduction of James Nasmyth's steam hammer in 1842 (vol IV, p 116) was a very notable advance, because it was able to deliver heavier blows and was also capable of much more sensitive control, hammers of 25 tons being in use at Sheffield in 1865 [1].

The hydraulic forging press was patented by Sir Charles Fox in 1847, and a press of 500 tons for forging Bessemer steel was erected at Platt Brothers, Oldham, in 1866 [9]. A hydraulic press of 4000 tons for forging the much larger open-hearth steel ingots was installed at Sheffield in 1887 [1].

In copper- and brass-working the shaping of ingots by forging was abandoned with the introduction of the rolling-mill at the beginning of the nineteenth century; billets for rolling were then produced in the required forms by casting. In this branch of the metallurgical arts the copper industry was greatly in advance of the iron industry, very much larger plates being available in copper than in wrought iron, at least until about 1865, when armour plate became important. By 1850 copper plates of over 1 ton were being rolled, and at the Vienna Exhibition of 1873 a plate 17 ft 7 in × 8 ft 7 in, and ¾-in thick, weighing more than 2 tons, was displayed. Copper-workers at this time employed the forge for the final hot-shaping of these large plates. In 1877 Swansea manufacturers offered hammered work comprising 'Pans—Heaters—Teaches—Crowns—Upper parts

—Collars and Domes' in diameters up to 10 ft 6 in, and with depths up to 39 in. For 'Round Raised Bottoms' diameters were up to 11 ft and depths up to 32 in; oval and rectangular bottoms could also be supplied. For shaping, the rolled plate would be heated to 850° C and the hammering continued until the plate was too cold to deform further, when it was reheated. Local thinning was carried out by the Nasmyth steam hammer, but most of the shaping was done by hand hammering. The operation is illustrated in plate 38 A. Both steam and hand hammering were practised without appreciable change until well into the twentieth century, and during this time the size of the pieces manipulated showed no great increase. In later years the locomotive fire-box became the principal product of the copper-workers' art.

III. ROLLING: BARS AND SECTIONS

The conception of the rolling-mill for the working of metals dates back at least to Leonardo da Vinci, and many of the basic principles and major variations in design and operation had been proposed in the eighteenth and early nineteenth centuries. For the most part these ideas were carried into effect only in the nineteenth century, with the development of the necessary machinery and skill for heavy engineering construction. The great bulk of the wrought metal required throughout the century was in the form of bars, plates, and sections for structural engineering, and of rails for the rapidly developing railways of the world. Consequently the most important developments in rolling-mills were aimed at satisfying these markets. In 1850 all the above products were made from wrought iron, but by the end of the century this had been completely superseded by mild steel, the main change of emphasis taking place between 1870 and 1880.

In the working of wrought iron the metal was first hammered to shape, then worked down in grooved or flat rolls according to whether bars or plates were required. A typical example of an early mill for the rolling of rails is illustrated in figure 321. The hammered bar is fed into the groove on the left and then successively through adjacent grooves. Since the mill is of simple 2-high[1] construction, and operates continuously in one direction only, the work-piece has to be returned over the top of the mill between each pass. The earliest wrought iron rails, produced in 1820, were 15–18 ft long. The first Bessemer steel rail appears to have been rolled at Dowlais in 1857,[2] while Siemens open-hearth

---

[1] In a 2-high mill there are two rolls, and the work normally moves in one direction. In a 3-high mill, with three rolls, the work can move in both directions simultaneously.

[2] This early success is explained by the exceptional purity of the iron employed. It was some years before Bessemer steel products became available commercially.

steel was being rolled by John Brown at Sheffield in 1867 [1]. The output of rails from Britain reached its zenith in 1870, when more than a million tons were exported, almost half going to the United States. From then onward, exports shrank progressively, until in 1877 they were only 500 000 tons, a mere 300 tons of this being taken by the United States.

An advanced mill installation of the mid-century, with facilities for many different types of product, is shown in figure 322. This had eight separate rolling trains driven from one steam-engine. The installation had two fly-wheels, each of 20-ft diameter, and all the rolling trains operated continuously, no reversing or stopping being possible. The group of rolls (A) were similar to those shown in figure 321, being of 2-high construction and capable of producing 80 tons of heavy angle-iron, slabs, or rails in 12 hours. At the other end of this shaft, the

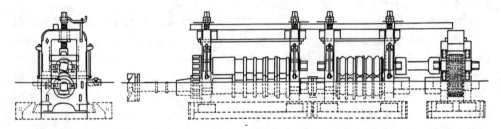

FIGURE 321—*Steam-driven rolling-mill installation, end and side views, in elevation. Dowlais, c 1850.*

train (B)—designed to roll H- and T-sections up to 12 inches in maximum depth and 50 ft in length—was equipped with duo-mills, the principle of which is shown in the diagram (F). The materials passed from right to left through the lower pair of rolls and were returned through the upper pair. The rolling-stand (C), which was for the preliminary blooming or rolling down of heavy bars for feeding the rail and section mills, was one of the earliest examples of the 3-high mill having three working rolls. In such a mill the product is rolled first between the bottom and centre rolls, being returned between the centre and top rolls. The rolling-stand (C) was also equipped with a lifting-carriage for raising the heavy bars for the return pass [8]. Both 3-high and duo-mills avoid the necessity of a 'blank' pass when the material is being returned over the top of the rolls, such an operation being non-productive as well as allowing the metal to cool unduly. Credit for the development of 3-high mills is usually given to John Fritz of Pittsburg, who in 1857 built a more extensive rolling-plant on this principle than that described above.

With the introduction of steel ingots the use of the hammer for shaping declined, and in 1884 the first universal mill was introduced. This was capable of taking a cast ingot and, without previous shaping, converting it at will to either plate or bar, the principle being the use of shaped rolls or of vertical edging rolls to control width. The trend continued, and by the beginning of the twentieth century universal mills employing this principle were already of

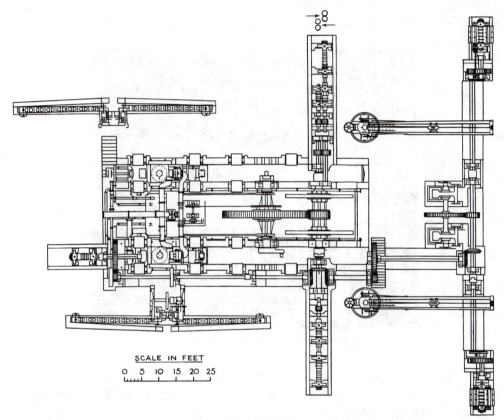

FIGURE 322—*Rolling mill for rails at Ebbw Vale Ironworks, in plan.* c *1850.*

SCALE IN FEET
0   5   10   15   20   25

tremendous power and complexity. For these mills the steam-engine was by then being rapidly displaced by the electric motor. This greatly increased flexibility, because the common drive could be replaced by separate motors driving each of the rolls, the screw-down gear, the roller-tables, and other auxiliaries, so that all operations could be controlled from a single station or pulpit.

IV. HEAVY PLATES

For the manufacture of large plates the ironmasters of the mid-century had perforce to use more complex methods than those used for copper (plate 38 B).

Sheet bars, the first product of sheet rolling, were, in the days of wrought iron, of only about 100 lb maximum weight. These were perfectly suitable for making light plate for the early iron merchantmen, but were quite inadequate for the protection of naval vessels against gun-fire. Laminated plate consisting of several thicknesses of plate bolted or riveted together proved ineffective. Armour plates of $4\frac{1}{2}$-in thickness were manufactured by roll-piling in Park Gate Ironworks,

FIGURE 323—*Rolling 20-ton armour plate, 1861.*

Sheffield, in 1856. In one example, five bars measuring 30 in × 12 in × 1 in were piled and rolled together to make a rough slab. Two such slabs were then rolled together to make a plate $1\frac{1}{4}$ in thick and 4 ft square. Next, four of these plates were piled and rolled into one plate 8 ft × 8 ft and $2\frac{1}{2}$ in thick. Finally, four of these large plates were rolled together to form the final product [8], [2]. This method of producing heavy armour plates from wrought iron was continued for the next twenty years, and by 1861 the rolling of a plate 12 in thick and weighing 20 tons was accomplished by John Brown & Sons. The rolling of this very special piece was witnessed by the Lords of the Admiralty and has been de-scribed in graphic terms. A bugle announced readiness for the final rolling operation, and the white-hot mass of metal was dragged from the furnace with chains and pincers, each requiring a dozen men for handling. The manipulation and rolling of this large ingot are illustrated by a contemporary drawing (figure 323), which indicates the heavy man-power involved because of the primitive means of handling available at that time [1]. Even in these great thicknesses, wrought iron soon proved inadequate for resisting the ordnance that could be brought to bear against it. The first counter move, in 1876, was to produce armour of wrought iron with a backing of steel, which was cast on to the partly rolled plate and consolidated by further rolling. By 1892 steel plates, produced from single steel ingots cast in the Siemens open-hearth furnace, were adopted by the Royal Navy, and by the turn of the century all heavy plates were rolled

FIGURE 324—*Sheet mills for tinplate rolling.*

from cast steel ingots. Massive pieces were handled; in 1902, for example, Krupp in Germany was able to produce plates measuring 43 ft × 11 ft × 12 in by rolling ingots of up to 130 tons in weight and 3 ft thick.

V. THIN SHEET

In the nineteenth century the rolling of thin sheets of iron or steel was undertaken entirely for tinplate manufacture, rusting being too great an obstacle to the use of uncoated sheet. The tinplate industry was already established at the beginning of the century (vol IV, ch 4), when records show that eleven mills were operating in Britain, mostly in south Wales and Monmouthshire; by 1825 the number had increased to eighteen, and the method of rolling evolved by that time was to endure for more than 100 years. Each rolling-unit consisted essentially of two stands of 2-high rolls. Roughing was carried out on one stand and finishing on the other, which had more carefully finished roll-surfaces. The unit also comprised shears and two or more reheating furnaces. A typical mill on the Welsh pattern is shown in figure 324; the reheating furnaces, close by, have been omitted. The starting-point was a sheet bar about 8 in wide and $\frac{1}{2}$-in thick, the length being sufficient to make the desired sheet width, with an allowance for

trimming. The weight varied from about 18 to 80 lb. Two such bars were taken
from the furnace, where they had been heated to about 790° C in a smoky reducing flame. With a man on each side of the rolls, one bar was fed with tongs by
the roller into the roll-bite, to be returned over the top by the catcher while
the second bar was fed in. After several rapid passes the bars had elongated
along their original 8-in dimension to form approximately square sheets. The
two were then 'matched', that is placed together, reheated, and rolled as a pair
until the thickness was reduced to about half. The sheets were then separated,
each doubled along its centre, matched again, and rolled in 'fours'. The process

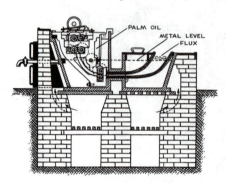

FIGURE 325—*Machine for tinning steel sheets, 1897.*

continued, the folds being sheared off
and the sheets separated from time to
time to prevent permanent sticking, and
to bring individual sheets in turn to the
outside [10]. Finally, rolling was completed in 'eights', although rolling in
'twelves' was sometimes practised and is
mentioned as far back as 1819.

The hot-rolled sheets were annealed
for 8 to 10 hours in wrought iron pots, and
then pickled to remove surface scale produced by the oxidation of the iron during
rolling and annealing. Early in the century pickling was carried out with pyroligneous acid (p 308) or dilute acetic acid from sour beer or other fermented
liquors, but sulphuric acid was employed from about 1830. In an account of
the tinning process published in 1883, Ernest Trubshaw described five operations [11]. The first was to immerse in palm oil; thence sheets were transferred
to the tin pot, in which the coating of tin was applied by an immersion of some
four minutes. Next, the washermen brushed the plates, to remove scruff, and
redipped them. The plate then went to the grease pot, where the tin was caused
to flow evenly, the thickness being regulated by passing the plates through
rollers. The plates were finally cleaned by rubbing with bran, using sheepskins.
Later the process was simplified by the introduction of machines of the type
shown in figure 325. In these, the sheet was introduced into the fluid tin on the
right through a layer of flux consisting of molten zinc chloride, and after passing
through immersed rollers emerged through a layer of palm oil, passing through
two further sets of rollers to remove surplus tin.

The best-quality tinplate was originally made from iron produced in the
charcoal-finery, and was known as charcoal plate. Coke plate prepared from iron

made in coal- or coke-fired puddling furnaces was of lower quality because of the sulphur contamination, which increased the tendency to rust at pin-holes in the tin coating. Although Bessemer steel replaced iron after about 1880, and open-hearth steel became the normal material before the end of the century, the terms charcoal plate and coke plate were retained and are still employed. Charcoal plates are the highest-quality material with a minimum specified coating of 32–46 oz of tin per basis box,[1] equivalent to a thickness of tin of 0·00012–0·00017 in. Coke plates have a tin coating of 17·7–28 oz per basis box, equivalent to 0·00006–0·0001 in per side. Three grades are distinguished in each of these categories.[2]

During most of the nineteenth century, Britain had a virtual monopoly of tinplate manufacture; production increased very rapidly during this time and a large proportion of the product was exported. Annual production rose from less than a million boxes in 1850 to some 14 m boxes in 1890, 60 per cent of the 1890 output being exported to the United States. In the same period the price was steadily reduced, from 27s 6d per box in 1850 to 14s 4d in 1890.

In 1890 the McKinley tariff imposed a duty of nearly 10s on every box of tinplate imported into America. Behind this protective barrier the American tinplate industry, which up to then had made little headway, rapidly established itself, using technologists from Wales and adopting the Welsh system almost in its entirety. By the end of the century the United States was self-supporting, although not until about 1910 did her output equal that of Britain.

The hot-rolling of thin copper sheets was undertaken in south Wales from early in the century. Records of 1828 indicate that the normal sizes of sheets for sheathing ships and for the Indian bazaar trade were 4 ft × 2 ft or 4 ft × 3 ft, with average weights of 10–32 oz per sq ft, corresponding to 0·013–0·044 of an inch in thickness. Sheets up to 10 ft long were produced for 'stem plates', however. To make this thin sheeting cast cakes were rolled with several reheatings, the final rolling generally being in 'twos'. The scale was removed by dousing with urine, reheating, and then quenching in water. Acid cleaning or pickling was more rarely employed. A contemporary record shows that finished sheared sheets amounted to 81 per cent of the starting weight of metal: there was a loss of 3½ per cent for scaling and pickling, and of 15½ per cent for trimming, a result which it would still be hard to better.

Hot-rolling of sheets left a matt uneven surface after scaling, and cold-rolling

---

[1] A basis box was defined in 1820 as 225 sheets 13¾ in × 10 in, but this was later redefined as 56 sheets 28 in × 20 in or 112 sheets 14 in × 20 in, all having the same total area. The most usual thickness for tinplate is 0·012 in, weighing 0·5 lb per sq ft. A basis box thus has a normal weight of about 110 lb, and there are some 20 boxes to the ton.

[2] Percy in 1880 quotes 8–8½ lb of tin as average on a basis box. The distinction between charcoal and coke plates was in quality of iron and not in thickness of tin.

was introduced later in the century in order to provide a better finish. This was particularly important for copper and brass, much of which was used for jewelry or plated ware on which a highly polished surface was required. The cold reduction of sheets exceeding 2 ft in width on 2-high rolls is laborious, and normally only sufficient reduction was carried out to give the necessary surface polish. Even so, the technical difficulties of cold-rolling were considerable. For example, the roll-barrels bend slightly under the heavy pressures involved in cold-rolling. If, therefore, they are initially prepared with parallel surfaces they will tend to roll the sheet to a greater extent on the edges, which consequently elongate disproportionately and become wavy. To counteract this effect the rolls were made with a slight camber at their centres. However, uneven wear occurs in rolling, and the heat produced in the working causes an expansion which affects the contour of the roll. Then, too, the sheet itself, especially if it has been previously hot-rolled, will have some slight variations in thickness. In consequence, when after hot-rolling a sheet is first put through a cold 2-high stand, it will assume an uneven shape owing to variations in the amount of elongation produced in different parts of the surface. This can be corrected only by the skill of the worker, who repeatedly and with careful control passes the sheet through the same mill until finally it assumes the same pattern of surface irregularity as the rolls, and so becomes flat. Depending on roll-conditions, this may require twenty or more passes through the rolls.

Birmingham brass-manufacturers overcame this difficulty of securing flatness by cold-rolling brass and copper in narrow widths in the form of long lengths which could be coiled, a practice which had been employed for centuries by rollers of the precious metals. Ingots were cast from 3 in to 6 in wide and about $1\frac{1}{2}$ inches in thickness, and cold-rolled through narrow mills. The sequence of operations was to reduce 50 per cent in thickness in about three passes through the rolls, anneal to soften, pickle, cold-roll to reduce a further 50 per cent, and so on. By the use of short heavy roll-barrels it was possible to apply sufficient pressure to give much heavier rolling than on wide sheet mills, and this avoided many of the difficulties arising from deformation of roll-shape, although careful control of roll-camber was still necessary. The successful rolling of flat uniform strip in coils depended on the skill of the craftsman, who maintained his roll-cambers by periodically scouring the surfaces with emery powder, using wooden laps cut to the shape of the roll-entry. Strip in coil form was in demand by the manufacturers of small articles of hardware, who were able to run presses fitted with automatic feeds for much longer continuous periods from coils than from short pieces of metal cut from a sheet.

The problem created by the bending of rolls under load was encountered at a very early date, and the first and most obvious solution was to increase barrel-diameter. However, this had the effect that, for the same reduction in thickness of the sheet being rolled, the power required to drive the rolls was increased. Berthard Lauth, in 1864, was the first to demonstrate the advantage of having a work-roll of small diameter, backed up by a support-roll of much larger diameter. The support-roll prevented deflexion without the necessity of increasing the driving-power. The 3-high Lauth mill had a single small-diameter roll with upper and lower rolls of larger diameter. The work was passed in one direction

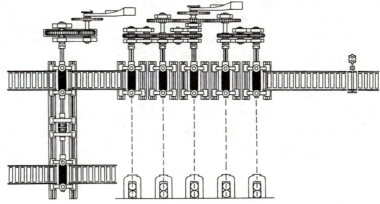

FIGURE 326—*Lay-out of Toeplitz mill, Austria.*

between the centre and upper rolls and in the other between the centre and lower rolls, all the rolls running continuously. The next logical step was the 4-high mill in which two smaller work-rolls were supported on the outside by much larger backing rolls. The engineering problems involved in the construction of the 4-high mill proved formidable, and although in the nineteenth century the 3-high mill found considerable application in both hot- and cold-rolling plants, wide 4-high mills for cold-rolling did not become a practical reality until well into the twentieth century.

The advantage sought in the 4-high design was the provision of a wide mill capable of cold-rolling down to thin gauges without the necessity of repeated passes, as in single-sheet rolling on 2-high mills. The more ambitious ideas visualized the production of tinplate sheets in continuous strip form using a whole series of rolling-stands operating in tandem, each capable of effecting a heavy reduction; the surface contours and cambers of any such series of rolls, however, would have to be controlled with great accuracy to maintain the surface of the strip flat throughout the complete series of rolling reductions.

The first serious attempt to carry out wide-strip rolling in a continuous mill was made at Toeplitz in Austria. The lay-out of the mill as described in 1902 is shown in figure 326. It had two 3-high stands driven by a single 1000-hp engine for breaking down the ingots, and a train of five 2-high stands operating in tandem, for finish-rolling, driven by a second 1000-hp engine. A metal slab, of 8-in maximum thickness and 1000-lb maximum weight, was first hot-rolled to 3-in thickness by passing it backwards and forwards through the 3-high mill shown in the lower left-hand part of the figure. After reheating, it was further rolled to 0·3-in thickness on the 3-high mill seen in the upper left-hand. Immediately afterwards, without further reheating, it was presented to the train of 2-high stands. These had rolls $24\frac{5}{8}$ in $\times$ 59 in and were spaced 9 ft apart. The speeds of these rolls were so arranged by gearing that the strip was being rolled by all five stands simultaneously, emerging at a thickness of 0·110 in and with a speed of 390 ft a minute. However, this mill was not a success because of its low speed and inadequate power [12]. These led to various difficulties—for example, the thickness of the finished strip showed unacceptable variations—and in 1907 the scheme was abandoned. It took another twenty-five years of intensive development before the continuous strip-sheet mill achieved full success.

VI. WIRE

The earliest method of wire-manufacture consisted in rolling bars of iron, copper, or brass into long flat strips, about $\frac{1}{4}$-in thick, which were then slit lengthwise into strips of square section. These were converted into round wire by drawing through a series of holes in a steel die-plate. For certain special requirements this method persisted throughout the century, and is indeed still used, but the great quantities of iron, steel, and copper wire which were of such vital importance to the progress of mechanical and electrical engineering required much more highly productive processes.

The rolling of hammered bars in grooved rolls was undertaken from the time of Henry Cort (vol IV, p 106), and by 1830 this method appears to have been well established, rod of $\frac{5}{16}$ to $\frac{9}{32}$ of an inch in diameter being readily available in coils of from 10 to 20 lb on the basis of the standard wrought iron practice. Up to that time there had been no great demand for wire in large quantities or great lengths, but the advent of the telegraph changed the situation abruptly. Urgent demands led to the founding of a complete new industry, with Warrington as its centre, within a remarkably short space of time. Grooved rolls, known as the 'Belgian train', were adopted generally; these presented a series of decreasing apertures of constantly changing section, from square successively to diamond, oval, and circular, the object being to work the metal right through its cross-section. In 1862 George Bedson invented and patented a continuous rolling-train, which was installed in the works of Johnson & Brothers at Manchester. The sixteen 2-high rolling-stands of the train were arranged with their axes alternately horizontal and vertical, thus avoiding the necessity of turning the rod periodically in its transit through the mill, as in the older Belgian mill. By means of a system of fixed gears the speed of rotation of each succeeding stand was higher than that of its predecessor, thus preventing the production of slack due to the elongation of the rod as rolling progressed. Wrought iron bars of $1\frac{1}{16}$-in square section, and up to 100 lb in weight, preheated in a continuous furnace, were rolled to $\frac{1}{4}$-in rod, and the mill was capable of turning out 20 tons in 10 hours [13].

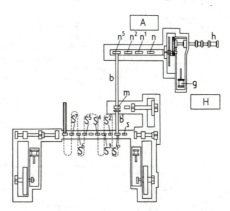

FIGURE 327—*Lay-out of early Garrett wire-rod mill.*

Rod-rolling plant of a much more productive and flexible character had its origin in the designs of William Garrett, who, with an engineer named Charles Hill Morgan, erected a number of plants in the United States from 1882 onwards.

A typical early Garrett mill is illustrated in plan in figure 327. Blooms 4 inches square are heated in the furnace (H), and passed to the bloom train (h) driven by the engine (g). The resulting billet, about $1\frac{1}{2}$-in square, is cut to length and reheated in the furnace (A), and is passed to and fro through the rolling-stands n to n^5. From n^5 the bar passes through a tube (b) to the stand (m) and thence to the series of stands (s^2) to (s^7). It passes between these separate rolls in grooves or tubes serving as repeaters, so that it is guided from one to the next: the catcher, who in earlier installations caught the end of the wire and turned it into the next roll groove, was thus dispensed with. Such a mill had more than one billet at a time in the rolling-train, and using billets of 120–180 lb weight would roll some 50 tons of rod of $\frac{5}{16}$-in to $\frac{1}{4}$-in diameter in 9 hours, the product being obtained in coil form. Mills of this type rolled mild steel made by either the Bessemer or the open-hearth process, as well as carbon steels made by the crucible process for the production of wires of high tensility. Wrought iron had by this time been largely superseded [13].

As already stated, the demand for wire in long lengths arose from the needs of the newly invented telegraph, which employed iron wires of $\frac{1}{6}$-in diameter. The first cable between Dover and Calais in 1850, and the first transatlantic cable of 1858, both had iron-wire conductors (vol IV, ch 22). Copper wire came into use shortly afterwards, and for making it steel-rolling practice was followed, using Garrett-type mills. Bars for wire-making were cast from tough pitch copper in flat open moulds, the section being normally 4 in square. Wire bars weighed 100–200 lb, and the ends were slightly tapered to facilitate entry into the rolls.

Drawing of rod into wire had been carried out from early times on a block.

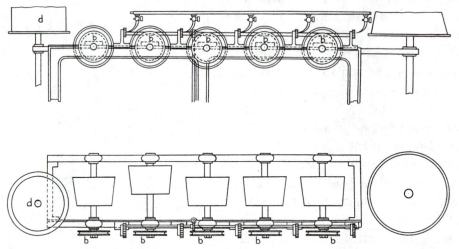

FIGURE 328—*Early continuous wire-drawing machine. The wire passed from right to left over the drums b, and was finally wound on the drum d.*

This block or drum on which the wire was coiled rotated on a vertical axis and provided the tension necessary to pull the wire through the die. Power-driven blocks were generally employed from the early nineteenth century. Steel die-plates were used for the larger sizes of wire, but for fine wires dies of diamond or other jewels were used from an early date. Iron wire was annealed in wrought iron drums and pickled in acid, sulphuric acid being in general use during the latter half of the nineteenth century. The value of a coating of lime in facilitating the drawing of iron was known as early as 1750, but does not appear to have come into common usage until about 1860. Heavier wire was drawn after drying the lime coat, using olive oil or soap as lubricant, but the finer sizes were more often drawn wet. The first multi-block machine appears to have been built about 1875, and copper wire drawn from 34 gauge to 48 gauge (0·0092 in to 0·0016 in) on a 14-die machine was shown at the

Glasgow Exhibition in 1888. Machines having more general application came into use following a patent lodged by S. H. Byrne in 1885 (cf figure 328). The wire was driven between each of the dies by passing over drums (b), and was finally wound on the drum (d). The dies were rotated by gears, a device intended to prevent unequal wear but subsequently found to be unnecessary, and a stream of soft-soap solution impinged on the mouth of the die. The speeds of the drums were carefully adjusted to accommodate the elongation of the wire, and drawing-speeds of 1000 ft a minute in the final die were attained as early as 1890 [14].

No history of the manufacture of steel wire can be complete without mention of the invention, by James Horsfall in 1854, of the process of 'patenting'. Before this date high-tensile steel wire was made from carbon steel by heat-treatment of the coil as a whole. Horsfall found that by using a continuous process, in which the wire passes in a single strand through a heating furnace, then a quenching bath, and finally a tempering bath of molten lead, the highest tensile strength could be obtained, combined with a high degree of ductility and ability to withstand twisting. A veil of secrecy was maintained over this process until well into the present century, but its use nevertheless spread until it eventually became standard practice. At the end of the last century high-tensile steel wire was known as plough wire because of its use in steam-ploughing (p 12). Stranded high-tensile steel wires were also employed extensively for aerial rope-ways, mine ropeways, and bridges, a notable early example being the Brooklyn suspension-bridge (p 509) in New York, erected in 1869–83. Cables for this bridge were each composed of some 6400 separate wires of '100 ton' high-tensile steel, the span being 1595 ft. Wire was also in great demand for musical instruments; the very considerable market and high prices offered for high-tensile steel piano-wire, capable of maintaining its tension without loss of pitch, created a tremendous rivalry between British and continental manufacturers [14].

Many ancillary trades of considerable importance were based on the use and manipulation of wire. In the early nineteenth century small nails were sheared from sheet. The sheet was cut to the width required for the length of the nail and was fed forward into a shear-blade set at a small angle, being turned over between each stroke of the blade. The tapered nail, of rectangular section, was headed in another machine. Iron nails were made for joinery, and copper nails for attaching the sheathing to ships' bottoms. Before the end of the century, however, nail machines using mild steel wire were capable of turning out 300 nails a minute, cutting and pointing being carried out simultaneously; heading was done in the movement which ejected the product [14].

Pins were generally made from brass wire; in Britain the industry was origin-ally located at Stroud, but its centre later moved to Birmingham. Writing in 1891, Bucknall Smith stated that current daily production of pins was 50 m, the wholesale price of ordinary pins varying from 1s 3d to 3s a lb, 16 000 being the average number to the pound [14]. Machines for the manufacture of needles were equally advanced at this date. These were made in pairs, the ends of the wire being pointed simultaneously and the eyes stamped out at the centre. The wire was then cut in half, the fractured surfaces ground smooth, and the two

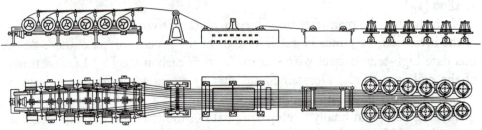

FIGURE 329—*Elevation and plan of continuous wire galvanizing plant, c 1880. Mechanically driven spoolers* (left) *pull wire from the coils* (right) *through the acid bath* (right centre) *and zinc bath* (left centre).

halves hardened and tempered. Cleaning, burnishing, and polishing followed, the wholesale value of the product being between 1s and 5s a thousand.

At the end of the century, too, the making of umbrella frames had become an important use for wire, a special grooved section being drawn for this purpose. Fox & Company of Sheffield carried out manufacture from the steel ingot to the finished umbrella frame, which weighed between 5 and 6 oz, and the business reached enormous proportions by the end of the century.

Mention must also be made of the many ingenious machines for producing woven wire products which were developed and perfected within twenty-five years of the first quantity-production of steel wire by means of Bedson's rolling-mill (p 621) in 1862. Products included wire netting, fencing, woven wire mat-tresses, and stranded wire rope.

VII. GALVANIZING

Reference to the zinc coating of iron occurs in the second half of the eigh-teenth century, but the industrial process dates from the invention of M. Sorel in 1836 of a practical coating process in which the iron is pickled in acid and fluxed with ammonium chloride before dipping in molten zinc. The protective action of zinc towards iron was well known from Faraday's researches on gal-vanic currents, and the practical success of galvanized iron in outdoor uses led to rapid growth of the industry from 1840 onwards. One of its earliest applications was for corrugated sheet, rolls for the production of which had been developed by John Spencer of West Bromwich in 1844. Corrugated galvanized iron sheeting was soon being made in considerable quantities for the roofing of buildings all over the world. The galvanizing of wire by dipping bundles or coils in molten zinc began with the introduction of the telegraph. In 1860 George Bedson invented a machine for continuously annealing and galvanizing iron and steel wire. The wire was passed as a continuous strand

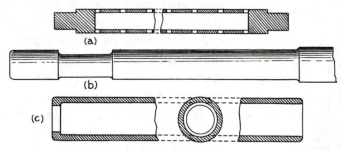

FIGURE 330—*Green's patent for solid-drawn tubes.*

through an annealing furnace, then through acid pickle, and so to the bath of molten zinc, being finally wound on a reel. A typical installation of the 1880s illustrating the principle is shown in figure 329. Galvanizing was soon being carried out on steel wires used for a great variety of outdoor purposes, including ropeways, guy-wires for suspension-bridges, and wire fencing.

Making galvanized wire for fencing became a very extensive industry in the last part of the nineteenth century. Modern methods of wire fencing, including the use of stranded galvanized wire tautened by means of ratchets, were established by about 1880. Barbed wire was introduced in the United States at about the same time, although it was not generally accepted in Europe until much later. Very large quantities of stranded and barbed wire for cattle-fencing were exported to the colonies and South America from British and German wire mills.

VIII. TUBES

In the early nineteenth century, tubes were mainly manufactured from wrought iron rolled out to narrow strip. This strip was folded across its width over a mandrel bar, with a suitable overlap which could subsequently be welded by hammering the joint while hot. Copper tubes were made in a similar manner with either a lap or a scarf joint, and the seam was then brazed with brass, using borax as a flux. Both iron and copper tubes were frequently sized by drawing through a die, but without any internal plug or mandrel; there was, therefore, no appreciable reduction in wall-thickness.

The making of seamed lead tube had been abandoned long before this period, seamless tube being made from the beginning of the century by casting the lead in a mould with a steel bar as core. The steel core was then used as a mandrel for rolling down or drawing out the lead tube, a method originating in a patent taken out by James Wilkinson in 1790. In 1838 Charles Green took out a patent for the manufacture of brass and copper tubes on a similar principle, but embodying a number of new features [15]. Green proposed to cast his hollow shell round a sand core formed over a perforated iron tube. This was used with a split cylindrical mould, made of cast iron, placed in a vertical position for casting. Figure 330 shows sections of the core bar (a), mandrel bar (b), and the hollow casting (c), taken from Green's subsequent patent of 1841 [16]. The casting is shown with a rim at one end to fit the shoulder of the mandrel. The tube was drawn down on a chain-driven draw-bench, and it is interesting to note that the die is specified as being of wrought iron 'with steel welded in to form a lining to the hole through it'. The tube was to be drawn down through a succession of dies of decreasing diameter, being withdrawn from the mandrel as necessary for annealing, and then returned for further drawing. The mandrel bar had an attachment for the draw-gear at both ends of the form illustrated, so that, by reversing the bar and tube on the draw-bench, the tube could be stripped off the bar by pulling through a dummy die-plate. Finally, the tube was annealed and pickled in acid ready for use. In a later patent (1851), Green proposed that the tubes should be left in the hard condition after the final drawing operation, the ends alone being annealed to facilitate fitting into the tube plate [17].

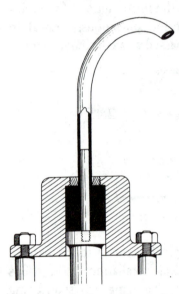

[1]FIGURE 331—*Burr's press for extruding lead tube (in section). 1820.*

Green's method of manufacturing tubes was widely adopted by Birmingham tube-makers, although some preferred to roll the cast shell on the mandrel bar using grooved rolls, the draw-bench being retained only for finishing. Rolling or drawing of cast shells became the principal method of making steam-engine condenser tubes of brass and other alloys, and remained so for more than half a century. Many features of the original patent, for example the design of the double-ended mandrel bar, became standard practice. Green's method of tube manufacture was well suited to the manufacture of narrow, thin-walled tubes, say of $\frac{1}{2}$ inch to 1 inch diameter and some 0·040–0·080 inch in thickness of wall. Such tubes were required in large numbers for steam-condensers. Green had proposed that the method should be used for the manufacture of textile printing-rolls, the diameters of which are generally some 4–6 in, with wall-thicknesses upwards of 1 in. It is obvious, however, that very heavy draw-benches would be required for this purpose, exceeding anything available at that time.

Extrusion, the second important method of tube manufacture to originate in the nineteenth century, also derived from the practice used for lead. The proposal that lead should be made into tube by squirting under hydraulic pressure through an annular orifice was suggested by Joseph Bramah in 1797, but the first practical machine on this principle was constructed and operated by Thomas Burr, a Shrews-bury plumber, in 1820. The arrangement of Burr's press is shown in figure 331. A cylindrical container is sealed at its lower end by the upper end of a hydraulic ram (c) into which is secured a short cylindrical bar serving as a mandrel (d). With the ram in its bottom position, lead is poured into the annular space around the mandrel. When it has solidified, the die (b) is screwed into position and pressure is applied, whereupon the lead pipe is extruded in a continuous length between mandrel and die. In later years many improvements to this simple machine were effected, but of special importance is the application of lead extrusion to the sheathing of electrical cables in order to protect them from damage and render them impervious to water. In 1879 a press for this purpose was designed in France by Barel, and this was immediately followed by others generally similar in conception. A section showing the vertical form of press generally adopted is shown in figure 332. Lead was poured into the container, and when solid was compressed by a descending ram. The lead flowed round the cable (which in the figure passes through the machine from left to right), emerging as a continuous coating. The two streams of lead weld together at the temperature, 200–250° C, at which the extrusion is carried out [18].

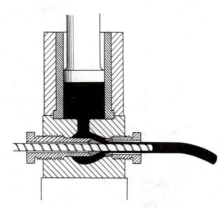

FIGURE 332—*Press for sheathing electric cable with lead (in section).*

Many efforts were made to adapt the extrusion technique to copper and copper alloys, but the type of equipment in use was quite unsuited to the high temperatures and pressures required for extruding these much more refractory materials. The first industrial application of extrusion to the production of copper tubes and cylinders was by the Broughton Copper Company in 1893: the arrangement of the press is shown in figure 333. The copper billet was separately heated to a temperature of about 850° C and placed in the vertical container; the hydraulic ram then descended and forced its way down through the centre of the billet, the copper being extruded upwards to form a short hollow cylinder. After removing this cylinder from the container, the base was sawn off and the shell was machined or cold-worked to the required dimensions. The method was particularly adapted to making very large copper tubes. It was much more suited than Green's process, moreover, to the manufacture of copper rollers for calico-printing, the demand for which had increased substantially with the development in Lancashire of the industry for making printed cotton fabrics.

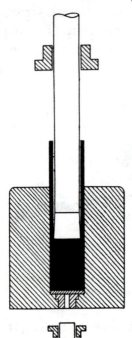

FIGURE 333—*Vertical press for making closed-end copper tube shell (in section).*

The above process was greatly improved upon by Everitt in 1902 (figure 334), who proposed to employ a horizontal container (a), open at its wider end to receive the billet (b), and having a narrow opening at the opposite end which was sealed by a secondary hydraulic ram with a short plug (c). The piercing bar (m), guided by the centring plate (n), was forced down almost to the base of the billet; at the last moment the plug (c) was withdrawn so that the piercer could travel right through, so making a complete cylinder. This avoided wasting the material which in the original method formed the base [19].

Further applications of extrusion to copper alloys had to await the inventions of Alexander Dick in the last decade of the nineteenth century. The importance of Dick's contribution was that the container for the hot billet, the die-holder, and the main hydraulic ram were all separately mounted components of the hydraulic press, so that they could be moved independently in relation to each other. The flexibility of operation to which these inventions gave rise enabled copper and a great variety of copper alloys to be readily extruded into a wide range of products. Some of these, such as tube shells, formed the basis for cold-drawing of small tubes, and superseded the use of Green's cast solid billets. Others, such as solid bars and sections in a great variety of sizes, were finished products. To consider the development of these processes, however, would take us beyond our period.

The production of seamless steel tubes depended on an entirely novel principle announced by the brothers Max and Reinhard Mannesmann in 1885 (p 63). In this process the hot billet is placed between rotating rolls, which compress it in one direction and produce a tension in another, the two opposing tensions tending to cause central rupture. The action of the rolls drives the hot billet forward, and by the insertion of a stationary piercing-bar the billet is caused to open out and form a tube, the diameter and wall-thickness of which can be varied

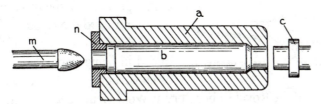

FIGURE 334—*Horizontal press for tube shell (in section).*

within considerable limits. The Mannesmann process was first operated by the Landore Siemens Steel Company of Swansea in 1887. The plant consisted of six Mannesmann machines, the largest being capable of piercing solid billets of up to 10-in diameter [20]. From the Mannesmann machines the tube stock was fed to Pilger mills, a process for which a British patent was granted to Max Mannesmann in 1891, following an earlier German application. In this process the tube is hot-forged over a steel mandrel-bar by the use of grooved rolls with diameters varying in the manner of cams. Between the compression phases, in which the tube is driven forward by the rolls, the actuating mechanism rotates and partially returns the tube, so that it progresses in a series of short steps. The Landore Siemens Steel Company maintained its position as the principal manufacturer of seamless steel tubes until almost the end of the century, when a plant designed and created at Youngstown, Ohio, by Stiefel, an engineer from Landore, became the principal world producer [20].

IX. DEEP DRAWING OF CARTRIDGE CASES

It has already been seen how the availability in large quantities of cheap cold-drawn wire, of high quality and uniformity, gave rise to great new industries in the period 1865–90. Cold-rolled sheet and strip have a similar history, although in the same period the scope of these developments was more restricted. The application to small articles of ornamental brass-ware, buttons, buckles, coins, and other typical Birmingham small wares was merely a matter of developing and improving existing types of machines, and no outstanding new techniques were called into being. The manufacture of deep-drawn products, however, merits comment, especially as it was an important landmark in the development of the basic infantry weapon, the rifle.

The first half of the nineteenth century had seen the muzzle-loader superseded by the breech-loader, and the introduction of a paper cartridge containing detonator, propellent, and projectile made up in a single package. The military consequences of this development were far-reaching. In existing systems the cartridge was relatively vulnerable to the weather and to the rigours of battle, while the sealing or obturation of the gases produced in firing depended on the accuracy of construction of the breech-block.

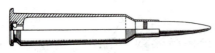

FIGURE 335—*Metal cartridge, showing components.*

E. M. Boxer, of the Royal Laboratory at Woolwich, developed the first metallic cartridge; the percussion cap was located in the base and the bullet sealed the nose of the cartridge. This cartridge had an iron base, and the walls were made from thin coiled brass wire. The Boxer cartridge was selected by the British Army in 1869 for use with the Martini–Henry rifle. Simultaneously with Boxer's work at Woolwich, George Kynoch had perfected a solid-drawn brass cartridge-case and manufactured many millions of such cases for foreign governments. It was ignored by the British, however, in favour of the Boxer type until 1882, when, in the Sudan campaign, trouble experienced with the jamming of the coiled cartridge-case led to its abandonment [21].

Kynoch's early solid-drawn cases were virtually of the same design and construction as those of today. The assembly of components in the rifle cartridge is shown in figure 335 and the various stages in the manufacture of the case are shown in figure 336. The starting-point is brass strip about 0·14-in thick, and the first stage is to blank out a disk and form it into a shallow cup; this involves the use of a double-acting crank-press. The tool which shears out the blank is actuated independently of the punch, which subsequently pushes the blank through the die plate to form the cup. After annealing to soften the metal and pickling to remove scale, the cups are further drawn, using smaller punches and dies, on a machine with automatic feed. So the process continues, with annealing, pickling, and further drawing. However, all operations from the fourth draw onwards are carried out without further annealing, so that the cartridge finally undergoes a considerable amount of cold-working, and thus has sufficient strength and elasticity to withstand the explosive force of the pro- pellent without deformation. The bullet is made, like the case, from a thin shell of cupro-nickel or copper-zinc alloy. Starting with a cup, the wall is drawn out in subsequent operations, and finally turned over the inner core of steel or lead.

Kynoch developed manufacture of this type of cartridge to such an extent that in the Boer War he was able to manufacture and load two million complete

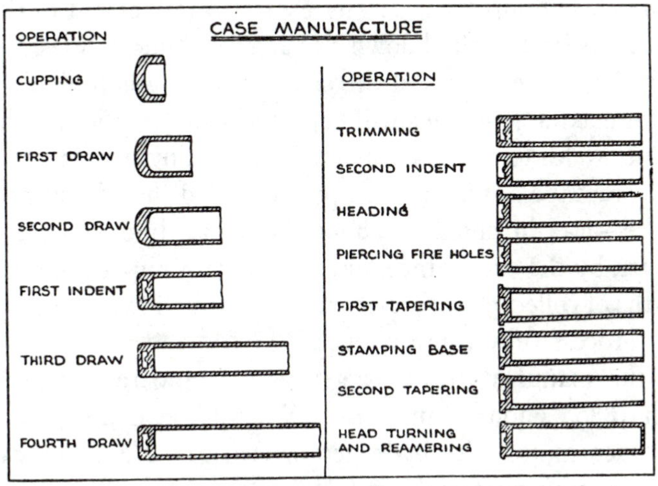

FIGURE 336—*Stages in manufacture of solid-drawn cartridge-case.*

rounds a week. Cupping-and-drawing became an important method for the pro- duction of small brass and copper tubular components, and was the cheapest and most economical method of making all types of small thin-walled tubes. It was thus complementary to the processes of piercing, extrusion, and draw-bench working which had been brought into being for larger and heavier products.

X. WELDING

Although the two principal methods of welding, by gas torch and electric arc, were introduced during the nineteenth century, they had little influence on the processes of metal fabrication until its last decade.

Brazing with brass of about 50 per cent copper content continued to be the normal method of making seams in copper, borax being employed as flux. Joints made in this way would normally have a copper content of about 60 per cent, the balance of the zinc having been lost by volatilization in making the joint. How- ever, silver solders, the use of which had for centuries been a closely guarded

secret of craftsmen in the precious metals, came into more general use for joining base metals. It is interesting to note that joints in the transatlantic cable of
1865, the first to employ copper for transmission, were made in mid-ocean by
silver soldering with a copper-silver-zinc alloy [22].

Carbon-arc welding was invented by Nicolas von Benardos, in 1885 [23]. One
terminal of the electrical generator was connected to the workpiece and the
other to a carbon rod; the arc drawn between the two produced local melting of
the iron or steel, and additional metal was provided from a steel wire, the tip of
which was introduced into the arc as necessary. Replacement of the carbon rod
by steel, which was itself melted down and acted as filler, followed shortly afterwards, and in the last ten years of the century there was limited application of
arc-welding for making joints in small engineering assemblies and in ornamental
iron-work. Butt-welding of rods—effected by striking an arc between the two
ends until they reached a sufficient temperature, and then forcing them together
under pressure—was invented at about the same time, but had found little
application even by the end of the century. Its main importance was for joining
together lengths of rolled rod preparatory to drawing down, in order to make the
wire-drawing process fully continuous [24].

Following the manufacture of oxygen as a commercial product by Brin's
process about 1880, Thomas Fletcher of Warrington in 1887 devised a blow-
pipe using oxygen mixed with hydrogen or coal-gas. He demonstrated the use
of this flame for melting metals and for cutting steel, a process whose first
application appears to have been in safe-breaking! The extensive employment
of the torch in welding had to await the commercial availability of acetylene at
the turn of the century [24].

XI. PLATING

The working of silver and gold had always been an important industry and
one quick to adopt new methods. Indeed, many methods of metal-working, such
as cold-strip rolling and wire-drawing on blocks, probably originated from the
methods employed for precious metals (vol III, ch 2). Silversmiths and gold-
smiths, ever conscious of the limited market for their wares because of high
cost, had developed plating as a means of reducing the requirement of
precious metal.

Close-plating was a centuries-old process. The base metal article was carefully tinned and a layer of tin was likewise applied to one or both sides of a piece
of silver foil cut to the required size. The two were then sweated together and
surplus tin or solder was removed by scraping and filing. Old Sheffield plate,

first made by Thomas Bolsover in 1743, consisted of copper with a coating of sterling silver on one or both sides, and was produced by rolling together carefully cleaned copper and silver plates (vol IV, p 130). However, the material was expensive and its success depended, at least during parts of its history, on the maintenance of an excise duty on solid silver ware [25].

The fire-gilding process of plating base metals, or more often silver, with a thin film of gold, had been practised from early times. The article was first cleaned and then placed in a solution of mercurous nitrate and nitric acid, so that it acquired a thin coating of mercury. The surface was next rubbed with an amalgam of gold and mercury, in the form of a stiff paste held in a porous fabric bag, until a smooth coating of the pasty mixture had been applied. Finally, the article was heated on a charcoal fire to drive off the mercury and the residual gold was burnished.

The process of plating base metals with silver and gold by electro-deposition was announced in a patent taken out by George Richards Elkington and Henry Elkington in 1840. This proposed the use of electrolytes prepared by dissolving silver and gold, or their oxides, in potassium or sodium cyanide solution. The articles to be coated were cleaned from grease and scale and immersed in the solution, current being supplied through a bar of metallic zinc or other electro-positive metal immersed in a separate fluid or electrolyte separated from the silver or gold solution by a porous diaphragm. Silver oxide was added from time to time to maintain the concentration of silver. Copper, brass, and German silver were suggested as the most suitable metals for plating [26].

A second patent, granted in 1842 to Henry Beaumont, an employee of the Elkingtons, covered some 430 additional salts of silver which might have application in electroplating. In the same year, John Stephen Woolrich obtained a patent for the use of a magneto-electric machine (p 183), the plating solution being the soluble double sulphite of silver and potassium. Licences were first issued by the Elkingtons in 1843, but Thomas Prime of Birmingham appears to have been the first to plate commercially by the use of the magneto-electric machine using Woolrich's patent; Dr Percy, the famous metallurgist, claims to have conducted Faraday himself round Prime's works in 1845 [27]. Subsequently, the Elkingtons took over Woolrich's patent and were able to command a minimum royalty of £150 from all who practised electroplating. In spite of this, however, electroplate rapidly supplanted Old Sheffield plate. According to Bradbury, the authority on Old Sheffield plate, the Sheffield directory of 1852 contained as the last entry under this heading one single representative remaining from the many practising the art five years previously [25].

Gold and silver plating had a tremendous effect on the jewelry industry of the later nineteenth century. Silver-plated ware, such as spoons, forks, tea-pots, urns, and cruets, was manufactured in very great quantities from brass or German silver. In the main the solid sterling silver and Old Sheffield plate designs were copied. The production of gold-plated jewelry, such as brooches, chains, buttons, and pins, developed and expanded to an even greater extent, and over the next twenty-five years Britain enjoyed a virtual monopoly in this field, goods being exported to all parts of the world. By 1890, however, British goods were being excluded from many countries by protective tariffs, and by the end of the century Germany had become the major manufacturer.

REFERENCES

[1] '100 Years in Steel.' Thomas Firth & John Brown, Sheffield. 1937.
[2] COOKSON, H. E. *Proc. Staffs. Iron St. Inst.*, **49,** 1–47, 1933–4.
[3] SHEPHERD, E. S. *J. phys. Chem.*, **8,** 421–35, 1904.
[4] SCHIB, K. and ONADE, R. 'Johann Conrad Fischer, 1773–1854.' Fischer, Schaffhausen. 1954.
[5] MACKAY, A. *Bull. Instn Metall.*, **3,** 15–27, 1951.
[6] DEBRAY, H. L. *C.R. Acad. Sci.*, Paris, **43,** 925–7, 1856.
[7] MONTEFIORE-LEVI, C. *J. Iron St. Inst.*, **7,** 408–13, 1873.
[8] PERCY, J. 'Metallurgy: Iron and Steel.' London. 1880.
[9] *Engineering*, **1,** 384, 1866.
[10] HOARE, W. E. *Bull. Instn Metall.*, **3,** 4–26, March 1951.
[11] TRUBSHAW, E. *J. Iron St. Inst.*, **22,** 252–60, 1883.
[12] "Austrian Continuous Sheet Mill." *Iron Age*, **70,** 20, 1902.
[13] BEDSON, J. P. *J. Iron St. Inst.*, **44,** 77–93, 1893.
[14] SMITH, J. B. 'A Treatise upon Wire, its Manufacture and Uses.' Offices of *Engineering*, London. 1891.
[15] British Patent No. 7707. 1838.
[16] British Patent No. 8838. 1841.
[17] British Patent No. 13,752. 1851.
[18] PEARSON, C. E. *Trans. Newcomen Soc.*, **21,** 109–22, 1940.
[19] British Patent No. 4132. 1902.
[20] EVANS, G. 'Manufacture of Seamless Tubes, Ferrous and Non-Ferrous.' Witherby, London. 1934.
[21] 'Textbook of Small Arms.' H.M. Stationery Office, London. 1929.
[22] BROOKER, H. R. and BEATSON, E. V. 'Industrial Brazing.' Iliffe, London. 1953.
[23] RÜHLMANN, R. *Z. Ver. dtsch. Ing.*, **31,** 863–7, 1887.
[24] FOX, F. A. and HIPPERSON, A. J. *Sheet Metal Ind.*, **28,** 465–72, 1951.
[25] BRADBURY, F. 'History of Old Sheffield Plate.' Macmillan, London. 1912.
[26] British Patent No. 8447. 1840.
[27] PERCY, J. 'Metallurgy: Silver and Gold.' London. 1880.

BIBLIOGRAPHY

BEVAN, G. P. (Ed.). 'British Manufacturing Industries' (2nd ed.). London. 1878.

COOK, M. "The Development of the Non-Ferrous Metal Industries in Birmingham." *Metal Ind., Lond.*, **48**, 485–90, 1936.

DAVIES, R. C. "The History of Electrodeposition." *Sheet Metal Ind.*, **28**, 477–81, 1951.

EPPELSHEIMER, D. "The Development of the Continuous Strip Mill." *J. Iron St. Inst.*, **138**, 185–203, 1938.

FORESTIER-WALKER, E. R. 'A History of the Wire Rope Industry of Great Britain.' Federation of Wire Rope Manufacturers of Great Britain, Sheffield. 1952.

GRIFFITHS, R. "History of Non-Ferrous Industries in South Wales." *Metal Ind., Lond.*, **60**, 90–93, 1942.

HAMMOND, G. B. "The Manufacture of Tin-Plates." *J. Iron St. Inst.*, **52**, 24–37, 1897.

LARKE, E. C. "The Rolling of Metals and Alloys. Historical Development of the Rolling Mill." *Sheet Metal Ind.*, **30**, 863–78, 989–98, 1081–91, 1953; **31**, 61–72, 241–8, 325–34, 338, 408, 411–25, 1954.

LEWIS, K. B. "The Shape of Things to Come." *Wire & Wire Prod.*, **17**, 15–23, 26–27, 56–60, 1942.

MORRAL, F. R. "A Chronology of Wire and Wire Products." *Ibid.*, **20**, 862–6, 885–7, 1945.

PEARSON, C. E. 'Extrusion of Metals' (rev. ed.). Chapman & Hall, London. 1953.

SHARMAN, J. C. and GARLAND, R. J. "Drop Forging." *Engng Insp.*, **10**, no. 2, 7–17, 1945.

THOMAS, L. "Development of Wire-Rod Production." *Wire Ind.*, **17**, 736–9, 743, 823, 825, 827, 903–5, 907–8, 1950.

TIMMINS, S. (Ed.). 'Birmingham and the Midland Hardware District.' London. 1866.

Lading refined copper in the form of flat cakes. These would be hot rolled to sheet.

26

MACHINE-TOOLS

D. F. GALLOWAY

I. GENERAL

THE development of machine-tools before 1850 was largely the work of a few men of outstanding vision and technical ability, who usually possessed in addition great tenacity and strength of personality. Such were Bentham (1757–1831) and M. I. Brunel (1769–1849) with their machines at Portsmouth dockyard for mass-producing pulley-blocks; Maudslay (1771–1831), the most gifted of all the early machine-tool makers; Bramah (1748–1814), with his range of special-purpose machines for making burglar-proof locks; Nasmyth (1808–90), with his inspired conception of the steam-hammer; and Sir Joseph Whitworth (1803–87), who was Britain's leading machine-tool maker in 1850 (vol IV, ch 14).

In comparison, the machine-tool builders of the second half of the nineteenth century appear less colourful, and it is often difficult to trace clearly the roles they played in the evolution of particular machines. Similar developments often occurred simultaneously in different factories, and the personalities of the designers tended to merge into the background as machine-tool firms grew in size.

An illuminating commentary on developments in the first half of the nineteenth century was made by William Fairbairn (1789–1874) in his inaugural address as president of the British Association at Manchester in 1861:

When I first entered this city [in 1814], the whole of the machinery was executed by hand. There were neither planing, slotting, nor shaping machines; and, with the exception of very imperfect lathes and a few drills, the preparatory operations of construction were effected entirely by the hands of the workmen. Now, everything is done by machine tools with a degree of accuracy which the unaided hand could never accomplish. The automaton or self-acting machine has within itself an almost creative power . . . [1].

By modern standards, however, the machine-tools of the period were still comparatively crude. Plate 41 B shows the interior of a factory for making locks, safes, and strong-rooms. All the machines are relatively simple and light in construction, and are belt-driven from overhead pulleys. None of them is fitted with guards to protect operators from moving machine-parts, driving-belts, and so on, and the high rate of accidents is thus not surprising. Machine operators are heavily outnumbered by the workmen at the benches in the background, suggesting that handwork was the greater element of factory activity.

The general-purpose machine-tools of this period could cut steel at a speed of about 50 linear ft per minute, but in general they lacked power, precision, and facility of operation. One consequence was that the accuracy of the work produced on early machine-tools was poor by modern standards. This inaccuracy is partly attributable to the crude measuring-equipment then used by machinists, but was mainly caused by deficiencies in the design of the machines, errors in the manufacture of lead-screws, slide-ways, and bearings, and a general lack of rigidity, arising in some cases from the use of wood in the construction of the machine.

Although machines of different make varied considerably in detail, D. K. Clark, superintendent of the machinery department at the International Exhibition held at South Kensington in 1862, could point out that:

Machinists are approximating to common types of structure and workmanship. Sliding surfaces are scraped; screws are uniform, frame-castings are hollow; all lathe-beds are of cast iron, they are all planed; headstocks are alike, they have back-gear, conical bearings, and sliding spindles. Screws are all cut by screws; wheel-lathes have all double face-plates, with circular racks on the back to drive them; and they are all adapted for working singly, simultaneously, or conjointly. Above all, machinists are unanimous in the application of self-acting feeds.

II. SIR JOSEPH WHITWORTH

Britain's lead in the construction of machine-tools in the middle of the nineteenth century was primarily due to Sir Joseph Whitworth. His exceptional displays of machine-tools at the Exhibitions of 1851 and 1862, his classic work on uniform screw-threads, his machine for measuring to one-millionth part of an inch, and his system of end-measurement, all show his incomparable skill in penetrating to the heart of mechanical problems and devising novel solutions to them. Among other things, Whitworth introduced the hollow or box casting for the frames of machine-tools, and this was considered so important an advance that Clark was moved to exclaim: 'The capacity of the box casting for resisting strains of every variety—longitudinal, transverse, and torsional—is amazing, and if it is not the most useful thing these exhibitors have done, it is certainly one of the happiest.' Whitworth had also given a lead to other machine-tool builders by casting small members of machine-tool frames integral with main castings, whereas the earlier practice, which tended to give machine-tools a fragmentary appearance, had been to bolt small castings on to large ones.

A vitally important factor in the superiority of Whitworth's machine-tools was his insistence on the application of rigorous principles of measurement. Early machine-tool builders encountered considerable difficulties because they lacked equipment for making precise measurements, and their problems were aggravated by the lack of consistent standards of measure. 'What exact notion', Whitworth asked, 'can any man have of such a size as a "bare sixteenth" or a "full thirty-second"?' These were normal statements of dimension in the mid-nineteenth century, until Whitworth rationalized workshop measurement by introducing a system of end-measurement based on the use of standard gauges with parallel ends. His machine for measuring to one-millionth part of an inch (figure 337) was designed to compare limit-gauges with his end-standards, and the words he spoke to the Institution of Mechanical Engineers when exhibiting this machine in 1856 are as universally acceptable today as they were revolutionary then:

FIGURE 337—*Whitworth's machine for measuring to one-millionth of an inch.*

We have in this mode of measurement all the accuracy we can desire; and we find in practice in the workshop that it is easier to work to the ten-thousandth of an inch from standards of end-measurement than to one-hundredth of an inch from lines on a two-foot rule. In all cases of fitting end-measure of length should be used instead of lines.

III. INFLUENCE OF VARIOUS FACTORS ON DEVELOPMENT

In the second half of the nineteenth century, machine-tool construction was profoundly affected by such developments as the wider application of the principles of interchangeable manufacture, improvements in cutting tool materials, the increased demand for small-arms as a result of wars in Europe and America, the introduction of new inventions, and the industrial application of electrical power. The influence of these factors penetrated into every aspect of machine-tool development.

Interchangeable manufacture. The basic principles of mass-production had been applied in Britain, France, and the United States in the late eighteenth and early nineteenth centuries, but there had been very little further progress in the production of large quantities of complicated components until Samuel Colt

(1814–62) and Elisha Root (1808–65) planned the manufacture of the Colt revolver at the Colt Armory, Hartford, Connecticut, in the years 1849–54. Root was a brilliant engineer who gave practical expression to Colonel Colt's determination to apply the principles of interchangeable manufacture at all stages of the production of the revolver. This implied the manufacture of standardized components, any proper selection of which could be assembled to make the finished product. Root designed and built numerous semi-automatic machine-tools (p 646), and made large numbers of gauges to ensure the accuracy of the work produced. He relied upon special jigs and fixtures to a far greater extent than ever before, their total cost being nearly equal to that of the machine-tools. The methods of manufacture adopted at the Colt Armory were brilliantly successful, and Root's principles were later adopted by other manufacturers.

Interchangeable manufacture in Britain was revolutionized when the small-arms factory at Enfield, Middlesex, was thoroughly reorganized after the visit to the United States of a British Royal Commission, including Whitworth and Nasmyth, appointed in 1853 to study the manufacture of small-arms (vol IV, p 441). Nasmyth was particularly impressed by the Springfield small-arms factory where, he wrote, 'by the use of machine tools specially designed to execute with the most unerring precision all the details of muskets and rifles, they were enabled to dispense with mere manual dexterity, and to produce arms to any amount'. Whitworth's report on the visit pointed out that:

The labouring classes [of the United States] are comparatively few in number, but this is counterbalanced by, and indeed may be regarded as one of the chief causes of, the eagerness with which they call in the aid of machinery . . . wherever it can be introduced, it is universally and willingly resorted to.

Many of the principles of the so-called American system of interchangeable manufacture were subsequently adopted in Britain, and some of the most useful machines developed in the United States for the production of small-arms were installed at Enfield. American procedures were evidently improved upon, for, according to Clark, the Americans had 'not attained the degree of nicety which has since been achieved at the Enfield factory'. An indication of the high standards of accuracy maintained at Enfield is given by the fact that 2000 rifles, each requiring more than 700 separate operations, were produced every week, the parts of each rifle being completely interchangeable with the corresponding parts of all other rifles made there.

New inventions. The history of the machine-tool industry after 1850 was also conditioned by new inventions such as those of the typewriter (p 689), sewing-machine (p 588), safety bicycle (p 416), and so on. As soon as public demand for the newly invented devices grew large, means had to be devised for producing great numbers of components accurately and economically. Throughout the second half of the century, as for seventy-five years previously, the commercial or technical success of new inventions was often delayed until improved machine-tools were developed. James Watt's steam-engine did not become fully practicable until Wilkinson built a more precise boring machine; the motor-car was an expensive luxury until Henry Ford revolutionized the production methods of the automobile industry; and though mechanical devices comparable to modern digital computers were designed in Britain in the nineteenth century the limitations of the techniques and machine-tools of the day prevented the manufacture of components of sufficient accuracy.

Influence of cutting tools. In 1850 the principal cutting tool material was plain carbon steel; tools made from this material did not have an economical working life at speeds greater than about 40 ft a minute. About 1868 Robert Mushet discovered that by adding tungsten and vanadium and increasing the manganese in tool steel, self-hardening or air-hardening tools could be produced (p 65). Mushet's steel reduced the uncertainties of heat-treatment and increased permissible cutting speeds from 40 ft a minute to about 70 ft a minute. The next major advance was the development of high-speed steel by Taylor and White at the end of the century. The new steel, which aroused world-wide interest at the Paris Exhibition of 1900, contained tungsten, chromium, and vanadium, and as it retained its hardness at red heat, cutting speeds of about 120 ft a minute could be attained. When both Mushet steel and high-speed steel were introduced, existing machine-tools could not fully exploit the merits of the new materials because they lacked rigidity, were under-powered, and tended to vibrate under heavy loads and at high cutting speeds. Much more robust and better proportioned machine-tools were then built, and greater attention was given to the design of spindle-bearings.

Development of the quick-change gear-box. The general quickening in the tempo of manufacture led to a widespread demand for machine-tools having broader ranges of speed and feed than could be obtained with stepped cone-pulleys and back-gears. With stepped pulleys, speed was changed by slipping the driving-belt from one pulley to another of different diameter; it was also often necessary to bolt the back-gear to the pulleys to obtain particular speeds. These deficiencies stimulated developments that eventually culminated in the introduction of the Norton gear-box in America in 1892. With the aid of this device various cutting speeds could be selected merely by moving a hand-lever.

Thus it greatly facilitated speed-changing while increasing the range of speeds available, and these advantages quickly led to its adoption by most machine-tool makers. Friction-drives, which gave infinitely variable spindle-speeds, were being developed in 1900, and one lathe had a friction-cone drive to the cross-slide to increase the spindle-speed in proportion to the reduction in diameter of the piece being worked during its machining, thus maintaining a uniform cutting speed throughout the operation.

Electrification of machine-tools. During most of the nineteenth century, power for driving machine-tools was derived from steam-engines which were often situated at a great distance from the machines. Factories were dark forests of belts, main-shafts, and counter-shafts. In 1873, however, a public demonstration of the use of electric power for driving machine-tools was given at the Vienna Exhibition. In the following year a visitor to the factory in Paris of the electrical engineer Gramme (p 188) saw:

> The whole of the lathes, tools and other machines driven by connecting one of his small lighting machines by means of a belt to the shafting, from which the steam engine was disconnected, which machine acting as a magnetic engine was driven at a speed of 815 r.p.m. by a derived current from one of his large machines which was producing on a second circuit at the same time a light of 2,400 candles.

By the end of the century, large electric motors were being used as a source of power, and soon afterwards machine-tool makers generally began to provide individual electric motors for driving their machines. At first the motors were usually mounted on a separate foundation some distance from the machine-tool, which was belt-driven in the usual way. Some makers were, however, already incorporating motors in the machine-tool structure, and one supplier prophetically stated that 'this construction gives rise to directly-connected machine-tools, a new line of machinery destined to be of great importance'. At the turn of the century a few machine-tools had two or more electric motors for separately driving the main spindle, feed-mechanisms, and other devices.

IV. DEVELOPMENTS IN PARTICULAR TYPES OF MACHINE-TOOL

Although detailed improvements in a particular family of machine-tools commonly reacted on the construction of most other types of machine, advances in general design usually occurred independently of developments in other machine-tools; hence it is convenient to consider each type separately.

Drilling machines. The general form and construction of drilling machines did not change radically between 1850 and 1900; the detailed improvements that were made arose mainly from the possibility of using higher speeds of rotation and feed following the introduction of Mushet steel and of improved twist-drills.

In 1862 Tomlinson described a drilling machine made by Whitworth & Company as 'one of the most complete tools of the kind ever constructed' (figure 338). The three-step cone-pulley B gave three spindle-speeds without the back-gear, and three lower speeds with the back-gear. Power-feed was applied to the spindle of the drill through two screw-wheels JJ, integral with the two small pulleys surrounded by friction-collars s. When the collars were clamped on to the pulleys, the screw-wheels were prevented from rotating; the stationary wheels acted as a nut for the screwed central section of the spindle, which was thus fed downwards as it rotated. When the friction-collars were released, the two wheels rotated with the spindle, which did not then move vertically. The feed-rate was adjusted by varying the amount of friction between the friction-collars and the screw-wheels. When the feed was disengaged, the spindle was returned to the top of its stroke by the balance-weight A. The circular work-plate K could be rotated round its axis by means of a worm and wheel, and could also be traversed towards or away from the frame by operating the crank which rotated, through gears, a screw engaging a stationary nut. The drill shown at the bottom of the spindle is the conventional flat drill of the period. The twist-drill was an innovation of the 1860s; it had an important influence on the development of drilling machines by permitting the use of higher speeds and feed-rates. By the end of the first decade of the twentieth century radial drilling machines had reached the stage of development illustrated in figure 339.

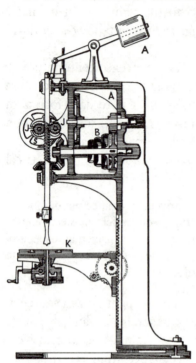

FIGURE 338—*Drilling machine made by Whitworth & Company in 1862.*

The advantages of drilling many holes simultaneously were obtained by the use of multiple-spindle drilling machines such as that shown in figure 340, which was described in a paper read to the Institution of Mechanical Engineers in 1860. This machine was constructed to drill holes 1 inch in diameter in the

$\frac{5}{8}$-in-thick plate used for the main side-girders of the Hungerford railway bridge over the Thames at Charing Cross. The drills rotated at 50 rpm, were hydraulically fed at approximately 0·040 inch a minute, and had an average life of 10 hours between re-grinds.

A slot-drilling machine was devised by Nasmyth for drilling or sinking slots or recesses in solid metal by traversing the drill or the work-piece laterally. One

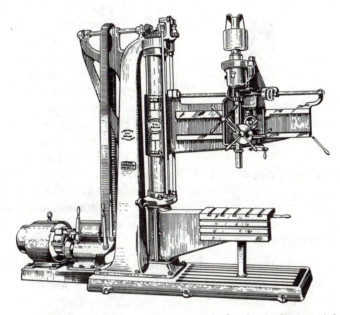

FIGURE 339—*Typical radial drilling machine made in the first decade of the twentieth century.*

of a range of slot-drilling and grooving-machines exhibited at the International Exhibition of 1862 is shown in figure 341. The headstock was reciprocated by means of a horizontal slotted disk and connecting-rod, and a nearly uniform velocity of translation was obtained through an eccentric gear. The machine was used not only for cutting slots but for drilling holes and key-ways, recessing solid metal, and so forth. The success of the slot-drilling machine was primarily due to the type of slot-drill devised by Nasmyth; this consisted of a flat-ended drill with the centre removed. Nasmyth described the development of the machine and drill as follows:

One of the most tedious and costly processes in the execution of the detail parts of machinery is the cutting out of Cottar Slots in piston rods, connecting rods, and key recesses in shafts. This operation used to be performed by drilling a row of holes through the solid body of the object, and then chipping away the intermediate metal between the

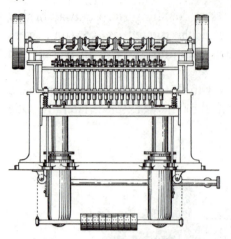

FIGURE 340—*Multiple-spindle drilling machine made for drilling girders of the Hungerford railway bridge.*

holes, and filing the rude slot so produced into its required form. The whole operation, as thus conducted, was one of the most tedious and irksome jobs that an engineer could be set to, and could only be performed by those possessed of the highest skill. What with broken chisels and files, and the tedious nature of the work, it was a most severe task to the very best men, not to speak of the heavy cost in wages.

In order to obviate all these disadvantages, I contrived an arrangement of a drilling machine, with a specially formed drill, which at once reduced the process to one of the easiest conducted in an engineer's workshop. The 'special' form of the drill consisted in the removal of the centre portion of its flat cutting face by making it with a notch. This enabled it to cut sideways, as well as down-wards, and thus to cut a slit or oblong hole. No labour, as such, was required; but only the intelligent superintendence of a lad to place the work in the machine, and remove it for the next piece in its turn. The machine did the labour, and by its self-action did the work in the most perfect manner [2].

Nevertheless, in using this type of machine difficulties were caused by chatter of the drill, which was subjected to fluctuating forces as the headstock was traversed. Methods used to prevent chatter included cutting slots simultaneously from opposite sides with two short drills.

Turret lathes. After the invention of the slide-rest by Maudslay, the most

FIGURE 341—*Slot-drilling and grooving machine, exhibited at the International Exhibition of 1862.*

radical improvement in lathe-construction was the development of a rotating turret which carried as many as eight cutting tools. Each of these could rapidly be brought into position for machining by turning the turret from one station to another. When the machine was set up, that is, when all the cutting tools were set and locked in position, large numbers of work-pieces could be machined by un-skilled operators until wear or breakage required some adjustment or replacement of the cutting tools. The turret lathe was

one of the first semi-automatic machine-tools; by increasing the speed of production and facilitating manufacture by unskilled labour it had an immediate
and widespread effect on interchangeable manufacture in the mid-nineteenth
century. Today the turret lathe is probably the most widely used machine-tool
for batch production.

The turret lathe is generally reputed to have been invented in the United

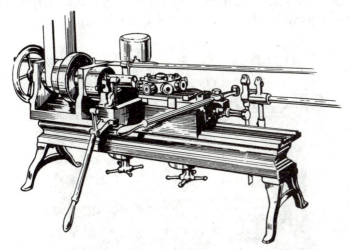

FIGURE 342—*Turret lathe built in 1855 by the Robbins & Lawrence Company, Vermont, United States. This machine was still in use in 1924.*

States, though it is claimed that an English patent for a capstan lathe with a
vertical turret was granted before 1840. Several turret lathes were certainly in
use in New England in the 1840s, but it has been suggested that English engineers
emigrating there either took with them actual machines or applied their knowledge of the principle of the turret on arrival. 'It is safe to say that these machines
were in either case an outcrop of the English design' [3]. There is, however, no
direct evidence of the use of capstan or turret lathes in Britain at this time, and
it is significant that such machines were apparently not shown at the International Exhibition of 1862.

In America, the first lathes with turrets appear to have been installed in the
works of Silver & Gay at North Chelmsford, Massachusetts. One had a six-
station turret on a vertical axis, and the other had a turret rotating on a horizontal
axis. The vertical-axis turret was mounted on a heavy carriage on the bed,
whereas the horizontal-axis turret was mounted on a slide which fitted directly
on the bed. Both turrets were rotated and locked in position by hand. Another

very early American turret lathe, used in 1845, had a self-revolving turret. About ten years later a lathe with a horizontal turret was built by Root for the production of revolver components at the Colt Armory. Undoubtedly an important part in the construction of the first commercial turret lathe, designed by Henry Stone and built by Robbins & Lawrence in 1854, was played by F. W. Howe, who was formerly employed by Silver & Gay when the two turret lathes were used in their machine-shop (vol IV, p 439). A turret lathe built by the same company in 1855 is illustrated in figure 342.

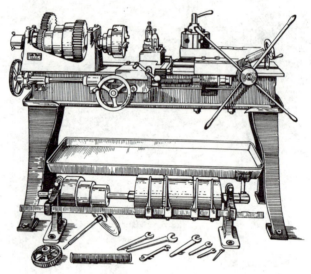

FIGURE 343—*Stage of development of the capstan lathe towards the end of the nineteenth century.*

Lathes with turrets that were automatically rotated by a ratchet-and-pawl mechanism were built in America in 1861, and a device for feeding and gripping bars of work-piece material while the spindle was rotating had also been introduced. Another important milestone in the evolution of the turret lathe was reached about 1889, when James Hartness of the Jones & Lamson Machine Company of the United States introduced the flat turret lathe. The turret of this machine was virtually a horizontal plate clamped at the outer edge; none of the tools bolted to the turret overhung the base. By the end of the nineteenth century the capstan lathe had reached the stage of development illustrated in figure 343.

Automatic lathes. The Civil War (1861–5) stimulated in the United States a need for higher output with less expenditure of labour, and this played an important part in the evolution of automatic machine-tools. Automatic lathes for the mass-production of screws were built during the war, but the machine having the most far-reaching influence on the development of automatic manu-facture was designed by C. M. Spencer shortly after the war. Spencer built a lathe which incorporated cylindrical cams, later known as 'brain wheels' (figure 344). Movement of the cutting tools and turret was controlled by adjust-able cams fitted on the cam-cylinders, which were geared to the spindle-drive. So long as the machine was fed with bar stock it automatically manufactured components until wear or breakage of the tools required them to be changed. Spencer's lathe was widely used in America for the production of screws and

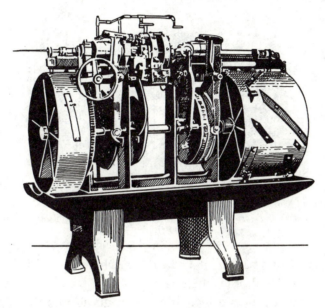

FIGURE 344—*Spencer's automatic lathe with cylindrical cams.*

similar components, and subsequently small automatic lathes have always been known in America as automatic screw-machines.

A British automatic machine for the production of screws was patented by C. W. Parker in 1879 and built by Greenwood & Batley (plate 40 B). The bar stock was fed through the headstock and turned to the correct size by stationary tools, which were then withdrawn to allow the screw-die to advance and cut the thread; the screw was cut from the bar by a parting-tool. The machine was originally designed to finish the head of the screw, an operation later carried out on a separate machine. The machine could produce screws one-eighth of an inch in diameter at the rate of 80–150 an hour, according to their length. The movements of the cutting tools were derived from a shaft carrying cams that

ran along the bed of the machine; a roller feeding-device for bar stock was incorporated in the machine.

By the end of the nineteenth century the automatic lathe had advanced considerably in size and power, and was being used for the automatic production of
a wide range of components required by the new industries springing up everywhere. Automatic feeding-devices were widely used, and magazines had been

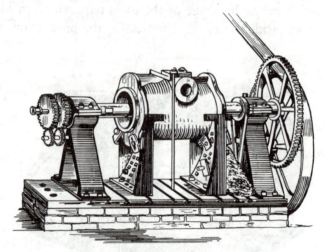

FIGURE 345—*Locomotive cylinders being bored at the Swindon works of the Great Western Railway in
1851.*

introduced for the automatic supply to the machine of small forgings, partly
finished components, and other materials.

In 1895 an important new principle was introduced into the construction of
the automatic lathe when a multi-spindle automatic was built in the United
States for the manufacture of components of sewing-machines. On a single-
spindle automatic lathe only one component is made at a time, the tools being
brought into successive operation by the movement of cross-slides and turrets.
On a multi-spindle automatic, however, several spindles in a main spindle-
carrier are periodically rotated to new stations and several components are
machined simultaneously. The multi-spindle automatic lathe thus finishes its
work on one component in the time required for the longest single operation.
One of the first multi-spindle automatics built in the United States had five
spindles, and by the end of the century four-spindle machines were commercially available there and in Sweden. The introduction of cam-operated
mechanisms, toggle-chucks and collets, and other devices enabled batteries of
automatic lathes to operate continuously with little more attention than was

needed for occasional tool-setting and for replenishing the machines with raw material.

Boring machines. The ironmaster John Wilkinson (1728–1808) built his horizontal boring machine for machining the cylinders of Watt's steam-engine in 1775 (vol IV, p 421). In 1851 such machines were still comparatively crude (figure

FIGURE 346—*Early vertical boring machine installed in Boulton & Watt's Soho foundry.*

345). By the end of the century many of the features that are characteristic of modern horizontal boring machines had been developed; both the size of work which could be bored and the accuracy of boring had greatly increased. The vertical boring machine was introduced about 1795; that illustrated (figure 346) was installed in Boulton & Watt's Soho foundry in its early days. The central column of the machine was supported by a structure fixed to the walls of the building in which it was housed. The vertical boring mill quickly came into general use after 1890 because of its superiority for machining large components, which could much more easily be clamped to a horizontal rotating table or face-plate than to a vertical one.

Planers. In the early nineteenth century, face-plate lathes of the type shown in figure 347 were used to machine flat surfaces. However, the superiority of the planing machine for rectilinear work was soon recognized after it was introduced by Roberts and others in the second decade of the century. An early wall planer

FIGURE 347—*Large face-plate lathe, capable of producing work up to 26 ft in diameter, installed in the Soho foundry before 1850.*

used in Watt's workshop is shown in plate 41 A; the cutting tool on this type of planer moved across stationary work, but gradually the planer with a reciprocating table was generally adopted.

The first American planer, built in 1836, had a bed of granite recessed to take cast iron slide-ways; the table was traversed along the bed by means of a flat chain and sprocket-wheel. By the middle of the century, however, planers were being built in Britain which had some of the characteristics of machines built quite late in the twentieth century. A self-acting Fairbairn planing machine, shown at the International Exhibition of 1862, was made for planing work 20 ft long by 6 ft wide (figure 348). The table was traversed by a rack and pinion; a power-feed and automatic quick-reversing gear were provided. Each of the tool-box saddles could be rotated through 360°; vertical surfaces also could be planed.

Considerable attention had been given before 1860 to the problem, in operating planers, of reducing the idle time during the reversal of the table. Some machines were fitted with cutter-boxes which were automatically reversed at the end of each movement of the table, so that the tools cut in both directions. The largest planers made by Whitworth had two reversing cutter-boxes and thus two sets of tools cut in both directions; small planers made by Whitworth and, with one or two exceptions, all planers made by other machine-tool builders, had non-reversing cutter-boxes that cut in one direction only, and a quick-return

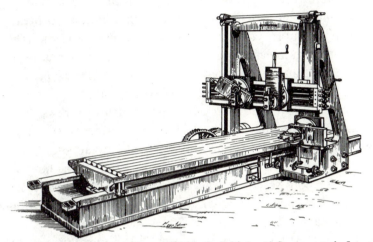

FIGURE 348—*Self-acting planing machine exhibited by P. Fairbairn & Company at the International Exhibition of 1862.*

motion was applied to the table. As early as 1860 the reversing cutter-box was gradually going out of favour, partly because the reversing mechanism sometimes failed.

The introduction of new cutting tool materials led to an increase in the cutting speeds used on planers and this in turn led to a further increase in the return speed of the table. By the end of the century the reversing cutter-box had apparently been abandoned. The ratio of the table's return speed to its cutting speed was fixed by the diameters of the forward- and reverse-motion pulleys. Thus an increase in the cutting speed effected a proportionately greater increase in the return speed, and serious difficulties were eventually encountered in reversing the table because of its own momentum and that of the driving mechanism. Reversing-gears were then developed which provided for the return of the table at a fixed speed, irrespective of the cutting speed. Many devices were also introduced for cushioning the shock of reversal, including buffers, spring-couplings, and a sliding rack.

At the time of the 1862 Exhibition there was still considerable controversy over the relative merits of screw and rack-and-pinion mechanisms for traversing. By about 1860 great improvements had been made in the shape of the teeth used in racks, and some makers had thus been led to abandon the use of 'repeating' racks with two, three, or even four sets of teeth in parallel rows. The repeating rack had been adopted in an attempt to reduce irregularities and jarring in the movement of the planing-machine table caused by badly formed teeth; this type of rack was nevertheless difficult to make with the precision required for smooth operation of the machine, and the teeth were apt to break. With the development of an improved form of rack-tooth, however, the table could be traversed smoothly by means of a single rack, which was readily made. Only Whitworth among the machine-tool builders who exhibited planing machines in 1862 continued to use a screw for traversing the table.

A similar controversy centred round the use of lead-screws and racks and pinions on lathes. Most machine-tool builders considered that the use of the lead-screw for all purposes would cause irregular wear and thus impair the accuracy of the screws produced by the lathe; Whitworth, however, adopted the lead-screw for both screw-cutting and traversing. Eventually, however, the opinion prevailed of those who advocated the use of a rack and pinion in conjunction with a lead-screw.

Milling machines. Although the American Eli Whitney (1765–1825) had built a milling machine in 1818, milling was still little practised in Britain forty years later, mainly because of the expense and difficulty of making milling cutters. D. K. Clark pointed out (1864) that while machines employing revolving cutters had long been used for some purposes, generally they had been confined to work for which single-point tools were not suitable:

In a few instances, shaping machines with circular cutters have been used for finishing the surfaces of machinery with marked success, doing, to the extent of their capacity, three times the work of a planing machine, [being] self-acting, requiring little management, and working six months without sharpening. The work turned off by properly made circular cutters is very superior, especially for intricate forms.

Several improvements had been made in the design of milling machines during the first half of the nineteenth century, and one with a vertically adjustable spindle and a simple device for indexing[1] was built in the United States as early as 1840. Milling machines of this period often had a wooden base to which were fixed cast iron slides carrying a table at a set height; the spindle and driving-mechanism were carried on posts and were adjusted vertically by means of screws and bevel-gears.

---

[1] That is, for rotating the work through any desired angle.

An improved plain milling machine was designed by F. W. Howe (p 646) for Robbins & Lawrence in 1848 (figure 349). The spindle was driven through cone-pulleys and back-gears. The table was traversed by means of a rack and pinion, and power-feed was obtained through a tilting worm-shaft similar to that used by Eli Whitney in his milling machine. The plain milling machine was followed in 1855 by the Lincoln miller, which incorporated a screw and nut for traversing the table and thus was not so liable to chatter at the start of a heavy

cut as was a machine with a rack-and-pinion traverse. The table of the Lincoln miller was mounted on a fixed bed and adjustments in height were made by moving the spindle. The design of the machine was basically sound from the beginning, and even at the end of the century it remained substantially unchanged.

Shortly after 1850, Howe built a milling machine with an adjustable cutter-slide and a swivelling chuck, which the British small-arms commission described as a universal miller. The cutter-spindle was carried in a headstock mounted on the table, and the work-piece was held in a vice supported by a column at the front of the machine. The column was

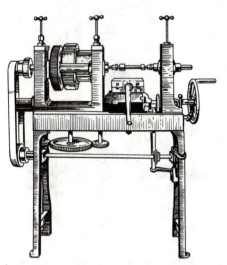

FIGURE 349—*Plain milling machine of improved design by F. W. Howe, made by the Robbins & Lawrence Company, Vermont, United States, in 1848.*

adjustable vertically and could be indexed by means of a drilled plate. The head-stock was traversed along and across the bed either by hand or by a power-feed.

A machine built in 1862 by the Brown & Sharpe Company of the United States has since been widely recognized as the first truly universal milling machine (figure 350). It was at first intended simply to eliminate the hand-filing of helical grooves in the tool-steel twist-drills that were then being used for the first time. When designing this machine J. R. Brown realized that its possibilities ranged far beyond the manufacture of twist-drills, and a machine was then developed that could be used for a variety of spiral milling operations, gear-cutting, and other processes previously effected by hand. Power-feed was applied to the table through a lead-screw, and work-pieces could be rotated in a fixed ratio to the transverse movement of the table by means of a universal head mounted on the table and geared to the lead-screw. Index plates fitted to the universal head enabled successive cuts to be made at determined intervals round circular blanks, when machining gear-teeth and so on. American engineers immediately perceived the many advantages of the universal milling machine, and the company at first had some difficulty in supplying the heavy demand for it. British engineers for many years continued to prefer the planer and shaper for machining plane surfaces.

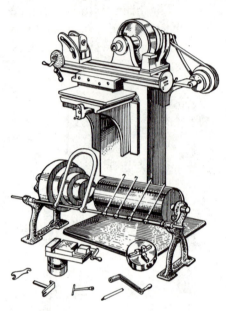

FIGURE 350—*First universal milling machine, made by the Brown & Sharpe Company, United States, in 1862.*

Improvements both in the construction of milling machines and in the manufacture and grinding of cutters eventually overcame this British conservatism, and by about 1910 British horizontal milling machines had reached a fairly advanced stage of development (figure 351). There was, however, still considerable discussion about the comparative merits of the milling machine and the planer and shaping machine. Ultimate acceptance of the milling machine was due primarily to a better appreciation of the economies to be made in machining large numbers of components having irregular profiles with gangs of formed cutters, and in removing large volumes of metal with spiral cutters.

As the milling machine became more widely used, wider ranges of speed and feed than could be obtained with cone-pulleys and back-gears were required; this encouraged makers to introduce quick-change gear-boxes (p 640) giving a wide choice of cutting conditions. Difficulties were encountered when milling machines were first fitted with gear-boxes because of vibrations resulting from inaccuracies in the gear-teeth, but improvements in the design and manufacture of gears gradually reduced such vibration to a tolerable level.

Grinding machines. The simple forms of grinding machine made before 1860 were mainly used for grinding cutting tools or for removing rough edges from castings and other metal parts. Grinding-wheels were made from natural materials such as emery and corundum, which wore rapidly and did not cut very freely; even sandstone wheels were occasionally used.

In 1864 D. K. Clark stressed the hazards of what he clearly considered to be the pernicious technique of surface grinding:

To appreciate rightly the importance and value of the method of scraping for obtaining true surfaces, it is necessary to revert for a moment to the antecedent process of grinding with emery. If a ground surface be examined, the bearing points will be found lying together in irregular masses, with extensive cavities intervening, and this defect is not under the control of the operator. A portion of the emery used for grinding becomes fixed in the pores of the metal, and causes a rapid and irregular wear of the surfaces. As grinding for a true surface is, in a manner, a self-acting process, it blunts the sense of responsibility in the operative as he slurs it over. So, at one time, the practice of grinding altogether impeded the progress of improvement in construction.

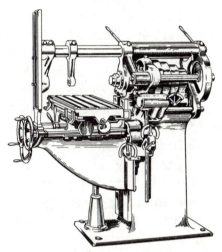

During the 1860s a simple production grinding machine was developed in America for the manufacture of sewing-machine components, and within a few years a universal grinder was introduced which incorporated a number of features found in modern grinding machines. The usefulness of grinding machines was still restricted, however, by the poor quality of the abrasives available for the manufacture of grinding-wheels. Silicon carbide

FIGURE 351—*Typical horizontal milling machine made in the first decade of the twentieth century.*

was synthesized, and the abrasive value of aluminium oxide was discovered, in the last decade of the nineteenth century; wheels made from these two abrasives completely revolutionized grinding techniques, both in the mass production of interchangeable components, and in the manufacture of jigs, precision gauges, and other devices in tool-rooms. Yet even at the end of the century there was considerable resistance in Britain to the practice of grinding machine-tool slide-ways, bearings, and so on in preference to scraping, as many makers and users of machine-tools believed that rapid wear would be caused by abrasive particles embedded in the ground surfaces. In the first years of the twentieth century these fears were shown to be unfounded, and the grinding machine quickly became indispensable in every workshop making components to close dimensional limits.

The production of gears. As the rotational speeds of prime movers, machine-tools, and mechanisms generally increased during the nineteenth century, the problems of producing satisfactory gears became more pressing. During much of the century the forms of teeth varied widely from one manufacturer to another, despite attempts to standardize them. An important advance was made when the cycloidal profile was introduced, but as the diameter of the rolling circle was usually based on that of the smallest pinion in a particular train of gears, full interchangeability was deferred until the involute form of gear-tooth was developed. In the last decade of the nineteenth century most gear-teeth were probably still being produced by formed milling cutters, although automatic gear-cutters had been built by the Brown & Sharpe Company in America as early as 1877. Other very important developments in gear-making techniques were, however, taking place.

Christian Schiele in 1856 conceived the hobbing process, in which gear-teeth are generated by a formed cutter rotating synchronously with a rotating gear-blank. The first hobbing machines were not built, however, until about 1887, when a patent application for a spur-gear hobbing machine was filed by G. B. Grant in the United States. Ten years later the first universal hobbing machine was constructed by the German, Hermann Pfauter, for hobbing spur- and spiral-gears. In the next few years hobbing machines were intensively developed, primarily in response to demands from the growing automobile industries (ch 18) of several nations for better and cheaper transmission-gears. However, inaccuracies in gear-teeth arising from errors in the manufacture of the hobs continued to cause difficulty until about 1910, when hobs finished by grinding began to come into general use. Previously, hobs had been machined to the correct form and dimensions in soft steel and then hardened, but were not ground before use, with the result that inaccuracies in the hob caused by variations in the metal and in its heat-treatment were reproduced in the hobbed gears. In 1896 F. W. Lanchester (p 430) built one of Britain's first hobbing machines for machining worms and worm-wheels for his cars, and in the same year an entirely new type of gear-shaper of complex design was invented in America by E. R. Fellows, a former window-dresser who had received virtually no technical or workshop training.

An early stage in the development of the bevel-gear shaping machine is exemplified in plate 40 A. This machine was developed by J. Buck in 1895, and was the first gear-shaper to machine both sides of the tooth simultaneously. The two cutting tools and tool-holders reciprocated simultaneously by crank motions; the tool-slides were pivoted about an axis to allow the tools to move along paths that converged at the apex of the pitch-cone. After each cutting stroke, the gear was indexed through one tooth-space until a series of cuts had been taken right round the blank; the saddle was then fed towards the tools for a further series of cuts. The tooth profile was a circular approximation to the involute.

For many years after 1900 there were few radical changes in machine-tool design and construction, but with the advent of transfer machines in the 1930s and of automation generally in the 1940s a revolution occurred in machine-tool engineering which immediately began to transform the whole pattern of mechanized production.

REFERENCES

[1] SMILES, S. 'Industrial Biography, Iron Workers and Tool Makers', p. 299. Murray, London. 1908.
[2] NASMYTH, J. 'James Nasmyth, An Autobiography' (ed. by S. SMILES), p. 422. London. 1897.
[3] HUBBARD, G. *Amer. Mach., Lond.*, **60**, 273, 1924.

BIBLIOGRAPHY

CLARK, D. K. 'The Exhibited Machinery of 1862: a Cyclopaedia of the Machinery represented at the International Exhibition.' London. 1864.
HUBBARD, G. "Development of Machine Tools in New England." *Amer. Mach., Lond.*, Vols **59** and **60**, 1923, 1924.
KIMBALL, D. S. "The Master Tools of Industry." *Ibid.*, **60**, 679–83, 1924.
NASMYTH, J. 'James Nasmyth, An Autobiography' (ed. by S. SMILES). London. 1883.
PARSONS, R. H. 'A History of the Institution of Mechanical Engineers, 1847–1947.' Institution of Mechanical Engineers, London. 1947.
ROE, J. W. 'English and American Tool Builders.' Yale University Press, New Haven. 1916.
SMILES, S. 'Industrial Biography, Iron Workers and Tool Makers.' London. 1863.
TOMLINSON, C. (Ed.). 'Cyclopedia of Useful Arts.' London. 1852–4.

Multi-spindle drilling machine, 1851.

27

CERAMICS

IREEN JAMESON

IN any industry the industrial revolution may be said to have begun when machinery took over much of the work done previously by hand. Lord Wedgwood (1872–1943) in his 'Staffordshire Pottery and its History' suggested that the 1870s can be taken as the date when machinery invaded the pottery industry. This statement has since been challenged on many sides and, on looking at the progress made in The Potteries (vol IV, ch 11) during the time of Josiah Wedgwood (1730–95), it must be admitted that the industrial revolution there should be placed a century earlier. Yet the ceramic industry underwent very profound changes during the period now under review, changes caused by new demands made upon the industry as well as by changes in production and materials. In turn, the output of the ceramic industry made possible new manufacturing processes in other fields. This interdependence is strikingly illustrated in the chemical, electrical, and metallurgical industries, for it should always be remembered that more and more ceramic products are not ends in themselves, as are table-ware or wall-tiles, for example, but are aids to other industries. Blast-furnaces require lining with refractory materials; the chemical industry requires large storage vessels, acid-proof pumps, and linings for reactors (figure 352); the electrical industry requires insulators and resistors, still largely made of ceramics and formerly almost entirely so.

The changes that came about during the second half of the nineteenth century can be described as a greatly extended field of use; an improvement in the quality and quantity of existing manufactures; a new range of products; and new or improved methods of manufacture.

The main change, however, was from an empirical period, roughly up to 1870, to an increasingly scientific period. This does not mean that even earlier than the 1870s many very precise 'philosophical' experiments and investigations were not carried out and applied in the pottery industry, or that even now, in the second half of the twentieth century, many a master potter will not judge his clay 'by the feel'. On the whole, however, it can be said that during the last quarter of the nineteenth century science played an increasingly important part in ceramics.

With this increasing use of scientific methods, there arose also a demand for a new type of potter—the ceramic engineer, ceramist, or whatever name may be given to a person who did not learn the subject only at the bench and in the pottery, but received a precise and specific training fitting him to investigate raw materials, and to provide the answers to the many problems of the works. Many of these problems had existed for centuries, but their nature had not previously been recognized. With the demand for trained workers came schools, colleges, and university departments dedicated to ceramics. Further specialization into a single circumscribed field of the ceramic industry did not, on the whole, take place until the very end of the century and even now has not yet reached its peak. Some of the old-established potteries, such as that of Wedgwood at Etruria and the manufactories of Vienna and Sèvres, had long had their own 'schools', but now separate institutes were founded all over the continent of Europe. By the end

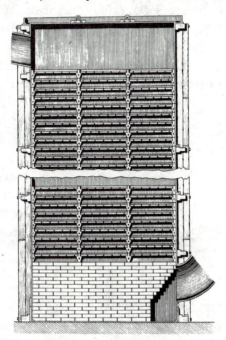

FIGURE 352—*Tower for sulphuric acid production.*

of the century the movement had spread overseas, and in 1894 Ohio University started its own small ceramic department.

I. SCIENTIFIC DISCOVERIES

Scientific researches in the ceramic industry were focused on three main subjects:

(i) the nature of the raw materials employed;
(ii) the manner of controlling the manufacture of articles;
(iii) the development of instruments to serve the first two purposes.

In early times searchers after truth often independently made the same, or very similar, discoveries at almost the same time, and the likelihood of this occurrence became much greater after the invention of printing and the consequent rapid dissemination of knowledge. It would, therefore, be invidious to ascribe all the glory of being 'father of scientific ceramics' to one man, but much of the credit should be ascribed to H. Seger (1839–94) who, after studying chemistry and working for some time in various industries, devoted the rest of his life to the clay industry, founding two technical journals and a famous laboratory.

Before Seger, others had made their name in this field; thus Thomas Graham (1805–69) of London can be considered the founder of colloid chemistry, which became known as such about 1861. In 1866 W. Rupert-Elsner of Vienna observed the change in the specific gravity of silica on heating, and work on the various forms of silica and its modifications was carried out, mainly in France by P. G. Hautefeuille (1836–1902), who published his results in the last two decades of the century. In Britain, A. W. Cromquist carried out the first microscopic investigations on silica and other refractory bricks, publishing his results in 1884. J. W. Mellor (1869–1938) did much to fill the gaps in scientific knowledge, investigating why particular ceramic materials produced specific effects under various conditions. In the field of instruments, C. W. Siemens (1823–83) first proposed electrical-resistance pyrometry to measure furnace temperatures in 1871, but, after initial interest the matter was forgotten, and revived only when Le Châtelier (1850–1936) developed his pyrometer in 1894. In the meantime the theoretical side was not forgotten, and Josiah Willard Gibbs (1839–1903), at Yale University, formulated the phase rule[1] in 1878.

FIGURE 353—*Seger's pyrometric cones.*

However, as mentioned above, it was Seger who did much of the pioneer work. Thus in 1872 he established a set of rules describing the way in which porous bodies must be altered in order to overcome their tendency to crazing, namely, by co-ordinating the coefficients of expansion of the body and the glaze. These rules included increasing the quartz-content; finer grinding of the quartz and all other constituents; calcining the quartz; increasing biscuiting temperatures; lowering the clay-content of the body; replacing china clay by ball clays; and increasing the proportion of non-plastic to plastic constituents.

Two years later Seger published the 'rational analysis', frequently called the 'Seger analysis', of clays, by which materials were classified as clay-substance, quartz, and felspar. The measure of his success is that, to a considerable degree, this method of representing composition is still used on the European continent.

---

[1] The phase rule describes the conditions of equilibrium between the 'phases', or distinct, mechanically separable, and homogeneous parts of a heterogeneous system. Ice, water, and water-vapour form such a system, consisting of three phases.

Another invention of Seger's is the pyrometric cone (figure 353) which was described in his article entitled 'The Composition of Standard Cones for the Measurement of High Temperatures in Kilns for the Ceramic Industry'. His invention was mainly concerned with the fusibility of ceramic materials, rather than with specific temperature measurement. The system is extremely simple. Cones of a specific composition are placed side by side on a refractory holder in a position inside the kiln, where they can be seen through a peep-hole from the outside. When the temperature reaches a certain point the relevant cone will bend over and finally fuse.[1] Orton followed suit with his cones, and so did many others in the United States and in Britain, and Lauth and Vogt introduced their own cones at Sèvres in 1882; but fundamentally these are all variations of, and improvements on, the Seger cone.

II. TABLE-WARE AND ART WARE

To the general public, ceramics means pottery and pottery generally means table-ware. Considering the many perfect pieces that have survived from the eighteenth century (vol IV, plates 16–19) it may at first sight seem as if improvements were hardly possible, yet there was very considerable progress in two main directions. On the one hand, better bodies and glazes became available as the scientific basis of the composition and firing became more widely understood; on the other, development of techniques for mechanical mass-production, together with greater facilities in transport, brought cheap, if not always very good, table-ware into every home. Among the factors leading to a better product must be mentioned first and foremost the battle—and often it really was a battle—against the inclusion of soluble lead in glazes, a movement in which England was foremost. The legislation relating to this problem was not passed by Parliament until 1913, and has since been modified, but by the end of the nineteenth century both the workers in the industry and those who used glazed ware were protected from lead poisoning.

Artistically, too, glazes made considerable progress. In Paris J. T. Deck (1823–91) produced the much prized Persian turquoise blue in 1861, a colour which eventually was called after him *bleu de Deck*. In Copenhagen, meanwhile, Clement was working on coloured crystal glazes for art ware, and the Royal Manufactory there is still famous for the beauty of its products. New colouring-agents were being employed, such as uranium (1853), while new effects of flame-mottling were deliberately induced by controlling the atmosphere in the kiln (Seger, 1890). Although transfer-printing on pottery had been introduced in

---

[1] Such cones are classified by 'cone numbers'; thus cone 1 fuses at about 1150° C and cone 42 at about 2015° C.

1756 (vol IV, p 354) it was at first in one colour only; 'picture printing' dates from 1846, when a patent was granted to Felix Edwards Pratt. By the time of the 1851 Exhibition gold border-printing had been developed, and among the ware much admired at the time were the charming little lids used for ointment- and pomade-pots (plates 1, 2). Ten years later Hughes of Stoke-on-Trent also introduced gold engraving for decoration on pottery.

Once china began to be imported from the Far East it was the aim of every potter to imitate it. Some came very near to success, others produced ware quite different from the original intention but nevertheless very acceptable to the public. Then the secret of true porcelain became known and various types of porcelain were developed (vol IV, p 336). Thus in 1862 Stellmacher in Bohemia produced a body, still called after him, which contained 0·8 per cent of potassium felspar and was fired at a cone number of 8–9. In 1879 Lenox, of Trenton in the United States, first produced Beleek porcelain, later known as Lenox china. The famous *pâte-sur-pâte* technique employed exclusively at Sèvres for over a century was finally copied successfully at Meissen in 1878. Up to 1866 European bone-china was produced exclusively in Great Britain. Then the factory at Odelberg in Sweden started production on a large scale and improved the body to such a degree that, whereas in Britain pieces had had to be fired singly, eight or even ten of the Swedish plates could be placed one above the other in the saggars. Curiously enough, Wedgwood did not take up the manufacture of translucent china until 1878.

It was only natural that, once manufacturers had learnt how to make porcelain and china, they should experiment on new articles made with these materials. Many such products were shown for the first time at the 1851 Exhibition, among them what was then the largest porcelain dish ever produced. This was made by Moritz Farkashagy-Fisher at Herend, Hungary. It had an imitation basket-work rim and was painted in the Chinese style, depicting scenes from Hungarian history. Queen Victoria was so much impressed with this dish that she ordered a whole dinner-set, and the Hungarian factory was able to stabilize its output, making 'Victoria' sets for many decades. In the meantime G. Donati in Italy brought out an 'ocarina' flute (1860), whose excellent and clear tone was greatly praised, though unfortunately it broke so easily that it never found great favour. As firing-techniques and kilns were improved it was possible to make bigger and bigger pieces, and in 1885 Andresen, a sculptor, designed a fireplace made entirely of porcelain; this was produced at Meissen. The model consisted of an elaborately decorated surround; on the mantelpiece stood a large mirror sur-rounded by figurines and angels and with four candle-holders. The climax was reached at the Universal Exhibition in Paris in 1900, where Sèvres showed a 'Ceramic Palace', made externally of the most highly refined architectural stoneware that had then been achieved, and internally constructed entirely of porcelain (plate 3). By that time, however, it was realized that porcelain was not in itself suitable for large-scale architectural purposes, though the Ceramic Palace showed what could be done had it been desirable.

III. ELECTRICAL AND CHEMICAL PORCELAIN AND STONEWARE

Meanwhile the electrical and chemical properties of porcelain were not overlooked, and in the corresponding industrial fields it and related materials made great strides. In the 1850s bell-shaped insulators for telegraph poles came into use throughout the world. With the rapid extension in the use of electricity for illumination, the demand for porcelain insulators of all sorts and shapes grew, and this in its turn brought about new problems of production. Mass production was essential, but it had to be combined with very great accuracy in size and a high standard of quality. Moulding by pressure was the obvious solution, and to avoid shrinkage and distortion dry-pressing was tried very extensively. Attention was mainly directed to lubrication of the dies, to their construction, and to the methods of using them. Vegetable and mineral oils were tried for lubricating purposes, but it was through an accident that one of the great forward steps was made. In 1878 Reissmann, at Saalfeld, Germany, dropped a quantity of so-called solar oil (an intermediate fraction obtained in distilling shale oil) into the dry porcelain body, with which it was mixed. The resulting pressed pieces were far more satisfactory than anything produced up to then, and though many difficulties had, and still have, to be overcome, lubricating oil has always been mixed with the body since that time.

Meanwhile in England, the United States, and to some extent Switzerland, both high- and low-tension porcelains were being manufactured on an ever-increasing scale. The soft natural mineral known as soapstone or steatite had been used for some time, but only in 1888 was it first employed for the electrical industry in its powdered form, mixed with fluxes, and treated like any other ceramic material. It has retained its place in the industry ever since.

In 1891 Voigt observed that gold in the form of decorative bands on porcelain retained its power of conducting electricity, and although resistors based on this principle use metals other than gold, it is due to this observation that another field was opened. In the meantime a new industry, based on the internal combustion engine, was making demands on ceramics. In 1888 H. K. Shank of Columbus, Ohio, obtained the first patent for insulating composites for sparking-plugs. Among the materials included as suitable for the insulation were mica, zircon, glass, porcelain, pure clay, and steatite.

The ceramic and chemical industries have long been of mutual assistance. Even today, although to a slightly lesser degree than formerly, many chemical processes can be carried out only in ceramic containers or in those lined with ceramic materials. This applies particularly to the production of acids (figure 352). Chemical stoneware is resistant to all cold acids at any concentration (with the exception of hydrofluoric acid), and against most hot acids. Tanks, pipes, pumps, exhausters (figure 354) were made of, or lined with, ceramic materials, mainly stoneware. Porcelain filters for drinking-water were patented by Nadoud de Buffon in 1861. Chemically resistant bricks and tiles for laboratories, factories, and workshops poured on to the market.

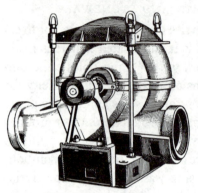

FIGURE 354—*Acid-resisting stoneware exhauster.*

IV. REFRACTORIES

In 1856 Bessemer announced his new process for the production of steel. All smelting-processes have to be carried out in furnaces, and furnaces have to be lined with materials resistant to heat and to the attack of slag, gases, acids, and molten metals. Ordinary clay is to some degree refractory and thus refractories of one sort or another have been employed since man first learnt to smelt, but between 1860 and 1914 Austrian magnesite became supreme among them. First used at Leoben in 1860 for converter-linings, bricks were soon being made from ground magnesite with a clay bond. Experiments were carried out simultaneously with local materials in France, England, and Germany, but the products were both rather unsatisfactory and much too expensive. Eventually crystalline Styrian magnesite conquered the entire market until the first world war cut off supplies. In 1885 the Otis Company of Cleveland, Ohio, imported the first 800 tons of Austrian magnesite into the United States; by the end of the century the trickle had turned into a flood.

Simultaneously dolomite, more abundant and much cheaper, was being investigated as a substitute for magnesite, but this material had many drawbacks which manufacturers partly could not overcome, and partly did not at that time consider worth overcoming. It was only when the supply of magnesite was interrupted that dolomite gained a great deal of ground, which it consolidated after magnesite had become available again, owing to the high price of the latter.

Carbon and pure silica also found application as refractories; thus carbon bricks were first produced in England in 1863, while French experiments led eventually to the manufacture of silica-carbon bricks from a synthetic amorphous or micro-crystalline material.

V. BUILDING-MATERIALS

It is perhaps not generally realized that many types of now familiar building-bricks and roofing-tiles have been in use for less than a century. With the exten-

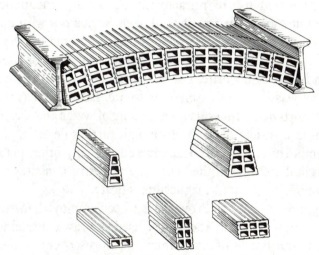

FIGURE 355—*Perforated bricks for lightweight partition walls, floors, and ceilings.*

sion of factories and the erection of taller buildings, the risk of fire increased, and regulations demanding floors and ceilings of non-inflammable materials were introduced (vol IV, ch 15). Ordinary bricks were much too heavy for this purpose, and hollow bricks were therefore increasingly employed (figure 355). They had been made before the 1850s, but no satisfactory mechanical method of production had been evolved. Antoine Félix Crotte had been making such bricks for some time, but it took him nearly ten years to evolve the ideal machine. His disappointment must have been great when he found that after all he had been forestalled by Carl Schlickeysen. The question of weight also entered into roof-construction, so that even the initially far from perfect interlocking tiles put on the market by Gilardoni in Alsace in 1841 had an immediate effect both on building costs and the change-over from thatch and slates to tiles.

At the same time, heavier and more vitrified bricks found favour with road- and bridge-builders. The United States, the Netherlands, and Germany were the countries that mainly employed brick surfaces for roads; in the United States special machinery was developed for laying them. Though the foundations of the main roads of a century ago are no longer able to stand up to the weight and vibration of modern road-traffic, the brick surfaces themselves have proved remarkably resistant to wear and weather.

VI. RAW MATERIALS

The use of new raw materials brought about a very considerable extension of the production and use of refractories. As already mentioned, there was Austrian magnesite, and experiments had been carried out with dolomite, silica, and carbon bricks. Three more refractories later became of very considerable importance. In 1888 William Taylor discovered, near Fort Benton, Montana, a mineral which he called taylorite, but as that name had already been employed the new mineral was eventually called bentonite. Bentonite has the property of being able to absorb many times its own volume of water and has found increasing application in a variety of fields. Although further deposits of this mineral, with various impurities, have been discovered in many other places, that from Fort Benton is still considered the best. The principal constituent of bentonite is montmorillonite, a hydrated magnesium silicate.

The rock around Les Baux in Provence has been employed, mainly as building stone, since Roman times. That it could be used as a raw material for the extraction of alumina, and finally of aluminium, was a discovery of the 1850s. This rock is no longer much mined in the place of its original discovery, but is still called bauxite. Although bauxite is chiefly used as a source of aluminium, very considerable quantities of alumina are used in the ceramic industry. Sintered alumina is one of the hardest materials produced, and is extensively used for cutting and grinding; it is resistant to very high temperatures and to chemical attack.

The third new raw material was moler. It was A. Poulsen of Copenhagen who in 1890 first recognized its insulating properties. Today it is one of the important raw-material exports from Denmark, although allied minerals are found in other parts of the world. Moler is a diatomaceous earth, and hollow blocks made from it are widely employed in building on account of their great mechanical strength and fire-resisting properties.

VII. KILNS

Originally, potteries established themselves near their supply of fuel. At the beginning of the nineteenth century $2\frac{1}{2}$ lb of coal were required to fire 1 lb of clay, so that the problem of fuel economy in the ceramic industry is not a recent one. Apart from the question of reducing the total quantity of coal required there were also those of more efficient firing and of smoke-abatement. The old-fashioned bottle kiln (figure 356) made the atmosphere of pottery districts very unpleasant, and from about 1855 onwards experiments were carried out in various countries to use coal- or producer-gas, and later electricity, for firing pottery and heavy clay ware, both in intermittent and in continuous kilns. The name of Friedrich Hoffmann is closely linked with the development of con-

FIGURE 356—*Bottle kilns, Staffordshire.*

tinuous kilns. In 1856 he designed his first continuous circular kiln, placing the hearth in the mouth of the kiln. Heating-flues were made by the unfired pieces themselves, and the fire was moved from opening to opening round the kiln .The first of these kilns was used industrially in 1857, and the first patent was granted in 1858. From the continuous round kiln, it was but a step to the continuous long-chamber kiln (figure 357), the first of which was built at Constance in 1864; with minor modifications and repairs this identical kiln has remained in use to the present day. Hoffmann was by no means the only one in the field of revolutionary kiln-design. That really great change in design, the development of the tunnel kiln, took place in a smaller country where fuel economy was an absolute necessity; the first was built in Denmark in 1839. It was not very satisfactory, but its potential usefulness was recognized and work continued. By 1873 there was a tunnel kiln fired by producer-gas, although coal also could be used: it was patented in 1877. The main disadvantage of this kiln was loss of heat through the movable floor, a difficulty which was finally overcome by insulating the floor with sand. A year later a factory in London set up its first annular tunnel kiln, designed for more economic use of the space there available; almost at the same time this design was used for another built in Hungary. The first tunnel kiln in the United States was built at Chicago in 1889 for firing dry-pressed bricks; Holland followed closely with even bigger examples.

Simultaneously with the above developments went a movement for better control of firing; down-draught kilns; continuous muffle kilns for decorating; and the first electrically heated kilns. It is not surprising that the newly acquired

FIGURE 357—*Continuous long-chamber kiln, late nineteenth century. The various compartments are heated in turn.*

knowledge was employed not only for the actual firing of ware, but for the preliminary drying. In 1881 humidity-drying of refractory materials was introduced in England: in this the drying-chambers were packed as closely as possible with the green ware, among which containers of water were set. The chamber was then sealed and heated from the outside. Only when the ware had reached a high temperature was the steam permitted to escape and hot, dry air introduced. The success achieved was remarkable, particularly with large pieces which in the ordinary way had been apt to crack easily. The process was soon made continuous, by piping the escaping superheated steam into an adjoining chamber. Tunnel driers had a much harder time in establishing themselves during the last quarter of the century, and even today lack the support that many consider they deserve. Needless to say, there was a close relationship between kiln-construction and engineering, the former demanding new and better devices for foundations, kiln-cars, hot-air pumps, gas-generators, heat-recuperators, valves, and other auxiliaries.

VIII. MACHINERY

During the period under consideration power began to be applied to a number of machines that had hitherto been worked by hand (figure 358). Steam-driven mills, breakers, and mixers for ceramic raw materials were introduced by James Watt, and made at the famous Soho Works, Birmingham. Shaping continued to be either by hand or by casting. Both methods were slow, and owing to the high water-content the bodies required longer drying, suffered greater risk of cracks and greater shrinkage, and needed more storage space.

The demands of other industries and of the general public upon the ceramic industry could be met only by vastly increased and standardized output, that is, by machine-made articles. It was at the 1851 Exhibition that some of the new ceramic machines were first introduced, among them being pipe-presses for

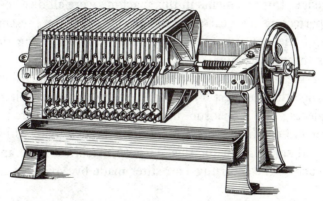

FIGURE 358—*Hand-operated filter press for removing surplus water from clay bodies.*

making stoneware pipes. These English presses and the early mechanical mixers were all of a vertical pattern. The pipe-presses found favour immediately, and were soon being installed in various continental countries. Meanwhile Boch in the Saar had also been working on presses, in this case for tile-making, and in 1852 he demonstrated a hydraulic press to replace the spindle-presses used up to that time. Herbert at Rheims, and Schlickeysen in Berlin, were both working on machines for the homogeneous mixing of materials, and the former first showed a screw-device for this purpose at the 1854 Paris exhibition; the latter, a year later, brought out the true auger machine for plastic bodies. It was vertical and driven by horses. Schlickeysen continued to work on his auger machines, and every few years new and improved models were offered to the industry, but years elapsed before they were changed from the vertical to the horizontal type. By 1874 rollers had been added, and water-fed mouthpieces followed a few months later. To the beginning of our period also belongs the introduction of profiles for use with the potter's wheel, shapes having up to then been copied by the skilled hand and eye of the master craftsman.

The grinding and crushing of raw materials by mechanical means had been one of the earliest problems of the industry. The early steam-driven grinders permitted potteries not situated on a suitable river to do their own crushing instead of depending on their more fortunate brothers in the trade to supply them with material of the correct grain-size and in the right quantities. In 1856 Blake, in the United States, constructed the first jaw-crusher. This had a wedge-shaped crusher-mouth enclosed by two jaws. One of these was fixed at its upper edge to a horizontal shaft and moved by means of a toggle-lever gear; the other jaw was fixed. The lower opening of the crusher-mouth could be adjusted by means of a wedge. Improvements in this machine were all directed towards one end, that of perfecting the gear-mechanism producing the pressure in order to use as much of the power as possible in the actual crushing process and to minimize loss through friction.

Others, working along different lines, produced pan mills for dry and wet grinding. In 1890 the Kuhnert Turbowerke introduced fine rollers, with interchangeable pieces, and Davidson in Copenhagen constructed a tube mill. Mere grinding and crushing were not enough; the raw material had afterwards to be sieved and sorted, and for this purpose machines large and small were constructed, such as the centrifugal air sifter made by Mumfort and Moodie in 1887.

As already mentioned, porcelain for electrical purposes was required in vast quantities and therefore suitable presses had to be constructed to fulfil the demand; the same applied to bricks, tiles, household ware, and so on. Thus Schmerber Frères in Paris first showed a revolving press for ceramic products in 1867; this was developed mainly for bricks and tiles, and had reached so satisfactory a stage ten years later that for nearly two decades it held its own against all comers. However, these presses and extrusion machines, good as they were in many respects, had one weak spot: the mouthpieces. Though all countries contributed to perfecting them, and though various materials were employed—such as steel, various alloys, glass, and porcelain, with or without lubricants—even today wear of the mouthpieces is still a problem.

BIBLIOGRAPHY

BOURRY, E. 'Traité des industries céramiques.' Gauthier-Villars, Paris. 1897. (See also Eng. trans.: 'Treatise on Ceramic Industries.' Scott, Greenwood, London. 1907.)
KERL, B. 'Handbuch der gesamten Thonwarenindustrie' (3rd ed.). Vieweg, Braunschweig. 1907.

28

GLASS TECHNOLOGY

R. W. DOUGLAS

I. NEW COMPOSITIONS FOR GLASS

BEFORE 1850, the glass industry was a craft with traditional recipes and secret processes, as has been indicated in earlier volumes, but by 1900 these were beginning to be replaced by chemical control and mechanical methods of manufacture. The part of the industry concerned with crystal glass, where artist and craftsmen work together to produce high-quality table-ware and decorative pieces, remained and remains exceptional, although the use of scientific methods of control in the preparation of this glass also is now well established.

Today the glass industry is almost entirely mechanized. Glass bottles are made at about 50 a minute, depending upon their size, in machines fed from furnaces that are, in effect, large tanks containing 100–200 tons of molten glass. Sheet glass for windows is pulled continuously from much larger tank furnaces, containing as much as 1000 tons of glass, in a strip 9 ft wide and at the rate of several hundred feet an hour. Plate glass is now made by causing glass to issue from the furnace as a wide, thin stream of glass, which passes between rollers and is subsequently annealed, ground, and polished in a continuous process. Bulbs for electric lamps are made at the rate of 800 a minute. Although the perfection of many of these devices lies beyond the end of the period we are now considering the beginnings of them were apparent within it.

At the beginning of the nineteenth century, the glass-maker often failed to differentiate between the alkalis. In districts near to forests the ashes of burnt wood were lixiviated with water and by recrystallization a crude potash was obtained (p 255); near the sea, however, the ashes of seaweed provided an alkali consisting chiefly of sodium carbonate. It appears that lime, although another major alkaline constituent of glass, had been included more often by accident than design, through the use of crude raw materials; some medieval glasses contained as much as 20 per cent calcium oxide.

In 1790 Leblanc devised his method of producing saltcake (sodium sulphate) and soda ash (soda) from salt (p 236). The difference in price was originally much in favour of the saltcake, so that with the introduction in 1860–70 of the Siemens furnace, which enabled much higher temperatures to be obtained in glass-making and the sulphate to be used correspondingly more easily, soda ash began to be displaced by saltcake. In 1863 the Solvay process for making soda ash was developed and this trend was reversed. To this day, however, a proportion of the sodium oxide in the glass is often added to the batch as saltcake, one reason being that it assists in preventing a scum of siliceous matter forming on the surface of the molten glass.

The growth of chemical science and the resulting increased purity of many manufactured chemicals paved the way for a systematic approach to glass compositions. In 1830 J. B. A. Dumas pointed out that soda-lime-silica glass became more resistant to attack by moisture as the composition approached one chemical equivalent each of sodium oxide or potassium oxide and lime for every six of silica. Benrath, in 1875, suggested that the most durable glass was one in which the molecular proportions were one part sodium oxide, one part lime, six parts silica. This corresponds to a glass having a composition by weight of 12·9 per cent sodium oxide, 11·7 per cent lime, and 75·4 per cent silica, very near the composition of modern window-glass. In fact, for bottle glass, for early automatic machines, the sodium oxide content by weight was usually about 16–17 per cent, lime 8–9 per cent, and silica 70–72 per cent, although modern glasses are near to Benrath's formula. It should be remarked, however, that small quantities of minor constituents, such as oxides of magnesium, aluminium, and boron, also play an important part.

Soda-lime-silica glasses have always constituted by far the largest fraction of glass made; the contribution of the last half of the nineteenth century was to provide the first steps to understanding and improving a recipe that had developed empirically over some three thousand years. One other composition of more recent introduction was in use: the lead glass used in the 'lead crystal' industry. This glass contains as main constituents 55 per cent silica, 32 per cent lead oxide, and 12 per cent potash. It had been used and known as 'English crystal' since the latter part of the seventeenth century. Merrett had translated Neri's 'Art of Glass' in 1662, and Ravenscroft, who was working under an agreement with the Glass Sellers' Company, may have drawn from this translation his inspiration to use lead as a flux (vol III, p 219). In 1675 he first produced the lead-potash-silica composition given above; its high refractive index and good working properties have resulted in its remaining to the present day the basis of all high-quality table and decorative glass.

The new compositions during the nineteenth century were developed in response to the growing demand for glass of controlled refractive index and dispersion for use in making lens-systems (vol IV, ch 12), and important developments in this field took place in the latter part of the century. Several famous men of science had been conducting experiments, among them Faraday, Fraunhofer, Harcourt, and Stokes, but in the period now under consideration pre-eminence must undoubtedly be given to the development which resulted from the collaboration of Ernst Abbé (1840–1905) and Otto Schott. In 1902, the firm in which they were associated produced a book describing their investigations and listing about 80 different optical glasses.

Abbé was interested in the improvement of microscopes, and in 1876 had produced a paper in which he showed that the existing limitations of the instrument were due to the lack of glasses having the refractive indices and dispersions called for by his calculations. In 1884 Schott persuaded Abbé to join him and Karl Zeiss (1816–88) in forming the Jena glass-works of Schott & Sons, and by July 1886 they were able to offer the new glasses commercially. When Abbé and Schott began their experiments the effects of the constituent oxides on the optical properties of a glass were known only for silicon, potassium, sodium, lead, and calcium. In a very few years the following 28 new elements had been introduced into various glasses in proportions of at least 10 per cent: boron, phosphorus, lithium, magnesium, zinc, aluminium, barium, strontium, cadmium, beryllium, iron, manganese, cerium, 'didymium', erbium, silver, mercury, thallium, bismuth, antimony, arsenic, molybdenum, niobium, tungsten, tin, titanium, uranium, and fluorine. Few of these experiments may have produced useful results, but this was the start of a new phase in the development of glass compositions. In addition to the optical properties, other properties of glass—such as ability to withstand sudden changes of temperature and resistance to attack by chemical reagents—were investigated. Problems such as these were to be subjects of intensive study in later years as scientific methods became more and more used by the industry.

An additional impetus to development and expansion was given to the glass industry in Britain in 1845, when the excise duties on glass were repealed. The following extracts from the regulations indicate the burden they were to the industry. 'Every annealing oven, arch or lehr for annealing flint glass . . . with a sufficient iron grating affixed thereto and proper locks and keys.' 'Four hours' notice to be given to the officer of the intention to heat any annealing arch.' 'Twelve hours' notice to be given before beginning to fill or charge any pot for making glass. . . .'

The duties included an annual payment by each glass-house for a licence to manufacture glass; a payment per pound on all glass melted in the pots and ready for use; and a payment per pound for the excess weight of manufactured glass over 40 per cent (later 50 per cent) of the calculated weight of molten glass. The excise officers were quartered in the glass-works and their activities were described by one manufacturer in these words: 'Our business premises are placed under the arbitrary control of a class of man to whose will and caprice it is most irksome to have to submit. We cannot enter parts of our own premises without their permission.' No wonder McCulloch in 1833 wrote: 'Not only does the duty operate to prevent competition with countries abroad, but it operates also to prevent all improvement because, to improve, experiments must be made, but a man with 125 per cent duty over his head is not very likely to make experiments.'

The increased demand that followed the repeal of the excise duties, and the pressure by the workers for increased wages, inspired attempts to reduce production costs by mechanizing the glass-working processes.

II. BOTTLE-MAKING

Various designs of semi-automatic bottle-making machines were the subject of patents granted from 1859 onwards. Initially, the patents originated in England, the first German patent appearing in 1889, and the first French one in 1893. In 1887 a semi-automatic bottle-making machine was used with commercial success for the first time. This was the Ashley machine, used at Castleford in Yorkshire.

In order to be able to give some indication of the nature of these developments it is necessary to recall the process of bottle-making by hand. The gatherer began the process by collecting on the end of a blowing-iron the desired amount of glass from the molten supply in the furnace. The blowing-iron is an iron tube about 5 ft long, 1 inch in external diameter, and $\frac{1}{4}$-inch in internal diameter. Next the blower took the iron and rolled the glass on the marver, a large flat stone. After this shaping, and suitable blowing, the blower had formed a gather of glass into a parison (or *paraison*), the latter being a hollow bulb with rather thick walls, approximating in size and shape to the finished bottle, but smaller. Much of the art of blowing a bottle lay in shaping the parison, which had to be varied according to the shape and distribution of glass required in the finished bottle. The parison was converted into a bottle by blowing it into shape in a hinged mould. After the blowing was completed, the iron with the attached bottle was handed to the wetter-off, who removed the bottle from the mould and cracked off the bottle from the iron by allowing water to fall on it from a knife-shaped piece of iron. This caused many small cracks near the point of application of the water, the part that would eventually be the mouth of the bottle; a sharp tap on the iron resulted in the bottle falling off. The bottle was then taken by the finisher, who held it by means of a split cylinder of iron on the end of a rod. He applied a thread of hot glass round the crack-off, and finished by using, with a pair of tongs (figure 359), a plug and external mould to form the mouth and neck of the bottle. Finally, a taker-in took the bottle to the annealing kiln, where it was cooled slowly to prevent its cracking. There were variations in the method of working from place to place, but the essential operations were much the same.

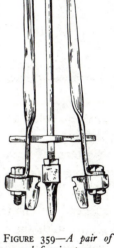

The semi-automatic machine needed only a gatherer and a taker-in. In Ashley's machine the gather of molten glass was dropped from an iron into the parison mould, where a plunger was pressed upwards into the glass to form the neck. This plunger was withdrawn and a puff of compressed air blew the glass up to fill the mould. The parison-mould was then opened and removed by hand. The parison, now held by the neck already formed, was inverted and the blow-mould closed around it. When in position the parison was blown up to form the finished bottle. The provision of a ring-mould to form the neck, and of parison- and blow-moulds, has been a feature of every successful machine since developed (plate 4 A).

FIGURE 359—*A pair of neck-forming tongs.*

Several variations of the original type appeared; in some the parison was pressed instead of blown into shape. This method was used for wide-mouth bottles and jars: after forming the neck, the glass was forced by a plunger to fill the space between it and the parison-mould.

The success of the semi-automatic bottle-machine created a need for some mechanical device to replace the gatherer for delivering molten glass to the machine. This step was accomplished by M. J. Owens, who built his first experimental machine in the United States in 1898. The method of operation is illustrated by the device with which he began his experiments; this was known as the Owens hand-gun (figure 360). The hollow cylinder of this gun was about $3\frac{1}{2}$ ft long: it was dipped into the molten glass and the piston withdrawn so as to suck glass up into the parison-mould. The glass was cut by a sliding knife, which then formed the bottom of the parison-mould, a plunger forming the neck. The entire gather was carried to a table where the parison, suspended by its neck in the neck-mould, was enclosed by a finishing-mould, in which the piston was pushed in and the bottle blown up. The diagram shows the gather with the finishing-mould around it.

In the automatic machine the moulds and the ancillary mechanism were mounted in sets or 'heads' round a rotating frame. To feed the glass to the machine a refractory saucer or pot about 10 ft in diameter and 9 inches deep was arranged so as to be continually fed by a stream of glass from the furnace, with part of it outside the furnace. The parison-moulds were arranged to dip into this reservoir of glass, and were filled automatically by suction. The removal of the parison-mould was effected automatically, leaving the parison hanging by the neck from the ring-mould. The finishing-mould closed around the parison and the bottle was completed by blowing.

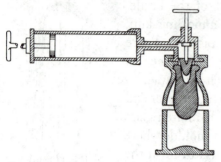

FIGURE 360—*The Owens hand-gun, 1898–1900.*

A team of five workers making bottles by hand could produce about 150 bottles an hour. The first Ashley machine, with two workers, produced about the same number. Two men working two later Ashley machines could make 200, while a 10-head Owens machine produced 2500 bottles an hour.

Although the Owens was the first successful completely automatic bottle-machine, the problem of eliminating the gatherer had been considered for some years. In 1885 the firm of Rylands, of Barnsley, designed a feeding-apparatus, which was only partially successful; it was probably a little before its time, for the advent of the multi-headed machine was needed to make the problem urgent. Homer Brooke produced the first successful 'feeder' in 1901, and feeders of this type were in use commercially for over twenty years. Here, a small projecting chamber was built at the working end of the furnace, and glass was allowed to run into the parison-mould through a hole in the bottom of this chamber. The stream was interrupted by a cup during the replacement of a full mould by an empty one: this resulted in chilling the glass, and bubbles or air-blisters were liable to be caused by the glass not filling the mould satisfactorily.

Subsequent developments treated the glass in a more viscous condition, and modern feeders form a gob of molten glass of suitable shape to go into the parison-mould. To obtain this gob the feeder is in the form of a long channel, about 15 ft long by 2 ft wide by 9 inches deep internally. This channel leads the glass from the furnace and allows its temperature to be adjusted, and by means of a plunger a column of glass of appropriate cross-section can be caused to issue from the orifice. The column is cut off at intervals by automatic shears, so that a succession of gobs of the desired shape can be fed to the moulds, which are brought in turn by the machine to the receiving position.

Similar developments took place in the methods of producing glass articles by pressing. This is a more simple process than bottle-blowing and is used in making pie-dishes, signal-lenses, bowls, and similar articles. It consists of dropping the correct amount of glass, at about yellow heat, into a mould, then thrusting a plunger into the glass and forcing it to assume the shape of the inside of the mould and the outside of the plunger.

III. FLAT GLASS

Flat glass had been made for many hundreds of years by processes (vol IV, ch 12) that were very little changed until the nineteenth century, when three methods of producing flat glass were in use. The first of these consisted in pouring the molten glass on to frames on which it was spread out evenly by rollers, the rough plate so formed being subsequently ground and polished. The description 'plate glass' is reserved for glass that has been thus ground and polished after casting.

The other two methods of making flat glass were the broad glass and the crown glass processes. Broad glass was made by blowing a large cylinder, which was cut along a line parallel to the axis, opened out, and flattened on a table. The crown method consisted of blowing a large sphere of glass which was subsequently opened out to form a bowl; this was then spun while still hot, so that a large flat disk of glass, about 5 ft in diameter, was formed. In England, most of the flat glass made was crown glass, which was of better quality than broad glass. In 1832, however, broad glass was taken up by Chance Brothers of Birmingham and the process was improved by blowing a larger cylinder—6 ft long and 16 inches in diameter—than had been the custom on the continent, and by allowing the cylinder to become cold before splitting it. When cold it could be cut cleanly with a diamond; it was subsequently flattened in a special heating-kiln. In starting work on this process in 1832 Lucas Chance showed great foresight, for when the excise duties were removed in 1845 the firm was in a good position to take advantage of the increased trade that followed. In 1851 the Chances were able to supply glass made by the cylinder process for the Crystal Palace. This work was done in co-operation with the French manufacturer, Georges Bontemps, who had brought French workmen over with him.

The cylinder-process remained essentially unchanged until 1903, when Lubbers in the United States succeeded in producing machine-drawn cylinders. In this process glass was ladled from the furnace and poured into a double crucible or pot mounted on the top of a kiln and heated by gas; the pots were about 42 inches in diameter, and each held about 500 lb of glass. The drawing-pipe was lowered by the machine into the glass; the glass did not stick to it, but solidified on the inside edge of the rim. The pipe was then drawn up, and at the same time air was blown down the pipe to blow the glass out to the diameter required. By controlling air-pressure and speed of drawing, a cylinder 40 ft in height and 40 inches in diameter could be made (figure 361). The pot from which the cylinder had been drawn was then turned over, thus presenting the under side, also in the form of a pot, in a condition ready to receive the next charge of molten glass. The cooled side, with the remains of the glass cylinder, was turned downwards over the heated kiln: the glass was melted off and the pot was reheated ready for the next cylinder.

FIGURE 361—*The Lubbers cylinder-blowing machine, 1903.*

The idea of drawing a flat sheet of glass direct from a furnace was considered for many years. The first patent was taken out in 1857 by William Clark of St Helens, but it was not until 1901 that Fourcault's successful process was patented. The general plan in all processes proposed was to dip a 'bait', in the form of a sheet of metal, into the molten glass; the glass adhered to the bait, which as it was drawn upwards withdrew the glass in the form of sheet. The difficulty to be overcome was that the nascent glass sheet gradually narrowed, because the glass coming from the furnace was hot enough to flow for some time afterwards. Fourcault solved this problem by forcing glass under hydrostatic pressure through a narrow slit in a fireclay float known as the *débiteuse* (figure 362). The *débiteuse* floats on the surface of the glass, and is depressed so that the slit is below the level of the glass. The glass is thus forced through the slit in the form of a sheet, and if it is drawn away as fast as it is formed the tractive force required is small: there is, therefore, little force tending to stretch the hot sheet, and thus the 'necking' is reduced. In addition, steel boxes through which water circulates are placed close above the slit to cool the sheet and solidify it as soon as possible. Fourcault's process had many teething troubles, however, and it was not until 1913 that it was operated commercially.

During this period I. W. Colburn in the United States was also working on a process for drawing sheet glass. In this process the flat sheet was drawn from the full surface of the glass, the width being kept constant by water-cooled knurled rollers operating on the edge of the glass sheet one or two inches above the surface of the molten glass. The sheet was drawn vertically for a few feet and then reheated enough to bend over a horizontal roller, whence it proceeded through a horizontal lehr or annealing oven.

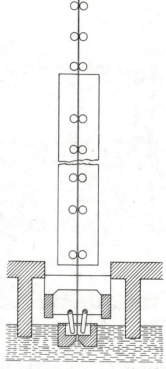

In making plate glass it had been the practice to remove some of the glass from the founding-pot in what was, in effect, a large ladle or iron box called a refining cuvette. This glass was left in the box for about six hours to finish refining, that is, to allow bubbles to escape, and it was then poured on the casting-table and rolled flat. In 1846 Bessemer, whose activities in glass-making did not equal his achievements in steel-making, had the idea of passing molten glass through a pair of rollers to produce a sheet. His experiments did not lead to a successful commercial process. He wanted to melt the glass in an open-hearth furnace instead of in crucibles, and to run the glass out of

FIGURE 362—*Diagram of Fourcault process for sheet glass.*

a rectangular slit at the bottom of the furnace. Although his process was unsuccessful, his new method of melting foreshadowed the development of the tank furnace, and in 1926 glass from a tank furnace was made to flow over a weir on to rollers, thus initiating the continuous plate-glass process. In 1884–7, the rolled-plate process was developed by Chance Brothers; in this process the molten glass was poured upon an inclined plate and then passed between a pair of rollers.

In whatever way the plates of glass were formed they had subsequently to be ground flat and polished. Machinery was gradually introduced for these processes; originally it was steam-driven, but in time gas-engines and electricity in turn provided the motive power.

IV. FURNACES

This mechanization of production of both flat glass and glass containers would not have been possible if there had not been a contemporaneous development in the furnaces used for melting glass. The furnaces in use in the glass industry in 1850 were direct-fired. The fuel burned in a grate underneath the floor on which stood the refractory pots in which the glass was melted, and flames from the burning fuel passed up through apertures to surround the pots. This furnace was situated in the centre of a large brick-work cone, open at the top, which in addition to forming the workroom around the furnace also acted as a chimney (vol IV, plate 21 B); the products of combustion passed out of the furnace-chamber through small flues into the wide outer conical chimney. These furnaces were not economical in fuel, but they had one advantage in that the draught of air drawn up by the cone kept the workers cool.

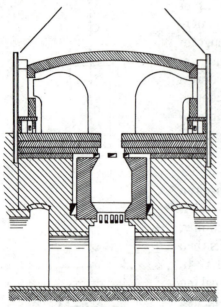

FIGURE 363—*Boetius furnace: an early example of the use of recuperation.*

Some improvements were made in direct-fired furnaces. The Frisbie feed was a mechanical device which fed the fuel upwards into the furnace-box instead of downwards. The products of combustion thus passed upwards through the hot fire; this resulted in the fuel being partially gasified and the gases burning inside the furnace. In the Boetius furnace can be seen the beginnings of the use of pre-heating of the air in the glass industry (figure 363). A large proportion of the air needed for combustion, termed secondary air, was passed through channels around the fire-boxes or producers. This method of pre-heating, in principle the same as that now known as recuperation, does not appear to have been used very considerably until the twentieth century.

The outstanding development in furnaces in the last half of the nineteenth century was the regenerative furnace of F. and W. Siemens (figure 364). In such a furnace two sets of chambers were provided, and by means of valves it was possible to arrange for the outgoing products of combustion to pass through one set of chambers while the incoming gas and air passed through the other. The direction of flow was reversed at intervals, so that the incoming gas and air

could take up the heat which had been
given up during the interval by the outgoing gases to the chambers through which
they were passing (figure 365). The first
patent taken out in England by Frederick
Siemens was dated 1856. The new furnace
was apparently first used in Atkinson's
steel-works at Sheffield, and in 1860–1 the

FIGURE 364—*Early Siemens regenerative tank furnace.*

regenerative system was tried out at the glass-works of Lloyd & Summerfield,
Birmingham. Chance Brothers had a furnace with a regenerative system in
operation in 1861. These furnaces used producer-gas as fuel.

This new method of heating enabled the glass-manufacturer to depart from
the traditional method of melting glass in fireclay pots. The gas-fired regenerative
furnace provided considerably higher temperatures than had previously been
available, and the useful life of the pots was consequently very much reduced.
This led to the tank furnace, possibly by accident. It is recorded that in a large
Rhenish factory, working four regenerative furnaces, the use of a considerably
higher temperature than usual resulted in all the pots in a furnace breaking.
The glass spread over the siege, or floor, of the furnace and pieces of broken pots
floated to the surface and were removed. The glass was well bubbled, another
batch was added to give the required working depth, and so the first tank
furnace was obtained.

References in the literature to the first introduction of regenerative tanks are
somewhat contradictory, but it is certain that they were in operation about 1870.
At first they were day-tanks; that is, the glass batch was melted overnight and
worked during the day. As the industry became increasingly mechanized, however, the tanks developed into continuous tanks; instead of glass-making operations being spread in time they were spread
in space. The batch was fed in at one end
of the tank and the temperature so arranged that, as the melting batch began
to form glass, it flowed down the tank to a
region where the temperature was higher
and refining could take place. Finally, it
moved on to a region where the temperature was somewhat lower and the glass
was in good condition for working.

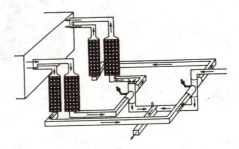

FIGURE 365—*Regenerative pre-heating system.*

BIBLIOGRAPHY

In the first half of the nineteenth century, England led in industrial development based on steam-power and railways. In the second half of the nineteenth century, the industrial application of chemistry and physics became more and more important. This was particularly so in Germany, and, as has been stated earlier, Schott and Abbé were foremost at this time in producing new fundamental knowledge about glass; similarly, the textbooks and literature in general about glass were mostly by German authors:

BENRATH, H. E. 'Die Glasfabrikation.' Vieweg, Braunschweig. 1875.
DRALLE, R. 'Die Glasfabrikation.' Oldenbourg, Munich. 1911.
HENRIVAUX, J. 'La verrerie au XXe siècle en France.' (2nd ed.). Geisler, Paris. 1911.
POWELL, H. J., CHANCE, H. and HARRIS, H. G. 'The Principles of Glass Making.' London. 1883.

A more recently published book that deals in some part with the period of this article is:

HODKIN, F. W. and COUSEN, A. 'A Textbook of Glass Technology.' Constable, London. 1925.

In the volumes of the *Journal of the Society of Glass Technology*, papers have frequently appeared dealing with historical aspects.

The growth of the American glass container industry, with particular reference to the Libbey–Owens partnership, is recorded in considerable detail in:

SCOVILLE, W. C. 'Revolution in Glass Making.' Harvard University Press, Cambridge, Mass. 1948.

Free-hand blowing of bottles in an eighteenth-century glasshouse.

29

PRINTING AND RELATED TRADES

W. TURNER BERRY

I. MECHANICAL TYPE-CASTING

BEFORE the period covered by this volume the methods of type-casting previously described (vol III, ch 15) were still being practised in many foundries. With the old ring-tailed casting-mould in one hand and a tiny ladle of molten metal in the other, the workmen still cast a single letter at each operation. In a 10-hour day one man might cast about 4000 pieces of type, which needed to undergo several other operations before they were ready for the compositor. Various attempts had been made in most countries to cast type by mechanical means, replacing hand-pouring by hand-operated pumps. In England such inventions were little encouraged, as the founders averred that their results were inferior to those of the old method; they also probably feared labour troubles, or were anxious to maintain agreed prices.

The first effective mechanical type-casting machine was the invention of David Bruce and was patented in the United States in 1838 (figure 366). In its action a pivoted frame rocked in such a manner as to move the mould to and from the nozzle of a melting-pot. In conjunction with this rocking there were combined movements for opening and closing the mould at the appropriate moments, and for tilting the matrix away from the face of the newly cast type in order to leave it clear for ejection. These machines could be worked by hand or by steam-power. They were soon in use in America and were quickly copied in Germany by F. A. Brockhaus, a leading printer of Leipzig, who exhibited his model at the Great Exhibition of 1851 together with books printed from type cast in the machine, for which he received a medal.

The Bruce caster was introduced into Britain shortly before 1850. The firm of Miller & Richard, progressive type-founders in Edinburgh, was using it in 1849 despite the combined opposition of the English foundries. Some of the larger printing-houses and newspapers were also casting by machinery before the 1851 Exhibition, including the firm of Clowes, which printed the voluminous Exhibition catalogues. Soon after this date the prejudice against mechanical casting broke down in England, and the general principles of the Bruce machine, with various modifications from time to time, are those upon which most subsequent type-casters have been modelled.

'The Times', which was responsible for important mechanical innovations in the printing trade, also achieved the record for speed in mechanical type-casting with its rotary caster, patented by Frederick Wicks in 1881, which had 100

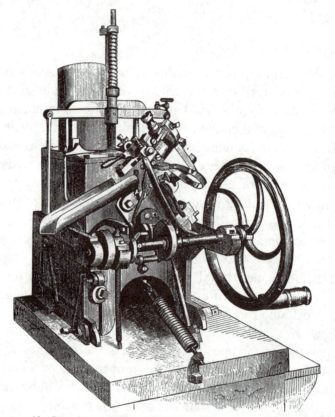

FIGURE 366—*Pivotal type-casting machine invented by David Bruce of New York.*

moulds and was capable of casting 60 000 characters an hour. For a newspaper, such rapidity of casting brought the advantage that the distribution of type after printing could be abandoned. The used type was simply thrown back into the melting-pot and the paper went to press each day with new type.

II. TYPE-COMPOSING MACHINES

Besides making attempts to mechanize type-casting, inventors were at work on the design of machines that would set type ready for printing at a greater

speed than was possible with hand-composition. There were two varieties
of these machines in the minds of inventors: one a type-setter that would
assemble ordinary founders' type, the other a machine that would actually
cast the type as well as assemble it. The first idea occurred to many minds, and
fortunes were spent in experiments. They all proceeded on much the same line,
which was to arrange a store of the various letters, figures, punctuation marks,
and so on, each in a separate magazine, from which the individual types could
be released as required by an operator by means of a keyboard resembling that
of a typewriter. As each letter was released from its magazine it slid down a
groove or channel to the place of assembly. In theory this was simple enough,
but in practice some letters fell more quickly than others, while the mechanism
for releasing only one piece of type at a time seems to have proved a major
problem.

The first record of such an invention is in 1822, when William Church, a
New Yorker living in England, announced that he had discovered a method of
composing type automatically; but apart from a wooden model of the machine
nothing was constructed. Eighteen years later a similar machine was designed
by Henry Bessemer (1813–98, inventor of the converter), and patented by J. H.
Young and A. Delcambre, both of Lille; it was known by the names of the
patentees and also as the Pianotype (figure 367). This machine required one
operator at the keyboard, while another gathered the types at the end of the
runway and 'justified' (spaced out) the lines to a given measure. On 17 December
1842 the type for the first number of the 'Family Herald' was set on this machine
at a speed of 6000 letters and spaces an hour. During the next thirty-five years
many type-setting machines were patented and some gave useful service. In
America the Mitchell (1853) and the Alden (1856)—which had 14 626 parts in
its construction—were used for a time in book-publishing houses. In England
the Hattersley (1857), the invention of a Manchester engineer, was successful
enough to be adopted by several provincial newspapers. In 1868 Alexander
Mackie, the proprietor of the 'Warrington Guardian', constructed an ingenious
automatic type-setter which was in two parts. One was a perforating machine
which in a narrow strip of paper punched holes corresponding to the letters
that it was desired to set. This strip was then fed into the main machine, which
at the top had little levers seeking to pass through the paper but unable to do so
save where the perforations appeared in line. When this happened a movement
of the machine extracted a type and dropped it upon a travelling belt, which
delivered it to a place of assembly ready for justifying by hand. This principle
was adopted in the Monotype machine some years later. The first type-setter to

be driven by electric power was the Hooker (1874), which was developed for Clowes and exhibited by that firm at the Caxton celebration in 1877.

An immense number of type-setters, some of them combining setting with the distribution of type after use, was put on the English and foreign markets

FIGURE 367—*The Young and Delcambre type-composing machine.*

before 1890. None of them, however, gave complete satisfaction in practice. They frequently became out of order, and their superiority in speed over hand-setting was not sufficiently marked to compensate for their various disadvantages. 'The Times', which did all in its power to encourage inventors, was reported to have cellars choked with discarded machines. Some would no doubt have reached greater perfection in course of time but for the epoch-making invention of the Linotype[1] machine, which nullified them all and opened a new era in the history of printing, especially newspaper-printing [1].

[1] Etymology: line o' type (!).

Type-setters had required three operators: one for the keyboard, one to keep up the supply of type, and a third to justify the line. The Linotype required one operator: the machine did the rest. Even skilled compositors who had been hostile to all mechanical setting-devices and had managed to keep them out of many printing-offices, particularly in London, eventually recognized that this new machine had come to stay, and many adapted themselves to the situation by becoming Linotype operators.

The Linotype was not a development of the type-setting machines. It was evolved from another line of thought altogether; in fact, those who devoted their time and money to its early development did not, in the first instance, have the printing trade in mind at all. The world owes this machine to the persistence of the stenographer James Clephane, who later became a practising lawyer in Washington. He wished for a machine which would save him the tedious business of writing longhand copies of his shorthand notes. He was one of the early users of the writing-machine invented by Densmore and Sholes (p 689) which eventually developed into the Remington typewriter (1873); but he wished to go further and own a machine that would mechanically reproduce his law reports in quantity without the cost of hand-composition. Clephane engaged Charles T. Moore, an inventor, who eventually devised for him a method of casting type-high 'slugs'[1] from a papier mâché mould.

In the following year (1879) Clephane arranged with Ottmar Mergenthaler (1854–99), a Württemberg watch-maker who had emigrated to America, to build a machine on the lines of Moore's. This was successfully accomplished and became known as the rotary impression machine. Mergenthaler followed this by another machine which consisted of vertical bars on each of which letters of the alphabet were engraved in relief. These bars were controlled by a keyboard, and when a line was in position a papier mâché strip was forced against them to form a matrix from which a whole line of copy could be cast. It then occurred to Mergenthaler that if he could assemble letters in relief from which a matrix could be struck, why should he not assemble a series of alphabetic matrices and cast a type-high slug direct? The new idea was to compose mechanically single-letter matrices which were released from magazines by a keyboard and moved to an assembly point by a blast of air. Justifying was to be done by wedge-shaped spaces which would extend the line to the measure required—an idea already patented by Schuckers in 1879 and eventually purchased by Mergenthaler's backers for half a million dollars. The Linotype 'blower' model was completed in 1885 and first used at the office of the 'New York Tribune' in 1886 (figure 368).

---

[1] A 'slug' is a line of type cast in one piece.

One of the major problems that the Linotype Printing Company, as it was first called, had to overcome was the rapid supply of some hundreds of matrices for each machine. These matrices had to be struck from punches which were laboriously hand-made by specially skilled workmen. In ordinary type-casting the founder, having cut his punch, needed only one or two matrices from which to cast vast numbers of a particular character: the Linotype needed hundreds of matrices and the difficulty was that the life of the punches was limited and duplicates were constantly necessary. Fortunately at this time Linn Boyd Benton, an inventor of Milwaukee, had just perfected a mechanical punch-cutting machine which worked on the pantographic principle and enormously simplified, cheapened, and speeded up the making of punches. In 1889 the Linotype Printing Company was able to purchase one of these machines, which not only solved their problem but improved the accuracy of their matrices. A perfected model of the Linotype was completed by 1890, and some hundreds were constructed—to find a ready sale in America, Great Britain, and later on the European continent. By 1900 twenty-one London dailies and 250 other newspapers and periodicals in London and the provinces were being set on these machines, of which the success was unparalleled in the mechanical history of printing. Today the Linotype is used throughout the world for the text-matter of newspapers and magazines, and in America for book-work also: its general principles are much as in the 1890 model.

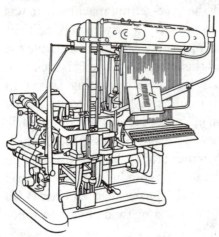

FIGURE 368—*The Linotype 'blower' composing machine, first used for the 'New York Tribune', 3 July 1886.*

One of the most fascinating features of the Linotype is the distribution mechanism. When a combination of matrices has cast its slug the matrices are taken by an arm and placed on a distribution bar. Each matrix is toothed like a key, and they hang from corresponding teeth on the bar, along which they are propelled by a worm-wheel. At intervals there are vacancies on the bar and, on reaching one of these, a matrix loses its grip and drops into its own compartment to line up behind the matrices of that same character, ready for further use when their turn arrives.

III. THE TYPEWRITER

Typewriters bear close affinity to type-composing machines and may be mentioned at this point. Their history begins with a patent granted in 1714 to Henry Mill, an English engineer, for 'an artificial machine, or method of impressing or transcribing of letters singly or progressively one after another, as in writing'. No drawings or descriptions of his machine exist and there is no record that one was ever constructed. If this was a typewriter in our modern sense, then Mill was well ahead of all others in this field; but there was little need for such machines in days when ill-paid clerks wrote legible hands and business houses were satisfied with duplicate records made with damp tissue and a copying-press. Even a century and a half later, when the Remington Company put the first reliable typewriter on the market (1873), sales were negligible for a time.

During the eighteenth and early nineteenth centuries many European inventors constructed writing-machines of various kinds, including a number which embossed paper for the instruction of the blind.

The first typewriter patented in the United States was the 'Typographer' invented by William Austin Burt of Detroit (1829). The type characters were mounted on a small semicircular band of metal which was moved to bring any desired letter to the printing position. In subsequent inventions this band of type was often replaced by a wheel with the type characters round the rim, or by a sleeve of small diameter with rows of characters round its surface. In all machines of this kind, when the required letter was in register, the impression was made by striking the band, wheel, or sleeve against the paper, or by a small hammer that struck the paper against the type. Two great advantages of such machines were that perfect alignment was easily obtained and that the type could be changed from one face to another. The sole surviving machine of this kind is the 'Varityper', which has the type characters on a curved band easily changeable for different alphabets or languages. It is chiefly used for the making of type-plates for the offset printing process.

The progenitor of the type-bar machines, having each character mounted on a separate bar which can be brought to the printing position independently of the others, was the invention of Xavier Progin, a printer of Marseilles (1833). He called it a *machine kryptographique* and maintained that it would write 'almost as fast as a pen'.

Christopher Latham Sholes, an American printer, is generally accepted as the father of the modern typewriter. With various associates he invented a machine for numbering which led to a writing-machine of the type-bar variety with a horizontal platen, whose movement was actuated by a weight. The impression was made by means of an inked ribbon. This working model was finished in 1867. During the next five years, encouraged by James Densmore, a capable business man, Sholes made some thirty different models before a machine capable of rapid fingering was constructed. His chief difficulty had been to over-come the clashing of the type-bars when fast typing was attempted. He eventually arranged a keyboard in which the letters that most frequently came together were placed as far apart as possible in the type-basket. This arrangement of the key-board was adopted in nearly all subsequent machines and became known as the

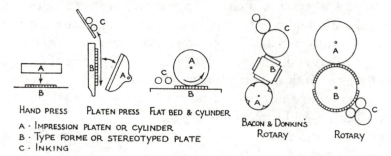

HAND PRESS   PLATEN PRESS   FLAT BED & CYLINDER

A · IMPRESSION PLATEN OR CYLINDER
B · TYPE FORME OR STEREOTYPED PLATE
C · INKING

BACON & DONKIN'S ROTARY   ROTARY

FIGURE 369—*Diagrammatic illustration of the principles of operation of various types of press.*

'Universal'. The machine was placed on the market in 1876 and, although sales were slow for a year or so, it eventually proved a commercial success because it was fully capable of doing good and rapid work and the time was propitious for its introduction.

Before the end of the nineteenth century, some forty other famous typewriters were introduced which embodied many improvements, including fully visible writing on the bar machines (Yöst 'Caligraph', 1880); portable machines (Blick, 1893); the tabulator as part of the mechanism (Underwood, 1897); and many other valuable innovations.

IV. THE IRON PRESS

Although mechanical composition was not fully accomplished until the 1890s, machinery for reproducing type-matter had made great strides by the middle of the nineteenth century. Clowes, who printed the weighty 'Reports of the Juries' of the 1851 Exhibition, had at that time twenty-six printing-machines driven by steam-power, and 'The Times' was producing 35 000 copies a day on a great rotary press, a replica of which was one of the most popular features of the exhibition. Various stages in the evolution of the press are shown in figure 369.

The wooden hand-press described earlier (vol III, p 400) offered the only method of reproducing type-matter before the end of the eighteenth century, except for minor improvements to obtain greater pressure introduced by M. Anisson for the Imprimerie Royale (1783), Firmin Didot of Paris (1795), Adam Ramage (a Scotsman of Philadelphia) (1790), and one or two others. While the main parts of the hand-press were of wood, the necessary pressure to print large formes of type-matter at a single impression was unattainable. The limitations

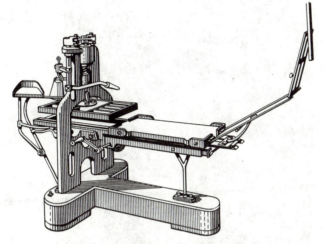

FIGURE 370—*The first English iron press. Invented by Lord Stanhope, 1800.*

of the wooden press were also a serious handicap in obtaining good impressions from the wood-engravings executed by the new technique of Thomas Bewick and his school, who excelled in the delicacy of their design.

The first major improvement in the press was made not by a printer or press-maker but by Charles Mahon, Earl Stanhope (1753–1816), amateur scientist and mathematician. He conceived of a means of producing a tremendous pressure at the moment of impression by a combination of lever- and screw-motion. The other parts of the press, including the mechanism for running the bed under the platen, were similar in principle to those of earlier presses, but all were made of iron except for the stout wooden tee upon which the bed rested. The extra power and stability of the Stanhope press made possible, for the first time, a full-sized platen which allowed an impression to be taken of the whole type-surface at one pull (figure 370). William Bulmer and other leading printers experimented with the new press and proved it to be superior in every way to the older presses. 'The Times' promptly installed a battalion of Stanhopes and so did those other newspapers and printers who were willing to pay the price of 90 guineas. This price, double that of a wooden press, encouraged several inferior imitations and a number of press-makers attempted to graft Stanhope's principles upon wooden presses—with disastrous results.

The first American iron press was the invention of George Clymer of Phila-

FIGURE 371—*The Columbian press, the first to eliminate the screw, was invented by George Clymer of Philadelphia, and was available in America in 1813. It was manufactured by R. W. Cope from 1818 for the English and continental markets.*

delphia, a cabinet-maker who in his younger days had attempted to make improvements to wooden presses. It is doubtful if Clymer had the opportunity of examining a Stanhope press. If he had, it certainly exerted little influence on the design and mechanism of his famous Columbian press, which was completed about 1813 (figure 371). A distinguishing feature of the Columbian was its elaborate ornamentation, and particularly the large metal eagle, perched on top, which jumped into the air at each pull of the bar. It was the first hand-press to

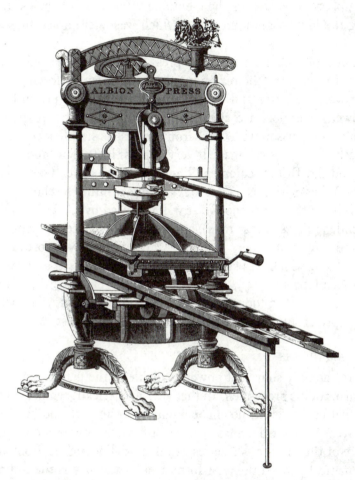

FIGURE 372—*An early form of the Albion press invented by R. W. Cope. In later models the counterweight bearing the royal arms at the head of the press—an idea derived from the Columbian press—was eliminated and the raising of the platen was effected by a spring.*

eliminate the screw, employing a well balanced system of levers and counter-weights (the eagle among them) to communicate the power to a straight plunger which forced down the platen. The action was smooth and required no great effort to obtain a good impression. The American newspapers, and book- and jobbing-printers who could afford to expend 400 dollars, quickly adopted the new press. In 1817 Clymer came to England and arranged that a press-maker, R. W. Cope, should manufacture the Columbian for the English market, where it was soon preferred to the Stanhope—particularly by printers specializing in the printing of wood-blocks. John I. Wells, another American, who took out a patent for a press in 1819, must be mentioned, for to him belongs the credit for introducing the first toggle-joint press, which was later copied by several other inventors.

R. W. Cope brought out his own press in 1820 and called it the Albion (figure 372). In this press the platen was brought down by forcing a steel bar to become vertical, the lower end of the bar sliding over the platen head and the greatest power being obtained at the moment it reached the perpendicular. Its light weight in comparison with other iron presses, its simplicity of action, and its great strength of impression, made it very popular in England and to some extent in Europe and the British colonies. The Albion has never been wholly superseded. When William Morris set out to revive fine printing he chose the Albion for use at his Kelmscott Press (1890–8). It was also used by C. H. St John Hornby at his Ashendene Press (1894–1914), and at the Doves Press (1900–17) by T. J. Cobden-Sanderson and Emery Walker. Many other private presses have preferred the Albion, which was subsequently made in thirteen sizes ranging from half-sheet folio platens ($15 \times 9\frac{3}{8}$ in) and sold in the 1860s at £12, to double royal (40×25 in) at £75. Even today many enthusiastic amateurs, who make printing their hobby, prefer an old Albion to any other hand-press.

V. THE STEAM PRESS

Until 1810 the only source of power available to the printer was provided by the strong arms of his press-men. In that year Frederick Koenig, a Saxon printer with ideas that had received no encouragement in his own country, constructed a power-driven press for Thomas Bensley, a famous London book-printer. The chief feature of the press was a series of inking-cylinders, fed from an ink-box, which automatically inked the type-forme: otherwise it was the ordinary hand-press adapted to power instead of manual operation. It was not very successful, although some of the 'Annual Register' was printed by it in Bensley's office at the rate of 800 sheets an hour.

Koenig was not long in realizing that a machine in which two flat surfaces came together—one to support the type and the other the paper—could never achieve the speed of production at which he was aiming; furthermore, to increase the size of these two surfaces, so that a larger area could be printed at a single impression, seemed impracticable. Encouraged and financed by Thomas Bensley and other eminent master printers, Koenig and a young fellow-countryman, Andrew Bauer, then turned their inventive minds to fresh experiments.

It must be recorded here that William Nicholson (1753–1815), scientist, engineer, schoolmaster, and author, had as early as 1790 taken out a patent which included details of printing machinery. His ideas included a method of inking with a roller and of making the impression by a cylinder carrying the paper, which rolled over the inked type. He further described a method by which the paper was to pass between two cylinders, one of which had the type-forme attached to its surface while the other served to press the paper against the forme, which had been inked by a third cylinder. Through lack of the necessary capital or through his failure to find a patron for his inventions, Nicholson's ideas lay dormant for some years. Some time later, being in need of money, he acted as a patent agent, and when Koenig and Bensley sought to take out a patent for the mechanized screw-press of 1810 already described, Bensley visited Nicholson for advice on the necessary procedure. He found him in the Queen's Bench prison, a broken man of fifty-seven, and learned of the patents which the unfortunate Nicholson had taken out twenty years before. Whether Koenig hit on the idea of using a cylinder as the impression surface before Bensley and Nicholson met is a controversial matter into which we cannot enter [1]; but by 1811 Koenig had actually constructed the first flat-bed cylinder-machine, the principle of which formed the basis of so many subsequent machines and was another important milestone in the history of printing technology.

Koenig's first cylinder-machine consisted of a type-bed propelled backwards and forwards under a large cylinder which had a three-stop motion. The cylinder had three separate printing surfaces and printed three sheets for each complete revolution. The paper was inserted at the top of the cylinder while it was stationary, the sheet being secured by a frisket frame. The cylinder then made one-third of a revolution, which brought a second impression surface to the top, and after a second sheet had been laid the cylinder again revolved one-third, which made the impression on the first sheet and allowed it to be removed by hand. A third sheet was then laid on the third impression surface and the cylinder completed its revolution bringing number one surface to the top, and so on. The inking-apparatus was similar to that of his first machine, the rollers being leather-covered and fed from an ink-box.

With the idea of doubling the speed of production Koenig then built a machine with a cylinder at each end, in order to utilize both motions of the type-forme. The trade was invited to see these machines in Bensley's office, but neither printers nor newspaper proprietors were very impressed, with the exception of

John Walter of 'The Times', who ordered two of the double-cylinder type to be erected in Printing House Square. They were completed with the help of 'The Times' engineers in 1814, and on 29 November readers were told that this issue was the first newspaper ever printed on a steam-driven machine at a speed of 1100 impressions an hour.

In Koenig's last machine designed in England an attempt was made to print both sides of a sheet at once. This first 'perfecting' machine was the natural out-

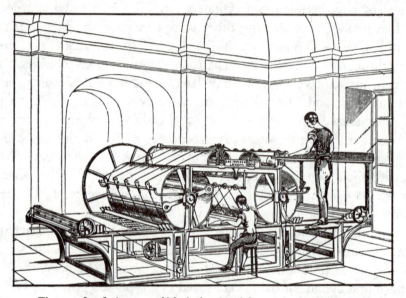

FIGURE 373—*The type of perfecting press which Applegath and Cowper developed from the Koenig machine. Various models were made for newspaper and book printing in the 1820s and 1830s for England and continental Europe.*

come of the single-cylinder type, being in fact a combination of two of these under one motive power. A machine of this kind was made for Bensley in 1815, but it was too large and clumsy for book-work. 'The Times' adopted the perfector and, after many modifications had been made to it by that newspaper's new engineers, Applegath and Cowper, it gave satisfaction until 1828 (figure 373). In that year, to keep pace with expanding circulation, 'The Times' put in a new machine, designed and built by their two engineers, which printed four sheets at a time on four cylinders from one type-forme at a speed of 4000 impressions an hour. This machine printed on one side of the sheet only, so that later news might be printed on the reverse.

The perfector type of machine was greatly improved by David Napier, an English press-manufacturer. He invented a system of grippers, or fingers, which took hold of the paper at the feed-board, held it while the impression was made, and then released it as the grippers of the perfecting cylinder took it over. These cylinders made two revolutions for each sheet printed, and during the second revolution a system of toggles raised the cylinder to permit the type-forme to run back without touching (figure 374). Later, this type of machine was greatly

FIGURE 374—*The Rutt flat-bed cylinder made by the firm of Napier, c 1819. This was a simple hand-operated machine used for book and jobbing work.*

improved in France and was known as the Anglo-French machine. In America, Robert Hoe of New York also perfected the English inventions, and developed single- and double-cylinder presses which, with subsequent improvements, are still in use. These early Hoe machines were capable of 2000 impressions an hour (the double-cylinders, 4000), which was as fast as a competent feeder could lay on the sheets.

VI. THE ROTARY PRESS

As the circulation of newspapers and other periodicals increased it was realized that faster production could never be achieved if the type-matter was to remain on a flat bed of great weight which had to be propelled backwards and forwards for each impression. The solution was obviously to adopt a rotary principle in which type and paper, each on separate cylinders, revolved together in mangle fashion with a continuous movement. Nicholson's patent of 1790 had suggested the possibilities of this principle, and in 1813 Richard M. Bacon, proprietor and printer of the 'Norwich Mercury', in partnership with Bryan Donkin, an engineer of Bermondsey, took out a patent for a machine of this type (figure 369). These inventors used four trays arranged on the four sides of a revolving spindle; in each tray a page of type was secured. This four-sided prism revolved between an inking-cylinder—which rose and fell to adapt itself to the four flat type-formes—and the impression-unit, which was quatrefoil in section. The machine was a wonder of ingenuity; but although the Cambridge University Press took it up, with the idea of using it for Bible-printing, it failed to give satisfaction. The great feature of this machine, which gives it an important place in the history of printing, was its use of inking-rollers made from glue and treacle. The machine itself was a failure, but the composition rollers soon became universal and the printing trade owes much to this innovation.

It was not until 1846 that a successful rotary press was built. This was the Hoe type revolving press, installed at the office of the 'Philadelphia Public Ledger'. In this machine the type was secured round a horizontal cylinder in cast iron beds, one for each page. Wedge-shaped metal rules locked between the columns of type prevented them from flying out through centrifugal force —although this mishap seems to have happened occasionally. Round the central cylinder four smaller impression-cylinders were grouped. As the sheets were fed automatic grippers carried them between the impression-cylinders and the revolving central type-cylinder. Meanwhile Applegath had built for 'The Times' a machine on much the same lines, except that the great type-cylinder, $5\frac{1}{2}$ ft in diameter, was in a vertical position and had eight vertical impression-cylinders grouped round it. This press needed eight men to feed it and eight to take off the printed sheets. A similar press of smaller size, which printed the 'Illustrated London News', was one of the sights at the exhibition in Hyde Park in 1851. The first Hoe type revolving press erected outside the country of its birth was bought for *La Patrie* (Paris 1848). In England it was installed for 'Lloyd's Weekly' (1857); and 'The Times', appreciating its superiority to their vertical model, changed over to a ten-feeder Hoe in the same year. This machine was capable of 20 000 impressions an hour, but required the attention of twenty-five men and boys to feed and take off the sheets (figure 375).

Despite this astonishing progress in speed there was still an urge for greater production. The taxes on knowledge which had kept British newspapers at a high price and hindered the establishment of new ones—especially in the provinces—were all repealed during the mid-nineteenth century. The newspaper tax of 1*d* on each copy was abolished in 1855; the advertisement tax, imposed in 1815 at 3*s* 6*d* (whatever the size of the advertisement) and reduced to 1*s* 6*d* in 1834, was repealed altogether in 1853; while the duty on

FIGURE 375—*The Hoe ten-feeder, sheet-fed rotary press, which was capable of 20 000 impressions an hour. Hoe machines with four, six, eight, or ten feeder stations were used by many newspapers during the 1860s and 1870s.*

paper, which had been 1½*d* a pound since 1837, was cancelled in 1861. The removal of these taxes encouraged greater sales and made possible the launching of a vast number of periodicals for a great variety of readers.

Experiments had been conducted for some time with the object of casting, from the type-formes, curved stereotype plates which would fit round the type-cylinders in place of loose type. Stereotyping was by no means a new invention, for it is believed that castings of type-matter were attempted experimentally in Holland and France as early as the sixteenth century. By 1725 William Ged, a goldsmith of Glasgow, was making them by means of plaster moulds, and Andrew Foulis, also of Glasgow, took out patents for a similar method, which by the early nineteenth century had become an established practice in the book-printing section of the trade. Stereotyping offered most obvious advantages for the printing of books that were being constantly reprinted, such as Bibles, prayer-books, school-books, and so forth. It reduced the wear of type and the need to keep vast quantities of set type standing for future use. About 1830 papier mâché replaced plaster, and it eventually became the normal practice to take a mould in 'flong' (several layers of paper pasted together with a mastic compound) from the type of any book of which a second impression seemed likely to be needed. Before this period such duplicate plates had been made flat for use on flat-bed machines. In 1854 Charles Craske succeeded in casting plates for the entire page of the 'New York Herald', each of them conforming to the curvature of the cylinder. James Dellagana, an Italian working in England,

FIGURE 376—*The press constructed by William Bullock of Philadelphia in 1865, which printed from a continuous web or roll of paper.*

who became the most successful stereotyper of his day, also made curved plates of the separate columns of 'The Times', for use on their Hoe machine in place of the loose type secured with wedge rules. These innovations enabled the newspapers to cast two or more sets of duplicates from one setting of type, which proved an important economy.

The feeding of single sheets of paper was now the main factor retarding speed of production: the solution was to print from an endless roll of paper. Fourdrinier had invented a machine that made paper in endless rolls as early as 1802, and Rowland Hill (1795–1879), of penny postage fame, had printed from a roll at 44 Chancery Lane in 1835; but the duty on paper at that time had demanded a stamp on each sheet, and therefore printing from the roll was considered impracticable by the taxing authorities. In 1865 William Bullock of Philadelphia invented the first newspaper rotary to use a continuous web (figure 376). It was first employed in the office of the 'Philadelphia Inquirer'.

Almost at the same time 'The Times' completed experiments in the same

ILLUSTRATION   701

direction. In 1866 they patented the famous Walter press, which first printed that newspaper in 1868. The main difference between the two machines was that whereas the Bullock machine cut the roll into sheets as it entered the press and actually printed on single sheets, the Walter press printed on the roll which was automatically cut after printing.

These machines were a challenge to the firm of R. Hoe & Company, who offered encouragement to the manufacture of faster-drying inks that would not 'set-off' in rapid printing. They also persuaded the paper-makers to produce rolls of more uniform quality and at lower prices. The Hoe 'perfecting web' press fully justified their efforts, and embodied in one machine all the improvements of the others. In France the firm of Marinoni had developed a rotary press with important features of its own, including the delivery of the sheets in four neat piles ready for folding, and the joining of the end of the roll to a new one without stopping the press.

The next step forward was a rotary press that, after printing and cutting the roll, folded the sheet ready for handling by the newsagent. This was achieved by Duncan & Wilson of Liverpool with their Victory rotary press, built in 1870 for the 'Glasgow Star'.

From this period the chief problem was the growth in size of newspapers, which resulted

FIGURE 377—*A woodcut from the news-pamphlet 'Trewe Encountre', London, 1513.*

in the construction of machines that would print, insert, and fold papers of a varying number of pages. These machines were really several units combined, each printing from its own roll, but all conveying the printed sheets to a single point where they were folded and inserted to make one newspaper.

VII. ILLUSTRATION

Picture-papers, or newspapers that made illustration their chief feature, originated in England with the 'Daily Graphic', which first appeared on 4 January 1890.

There had been occasional pictures in news-sheets many years before. As early as 1513 a pioneer news-pamphlet, bearing the title 'Trewe Encountre' and describing the defeat of the Scots at Flodden, was illustrated by a woodcut of a scene from this battle (figure 377). Similar woodcuts appeared from time to time in couriers' news-letters and news-pamphlets which were *ad hoc* publications concerned with one event of topical interest. On the continent, however, they became more general in character and more regular in publication, and were the forerunners of the newspapers we know today.

Advertisers were quick to appreciate the value of illustrations, and by the early eighteenth century tiny woodcuts appeared which drew attention to the very wordy announcements concerning the merits of various medicaments, surgical belts, and beautifying lotions.

By the 1790s the 'Morning Chronicle' and the 'Observer' were illustrating important events, but in this practice they remained almost alone for some years. By the 1820s wood engravings were a special feature of the broadsheets issued by J. Catnach and others, which pictured and described royal marriages, disasters at sea, public executions, and the like, to satisfy the cravings of the common people for details of the latest events of the day. These sheets—a penny plain and twopence coloured—demonstrated the value of illustration, even if they were crude and usually inaccurate. They undoubtedly had great influence on the newspapers and weekly periodicals that followed.

One important reason why so few illustrations had appeared was the difficulty of printing them on the old hand-presses when they were surrounded by a mass of small type. The iron hand-presses and still more powerful machines solved this problem.

Between 1820 and 1840 at least 2000 new newspapers and periodicals, many with illustrations, made their appearance in Britain, and in other countries there was similar enterprise. The 'Penny Magazine', founded in 1832 by Charles Knight, which gave 'tabloid' information on a wide variety of subjects, was excellently illustrated with wood engravings of portraits, views, and great works of art. It soon reached a sale of 180 000 copies a week. 'Punch' (1840), the 'Illustrated London News' (1842), the 'Penny Illustrated Paper' (1862), and the weekly 'Graphic' (1869) all made illustration their chief feature.

By the last quarter of the nineteenth century methods of illustration were revolutionized by photo-process engraving. Nicéphore Niépce (p 719) took what is believed to be the first photograph (1822); Fox Talbot (p 722) was the first to produce a photographic negative from which any number of positive prints could be made (1835); but it was not until the 1880s that photo-mechanical blocks were made which could be successfully printed in the same way as the hand-engraved wood-blocks (figure 378). The 'Daily Telegraph' (1881) was one of the first newspapers to use a photographic line-block, or 'zinco' as it would be

ILLUSTRATION   703

called today, but such illustrations made their first appearance in bulk in the
'Daily Graphic'. Artists' line-drawings in black on white paper, with no tones
other than those that could be achieved by variation of line-structure, such as
line-hatching, dotting, and so on, were the only suitable copy for this process.
From these drawings a negative was made which was placed in contact with a

FIGURE 378—*A wood-engraver at work.*

zinc plate previously rendered sensitive. After exposure to powerful lamps the
plate was taken to a dark room and lightly rolled with printers' ink. When
immersed in water and rubbed with cotton-wool the soluble parts were washed
away, while the insoluble parts—which were the lines of the drawing—remained
fixed to the zinc. The plate was then etched to leave these lines in relief and
finally mounted on a block of wood to make it the same height as the type
(0·918 in).

Half-tone. Neither the wood-block nor the line-zinco could reproduce the
tones of a photograph or an artist's wash-drawing. The half-tone process, which
turned the graduated tones of a photograph into a printing-block, made such

reproduction possible for the newspapers. In making these blocks the original was copied by a process-camera in which a cross-line screen had been interposed in front of the negative plate. This screen broke up the picture into thousands of dots varying in size from heavy ones in the shadows to pin-points in the high-lights. When the resultant print was viewed from the normal distance the dots merged into areas of different tones to make the picture. The screen used varied from about 80 to 135 lines to the inch, according to the smoothness of the paper on which it was intended to print. Today the range is from 55 to 200. The coarser screens were used in newspapers, but for whole-sheet illustrations in books, printed separately from the text, the finer screens were used to obtain the highest pictorial qualities. Blocks made with these fine screens demanded a very smooth, clay-coated paper to obtain a good result; such 'art paper' is an unwelcome legacy still with us.

The use of half-tone blocks in newspapers dates from 1877 when, according to J. M. Eder in his 'History of Photography' [2], the brothers Moritz and Max Jaffé of Vienna produced half-tone plates with a gauze screen. In America, Stephen Horgan was responsible for the first half-tone in the 'New York Daily Graphic' (1880), and four years later 'Harper's Magazine' followed and pioneered many improvements. Georg Meisenbach of Munich may be described as the founder of the commercial half-tone process. He first used a single line-screen which he turned during the exposure of the negative plate; but the English branch of his company took advantage of the Max Levy screen which consisted of two sheets of glass each engraved with parallel lines, filled with a black pigment, and cemented together crosswise to form tiny transparent squares. The 'Daily Graphic' was using half-tones by 1894, and by 1900 they were common in most weekly newspapers. In quality, however, they were rather dull and muddy, and considerable hand-engraving was necessary to give them 'life'. During the past fifty years vast improvements have been made in their manufacture and printing methods, and practically every newspaper in the world makes use of them. The half-tones on the back page of 'The Times' are today among those of the highest standard.

Colour. Not long after the half-tone process was invented attempts were made to apply it to colour-printing. Some progress had already been made in the application of the three-colour theory of photography, and it was soon realized that if three half-tone negatives could be made to represent the yellows, reds, and blues of an original, it would be possible to make three separate printing plates which, if inked with their appropriate colours and printed successively in register on the same sheet of paper, would produce colour-prints closely resembling the

ILLUSTRATION 705

original. This was eventually achieved by using colour-filters which were complementary to the colour to be recorded on the negative. To obtain a negative of all the blues in the picture the complementary orange (red+yellow) filter was used, for the red a green filter, and for the yellow a purple filter. At the time of making the colour-negatives the half-tone screen was used to break up the picture into dots. The theory of the process was sound enough, but a vast amount of research was necessary with filters, colour-sensitive plates, suitable coloured inks, and the problem of correct register before any real progress was made.

Chromo-xylography was one of the most interesting colour-processes of the nineteenth century. The illustration was printed in colour from a series of hand-cut wood-blocks—one for each colour. This process gave the print a pleasing transparent quality that cannot be obtained by most other methods. It was carried to a considerable pitch of excellence by Savage about 1820, but did not become popular before the mid-century. The two most effective workers in this process were Edmund Evans and Benjamin Fawcett, the latter being a striking instance of unaided genius working alone and producing excellent work. His illustrations to Morris's 'British Birds' were a superb achievement. Evans is chiefly remembered for the colour-blocks he cut of drawings made by Walter Crane, and for the children's books of Kate Greenaway and Randolph Caldecott. Chromo-xylography was not practised much on the European continent except by the firm of Knöfler of Vienna, founded in 1856. This firm produced work of the very highest quality, chiefly of saints, apostles, and other religious subjects, in many colours including gold. Their work still adorns the walls of churches and the prints have lost little of their original beauty.

The Baxter process, patented in 1835, belongs to this group. Baxter used as many as twenty wood-blocks to apply his oil colours to steel outline-engravings. His delicacy of treatment and pleasing combination of colours put him in a class by himself. The prints that he and his patentees produced are today highly esteemed collectors' pieces.

Among the lesser-known processes of the 1890s was Orsoni's 'Aquatype'. The colouring of pictures and playing-cards by means of stencils was practised before the invention of typography, and this method has found applications in many decorative arts since. Orsoni harnessed stencilling to a machine largely used in France for colouring ladies' fashion papers, early 'comics', and the cheaper picture postcards for which there was a craze at the turn of the century. After printing the outline of the pictures in black from line-process plates, the sheets were fed on a travelling band which carried them in turn under as many stencils as there were colours to be applied. When in position the mechanism passed large circular brushes over the stencils. The results were crude and the register was seldom perfect, but the water-colour inks were bright and transparent and the effects satisfactory enough for such ephemeral publications. The silk-screen process of stencilling, used extensively today for show-cards, is a twentieth-century invention.

Lithography. The chief nineteenth-century process of colour-printing was lithography, a method of printing from a prepared slab of stone invented by J. A. Senefelder, a native of Prague, a few years before the century opened. Lithography still ranks high among the graphic arts. Unlike the wood-block and the process-blocks, which are in relief and mechanically produced, lithography was a planographic or flat-surface process of a chemical nature. There were two modes of procedure. The artist could either draw directly on the stone with lithographic ink or crayon—both mixtures of tallow, beeswax, soap, and sufficient pigment to render the drawing visible to his eye—or his drawing on specially prepared paper could then be transferred to the stone. When working direct on the stone it was necessary to reverse the drawing. In printing, the stone was thoroughly damped, but as the greasy ink- or crayon-lines constituting the drawing naturally repelled water, only those parts of the stone not covered by them retained the moisture. While the stone was still wet the printer rolled a thick ink of the appropriate colour over the whole surface, which adhered to the greasy lines of the drawing but was repelled by the wet parts of the stone.

Printing in colour by the lithographic process (*chromolithography*) demanded a stone for each colour or tone, as many as twenty being used for the reproduction of oil and water-colour paintings. It was an art medium that connoisseurs and publishers of fine prints had been waiting for, and it attracted eminent artists by its great potentialities for reproducing studio pictures and, to some extent, for book-illustration. The latter were often printed on thin stock and mounted on leaves left blank to receive them, as they could not be printed with the text. Achievements of very special distinction were an edition of Thomas à Kempis's *Imitatio Christi* with decorated borders from early manuscripts, lithographed by Lemercier of Paris (1856–7); Owen Jones's 'Grammar of Ornament', printed by Day & Son, who were the leading chromolithographers in London (1856); and the Arundel Society's prints of Italian frescoes produced in England and Germany from 1856 onwards. Chromolithography was also extensively used for commercial work of all kinds, from menus to bottle-labels; while Germany, with her usual enterprise, flooded the markets with the cheap greetings-cards dear to the heart of that generation.

Impressions from the stone, in the early days of the process, were taken with

ILLUSTRATION   707

copper-plate presses of the mangle variety, but later a press was devised in which the paper was given greater pressure against the stone as it passed on a bed under a 'scraper' device. The adoption of machines for printing was slow, owing to the stubborn attitude of lithographers, who were fearful of commercializing the art. G. Sigl of Vienna was the first to build a power-press (1852), which M Engues, a French engineer, improved and sold in England and the United States. The first useful flat-bed machines especially built for the process were generally available about 1870. During the next ten years grained zinc plates were much used in place of the more cumbersome stones, and machines were so greatly improved in precision and speed that lithographic firms increased in number all over the world. The last ten years of the century saw the general application of the half-tone process to lithography, the introduction of the aluminium plate as a printing-surface, and then a race between the leading countries of the world to build the perfect rotary on which the thin plates could be used round a cylinder for still faster production. The development of offset-lithography, in which the impression is first made on a rubber-covered cylinder and then transferred to the paper, board, or other material, belongs to the present century.

Collotype, another planographic process which depends on the natural antipathy of grease and water, must be mentioned here. It was commercialized in the latter part of our period, first on the continent—especially in Germany and France—and later in England; a fact mainly due to the more stable climatic conditions abroad, for the rapidly varying temperatures and humidity of Britain were not conducive to good work. Collotype is more purely photographic than any of the other processes. It requires no screen, and it reproduces the most delicate tones and gradations of a photograph, an artist's drawing, or a painting. As the printing surface is gelatine the number of prints obtainable from a plate is limited, and the process is therefore suitable only for illustration in small, finely printed editions or for wall-pictures. The printing surface was a sheet of glass coated with an emulsion of gelatine and potassium dichromate. This was exposed to light under a reversed (left to right) negative, which might be in line or tone or both. The effect was to harden the gelatine in proportion to the amount of illumination it received. The shadows of the original, represented by the light parts of the negative, were hardened most, while the high-lights of the original—the dark parts of the negative—prevented the light from reaching the sensitive dichromate and in these parts the gelatine remained soft. Between these two extremes a complete gradation of tones was represented by varying degrees of softness. After washing to remove the unexposed dichromate, the plate was soaked in a mixture of glycerine and water, which the gelatine absorbed in proportion to its hardness, the softer parts absorbing most. When ink was applied to the plate it was deposited more thickly on the hardened parts, the shadows of the picture, and repelled in other parts according to the amount of dampness that the gelatine was holding. Various presses and machines were utilized to produce the impression, from the hand-press to the giant lithographic machines; but special collotype presses were put on the market, first in France and then in Germany, and several of them were imported into Britain. The first British machine, made by Furnival & Company, was introduced in 1893. Colour-plates were produced by this process with exquisite effects. The three-colour process was not applicable to collotype, and eight or more plates were often necessary to obtain all the colours of the original; this fact made the cost prohibitive for general book-illustration.

Photogravure (Fox Talbot, 1852), which came to commercial fruition at the close of our period, was neither a relief nor a planographic but an intaglio process, using etching below the surface of the plate. A positive of the subject was first printed photographically on a plate of polished copper, and then a screen of crossed lines was printed on top of the image and the plate was etched. The screen, usually about 150 lines to the inch, was completely protected from the action of the acid, but the spaces between the lines of the screen were eaten away to varying depths, the heaviest shadows of the picture being the deepest. In printing, the dissolved pits were filled with a thin ink and the surplus ink on the surface was removed with a scraper-blade which pressed on the crossed lines. Originally, flat copper plates were used, but eventually copper cylinders were etched directly and then printed on fast rotary machines. In recent years rotary-photogravure has become the process *par excellence* for illustrated magazines with wide circulations.

VIII. JOBBING PRINTING

In addition to the firms specializing in the printing of books or the publication of newspapers there was another section of the printing trade which, in the nineteenth century, was known as general jobbing (plate 39). In size, if not in importance, it was easily the largest group. It is estimated that at the close of the century there were at least 8000 firms in Britain alone engaged in work of this kind, which included anything from visiting-cards and bill-heads to catalogues and time-tables. For comparison, it may be mentioned that there were about 2000 newspaper establishments, while book-printing was carried on in not more than two dozen towns.

There has always been a certain amount of jobbing, although the histories of printing say little about it. Its products were of ephemeral interest only, and usually failed to survive when their content became out of date. With the increase of trade and commerce, railways and shipping, entertainment and sport, the variety and volume of jobbing increased, and many one-man businesses developed into important firms as villages grew into towns and coastal hamlets into popular health-resorts.

During the first half of the century jobbing printers used iron presses, which were so simply and soundly constructed as to be almost indestructible; many of them continued in use throughout the whole century. But some, perhaps most, of the smaller offices used the old wooden presses exclusively because they were cheapest, and repairs and modifications could be effected by a local joiner. The hand-press was, however, ill adapted to the requirements of a printer receiving large orders, even if they were only for bill-heads, cards, and labels. The hand-press, whatever its size, could rarely exceed a yield of 250 impressions an hour and profits were small; around the middle of the century hand-bills often sold at less than 5s a thousand. The general practice was to allow jobs to accumulate, sometimes by sending a traveller out for a whole week at a time, and then to impose several small commissions on the same press so that they could be pulled together. The sheets could then be cut up as required with a knife and rule, or with the guillotine used by book-binders. Hand-bills were at this time the most usual form of advertising, and bill-deliverers were very common in the streets. William Smith, in his book on advertising, states that he took a walk round the City and West End of London in 1861. During his walk he was handed bills, pamphlets, and booklets at every street corner and at the end of his walk had collected in all 250 [3].

The ideal machine for the jobbing-printer came in 1851, the year of the Great Exhibition. Stephen Ruggles, an inventive printer of Boston, Massachusetts, had been experimenting with mechanical presses for some years. In 1839 he finished his so-called 'engine press', which was the first self-inking treadle job-press to be manufactured. It was on the pattern of the hand-press, both bed and platen being horizontal, but the type was above and the platen below. Although it worked well and sold without difficulty in the United States, it had several disadvantages, especially the danger that a loose type might fall from the hanging forme. In 1851 Ruggles built a press of much simpler construction, which had the distinction of being the first press with a vertical bed—an innovation that has been followed for jobbing-presses to the present day. The platen was hinged at the base of the press, and rocked back and forth to make the impression on the forme, which was a flattened section of a cylinder. The inking-rollers travelled round this cylinder, and the portion not occupied by the forme served as a table for evenly distributing the ink. This 'card and bill-head press' had the great advantage that the type-forme and the paper were always in sight except at the moment of impression. It was very small—the chase holding the type was only $4\frac{1}{2}$ by $7\frac{1}{2}$ in.

George Phineas Gordon, a small master-printer of New York, was influenced

FIGURE 379—*H. S. Cropper & Company's 'Minerva', the first English-made treadle jobbing platen, 1860. It could be worked by hand, foot, or steam-power.*

by Ruggles's design and in the same year (1851) put his Alligator press on the American market. His platen stood fixed at an angle of 45° and the bed, which was vertical when at rest, tipped forward to make the impression. There was, however, no warning when this quick action would occur and an unwary feeder was certain, sooner or later, to have his fingers trapped between platen and forme. Later in the year Gordon took out a further patent describing the basis of all his subsequent designs, in which the bed was in a fixed vertical position while the platen moved from an almost flat position in front of the operator. After various modifications Gordon put his press on the market under the name of the Franklin, and it proved a great success. It was introduced into Europe at the International Exhibition in London in 1862, and was immediately popular. Arrangements were soon made for its manufacture in London, under the name of the Minerva, by Cropper & Company (figure 379)—whence a generic term among printers, who called all treadle-platens 'croppers', no matter who made them. These machines had a great vogue and for a time satisfied all the demands made upon them. Other makers soon entered the market with new designs embodying improvements to keep pace with new requirements. These included the Liberty, one of the first offered to the trade, which had the disk or inking-slab placed at the back; the Universal for heavier work and with a greatly improved inking-mechanism especially suitable for wood-block printing; the Mitre, in which the platen was guided strictly in a parallel position to the face of the forme and so avoided the slurring sometimes experienced in earlier machines; and many others. Some of the more powerful platen presses were extensively used for embossing and card-creasing and for making cut-outs, until special presses for these processes came on the market.

Up to the last years of the eighteenth century there was no style of type generally available for 'display' in jobbing-printing, other than the large sizes of those types used for the printing of books. In the first decade of the nineteenth century, for no single obvious reason, the appearance of book-types underwent a rapid revolution, becoming more heavily stressed, with thin serifs and hair-lines. Paper with a smoother surface, made on a woven-wire mould, was more generally available, and the tendency in type-design was towards a greater contrast of thick and thin strokes. The comfort of the reader naturally restricted the development of this movement in book-types; in the field of the jobbing-printer a new market was either found or created for types in which the proportion of thick and thin strokes earned them the name of 'fat face'. For thirty years these display types were bold and vigorous. About 1840, perhaps in reaction against the prevailing style, display types and ornaments became steadily more delicate and lighter in weight, and this movement had its parallel in book-types, which now economized both ink and space by becoming lighter and narrower. The success of litho-graphy in emulating the flourishes of the engraver was also a threat that helped to dictate the new styles; many of the new types were close copies of drawn lithographed letters and their vast variety must have been a great strain on the resources of those printing firms ambitious to keep up to date. The simple platen presses, already referred to, proved ideal for the delicate types, borders, corner-pieces, and fancy rules of this 'artistic' jobbing.

IX. BOOK-PRINTING

Type for books was set by hand throughout the whole of our period, apart from experiments with the many type-setting machines. During the last few years of the nineteenth century some books in America were set on the Monotype machine, which has since been adopted by most British, and to a lesser extent by other, printers for the setting of books, thanks largely to the fine range of classic type-faces which the Monotype Corporation has made available. The Monotype machine (cf p 685) casts separate types and is actuated by a perforated roll of paper. A keyboard is used for perforating the paper, and the keyboard operator has nothing to do with the caster, which may be in another room or another country. Both the keyboard and the caster are worked by compressed air, and the action of the paper on the caster can be compared with that of the same kind of perforated paper in a pianola. The matrix is a plate of steel about 4 in square on which is the full alphabet together with the various necessary 'sorts'. It is operated by a wonderful series of levers, which enable it to take position so that any letter or figure may be cast. The work is very rapid and corrections can be made by replacing single types, whereas in the Linotype the complete line has to be recast.

Before 1850 the inventors working on flat-bed cylinder-machines had concentrated their energies on the perfection of machines for the rapid printing of newspapers. Book-printers, who were more concerned with good press-work, had been content with the hand-presses or with steam-driven platen-presses which were little more than the hand-press harnessed to power. However, a few small cylinder-presses of simple construction and usually worked by hand, such as the Rutt, had been tried out for a time. After the 1850s this type of machine was vastly improved in America, on the European continent, and in Britain, and it was gradually adopted by the book-printers. The speed of such machines was obviously much slower than that of the rotary presses, since half the time was taken up by the backward travel of the bed, and the repeated change of direction meant a heavy strain on the mechanism if too rapid a motion was attempted. Speed, however, continued to improve and the complete control of pressure, inking, feeding, and delivery made this type of machine the ideal one for the perfect press-work of book-pages.

Until about 1870 all paper before printing had to be damped to yield a good impression, and afterwards dried. The drying caused much delay and incidentally added greatly to the risk of fire in printing-offices. This practice continued until Theodore de Vinne of New York succeeded in printing the 'Century Magazine' on a dry calendered paper; his methods were quickly followed in other countries.

X. PAPER

The demand for paper by printers, stationers, and other tradesmen had increased to such an extent by 1850 that the paper-maker was finding it difficult to obtain sufficient linen and cotton rags—his chief raw materials—to satisfy the needs of his ever-increasing market (vol III, pp 411–16). The addition of straw to the rags had helped to some extent; but other raw materials were vital, particularly in Britain, which was leading the world in the consumption of paper. About 1855 the position was eased to some extent by the introduction of esparto grass from Spain and North Africa, but this proved only a palliative. The real solution was found in a material which had been the subject of experiment over the past two centuries, namely wood-pulp. Soon after esparto had been introduced the first attempts were made to employ wood-pulp on a commercial scale. Trees were cut into logs, which were pulped by friction against grindstones revolving in water. The paper made from this mechanical pulp was, however, of very poor quality owing to the large amount of impurity, such as resins, incorporated with the cellulose fibres. By 1873 chemical methods of extracting the bulk of the impurities by boiling wood-chips with various alkaline or acid reagents had been perfected. From this chemical wood-pulp the great proportion of papers was being made by 1890, and its mixtures with mechanical wood- and esparto-pulps formed the ingredients of the many special papers demanded by the stationery and printing trades [4]. Noteworthy among these were the spongy, featherweight 'antique wove' which was introduced for books when the old three-decker novel went out of fashion; the pleasing, silky, thin, but opaque and strong 'India' papers, used for books of small compass; and the highly glazed 'art papers' (p 704) coated with china clay, which were demanded for fine half-tone reproduction.

XI. BOOK-BINDING

In the book-binding trade machines were introduced for almost every section of the business. The trade practice in the eighteenth century had been to sell books either in sheets for individual binding, or in cheap 'sheep' or calf covers. During the Napoleonic wars, when the price of books rose sharply, a binding in boards backed with paper was accepted. A revolution in the method of binding was the introduction of the 'case' as a substitute for the more elaborately attached leather binding (c 1825). This cheaper method, together with the use of cloth, is said to have been begun by the publisher William Pickering, who used it on his popular series of poets. The case, made separately and glued to the sewn sheets by means of tapes, made the use of machinery practicable. Individual tooling, both blind and gilt, was replaced by the use of the blocking-press which decorated the whole cover in one operation (c 1832). Many machines were devised for sewing and casing. Unfortunately the trade could not wait for the thread-sewing machines which were on general sale about 1878, and a much baser and cheaper means of stitching with iron wire was introduced from America about 1875. One of the first to use this type of machine was the great publisher of guide-books, Baedeker. The wire quickly rusted and soon caused the book to disintegrate. Another deplorable method was to cut off the back folds of the book and coat the flat surface with a flexible 'glue'—often a rubber solution: this soon perished and the book fell to pieces. Plastic adhesive, which may have a longer life, is being used for 'unsewn' binding today, but sewing with thread was, and is, the most common and reliable method. The last few years of the nineteenth century saw an invasion from America of many fast-running machines for the binding trade, with automatic feeds and all especially designed for intensive mass-production.

XII. WAGES AND TRAINING

Wages in the printing and allied trades during our half-century were a little higher than in most others. There was, however, much unemployment, caused chiefly by the vast number of boys engaged in the trade at low wages—some as young as nine and ten years of age. The excessive proportion of apprentices indentured for seven years, often with perfect indifference to their future prospects in the trade at the expiration of their servitude, also tended to depress the skilled journeyman's wage. Many of these apprentices had very little tuition and were scarcely more than labourers.

The first technical schools were founded in Vienna in 1875, in Berlin in 1876, and at Antwerp in 1880. In this country the germ of technical education may be traced to the Glasgow Mechanics' Institution (1823) (ch 33). The same idea spread to other cities and led, on the one hand, to the public library movement and, on the other, towards the modern technical college, of which those of Manchester (1883), Birmingham, and Leeds are examples. In London, ancient guild funds were pooled to finance the City and Guilds of London Institute (1878). The Regent Street Polytechnic was founded in 1883. The St Bride Printing School was established in 1894 with the aid of money derived from charitable bequests, made long before, by residents of that City parish. It developed into the vast 'monotechnic' known as the London School of Printing and Graphic Arts, which now has some 7000 students of printing and related subjects.

The apprentice to printing may still retain his centuries-old nickname of 'printer's devil', but the prospects before him would surely seem, to his nineteenth-century forerunners, a paradise of opportunity.

REFERENCES

[1] See 'Friedrich Koenig und die Erfindung der Schnell-presse. Ein biographisches Denkmal' by THEODOR GOEBEL (Stuttgart, 1883), which attempts to prove that to Koenig alone the world is indebted for the invention of the steam printing-press. For a criticism of this work see "The Invention of the Steam-press" by WILLIAM BLADES, a series of articles contributed to the *Printer's Register*, **23**, 1883–4.

[2] EDER, J. M. 'History of Photography.' Columbia University Press, New York. 1945.

[3] SMITH, W. 'Advertise. How? When? Where?' London. 1863.

[4] The growth of the paper industry between 1850 and 1900 was computed by A. DYKES SPICER in 'The Paper Trade' (Methuen, London, 1907) to be:

1850. Vats for hand-made papers 200 = 5426 tons; machines 267 = 57 535 tons.
1900. Vats for hand-made papers 104 = 3886 tons; machines 539 = 647 746 tons.

BIBLIOGRAPHY

BLAND, D. 'The Illustration of Books.' Pt I: 'History of Illustration'; Pt II: 'The Processes and their Application.' Faber & Faber, London. 1951.

BURCH, R. M. 'Colour Printing and Colour Printers' (with a chapter on "Modern Processes" by W. GAMBLE). Pitman, London. 1910.

GREEN, R. 'History of the Platen Jobber.' Privately printed, Chicago, Ill. 1953.

Idem. 'The Iron Hand Press in America.' Privately printed, Rowayton, Conn. 1948.

ISAACS, G. A. 'The Story of the Newspaper Printing Press.' Co-operative Printing Society, London. 1931.

LEGROS, L. A. and GRANT, J. C. 'Typographical Printing Surfaces: the Technology and Mechanism of their Production.' Longmans, Green, London. 1916.

LEIGHTON, D. 'Modern Bookbinding: a Survey and a Prospect.' Fifth Dent Memorial Lecture. Dent, London. 1935.

NIEPP, L. 'Les machines à imprimer depuis Gutenberg.' Club Bibliophile de France, Paris. 1951.

PLANT, MARJORIE. 'The English Book Trade: an Economic History of the Making and Sale of Books.' Allen & Unwin, London. 1939.

SOUTHWARD, J. 'Progress in Printing and the Graphic Arts during the Victorian Era.' London. 1897.

'The Times. Printing Number' (reprinted from the 40 000th issue, September 10th, 1912). The Times Publishing Company, London. 1912.

WILSON, F. J. F. and GRAY, D. 'Practical Treatise upon Modern Printing Machinery and Letterpress Printing.' London. 1888.

Typewriters

MINISTRY OF EDUCATION: SCIENCE MUSEUM. 'A Brief Outline of the History and Development of the Correspondence Typewriter with Reference to the National Collection and Description of the Exhibits' by G. TILGHMAN RICHARDS. H.M. Stationery Office, London. 1955.

30

PART I
THE PHOTOGRAPHIC ARTS:
PHOTOGRAPHY

HELMUT AND ALISON GERNSHEIM

THE publication in 1839 of the first practicable process of photography fired the imagination of the public everywhere. 'From today, painting is dead!', exclaimed the artist Paul Delaroche on first examining a daguerreotype. Photography was considered only as 'the new art', and none foresaw the essential role it would come to play in modern civilization. Before the close of the nineteenth century, however, photography had become indispensable to science, medicine, industry, commerce, the illustrated press, book-illustration, and its own offshoot—cinematography.

Why photography was not invented before the nineteenth century remains the greatest mystery in its history, for knowledge of both the optical and the chemical principles on which it is based was widespread in the eighteenth century. Its late arrival must be ascribed not to a lengthy period of abortive attempts, but to the fact that before 1800 no one even conceived the idea.

I. THE PRE-HISTORY OF PHOTOGRAPHY

(i) *The Camera obscura.* The photographic camera derives directly from the camera obscura, which was originally, as its name implies, simply a dark room, with a tiny hole in the wall or window-shutter through which the view outside was projected, upside-down, on to the opposite wall or a white screen. The principle of the camera obscura was described over 900 years ago by Alhazen (? 965–?1039), who proposed it for observing solar eclipses, and for over five centuries its use remained confined to this purpose (figure 380). Designed originally to avoid harming the eyes by looking directly at the sun, observers also found it amusing to watch the projected image of what went on in the street outside.

During the sixteenth century, optical improvements resulted in brighter and sharper images: Girolamo Cardano (1501–76) inserted a bi-convex lens in the hole (1550) and Daniele Barbaro (1528–69) introduced a diaphragm in front of the lens (1568). The reversal of the image was corrected by Ignatio Danti (1536–86) by interposing a concave mirror (1573). In 1558 Giovanni Battista della Porta

(1538–1615) advised artists to lighten their labours and obtain perfect perspective by tracing the outlines of the projected view or portrait.

For topographical views a transportable camera was necessary, and one in the form of a light-weight hut was recommended before 1580 by Friedrich Risner. Athanasius Kircher (1601–80) (p 736) illustrated in *Ars magna lucis et umbrae* (1646) a little hut carried between poles, like a sedan chair. Before this, Johann Kepler (1571–1630) had used a tent-type camera when making a topographical survey of upper Austria in 1620.

The truly portable box-camera dates from the middle of the seventeenth century. Kircher's pupil Caspar Schott (1608–66) in 1657 made a small camera consisting of two boxes, one slightly smaller to slide within the other to adjust the focus. In the first reflex camera, introduced in 1676 by J. C. Sturm (1635–1703), the image was reflected the right way up, by a plane mirror set at 45° to the axis of the lens, on to an oiled-paper screen. Johann Zahn in 1685 replaced this by a ground-glass screen like those

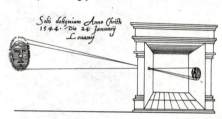

FIGURE 380—*The first illustration of a camera obscura, published by Gemma Frisius in 1545.*

still used. The small cameras that he illustrated in *Oculus artificialis* (1685) (figure 381) measured only 22·5 × 22·5 × 60 cm. They had a tele-lens combination consisting of a convex lens of longer, and a concave lens of shorter, focal length, giving an enlarged image. This was the first time that such a tele-lens combination, known to Leonard Digges over a century earlier, was incorporated in the camera obscura. By 1685 the camera obscura was ready for photography, long before the chemical side of photographic picture-making had received any attention. The only further improvements introduced before the photographic camera were John Dollond's achromatic lens (vol IV, p 358), originally designed for the telescope (1758), and W. H. Wollaston's achromatic meniscus prism lens introduced for the camera obscura (1812).

(ii) *Photochemistry*. The darkening of silver salts had long been observed, but was attributed to the effect of air or the heat of the sun. The first person clearly to indicate that the sun's light has a chemical effect on silver salts was Johann Heinrich Schulze (1687–1744), who communicated his observations to the Imperial Academy at Nuremberg in 1727. Schulze was the first to produce images by the action of light on silver salts. He covered a glass bottle containing a mixture of chalk and silver nitrate solution with paper from which he had cut out letters. Where this stencil protected the liquid from the sun's rays it remained white, while in all other parts it darkened. Though Schulze did not make any practical application of his experiment, it is nevertheless the root of the genealogical tree of photochemistry, which within a hundred years began to blossom into photography.

A number of scientists, including C. W. Scheele (1742–86), J. Senebier, the elder Herschel, J. W. Ritter, and W. H. Wollaston, made researches on the relative speed of the darkening of silver salts by the various components of the solar spectrum, but none of them thought of applying this knowledge to the production of pictures.

Meanwhile, many French, English, and German books on popular scientific

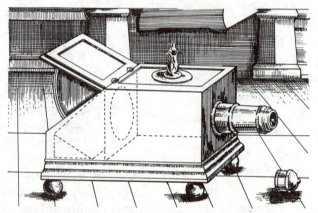

FIGURE 381—*Johann Zahn's reflex box camera obscura, 1685.*

amusements contained a description of Schulze's experiment, included as a kind of chemical conjuring-trick. Moreover, during the eighteenth century the camera obscura was exceedingly popular with artists, travellers, and scientists as an aid to sketching in accurate perspective. It is surprising, therefore, how long it was until someone thought of combining the widely disseminated optical and chemical knowledge to make photographs.

The earliest attempt at photography was made about 1800 by an amateur scientist, Thomas Wedgwood (1771–1805). He tried to fix the images of the camera obscura upon paper or white leather coated with a solution of silver nitrate, but finding it impossible to produce an effect in a reasonable time resorted to the simpler technique of laying leaves, wings of insects, and paintings on glass (then fashionable) on the sensitive material. White images on a dark ground could be formed in two or three minutes in sunlight, but Wedgwood found no method of preserving the pictures, which darkened all over when further exposed to light. His friend Sir Humphry Davy (1778–1829), who repeated the experiments with silver chloride, had no better success in rendering the images permanent. Their joint results were communicated to the Royal Institution in June 1802.

II. PHOTOGRAPHY ON METAL

The image of the camera obscura was first permanently fixed by Joseph Nicéphore Niépce[1] (1765–1833). In the spring of 1816 Niépce succeeded in taking views from the window of his workroom in the family mansion, near Chalon-sur-Saône, on paper sensitized with silver chloride. The lights and shades were, as he anticipated, reversed, but as they were only partially fixed with nitric acid, an attempt to print positives from these negatives failed. Over a period of several years Niépce experimented with a large number of light-sensitive substances. Eventually, he tried bitumen of Judea, which he had earlier used in lithography; employing this asphalt, which hardens—instead of changing colour—under the influence of light, Niépce took the world's first photograph (plate 43) in 1826. In this the sun appears to be shining on both sides of the courtyard, owing to the extremely long exposure of eight hours.

A thin layer of bitumen of Judea dissolved in white petroleum was spread on a polished pewter plate (Niépce at various periods also used plates of copper, zinc, glass, and finally silvered copper). After exposure in the camera obscura, the latent image was rendered visible—that is, developed—by washing the plate with a mixture of oil of lavender and white petroleum, which dissolved away the parts of the bitumen that had not been hardened by light. The result was a direct positive picture, in which the lights were represented by bitumen and the shades by bare metal. After rinsing and drying, the picture was permanent.

Some of Niépce's apparatus at Chalon-sur-Saône proves him to have been also a pioneer in camera design. The bellows-camera originated with him, and so did the iris diaphragm, made of laminated zinc. He was also the first to use a metal camera.

Niépce was the inventor of photo-etching as well as of photography, both of which he called heliography. An ordinary copper-plate engraving was made transparent by oiling, laid on a bitumenized plate, and exposed for two or three hours to sunlight. The bitumen under the transparent parts of the engraving hardened, while that under the dark lines remained soluble. After the dissolving process, the plate was etched and prints were pulled in the usual way. Niépce's most successful photo-etching was of a portrait of Cardinal d'Amboise, of which two plates were made in 1826 and a print pulled from each in 1827 (plate 42 A).

[1] Niépce himself used the accent, but some modern authorities have mistakenly omitted it.

In that year Niépce unsuccessfully tried to interest the Royal Society in his invention. In December 1829 he entered into partnership with L. J. M. Daguerre (1787–1851), a Parisian theatrical designer and inventor of the diorama, who offered to perfect heliography, but it was not until 1837 that Daguerre succeeded in making clear and permanent photographs with a comparatively short exposure. Though Daguerre built on Niépce's knowledge, he considered that his system of development with mercury vapour, making it possible to reduce the exposure to 20–30 minutes, rendered the final process sufficiently different from heliography to justify his naming it 'daguerreotype'.

On the advice of the astronomer D. F. Arago, the French government acquired the daguerreotype process by act of Parliament, granting pensions to Daguerre and to Niépce's son. Details of the method of manipulation were revealed on 19 August 1839—the official birthday of photography—at a joint meeting of the Académie des Sciences and the Académie des Beaux-Arts.

A polished silvered copper plate was exposed to the vapour of iodine, which formed a microscopically thin layer of light-sensitive silver iodide on its surface. After exposure, the plate bearing the latent image was developed in a box containing mercury, which was heated to 60° C to vaporize it. During development, which lasted about 20 minutes, tiny globules of mercury settled on the parts of the plate which had been affected by light, forming the lights of the picture. The unchanged iodide was then dissolved away by washing the plate with a solution of sodium 'hyposulphite' (more precisely thiosulphate, although the name 'hypo' persists to this day) to make the image permanent, leaving the bare polished silver to form the shades of the picture. As the mercury adhered only lightly to the plate, it had to be protected by glass.

The 'official' daguerreotype outfits, bearing Daguerre's signature and manufactured exclusively by his relative Alphonse Giroux, consisted of a wooden camera, plate box, iodizing box, mercury box and spirit-lamp, various bottles of chemicals, and buffers and powders for polishing the plates (figure 382). The whole outfit weighed 50 kg. The camera consisted of two boxes, the rear one, with a ground-glass screen for focusing, sliding within the front box containing the lens. Made for taking whole plate ($16\cdot4 \times 21\cdot6$ cm) pictures, the camera's external dimensions were $31 \times 37 \times 26\cdot5$ cm, increasing to 51 cm when fully extended. By means of a mirror fixed behind the ground-glass at 45° to the optical axis the photographer could see the image right way up. The lens, manufactured by Chevalier, was of the Wollaston achromatic meniscus type with a focal length of 38 cm, contained in a brass mount with a simple brass disk to act as shutter. Though its diameter was $8\cdot1$ cm, the effective aperture was reduced to f/14 by a 2·7 cm stop fixed inside the lens tube to sharpen the image. The focal length was longer than was necessary for the plate size, and this, combined with the small lens opening, was the cause of the rather long exposures. This type of camera—though with greatly improved lenses—remained the standard for several decades.

At first the new art could be used satisfactorily only for recording architecture, sculpture, and views. Portraiture remained for the time being outside its scope,

FIGURE 382—*Daguerreotype outfit, 1847.*

since sitters would have had to pose motionless for at least a quarter of an hour in full sunshine.

Various optical and chemical improvements soon changed this state of affairs. Alexander Wolcott (1804–44) of New York, assisted by Henry Fitz, devised an ingenious camera without a lens, the image of the sitter being reflected on to the sensitive plate by a concave mirror. In this way several times as much light reached the plate, but the image was limited to 2 in square and was not very sharp. Nevertheless, this fast camera enabled Wolcott to open the world's first photographic portrait studio in New York in March 1840. A year later Richard Beard, English patentee of the mirror camera (figure 383), opened the first portrait studio in Europe at the Royal Polytechnic Institution in London.

A far more important improvement was J. M. Petzval's portrait lens introduced by J. F. Voigtländer (1779–1859) in 1840. This double combination lens was characterized by a large aperture (f/3·6) and a fairly short focal length

(15 cm), and gave excellent definition at the centre of the picture without the use of a stop. It could therefore be employed at full aperture, which made it thirty times as fast as the lenses in the original Daguerre–Giroux camera. Indeed, its high qualities made this design of lens the most popular until the introduction of Paul Rudolph's anastigmat by the firm of Karl Zeiss in 1889.

Contemporaneously with Petzval's optical improvement, Goddard and Claudet in London and Kratochwila and Natterer in Vienna worked on chemical acceleration of the daguerreotype plate by sensitizing it with vapours of bromine or chlorine as well as of iodine. By these methods exposures were brought within the range 10–90 seconds, according to lighting conditions.

After 1841 no significant modification of daguerreotype technique took place. The process flourished in Europe until the late fifties, in America until the mid-sixties. It was free from patent restrictions in all countries except England and Wales, where Daguerre had patented his invention five days before the French government presented it to the world. Hence in England and Wales the daguerreotype was practised only by a few licensees.

FIGURE 383—*Alexander Wolcott's mirror camera, as used in Richard Beard's studio, 1840–3.*

III. PHOTOGRAPHY ON PAPER

In 1835 W. H. Fox Talbot (1800–77) had achieved a fair measure of success in taking photographs on paper coated with silver chloride. Good results were obtained in making copies of botanical specimens, lace, and engravings laid direct on the paper and exposed to sunlight; and enlarged pictures of objects were taken with the solar microscope. Talbot's camera views of his house, Lacock Abbey, were less satisfactory, however. He took them with tiny (2½ in square) cameras fitted with fixed-focus microscope lenses of 2-in focal length, the exposure being half an hour. On hearing of the announcement of the daguerreotype on 7 January 1839, Talbot hastened to exhibit specimens of his 'photogenic drawings' at the Royal Institution and to the Royal Society in order to claim priority. Incidentally, a number of independent inventors of photography came forward at this period.

Though not giving fine detail like the daguerreotype, Talbot's process had nevertheless one great advantage over it. Whereas each daguerreotype was a unique positive picture from which no copies could be made, Talbot's were paper negatives from which a large number of positives could be printed. This is the principle on which modern photography is based. One of the disadvantages of paper photographs was, however, their liability to fade; this cannot happen to daguerreotypes, although the silvered plate may become oxidized if not properly sealed against contact with air.

The essential point in Talbot's improved calotype process, patented in England and Wales in February 1841, was the system of developing the latent image with gallic acid; this greatly reduced the necessary time of exposure. Another inventor of photography, J. B. Reade (1801–70), had used an infusion of nut-galls as an accelerator as early as 1837, and Talbot had learned of this from a common acquaintance.

FIGURE 384—*Willats's folding camera, 1851.*

To prepare the calotype, good-quality writing-paper was brushed over successively with solutions of silver nitrate and potassium iodide, forming silver iodide. The iodized paper was then rendered more sensitive by brushing it over with solutions of gallic acid and silver nitrate; it was exposed for 1–5 minutes, according to lighting conditions and the size of negative. The latent image was developed by a further application of gallic acid and silver nitrate solution, and became visible when the paper was warmed by the fire for a minute or two. The picture was fixed with a solution of potassium bromide, which Talbot later abandoned in favour of sodium 'hyposulphite'—still the most widely used fixing-agent—the properties of which as a solvent for silver salts had been described by Sir John Herschel in 1819.

The grain of the paper gave broad effects of light and shade, and for this reason the calotype was, on the whole, found more suitable for views than for portraits. On account of the patent it never achieved a great measure of popularity in England, though the beautiful calotypes of the Edinburgh painter David Octavius Hill (1802–70), taken in collaboration with Robert Adamson between 1843 and 1847, were, and still are, much admired.

As there were only about a dozen calotypists in the early and middle forties, Talbot made special efforts to popularize his process. He set up the first photographic printing establishment, at Reading, where 'sun pictures' were made for sale at print-sellers' and stationers' shops. Talbot also published the first photographically illustrated book in the world, 'The Pencil of Nature' (1844), containing original photographs. Until about 1875, pasting photographs on or between the text pages remained the only way of illustrating books photographically (p 706).

Cameras for the calotype differed little from those used for the daguerreotype process, but Richard Willats's collapsible camera (1851) (figure 384) broke new ground in camera design by introducing light-weight cloth for the centre part.

A modification of the calotype was introduced by Blanquart-Evrard in 1847. It reduced exposures to about a quarter of those necessary for a calotype or a daguerreotype, and led to the gradual superseding of the daguerreotype by the paper process in France for all purposes except professional portraiture.

At Blanquart-Evrard's printing establishment, opened at Lille in 1851, the printing of positives from amateurs' negatives and for book-illustration was carried out on mass-production lines. Developing the positive prints like negatives enabled the firm to turn out 200 to 300 copies from each negative daily, whereas the slow printing-out method with calotype or albumen paper, used everywhere else, limited the daily output per negative to about five or six. The permanence of the prints was assured by greater care in fixing and rinsing than was exercised at Talbot's Reading works, followed by a gold chloride toning-bath.

In the same year another Frenchman, Gustave Le Gray, brought photography on paper to its culmination with his invention of the waxed-paper process. Calotype negatives were sometimes waxed before printing to make them more transparent, but in Le Gray's process the paper was waxed before iodizing, and many of the chemicals employed were different. The waxed-paper process proved ideal for the travelling photographer, because the paper could be prepared ten to fourteen days beforehand instead of on the day before as with the calotype, and did not need to be developed until several days after the picture had been taken, whereas the calotype had to be developed on the same day. Exposures were, on the whole, about the same as with the calotype, but development needed one to three hours. Le Gray's method soon superseded Talbot's and Blanquart-Evrard's paper processes, for, besides the above-mentioned advantages, waxing suppressed the grain of the paper and the picture had almost as fine detail as one made from a glass negative.

IV. PHOTOGRAPHY ON GLASS

(i) *The albumen process*. It is surprising that the first practical photographic process on glass was invented as late as 1847, for glass was cheaper than a silvered copper plate and more transparent than paper. The advantages of glass had in fact previously been recognized by Niépce and Daguerre, but the problem of finding a vehicle for the silver salts that would not dissolve or float off during development, fixing, and rinsing was not solved until 1847. In that year Abel Niepce de Saint-Victor found that white of egg (albumen) formed a satisfactory base for the silver salts.

The glass plate was coated with a thin layer of beaten-up white of egg containing a few drops of potassium iodide solution, and when dry was washed with an acid solution of silver nitrate, which formed silver iodide. After exposure the latent image was developed with gallic acid.

On account of its slowness—5 to 15 minutes' exposure—the albumen process could not be used for portraiture, but it served well for architecture, sculpture, and art reproductions. Though soon superseded for ordinary purposes, it remained in favour for several decades for the production of magic-lantern slides and stereoscopic glass positives, on account of its fine detail. The former were introduced by the brothers Langenheim of Philadelphia in 1849 under the name hyalotypes; the latter by C. M. Ferrier of Paris in 1851.

(ii) *The collodion process.* The wet collodion process introduced by Frederick Scott Archer (1813–57) in London in March 1851 ousted within a few years all existing techniques—daguerreotype, calotype, waxed paper, and albumen. It was the fastest photographic process so far devised, and the first in England legally proved not to come under Talbot's patent. It was universally used for nearly thirty years.

Collodion (gun-cotton dissolved in ether) containing potassium iodide was poured on to the glass plate, which was tilted until the solution formed an even, sticky coating all over it. Immediately afterwards, the plate had to be sensitized by dipping it in a bath of silver nitrate solution. Exposure had to be made while the plate was still moist (hence the process is also called the wet-plate process) because the sensitivity deteriorated progressively as the collodion dried. Development, too, had to be done before the plate dried, using either pyrogallic acid or ferrous sulphate. The picture was fixed with hypo or potassium cyanide.

The making of ambrotypes, or collodion positives on glass, was a modification of the wet collodion process worked out by Archer in collaboration with Peter W. Fry. By bleaching a slightly under-exposed or under-developed collodion negative with nitric acid or mercuric chloride, the blackened silver iodide was transformed into white metallic silver, and the negative image was converted into a seemingly positive one by mounting it over a black background (plate 42 B). This technique was quick and easy, and ambrotype portraits soon displaced daguerreotypes. Ambrotypes were exceedingly popular for cheap portraiture from 1852 until about 1865, when the *carte de visite* fashion was at its height. A variant of the ambrotype, the tintype or collodion positive on metal, is still occasionally made by seaside and fair-ground photographers.

The popularity of the collodion process should not convey the false impression that photography had become easier. On the contrary, the manipulation demanded more skill, but the extremely fine detail, improved half-tones, and greatly increased sensitivity compensated for the difficulty. For the portrait photographer, work was eased by the faster sensitive material, but for the landscape photographer the heavy additional burden of equipment almost outweighed

FIGURE 385—*Travelling photographer's dark-tent*, c *1865*.

the advantages of shorter exposures, since the plate had to be prepared and processed on the spot.

In addition to the camera and several lenses, and a sturdy tripod, the landscape photographer was burdened with bottles of solutions for coating, sensitizing, developing, and fixing the negatives; a number of dishes; a good supply of glass plates; glass measures, funnels, and other impedimenta, including a pail to fetch the rinsing water—and occasionally the water itself. Above all, he needed a portable dark-tent, in the suffocating atmosphere of which the chemical manipulations were performed (figure 385). The over-all weight of equipment for a day's outing was 100–120 lb. Some photographers pushed a wheelbarrow or 'photographic perambulator'; the more affluent had a carriage. Often the latter served merely to carry the photographer and his equipment to the scene, but sometimes it was fitted up as a travelling dark-room.

Because the albumen positive paper introduced in 1850 was not very sensitive, enlarging was little practised. In consequence, negatives were very large, 8 × 10, 10 × 12, and 12 × 16 in being the usual sizes. The bulk and weight of the cameras taking these large plates were proportionately great. In an attempt to reduce the equipment for travelling photographers, combined darkroom-cameras were invented in which the chemical manipulation took place inside the camera box or in a tank beneath it, but these were makeshift devices; the serious photographer could not do without a tent.

At the Great Exhibition of 1851 Sir David Brewster's lenticular stereoscope, and stereoscopic daguerreotypes giving a three-dimensional effect, aroused much interest, and within six months the stereoscope became the craze of the day. The first stereoscopic photographs were taken with two cameras side by side, or with cameras designed to be moved laterally along a groove to allow the same view to be taken from slightly different viewpoints. The necessity for consecutive exposures naturally precluded the photographing of any but inanimate objects. The binocular or twin-lens camera constructed to Brewster's design by J. B. Dancer in 1853 made possible the taking of both pictures simultaneously. The short-focus lenses ($4\frac{1}{2}$–5 in) and the small plate-size (the two pictures each measured $3 \times 3\frac{1}{4}$ in) gave a sharp picture at almost full aperture, thus cutting down exposures to a fraction of a second. For the first time 'life' and motion came within the scope of photography. Street-scenes with moving pedestrians and traffic could be photographed if taken from a window above ground-level and with the camera pointing towards the traffic, for then the apparent movement was slow.

Besides stereoscopic cameras there were still smaller instruments, such as Skaife's pistol camera (1856), Bertsch's *chambre noire automatique* (1860), and Dubroni's hand-camera (1864), but these forerunners of the modern miniature camera were exceptions made to meet special needs. The great majority of photographers worked with large plate cameras of the wooden box type. The lighter bellows-camera began to establish itself only slowly, probably because it was not rigid enough for the comparatively long exposures needed with large plate sizes.

Carte de visite photographs, patented by Disderi and fashionable between 1859 and the end of the century, were usually taken with a special camera having four identical lenses of $4\frac{1}{2}$-in focal length. By means of a repeating back, eight pictures were taken on one $10\frac{1}{2} \times 8\frac{1}{2}$ in plate in two exposures. The contact print was cut up into the separate portraits and mounted on cards.

The inconvenience of working with wet collodion, the necessity for dark-tents, and so forth, naturally led to a desire for dry plates. A great variety of substances was introduced to preserve the collodion coating in a sensitive state for several days or even weeks, but all these preservative techniques were complicated and considerably slower than using wet collodion.

Richard Hill Norris recognized that one important function of the preservative coating was to fill up the pores of the collodion while they were wet and open. He contrived this by pouring over the sensitized collodion plate liquid gelatine, or some other viscous substance which would soften in water so that the developer could pass into the collodion. As the plates were dry, they could be packed in boxes for sale—a revolutionary idea in photography—and from 1856, when Norris's plates were first commercially introduced, until 1866, they enjoyed great popularity among amateurs.

In 1864 W. B. Bolton and B. J. Sayce of Liverpool made an important advance in dry-plate photography with the introduction of collodion and silver bromide emulsion. The sensitizing substance silver bromide—which was much faster than the iodide—and the preservative, tannin, were incorporated in the emulsion. All the photographer had to do was to pour the ready-made emulsion over his glass plate. From early in 1867 even this was unnecessary, for the commercial production of collodion emulsion dry plates was started by the Liverpool Dry Plate and Photographic Company.

(iii) *Gelatine emulsion*. The invention of gelatine emulsion is usually attributed to Richard Leach Maddox (1816–1902), who published his experimental results in September 1871. He formed an emulsion of gelatine containing nitric acid, cadmium bromide, and silver nitrate, and developed with a solution of pyrogallol containing a trace of silver nitrate. Maddox's gelatine emulsion was slower than wet collodion, but other experiments—chiefly those of John Burgess and Richard Kennett—brought about such vast improvements that photographers invariably over-exposed the gelatine dry plates which the Liverpool Dry Plate Company put on the market in 1876. Their great sensitivity—twenty times faster than wet collodion—was due to 'ripening' or 'cooking' the emulsion by heat, a process first revealed by Charles Bennett in March 1878.

Early in that year large-scale production of gelatine dry plates was being carried on by four British firms, and by the autumn of 1879 their number had increased to fourteen. British dry plates were exported all over the world. Within a year or so automatic machines had been invented for coating glass plates with gelatine emulsion at the rate of 1200 an hour in any size up to 20 × 24 in.

By 1880 the change-over from wet collodion to gelatine dry plates was in full swing. With them, truly instantaneous photography can be said to have begun, and as they were ready-made, photography had become—at least, according to the plate manufacturers—so simple that 'a person of average intelligence could master it in three lessons'. This was the beginning of the amateur movement, which in the nineties grew to previously undreamt of proportions.

Before this time photographic material was both over-sensitive to blue and violet light and hardly sensitive at all to red, with the result that the tone-rendering was incorrect and had to be adjusted by the use of filters. During the eighties and nineties a number of scientists investigated orthochromatism on the lines of the pioneer work of H. W. Vogel (1834–98), who in December 1873 found that treating a photographic emulsion with certain dyes made it sensitive to the colours absorbed by them. In 1883 appeared the first isochromatic plates, which were supposed to render all colours equally well—but even the first panchromatic plates (1904) were far from perfect in this respect.

V. PHOTOGRAPHY ON FILM

Since glass plates were both heavy and fragile, the use of flexible film as a support was long sought. The various kinds of stripping and other film tried out before celluloid film were, on the whole, not very satisfactory. Celluloid (nitro-cellulose plasticized with camphor), invented by Alexander Parkes in 1861 and first named 'Parkesine', was registered in 1873 with the trade-mark 'Celluloid' by John Wesley Hyatt of Newark, New Jersey, who used it for the manufacture of solid objects (p 747). At the request of John Carbutt, a Philadelphia plate manufacturer, Hyatt produced in 1888 clear sheets of celluloid with a uniform thickness of a hundredth of an inch, which fulfilled perfectly the demand for a new photographic base. The same year Carbutt put on the market sheets of this film coated with emulsion. Its thickness and imperfect flexibility precluded its use for roll-film.

A little earlier, in May 1887, Hannibal Goodwin (1822–1900), also of Newark, applied for a patent for a transparent roll-film made of celluloid, but it was not granted until September 1898, the specification being considered insufficient. In the meantime a similar film invented by H. M. Reichenbach was put on the market by the Eastman Company, for which the firm was granted a patent in December 1889. For the next fifteen years they had practically a world monopoly in the manufacture of roll-film, producing 80 to 90 per cent of the total output.

Simultaneously with the manufacture of gelatine dry plates came the introduction of a wide range of gelatine printing-papers, of which the most important was the fast gelatine bromide-paper which was sensitive enough to permit the enlarging of small negatives by artificial light. This revolutionized photographic apparatus, for it was now feasible to use small negatives in hand cameras, and to make enlarged prints.

The characteristics of apparatus after 1880 were, therefore, compactness, simplicity of manipulation, and light weight. The photographer's equipment was reduced to approximately what it is today. There were four main types of camera: change-box, magazine, roll-film, reflex. In all these it was possible to use a large number of plates or films in quick succession. The quarter-plate ($4\frac{1}{4} \times 3\frac{1}{4}$ in) size established itself as the favourite of amateurs in Britain and the United States, 9×12 cm being the equivalent on the European continent.

The change-box, which was attached to the camera and enabled the plates to be changed in daylight, was usually fitted with an automatic counter indicating the number of plates used. Each of the dozen plates was contained in a separate sheath, and after exposure the plate was lifted into a soft leather bag on top of

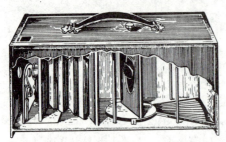

the box, and then manipulated into a place behind all the other plates, which meant that the next plate was now pushed into the focal plane. Change-boxes were made in various sizes to fit the backs of all standard cameras.

In magazine cameras twelve to forty plates or sheets of cut film were stored in a magazine inside the camera, the plate being changed after exposure by

FIGURE 386—*Marion & Company's 'Radial' magazine camera, 1890.*

a mechanism which differed in almost every model. The most usual was a spring attachment (figure 386).

Roller-slides and roll-film cameras used flexible bands of film wound on two spools, the action of winding up the exposed portion unwinding a fresh portion for the next exposure. Originally the film was in a separate box—the roller-slide or roll-holder—made in different sizes for attachment to the back of standard plate cameras. Invented in 1854 by Spencer and Melhuish for use with calotype paper, the roller-slide became popular when in 1885 George Eastman (1854–1932) and W. H. Walker introduced it as a mass-produced article, carrying a roll of fast negative-paper sufficient for 24 exposures. In 1888 it was loaded with stripping film for 48 exposures, and the following year with Reichenbach's celluloid film for 24 or 48 exposures.

The invention that gave the greatest stimulus to amateur photography was the Kodak camera (figure 387), introduced by George Eastman in August 1888. It reduced to three the ten or more operations hitherto necessary to make an exposure, reduced the weight and bulk in the same proportion, and permitted the taking of one hundred pictures without reloading. A simple mass-produced hand camera measuring only $6\frac{1}{2} \times 3\frac{1}{2} \times 3\frac{1}{2}$ in, and weighing 2 lb 3 oz, the Kodak was the first apparatus with a built-in roll-film arrangement. Fitted with a rectilinear fixed-focus lens giving sharp definition of everything beyond 8 ft, and having one speed and a fixed stop, the camera was the embodiment of simplicity. The Kodak's enormous appeal to the amateur was enhanced by Eastman's processing service. The camera could be sent to the firm for the

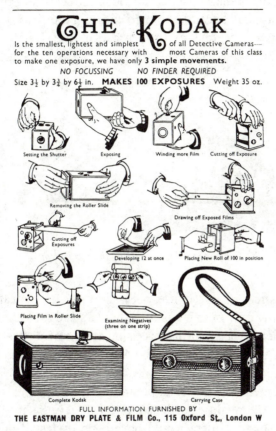

FIGURE 387—*Advertisement of the first Kodak camera, 1888.*

development and printing of the film, and was returned loaded with a new film, together with mounted prints of all successful pictures. In this way Eastman's famous slogan, 'You press the button—we do the rest', was put into effect.

Single- and twin-lens reflex cameras form a group of their own, for although they were variously made with change-box, magazine, or roll-film attachment, they are basically of different construction from all others. Reflex cameras incorporate a plane mirror, fixed at an angle of 45° to the base of the camera, which reflects the image upon the ground-glass screen, allowing observation of the scene up to the moment of taking the picture without the need for a focusing cloth. This old camera obscura principle was first applied to a photographic camera in 1861 by Thomas Sutton, but failed to establish itself until the eighties.

'Detective' was an apt description for the kind of disguised magazine hand cameras that Thomas Bolas designed for Scotland Yard in January 1881. In the 1890s detective cameras became the rage with dilettanti who, like many people today, were attracted by toys of little practical use. They were in the form of opera-glasses, field-glasses, revolvers, guns, books, watches, or concealed in

FIGURE 388—*Adams's hat detective camera, 1891.*

purses, walking-sticks, hats (figure 388), cravats, or beneath the waistcoat. They are interesting only in so far as they show a steady trend towards the miniature camera, which as a scientific precision instrument was first designed by Oskar Barnack in 1914. They were always of the fixed-focus type, and usually had lenses of inferior quality.

Since by that time the majority of photographers used hand cameras and fast negative material, the qualities of lenses and fast-acting shutters assumed great importance, for a hand camera would have been useless if one had had to use a small stop in order to obtain a sharp picture. According to the degree to which the various imperfections had been overcome, lenses were classified as aplanats, anastigmats, and double anastigmats, terms introduced by Steinheil (1866), Zeiss (1889), and Goerz (1893) respectively.

Of the many types of shutter that could be set for exposures of a fraction of a second, the roller-blind and focal-plane shutters are the most important of those invented before 1900. The latter type, invented in 1861 by William England for taking instantaneous street views, is still incorporated in all modern high-speed cameras.

BIBLIOGRAPHY

EDER, J. M. 'The History of Photography' (trans. by E. EPSTEAN). Columbia University Press, New York. 1945.

GERNSHEIM, HELMUT and GERNSHEIM, ALISON. 'The History of Photography, from the Earliest Use of the *camera obscura* in the Eleventh Century to 1914.' Oxford University Press, London. 1955.

LECUYER, R. 'Histoire de la photographie.' Baschet, Paris. 1945.

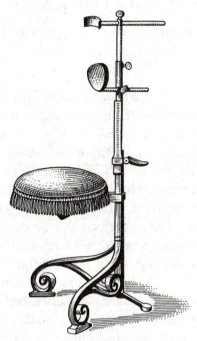

Posing chair, 1882.

30

PART II

THE PHOTOGRAPHIC ARTS:
CINEMATOGRAPHY:

ANTHONY R. MICHAELIS

I. INTRODUCTION

THE cinema, one of the few art-forms born of the machine age, has become a world-wide medium of entertainment and a major industry. As a teaching aid, it has brought the outside world to the class-room. As a research instrument it has been used in all the experimental sciences, enriching our knowledge and increasing our mastery over nature. These numerous and valuable applications of cinematography are not due to a single person, nor can they be credited to one country. Much toil and research were needed to bring cinematography to its present state of perfection, a process that took three-quarters of a century to mature: here we are concerned only with its first twenty-five years. In 1874, the first moving object was intermittently photographed on a single plate, and in 1895, the first film, as we know it today, was publicly screened (plate 44 B). By 1900 the cinema was well established in all European and American cities, by no means as glamorously as today, but already as a profitable and much-discussed form of entertainment.

The word *cinématographe* was first used by G. Bouly in 1892 in a French patent specification for a camera, and has since found its way, in one form or another, into nearly all languages. Its meaning has been widened and 'cinematography' now includes all the applied sciences that are concerned with the recording and reproduction of 'moving pictures'.

Cinematography may well be defined as follows. A series of separate images, recorded on the same continuous light-sensitive ribbon, is exposed at standard intervals of time to represent successive phases of a movement. When exhibited in rapid sequence, above the fusion frequency of human vision, the separate images persist long enough in the mind of the observer to reproduce the appearance of continuous motion.

This definition embodies the mechanical, the chemical, and the physiological principles of cinematography. First, the recording of separate images at standard intervals of time demands an intermittent mechanical movement of the ribbon on which the images are registered. Secondly, this ribbon must be light-sensitive, and, from the beginning of cinematography until the present day, the photographic emulsion with its chemical changes has been found most suitable, though current research is seeking to replace the emulsion by magnetic tape. Thirdly, in order to reproduce the appearance of continuous motion, the separate images must be projected at such a frequency that the physiological phenomenon of persistence of vision is brought into play and the parts fuse into a whole.

In this technological history of cinematography, our main concern is with the first basic principle, namely, how the intermittent movement of the ribbon was achieved in both the cine-camera and the film projector. The discovery and the history of the photochemical reactions of silver halides, the second basic principle which makes cinematography possible, has already been described in the first part of this chapter. The third principle, the physiological phenomenon of persistence of vision, is the oldest of the three; a brief consideration of it will lead us logically to our main subject.

II. THE FORERUNNERS

An image on the human retina remains unchanged for a period of one-twentieth to one-tenth of a second, depending on the object's colour, shape, and distance from the eye. This phenomenon of persistence of vision must have been noticed by prehistoric men. When a stick with lighted or glowing end is whirled rapidly in a circle, a luminous and continuous path is seen. In Ptolemy's second book on optics, written about A.D. 130, he remarks that if a sector of a disk be coloured, then the whole disk appears of that colour if rapidly revolved. Others discussed persistence of vision: Alhazen in the eleventh century, Leonardo da Vinci in the fifteenth, and later Newton and Boyle—all from a theoretical point of view. The first to apply this phenomenon and use it in a philosophical toy was an English doctor, J. A. Paris, who in 1826 described his 'thaumatrope' or 'wonder-turner' (tailpiece). A small cardboard disk, having different images on each surface, was suspended between two pieces of silk; these threads, held between the thumb and forefinger of each hand, were rapidly turned, thus spinning the card. The result was that the two images appeared simultaneously. From this achievement it was but a short step to produce the illusion of motion by looking at a sequence of drawings passing rapidly in and out of the field of view.

The achievement of this illusion was the one and only fundamental discovery in the field of cinematography. Both J. A. F. Plateau, a blind Belgian physicist, and S. von Stampfer, an Austrian geologist, succeeded in 1832 in demonstrating their solution. Disks with a varying number of slots at their periphery were spun in front of a mirror; at the centre of each disk was a series of drawings each progressively different from its neighbour, yet, when viewed through the slots, fusing into a moving whole. These spinning wheels have been called 'magic disks', fantascopes, phenakistiscopes, and stroboscopes. Two years later,

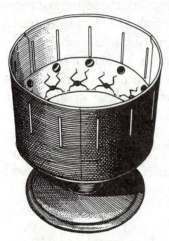

W. G. Horner, an Englishman, improved the design by placing the drawings on a ribbon inside a slotted horizontal wheel and thus made it possible for several people, instead of a single viewer, to enjoy the entertainment. This was the so-called zoetrope or wheel-of-life (figures 389, 390). In 1839, W. H. Fox Talbot in England, and L. J. M. Daguerre in France, announced practical photographic processes, yet it took another thirty-five years to combine photography and these primitive moving pictures.

FIGURE 389—*The wheel-of-life, with ribbon drawing in place.*

Let us now turn briefly back to the middle of the seventeenth century, to 1645, two years after Louis XIV began his reign in France, and four years before Charles I was executed in England. At that time there lived in Rome a German Jesuit, Athanasius Kircher (1601–80), who was professor of mathematics at the Collègio Romano. A scholar of many attainments, he was the first to project a picture on to a screen. His apparatus was crude, yet contained all the essentials: a source of light with a reflector behind and a lens in front of it, a painted glass slide, and a screen. His audience was astonished, somewhat perturbed, and talked of black magic. Undismayed, he published his experiments, and they have never been forgotten. Throughout the next two centuries, improved versions of his 'magic' lantern were used to entertain and even to instruct. Of the many who developed his idea, P. van Musschenbroek (1692–1761) deserves mention here; in 1736 he was able to introduce motion on the screen by using a stationary slide as background and a moving one as a foreground, thus producing an effect miraculous for that period. Painted glass slides of this kind were still a popular toy at the end of the nineteenth century.

By 1850 the time was ripe for a synthesis of Kircher's magic lantern and the rotating disks of Plateau and von Stampfer, thus achieving projection of moving pictures. An Austrian artillery officer, Baron F. von Uchatius (1811–81), was the first, in 1853, to publish a successful solution. He was asked to develop a method for military instruction that would show moving pictures to a large audience. Uchatius first solved this problem by making projection on to a screen through a rotating glass slide, a rotating shutter, and a fixed lens. His second, and improved, version contained a rotating light-source, fixed slides, and a series of slightly inclined lenses whose optical axes met on the centre of the screen. The limited number of consecutive drawings that could be put on one slide did not allow a projection period longer than 30 seconds. This time was not exceeded in any subsequent projectors until 1895.

FIGURE 390—*Two typical ribbon drawings for the wheel-of-life (figure 389).*

Many other incidental improvements were required before one can speak of cinematography proper. F. and W. Langenheim, two Germans living in Philadelphia, in 1850 perfected a process for making photographic positives on glass slides, suitable for projection in a magic lantern. T. H. Dumont and P. H. Desvignes in France in 1860, W. T. Shaw in England in 1861, and C. Sellers in the United States in the same year, all published papers and obtained patents on improved methods of viewing and projecting moving pictures. By 1865 J. Laing had announced his 'Motorscope' in England; L. Foucauld, the famous French astronomer, had described his stereophantascope or bioscope; and H. Cook and G. Bonelli had obtained a patent in England for seeing through a microscope a series of small views mounted on the edge of a disk, this being rotated in unison with a perforated eye-piece. 1868 is an important date, for in that year J. W. Hyatt invented celluloid while seeking a substitute for ivory in making billiard balls. J. Clerk Maxwell, famous for his contribution to the mathematics of electro-magnetic waves, published in 1869 an improvement to the then popular zoetrope; he substituted concave lenses for slots. In the following year, J. P. Bourbouze, a French scientist, used the first moving pictures to demonstrate to his students the action of pistons, pumps, and compressors.

Had Janssen, Muybridge, and Marey—the three pioneers next to be discussed —realized their importance in the technological development of cinematography, they might well have echoed Newton's words: 'If we have seen a little farther than others, it is because we have stood on the shoulders of giants.'

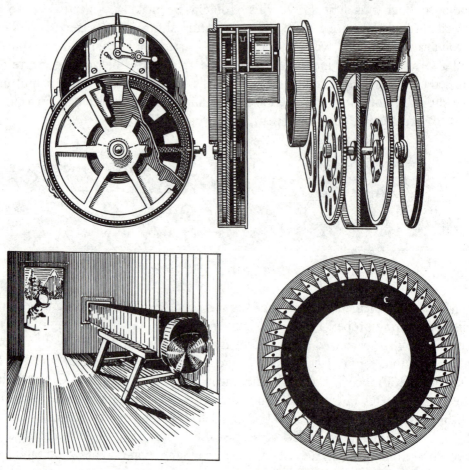

FIGURE 391—*Janssen's* revolver astronomique, *for observation of successive phases of the transit of Venus in 1874.*

III. THE PIONEERS: JANSSEN, MUYBRIDGE, MAREY

By 1870, then, it had become possible to view moving pictures painted on glass slides, and also to project photographs on to a screen. No one, however, had as yet taken a series of photographs in order to dissect a consecutive movement into its constituent fractions; this step is an essential preliminary to their synthesis and subsequent reproduction as lifelike movement.

For 8 December 1874, an extremely rare astronomical event was predicted: a transit of Venus across the Sun. To record it permanently, P. J. C. Janssen

(1824–1907), director of the Meudon observatory near Paris, designed and used the first apparatus that photographed consecutive phases of a single movement. He was guided by Plateau's magic disks, and simply reversed the process. He placed a circular plate, covered with a photographic emulsion, behind another disk, perforated by radial slits. The two disks were moved intermittently by a clockwork mechanism, and the complete apparatus was attached to the

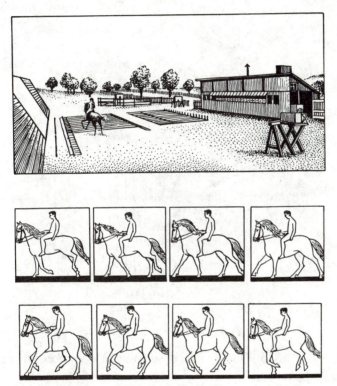

FIGURE 392—*Muybridge's photographic installation* (above) *and an example of his results.*

eye-piece of his astronomical telescope, focused by means of a heliostat on the Sun. Thus the first 'film' was made, showing clearly to this day, in 48 consecutive pictures recorded on the same photographic emulsion, the slow movement of Venus across the Sun (figure 391).

In California, another pioneer, E. Muybridge (1830–1904), a native of Kingston upon Thames, was hard at work. In 1872 he was asked to settle a bet by photographic methods and succeeded in recording the individual paces of a galloping horse; he proved that for an instant all four legs were off the ground. This was not new knowledge, for E. J. Marey (1830–1904) had proved the same fact in Paris in 1870 by means of kymograph records (p 741), but he had not then obtained any photographic proof. Through the years, Muybridge and Marey were in correspondence, each influencing the other. Muybridge at the beginning took many photographs to help Marey's investigation of the flight of birds; later on, when Marey saw these photographs, he became convinced that photographic techniques were superior to his own kymographic results, and he himself turned to photography and built the first modern cine-camera in his

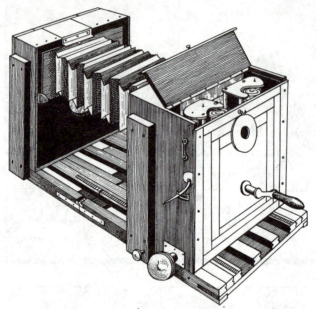

FIGURE 393—*Marey's* chambre chronophotographique.

Paris laboratory in 1888. But before describing Marey's equipment we must consider that of Muybridge.

Muybridge required his objects to move in front of a series of 12–30 photographic cameras a foot apart, all facing a white wall. Between wall and cameras was a series of strings, each of which triggered an electromagnetic shutter of the camera to which it was attached (figure 392). This work was begun in 1878 and continued with improvements until the death of its originator; it led to the publication of 11 volumes containing 20 000 photographs of animal and human locomotion, recording the performance of men, women, and children and of a very wide range of animals. His technique is open to the criticism that his early records were equidistant in space but not in time; he overcame this defect later, by triggering the shutters of his cameras from a rotating commutator; he could then set up three banks of cameras and use them synchronously.

Marey started his photographic work in 1882; his idea, following Janssen's suggestion, was to record all movement through a single photographic lens. His first equipment, the *fusil photographique*, was in fact closely inspired by, and indeed very similar to, Janssen's rotating disk-and-shutter mechanism. A circular glass plate received 12 consecutive images in one second, and for each exposure the plate was brought to complete rest behind the opened shutter for $\frac{1}{720}$-sec. With it, Marey carried out a number of interesting investigations about the flight of birds (plate 44 A), but it had grave limitations. The mass of the glass plate, which had to be accelerated and brought to rest 12 times a second, and the smallness of the individual pictures, greatly limited the analysis of motion.

Marey then had a brilliant idea. For many years he had employed a kymo-

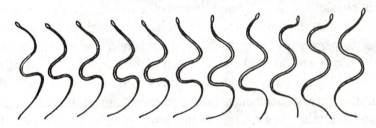

FIGURE 394—*Example of results of Marey's* chambre chronophotographique: *snake in motion.*

graph as his principal instrument for recording all aspects of the motion of animals. On its slowly revolving drum, covered with smoked paper, a stylus scratched a white line; by suitably connecting the movement under investigation to the stylus, a corresponding trace could be inscribed on the paper. Marey's idea was to use a ray of light instead of the stylus, and to replace the smoked paper by one of the lengths of photographic paper which by 1887 had become available. At first he tried continuous movement of the photographic emulsion, but he realized almost at once that he had to employ the intermittent movement of his *fusil photographique* if he wanted to obtain clear and sharp images on development. This was indeed the birth of cinematography, which Marey communicated to the Académie des Sciences on 29 October 1888. On this historic occasion Janssen was in the chair, but few of the other members could have realized that these small strips of photographic paper marked the foundation of a new art and a new industry.

Marey's camera, the so-called *chambre chronophotographique*, was by no means perfect, although it embodied all the principles of a modern cine-camera (see figures 393, 394). A ribbon of light-sensitive paper, made by Eastman or Balagny and about 4 m long, moved intermittently past the lens of the camera, from a supply-spool to a take-up spool. A shutter, with a window 1 cm square, was rotated between the lens and the emulsion and cut off the illumination while the paper was moved; images were recorded at the rate of 10–12 per sec. Intermittent motion of the film, the crux of the camera, was achieved in a rather complex manner. A hand-crank, which also turned the shutter, drove the take-up spool continuously, but through a friction clutch; when the starter-button of the camera was pressed, a brake on the take-up spool was removed and the film was thus pulled through the camera. It was intermittently arrested behind the lens by a second brake, actuated by a cam, and a loop in the film and a weak spring ensured that the film was not torn during its momentary arrest. Each camera was made by hand in the workshops of the Collège de France, where Marey was professor of physiology. Wood, brass, and steel cams were the main raw materials, the bellows between the shutter and the film being of leather. The concept of the camera was by no means perfect: the frictional forces relied on for the movement of the film were not sufficiently controllable, and the width of the film, 9 cm, allowed only a limited series of pictures to be taken, normally about 40. Two of these historic cameras have been preserved, one at the Science Museum, London, and the other at the Conservatoire des Arts et Métiers, Paris. Marey proceeded to the projection of his films only many years later, in 1898.

IV. THE CONTRIBUTORS

No one would claim today that cinematography was invented by one person, although the greatest single impetus came from Marey, who was the first to demonstrate successfully the basic principle and to publish it in a way accessible to all. Many others had to develop his ideas before the initial *première* could be staged. The work of some of these contributors has long been forgotten; other ideas were tried towards the end of the last century, given up, and lay dormant for many decades until perhaps a high-speed cinematograph camera or a special gun-camera posed extreme demands that could be met only by having recourse to forgotten inventions. Examples are F. Jenkins's optical compensation by a ring of rotating lenses, and G. Demeny's beater-mechanism (p 743) for film-transport. Other contributors, such as T. A. Edison and A. and L. Lumière, have their names linked with final success and will always be remembered. Unfortunately, the question of the nationality of the 'inventor' of cinematography has also arisen, and from time to time extravagant claims have been made by his native country for one single person; it is hoped that this short chapter will show the true character of the origin of cinematography to be as international as are its benefits to mankind.

The period up to 1895 was one of intense activity in the field of moving pictures, but only a few of the more outstanding contributors can here be briefly mentioned. In England, W. Friese-Greene, M. Evans, and J. A. R. Rudge demonstrated their cine-camera to the Bath Photographic Society in 1890. An unperforated film, 63 mm wide, was intermittently moved from supply to take-up spool by an ingenious spring-mechanism which alternately was wound by the main shaft and unwound itself to move the film forward one frame. Three hundred frames could be exposed at a rate of 10 a second, but the series of pictures so obtained was never projected. The name of W. Donisthorpe and his patent of 1889 may also be recalled; he proposed intermittent movement by cranking the whole camera upwards and downwards, with the film running continuously behind it. In 1893, G. Demeny, an assistant of Marey's, patented a camera which he called a bioscope; his film was moved intermittently by two eccentrically mounted pins used as film-spools, between which a 'dog' or beater operated, thus pulling the film into a loop at one-frame intervals.

While these and similar other inventions were discussed in European photographic and scientific circles, the Kinetoscope Parlor on Broadway, New York, became the centre of interest on the other side of the Atlantic when it was opened on 14 April 1894. There T. A. Edison demonstrated to the public for the first time his contribution to cinematography. Edison's work, with that of his assistant K. L. Dickson, is said to date back to 1887, when a project to combine the sound of the phonograph with moving pictures was discussed between them. At first Edison tried to record pictures in a spiral around a cylinder, as sound was recorded on phonograph drums. Two years later, in 1889, he visited Paris, and there met Marey and saw his films. But in his famous American patent filed in 1891, Edison described a different intermittent movement for his camera, the kinetograph; for his projector, the kinetoscope, he followed closely the lines of Anschütz's electrical tachyscope of 1889. Intermittent movement in the kinetograph was achieved by means of two toothed wheels, with shafts at right-angles to each other, which periodically interlocked and arrested the movement of the film from spool to spool. This arrangement became public knowledge only when the patent was issued in 1897. The great and lasting contribution of Edison was his use of celluloid film, 35 mm wide, with four perforations for each picture, a practice still standard sixty years later. Perforations had been used previously by E. Reynaud in his picture-series hand-painted on gelatine, which he projected successfully in Paris from 1888 to 1900 and which Edison may have seen on his visit to Paris in 1889; Edison was the first, however, to employ perforations on photographic films. These regularly spaced holes on both sides of the photographic image allow precise alignment and transport of the film from picture to picture: toothed sprocket-wheels can be employed to move the film through either the camera or the projector.

Edison's projector used a small electric motor for the continuous movement of the films (figure 395). It was a wooden cabinet, furnished with a peep-slit and an inspection-lens through which a single person could view the endless loop of film which passed below it; the film was illuminated from behind by an electric

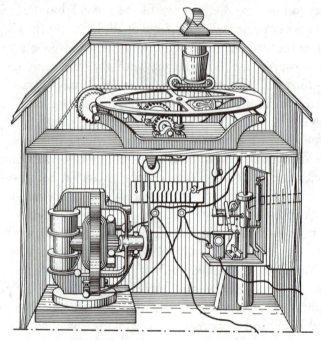

FIGURE 395—*Edison's kinetoscope.*

lamp. In order to allow the individual pictures recorded on the film to be seen, and to let them be fused into a continuous movement by the phenomenon of persistence of vision, a one-slot rotating shutter was interposed between film and lens. Edison employed a frequency of 46 pictures a second, requiring a shutter-speed of 46 revolutions a second. Although this system worked well for a single viewer, it was quite uneconomical for purposes of projection, as only 1/46th of the available light was utilized. Edison was at first unconvinced of the need for projection to large audiences, although the ready and widespread success of his kinetoscopes in Europe and America should have convinced him of the existence of a great public demand for moving pictures.

The final step in the early history of cinematography takes us back again to

France; to Lyons, where Auguste and Louis Lumière were conducting a flourishing photographic business. They had seen both Edison's kinetoscope, and Reynaud's *théâtre optique*, in which a long series of hand-painted pictures was projected life-size on to a screen. The combination of these two ideas—the development of a satisfactory camera and projector, and the projection on to a screen of life-size photographic pictures of movement for several minutes at a time—is the basis of the undying fame of the Lumières. They borrowed from Edison the idea of perforations, although they used only one per picture instead of four, and they reduced the frequency to 16 a second, a figure perfectly satisfactory for achieving persistence of vision and today still the standard for silent films. They engaged an engineer, C. Moissant, to design for their camera a claw-movement which allowed two pins to enter the perforations and pull down the film while a semi-circular shutter cut off the light between lens and film. While the picture was either exposed in the camera, or projected on to the screen, the two pins of the claw-movement returned to their original position, ready to repeat the process of intermittent movement of the film. This technique, too, is still a standard today in nearly all cine-cameras, and in some projectors. The claw-movement itself was actuated by a sectoral cam, driven by a shaft mounted on its apex.

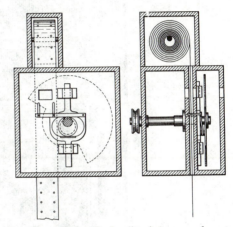

FIGURE 396—*The Lumière* cinématographe.

The Lumières had their machines (figure 396) manufactured by J. Carpentier's firm. Their first patent was filed in France on 13 February 1895, and in England on 8 April of the same year. On 22 March the first demonstration was given at Lyons, and on 10 and 12 June they created a sensation by filming the arrival of delegates at the Congress of the National Union of French Photographic Societies and projecting this same event to them two days later. Finally, on 28 December 1895, in the Grand Café on the Boulevard des Capucines, Paris, thirty-three inquisitive people walked in from the street and paid a franc each to see on the screen 'The Baby's Meal', 'The Arrival of a Train' (plate 44 B), 'Scenes from the Bourse of Lyons', and similar events. A week or so later, the audiences numbered some 2000 each night. Cinematography as we know it today had arrived, to begin its triumphant march of the next six decades.

It would be entirely wrong to suppose that from that day onward the Lumières' equipment was universally employed to record and project cinematograph films, although it was widely hailed and used all over the world. In London, R. W. Paul followed close behind the Lumières when on 20 February 1896 he showed his first moving pictures at the Finsbury Technical College. His camera at first used a clamping and unclamping action which was rather hard on

FIGURE 397—*The Prestwich camera, one of a wide range of instruments that appeared at the end of the nineteenth century.*

the film; this he replaced soon afterwards by the well known Maltese-cross movement. He was the first to introduce it to cinematography, and it still remains the standard method of producing intermittent motion in 35-mm projectors. The name of Paul must be associated with that of B. Acres, his colleague, camera man, and commercial showman. One of their outstanding successes was the filming of the Derby in 1896 and the projection of the film on the same night at the Alhambra Theatre in Leicester Square.

This story has followed the main current only, but it must be concluded by showing some of the many eddies that swirled around cinematography during the period 1895–1900. Theoretically at least, film can be moved continuously, but must be seen for a very short period only, as in Edison's kinetoscope; it can also be rendered relatively stationary, or optically stationary. In addition, film can be moved intermittently by rollers through the interaction of toothed wheels with worms or cams; by changing the position of the sprocket-wheels; by ratchet-gearing; or by the periodic grip of two rollers. Furthermore, film can be moved intermittently by teeth always in contact with it (spring-teeth); by teeth inserted and withdrawn (claws); or by such substitutes as gripping fingers. Alternatively, it can be moved intermittently by pressure of eccentrics; by reciprocating arms; or by spring-arms which act when a braking-clamp is removed. All these methods had been tried by 1900. The names of their inventors and the titles, often bizarre, of their equipment have been preserved to us in the patent literature of the period, although few of the machines have survived. Most of the various types were described in detail by H. V. Hopwood in 1899 (figure 397, and Bibliography). Hopwood suggested that 'animatography' might be used to describe the subject, remarking that the terms 'kinetoscopy' and 'cinematography' had not been generally approved.

V. THE FILMS

It has already been mentioned (pp 729, 737) that J. W. Hyatt was the first to make celluloid,[1] in 1868, although at that time it was used merely for the production of solid mouldings. It was not until twenty years later that celluloid in sheet form became available; a number of people then simultaneously realized that this was the ideal material to use in strip form, sensitized to light, for the recording of movement. Apparently the first to have this idea was H. Goodwin, who filed a United States patent on this subject on 2 May 1887; it was not granted until 13 September 1898. George Eastman, at Rochester, New York, was the first to put the idea into practice and to manufacture a celluloid film coated with a light-sensitive photographic emulsion. A long legal battle between him and the heirs of Goodwin resulted in a settlement. In France, the Lumière brothers made their own film from the outset; other manufacturers were Balagny and the Blair Company.

Before 1900, film was invariably manufactured in batches; continuous production did not occur until much later. The principle, however, has remained the same; cellulose nitrate was dissolved in a suitable aromatic solvent, mixed with camphor or other ingredients, and poured on to glass-topped tables, up to 30 m long. After evaporation of the solvent, the emulsion—a mixture of silver halides in gelatine—was applied. It remained only to cut the sheet into ribbons

---

[1] Alexander Parkes of Birmingham had taken out a patent for the same or a similar product in 1865, but failed to manufacture it successfully (p 729).

of the required widths by means of roller-shears—but at this point the troubles of the first film-makers and cinematographers began.

A remarkable diversity of sizes was in use. Mutograph film was 70 mm wide; Skladanowsky's camera took 65-mm film; the Demeny and the Prestwich cameras employed 60-mm film; the Lumières' gauge was 35 mm and Edison's 34·8 mm. The 'Birtac', probably the first to introduce narrow-gauge film, used 17·4 mm material, the same size as was required for the 'Junior' Prestwich. But besides variations of width, each camera had a different method of propelling the film through the gate; in some, there was no need for perforations, and the film

FIGURE 398—*A typical film laboratory of the period.*

was used in its entire width. Those who perforated their film could not at first agree on the dimensions of the perforation, or on the number of holes or their exact shapes. It therefore became essential to issue with each camera a perforating machine, through which all film had to pass—naturally in the dark—before it could be used. Evidently, therefore, a film made with one camera could be projected only with a machine having precisely the same film-gauge and sprocket-wheels. Furthermore, as the film exposed in the camera was necessarily a negative, and a positive copy had to be made before projection, a printing-apparatus had to be available, again of precisely the same dimensions.

No wonder, therefore, that in those early days many inventors claimed to have perfected a machine that could be used as camera, projector, or printer, according to the need of its operator. This idea was never acceptable. It is evidence of the rapid and successful expansion of cinematography that soon after the turn of the century the 35-mm width, with four rectangular perforations per picture, was adopted as standard. Though the emulsion-support has been changed from the highly inflammable and unstable cellulose nitrate to the stable and safe cellulose acetate, the standard dimensions and perforations have now remained unaltered for the last fifty years.

After exposure, the film had to be developed, and the most primitive method was to pass the film from hand to hand in a large bucket. A great improvement

FIGURE 399—'L'homme à la tête de caoutchouc', *from a film by Méliès*.

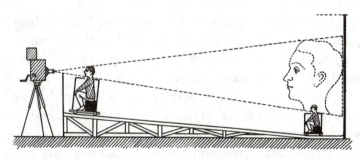

FIGURE 400—*Apparatus used in making Méliès's film (figure 399)*.

was to wind the film on to a frame, circular or rectangular, and immerse it thus supported into tanks of developer, washing water, and fixing solution. The best method for developing film batches up to 30 m long—and before the end of the nineteenth century these were the only techniques employed—was to wind the film on to large drums (figure 398). These drums were about 1 m in diameter and just over 2 m long, constructed of lattice-work and fitted with a horizontal shaft, supported loosely from upright stands at the ends of shallow troughs. The drum could be turned easily by the operator. When the desired density of the negative had been reached, the drum could be lifted off the stands of one trough and moved on to the next; thus the whole film was evenly and uniformly exposed to the action of the various solutions. Final drying was also carried out while the film was still rolled on the drums. The production of film, the manufacture of cameras, and film development were by 1900 still in the tentative stages, and mass-production methods were not introduced until several decades later.

Limitations of technique do not, however, imply that the subjects recorded on films at that time were also few and limited. The difficulties of a camera man during the last four years of the century were indeed formidable. His only illumination was sunlight, and his camera had to be laboriously cranked by hand. He employed a wooden tripod to steady the camera, but exposure, distance, and duration of filming had to be judged by his own experience. Ingenuity in choice of subject, coupled with great determination, was his main qualification for success. As soon as the Lumières had proved that films were able to show a profit, camera men set out to the farthest corners of the world, and by the middle of 1896, a bare six months after the world *première*, a camera man was filming events in Australia. The most obvious subjects were public and sporting events. The military campaign in the Sudan of 1898 provided what was probably the first war film, but industrial subjects were not neglected, provided they could be filmed in the open or were self-luminous.

Above all others, we must record the name of one French cinematographer whose brilliant imagination and superb technical skill gave the young art of the cinema a line to follow whose end is yet to be reached. Georges Méliès set out to entertain, and he was so successful that by the end of 1896 he had made 17 films; his famous company, Star Films, had completed 4000 by 1910. A great number of these short masterpieces have survived and still bring enjoyment to modern audiences. In his little sunlit studio at Montreuil he created the most fantastic scenes and characters: devils, macabre spirits, clowns, giants, strange animals, and personified machines. Not content with these, he was the first to use such cinematographic tricks as double exposure, tracking-cameras, animated models, and silhouettes (figures 399, 400). Perhaps it was no wonder that Georges Méliès, the expert conjuror, saw in the cinema an extension of his gifts sufficient to provide his imagination with unlimited opportunities.

And so the cinema was launched, as the twentieth-century entertainment, to show the world imaginative stories from the past, the present, and the future, to bring reality and news from the corners of the world, to document our own and our neighbours' social conditions, to teach in the schools and in the universities, and to aid the scientist in his research work to see events that his unaided eye could never hope to discover.

BIBLIOGRAPHY

COISSAC, G. M. 'Histoire du cinématographe de ses origines jusqu'à nos jours.' Gauthier-Villars, Paris. 1925.

HOPWOOD, H. V. 'Living Pictures: their History, Photo-Reproduction and Practical Working.' London. 1899.

LIESEGANG, F. P. 'Zahlen und Quellen zur Geschichte der Projektionskunst und Kinematographie.' Deutsches Druck- und Verlagshaus, Berlin. 1926.

QUIGLEY, M. (Jr.). 'Magic Shadows. The Story of the Origin of Motion Pictures.' Georgetown University Press, Washington. 1948.

RAMSAYE, T. 'A Million and One Nights. A History of the Motion Pictures.' Simon & Schuster, New York. 1926.

VIVIÉ, J. 'Traité général de technique du cinéma', Vol 1: 'Historique et développement de la technique cinématographique.' Bureau de Presse et d'Informations, Paris. 1946.

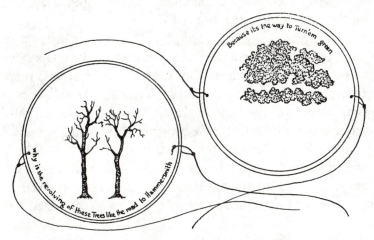

The 'Thaumatrope' or 'Wonder-turner', 1826 (front and back view).

31

PRODUCTION AND UTILIZATION OF RUBBER

S. S. PICKLES

I. NATURE OF RUBBER

CAOUTCHOUC (a native word meaning 'weeping wood') occurs in the form of very fine particles, or globules, suspended in an aqueous liquid found in the bark of certain tropical plants. There are many types of rubber-bearing plants, deriving from a large range of genera and species, and widely distributed over the surface of the globe. The principal one is that known as *Hevea brasiliensis* or Para rubber, indigenous to South America but now largely cultivated in Malaya, Ceylon, and Indonesia. Other types occur in Mexico, Africa, India, the East Indies, and elsewhere.

Rubber latex is a white, milky liquid secreted in a system of cells situated in the inner portions of the bark; it is not the true sap of the tree, but a separate secretion the function of which is unknown. Within the laticiferous system there is some pressure, varying according to the season, so that when the cells are opened up by cutting away portions of the bark, the liquid exudes into the cut thus formed, whence it can be collected for further treatment. This cutting process is known as 'tapping', and in South America the native method was to cut the bark with small axes known as *machadinhas*, the latex being collected in cups attached to the tree by moist clay (figure 401). From these it was transferred to larger vessels, before being converted into solid rubber by a process of combined heating and smoking.

In the latex the rubber exists in the form of minute particles about one sixteen-thousandth of an inch in diameter, suspended in a liquid which consists of water with small quantities of sugars and proteins in solution. When certain substances, such as acids or certain salts, are added, the particles of rubber aggregate and coalesce to form a clot of solid rubber, which separates from the mother liquid. This process, known as coagulation, is brought about, in Brazil, by heating the latex, in the form of a thin film carried on a wooden paddle, in the smoky fumes obtained by burning wood in a kind of brazier. As the film dries, more latex is applied and the process is continued until a large ball of solid rubber accumulates; this is afterwards removed by cutting. In the modern process, as practised in the Eastern plantations, the latex is collected in aluminium or glass cups from sloping cuts made in the bark by special tapping-knives. The cups are emptied into larger receptacles which are taken to the estate factory; here the latex is first passed through strainers to remove any foreign matter and then suitably diluted and mixed with acetic acid to bring about coagulation. This process takes place in coagulating-tanks, the upper portions of which are divided into partitions by laths. When coagulation is complete, the coherent clot is passed between rollers to remove the serum, and then washed and rolled until uniform sheets about $\frac{1}{8}$-in thick are obtained; these may be air dried to give 'pale crêpe' or dried in smoke-houses to give 'smoked sheet'.

FIGURE 401—*Method of extracting india-rubber from the para trees in Brazil.*

Physically, rubber is an easily deformable, elastic solid; its intrinsic and characteristic property is that of recovering its shape after deformation. Many materials, including glass and steel, are highly elastic, but the extent to which they can be deformed within elastic limits is small compared with that of rubber. Rubber has no elastic limit in the sense that metals have, for after stretching a piece to about seven times its original length, it will recover, and even on breaking it, the segments will tend to return to their original dimensions. Rubber may also possess remarkable strength; it can now be prepared with a tensile strength of about 20 tons per sq in, calculated on the cross-section at the breaking-point. Although rubber cannot be melted without decomposition, it can be rendered plastic and workable, and in this condition can be moulded or sheeted into any desired form and the shape thus impressed upon it can afterwards be rendered permanent. We thus have a material of vegetable origin which, within limits, is susceptible to treatment similar to that applied in metallurgical operations. Its elasticity, its stability, its resistance to atmospheric influences, and its adaptability in working, together form a unique combination of useful properties possessed by no other natural material. In addition, by various methods of treatment the consistency of the product can be varied from that of the extreme softness and pliability of rubber thread to the great hardness of ebonite.

II. EARLY REFERENCES

Very early information concerning India rubber or caoutchouc is given by Spanish historians of the period following the discovery of America towards the end of the fifteenth century. They refer to the use of rubber balls by natives of the West Indies in their national games and pastimes. Recent researches into the life and customs of the ancient Aztec and Maya peoples have revealed that various rubber articles were in common use 700 years ago, and that organized games with rubber balls were even then a feature of social life [1].

Since the sixteenth century there have been many references to the rubber-yielding trees with which the South American natives were acquainted: when the bark of these was cut, the milky latex was liberated. From this they prepared films—probably by evaporation—which, when placed on shaped moulds fashioned in clay or some similar material, gave them articles of various shapes and sizes. They were thus able to make protective clothing, shoes, syringes, bowls for containing liquids, and other useful domestic articles.

III. INTRODUCTION OF RUBBER INTO EUROPE

Although the Spanish settlers in the New World soon became acquainted with rubber and, in fact, used it for weather-proofing their soldiers' cloaks as early as 1615, there seems to have been little attempt to extend and develop its application in the countries of Europe for more than 200 years. It is to the French that we owe the first attempts to study the properties and sources of the material and the possibilities of importing it for the manufacture of useful articles in Europe. In 1736 Charles de La Condamine (1701-74), a member of a scientific expedition sent by the Académie des Sciences to Peru, forwarded an account of a journey he had made, following the course of the Amazon, across the South American continent. With this report he enclosed some rolls of dark, resinous caoutchouc which he had obtained during the course of his journey. In a later communication to the Académie in 1751 La Condamine [2] gave further interesting particulars of this material, and at the same time submitted a memoir by his compatriot Fresneau on the same subject.

Caoutchouc was stated to be obtained from a tree known as *Hhévé*, which on incision yielded a milky white liquid that hardened and darkened on exposure to the air. From the resin the natives made boots in one piece; these were waterproof and when smoked had the appearance of leather. By using clay moulds they obtained bottles for containing all sorts of liquids, and by coating canvas with the latex they produced protective fabrics.

Fresneau identified and described the tree which yielded caoutchouc. He also secured a small quantity of the material and, using native methods, made for himself a pair of boots, some bracelets, and other objects, all of which were elastic. Although Fresneau realized the possibilities of rubber for the manufacture of useful objects, he clearly recognized the difficulties that would have to be surmounted before its use could be extended beyond the crudely fashioned articles prepared by the natives from freshly collected latex. In his memoir he expressed the view that the preparation of rubber articles by native methods was possible only where the trees were found and before the latex coagulated. Methods of stabilizing the latex in liquid form had not then been discovered, and in fact it was not until many years later that the satisfactory transportation of latex over long distances became a normal procedure. Because of this tendency to undergo spontaneous coagulation most of the rubber subsequently imported into Europe was in the solid form in the shape of native-prepared bottles or large balls.

The publication of the reports of La Condamine and Fresneau in 1751 almost immediately aroused and stimulated the interest of European scientists and technicians, who quickly perceived the potential importance of the flexible and elastic properties of the newly introduced material. Communications began to appear in the scientific journals, and samples of the product were taken for scientific and experimental purposes. Many of the early investigations had as their object the discovery of a satisfactory solvent for the solid rubber which, being tough and resilient, did not lend itself to manipulation by any of the processes of manufacture then available. In 1763 the French chemists L. A. P. Herissant (1745–69) and P. J. Macquer (1718–84) proposed the use of rectified turpentine, and in 1768 the latter also found that purified ether was a suitable solvent for rubber.

IV. EARLY TECHNIQUE

Although Macquer had made small rubber tubes by repeatedly dipping a wax core into the ether solution and allowing the solvent to evaporate, afterwards removing the core by melting it in hot water, these were merely scientific demonstrations to draw the attention of surgeons and others to the possible applications of the new material. They pointed the way, however, to further developments, and in 1791 Grossart [3] introduced a new method for the production of tubes and other small articles that had far-reaching consequences on the subsequent progress of manufacture. In this method, the volatile solvent was used merely to soften the solid rubber and render it adhesive. Using native 'bottle' rubber from Brazil, Grossart obtained strips or layers by cutting the rubber to a convenient size, and after swelling and softening them by a short exposure to a volatile oil, wrapped them around a mandrel and applied a spiral bandage with suitable pressure. On drying, the rubber, now united and consolidated, retained the shape that had been given to it. The articles thus made had a considerable vogue and were apparently much appreciated by the surgeons of the period.

In 1770 Joseph Priestley (1733–1804) drew the attention of draughtsmen to the advantages of pieces of caoutchouc for erasing pencil marks from drawing-paper, and to this application it owes the name of 'rubber' or 'indiarubber' which it has since borne in this country. The material was soon to be found in the stationers' shops, and a regular and popular demand was thus established.

During the remainder of the eighteenth century experiments continued to be made, but without any results striking enough to foreshadow the foundation of a new industry. One concludes from the literature that, in France, efforts had been mainly concentrated on medical and surgical applications. Grossart had drawn attention to the advantages of a flexible and elastic material for surgical purposes, for such articles as tourniquets, bandages, stomach-pumps, ice-bags, and catheter-tubes; and an article on elastic bandages by J. Lucas appeared in the 'London Medical Journal' of 1788. In England, however, probably owing to the increasing popularity of coaching and road-travelling, early attention was given to the rain-proofing of materials such as leather, cotton, and other fabrics.

One of the earliest rubber patents was that of Samuel Peal (1791) for an improved method of making and rendering waterproof all kinds of leather, cotton, linen, wool, and so on, to be worked up into shoes, boots, and other wearing-apparel. The method consisted in 'making a solution of rubber in turpentine or other spirits or by using rubber in its natural state and applying the liquid by means of a brush or other utensil capable of giving a regular thin coating, then leaving the article in a hot room or store until properly dry'. Waterproofing patents continued to be applied for until well into the following century, but the wide extension of the applications of rubber, including the production of solid articles and the development of practical manufacturing processes, dates from the early 1800s.

Rubber-impregnated fabric was used for balloons, and in 1783 ascents were made in a rubberized balloon filled with hydrogen (p 395). Grossart's strip method is said to have been applied in 1803 at St-Denis, near Paris, in the making of garters and 'elastic' by causing stretched pieces of raw rubber to adhere to woven ribbons. In 1813 John Clark took out a patent (B.P. No 3718) for a method of making inflated beds, pillows, and cushions by impregnating the inner casings with a solution of rubber in a mixture of turpentine and linseed oil.

V. INTRODUCTION OF MECHANICAL PROCESSES

The year 1820 is a particularly memorable one in the annals of the rubber industry, for on 29 April of that year a patent was granted to Thomas Hancock (1786–1865) for 'an application of a certain material to various articles of dress and other articles, that the same may be rendered more elastic'. The object of the invention was the application of caoutchouc for the purpose of making 'a better kind of spring than any then in use'. Strips of raw caoutchouc of a convenient length and thickness were enclosed in a case or pipe of leather, cotton, or similar material. The extremities of the strip were fastened to the case by sewing or other means in such a manner that the case could contract or gather up very considerably. 'Springs so made, may be applied to the wrists of gloves, braces, garters, etc., or to boots and shoes when the desire is to take them off without any unlacing.' The patentee also applied caoutchouc to the soles of boots, shoes, and clogs to make them elastic to the foot. This is the first published reference to the remarkable man who played so important a part in the foundation of the rubber industry as we now know it; who invented and introduced machinery and processes for the elaboration of the raw material; and who did so much to extend its applications and popularize its products.

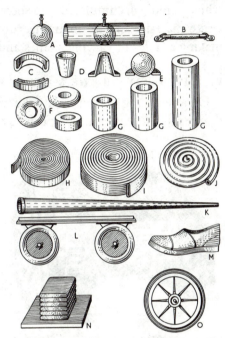

FIGURE 402—*Illustration of rubber articles for use in mechanical applications, manufactured in 1856 (Hancock).* (A) *Gas bag for repairing mains (shown also inside a pipe);* (B) *door spring;* (C) *hydraulic ram packing;* (D) *pump bucket (shown also in section);* (E) *plug ball valve;* (F) *buffer rings;* (G) *cylinders;* (H) *machinery banding;* (I) *hose pipe;* (J) *tubing;* (K) *flexible taper hose pipe for the end of fire-engine pipes;* (L) *rubber tyres for noiseless truck wheels;* (M) *malting shoe;* (N) *gig spring block;* (O) *carriage-wheel tyre.*

Hancock became interested in rubber about 1819 and, noting its exceptional qualities, was surprised that such a substance had remained so far neglected that no means had been discovered of converting it into solid masses or of facilitating its solution. His first experiments, using turpentine as a solvent, yielded only weak solutions that dried badly. It occurred to him that the rubber could be applied directly for many uses where elasticity was desirable, and the results of his efforts in this direction form the subject of his patent quoted above. For his raw material Hancock used the native 'bottle' rubber. Selecting the small, thin bottles, he cut them into rings, which he used chiefly for the wrists of gloves and sleeves. In this way he conveniently obtained the materials for his applications, but as the business in these articles increased, difficulties arose; first in getting supplies of bottles of convenient size, and secondly in disposing of the cuttings, which rapidly accumulated. He soon had to seek some means of working up his waste material and of obtaining rubber in quantity and condition suitable for making articles of varying shapes and sizes (figure 402).

VI. DISCOVERY OF THE MASTICATOR

On attempting to consolidate the waste by pressure, it was found that although the freshly cut edges united perfectly the previously exposed surfaces would not

do so. In order to get over the difficulty caused by the non-adhesiveness of the exposed surfaces Hancock decided to try shredding the rubber, and with this in view he devised an experimental machine which he hoped would effect the disintegration. This consisted of a hollow wooden cylinder internally studded with teeth, in the central cavity of which revolved a solid roller also fitted with teeth or spikes on its outer surface. There was thus an annular space between the two into which scraps of rubber could be fed. It was expected that, on rotating

FIGURE 403—*Old-type Bridge single-roll masticator; this was later replaced by open two-roll mixing machines.*

the internal roller, the rubber would be torn into shreds by the teeth of the machine, but the effect produced was in fact quite different. On making the experiment, Hancock found that as the treatment continued, the effort required to operate the machine became progressively greater, and when he came to open the cylinder he found to his surprise that the rubber, instead of being in shreds, had agglomerated into a ball. Further working somewhat improved the dispersion, and a homogeneous mass of solid rubber was obtained.

The capacity of this simple device was only 2 oz of strip rubber, but larger and more powerful machines were soon constructed which produced the rubber in cylindrical form (figure 403). By compressing the cylinders in iron moulds Hancock was able to obtain blocks of any shape and size, and these could be cut up as desired for the manufacture of his various articles.

This process, discovered in 1820, became known as 'mastication' and the machine as a 'masticator', although it was at first referred to as a 'pickle' for reasons of secrecy. It was the prototype of modern mills and masticators (figure 404). In the larger machines used by Hancock the principle remained the same, except that the teeth in the hollow cylinder were omitted as they were found to be unnecessary. Ultimately it became possible to operate with batches of rubber weighing 180–200 lb.

In his 'Narrative' [4], published in 1856, Hancock states 'that the discovery of this process [in 1820] was unquestionably the origin and commencement of the

FIGURE 404—*Large masticating machine, showing the removal and cutting of the rubber after processing.*

india-rubber manufacture, properly so called'. Other developments were quickly to follow; these included the production of cut sheet and thread, and the intro-duction of the mixing process.

VII. THE PRODUCTION OF CUT SHEET RUBBER

The shaped blocks of masticated rubber that Hancock now had at his dis-posal provided the material for his patented elastic articles, and it occurred to him that blocks might easily be cut into sheets and used for a variety of other purposes. A simple device [5] was constructed consisting of a wooden box capable of holding a square block of rubber of suitable size. Smooth steel plates were attached to the upper edges of the sides of the box, and, in the lower portion, a movable bottom was fixed which, by means of four long screws acting in the fitted bottom, could be raised or lowered as required. The block of rubber, well soaped at the sides, was placed in the box, and its height adjusted by means of the screws until the upper surface rose a little above the steel plates on the upper edges of the box. A long, straight knife, kept wet by dripping water, was then inserted at the right-hand end and, by a steady cutting and thrusting motion, passed through the block to the other end. By repeating this operation and adjusting the screws to give the thickness of sheet required, excellent sheet rubber was produced; the block could, by this machine, be cut so thin as to give a semi-transparent sheet. When warm, the sheets could very easily be joined edge to edge, and large sheets were made in this way.

This 'cut sheet' became a standard commodity, and was used by Hancock for a number of purposes, including the manufacture of flexible tubing and even of elastic thread, although for this latter application he preferred to use the bottle rubber, as imported, on account of its superior strength.

VIII. CUT THREAD

For making thread [6] the largest and thickest bottles were selected; after softening in hot water they were cut lengthwise into halves which were pressed between plates to flatten them. When cool, they were cemented to a board and passed to the cutting machine, a kind of lathe carrying a revolving circular knife, the edge of which just came into contact with the surface of the board on which the flattened halves were cemented. A sliding motion carried the board and rubber past the knife, which made a clean cut through the rubber; this motion was repeated until the whole breadth of the rubber carried these cuts, usually about $\frac{1}{16}$-in apart.

The board and the rubber were then placed in a device similar to that used in cutting sheets; here, by means of a knife, the rubber was cut horizontally and threads were obtained with a square section and about 5 inches in length. The short lengths were then united by cutting the ends with scissors and pressing them together while still warm. In this way threads of almost any length could be produced for use as warps in the manufacture of elastic fabrics and webbing.

Later, Hancock made a tube or cylinder from masticated rubber and sent it to Para as a pattern for the natives, who made up similar tubes, presumably from latex, by the native smoking process. A large number of these were imported; they were placed on a mandrel in a lathe and by means of a circular knife and a screw-and-slide motion a long tape-like strip was obtained. This was then cut into square thread in another machine, and longer threads with fewer joints were thus obtained.

IX. THE MIXING PROCESS

The introduction of mastication had provided the way for further development. The next important step in the progress of manufacture was that of blending rubber with other materials. Hancock had already found that mastication greatly facilitated the solution of rubber in the usual solvents, and in 1823 he patented a process for mixing pitch and tar with rubber by first dissolving the rubber in turpentine and then adding the other ingredients to the solution. He later discovered that pitch would readily commingle with rubber in the masticator without the use of solvents [7], thus

FIGURE 405—*Early type of open mixing mill, consisting of two horizontal rollers revolving in opposite directions at different speeds. It was used for mixing rubber with other ingredients.*

effecting a considerable saving in cost. It therefore appears that the first dry mixing was done in the masticator, the same machine being used by Hancock for both purposes.

At an early date, however, it became the practice in the industry to use the two-roller open type of mixing machine and this continued almost unaltered until the advent of the internal, or enclosed, type of mixer at the end of the nineteenth century.

The open type of mixer consists of a pair of iron rollers placed horizontally and revolving in opposite directions, and at different speeds, the distance between them being capable of adjustment (figures 405 and 406). The rollers are hollow, so that steam or water can be admitted into the interior for heating, if required. In passing through the rollers the rubber is not only heated and compressed, but subjected to a tearing action owing to the different speeds of the two rollers. After a few passages through the machine the rubber forms itself into a continuous band which envelops the front roller and revolves with it, passing through the 'nip' at each revolution. It gradually becomes dough-like in consistency and is then in a suitable condition for receiving the various compounding ingredients. By means of a scoop these are spread evenly over the revolving rubber, and to obtain uniform distribution the rubber sheet is repeatedly cut and doubled over. On leaving the machine the mixed rubber batch is cut into thick sheets and allowed to cool before passing on for further processing.

FIGURE 406 — *Mixing mills arranged in line.*

X. FOUNDATION OF THE RUBBER-PROOFING INDUSTRY

About this period Charles Macintosh (1766–1843), a Glasgow chemical manufacturer, discovered that coal-tar naphtha—a by-product of the gas industry—was an efficient and satis-factory solvent for rubber. Cutting the raw 'bottle' rubber into strips and immersing them in the volatile liquid, he obtained a solution or varnish which, by means of a brush or other suitable instrument, could be applied to the sur-face of cloth to render it impermeable to air and water. On evaporation of the solvent, the rubber was left as a viscous layer. By folding two pieces of cloth together, with the varnished surfaces inside, and applying pressure, a com-pound fabric was obtained, which later became known as a 'double texture'. On 17 June 1823 Macintosh obtained a patent for this process, which included (*a*) the use of the particular solvent, and (*b*) the method by which the cement was prevented from appearing on the surface of the fabric.

FIGURE 407—*Rubber spreading and proofing machine with 'feeding' and 'take-up' rollers for cloth, spreading knife, and steam-heated drying table.*

These compound fabrics appear to have been immediately successful for the manufacture of waterproof garments, air-cushions, and many other useful articles. The garments became known as 'macintoshes', a name still in general use, and in 1824 a factory was opened at Manchester for their production.

In 1825 Thomas Hancock obtained a licence under Macintosh's patent, in-cluding the use of coal-tar naphtha. Using the latter in conjunction with his own masticated rubber he was able to effect great economies in the use of solvent, and arrangements were made for him to prepare the solution at the works of Macintosh & Company. He personally superintended the installation of the new plant, and subsequently, from 1834 onwards, acted as a partner in and director of the Macintosh firm. It was during this period, in 1837, that he invented the spread-ing machine [8] which, with slight modifications, is in general use today for proofing fabric. This machine (figure 407) made it possible to manufacture proofed cloth very efficiently in long lengths, which could be cut up as required.

The cloth to be proofed is delivered on to the surface of a flat metal bed or, alternatively, of a hollow revolving roller of a length greater than the width of the cloth. The spreader, a long metal box, the lower part of which is tapered off nearly to an edge, is adjustably supported so that the edge lies above the bed and parallel to it. The cloth to be treated is drawn between the bed and the edge of the spreader, and on the incoming side is placed a bank of rubber dough previously suitably softened by the admixture of solvent. As the cloth is slowly drawn through, the dough is uniformly distributed over the cloth, to which it firmly adheres.

The rubberized fabric is then passed over a heated metal table which forms part of the machine; here the solvent evaporates and a film of dry rubber remains. The process is repeated until the required thickness of film is obtained. If the cloth is required for double textures, the two textures are coated with rubber as described, and united by passing them with sufficient pressure between rollers, with the coated surfaces in contact.

XI. THE CALENDER

The next important step was the introduction, in 1836, of the process of calendering; the main object of this process is the production of rubber in sheet form, the basis of the manufacture of very numerous and diverse articles.

About 1830 rubber manufacture was started in the United States, for the production of rubber shoes. The original calender patented in 1836 was the invention of E. M. Chaffee of the Roxbury Rubber Company, one of the early pioneers, whose object was to obtain rubber sheet without the use of solvents.

The calender machine, known as the 'Mammoth' on account of its size, consisted of three heavy steel rollers mounted vertically one above the other in a stout iron frame. It was fitted with means for adjusting the distances between the rolls, and with gear-wheels for controlling the direction and relative speed of rotation of the different rolls. Central cavities in the rollers permitted the admission of steam or water for controlling the temperature.

For the production of plain sheet, the mixed rubber, after being warmed and softened, is placed between the two upper rollers running at equal speeds. It is there sheeted and passed round the central roller and under the lower roller. The sheet is then run between wrapping-cloth, to prevent the individual layers from sticking together, and on to a wooden roller, where it remains until required for further processing.

By a modification of this procedure, the machine can be used for a type of spreading known as frictioning. In this case the lower roller is caused to revolve at a speed different from that of the central roller. A length of fabric is fed between the bottom roller and the central one carrying the rubber, when, owing to the combined effect of pressure and the differential speeds of the two rollers, the fabric becomes firmly united to the rubber and a strongly adhering film is thus obtained.

Chaffee's machine was the prototype of the modern calender, a most important item of rubber-works equipment, now used throughout the world. One of the earliest specimens in Britain is that erected by Stephen Moulton, from the American drawings, in 1849. This machine is still in operation at Bradford-on-Avon, Wiltshire (plate 5).

XII. THE FORCING OR EXTRUSION PROCESS

When a rubber article can be made in continuous lengths of uniform cross-section, as with tubing, rubber cord, cable-covering, and so on, the process of extrusion is commonly employed. In this process the plastic rubber is forced through an orifice or die (figures 408, 415).

FIGURE 408—*Machine by* Friedrich Krupp Akti-engesellschaft Grusonwerk, *Magdeburg-Buckau, for making tubing by extrusion. The strong steel barrel contains a revolving spiral, which forces the rubber through a shaped die or nozzle.*

One of the earliest mechanical devices for extrusion was that described by H. Bewley in his patent application of 1845 for improvements in such articles as tubes and hoses, made not in rubber but in the closely allied material gutta-percha. This resembles rubber, but contains more resin. The gutta-percha, in a plastic state, is put into a cylinder, and a piston working in the cylinder presses the gutta-percha against a heated disk. In the disk there are holes through which the material is pressed into a cup; from this it passes out round a core and descends, in the desired tubular form, into a receiver containing cold water.

In the machines subsequently made by Shaw, Royle, and others for use in the rubber industry, the piston was replaced by a power-driven centrally situated worm-shaft fitting closely to the walls of the cylinder. This carries the rubber forward towards the front portion of the cylinder, where it is forced through a heated die of the desired shape. After passing through the die the strip or tube is delivered into trays containing French chalk, or on to a travelling conveyer-belt for further working-up.

By 1838 the manufacture of rubber goods in Britain was well established. Water-proof garments, hose-pipes for use in breweries and on fire-engines, rubber blankets for printers, elastic fabrics, air-cushions for beds, pillows, and many other articles were produced in considerable quantities. Rubber shoes were also made, mostly by outside manufacturers who bought their materials from Hancock or Macintosh. There was also an appreciable demand for rubber for surgical purposes, which John Hancock met by opening a factory at Fulham where he made articles from cut sheet supplied by his brother Thomas. In addition, Hancock had made extensive experiments with latex, but apparently the use of this form of rubber was discontinued on account of the difficulty in obtaining the material in satisfactory condition. Hancock had also been instrumental in introducing rubber manufacture into continental Europe, for in 1828 he had personally supervised the inauguration of his process at the works of Rattier and Guibal in Paris.

By this time most of the standard processes for the manufacture of rubber had already been introduced. Hancock had invented the masticator and the spreading machine, and had developed the use of compounding ingredients and the processes of moulding. The processes of preparing cut sheet and rubber thread had been worked out, and the manufacture of elastic woven fabrics was the subject of many patents. The calender in the form we now know it had been invented in the United States by Chaffee, and an extrusion-machine for tubing was patented a few years later by Bewley.

It is noteworthy that this remarkable progress had almost all occurred before the discovery of vulcanization, the next milestone on the road of the industry's development.

XIII. THE DISCOVERY OF VULCANIZATION

'Vulcanization' or 'curing' is the name applied to the change that occurs when rubber is mixed with sulphur and the mixture heated. It is essentially a chemical action, but is accompanied by profound physical changes; the rubber after 'curing' becomes less susceptible to the action of solvents and to the effects of changes in temperature.

It had long been realized that raw rubber had a natural tendency to become hard and inelastic on prolonged exposure to cold; and also that, especially after mechanical working or softening by solvents like turpentine, it was liable to be detrimentally affected by heat, strong sunlight, and other factors, becoming soft and tacky.

In Britain, these were regarded as natural defects of the material, limiting its use to suitable applications; in certain cases, undesirable results had been avoided or mitigated by enclosing the rubber in fabric, as in double-texture proofing and elastic webbing. But in the early days of the industry in the United States, where the manufacture had been embarked upon without due regard to these tendencies, difficulties were quickly encountered. In 1835 a very large proportion of the rubber goods that had been placed on the market became hard and unyielding in the winter, and decomposed or 'perished' in the hot months of summer. The results were disastrous; many firms had to close down and the reputation of rubber manufacture in America received a set-back from which it took many years to recover. It was at this critical stage of the industry's progress that Charles Goodyear (1800–60), a former hardware merchant of Philadelphia, became interested in rubber manufacture. Goodyear determined to devote himself to the discovery of some means of overcoming or of preventing the unfortunate tendency of rubber to harden or 'perish' after manufacture. The remedy was not obvious, for these properties were apparently inherent in the material.

Goodyear encountered many difficulties, both financial and personal, before he decided to try the effect of heat upon a mixture of rubber, sulphur, and white lead [9]. An accidental over-heating of one of the specimens produced charring but no melting. When he repeated the process before an open fire, again charring occurred in the centre, but along the edges there was a border which was not charred but perfectly cured. Further tests showed that the new substance thus obtained did not harden in the winter cold and was not softened by the heat of summer; it was also proof against solvents that dissolved the native gum. He had thus attained the object of his long search.

Obtaining financial and other assistance from William Rider, a New York rubber manufacturer, Goodyear continued his experiments and in 1841 succeeded in making the elastic compound uniformly in continuous sheets, by passing it through a heated cast iron trough. This was the first successful operation of vulcanization as an industrial process.

On 6 December 1841 Goodyear had a specification prepared and this was deposited in the Patent Office of the United States as a claim for invention instead of as an application for a patent, as was at first intended. The application for an English patent was not lodged until 1844, the reasons for the delay being mostly financial.

Public opinion in the United States was still very hostile to rubber, and Goodyear was anxious to interest manufacturers abroad in his discovery. With this object in view he enlisted the services of Stephen Moulton (p 764), an Englishman then resident in the United States, who was about to make a visit to England. Goodyear requested Moulton to take with him samples of his 'improved rubber' and instructed him to show them to suitable people, and especially to Macintosh & Company, with the object of selling the secret of manufacture.

Moulton arrived in England in August 1842 and was introduced to Macintosh & Company, with whom he discussed Goodyear's proposal and left samples of the improved rubber. He could not, however, disclose the process and no agreement to purchase was arrived at. Macintosh & Company reasonably suggested that Goodyear should take out a patent, so that they could better judge the nature of the process.

The samples that were left aroused great interest, for the following reason. The use of double textures in proofing by the Macintosh firm had resulted in comparative immunity from the grosser manifestations of the hardening and perishing tendencies of uncured rubber. When, however, it became desirable, about 1842, to produce lighter, single-texture garments, difficulties arose owing to the adhesiveness of the exposed rubbered surfaces and to the stiffening of the rubber on exposure to cold. A means of overcoming these natural defects had long been desired, and unsuccessful attempts to prevent cold-stiffening had been made by Hancock some twenty years previously.

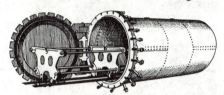

FIGURE 409—*Live steam 'open cure' vulcanizer. This consists of a cylinder heated internally by steam and fitted with a metal frame, running on rails, on which various articles can be carried. The door is secured by bolts.*

Some of the samples sent by Goodyear had been given to Hancock, who found that one of them had a little dusty powder on the surface. The rubber had a slight smell of sulphur, and Hancock states that he thought a little powdered sulphur had been rubbed in to mislead. He found the samples were, as stated, not affected by cold and, in his own words, 'finding now that this object appeared to have been somehow or other effected . . . I set to work in earnest, resolved, if possible, not to be outdone by any'.

Later he states that 'the little bits given me by Mr. Brockedon [who had introduced Moulton] certainly showed me for the first time that the desirable changes in the condition of rubber of not stiffening by cold, had been attained, but they afforded no clue to the mode by which it had been brought about. . . . I made no analysis of these little bits nor did I procure either directly or indirectly, any analysis of them . . . and I considered the small specimens given me simply as proof that it was practicable. . . . I knew nothing more of the small specimens than I or any other person might know by sight and smell.'

Hancock describes how he then set to work in his private laboratory, working often till midnight. He compounded rubber, sometimes in solution, sometimes softened by heat, with innumerable substances, including sulphur both free and dissolved in turpentine, using various degrees of heating.

Eventually he found that by melting sulphur in an iron vessel at 240° F and immersing strips of cut sheet rubber in it, the rubber first absorbed the sulphur; and on raising the temperature and prolonging the time of exposure, the rubber

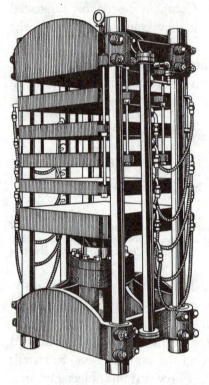

became perfectly changed throughout [10]. For this process he applied for and obtained a provisional patent on 21 November 1843, some two months before the belated arrival of the Goodyear application on 30 January 1844. From that time, American firms manufactured vulcanized rubber under licence from Goodyear, but in England most firms using the process did so under licence from Thomas Hancock or Macintosh & Company, the owners of the English patent.

For the ordinary process of vulcanization, the sulphur, in finely divided condition, is added to the rubber along with the other ingredients, such as litharge, zinc oxide, and various pigments, in the mixing machine. After thorough incorporation, the mixed batch is sheeted and allowed to cool. The rubber is then cut up into shape appropriate for the article it is intended to make, and is placed in metal moulds ready for the heating process. The heating takes place in cylindrical heaters to which live steam can be admitted (figure 409); or alternatively, the moulds can be placed between steam-heated platens in a vertical press (figures

FIGURE 410—*Hydraulic vulcanizing press, by David Bridge & Company, Castleton. Articles to be vulcanized are enclosed in accurately shaped steel moulds placed between steam-heated platens. During the processing, hydraulic pressure is maintained by means of a ram.*

410 and 411). The heat of the steam is thus communicated to the moulds and from them to the rubber. Here the change takes place, the rubber being converted into a permanently elastic, solid article. In some early vulcanizers other sources of heat were used; that shown in figure 412 was heated by petroleum.

XIV. OTHER METHODS OF VULCANIZATION

Two years later, in 1846, Alexander Parkes (1813–90) made the interesting discovery that thin strips of rubber could be cured very quickly by immersion in a dilute solution of sulphur chloride in naphtha or carbon disulphide. This method, suitable only for the vulcanization of thin-walled rubber articles or rubber layers, has become well known as the 'cold cure' process. It was soon employed in the treatment of single-texture rubber-proofed garments, and a factory for this purpose was erected at Birmingham. Later the patent was acquired by Macintosh & Company, and the operations were transferred to Manchester.

This method of vulcanization also found useful application in conjunction with the 'dipping' process for the production of toy balloons, rubber teats, seamless rubber gloves, and so on. A subsequent development, introduced by W. Abbott in 1878, consisted in the use of sulphur chloride vapour instead of the solution formerly used. It is sometimes known as the 'vapour cure'.

A further process, in reality a modification of the hot curing process, was that patented by Stephen Moulton in 1847; in this method, lead hyposulphite was employed in place of sulphur as the curing agent. This method was used principally in the manufacture of waterproof capes and similar objects.

The discovery of vulcanization gave great impetus to the rubber industry at a very opportune moment. For various reasons the sale of heavy waterproof garments had fallen considerably. The unsuitability of raw rubber for many mechanical purposes had restricted its application in this direction, and its susceptibility to climatic conditions had also been a deterrent to its wider use.

The fundamental change in properties produced by vulcanization removed most of these disabilities and tremendously increased the field for further development. It was not long before articles made of vulcanized rubber began to appear on the market. The new material attracted the attention of inventors and others whose ideas were embodied in patents for various articles, often manufactured for them by Macintosh or Hancock.

FIGURE 411—*Autoclave tyre press for vulcanization of tyres, early twentieth century. The tyres, fitted with air bags, are placed in hollow steel moulds ranged one above another on the ram table inside an autoclave pan. The pan is closed and steam is admitted: hydraulic pressure is provided by the ram.*

FIGURE 412—*Oil-heated mould and press for vulcanizing small rubber articles.*

Until about 1840, owing to the protection provided by the Macintosh patent and the secrecy by which Hancock's processes had been safeguarded, the rubber industry in Britain had been largely a monopoly, but about this time several other firms entered the manufacturing field. The next twenty-five years proved a time of rapid expansion, and the foundations of many firms, now well known in the industry, date from this period of great industrial activity. Until the expiration of Hancock's patent in 1858 much of the vulcanized rubber was manufactured under licence, but subsequently the process became available without

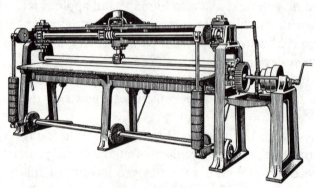

FIGURE 413—*Hose-making machine. The hose, consisting of a central rubber lining surrounded by layers of rubberized fabric, is assembled on a metal mandrel. This is placed on the table and caused to revolve below the weighted circular roller to obtain consolidation and adhesion of the plies.*

restriction and the number of manufacturing firms increased rapidly, some entering the proofing business, some the manufacture of rubber shoes and other forms of footwear; many afterwards specialized in more limited directions. The engineering industries were also in a state of active development, and a considerable demand arose for rubber for various mechanical applications, such as valves, packing for steam-joints, rubber belting for conveyers and power transmission, and hose of various types (cf figure 413).

XV. THE EXPANSION OF USE OF RUBBER

An idea of the expansion of the industry in the early days may be gathered from the returns for raw rubber imports into Britain (see also p 773):

1830	23 tons	1874	6458 tons
1840	332 tons	1888	11 018 tons
1857	1100 tons	1897	19 816 tons

The trend of rubber manufacture has been largely influenced by the social conditions prevailing at the various stages of its development. In the pre-railway days the main concentration was on clothing, shoes, and the like, for protection against the weather. With improvements in the methods of transport, attention was directed to shock-absorption and vibration-damping devices for both road and railway vehicles. The development of the electrical industry opened up a new field of application in the insulation of cable (figures 414 and 415).

As early as 1826 a patent was granted to H. C. Lacy for the use of cubical blocks of caoutchouc in place of the steel spring commonly used for suspending road-carriages, and in 1845 vulcanized rubber was used by Fuller for cushions and for the ends of railway carriages, to diminish the effects of concussion. Later, Charles de Bergue used vulcanized rubber rings between metal plates in buffering and traction apparatus. George Spencer patented his first rubber railway springs in 1852, the first of a long line of inventions and rubber developments extending over many years.

The most spectacular development in the field of transport, however, was the rubber tyre for road vehicles. From this has grown the great tyre industry, which now absorbs about 75 per cent of the world's total raw rubber production. It

FIGURE 414—*Extruding machine for forcing rubber through dies to form rods, tubes, or insulation for electric cables.*

seems probable that the first solid rubber tyres were not the subject of a patent; Hancock has described their manufacture by his firm in 1846 [11]. He states that these tyres were about $1\frac{1}{2}$ in wide and $1\frac{1}{4}$ in thick. The vulcanized rubber was firmly attached to a metal hoop or tyre, or an endless band of rubber was sprung on to an ordinary wheel and kept in position by a flange on either side; the rubber projecting from the flanges rested on the ground, thus preventing the concussion to which the wheels are ordinarily subject. From about 1870, solid rubber tyres became very popular for bicycles (p 418) and remained so for twenty years.

In 1845 R. W. Thomson (1822–73) took out the first patent (B.P. No 10 990) for pneumatic rubber tyres. Thomson's invention was described as a 'hollow belt composed of indiarubber or gutta percha and inflated with air to present a cushion of air to ground, rail, or track'.

The air-tube consisted of several layers of canvas saturated with rubber solution and vulcanized. This was encased in leather to provide strength and resistance to wear, the leather being secured to the wheel by rivets. The tube was inflated by a pump or 'condenser'. Carriages fitted with these tyres or 'aerial wheels' were tested in Hyde Park, and one carriage fitted with them was said to have run quite successfully for 1200 miles. The idea was, however, before its time; it never achieved commercial success and was forgotten for nearly fifty years.

In 1888 John Boyd Dunlop (1840–1921), a Belfast veterinary surgeon, wishing to obtain an improved bicycle for his ten-year-old son, conceived, or recon-

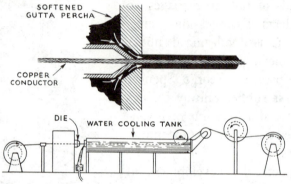

FIGURE 415—*Covering electric cables with rubber or gutta-percha insulation by the extrusion process.*

ceived, the idea of using a cushion of compressed air, instead of solid rubber, to lessen vibration. Dunlop's pneumatic bicycle tyre (B.P. No 10 607) contained an all-rubber inner tube surrounded by a canvas jacket, protected on the outside by rubber strips which were thickened to form the tread. Protruding flaps from the canvas jacket served to attach the tyre to the rim of the wheel, rubber solution being used as the adhesive. The first tests gave good results, and in subsequent trials on roads and on racing-tracks the pneumatic tyre attained almost instant success and general approval.

Improvements were later made in the design of the tread, and new methods of attachment to the rim of the wheel were introduced by Welch (wired-on tyre and curved rim) and by Bartlett (the well known 'Clincher' tyre with beaded edges), and in a very few years almost every bicycle in Britain was equipped with pneumatics [12].

XVI. MOTOR TYRES

The adaptation of the pneumatic principle of the bicycle tyre to tyres for mechanically propelled vehicles occurred a few years later. In the first instance it was simply a matter of increasing the number of canvas plies and the thickness of the tread. Clincher-type beads and rims were at first used. Apparently pneumatic tyres were first used on motor-vehicles by André and Edouard Michelin in 1895, when competing in the Bordeaux–Paris motor-car trials. The Dunlop Company produced their first motor tyre in 1900. At first, square-woven fabric was used for the canvas plies, but this was later replaced by cord fabric. The strength and wear-resisting properties of the tread were greatly increased by the application of scientific methods of compounding. Since the introduction of motor transport, the progress of the tyre division of the rubber industry has been colossal, and it now surpasses all other branches combined in the amount of rubber consumed (p 771).

It would, however, have been extremely difficult, if not impossible, to meet the tremendously increased demands for raw rubber consequent upon the growth of the tyre industry had it not been for another and most opportune development, that of the plantation-rubber industry.

XVII. THE DEVELOPMENT OF THE PLANTATION-RUBBER INDUSTRY

In 1840 most of the raw rubber imported into the United Kingdom came from the forests of South and Central America. The increased demand due to the rapid growth of the industry in England and America between 1840 and 1850 stimulated the search for the raw product not only in America but in the Far East, India, Malaya, and Java, and later in the forests of Africa. Until the close of the nineteenth century these 'wild' or forest rubbers were the main sources of supply available to manufacturers.

Obtained from a variety of botanical sources, the different types of wild rubber differed from each other in composition, in appearance, and in their content of extraneous material. In nearly all cases washing was essential before manufacture. With a rapidly increasing demand, supplies of rubber from the forest sources became more and more difficult to maintain, because of the exhaustion of easily accessible areas and the use of destructive methods of tapping. It was extremely fortunate, therefore, that some steps had already been taken to provide an alternative and rapidly expansible supply of a more uniform product.

Suggestions had been made as early as 1855 regarding the possibility of cultivating in the East and West Indies the best kinds of rubber-producing plants, but it was not until 1870 that official attempts were made to cultivate rubber-trees within the British Empire. The initiative was apparently taken by the India Office [13], whose assistant secretary, Sir Clements Markham (1830–1916), had already succeeded in introducing the cultivation of cinchona into India. Steps were first taken to obtain information concerning the rubber-trees most suitable for cultivation in British India. Having obtained this, it was decided that attention should first be paid to the trees indigenous to the country, but that, in view of the superiority of the rubber from *Hevea* and other South American trees, these should be introduced as soon as possible.

In 1873 the India Office purchased 2000 *Hevea* seeds, and from them seedlings were raised at Kew Gardens and sent to Calcutta. The climate there proved unsuitable, and the plants failed. Later, Robert Cross, a well known botanist, was sent out to Para to collect live plants. He returned with 1080 seedlings, of which 3 per cent survived, and from these plants others were propagated by cuttings and sent to Ceylon, Singapore, and Java.

Meanwhile, Sir Joseph Hooker, Director of Kew Gardens, who had taken a keen interest in the enterprise, commissioned H. A. (later Sir Henry) Wickham, an English planter, then resident at Santarem on the Amazon, to collect *Hevea* seeds at the rate of £10 a thousand. Wickham collected his seeds from trees which were then being tapped in the forests covering the broad plateau dividing the Tapajos and the Madeira rivers. The seeds were shipped immediately and reached Kew on 14 June 1876. The seeds were sown the next day, and of the 70 000 collected some 2700 subsequently germinated. In the following August about 2000 plants were sent to Ceylon for establishment and subsequent distribution, and approximately 90 per cent arrived in good condition. Some plants were sent to Singapore and other places abroad (tailpiece).

The total cost of the whole introduction appears to have been roughly £1500, a moderate price for an exceedingly valuable enterprise. From these plants has grown the great plantation industry which, from Malaya, Ceylon, the East Indies, and Indo-China, now supplies over 90 per cent of the world's requirements of raw rubber. The introduction of the plants, however, was only the beginning of the plantation development. Much work had to be done on the clearing and weeding of the sites, the planting and cultivation of the trees, the introduction of suitable methods of tapping and coagulating the latex, and the drying of the rubber and its preparation for the market. Great credit for this is due to the staffs of the Government Agricultural and Botanical Gardens in Ceylon and Malaya, where the original trees were planted and tended, and from which distributions were subsequently made. Here also, tapping experiments were conducted. The phenomenon of 'wound response' was discovered by H. N. Ridley about 1889. Often when an oblique cut is made in the bark of a tree for the first time very little latex exudes. If, however, the tree is left for a time, and the wound is then reopened by shaving off a further layer of the bark, a more plentiful flow of latex results. This process can be repeated at intervals, say every second day, and thus a regular flow of latex is obtained at the expense of very little bark, which in any case is slowly renewed by the tree. This discovery was of great value from the point of view of latex production.

The establishment of the plantation industry was necessarily gradual, and it took some time to convince planters of the prospective advantages of replacing existing crops by one of which they had had no previous experience. Increasing demands and the high prices obtainable, however, supplied the necessary stimulus, and by 1900 sizable consignments of plantation-rubber were being exported.

REFERENCES

[1] JONES, F. "Early History to 1826" in 'History of the Rubber Industry' (ed. by P. SCHIDRO-WITZ and T. R. DAWSON), p. 2. Heffer, Cambridge, for the Institution of the Rubber Industry. 1952.

[2] CHAPEL, E. 'Caoutchouc et la Gutta Percha', pp. 8–12. Paris. 1892.

[3] GROSSART, C. *Ann. Chim. (Phys.)*, **11**, 143–55, 1791.

[4] HANCOCK, T. 'Personal Narrative of the Origin and Progress of the Caoutchouc or India-Rubber Manufacture in England', p. 13. London. 1857.

[5] *Idem. Ibid.*, p. 17.

[6] *Idem. Ibid.*, p. 70.

[7] *Idem. Ibid.*, p. 20.

[8] *Idem. Ibid.*, p. 224.

[9] GOODYEAR, C. 'Gum Elastic and its Varieties, with Detailed Account of its Applications and Uses, and of the Discovery of Vulcanisation', pp. 119–27. New Haven. 1855.

[10] HANCOCK, T. See ref. [4], p. 103.

[11]. *Idem. Ibid.*, pp. 115, 170.

[12] LAMBOURN, L. J. and PERRET, A. G. "Tyres." See ref. [1], p. 216.

[13] PORRITT, B. D. 'The Early History of the Rubber Industry.' McLaren, London. 1926. (Reprint from *India Rubb. J.*, **71**, 404, 444, 483, 1926.)

One of the 38 Wardian cases in which were dispatched from Kew to Ceylon the two thousand plants that initiated the Para rubber plantation industry in the Far East.

32

EDUCATION FOR AN AGE OF TECHNOLOGY

SIR ERIC ASHBY

THE greatest invention of the nineteenth century', wrote A. N. Whitehead, 'was the invention of the method of invention.' During the nineteenth century the tradesman replaced the craftsman and the applied scientist replaced the inventor. With this change, education began to influence industry. Today education has become the pacemaker for technological progress, but this did not happen quickly or easily: science had to fight its way into the schools and universities, and schools and universities had to fight their way into the factory and the workshop. There has been a long struggle to establish education as an essential ingredient in industry. It is the purpose of this chapter to describe the struggle, with special emphasis on technical and scientific education in Britain in the critical years between the Great Exhibition of 1851 and the Education Act of 1902.

I. THE STATE OF TECHNICAL EDUCATION IN BRITAIN BEFORE 1851

In 1841, 33 per cent of the men and 49 per cent of the women marrying in England and Wales signed the marriage-register with a mark [1]. Even those who had attended schools learnt little or no science. Mathematics had been introduced at Shrewsbury in 1836 and physics at Rugby in 1837. A few schools, inspired by the dissenting academies of the eighteenth century, had comparatively enlightened courses, but the great majority of schools were offering a curriculum indistinguishable from that pursued by Samuel Johnson at Lichfield over a century earlier, or indeed by John Milton in London two centuries earlier. Latin grammar, translation, and composition, some Greek, and the catechism: this was the education enjoyed by sons of the upper classes, merchants, and professional men. As to the working classes, it was estimated that in 1833 only some 800 000 of them were receiving any sort of schooling and this in dames' schools where only reading and writing were taught, or in schools maintained by churches where children paid a penny or twopence a week [2]. The Factory Act of 1833 provided that children between 9 and 13 were to be employed only if they had a voucher certifying that they had attended school two hours daily on six days in the preceding week, but this applied solely to textile factories and even there it was not everywhere enforced.

It is remarkable that such a barren soil as this should have supported one of the great educational movements in British history, the mechanics' institutes. They arose in the 1820s. They survived, with many vicissitudes, until the Technical Instruction Act of 1889; even today there are no fewer than thirty-four working men's clubs and libraries which are the direct descendants of mechanics' institutes founded before 1851. The most recent historian of the mechanics' institutes, Kelly [3], describes how their fortunes fluctuated with the ups and downs of trade cycles. In times of good employment they flourished. In times of depression, when political science obviously became more important than natural science, they languished, because it was the policy of mechanics' institutes to discourage any talk about such controversial issues as politics or economics: they were anxious not to get mixed up with trade unionists or Chartists. This policy is not surprising, for it was the well-to-do manufacturer or merchant who took the initiative in founding most (though not all) of the mechanics' institutes. The Glasgow Gas Workmen's Institution, for example, was started in 1821 by a manager, James Neilson (vol IV, p 109). The members paid $1\frac{1}{2}d$ weekly; there were two meetings a week. Members took it in turn to give talks prepared by themselves or to lecture from Murray's 'Chemistry' or Ferguson's 'Mechanics'. Other institutes had more democratic beginnings; at Keighley a joiner, a tailor, a painter, and a reed-maker combined for 'mutual instruction and to establish a library for that purpose', and the institute at Stalybridge began when a group of working men held meetings in a garret.

One can imagine the ferment of these early meetings. The manager, with an eye to an improvement in productivity, hoped the classes would throw up another Arkwright or a Brindley. The workmen (among whom there must have been many who today would gain places in grammar schools) saw dimly both that knowledge was worth having for its own sake and that it might open a door to personal advancement. In an address to the Manchester Mechanics' Institution (tailpiece) in 1827 Benjamin Heywood said:

... the object of this Institution is to teach the workman (be his trade what it may), those principles of science on which his work depends; to show him their practical application, and how he may make his knowledge of them profitable; to enable him thoroughly to understand his business, and to qualify him for making improvements in it; to teach him how he may advance himself in the world, and to give him an honourable and delightful employment for his leisure [4].

The enthusiasm did not last. By 1830 the mechanics' institutes were sick. There had been a depression, which rendered managers querulous and workmen disheartened. Tories denounced the institutes as hotbeds of radicalism ('I had rather see my servants dead drunk than I would see them going to the mechanics' institutes', wrote one critic); radicals denounced the institutes as an exercise in paternalism designed to exploit the workers. The chief cause of the decline was more fundamental still: there was no foundation of primary schooling on which this further education could be built, and very little of what was being taught in the institutes was relevant to day-to-day work in the mill. Nearly forty years later (in 1868) the chairman of the Nottingham Chamber of Commerce said in evidence before a Select Committee on Scientific Instruction:

The ability to read a very simple paragraph is not possessed by nearly 50 per cent. of the people employed in our large factories in Nottingham . . . in the lace factories, in the hosiery factories, in the bleaching works, and in the dye works; in the brickyards . . . the people cannot read at all. Two of our largest brickmakers returned only 12 people who were able to read, out of all who were in their employment, and they were the sons of foremen [5].

Nevertheless the movement did revive: by 1841 there were some 50 000 members in over 200 institutes. But its character had changed: systematic instruction in the scientific principles of various trades had been replaced by popular science, music, and even mesmerism and ventriloquism. Many institutes became working men's clubs, devoted to innocent amusement rather than to education. There were important exceptions [3]. At Stourbridge, for instance, the institute library issued 3900 books in a year. At Manchester there were over a thousand students attending night classes in subjects as serious as arithmetic, algebra, geometry, grammar, and drawing. In 1835 the Liverpool Institution opened a day school for boys, which had a long and distinguished career. Even the original objectives were by no means forgotten, for in 1868 the Select Committee on Scientific Instruction received the syllabus for a course of sixteen classes in the chemistry of dyeing, with practical work, arranged by the Huddersfield Mechanics' Institution [5, appendix 5]. There was a fee of 5s for artisans and 15s for others. Still more significant was a memorial, signed by 5000 working men and presented in 1856 to the Council of Education, which came from the London Mechanics' Institution and other similar bodies, asking for government financial backing for the mechanics' institute movement [5, appendix 19].

When Britain emerged from the bad times in the 1840s to the effulgence of the 1851 Exhibition, the mechanics' institutes again revived. There was scarcely a town without one. The institutes in Yorkshire had banded themselves into a union, with 100 affiliated branches and 20 000 members. James Hole, secretary of the Yorkshire Union, in a memorable essay that was awarded a prize by the [Royal] Society of Arts [6], suggested that the institutes should become constituent colleges of a national industrial university. The Society of Arts itself gave great encouragement to the movement; in 1852 it called a conference of unions of mechanics' institutes to discuss the promotion of technical education. It organized examinations and awarded diplomas, and so for the first time provided a tangible incentive for evening classes. This was something the institutes needed; but it was not enough, for managers were not yet convinced that industry needed technically trained men, let alone men with some knowledge of science. A few holders of Society of Arts diplomas found their way into technical posts, but the majority were employed as clerks [7].

What is the judgement of history on the mechanics' institutes? On the debit side they failed to meet the need for popular technical education in Britain and they failed to have any immediate and contemporary impact on British industry. The reasons for these failures lay outside the control of the institutes: it could not be expected that further education would take root where there was practically no primary education, and it could not be expected that many artisans would persist at evening classes after working from 6 a.m. to 7 p.m. in a factory, unless employers offered some recognition and reward. (A clergyman, James Booth, of the Society of Arts, conducted in the 1850s a vigorous campaign to persuade manufacturers of the need to encourage technical education in the institutes, but there was very little response.) On the credit side the mechanics' institutes have much more to show. They put a few men on the road to distinction; James Young (1811–83), for instance, who began at the Andersonian Institution, Glasgow, and ended as the father of the petroleum industry. In founding unions in Lancashire, Cheshire, and Yorkshire they took the first steps towards the organization of technical education in Britain. They co-operated with the Society of Arts in the first nation-wide examination system for a technical qualification by evening study. If in the second half of the nineteenth century they appeared to dissolve, it is because they became part of the national system of technical education which was the dream of some of their founders. The examinations of the Department of Science and Art (p 782); the Technical Instruction Act of 1889 and all the technical education by local authorities which stems from it; the Glasgow Royal Technical College, the Heriot-Watt College in Edinburgh, the Huddersfield Technical College, and the Manchester Technical College: in all these there flows the blood of the mechanics' institute movement.

Up to 1851 the schools and mechanics' institutes had made little impression upon technology in Britain. The universities had made even less. Oxford and Cambridge still lay entrenched behind their medieval statutes. Their obsolete curricula were being vigorously attacked by Sir William Hamilton in the 'Edinburgh Review' [8], but it was not until the 1850s, following two royal commissions, that they were reformed [9]. However, it is a mistake to underestimate the value of a Cambridge degree in the 1830s. Although it was still true in those days that about one in ten of the matriculants was 'privileged', nevertheless a revival of scholarship had already begun. The classical tripos was established in 1822. It was for its time a liberal education, for it had to be preceded by a mathematical tripos, which included a rigorous training in Newtonian physics [7]. Therefore the judges, the statesmen, and the bishops of that day who were Cambridge graduates in classics were more familiar with concepts such as mass, velocity, and inertia, and with the principles of mechanics, than most modern classicists are. The Oxford classical degree also had a leaven of mathematics; and to the credit of Oxford it has to be recorded that in 1832, on the occasion of the first visit there of the British Association, the university gave the honorary degree of D.C.L. to four scientists: Brown, Brewster, Faraday, and Dalton. All four were dissenters and as such not eligible even to matriculate at the university. For the most part, however, science professors at the ancient universities were virtually unemployed in teaching,[1] and those few industrial managers who received their education in early Victorian Oxford or Cambridge certainly had little encouragement to study aspects of natural science relevant to technology.

Apart from the insufficiency of their curricula for the industrial revolution, Oxford and Cambridge were not accessible to enough students. In 1840, for instance, there were only 396 matriculants at Oxford and 345 at Cambridge [11]. The only other universities in the United Kingdom were a struggling new one at Durham (the last episcopal foundation for higher learning), London University, and the universities of Scotland and Ireland.

The Scottish universities had for a long time included both science and engineering in their curricula. At Glasgow, for example, the distinguished Joseph Black (1728–99) persuaded the university to provide him with a chemical laboratory in 1763, and it was there that much of his classic work was done. John Anderson, who was elected to the chair of natural philosophy in 1757, lectured not only to his formal classes[2] but initiated what he called his 'anti-toga' evening classes in physics for mechanics and artisans. Even engineering was established at Glasgow eleven years before the Great Exhibition. The chair was set up by royal warrant and it is said to be the oldest university chair of

---

[1] In 1839 the professors of physics, chemistry, geology, and botany petitioned the university of Oxford that they might be excused from lecturing because there were so few students [10].

[2] The very fact that he was known as 'Jolly Jack Phosphorus' is a sign that his classes were attended by students.

engineering in the kingdom. The first professor of engineering had to give assurances that he would not encroach on other studies in the university. The Senate would not provide him with a classroom until the Lord Advocate of Scotland intervened on his behalf. Nevertheless some technology was being taught at Glasgow in the early 1840s, although even as late as 1861 engineering was not considered 'a proper department in which a degree should be conferred' and it remained for years in the faculty of arts. More significant still is the influence of Glasgow's engineering professors on contemporary technology. The first professor, L. D. B. Gordon, practised as a very successful consulting engineer and eventually resigned his chair to make and lay submarine cables. The second professor, W. J. M. Rankine (1820–72), who succeeded Gordon in 1855, was also a practising engineer, although later he gave his attention to the study of heat and to the writing of textbooks. It was in Scotland, therefore, that the first contacts between technology and the universities were made [12].

University College, London, too, had from the very beginning chairs in science (chemistry, experimental philosophy, and botany), and a chair in engineering was established in 1841. Students were encouraged to take a four-year 'general' course (which included classics, science, economics, jurisprudence, and philosophy) or professional courses in law, medicine, and engineering. The London B.A. from its establishment required a knowledge of mathematics, natural philosophy, and biology, besides classics, logic, and ethics.

There was, therefore, an opportunity as long ago as 1837 (when University College was incorporated in a University of London) for managers and industrialists in England to give their sons a balanced and liberal education in science. Doubtless a few individuals took advantage of this opportunity, but there is no evidence that the universities at this time were making any impact on industry or technology. Yet there were, throughout the first half of the nineteenth century, far-sighted men who realized that British industry could no longer rely on its early monopoly of trade and commerce, nor on its untutored inventors and its craft-engineers. The very fact that Britain would not part with the secrets of her industrial processes stimulated continental countries to promote technology more systematically than Britain had ever done. British travellers brought back ecstatic reports of the state of science in Germany. British scientists lamented (sometimes querulously) the decline of science in England. England alone (said Brewster in 1830) had hesitated to take a part in the revival of industry after the wars that had molested Europe [13]. Augustus De Morgan wrote in 1832 that among a people 'who depended for their political greatness on trade and manufactures there was not, generally speaking, in the education of their youth one atom of information on the products of the earth . . . nor any account of the principles whether of mechanics or chemistry which, when applied to these products, constituted the greatness of their country' [14].

In this state of buoyant reliance on her industrial supremacy, and undeterred by a handful of critics calling for more science and more technical education, the people of Britain flocked to the Great Exhibition of 1851.

II. AWAKENING TO THE NEED FOR TECHNOLOGICAL EDUCATION, 1851–67

The Great Exhibition was a vindication of British technology and a unique occasion for national self-congratulation. There were a hundred categories of manufactures to be assessed by the international jury. Britain won prizes in most of these categories. Nevertheless, thoughtful observers were alarmed by the evidence of competition from abroad: it was clear that Britain's easy supremacy in trade and commerce was threatened, and it appeared that other countries were overtaking her because their craftsmen were better educated and their governments were giving liberal support to scientific and technological research. In the winter following the Exhibition the Society of Arts summarized in a series of lectures the lessons that were to be learnt from it. Lyon Playfair (1818–98), who had been closely associated with the Prince Consort during the planning of the Exhibition, made an eloquent plea for scientific research and instruction: 'Raw material, formerly our capital advantage over other nations, is gradually being equalised in price, and made available to all by improvements in loco-motion, and Industry must in future be supported, not by a competition of local advantages, but by a competition of intellects' [15]; and 'the cultivators of abstract science . . . are . . . the "horses" of the chariot of industry. . . . In the establishment of institutions for industrial instruction you, at the same time, create the wanting means for the advancement of science in this country.'

The beneficent influence of the Prince Consort ensured that sentiments such as these did not fall on stony ground. In 1853 the Speech from the Throne contained a promise of government support for systematic scientific instruction having a bearing upon industry, and a year later the Department of Science and Art was founded. It was initially under the Board of Trade and its purpose was to promote scientific and technical education. Its first educational responsibility was to control the Government School of Mines, which had been opened two years earlier, and which was to absorb the Royal College of Chemistry—a private venture that had been launched in 1845.[1] This (if one excepts the government-

---

[1] This college admitted about 40 new students a year. Its first professor was A. W. von Hofmann (p 269). For

subsidized chairs for science and engineering in Scotland and the Queen's Colleges in Ireland) was the beginning of state-supported education in higher technology.

It is not surprising that the Department of Science and Art was a clumsy instrument for stimulating industrial instruction, for England had no experience of national schemes of education, and her leaders were still faithful to the doctrine of free enterprise in education as in trade. A system of compulsory primary schooling, run by the state, was still two decades away. The wonder is that the Department accomplished so much. Since 1837 the Board of Trade had administered grants for schools of design, but, as the Exhibition demonstrated with cruel clarity, these schools had little influence on taste in industry. In 1854 the new Department inherited this responsibility for art and design, together with responsibility for science.

Early efforts to establish in London 'a Science School of the highest class capable of affording the best instruction . . . ' did not succeed; but in 1859 the Department established a payment-by-results scheme for stimulating science teaching in schools. This provided for financial aid to be given to any place which established classes in mathematics, physics, chemistry, geology, or natural history. Teachers, if they had themselves passed the Department's examination, were paid according to the number of their pupils who passed examinations. There were rewards for the pupils also—prizes, exhibitions, and scholarships— and grants were made to schools for books and apparatus. This system of encouraging scientific education by holding state inducements before the eyes of both pupils and teachers went on without much change for fourteen years; not till 1873 was there any relaxation of payment-by-results. The scheme was undoubtedly successful. In 1862 there were only 2543 pupils in 70 schools: ten years later there were 36 783 students in 948 schools [11]. As years went by the subjects in which examinations could be taken increased to twenty-five.

There were obvious drawbacks to the state encouragement of science simply by rewarding teachers on examination results, especially when there was no state control over places where science was taught. But the policy, for all its drawbacks, accomplished its purpose; it was (said T. H. Huxley years afterwards) an 'engine for forcing science into ordinary education'.

The Department of Science and Art was not the only stimulus to science and technology that arose out of the Great Exhibition. The Society of Arts, which had come to the help of mechanics' institutes by amalgamating them into a

years he and his successors ran a research school on the German model, and by 1875 the college had placed over a hundred of its students in chemical industry.

nation-wide Union (p 779), started examinations for Union members. These examinations were in scientific as well as literary subjects, for factory workers who had left school and who had attended classes at mechanics' institutes. The questions were quite formidable. The 1856 papers, for example, included the following questions [16]:

Principles of Mechanics (26 questions in a 3-hour paper). 'What is meant by the moment of a statical pressure? Apply the principle of moments to explain the uniformity of action of a three-throw crank in pumping machines.'

Practical Mechanics (26 questions in a 3-hour paper). 'Describe the processes of annealing and welding and explain the physical processes upon which they depend.'

Chemistry (9 questions in a 3-hour paper). 'Enumerate and describe shortly the various acid compounds of sulphur and oxygen including under sulphuric acid the manufacture of that acid in the leaden chamber, with the theory of the process.'

It is little wonder that the rate of failure in these examinations was over 80 per cent. In later years the examinations of the Department of Science and Art displaced the Society's examinations in science, but the Society continued to offer a valuable service to technological education through examinations for certain technical skills and trades.

For some years after the Exhibition these two organizations to promote technological education—the Society of Arts representing private endeavour and the Department of Science and Art representing the first stirring of parliamentary responsibility—battled against prejudice, inertia, and complacency. But at every level of education the ferment sown by the Exhibition was at work. In schools here and there over the country science classes were being started. Even some of the endowed schools began to teach a little science. The Public Schools Commission under Lord Clarendon, which inquired into the administration of the nine great public schools, recommended that all schools should devote one hour out of twenty-eight each week to natural science [17]. This was for the upper classes, for whom science was not considered really necessary. Schools for the middle classes were the subject of inquiry by another body, the Schools Enquiry Commission under Lord Taunton, which suggested an imitation of the Prussian school system: a classical *Gymnasium* for those proposing to go on to Oxford or Cambridge, and a *Realgymnasium*, together with trade schools, for the middle and lower middle classes, with science as an integral part of their curriculum [18]. It is clear from the evidence given to these two commissions that even ten years after the Exhibition it had not dawned on headmasters and politicians that science or technology was relevant to the education of the upper and middle classes. At Eton there were 24 classical masters, 8 mathematics masters, and 3 to teach all other subjects. 'It is plainly out of the question', said Moberly of Winchester, 'that we should teach chemistry. . . .' Only for the education of children belonging to the class who support themselves by manual labour (as the Code of 1860 put it) was science thought to be appropriate, and there was provision in the Code—administered by the new Education Department founded in 1856—to give grants to schools for the lower classes to cover two-thirds of the cost of scientific apparatus.

Even the older universities did not escape the stimulus of the Great Exhibition. In 1851 the natural sciences tripos at Cambridge was instituted, and in 1853 Oxford established honours schools in science, though for some years very few students took advantage of these new opportunities. Both universities had, after bitter opposition, succumbed to the attentions of royal commissions, which published reports in 1852. The Oxford Commissioners' report included strong recommendations for an increased allocation of fellowships and prizes to physical science, and they published an ironic comment from the great German chemist Liebig: 'That it is a requirement of our times to incorporate the natural sciences as means of education into the university course is not perhaps doubted anywhere except in England' [19]. The report of the Cambridge Commission included an enlightened statement about the need to teach the scientific principles of engineering:

It may be quite true, that many of the practical and technical details of civil engineering may be best learned in the offices of engineers engaged in the execution of important works; but the knowledge of mathematics and of mechanical principles, as involved in the estimate of the strength and distribution of materials, the effects of elasticity, and generally of the operations of forces and pressures, is so necessary in all the more important and difficult applications of this science, that no amount of practical skill and experience can ever replace the want of this theoretical knowledge.

Throughout this period fear of competition from the European continent became the mainspring for educational reform in England. The École Centrale of Paris and the polytechnics in Germany and Switzerland were producing a new kind of industrialist. Men like the Prince Consort and Lyon Playfair (p 782) wished to see established in London a great industrial university which would incorporate the School of Mines and the Royal College of Chemistry. But one frustration after another prevented this, and such other facilities as London afforded for higher study in science or technology did not attract many students. Outside London the opportunities were very meagre. There was Owens College at Manchester which in 1861, ten years after its foundation, had only eighty-eight day students; there was Durham; there were the Scottish universities; and there were the Birmingham and Midland Institute and such of the mechanics' institutes as still sustained serious work. That was all. The buoyant hopes that had germinated in the lambent atmosphere of the Crystal Palace were not thriving. The hierarchical nature of English society sheltered the upper classes from all educational influences except those prevailing at the public schools and the older universities. A few of the proprietors and managers in industry had pursued courses in science in London or Scotland; the great majority of them had no knowledge of scientific principles except the fragments they had picked up through solitary reading. The deficiency was being perpetuated because mill-owners and ironmasters were not yet convinced that anything so novel and expensive as technological education was necessary for their sons. The smaller manufacturers and managers were commonly self-made men with little more than an elementary or commercial education. Most of the workmen had left school so early that they could scarcely read or write and thus were beyond the reach of further education in science and technology, though a few of them—mostly foremen or skilled craftsmen in the big centres of population—could enjoy the strenuous opportunity, denied to most of their betters, of sitting in a dingy room after a long day's work, studying the elements of mechanics and physical science [20]. Every year the contrast between technical education in England and abroad became more alarming to informed observers.

III. TECHNICAL EDUCATION ON THE CONTINENT

It seems at first sight puzzling that, at the time of the Great Exhibition, England was leading the world in industry and trade and yet was so backward in general and technical education. The explanation cannot be better expressed than in the words of the Royal Commissioners on technical instruction in 1884:

The beginnings of the modern industrial system are due in the main, as we have indicated, to Great Britain. Before factories founded on the inventions of Watt, or Arkwright, and Crompton, had time to take root abroad, and whilst our own commerce and manufactures increased from year to year, the great wars of the early part of this century absorbed the energies and dissipated the capital of Continental Europe. For many years after the peace we retained almost exclusive possession of the improved machinery employed in the cotton, woollen, and linen manufactures. By various acts of the last century, which were not repealed till 1825, it was made penal to enlist English artisans for employment abroad; the export of spinning machinery to foreign countries was prohibited until the early years of Your Majesty's reign. Thus, when less than half a century ago, Continental countries began to construct railways and to erect modern mills and mechanical workshops, they found themselves face to face with a full-grown industrial organization in this country, which was almost a sealed book to those who could not obtain access to our factories.

To meet this state of things, foreign countries established technical schools like the École Centrale of Paris, and the Polytechnic Schools of Germany and Switzerland, and sent engineers and men of science to England to prepare themselves for becoming teachers of technology in those schools.

Technical High Schools now exist in nearly every Continental State, and are the recognised channel for the instruction of those who are intended to become the technical directors of industrial establishments. Many of the technical chemists have, however, been, and are being, trained in the German Universities. Your Commissioners believe that the success which has attended the foundation of extensive manufacturing establishments, engineering shops, and other works, on the Continent, could not have been achieved to its full extent in the face of many retarding influences, had it not been for the system of high technical instruction in these schools, for the facilities for carrying on original scientific investigation, and for the general appreciation of the value of that instruction, and of original research, which is felt in those countries.

The continental countries which had this enviable system of technical education were able to base it upon state-supported compulsory schooling: indeed, the reforms introduced by the Education Act of 1870 in Britain had already existed in most of the German states since the 1820s. In Prussia, for instance, a regulation was introduced in 1826 that obliged all children between the ages of 7 and 14 to attend school full time. Attendance was enforced by school committees backed by the police, and 2 021 000 out of Prussia's 2 043 000 children were at school in the 1830s [21]. In other European countries children were not allowed to work until they had completed a course of elementary education. At about the age of 14 they could go into factories, but in many parts of Europe they had to continue their education by compulsory day-attendance (for half the working week in Switzerland) in trade schools up to the age of 16. These day-release trade schools conferred great benefit on the worker: they not only taught the scientific principles behind many trades but obliged young people to continue to read and to think, and so consolidated the elementary education received in primary schools. At the time of the Great Exhibition there were twenty-six *Gewerbeschulen* in Prussia alone. The royal commission of 1884 found continuation schools in nearly all towns in the countries they visited. All schools taught science and geometrical drawing, and some were highly specialized for the weaving, mining, building, brewing, and similar trades.

The purpose of this widespread system of technical education abroad was not humanitarian; it was to enable continental countries to compete with one another and to catch up with and overtake British industry. Accordingly, emphasis was laid on the training of managers and others who would direct technical policy. Three examples illustrate how this was done. In Rhine-Westphalia there was a metallurgical school at Bochum, supported by government, town, and local industry. The course occupied three years, with over thirty-six hours of formal instruction a week. Men with at least four years' practical experience were given full-time release from industry to take the course. The syllabus included pure and applied mathematics, physics, chemistry, drawing, metallurgy, machine construction, accountancy, and German. The students were aged 18 to 34. They included moulders, puddlers, fitters, turners, boiler-makers, and pattern-makers. They paid a fee of 30s. for the entire course. In Holland there was a Polytechnic School at Delft as early as 1864. Its purpose was to train works managers, engineers, architects, mining experts for the Dutch Indies, and even schoolmasters. It, too, was supported by the state. At Chemnitz there was a Higher Trade Institute which included not only a school for foremen but a much more advanced school for potential managers, who entered it at sixteen and worked, mainly at science, for as long as four and a half years before 'graduating'.

For leadership in the chemical industry Germany turned to her universities. The German universities had a long start over those in England. As early as 1830 there were nearly 16 000 university students in Germany, and even as late as 1885 it was estimated that Germany still had two and a half times as many students in proportion to her population as England had for hers. The historian Ranke and the scientists Helmholtz and Liebig had introduced the spirit of research into universities, and it was the research laboratories, not the under-graduate classes, that became the nurseries for industrial chemists. Kolbe, at Leipzig, had forty places for research workers in his laboratory; Baeyer, at Munich, had fifty research students. Liebig at Giessen, Bunsen at Heidelberg, Kekulé at Bonn, Wöhler at Göttingen: all these distinguished chemists trained men who were accepted for industrial posts, and all found themselves in close touch with German chemical industry. It is little wonder that British visitors to the continent were impressed and even alarmed at the ties they found there between science and production. In Germany, particularly, the organization of industry was favourable to such ties, for the railways, the mines, and some of the bigger industries were not in the hands of private enterprise but were state monopolies or cartels.

Even in the United States education was more firmly established than in England, and the dissemination of technical education was greatly facilitated by the endowment of land grant colleges in 1862. By the 1880s there was not a settlement of farmers or a mining camp without its state school [26], and the Massachusetts Institute of Technology, founded in 1865, was already famous as a place 'intended for those who seek administrative positions in business . . . where a systematic study of political and social relations and familiarity with scientific methods and processes are alike essential' [22].

In contrast to this, England, sixteen years after the Exhibition, still had no compulsory education, no widespread science teaching in schools, no new university since the foundation of Durham in 1832, and no institution to perform the functions of the continental polytechnics. The movement for scientific and technological education was not at a standstill, but it needed a fresh impulse to give it momentum.

IV. YEARS OF ACCOMPLISHMENT IN SCIENTIFIC AND TECHNICAL EDUCA-
TION, 1867–89

That impulse was provided by the Paris Exhibition of 1867. Britain, which in 1851 had won awards in nearly every division of the Exhibition, had to be content in 1867 with a bare dozen awards. Lyon Playfair, who had been in charge of the juries for assessing awards in 1851 and who was one of the jurors in 1867, summarized his anxieties in a memorable letter, published in the 'Journal of the Society of Arts' [23]. He discovered in Paris that:

a singular accordance of opinion prevailed that our country had shown little inventiveness and made little progress in the peaceful arts of industry. . . . The one cause upon which there was unanimity of conviction is that France, Prussia, Austria, Belgium, and Switzerland possess good systems of industrial education for the masters and managers of factories and workshops, and that England possesses none.

This letter, reinforced by another conference called by the Society of Arts, at last ignited public opinion and stirred Parliament to inquire into the desperate need for industrial education. Ambassadors and consuls were instructed to report on technical education abroad [7], and a Select Committee under the chairmanship of the progressive industrialist, Bernhard Samuelson (1820–1905), was appointed 'to inquire into the Provisions for giving Instruction in Theoretical and Applied Science to the Industrial Classes'. The report of this Committee is a turning-point in the history of technology in Britain, for it set technical education on the course that led to twentieth-century industrial Britain.

The evidence given to the Committee brought out two points. The first was that lower wages and absence of industrial unrest on the continent enabled manufacturers to compete successfully with Britain for markets; the second, that in some industries this successful competition depended on a grasp of applied science among the managers which had no parallel in England. For example, it was disclosed to the Committee that Belgian iron girders were being used for a building in Glasgow on the grounds of cheapness, and that these girders were cheaper because the Belgians had introduced economies depending on chemical analysis of the ore, limestone flux, and fuel. It was disclosed, too, that British fabrics were being sent to France to be dyed, on the grounds that the techniques of the French were superior to our own. This superiority was attributed to their schools for applied science: 'the foreigner thinks it is our water and our sunshine, but we say it is our chemistry.'

Evidence of defects in English education faced the Committee from all sides: no compulsory primary schooling and consequential widespread illiteracy; very little opportunity for any secondary education except at public schools (only four of which taught any science) and endowed grammar schools (only eighteen of which devoted as much as four hours a week to science); such a scarcity of science teachers and other science graduates that the Department of Science and Art had to borrow officers of the Royal Engineers from the War Office to supervise the Department's examinations; laboratories in the School of Mines not filled because the schools could not produce enough qualified applicants. Meanwhile continental Europe had built up a substantial school system which was feeding its polytechnics with future managers and industrialists. In the Zürich Polytechnic alone there were 60 professors and lecturers, compared with 12 at South Kensington.

The most vivid evidence for the potentialities of the teaching of science in schools came from Edwin Abbott (1838–1926), headmaster of the City of London School. He was a very enlightened headmaster. Every boy, all the way through the school, did one hour a week of science, and sat for the examinations of the Department of Science and Art. There was no laboratory, but the boys were 'accustomed to make workshops in their homes, and their doing so is encouraged in every possible way'. The master in charge of science there was Thomas Hall, a graduate of London University. It was from Hall's teaching at this school that W. H. Perkin (1838–1907) became interested in chemistry and was encouraged to start the experiments that led to the discovery of coal-tar dyes.

Higher education in science and technology in Britain was frustrated by two circumstances: the inadequacy of secondary education and the prejudices of the older universities. On this latter point T. H. Huxley offered incisive and ironic evidence. 'If I intended my own son for any branch of manufacture', he said, 'I should not dream of sending him to the university. . . . At present the universities make literature and grammar the basis of education: and they actually plume themselves upon their liberality when they stick a few bits of science on the outside of the fabric. Now that, in my apprehension, is not real culture, nor is it what I understand by a liberal education' [20].

The Committee's recommendations were a model of reasonableness and prescience: compulsory schooling within reach of every child; scientific instruction in all elementary schools; a completely reorganized system of secondary education, incorporating science teaching; the reconstitution of some endowed schools to serve as regional science schools; the establishment of open exhibitions to these science schools 'so that children of every grade may be able to rise from the lowest to the highest school'; state support for higher education in science and technology; courses in theoretical and applied science for students in teachers' training colleges; and co-ordination of government institutions for scientific instruction in London. It was a blueprint for the rest of the century. Indeed, it has required nearly three generations of committees and the challenge from the continent of two wars to persuade the British public to implement all these recommendations.

After the sharp lesson of the Paris Exhibition of 1867 it was not only the savants, as they were commonly called, whose voices were raised in advocacy of scientific and technical education; it was the industrialists too. On 18 March 1868 Sir Joseph Whitworth (1803–87) wrote to Disraeli offering to found thirty scholarships of £100 each to bring 'science and industry into closer relation with each other than at present obtains in this country'. The scholarships were open on equal terms 'to the student who combines some practice with his theory, and to the artisan who combines some theoretical knowledge with perfection of workmanship'. British technology is doubly indebted to Whitworth: on the one hand he introduced precision of measurement into tool-making; on the other hand he established for all time a practical way to combine in the technologist the experience of factory and university, of shop-floor and laboratory [24]. His evidence before the Select Committee on Scientific Instruction reveals a man whose thinking had penetrated to the heart of the problem of technical education. He wanted boys to learn the use of tools from the very beginning of their school careers:

First of all I would give notice that there would be competition of half-a-dozen boys in the use of the knife, and I would have a carpenter prepare half-a-dozen cylindrical pieces of wood eight inches long, and one inch in diameter, and I would ask those boys to make it square by the use of the knife. In the first trial I would have a piece of white deal. . . . On the second trial I would have red deal, and, on the third trial, beech, or ash, or oak. That would be teaching those little boys the different natures of woods, at the same time that they would be learning to sharpen the knife according to the wood they would be operating upon. You would want a very different edge for oak and for white deal. Then, if you found a boy with a very good intellect he might, perhaps, be a surgeon, while a boy with less brain might be a butcher or a shoemaker; but this knowledge of the use of the knife must do good to all of them [20].

Here is the quintessence of technical education.

The Select Committee's recommendations implied state support for education and especially for higher education in pure and applied science. But in the 1860s political thinkers had already fastened on that dangerous misinterpretation of Darwinism which elevated competition and survival above co-ordination and interdependence, and the climate was not yet favourable to the idea of state subsidies for education or science. Fortunately pressure came from another direction. In 1868 a powerful committee was set up by the British Association for the Advancement of Science to discuss provision for research and education in science. The Committee's report was followed by a deputation to the Lord President of the Council, urging upon him a thorough inquiry into the relation of the state to science. The deputation was successful and in 1872 a royal commission was appointed [25].

The reports of this royal commission are a monument of thoroughness. The evidence includes such diverse information as a catalogue (with prices and illustrations) of the apparatus needed to teach elementary science, the curricula for science in German universities, and a list of members of the academic staffs at Oxford and Cambridge together with their teaching duties. The commission's recommendations ranged from the maintenance of London museums to the encouragement of science in the Queen's Colleges of Ireland.

It is clear from the evidence that, since the Clarendon Commission ten years earlier, there had been some change of heart in the public schools but not a corresponding change in practice. Eton, Rugby, Winchester, and Marlborough (to mention only a sample) were all in favour of a little science: 'I introduced it into the classical sixth' (said the Master of Wellington College) 'solely with the view of increasing the boys' interest in life (there is not enough to produce results in the external examinations) and of improving their literary work by widening their interests.' Nevertheless the commission felt compelled 'to record our opinion that the Present State of Scientific Instruction in our Schools is extremely unsatisfactory. The omission from a Liberal Education of a great branch of Intellectual Culture is of itself a matter for serious regret; and, considering the increasing importance of Science to the Material Interests of the

Country, we cannot but regard its almost total exclusion from the training of the upper and middle classes as little less than a national misfortune.' And the commission goes on to recommend:

1. That in all Public and Endowed Schools a substantial portion of the time allotted to study, should, throughout the School Course . . . be devoted to Natural Science; and we are of opinion that not less than Six hours a week on the average should be appropriated for the purpose.

2. That in all General School Examinations, not less than one-sixth of the marks be allotted to Natural Science.

3. That in any Leaving Examination, the same proportion should be maintained [25, 6th report, 1875, p 10].

It is ironical that today, three generations later, these recommendations would be regarded as too drastic for most British schools.

The Commission's recommendations for the encouragement of science in universities were no less drastic. But the climate of opinion was changing. The idea of the university as a research institute, pushing out the frontiers of knowledge, had been imported from Germany and enthusiastically accepted by the London colleges and by Owens College, Manchester. Other colleges, inspired by the same idea (but, unlike the German universities, with strong regional ties), were founded at Birmingham (1880), Bristol (1876), Leeds (1874), Liverpool (1881), Newcastle (1871), Nottingham (1881), and Sheffield (1879). All these except Newcastle, which was attached to Durham, prepared students for external degrees in the university of London.

The rapid expansion of science and the influence of German scholarship influenced not only the new civic colleges but the older universities too. In 1870 the first physics classes were held in the Clarendon Laboratory at Oxford, and in 1871 Clerk Maxwell began to supervise the building of the Cavendish laboratory at Cambridge. In 1881 the Cambridge natural sciences tripos was divided into two parts, and Part II of this tripos, as of others, began its development into the highly specialized training that we know today.

Meanwhile there had been drastic changes in primary education. The Education Acts of 1870, 1876, and 1880 set up school boards, charged them with a statutory duty to establish and maintain elementary schools, and provided machinery to enforce attendance. Between 1871 and 1881 the numbers attending public elementary day schools rose from 1 231 000 to 2 864 000. The London School Board, more enlightened than most, had in 1879 over 1300 teachers holding advanced science certificates, and in more than half the schools some science—if only natural history—was taught. The Liverpool School Board appointed a peripatetic demonstrator in mechanics who toured the schools, accompanied by a load of apparatus which was transported from school to school in a hand-cart [27]. But it was not until 1890 that obligatory science and manual training were incorporated into the elementary school code.

At long last the foundation was laid on which technical and technological education in Britain could be built. There was still a dearth of secondary schooling; there were still no institutions for higher technological education corresponding to the polytechnics of the Continent; and there was still no firm bridge between pure and applied science. Nevertheless the massive inertia against educational change, which Victorian England inherited from the eighteenth century and which had so long withstood the pressure of reformers, was now overcome. Every year saw some new plan come to fruition and some old prejudice wither away.

Among the last prejudices to go was the idea that technical skill could not be taught in a trade school or technical college but only 'on the job'. Despite the unanimous praise for such institutions as the school for watch-makers' apprentices in Paris and the Higher Trade Institution at Chemnitz, Parliament refused to support similar institutions in Britain; governments were prepared to subsidize the study of scientific principles but not the study of technologies or trade techniques. It was the Livery Companies of London that began to assume this responsibility. In 1876 the City and Guilds of London Institute for the Advancement of Technical Education was set up. The Institute made an enduring contribution to the cause of technical education. It bridged the gap between the enlightened prescience of Samuelson's Select Committee of 1868 (p 789) and the Technical Instruction Act of 1889. In the first place the Institute conducted examinations, on the principle of payment by results, in subjects too technical to be covered by the Department of Science and Art. The Society of Arts had for some years been trying to serve this need, but was not able to provide a sufficient financial incentive. In the second place the Institute built in 1881–3 at Finsbury the first genuine technical college where emphasis was laid on the practical applications of science to trade and commerce.[1] In the third place the Institute founded the famous City and Guilds College in South Kensington, where emphasis was laid on the scientific basis for higher technology not only in engineering (its present specialism) but in the physical sciences also.

All these enterprises of the City and Guilds Institute met with success. By 1890, for example, over 6000 candidates offered themselves for examination in 49 technical subjects. On all sides there was evidence of a demand from the

---

[1] Similar colleges had existed on the continent for over half a century.

workers for technical education. When, in 1882, the Regent Street Polytechnic opened its doors to provide trade instruction to apprentices, over 6000 students attended, and other London polytechnics, established with funds accumulated from the parochial charities, met with similar success. But it was not enough that the pioneers of technical education had set up facilities and created a small but annually increasing supply of technically trained men. The pioneers had to create a demand as well, for many managers were still prejudiced against the college-trained technologist or the artisan from a trade school; they still had to be convinced that in many industries it was no longer sufficient to rely on sturdy individualism without science, and amateur inventiveness without technology.

Once more the stimulus for overcoming these prejudices came in the form of renewed fear of competition from abroad. Another royal commission was appointed [26]. Its report contains vivid evidence of the change in heart that had come over British industry since the 1860s. In the Nottingham of 1868 half the operatives in the lace factories had been described as illiterate (p 778): in 1884 Nottingham lace manufacturers obliged their apprentices to attend the School of Art and some employers even paid the fees. 'They used to send to France for designers', the evidence ran, 'but latterly the great majority of designers were Nottingham men who had received their training in the Nottingham school' [26]. In some branches of industry—especially heavy engineering—Britain was holding her own and the skill of her craftsmen was still unrivalled. But the commission produced devastating evidence that in other branches—especially the chemical and electrical industries—the continent had gained the lead. For example, the dyestuff industry had been founded by Perkin in England (p 270), and its raw material—coal—was abundantly available; nevertheless by 1884 there were only five dye-works in Britain, with a production worth only £450 000. By contrast there were seventeen dye-works in Germany with a production worth £2 m per annum, four-fifths of which was exported. Faraday's discoveries were being exploited in factories on the continent. Mathematics applied to bridge-building was enabling the Germans to excel in combining stability with economy. Antwerp was displacing Liverpool as a market for woollen yarns.

The Commission's exhaustive inquiries (which included a detailed survey of the state of technical education on the continent) did not lead to very bold conclusions but they did provide a clear analysis of a very complicated situation. British technical education was suffering because there were insufficient and inadequate secondary schools, and therefore the foundations for higher technological education were weak; it was suffering, too, because opportunities for the managers and masters to receive education in applied science were far too few.

While Germany was estimated to have in industry 4000 chemists trained in universities or polytechnics, Britain had only a handful. The belated system of compulsory education (by then fourteen years old) was beginning to show results. Emphasis was no longer on illiteracy among the workers: it was now on ignorance of applied science among the managers.

Out of this royal commission came the Technical Instruction Act of 1889. It remedied at any rate one of the ills of British technical education, for it empowered local authorities to set up technical schools and to subsidize science in secondary schools. But the only effective remedy—the establishment of a state system of secondary education—still had to wait until 1902. A year later, in 1890, the local Taxation (Customs and Excise) Act was passed which made available to local authorities a large sum from customs and excise duties (the so-called 'whisky money') for technical education. At long last the battle for technical education in Britain was won. All over the country technical colleges came to life. Some, such as the Leicester College of Art and the Brighton Technical College, were founded soon after the Act was passed. Others, such as the Lancaster and Morecambe College of Further Education, were taken over by the local authority when the Act was passed, after a long and honourable history as mechanics' institutes.

The royal commission put on record, too, evidence for the respectability of applied science in the universities. Roscoe at Manchester had established a course in technological chemistry in no way inferior to that in the Zürich Polytechnic. In University College, London, Graham was giving courses in chemical technology which included brewing, metallurgy, bread-making, the alkali trade, soap, glass, pottery, and agricultural chemistry; Kennedy was giving the first practical course in the country on the principles of civil engineering; and in Foster's physics course students had to make their own apparatus. But as research centres the British universities still lagged behind the universities of Germany and Switzerland, and financial support from Westminster was niggardly compared with the scale of state support for laboratories on the continent. The spur to reform was still fear of foreign competition. For example, the National Physical Laboratory was set up in 1900 to emulate the *Physikalisch-Technische Reichsanstalt*, and even as late as 1903 one of the arguments used in favour of uniting the Royal College of Science, the Royal School of Mines, and the City and Guilds Engineering College into an Imperial College of Science and Technology was that such a college would be a 'Charlottenburg' for London.

The Education Act of 1902, establishing a state system of secondary education, and the emergence of half a dozen civic universities,[1] completed the pattern for

---

[1] Belfast (1908), Birmingham (1900), Bristol (1909), Leeds (1904), Liverpool (1903), Sheffield (1905).

technological education in Britain. Two world wars and renewed anxieties about foreign competition for markets have etched the pattern more deeply, but they have not substantially changed it. The 1880s saw the exit of the amateur in science and technology and the entry of the specialist. In England the specialist did not arise in response to demands from industry: he was a product of the growing complexity of science itself, and it is only since the turn of the century that industry has discovered his value. Now the specialist has displaced the inventor and in many industries he has displaced the craftsman, for he has transformed invention and craft into exact sciences.

ACKNOWLEDGEMENT

The author is indebted to Mrs D. Feyer and Mr M. D. Forster for assembling some of the material from which this chapter has been written.

REFERENCES

[1] PORTER, R. G. 'Progress of the Nation.' London. 1847; quoted by DODDS, J. W. 'The Age of Paradox.' Gollancz, London. 1953.

[2] SADLER, M. E. and EDWARDS, J. W. 'Special Reports on Educational Subjects', No. 2. London. 1898.

[3] KELLY, T. 'George Birkbeck, Pioneer of Adult Education', pp. 207–77. University Press, Liverpool. 1957.

[4] HEYWOOD, SIR BENJAMIN. 'Addresses at the Manchester Mechanics' Institution.' London. 1843; quoted by KELLY, T. Ref. [3].

[5] 'Report of the Select Committee on Scientific Instruction.' London, Parliamentary Papers, Session 1867–8, Vols 15, 50.

[6] HOLE, J. 'An Essay on the History and Management of Literary, Scientific, and Mechanics' Institutes.' London. 1853.

[7] CARDWELL, D. S. L. 'The Organization of Science in England.' Heinemann, London. 1957.

[8] HAMILTON, SIR WILLIAM. 'Discussions on Philosophy and Literature, Education and University Reform. . . . ' (3rd ed.). Edinburgh. 1866.

[9] ARMYTAGE, W. H. G. 'Civic Universities.' Benn, London. 1955. This book contains a full and well-documented account of the history of English universities. For the state of universities before 1851, see chap. 8. See also: CARDWELL, D. S. L. Ref. [7], chap. 3.

[10] TURNER, DOROTHY M. 'History of Science Teaching in England.' Chapman & Hall, London. 1927.

[11] BALFOUR, G. 'The Educational Systems of Great Britain and Ireland' (2nd ed.). Clarendon Press, Oxford. 1903.

[12] 'Fortuna Domus. A Series of Lectures Delivered in the University of Glasgow in Commemoration of the Fifth Centenary of its Foundation', see lectures by J. W. COOK, P. I. DEE, and J. SMALL. University Press, Glasgow. 1952.

[13] BABBAGE, C. Quart. Rev. 43, 305, 1830.

[14] DE MORGAN, A. Quart. J. Educ. 3, 1832; quoted in ref. [7], p. 49.

[15] PLAYFAIR, L. In 'Lectures on the Results of the Great Exhibition of 1851.' London. 1852.

[16] BOOTH, J. *Trans. nat. Ass. Prom. soc. Sci. for 1857*, 145, 1858.

[17] 'Report of the Public Schools Commission.' Parliamentary Papers, Sessions 1862, Vol. 43; 1864, Vol. 20.

[18] 'Report of the Schools Enquiry Commission.' London, Parliamentary Papers, Session 1867–8, Vol. 28.

[19] 'Report of the Royal Commission on the University of Oxford.' London, Parliamentary Papers, 1852.

[20] 'Report of the Select Committee on Scientific Instruction', especially pp. iii–vii. London, Parliamentary Papers, Session 1867–8, Vols 15, 54.

[21] BACHE, A. D. 'Report on Education in Europe.' Philadelphia. 1839.

[22] MACK, H. T. 'Special Reports on Educational Subjects', No. 11, pp. 101–229. London. 1902.

[23] PLAYFAIR, L. *J. Soc. Arts*, **15**, 477, 1867.

[24] LOW, D. A. (Ed.). 'The Whitworth Book.' Longmans, London. 1926.

[25] 'Reports of the Royal Commission on Scientific Instruction and the Advancement of Science.' London, Parliamentary Papers, Sessions 1872, Vol. 25; 1873, Vol. 28; 1874, Vol. 22; 1875, Vol. 28. The Chairman was the Duke of Devonshire. The Commission included T. H. Huxley, Norman Lockyer, Sir John Lubbock, and Bernhard Samuelson.

[26] 'Reports of the Royal Commission on Technical Instruction.' London, Parliamentary Papers, Session 1884, Vols 29, 30, 31. The Chairman was the same Bernhard Samuelson who had presided over the Select Committee on Scientific Instruction sixteen years earlier.

[27] GLADSTON, H. 'Report of the British Association for the Advancement of Science', 1879, Section F, p. 475.
   HANCE, E. M. *Ibid.*, p. 477.

The Manchester Mechanics' Institution, 1824.

33

TECHNOLOGY AND INDUSTRIAL ORGANIZATION

CHARLES WILSON

THE relations between technology and industrial organization in the nineteenth century can best be regarded as a set of variations on the theme of specialization. If industrial organization be defined as the means for producing and distributing goods and services, it is evident that fundamental changes in its character took place in the nineteenth century; evident, too, that these changes were, in important respects, consequences of the development of the technology which lay at the dynamic centre of many—though not of all—industries. The complex of techniques which in a modern concern begin with the production engineer or the chemical engineer, and continue through a series of specialists to end with the advertising agent and the market research team, were represented in the early stages of the industrial revolution by one, or more often, two men. Entrepreneurs like Josiah Wedgwood, Matthew Boulton, Benjamin Gott, or Josiah Mason surveyed and encompassed the entire industrial process, as no previous economic agent had done. Estimating some existing need or potential demand, they so moulded the machinery of production as to provide for its satisfaction. Invention, technology, the factory system, even primitive forms of advertisement (like Wedgwood's famous catalogues) were all instruments to their hand. The primitive character of those common services, such as transport, which modern producing industry expects to be provided independently by private or public enterprise, took them into ventures that went far beyond the interests of their own factories. Wedgwood and Boulton were both concerned with canal building: the ironmasters of the north-east were intimately concerned with early railway construction. The early textile manufacturers had themselves to make the machinery needed for their factories. The functions of the early entrepreneurs were socially pervasive and economically all-embracing.

Nevertheless, even at this earliest stage, there are signs of a necessary specialization within industry—a germ from which many later things were to grow. It is true that business acumen and organizing ability were, and were to continue to be, the basis of success for many firms. Even the new machinery in the textile industry involved no principles that an intelligent merchant could not grasp.

Indeed, much of the mechanical invention of these years was simply the result of the harnessing of the traditional skills of clockmakers, millwrights, black-smiths, and the like to the needs of the entrepreneur. In such industries the dynamic factor continued to be the sense of commercial opportunity of the directing entrepreneur. These were, in general, industries which manufactured consumer goods for a mass market, where the need to pursue or even anticipate fashion, to attend to matters of design and economy—to produce, in fact, an appropriate article in quantity at a steady price and of a consistent quality—was paramount. The commercial flair needed in such markets was not absent from the new capital-goods industries such as the metal and chemical and nascent engineering industries.

The commercial talents of Boulton have been emphasized, but they were directed to a rather different end from those of Wedgwood. In the matter of the steam-engine, Boulton's talents were combined with the scientifically inventive genius of Watt to develop a serviceable engine and modify it for the various purposes to which it was put in ironworks, spinning-mills, breweries, and mines. The most striking contrast between Britain and France at this period is the higher rate at which, in Britain, inventions were adopted, developed, and passed into industrial application. No nation in the world showed more vivid inventive genius than the French, but a high proportion of their inventive talent proved abortive or was put to profitable use elsewhere—notably in England and Scotland.

As the nineteenth century proceeded, the number of those industries within which technology was a—we might say almost the—dynamic force, increased. Foremost, perhaps, in this second phase of industrial revolution was the engineer-ing industry. When Watt's patent finally expired in 1800, only about 500 engines had been built (vol IV, p 163). Patent or no patent, it would have been difficult to build at any greater rate because of the shortage of even moderately skilled engineers. Two of the fundamental changes affecting industrial growth and organization between 1800 and 1851 were the training of an army of engineers and the invention of automatic tools, which made it possible to repeat, accurately and indefinitely, the manufacture of a piece of machinery. Here was one point at which mass production already surpassed the hand and eye of the craftsman. 1851 saw both the formation of the Amalgamated Society of Engineers and the Great Exhibition, which was above all a tribute to the skill of engineers. Their ancestry may be traced back to Joseph Bramah, who was the first to apply the machine-tool to the making of locks. Henry Maudslay, his pupil, made the lathe self-acting, and from his workshops came work more precise than the world had yet seen and a succession of pupils who carried on his traditions—James Nasmyth and Joseph Whitworth especially. The London engineering industry became a training ground to which enterprising Northerners, especially Scots, flocked to perfect their skill and broaden their knowledge of the world of machines: hence the Rennies, the Fairbairns, the Bells, the numerous Napiers, engineers of every type. Their devices and refinements diffused a new and greater surge of energy through the nation's industry, sweeping away the obstacles that had delayed Watt and the early machine-makers. 'How could we have had good steam engines, if we had no means of boring a true cylinder or of turning a true piston rod or of planing a valve face?' asked Nasmyth in his autobiography [1]. The new methods created new industries—especially in London, Manchester, and Leeds—so accustomed to accurate standardizing that by the middle of the nineteenth century it was possible to have different parts of the same machine made in Manchester, Glasgow, Liverpool, and London, and yet be sure that they would function together perfectly when assembled.

Most of these engineering firms were small or medium-sized concerns employing anything between half a dozen and three or four score men. But a few became very large by the standards of the time—Kitsons of Leeds (who specialized in locomotives), Platts of Oldham (spinning-machinery), Whitworths of Manchester—and they grew swiftly towards the middle of the century. Whitworths employed 172 men in 1844, and 636 ten years later. Kitsons had 259 men in 1845, and 431 in 1851.

The iron industry was another activity where the technologist could claim to rank very high amongst the dynamic elements that went to give the industry its momentum. In 1850 the north-eastern area came well behind Scotland, Staffordshire, and south Wales as a maker of pig iron. Within the next quarter of a century the Middlesbrough area came to account for a third of the whole British output of that commodity. Not the least of the reasons which explain the rise of Middlesbrough lies in the technological progress of the local ironmasters. Two in particular made a unique contribution. John Vaughan (of the firm of Bölckow, Vaughan) not only discovered the main seam of the lias ironstone that emerged in the Cleveland Hills but led the attack on wasteful and inefficient methods of iron production. Waste gases were used to raise steam and heat the blast. The size of furnaces was increased from 5000 to 20 000 cu ft. The consumption of coal was made more economical. Output rose to 500 tons a day. Vaughan's neighbour, Lowthian Bell (of Bell Brothers) was another innovator. More literate than Vaughan, his accounts of his experiments and opinions, especially his 'Principles of the Manufacture of Iron and Steel' (1884), have come down to us as one of the basic sources of knowledge of Victorian industry. Men like Vaughan and Bell drove up the iron output of the north-east, but until 1879 the phosphoric ores of the region could not be used in the new methods of making cheap steel. The discovery by Gilchrist and Thomas in that year of a method of eliminating the phosphorus revolutionized the character of the north-east, which became a large steel-producing as well as an iron-producing area.

The guiding effects of technology on the character of industry were nowhere more evident than in the chemical industry. In one branch especially—the manufacture of soda, vital to glass, soap, textiles, and many other industrial processes—technology effected a notable revolution. Leblanc showed how soda could be made cheaply from common salt, and from the late twenties Muspratt and Gamble were manufacturing on his principles at Widnes and St Helens. The main disadvantage of the process was its crop of corrosive by-products, and a long history of trial and error was needed before a superior alternative, the ammonia-soda process, was perfected. Of this process Ernest Solvay, the successful Belgian discoverer, said: 'Never before was the industrial realization of any process attempted so frequently and for such a long period of time' [2]. It had taken well over half a century to perfect the industrial application of a scientific principle. This was the process introduced into England in 1873 by Ludwig Mond. Yet even at this stage, teething troubles were by no means at an end. The apparatus was complex; a single fault could bring a whole plant to a standstill and falsify all calculations of costs and profits. Mond and his partner Brunner, like Solvay, had their explosions and disasters. Everything, it was plain, hinged on plant construction; and though Ludwig Mond was a shrewd entrepreneur well able to calculate the economic value of his inquiries and discoveries, his real genius lay in his ability to translate formulae into plant. His process for the recovery of sulphur from the Leblanc waste, the ammonia-soda process, power gas, and nickel-refining all point to the same conclusion. Mond, joint founder of one of Britain's largest modern industries, himself defined the role of the industrial scientist in a presidential address to the Society of the Chemical Industry in 1889:

... we can now foresee ... in what direction progress in technology will move and in consequence the inventor is now frequently in advance of the wants of his time. He may even create new wants, to my mind a distinct step in the development of human culture. It can then be no longer stated that necessity is the mother of invention; but I think it may truly be said that the steady methodical investigation of natural phenomena is the father of industrial progress [3].

Mond's words are really a *credo* in which enterprise and technology come together more closely than they had ever done, and he was perhaps hardly aware that he himself combined those qualities to a unique degree. In industries less fortunate in marrying the two, the gap often remained wide—as it did, for example, among Brunner, Mond's competitors who stuck to the Leblanc system of soda manufacture. The impact of the new technology on the structure of this older industry was plain: the Leblanc makers were driven into combination for self-preservation. Collective action was no novelty to the older generation of chemical manufacturers; and the United Alkali Company, floated in the winter gloom of 1890, was the culmination of years of experience of the value of what was politely known as the 'principle of association'. The demands of the First World War prolonged Leblanc manufacture, but by 1920 it was dead, the victim, in part at any rate, of a superior technology.

That the character of some vital industries was changing under the impact of technology and enterprise is not in doubt. But a glance at some social and economic statistics acts as a useful check on exaggeration. The beginning of the industrial revolution is frequently set at about 1760. Yet Sir John Clapham has pointed out that 'outwork' was still the predominant form of capitalistic industrial organization in the England of George IV [4]. The technology and organization of the cotton industry and the iron industry had been revolutionized, but none other. The metal industries of the midlands and West Riding demonstrated every kind of transitional stage between the independent master craftsman and the complete factory. The amount of steam-power used here was small, as it was in most industries other than cotton. The worsted industry of the West Riding was using 10 000 hp by 1850, mostly for power looms, but in woollens the hand loom kept its grip until after 1851. These impressions—of a country not yet an 'industrial state'—are supported by the figures of the occupational census of 1851. By far the largest employing industry was agriculture, which kept 1¾ million people active. Other traditional occupations followed: domestic service occupied over a million and the varied skills needed in building nearly half a million. Truly industrial occupations like cotton manufacture accounted for about half a million, woollen cloth manufacture for rather more than a quarter-million. But the quality of early Victorian England may be sensed more accurately from the fact that there were twice as many tailors as there were railway employees, while the number of blacksmiths exceeded the number of iron workers by nearly 50 per cent.

By the third quarter of the century, there had been a further substantial change. The size of the average cotton-spinning factory had grown by 30 per cent, the average worsted mill by 80 per cent. Steam-power and better machinery were thrusting the factory system into industries previously held by hand-workers—like hosiery and boot-making—and increasing the size of the firm in industries where large-scale organization had taken hold earlier, such as iron manufacture and shipbuilding. The average shipyard in 1870 employed nearly the 600 men that represented the peak total of the very largest yard in the 1820s. Ancient handicrafts persisted—wheelwrights, saddlers, carpenters, dressmakers —but they tended to draw on factory industry more and more for their half-finished goods—axles, ironmongery, sawn plank, sewing thread, and so on.

Specialization, the division of labour, and concentration were fostered throughout industry by the spectacular improvements in transport of the 1830s and 1840s, when an enterprising York draper, George Hudson, engineers like Stephenson, and armies of navvies covered Britain, ingeniously if expensively, with a network of railways that spelt the end of the canals. From the 1850s an increasing proportion of railway revenue came from freights, and no industrial structure was more affected than that of brewing. Competition had already brought about a high degree of concentration in the London brewing industry in the eighteenth century. By the early nineteenth century, a dozen or so great breweries, representing unique aggregations of capital for the time, brewed most of the Londoner's beer. Railways now helped to extinguish the handicraft brewer in the provinces and drive on the process of amalgamation. At Burton-on-Trent four different railway systems ran into the town to convey the products to market, especially to the newly built London terminus at St Pancras, which had, below the goods depot, accommodation for 8000 butts. At every point of manufacture and carriage—malting, hopping, brewing, bottling, carrying—the brewing industry was shaped by technological influences.

Conversely, this and many other industries whose markets were enabled to expand by the revolution in transport were indirectly influenced by the technological changes in the metal industries. The railways that broke up and united the parochial areas into which many industrial markets were earlier divided were the products of an industry itself revolutionized by Cort, Neilson, Nasmyth, and numerous others, and brought to fruition by industrialists like Bell and Vaughan. Between 1855 and 1885 the total output of pig iron rose from just over 3 million to $7\frac{1}{4}$ million tons. Railways, engines, and locomotives were made from this expanding output of iron; so were steamships increasingly in the 1870s. Long after cheap steel was a possibility, many ships were built of iron plates and angles, the manufacture of which kept a large part of the north-eastern industry busy. Yet ultimately Bessemer, Siemens, and Gilchrist and Thomas wrought a second revolution. In 1884 Lowthian Bell, the voice of the iron industry, stated that steel 'must be henceforward looked upon as the proper material for rail-roads', though John Brown had been rolling steel rails at Sheffield for nearly a quarter of a century. By that time, Lloyd's surveyors had accepted steel as building material for ships. Thus behind the 386 000 miles of railway which had revolutionized the world's communications by 1890, and behind the 75 million tons of shipping which entered and left United Kingdom ports in that year, lay basic industries transformed by technological progress.

Enterprise and technology had so far combined, first in the textile and metal industries, then in engineering and shipping, to bring the industrialization of Britain to full fruition. In the last quarter of the century, the needs of a growing population for food, and of an expanding industry for raw materials, had far out-run her domestic resources. Yet what was required was easily paid for by the combined visible and invisible exports generated by the new industrial and commercial system. There was even a substantial surplus for reinvestment abroad, which helped in turn to swell the nation's invisible income.

This basic change in the character of the British economy involved consequen-tial changes in the machinery by which industry was financed. These were not sudden. The private, informal borrowings between relations or friends or members of the same chapel, which had supplemented the ploughing-back of profits in the early stages of change, continued to suffice in many industries for a surprisingly long time. Before 1825 a public joint-stock company was a rare industrial phenomenon. The 1840s saw the beginning of a substantial relaxation in the laws that reserved to the few the privileges of corporateness and limited liability. Acts of 1844 and 1856 pushed the process a long way farther by making it easier to register a public company, to get it incorporated, and to limit the liability of shareholders. Down to the 1850s the only industries of such a size as to need finance by joint stock methods were the canals and railways. Before 1855, some £300 m had been invested during the several manias in railway building. Most of it came from provincial middle-class savers. Even in 1845 the London Stock Exchange was said to have quotations for 260 different kinds of railway shares, some of it debentures and fixed-interest stocks, but the great majority risk-bearing ordinary shares.

The change brought about by the needs of railway finance can be followed from the City columns of 'The Times'. In 1845 government stocks and some 60 railway companies were quoted. In the 1860s a growing number of large firms in coal-mining, iron-making, and engineering took advantage of the new laws to raise from the public the capital required by the new technology and expanding output. Yet the proportion of industry organized in this way was still small. In 1875 'The Times' City column (still headed, significantly, 'Stocks, and Railway and Other Shares') quoted only a few telegraph companies and some half-dozen industrial concerns with English works. In the last quarter of the century, things moved a good deal faster. The City columns of 1900 have a modern and familiar look. Gilt-edged, railways, and telegraphs have been joined—very prominently—by the great and capital-consuming mining enterprises of South Africa, but the columns record that business was done in shares in some fourteen large brewery companies, and in seven large coal, iron, and steel firms. There were, besides, quotations for some 50 miscellaneous industries whose activities illustrate the growing variety and range of an economy that was adding semi-necessities and even luxuries to basic necessities. The chemical industry was represented by Brunner, Mond; the cotton industry by J. and P. Coats; the iron and steel industry by Dorman, Long. But most typical of the age, perhaps, were the great stores—Harrods, Waring and Gillow, D. H. Evans—and the 'multiples' like Liptons and the Maypole. Industry in 1900 meant many things it had not meant in 1875, including Sunlight soap, margarine, cheap jam, and Bovril. The extent to which these new industries sought their customers in the working-class market is an important pointer to the social changes that were taking place in this increasingly industrialized community.

Technology had made it necessary to fashion a new kind of finance for industry. The new finance in turn helped to refashion the organization of industry—or at any rate that part of it which invited public subscriptions, for we must not forget that much industry continued to finance itself after the old informal and private manner. The consequences of conversion to a public company varied from company to company. In many instances the effects were postponed by the resolute policy of the former owner or partners in retaining ownership of the equity, and selling to the public only preference shares with limited voting rights. William Lever, the founder of Lever Brothers of Port Sunlight, followed this policy from 1894 until his death in 1925, and thus retained effective control of policy and management. But in other companies, it was not possible to do this: or at any rate, it was not done. Ownership and management often became divided. Salaried managers appeared, yet their relationship on the one hand to those members of the family who had previously been sole owners, and on the other to the shareholders, followed no general pattern. Certainly, few of this new class could yet speak with the undivided authority of the older owner-managers, and herein lies part of the explanation of the vicissitudes of British industry in the later nineteenth and early twentieth centuries. This was a transitional age in management.

In other firms, management was hampered by boards of directors loaded with spokesmen for those fixed-interest shareholders whose instinct was to play for safety; they were apt to regard technological innovations with suspicion. Not all the troubles were attributable to the public company form of management. Alfred Marshall in 1903 castigated—rightly or wrongly—the lethargy of those manufacturers' sons who were 'content to follow mechanically the lead given by their fathers. They worked shorter hours and they exerted themselves less to obtain new practical ideas than their fathers had done, and thus a part of England's leadership was destroyed rapidly' [5]. Whether this is fair or not—for there were also problems arising from restrictive practices by labour and competition from foreigners starting under more favourable conditions—the pace of technological change seems to have slowed down in the nineties. Not only professional critics of capitalism, but economists of moderate opinions and even thoughtful business men, were coming to think that virtue was going out of the old system. New industrial methods were developed abroad rather than in Britain: ring-spinning and mechanical coal-cutting, the mechanical handling of grain and other cargoes, the use of steel-framed buildings—all came from America and penetrated British practice either very slowly or not at all. Britain electrified her factories only very slowly. The pioneers of the new internal combustion engine were mainly French or German; the aeroplane was an American invention, developed mainly in France. Some of Britain's leading industrial scientists, like Mond and Siemens, were of foreign origin, and the continent of Europe had in many respects taken from Britain her lead in some important branches of the chemical industry, such as those concerned with coal-tar products and the chemistry of oils and fats. The one major invention of the nineties was the Parsons turbine, and it is significant that this was in the field where Britain remained well ahead—shipbuilding and machinery—long after her lead had begun to shorten in textiles and iron and steel.

It is important to preserve a sense of balance in dealing with the problem of 'decline' in Britain. It would be futile to expect the primacy of the mid-Victorian age to be continued for ever, and in any case there were to be marked signs of renewed vitality after 1900. Even at the height of its prosperity the *laissez-faire* system of industrial development had placed heavy burdens on certain groups in British society, but so rapid had been the advance in national wealth at large that these had been quickly forgotten. Now the industrial mechanism itself represented such a large accumulation of capital and technical methods that it was becoming more and more rigid, more and more difficult to adapt and adjust. What was really serious was not so much that fewer inventions were being generated but that fewer were being incorporated into industrial practice. It is difficult to know how far the apparent rigidity in older industries was compensated for by the arrival of new ones, how far capital and intelligence were going (as G. M. Young has said) into 'light industry, distribution, salesmanship' [6]. It certainly seems true that the Age of the Engineer had been superseded by the Age of the Advertiser. What the resulting balance sheet was is more difficult to say.

Meanwhile the industrial potential of other nations was being rapidly developed. By the last quarter of the century Germany, the United States, and France were all launched into full-scale policies of industrialization. In each, the local circumstances—of geography, natural resources, national psychology, and tradition—coloured the process of industrial change. In France the great age was that of the Second Empire: after 1870 growth was retarded and the valuable resources of Alsace and Lorraine were lost. In general, France was better at light industries than at heavy. Even in 1900 the workshop rather than the factory was the typical unit of her industry. Germany's great age of expansion followed upon that of France. From 1870 the cumulative effects of the customs union, railways, and the gain of Lorraine ores and industries all made themselves felt, and mining, metallurgy, shipbuilding, engineering, and chemical manufacture developed rapidly. In the United States, large-scale industry was no novelty: on the eve of the Civil War a Southern commentator could deride his Northern foes as 'greasy mechanics and filthy operatives'. But all previous growth seemed negligible when compared with the expansion of the period between the Civil War and the 1890s.

Industrialization amongst the newcomers showed certain common characteristics and some analogies with British experience. In France, Germany, and the United States, the transport revolution formed an indispensable prelude to major economic change. In France and Germany, the railway network created the demand for iron (and later steel), provided markets for agricultural producers, and distributed industrial manufactures. In no country did the new transport play a more vital role than in the United States, where an important section of the iron industry depended on the thousand miles of railroad that brought the ores of Lake Superior to the coal of Pittsburgh. By the 1880s the great transcontinental lines were complete. By 1900, America had 200 000 miles of railroad in operation. And she, like the European countries, paid tribute to Britain's technological experience by borrowing British engineers, skilled labour, materials, and capital.

Nor was railway technology the only form of skill to be borrowed. Since the mid-eighteenth century, British engineers and artisans were to be found migrating to continental Europe. In the nineteenth, Lancashire operatives and machine-makers played an important role in developing New England industries. The German industrialists from 1820 likewise enticed British workmen as well as capital into their undertakings: contrariwise, German scientists and technologists contributed in vital respects to British industrial progress. Long after Germany had an up-to-date engineering industry she continued to obtain textile machinery from Lancashire. Britain made no more valuable gift to Germany than the Gilchrist and Thomas process of steel-making, for Lorraine, Germany's spoils in the war with France, contained one of the world's most important beds of phosphoric ore. When the patent expired in 1894 German output of iron and steel had surpassed that of Britain. The French steel industry also benefited, as, of course, did that of the United States, from the inventions of Bessemer, Siemens, and Gilchrist and Thomas.

The world's basic industries grew, then, to a considerable extent from common technological roots: they were influenced, and differentiated, by local considerations. For example, the part played respectively by state and individual varied from country to country. In Germany, the role of the state had, from the beginning, been large, and so it continued. Although Germany began to produce her great entrepreneurs, the state gave its blessing to industrial development, set up tariffs to protect nascent industry, shaped railway rates to help exports, assisted the spread of technological education, and encouraged the organization of *Kartells*—in coal, steel, and chemicals—as stabilizers of prices and employment.

In Germany, and in France too, industry was financed by methods different from those that ruled in Britain and America. Although France, in 1867, and Germany, in 1870, followed Britain's lead and moved towards limited liability, a great part of industry was financed through the banks. In France, the *Crédit Mobilier* and the *Crédit Foncier* had played an important part in the economic schemes of Napoleon III. In Germany, from the 1850s to the 1870s, the banks—*Darmstädter, Diskontogesellschaft, Deutsche, Dresdner*, and *Reichsbank*—helped to canalize industrial investment. Hence, some British observers believed, the greater coherence and drive of German industry. On the whole, German opinion approved the measures taken to finance and encourage industry, to protect it from the keenest winds of competition. There was no tradition of liberal individualism to revolt against business consolidation, as an important section of American opinion revolted in the last years of the century. In the United States, the pools, trusts, holding companies, and mergers of those years were represented—with a greater or less degree of truth—as the devices of robber barons to obtain monopoly profits behind a tariff screen. By 1890 critical opinion had secured the passing of the Sherman Anti-Trust Act: but this was only the beginning of a campaign that was joined and promoted by 'progressives' of all kinds.

By 1900, the entrepreneurs of Britain's principal industries had endowed her with a legacy of specialization. Britain's economy was specialized by regions: and within those regions industrial processes also were specialized. Technology was a basic factor in the creation of regional industries: industry tended to grow where fuel and raw materials were most easily available. The most obvious example was the iron industry. Darby and Cort, by introducing smelting with coke, transferred the iron industry to those areas where coal and ore were most conveniently exploited. The hot blast helped to create a great Scottish iron industry. Vaughan and Bell were among the authors of Middlesbrough's rise to supremacy. Bessemer and Siemens transferred the emphasis from areas like south Staffordshire to the coastal areas. Gilchrist and Thomas removed the threat of the new steel-makers to Middlesbrough iron by enabling steel to be made of phosphoric ores, but at the same time helped to raise Germany to the position of chief European steel-producer. In these and other ways technology helped to shape the regional pattern of specialization in iron and steel.

Similarly, the cotton industry became more and more strongly localized in east Lancashire and north Cheshire; while between Liverpool (which handled the raw cotton) and Manchester (which distributed the finished goods) came further degrees of specialization. The north-east wove and the south-east spun, while each of the cotton towns had its speciality of spinning or weaving, fine or medium or coarse, shirtings or furnishings or apparel cloths. The wool-using industry was likewise localized in the West Riding as the older competing areas of the west country and East Anglia dwindled away. Here, as in Lancashire, there was some degree of regional sub-specialization by product, the north and west (centred on Bradford) concentrating more on worsteds, the south and east (centred on Leeds) concentrating on woollens; Huddersfield stood for quality, Dewsbury for cheapness.

The change of constructional methods in shipbuilding from timber to iron brought with it a change of location from the Thames to the Clyde, the Tyne, the Wear, and the Tees. Of the great industries of the late nineteenth century, engineering remained widely scattered because it was in fact not one industry but a congeries of industries, and its branches remained close to the parent industries they served. Thus textile engineering remained focused on Yorkshire and Lancashire, marine engineering on the Clyde and the north-east coast, agricultural engineering in East Anglia. Motor and cycle manufacturers were concentrated in the midlands, partly by accident, partly because this was already the place where there were plenty of small producers able to make the numerous components needed.

Throughout the textile industries the process of specialization affected the structure of the firm itself, so that while firms tended to grow larger, employing more people and capital, each tended to concentrate on a narrower productive task. Down to the 1840s many cotton manufacturers engaged in spinning and weaving and even sold their own goods. From that time onwards, however, the manufacturing processes tended to separate as techniques and machines became more complex and demand more varied. Even in the 1880s, about half the total number of cotton firms both spun and wove: by 1911 the proportion had fallen to 30 per cent. The finishing section, where large plants are required for economical working, necessarily tended to be separately operated. A similar pattern was increasingly found in the worsted industry, where producers tended to confine themselves to a single process. For this, too, there were obvious technological reasons. Worsted spinning went into mills before the weaving, and therefore became separately organized. Combing, a key process, became specialized with the advent of mechanical combing because this was governed by patents and, again, most economically done on a large scale. By and large this specialization was the mark of an industry working for quality trades. The American woollen manufacturers, who worked for cheaper markets, frequently carried out all the processes in a single plant.

The textile industries were thus able to work out the logic of their situation in the nineteenth century undisturbed by fundamental technological change. It was otherwise with iron and steel, where such change continued throughout the nineteenth century. Initially the new technology made for specialization; blast-furnaces, puddling-furnaces, and rolling-mills were sometimes combined in one firm but often separate. In one sense specialization persisted, in that iron and things made of iron, whether ships or cutlery, continued to be made by different firms. Yet the size of the business unit tended inevitably to increase (as Marshall said) by reason of 'the magnitude of the aggregate volume of the homogeneous fluid material which has to be produced and by the magnitude of the individual masses to be handled' [7].

It appeared that both economy and convenience would be served by lateral and, especially, vertical combination. Some of the Cleveland firms owned their own ore supplies from the start, and in most other areas there was common ownership of coal and ore supplies. By the 1870s Bölckow, Vaughan owned a dozen collieries, ore mines in Spain, Portugal, and Africa, and a fleet of steamers, employed 10 000 men, and were moving from iron into steel production. The impulse to combine was strong, yet many kinds of specialization remained. Vaughan's neighbours, Bell Brothers, who likewise owned raw material supplies, continued as iron makers until 1899, when they combined with Dorman, Long, who by this move were, as Clapham says, 'pushing back towards that control of raw material which, before the age of steel, iron masters using coal measure iron ore on the coal measures had enjoyed automatically' [8]. Such amalgamations, suggested by technological considerations, were facilitated by the financial flexibility of the limited company system. One area—Staffordshire—was slower to join the movement. Here, in the 1870s, the firm with a single blast-furnace and the small iron-mill remained common.

Thus, while vertical 'integration' was usually in some measure a response to technological possibilities, the horizontal extensions found in the textile and chemical industries proceeded largely from commercial reasons—extensions, as Clapham has said, 'of that buying up by the strong man of useful neighbours or possible competitors . . .' [9]. Towards the end of the century they were frequent and large: Coats's Thread, Yorkshire Woolcombers, Yorkshire Indigo Dyers, the Calico Printers' Association, the Fine Cotton Spinners, and Bradford Dyers. As the names record, they were 'process combinations', the members being concerned with only one stage in production, and they reflect largely the need for protection against the extremities of competition in the storms into which British industry had run. The danger—though by no means certain danger— was that they would retard technological progress rather than promote it.

If some saw dangers in the attempts of organized capital to influence the price of goods, others were disturbed by the efforts of organized labour to influence the price of labour. Both seemed to be ominous threats to the free economy and the working of economic laws. In Britain, however, neither the conditions nor price of labour had ever been entirely a matter of *laissez-faire*. From 1802 there had been Factory Acts, and though there was still plenty of sweated labour in 1900, industrial regulation had steadily grown in efficiency. Continental Europe was slower, and until the 1890s there was little serious intervention in working conditions. On the other hand, Germany was ahead in industrial insurance, with sickness and accident insurance by 1884. If the coming of factories made it more urgent to organize labour and secure fair remuneration, it also made it easier to do so, though even so the struggle to get collective bargaining recognized and to standardize wages, hours, and conditions was long and bitter. In Britain down to 1890, unionism covered mostly the skilled crafts. In the 1890s labour began to be organized by industries rather than by crafts, and in 1900 union membership exceeded 2 million for the first time. Incomplete and legally insecure as it still was, British labour organization far surpassed the achievements of labour elsewhere. In France restrictions did not disappear until 1884 and the *Confédération Générale du Travail*, formed in 1895, did little to realize its ambition of seizing control of industry. In Germany the ban on unionism survived until 1890, when the large 'free unions' made some progress with practical measures to better labour's lot. In the United States organized labour had a longer history and met less official resistance: here the problems arose more from the rapidity of economic growth, immigration, and the social mobility of a new society. The record is one of instability until the formation of the American Federation of Labor in 1881: unlike its more idealistic forerunners, this was severely practical in outlook. Yet even the Federation of Labor had only about half a million members when the century closed, and its work had only just begun.

The century ends, then, in Britain, on a note of doubt and hesitation. The older industries—coal, iron, and textiles—seemed to have come to a technological standstill, while competitors in the United States and Germany were still moving fast. Industrial organization often seemed designed to hinder rather than to facilitate change. But there were newer industries where the picture was brighter, enterprise sharper, inventiveness more prevalent. Sir John Clapham has summarized the position: 'Britain . . . was yet not so stirring industrially as America or Germany, not so stirring as she had herself once been: but her conservatism had been shaken and she was preparing, at her own pace, in those last years, to prove that she was not decadent, though both enemies and desponding friends often said that she was.' [10]

REFERENCES

[1] NASMYTH, J. 'James Nasmyth . . . An Autobiography', ed. by S. SMILES. London. 1883.
[2] COHEN, J. M. 'Life of Ludwig Mond', p. 131. Methuen, London. 1956.
[3] *Idem. Ibid.*, pp. 181–2.
[4] CLAPHAM, SIR JOHN (HAROLD). 'An Economic History of Modern Britain', Vol. 1, ch. 5. University Press, Cambridge. 1926.
[5] MARSHALL, A. Memorandum of 1903, printed as a White Paper in 1908 (No. 321).
[6] YOUNG, G. M. 'Victorian England. The Portrait of an Age', p. 159. Oxford University Press, London. 1936.
[7] ALLEN, G. C. 'British Industries and their Organization', p. 108. Longmans, London. 1956.
[8] CLAPHAM, SIR JOHN (HAROLD). See Ref. [4], Vol. 3, p. 223. University Press, Cambridge. 1938.
[9] *Idem. Ibid.*, p. 223.
[10] *Idem. Ibid.*, p. 71.

34

TECHNOLOGY AND ITS SOCIAL
CONSEQUENCES

SIR ALEXANDER FLECK

I. INTRODUCTION

To those who spend most of their energies dealing with technical affairs, it is tempting to conclude that history is, in contrast, an untidy business. But if it be allowed that our subject can best be treated by an author who, while not ignorant of history, is biased in approach in favour of technology, then so far as history is ever amenable to a division into discrete and tidy periods, the last years of the nineteenth century can be said to be the end of an era. To have proceeded beyond would have been to advance into a technological realm of which the social consequences cannot yet be seen in their proper perspective. Although the originators of the internal combustion engine, the cinema, wireless, new methods of agriculture, refrigeration, and comparable devices were at work before the end of the nineteenth century, the massive development of these enormously influential inventions has been reserved for the twentieth century. It is now commonplace to say that nuclear power, the gas turbine, and electronics—together with all the new materials which these developments demand—have brought us to the threshold of a second Industrial Revolution.

Yet, to a reflective observer of the mid-eighteenth century, the 300 years since the fall of Constantinople in 1453 must themselves have seemed to have generated radical changes in the way men lived and thought. The twin authority of Church and State had been challenged: the Church by the forces of science and humanism, the State by the growing spirit of freedom which these forces helped to liberate. In an age of urbane scepticism our eighteenth-century observer, given prophetic powers, could not but have marvelled at the transformation in social and political life which was to follow the revolution in technology, beginning about 1750. The fundamental change in the way men lived their lives was the direct result of the great wave of technological invention which swept western Europe and North America in the years spanned by the last two volumes of this History. From 1750 onwards, for the first time in history, a predominantly agricultural society was to become predominantly industrial. This chapter will say something of what this change meant to both the community and the individual.

II. GENERAL IMPACT OF TECHNOLOGY ON THE SOCIAL AND ECONOMIC STRUCTURE, 1750–1850

It is in Britain, in the hundred years after 1750, that the first steps towards an industrial society can most vividly be seen. It may be thought that to describe Britain as an agricultural society in the mid-eighteenth century does scant justice to the importance of its mercantile activities. British merchant adventurers provided the essential conditions in which industry was to grow so rapidly: they had opened new markets; they had capital and, above all, they had a spirit of enterprise and a willingness to take risks. Anthony Bacon, ironmaster of the Rhondda Valley, and John Glassford, one of the Glasgow 'tobacco lords', who backed both Roebuck's venture in vitriol-making and the Gordons' manufacture of cudbear, were first and foremost merchants. The difficulties of war-time trade, particularly when the revolt of the American colonies closed an important outlet for British merchandise, helped to turn merchants' attention to the commercial possibilities of industry and gave them new scope for employing their accumulated mercantile capital. The wealth of Britain was in great measure due to her having the undisputed leadership of the world's carrying trade and her flexible banking system. Goods that lay in British ships insured at Edward Lloyd's Coffee House were mainly the products and by-products of an agricultural economy, native and colonial. Even exports of manufactures, such as hardware and textiles shipped to Africa in the great triangular trade with the West Indies, were mainly the output of cottage industry. By providing work for the farmer and his family when they were not busy on the land, cottage industry permitted the otherwise uneconomic working of small farms and was an essential feature of the agrarian economy.

Industrialization was a slow process in its early stages. During the first fifty years of the nineteenth century the new towns with their growing populations were concentrated in the coal-mining regions. At the same time the revolution in transport, the growth of the canal system and then the railway network, linked one manufacturing town with another and provided a succession of sites suited to development, all with ready access to raw materials and to markets for the finished goods. The dominant impression of the landscape of south Lancashire, the Tyne, the midlands, and the Clyde basin was one of industry. Built-up districts were tending to coalesce: the fields surviving in these areas assumed a smoky and apologetic air.

When we think of the difference that the aeroplane has made to our notions of travel to distant places, we have some idea of what the railways meant to people in the early nineteenth century. London to Birmingham 3 days, to Manchester $4\frac{1}{2}$ days, to Edinburgh nearly a week: such were the coaching times in the eighteenth century; and one might lose a wheel or turn over on the journey. Movement across the country in the railway age ceased to be the prerogative of the rich and leisured. Again, with the advent of Rowland Hill's penny postage in 1840 personal communication over distance was within the power of everyone who could read or write. Before 1839 some 76 million letters passed through the British post in a year; this increased to 169 million in the year of the inauguration of the penny post. Ten years later, one million letters were being posted a day; over 80 per cent of these were sent in envelopes folded in Thomas de la Rue's machine.

Despite these developments in communication, industry remained relatively localized. But it was not for this reason only that the structure of society remained predominantly agricultural. Many of the workers who moved into the new urban areas were small farmers, agricultural labourers, or hand-loom weavers who had been forced by enclosures, the 'Speenhamland Act', or the advent of textile machinery to seek a livelihood in the towns. Some who migrated to the towns with their parents could well remember with nostalgia the country life of their childhood. In certain areas flourishing non-agricultural industries lapsed: as timber resources dwindled, the charcoal furnaces of Sussex iron-smelters could not compete with the coal-based iron industry of south Wales, and by 1796 one single Sussex furnace remained working. The wool manufactures of East Anglia and the west country gradually diminished as the West Riding gained the ascendancy, though the leather trades to some extent took their place.

In Lancashire, south Wales, the Black Country, and on the Tyne and Clyde the trend was firmly set towards industrialization. Application of steam-power to coal and metal mining, and above all to the new textile machinery, effected what today would be called a rise in productivity on an unprecedented scale. It is estimated, for example, that between 1818 and 1823 the number of power looms operated in Great Britain increased from 2000 to not less than 10 000: by 1830 there were 60 000 and three years later 100 000. Chemical manufacture, which had relied on long-established empiricism, was beginning to draw on the capital of scientific discovery and quantitative work accumulated mainly in the eighteenth century. The synthesis of soda from common salt was developed commercially and greatly stimulated the production of sulphuric acid. The output of pig iron in 'Great Britain in 1806 was more than a quarter of a million tons, having doubled in ten years and nearly quadrupled in less than twenty. At the same time, to a surprising degree, the articles fabricated from iron were still manufactured in small workshops or were even 'put out' to cottage industry for finishing. This was particularly true of the manufacture of nails, chains, and small hand tools. On asking Peter Stubs of Warrington to show him the factory for the manufacture of his famous files, Nasmyth was surprised to be told that there was no such factory and that cottage workshops in Cheshire and Lancashire produced the files from metal supplied to them.

The rise in the gross national product did not benefit everybody. Hand-loom weavers—of whom there were still about 200 000 in Britain in 1835—suffered great hardship and degradation. Their wages fell by about a half or two-thirds during a period of rising prices, and as, in the production of textiles, female and child labour was cheap and effective, men sometimes suffered the indignity of ceasing to be the chief breadwinners in their families.

The period 1750 to 1850 was, then, one of far-reaching transition. It was, too, a period full of promise, but at the same time not without great suffering for those who had to bear the brunt of dislocation of the agrarian economy by the growth of urban industry.

III. 1851–1900

No event was more symbolic of the progressive optimism of the mid-nineteenth century than the Great Exhibition of 1851. It was the first international exhibition and the first to bring home to all classes of society the vast potentialities of the new Industrial Age. The Exhibition revealed the United Kingdom as the foremost manufacturing country of the world. The Queen wrote in her journal, 'God bless my dearest Albert, and my dear Country, which has shown itself so great today'. Her journal makes an interesting commentary on the exhibits of foreign countries. As well as noting with favour the superb Aubusson and Gobelins tapestries and Sèvres china, she remarked 'there was much French machinery, which the French themselves fear they will not shine in', a pessimistic attitude to which the slow development of industry in early nineteenth-century France lends colour. Of the American section the Queen wrote, 'it contains some very curious inventions: small maps on gutta percha—a reaping machine, &c.'. Other contemporary comment on the latter invention was more explicit: 'Mr. McCormick's reaping machine has convinced English farmers that it can be economically employed. . . . In agriculture, it appears that the machine will be as important as the spinning jenny and power loom in manufacture.' In general, the American exhibits seem to have created a considerable impression because of their simplicity and aptness; their emphasis was not on luxury but on utility. In this, the American exhibitors showed a remarkably sure grasp of the lines on which the manufactures of the Machine Age should develop. A contemporary German observer, Lothar Bucher, called attention to 'the grandfather clocks with their excellently contrived works and simple walnut cases; the chairs—from simple wooden work benches to easy chairs—with their freedom from the gingerbread carving which tears at our hands and clothing, and the absence of the right angles of those currently popular Gothic chairs which are hunching everyone's shoulders. All that we see of American domestic equipment breathes the spirit of comfort and fitness for purpose' [1].

As a result of the 1851 Exhibition, Whitworth's work in bringing standardization and precision to the manufacture of machinery first received universal recognition. Whitworth preached the gospel 'of the vast importance of possessing a true plane', and although his work derives from an earlier period it was only in the second half of the century that its effects were fully felt. The accurate machine-tools of Whitworth and his contemporaries had been produced mainly to make other machines. The range of these tools was soon to be enormously extended by the cheapening of steel, following the introduction of Bessemer's converter and Siemens's open-hearth process in 1856. From the time of the Great Exhibition, machine-tools began to be sold to manufacturers in many industries, and the way was opened to mass-production of consumer goods far beyond the field of textiles.

It is easy to slip into the use of the term 'mass-production' without realizing how revolutionary a departure in manufacture it represented. Mass-production is the greatest contribution of America to the development of technology. 'Detroit automation' is in direct line of descent from Henry Ford's Model T, the very symbol and embodiment of the American tradition, and, farther back, from Eli Whitney's small-arms factory in Connecticut. By his invention of the cotton gin in 1793, which led to a great increase in the size of cotton plantations, Whitney had already introduced a device which affected directly the lives of every man and woman, black and white, in the Southern States, and ultimately, through the slavery question and the Civil War, the whole of the North as well. Through the application of the 'American system', as it came to be known later in England, Whitney's genius made a second great contribution to technology. By this system, components of articles were produced with such precision that complete interchangeability of parts was made possible. The great accuracy of the new machine-tools, together with the 'American system' of manufacture, provided the essential basis for the mass-production of goods to cope with the tremendous growth of the American domestic market. The sewing-machines of Elias Howe and Isaac Singer were typical examples of early mass-production in the United States. By 1860 Singer's European agencies were selling more sewing-machines on this side of the Atlantic than three thousand salesmen were able to sell in the American domestic market.

Industrialization in America could not have proceeded as rapidly as it did without a widespread network of railways based on imports of British locomotives and rails. Once under way its progress was greatly accelerated by the Civil War. The Macedonian phalanx and the Roman legion, the bowmen of England and Cromwell's Ironsides, each formed a decisive contribution to the technology of warfare, but in the American Civil War, for the first time, the technological resources of a whole nation were ultimately mobilized to overwhelm an opponent. There was mass-production of weapons and ammunition, of uniforms and boots: canned food was supplied to armies transported for the first time by rail. In a famous dispatch to Lincoln in 1862, John Ericsson, who had designed the floating armoured battery *Monitor*, wrote: 'The time has come, Mr. President, when our cause will have to be sustained not by numbers, but by superior weapons. By a proper application of mechanical devices alone will you be able with absolute certainty to destroy the enemies of the Union. Such is the inferiority of the Southern States in a mechanical point of view, that it is susceptible of demonstration that, if you apply our mechanical resources to the fullest extent, you can destroy the enemy without enlisting another man.'

While the contribution made by the export of British railway equipment to the development of the United States brought wealth to British manufacturers, it had highly adverse consequences for British agriculture. American grain became cheap: as the railways expanded westwards and the vast prairie lands came under the plough, the use of agricultural machinery mitigated the shortage of labour and made arable farming profitable. Corn could be brought cheaply to America's eastern exporting seaboard. In the 1870s the improvement of the marine steam-engine permitted an increase in the size of transatlantic grain cargoes, and this was decisive in bringing ruin to the British farmer. Conversion to an industrial society was thenceforth inevitable in Britain.

The coming of the railway was to bring about important consequences in other lands. Two widely different examples must suffice, one from Asia, and one from Europe. In India the beginning of a railway network brought to Hindus the fear of a mixing of castes during travel and was a contributory factor to the outbreak of the Indian Mutiny. The present-day problem of assimilating

Eurasians into Indian or western culture is partly traceable to the coming of the railways: in the early days, the Indian railways were entirely manned by British technicians, many of whom married Indian women. In Germany the advent of the railway age resulted in the iron-ore deposits becoming, for the first time, economically linked with coal in that country. The era of 'blood and iron' was dawning. By 1866 Prussia had replaced Austria as leader of the German-speaking peoples. Four years later, a pretext had been found for war against France, and Bismarck's concept of a unified Germany had materialized. In achieving military victories the Prussian armies were considerably aided by their technological advantage in small-arms. An improved breech-loading rifle in the hands of the well trained Prussian soldier, combined with the efficiency of the Officer Corps and General Staff established by Scharnhorst and Gneisenau, proved too much for the armies of a still largely agricultural France.[1] Emergence of a united Germany and its acquisition by conquest of the low-grade phosphoric iron ores of Lorraine had a dominating significance in world events for the next three-quarters of a century. The Gilchrist and Thomas process, invented in England in 1879, permitted the first use of the iron ores of Lorraine and Luxemburg in the manufacture of steel. The new powerful and energetic Germany was not long in rivalling Britain's early lead in steel production. By 1895 the British output was surpassed by the German.

The rapid process of industrialization in Germany from 1870 onwards soon brought her up to and beyond the stage that Britain had taken about a century to reach. Germans have rightly a reputation for great organizing ability; they are systematic, painstaking, and ready to adopt what they admire. German banks modelled on the Péreires' *Crédit Mobilier*, the prototype of industrial banking, were efficiently organized to finance industry. Like many late starters, German industrialists had the benefits of their predecessors' newest processes without being burdened with obsolete plant inherited from earlier stages of development. The relative shortage of workshops, as compared with Britain, made the foundation of institutions for technical education essential. This involved association of scientific theory and technological training, rather than purely practical instruction in workshop and factory, and this later brought handsome rewards as the alliance of science and industry became ever more important. Britain, moreover, had little to compare with France's *École Polytechnique* (1794) or, more important, with the German technical colleges which

---

[1] On the other hand, an article in the 'Journal of the Society of Arts', 1867, describes the French Chassepot gun as superior to the celebrated Prussian needle-gun, which only carried 400 metres: 'The soldiers of the Chasseurs-à-pied, being now accustomed to the gun, have obtained wonderful results with it, especially at 1,000 metres range....'

proliferated in the decade 1820–30 to receive the influx of students leaving von Humboldt's *Realschulen*, and which developed into the great *Technische Hochschulen* towards the end of the century (pp 786–8).

Although in certain fields of pure research British scientists made outstanding contributions, there was nothing to parallel the centres of chemical research presided over by Liebig, Wöhler, Bunsen, Kolbe, and Kekulé—nothing, that is, until Hofmann, himself a German and Liebig's pupil, became professor at the Royal College of Chemistry in London (p 269). Hofmann, in his 1875 Faraday Lecture, could say, with justification, of Liebig's laboratory in the small university of Giessen that it 'marks an epoch in the history of chemical science'. Until Ferdinand Hurter, a Swiss trained by Bunsen at Heidelberg, founded at Widnes in 1892 the laboratory that was to bear his name, there was no organized industrial chemical research laboratory in Britain, if one excludes the modest laboratory established by Alfred Nobel in his explosives factory at Ardeer about 1873. In the United States a comparable trend can be discerned: the chemical firm of E. I. duPont de Nemours had been in existence for exactly one century before it founded its first formal research venture in 1902, and yet Éleuthère Irénée, the founder of the company, had himself been the pupil of Lavoisier, a principal progenitor of quantitative chemistry.

Wissenschaft, the systematic organization of every branch of human knowledge, was a peculiarly German concept. In Britain, Oxford and Cambridge, unlike University College, London, ignored the implications of their right to be called universities by not offering, until 1850 and 1851, formal facilities for the study of natural science. Equally, the English public and grammar schools, largely modelling themselves on Arnold's practice at Rugby, placed primary emphasis on teaching the humanities (pp 784, 792). Arnold's aim, and that of his imitators, was to produce in the sons of manufacturers, merchants, and farmers the qualities of a 'Christian Gentleman' who would take his place in that rising professional class which was needed to administer the complex structure of an industrialized nation and its colonial Empire. A bias remained against industry and trade, a bias that derived from the Platonic tradition which regarded money, and mechanical labour, as vulgar and degrading. The public school system, while producing first-class administrators, produced also an educational climate unfavourable to industrial advance. The second and third generations in manufacturing families were not always able or willing to maintain the single-minded drive of their fathers and grandfathers, preferring to devote themselves to public life or to establishing a position in society. Energy which might have gone into new ventures was diverted into more socially acceptable channels. In the United

States there was no such taboo on a career in industry or commerce; in Germany, owing to an implacably rigid caste system, the temptation to forsake industry and trade for loftier positions in the social hierarchy could not arise. As a result, industry in these latter countries was constantly being enriched by a much larger proportion of energetic and talented men than found their way into British industry.

During the closing twenty-five years of last century the technological initiative in Europe passed to Germany. There is reason to ascribe the ascendancy of Germany in large measure to the consequences of her educational system. The United Kingdom, on the other hand, was by then lagging technologically, especially in the newer fields of electrical engineering, organic chemical manufacture (particularly of dyestuffs), and the motor-car industry. The leading makes of motor-car in the 1890s were German, French, and American. On the other hand, there were at least two British inventions of major technical importance: Parsons's steam turbine and Dunlop's pneumatic tyre. Politically, at that time, German progress in arms manufacture—typified by the mighty Krupp works and great naval yards—seemed the most serious consequence of her industrial expansion. A new warship with a more powerful broadside could make a rival fleet obsolete overnight—a lesson the Confederate ship *Merrimac* had first demonstrated when she broke the Union blockade at Hampton Roads in 1862. The numerical superiority in ships that Britain had long enjoyed ceased to have primary importance.

To sum up, the second half of the nineteenth century saw the maturing of industrialization. Mass-production had made consumer goods cheap and universal; it had also become possible to clothe and equip armies on an unprecedented scale. Increased organization of research and production in industry, based in Germany at least on sound technical education, was paralleled by more systematic public administration. Urbanization proceeded apace: in both Britain and Germany by 1900 the urban exceeded the rural population, while in the United States the migration to the cities became, after 1890, when the westward drive had lost its force, the dominant feature of population movements.

IV. POPULATION INCREASES

About the middle of the eighteenth century, the population of the countries of western Europe and North America began to show remarkable increases. The statistics before 1800 are unreliable, but from the beginning of the nineteenth century it is possible to form an accurate assessment of the rate of growth. If 1800 is taken as the index year (100) the following table indicates the changes that took place:

Year	United Kingdom	France	Holland	Belgium	Spain	Switzer-land	United States of America
1800	100	100	100	100	100	100	100
1850	261	130	141	147	125	133	438
1900	395	142	236	223	157	183	1434
1950	507	152	459	287	233	261	2843

In North America, the increase was due initially to the greatly accelerated immigrations from Europe; in the Old World, the reasons for the substantial increase in the majority of western European countries and for the contrastingly slow rate of increase in France are less obvious and still not wholly clear.

In the United Kingdom contemporary opinion, officially expressed in the preface to the 1831 census report, ascribed the increase directly to the new factory system which was thought to encourage early marriage by providing opportunities for the lucrative employment of children, especially in textile manufacture. The astonishing increases in the population of some of the spinning towns, which were the largest employers of child labour, lent plausibility to this view. Oldham, with a population of some three or four hundred in 1760, had a population of 21 000 in 1801, and 38 000 twenty years later. During the same twenty-year period the number of Bolton's inhabitants increased from 29 000 to 50 000. Payments from the rates to supplement wages, following the practice begun by the Speenhamland magistrates in 1795, were also supposed to have had a contributory effect in promoting growth of population.

The increase in population, in Britain at least, was thus unequivocally attributed in the main to the impact of textile technology. But a critical study of the available statistics seems to indicate that, from about 1750, the birth-rate in the United Kingdom and in the countries of western Europe, excluding France, remained relatively stable until the 1870s, when a decline began. The striking increase in population appears to have been due to a fall in the death-rate as a result of greatly improved public health. Technology was indeed responsible for the increase in population, but it was the technology not of the textile industry but of medical practice.

In France exceptional, but not unique, conditions seem to have prevailed: a decline in the birth-rate is traceable from the end of the eighteenth century, and was due, as far as can be judged, to a deliberate policy to limit the size of families. The security of the peasant family—and the economy of France remained predominantly agricultural—was threatened if the limited amount of land had to be split into many portions. In fear of this, legislation was introduced to limit testamentary freedom according to the number of children. Although a Catholic country, France since the Revolution developed a tradition of free thought which could countenance the widespread practice of family limitation. In Britain, on the other hand, there were no such barriers to slow down the normal birth-rate. The apprentice system was yielding to factory working, with the result that early marriage tended to become more common. In this sense, industrial conditions, while not stimulating the birth-rate, at least created conditions in which no deliberate attempt was made to limit the size of families. So much might be claimed for the major part of the nineteenth century, but from the 1870s in the more highly industrialized countries of western Europe and in the United States there was a sharp decline in the birth-rate. For economic and social reasons, not least the growing emancipation of women, the small family became the rule.

For the majority of the period, changes in the birth-rate had much less significance than the remarkable decrease in the death-rate, especially that of infants. Improvement in medical practice had its origin in the eighteenth century, and physicians became recognized as members of a profession with a growing corpus of scientific and practical knowledge to apply in their calling. Hospitals were founded in increasing numbers not only for the treatment of illness and disease but for childbirth. Vaccination and inoculation, anaesthetics and antiseptics, all contributed to reduce the rate of mortality, while the reforming zeal and driving force of Elizabeth Fry and Florence Nightingale helped to create eventually a nursing profession to replace the often hazardous ministrations of contemporary Mrs Gamps. No less important was the improvement in sanitary conditions and personal hygiene initiated by Sir Edwin Chadwick.

Colonel Coote-Manningham's 'Regulations for the Rifle Corps', published in 1800, laid down: 'in the soldier's dressing well and with smartness, the principal object is first cleanliness (and cleanliness is at all times health), and a certain degree of self-pride. . . .' No doubt Robert Jackson was thinking of these improvements when he wrote in 1804, 'A soldier, until lately, notwithstanding he might be incrusted from head to foot, was said to be clean if his small-clothes and facings were covered with pipe-clay, and the head was said to be dressed, if the hair was matted with a paste of grease and flour' [2]. Coote-Manningham's regulations, based on comradeship, humanity, and common sense, reflected the teaching of Sir John Moore,[1] and were astonishingly far in advance of contemporary military doctrine, which relied heavily on flogging and hanging to

[1] It is interesting to note that as a young man Sir John Moore had been employed in the Gordons' cudbear factory which George Macintosh, his aunt's husband, had taken over [3].

instil discipline. It was not, however, until the work of Pasteur in the later 1860s that the true relationship between dirt and disease began to be more fully understood. In the meantime, availability of cheap cotton clothes and soap led to greater cleanliness and reduced infection. Improved public water-supplies greatly reduced the incidence of such deadly diseases as cholera and typhoid.

V. POPULATION MOVEMENTS

It is now necessary to examine some of the causes leading to the extensive population movements of the nineteenth century, which themselves provided in part the basis of local population increases. Population movements resulting from religious or political persecution lie outside our range. Such migrants sought greater freedom and, if anything, they influenced rather than were influenced by technological advances: there must be few countries that have not gained immeasurably from opening their gates to the refugee.

The emigration resulting from simple famine in Ireland is more relevant to our theme. Before the end of the eighteenth century the Irish were making the short sea crossing to Liverpool because of the immediate prospect of work in the cotton-mills of Lancashire or as 'navigators' on the construction of the growing system of canals. In the terrible years that followed the famine of 1846, when nearly 200 000 Irishmen annually left their country, the increase in transatlantic shipping brought the limitless labour market of the United States within reach. After the American Civil War, more Irishmen left home to build the Union Pacific railroad, joined by a golden spike to the track of the Central Pacific, for which Chinese coolies provided the labour force. It was said that the eastern half of the transcontinental line was built on whiskey and the western half on tea.

There were other immigrant movements into the New World which are of more direct interest to the student of the history of technology. These might be called 'voluntary' and 'involuntary' immigrations; the first were stimulated by the technical opportunities offered by new territories; the second resulted sometimes from the collapse of domestic industries, as a consequence of technological change, and sometimes from sheer pressure of population. Even here there is not always a clear-cut distinction. Just as the motives of those who emigrate from Britain today cannot with certainty be ascribed to the attractions of undeveloped territories or to dissatisfaction with conditions at home, so the motives of the Cornish miners who emigrated may have been mixed. They, like countless others, were undoubtedly attracted by the discovery of gold in California in 1849. So pronounced was the skill of these 'Cousin Jacks', as the Cornishmen were known in the United States, that their prowess was recorded in song by the 'forty-niners':

> *They come from distant Tombstone*
> *And Virginia on the hill,*
> *You ne'er can beat a Cousin Jack*
> *For hammering on the drill.*
>
> *Amongst you other Irishmen*
> *Do justice if you can,*
> *For there's none that can compete*
> *With the good old Cornishman.*

On the other hand, the movement of iron puddlers from south Wales to Germany and Sweden took place, surprisingly enough, mainly in the second quarter of the nineteenth century, when their skill was still much in demand in the United Kingdom. In contrast, the collapse of the kelping industry in the Celtic fringe of the British Isles, due to the manufacture of synthetic alkali from salt, brought additional hardship in an already precarious economy. Those of the German hand-spinners ruined by competition from English mill yarn who did not die in the years of bad harvest and poor trade before 1848 sought their future in the United States. The button-makers of Dorset—at Shaftesbury alone there were some 4000 women and children in that trade in 1793—flourished until John Aston's button-making machine drove the hand-made horn button from the market. For a time, conditions of near-starvation prevailed in Shaftesbury until the local landed families helped several hundreds to emigrate to America and Australia. Henry Bellairs, sailor, soldier, and priest,[1] financed the emigration to New Zealand of a large number of his parishioners at Bedworth in Warwickshire when their lace-making could no longer support them. When the depression in the silk trade hit the ribbon weavers of neighbouring Coventry, the population of the town dropped by 7 per cent between 1861 and 1871; in that city, however, many stayed to work in the new light-engineering industries, which have flourished there ever since.

Emigration to the New World was both numerically and historically the most significant of the population shifts in this period. Absence of political and religious prejudice, and the freedom of a society much less encumbered with class distinctions, where the successful entrepreneur was an object of admiration rather than deprecation, all added, then as now, to the attraction of the United States for the emigrant. The natural resources and the sheer vastness of the country kindled the imagination of all those who had energy and ingenuity to offer.

---

[1] He had the unusual distinction of fighting as a 'first-class volunteer' at Trafalgar at the age of fifteen, obtaining a commission in the Fifteenth Light Dragoons, and subsequently taking Holy orders.

VI. SPREAD OF TECHNOLOGY BEYOND EUROPE

The spread of technology in North America was stimulated by, and helped to stimulate, this movement. America was a fertile field for the development of the use of machinery. The working population was thinly spread over a large area and the shortage of labour was thus a perpetual problem. It is not surprising that the advent of machinery was as welcome to Americans as it was at first feared and resisted by certain sections of the workers in crowded Britain. The receptiveness of the American mind to technological innovation provided an ideal climate for its rapid development. To this day, the American workman likes machinery for its own sake, while the Englishman, with an atavistic but suppressed Luddism, is apt to fear its continuing advance. This is not to suggest that it was left solely to the nineteenth-century immigrants to bring about rapid technological expansion in the United States. Although this expansion was based on the conquest of great distances by the building of the railroads, on the British pattern and with British equipment, there was, as we have seen, a strong tradition of native talent handed down from earlier generations of immigrants. This indigenous mechanical trend had made the United States substantial exporters of pig iron to the United Kingdom from 1750, and brought American shipbuilding to its full flowering in the construction of the clippers which almost monopolized the carriage of certain commodities, like tea, even when steam was replacing sail. American-built locomotives in the 1840s began to compete in export markets with those of British manufacture.

The growing industrialization of the north-eastern States presented a sharp contrast to the agrarian economy of the South, where wealth was concentrated in 'King Cotton'. The specific causes of the Civil War were complex; but whatever they were, the disparity of the two economies was a potential source of conflict. The maintenance of slave labour was considered to be essential to the economy of the Confederate States, and they were prepared to secede rather than countenance their own ruin. Nearly four grim years of civil war were necessary to decide the issue between the interests of the rural South and those of the industrial North.

While, in the 1860s, at a critical phase in technological history, the Negroes of the southern American States found themselves the centre of a conflict between two economies, their African cousins were destined in more recent times to leap straight from stone age techniques to those of modern industrialism. The demand for raw materials stimulated the growth of underdeveloped territories. Mining and quarrying techniques found their way to the phosphate rock deposits in the deserts of north Africa, and exploitation of the mineral wealth of South

Africa soon gave Johannesburg and Kimberley the air of industrial towns, complete with slum districts. Palm oil from West Africa for the soap industry, rubber from Brazil and later Malaya, and petroleum from the desert, brought to primitive peoples their first contacts with the mechanized civilization of the west. It was not only the technology of extractive industries that penetrated to the less developed areas of the world. In a later era, Soviet Russia was to rely extensively on the technology of the west to implement a series of five-year plans. Lenin left the world in no doubt as to the importance he attached to technological development by propounding in his report to the Eighth All-Russian Congress of Soviets the equation 'Electrification plus Soviet power equals Communism'. In Japan also, western manufacturing techniques were rapidly assimilated, so that by 1914 Japan had become a net exporter of textiles. In the long run, the disappearance of traditional markets because of the rise of indigenous domestic manufacture was an inevitable consequence of technological progress, but at the same time it tended to force the older manufacturing countries to apply their technical inventiveness and enterprise to new fields.

VII. EFFECTS OF TECHNOLOGY ON THE CONDITION OF THE PEOPLE

So far we have considered the general impact of technology upon the social structure of western European countries and of North America. Let us now examine its effect on the day-by-day life of the people. Writers on the Industrial Revolution in the United Kingdom in the nineteenth century have either, like Andrew Ure, tended to see it as the dawn of the millennium or, like Friedrich Engels, as bringing a nightmare of squalor and degradation which could end only in violent revolution.

It cannot be doubted that Engels's picture in 'Conditions of the Working Class in England in 1844' has at least partial truth. 'More filth, worse physical suffering and moral disorder than Howard described [in his report on English prisons] . . . are to be found amongst the cellar population of the working people of Liverpool, Manchester, or Leeds and in large portions of the Metropolis.' These are Chadwick's words from his 'Report on the Sanitary Conditions of the Labouring Population' published three years before the appearance of Engels s book. But Engels was concerned to produce a deliberately political tract and this precludes its acceptance as entirely reliable evidence.

The influx of labour, whether from the English countryside or from Ireland, into unplanned new towns at a time when administration had not effectively caught up with industrialization, resulted in appalling housing and sanitary conditions. The Prince Consort was himself interested enough in the problem to design a model home for working-class families: it was built to hold four families, and can still be seen in Kennington Park, where it was re-erected after the 1851 Exhibition. But the blame for bad housing should not be laid exclusively on the Industrial Revolution: we have Chadwick's testimony that rural housing conditions were no better than those in the industrial towns.

It would be a mistake also to attribute exclusively to the Industrial Revolution all the horrors connected with the employment of women and children in mines and factories at this time. No exaggeration of the conditions is needed to make them seem intolerable today: but the charge—not so much of wilful cruelty as of callous indifference—could more justly be levied against contemporary society as a whole, and its tolerance of other abuses no less reprehensible, than against the class of industrial employers. Householders had employed little boys to sweep chimneys since the beginning of the eighteenth century, while Defoe in 1724 described with admiration the use of child-labour in the homes of Yorkshire clothiers: 'scarce any Thing above four Years old, but its Hands were sufficient for its own Support.' The employment of children in agriculture and at sea was an established commonplace, and the system of apprenticeships had long been open to abuse.

What to our age appear harrowing conditions of child-labour were common long before the factories were built. The particular effect of the Industrial Revolution was to destroy the immediate personal relationship between employer and employed and to substitute the factory overlooker for the master himself. It thus becomes a question whether personal or impersonal cruelty was the greater evil. By no means all employers were equally guilty of inhumanity. It is proper, for example, to recall the Gregs' model mill at Styal, which employed seventy to eighty workhouse children from Liverpool. The children were well looked after, and their education, which included drawing and singing, was supervised by the Gregs themselves. Yet even at Styal the working hours were over twelve a day, including Saturdays.

Many of those employers who were genuinely interested in their workpeople, and who made serious efforts to improve working conditions, were to be found amongst the Quakers and other nonconformist bodies. Barred by the Test Acts from the English universities and from government office, the Dissenters found scope for their talent and energy in industry and commerce. More important, they constituted the better-educated section of the middle class. A letter by William Penn to his wife and children attests the importance that the Quakers always attached to education, and especially to technological education. He wrote in 1682: 'For their learning be liberal . . . but let it be useful knowledge, such as is consistent with Truth and Godliness. . . . I recommend the useful parts of mathematics, as building houses or ships, measuring, surveying, dialing, navigation; but agriculture is especially in my eye.' Later generations of Quakers, while recognizing the importance of education, concentrated less on husbandry and more on manufacturing, merchanting, and banking. The Darbys and the Reynolds's at Coalbrookdale built houses and schools on the works estate, a tradition upheld in recent times by the Cadburys at Bournville and the Rowntrees at York. Personal example also played its part: Alexander Chance cured drunkenness in his Oldbury chemical works by founding a temperance club and himself signing the pledge. In contrast to the education and religious background of the Quakers and nonconformists, Robert Owen, one of the most celebrated of all enlightened employers, left school at the age of nine and subscribed to no specifically Christian principles. In Owen's New Lanark mill, hundreds of children, none under the age of ten, were employed in humane and enlightened conditions.

Though poverty was no new phenomenon, the growth of population in urban districts made it more glaringly obvious. Benjamin Thompson (Count Rumford) was one who received wide recognition for his philanthropic work. In his capacity as administrator and adviser to the Elector of Bavaria, he had set up in Munich 'houses of industry' in an attempt to cope with the problem of mendicancy. Rumford soup-kitchens equipped with Rumford boilers and Rumford roasters were widely used. Such were his extraordinary services to the poor that he was elected on 24 February 1797 to the general committee of the Society for Bettering the Condition and Increasing the Comforts of the Poor, and to life membership. This Society was a philanthropic organization founded the previous year by Sir Thomas Bernard, William Wilberforce, and Edward James Eliot, under the presidency of the Bishop of Durham and the patronage of the King. Its general committee included no fewer than twenty-one Members of Parliament. Its importance lies in its systematic attempt to impart practical information for the benefit of the poor. In his preliminary address to the public, Sir Thomas Bernard said: 'Let us therefore make the enquiry into all that concerns the POOR, and the promotion of their happiness, a SCIENCE. . . .' The diversity of the Society's interests is revealed in its published reports: 'Dr. Haygarth's rules to prevent infectious fevers' are found next to 'Mr. Millington's letter on a mode of preserving potatoes'. An early statistical approach is clearly in evidence from the wish of some of the committee to visit the house of every individual who received the benefit of a charity in Spitalfields, 'to inquire into circumstances and situation and to record each particular case. This, it was presumed, might contain a valuable body of information relative to the situation of the poor'.

In 1799, having conferred with a committee of the Society, Rumford founded the Royal Institution with the object, among others, of directing 'itself to the improvement of the MEANS OF INDUSTRY AND OF DOMESTIC COMFORT AMONG THE POOR'. Rumford's great interest in fuel efficiency is illustrated by the intention to exhibit models 'of improved fireplaces and kitchens, and of flues and louvres for supplying rooms either with tepid or fresh air; so as to produce a considerable saving in the quantity of food and fuel consumed, either in cottages, or in public establishments'.

Although the later development of the Royal Institution deviated from the original conception, its foundation was symptomatic of the growth of planned philanthropy and humanitarianism which became a marked feature of nineteenth-century life.

The reforms in military service under Sir John Moore's influence at Shorncliffe have already been noted. In 1806 Sir Samuel Romilly began his crusade to reform the criminal law of England, under which a very large number of offences were punishable by death. Although at the time his endeavours were largely frustrated, they demonstrated to a wide public the urgent need for a revision of the penal code, which was ultimately brought about. In general, philanthropy and social reform were prompted by the enthusiasm of private individuals; it took time for the public conscience to be stirred to action by feelings of humanity.[1] Death, especially the death of young children, was a familiar event in the families of rich and poor alike, and, if it happened in rather more unpleasant circumstances in the families of the factory worker or miner, comfort was to be gained from the strongly evangelical thought of the time that suffering was good for the soul, especially the soul of the poor. The passing of Lord Shaftesbury's Mines Act in 1842 and of a series of Factory Acts from 1802 onwards helped to prevent some of the worst abuses.

Outside the factories, bad working conditions were untouched by legislation. Thomas Hood made it his vocation to plead the cause of the young girls employed in the dressmakers' and milliners' establishments of London: his 'Song of the Shirt' first appeared anonymously in 'Punch' in 1843. The picture it gave was not overdrawn. On Mary Anne Walkley, aged 20, employed by a court dressmaker, the jury returned a verdict 'that the deceased died of apoplexy; but that there is too much reason to fear that her death was accelerated by working long hours in a crowded workroom, and sleeping in a close, badly ventilated bedroom'.

---

[1] The high degree of indifference to death and injury in road-accidents in the twentieth century serves as a reminder that the public conscience, in comparable circumstances, is not always more acute now than it was formerly.

In the end it was not legislation that improved the lot of the seamstress but the mass-produced sewing-machine from the United States.

New industries brought new health hazards; typhus, already known by a variety of names, appeared as 'factory fever' and 'prison fever'. We now know it to be spread by lice. Industrial diseases previously unknown, such as grinders' asthma amongst the Sheffield cutlers and the dreaded phosphorus necrosis of the jaw in the match industry, took their toll. Improvements in the technology of phosphorus manufacture eventually reduced the incidence of the latter ('phossy jaw'). In the 1890s, Albright & Wilson, a company with strong Quaker ties, built a dental clinic, and regular dental treatment for their operatives was introduced as a precaution against the disease. Women and children employed in the textile factories often suffered from bone malformation as a result of the unsuitable design of textile machinery. On the other hand, the concentration of free chlorine in the Widnes atmosphere was commonly believed to have given the town, on the whole, a good health record, even if the hydrochloric acid vapour destroyed vegetation and rotted the men's teeth.

To combat other occupational risks, science and technology were ultimately summoned to the rescue. Sir Humphry Davy, among others, was urged to design a safety lamp for miners. In an attempt to strike at the roots of the problem of danger from mine gases, mechanical fans were introduced to give improved ventilation. William Bickford of Tuckingmill had long deplored the terrible frequency of fatal explosions in the Cornish tin-mines due to primitive methods of blasting. His invention of the safety fuse was inspired by humanitarian feelings. It was left to his son-in-law, George Smith, and partner, Thomas Davey, to develop the invention commercially throughout the world. Processes and machinery were increasingly adapted to give safer working conditions. Nasmyth, for example, introduced a simple wormwheel mechanism on his foundry ladle to save his men from the burns for which the old equipment was frequently responsible. The introduction of gas-lighting into Phillips & Lee's cotton-mill at Salford, however, was a mixed blessing for the workers: while it lowered the risk of fires caused by candle-flames, it also effectively lengthened the hours of an already long working day.

Apart from its application in these humanitarian attempts to increase the safety of labour, technology helped to relieve its drudgery. New methods of producing steel replaced the arduous task of puddling iron. Mechanical stokers lightened the burden of manual fuelling, and the use of sewing machinery throughout the clothing trade brought immeasurable relief to weary thousands. At the same time, the balance was partially redressed by new heavy and dangerous jobs. As Sir John Clapham puts it, 'an hour's work in the caissons [under raised atmospheric pressure], or on the cantilevers, of the Forth Bridge may well be called heavier than one put in under Rennie on Waterloo Bridge' [4].

In Britain the Factory Act of 1802 limited the working hours of pauper children, and that of 1819 of all children, employed in the cotton factories. The Act of 1850, by ordering that their work should cease at 2 p.m. on Saturdays, was a first step towards bringing the *semaine anglaise* to a large section of the British working population; by 1874 most factory day-workers were not working more than $56\frac{1}{2}$ hours a week. Nevertheless, shift-workers and those outside the scope of the Factory Acts continued to work much longer hours. Although, for example, Brunner, Mond & Company had put an end to the 12-hour shift for their chemical workers as early as 1889, the 84-hour week, especially in the iron and steel industry, was common up to the First World War.

It should be remembered that prosperity was intermittent: in many trades a period of enforced idleness through lack of work occurred in most years. While the shortening of the working day was brought into effect by legislation inspired by the demands of social justice, the possibility of shorter working hours was mainly a result of technological developments which greatly increased the distributable wealth of industrial countries.

The gradual improvement in industrial working conditions in Britain did not include until as late as 1897 a compensation act for injuries to workmen, although the Employers' Liability Act of 1880 had gone some of the way. Over sixty years earlier, in America, those widowed or orphaned by an explosion at duPont's Eleutherian Mill had been pensioned for life. A week's holiday with pay, an extremely advanced step for industrial management to have taken in 1884, was instituted by Brunner, Mond & Company: it was made conditional on good time-keeping, but nearly all the workers qualified year after year.

These were undoubted gains, but some of them were, in the jargon of today, 'fringe benefits'. What of real wages? This is a complex question; its technical difficulties must keep it within the province of the economic historian. Regional variations, among other factors, make generalizations misleading: for example, in the north of England, where there was stronger competition from the factories for labour, agricultural wages tended to be higher than in the south. Widespread employment of women and children and the practice of payment in kind also confuse the issue by making it virtually impossible to estimate family incomes.

Some general conclusions on wages can, however, be drawn. Of the period up to the 1840s Woodward writes: 'the average wage-earner in employment could live a little better than he had been able to live during the war period, and better, in most years, after 1815 than his father and grandfather had lived in the years of peace. On the other hand, in the new industries he was more subject to unemployment, and if he were one of the thousands of handloom-weavers of 1840 his fate was harsh beyond tears' [5]. In the period of 1850–75 wages did not quite keep pace with the rise in the cost of living, but 'by 1870 most working-class families were absolutely, as well as relatively, better off by about ten per cent than in 1850' [6]. From 1850 there was also a decrease in the number of paupers and a rise in savings. From 1873 prices fell more rapidly than wages, so that the standard of living of the working population in that period steadily improved.

The indexes on which most calculations of real wages are based take account of an improvement in dietary standards. Such improvement was partially due to the analytical work of Arthur Hassall, following the trail blazed by the unfortunate Friedrich Accum. Accum's 'Treatise on the Adulteration of Food and Culinary Poisons' (1820) made him powerful enemies, especially among the brewers; he fled the country to avoid a trumped-up charge of mutilating books in the Royal Institution, of which he was librarian. Until the middle of the century tradesmen had with impunity adulterated bread with alum, sold rancid bacon after first treating it with boric acid, and coloured sugar confectionery with lead chromate or gamboge. All these and other malpractices revealed by Hassall's investigations were fearlessly published by 'The Lancet' Analytical Sanitary Commission, whose work led to the Adulteration of Food and Drink Act of 1860.

The conditions of the working people improved in other ways. The tax on soap was abolished in 1853: consumption per head in Britain rose steadily from 3·6 lb per annum in 1801, to 8 lb per annum in 1861; by 1891 it had nearly doubled again [7]. Cotton garments were within reach even of the poorest. Proper attention was at last paid to sanitation; water-supplies were improved by the use of cast iron water mains; the streets became cleaner. Sewage was dealt with, but a cholera epidemic was needed to put a public health act in the Statute Book for the first time in 1848.

The working man and his family began to accumulate possessions. Cutlery, table-ware, and cooking utensils were turned out cheaply and in large numbers. Iron bedsteads, proof against the ubiquitous bed-bug, became almost universal. The Staffordshire potteries produced cheap decorative ware which has not, even today, lost its attraction. Many households could afford to buy brightly glazed figurines of the Queen and her Consort, who was himself a most earnest devotee of the new technologies. New methods of printing brought reproductions of popular pictures into every home; Landseer's 'Highland Cattle' cast their ruminative glance into many front parlours.

The alteration in working hours and in the burden of work brought time for leisure at the end of the day, and the day itself was extended by gas-lighting and, towards the end of the century, by electricity. The leisure pursuits of the upper classes were relatively untouched by the progress of technological development, except that the railways had brought new accessibility to their country houses. A whole new pattern of life, however, lay before the working man and his family. There was an increase in literacy, which became almost universal when Forster's Elementary Education Act of 1870 made education in England compulsory. Abolition of the newspaper tax in 1855 was followed by the abolition of the duty on paper in 1861. Newnes, for example, found a ready public for 'Tit Bits' in 1880: this was the beginning of mass journalism. Public libraries were established in England by an Act of 1850, but they were limited to boroughs of more than 10 000 people, a limitation removed by an Act of 1892. The Local Government Act of 1894 made it possible for even remote rural parishes to have a public library.

A marked change in the social *mores* of the lower classes in England had become manifest by the mid-century. In 1852, a Mr Oliviera remarked to a meeting summoned to prevent the demolition of the Crystal Palace: 'Let anyone observe the different aspect of the character of the population to what it was twenty years ago. We all know, twenty years ago, if you admitted some of these unfortunate people in a public place, there would be drunkenness, impropriety and misconduct.' These evils persisted, but the Victorian emphasis on sobriety and decorum, endorsed by legislation, was effective at all levels of society.

The 1851 Exhibition led both to the introduction of the double-decker bus and the day excursion. The railways offered special tickets to London at cheap rates. On 14 June 1851 Queen Victoria recorded in her journal: 'Quite forgot to mention that on the morning of the 12th we saw 3 whole parishes Crowhurst, Linchfield and Langford, from Kent and Surrey (800 in number) walking in procession 2 and 2, the men in smock frocks, with their wives looking so nice. It seems that they subscribed to come to London, by the advice of the clergyman, to see the Exhibition, it only costing them 2s and 6d.' Day trips to Windermere and Llandudno from the industrial towns of the north and midlands became common: Blackpool achieved sufficient importance to be made a borough in 1876. To the elegant watering-places of the eighteenth century were added numerous popular seaside resorts. Tourism abroad, once the preserve of the aristocracy, became open to the middle classes, though no one could say with any conviction that the intermingling of nations was leading to greater international friendship.

VIII. TECHNOLOGY AND THE ARTS

The drab ugliness of *laissez-faire* industrial development produced among painters a general revulsion from the contemporary scene. This disenchantment helped to accentuate an unfortunate trend, begun in the eighteenth century, which distinguished certain arts as 'fine arts' and confined them to the Academy and Salon. The Pre-Raphaelites escaped into an imaginary world of the past where they could forget the soot and grime of contemporary England and from which they emerged from time to time to execute commissions for portraits from the wealthy middle class. Art became divorced from life; it was left to the great illustrators and poster artists, given scope by improved methods of printing and engraving, to redress the balance. Daumier and Doré, Cruickshank and the masterly 'Punch' artists, portrayed the contemporary social scene, while the lithographed masterpieces of Toulouse-Lautrec and his contemporaries reached a vast new public from the hoardings of Paris. The growing literacy of the masses had inaugurated the era of the widespread advertisement.

The invention of the camera and photographic plate, and their use in the hands of early masters like Fox Talbot, seemed to some people to presage the end of the artist as portrait and landscape painter. The sight of a daguerreotype moved Elizabeth Barrett Browning to write to Miss Mitford in 1843: 'the fact of *the very shadow of the person* lying there fixed for ever! It is the very sanctification of portraits, I think.' But photography proved salutary in its effect. It stimulated painters to a new creativeness. In France the Impressionists experimented with light and colour to catch, as with the camera, the fleeting image on the retina and preserve it for all time. Photography brought about a movement away from purely representational art: interest in abstract design was to steer the pictorial and plastic arts into new creative directions.

Musicians, too, felt the impact of mechanical invention. Manufacture of the barrel-organ from the end of the eighteenth century and of the harmonium from 1840 brought about the downfall of the church orchestra in villages like Thomas Hardy's 'Mellstock', and with it went something of the corporate feeling that these orchestras brought to the life of church and parish. In compensation for this loss, some enjoyment was to be derived from the village and miners' bands whose brass instruments were now manufactured with a much greater range and accuracy. In middle-class homes pianos, produced in quantity, made the musical evening a universal entertainment until the sometimes exiguous sparks of amateur talent were extinguished by the gramophone and wireless.

If Dickens, Disraeli, Mrs Gaskell, George Eliot, and a few others are excepted, the majority of the nineteenth-century novelists, no less than the painters, averted their eyes from the industrial scene. The chairman of the Edinburgh Gas Light Company, Sir Walter Scott, chose to write historical novels. Trollope and Hardy set their characters in small country towns. For the same reason Thackeray preferred to write about an earlier period than his own. It seems hard to believe that the England of Jane Austen and that of H. G. Wells lie within the same hundred years.

The Gothic romanticism of Byron and Heine found its parallel in the architecture of the period. Consciously or unconsciously architects attempted to escape from industrialization. In particular they took refuge in the romantic and religious character of neo-Gothicism, which derived its inspiration from the supposed simplicity of life in the Middle Ages. A misconceived reverence for the piously or romantically beautiful encouraged them to disguise factories as Gothic cathedrals and railway stations as medieval strongholds. With a fine disregard for consistency, architects and decorators made full use of all the resources of the factories and services that their finished work was designed to conceal. Some architects and engineers, however, were quick to appreciate the potentialities of new structural materials for original work. Nash made effective use of cast iron columns in the Royal Pavilion at Brighton. Boulton & Watt's design for a seven-storey cotton-mill at Salford was extraordinarily bold for the year 1801. Followed seventy years later in direct line of succession by the load-bearing iron skeleton of Saulnier's chocolate factory at Noisiel-sur-Marne, it foreshadowed the steel skyscrapers of the 1880s built by the Chicago architects. Fontaine's Galérie d'Orléans in Paris and Paxton's Crystal Palace in England showed a wonderful grasp by their designers of the relation of materials to form.

In the main, despite the precept of Ruskin and the practice of William Morris, Art and Life, with capital letters, obstinately remained in separate compartments. Although Emil Rathenau, the creator of the *Allgemeine Elektrizitäts Gesellschaft*, employed an architect, Peter Behrens, to deal with all aspects of design from new plants to the company trade-mark, it was Behrens's pupil Walter Gropius who inaugurated a new epoch by founding the Weimar *Bauhaus* in 1919. In Gropius's own words, it was established to realize 'a modern architectonic art, which like human nature should be all-embracing in its scope' [8]. The influence of the *Bauhaus* not only did most to emancipate the whole field of design from traditions antedating the Industrial Revolution, but also to realize the full potentialities of materials and methods of production which the progress of technology put at the architect's disposal.

IX. POLITICAL AND PHILOSOPHICAL TRENDS

Harmony in the relations of employer to employed was one of the earliest casualties of the new machine age. Though it would be absurd to pretend that the dawn of the industrial era corrupted what had been an ideal relationship between master and man, the dislocation of an agricultural society brought problems and tensions between them that were new in character. The family, the basic unit of society, was first uprooted and then scattered. There was no immediate substitute for the local loyalties that had grown up over centuries. In the towns and cities men lost the sense of personal touch which they had had with those for whom they formerly worked in the villages and on the land. Men who had enjoyed the status and the skill of craftsmen found themselves forced into repetitive processes in mill or factory along with hundreds of others. A sense of 'belonging' was largely destroyed, and only restored in those works, like Nasmyth's foundry at Patricroft, where pride of craftsmanship was encouraged and an opportunity given for any man of ability to accept responsibility.

The chronic problem that the age of machinery posed was not so much the immediate impact of unemployment, though this was harsh enough for the handloom worker, but the failure of employers to recognize that their workmen were more than just so many 'hands'. Luddism was never more than a local problem, but the treatment of workers as chattels, much more than the actual suffering and hardship of early working conditions, left an indelible mark on our society that no amount of paternalistic welfare schemes could erase.

In the twentieth century the industrial psychologist has been invoked to demonstrate what the good employer, without analysis, grasped instinctively, namely that it was necessary to capture the workman's interest in the full implications of his job and to stimulate his sense of responsibility to his fellow men whether employer, work-mates, or the community at large. Now, in the mid-twentieth century, the increasing use of automatic processes once again brings the same problem into prominence. The social tensions arising from the resulting redeployment and retraining of labour constitute a major challenge to industry, and much attention has to be paid to the mental stresses and strains of the worker in those industries where the expenditure of purely physical human energy is reduced almost to disappearing point. Nineteenth-century employers, so far from meeting the challenge of machinery to the personality of the individual, scarcely even recognized it as a problem.

G. D. H. Cole has said with justification: 'the Industrial Revolution gave birth to the Labour movement' [9]. In England, Chartism, the protest of a 'lapsed peasant' society, gave way to a period of consolidation during which, in accepting industrialization, the movement made no attempt to reject capitalism as a system, until finally in the 1880s it became preoccupied with orthodox socialism. In all industrial countries a working-class emerged, possessing a sense of solidarity given to it by a common interest in improving its social and political condition.

Nevertheless, the antagonism between capital and labour was not the most important of the political conflicts stimulated directly or indirectly by the growth of technology. The fiasco of the Kennington meeting which ended when the Chartists trundled the Great National Petition to the House of Commons on the roofs of three hackney cabs was a poor flicker of the revolutionary flame that burnt in half the capitals of Europe in 1848. The explanation may be that continental revolutionary movements received strenuous bourgeois support, whereas in England the Reform Bill of 1832 had already recognized the claim of the middle class to a stake in the government of the country. On the continent the entrenched ruling class was assailed not only by discontented workers but by an educated middle class of university professors and bankers, merchants and manufacturers, made rich and potentially powerful by the growth of industry. This conflict thus had a far greater political significance than a direct issue between capital and labour. The later decline of German liberalism and the rise, in its place, of German nationalism—foreshadowed years before the rise of Prussia—was to have portentous consequences.

Liberal and radical thought was directed also against orthodox religion. In continental Europe the onslaught was conducted mainly in philosophical terms, though from it emerged in due course the 'scientific socialism' of Marx and Engels. In Britain, however, the conflict was more directly between science and religion, reaching its height in the Darwinian controversy. There was nothing new as such in the conflict of science and religion: what was new and remarkable was the informed interest in scientific matters taken by a wide public which, though powerfully influenced by the forces of orthodox religion, had become conditioned to the increasingly important part played by science and technology in their daily lives.

X. CONCLUSION

An attempt has been made here to examine the social consequences of the progress of technology in the years 1750–1900. Is there any conclusion that can be drawn from this survey? As the critics of Utilitarianism were quick to point out, there is an inherent difficulty in measuring pleasures and pains, either quantitatively or qualitatively. In that sense, it is pointless to ask the question whether the sum of human happiness was greater or less as a result of the invention of Arkwright's water-frame or Watt's steam-engine.

It is, however appropriate to point to some of the gains and losses in terms of human happiness. High on the debit side must be placed the loss of that peacefulness of mind which the gentle and unaltering rhythm of country life can bring. With that loss must be set the irretrievable destruction of much of the beauty of the countryside. But the very remoteness of country places imposed its own limitations. The accessibility conferred by railways and improved roads widened the frontiers of the mind by bringing to many something better in the way of education than the village school could offer. The Industrial Revolution brought poverty and misery to many who could not adapt themselves to technical change, but to many more it gave a higher standard of living than any agricultural economy could have supported. If the factories for a time brought cruel and degrading conditions to the workers, especially to the women and children, the public conscience at last was shocked into remedying some of those malpractices, which could themselves be traced to an era before 1750. Autocratic exploitation of labour by employers who had lost all personal touch with their men had in the end the salutary effect of creating an organized working class with the proper ambition of improving their conditions and securing representation in the affairs of the nation. The substitution of the concept of class for the rigid caste system of 'orders and degrees', where every man knew his place and stayed in it, tended to give the new social structure a much greater stability.

To ask the question whether the effects of the revolution in technology were or were not socially beneficial is, then, inappropriate. Moreover, it seems to miss a central feature of the Industrial Revolution, that it was, and indeed continues to be, a revolution in power, but not only in the power of the machine. It revolutionized the power of the middle-class employer and the power of labour, the economic power of nations and the power of armaments. But power in itself is neither good nor evil: in the last analysis, its uses are subject to man's good sense or his stupidity. If this is a truism, it is one that man, in the age of nuclear energy, can scarcely afford to ignore.

REFERENCES

[1] BUCHER, L. 'Kulturhistorische Skizzen aus der Industrieausstellung aller Völker', pp. 146 ff. Frankfurt a. M. 1851. (Quoted in S. GIEDION. 'Space, Time, and Architecture', p. 259 n. Harvard University Press, Cambridge, Mass. 1947.)
[2] JACKSON, R. 'A Systematic View of the Formation, Discipline, and Economy of Armies', p. 262. London. 1804.

[3] HARDIE, D. W. F. "The Macintoshes and the Origins of the Chemical Industry" (Hurter Memorial Lecture). *J. Soc. Chem. Ind.*, 607, 1952.

[4] CLAPHAM, SIR JOHN (HAROLD). 'An Economic History of Modern Britain', Vol. 2, p. 447. University Press, Cambridge. 1932.

[5] WOODWARD, SIR ERNEST (LLEWELLYN). 'The Age of Reform 1815–1870', p. 11. Clarendon Press, Oxford. 1938.

[6] *Idem. Ibid.*, p. 586.

[7] WILSON, C. E. 'The History of Unilever. A Study in Economic Growth and Social Change' (2 vols). Cassell, London. 1954.

[8] GROPIUS, W. 'The New Architecture and the Bauhaus' (Eng. trans. by P. M. SHAND), p. 43. Faber, London. 1935.

[9] COLE, G. D. H. 'A Short History of the British Working Class Movement, 1789–1947' (rev. ed.), p. 3. Allen & Unwin, London. 1948.

A HISTORY OF TECHNOLOGY

CONTENTS

VOLUME I

FROM EARLY TIMES TO FALL OF ANCIENT EMPIRES

VOLUME II

THE MEDITERRANEAN CIVILIZATIONS AND THE MIDDLE AGES
c 700 B.C.–*c* A.D. 1500

CONTENTS

VOLUME III

FROM THE RENAISSANCE TO THE INDUSTRIAL REVOLUTION
c 1500–*c* 1750

VOLUME IV

THE INDUSTRIAL REVOLUTION
c 1750 TO *c* 1850

CONTENTS

I. INDEX OF PERSONAL NAMES

See also Index of Companies

II. INDEX OF COMPANIES

(See also Index of Personal Names for names of manufacturers)

III. INDEX OF PLACE-NAMES

IV. GENERAL INDEX OF SUBJECTS

PLATE I

A

B

The Great Exhibition of 1851 as depicted on Victorian pot-lids, further examples
of which are shown in plate 2. (p 662)

PLATE 2

A

B

C

D

E

F

Examples of 'picture printing' on pottery, dating from F. E. Pratt's patent of 1846 (p 662). The various designs shown here have been chosen because they relate to subjects discussed in this work. (A) Flaying a bear; (B) Royal Harbour, Ramsgate; (C) fishing boats taking in nets; (D) view of Strasbourg; (E) the new Houses of Parliament; (F) the new Blackfriars Bridge.

PLATE 3

Façade of 'Ceramic Palace' of Sèvres architectural stoneware. Universal Exhibition, Paris, 1900. (p 663)

PLATE 4

A. *Parison and milk bottle, as produced on a modern bottle-making machine.* (p 674)

B. *Veal can, taken by Parry on his 1824 and 1826 expeditions to the Arctic.* (p 39)

C. *Norton's improved automatic machinery for making tin cans. The processes are: cutting can bodies, B, G; folding, forming, and sealing bodies, F; soldering side seams, C; putting on ends (capacity 3600 per hour), A; soldering tops and bottoms, D; testing, E; finished can, top inset.* (p 44)

PLATE 5

Three-roll calender (Chaffee) for producing rubber in sheet form without the use of solvents, (p 764)

PLATE 6

A. *7000-amp Héroult cell, Neuhausen, Switzerland.* c *1890.* (p 94)

B. *Poineer Run oil wells,* c *1870.* (p 110)

PLATE 7

A. *Model of Hornsby's horizontal steam-engine,* c *1880. Diameter of fly-wheel 8 ft.* (p 131)

B. *Model of a horizontal tandem compound mill-engine. Diameter of fly-wheel 10 ft.* (p 132)

PLATE 8

A. *Model of Babcock & Wilcox water-tube boiler with mechanical stoker. Boiler drum 20 ft × 4 ft.* (p 138)

B. *The first Belliss & Morcom engine with forced lubrication, 1891. Fly-wheel 20 inches in diameter.* (p 136)

PLATE 9

A. *The original Parsons axial-flow steam-turbine and electrical generator, 1884. Overall length 5 ft 8 in.* (p 139)

B. *The first condensing Parsons radial-flow steam-turbine, 1891. Overall length 13 ft 6 in.* (p 139)

PLATE 10

B. Magneto-electric generator made by F. H. Holmes for Souter Point lighthouse in 1867. Height 5 ft 6 in. (p 191)

A. Horn's compound beam engine, c 1860. Fly-wheel 10 ft in diameter. (p 133)

B

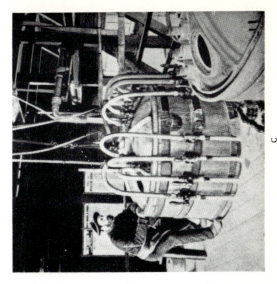

C

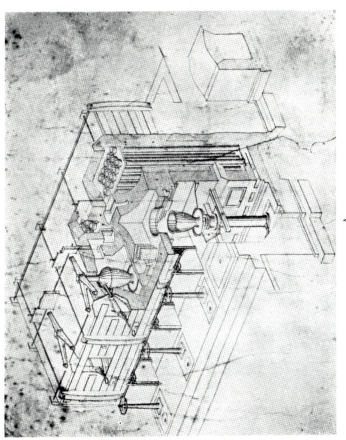

A

A. Castner's sodium furnace. (p 249)

B. The original battery of rocking cells set up at Oldbury for the manufacture of caustic soda by Castner's process. (p 251)

C. Nitration of glycerine at Ardeer factory, c 1890–1900. The operator sits on a one-legged stool to ensure that, through having to preserve his balance, he never falls asleep even momentarily and remains alert during the whole period of nitration. (p 287)

PLATE II

PLATE 12

A. *Sectional model of side-lever marine engine, c 1840.* (p 145)

B. *Model of marine 'steeple' engine, c 1837.* (p 145)

PLATE 13

A. *Model of oscillating paddle engines of the* Great Eastern, *1858.* (p 146)

B. *Model of inclined engines of P.S.* Princesse Henriette, *1888.* (p 146)

PLATE 14

A. *Model of geared engines of S.S.* Great Britain, *1843.* (p 147)

B. *Model of trunk engines of H.M.S.* Northumberland, *1868.* (p 148)

PLATE 15

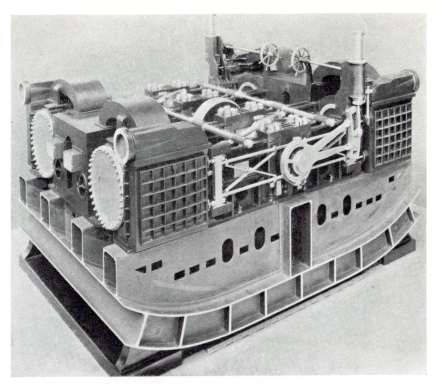

A. *Model of horizontal screw engines of the* Great Eastern, *1858.* (p 148)

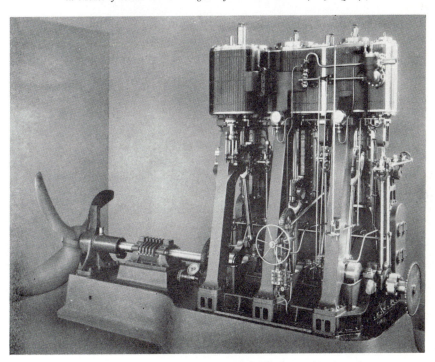

B. *Model of triple expansion engines of S.S.* Flamboro, *1885.* (p 149)

PLATE 16

A. *'Geared Facile' bicycle, c 1888.* (p 416)

B. *Rear view of Benz dog-cart of 1900, showing the engine and driving belts.* (p 427)

PLATE 17

A. *Rear view of an early Benz three-wheeled motor car, with back cover off, c 1888.* (p 427)

B. *Rear view of Cannstatt-Daimler car, c 1896, showing the engine and belt transmission system.* (p 428)

PLATE 18

A. *Model of Siegfried Markus's second car, c 1875. (p 426)*

B. *Stanley steam-car of 1899. The tiller is in the raised position to allow for entrance. (p 425)*

PLATE 19

A. *The first Lanchester car, 1896, as afterwards converted to wheel steering.* (p 431)

B. *The earliest type of Coventry-built Daimler car, a dog-cart of 1897 fitted with a 4-hp twin-cylinder engine.* (p 428)

A. The first passenger railway in the world; the engine is the 'Catch-me-who-can'. Designed by Trevithick, it was demonstrated at Bloomsbury. (p 322)
B. and C. Interior and exterior views of 'Number Nine', the first Pullman sleeping-car, converted from a Chicago and Alton Railroad day coach in 1859. (p 342)

PLATE 21

A. The 'Swallow', built for the Great Western Railway in 1849, renewed 1871, condemned 1892. The photograph shows the engine in its last years, but the design had been very little altered. (p 325)

B. North Eastern Railway 4–4–0 compound locomotive No. 779, built in 1887 to designs of T. W. Worsdell. Subsequently converted to simple, it was in use until 1930. This well exemplifies the elegance of late Victorian locomotive design. (p 338)

C. London, Brighton, and South Coast Railway engine, the 'Lewes', one of William Stroudley's famous 'D' class, the first of which was built in 1873. (p 326)

PLATE 22

A. *Engine siding*, c *1870*. (p 333)

B. *Baker Street Station, London, 1863*. (p 333)

PLATE 23

A. *Garnerin's parachute, with which the first descent from a balloon was made in 1797.* (p 399)

B. *The Wright brothers' first flight, 17 December 1903.* (pp 391, 392)

PLATE 24

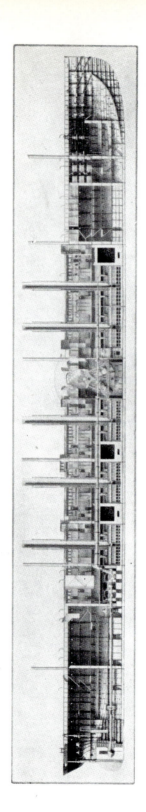

The Great Eastern. (Above) Elevation, (below) plan of fifth deck. Note the large amount of space reserved for fuel. (pp 363, 377)

PLATE 25

The Campania of 1893. (pp 374, 377)

PLATE 26

B. *The British Museum Reading Room during construction, c 1855, showing wrought iron ribs and beams on cast iron columns. The Reading Room was built within the courtyard of the older museum galleries.* (p 476)

A. *The Coal Exchange, London, showing cast iron constructional work.* (p 471)

PLATE 27

B. *The cast iron spire of Rouen Cathedral, built 1876. (p 472)*

A. *Queen Anne's Mansions, London's first skyscraper. Building was begun in 1873, with brick walls and for the most part fire-resisting concrete floors. (p 478)*

PLATE 28

Erection of cantilevers proceeding on the Forth bridge, c 1890. (p 507)

PLATE 29

One of the 450-ft tubes of the Britannia bridge being floated into position, 1849. (p 504)

PLATE 30

The Clifton suspension bridge over the gorge of the river Avon. (p 507)

B. *Hydraulic erector mounted on travelling carriage used in the Hudson River tunnel, constructed between 1874 and 1908.* (p 520)

A. *Steel tunnel shield and cast iron lining used in the Hudson River tunnel.* (p 520)

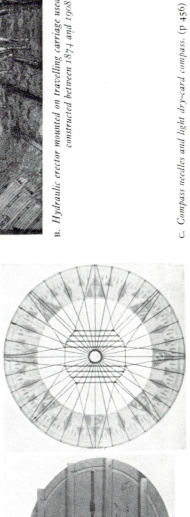

c. *Compass needles and light dry-card compass.* (p 456)

PLATE 31

PLATE 32

A. *The first regular chlorination of a British water supply, at Lincoln, in 1905. A solution of sodium hypochlorite was made up in the stone jars and fed into the water.* (p 567)

B. *Cleaning a slow sand filter at the Hampton works of the Southwark and Vauxhall Water Company, c 1890. After draining the water from the filter, the top layer of sand, up to about an inch thick, was scraped off and removed by hand.* (p 563)

PLATE 33

A. *A 44-in riveted steel water-line as installed at San Francisco, 1885. The line is in service at the present time.* (p 559)

B. *Vyrnwy Dam, north Wales, built 1881-91. The dam is 1172 ft long at the crest, and has a maximum height from foundations to water level of 144 ft. It impounds a maximum of 12,131 m gallons of water.* (p 557)

PLATE 34

B. *Heathcoat's bobbin-net machine. The warp threads are carried from the bottom to the top roller. The gaits for the bobbin carriages can be seen behind the bar, with handle, and above is the comb-like point bar. The bobbin threads pass through the vertical warp threads, and are twisted round them. The net is closed up by the movement of the point bar and wound up on the top roller. Several parts of the machine, including the treadle, are missing. (pp 601, 603)*

A. *Stocking-frame built on Lee's principles. The sinker bar and the tops of the sinkers can be seen above the fabric. The needles are set horizontally. Depression of the right and left pedals, alternately, draws the slur bar across the back of the sinkers so as to bring them down between the needles, on which the thread is laid, and form the loops. The presser bar, seen in front of the sinkers, is brought down on to the needle beards by depressing the middle pedal. In this way the loops are cast off the needles to form the fabric. (p 596)*

PLATE 35

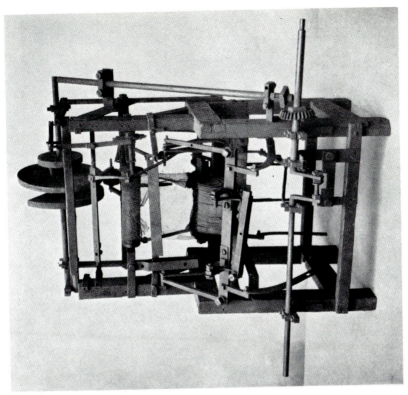

B. *Early Leavers lace machine. Many parts are missing, but the bobbins and carriages are clearly shown. The cams at the top of the machine worked the point bar. The mechanism connecting them with the treadle is incomplete.* (p 602)

A. *Small manually-operated Leavers lace machine with jacquard attachment (right). The vertical threads pass through the guide bars (left), which move horizontally. As the jacquard cards revolve, their perforations act on the rods connected to the guide bars.* (p 603)

PLATE 36

A. *Leavers lace machine, on which wide lace is being made. The jacquard apparatus, not fully shown in the photograph, is on the right of the machine. When narrow breadths are made, the pieces are separated by drawing out the joining threads after the lace has left the frame. The machine illustrated is modern, but all its essential features had been developed by the end of the nineteenth century.* (p 603)

B. *Nottingham lace curtain machine. The jacquard apparatus is overhead and the strings connecting it with the jacks are shown.* (p 603)

PLATE 37

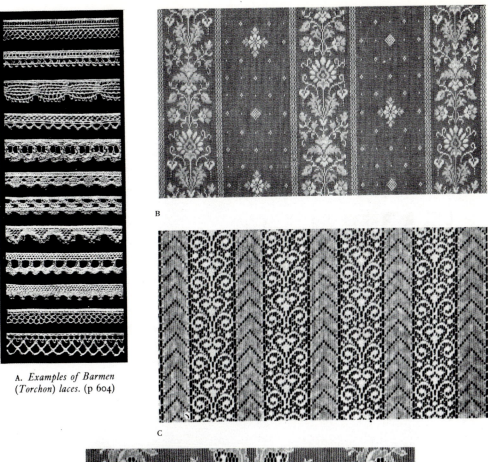

B

C

A. *Examples of Barmen (Torchon) laces.* (p 604)

B, C, *and* D. *Examples of curtain lace. Note the characteristic square mesh of the base fabric.* (p 604)

PLATE 38

B. *Rolling large copper locomotive plate.* (p 613)

A. *Shaping copper plate on a steam-hammer.* (p 611)

PLATE 39

A typical jobbing printing-office, using Columbian press, in Early Victorian days. (p 708)

PLATE 40

A. *Bevel-gear shaping-machine developed by J. Buck in 1895.* (p 656)

B. *British automatic machine, patented by C. W. Parker in 1879, for the production of screws.* (p 647)

PLATE 41

A. *An early planing machine fixed to the wall in James Watt's workshop at the Soho foundry.* (p 650)

B. *Interior of Chubb & Son's London factory for making locks, safes, and so on, 1868.* (p 636)

PLATE 42

B. *Ambrotype, c 1855, with half the backing removed to show positive and negative effect.* (p 725)

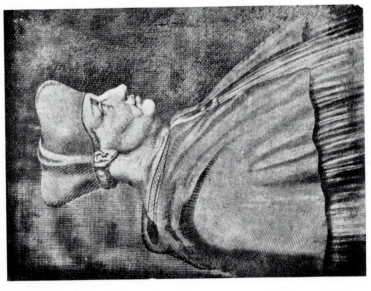

A. *Photo-etching of Cardinal d'Amboise by Nicéphore Niépce. A print 5½ × 8 in, pulled in 1827 from a plate made in 1826.* (p. 719)

PLATE 43

The world's first photograph by Nicéphore Niépce. View from his window at Chalon-sur-Saône, 1826. (p 719)

PLATE 44

A. *Flight of pigeons recorded by Marey's* Chambre Chronophotographique. *Marey filmed many experiments with birds as he hoped that a closer understanding of their flight would help the development of powered flying machines. This particular film was taken in 1892, and the illustration is directly reproduced from the original.* (p 741)

B. *'Arrival of a train', Lumière, 1895. This is the first cinematograph record ever made, and was shown to the public in Paris at the first screenings of films.* (p 745)